THE OXFORD HANDBOOK OF

ENGLISH PROSE

1500–1640

The Oxford Handbook of English Prose 1500–1640 is the only current overview of early modern English prose writing. The aim of the volume is to make prose more visible as a subject and as a mode of writing. It covers a vast range of material vital for the understanding of the period: from jestbooks, newsbooks, and popular romance to the translation of the classics and the pioneering collections of scientific writing and travel writing; from diaries, tracts on witchcraft, and domestic conduct books to rhetorical treatises designed for a courtly audience; from little known works such as William Baldwin's *Beware the Cat*, probably the first novel in English, to The Bible, *The Book of Common Prayer* and Richard Hooker's eloquent statement of Anglican belief, *The Laws of Ecclesiastical Polity*. This book not only deals with the range and variety of the substance and types of English prose, but also analyses the forms and styles of writing adopted in the early modern period, ranging from the Euphuistic nature of prose fiction inaugurated by John Lyly's mannered novel, to the aggressive polemic of the Marprelate controversy; from the scatological humour of comic writing to the careful modulations of the most significant sermons of the age; and from the pithy and concise English essays of Francis Bacon to the ornate and meandering style of John Florio's translation of Montaigne's famous collection. Each essay provides an overview as well as comment on key passages, and a select guide to further reading.

Andrew Hadfield is Professor of English at the University of Sussex and visiting Professor at the University of Granada. He is the author of a number of works on early modern literature, including *Literature, Travel and Colonialism in the English Renaissance, 1540–1625* (Oxford University Press, 1998), and *Spenser's Irish Experience: Wilde Fruyt and Salvage Soyl* (Oxford, 1997). He has also edited a number of volumes, with Raymond Gillespie, including, *The Oxford History of the Irish Book, Vol. III: The Irish Book in English, 1550–1800* (Oxford, 2006). He was editor of *Renaissance Studies* (2006–11) and is a regular reviewer for *The Times Literary Supplement*.

THE OXFORD HANDBOOK OF

ENGLISH PROSE 1500–1640

Edited by
ANDREW HADFIELD

Great Clarendon Street, Oxford, OX2 6DP,
United Kingdom

Oxford University Press is a department of the University of Oxford.
It furthers the University's objective of excellence in research, scholarship,
and education by publishing worldwide. Oxford is a registered trade mark of
Oxford University Press in the UK and in certain other countries

© Oxford University Press 2013

The moral rights of the authors have been asserted

First published 2013
First published in paperback 2016

All rights reserved. No part of this publication may be reproduced, stored in
a retrieval system, or transmitted, in any form or by any means, without the
prior permission in writing of Oxford University Press, or as expressly permitted
by law, by licence or under terms agreed with the appropriate reprographics
rights organization. Enquiries concerning reproduction outside the scope of the
above should be sent to the Rights Department, Oxford University Press, at the
address above

You must not circulate this work in any other form
and you must impose this same condition on any acquirer

Published in the United States of America by Oxford University Press
198 Madison Avenue, New York, NY 10016, United States of America

British Library Cataloguing in Publication Data
Data available

Library of Congress Cataloging in Publication Data
Data available

ISBN 978-0-19-958068-2 (Hbk.)
ISBN 978-0-19-877834-9 (Pbk.)

Links to third party websites are provided by Oxford in good faith and
for information only. Oxford disclaims any responsibility for the materials
contained in any third party website referenced in this work.

Acknowledgements

My thanks are due to a number of people and institutions who helped make this work possible. The research committee in the School of English, University of Sussex, provided support and money for the illustrations; The Bodleian Library, Oxford, supplied pictures swiftly and efficiently; Amy Kenny laboured hard to produce the bibliography; the team at Oxford University Press have been reassuringly professional, a great support and a pleasure to work with—the volume was originally commissioned by Andrew McNeillie, and carried through by Jacqueline Baker, who also commented helpfully on the introduction, along with Ariane Petit and Rachel Platt; Jo North has been an excellent copy editor. Moreover, the contributors to the volume have been models of patience, as well as scholarly and critical expertise, reminding me how enjoyable a collaborative project such as this often can be.

For Mary Yarnold,
a great reader of prose

Contents

List of Figures   xi
List of Abbreviations   xii
List of Contributors   xiii

Introduction   1
ANDREW HADFIELD

PART I TRANSLATION, EDUCATION, AND LITERARY CRITICISM

1. Englishing Eloquence: Sixteenth-Century Arts of Rhetoric and Poetics   9
   CATHERINE NICHOLSON

2. All Talk and No Action? Early Modern Political Dialogue   27
   CATHY SHRANK

3. Commonplacing and Prose Writing: William Baldwin and Robert Burton   43
   JENNIFER RICHARDS

4. Romance: *Amadis de Gaule* and John Barclay's *Argenis*   59
   HELEN MOORE

5. Montaigne and Florio   77
   PETER MACK

6. Italianate Tales: William Painter and George Pettie   91
   NEIL RHODES

7. Classical Translation   106
   GORDON BRADEN

8. *Lazarillo de Tormes* and the Picaresque in Early Modern England   121
   ALEXANDER SAMSON

PART II PROSE FICTION

9. William Baldwin's *Beware the Cat* and Other Foolish Writing — 139
   THOMAS BETTERIDGE

10. The Adventures Passed by Master George Gascoigne: Experiments in Prose — 156
    GILLIAN AUSTEN

11. 'Turne Your Library to a Wardrope': John Lyly and Euphuism — 172
    KATHARINE WILSON

12. Robert Greene — 188
    R. W. MASLEN

13. Nashe's Stuff — 204
    JASON SCOTT-WARREN

14. Sir Philip Sidney's *Arcadia* — 219
    GAVIN ALEXANDER

15. Topicality in Mary Wroth's *Countess of Montgomery's Urania*: Prose Romance, Masque, and Lyric — 235
    MARY ELLEN LAMB

PART III VARIETIES OF EARLY MODERN PROSE 1: PUBLIC PROSE

16. *Utopia* and Utopianism — 253
    ROBERT APPELBAUM

17. English Scientific Prose: Bacon, Browne, Boyle — 268
    CLAIRE PRESTON

18. Richard Hakluyt — 292
    NANDINI DAS

19. Raphael Holinshed and Historical Writing — 310
    BART VAN ES

20. Astrology, Magic, and Witchcraft — 326
    P. G. MAXWELL-STUART

21. Jest Books 343
IAN MUNRO AND ANNE LAKE PRESCOTT

22. Political Prose 360
NICHOLAS MCDOWELL

23. Modes of Satire 380
DERMOT CAVANAGH

24. News Writing 396
JOAD RAYMOND

PART IV VARIETIES OF EARLY MODERN PROSE 2: PRIVATE PROSE

25. Letters 417
ALAN STEWART

26. Diaries 434
ADAM SMYTH

27. Life Writing 452
DANIELLE CLARKE

28. Essays 468
PAUL SALZMAN

29. Domestic Manuals and the Power of Prose 484
CATHERINE RICHARDSON

PART V RELIGIOUS PROSE

30. Immethodical, Incoherent, Unadorned: Style and the Early Modern Bible 505
KEVIN KILLEEN

31. The Style of Authorship in John Foxe's *Acts and Monuments* 522
THOMAS S. FREEMAN AND SUSANNAH BRIETZ MONTA

32. The Marprelate Controversy 544
JOSEPH L. BLACK

33. Sermons 560
PETER MCCULLOUGH

34. The Book of Common Prayer 576
DANIEL SWIFT

35. Richard Hooker's *Of the Lawes of Ecclesiasticall Politie* 592
RUDOLPH P. ALMASY

PART VI MAJOR PROSE WRITERS

36. Gabriel Harvey 611
H. R. WOUDHUYSEN

37. John Knox, George Buchanan, and Scots Prose 631
CAROLINE ERSKINE

38. Robert Burton and *The Anatomy of Melancholy* 646
ANGUS GOWLAND

39. 'When all things shall confess their ashes': Science and Soul in Thomas Browne 669
KEVIN KILLEEN

Bibliography 686
Index 733

List of Figures

4.1	John Barclay, *Argenis*, trans. Robert Le Grys (1628), title page	65
7.1	Xenophon, *Cyropaedia*, trans. Philemon Holland (1632), title page	108
8.1	*The Pleasant History of Lazarillo de Tormes* (London: E. Griffin, 3rd edn., 1639 [1st edn., John Haviland, 1624]), frontispiece and title page. © British Library. C62.aa.18(1)	128
8.2	*Libro de entretenimiento, de la Picara Iustina* (Brussells: Olivero Brunello, 1608), sig. †1r, frontispiece after title page. © British Library. 1074.d.17	133
10.1	George Gascoigne, self-portrait, *The Steele Glas and the Complaynte of Phylomene* (1576), frontispiece	167
17.1	Chameleon, in Ulisse Aldrovandi, *De Quadrupedibus Digitatis Oviparis* (1637), p. 670	280
18.1	Richard Hakluyt, *Principal Navigations* (1599), title page	294
21.1	Anon., *The Cobler of Caunterburie* (1590), title page	353
28.1	Francis Bacon, *Essays* (1625), title page	470
30.1	*King James Bible* (1611), title page	507
31.1	John Foxe, *Actes and Monuments of the Christian Church* (1570), title page	531
31.2	John Foxe, *Actes and Monuments of the Christian Church* (1570), image of Elizabeth as Constantine (p. 1)	534
38.1	Robert Burton, *The Anatomy of Melancholy* (1621), title page	654
39.1	Thomas Browne, *Religio Medici* (1642)	673

Figures 8.1 and 8.2 are reproduced with the kind permission of the British Library Board. All other figures are reproduced with the kind permission of the Bodleian Libraries, Oxford.

List of Abbreviations

ODNB *Oxford Dictionary of National Biography*
OED   *Oxford English Dictionary*

List of Contributors

Gavin Alexander is University Senior Lecturer in the Faculty of English, University of Cambridge, and a Fellow of Christ's College. His recent publications include *Writing After Sidney: The Literary Response to Sir Philip Sidney, 1586–1640* (Oxford University Press, 2006); *Sidney's 'The Defence of Poesy' and Selected Renaissance Literary Criticism* (Penguin Classics, 2004); *Renaissance Figures of Speech* (Cambridge University Press, 2007), co-edited with Sylvia Adamson and Katrin Ettenhuber; and numerous articles and book chapters on literary and musicological topics. An edition of *The Model of Poesy* by William Scott, a manuscript treatise on poetics from c.1600, is forthcoming from Cambridge University Press.

Rudolph P. Almasy is Professor of English at West Virginia University. His scholarly interest is sixteenth-century English religious polemical literature, and he has published on William Tyndale, John Bale, Anne Askew, John Knox, and Richard Hooker, as well as Phillip Sidney and William Shakespeare. At WVU, he has also served as Dean of the Eberly College of Arts and Sciences, as well as Dean of the Davis College of Agriculture, Natural Resources, and Design. His current scholarly project focuses on Knox's exilic writings. He is an active member of the Society for Reformation Research.

Robert Appelbaum received his Ph.D. from the University of California, Berkeley, and is currently Professor of English Literature at Uppsala University, Sweden. His publications include *Literature and Utopian Politics in Seventeenth-Century England* (Cambridge University Press, 2002), *Aguecheek's Beef, Belch's Hiccup and Other Gastronomic Interjections: Literature, Culture and Food Among the Early Moderns* (University of Chicago Press, 2006), and *Dishing It Out: In Search of the Restaurant Experience* (Reaktion, 2011). A Leverhulme and AHRC Fellow, his most recent research focuses on terrorism and the literary imagination.

Gillian Austen did her research at Lincoln College, Oxford, and is currently a Visiting Fellow in the Department of English, University of Bristol. Her book *George Gascoigne* (Studies in Renaissance Literature, 24; D. S. Brewer, 2008) is the first on Gascoigne to discuss all of his work, including his illustrations. She has published several articles on Gascoigne, as well as other early Elizabethan authors, including Turberville and Whetstone. She convened three small-scale international conferences at Lincoln College, Oxford, under the title The Gascoigne Seminar, and is currently preparing a fully annotated *Gascoigne Bibliography* and editing the collection *New Essays on George Gascoigne*, both for AMS Press in New York.

Thomas Betteridge is Professor of Theatre at Brunel University. He has published numerous pieces on English Reformation drama, literature, and history. His books include *Tudor Histories of the English Reformations* (Ashgate, 1999), *Literature and Politics in the English Reformation* (Manchester University Press, 2004), and *Shakespearean Fantasy and Politics* (University of Hertfordshire Press, 2005). His monograph on Sir Thomas More will be published in 2013 by the University of Notre Dame Press. He is also co-editor, with Greg Walker, of *The Oxford Handbook of Tudor Drama* (Oxford University Press, 2012).

Joseph L. Black is Professor in the Department of English at the University of Massachusetts, Amherst. He has published on various aspects of Renaissance literature, pamphlet warfare, and book history, and his books include *The Martin Marprelate Tracts* (Cambridge University Press, 2008) and co-edited collections and anthologies: *Private Libraries of Renaissance England*, vol. 7 (MRTS, 2009), *The Broadview Anthology of British Literature*, vol. 2: *The Renaissance and Early Seventeenth Century* (Broadview, 2006), and *The Broadview Anthology of Seventeenth-Century English Verse and Prose* (Broadview, 2000). He is currently co-editing *The Library of the Sidney Family of Penshurst Place* and further volumes in the Private Libraries of Renaissance England series.

Gordon Braden is Linden Kent Memorial Professor of English at the University of Virginia. He is author of *Renaissance Tragedy and the Senecan Tradition* (Yale University Press, 1985), *Petrarchan Love and the Continental Renaissance* (Yale University Press, 1999), and (with William Kerrigan) *The Idea of the Renaissance* (Johns Hopkins University Press, 1989), and (with Robert Cummings and Stuart Gillespie) editor of the second volume (1550–1660) of *The Oxford History of Literary Translation in English* (Oxford University Press, 2010).

Dermot Cavanagh teaches literature at the University of Edinburgh. He is the author of *Language and Politics in the Sixteenth-Century History Play* (Palgrave Macmillan, 2003) and co-editor (with Stuart-Hampton Reeves and Stephen Longstaffe) of *Shakespeare's Histories and Counter Histories* (Manchester University Press, 2006). He is currently editing *King John* for the third edition of the Norton Shakespeare.

Danielle Clarke is Professor of English Renaissance Language and Literature at University College Dublin, and has published widely on early modern women's writing, as well as gender, sexuality, and language in the Renaissance. Her most recent book is *Teaching the Early Modern Period*, edited with Derval Conroy (Palgrave Macmillan), and she is currently working on a book-length project on the negotiation and form, genre, and language in women's poetry of the Renaissance.

Nandini Das is Professor of Renaissance Literature at the School of English, University of Liverpool. She has written on a range of subjects, from Renaissance prose fiction and cross-cultural encounters, to the development of early eighteenth-century Orientalism. Her recent publications include *Robert Greene's Planetomachia* (Ashgate, 2007) and *Renaissance Romance: The Transformation of English Prose Fiction, 1570–1620* (Ashgate,

2011), along with essays on Richard Hakluyt and early modern travel. Das is volume editor of 'Elizabethan Levant Trade and South Asia' in the forthcoming complete edition of Richard Hakluyt's *The Principal Navigations, Voyages, Traffiques and Discoveries of the English Nation (1598–1600)*, ed. Daniel Carey and Claire Jowitt (Oxford University Press) and is currently working on a project on Renaissance travel and cultural memory.

Caroline Erskine has recently co-edited, with Roger Mason, a volume on *George Buchanan: Political Thought in Early Modern Europe and the Atlantic World* (Ashgate, 2012), and is also co-editor of *Scotland: The Making and Unmaking of the Nation, c.1100–1707* (Dundee University Press, 2007). Her interests lie primarily in political traditions and historical narratives of resistance as an aspect of the Scottish Reformation, and the transmission and reception of these through to the seventeenth century. Her current research focuses on John Knox's *History of the Reformation* and George Buchanan's *Rerum Scoticarum Historia* as particularly important repositories of this line of thought.

Thomas S. Freeman was Research Officer for the British Academy John Foxe Project. He is currently a Research Fellow with the Faculty of Divinity at Cambridge University and a Visiting Lecturer at the University of Essex. He is the co-author (with Elizabeth Evenden) of *Religion and the Book in Early Modern England: The Making of Foxe's 'Book of Martyrs'* (Cambridge University Press, 2011) and the co-editor of four books on early modern British history.

Angus Gowland is Reader in Intellectual History at University College London. He is the author of *The Worlds of Renaissance Melancholy: Robert Burton in Context* (Cambridge University Press, 2006), and of articles on the early modern understanding of melancholy.

Andrew Hadfield is Professor of English at the University of Sussex, Visiting Professor at the University of Granada, and Founding Director of the Centre for Early Modern Studies at Sussex. He is the author of a number of works on early modern literature, including *Shakespeare and Republicanism* (Cambridge University Press, 2005; paperback, 2008); *Literature, Travel and Colonialism in the English Renaissance, 1540–1625* (Oxford University Press, 1998; paperback, 2007); *Spenser's Irish Experience: Wilde Fruyt and Salvage Soyl* (Oxford University Press, 1997); and *Literature, Politics and National Identity: Reformation to Renaissance* (Cambridge University Press, 1994). He has also edited, with Matthew Dimmock, *Religions of the Book: Co-existence and Conflict, 1400–1660* (Palgrave Macmillan, 2008); with Raymond Gillespie, *The Oxford History of the Irish Book, Vol. III: The Irish Book in English, 1550–1800* (Oxford University Press, 2006); and with Paul Hammond, *Shakespeare and Renaissance Europe* (Cengage, Arden Critical Companions, 2004); and *Literature and Censorship in Renaissance England* (Palgrave Macmillan, 2001). He was editor of *Renaissance Studies* (2006–11) and is a regular reviewer for *The Times Literary Supplement*.

Kevin Killeen is Lecturer in Renaissance Literature at the University of York. He is the author of *Biblical Scholarship, Science and Politics in Early Modern England: Thomas Browne and the Thorny Place of Knowledge* (Ashgate, 2009) and the co-editor of *Biblical Exegesis and the Emergence of Science in the Early Modern Era* (Palgrave Macmillan, 2007). He has published on early modern science, intellectual history, and the uses of the Bible in early modern England.

Mary Ellen Lamb is Professor of English at Southern Illinois University, Carbondale. She is the author of *The Popular Culture of Shakespeare, Spenser, and Jonson* (Routledge, 2006), and co-editor of *Staging Early Modern Romance: Prose Fiction, Dramatic Romance, and Shakespeare* (Routledge, 2009) and *Oral Traditions and Gender in Early Modern Literary Texts* (Ashgate, 2008). She has published essays in such journals as *English Literary Renaissance, Shakespeare Quarterly, Shakespeare Survey, Criticism,* and *Review of English Studies*. She is the editor of the *Sidney Journal* and serves on the editorial board of *English Literary Renaissance*. Her abridgement of *The Countess of Montgomery's Urania* (2011), with modernized spelling, is now available from the Arizona Center for Medieval and Renaissance Studies.

Peter McCullough is Fellow and Tutor in English at Lincoln College and Professor of English at Oxford University. He specializes in the religious and literary history of early modern England. In addition to articles on Andrewes, Donne, Milton, Shakespeare, and the London book trade, he is author *of Sermons at Court: Politics and Religion in Elizabethan and Jacobean Preaching* (Cambridge University Press, 1996), editor of *Lancelot Andrewes: Selected Sermons and Lectures* (Oxford University Press, 2005) and *The Oxford Handbook of the Early Modern Sermon* (Oxford University Press, 2011, with Hugh Adlington and Emma Rhatigan), and General Editor of *The Oxford Edition of the Sermons of John Donne*. He is also Lay Canon of St Paul's Cathedral, with Chapter portfolio for cathedral history and its interpretation.

Nicholas McDowell is Professor of English at the University of Exeter. His visiting positions have included Membership of the Institute for Advanced Study, Princeton (2009). He is the author of *The English Radical Imagination: Culture, Religion, and Revolution, 1630–1660* (Oxford University Press, 2003) and *Poetry and Allegiance in the English Civil Wars: Marvell and the Cause of Wit* (Oxford University Press, 2008). He is the co-editor of *The Oxford Handbook of Milton* (Oxford University Press, 2009; paperback, 2011) and *The Oxford Complete Works of John Milton. Volume VI: Vernacular Regicide and Republican Tracts* (Oxford University Press, 2013), for which he has edited *The Tenure of Kings and Magistrates, Articles of Peace Made and Concluded with the Irish Rebels,* and *Eikonoklastes*. He is currently writing an intellectual biography of Milton for Princeton University Press and editing *The Oxford Handbook of English Prose, 1640–1714*. In 2007 he was awarded a Philip Leverhulme Prize by the Leverhulme Trust.

Peter Mack is Director of the Warburg Institute, Professor of the History of the Classical Tradition, University of London, and Professor of English, University of Warwick. His books include *Renaissance Argument: Valla and Agricola in the Traditions of Rhetoric and Dialectic* (Brill, 1993), *Elizabethan Rhetoric: Theory and Practice* (Cambridge University Press, 2002), *Reading and Rhetoric in Montaigne and Shakespeare* (Bloomsbury, 2010), and *A History of Renaissance Rhetoric, 1380–1620* (Oxford University Press, 2011).

R. W. Maslen is Senior Lecturer in English Literature at the University of Glasgow. He has published books on early modern prose fiction and Shakespeare's comedies, edited Sidney's *Apology for Poetry* and Middleton and Dekker's *News from Gravesend*, and written many essays on Renaissance literature and drama. He is also interested in fantastic fiction of the twentieth century.

P. G. Maxwell-Stuart is Reader in Mediaeval and Early Modern History at the University of St Andrews. He specializes in the field of the occult sciences and his recent publications include *Astrology: From Ancient Babylon to the Present* (Amberley Publications, 2010) and *Witch Beliefs and Witch Trials in the Middle Ages* (Continuum, 2010). He has just finished a book on poltergeists and is working on a study of the Evil Eye.

Susannah Brietz Monta is John Cardinal O'Hara, C.S.C. and Glynn Family Honors Associate Professor of English and Editor of *Religion and Literature* at the University of Notre Dame. Her book, *Martyrdom and Literature in Early Modern England* (Cambridge University Press, 2005; paperback, 2009), won the Book of the Year award from the MLA-affiliated Conference on Christianity and Literature. With Margaret W. Ferguson, she edited *Teaching Early Modern English Prose* (MLA, 2010), and is preparing an edition of Anthony Copley's *A Fig for Fortune* (1596), the first published response to Edmund Spenser's *Faerie Queene*, for Manchester University Press. Her current project examines the devotional and aesthetic uses of repetition in early modern prayer, poetry, and rhetoric. Her published articles focus on history plays, early modern women writers and patronesses, martyrology, hagiography, devotional poetry and prose, and providential narratives.

Helen Moore is Fellow and Tutor in English at Corpus Christi College, Oxford, and CUF lecturer in the Faculty of English, University of Oxford. She works at the interface of early modern English and continental literary cultures, and has published on romance, drama, translation, and reception. Most recently she has co-edited *Classical Literary Careers and their Reception* (Cambridge University Press, 2010) and *Manifold Greatness: The Making of the King James Bible* (Bodleian Library Publishing, 2011).

Ian Munro is Associate Professor of Drama at the University of California, Irvine. He is author of *The Figure of the Crowd in Early Modern London: The City and Its Double* (Palgrave Macmillan, 2005) and editor of *'A womans answer is neuer to seke': Early Modern Jestbooks, 1526–1635* (Ashgate, 2007), part of the 'Early Modern Englishwoman' facsimile series. He is currently working on a project about early modern wit and jesting.

Catherine Nicholson is Assistant Professor of English Literature at Yale University. She teaches and writes about sixteenth-century literature and literary criticism, especially the intersection of classical rhetorical theory and experiments in vernacular style. She has published essays on Spenser, Shakespeare, and Marlowe, and her book, *Uncommon Tongues: Eloquence and Eccentricity in the English Renaissance*, is forthcoming from the University of Pennsylvania Press.

Anne Lake Prescott is Helen Goodhart Altschul Professor of English Emerita at Barnard College, Columbia University. A former president of the Sixteenth Century Society and of the Spenser Society, she is the incoming president of the John Donne Society. The author of *French Poets and the English Renaissance* (Yale University Press, 1978) and *Imagining Rabelais in Renaissance England* (Yale University Press, 1998), she is editing (with Andrew Hadfield) the new *Norton Critical Edition of Spenser*. She and Betty Travitsky co-edited an Ashgate series of texts by early modern Englishwomen. Two recent essays won prizes: '"Formes of Joy and Art": Donne, David, and the Power of Music' (*John Donne Journal*, 2006) and 'Mary Sidney's Ruins of Rome' (*Sidney Journal*, 2006). Her most recent essays include two on Thomas More and one on the English Sidneys and the French Chéron siblings as interpreters of the psalms (in *Psalms in the Early Modern World*, ed. Linda Austern et al., Ashgate, 2011). Forthcoming essays include two on Saul in the Renaissance and another on David and upward mobility for *Renaissance Quarterly*, as well as work on Ronsard, jest books (for the *Oxford Guide to Tudor Prose*), Du Bellay and Shakespeare's sonnets, and early modern polemics' contribution to the creation of public space.

Claire Preston is Professor of Early Modern Literature at the University of Birmingham. She has published widely on early modern topics (including the literary-scientific, word and image studies, and Renaissance rhetoric) and on American Gilded Age fiction (including Edith Wharton, Theodore Dreiser, and William Dean Howells). Her recent work includes essays on Spenser and the visual arts, seventeenth-century scientific correspondence, the Renaissance reception of classical scientific and speculative writing, and the poetics of early modern drainage; her recent books include *Thomas Browne and the Writing of Early-Modern Science* (Cambridge University Press, 2005), *Bee* (Reaktion, 2006), and (with Reid Barbour), *Sir Thomas Browne: The World Proposed* (Oxford University Press, 2008). She is completing a study of literature and scientific investigation in the long seventeenth century, and is general editor of the Oxford complete works of Sir Thomas Browne (8 volumes, forthcoming 2015–18), a project for which she currently holds major AHRC funding. She is the recipient of the British Academy's Rose Mary Crawshay Prize, a Guggenheim Foundation Fellowship, and a British Academy Research Development Award.

Joad Raymond is Professor of Renaissance Studies at Queen Mary, University of London. In addition to articles on early modern literature, politics, and print culture, he is the author of *The Invention of the Newspaper* (Oxford University Press, 1996), *Pamphlets and Pamphleteering in Early Modern Britain* (Cambridge University Press, 2003), and *Milton's Angels: The Early Modern Imagination* (Oxford University Press, 2010), and editor of *The Oxford History of Popular Print Culture*, vol. 1: *Cheap Print in Britain and Ireland to 1660*

(Oxford University Press, 2011). He is currently editing Milton's Latin defences for the Oxford *Complete Works of John Milton* and directing an international collaborative project on news networks in early modern Europe.

Neil Rhodes is Professor of English Literature and Cultural History at the University of St Andrews. He is co-General Editor, with Andrew Hadfield, of the MHRA Tudor and Stuart Translations. His publications include, with Chris Jones, *Sound Effects: The Oral/Aural Dimensions of Literature in English*, a special issue of *Oral Tradition* (2009), and *Shakespeare and the Origins of English* (Oxford University Press, 2004).

Jennifer Richards is Professor of Early Modern Literature and Culture at Newcastle University. She is the author of *Rhetoric and Courtliness in Early Modern England* (Cambridge University Press, 2003), and *Rhetoric: The New Critical Idiom* (Routledge, 2007) as well as essays on sixteenth-century literature and culture in *Criticism*, *Renaissance Quarterly*, *Huntington Library Quarterly*, and *The Journal of the History of Ideas*. She has edited several collections of essays, including *Early Modern Civil Discourses* (Palgrave Macmillan, 2003), and most recently, with Fred Schurink, *The Textuality and Materiality of Reading* (a special issue of *Huntington Library Quarterly*, 2010). With Professor Andrew Hadfield she is editing the works of Thomas Nashe for a new edition to be published by Oxford University Press in 2015 and she is writing a new monograph, *Useful Books: Literature and Health in Early Modern England*.

Catherine Richardson is Reader in Renaissance Studies at the University of Kent. Her research focuses on the material experience of daily life in early modern England—on the way material and textual cultures relate to one another; on things and the stories people tell about them. She writes about the household and its furniture and furnishing and about the social, moral, and personal significance of clothing. She is the author of *Domestic Life and Domestic Tragedy: The Material Life of the Household* (Manchester University Press, 2006) and *Shakespeare and Material Culture* (Oxford University Press, 2011), as well as the editor of *Clothing Culture, 1350–1650* (Ashgate, 2004) and, with Tara Hamling, *Everyday Objects: Medieval and Early Modern Material Culture and its Meanings* (Ashgate, 2010).

Paul Salzman is Professor of English Literature at La Trobe University, Melbourne, Australia. He has published widely in the area of early modern prose fiction, women's writing, and literary history. Recent books include *Reading Early Modern Women's Writing* (Oxford University Press, 2006), and he has also just completed an online edition of Mary Wroth's poetry <http://wroth.latrobe.edu.au/>. He is currently writing a book on literature and politics in the 1620s.

Alexander Samson is a Lecturer in Golden Age Literature at University College London. His research interests include the early colonial history of the Americas, Anglo-Spanish intercultural relations, and early modern English and Spanish drama. His recent publications include edited volumes on *The Spanish Match: Prince Charles's Journey to Madrid, 1623* (Ashgate, 2006), with Jonathan Thacker, *A Companion to Lope de Vega* (Tamesis, 2008) and *Gardens and Horitculture in Early Modern Europe*, a special issue of *Renaisance Studies* (2011), as well as articles on the marriage of Philip II and Mary Tudor, historiography and royal chroniclers in sixteenth-century Spain, English travel writers, firearms, maps, John Fletcher and Cervantes, and female Golden Age dramatists. His book *Mary Tudor and the Habsburg Marriage: England and Spain 1553–1557* and an edition of Lope de Vega's *Lo fingido verdadero*, with Manchester University Press, are forthcoming. He runs the Golden Age and Renaissance Research Seminar and is co-director of UCL's Centre for Early Modern Exchanges.

Jason Scott-Warren is a Senior Lecturer in the Faculty of English, University of Cambridge, and a Fellow of Gonville and Caius College. He is the author of *Sir John Harington and the Book as Gift* (Oxford University Press, 2001), *Early Modern English Literature* (Polity Press, 2005), and numerous studies of early modern textual circulation and cultural history. In 2009 he co-founded the Cambridge Centre for Material Texts <http://www.english.cam.ac.uk/cmt/>, of which he is currently the Director.

Cathy Shrank is Professor of Tudor and Renaissance Literature at the University of Sheffield. Her publications include *Writing the Nation in Reformation England, 1530–1580* (Oxford University Press, 2004, 2006) and essays and articles on various sixteenth- and early seventeenth-century topics, including language reform, civility, travel writing, cheap print, and mid-sixteenth-century sonnets. She is the co-editor, with Mike Pincombe, of the *Oxford Handbook of Tudor Literature, 1485–1603* (Oxford University Press, 2009). Current projects include a monograph about non-dramatic dialogues and, with Raphael Lyne, an edition of Shakespeare's poems for Longman Annotated English Poets.

Adam Smyth is a Senior Lecturer in English Literature at Birkbeck College, University of London, specializing in sixteenth- and seventeenth-century literature and culture. His latest book is *Autobiography in Early Modern England* (Cambridge University Press, 2010). He has also published *Profit and Delight: Printed Miscellanies in England, 1640–82* (Wayne State University Press, 2004) and edited *A Pleasing Sinne: Drink and Conviviality in Seventeenth-Century England* (Boydell and Brewer, 2004), in addition to writing many articles on the literature and history of early modern England. He is currently working on a book on the ways in which early modern readers cut up, burnt, recycled, and variously remade their books.

Alan Stewart is Professor of English and Comparative Literature at Columbia University, and International Director of the Centre for Editing Lives and Letters in London. He is the author of *Close Readers: Humanism and Sodomy in Early Modern England* (Princeton University Press, 1997); *Hostage to Fortune: The Troubled Life of Francis Bacon* (with Lisa Jardine, Victor Gollancz, 1998); *Philip Sidney: A Double Life* (Chatto & Windus, 2000); *The Cradle King: A Life of James VI and I* (Chatto & Windus, 2003); *Letterwriting in Shakespeare's England* (with Heather Wolfe, Folger Shakespeare Library, 2004); and *Shakespeare's Letters* (Oxford University Press, 2008). Recent publications include his edition of Bacon's early writings from 1584–1596 for the Oxford Francis Bacon (Oxford University Press, 2012) and the three-volume *Encyclopedia of English Renaissance*

Literature, co-general edited with Garrett Sullivan (Blackwell, 2012). He is currently working on a new project entitled *French Shakespeare*.

Daniel Swift is Senior Lecturer for English at the New College of the Humanities, London. He is the author of *Bomber County* (Hamish Hamilton) and *Shakespeare's Common Prayers* (Oxford University Press).

Bart van Es is Fellow and Lecturer in English at St Catherine's College, University of Oxford. He is the author of *Spenser's Forms of History* (Oxford University Press, 2002) and *A Critical Companion to Spenser Studies* (Palgrave Macmillan, 2006). In addition to his work on Spenser he has published articles on Shakespeare, Daniel, Drayton, Renaissance historiography, and pastoral poetry. Essays by him appear in various Oxford Handbooks, including that on *Holinshed's Chronicles*. He is also the author of the chapter on Classical history and biography in the forthcoming *Oxford History of Classical Reception in English Literature*. His book on Renaissance drama, *Shakespeare in Company*, was published by Oxford University Press in 2013.

Katharine Wilson has taught at Newcastle University and the University of Oxford. She is the author of *Fictions of Authorship in Late Elizabethan Narratives: Euphues in Arcadia* (Oxford University Press, 2006). She has written essays on early modern fiction, especially the works of Lyly and Greene, and has contributed to *Writing Robert Greene*, edited by Kirk Melnikoff and Edward Gieskes (Ashgate, 2008), and *The Oxford Handbook of Tudor Literature, 1485–1603*, edited by Mike Pincombe and Cathy Shrank (Oxford University Press, 2009).

H. R. Woudhuysen is Rector of Lincoln College, Oxford. He has edited *The Penguin Book of Renaissance Verse, 1509–1659* (Penguin, 1992) with David Norbrook and has published a study of *Sir Philip Sidney and the Circulation of Manuscripts, 1558–1640* (Oxford University Press, 1996). One of the General Editors of the Arden Shakespeare Third Series, he edited *Love's Labour's Lost* (1998) and, with Katherine Duncan-Jones, *Shakespeare's Poems* (2007) for the series. In 2010, *The Oxford Companion to the Book* was published, for which he and Michael F. Suarez, SJ, acted as General Editors. He has been closely involved in the Catalogue of English Literary Manuscripts, 1450–1700, a project which has created a freely accessible online record of surviving manuscript sources for over 230 major British authors, including Gabriel Harvey.

INTRODUCTION

ANDREW HADFIELD

THIS handbook is designed to fill an obvious need: the lack of a comprehensive guide to early modern prose. The volume consists of thirty-nine substantial essays, providing a reader with a guide to the varieties of early modern prose, from the reign of the first Tudor, Henry VII, to just before the Civil War, a crucial period of about 150 years. In 1485, printing had only just been introduced to the British Isles, and most material circulated in manuscript form. Many types of non-fictional narrative, such as history, were produced in verse as well as prose and reached a limited audience of the literate. Virtually all literature of high status was written in verse. By 1640 far more people could read and were eager to participate in the public sphere of print, whether as readers or writers, consumers and/or producers, and prose had become the most established medium of written communication. Moreover, an explosion in the production of printed texts, as pamphlets from every quarter and from every possible point of view, written by a wider spectrum of English society than ever before, changed the nature of public culture for ever. Prose was now the dominant form of the written word, as it has been ever since. Literary forms such as the novel, which developed out of the varieties of prose fiction and romance produced in the sixteenth and seventeenth centuries, and the newspaper were about to transform the habits and horizons of a nation of newly educated readers, methods of communication for a new, vastly expanded public sphere. Both forms had a common origin in the news books and journalism that was also proliferating as the printing press became ever more technologically sophisticated and adept at producing text quickly and easily.

This handbook cannot claim to be comprehensive, despite its obvious bulk. There is simply far too much material to cover adequately and decisions have been taken to make this work as representative as possible. Furthermore, prose can be envisaged in two overlapping ways. First, and more obviously, as the bulk of material produced in prose, defined by the *Oxford English Dictionary (OED)* as 'Language in the form in which it is typically written (or spoken), usually characterized as having no deliberate metrical structure (in contrast with *verse* or *poetry*)'; second, as the ways in which non-metrical language can be and was employed in the period. An approach to the first definition would look at historical narrative, legal material, conduct manuals, theological tracts, literature, and so on; and an approach to the second, the style and form of prose produced, explaining what defined its character and made it distinctive. The writers in this volume have all attempted the challenging task of including comment on each aspect of the material under discussion in their essays so that the handbook contains a balance of an explanation of the varieties of prose writing and an analysis of its various forms, styles, and possibilities.

The essays cover an extraordinary range of material, from the most sophisticated and intricate sermons by the finest theological minds of the age (John Donne and Richard Hooker), analysed in Peter McCullough's essay, to domestic manuals detailing household tasks, the very stuff of life, explored in Catherine Richardson's; from rhetorical treatises designed to produce the highest artistic forms (Catherine Nicholson) to tracts on witchcraft (P. G. Maxwell-Stuart), intended to reveal the true extent of a problem and so to protect individuals from harm; and from the most personal devotions to public acts of collective responsibility. Indeed, what invariably emerges from the study of these diverse forms of writing is the wealth of connections between types, styles, and modes of thought and writing. The functional and the ornamental are often not as far apart as might be assumed. As Alan Stewart points out in his essay on letter-writing, letters might look like intimate and private communication between two individuals, but are almost always highly crafted works that were designed in terms of well-established models and reached a wider audience than we often realize. And, as R. W. Maslen argues in his essay on the career of Robert Greene, the first professional writer in England who transformed our understanding of the possibilities of prose writing, what looks like something new and different was often written with an acute understanding of the culture from which it emerged. Greene's prose can seem anarchic and to bear little relation to the moral treatises that were in general circulation, but that is because the moral of his tales is that real life teaches us lessons that qualify and transform what we think we will learn in books. Prose was ordered, regimented, and carefully designed, but was never easy to control. Moreover, the relationship between theory and practice was often complicated and confusing. In large part this was due to the ways in which ideas were transmitted and stored. People wrote out notable pieces of wisdom and startling expression in their commonplace books, and Jennifer Richards shows us that these intellectual practices and habits of mind link the prose of such apparently diverse figures as the mid-Tudor intellectual, William Baldwin, and the author of *The Anatomy of Melancholy*, Robert Burton. Choice phrases and maxims were extracted from major works and then recycled either as the central part of an argument, or as useful supporting evidence.

The volume also reveals a series of struggles between different types and forms of writing. On the one hand, we have the proliferation of prose romance in its various guises, as the essays of Helen Moore, Neil Rhodes, Gavin Alexander, and Mary Ellen Lamb demonstrate, a form of writing that always threatened to get out of hand, travelling beyond established boundaries of sense and taste and 'dilating' outwards away from its narrative core into new and sometimes bizarre areas. It is easy for us to undervalue, or even to dismiss romance as a vulgar and debased literary form, but it was taken seriously and undertaken by some of the most incisive writers in early modern England, and served to define the scope and nature of women's writing. On the other hand, there is the heavily didactic and ordered prose of John Foxe's *Acts and Monuments of the Christian*

Church, its repetitive structures working to produce an apparently inescapable series of conclusions, as Thomas S. Freeman and Susannah Brietz Monta's essay reveals; or the equally controlling cadences of John Knox and George Buchanan, made visible in Caroline Erskine's analysis. Yet even—or perhaps especially—in religious debate chaos threatens to overwhelm order, as readers of Joseph L. Black's essay on the Marprelate Controversy and Kevin Killeen's on the translations of the Bible will soon realize. The need to explain and define the truth and to banish evil and falsehood invariably produced complex and messy texts. Put another way, the conflicting demands of accurate brevity and expansive copiousness pull writers of prose in opposite directions, a contrast that will be obvious to readers of Paul Salzman's essay on the variety of essay forms in the early modern period, from Bacon's brief and controlled interventions to the sustained and wandering explorations of Sir William Cornwallis, a writer very much in the mould of the significantly more prolix Michel de Montaigne.

Any survey of prose has to include more types and forms than any other category of writing used to quantify and explain the variety of writing in the early modern period. Essays in this handbook deal with apparent ephemera such as news pamphlets and news books (Joad Raymond), and cheap and popular print forms such as jest books (Anne Lake Prescott and Ian Munro), to the eloquent expansiveness of Richard Hooker's *Laws of Ecclesiastical Polity* (Rudolph Almasy), Robert Burton's brilliant, highly individual exploration of contemporary culture, *The Anatomy of Melancholy* (Angus Gowland), and the sustained meditations of Thomas Browne (Kevin Killeen). Following Peter Burke's insight, we need to acknowledge that although high culture was designed to reach a restricted audience, popular culture was everyone's culture and was consumed by monarchs as well as the general public. Queen Elizabeth, like most aristocrats, had a robust and vulgar sense of humour and enjoyed the bawdy nature of jest books, with their emphasis on bodily functions. Equally, what might be imagined as a clear-cut contrast between the ordered and precise and the anarchic and transgressive, proves to be anything but, as Claire Preston's essay on the scientific prose of Francis Bacon, Thomas Browne, and Robert Boyle demonstrates. Jacques Derrida and Tzvetan Todorov pointed out some time ago that genres are inescapably in discourse. They have markers that persuade the reader to consume them in a particular way while always containing traces of other forms of writing, residues that cannot be eliminated from our understanding of how such texts work and how they were read. Nandini Das's essay on Richard Hakluyt the younger, the most famous armchair traveller in early modern England, shows how there was an extensive interaction between travel writing and prose fiction, each type of writing borrowing style and content from the other so that voyage narratives were often imagined in terms of chivalric romance and heroic tales narrated as mercantile quests for survival and profit, as much as glory and honour.

A major part of the handbook explores the literary prose of the period. Again, this reveals the close links between apparently diverse forms of writing. Tom Betteridge and Gillian Austen show how both William Baldwin, author of the first sustained prose fiction in English, *Beware the Cat*, and George Gascoigne, among the most prolific, brilliant, and underrated of Elizabethan writers, looked back to Chaucer in order to determine how they should write English prose, conscious of their place within a distinctly English tradition of writing. Gascoigne could never leave his intellectual coordinates to one side and his true report of the devastation of Antwerp 'reveals a considerable amount of rhetorical structuring and formal organisation'. Even when experimenting in what might appear to us to be a literary vacuum, writers such as John Lyly (Katharine Wilson) and Thomas Nashe (Jason Scott-Warren) were acutely aware of their intellectual heritage. In turn, Lyly's distinctive contribution to English prose style, the heavily balanced rhetorical parallels known as 'Euphuism' from his most important prose work, had a major impact on the development of English prose in the next two centuries, even after his initial dominance had been challenged by writers eager to break free from his spell. Nashe's contribution was not confined to *The Unfortunate Traveller* and his prose works, which often remained as single editions after his work was censored in 1599, defined a very different mode of writing, one based on startling juxtapositions, capable of joining the 'disgusting and miraculous'. The complicated and often tortuous attempt to think through the eloquence that could be achieved in prose, simultaneously demonstrating an acute understanding of literary traditions and the desire to break free and establish new forms of writing, characterizes the career of Gabriel Harvey, in many ways a typical figure, as well as an important innovator (Henry Woudhuysen). Harvey is all too often remembered as Nashe's victim in their pamphlet war, but there is far more to Harvey's prose than this exchange indicates, and Harvey was often as innovative as Nashe, especially in his manuscript *Letter-Book*.

There is also a significant concentration on English translation in this volume, a vital part of the works produced in prose and one of the most widely consulted, but all too often omitted from serious analyses of early modern writing. This omission has seriously limited our understanding of the culture of the early modern period. Gordon Braden's essay provides us with a snapshot of the types of prose translation through a series of paradigmatic examples and judiciously selected quotations, while Peter Mack concentrates on probably the most famous prose translation in Renaissance England, John Florio's brilliant attempt to capture the style and spirit of the *Essays* of Michel de Montaigne. Neil Rhodes explores the significance of the bawdy, irreverent, but often politically astute and challenging Italian tales which helped to define a culture for the English, which was simultaneously ennobling, disgusting, and threatening, while Alexander Samson analyses the most significant element of Spanish culture that reached these shores. *Lazarillo de Tormes* was translated in 1576 and helped to define an English understanding of Spanish literature and culture as concerned with the struggle to overcome the cruel and hostile forces that besieged the peasant in an authoritarian society. Such a world encouraged sly cunning and militated against moral probity, at least until the good fortune of the 'picaro' ran out. It is easy to see how such a work had a major impact on the course of English fiction, notably Thomas Nashe's *The Unfortunate Traveller*, published just over a decade later, as well as the earthy style of prose and drama. At the opposite end of the scale was Thomas More's *Utopia*, translated into English by Ralph Robinson in 1551. Robert Appelbaum's essay charts the variety and complexity of the Utopian tradition in English, one that embraced both political and scientific experiment, looked towards a better future, satirized the present, and produced a distressing vision as often as a hopeful one.

Prose defined and established the character of English life and thought. Probably the most influential book produced in this period, having even more impact than the Bible, was the Book of Common Prayer, first produced under the aegis of Thomas Cranmer in 1549, and then undergoing significant changes in the next 120 years. As Daniel Swift demonstrates, we owe more than our understanding of the liturgy and forms of religious ceremony to Cranmer's project. It also gave us a vast number of everyday phrases which have characterized the nature of colloquial English to the present day, even though most native speakers are unaware of the origins of the phrases they use. Other essays show how this common language was used by a vast array of ordinary people, in diaries (Adam Smyth) and the various forms of life writing (Danielle Clarke). Again, we find that what looks as if it is an intimate, private form of writing that opens a window into the author's soul is in fact carefully crafted and structured. As Adam Smyth suggests, diaries, like that of Lady Margaret Hoby, were 'less a path to inwardness, and more a log-book of actions across several spheres', most closely related to one of the most popular forms of print culture, the almanac. Life writing as a category did not exist in this period and we have to construct a category from miscellaneous writings after the event, one reason why so many inexperienced readers are surprised at the lack of biography and autobiography, as well as materials for constructing a life that survive from the sixteenth and, to a lesser extent, the seventeenth century. What emerges is an interesting difference between the life writings of men and women, the latter willing to 'exploit the fluidity of the discourses of the self in order to fashion subjectivities strongly rooted in the private world, whilst reflecting on and affecting the public one' (Danielle Clarke).

Prose had a major role in exhorting, persuading, and forcing people to act, from the proclamations, treatises, and political arguments discussed in Nicholas McDowell's essay, to nuanced discussions and staged dialogues on major issues analysed in Cathy Shrank's, a seriously under-explored genre that enabled writers to carry on debates that had often started in conversation, the staple form of education in a period in which communication was still predominantly oral. After all, 'political argument and change are registered and initiated in prose' (Nicholas McDowell). Of course, a number of genres and modes of writing can accommodate widely divergent purposes, styles, and methods, as Bart Van Es's essay on history writing demonstrates, showing the differences between the inclusive, apparently non-evaluative nature of the chronicle and the controlled, focused direction of the historical narratives produced by a Bacon or a Daniel. In his equally wide-ranging essay, Dermot Cavanagh follows the course of the sixteenth century through three major satirists: Erasmus in his *Praise of Folly*, a Menippean satire designed to expose and correct vice; Stephen Gosson's rather more vigorous polemic against the theatres, *The School of Abuse*; and Thomas Nashe's disorienting and disturbing polemical fiction, *The Unfortunate Traveller*, in which 'the narrator learns the full extent of the theatrical imposture that passes for reality in the world around him and that sustains the appearance of reality'.

The significance of prose has at last been re-recognized after a long hiatus when it was only sparingly taught in schools and universities. Major new editions of the works of Sir Francis Bacon, Robert Burton, Sir Thomas Browne, and Richard Hakluyt are well underway; there has been a great deal of serious work on sermons, especially Lancelot Andrewes and John Donne; there is renewed interest in Lady Mary Wroth, Sir Philip Sidney, William Baldwin, and Raphael Holinshed; as well as major new works on types and forms of writing, notably letters, jest books, popular romance, and print culture. The danger is not that this handbook will fail to find an audience but that the amount of work may leave it in need of revision and updating in the near future.

Further Reading

Barbour, Reid. *Deciphering Elizabethan Fiction* (Newark: University of Delaware Press, 1993).

Black, Joseph L., ed. *The Martin Marprelate Tracts: A Modernized and Annotated Edition* (Cambridge: Cambridge University Press, 2008).

Fowler, Elizabeth, and Roland Greene, eds. *The Project of Prose in Early Modern Europe and the New World* (Cambridge: Cambridge University Press, 1997).

Mander, Jenny, ed. *Remapping the Rise of the European Novel* (Oxford: Voltaire Foundation, 2007).

Monta, Susannah Brietz, and Margaret W. Ferguson. *Teaching Early Modern English Prose* (New York: Modern Language Association, 2010).

Newcomb, Lori Humphrey. *Reading Popular Romance in Early Modern England* (New York: Columbia University Press, 2002).

Pooley, Roger. *English Prose of the Seventeenth Century, 1590–1700* (London: Longman, 1993).

Raymond, Joad, ed. *The Oxford History of Popular Print Culture: Vol. 1, Cheap Print in Britain and Ireland to 1660* (Oxford: Oxford University Press, 2011).

Rhodes, Neil, ed. *English Renaissance Prose: History, Language and Politics* (Tempe, AZ: Medieval and Renaissance Text Society, 1997).

Salzman, Paul, ed. *An Anthology of Elizabethan Prose Fiction* (Oxford: Oxford University Press, 1998).

—— ed. *An Anthology of Seventeenth-Century Fiction* (Oxford: Oxford University Press, 1991).

—— *English Prose Fiction, 1558–1700: A Critical History* (Oxford: Oxford University Press, 1985).

Travitsky, Betty S. 'The Possibilities of Prose', in Helen Wilcox, ed., *Women and Literature in Britain, 1500–1700* (Cambridge: Cambridge University Press, 1996), 234–66.

PART I

TRANSLATION, EDUCATION, AND LITERARY CRITICISM

CHAPTER 1

ENGLISHING ELOQUENCE: SIXTEENTH-CENTURY ARTS OF RHETORIC AND POETICS

CATHERINE NICHOLSON

1.1 Ineloquent England

IN 1531, when Sir Thomas Elyot surveys England's linguistic landscape, he discerns in its contours only 'a maner, a shadowe, or figure of the auncient rhetorike'. That shadow or figure inheres in the law school ritual of 'motes' or moot courts, mock trials at which students debated 'some doubtfull controversie' before a court of their faculty and peers. As Elyot notes in *The Boke named the Governour*, the moot courts required students to generate a set of plausible arguments, arrange them persuasively for a judge or jury, and present them in a public setting, and so they trained young lawyers in the rudiments of invention, disposition, and memory, the first three parts of the classical art of rhetoric. But according to Elyot, the moot courts did not, and could not, revive the whole of the ancient art: because 'the tonge wherin it is spoken is barberouse, and the sterynge of affections of the mynde in this realme was neuer used, there lacketh Eloqution and Pronunciation, the two principall partes of rhetorike'.[1] In other words, it isn't simply the English language to which eloquence is foreign, it is England itself, identified here as a realm where persuasion—the stirring of the affections through language—was never used.

Elyot's critique of English legal discourse highlights a more pervasive dilemma for sixteenth-century vernacular writers. The eloquence enshrined in ancient Greek and Latin oratory was revered as the epitome of linguistic achievement: as Roger Ascham

---

[1] Thomas Elyot, *The Boke named the Governour* (1531), repr. and ed. R. C. Alston (Menston: Scolar Press, 1970), fos. 56ʳ–57ᵛ.

writes in *The Scholemaster* (1570), 'in the rudest contrie, and most barbarous mother language, many be found [that] can speake verie wiselie, but in the Greeke and Latin tong, the two onelie learned tonges, we finde always wisdome and eloquence, good matter and good vtterance, neuer or seldom asunder'.[2] But the gap between these tongues and English was vast, perhaps insuperably so: as Ascham bluntly observed in 1545, 'in the Englysh tonge contrary, euery thinge in a maner so meanly, bothe for the matter and handelynge, that no man can do worse'.[3] Given this extreme disparity, eloquence itself could seem a hopelessly alien quality, even a threat to the integrity of what Thomas Nashe dubs 'our homely Iland tongue'.[4] Thus, in 1578, when Richard Harrison takes stock of the linguistic refinements of the past several decades, he describes English as a tongue simultaneously 'perfect[ed]' by the efforts of 'sundry learned and excellent writers' and 'corrupted with external terms of eloquence'.[5]

How to craft an English language that is eloquent without ceasing, in the process, to be English: this is the challenge taken up by many poets, playwrights, and prose writers of what we now call the English Renaissance, but it is a challenge that is confronted most directly in the pages of vernacular treatises on rhetoric and poetics, practical guides to the domestication of a theoretical discourse identified powerfully and often exclusively with what was written and spoken elsewhere. As Elyot's comments in *The Governour* suggest, early Tudor England laid claim to only a very partial remnant of that ancient discourse. Indeed, the sole printed vernacular text on rhetoric, Leonard Cox's *Art or Crafte of Rhetoryke* (c.1524–30), begins with the author's explanation that he has taken a deliberately truncated approach to the material in his Latin source texts, devoting the bulk of his attention to invention, some to disposition and arrangement, and none at all to elocution and pronunciation. Those who have read Cicero or Quintilian will, he acknowledges, perceive that 'many thynges be left out of this treatyse that ought to be spoken of'—but not, he insists, in an English handbook. For his intended audience, defined by its linguistic incompetence, he writes for 'yonge beginners' and 'suche as haue by negligence or els fals persuacions' failed to 'attayne any meane knowlege of the Latin tongue'—what Ascham calls 'good utterance' is no plausible object.[6] In the decades following the publication of *The Boke named the Governour*, however, an increasing number of English authors challenged this assumption: in texts that attempt to translate the precepts of classical rhetoric and poetics into principles meaningful for a vernacular audience, they represent eloquence as a refinement rather than a repudiation or transcendence of Englishness.

In this regard, it is Thomas Wilson rather than Leonard Cox who deserves the title of the first English rhetorician. Cox may write the first English art of rhetoric, but Wilson's

---

[2] Roger Ascham, *The Scholemaster* (1570) (repr. Menston: Scolar Press, 1967), 46.

[3] Roger Ascham, *Toxophilus: The Schole of Shoting* (1545), in *English Works*, ed. William Aldis Wright (Cambridge: Cambridge University Press, 1904), xiv.

[4] Thomas Nashe, *Have With You to Saffron Walden* (London: John Danter, 1596), sig. M2^v.

[5] William Harrison, 'The Description and Historie of England', in Raphael Holinshed, *The first and second volume of Chronicles* (London, 1587; 2nd edn.), 14.

[6] Leonard Cox, *The Arte or Crafte of Rhetoryke* (London, 1532), sig. [F6]^r.

Arte of Rhetorique (1553, 1560) is the first art of *English* rhetoric: a treatise that takes for granted its interest and value as an analysis of vernacular norms and practices. Where Cox envisions an audience of schoolboys or poor Latinists, Wilson's treatise addresses itself on its title page to '*all suche as are studious of Eloquence*'. 'Boldly...may I aduenture, and without feare step forth to offer that...which for the dignitie is so excellent, and for the use so necessarie', Wilson proclaims in his Prologue to the revised and expanded edition of 1560.[7] This boldness has much to do with Wilson's ability to imagine a mutually enriching relationship between eloquence and Englishness. Cox expects that an educated readership will greet his English rhetoric as 'a thyng that is very rude and skant worthe the lokynge on' and reassures himself with the thought that his partial accounting of the art 'shall be sufficyent for an introduction to yonge beginners, for whome all onely this booke is made' (sigs. F6ᵛ–F7ʳ). Wilson, by contrast, courts an educated readership, prefacing the first edition of his *Arte* with Latin poems by university men. He dedicates both editions to his patron John Dudley, the Earl of Warwick, whose 'earnest...wish' that he 'might one day see the precepts of Rhetorique set forth...in English' Wilson attributes not to his defects as a Latinist, but to the 'speciall desire and Affection' he 'beare[s] to Eloquence'. Indeed, for Wilson, Dudley's Englishness is a rhetorical asset: he anticipates a time when the 'perfect experience, of manifolde and weightie matters of the Commonweale, shall haue encreased the Eloquence, which alreadie doth naturally flowe' in Dudley to such an extent that his own *Arte* will be 'set...to Schoole' in Dudley's home, 'that it may learn Rhetorique of...daylie talke'.[8]

This fancy, that eloquence might be schooled by an English nobleman's 'daylie talke', upends Thomas Elyot's conception of England as a realm where persuasion was never used, and it offers a radical challenge to Roger Ascham's conviction that the 'trewe Paterne of Eloquence' must be sought not in 'plaine naturall English', but in 'the unspotted proprietie of the Latin tong...at the hiest pitch of all perfitness'—that is, 'not in common taulke, but in priuate bookes' (*The Scholemaster*, 146). Like Elyot and Ascham (whose friend and peer he was), Wilson identified with the cause of English humanism, but in *The Arte of Rhetorique*, he is at pains to expose what he sees as the unintended cost of that movement's lack of faith and interest in the mother tongue: a slavish devotion to Latin and Greek that has prevented English from fulfilling its own potential for eloquence.

Indeed, the chief objects of concern in Wilson's *Arte* are not the unlearned, ineloquent English, but those among them who have forsaken common talk for the pleasures of

---

[7] Thomas Wilson, *The Arte of Rhetorique* (London: Richard Grafton, 1553; 1560); expanded 1560 edition reprinted as *Wilson's Arte of Rhetorique*, ed. G. H. Mair (Oxford: Clarendon Press, 1909), sigs. Aiiᵛ–Aiiiʳ.

[8] Gabriel Harvey echoes this wish when discussing the success of Wilson's *Rhetorique* in the latter half of the sixteenth century: a handwritten note on the final page of his copy of Quintilian observes that the *Rhetorique* had become the 'daily bread of our common pleaders and discoursers' (quoted in Peter E. Medine, *Thomas Wilson* [Boston: Twayne Publishers, 1986], 55)—whether Harvey, no proletarian in matters of eloquence, meant this as a compliment is uncertain, but both the dailiness of use and the commonness of the users would have pleased Wilson himself.

private books and foreign travel: modish young men so enamoured of foreign literature that they mistake foreignness itself for a linguistic virtue, 'seek[ing] so far for outlandish English, that they forget altogether their mothers language'. Orphaned and alienated by their own affectations, they 'will say, they speake in their mother tongue', but, Wilson remarks, 'if some of their mothers were aliue, they were not able to tell what they say'. Having forsaken their mother country and mother tongue, these 'farre jorneid jentlemen at their returne home, like as thei loue to goe in forraine apparel, so thei will pouder their talke with oversea language'. Actual foreign loan-words are merely the most obvious marks of rhetorical error: worse still are the 'farre fetcht colours of Antiquitie', the pseudo-archaisms and pretentious classicisms that force the speaker to transgress the bounds of community (162).

Wilson's sense of the vernacular thus depends on the same equation of geography and language that, for Elyot, condemns England to rhetorical mediocrity: he too treats English as an insular tongue, remote from Latin, Greek, and the modern Romance languages. But Wilson draws a strikingly different conclusion from that equation; for him, English is not the rude speech of a rude country, but the uncorrupted tongue of a nation whose insularity and remoteness have preserved it from moral degradation, political coercion, and 'oversea language'. Its peculiar geography is not the impediment to England's literary ambition, but the condition necessary for its fulfilment, the guarantee of its linguistic purity. As Wolfgang Müller observes, 'Compared to contemporary rhetoric books'—like Richard Sherry's *Treatise of Schemes and Tropes* (1553), which opens with an extended defence of its author's reliance on Greek and Latin terms of art—'Wilson seems to have deliberately made his book look as English as may be', even as he continues to draw on classical and continental models.[9] Not only does he eschew Greek, Latin, and French terminology wherever possible, he populates his treatise with vividly drawn characters from English life: the effete Italianate courtier, the country bumpkin, the pretentious Lincolnshire clergyman. Often these are figures of fun, but they also represent Wilson's conviction that vernacular eloquence is the stuff of daily talk.

Instead of fretting over England's infelicitous isolation or the distinctions between its speech and the language of classical authors, then, Wilson worries about preserving that isolation and honouring those distinctions, forestalling the needless contamination of English by alien influences.[10] But in his determination to rise to the challenge set by Thomas Elyot, Wilson ends up promoting an ideal of vernacularity whose boundaries

---

[9] Wolfgang G. Müller, 'Directions for English: Thomas Wilson's *Art of Rhetoric*, George Puttenham's *Art of English Poesy*, and the Search for Vernacular Eloquence', in Mike Pincombe and Cathy Shrank, eds., *The Oxford Handbook of Tudor Literature, 1485–1603* (Oxford: Oxford University Press, 2009), 311.

[10] We might compare this insistence on eloquence's native provenance with Wilson's treatment of logic in his 1551 treatise, *The Rule of Reason*, the preface to which confesses that the 'fruit' of logic is 'a straunge kind (soche as no Englishe ground hath before this tyme, and in this sort by any tillage brought forthe)' and that 'it maie perhaps in the firste tastyng, proue somewhat rough and harsh in the mouthe, because of the straungenesse' (sig. A2ᵛ). *The Arte of Rhetorique* contains no such disclaimers.

are necessarily more fluid. In the final section of his *Arte*, he identifies elocution as 'that part of *Rhetorique*, the which aboue all other is most beautifull': in its absence reason 'walk[s]...both bare and naked'. And elocution depends not simply on plainness and commonness of diction, but on 'delitefull translations, that our speech may seeme as bright and precious, as a rich stone is faire and orient', on 'beautifying of the tongue with borowed wordes', and on 'change of sentence or speech with much varietie': such rhetorical values are not easily distinguished from the vices of Wilson's far-journeyed gentlemen with their oversea language. His *Arte* therefore marks an important turn in the vernacularization of rhetoric, but it also exposes the contradictory visions of Englishness that underwrite the new vernacular rhetorics. Treatises like Wilson's testify to the changes wrought upon a classical ideal of eloquence when it is identified with England's daily talk, but they also testify to the changes wrought upon sixteenth-century ideals of Englishness as they assimilate an alien theory of eloquence.

1.2 Words in Their Place

Wilson's desire to challenge the exclusively foreign provenance of eloquence is not simply an expression of nationalist fervour. More importantly, his effort to promote a thoroughly English art of eloquence derives from the conviction that any approach to rhetoric that privileges unfamiliar language over ordinary speech violates the essence of the art. 'I know them that thinke *Rhetorique* to stande wholie vpon darke wordes, and hee that can catche an ynke horne terme by the taile, him they coumpt to be a fine Englisheman, and a good *Rhetorician*', he writes, but such affectation is 'foly', for it fails to accomplish the most fundamental purpose of speech. 'Doeth wit rest in straunge wordes', Wilson demands, 'or els standeth it in wholesome matter, and apt declaring of a mans minde? Doe wee not speake because we would haue other to vnderstande vs, or is not the tongue giuen for this ende, that one might know what an other meaneth' (163–4)?

In his emphasis on shared understanding, Wilson is not so far from his predecessor Cox, who argues that rhetoric teaches men to speak 'in suche maner as maye be moste sensible and accepte to their audience' and justifies his own vulgarization of rhetoric on the principle that 'euery goode thynge,...the more commune that it is the better it is' (sigs. A.ii^v, Aiii^r). But for Cox, commonness is all English has to recommend it— eloquence he regards as the sole property of the classical tongues. For Wilson, commonness is at the heart of 'an Orators profession', which is fulfilled when he 'speake[s] only of all such matters, as may largely be expounded...for all men to heare them' (1). The wanton misuse of foreign terms and 'darke wordes' is thus not simply a stylistic or even political concern: to Wilson's mind, it alienates eloquence from its primary orientation towards understanding and community.

Wilson begins his *Arte* with a fable designed to illustrate this point, a fable adapted from the myth recounted by Cicero at the beginning of *his* first treatment of the art of rhetoric, *De Inventione*.¹¹ The myth credits eloquence with the creation of meaningful bonds between men and the places they inhabit. Before eloquence was known or used, Cicero writes, men were like beasts in their relation to the earth: they 'wandered at large [*vagabantur*]' and 'were scattered [*dispersos*] in the fields and hidden in sylvan retreats'. This vagabond existence persisted until one man (traditionally identified with the poet and musician Orpheus), by the force of his words, 'assembled and gathered them in a single place [*compulit unum in locum et congregavit*]'.¹² From this original gathering place, Cicero writes, sprang civilization: homes, cities, nations, and empires founded on the banishment of error, of wandering and unreason. Later accounts of rhetoric often featured versions of the same myth, reiterating the role of eloquence in the foundation of human communities. In the *Institutio Oratoriae* Quintilian writes, 'I cannot imagine how the founders of cities would have made a homeless multitude [*vaga illa multitudo*] come together to form a people, had they not moved [*commota*] them by their skillful speech.'¹³ This formulation contrasts the vagrancy of the homeless multitude with the purposeful solidarity of a people 'moved' by eloquence. Rhetoric counteracts man's natural tendency to *err* with the attractive power of words and ideas.¹⁴

For Wilson, reading this myth through the lens of Protestant Christianity, the errant proclivity of man is not only a sign of savagery, but a mark of sin. Aligning the founding myth of eloquence with biblical history, he makes a case for rhetoric as an instrument of salvation. After Adam's fall, he writes, the 'eloquence first giuen by God' was lost, and the immediate consequence was the demise of human community: 'all things waxed sauage, the earth vntilled, societie neglected'. Lacking a productive relation to the land, or to each other, men 'grased vpon the ground' and 'roomed' like wild beasts. They 'liued brutishly in open feeldes, hauing neither house to shroude them in, nor attire to clothe their backes'.¹⁵ Thus far, Wilson's narrative recapitulates the Old Testament history of mankind's fall, whereby Adam and Eve are cast out of the garden, Cain becomes, in the words of the 1560 Geneva Bible, 'a vagabond and a runnagate in the earth' (Gen. 4:12), Noah's sons are 'deuided in their lands, euery one after his tongue; [and] after their fami-

---

[11] Wayne Rebhorn provides a lengthy consideration of classical and Renaissance accounts of the origins of rhetoric, paying particular attention to the distinctive political ideologies that inflect versions of the foundational myth offered in republican and monarchic societies. See *The Emperor of Men's Minds: Literature and the Renaissance Discourse of Rhetoric* (Ithaca: Cornell University Press, 1995), 23–9. Neil Rhodes likewise reflects on Renaissance ideas of eloquence in the first chapter of *The Power of Eloquence and English Renaissance Literature* (New York: St. Martin's Press, 1992).

[12] Marcus Tullius Cicero, *De Inventione*, trans. H. M. Hubbell (Cambridge, MA: Harvard University Press, 1949), 5–7.

[13] Quintilian, *Institutio Oratoria*, 4 vols., trans. Donald Russell (Cambridge, MA: Harvard University Press, 2001), 1:373.

[14] Cicero's *De Officiis* highlights the significance of this communal function of rhetoric. In the words of Grimald's 1556 English translation, '[O]nlesse the felowshippe of mankinde, dothe meete with the knowledge of thinges: it may seeme a very bare, and alonewandering knowledge: and likewise greatnesse of corage, severed from common feloushippe, and neybourhod of men, muste needes bee a certein savagenesse, and beastly crueltie' (1.157, 109).

[15] Wilson, *Rhetorique*, sig. [A6]ᵛ.

lies, in their nations' (Gen. 10:5), and, at last, at Babel, God resolves to 'confound the language of all the earth... [and] scatter them vpon all the earth' (Gen. 11:9).[16] This state of alienation and confusion persists, according to Wilson, until God's 'faithfull and elect... called [men] together by vtteraunce of speech', persuading them 'to live together in fellowship of life' and 'to maintain Cities'. By no 'other meanes', he asserts, could men have been brought to submit to the authority of God and his ministers. Man's natural vagrancy and errancy would lead him to seek to move to a higher station, he writes, 'were [he] not persuaded, that it behoueth [him] to liue in his owne vocation: and not to seeke any higher roume' (sig. [A7]$^{r-v}$).

Eloquence creates community, but it also maintains, according to degree, the natural boundaries between peoples, classes, nations, and all other entities otherwise vulnerable to motion, error, and change. Wilson's stylistic, syntactic, and formal prescriptions are thus repeatedly cast in geographical terms, as warnings against departure from the space of common knowledge and shared understanding. Orators are urged to avoid 'straunge woordes, as thou wouldest take hede and eschue greate Rockes in the Sea', and to guard against 'roving without reason' from the plain statement of their arguments (2–3, 87). 'Would not a man thinke him mad, that hauing an earnest errande from London to Dover, would take it the next way to ride first into Northfolke, next into Essex, and last into Kent?' Wilson asks. So much the greater, he argues, is the folly of those who treat rhetoric as an art of evasion and circumlocution. He offers the cautionary example of an Anglican preacher who, intending to speak 'of the generall resurrection', instead 'hath made a large matter of our blessed Ladie, praysing her to bee so gentle, so curteous, and so kinde, that it were better a thousand fold, to make sute to her alone, then to Christ her sonne'. Such rhetoric is, Wilson argues, 'both vngodly, and nothing at all to the purpose'; like the savage men of the pre-rhetorical world, it 'roomes'. The pun on 'Rome' and 'roaming', which the text's orthography invites, emphasizes the conflation of linguistic, moral, and geographic errancy: rhetorical laxity, like the pursuit of strange words, leads to heresy. '[A]ssuredly', Wilson concludes, 'many an vnlearned and witlesse man, hath straied in his talke much farther a great deale, yea truly as farre as hence to Roome gates' (87–8).

Wilson's *Rhetorique* thus paves the way for a new approach to the vernacular, one founded on the virtues of familiarity, proximity, and even insularity. In the latter half of the sixteenth century, a number of writers follow Wilson in arguing that England's national integrity—the security of its place in the world—demanded that English be put on equal footing with all other tongues. They adopt both his confidence in the mother tongue and his conviction that insularity makes an ideal landscape for eloquence. One of the most radical attempts to challenge the hegemony of the classical tongues is Ralph Lever's 1573 vernacular art of logic. Pointedly titled *The Arte of Reason, rightly termed Witcraft*, Lever's treatise excludes as many Latinate words as possible, replacing even

---

[16] *The Geneva Bible: A Facsimile of the 1560 Edition*, with an introduction by Lloyd E. Berry (Madison: University of Wisconsin Press, 1969), fos. 2^v, 5^r, 5^v.

familiar terms—like 'logic' itself—with invented Anglo-Saxon equivalents like 'witcraft'. 'We who devise understandable terms, compounded of true and ancient English words', Lever explains, 'do rather maintain and continue the antiquitie of our mother tongue.' By contrast, he argues, 'they, that with inckhorne termes soe chaunge and corrupt the same, mak[e] a mingle mangle of their natiue speech,... not observing the propertie thereof'.[17] That English has an 'antiquitie' and 'propertie' of its own is precisely what Thomas Elyot does not allow when, in *The Boke named the Governour*, he attributes England's rhetorical limitations to its 'infilicitie of tyme and countray' (fol. 18ʳ): if English can claim for itself a place worth having, both in history and on the globe, then its alienation from the classical world no longer matters. Indeed, Latin, Greek, and their modern heirs may be regarded not as remote ideals, but as unwanted interlopers, trespassers on the vernacular's rightful territory.

This is precisely the position taken by Samuel Daniel in his *Apologie for Ryme* (1603), which likens the importation of foreign words into English to an influx of undesirable immigrants. '[W]e always bewray our selues to be bothe vnkinde and vnnaturall to our owne natiue language, in disguising or forging strange or vnusuall wordes, as if it were to make our verse seeme another kind of speech out of the course of our vsuall practice, displacing our wordes', Daniel declares. The boundaries of English, he implies, are no less fixed than those of England itself and ought to be guarded with as much zeal: the vernacular constitutes a finite territory, in which the presence of foreigners necessarily threatens to 'displace' the native inhabitants. 'I wonder at the strange presumption of some men', he writes, 'that dare so audaciously aduenture to introduce any whatsoeuer *forraine* wordes, be they neuer so *strange*, and of themselues, as it were, without a Parliament, without any consent or allowance, establish them as Free-denizens in our language.'[18]

In reality, the borders of the English language could not be sealed any more than the borders of England itself: both the country and its vernacular were heavily dependent on foreign imports. Even the word 'denizen', which Daniel uses to scold those who presumptuously introduce foreign terms into English, is a legal term borrowed from Norman French[19]—a remnant of William the Conqueror's invasion of England. The presence of such words was a constant reminder of the permeability of England's geographic borders, its heritage of repeated conquest by foreign nations.[20] But however ignominious this history might be, it had made English into a much richer and more diverse tongue than it otherwise might have been. Certainly Thomas Wilson recognizes this fact—unlike Lever, he is no Anglo-Saxon purist. Wilson allows that, when foreign terms are required 'to set forth our meaning in the English tongue, either for lacke of

---

[17] Ralph Lever, *The Arte of Reason, rightly termed Witcraft* (London: H. Bynneman, 1573), sig. [*7]ᵛ.
[18] Samuel Daniel, *The Defence of Ryme* (London: Edward Blount, 1603), sig. H7ʳ.
[19] See *OED* s.v. 'denizen', *OED* <http://www.oed.com> accessed 18 March 2013.
[20] As Richard Foster Jones observes, 'five times strangers had invaded England, and each time had changed the language' (*The Triumph of the English Language* [Palo Alto, CA: Stanford University Press, 1953], 5).

store, or els because we would enrich the language: it is well doen to vse them', provided that 'all other are agreed to followe the same waie'. Such words, 'being vsed in their place', should cause no one to be 'suspected for affectation', he writes, as long as they are 'apt and meete... to set out the matter' (165). Here, as always in Wilson's *Arte*, the concern is with place: that words be accommodated to the place in which they are written or spoken, and that they do not displace more familiar and proper terms.

Keeping words 'in their place' was not simply a matter of policing the incursion of foreign terms into English; it was also a matter of managing the vernacular's worrisome *internal* heterogeneity. To call English an 'island tongue' was to ignore the many differences of dialect that divided one region from another.[21] This internal heterogeneity represented a serious obstacle to claims for vernacular eloquence: England was understood to be full of places that engendered corrupt or barbarous versions of the mother tongue. George Puttenham's *Arte of English Poesie* (1589) precisely enumerates these places in an effort to pinpoint the site of true eloquence. The best speech in any language, Puttenham writes, is not that which is spoken 'in the marches or frontiers, or in port townes, where straungers haunt for traffike sake, or yet in Vniuersities where Schollers vse much peeuish affectation of wordes out of the primatiue languages, or finally, in any vplandish village or corner of a Realme, where there is no resort but of poore rusticall or vnciuill people', rather, it is strictly that dialect that is used 'in the kings Court, or in the good townes and Cities within the land'. This dictum bars 'any speech vsed beyond the riuer of Trent', which, although it may reflect more of the pure 'English Saxon' is 'not so Courtly nor so currant as our Southerne English'. According to Puttenham, proper English corresponds to exact geographic coordinates: it is found 'in London and the shires lying about London within lx. myles, and not much aboue'.[22]

Puttenham's strict mapping of acceptable vernacular usage echoes in another form Wilson's warnings against 'roaming' language, but Puttenham—writing for an audience of courtiers—disregards Wilson's sense of the contextual nature of propriety. For Puttenham, the English of the court is inherently preferable to that spoken elsewhere— the burden of barbarous marginality is simply shifted to England's own periphery, while the privileged centre of learned speech is transferred from Rome to London. Wilson, by contrast, regards courtly speech as proper only to the court; spoken outside of that setting, it is as ludicrous as any other foreign usage. The distinction is crucial, for it highlights the central feature of Wilson's whole theory of vernacular eloquence: the notion that eloquence is a local rather than a universal quality.

Given his urgent desire to protect English from the strange speech of other nations, we might expect Wilson to share Puttenham's anxiety about the internal peculiarities of

---

[21] This internal difference of language is the subject of Paula Blank's *Broken English: Dialects and the Politics of Language in Renaissance Writings* (London and New York: Routledge, 1996), which examines the role of dialects in various efforts to standardize vernacular usage and to represent English identity in literary form.

[22] George Puttenham, *The Arte of English Poesie*. In *English Reprints*, vol. 4 (New York: AMS Press, 1966), 156–7.

the mother tongue. In fact, however, Wilson regards the variation of speech within England's borders as an obstacle to eloquence only when the rhetorical proprieties of one social or geographic context come into conflict with those of another. He repeatedly tells stories of low-born men from the provinces whose upper-class pretensions lead them into comic rhetorical errors—the 'ignorant fellowe' who calls a flock of sheep 'an audience' or the yokel who refers to a house as a 'phrase of building'. But Wilson makes clear that such abuses of language occur not because the vernacular itself needs reform, but because speakers fail to consider what is proper to a given context: they 'vs[e] words out of place'. The solution, he argues, is to map the vernacular with as much care for internal divisions as for external boundaries: '[W]e must make a difference of English, and say some is learned English, and other some is rude English, or the one is court talke, the other is countrey speech', he advises, 'or els we must of necessity banish all such *Rhetorique*, and vse altogether one maner of language' (164, 166).

The inability to draw such distinctions deprives rhetoric of its most basic stylistic and persuasive virtues, those of familiarity and clarity. Unless speakers abide by the law of proximity, avoiding that which is strange or far-fetched, they cannot hope to win the assent of their audience. Those who would 'acquaint themselues with the best kind of speech', Wilson writes, 'must seeke from time to time such wordes as are commonly receiued, ... what wordes we best vnderstande, and knowe what they meane: the same should soonest be spoken' (165). Wilson's respect for the local permutations of style and usage within England's borders thus derives, as do all his precepts, from the conviction that eloquence is a communal art. Men, he writes in his 'Preface', should learn how to speak by following 'their neighbours deuise' (sig. [A7]^v). Such an assertion is a profound departure from the view that England could only learn eloquence from strangers: Wilson's *Rhetorique* not only frees English rhetoric from its thraldom to Latin and Greek, it roots the art of persuasion in the most intimate and familiar of relationships, asserting that 'the best kind of speech' is that which is literally closest to hand.

1.3 Fair and Orient Figures

His emphasis on the locally particular character of linguistic decorum allows Thomas Wilson to stake England's claim to a native art of eloquence, but it leaves readers of *The Arte of Rhetorique* with an unresolved paradox. As the epitome of rhetorical decorum, eloquence ought to be the form of speech most in accord with local custom and circumstance, but the definition of eloquence depends on the perception of its *difference* from ordinary or common speech. As Wilson allows, familiarity may be the basis of persuasive power, but the best orator does not blend into the crowd: 'among all other, I thinke him most worthie fame', he writes, 'that is among the reasonable of al most reasonable, and among the wittie, of all most wittie, and among the eloquent, of all most eloquent: him thinke I among all men, not onely to be taken for a singuler man, but rather to be coumpted for halfe a God' (sig. A7^v). The singularity and near divinity of the eloquent man—his reputation or fame as an orator—derives not from his speaking commonly, but extraordinarily. True eloquence not only justifies departures from common usage; it demands them.

Even as Wilson founds his vernacular *Arte* on an identification of eloquence with proximity to common use, then, that proximity does not dissolve into identity: the persuasive force of rhetoric depends as much on singularity as it does on familiarity. Thus, Wilson turns in the final section of his *Arte* to 'exornation', the practice by which '[w]hen wee haue learned apte wordes, and vsuall phrases to set foorth our meaning, and can orderly place them... wee may boldely commende and beautifie our talke'. 'Apt' and 'usual' terms set in 'orderly' places may be the standard for which the novice orator strives, but boldness and beauty are the marks at which the truly expert speaker aims—even if they necessitate violations of aptness, order, and use. That boldness and beauty may require such violations is plain from Wilson's account of exornation, which he defines as 'a gorgeous beautifying of the tongue with borrowed wordes, and change of sentence or speech with much varietie', so that 'our speech may seeme as bright and precious, as a rich stone is faire and orient' (169). This last simile highlights a shift in Wilson's sense of the relationship between eloquence and familiarity. What, after all, could be more distant and alien, more 'far-fetched', than the gem-rich Orient evoked by Wilson's comparison? The contrast to his earlier prohibitions on strange words grows more marked as Wilson's discussion of exornation proceeds: ornament, he writes, is most often achieved by figures of speech, which are 'vsed after some newe or straunge wise, much vnlike to that which men commonly vse to speake'. Without such new and strange figures, Wilson claims, 'not one can attaine to be coumpted an Oratour, though his learning otherwise be neuer so great' (170). Among the most skilled speakers, he observes, '[m]en coumpt it a point of witte, to passe ouer such words as are at hand, and to vse such as are farre fetcht and translated'—by such diversions from common use, he concludes, '[a]n Oration is wounderfully enriched' (171–2).

This is a striking reversal of the relationship hitherto presumed to exist between place and eloquence: now rhetoric leads away, to the alien and exotic, rather than sustaining the common and usual. The shift points to a tension within the project of vernacular rhetoric. That is, for those who seek to establish guidelines for the eloquent use of English, it is essential either to close the gap between English and Latin or to propose alternative, vernacular standards for rhetorical propriety. However, such efforts at uniformity and standardization must give way to the imperative to distinguish rhetorical speech from its mundane counterparts. Eloquence cannot be so closely tied to common usage that it disappears altogether. Thus, even as Puttenham insists that proper diction must correspond to that of London, he too encourages vernacular authors in the use of 'the rich Orient coulours' of 'figures and figurative speech' if they hope to attain eloquence (143).

In treatises like Wilson's and Puttenham's—often heralded as markers of burgeoning national pride and linguistic self-confidence—Elyot's perception of rhetoric (and, especially, of style) as an essentially exotic commodity is not so much dispelled as displaced onto a territory internal to the supposedly homely mother tongue: as eloquence is redefined on English terms, the shadows and figures of the native linguistic landscape assume an increasing prominence and value. Here it is worth turning back to a handbook I earlier contrasted to Wilson's *Arte* in its self-conscious reliance on classical terminology. The title page of Richard Sherry's 1550 *Treatise of Schemes and Tropes*, the first vernacular guide to what Elyot dubbed the 'principall partes of rhetorike', advertises it as an aid 'for the better vnderstanding of good authors', and those who picked it up probably assumed that the authors in question were classical writers: here was a handbook to help schoolboys recognize a Ciceronian *paraphrasis* or a Virgilian *metalepsis*. Sherry's preface initially reinforces the assumption that his object is the demystification of a foreign discourse. He apologizes for the fact that his title must sound 'all straunge unto our Englyshe eares', causing 'some men at the fyrst syghte to marvayle what the matter of it should meane', and urges readers to consider that 'use maketh straunge thinges familier'. With time, he suggests, alien terms like 'scheme' and 'trope' may become as common 'as if they had bene of oure owne natiue broode'.[23]

But as Sherry soon reveals, the strangeness his treatise seeks to make familiar is less a property of Latin and Greek than it is of English itself. 'It is not vnknowen that oure language for the barbarousnes and lacke of eloquence hathe bene complayned of', he writes,

> and yet not trewely, for anye defaut in the toungue it selfe, but rather for slackenes of our countrimen, whiche haue always set lyght by searchyng out the elegance and proper speaches that be ful many in it: as plainly doth appere not only by the most excellent monumentes of our auncient forewriters, Gower, Chawcer and Lydgate, but also by the famous workes of many other later: inespeciall of ye ryght worshipful knyght syr Thomas Eliot,... [who] as it were generallye searchinge oute the copye of oure language in all kynde of wordes and phrases, [and] after that setting abrode goodlye monumentes of hys wytte, lernynge and industrye, aswell in historycall knowledge, as of eyther the Philosophies, hathe herebi declared the plentyfulnes of our mother tounge. (sigs. A2^v–[A3]^r)

The 'good authors' of the title page thus include not simply Cicero and Virgil, but Elyot, Thomas Wyatt, and the 'manye other...yet lyuyng' (sig. [A3]^v) whose very familiarity—whose Englishness—has obscured the 'copye' or riches of their speech.

In truth, it is hard to imagine any reader consulting the litany of arcane tropes and figures that ensues and finding Elyot's prose or Wyatt's verse easier to read as a consequence: the aim is not clarification, but complication. We—and, presumably, sixteenth-century readers—do not need Sherry's definition of the figure he calls 'Metaphora' or 'translacion'—'a worde translated from the thynge that it properlye signifieth, vnto another whych may agre with it by a similitude' (sig. C4^v)—to understand what Elyot means when he describes moot court exercises as the 'shadow or figure' of an ancient rhetoric, but the label and the definition call our attention to the artfulness of the phrase, its capacity to suggest the way time has attenuated and flattened a once substantive art.

---

[23] Richard Sherry, *A Treatise of Schemes and Tropes* (London, 1550), sigs. A1^v–A2^r.

When Sherry promises his readers 'better understanding' of authors like Elyot, he offers them a mode of access to their mother tongue that is also a process of alienation from it: the domestication of classical rhetoric brings with it a deliberate and profitable estrangement from the mother tongue.

Indeed, Sherry's *Treatise* extends to English readers the possibility that the strangeness of eloquence might be its chief asset for the vernacular: although he worries that some readers will scan the title of his book, 'marvayle' and cast it aside as 'some newe fangle', he imagines 'other[s], whiche moued with the noueltye thereof, wyll thynke it worthye to be looked vpon, and se what is contained therin' (sig. A2^r). In appropriating wonder as a productive response to the foreign terminology of style—schemes and tropes, metaphors, zeugmas, and antistrophes—Sherry doesn't simply make good on an inevitable feature of his rhetorical project, the need to reckon with Greek and Latin terms of art and odd linguistic technicalities, he also recovers for the vernacular a central, and often problematic, feature of what Elyot calls 'the ancient rhetoric': the counter-intuitive premium it placed on the orator's ability to impress his audience with the unlikelihood of his expressions. For as much as classical rhetoricians urged their pupils to conform their speech to the experiences and expectations of their audience—the orator, writes Quintilian, must discern 'those things about which there is general agreement,...if not throughout the whole world, at any rate in the nation or state where the case is being pleaded'[24]—they also remained sensitive to the particular power of language that alters or departs from ordinary usage. 'To deviate [from prevailing (*kyrios*) usage] makes language seem more elevated; for people feel in the same way in regard to *lexis* as they do in regard to strangers compared with citizens', writes Aristotle in Book Three of the *Art of Rhetoric*. 'As a result, one should make the language unfamiliar, for people are admirers of what is far off, and what is marvellous is sweet.'[25] The sixteenth-century Englishing of classical rhetoric thus recapitulates a debate that structures the very foundation of classical theories of eloquence: does persuasion inhere in the fashioning of an argument that comes closest to what an audience will recognize as the truth of their own experience, or does it operate most powerfully in those rhetorical shadows and figures that entice us with their strangeness?

Within vernacular treatises on rhetoric and poetics, this ancient uncertainty produces a conspicuous metaphorical volatility: the geographic language of distance and foreignness that is used so often to stigmatize bad rhetoric or affected speech is therefore equally available to positive representations of vernacular eloquence. Metaphor itself, as all of these writers well knew, means 'to carry across'—as Puttenham says, it might be dubbed 'the figure of *transport*', since it entails 'a kind of wresting of a single word from his own right signification, to another not so naturall' (148). That less 'naturall' signification might imply a transgression of decorum—Jonson warns readers that '*Metaphors* farfet

---

[24] Quintilian, *Institutio Oratoria*, ed. and trans. H. E. Butler (Cambridge, MA: Harvard University Press, 1966), 5.10.11–13; vol. 2, 209.

[25] Aristotle, *On Rhetoric: A Theory of Civic Discourse*, ed. and trans. George A. Kennedy (Oxford: Oxford University Press, 1991), 3.2.2–3; 221.

hinder to be understood' and that a speaker should take care not to 'fetcheth his translations from a wrong place' (95)—but it also opens language up to exotic delights and strange riches. Thomas Nashe might mock Gabriel Harvey for speaking English like a stranger and insist that true Englishmen are 'the plainest dealing souls that ever God put life in',[26] but even plain dealing souls are not immune to the allure of the distant and rare. Indeed, it just this allure that draws writers to the study of rhetoric, as Nashe himself allows: perfecting the art of speech, he jokingly observes, entails a perpetual hunt for 'a more Indian metaphor'.[27] As a character in Nashe's *The Unfortunate Traveller* (1594) remarks, far-flung travels and exotic adventures may have corrupted Ulysses's morals, but they refined his skill as an orator: '*Non formosus erat, sed erat facundus Ulysses*; Ulysses, the long traveler, was not amiable but eloquent' (343).

Not just rhetorical excess, then, but rhetoric itself continued to be associated with travel and exoticism, even by those early modern English authors who took it upon themselves to counter Elyot's notion of eloquence as definitively un-English. In part, this association reflected the persistence of the belief that the vernacular as it was commonly spoken was inadequate as a vehicle for eloquence—the 'homely Iland tongue' might be too narrowly provincial after all—but it also reflects a belief that eloquence demands liberal bounds: the rusticity of the vernacular might as well be blamed on lack of industry and daring as on any necessary restrictions. This, according to George Puttenham, was the function of all figurative language: 'As figures be the instruments of ornament in euery language, so be they also in a sorte abuses or rather trespasses in speech, because they passe the ordinarie limits of common vtterance', becoming a 'manner of forraine and coloured talke' (159–60). Ultimately, Puttenham suggests, the effect of rhetoric on an audience is not to confirm their sense of place in the world, but to provide the illusion of leaving it: figures of speech, he writes, 'carieth [the listener's] opinion this way and that, whither soeuer the heart by impression of the eare shalbe most affectionately bent and directed', 'drawing [the minde] from plainnesse and simplicitie to a certain doublenesse' (159–60). This 'doublenesse', the 'inuersion of sense by transport', serves as yet another response to the relationship understood to exist between English language and England's place. Here neither the vernacular nor the foreign are shunned, since figuration allows for the coexistence of the two in a single discourse: 'euery language' has the capacity to become a 'manner of forraine...talke'.

In other words, every language is capable of poetry: Puttenham's treatise begins with the assertion that eloquence is bred only by the influence of poets upon a language. Poetry, he writes

> is...a maner of vtterance more eloquent and rhethoricall then the ordinarie prose which we vse in our daily talke, because it is decked and set out with all maner of fresh colours and figures...The vtterance in prose is not of so great efficacie, because...it is dayly vsed, and by that occasion the eare is ouerglutted with it. (9)

---

[26] Thomas Nashe, *The Unfortunate Traveller*, in *The Unfortunate Traveller and Other Works*, ed. J. B. Steane (New York: Penguin Books, 1973), 342.

[27] Nashe, *The Unfortunate Traveller*, 293.

Whereas Wilson cautioned orators against adopting the extravagant style of the poet, Puttenham offers poetry as the ideal model for rhetorical excellence: 'the Poets were...from the beginning the best perswaders, and their eloquence the first Rhethoricke of the world' (9). The division between poetry and 'ordinarie prose' thus becomes another boundary to be trespassed in the pursuit of eloquence.[28] Indeed, as Paula Blank argues, 'words usually characterized as examples of Renaissance "poetic diction"' may be 'better understood as dialects of early modern English'. Blank cites Alexander Gill's Latin history of the English language, *Logonomia Anglica* (1619), which places the 'Poetic' alongside 'the general, the Northern, the Southern, the Eastern, [and] the Western' as one of the 'major dialects'. 'Along with regional languages implicitly defined, geographically and socially, by their relation to the "general" language (i.e., an elite variety of London English)', Blank writes, we might consider ' "Poetic" language as a province of the vernacular'.[29]

For most rhetorical and poetic theorists, however, the place of poetry in relation to the ordinary vernacular is represented not by reference to internal regions, but to more exotic locales: Nashe's 'Indian metaphor', Wilson's 'faire and orient' speech, or Puttenham's 'Orient colours'. In the case of poetry, foreignness derives not from the words themselves (although these may be foreign in origin), but primarily from what Chapman calls the 'beyond sea manner of writing'. How is it that poetic language accomplishes this estrangement of the vernacular from itself? George Gascoigne offers one explanation in 'Certayne Notes of Instruction Concerning the Making of Verse', an essay appended to his 1575 anthology *The Posies*. Gascoigne begins the essay by urging his fellow vernacular poets *not* to regard poetic diction as alienated from ordinary speech, encouraging them rather to hew to 'playne Englishe' in the composition of their verses.[30] Take care, he writes, that 'you wreste no woorde from his natural and vsuall sounde' and, when possible, choose simple words, for 'the more monosyllables that you vse, the truer Englishman you shall seeme'.[31] Gascoigne particularly urges vernacular poets to 'eschew straunge words, or *obsoleta et inusitata*', and to 'use your verse after theenglishe phrase, and not after the maner of other languages' (52–3).

Nevertheless, it is by no means obvious to Gascoigne that poetic language always can or should adhere to the boundaries of 'playne Englishe'. Indeed, he quickly qualifies his own ruling, allowing that archaisms and other 'unnatural' words are sometimes permitted to verse by 'poetic licence':

---

[28] For a discussion of the 'generic intertextuality' enacted by Puttenham's conflation of poetry and eloquence, see Heinrich F. Plett, *Rhetoric and Renaissance Culture* (New York: Walter de Gruyter, 2004), 151–2, 162–73.

[29] Blank, *Broken English*, 3.

[30] George Gascoigne, 'Certayne Notes of Instruction Concerning the Making of Verse or Ryme in English', in *Ancient Critical Essays Upon English Poets and Poesy*, ed. Joseph Haslewood (London: Robert Triphook, 1815), vol. 2, 53.

[31] Gascoigne, 'Certayne Notes of Instruction', 50–1.

> Therefore even as I have advised you to place all wordes in their naturall or most common and usuall pronunciation, so would I wish you to frame all sentences in their mother phrase and proper Idioma, and yet sometimes (as I have sayd before) the contraries may be borne, but that is rather where rime enforceth, or *per licentiam Poeticam*, than it is otherwise lawfull or commendable. (53)

But Gascoigne's own language at this moment ironically and rather playfully enacts the permeability of that supposedly lawful and commendable boundary between 'the englishe phrase' and 'the maner of other languages', even in prose: 'straunge words' is glossed with the Latin '*obsoleta et inusitata*', 'the mother phrase' is elaborated—gratuitously—by the Greek 'Idioma', and '*per licentiam Poeticam*' substitutes for the perfectly serviceable vernacular equivalent. Recourse to language outside of the common usage, it seems, is not simply a freedom allowed to English verse: prose stylists too may find themselves straying into foreign tongues, either where the paucity of the vernacular 'enforceth' such transgressions or simply where the whim of the author makes them desirable.

As Gascoigne unfolds his theory of '*licentiam poeticam*', he further multiplies the qualifications to his own rule against 'straunge words'. 'This poeticall license', he writes, is 'a shrewde fellow', which 'covereth many faults in a verse'. Poetic licence, he observes, has the procrustean ability to 'maketh words longer, shorter, of mo syllables, of fewer, newer, older, truer, falser, and to conclude it turkeneth all things at pleasure' (53–4). Here, again, Gascoigne's own language partakes of the licence he describes: 'turkeneth', according to the *Oxford English Dictionary*, is emphatically a 'newer' word in 1575, perhaps even Gascoigne's own coinage. The twofold connotation of the word preserves a sense of Gascoigne's ambivalence about poetic licence: on the one hand 'to turken' (or, to use an earlier, related form of the word, 'to turkesse') means either 'to transform or alter for the worse; to wrest, twist, distort, pervert' or—much less negatively—'to alter the form or appearance of; to change, modify, refashion (not necessarily for the worse)'.[32] Which definition applies to the 'turkening' of that shrewd fellow, poetic licence, is uncertain in Gascoigne's account. Are the alterations wrought in the common language by poetic usage 'perversions' of that language, or are they simply acts of 'refashioning' and 'modification'? Is poetic licence an invitation to poetic licentiousness?

There is, of course, another ambiguity residing in Gascoigne's uncommon turn of phrase: its etymological relation to early modern England's pre-eminent figure for *global* difference and licentious excess: the Turk. According to the *OED*, while 'turken' and 'turkesse' are understood by some as versions of the French 'torquer' or the Latin 'torquere', meaning 'to twist', this etymology presents 'difficulties both of form and sense'. An alternative derivation is suggested 'from Turk and Turkeys, [or] Turkish', since, as the *OED* observes, 'they were often associated with these words'. A survey of the citations provided in the *OED* suggests that these two etymologies converged in the early seventeenth century, when 'turken', 'turkesse', and 'turkize' were used to describe the transformation or conversion of sacred language or objects or individuals from Christian truth

---

[32] *OED*, s.v. 'turkesse', *OED* <http://www.oed.com> accessed 18 March 2013.

to Islamic error. In *Purchas His Pilgrimage* (1613), for instance, Samuel Purchas describes how 'the Turkes, when they turkeised it [St Sophia], threw downe the Altars, [and] turned the Bells into great Ordinance', while a citation from 1648 deplores 'those... which are so audacious as to turcase the revealed, and sealed Standard of our salvation... to the misshapen models of their intoxicated phansies'. Gascoigne's use of 'turkeneth' does not explicitly invoke the presence of Islam, but his witty coinage does invite readers to locate his discussion of poetic licence within a larger conversation about the boundary between the native and the foreign, the natural and the unnatural, the lawful and the unlawful. The link between the foreign and the poetic, Gascoigne suggests, inheres in the (dangerously) transformative power of each.

Insofar as it signifies a potentially illicit 'turning' of language, 'turken' is also a synonym for 'trope', the operation by which words, as Puttenham says, 'haue their sense and understanding altered and figured... by transport, abuse, crosse-naming, new-naming, change of name' (189). For all his anxieties about the English spoken outside of London, Puttenham does not regard this tendency to wander from the proper idiom as a defect of tropological language; on the contrary, he understands the appeal of figuration to reside precisely in its ability to 'delight and allure as well the mynde as the eare of the hearers with a certain noueltie and strange maner of conueyance, disguising it no little from the ordinary and accustomed' (147). Such conveyance forces both language and listeners from their common uses: when speech is ornamented with 'figures rhethoricall', Puttenham writes, it possesses, in addition to the 'ordinarie vertues' of 'sententiousnes, and copious amplification', an 'instrument of conueyance for... carrying or transporting [meaning] farther off or nearer' and for making the mind of the listener 'yielding and flexible', susceptible to persuasion in any direction (207). Figuration invests language with the power to transport listeners, while remaining within the confines of the mother tongue. And in texts like Puttenham's *Art*, Gascoigne's *Notes*, and even Wilson's emphatically domestic *Rhetorique*, eloquence finds a place within the vernacular that is as far-fetched and extravagant as it is English.

Further Reading

Blank, Paula. *Broken English: Dialects and the Politics of Language in Renaissance Writings* (London and New York: Routledge, 1996).

Jones, Richard Foster. *The Triumph of the English Language* (Palo Alto, CA: Stanford University Press, 1953).

Keilen, Sean. *Vulgar Eloquence: On the Renaissance Invention of English Literature* (New Haven: Yale University Press, 2006).

Kennedy, George. *Classical Rhetoric and Its Christian and Secular Tradition from Ancient to Modern Times*, 2nd edn. (Chapel Hill: University of North Carolina Press, 1999).

Mann, Jenny. 'The "Figure of Exchange": Shakespeare's "Master Mistress," Jonson's *Epicoene*, and the English Art of Rhetoric', *Renaissance Drama*, 38 (2010): 173–98.

—— 'Sidney's "Insertour": Arcadia, Parenthesis, and the Formation of English Eloquence', *English Literary Renaissance*, 30.3 (Autumn 2009): 460–98.

Müller, Wolfgang G. 'Directions for English: Thomas Wilson's *Art of Rhetoric*, George Puttenham's *Art of English Poesy*, and the Search for Vernacular Eloquence', in Mike Pincombe and Cathy Shrank, eds., *The Oxford Handbook of Tudor Literature, 1485–1603* (Oxford: Oxford University Press, 2009), 307–22.

Rebhorn, Wayne. *The Emperor of Men's Minds: Literature and the Renaissance Discourse of Rhetoric* (Ithaca: Cornell University Press, 1995).

Rhodes, Neil. *The Power of Eloquence and English Renaissance Literature* (New York: St. Martin's Press, 1992).

CHAPTER 2

....

ALL TALK AND NO ACTION? EARLY MODERN POLITICAL DIALOGUE

....

CATHY SHRANK

> There was then to be hearde pleasaunte communication and merye conceytes, and in every mannes countenaunce a manne might perceive peyncted a lovynge jocoundenesse. So thys house truelye might be called the verye mansion place of Myrth and Joye. And I beleave it was never so tasted in other place, what maner a thynge the sweete conversatyon that is occasyoned of an amyable and lovynge companye, as it was once there.[1]

THE opening of Baldassare Castiglione's *Il Cortegiano* (1528) paints an idyllic—and nostalgic—picture of the court of Urbino in the first decade of the sixteenth century. As he endeavours to recapture a community, now lost, Castiglione focuses above all on conversation: the text in which Castiglione memorializes the former court is a dialogue (that is, in the form of a reported conversation); and the society described is one which expresses itself, and is manifested through, the manner and variety of its verbal communication: the 'disputations', 'jestings', 'talke & debating of matters', which brought 'wonderous great pleasure on all sydes' (A4ᵛ).

This essay examines sixteenth- and early seventeenth-century dialogue, one of the commonest literary forms in the period, thinking about why so many writers chose to convey opinions or explore ideas in works laid out as conversations, and—having selected that form—the uses to which they put it. Whilst sixteenth-century English writers were less prone to theorizing dialogue than their Italian counterparts, the form was

---

[1] Thomas Hoby, trans., *The Boke of the Courtier* (1561), sig. A3ᵛ.

as prominent in England as elsewhere in early modern Europe.[2] Roger Deakins estimates that there are 'some two hundred and thirty' sixteenth-century English prose dialogues extant in print;[3] to this figure we need to add dialogues in manuscript, in Latin, and (although this area is beyond the remit of this volume) in verse. The pervasiveness of the form is also apparent in the sheer gamut of topics discussed 'dialogue-wise': subjects stretch from worshipping saints to the proper behaviour of women; from music to the art of warfare.[4] Dialogue (like conversation in Castiglione's Urbino) comes in many guises: descriptors on printed title pages range from the neutral 'colloquy' or 'discourse' to the more formal 'debate' and 'dispute'. The conversations depicted vary in the number of speakers, and the relative authority of the interlocutors. In discussions between two speakers (the most usual formulation) one frequently plays the 'straw-man', feeding lines for the superior speaker to refute, or acting the ignoramus, asking for clarification on specific issues or instruction in particular skill-sets (such as physic or fishing).[5] Alternatively, these two-handed conversations might offer views for and against a position, or allow speakers to endorse each other's opinion, emphasizing a shared outlook.[6]

There is, in other words, enormous diversity within early modern dialogue: in subject, tone, structure, style, and intent. What holds together this heterogeneous body of writing is the way it sets itself up as conversation.[7] Nonetheless, after an initial scene-setting, many dialogues abandon that conversational mode: turn-taking falls away and dominant characters hold sway, uninterrupted for pages on end. However, it is not simply that conversation recurrently makes way for oration (a more formal but still speech-based genre); dialogues are often based more firmly in literary than spoken practices. Take the opening sentence of Book 2 of *Utopia* (in Ralph Robinson's 1551 translation):

> The Ilande of Utopia, conteyneth in breadthe in the myddell part of it (for there it is brodest) CC. miles. Whiche bredthe continueth through the moste parte of the lande. Savyng that by lytle and lytle it commeth in, and waxeth narrower towardes

---

[2] Key cinquecento Italian theories of dialogue are: Carlo Signonio, *De dialogo liber* (1561); Lodovico Castelvetro, *'Poetica' d'Aristotele* (1567); Sperone Speroni, *Apologia dei Dialoghi* (1574); and Torquato Tasso, *Discorso dell'arte del dialogo* (1585). See Jon R. Snyder, *Writing the Scene of Speaking: Theories of Dialogue in the Late Italian Renaissance* (Stanford: Stanford University Press, 1989). The lack of explicit theorizing by English writers may explain why the English dialogue tradition has attracted less critical attention than its Italian counterpart.

[3] Roger Deakins, 'The Tudor Prose Dialogue: Genre and Anti-Genre', *Studies in English Literature*, 20 (1980): 5–23 (9).

[4] Thomas More, *A dyaloge of syr Thomas More, knyght* (1529); Walter Lynne, *A Watch-word for wilfull women* (1581); Robert Barret, *The Theorike and practike of moderne warres* (1598); Thomas Morley, *A plaine and easie introduction to practicall musicke* (1597).

[5] William Bullein, *The governement of healthe* (1558); [William Samuel?], [*The arte of angling*] (1577).

[6] John Coke, *The debate betwene the heraldes of Englande and Fraunce* (1550); [William Roy?], *A proper dyaloge betwene a gentillman and an husbandman* (?1529).

[7] For an attempt to recover early modern spoken interaction using a corpus of didactic dialogues, personal correspondence, trial proceedings, and plays, see Jonathan Culpeper and Merja Kytö, *Early Modern English Dialogues: Spoken Interaction as Writing* (Cambridge: Cambridge University Press, 2010).

both the endes. Whiche fetchynge about a circuite or compasse of .v c. myles, do fassion the hole Ilande lyke to the newe mone.[8]

There is little about this passage that indicates orality: there is no colloquial language, non-standard grammar, direct addresses to interlocutors, discourse markers (such as 'well'), or politeness formulae. Admittedly, textual scholarship on *Utopia* suggests that Book 2 was composed first, and afterwards transformed into a dialogue by the addition of Book 1 and the final coda.[9] Nevertheless, this example reminds us that the genesis of many of these texts—not just *Utopia*—is a written one and their later metamorphosis into an apparently more oral form is often only partial and incomplete. Thomas Smith's dialogue on spelling reform, *De recta et emendata anglicae scriptione* (1568), captures this process of transition: its preamble establishes a scenario in which a manuscript treatise, written twenty years previously, is read out and discussed with the interlocutor, transforming a handwritten artefact into a 'conversation' even as the work moves into print. Like *Utopia*, Smith's *De recta* is in Latin, an additional reminder of the bookishness of such enterprises. Scholars like Smith and More would have been able to communicate orally in Latin quite comfortably, but—even for them—it is not the language of everyday conversation; Robinson's translation of *Utopia* is even further removed from an oral world, not least because of his 'smale lerning', for which he apologizes in the 1556 edition (sig. A3^v).

The orality of many dialogues is thus, to some extent, a veneer. Some writers do attempt to capture individual voices, but it is debatable as to what degree this endeavour to individuate character is truly oral. William Baldwin's *Beware the Cat* is an instructive example (composed in 1552, printed in 1570). G.B.'s (Guilemus Baldwinus's) dedicatory epistle playfully boasts of the verisimilitude of the work, declaring that he has 'so neerly used bothe the order and woords of him that spake them, which is not the least vertue of a reporter, that [he] doubt[s] not but that he and Master willot shal in the reading think they hear Master Streamer speak, and he him self in the like action, shal dout whether he speaketh or readeth'.[10] Streamer's resulting verbal style is indeed distinctive, as his opening lines illustrate:

> Being lodged (as I thank him I have ben often), at a frends house of mine, which more rowmish within then garish without, standing at Saint Martins lane end, and hangeth partly upon the towne wall that is called Aldersgate, either of one Aldrich, or els of Elders, that is to say, auncient men of the Cittie which among them builded it, as Bishops did Bishopsgate, or els of eldern trees, whiche perchaunce as they doo in the gardins now there about. So while the common there was vacant: grew

---

[8] Thomas More, *A fruteful, and pleasaunt worke of the beste state of a publyque weale, and of the newe yle called Utopia*, trans. Ralph Robinson (1551), sig. G5^r. The first sentence is the first full grammatical unit, rather than the unit marked by Robinson's punctuation.

[9] J. H. Hexter, *More's Utopia: The Biography of an Idea* (Princeton: Princeton University Press, 1952).

[10] William Baldwin, [*A marvelous hystory intitulede, beware the cat*] (1584), sig. A3^r; quotations are from the 1584 edition because the 1570 edition is incomplete.

abundantly in the same place where the gate was after builded, and called therof Eldern gate, as Mooregate took the name of the feeld without it, which hath bene a very Moore. Or els because it is the most auncient gate of the Cittie, was therof in respect of the other, as Newgate called the eldergate [. . .] (sig. A5^v)

Streamer's musings on Aldersgate continue past this point; yet, for all their garrulity and pedantry, are Streamer's digressions really speech-like? Rather, they function as a learned joke, gently mocking the antiquarian sport of uncovering historical origins through etymological speculation, and help characterize Streamer as a narrator who is unable to distinguish between what is, and is not, significant, a failing which undermines his authority in the subsequent account. Moreover, as G.B. attempts to ventriloquize Streamer's verbal tics, we must remember that the conversation recorded is entirely and quite obviously imagined—a fantasy in which magic and medicine allow Streamer to understand the language of cats with the aid of pastilles (manufactured, in part, from cat turd) and some furry ear muffs: a pair of cats' ears, scalded of hair and fried in 'good' olive oil (we are assured of the quality). Of course Streamer will be unable to tell whether he is reading or speaking, because he is a fiction: both he and his speech only exist on paper, only exist to be read.

Baldwin's *Beware the Cat* might be an extreme example of the distance between prose dialogue and speech, but it is not an example that I have scoured the corpus to find. It is particularly striking that a dialogue which seemingly pays such careful (and rare) attention to voice should also be, on closer examination, so far removed from orality. There is, in other words, a gulf between the potential of the medium and the performance of it. This gap is not due to authorial incompetence. Anyone who has read Baldwin's works can testify to his artful self-consciousness; similarly writers like More or Thomas Smith. This begs the question which occupies the rest of this essay: if writers of dialogues are not necessarily or primarily concerned with replicating speech, why choose a medium that pretends (at least superficially) to do so?

In part, the answer lies with educational practices, such as the medieval use of catechism—question and answer—for religious instruction and teaching points of law,[11] and the increasing dominance of humanist education from the early decades of the sixteenth century. Humanist education raised schoolboys to admire and emulate writers of dialogues, such as Cicero; and, as we will see from examples in the body of this essay (which habitually address specific issues), English dialogue is much more akin to what C. S. Baldwin identifies as a Ciceronian 'exposition of something already determined' than to a Platonic 'quest' for enlightenment.[12] Following the advice of Cicero and other

---

[11] See, for example, *A dialogue between a doctor and his disciple, in which several passages of Holy Scripture are illustrated, and various points of Christian doctrine and practice explained*, BL Add MS 14,537 (7th–8th century); *Dialogue between Rogerius and Jurisprudentia on tit. xiv of lib. i of the Codex*, BL MS Royal 11.B.XIV (13th century).

[12] C. S. Baldwin, *Renaissance Literary Theory and Practice: Classicism in the Rhetoric and Poetic of Italy, France and England, 1400–1600*, ed. Donald L. Clark (New York: Columbia University Press, 1939), 43.

classical authorities, humanist education also trained students to argue *in utramque partem* (for and against) to explore issues and refine rhetorical skills, equipping and conditioning pupils to argue from different positions, an important facility for dialogue writing.

Yet the appeal of dialogue has to rest in more than its Ciceronian associations or status as a long-established mode of instruction. Plenty of other classical forms were adopted by the vernacular cultures of early modern Europe, but none with quite the same enthusiasm, variety, or quantity as dialogue.[13] What, then, is the attraction of this form? This essay addresses that question by focusing on political dialogues: dialogues which mull over a particular problem of state, or which (more abstractly) endeavour to analyse the best form of government. This subgroup has been chosen for the test case because of the iconic status given to oral communication in early modern political thought and culture. Focusing on one type also allows us to consider how the form adapted to the pressure of differing political circumstances, in particular the shift between the Elizabethan and Jacobean regimes.

It was a humanist commonplace, underpinning educational aims and practices, that eloquence (the art of persuasion) was an essential factor in the creation and maintenance of civil societies; this notion invested huge significance in the effective use of language. The Henrician humanist and statesman, Thomas Elyot, epitomizes this outlook, writing in 1531 that:

> noble autours do affirme/that in the firste infancie of the worlde/men wandring like beastes in woddes and on mountains/regardinge neither the religion due unto god/ nor the office pertaining unto man/ordred all thing by bodily strength: yntill Mercurius (as Plato supposeth) or some other man holpen by sapience & eloquence/ by some apt or propre oration assembled them togeder/& perswaded to them/what commodite was in mutual conversation & honest maners.[14]

Versions of this passage crop up again and again in the pages of sixteenth-century works of a humanist bent. Society, in other words, is built, and reliant, on language. In 1531, 'conversation' had not yet acquired its dominant modern meaning of 'talking with' (for which the first citation in the *Oxford English Dictionary* is Philip Sidney's *Arcadia*, c.1580). Rather, derived from the late Latin *conversare* (to dwell), the word at this point was more likely to mean 'The action of living or having one's being in a place or among persons', 'The action of consorting or having dealings with others; living together; commerce, intercourse, society, intimacy'.[15] Nonetheless, the fact that within no more than fifty years the word had evolved—so that co-habitation became synonymous with verbal communication—indicates its perceived importance as the critical factor which enables the founding and proper functioning of society; an earlier model for these overlapping senses was also provided by the word 'common' (to talk, share, associate, or eat

---

[13] See Baldwin, *Renaissance Literary Theory*, 42–3.
[14] Thomas Elyot, *The Boke named the Governour* (1531), fol. 48ʳ.
[15] 'conversation, *n.*', senses 1, 2, *OED* <http://dictionary.oed.com> accessed 18 March 2013.

together), multiple meanings which Thomas Starkey puts at the core of his *Dialogue between Pole and Lupset*, composed in the early 1530s, in which Lupset wishes to 'commyn & talke' with Pole to convince him to 'commyn such gyftys as be to [him] gyven', 'to the profyte of other'.[16]

Talking, being a social being: these concepts are closely intertwined. As George Pettie writes in *The civile conversation of M. Steeven Guazzo* (1581), which he was translating contemporaneously with Sidney's composition of *Arcadia*: 'the tongue serveth us to teache, to demaunde, to conferre, to trafficke, to counsaile, to correct, to dispute, to judge, and to express the affection of our heart: meanes whereby men come to love one another, and to linke themselves together'.[17] Here the twin meanings of 'conversation'—as dwelling among, and verbal interaction with, other people—are closely aligned: talking with others is exactly what the doctor, Annibal, understands by living with and alongside them; and it is through talking that Annibal manages to cure the melancholic outsider, 'Maister Guazzo' (the author's brother), and draw him back into society. Conversation (discussion) enables Guazzo's brother to be conversant (live) with others. In short, in *The civile conversation*, dialogue is efficacious in the extreme: the very process of talking achieves something, rehabilitating and reintegrating Guazzo, transforming him from an inactive person, of no use to the wider community, into a fully functioning member of society. Guazzo thinks that he is simply being told about the benefits of conversation, but he is actually experiencing them at the same time. In this case, talking is doing.

That same confidence in the effectiveness of dialogue can be found in a more obscure and politically targeted example: a manuscript dialogue featuring Historagraphus and Politicus, excerpted and translated from a French source, *Le Reveille-Matin des Francois, et de Leur Voisines* ('The wake-up call for the French and their neighbours'), printed in Geneva in 1574 with a false Edinburgh imprint, and probably written by the Huguenot refugee Nicholas Barnaud. The English extract focuses on the problem of Mary Queen of Scots, then captive in the north of England. The two interlocutors do not disagree that Mary poses a severe threat; both concur that her accession would cause 'the sudayn and fearfull destruction both of state and of religion'.[18] Where they differ is in their mode of argumentation. At the outset Politicus's speech is emotive; as he castigates Mary as 'this furie', 'this fatall Medea', 'this deadlie & mischevous Clytemnestra' (fos. 341^v–342^r), he recycles the type of gendered abuse underpinning much of the anti-Marian propaganda (found, for example, in ballads produced by the Scottish printer, Robert Lekpreuik, in the late 1560s).[19] To induce Politicus to abandon such insults and to adopt a more robust line of reasoning, based on legal and historical precedent, Historagraphus instigates an

---

[16] Thomas Starkey, *A Dialogue between Pole and Lupset*, ed. T. F. Mayer, *Camden Fourth Series*, 37 (1989), 1.

[17] George Pettie, trans., *The civile conversation of M. Steeven Guazzo* (1581), fol. 12^r.

[18] British Library MS Stowe 159, fol. 341^r.

[19] Cathy Shrank, '"This fatall Medea", "this Clytemnestra": Reading and the Detection of Mary Queen of Scots', *Huntington Library Quarterly*, 73 (2010): 523–41.

argument *in utramque partem*, where he 'as an Attorney to the Quene of Scottes will alledge every thinge that maie maintaine her innocencie or wipe awaye the crymes that are laide gainst her'; Politicus 'on the contrarie parte shall playe the accuser, that with like trustiness shall showe everye thinge which apperteyneth to the ouerthrowing of her wickednes and the saftie of the nacion' (fol. 343ʳ). As with Annibal in Guazzo's *Civile conversation*, the exchange with Historagraphus cures Politicus, purging him of his inflammatory rhetoric: in the French version, Historagraphus ultimately declares himself 'most satisfied' with his interlocutor's now 'grave and prudent speech' (the English extract ends just before this point).[20]

That Politicus instructs Historagraphus to relay 'the cheifest pointes of our disputations' to 'the peeres which you knowe' (fol. 351ʳ) is further indication of why dialogue had such ideological import. The dominant conception of the English polity in the sixteenth and early seventeenth centuries was that it was a 'mixed' constitution, whereby England was not purely a monarchy, but had ancient checks and balances—such as parliament and council—circumscribing the power of its sovereign and compensating for any shortcomings. As Thomas Smith wrote in 1549 in *A Discourse of the Commonweal*, 'that kinde of reasoning seems to me best for boultinge out of the truth, which is used by waye of Dialogues or colloquyes, where reasons were made too and froe, as well for the matter intended as against it'.[21] Or, as the author Thomas Norton put it during Elizabeth's reign: 'where manie men be, there must be manie myndes, and in consultacions convenient it is to have contrary opinions, contrary reasoninges and contradiccions, thereby the rather to wrest out the best'.[22] Yet, despite the onus put on debate and discussion (and the institutions of council and parliament where such debates should occur, to the benefit of the commonweal), what we recurrently find in English dialogues is not that happy marriage between talk and action seen in Pettie's translation of Guazzo or the Barnaud extract; instead, what we encounter is a sense of impasse, of words having little effect, a concern which can be traced to one of the first, and certainly the most important, political dialogues written by an Englishman: More's *Utopia* (1516).

Although originally composed in Latin, *Utopia* overshadows the later vernacular tradition. Over and over, Tudor writers pay homage to More's *Utopia*, through allusions or parody—be it the vision of Ireland as 'another *Eutopia*' in Thomas Smith's *A Letter sent by I.B. Gent.* (1572), or William Bullein's depiction in *A Dialogue against the Fever Pestilence* (1564) of the through-the-looking-glass land of Taerg Nattirb (Great Britain) and its capital, Nodnol, 'the best reformed Cittie of this worlde', an account placed in the

---

[20] 'Je suis tant satisfaict en ton discourse, grave & prudent', [Nicholas Barnaud], *Le Reveille-Matin des Francois, et de Leur Voisines* (1574), 49.

[21] Printed and ascribed to William Stafford in 1581 as *A compendious or briefe examination of certayne ordinary complaints of divers of our country men in these our dayes*, sig. A2ʳ. The work is also attributed to John Hales. For evidence of Smith's authorship, see Mary Dewar, 'The Authorship of the "Discourse of the Commonwealth"', *Economic History Review*, 2nd series, 19 (1966): 388–400.

[22] T. E. Hartley, ed., *Proceedings in the Parliaments of Elizabeth I, 1558–1581* (Leicester: Leicester University Press, 1981), 241.

mouth of Mendax (liar), a debased version of More's Hythloday, a teller of nonsense.[23] Even as they invoke *Utopia*, both these texts illustrate the tendency of many sixteenth-century political dialogues to be reactive, stimulated by a particular issue or set of circumstances.[24] Bullein's neverland is viewed through the prism of religious reformation and is almost entirely concerned with shaming readers into amending their ways. Smith's pamphlet, which amends 'no-place' (Utopia) to an attainable and desirable 'good place' (Eutopia), ripe for colonization, was printed as a means of recruiting volunteers for his projected plan to settle the Ards Peninsula.[25] Appended to the dialogue is 'The offer and order given forthe by Sir Thomas Smyth Knighte, and Thomas Smyth his sonne, unto suche as be willing to accompanie the sayd Thomas Smyth the sonne, in his voyage for the inhabiting some partes of the North of Irelande' (sig. G3^v); interested readers are further directed to view originals of the relevant documents, including letters patent, at Anthony Kitson's shop 'at the signe of the Sun' in St Paul's Churchyard, where the *Letter* is itself on sale (sig. H2^r).

The form and title of Smith's *Letter* also highlight a recurrent feature of many English dialogues: their existence within an epistolary framework, an often liminal space in which the dialogue blurs with the 'real' world. This facet owes much (again) to the influence of More's *Utopia*, where the prefatory epistle addresses the work to Peter Giles, one of the interlocutors of the text that follows, and requests his help with supplying some of the alleged lacunae in Hythloday's discourse. However, these epistolary frameworks are additional indication of the way in which these dialogic texts frequently highlight their own hybridity, as they gesture towards writing that sits on the boundaries of the oral: letter-writing in this period is habitually described as 'a mutual conversation between absent friends', a conversation which, like dialogue, is an artificial and literary one.[26]

If More's *Utopia* inspires some of the persistent motifs of subsequent English dialogues—such as epistolarity and metafiction—then it also sets up some of the key philosophical problems that reverberate throughout political dialogues of the sixteenth and early seventeenth centuries: namely, the effectiveness or not of communication and the problem of resolution. At the core of Book 1 of *Utopia* is the debate of counsel, about whether or not learned men should accept the role of royal counsellor and the degree to

---

[23] William Bullein, [*A dialogue both pleasant and piety-full, against the fever pestilence*] (1564), fol. 83^r. Note that this section does not appear in the other 1564 edition (STC2 4036.5); the edition cited here is STC2 4036.

[24] This impetus begins early in the English tradition and is certainly underway by the 1530s: witness texts like John Rastell's *New boke of Purgatory* (1530). For a persuasive reading of Thomas Elyot's *Pasquil the Playn* and Giles Du Wes's *Introductorie for to lerne to pronounce and speke Frenche trewly* as dialogues about the Henrician Reformation, see Greg Walker, 'Dialogue, Resistance and Accommodation: Conservative Literary Responses to the Henrician Reformation', in N. Scott Amos, Andrew Pettegree, and Henk van Niewp, eds., *The Education of a Christian Society* (Aldershot: Ashgate, 1999), 89–111.

[25] [Thomas Smith], *A letter sent by I.B. Gentleman* (1572), sig. E1^r.

[26] Desiderius Erasmus, *De conscribendis epistolis*, ed. and trans. Charles Fantazzi, *Collected Works of Erasmus* (Toronto: University of Toronto Press, 1985), vol. XXV, 20.

which, having done so, they should be prepared to compromise their ideals. Whereas Hythloday refuses to sully his hands with politics, for Morus, there is a time and place for offering advice, and holding back to preserve one's ideals is, potentially, much more damaging to the commonweal. Morus argues for 'an other philosophye more cyvyle, whyche knoweth as ye wolde saye her owne stage'; he admits that 'evell opynyons and noughty persuasions can not be utterly and quyte pluckede owte of their hartes', but insists that 'if you can not even as you wold remedye vyces, whiche use and custome hath confirmed: yet for this cause yow must not leave and forsake the commonwealth'. Instead, 'you must with a crafty wile & a subtell trayne studye and endevoure your selfe asmuch as in yow lyethe to handle the matter wyttelye and handsomelye for the purpose and that whyche yowe can not turne to good, so to ordre it that it be not very badde' (sig. F5ʳ). This crucial (and still pertinent) debate never reaches a conclusion: Hythloday asserts that it is pointless participating unless you have a polity receptive to rational reform and the discussion segues into a description of what Hythloday regards as the perfect state. No one has changed their minds; they have simply changed topic.

That sense of incompletion is also present at the end of the dialogue. Morus, the self-professed champion of compromise—the man who believes in fitting his words to audience and occasion—wants to challenge Hythloday about some of the Utopian customs he has lauded. However,

> bicause I knew that he was wery of talkinge, and was not sure whether he coulde abide that any thing shoulde be said againste hys minde: speciallye bicause I remembred that he had reprehended this fault in other which be, aferd least they shoulde seme not to be wise enough, onles they could find some fault in other mens inventions: therfore I praising both their institutions and his communication, toke him by the hand and led him into supper: saying that we wold chuse an other time to way and examine the same matters, and to talke with him more at lardge therin. (sig. S3ᵛ)

More as author signals the self-censorship (and even sycophancy?) practised by his alter-ego, as Morus tells Hythloday what he wants to hear, curtailing debate, partly through consideration for others, partly to save face.

Dialogue, though, is a form with two audiences: one figured within the text; one external to it. If we think back to the Historagraphus/Politicus piece, the choice of dialogue had additional efficacy, in that (to readers) it creates the impression that Mary has only been condemned after a fair hearing. In More's *Utopia*, debate might have collapsed within the work, but the questions left hanging as to which Utopian policies Morus would wish implemented in England can be seen as a prompt to further discussion, beyond the confines of the text. In some ways, the breakdown of dialogue within the text is necessary precisely to encourage conversation back in the 'real' world, conversation that will (ideally) lead to self-reflection and, perhaps, even action. Nonetheless, even as it does so, the work raises questions about the effectiveness of such debates, by featuring a protagonist (Hythloday) who is impervious to the arguments of others and who cows them into silence, and an interlocutor (Morus) who proves reluctant to rock the boat.

Certainly, it is the shutting down of dialogue that attracts Baldwin's attention in *Beware the Cat*, which can be read as an early response to the first English translation, printed the previous year in 1551.[27] Sixteenth-century readers would have been oblivious to the retrospective evolution of More's text into dialogue, and Streamer's verbosity and hostility to interruption produces a more exaggerated rendering of the way in which Hythloday's extended oration in Book 2 stifles dialogue. Streamer instructs his audience:

> If that I thought you could be content to hear me, and without any interruption til I have doon to mark what I say: I would tel you such a story of one peece of myne own experimenting, as should bothe make you wunder and put you out of dout concerning this matter, but this I promise you a fore if I doo tel it, that assoon as any man curiously interrupteth mee: I wil leave of & not speak one woord more. (sig. A5ʳ)

That Baldwin's fiction critiques Hythloday's attitude to dialogue indicates the significance invested in the ethos of conversation (which Hythloday is perceived to have breached). The conversations staged in *Beware the Cat* reveal little, beyond adulterous alliances and the widespread existence of superstitious practices. Their very triviality exposes a complacent society which has failed to root out the Catholic faith and in which a divine-like Streamer is not leading his flock as he ought, but frittering away his knowledge. The political bite of Baldwin's dialogue lies in its inconsequentiality; however, transpose its examination of the fault-lines in the dialogic process to more straightforwardly 'serious' works, then dialogue becomes a tool for interrogating assumptions about the power of eloquence and the mechanisms of debate and decision-taking which lie, as we have seen, at the heart of Tudor conceptions of successful governance. As Virginia Cox suggests, 'when any age adopts on a wide scale a form which so explicitly "stages" the act of communication, it is because that act has, for some reason, come to be perceived as problematic'.[28]

Failed persuasion haunts English dialogues, including those of More's immediate successors, Thomas Elyot and Thomas Starkey, whose works replay the dilemma of counsel: namely, how a good man should serve his monarch in a corrupt and corrupting system. Starkey's Pole, for example, sounds remarkably like More's Hythloday, as Lupset (like Morus and Giles) urges him to employ his learning and experience for his compatriots' benefit:

> I have much & many tymys marveyld, reasonyg with my self, why you mastur pole aftur so many yerys spent in quyet studys of letturys & lernyng, & aftur such experience of the manerys of man, taken in dyvers partyss beyond the see, have not before thys settylyd your selfe [...] applyd your mynd to the handelyng of the materys of the common wele. (1)

---

[27] Robert Maslen, 'William Baldwin and the Tudor Imagination', in Mike Pincombe and Cathy Shrank, eds., *The Oxford Handbook of Tudor Literature, 1485–1603* (Oxford: Oxford University Press, 2010), 291–306 (299–300, 305 n).

[28] Virginia Cox, *The Renaissance Dialogue: Literary Dialogue in its Social and Political Contexts, Castiglione to Galileo* (Cambridge: Cambridge University Press, 1992), 10.

At the end of the dialogue, we find Lupset still trying to convince his companion: his final speech insists that where 'sluggysh myndys lyve in cornarys & content themselfys with pryvate lyfe', 'veray nobul hartys ever desyre to governe & rule, to the commyn wele of the hole multytude' (143). Lupset's disappointment within the dialogue is underscored by Starkey's own seeming failure to reach a sympathetic readership. As T. F. Mayer argues, Starkey's initial target was his patron, Reginald Pole; by presenting a vision of what Pole could be, Starkey hoped to convince him to enter royal service.[29] Yet the fictional Pole proves no more tractable than the real-life Pole, who by the mid-1530s had become one of the highest profile opponents of Henry VIII's religious policy. At this point, Starkey appears to have redirected the text to Henry VIII, presumably hoping to find there a receptive audience for his analysis of the English commonweal and the problems it faced. He no more succeeded in that aim than he did in persuading Pole to sign up to the royal meal-ticket: the work exists in one copy, which bears no evidence (such as marginalia) of reading, besides Starkey's own emendations; nor are there any known allusions to Starkey's work and the often radical ideas it expounds (including the concept of an elective monarchy). Lupset's efforts at persuasion, Starkey's dialogue: both fall on deaf ears.

The limitations of counsel are similarly written in to the fabric of Elyot's *Pasquil the Playn* (1533), which reworks More's debate of counsel in a three-way conversation between the flattering Gnatho, the taciturn Harpocrates, who represents complicit silence (that is, standing by and letting bad things happen), and the bluntly spoken Pasquil, who refuses to compromise and adapt his language to suit the audience and occasion. The debate breaks into two parts: the first examines what is meant by opportune speech; the second explores the related topic of when a servant should break silence and warn his master of danger. Neither discussion is conclusive; none of the interlocutors alters their opinion one jot and the situation at the end of the dialogue is exactly the same as it was at the outset. Pasquil, despite his undoubted integrity, has not learned the value of tact and continues to be excluded from the circles of power (all his virtues thus going to waste); Gnatho and Harpocrates return to court, their consciences untouched by Pasquil's forthright arguments, confident that flattery and complicit silence are the way to preferment, as their success at court confirms.

Whilst such deadlock is a recurrent feature of early modern English dialogue (found, for example, in Elyot's other 1533 dialogue, *Of the knowledge which maketh a wise man*), it is far from a uniquely English motif. *A pleasant dialogue betweene the cap and the head* (1564) is an anonymous translation of Antoine Geuffroy's French version of Pandolfo Collenuccio's Italian *Dialogo tra la beretta e la testa* (1497). It is a satirical piece, critiquing worldly vanities and examining what constitutes true nobility. Curiously, the head is denied the faculty of reason with which it is habitually endowed; instead the cap is granted moral authority and the role of instructing the head. Like Elyot's Pasquil, the acerbic cap fails to reform his interlocutor; and, like Pasquil excluded from court, the

---

[29] T. F. Mayer, *Thomas Starkey and the Commonweal: Humanist Politics and the Religion of Henry VIII* (Cambridge: Cambridge University Press, 1989), 105.

cap's possibility of future influence is also shown to be negligible. Although the head acknowledges that the cap has 'spoken reason', its arguments are 'contrarye to the common opinion'.[30] Unwilling to risk being 'counted fantasticall' (sig. B5r), the head ends the dialogue deciding to purchase a new, less troublesome hat, which will allow him 'to frame [him] selfe according to the tyme and the company' (sig. B6v). The principles of compromise and tact debated in *Utopia* and *Pasquil* are here evoked not to try to oil the political machine and make things in a bad world a little better, but in order to justify the head's desire to blend in. There is, in other words, a debasement of a quality—decorum—that can be a political virtue, as Elyot himself indicates, writing in *The Governor* that 'thre thinges be required in the oration of a man havyng autoritie; that it be compendious/sententious/& delectable: havyng also respecte to the tyme whan/the place where/ and the persones to whom it is spoken' (sig. O2v).

As with *Utopia*, these instances of unsuccessful persuasion can be seen as anti-models: recalcitrant interlocutors are figured to provoke right-minded readers to further debate or even action (including self-correction) by depicting patterns of erroneous behaviour to eschew. Nonetheless, as we move through the century, it is possible to detect an increased cynicism about the ability of dialogue to change people's minds. Thomas Wilson's *Discourse upon Usury* is a pertinent example. Printed in 1572, after fruitless attempts in parliament to strengthen laws against usury, Wilson's text acknowledges its own futility. The characters within it are only converted from usury by a miracle, a sudden *volte-face* which the author immediately undercuts as he lays bare the artifice on which the work is founded:

> An easie matter it is, to tell a tale, or to make a tale of any man, or any matter eyther to or fro. [...] I have concluded of these men, as I woulde it were [...] and so al things after much talke are lapped up as you see. [...] What yf I sayde, that these merchauntes and lawyers, notwithstanding their solempne vowes, will not be so good, as they say they seme to have made promyse upon this last agreement? I thinke yf I layd a good round wager upon this matter [...] there be thousands in England, that woulde bee my halfe.[31]

Examples of this sense of stalemate abound, and yet some comfort can be found in the manner in which conversations are conducted. T.F.'s *Newes from the North* (1578), for instance, features an impasse between Piers Plowman (displaced from his agrarian lifestyle and bankrupted by the expense of the lawsuits he has foolishly pursued) and the innkeeper, Sim Certain, as they argue about whether the law and its officers are benevolent or malevolent. The debate never reaches a conclusion and fragments into a tale-telling competition, but the metropolitan author finds inspiration in the civility with which the company has handled the disagreement: if there is any solution to the exponential increase in litigation experienced in later Elizabethan England, then it is in the sort of neighbourly civility witnessed in Sim's Yorkshire hostelry.

---

[30] *A pleasaunt dialogue or disputation betweene the cap, and the head* (1564), sigs. B6r, B5r.
[31] Thomas Wilson, *A discourse uppon usurye* (1572), sig. 2D4r.

Dialogues might not reach a conclusion, that is, but it matters that issues are discussed and it matters how they are discussed. Under Elizabeth, dialogue accorded with the ethos of those at the centre of power, not least Elizabeth's chief minister, the Cambridge-educated William Cecil, whose own papers witness his tendency to think through issues dialogically, drawing up tables *pro* and *contra*. This was a generation of statesmen, including Smith and Wilson, who cut their political teeth during the reigns of two queens (Mary and Elizabeth) and an under-age boy (Edward VI). Dialogue represents on paper the sort of discussion and advice-giving that they regarded as essential to the proper functioning of a realm governed by women or children, whose rule (as Smith put it in 1565) is tolerable only because it is 'by common intendment understood, that such personages never doe lacke the counsell of such grave and discreete men as be able to supplie all other defecte'.[32] Certainly, many of the political dialogues of the 1570s and 1580s—those reacting to specific issues, be it the problem of Mary Queen of Scots, or the threat of the Spanish—show signs of Cecil's sponsorship and even authorship: Christopher Warner attributes to Cecil *A Packe of Spanish Lyes* (1588), in which propositions and their rebuttals are laid out in two columns, like Cecil's private memoranda.[33] Dialogue thus endorses both the policies of those at the heart of government and the ideology of counsel and debate to which they adhered. Further to that, by composing dialogues addressing affairs of state (often on topics which Elizabeth had declared off limits, such as foreign policy, her marriage, and Mary Queen of Scots) these writers-cum-statesmen represented as normative such debate and discussion.

The final part of this essay considers what happens to this dialogic culture once an adult male sovereign, James I, ascended to the throne, by examining Walter Ralegh's *Dialogue betweene a Counsellor of State and a Justice of the Peace*, written in the wake of the Addled Parliament of 1614, which was held during Ralegh's long incarceration in the Tower of London. There Ralegh would have had some opportunity to interact with his fellow prisoner John Hoskins, whose attack in the House of Commons on royal financial policy had provided the excuse for James's dissolution of parliament.[34] Ralegh's dialogue features a Justice of the Peace and a royal counsellor; the JP dominates, arguing that James should not be afraid of summoning parliament (an institution in which Ralegh sat as MP, three times during Elizabeth's reign). The dialogue was widely circulated in manuscript during Ralegh's lifetime and was printed posthumously, entitled *The Prerogative of Parliaments*, in 1628, 1640 and—as part of Ralegh's *Remains*—in 1661 and 1669 (all key dates in the history of relations between parliament and monarch). Much of the work is devoted to a reign-by-reign account of parliamentary taxation, a selective version of constitutional history in which parliament does not curb, but

---

[32] Thomas Smith, *De Republica Anglorum*, printed as *The common-welth of England* (1589), 28.

[33] John D. Staines, *The Tragic Histories of Mary Queen of Scots, 1560–1690* (Farnham: Ashgate, 2009), 27–39; Christopher Warner, 'Thomas More's *Utopia* and the Problem of Writing a Literary History of English Renaissance Dialogue', in Dorothea Heitsch and Jean-François Vallée, eds., *Printed Voices: The Renaissance Culture of Dialogue* (Toronto: University of Toronto Press, 2004), 63–76 (69).

[34] Wilfred Prest, 'Hoskins, John (1566–1638)', www.oxforddnb.com.

enables, monarchical power. Despite this undeniably dry topic and the work's reputation for tedium (it is dismissed as 'often quite boring' by Mark Nicholls and Penry Williams), it is nonetheless deserving of study for the light it can shed on both early modern political culture and the role of dialogue within that.[35]

Like many of its sixteenth-century counterparts, Ralegh's dialogue addresses a very particular political issue; yet as it does so, it belongs to, and expresses, a rather different political context, in which the very form that Ralegh adopts assumes an oppositional resonance. Ralegh does not write a monologic treatise defending parliament: he styles it as a dialogue, which—by including a JP—extends the debate beyond the organ of the royal council; as such, the form of the work enacts the conception of wider political participation which its support for parliament also epitomizes. That Ralegh's dialogue so obviously attacks the institution of the royal council is, moreover, a measure of just how far we are from the Cecilite dialogues of Elizabeth's reign, which lauded and endorsed the role of counsel/council. The abbreviated forms of the JP's title used through much of the dialogue (JUSTICE/JUST) imbue him with some of the virtue of that abstract, unimpeachable principle, in contrast to the counsellor, whose virtue is much less absolute or assured. Ralegh's dialogue thus erodes the integrity of the counsellor (and with him, all of James's council). Early on, for instance, the Justice hints that the counsellor and his peers resemble 'the late Duke of Alva', 'who was ever opposite to all resolutions in business of importance; for if the things enterprized succeeded wel, the advice never came into question: If ill [. . .] he then made his advantage by remembring his count[ra]ry councell.'[36] These suspicions are proven true towards the end of the dialogue, where the counsellor reveals that he does follow Alva's line, and is more concerned with covering his back than profiting the commonweal. Although the Justice has by now produced a convincing argument for summoning parliament, the counsellor prevaricates, admitting that 'notwithstanding wee dare not advise the king to call a parliament, for if it should succeed ill, we that advise, should fall into the kings disgrace' (62). This moral and political cowardice is then compounded by the counsellor's revelation, once again, that benefiting the commonweal takes secondary importance to the council's endeavours to protect its own status: 'you may well assure your selfe, that wee will never allow of any invention how profitable so ever, unlesse it proceed, or seeme to proceed from our selves' (63).

In its anxieties about the integrity of royal counsellors and in its sense of defeatism, Ralegh's dialogue shares much common ground with a work like Elyot's *Pasquil the Playn*. Like Pasquil, Elyot's honest but problematically outspoken interlocutor, the Justice is left impotent on the margins of power. As the counsellor pointedly reminds him, 'you [. . .] have no interest in [i.e. claim upon][37] the kings favour, nor perchance in his opinion' (64). He then proceeds to attempt to frighten the Justice into silence: 'Howsoever his Majesty may neglect your informations, you may be sure that others

---

[35] Mark Nicholls and Penry Williams, 'Ralegh, Sir Walter (1554–1618)', www.oxforddnb.com.
[36] Walter Ralegh, *The prerogative of parliaments in England* (1628), 2.
[37] 'interest, *n.*', sense 1, *OED* <http://dictionary.oed.com> accessed 18 March 2013.

(at whom you point) wil not neglect their revenges [...]. Remember Cardinall *Wolsey*, who lost all men for the Kings service, and when their malice (whom hee grieved) had out-lived the Kings affection, you know what became of him as well as I.' The Justice does not bow to the threat, but his final words are hardly a resounding assertion of purpose: 'Neither riches, nor honour, nor thankes [do I seek], but *I* only seeke to satisfie his Majestie (which *I* would have bin glad to have done in matters of more importance) *that I have liv'd, and will die an honest man*' (65). The desire to serve the king is expressed in an unrealized past tense ('*I* would have bin glad'). This parenthetical, conditional comment also disrupts the sentence, a disjunction in which the matter which the Justice wishes to communicate to his sovereign ('to satisfie' him of) has shifted from policy (what we would expect) to a statement of personal ethics (italicized in all the printed texts): '*that I have liv'd, and will die an honest man*', a juxtaposition of past and future tenses which squeezes out the possibility for present action. In every printed edition, the Justice's last words are followed by Ralegh's self-epitaph ('Even such is time'), which compounds the sense that this finale does indeed represent the end of any ambitions that the Justice might have had of influencing policy; he is left with nothing but the hope of making a good death.

In choosing to convey their ideas and opinions in a dialogue, early modern writers selected a form that had ideological resonances; it was a form which gestured towards the debate and verbal interaction that they believed should lie at the heart of successful governance and a healthy society: for many dialogues, the very solution lies in talking, be it curing Guazzo's brother in *The civile conversation*, or healing a fractious society in T.F.'s *Newes from the North*, which finds hope for a polity riven with legal disputes in the type of 'charitable' discourse achieved in an idealized Yorkshire inn. Nonetheless, despite the ideological freight placed on discussion as the best means of deciding policy, these texts frequently highlight their potential failure to convince or engage their projected audience. Repeatedly, these dialogues reach deadlock, or stutter into silence. They self-consciously stage failed communication: the interlocutor who cannot contribute to Thomas Smith's *Communicacon of the Quenes Highnes Mariage* (c.1561) because he has a profound stammer; and the usurious merchant in Wilson's *Discourse uppon Usurye* who falls asleep and misses most of the arguments aimed at his reformation.[38] Recurrently, there is a sense in which these texts are paper-Pasquils, railing from the margins, like Ralegh, imprisoned in the Tower of London, writing Pasquil-like from a position of no influence, and transformed in print into a martyr for the parliamentary cause. In such cases, failure—it seems—speaks louder than words. If, as we saw earlier, civil society rests on persuasive language, then a lurking awareness that language does not always persuade is a scab itching to be picked. It is this scab that early modern political dialogues worry at.

---

[38] Smith's *Communicacion* only exists in manuscript; BL Add MS 4,149, BL Add MS 48,047. For fuller discussions of dialogues by Wilson and Smith, see Cathy Shrank, *Writing the Reformation, 1530–1580* (Oxford: Oxford University Press, 2004), 155–65, 205–18; and Phil Withington, '"For This is True or els I Do Lye": Thomas Smith, William Bullein, and Mid-Tudor Dialogue', in Pincombe and Shrank, eds., *The Oxford Handbook of Tudor Literature*, 455–72.

Further Reading

Cox, Virginia. *The Renaissance Dialogue: Literary Dialogue in its Social and Political Contexts, Castiglione to Galileo* (Cambridge: Cambridge University Press, 1992).

Deakins, Roger. 'The Tudor Prose Dialogue: Genre and Anti-Genre', *Studies in English Literature*, 20 (1980): 5–23.

Heitsch, Dorothea, and Jean-François Vallée, eds. *Printed Voices: The Renaissance Culture of Dialogue* (Toronto: University of Toronto Press, 2004).

Richards, Jennifer. *Rhetoric and Courtliness in Early Modern Literature* (Cambridge: Cambridge University Press, 2003).

Shrank, Cathy. 'Disputing Purgatory in Henrician England: Dialogue and Religious Reform', in Andreas Höfele, Stefan Laqué, Enno Ruge, and Gabriela Schmidt, eds., *Representing Religious Pluralization in Early Modern Europe* (Berlin: Lit Verlag, 2007), 45–61.

—— '"This fatall Medea", "this Clytemnestra": Reading and the Detection of Mary Queen of Scots', *Huntington Library Quarterly*, 73 (2010): 523–41.

Walker, Greg. 'Dialogue, Resistance and Accommodation: Conservative Literary Responses to the Henrician Reformation', in N. Scott Amos, Andrew Pettegree, and Henk van Niewp, eds., *The Education of a Christian Society* (Aldershot: Ashgate, 1999), 89–111.

—— *Writing Under Tyranny* (Oxford: Oxford University Press, 2005), chapter 9.

Wilson, K. J. *Incomplete Fictions: The Formation of English Renaissance Dialogue* (Washington, DC: Catholic University of America Press, 1985).

Withington, Phil. '"For This is True or els I Do Lye": Thomas Smith, William Bullein, and Mid-Tudor Dialogue', in Mike Pincombe and Cathy Shrank, eds., *The Oxford Handbook of Tudor Literature, 1485–1603* (Oxford: Oxford University Press, 2009), 455–72.

CHAPTER 3

COMMONPLACING AND PROSE WRITING: WILLIAM BALDWIN AND ROBERT BURTON

JENNIFER RICHARDS

'[E]VERYBODY used them.'[1] So claimed Walter J. Ong, thinking of Renaissance commonplace books: collections of quotations 'culled from authors held to be authoritative' and organized under headings to facilitate their retrieval.[2] Their ubiquity will be clear to anyone who has trawled through the manuscript collections of research libraries. Some readers stored information in different 'collecting' books. Lady Margaret Hoby kept a commonplace book and a pocket notebook or 'table book'; she also recorded notes in her 'testament' or Bible.[3] Ready-made print collections of sayings were popular too.

The reason for their ubiquity is not hard to guess. Like electronic databases today, these books were useful; they helped Renaissance readers to cope with 'information overload'.[4] Large, scholarly commonplace books like the one compiled by the lawyer Julius Caesar, with its marginal instructions of '*vide*' or 'see' and accompanying page numbers, seem to anticipate the 'relational database that works as...hypertext'.[5]

Thanks to Mike Pincombe, Fred Schurink, and colleagues at the International Society for the History of Rhetoric, Bologna, 2011, for advice and guidance.

[1] Walter J. Ong, SJ, *Rhetoric, Romance, and Technology: Studies in the Interaction of Expression and Culture* (Ithaca: Cornell University Press, 1971), 60.

[2] Ann Moss, *Printed Commonplace-Books and the Structuring of Renaissance Thought* (Oxford: Clarendon Press, 1996), v.

[3] Lady Margaret Hoby, *The Private Life of an Elizabethan Lady: The Diary of Lady Margaret Hoby 1599–1605*, ed. Joanna Moody (Stroud: Sutton Publishing, 1998), xxxviii, xl.

[4] Ann Blair, 'Reading Strategies for Coping with Information Overload ca. 1500–1700', *Journal of the History of Ideas*, 64.1 (2003): 11–28.

[5] William H. Sherman, *Used Books: Marking Readers in Renaissance England* (Philadelphia: University of Pennsylvania Press, 2008), 148.

However, they also undoubtedly helped men and some women to find something to say, especially in written compositions; they are also, then, literary tools.

The origins of the commonplace book lie in the classroom. Desiderius Erasmus's print publications of 1512, his educational writings *De ratione studii* and *De copia*, represent 'something of a watershed' in the history of the commonplace book, Ann Moss argues, because they shift 'the emphasis from reading and memorizing' sayings, the purpose of medieval *florilegia*, 'to production'.[6] Commonplacing is the method Erasmus advocates to develop an abundant style (*copia*) on any topic in Latin, and his *De copia* is little more than a 'phrase-book', 'a resource for the expressive variation of any proposition'.[7] One hundred years later, the provincial schoolmaster John Brinsley advises in *Ludus Literarius* (1612) that schoolboys should not only keep a commonplace book to manage their reading, but also use Latin print collections so they have ready to hand 'the matter of the best Authors'. These books give readers a store of 'the choicest sayings of the very wisest of all ages' that they might plunder when composing 'themes' or preparing for disputation just 'as it is in Divinity, Law, Physick, and whatsoever Artes'.[8]

These methods carry over to English literary composition too, especially of prose.[9] If we want to understand English Renaissance prose and its most distinctive feature, its '[e]pisodic, loosely serial organization', Ong suggests, then we need to take note not only of its authors and genres, but also of this, its most basic building block: the commonplace.[10] 'It is easy to imagine how such a method [as commonplacing]', writes Sherman, 'might lie behind a text such as Sir Philip Sidney's *Apology for Poetry*' (c.1579). It 'would almost be possible', he proposes, 'to work in reverse and reconstruct entries in a commonplace book that Sidney no doubt created and used as preparation for his writing'.[11] The assumption is that Sidney wrote *Apology for Poetry* with his commonplace book to hand, writing to headings, lifting out suitable excerpts for inclusion. The same

---

[6] Moss, *Printed Commonplace-Books*, 102–3.

[7] Moss, *Printed Commonplace-Books*, 107. See Desiderius Erasmus, *Collected Works of Erasmus: Literary and Educational Writings 2, De Copia/De Ratione Studii*, trans. Betty I. Knott, ed. Craig R. Thomson (Toronto: University of Toronto Press, 1978), 638, 644. On the collection of sayings in sixteenth-century educational writings in England see Mary Thomas Crane, *Framing Authority: Sayings, Self, and Society in Sixteenth-Century England* (Princeton: Princeton University Press, 1993), esp. chap. 3.

[8] John Brinsley, *Ludus Literarius: or, The Grammar Schoole* (London, 1612), sig. 2B2ᵛ.

[9] Ong argues that the 'doctrine' of the places, though 'applied to poetry, too ... was developed mostly for prose use', *Rhetoric, Romance, and Technology*, 35. See also Peter Mack, *Elizabethan Rhetoric: Theory and Practice* (Cambridge: Cambridge University Press, 2002), 135–75. On the relationship between commonplacing and drama see: Paul Hammond, 'The Play of Quotation and Commonplace in *King Lear*', in Lynette Hunter, ed., *Toward a Definition of Topos: Approaches to Analogical Reasoning* (Basingstoke: Macmillan, 1991), 78–129; Peter Mack, 'Rhetoric, Ethics, and Reading in the Renaissance', *Renaissance Studies*, 19 (2005): 1–21; Neil Rhodes, *Shakespeare and the Origins of English* (Oxford: Oxford University Press, 2004).

[10] Ong, *Rhetoric, Romance, and Technology*, 38–41.

[11] Sherman, *Used Books*, 131.

assumption applies to other writers whose works appear little more than 'strategically assembled' sayings on different topics.[12] 'Disingenuous as ever', Michel de Montaigne may deny keeping notebooks, Moss writes, but his book of *Essais* is 'that most uncommon of commonplace-books'. Montaigne, she argues, transcribes quotations from his reading directly into them.[13]

This chapter takes up this very topic, arguing that the 'commonplace' is as foundational to the practice of early modern prose fiction as literary devices with a more familiar resonance: such as point of view, unreliable narrators, and heteroglossia. However, it is not the commonplace as 'building block' that interests me so much as its creative use to make the reader *think*, and thus what this tells us about the composition and reception of literary prose.[14]

We have come, with Moss, to value the commonplace as authoritative quotation, but as Terence Cave argued previously, Erasmus's *De copia* actually offers not 'static collections of materials' but 'a dynamic method' to achieve a copious style that is 'rooted in generative principles'; it encourages the transformation of sayings.[15] It is this use that interests me, and in particular how Latin *sententiae* are transformed in plain English. Thus, I take as my starting point not the ubiquitous and revered school text *De copia*, but William Baldwin's rushed, flawed, but very popular *A Treatise of Morall Phylosophie, contaynyng the sayinges of the wyse* (1547).[16] Flawed this work may be, but the liberties Baldwin takes with the ancient wise sayings he claims to have collected make this work an important contribution to our understanding of this rhetorical habit. Baldwin has no reverence for unmodernized antiquity; he freely adapted and reworked Greek sayings which he derived second- or even third-hand, often from English sources.[17] Baldwin does this both to give advice that is prosaic and indeed rather ordinary, but also to make the reader think about what is really wise.

More broadly, I will suggest, it is the loose citation and free adaptation of sayings 'from authors held to be authoritative' in English that paves the way for some of the most experimental and challenging prose writing, including by Baldwin himself. Thus, I am making a case for the importance of *vernacular* commonplacing. As Baldwin and my

---

[12] Ong, *Rhetoric, Romance, and Technology*, 77–8.
[13] Moss, *Printed Commonplace-Books*, 213.
[14] On this see especially Mack, 'Rhetoric, Ethics, and Reading', 17–18, 1.
[15] Terence Cave, *The Cornucopian Text: Problems of Writing in the French Renaissance* (Oxford: Oxford University Press, 1979, repr. 2002), 11.
[16] William Baldwin, *A Treatise of Morall Phylosophie, contaynyng the sayinges of the wyse* (London, 1547). All citations are to this edition unless otherwise stated. This book was first printed in 1547. Thereafter there were twenty-four editions by 1610, including Thomas Palfreyman's pirated edition. *Morall Phylosophie* was undoubtedly one of the most successful vernacular printed books in sixteenth-century England.
[17] On some of Baldwin's possible sources, Thomas Elyot's *The Boke named the Governour* and Antonio de Guevara's *The Golden Boke*, see Mack, *Elizabethan Rhetoric*, 165. See also the introduction to Baldwin, *A Treatise of Morall Philosophie by William Baldwin. Enlarged by Thomas Palfreyman. A Facsimile Reproduction of the Edition of 1620*, ed. Robert Hood Bowers (Gainesville, FL: Scholars Facsimiles and Reprints, 1967); Curt C. Bühler, 'A Survival from the Middle Ages: William Baldwin's Use of the *Dictes and Sayings*', *Speculum*, 23 (1948): 76–80; and D. T. Starnes, 'Sir Thomas Elyot and the "Sayings of the Philosophers"', *Texas University Studies in English*, 13 (1933): 5–35 (13–17).

second collector, discussed later in this chapter, the seventeenth-century divine, Robert Burton, understood, digesting the wise sayings of the ancients in plain English makes them 'ours' at the same time that it creates healthy citizens. It gives them a healthy dose of scepticism.

3.1 Commonplaces Englished: William Baldwin

The 'Ethicke' part of philosophy, writes William Baldwin, is 'the knowlege of preceptes of al honest maners, whiche reson acknowledgeth to belong and appertayne to mans nature' and which are 'necessary for the comly governance of mannes lyfe'. In his *A Treatise of Morall Phylosophie*, Baldwin gathers and provides English translations of selected precepts from a range of ancient philosophers, including Socrates, Plato, Aristotle, and Plutarch, organizing them according to the three ways in which he says this subject is usually taught: first, by counsels, laws, and precepts; secondly, by proverbs and adages; and thirdly, by parables, examples, and semblables (or analogies) (A3^{r-v}; A5^v–A6^r).

Nonetheless, despite Baldwin's ambition to share ancient wisdom with his compatriots and despite the popularity of this book, *Morall Phylosophie* may seem an unpromising starting point, not least because it is in 'English'. When Erasmus describes the benefits of commonplacing in *De copia* he is imagining a reader who aspires to speak Latin fluently, not 'his' native tongue. Moreover, as Ann Moss observes, most extant manuscript and print commonplace books collect 'Latin quotations' from authors who are 'regarded as exemplary in terms of linguistic usage and stylistic niceties'.[18] In this respect, Baldwin's *Morall Phylosophie* is one of the poor relations. The material in books like this one was 'often of much coarser stuff than the quality quotations from good authors on offer in the Latin commonplace-book'; Baldwin and other vernacular compilers aim only to give 'popular culture […] a certain veneer'.[19]

Moss's reservations are not unfounded: the sayings collected by Baldwin in *Morall Phylosophie* are made of coarser stuff, if we accept her conception of a commonplace as a 'quality quotation'. Baldwin appears to play fast and loose with the adaptation of ancient *sententiae*; he also quite shamelessly makes some of them up. Readers may be surprised to find the following quotations attributed to Socrates in Baldwin's second book:

> Neyther flatter, nor chyde thy wyfe before straungers.
> Be not proude in prosperitie, neyther disprayse in adversitie. […]
> Moderate thy lustes, thy tongue, and thy belly. (L5^r)

---

[18] Moss, *Printed Commonplace-Books*, v.
[19] Moss, *Printed Commonplace-Books*, 207–8.

One would be hard-pushed to ascribe these absolutely to Socrates. After all, Socrates was not given to moral pronouncements and he left behind no written record of his teachings. Indeed, at the end of this book Baldwin pauses to acknowledge that some readers will 'muse why I haue attributed so many sentences to Socrates, whiche they perhaps knowe to have be[en] wrytten of other men' (M5^v). Then he offers this disarming excuse: he has followed the proverb 'Doubtefull thynges ought to be interpreted to the best'. And then adds: 'suche thinges as I have founde wrytten, without certaynty of any certayne authour, I have ascrybed unto hym, not onelye because they be thynges meete for hym to speake, but because they be wrytten by some of his scholers, which learned them of hym'. More provocatively, Baldwin confesses that he hoped 'the authoritie of the speaker, myght cause the matter to be more regarded' (M5^v–6^r).

We might also be puzzled by Baldwin's account of the usefulness of the analogies that he has drawn from Erasmus's *Parabolae* (1514) in the fourth book of this treatise. There is no reason to explain in detail how they might be used, he explains, 'seyng theyr owne playnnesse declare theym so plainly, as no man maye do it playnlyer'. As proof he offers an example in his preface of one analogy taken from Erasmus's letter to Pieter Gilles in *Parabolae*:

> Lyke as Humlocke [hemlock] is poyson to man, so is wyne poyson to Humlocke.
> What declaracion neadeth this nowe, to be better understanded, except a man phisicallye shoulde shewe the properties of wyne and Humlockes? Nowe as for the use of this in perswasion, it may be thus applyed.
> Lyke as Humlocke is poyson to man, and wyne poyson to Humlocke: So is Flattery poyson to frendship, and license to be flattered, poyson unto flattery.
> Loe here the exaumple that Erasmus useth, wherin is contayned great councel, great wyt, and great learnyng. Fyrste it teacheth that Humlocke is poyson, & mortall whan it is myngled with wyne ... Then counsayleth he to beware of flatterye, and in shewyng what maketh flattery deadly poyson, he teacheth a remedy howe to avoyde flattery. For yf we regard not a flatterer, nor geve hym lice[n]ce to flatter us, we shall never be hurte by flatterye. (Q2^v–3^r)

Yet, this is hardly plain. To begin with, Baldwin's suggestion that 'license to be flattered' is 'poyson unto flattery' does not make sense, unless he means that if one is open to being flattered then it is no longer 'flattery'. But *if* this is what he means, it is contradicted a few lines later when he argues that 'yf we regard not a flatterer, nor geve hym lice[n]ce to flatter us, we shall never be hurte by flatterye'.

Part of the problem is that Baldwin seems to have misunderstood his source. Erasmus takes this example from the essay of the moral philosopher Plutarch, 'How to Tell a Flatterer from a Friend', to illustrate a rather different point in his letter to Pieter Gilles, that the analogies on show in *Parabolae* are 'precious stones' drawn 'from the inner treasure-house of the Muses'; the point in using them is to win 'double praise'.[20] In Plutarch's essay, the wine–hemlock analogy is used to explain a particular conundrum,

---

[20] Erasmus, *Parallels/Parabolae sive similia*, trans. R. A. B. Mynors. In *Collected Works of Erasmus*, ed. Craig R. Thompson (Toronto: University of Toronto Press, 1978), 131.

that *parrhesia*, bold or frank speech, ostensibly the opposite of flattery, can in fact be used to flatter. Flatterers, Plutarch recognizes, 'also use a certain kind of plain and free speech [*parrhesian*].'[21] (The example he gives is Antony's admonishment by his friends for his hard-hearted treatment of his smitten mistress, Cleopatra. As Plutarch observes, this chiding was in fact pleasing to Antony; it confirmed Cleopatra's love for him and so served further to debauch him.) Erasmus explains this analogy thus: flattery is likened to a poison, hemlock; frank speech is likened to its antidote, wine; *but* the dangerous blending of wine and hemlock is likened to the deadliest of all poisons, i.e. flattery dressed up as frank speech. Here is Erasmus's account of it in a modern translation:

> Hemlock is poisonous to man, and wine neutralises hemlock; but if you put an admixture of wine into your hemlock, you make its venom much more immediate and quite beyond treatment, because the force and energy of the wine carries the effect of the poison more rapidly to the vital centres. Now merely to know such a rare fact in nature is surely both elegant and interesting as information. Suppose then one were to adapt this by saying that adulation poisons friendship instantly, and that what neutralises that poison is the habit of speaking one's mind, which Greek calls *parrhesia*, outspokenness. Now, if you first contaminate this freedom of speech and put a touch of it into your adulation, so that you are flattering your friend most insidiously while you most give the impression of perfect frankness, the damage is by now incurable.[22]

Baldwin seems to be struggling to understand a crucial sentence in Erasmus's original text: 'verum ei rursum veneno venenum esse libertatem admonendi, quam Graeci vocant παρρησια' ('what neutralises that poison is the habit of speaking one's mind, which Greek calls *parrhesia*, outspokenness').[23] He mistranslates *libertatem admonendi*, literally the liberty of admonishing (a gerund)—that is, *parrhesia* in Greek; *licentia* in Latin—as 'license to be flattered' (a gerundive) and in so doing, he appears to miss the main point of Erasmus's analogy *and* of Plutarch's essay, that flattery can be poisonous *and* difficult to detect.

And yet, it is surely odd that Baldwin should make such a mess of the hemlock and wine analogy. Baldwin, who probably never went to university, was nonetheless a reasonable Latinist: he translated the anti-papal satire *Epistola de morte Pauli tertii* ('A letter on the death of Paul III') as *Wonderful News* (c.1552).[24] It is odd, moreover, that he should

---

[21] Plutarch, *The Philosophie, commonlie called, the Morals*, trans. Philemon Holland (London: Dent, 1911), 43; cited in David Colclough, 'Parrhesia: The Rhetoric of Free Speech in Early Modern England', *Rhetorica*, 17 (1999): 177–212 (191).

[22] Erasmus, *Parallels*, 131–4. For discussion of this analogy see Colclough, 'Parrhesia', 190–4.

[23] Erasmus, *Parabolae, sive similtudines* (London, 1587), sig. A3ʳ.

[24] John N. King notes that 'Anthony à Wood's claim that [Baldwin] supplicated for the M.A. degree from Oxford University carries no authority', *English Reformation Literature: The Tudor Origins of the Protestant Tradition* (Princeton: Princeton University Press, 1982), 359. For recent discussions of *Wonderful News* see Mike Pincombe, 'Truth, Lies, and Fiction in William Baldwin's *Wonderful News of the Death of Paul III*', *Reformation*, 15 (2010): 3–22; also Anne Overell and Scott C. Lucas, 'Whose Wonderful News? Italian Satire and William Baldwin's *Wonderfull Newes of the Death of Paule the III*', *Renaissance Studies*, 26.2 (2012): 180–96.

try to conceal the difficulties he has with this analogy by emphasizing its plainness: 'seyng theyr owne playnnesse declare theym so plainly, as no man maye do it playnlyer'. Unless of course the intention is to reveal a problem: that the analogy is overly elaborate. In fact, in contrast to Plutarch and Erasmus, Baldwin offers a very simple 'remedy' for dealing with flatterers whatever shape they come in: just ignore them.

It is equally likely, of course, that Baldwin, working in Edward Whitchurch's print shop at the time that he brought this work to completion, has just been careless and hasty. Yet, even if that is true we might *still* want to ask whether his inaccuracies actually matter. Arguably, we will always suppose that Baldwin is only offering 'coarser stuff' if we assume that the purpose of the commonplace book is to offer 'quality quotations' from recognized ancient authorities that can be lifted and reused. To be sure, this is not a presumptuous assumption. For many vernacular compilers this was their purpose. As Francis Meres, the compiler of *Witt's Academy: A Treasurie of Goulden Sentences, Similes and Examples* (1598, 1634, 1636), argues in his preface: 'he that would write or speake pithily, perspicuously and persuasively must use to have at hand in readiness ... Sentences, Similitudes and Examples'.[25] Later editions of *Morall Phylosophie*, notably Thomas Palfreyman's pirated edition (c.1555), turn it into just this kind of resource. Palfreyman expands Baldwin's four books into seven, adds more sentences of his own, mainly from the Bible, but also places the 'precepts, counsailes, parables & semblables' that he says he 'found dysplaced' in Baldwin 'in the right chapter', so that 'man wold familiarly tell a tale' of them.[26]

However, this was not the only use of the commonplace book. Recently, the utilitarian account of commonplacing has been challenged by historians of reading whose studies of manuscript collections emphasize the 'variety of readers'. Commonplacers may be collecting quotations for reuse in their own speech or writing, some of which may be politically directed, though not all; they might also be collecting literary passages for 'recreation'; or they may do all of these things.[27] Baldwin, I would like to suggest, is different yet again: he urges his readers to think about so-called 'wise' sayings in order to make them wise.

The wine–hemlock analogy is only one possible piece of evidence for Baldwin's attempt to alert the reader to problems of interpretation and even then it needs to be

---

[25] Francis Meres, *Witt's Academy: A Treasurie of Goulden Sentences, Similes and Examples* (London, 1636), sig. A2ᵛ.

[26] I am quoting from Thomas Palfreyman, *A Treatyce of Morall Philosophy* (London, 1557), sig. A4ᵛ. On Baldwin and Palfreyman see R. W. Maslen, 'William Baldwin and the Politics of Pseudo-Philosophy in Tudor Prose Fiction', *Studies in Philology*, 97 (2000): 29–60 (33–5). Baldwin objected to Palfreyman's reorganization of his work; see the preface to *The Tretise of Morall Phylosophy ... Newly perused, and augmented by William Baldwyn* (London, 1556). For a quick summary of Palfreyman's changes across several editions see Jill Kraye's entry on Thomas Palfreyman in the *Oxford Dictionary of National Biography* (*ODNB*) <http://www.oxforddnb.com> accessed 2 August 2011.

[27] Heidi Brayman Hackel, *Reading Material in Early Modern England: Print, Gender, Literacy* (Cambridge: Cambridge University Press, 2005), 142–9, 175–95; Fred Schurink, 'Manuscript Commonplace Books, Literature and Reading in Early Modern England', *Huntington Library Quarterly*, 73 (2010): 453–69, esp. 453–7.

used with caution. But his concern with the thoughtful use of sayings is signalled unmistakably in the preface to *Morall Phylosophie* and once again it rests on adaptation and reinterpretation rather than exact reuse. It cannot be an accident that the first sentence of 'The Prologue to the Reader' is also adapted from Erasmus: on this occasion, an anecdote the latter drew from Plutarch's life of Pericles and cited in his *Apophthegmata* (translated by Richard Taverner in *The Garden of Wisdom* (1539)).[28] As Baldwin relates, Pericles persuades the governor of his ship to sail against the Peloponnesus in spite of his fear of a solar eclipse. By covering the governor's eyes with a cloak, Pericles is able to convince him that an event which appears to be an ill omen is a natural occurrence. At least, this is the point of the anecdote as told by Erasmus. However, Baldwin's use of it is different. Unlike Erasmus, Baldwin remains true to Plutarch's history by affirming that Pericles's navy *was* destroyed. Pericles dismisses 'a good admonicion sent [...] by god' and so sends his sailors to their deaths. Baldwin's example is instructive in other ways that Erasmus does not note:

> In lyke maner there be manye nowe a dayes, which as Pericles despysed Astronomye, despyse all other sciences: devysyng proper toyes (as he dyd) to dasshe them out of countenaunce, runnyng headlyng through Ignoraunce, into contempt of all good learnyng: Not only inventyng tryfelyng toyes, but also wrestyng the holy scriptures whiche they understand not to serve for their pyvish [peevish] purpose. For yf it chaunce them to be improued with any of the good sayinges of the auncient philosophers, which so playnly impugneth theyr vices, that they be unable by good reason to refell it, than on goeth the brasen face, and a cloke must be sought oute of Scrypture eyther to deface all Phylosophye, or els to blynde mens eyes withall (A4^v).

In Baldwin's hands, this anecdote becomes, firstly, a warning to those who condemn all good learning and, secondly, an admonition to those who manipulate the 'holy scriptures' to serve their turn, mainly because they feel rebuked by the advice they find in ancient moral philosophy. For Baldwin, the 'cloke' is a metaphor, not for superstition, but for the obscuring of pagan advice.

Most obviously, this observation underpins Baldwin's purpose in his treatise, which is not just to offer pagan precepts that advise on governance in the broadest sense, but to recover and defend their value against those who use scripture as a 'cloke'. He goes out of his way to emphasize that ancient moral philosophy is compatible with the Bible. In the first book he emphasizes that God is the origin of wisdom (*sophia*) and then traces, albeit quickly, the history of philosophy from the sons of Seth to Pythagoras and beyond. In the second book he begins by listing the precepts of Greek philosophers that reflect on 'God' and the 'soul', so that readers might 'understand what [they] thought' (I2^v).

But there is more too. The source that Baldwin cites for this approach is St Augustine. In book II of *De doctrina Christiana*, Baldwin notes, Augustine argues that if 'they

---

[28] I am grateful to Mike Pincombe for this example. See Richard Taverner, *The Garden of Wisdom* (London, 1539), E5^v–E6^r.

whiche be called Phylosophers, specially of Plato his secte, have spoken ought that is true, and appertinent to our faythe, we ought not onely not to feare it, but also to chalenge it as our owne, from them whiche are no ryght owners therof' (A5ʳ). This again is an interesting adaptation. In fact, in book II of *De doctrina Christiana* Augustine identifies the Bible as the source of wisdom, not Plato and his sect, whose moral insights, he argues, derive from the early Christians. To claim otherwise is 'a quite crazy idea [*quod dementissimum est credere*]'.[29] But at the start of his preface Baldwin is worrying instead that scripture is used to obscure the wise advice of ancient philosophers. Then he invites the reader, *pace* Augustine, to 'chalenge' the precepts of the moral philosophers 'as our owne'. For Baldwin, wisdom already belongs to us. Making wisdom 'our owne' means thinking about, adapting, and using precepts, and he shows us how. Baldwin's precepts may be made of 'coarser stuff' or, as he puts it himself, 'simply & rudely declared' rather than 'reasoned to the tryall' (A3ᵛ). But that makes them *good*. Here is the final warning he gives the reader, again adapting Augustine's *De doctrina Christiana*:

> I humblye beseche the[e] (most gentle Reader) to take in good part this simple philosophycal treatyse, & so to use it as sainct Augustine hath taught us, takyng the good, and leavyng the bad, neyther reverencying it as the gospel, neyther yet despysing it as a thing of no value. (A6ᵛ)

What matters for Baldwin is that the counsels of *Morall Phylosophie* should be used carefully and thoughtfully. Not all sayings, Baldwin implies, are equally good. One needs to sift the wheat from the chaff and it is the reader's judgement, not an authoritative original, that is the touchstone for this work's wise use.

3.2 Baldwin's *Beware the Cat*

Baldwin's *Morall Phylosophie* may disappoint scholars who have little time for vernacular impostors. Yet, many of its inaccuracies or infelicities make good sense. Most refreshing, though, is the trust Baldwin places in the reader's judgement and in relation to this his warning not to treat all sayings with reverence. We do not need to rely on Baldwin's preface to his commonplace book to see how seriously he valued the judging of supposedly wise counsel. It also structures, in a different way, the experience of reading his prose fiction too, notably *Beware the Cat* (1561; 1570; ms 1553).[30] *Beware the Cat* was no doubt written with the help of a commonplace book, but it is also best read, I would now like to argue, with Baldwin's directions in his treatise in mind.

---

[29] Augustine, *De Doctrina Christiana*, ed. and trans. R. P. H. Green (Oxford: Clarendon Press, 1995), II. 107–8.

[30] On the reworking of some of Baldwin's advice in prose writing later in the century, notably Lyly's *Euphues*, see Mack, *Elizabethan Rhetoric*, 166–7.

This curious work, arguably 'the first original piece of long prose fiction in English',[31] is a first-person narration, organized as three orations; it relates the adventures of the fictional Gregory Streamer. In the first oration, Streamer recounts how he was kept awake at night by the mewing of rooftop cats and he recalls the conversation he had the next day at the fireside with fellow lodgers. Following his complaint, Streamer explains that 'we fell in communication of cats' and that some in that company insisted that cats 'had understanding' (11). The first proof of this bizarre claim is the strange story told of Grimalkin, an Irish cat who ate a whole man (and much else), and the loyalty of a 'kitling' who fatally wounded her owner when she heard that he had killed Grimalkin with a dart. To prove that cats really do have reason, Streamer then concocts and consumes a magical-medical potion that will purge his ears of excess humours so he can understand cat-talk. The second and third orations explain the recipe and recall his adventures. With his ears purged, Streamer gains insight into the strange laws of cats: 'our holy law ... forbiddeth us females to refuse any males not exceeding the number of ten in a night' (47). More to the point, he also gains insight into the secrets of men and women.

On this description, *Beware the Cat* will seem a long way from the more sober *Morall Phylosophie*. In fact, both works share a concern with how wisdom is used. Its title, for instance, is another 'made-up proverb'.[32] Baldwin's instructs the reader in his dedicatory epistle to 'learn to Beware the Cat' (4), and in his moral conclusion he offers some guidance: he advises the reader to 'mind this proverb, *Beware the Cat*; not to tie up thy cat till thou have done, but to see that neither thine own nor the Devil's cat (which cannot be tied up) find anything therein whereof to accuse thee to thy shame' (54–5). As John N. King explains, the 'special meaning' Baldwin 'attaches to the phrase treats the cat as a figure for Protestant conscience'.[33] Quite simply, cats can see and talk about our secrets. However, this is not the only lesson this remarkable fiction teaches. It also establishes the importance of thinking about advice.

Beware the Cat is often interpreted as an anti-Catholic satire, as the world of the Catholics is revealed: the cats discover the secret lives of recusants. Even the absurd stories of this work seem to support this argument. As this text's modern editors, William A. Ringler and Michael Flachmann suggest, the 'general thrust' of its 'fictional argument' is that 'only a person gullible enough to believe a character as outrageous as Gregory Streamer would believe in the "unwritten verities" handed down by the "traditions" of the Church'.[34] Indeed, anti-Catholicism plays heavily in this fiction. Yet, it is also concerned more broadly with gullibility, including of those who believe too readily in anti-papist slurs, and in the authority of disciplines like medicine. To establish this Baldwin pays attention to the nonsensical use of proverbs and analogies.

---

[31] William Baldwin, *Beware the Cat: The First English Novel*, ed. and intro. William A. Ringler, Jr. and Michael Flachmann (San Marino, CA: Huntington Library, 1988), xxi.

[32] King, *English Reformation Literature*, 388.

[33] King, *English Reformation Literature*, 388.

[34] Baldwin, *Beware the Cat*, xxv. Robert Maslen suggests there is a close link between Baldwin's treatise and the anonymous *Image of Idlenesse*, and persuasively argues that Baldwin is the likely author of the *Image*, see Maslen, 'William Baldwin'.

This fiction is full of proverbs and sayings, supposedly wise counsel. Sometimes proverbs are cited by a character to 'prove' a particularly wild claim. One 'well-learned man and one of excellent judgment', Streamer recounts, supports the case that cats are reasonable by advising that Grimalkin was likely 'a hagat or a witch'. Many witches have taken on the likeness of a cat, he adds, offering as proof of this 'the proverb, as true as common, that a cat hath nine lives (that is to say, a witch may take on her a cat's body nine time)' (16). Yet, this proverb, like the story of Grimalkin, is no 'proof' at all; and, moreover, this interlocutor is clearly rather free in his interpretation of it.

There are many other examples which show that good judgement is lacking. During the same conversation another of the fireside companions notes that Grimalkin is esteemed in much the same way as the 'master' (i.e. queen) bee, 'at whose commandment all bees are obedient'. He then offers a second, more elaborate analogy: 'or as the Pope hath had ere this over all Christendom, in whose cause all his clergy would not only scratch and bite, but kill and burn to powder ... whomsoever they thought to think but once against him—which Pope, all things considered, devoureth more at every meal than Grimalkin did at her last supper'. Is this evidence of the work's anti-Catholic stance? This elaborate analogy is diffused by a literal-minded Streamer who argues that, on the contrary, the Pope 'eateth and weareth as little as any other man'; he then introduces yet another saying that provides a different perspective, commending the Pope's easily misunderstood virtue, his liberality:

> And I have heard a very proper saying in this behalf of King Henry VII: When a servant of his told him what abundance of meat he had seen at an abbot's table, he reported him to be a great glutton; he asked if the abbot eat up all, and when he answered no, but his guests did eat the most part, 'Ah', quod the king, 'thou callest him glutton for his liberality to feed thee and such other unthankful churls'. (15)

Streamer is a distinctly unreliable narrator and he is certainly naïve enough to 'believe in the "unwritten verities" handed down by the "traditions" of the Church'. Yet, it is not clear that anti-Catholic satire is Baldwin's only purpose, for the attacks are not entirely rational either. Just like the interlocutor who offers a rather unexpected analogy—that Grimalkin is like the master bee *or* a cruel, greedy pope—so the printer, or author ('Baldwin'), provides some surprising commentary in the margins that both reveals his anti-popery with asides such as 'Railing and slandering are the Papists' Scriptures' (38), but also his credulousness. For example, on the same page we find: 'No such persuasions as miracles chiefly in helping one from grief' (38). On another page the marginalium states 'Cat's grease is good for the gout' next to Streamer's clear admission that he has tricked 'Thomas': 'after I had taken some of the grease ... to make (as I made him believe) a medicine for the gout' (27).

More broadly, this fiction teaches us by bad example how important it is to be careful and alert. As these last examples suggest, one of the ways in which Baldwin does this is by sending up the kind of reader who is eager to find some useful snippet of information or wise saying from a text, regardless of its meaning or context. The fictional Streamer is introduced to us as a medical authority; he is a divine and also a translator of an Arabic medical treatise, *Cure of the Great Plague* (3). But the weird potions he creates are clearly one of the jokes of this fiction. Streamer pounds and cooks various bits of animals—hare, fox, cat, and hedgehog (or 'urchin')—creating what 'Baldwin' calls in the margin 'The intelligible diet' (28). After its consumption, his nose oozes a pint of 'such yellow, white, and tawny matters as I never saw before' (28). He then makes pellets out of the ears and tongues of these animals and, he narrates, 'I fried [them] in good olive oil and laid them hot to mine ears [...] and kept them thereto till nine o' clock at night, which holp exceedingly to comfort my understanding power' (29). Aside from the ridiculous image of this learned man with pellets of disgusting gunk in his ears, we also have 'Baldwin's' absurd effort to make sense of it: 'A good medicine for aching ears' (29). And when Streamer reheats these 'pillows', lays them to his ears, ties 'a kercher about my head', and then goes among the servants 'with my lozenges and trochisks in a box', the author solemnly notes: 'Heat augmenteth the virtue of outward plasters.' There is another response detailed in the text and we would do well to keep it in mind. A shrewd servant tastes one of Streamer's lozenges, 'chewed it apace, by means whereof when the fume ascended he began to spattle and spit, saying "By God's bones, it is a cat's turd"' (30).

3.3 Taking Liberties: Robert Burton's *Anatomy*

Commonplace books, I explained at the start of this chapter, quoting Ann Moss, are collections of quotations 'culled from authors held to be authoritative' and organized under headings to facilitate their retrieval. This now-familiar definition has shaped the way in which these collections have been valued by historians of reading and it also reinforces the conception of the purpose of humanist education as career-orientated and pragmatic. William Drake's commonplace book, argues Kevin Sharpe, discovers a resolutely utilitarian reader and political operator. 'All social relationships', writes Sharpe, like the books that Drake avidly digested, 'were pursued for gain.'[35] Historians like Sharpe have provided an alternative approach to those literary scholars who worried that commonplacing created, not savvy politicians, but unthinking subjects. Thomas Greene's observation that the notebook method could not 'produce sensitive understanding and creative imitation' is echoed by Mary Crane: 'English theorists in the sixteenth century wanted to believe that the commonplace book led to assimilation and understanding', she argues, but 'they were unable to describe how this actually worked.'[36]

---

[35] Kevin Sharpe, *Reading Revolutions: The Politics of Reading in Early Modern England* (New Haven: Yale University Press, 2000), 84–5, 99. See also Sharpe, 'Uncommonplaces? Sir William Drake's Reading Notes', in Sabrina Alcorn Baron, ed., *The Reader Revealed* (Seattle and London: University of Washington Press, 2001), 59–65.

[36] Thomas Greene, *The Light in Troy: Imitation and Discovery in Renaissance Poetry* (New Haven: Yale University Press, 1982), 318, n. 1, cited in Crane, *Framing Authority*, 61. See also Fred Schurink's study of one schoolboy's pedestrian use of Thomas of Ireland's *Manipulus florum* in 'An Elizabethan Grammar School Exercise Book', *Bodleian Library Record*, 18.2 (2003): 174–96 (182–3).

However, this chapter takes note of yet another use of print commonplace books, one which understands that collected quotations are not really authoritative and that users of them are often encouraged to think about them, to challenge and rework them. The recognition of this structures so much literary prose fiction and drama.[37] Thus, I value all that seems coarse or poor about the contents of *Morall Phylosophie*: the insinuation that Baldwin is making things up as he goes along, for example, when he ascribes quotations to Socrates simply 'because they be thynges meete for hym to speake' and also his advice to the reader to take 'the good' and leave 'the bad', 'neyther reverencying it as the gospel, neyther yet despysing it as a thing of no value'.

Baldwin may be idiosyncratic, but he is not exceptional, and I want to conclude with some examples that make this clear. Many compilers explicitly encourage the absorption *and* transformation of the advice they collect, not least by using the same corporeal metaphor to represent this process: digestion. To 'digest' a book means primarily 'to divide and dispose' and 'distribute' its contents (*OED* 3). Thus, a well-organized commonplace book, Michael Schoenfeldt observes, is 'a very literal form of a reader's digest'.[38] However, the metaphor of 'digestion' carries another meaning too: 'rumination'. When Thomas Elyot recommends that the sentences he has collected in *A bankette of sapience* (1539) are 'holsome' only if they are 'wel masticate, and not hastily devoured' at the dinner table, he is advising us not only to absorb the precept, but also to debate it.[39] The same is meant when a character in Stefano Guazzo's *Civil Conversation* wisely observes that 'Because a hastie sentence is a manifest note of a rash Judge, it behoveth us therefore ... to chew it well in our mindes before, least it be thought to be degorged againe, as altogether raw and undigested.'[40]

This alimentary metaphor is useful to note not only because it shows us another way in which commonplaces might be used, but also because it suggests a different way of thinking about literary prose, as a digestion, a testing and reworking of sayings. Elyot's educational tract, *The Boke named the Governour* (1531), for example, is full of quoted sayings, but not all of them are well illustrated by the examples he offers and in this way Elyot makes the reader think about them, inviting us to test the relationship between precept and example, and to relate ideal to practice.[41] Guazzo's *Civil Conversation*, a prose dialogue running to four books, shows its interlocutors ruminating sayings. The junior interlocutor in this dialogue, William, is suffering from melancholy, and he is

---

[37] See above, n. 9.

[38] Michael Schoenfeldt, 'Reading Bodies', in Kevin Sharpe and Stephen Zwicker, eds., *Reading, Society, and Politics in Early Modern England* (Cambridge: Cambridge University Press, 2003), 215–43 (220).

[39] Thomas Elyot, *The Bankette of Sapience* (London, 1539), sig. A3^r.

[40] Stefano Guazzo, *The civile conversation of M. Stephen Guazzo, written first in Italian, diuided into foure bookes, the first three translated out of French by G[eorge] pettie......the fourth[is] now translated out of Italian into English by Barth[olomew] Young* (London, 1586), fol. 4, 181^v.

[41] For discussion of this see Jennifer Richards, 'Male Friendship and Counsel in Richard Edwards' *Damon and Pythias*', in Thomas Betteridge and Greg Walker, eds., *The Oxford Handbook of Tudor Drama* (Oxford: Oxford University Press, 2012), 293–308.

slowly cured by being brought into company. This means teaching him to avoid being a 'rash judge' in social situations and that involves turning over, 'chewing', and rethinking commonplaces values and opinions.[42]

However, it is with my last example that we will find our clearest defence of the importance—the healthiness—of ruminating advice in the vernacular, as well as a deep-rooted and lasting scepticism of quoted authority. This is *The Anatomy of Melancholy* of the seventeenth-century divine, Robert Burton, and it is to his lengthy prose preface 'Democritus Junior to the Reader' that I quickly turn.

If Moss was unpersuaded by Baldwin's contribution to the genre of the print commonplace book, then it is hard to imagine that she would be impressed by Burton's *The Anatomy of Melancholy* (1621–76). For the *Anatomy* is an unruly work. It is variously categorized as a medical work, an encyclopaedia, and also described as a sermon and Menippean satire. Indeed, so complex is its generic identity that Mary Ann Lund no doubt wisely chooses to emphasize rather this text's 'flexibility', arguing that it is part of its 'curative purpose'. Burton understands that given the complexity of the malady, then 'the "whole physitian" needs to be both priest and doctor, so Burton's text must vary in its aims, applying different forms of treatment to the melancholic reader'.[43]

However, there is another reason why we might be unimpressed. As so many scholars have noted, 'deliberately or otherwise, Burton overwhelmed his readership with torrents of authoritative quotations'. Burton gives us quotations from authorities, lots of them, but many are contradictory and he never offers any guidance or resolution.[44] In this respect, the *Anatomy* is best understood not in terms of medical or literary genres, but rather as a sprawling, ever-expanding commonplace book. Or, as Grant Williams puts it more kindly, as an 'extraordinary commonplace book'. Like his 'namesake' in the preface, 'the pre-Socratic philosopher Democritus, who dissected animals to find the seat of *atra bilis*', black bile, Williams argues, so Burton dissects books to a similar end, to locate the source of melancholy, arranging textual 'fragments [...] under headings corresponding to the Galenic rubric for examining diseases: symptoms, causes, and cures'.[45] Of course, there is no single cause; the *Anatomy* is testimony to the complexity both of the malady and debate about it.

To be fair, Burton recognizes the problems. In his preface, 'Democritus Junior to the Reader', he confesses that he did not have time to organize this work properly, and that it grew 'out of a confused company of notes'. He also admits that he wrote it 'with as small a deliberation as I doe ordinarily speak, without all affectation of big words, fustian

---

[42] For discussion of this see Jennifer Richards, *Rhetoric and Courtliness in Early Modern Literature* (Cambridge: Cambridge University Press, 2003), chap. 1.

[43] Mary Ann Lund, *Melancholy, Medicine and Religion in Early Modern England: Reading* The Anatomy of Melancholy (Cambridge: Cambridge University Press, 2010), 126–7.

[44] Angus Gowland, *The Worlds of Renaissance Melancholy: Robert Burton in Context* (Cambridge: Cambridge University Press, 2006), 115.

[45] Grant Williams, 'Textual Crudities in Robert Burton's *Anatomy of Melancholy* and Thomas Browne's *Pseudodoxia Epidemica*', in Christopher Ivic and Grant Williams, eds., *Forgetting in Early Modern English Literature and Culture: Lethe's Leg* (London: Routledge, 2004), 67–82 (67, 79).

phrases, jingling termes, tropes'. 'I am *acqæ potor* [a drinker of water]', he confesses, 'a loose, plaine, rude writer [...] I call a spade a spade [...] I respect matter, not words'.[46] 'My translations', he adds, 'are sometimes rather Paraphrases, then interpretations, *non ad verbam* [not word for word], but as an Author, I use more liberty, and that's only taken, which was to my purpose: Quotations are often inserted in the Text, which make the stile more harsh [...] I have mingled *Sacra prophanis* [sacred things with profane]' (1. 19; 4. 41–2).

The *Anatomy* also leads Burton to worry about the value of collecting quotations. There are too many writers, he complains, and all they do is 'skim off the Creame of other mens Wits, pick the choyce Flowers of their tild Gardens to set out our owne sterill plots' (1: 9). Filching from others' works is no way to help English style or English readers. 'Amongst so many thousand Authors', he laments, 'you shall scarce finde one by reading of whom you shall be any whit better', an insight he reinforces rather cheekily with a quotation from Palingenius:

> *What has anyone learnt, what does he know, who reads works like that, but dreams, trifles?* (1: 10; 4. 24).

It is not surprising, then, that Williams should regard the *Anatomy* as marking the 'death of Renaissance humanism and the birth of the modern episteme', that is, the rise of scientific methodology, even as it shares with us 'an extraordinary surplus enjoyment'.[47] Each new edition of the *Anatomy* adds more examples and quotations; Burton cannot stop himself it seems. Yet, because Williams understands the commonplace book only as a 'digest',[48] an orderly organization of one's reading, he misses Burton's preoccupation with *digesting*. 'I have only this out of *Macrobius* to say for my selfe, *Omne meum, nihil meum*, 'tis all mine and none mine', he declares:

> As a good hous-wife out of divers fleeces weaves one peece of Cloath, a Bee gathers Wax and Hony out of many Flowers, and makes a new bundle of all,
> *Floriferis ut apes in saltibus omnia libant*,
> [*As bees sip everything in flowery glades*]
> I have laboriously collected this *Cento* out of divers Writers, and that *sine injuriâ* [without injury], I have wronged no Authors, but given every man his owne [...]
> The matter is theirs most part, and yet mine, *apparet unde sumptum sit* [It is apparent where it was taken from] (which Seneca approves), *aliud tamen quàm unde sumptum sit apparet* [but it appears as something different from its source], which nature doth with the aliment of our bodies, incorporate, digest, assimilate.

Burton is not simply justifying the fact that he has changed what he has read and collected. By incorporating it, he gently suggests, he may even have improved it:

---

[46] Robert Burton, *The Anatomy of Melancholy*, ed. Thomas C. Falulkner, Nicholas K. Kiessling, and Rhonda L. Blair, 6 vols. (Oxford: Clarendon Press, 1989–2000), 1. 17, 4. 38. All citations are to this edition. Translations of Latin quotations are from volume 4.
[47] Williams, 'Textual Crudities', 81.
[48] Williams, 'Textual Crudities', 68.

> Though there were many Giants of old in Physicke and Phylosophy, yet I say with *Didacus Stella: A Dwarfe standing on the shoulders of a Giant may see farther than a Giant himselfe*; I may likely adde, alter, and see farther than my Predecessors. (1. 11–12; 4. 26–7)

Burton's preface is a good point on which to end because it draws together so many of the themes in this chapter and because in it he digests his own reading. Burton turns over, chews, and thinks around stock ideas. His preface is full of reversals, as he slowly leads the reader to understand that things may be seen differently. His namesake, Democritus, for example, turns out to be wisely sceptical rather than sick or mad (1. 37). Burton has a fine sense of the reversibility of judgements. The philosopher Seneca—a reassuring presence in many Renaissance commonplace books—may be admired for his sententiousness by some readers, including Burton, but he was once jeered at by others, dismissed for his '*dicaces & ineptæ sententiæ, eruditio plebia*', his 'facile and out-of-place sentiments, plebeian learning' (1. 15; 4. 34). But Burton values this reversibility, for it can work in his favour too; *his* plebeian learning can be re-evaluated too. Burton may not be interested in quality quotations, but this is because 'I respect matter, not words' (1. 19). Just as in Baldwin's treatise, so in this readers are warned they will find material that is 'sometimes faire, sometimes foule' (1. 18). We need to sift the wheat from the chaff.

Further Reading

Baldwin, William. *A Treatise of Morall Philosophie by William Baldwin. Enlarged by Thomas Palfreyman. A Facsimile Reproduction of the Edition of 1620*, ed. Robert Hood Bowers (Gainesville, FL: Scholars Facsimiles and Reprints, 1967).

Cave, Terence. *The Cornucopian Text: Problems of Writing in the French Renaissance* (Oxford: Oxford University Press, 1979, repr. 2002).

Gowland, Angus. *The Worlds of Renaissance Melancholy: Robert Burton in Context* (Cambridge: Cambridge University Press, 2006).

King, John N. *English Reformation Literature: The Tudor Origins of the Protestant Tradition* (Princeton: Princeton University Press, 1982).

Lund, Mary Ann. *Melancholy, Medicine and Religion in Early Modern England: Reading The Anatomy of Melancholy* (Cambridge: Cambridge University Press, 2010).

Mack, Peter. *Elizabethan Rhetoric: Theory and Practice* (Cambridge: Cambridge University Press, 2002).

Maslen, R. W. 'William Baldwin and the Politics of Pseudo-Philosophy in Tudor Prose Fiction', *Studies in Philology*, 97 (2000): 29–60.

Moss, Ann. *Printed Commonplace-Books and the Structuring of Renaissance Thought* (Oxford: Clarendon Press, 1996).

Ong, Walter J., SJ. *Rhetoric, Romance, and Technology: Studies in the Interaction of Expression and Culture* (Ithaca: Cornell University Press, 1971).

Sherman, William H. *Used Books: Marking Readers in Renaissance England* (Philadelphia: University of Pennsylvania Press, 2008).

Williams, Grant. 'Textual Crudities in Robert Burton's *Anatomy of Melancholy* and Thomas Browne's *Pseudodoxia Epidemica*', in Christopher Ivic and Grant Williams, eds., *Forgetting in Early Modern English Literature and Culture: Lethe's Leg* (London: Routledge, 2004), 67–82.

CHAPTER 4

ROMANCE: *AMADIS DE GAULE* AND JOHN BARCLAY'S *ARGENIS*

HELEN MOORE

EVIDENCE for the readership of early modern prose fiction—and, indeed, for a taxonomy of the genre—is often to be found in the links between books that are articulated by commentators of the period. As a romance blessed with an extended longevity in England thanks to its multilinguality (being read first in French from the 1540s, then in English from the 1590s), *Amadis de Gaule* features in many such rhetorical alliances and is frequently paired with Sidney's *Arcadia* in particular. Such judgements on romance readership manifest their own generic characteristics: they are often negative and are just as likely to be heavily gendered. This is certainly true of the occurrence of *Amadis* alongside John Barclay's Latin romance *Argenis* (1621) in a prohibition emanating from Queen Henrietta Maria's confessor that stereotypically places the romances in a negative contrast with religious reading:

> Besides the Queens confessor and other priests will not endure that she or they should read Barclaies Arginis, Amadis de Gaule, or any such like bookes but only St Katherine's life, St Brigetts prophecy or other such like holy tales of that stile...[1]

While this may well refer to the Queen's actual preferences, it is also potentially another version of the traditional 'good' and 'bad' books advice that was doled out to both men and women by clerics and humanists throughout the early modern period. It was expressed particularly forcefully in Catholic Spain thanks to the popularity of the *libros de caballaría*, or books of chivalry, of which *Amadis* is the most notable example.[2]

---

[1] Cited in Danielle Clarke, *The Politics of Early Modern Women's Writing* (Harlow: Pearson Education, 2001), 236.

[2] Foundational texts are Erasmus's *Education of a Christian Prince* (1516) and Juan Luis Vives's *Education of a Christian Woman* (1524). On the role of Spain see B. W. Ife, *Reading and Fiction in*

Drawing its roots from the Platonic distrust of fiction, such advice often sought to legislate against the personal effects of reading fiction, such as vicarious emotion and elevated sensuality. Despite the conventional rhetoric of repudiation, the contrastive prohibition as used here is actually an acute piece of genre criticism that implicitly recognizes the many similarities between 'bad' fiction (romance) and 'good' fiction (hagiography), such as exemplarity, the rhetoric of affect, and the marvellous: the defining difference between 'good' and 'bad' fictions, of course, lies in the ends to which this material is, or can be, directed.

All three of these elements and others, such as stylized violence and latent or implicit Catholic piety, are certainly found aplenty in both *Amadis* and *Argenis*, and they accord with what we know from other contexts about the literary tastes of the Stuart courts and specifically of Henrietta Maria's circle. Linda Levy Peck's characterization of the Jacobean court as a world of 'court scandal and court reform, chivalric nostalgia and classicism, mannerist excess and baroque grandeur' certainly chimes with the matter and style of *Argenis* and *Amadis*, both of which were praised throughout Europe for their rhetorical elegance and courtly sophistication and which certainly manifest plenty of excess and grandeur. Both romances also tapped into, and in the case of the earlier *Amadis* helped to formulate, the Jacobean celebration of 'family and uxoriousness', and like the Stuart houses discussed by Peck, they express the culture's 'changing conceptions of the role of the nobility, from magnate to courtier and from courtier to virtuoso'.[3] Amadis, for example, is a poet and exemplar of courtly sentiment as well as a marvel of chivalric prowess. Other reasons to link the two works abound: they are both extremely long translated texts that stem from a pan-European fictional tradition rooted in Greek romance (from which the *Argenis* is derived) and thirteenth-century French prose romance (the origins of *Amadis*). Both had been or were popular reading matter at the English court. The aristocratic heyday of *Amadis* in England was during the Elizabethan period, when it was widely read in its French incarnation, but it retained sufficient purchase during James's reign for Jonson and others to continue to use the name of its heroine, Oriana, for Anna of Denmark, as had been done for Elizabeth in the madrigal tradition.[4] Translated in parts by Anthony Munday during the 1590s, the central four-book narrative of Amadis himself (as opposed to his descendants, whose deeds fill out the rest of the cycle) was completed and repackaged in a substantial folio dedicated to Philip Herbert in 1618–19. Barclay's *Argenis*, originally published in Latin in 1621, was available in English from 1625. Unlike Munday's *Amadis*, it did not have a 'popular' readership, but it was nevertheless read late into the seventeenth century and beyond, and indeed initiated the mid-century fashion for lengthy romances of elevated sentiment that also engaged topically with the matter of politics.

Golden-Age Spain: A Platonist Critique and some Picaresque Replies (Cambridge: Cambridge University Press, 1985).

[3] Linda Levy Peck, 'Introduction', in Linda Levy Peck, ed., *The Mental World of the Jacobean Court* (Cambridge: Cambridge University Press, 1990), 1–17 (2, 6, 10).

[4] C. H. Herford and Percy and Evelyn Simpson, eds., *The Works of Ben Jonson*, 11 vols. (Oxford: Clarendon Press, 1925–52), vol. VII: 124–5, 139.

In their different ways, *Amadis* and *Argenis* are participants in, and indicative of, the internationalism of Jacobean culture and the intensely self-conscious engagement of its fictional prose genres with the precedents of the ancient and medieval pasts as well as the modern novelistic fictions emerging in France and Spain. The earliest fragments of the Spanish *Amadís de Gaula* date from the fifteenth century, but it was the four-book redaction by Garci Rodríguez de Montalvo (1508) that took Europe by storm during the early modern period, being translated into French, Italian, Dutch, English, German, and Hebrew, and inspiring a frenzy of imitation and continuation that eventually extended the cycle to twenty-four books.[5] Crucial to this success was Nicholas de Herberay, who under the patronage of Francis I translated the first eight books into French between 1540 and 1548. Herberay's *Amadis* is an act of wholesale cultural as well as linguistic *translatio* that relocates Montalvo's intensely peninsular romance (deeply Catholic, embedded in the politics and language of the Reconquest, prophetic, and austere, yet fantastical) into the world of the Valois court. Herberay updated the military elements, swapped peninsular politics for courtly spectacle, expanded the amorous action, and achieved a heightening of the French language that was so elegant, eloquent, and sophisticated that he was praised by du Bellay as 'l'Homère François'.[6] Herberay's *Amadis* served as the source text for Anthony Munday's translations of the first four books of the romance (1590, 1595, 1618–19) and also for the translations of books five, six, and seven that were published in 1598 (reprinted 1664), 1652, and 1694 respectively. The letters and speeches of the romance were so highly regarded that they were extracted and gathered together for the purposes of rhetorical self-instruction in a succession of books calling themselves 'treasuries' (*Thresors*) of *Amadis*: an English translation by Thomas Paynell of one of these compendia, *The Treasurie of Amadis of Fraunce*, was published c.1572.

The origins of Barclay's *Argenis* are similarly cosmopolitan. Barclay was born in France of Scottish-French parentage, was educated in France, and himself married a Frenchwoman. He spent the years 1606 to 1615 in England at the court of James I where he wrote satirical and political works in Latin and assisted the King in his own literary endeavours. In 1615 he moved to Rome for the sake of his Catholic family, where he composed the *Argenis*, 'beyond any doubt the most accomplished novel written in Latin'.[7] *Argenis* was published in Paris in 1621 and Barclay died of a fever in Rome the same year, aged 39.[8]

---

[5] See Sir Henry Thomas, *Spanish and Portuguese Romances of Chivalry* (Cambridge: Cambridge University Press, 1920).

[6] On Herberay's *Amadis* see Luce Guillerm, *Sujet de l'écriture et traduction autour de 1540* (Paris: Aux Amateurs des Livres, 1988) and Mireille Huchon, '*Amadis*, "Parfaicte idée de nostre langue françoise"', in Nicole Cazauran and Michel Bideaux, eds., *Les Amadis en France au XVIe siècle* (Paris: Éditions Rue d'Ulm—Presses de l'École normale supérieure, 2000), 183–200.

[7] Jozef Ijsewijn, *Companion to Neo-Latin Studies Part I: History and Diffusion of Neo-Latin Literature*, 2nd edn. (Louvain: Leuven University Press and Peeters Press, 1990), 131.

[8] Nicola Royan, 'John Barclay', *ODNB* <http://www.oxforddnb.com/view/article/1342?docPos=10> accessed 18 March 2013.

4.1 Transformations in Narrative Prose

Amadis is a neo-Arthurian romance, descended from the thirteenth-century French prose romances of Lancelot and Tristan that were well known, translated, and adapted in the Iberian peninsula. Amadis, the son of Perion and Elisena, is raised outside his family and known as the 'Gentleman of the Sea', but his royal parentage is manifested in his remarkable early adventures and deeds of arms. Drawn to the court of Lisuart, King of Great Britain, Amadis falls in love with Lisuart's daughter Oriana; their love is secretly consummated and a son, Esplandian, is born. But the secrecy of their liaison renders it vulnerable to misunderstanding and jealousy: troubled by fears of a rival, Queen Briolania, Oriana banishes Amadis, who, under the sobriquet of the 'Faire Forlorne', continues his chivalric adventures. Meanwhile, Lisuart, his family, and his kingdom are constantly subjected to the machinations of the enchanter Archalaus, which include orchestrating insurrection in Britain and abducting Lisuart and Oriana. A more worldly threat to the lovers arises from Lisuart's errors of kingship, such as his attempt to secure the marriage of Oriana to Patin, Emperor of Rome. The intervention of Amadis and his allied knights and the rescue of Oriana to the 'Firme Island' ruled by him, sets up an alternative locus of power that threatens the stability of Lisuart's kingdom yet further. Ultimately, however, Lisuart comes to recognize his dependence on Amadis, and both political and familial harmony are restored by the revelation of Esplandian's identity.

Montalvo's *Amadis* is rightly viewed as a bridge between the medieval and the Renaissance, 'a work of medieval inspiration, composition and themes' that through the intervention of Montalvo—most notably in his updating and refining of the romance's language and its treatment of arms and love, a process continued further by Herberay—became the pattern for the genre of the *libros de caballería* that dominated European fictional prose during the sixteenth century.[9] As far as developments in early modern prose are concerned, *Amadis* refashions for the modern age the technique of interlaced narrative and the 'cyclic imagination' of medieval prose romances.[10] It is typical of cyclic narrative in having no beginning, middle, or end; it interweaves the narratives of subordinate characters and descendants (such as Amadis's brother Galaor and his son Esplandian) into the narrative of the hero (some of these narratives, such as that of Esplandian, become separate 'branches' emanating from this 'trunk'); and it employs digressions. Following Horace, discussions of cyclic narrative often debate its capacity for internal coherence and its strategies for managing its inherent diffuseness. A strict control of chronology is important here (chronology being the primary means of structuring a cyclic narrative), as are, paradoxically, the digressions: as well as contributing to the diffuse character of the cyclic romance, they bestow coherence upon its *sens* (meaning) by

---

[9] Daniel Eisenberg, *Romances of Chivalry in the Spanish Golden Age* (Delaware: Juan de la Cuesta, 1982), 30–1.

[10] Douglas Kelly, 'Interlace and the Cyclic Imagination', in Carol Dover, ed., *A Companion to the Lancelot-Grail Cycle* (Cambridge: D. S. Brewer, 2003), 55–64.

showing how the narratives of its diverse *matière* (substance) 'harmonize or clash'.[11] Chronology is indeed the determining feature of the narrative in *Amadis*: it has a beginning of sorts, in the story of the encounter between his parents that leads to the hero's birth, but the four-book 'trunk' of the narrative does not end: after the reconciliation of Amadis and Lisuart, adventures continue to proliferate into the next generation, often reprising established 'memes' such as the abduction of Lisuart, an event which recurs in the final chapters and triggers the branching out of the Esplandian narrative.[12] Having said that, Montalvo is successful in imparting a high level of coherence to his *Amadis*. This is achieved primarily through the unifying effects of the love narrative and the extension of this amorous theme into the realm of politics by means of the fact that Amadis's devotion to Oriana and his lordship of the Firme Island set up an alternative power base in the romance that makes amorous loyalty the scenario for knightly disobedience. Lisuart is not a tyrant, but he is prone to kingly folly: during the episode of Barsinan's rebellion he fails to discern bad advice and acts rashly.[13] The (only partially successful) re-education of Lisuart in the art of good government and Amadis's own entry to the 'higher felicities' of rule (961) establish a thematics of kingship that unifies the narrative and (like Barclay's *Argenis*) sets up many typically Renaissance similarities between the prose romance and the mirror for policy. As Robert Cummings notes concerning English translations of the latter in this period, there is a tendency to 'leave behind the empirical and the historical to propose models and offer critiques for princes and states'.[14] The modelling and critiquing of statehood certainly underpins *Amadis*, which in its Spanish incarnation addresses itself directly to the personalities and peninsular politics of Ferdinand and Isabella, the *Reyes Católicos*. In his preface (not found in either French or English translations) Montalvo praises the 'santa conquista' (holy conquest) of Granada using the terminology of his own romance, invoking the dangerous combats, grand speeches, and great praise accruing to the King from his deeds.[15] Although the intense geopolitical ambitions of Reconquest Spain are displaced by the Valois obsession with courtly government and cultural supremacy in Herberay's version, the essential function of *Amadis* as a critique of princeliness, action, loyalty, and obedience (virtues that map conveniently onto both the amorous and political worlds) nonetheless remains intact.[16]

---

[11] Kelly, 'Interlace', 58.

[12] On romance 'memes' and their role in mediating medieval romance to the Renaissance see Helen Cooper, *The English Romance in Time: Transforming Motifs from Geoffrey of Monmouth to the Death of Shakespeare* (Oxford: Oxford University Press, 2004).

[13] Anthony Munday, *Amadis de Gaule*, ed. Helen Moore (Aldershot: Ashgate, 2004), book I, chapters 30–39. Subsequent citations will be given in the text, either as page or book and chapter numbers.

[14] Robert Cummings, 'Mirrors for Policy', in Gordon Braden, Robert Cummings, and Stuart Gillespie, eds., *The Oxford History of Literary Translation in English, vol. 2, 1550–1660* (Oxford: Oxford University Press, 2010), 408–17 (408).

[15] Garci Rodríguez de Montalvo, *Amadís de Gaula*, ed. Juan Manuel Cacho Blecua, 2 vols., (Madrid: Ediciones Cátedra, 1991), I:220.

[16] I discuss this cultural re-visioning of Amadisian geopolitics further in 'The Eastern Mediterranean in the English *Amadis* Cycle, Book V', *Yearbook of English Studies*, 41 (2011): 113–25.

Barclay's *Argenis* is even more overtly engaged with questions of statehood and kingship. It was published in Latin in 1621; over thirty Latin editions have been identified and it was translated into all the major European vernaculars.[17] English translations were made by Kingsmill Long (1625), with verses by Thomas May and by Robert Le Grys (1628), using the same verses by May. These verses are themselves notable for being May's first published foray into the translation of politically resonant Latin texts. His translation of Lucan's *Pharsalia* (of which the first three books were published in 1626 and the whole in 1627) has earned him a significant place in the narrative of English republicanism. The *Pharsalia*, like *Argenis*, is deeply critical of courtly corruption, but unlike Barclay's romance, it extends that scepticism into a questioning of absolute royal power. *Pharsalia* and *Argenis* are linked by their shared interest in the limitations of monarchical absolutism, the element of the subject that was of most topical interest in England. May's choice of dedicatees for the *Pharsalia* signals 'a gesture of support for an anti-absolutist alliance', but its position is not ultimately a republican one, May preferring instead to close with 'a generalized appeal to monarchical nationalism'; it is not, then, surprising to find him engaging with the decidedly un-republican *Argenis* in the same period.[18] *Argenis* is rooted in the societies and discourses of early modern monarchy. The version by Le Grys declares itself on the title page (Figure 4.1) to be 'translated . . . upon His Majesties Command' and Le Grys states in his dedication to Charles I that Barclay was 'long bred under your Royall Father'; although *Argenis* had 'a forraine birth, it was first conceived in this your Kingdome' and is now 'cherish[ed]' of the King.[19] According to Sir Dudley Carleton, James I commissioned Jonson to translate it; although entered in the Stationers' Register in 1623, Jonson's translation of three books of *Argenis* was lost in the fire that consumed his library that same year, as remembered in the poem 'An Execration upon Vulcan'.[20]

Argenis opens amid 'broyles and civill dissension' (107) arising from the rebellion of Lycogenes against Meleander, King of Sicily.[21] Meleander is a weak king, principled but indecisive, whose inaction means that he is assailed at home by 'civil dissensions' arising from a destabilizing concoction of noble conspiracies and the innate tendency to disobedience of the 'unruly vulgar' (247). A lack of effective action against his domestic rebels renders Meleander vulnerable on the international stage as well: the Sardinian prince Radirobanes exploits Meleander's dependence on his military aid in order to

---

[17] Listed in John Barclay, *Argenis*, ed. Mark Riley and Dorothy Pritchard Huber, *Bibliotheca Latinitatis Novae/Medieval and Renaissance Texts and Studies*, 273, 2 vols. (Assen: Royal van Gorcum and Tempe, AZ: Arizona Center for Medieval and Renaissance Studies, 2004), I:51–8.

[18] David Norbrook, *Writing the English Republic: Poetry, Rhetoric and Politics, 1627–1660* (Cambridge: Cambridge University Press, 1999), 43 and 50.

[19] Robert Le Grys, trans., *John Barclay his Argenis* (London, 1628), A2^v.

[20] Barclay, *Argenis*, I:30–1.

[21] Citations from *Argenis* are from the translation by Kingsmill Long, *Barclay his Argenis: or, the Loves of Poliarchus and Argenis* (London, 1625) and take the form of either page or book and chapter numbers. Riley and Huber print a translation based on Long's in their edition of the Latin original, but the level of their textual intervention makes it unsuitable for citation in this context.

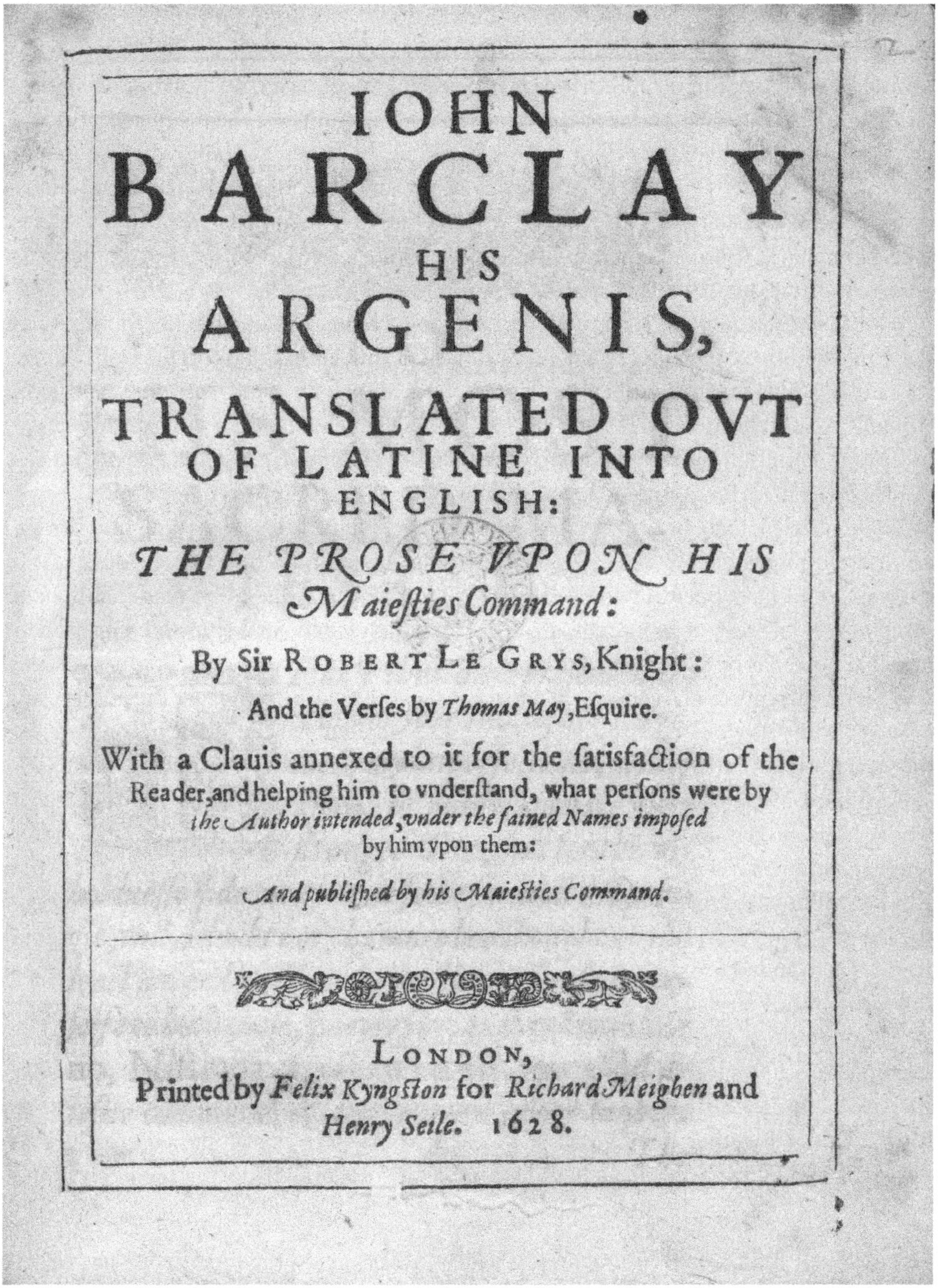

IOHN BARCLAY HIS ARGENIS,

TRANSLATED OVT OF LATINE INTO ENGLISH:

THE PROSE VPON HIS Maiesties Command:

By Sir ROBERT LE GRYS, Knight:

And the Verses by *Thomas May*, Esquire.

With a Clauis annexed to it for the satisfaction of the Reader, and helping him to vnderstand, what persons were by the *Author intended, vnder the fained Names imposed* by him vpon them:

And published by his Maiesties Command.

LONDON,
Printed by *Felix Kyngston* for *Richard Meighen* and Henry Seile. 1628.

FIGURE 4.1 John Barclay, *Argenis*, trans. Robert Le Grys (1628), title page

mount his own political and sexual assault on Sicily, culminating in the attempted abduction of Meleander's daughter Argenis. As so often in Jacobean literature, Sicily's tumults are a reflection of, and themselves pattern, the domestic turmoil of Meleander's family: his daughter's attendant Theocrine has turned out to be the disguised prince of France, Poliarchus, whose real identity is known only to Argenis, and whose potential aid to Sicily is thereby squandered by Meleander's vengeful pursuit. Meleander is a master of political *mésalliance* who, apart from his ill-advised compact with Radirobanes, seeks an alliance for his daughter with Archombrotus, incognito prince of Mauritania, who turns out to be Argenis's half-brother.

Like *Amadis*, *Argenis* also circulated in a reduced form. In this case, the focus was on the core narrative of the lovers Argenis and Poliarchus, rather than on the utility of the romance as a rhetorical pattern book, as it had been with the *Treasurie* culled from *Amadis*. Again, though, the generic paradigm is a French one, that of the abridgement, or 'epitome'. Judith Man's *An Epitome of the History of Faire Argenis and Polyarchus* was published in 1640; it is a translation of the abridgement *Histoire de Poliarque et d'Argenis* by Nicolas Coëffeteau, bishop of Marseille. Coëffeteau's motives in making his abridgement are difficult to discern: as Amelia Zurcher has pointed out, the abridgement of *Argenis* could have been intended either to increase the range of its readership, or to remove the defences of monarchical authority which Coëffeteau (himself a proponent of papal power) opposed.[22] Certainly, in the prefatory material to the English version, there is no indication of the political nature of Barclay's work, as the reading and writing of the epitome is relocated into an entirely female world of paradigmatic heroism, virtuous aristocracy, and obedient translation. Casting herself as a grateful and diligent subordinate, Man's dedication to Anne Wentworth, daughter of the Earl of Strafford (in whose household Man was educated), draws a parallel between her patron and Argenis, 'the Fairest, most Vertuous, and Constant Princesse of Her time' and hopes that Anne will herself be matched with an equivalent to Poliarchus, 'the most Compleat Prince of the Earth' (sigs. A3^r and A4^v). Thus, the regal biopolitics on which the plot of the original *Argenis* is founded are themselves 'epitomized' into a local form of dynastic romance, the aristocratic marriage.[23]

Although not a cyclic narrative like *Amadis*, Barclay's *Argenis* still has to manage its multiple narratives, protagonists, and speakers very carefully. The beginning *in medias res* pays tribute to the foundational influence of Heliodorus's *Aethiopica*, but at the same time it brings together in friendship the men who will later become competitors for Argenis's hand (and throne), as Archombrotus aids Poliarchus during the latter's flight

---

[22] Amelia A. Zurcher, 'Introductory Note' to Judith Man, *An Epitome of the History of Faire Argenis and Polyarchus (1640)*, *The Early Modern Englishwoman: Series 1, Printed Writings, 1500–1640: Part 3*, volume 2 (Aldershot: Ashgate, 2003), xii.

[23] Coëffeteau adds a monologue on constancy and virtue uttered by Argenis, a change that clearly facilitated Man's rhetorical fusing of the amorous identities of Argenis and Anne Wentworth (*An Epitome*, p. xiii). Jacobean romance frequently invokes royal and aristocratic 'biopolitics'; for a case study see Mary Ellen Lamb, 'The Biopolitics of Romance in Mary Wroth's *Urania*', *English Literary Renaissance*, 31 (2001): 107–30.

from the vengeful pursuit of Meleander. The cause of this strife lies in Poliarchus's abuse of the laws of hospitality and his potential treason in having disguised himself as a woman, thereby gaining access to Argenis. This explanation remains hidden, however, until it is revealed maliciously in flashback to the third suitor, Radirobanes, by Argenis's waiting woman, Selenissa, in Book III. Both romances use the techniques of prospection and retrospection, but chronology is disrupted like this more frequently in *Argenis* than in *Amadis*, via the use not only of flashback, but also of explanation. For example, Poliarchus's account for Archombrotus of the origins of the rebellion gathers up into a coherent political narrative otherwise disconnected events spread over a considerable period of time (I.2). Information is also presented incrementally: Poliarchus's identity as a great man is trailed long before his history is revealed and the minutiae of Lycogenes's plots emerge over several chapters; such incremental narrative progress and the gradual elucidation of meaning to events is a descendant of the riddling withholding of information (usually a name) that is seen frequently in medieval prose romances such as those from which *Amadis* is descended.

Barclay maintains an impressive command over the intersecting narratives and conventions that make up *Argenis*; while drawing freely and unselfconsciously on his stock of inherited narrative motifs, he is also careful to habilitate them to the needs of his own story. Arsidas's capture by Gobryas's fleet (a version of the capture by pirates found in Greek romance) turns out to be a highly effective means of infilling the story of Poliarchus's earlier life, as the enforced cessation of Arsidas's active narrative thread—his search for Poliarchus—enables him to 'find' Poliarchus in a more abstract sense, by learning of his past deeds and royal identity from Gobryas's inset narration (IV.8–14). The trickster-servant motif is given new life, too, in the theft of Arsidas's precious cargo, a letter from Argenis to Poliarchus. This serves as an excellent means of getting Argenis's letter into Poliarchus's hands and thus accelerating the progress of the plot whilst providing some incidental comedy as Arsidas and Poliarchus talk at cross-purposes thanks to the confusion the thief has introduced in an effort to exculpate himself (V.6–8).

The narratives of *Amadis* and *Argenis* are also punctuated by incursions from other genres. Both romances include examples of prose genres such as the letter, the oration, and the prayer, and as discussed below, both stage debates on kingship through dialogue and scenes of counsel. Soliloquies are frequently deployed in *Amadis*, interrupting and yet amplifying the plot in the same way as does a letter or oration: they proliferate in the emotionally intense section of Book II that deals with Oriana's jealousy and Amadis's exile. The soliloquy on Fortune in II.4 is a set piece lament that elaborates cosmic woe out of individual misfortune, as repeated references to the self ('I', 'me', 'my') rub shoulders with proverbial sentiments castigating Fortune for 'flatteries and wanton intisements' and warning of the 'labyrinth of all desolation' that awaits those who trust in her (326).

Inset verses perform much the same function of elaboration and commentary. In *Amadis*, the poetry is exclusively amorous, but in *Argenis* it embraces public genres and is frequently occasional. There is pastoral (99–100), protest poetry (88–9), lament (114–15), epithalamium (335–6), and epic (328–32), for example. Verses can also serve a narrative function: in one particularly self-aware moment in *Amadis*, an inset verse becomes entangled in the plot, as Amadis and his squire Gandalin overhear the song of praise to Oriana uttered by his soon-to-be-rival, Patin. Full of despair, Amadis has to be nagged and shamed by Gandalin into rebuking this poetic 'presumption': doing so, however, places him back on the path to emotional and chivalric recuperation (329).

4.2 STATELY FABLING

In *Argenis* II.2, the poet and courtly commentator Nicopompus (a figuring forth of Barclay himself) describes his intention to write 'some stately Fable, in manner of a History' in which he will 'fold up strange events; and mingle together Armes, Marriages, Bloodshed, Mirth' that will delight and then 'with the shew of danger' 'stirre up pitty, feare, and horrour'. Some readers will meet with themselves in the fiction, but in a concealed form and mingled with 'imaginary names' to resist over zealous glossing. Located somewhere between factuality and fiction, Nicopompus's 'new kind of writing' (a thinly veiled description of *Argenis*) defies both (109).

When *Argenis* first began to command some degree of critical attention in the later twentieth century, studies were dominated by its identification as a *roman à clef*. In an influential reading that located *Argenis* within the 'royal romance' of Stuart (specifically Caroline) self-presentation, Annabel Patterson asserted that the Latin *Argenis* was 'quickly recognized as an encoded and fictionalized account of European history': Queen Hyanisbe 'represents' Elizabeth I, Meleander is Henri III of France, and Argenis herself is 'an allegorical concept, the crown of France'. Paul Salzman's overview of early prose fiction adopts a similar line: it is 'a political allegory depicting the religious and political turmoil in France under Henry III and Henry IV'.[24] Both Patterson and Salzman take their cue from the tradition of providing a *clavis*, or key, to *Argenis* that identifies the historical personages who can be linked to Barclay's fictional creations. The *clavis* appeared in the Latin edition of 1627 and was translated for the 1636 second edition of Long's translation; a shorter version was included in Robert Le Grys's translation of 1628. It is important to note that in both of its English incarnations the *clavis* prioritizes the act of reading over that of writing: it advertises itself as a satisfaction to readerly curiosity, an 'unlock[ing]' of 'the intentions of the Author': it is a scratch to a hermeneutic itch.[25]

---

[24] Annabel Patterson, *Censorship and Interpretation: The Conditions of Writing and Reading in Early Modern England* (Madison, WI: University of Wisconsin Press, 1984), 180, 182, 184 and Paul Salzman, *English Prose Fiction, 1558–1700: A Critical History* (Oxford: Clarendon Press, 1985), 150. Salzman continues the allegorical line in his discussion of *Argenis* in *Literary Culture in Jacobean England: Reading 1621* (New York and Basingstoke: Palgrave Macmillan, 2002), 75–80. In contrast, Amelia A. Zurcher's reading of self-interest and rivalry in *Argenis* emphasizes political philosophy over political allegory: see her *Seventeenth-Century English Romance: Allegory, Ethics and Politics* (New York and Basingstoke: Palgrave Macmillan, 2007), 61–103.

[25] As in the introduction to the *clavis* in Le Grys, *Argenis*, 485.

The 1636 Long edition also included the elegant illustrations by Mellan and Gaultier first used in the French edition of 1623: in this edition, *clavis* and illustrations work together paratextually to enforce a particular kind of reception that is cognizant of the purposeful dignity and continental aesthetics attributed to Barclay's romance. The self-description in the 1636 subtitle—'beautified with pictures together with a key præfixed to unlock the whole story'—indicates that by the 1630s the act of reading *Argenis* was firmly allied with visual pleasure and the heavily managed hermeneutic satisfactions of a particular kind of elite readerly 'unlocking'. Encountering the English *Argenis* in this decade was of necessity a cross-cultural activity, framed and directed paratextually by continental, aristocratic norms of reading that insistently and self-referentially invoked art, history, and politics alongside fiction.

As Danielle Clarke has pointed out, the use of a *clavis* does not necessarily lead to the successful literary decoding that is being advertised. Rather, 'it may be that the clavis merely serves to restrict access to the subtext by providing an interpretation that *gestures* at closure'.[26] Even assuming that the identifications proposed in the *clavis* have some validity (and it should be noted here that Nicompompus's description expressly resists undue allegorization), they represent only a partial story, one that is notably (perhaps deliberately, as Clarke argues) dismissive of alternative modes of romance reading typically characterized as wanton or pleasurable. While *Argenis* does undoubtedly contain allusions to contemporaneous European history such as the rise of Calvinism (II.5) and to Jacobean politics (for instance the Overbury scandal [I.6] and tax controversies [IV.18]), these elements do not exert a structural or determining influence on its plot, which functions independently of history and possesses its own internal viability.[27] This is manifestly clear in the triangulated relationship of Argenis and her two suitors Poliarchus and Archombrotus. Argenis has no historical identity (she is typically glossed as an anagram of 'Regina', with an added 's' to make a Greek-sounding name); the deftly realized hatred of Archombrotus for Poliarchus as Argenis's preferred suitor (expressed for example in IV.4) is rooted in an intense male sensibility that is literary rather than historical in its origins; and the *deus ex machina* solution to the problem (Archombrotus turns out to be Argenis's half-brother) has a double heritage in both Greek and medieval French romance (not to mention *Amadis* itself).

Over-reliance on the *clavis* should also be qualified by a recognition that *Argenis* addresses political matters directly through inset dialogues and digressions, in which policy can be discussed in isolation from the matter of the plot itself (as exemplified by the discussion of forms of government in I.18). Hence, *Argenis* is not properly allegorical romance in a sustained sense, but a flexible and historically self-aware mode of fiction that references and recasts contemporaneous events, personality types, gossip, and scandal as part of its capacious receptivity. The anti-hero Radirobanes, for instance, exemplifies the dangers to the princely person and the commonweal that are attendant upon

---

[26] Clarke, *Politics*, 234.
[27] See Barclay, *Argenis*, I: 16–26 on the romance's political and historical allusions.

solipsism, delusion, misplaced lust, and the treacheries they generate. This function is enhanced, not effaced, by his identification in the *clavis* as Philip II of Spain, which adds a frisson of recognition and serves as an argumentative proof, an *exemplum* cut from the real world, to demonstrate the truth of Barclay's wider moral-philosophical point about the perils of excess as practised by the mighty (in other words, tyranny).

Easy as it is to see the 'unlocking' act of the *clavis* as operating on the narrative by revealing a political (and by implication more true and serious) *sous-texte*, it should instead be viewed in a horizontal, rather than vertical axis, as 'unlocking' the purposeful links between the matter of romance and the incident of history: it makes correspondences, rather than negates the matter of fiction, amplifies significations, rather than reduces them. The writers and translators of the different keys knew this, as revealed in the ways they negotiate around *Argenis*'s innumerable historical inconsistencies. The 1628 *clavis*, in discussing Radirobanes, acknowledges that his historical alter-ego did not of course 'dye upon Poliarchus his sword' as Radirobanes does (sig. 2K1ᵛ) and the 1636 version prefaces its discussion of Radirobanes as Philip II by expressing some doubt 'whether that may in all things suit to his person'. The problem is finessed by a pragmatic acknowledgement of the fact that 'all things in this Booke are not to be drawne to an Historicall truth', as Nicopompus himself had dictated (sig. B1ʳ). That observation is nowhere more true than in the chapters in which Radirobanes becomes separated from his army during the wars against Hyanisbe and her ally Poliarchus in Mauritania. As the aggressor, Radirobanes is fatally in the wrong during this conflict, but Barclay nonetheless manages to inject a moving and individualized sense of his vulnerability, fear, and courage as he seeks to hide amongst the Mauritanian troops and then escapes back to his army by swimming his horse across a lake (IV.19–20). Within two chapters he is dead at the hands of Poliarchus, an outcome that is very nearly regrettable following the insight this episode provides into Radirobanes's version of the 'great spirit' (9) that is both the virtue and the potential undoing of all the rulers in *Argenis*.

Barclay's combining of romance fiction with historical particularity and broader political instruction was influenced by the writings of his father William in support of absolute monarchy and against papal power, and also by classical texts that did not observe a strict distinction between the prose of instruction and that of fiction.[28] One he must have read with particular assiduity is Xenophon's *Cyropaedia* ('Education of Cyrus'), in which the education and achievements of Cyrus the Great are expounded through a mixture of narrative and politico-philosophical dialogues. Xenophon was highly valued by Spenser and Sidney, Barclay's predecessors in writing politically inflected romance, because of his skill in 'feigning' history and philosophy—that is, turning them into the 'poetry' (meaning literature/fable/fiction) that can best teach 'the sound of virtue', as Sidney puts it in his *Defence of Poetry*. In the *Defence*, Sidney

---

[28] For the influence of his father's political writings and his own classical reading (primarily Statius, Petronius, Heliodorus, and Xenophon), see Barclay, *Argenis*, I: 3, 6–8, 28–30.

repeatedly cites Xenophon's 'feigned Cyrus' as 'doctrinable' (instructive), a demonstration of how poetry is better for directing a prince than 'philosopher's counsel', and an embodiment of 'each thing to be followed', a 'perfect pattern'. These sentiments are echoed in Spenser's letter to Ralegh, appended to the 1590 *Faerie Queene*, in which Xenophon is to be preferred to Plato because in Cyrus he 'fashioned a government such as might best be'.[29] Xenophon's feigned history bears fruitful comparison with Barclay's techniques: his Cyrus is only loosely based on the Cyrus of history, and historical geography and politics have been adjusted to suit Xenophon's own 'doctrinable' ends (for example, Persia is geographically more like Sparta and its politics is actually closer to that of the Greek *polis*).[30] The *Cyropaedia* was read as a combination of travelogue and mirror for policy throughout the sixteenth century: according to William Barker, whose translation was published in 1552, it offers 'preceptes' that instruct in good government, virtue, and policy.[31] Exactly the same vocabulary of political example and principle is used in the 1636 *clavis* to *Argenis*, which is just as concerned to identify the political direction of Barclay's 'counsailes and precepts' (sig. A6^v) as it is to name names: unfortunately, the perpetuation in the English *clavis* of this mid-Tudor language of political engagement has been obscured by the tendency to read *Argenis* retrospectively from the allegorical high ground of 1650s romance, rather than as the inheritor of a classical and Tudor discourse of governmental precept that was shared across poetical and political texts. Barclay was certainly not the only writer contemplating the ancient and modern 'feigning' of history for the purposes of political instruction at this time: Philemon Holland, translator of Livy, Pliny, and Plutarch, completed his first draft of the *Cyropaedia* in 1621 as well, although it was not published until 1632.[32]

The most obviously 'doctrinable' element of *Argenis* is the insight it provides into good and bad government by kings, whether of their own 'great spirit', of their nobles, or of the commonweal. Meleander is the indicative negative example: he is certainly 'doctrinable' in his deficiencies, but at the same time Barclay's great skill in articulating the psychology of kingship renders him far more than an exemplary failure. Early on Meleander is tellingly described as 'perplexed' by faithlessness (6): the primary meaning here is the political one ('perplexed' as used of a state meaning 'troubled'), but it is indicative of Barclay's method that there should also be a psychological dimension. The perplexities of Sicily that dominate the plot of *Argenis* are also the perplexities of a king and a father who is repeatedly confounded (another word with both political and psychological resonances) by the machinations of the people around him, whether subjects, allies, enemies, or

---

[29] Brian Vickers, ed., *English Renaissance Literary Criticism* (Oxford: Clarendon Press, 1999), 353–4 for Sidney and 299 for Spenser.

[30] Xenophon, *The Education of Cyrus*, trans. Wayne Ambler (Ithaca, NY and London: Cornell University Press, 2001), 3–5.

[31] *The Bookes of Xenophon contayning the discipline, schole and education of Cyrus the noble Kyng of Persie*, trans. William Barker (London, 1552), sig. A5^r.

[32] John Considine, 'Holland, Philemon', *ODNB* <http://www.oxforddnb.com/view/article/13535> accessed 18 March 2013.

family. As the narrative unfolds we learn from many different sources about Meleander's weaknesses: these include an undue interest in pleasures such as hunting, a failure to grasp the realities of courtly self-interest, a lack of decision (in a further overlaying of politics and psychology he is described as troubled by 'conflict of his thoughts' [11]), a failure to discern the trustworthy from the deceitful, and an undignified willingness to 'covenant' (62) with a subject as shown by his consideration of a pact with the rebel Lycogenes.

Meleander is also, however, a rhetorical participant in his own 'doctrinable' function: by granting him the opportunity for self-analysis he can also be used to model that most notoriously difficult of political desiderata, royal self-correction. An important exchange between the King and Cleobulus in III.4 shows Barclay's dialogic method at its best, interweaving theoretically driven political dialogue with plot-driven conversation. Debating how to mop up the pockets of resistance left over from Lycogenes's rebellion, Meleander asks Cleobulus to outline his own faults, as 'a warning, that I fall not into the same lapse'. Ever the courtly pragmatist, Cleobulus evades the pitfall of 'saucy freedom' and 'prepare[s] the king's mind' for counsel by blaming 'his enemies, the times, and the Fates' before launching into a lengthy rebuke to his 'clemency' (158) that addresses both the specifics of Meleander's dilemma and the wider principles of absolute power dear to Barclay's heart. Overtly and carefully chary of tyranny, Cleobulus's advice nonetheless advocates firm measures to quell the 'restless dispositions' of a factional nobility (159), such as removing their royally given estates and powers. Sighing and striking his breast in reply (itself a telling demonstration of the way in which the gestural languages of amorous and political emotion overlay one another in *Argenis*), Meleander resists the daily 'rigour' in government that is implied, by personalizing Cleobulus's theory: 'Shall I make All, my enemies, by my strictnesse? Or shall I live like a beast in the Desart? Or rather, furnish my Court with new men?' (161). The personal frustrations of kingship are clearly audible here alongside the political theorizing.

The use of romance to exert political traction such as this was by no means the invention or even the preserve of the seventeenth century, however. *Amadis* is equally concerned with the theorization of kingship, although its analysis is delivered not through philosophical dialogue, but elaborated scenes of royal counsel that are derived from the medieval tradition of the *quaestio* in which arguments for and against a particular thesis are rehearsed. Two such debates occur at moments of crisis in Lisuart's kingdom—in the lead up to the rebellion of Barsinan in Book I (I.32) and during the early stages of the hostilities between Lisuart and Amadis's Knights of the Firme Island in Book III (III.1). The first crisis, in which the threat is an external one emanating from the malevolence of Archalaus the enchanter, is moralized by the narrator as a reminder of the dependence of worldly power upon divine favour: Lisuart's misfortunes are attributable either to his forgetting 'the author of his good' or as a consequence of 'divine permission' (219). In the second instance, Lisuart is rendered more overtly culpable because it is his unreasonable hostility to Amadis, sown in his mind by the hypocrites Gandandell and Brocadan in hope of gaining the kingdom, that precipitates war. Gandandell plays on Amadis's importance to Lisuart's court in order to plant the fear of treachery and alien influence

(Amadis being a prince of Gaule) in the King's mind. This in turn generates a desire in Lisuart to reassert his authority by refusing to grant the Isle of Mongaza to one of Amadis's allies. In a process of incremental despotism, Lisuart quarrels with Amadis (II.20), refuses reasonable supplications, and even ignores what ought within the moral framework of the romance to be the overwhelming evidence provided via judicial combat (II.22). His knowing repudiation of advice that even he acknowledges to be 'verie good' and his reliance on military might ('their strength is in no way equall to mine' [521]) accelerate his decline from good to bad king.

Unlike *Argenis* (and behind it the *Cyropaedia*), or, indeed, Sidney's *Arcadia*, *Amadis* does not attribute particular agency to the populace, or construe them as a threat to monarchy. In *Amadis*, the knightly class is both the origin of instability and the source of a king's protection: the fact that Lisuart has been captured and therefore removed from the military action (I.36) prior to Barsinan's assault on London (I.38) very much throws the focus onto the role of King Arban, Lisuart's relative and ally and a member of his court. It falls to Arban to deliver one of the romance's typically stirring military orations in opposition to usurpation and tyranny, and in defence of ordained monarchy:

> Remember the cause of your fight, not onely to maintaine your good king, but your owne liberty: against a tirant, a traitour, and what worse? . . . Beholde you not the end of his purpose? Which is to ruinate this noble Realme, that hath (by divine providence) beene so long time preserved, and ever-more continued in reputation, flourishing with loyal subjects to their Prince? (260)

The political commentators of *Amadis* and *Argenis* are united in their abhorrence of flattery. Here in *Amadis* the anti-flattery rhetoric invokes Edenic treachery ('Heard you not the flattering perswasions, which the Rebell used before the assault, thinking to conquer us by his golden tongue?' [260]). In *Argenis* the focus is on the practical, deleterious effects of flattery and favouritism upon the courtly polity and the way it undermines monarchical government. The vulnerability of a monarch to being 'spoil'd with flattery' (49) is a key weakness in this system, one that Barclay advertises at every turn. In this *Argenis* is reminiscent of the 1620s satires that excoriated the corrupt counsel, sexual immorality, and profligacy that stemmed from favouritism.[33] In both romance and satire, flattery is dangerous because it traduces good government and imperils the legitimacy of monarchical rule, leading to dangerous political speculations. During the inset debate on forms of government in I.18, for example, Anaximander expresses his preference for government 'in which the people or the Nobles governe: for why should all things depend upon one man's will', especially if it can be turned so that the people's money is 'lavishly powred [poured] upon Favourites' (49).

---

[33] On 1620s court satire see Andrew McCrae, *Literature, Satire and the Early Stuart State* (Cambridge: Cambridge University Press, 2004), 114–27.

4.3 'Worthy of wonder'

Recent work on ancient prose has noted with interest the links between political philosophy and the Greek novel, itself a paradigm of narrative discourse for Barclay.[34] Cyrus is described, for example, in the language of a romance marvel, being 'worthy of wonder' for bringing so many nations under his rule.[35] Such articulation of wonder (astonishment and admiration) is also a very Jacobean enterprise found in travel writing, history, and drama. *Argenis* and *Amadis* are replete with wonders, whether of the human or the magical kind. Indeed, the evocation of wonder is in many ways both the downfall and the apotheosis of prose romance in this period, paradoxically laying it open to the charges of extreme fabulation and imaginative ravishment so often directed at *Amadis*, or alternatively rescuing it from those very accusations of idleness by pointing to a higher plane of human aspiration in politics, art, or architecture. The hybrid identity of *Amadis* as both medieval and modern, Spanish and French, means that it juggles wonders such as the Endriagus—a monstrous concatenation of medieval horrors (scaly, hairy, red-eyed, smoking, stinking, howling, and winged) who inhabits the Devil's Island—and Apolidon's enchanted palace, which is recast by Herberay into an astoundingly modern architectural marvel based on the château de Chambord, the construction of which was begun by Francis I in 1519.[36]

As well as supplying wonder to the reader in these diverse ways, *Amadis* also deploys wonder internally as a spur to action and an index of courage. When shipwrecked on the Devil's Island, for example, Amadis is surprised by the terror of his shipmates, observing that 'I see nothing yet that should thus amaze ye' (631); having heard the story of the Endriagus's origins and deeds he is duly 'amazed' (632) and enacts the drama of (in)comprehension that features so often in romance from Chrétien de Troyes onwards, in this instance questioning internally how such a thing could be born and externally how the monster could have been permitted to live so long. The task of explanation is undertaken by Master Elisabet, physician and repository of knowledge in *Amadis*, and the hero's amazement thereby serves a useful purpose in terms of narrative diversification by generating an inset tale of archetypal vice that mingles detailed conversational exchanges, moral commentary, and folkloric descriptions of grisly matricidal and patricidal violence. Amadis is duly amazed for a second time ('you have told me wonders',

---

[34] See, for example, J. R. Morgan and Richard Stoneman, eds., *Greek Fiction: The Greek Novel in Context* (London: Routledge, 1994). The *Aethiopica* of Heliodorus was highly influential upon *Argenis*, as it was upon Sidney's *Arcadia*; for the context of its sixteenth-century revival see Victor Skretkowicz, *European Erotic Romance: Philhellene Protestantism, Renaissance Translation and English Literary Politics* (Manchester: Manchester University Press, 2010).

[35] Xenophon, *The Education of Cyrus*, trans. Ambler, 23.

[36] *Amadis*, III.10 (631–6) and IV.2 (745–51); on Chambord see André Chastel, *The Palace of Apolidon*, The Zaharoff Lecture for 1984–85 (Oxford: Clarendon Press, 1986), 11–12.

634) and enacts a conceptual leap that amplifies the coming combat into a battle of moral dimensions by stating his intention to revenge wrong and restore Christian religion to the island. Amazement, and the lack thereof, shifts at this point from being the trigger for an interpretative dilemma that generates an inset narrative and moral digression to being an index of heroism. The 'admirable maner' of the monster's dreadful appearance 'could not daunt our knight a jote' (unlike his squire Gandalin, who rather pointedly runs to hide): the hero's *not* being amazed or admiring thus becomes a marker of spiritual resistance, heroic agency, and exemplary purpose (636).

The sources of admiration in *Argenis* tend to be more like those found in Heliodorus, typically invoking wonder by some kind of alterity, whether ethnographic (for example religious rites, I.20) or mythological (the discovery of Cyclops's bones, II.22). One remarkable feature of the romance is its lack of the kinds of amorous wonder that characterize *Amadis*: there is no Arch of Loyal Lovers to enthrone Argenis and Poliarchus, no consummation scene, nor even a chaste embrace. The lovers rarely encounter one another and their energies are directed far more towards the evasion, deflection, and subversion of Meleander's patriarchal authority than the traditional love-business of romance. Argenis emerges as a new kind of heroine in this rescription of love as dynastic pragmatism: the very lack of amorous encounters renders her a much more active and strategizing, indeed subversive, agent even than Oriana, who herself rebukes and resists her father (III.18).

Barclay seems remarkably at ease with the idea of the governing mother who overcomes defective or absent husbands and rebellious nobles: both Hyanisbe, Archombrotus's adoptive mother, and Timandra, Poliarchus's mother, rule alone and take command of their armies. For much of the romance, it looks as though Argenis is being schooled in the traits of this romance gynocracy, as manifested particularly in her mastery of emotion: she becomes expert in managing 'the combat of griefe and dissimulation' such that 'her words and gestures might fall into a just temper' (25). Temperance, or emotional balance, is an indispensable attribute for a monarch, but an unusual aspiration for a romance heroine. Also unusual is the way in which Barclay recasts female dissimulation as a form of legitimate resistance to a flawed king: Argenis in her own way is just as much a threat to the stability of Meleander's throne as are Lycogenes or Radirobanes. She has her own epithet, too—as 'quicke-witted Argenis' (187), she is far better than her father at scenting out treachery and casting her own counter-plots. In a splendid speech comparing herself to Iphigenia, Argenis articulates the frustrations of a woman at the heart of political events, yet without political influence. The letter she writes to Poliarchus binding him to revenge upon Radirobanes for his plots against her and outlining her plans for the 'ghastly spectacle' of her suicide on her forced wedding day is lucid, dignified, and magisterially 'violent', the public-private prose of a princess and an implicit rebuke to the men who command and, so she fears, fail her (IV.5; 256). In its rhetorically charged 'admirable maner' it encapsulates one of the many common threads linking *Argenis* and *Amadis*, both of which, like Argenis's letter, are exhortations to the mighty born of an insistent sense of the dangers and opportunities inherent in the exercising of power.

Further Reading

Barclay, John. *Argenis*, ed. Mark Riley and Dorothy Pritchard Huber, *Bibliotheca Latinitatis Novae/Medieval and Renaissance Texts and Studies*, 273, 2 vols. (Assen: Royal van Gorcum and Tempe, AZ: Arizona Center for Medieval and Renaissance Studies, 2004).
Munday, Anthony. *Amadis de Gaule*, ed. Helen Moore (Aldershot: Ashgate, 2004).
Patterson, Annabel. *Censorship and Interpretation: The Conditions of Writing and Reading in Early Modern England* (Madison, WI: University of Wisconsin Press, 1984).
Salzman, Paul. *English Prose Fiction, 1558–1700: A Critical History* (Oxford: Clarendon Press, 1985).
—— *Literary Culture in Jacobean England: Reading 1621* (New York and Basingstoke: Palgrave Macmillan, 2002).
Zurcher, Amelia A. *Seventeenth-Century English Romance: Allegory, Ethics and Politics* (New York and Basingstoke: Palgrave Macmillan, 2007).

CHAPTER 5

MONTAIGNE AND FLORIO

PETER MACK

MICHEL de Montaigne (1533–92) was one of the great originals of world literature. He perfected a new literary genre in which he asked himself whether the teachings of past generations really corresponded to his own experience of the world and what he discovered through his critical reading. Montaigne's *Essais* question and test (*essayer*) received wisdom. He was sympathetic to scepticism, and his longest chapter, the 'Apologie de Raimond Sebond', gives a careful account of the sceptical position, but far from suspending judgement, as the sceptics advised, Montaigne's aim was to make judgements which better suited his own experience of the world. He was also sympathetic to the epicurean position, intent on valuing the pleasures of life, intellectual as well as physical. He discusses a wide range of subjects, including: proper conduct in politics and war, attitudes to death, pain, and poverty, the advantages and disadvantages of habit, the differences between the old world and the new, sex, friendship, education, reading, travel, vanity, pride, and family life. Since many of his arguments are illustrated with stories about his own life, the *Essais* also provide a self-portrait of a thoughtful man living in times of civil war and suffering the terrible pain of kidney stones. Because Montaigne is so engaging and frank, and because he discusses so many subjects in such original ways, his readers usually feel that they have come to know him personally. The French learned society dedicated to his work is called the Société des Amis de Michel de Montaigne.[1]

Montaigne's method of writing is based on reading, taking a received idea, finding stories and opinions to support that view, and then making counter-arguments which

---

[1] Books in English which offer a starting point on Montaigne include: Sarah Bakewell, *How to Live: A Life of Montaigne* (London: Chatto & Windus, 2010); D. Frame, *Montaigne: A Biography* (London: Hamish Hamilton, 1965); R. A. Sayce, *The Essays of Montaigne: A Critical Exploration* (London: Weidenfeld & Nicholson, 1972); H. Friedrich, *Montaigne* (Berkeley: University of California Press, 1991); U. Langer, ed., *The Cambridge Companion to Montaigne* (Cambridge: Cambridge University Press, 2005); T. Cave, *How to Read Montaigne* (London: Granta, 2007); and P. Mack, *Reading and Rhetoric in Montaigne and Shakespeare* (London: Bloomsbury, 2010). Philippe Desan, ed., *Dictionnaire de Michel de Montaigne*, 2nd edn. (Paris: Champion, 2007) provides up-to-date entries on many important issues related to the study of Montaigne.

were prompted or supported by examples taken from his reading or narratives of his own life. He aimed to be as frank as possible about his opinions and experiences. Typically his chapters grew by accretion. He would reread a section of his text and ask himself whether he really agreed with what he had written. Sometimes his new reading in oriental history or accounts of the conquest of the New World would lead him to add new comments and examples. Above all, he frequently reread a few favourite classical authors (Plutarch, Seneca, Horace, Virgil, Lucretius, and Catullus) and inserted numerous quotations or paraphrases of them in his work, often in Latin, rather than French.

This method of writing, which includes so many sentences from other writers and so many changes of mind, leads to a quality of changeability in the text which both serves to represent the twisting and turning of a mind in motion and enables many different people to feel that Montaigne speaks directly to their experience. Montaigne notices this feeling himself, writing of changeability in his own reading of texts, and of finding different meanings in his own book:

> I pick up some book: I may have discovered outstanding beauties in a particular passage which really struck home: another time I happen on the same passage and it remains an unknown shapeless lump for me ... Even in the case of my own writings I cannot always recover the flavour of my original meaning; I do not know what I wanted to say and burn my fingers making corrections and giving it some new meaning for want of recovering the original meaning which was better. I go backwards and forwards: my judgement does not always march straight ahead, but floats and bobs about,
>
> > Velut minuta magno
> > Deprensa navis in mari vesaniente vento
> > (Like a tiny boat buffeted on the ocean by a raging tempest, Catullus 25.12)
>
> Many's the time I have taken an opinion contrary to my own and (as I am fond of doing) tried defending it for the fun of the exercise: then, once my mind has really applied itself to that other side, I get so firmly attached to it that I forget why I held the original opinion and give it up. (II, 12, P600, S637–8)[2]

Two years after the death of his father, in 1570 Montaigne gave up his magistracy in Bordeaux and went to live on and manage the family estate in Montaigne in the Dordogne. Around 1572 he began to compose his *Essais*, in order to tame the wild fantasies of his idle brain by recording them, as he jokingly claims (I.8, P54–5, S28–9). He sent a first version, in two books, with a total of ninety-four chapters, to the Bordeaux printer Simon Millanges in 1580. He added a few short passages (including one on visiting the poet Tasso, confined in his madness, during his trip to Italy in 1580–1) to the second Bordeaux edition of 1582. The 1588 Paris edition contained a new third book of thirteen generally long chapters and large additions to most of the previous ones. Together these changes doubled the size of

---

[2] Montaigne, *Les Essais*, ed. J. Balsamo, M. Magnien, and C. Magnien-Simonet (Paris: Gallimard, 2007), hereafter P; Montaigne, *The Complete Essays*, trans. M. Screech (Harmondsworth: Penguin, 1991), hereafter S.

the book. At the time of his death he had already made extensive further revisions (mostly additions) which are incorporated in the posthumous 1595 edition, seen through the press by Marie de Gournay, and are represented in a copy of the 1588 edition with manuscript additions by Montaigne and his secretaries, known as the Bordeaux copy.

This process of continual revision has caused problems for editors, readers, and translators. For about three centuries (and for Florio) editions of Montaigne were based on the 1595 edition. Most twentieth-century editions, including the long-standard Villey-Saulnier edition (3rd edition, Paris, 1965) are based on the Bordeaux copy and divide the text into three layers, text originating in 1580 (A), additions in 1588 (B), and new material in the Bordeaux copy (C), which was believed to be more authentic than the 1595 edition. This method of representing the text is very helpful to readers in showing how the text developed, but the editors were at times selective in the changes they recorded, rarely noting single word changes, for example. The Villey-Saulnier text is the basis for the two best-known modern English translations, by Donald Frame (Stanford: Stanford University Press, 1957) and Michael Screech (Harmondsworth: Penguin, 1991). Subsequent bibliographical studies have tended to vindicate the text of 1595, which is now generally believed to be a faithful representation of a second copy of the 1588 edition with manuscript additions sometimes different from those in the Bordeaux copy, which has not survived.[3] The most recent edition by J. Balsamo, M. Magnien, and C. Magnien-Simonet (P) presents the printed text of 1595 but reports all previous versions, and variants from the Bordeaux copy, in notes printed after the text. For readers concerned with English versions of Montaigne, this new edition corresponds to the edition which Florio translated from, but sometimes differs from the text translated by Frame and Screech.[4]

It is easy to exaggerate the extent to which Montaigne retired from the world in 1570. He managed his estates. He took part in various negotiations between Henri III and the Protestant Henri de Navarre, who was eventually in 1593 to convert to Catholicism and become King of France as Henri IV. At the King's command, he became Mayor of Bordeaux in 1581 and served a rare second term up to 1585.[5] His observations on the best manner of conducting oneself in military and political affairs reflect serious personal experience as well as wide reading and deep questioning. It has been suggested that writing and publishing the *Essais* was partly motivated by the desire to improve his political and social standing. At any rate, there is no doubt that the book was successful from the first, drawing compliments from Henri III and making Montaigne much more widely known.[6]

---

[3] R. Sayce, 'L' édition des *Essais* de Montaigne de 1595', *Bibliothèque d'Humanisme et Renaissance*, 36 (1974): 115–41; D. Maskell, 'Quel est le dernier état authentique des *Essais* de Montaigne?', *BHR*, 40 (1978): 85–103; R. Sayce and D. Maskell, *A Descriptive Bibliography of Montaigne's Essais* (London: Bibliographical Society, 1983).

[4] Readers of Frame and Screech's excellent translations will also want to be warned that their (Bordeaux copy based) chapter I.14 ('That the taste of good and evil . . .') becomes I.40 in the 1595 edition, so that their chapters between 15 and 40 will be numbered 1 higher than in 1595 and in Florio.

[5] Frame, *Montaigne*, 223–45, 266–88; Bakewell, *How to Live*, 245–73. G. Hoffmann, *Montaigne's Career* (Oxford: Oxford University Press, 1998).

[6] O. Millet, *La première reception des* Essais *de Montaigne* (Paris: Champion, 1995).

Some of Montaigne's earliest readers were English, including Anthony Bacon, who twice met Montaigne, and his brother Francis, whose somewhat different *Essays* first published in 1597, pay Montaigne the compliment of copying his title and of a few silent borrowings.[7] Soon other writers were copying Montaigne's titles and in 1600 Sir William Cornwallis published his *Essays*, which openly acknowledged a debt to Montaigne, acquired by reading some of them in English translation.[8] On 20 October 1595 'The Essais of Michaell Lord Mountene' was entered in the Stationers' Register of books due to be published by Edward Agger.[9] This probably implies that an English version was being considered, but nothing appeared from that source. On 4 June 1600 'The Essais of Michell lord of Montaigne, translated into Englishe by John Florio' were licensed to Edward Blount, who was involved in the eventual publication of Florio's version in 1603.

John Florio (1553–1626) was born in London to an English mother. His father Michelangelo, an Italian Protestant pastor, left England with the family in 1554 on the accession of Mary, to live first in Strasbourg and then in Soglio in the Val Bregaglia in Switzerland. By 1563 John was at school in Tübingen, staying with the Italian Protestant bishop Pietro Paolo Vergerio. John Florio returned to England in the first half of the 1570s. In 1576 he was tutoring in Italian at Oxford.[10] His first book, *First Fruits*, a bilingual edition of conversational phrases, extracts from poetry, and moral dialogues, intended to teach Italian to the English, and English to Italian merchants, was published from London in 1578. Frances Yates has shown that in places Florio's text relies on Antonio de Guevara and on moral axioms taken from Lodovico Guicciardini's *Hore di Ricreatione* and translated into English in James Sanford's *The Garden of Pleasure* (London, 1573).[11] In 1580, commissioned by Hakluyt, Florio translated the *Navigations and Discoveries* of the French sailor Jacques Cartier, from the Italian version by Ramusio.[12] From 1583 onwards he was employed at the French embassy in London as a tutor and an interpreter. While working there he met and befriended the Italian philosopher Giordano Bruno.[13] In 1591 he published his *Second Fruits*, a series of twelve dialogues for language teaching which are less moralistic and offer a more dramatized portrayal of the social life of privileged young men than the *First Fruits*. The *Second Fruits* are also studded with Italian proverbs which are collected in Florio's *Giardino di Recreatione* (1591).[14] At about this time or soon after, certainly by 1594, Florio entered the service of the Earl of Southampton as his Italian tutor. Florio dedicated his Italian–English dictionary, the *Worlde of Wordes*, to Southampton in 1598, saying that he had been living under his patronage for several years.[15]

---

[7] F. Bacon, *The Essayes*, ed. M. Kiernan (Oxford: Oxford University Press, 1985), 180, 182, 192, 254, 264, 275, 314.

[8] F. O. Matthiessen, *Translation: An Elizabethan Art* (Cambridge, MA: Harvard University Press, 1931), 105–6; D. C. Allen, ed., *Essayes by Sir William Cornwallis the Younger* (Baltimore: Johns Hopkins University Press, 1946), 44.

[9] F. A. Yates, *John Florio* (Cambridge: Cambridge University Press, 1934), 214.

[10] Yates, *Florio*, 13–22.   [11] Yates, *Florio*, 36–41.   [12] Yates, *Florio*, 55–6.

[13] Yates, *Florio*, 61–2, 112–25.   [14] Yates, *Florio*, 124–38.   [15] Yates, *Florio*, 188–91.

An Anglo-Italian Protestant who had been educated in Germany and had worked in the French embassy, Florio was a language teacher who composed and compiled moral dialogues, collections of proverbs, and the first large-scale Italian–English dictionary (which defined 46,000 words, expanded in the second edition of 1611 to around 74,000)[16] and translated a travel narrative. It is easy to understand how reading Montaigne's *Essais*, which also used classical ethical writings and their modern compilations, proverbs, and histories of the New World, might have appealed to Florio. In his dedicatory epistles Florio thanks Sir Edward Wotton as his 'not-to-be-denied Benefactor', while recalling the way in which Lady Anne Harrington had encouraged him from the point when he had completed only one chapter of the work.[17] He explains that he was attracted above all by the work's

> so pleasing passages, so judicious discourses, so delightsome varieties, so persuasive conclusions, such learning of all sortes, and above all, so elegant a French stile, as (I thinke) for ESSAYES, I may say of him, as he in this Booke, did of Homer: Heere shines in him the greatest wit without example, without exception, deserving for his composition to be entituled, Sole Maister of Essayes. (Florio, II, 4)

He also mentions the help which he has received from the learning of Thomas Diodati and John Harrington in unravelling the difficulties of the text, and from Dr Matthew Gwinne, who has translated and as far as possible identified for him 'what Latine prose, Greeke, Latine, Italian or French Poesie should crosse my way',[18] thus allowing Florio to provide English versions of almost all the foreign language quotations, a help which Montaigne did not provide for his French readers.

In a slightly paradoxical consensus, critics who have compared the translation to Montaigne's original in detail agree that Florio's work contains omissions, mistakes, misunderstandings, and additions, and yet that it is a highly successful translation, which nevertheless retains 'the essential spirit' of Montaigne's book.[19] Matthiessen and Yates have collected representative examples of Florio's errors;[20] some derive from misunderstanding of the sentence structure or of vocabulary. Several involve mistakes of number or tense. Some are easy for the reader to correct, while others create nonsense for a sentence or two. (We will come across a few instances below.) This is regrettable, but it doesn't matter a great deal. Montaigne is so rich, he says so many different things, that it is impossible for a reader to respond to and remember every aspect of a twenty-page segment, never mind of the whole. If Florio fluffs some of the lines, he conveys enough of the others with vitality and expressiveness to justify any reader's attention. For such a long and difficult text there are surprisingly few errors. Indeed, there are some French scholars of Montaigne who, when they are in doubt about Montaigne's meaning, consult Florio as one source of possible resolutions.

---

[16] Yates, *Florio*, 265, 188–213, 265–76.
[17] Montaigne, *The Essayes of Michael Lord of Montaigne, Translated by John Florio*, ed. A. R. Waller, 3 vols. (London: Everyman's Library, Dent, 1910), hereafter Florio, I, 3–4.
[18] Florio I, 4–5; Matthiessen, *Translation*, 155–6.
[19] Matthiessen, *Translation*, 130–4.   [20] Matthiessen, *Translation*, 130–4 ; Yates, *Florio*, 237–9.

Florio also adds to the text. On most pages there will be several examples of Florio doubling a verb or a noun, but doubling is also a very strong characteristic of Montaigne's own style. Sometimes Montaigne used to remove doublets in the process of revision, but he also used to add others.[21] Florio's preference for alliteration in his doublets is not shared by Montaigne, but it is very characteristic of sixteenth-century English prose and would have seemed very natural to Florio's readers. Florio likes to add in proverbs and idiomatic English expressions; Montaigne too liked proverbs and idioms. Thus, for example, when Montaigne explains that since all men are unfaithful it is only just that most of them should also be cuckolds,

> Chacun de vous a fait quelqu'un coqu: or nature est toute en pareilles, en compensation et vicissitude. La frequence de cet accident en doibt mes-huy avoir moderé l'aigreur: le voylà tantost passé en coustume. (III, 5, P913)

Florio adds a pair of proverbs to reinforce the point, but manages to recover the brevity and force of the conclusion.

> There is none of you all but hath made one Cuckold or other. Now nature stood ever even on this point, *Kae mee Ile kae thee*, and ever ready to be even always on recompences and vicissitude of things and to give as good as one brings. The long-continued frequence of this accident, should by this time have seasoned the bitter taste thereof. It is almost become a custome. (Florio, III, 97)

Here, as often, Florio retains some of Montaigne's key words (nature, compensation, vicissitude, frequence, and custome), while adding native English phrases which clarify the meaning. Many of Florio's importations have become naturalized English words, but some, as Matthiessen shows, have not (*Translation*, 120–1). Florio sometimes adds explanations which a French reader would not have needed (noting, for example that the Louvre is 'the pallace of our Kings in Paris');[22] so much the better for the English reader. Sometimes he adapted cultural references, replacing 'les Basques et les Troglodytes', with 'the Cornish, the Welch, or Irish'. Sometimes he elaborates to convey a London flavour, as when 'la tourbe des escrivailleurs' becomes 'the common-rabble of Scriblers and blur-papers which now adayes stuffe Stationers shops'.[23] Matthiessen uses italics to show how Florio elaborates the detail of Montaigne's anecdote about the bearded old man he once met, who had, until the age of 22, been the woman Marie Germain:

> He saith, that *upon a time* leaping, and straining himselfe *to overleape another, he wot not how, but where before he was a woman he suddenly felt* the instrument of a man to come out of him; and to this day the maidens of *that towne and countrie* have a song in use, by which they warn one another, *when they are leaping*, not to *straine themselves overmuch, or* open their legs too wide, for feare they should be turned to boies, as Marie Germane was. (Florio I, 94; Matthiessen, *Translation*, 137)

---

[21] P. Iemma, *Les Repentirs de l'Exemplaire de Bordeaux* (Paris: Champion, 2004), 91, 92, 103 144–5 ; Mack, *Reading and Rhetoric*, 50–1.

[22] III, 9, P1042, Florio III, 246; earlier he had translated 'Louvre' as 'the court', III, 3, P864, Florio III, 43.

[23] I owe these two examples to Yates, *Florio*, 237.

Florio's additions here, which almost seem inspired by Erasmus's methods for producing *copia* of things, make the story more vivid and enjoyable. More than for most writers, Montaigne's was an open text, which he added to when he pleased; for Florio to add a little more, even if sometimes it is more English than Montaigne, does not harm the translation in any important way. Indeed, it may help naturalize the text for English readers.

Florio's longest addition, noted by Frances Yates, inserts twelve lines or so to 'On the Education of Children' (II.25):

> Madame, Learning joined with true knowledge is an especiall and graceful ornament, and an implement of wonderfull use and consequence, namely in persons raised to that degree of fortune, wherein you are. And in good truth, learning hath not her owne true forme, nor can she make shew of her beauteous lineaments, if she fall into the hands of base and vile persons. For, as famous Torquato Tasso saith: 'Philosophie being a rich and noble Queene, and knowing her own worth, graciously smileth upon and lovingly embraceth Princes and noble men, if they become suitors to her, admitting them as her minions, and gently affording them all the favours she can; whereas upon the contrarie, if she be wooed, and sued unto by clownes, mechanicall fellows, and such base kind of people, she holds herself disparaged and disgraced, as holding no proportion with them. And therefore see we by experience, that if a true Gentleman, or nobleman follow her with attention, and woo her with importunitie, he shall learne and know more of her, and prove a better scholler in one yeare, than an ungentle or base fellow shall in seven, though he pursue her never so attentively.' (Florio, II, 153–4)

We are quite justified in condemning these sentiments, but we need to put them in context. Montaigne, in the first five lines, is urging an aristocratic lady to give her son a liberal and literary education; he wants to assure her that it will be worthwhile. Florio, no doubt thinking of the aristocratic ladies to whom his edition is dedicated, adds the long supporting quotation from Tasso. Montaigne would probably not have quoted this passage at such length, but to back up an opinion expressed in his own voice with a quotation found later through his reading is absolutely characteristic of the way he revises his text. It is quite understandable that Florio, as a commoner seeking to renew aristocratic patronage, should add to the flattery which Montaigne, more conceitedly in view of his own social standing, had begun. In the literal sense, this is not translation, but neither does it falsify the original.

Matthiessen and Yates have drawn attention to a change which Florio made on the grounds of his religious beliefs. Where Montaigne wrote 'des erreurs de Wiclef' (I.3, P41), Florio referred to 'Wickliff's opinions' (I, p. 28). On other occasions, though, Florio translated Montaigne's criticism of Elizabethan policy or the Protestant religion without alteration. In the eighteenth chapter of the first book ('That we should not judge of our happiness until after our death'), Montaigne gives as one of his examples of an honourable life ended by a miserable death an unmistakeable condemnation of the execution of Mary Stuart.

> La plus belle Royne, vefve du plus grand Roy de la Chrestienté, vient elle pas de mourir par la main d'un Bourreau? Indigne et barbare cruauté! (I.18, P80)

Florio translates this directly, with the slight alteration of widow to wife:

> The fairest Queene, wife to the greatest King of Christendome, was she not lately seene to die by the hands of an executioner? Oh unworthie and barbarous crueltie! (Florio, I, 71)

Florio makes no attempt to soften Montaigne's criticism of Elizabeth. Expressing his sorrow at changes of religion on the other side of the channel, Montaigne writes:

> Depuis que je suis nay, j'ay veu trois et quatre fois, rechanger celles [i.e. les loix] des Anglois noz voisins, non seulement en subject politique, qui est celuy qu'on veut dispenser de constance, mais au plus important subject qui puisse estre, à sçavoir de la religion. (II.12, P614)

Florio makes some small expansions but reports this without altering the charge of flightiness which a Protestant subject of Elizabeth would presumably have resented:

> I have since I was borne, scene those [i.e. the laws] of our neighbours the Englishmen changed and rechanged three or four times, not only in politike subjects, which is that some will dispense of constancy, but in the most important subject, that can possibly be, that is to say, in religion. (Florio I, 296)

If anything, Florio's habit of doubling verbs here ('changed and rechanged') makes the accusation seem worse. He spoils the effect of Montaigne's throw-away summary of this section, through not quite grasping the implication. Montaigne wrote

> Quelle bonté est-ce, que je voyois hyer en credit, et demain ne l'estre plus: et que le traject d'une riviere fait crime? (II.12, P615)

Florio gives

> What goodnesse is that, which but yesterday I saw in credit and esteeme, and tomorrow to have lost all reputation, and that the crossing of a river is made a crime? (II, 297)

The sense here needs to be 'and the crossing of a river makes something a crime'. Screech translates

> What kind of good can it be which was honoured yesterday but not today and which becomes a crime when you cross a river! (S653)

which alters the original a bit more than Florio does but conveys the throw-away tone much better. In this case, apart from the misunderstanding, Florio's tendency to make things longer and heavier works against what Montaigne writes. The first chapter of the second book ends with phrases of self-conscious brevity, making a joke of the paradoxical recommendation that people should give up making judgements.

> Il faut sonder jusqu'au dedans, et voir par quels ressors se donne le bransle. Mais d'autant que c'est une hazardeuse et haute entreprinse, je voudrois que moins de gens s'en meslassent. (II.1, P358)

Florio takes his often successful approach of making things clearer and more concrete, but loses the wit and ironic force of the conclusion.

> A man must thorowly sound himselfe, and dive into his heart, and there see by what wards or springs the motions stirre. But forasmuch as it is a hazardous and high enterprise, I would not have so many meddle with it as doe. (II, 15)

The first sentence here is very forceful and concrete, though without the concision of the original. The second suffers by staying too close to Montaigne's vocabulary and word order until the end, when English grammar requires an addition. Reluctantly, but for the sake of honesty, I'll give one more example of Florio not quite conveying the sense of his original. In book III chapter 5, Montaigne is discussing the importance of the phallus in religions and folk customs:

> Les plus sages matrons à Rome, estoient honorées d'offrir des fleurs et coronnes au Dieu Priapus: Et sur ses parties moins honnestes faisoit-on soir les vierges au temps de leurs nopces. (P901)

Florio translates:

> The greatest and wisest matrons of Rome were honoured for offering flowers and garlands to God Priapus. And when their virgins were married, they (during the nuptials) were made to sit upon their privities. (III, 83)

Florio here seems to mistake the interpretation of both the preposition in the first sentence and the singular possessive pronoun in the second. Screech conveys the meaning of both words more accurately:

> The wisest of the Roman matrons were granted the honour of offering crowns of flowers to the God Priapus; when their maidens came to marry, they were required to squat over its less decent parts. (S969)

But when you take the opposite approach and turn to your favourite passages of Montaigne, most of the time Florio conveys Montaigne's meaning very well and sometimes he writes superb English, largely as a result of his small changes in focus. Here, for example, Florio translates Montaigne on the contrast between man's large ambitions and his wretched nature:

> Let us now but consider man alone without other help, armed but with his owne weapons, and unprovided of the grace of God, which is all his honour, all his strength, and all the ground of his being. Let us see what hold-fast, or free-hold he hath in this gorgeous, and goodly equipage. Let him with the utmost power of his discourse make me understand, upon what foundation, he hath built those great advantages and odds, he supposeth to have over other creatures. Who hath perswaded him, that this admirable moving of heavens vaults; that the eternal light of these lampes so fiercely rowling over his head; that the horror-moving and continuall motion of this infinite vaste Ocean, were established and continue so many ages for his commoditie and service? Is it possible to imagine any thing so ridiculous, as

this miserable and wreched creature, which is not so much as master of himselfe, exposed and subject to offences of all things and yet dareth call himselfe Master and Emperour of this Universe? (II, 139)

The force of this passage is built on contrasts, particularly in the first, fourth, and fifth sentences. In the first sentence, announcing the idea to be explored, man alone, without help and armed only with his own weapons, is contrasted with God, as the source of honour, strength, and being. The fourth sentence encompasses a triple description of the grandeur of the universe, which is the main focus of the sentence, within a mocking question (Who has persuaded man that the whole world exists only for his benefit?). The fifth sentence contrasts the miserableness and wretchedness of man, not even master of himself, with his claim to be master and emperor of the world. The contrast is introduced as the most ridiculous proposition that could be entertained.

The architecture of this passage and the structure of the individual sentences are all Montaigne's (P470–1). Florio's only significant additions are the alliterated doublings in the second sentence where 'tenue' becomes 'hold-fast or free-hold' and 'bel equipage' becomes 'gorgeous, and goodly equipage', which together slightly spoil the terseness of Montaigne's second sentence, in contrast to the other four sentences and the expansion in the third sentence of 'avantages' to 'advantages and odds'. The moments of contrast, the triplings, and the build-up to the rhetorical questions are all Montaigne's. And yet, thanks to Florio's choice of apt and concrete equivalents this is an extraordinary passage of English prose, at the same time more restrained and more magnificent than Lyly or Sidney could have managed. Florio had the taste to recognize the superb formal shape which Montaigne had created and he had the breadth of vocabulary from which to choose equivalent terms which could fit into Montaigne's structure and deliver a similar combination of the descriptive and the expressive. Here is Florio's version of one of the central arguments of 'On Vanity' (III, 9):

You will say, there is vanitie in this amusement. But where not? And these goodly precepts are vanitie, and *Meere vanitie is all worldly wisedome. Dominus novit cogitationes sapientum, quoniam vanae sunt* (Psalm 93.11). *The Lord knows the thoughtes of the wise, that they are vaine.* Such exquisite subtilities are onely fit for sermons. They are discourses that will send us into the other world on horsebacke. *Life is a materiall and corporall motion, an action imperfect and disordered by its owne essence*: I employ or apply my selfe to serve it according to it selfe . . . To what purpose are these heaven-looking and nice points of Philosophie, on which no humane being can establish and ground it selfe? And to what end serve these rules that exceed our use and excell our strength? I often see that there are certaine Ideaes or formes of life proposed unto us, which neither the proposer nor the Auditors have any hope at all to follow; and which is worse, no desire to attaine. *Of the same paper, whereon a Judge writ but even now the condemnation against an adulterer, hee will teare a scantlin, thereon to write some love-lines to his fellow-judges wife. The same woman from whom you have come lately, and with whom you have committed that unlawfull-pleasing sport, will soone after even in your presence, raile and scold more bitterly against the same fault in her neighbour than ever* Portia *or* Lucrece *could. And some condemne men to die for crimes that themselves esteeme no faults... Human wisedome could never reach the duties, or attaine the devoirs it had prescribed unto it selfe.* And had it at any time attained them, then would it doubtlesse prescribe some others beyond them, to which it might ever aspire and pretend. So great an enemy is our condition unto consistence. (Florio, III, 236–7, 239, italics as in original; P1034–5, 1036)

This passage combines unsettling reversals of perspective, general statements about human life, rhetorical questions, and detailed dramatic vignettes. It advances a profound critique of existing ethical teachings, arguing that they are no less vain than all other human activities, that indeed there may be something in human nature that causes people to establish moral rules which they can never live up to. It is dizzyingly impressive as a piece of thought and extraordinarily effectively expressed.

The rhythm and arrangement of Florio's prose here owe everything to Montaigne. Florio's extremely compressed second sentence exactly reproduces Montaigne's 'Mais où non'. The near-chiasmus in the third sentence (Precepts.vanity/Vanity.wisdom) is Montaigne's. The Bible quotation is Montaigne's, though, as usual, he does not add a translation into French. The move to the literal in the seventh sentence ('on horseback') exactly reproduces Montaigne's 'basté' (saddled up). The first two doublings of the eighth sentence (material and corporal; imperfect and disordered) are Montaigne's, though the third (employ or apply) is Florio's addition; as is 'heaven-looking and nice' for Montaigne's 'eslevées'. 'Scantlin' is a magnificent equivalent for 'lopin'. 'Unlawfull-pleasing sport' is less physical and more obvious in its opposition of morality and pleasure than 'vous frotter illicitement', but its overriding moral tone follows its original, as it needs to do in view of the opposition of ideas with 'Judge' in the previous sentence and Portia in this one. Florio doubles 'raile and scold' for 'criera', and adds Lucrece beside Portia. His 'could never reach the duties or attain the devoirs' is somewhat redundant for 'n'arriva jamais aux devoirs', but it explains the retained French word. 'Aspire and pretend' copies Montaigne's words, while the final sentence is an exact and forceful rendition of 'Tant nostre estat est ennemy de consistance'. Perhaps Montaigne's passage is stronger for being slightly briefer than Florio's, but Florio gives English readers almost everything they could want from a quite exceptional passage of writing. None of the English moralists of the period can come close to this.

My final example is a passage which I had thought would be impossible to do well in English, where Montaigne examines the vocabulary which produces the particular gravity of a passage in Lucretius describing the love making of Mars and Venus and continues to reflect on the special qualities of the greatest Latin poetry:

Their speech is altogether full and massie, with a naturall and constant vigor. They are all epigram, not only tail, but head, stomach and feet. There is nothing forced, nothing wrested, nothing limping; all marcheth with like tenour. *Contextus totus virilis est, non sunt circa flosculos occupati.*[24] *The whole composition or text is manly, they are not bebusied about Rhetoric flowers.* This is not a soft quaint eloquence, and

---

[24] Seneca, Letters to Lucilius, 33.1; Florio (or Gwinne) does not identify this quotation.

only without offence, it is sinnowie, materiall, and solid; not so much delighting, as filling and ravishing, and ravisheth most the strongest wits, the wittiest conceits. When I behold these gallant forms of expression, so lively, so nimble, so deepe: I say this is not to speake well, but to think wel. It is the quaintnesse or livelinesse of the conceit, that elevateth and puffes up the words. *Pectus est quod disertum facit.*[25] *It is a mans owne brest, that makes him eloquent.* Our people terms judgement, language; and full conceptions, fine words. This pourtraiture is directed not so much by the hands dexterity, as by having the object more lively printed in the minde. *Gallus* speaks plainly, because he conceiveth plainly. *Horace* is not pleased with a sleight or superficiall expressing; it would betray him; he seeth more cleere and further into matters; his spirit pickes and ransaketh the whole store-house of words and figures to shew and present himselfe; and he must have them more then ordinary, as his conceit is beyond ordinary. *Plutarch* saith that he discerned the Latin tongue by things. Here likewise the sense enlighteneth and produceth the words; no longer windy or spongy, but of flesh and bone. They signifie more then they utter. (Florio, III, 100–1, P915–16)

The passage both describes and accounts for the forcefulness of the best Latin poetry. Montaigne regards such inspiring writing as a product of sharp perception and strong thought. The style he describes is lively, weighty, and thoughtful. The passage is characterized by vocabulary which is vivid and concrete, embodying some of the qualities it admires in the passage from Lucretius. It is as if Montaigne as reader claims for himself the same qualities which he finds in the passages he quotes, supporting the implication with the claim that the strongest intellects respond best to such powerful language. The idea that striking thought is required to produce forceful language is developed through a metaphor from painting, a comparison between Gallus and Horace, a justifying quotation from Plutarch, and a development of Plutarch's idea in his own voice.

Florio follows Montaigne's structures very closely in this passage. His wide vocabulary enables him to choose English words which have the physicality and gravity of the French words he is translating. Much of the weight of the passage derives from these carefully chosen words, but he enhances the effect by adding to Montaigne's lists of qualifiers and adjectives (for example 'nothing limping' [l. 3], 'quaint' [l. 5], 'materiall' [l. 6], and 'nimble' [l. 8] are Florio's additions). He supports 'the strongest wits' in line 7, translating 'les plus forts esprits', by the appositional addition of 'the wittiest conceits'. He translates 'gailliardise', with the doubling 'quaintnesse or livelinesse' (line 9). Some of these additions look like alternative translations, helping to clarify Montaigne's meaning, but their effect is to make the opening section of the passage even weightier. There are only two additions in the second half of the passage, when he offers the alternatives 'shew and present' (l. 17) for 'representer', and 'windy or spongy' (l. 19) for 'de vent'. In lines 11–12, he inverts the order, possibly to clarify the logic of the sentence, but in so doing, he loses the near-chiasmus of Montaigne's 'jugement, langage, et beaux mots, les pleines conceptions'.

---

[25] Quintilian, *Institutio oratoria*, X.7.15; not identified by Florio.

The argument of this passage, that strong thoughts produce an effective style, could be applied to Florio, who writes a strong, forceful English by following the movement of Montaigne's French arguments very closely and by choosing English words which convey the same qualities of weightiness, sharpness, and liveliness. Some of Florio's additions give his sentences the sort of balance which contemporary English prose stylists sought for, as in the last phrase of 'his spirit pickes and ransaketh the whole store-house of words and figures to shew and present himselfe', but, in general, by following Montaigne so closely, he achieves an English prose style which is neither Ciceronian, nor Euphuistic, nor Senecan, though epigrammatic phrases can play a part in it. More importantly, he brings over for his English audience the thought and much of the tone of his original.

Florio's translation of Montaigne was successful almost from its first publication in 1603. New editions appeared in 1613 and 1632. The book was owned by Ben Jonson, who borrowed from it in *Timber*, and Sir Walter Ralegh.[26] It was extensively quoted in Robert Burton's *Anatomy of Melancholy*. Shakespeare used a section of 'Des cannibales' in *The Tempest* (1611) and may well have borrowed from Montaigne's ideas, through Florio, in earlier plays. Marston (especially in *The Dutch Courtesan*) and Webster used phrases taken from Florio's translation in their plays, both for the pithiness of the expression and for the frankness of some of his remarks on sexual behaviour.[27] William Hamlin has collected the marginal notes of numerous readers of the first three editions of Florio and has noted its use in Samuel Daniel's *The Queen's Arcadia* (1605) and Richard Younge's *Drunkard's Character* (1638).[28] He has edited a seventeenth-century English compilation of moral axioms which evidently draws on Florio.[29] Warren Boutcher has shown that James Cleland borrowed from Florio in his *Institution of a Young Nobleman* (1605).[30]

Florio's translation owes its success primarily to the quality of the original. Montaigne was an engaging writer and a perceptive critical thinker. His questioning attitude and his determination to test received ideas against the problems of living in the practical world, as well as his willingness to write about subjects which most other writers passed over, attracted early modern English readers. But Montaigne's text is often difficult and his habit of adding in new stories, quotations, and reflections can make the line of the

---

[26] A. H. Upham, *The French Influence in English Literature* (New York: Columbia University Press, 1911), 524–8, 537–44.

[27] Yates, *Florio*, 240–4; Matthiessen, *Translation*, 156–68; R. W. Dent, *John Webster's Borrowing* (Berkeley: University of California Press, 1960), 41–2, 78–85, 125–6, 133, 164, 169, 177, 179, 192, 194–5, 238, 246, 256–7; P. Mack, 'Montaigne and Shakespeare: Source, Parallel or Comparison', *Montaigne Studies*, 23 (2011): 151–80. Hamlin (see next note) pp. 510–11, Mack, 'Marston and Webster's Use of Montaigne', *Montaigne Studies*, 24 (2012): 67–82.

[28] W. M. Hamlin, 'Florio's Montaigne and the Tyranny of "Custome": Appropriation, Ideology and Early English Readership of the *Essayes*', *Renaissance Quarterly*, 63 (2010): 491–544.

[29] W. M. Hamlin, '*Montagne's Moral Maxims*: Seventeenth-Century English Aphorisms Derived from the *Essayes* of Montaigne', *Montaigne Studies*, 21 (2009): 209–24.

[30] W. Boutcher, 'Marginal Commentaries: The Cultural Transmission of Montaigne's *Essais* in Shakespeare's England', in P. Kapitaniak and J.-M. Maguin, eds., *Shakespeare et Montaigne* (Montpellier: Société Française Shakespeare, 2004), 13–27 (25–6). Both Boutcher and Hamlin are preparing books on the influence of Florio's Montaigne in the seventeenth century.

argument hard to follow. Florio's translation is almost always lively, generally accurate, and it reads well in English. For the most part, the excellence of Florio's English prose derives from the closeness with which he followed Montaigne's sentence structures. Florio's vocabulary usually has just the right mixture of concrete, physical objects and abstract concepts. Sometimes he finds breath takingly suitable English equivalents for difficult French words. Florio never wrote anything as good as his translation of Montaigne, though he did compile a superb dictionary; from the point of view of his English reception, Montaigne was fortunate to find a translator who appreciated the power of his sentence structures and had the breadth and liveliness of vocabulary to match his own 'sinnowie, materiall, and solid' language.

FURTHER READING

Boutcher, W. 'Marginal Commentaries: The Cultural Transmission of Montaigne's *Essais* in Shakespeare's England', in P. Kapitaniak and J.-M. Maguin, eds., *Shakespeare et Montaigne* (Montpellier: Société Française Shakespeare, 2004), 13–27.

Cave, T. *How to Read Montaigne* (London: Granta, 2007).

Friedrich, H. *Montaigne* (Berkeley: University of California Press, 1991).

Hamlin, W. M. 'Florio's Montaigne and the Tyranny of "Custome": Appropriation, Ideology and Early English Readership of the *Essayes*', *Renaissance Quarterly*, 63 (2010): 491–544.

Langer, U., ed. *The Cambridge Companion to Montaigne* (Cambridge: Cambridge University Press, 2005).

Mack, P. *Reading and Rhetoric in Montaigne and Shakespeare* (London: Bloomsbury, 2010).

Matthiessen, F. O. *Translation: An Elizabethan Art* (Cambridge, MA: Harvard University Press, 1931).

Montaigne, *The Complete Essays*, trans. M. Screech (Harmondsworth: Panguin, 1991).

—— *Les Essais*, ed. J. Balsamo, M. Magnien, and C. Magnien-Simonet (Paris: Gallimard, 2007).

—— *The Essayes of Michael Lord of Montaigne, Translated by John Florio*, ed. A. R. Waller, 3 vols. (London: Everyman's Library, Dent, 1910).

Sayce, R. A. *The Essays of Montaigne: A Critical Exploration* (London: Weidenfeld & Nicolson, 1972).

Yates, F. A. *John Florio* (Cambridge: Cambridge University Press, 1934).

CHAPTER 6

ITALIANATE TALES: WILLIAM PAINTER AND GEORGE PETTIE

NEIL RHODES

6.1

In 1566, exactly a decade before 'The Theater' opened in Shoreditch, William Painter, Clerk of the Ordnance at the Tower of London, published the first collection of prose short stories in English, promisingly called *The Palace of Pleasure*. Reading these stories now, it is difficult to avoid seeing them either as antecedents of the drama, or as antecedents of the novel, and in both cases as rather lumbering prototypes of a more sophisticated literary form. Yet, this is clearly not how Boccaccio stands in relation to subsequent Italian literature and it is Boccaccio who determines the ultimate character of Painter's landmark collection. He tells us in his preface that he has translated a good deal from the *Decameron*, but only intends to include ten stories in the present volume and will save the rest for 'another tome', unless somebody else 'with better stile to express the author's eloquence' beats him to it. He anticipates and claims to welcome competition because 'the works of Boccaccio for his stile, order of writing, gravitie, and sententious discourse, is worthy of intire provulgation' (1: 11). There is an air of defensiveness about this, since Painter is well aware of how the subject matter of his stories is likely to be interpreted by his more high-minded English readers and he wants to assert Boccaccio's status as an elevated author and a master of vernacular prose style. This is why he opts for the rather pompous term 'provulgation' to describe his Englishing of these tales. He is anxious to explain why they should be made common, but doesn't want them to sound too common; nonetheless, in a later century C. S. Lewis was to rate them as common as muck when he described the *Palace* as 'dung or compost for the popular drama'.[1]

---

[1] C. S. Lewis, *English Literature in the Sixteenth Century* (Oxford: Clarendon Press, 1954), 309.

Painter was absolutely right in anticipating both the popularity that this new literary form would enjoy with English readers and the odium it might attract from the custodians of good taste and public morals. The second volume he had planned appeared in 1567 and almost immediately Geoffrey Fenton published a competing collection, *Certain Tragicall Discourses*, which had four stories on exactly the same subjects as those of Tome 2 of the *Palace*. A complete *Palace* came out in 1575 and in the following year George Pettie produced his slimmer variation on the winning formula, *A Petite Pallace of Pettie his Pleasure*, which went through six editions to 1615. There were similar offerings from Thomas Fortescue (1571) and Robert Smythe (1577), while George Whetstone and George Turberville both published collections of verse stories in 1576. Whetstone's book, *The Rock of Regard*, versified some of Painter's tales and he followed this with a prose collection called *The Heptameron of Civil Discourses* (1582), which was successful enough to reappear in 1593 with the new title, *Aurelia: The Paragon of Pleasure and Princely Delights*. So Painter's initial volume let loose a spate of publications in the genre of short prose fiction, with a particular concentration around the time that the new playhouse opened in 1576, and it was not long before the fashion for this kind of literature met with a backlash from the likes of the pedagogue Roger Ascham (Queen Elizabeth's former tutor) and the playwright-turned-Puritan Stephen Gosson. The grounds of Ascham's attack on 'Italianate tales' has been wittily analysed by R. W. Maslen, but the gist of his and Gosson's censure is that this material is morally corrupting and socially subversive.[2] What is not in doubt is the impact that the new prose fiction made. When Lewis called it 'dung' he meant of course that it was a fertilizing agent, so his remark is not entirely contemptuous, but he underestimated the importance of the genre in its own right. What Painter introduced to English from Boccaccio was exactly the kind of generic and stylistic flexibility that is traditionally associated with Shakespeare: the mixing of comedy and tragedy and the moving between high and low stylistic registers. What he introduced from his classical models (especially Livy) was the kind of controversial ethical framework that characterizes much of Elizabethan literature, both dramatic and non-dramatic; and what he took from his other modern sources was an inventory of plot material that could be rhetorically deployed by resourceful characters to serve their own ends, as Lorna Hutson has argued.[3] This volatile mix ensured that the new prose fiction was innovative, experimental, and explosive, as one might expect a keeper of munitions to appreciate. It is no wonder that Ascham was alarmed.

But how do we read these stories now, in view of their later eclipse first by the drama and then by the novel? One of the difficulties of getting a purchase on them is that Painter himself is uncertain as to the genre he is working in. The genesis of the *Palace* has been well described by Andrew Hadfield, who points out that its original title had been 'The City of Civility' and that Painter had initially gone to Livy for his material, a choice that

---

[2] R. W. Maslen, *Elizabethan Fictions: Espionage, Counter-Espionage, and the Duplicity of Fiction in Early Elizabethan Prose Narratives* (Oxford: Clarendon Press), 6–7.

[3] Lorna Hutson, *The Usurer's Daughter: Male Friendship and Fictions of Women in Sixteenth-Century England* (London: Routledge, 1994), 91–151.

was 'a bit subversive because of [Livy's] republican sympathies'.[4] Livy is the source for the first five stories in the *Palace*, and other classical authors (Aelian, Aulus Gellius, and Plutarch) dominate up to tale 30, when Boccaccio first appears. There is no doubt that the genre represented by Livy is 'history'. But the term 'history' is used very flexibly in sixteenth-century English to cover both fact and fiction and fiction masquerading as fact. There is a rough equivalent in modern Italian *la storia*, which means history in the modern sense, but also a fictional story and even (as in modern English 'just telling a story') a load of rubbish. The veracity or otherwise of this kind of material is a hugely sensitive issue, not just for Painter, but for other writers of fiction in the period, and it culminates in Sidney's assertion in the *Apology for Poetry* that for the poet 'nothing affirms, and therefore never lieth' (103). All are aware that fiction is fraught with moral danger. In the case of Painter, this anxiety is evident in the ambiguous way he refers to the stories in his collection. In the dedication to the Earl of Warwick he explains that it all started when he chanced upon a copy of Livy in the meagre holdings of the armoury library and decided to translate some of these 'straung Histories' into English. But when he moves on to the more modern writers, his terminology starts to shift, as he refers to 'these histories (which by another terme I call Novelles)', and in the dedication to the reader that follows, he uses 'histories' and 'novelles' interchangeably, though with the order reversed, because he is now addressing the reading public rather than an aristocratic patron: '[t]hese novelles then... [are] profitable and pleasaunt Histories, apt and meete for all degrees...' (1: 13). Painter seems to have been the first person to use the term 'novel' in English to refer to short prose fiction and he takes it from Boccaccio, who is even more elastic in his generic description of the stories in the *Decameron*, calling them 'a hundred stories or fables or parables or histories' ['cento novelle o favole o parabole o istorie'] (1995: 3). Though Painter starts out with Livy, it is Boccaccio, along with his followers, Marguerite of Navarre and Matteo Bandello, who determines the direction that *The Palace of Pleasure* would eventually take.[5]

Painter's change of direction is extremely significant and this is apparent in his change of title as well as his change of terminology. When the book was entered in the Stationers' Register as 'The Cytie of Cyuelitie' in 1562, Painter clearly had in mind a work of political counsel, where 'civility' is almost tautological since it points to issues of civil order or justice within a state or 'city'. At least, that is how the stories from Livy that begin the volume might be described and Painter's original title seems to have been chosen with those in mind. 'The Palace of Pleasure', on the other hand, gestures to the very different, aristocratic milieu of the *Decameron*, or rather of its *cornice* or narrative frame, where seven ladies and three young men escape from plague-ridden Florence to a country estate, 'a palace, built round a fine, spacious courtyard, and containing loggias, halls, and sleeping apartments', where they tell their stories (19). The Italian *novelle* are quite deliberately

---

[4] Andrew Hadfield, *Literature, Travel, and Colonial Writing in the English Renaissance, 1545–1625* (Oxford: Clarendon Press), 149.

[5] On sixteenth-century English translation of Boccaccio see Giovanni Boccaccio, *Boccaccio in English, 1494–1620*, ed. Guyda Armstrong (London: MHRA, forthcoming).

not 'of the city'. Where the 'city of civility' template would have required readers to focus uncompromisingly on the rigours of civic duty, its redesignation as the 'palace of pleasure' releases them into an environment that allows the possibility of social experiment and a more flexible understanding of identities determined by rank and gender. In a word, Painter's move from the city to the palace redirects the genre from the political to the social and this is in turn reflected in his shift of terminology from history to 'novelles'. But while he may he may have been the first English writer to use that term to refer to the prose short story, the word was already available to mean 'news' or 'gossip' as a Gallicized version of Old English 'tidings'.[6] In that respect, 'novelles' originate in oral reports and can be understood as operating within the social framework of conversation. So one way of understanding Painter's choices is to see them in terms of a shift in the meaning of 'civility': from the fundamentally political sense of the civic to the more social sense that is represented by the term 'civil conversation'. This is roughly how short prose fiction in English develops in the decade before the theatre.

The last reason why Boccaccio was important to Painter is that he was able to confer status on a deeply suspect genre that might have been seen as little more than pulp fiction, as it were, without any of the sophisticated referencing of a Quentin Tarantino. The classical histories were not in need of an apology: as Painter points out, Cicero had described 'what difference of commoditie, is between fained fables, and lively discourses of true histories' (1: 14). The Boccaccian *novella*, on the other hand, while not mythological, was certainly of dubious authenticity and far from being concerned only with the ruling classes and with momentous political events. At the same time, Boccaccio had the status of being one of a triumvirate of Italian vernacular writers, along with Dante and Petrarch, and in England was sometimes given the title 'Poet Laureate'. What Painter is trying to do in his 'provulgation' of Boccaccio and his followers is to create a new kind of prose fiction which is more socially inclusive ('meete for all degrees') but which has behind it the authority of the premier vernacular stylistic model for prose in early modern Europe.

6.2

The most obvious way in which the stories of *The Palace of Pleasure* are more socially inclusive is in the prominence they give to women. However, Painter begins with the 'true history' of Livy, not the *novelle* of Boccaccio, and his first story comes with an austere warning that it will have none of the feminine trappings of chivalric romance. The story concerns the wars between the Romans and the Albans and their agreement to settle matters in a combat between three men from either side, who will fight 'not for sportes of Ladies, or for precious prises, but for Countrie quarell and libertie of Native

---

[6] As does the English translator of Christine of Pisa, reporting 'euyll tydyngs and nouelles', *The C Hystoryes of Troye* (1549), EEBO image 81.

soyle'. The wars themselves are described as 'much like to a civile contention almost, betwene the father and the sonne' (1: 15, 17). So this is political territory, and designated masculine, but the story also redefines affairs of state in terms of kinship and views civil issues from a familial and personal perspective. After the combat, the surviving champion, Horatius, discovers that his sister has been betrothed to one of the slain opponents, whereupon he kills her for what he calls her 'unreasonable love'. He is condemned to death for this act, but his father pleads eloquently that he should be spared for both public reasons (his son's service to the state) and private ones (he doesn't deserve to lose both his children). The outcome is that Horatius is acquitted 'rather through the admiration of his [father's] vertue and valiance, than by justice and equity of his cause' (1: 21). The reader is invited to marvel at the strictness of Roman law, but is also allowed the satisfaction of knowing that the father's 'valiance' will ensure that he doesn't lose his other child. The lesson to be drawn, as Painter has already told us in his preface, is that you should 'learne how to behave thy selfe with modestie after thou hast atchieved any victorious conquest' and avoid 'committing a facte unworthy of thy valiaunce' (1: 11). 'Immodest' hardly seems an adequate way of describing the murder of a sister and the woman in this story is clearly expendable and her role negligible. Yet even here, at the gate of the palace, there are signs of a contrary direction, and the outcome doesn't quite have the effect Painter claims for it. After all, the rigour of the law is softened by the eloquence of a suppliant and the decision to relax it is taken not by a judge but by 'the people'. This is clemency by popular decree.

Painter's second tale is a version of the tragic subject of Shakespeare's *The Rape of Lucrece* and the third is about the lifting of a siege of Rome. Novel 4 concerns Coriolanus, also familiar to us from Shakespeare, though he went to Plutarch rather than Painter for his plot and there are some significant differences in emphasis in the Livy–Painter, Plutarch–Shakespeare versions of the story. This is not the place to rehearse those differences, but it is worth noting here that Painter's head-note provides a more partisan interpretation of events than we get in Shakespeare, with its succinct opening, 'Martius Coriolanus goinge aboute to represse the common people of Rome with dearth of Corne was banished' (1: 29). In the story itself, Painter shows that since the people are reluctant to fight because they need to till the land, Coriolanus's actions explicitly deny them the fruits of their labour. The effect of this injustice is to create a sense of the need for cooperation between patrician and plebeian, as we see after Coriolanus's banishment and defection to the Volscians. Despite previous contention 'betwene the people and the fathers', fear of invasion has now united them and 'linked their mindes together, in the bands of concord'. It is agreed that Coriolanus's mother and wife should be delegated to plead with him not to attack Rome, as happens in Shakespeare, though here Painter adds, interestingly: 'whether the same was done by common consent, or by the advise of the feminine kind, it is uncertaine' (1: 32–3). Coriolanus's mother, who is called Veturia in this version (Volumnia is his wife), does indeed make an impassioned speech, but Coriolanus is also moved by the tears of the suppliant women who have come to support Veturia and Volumnia. This is very much a female group effort and it is recognized as such by the city: '[t]he Romains disdaigned not to attribute to women, their due prayse:

for in memorie of this deliverie of their Countrie, they erected a Temple, Fortunae Muliebri, to Womens Fortune' (1: 34). And not only that, but a group effort that identifies the interests of women with those of the common people, as the values of the peaceable, agrarian social stratum win out over those of the elite warrior class.

The last of the sequence of five stories from Livy concerns Appius and Virginia, later tuned into a play by one 'R.B.' and then by Webster. This is a tale about the abuse of the law, but it is also about class struggle. Appius is one of a new kind of Roman official called Decemviri, who have been appointed to draft revisions to the law, and having conceived a violent desire for a maiden, Virginia, whose father is away fighting with the Roman army, he contrives a legal fraud to have her identified as the daughter of his bondswoman and therefore his property. Virginia is defended by Icilius, her betrothed, and her father, Virgilius, is recalled from the army to rescue her. However, when the latter gets back to Rome he realizes that she is in a hopeless position and decides to kill her rather than allow her to be 'ledde to the rape *like a bondswoman*' (1: 40, my italics). It is this last point that turns out to be the central issue: not the rape or the honour killing, but the enforced servitude. Eventually, Appius is put on trial and charged that 'against the order and forme of lawe (thou thy selfe being judge) wouldest not suffer the freman, to enjoye the benefite of his freedome, during the processe made of servitude' (1: 44). So this is a prototype of the 'corrupt magistrate' motif, but the wording of the charge (with its reference to 'the freman') gives it a political dimension at the same time as it obliterates the memory of Virgilia herself. That political dimension supplies the wider context for the story. Icilius and Virgilius are supported by 'the multitude' and it is popular hatred of the corrupt and arbitrary power of the Decemviri that leads to a stand-off between the people and the senate. The senators, who are known as the 'fathers conscript' of the city, recognize that the Decemviri must be purged, but they also recognize that their malpractices have shifted the balance of power, ruefully observing that '[w]e shall soner wante our Fathers and Senatours, than they their plebeian officers. They bereved and toke away from us the fathers a newe kind of authoritie, which was never sene before, who now feeling the sweetnesse thereof, will never geve it over' (1: 42). This 'new kind of authority' is democracy.

Painter does not use the D-word, but Hadfield is certainly right to suggest that the classical stories at the start of the *Palace* are 'a bit subversive'. While the moralistic glosses that Painter inserts from time to time show him trying to steer the reader in a safe direction, they completely fail to put a cap on the democratic energies that his subject matter releases. In one sense, then, his aim of being socially inclusive is over-fulfilled. In another respect, however, it certainly isn't, since the status of women in these stories is inconsistent, to say the least. It is when Painter moves to Boccaccio that women in turn move to central narrative positions: many of these tales might in fact be grouped under the title 'Women's Fortune', to borrow the tag from the Coriolanus story, and they feature women in roles that are to some degree independent of the authority of father or husband. The switch from classical to Italian material, or from the city of civility to the palace of pleasure, may seem abrupt, and there is no doubt that it represents a change in Painter's interests and in his plan for the volume as a whole. The austere political culture of freedom and bondage, of 'valiaunce' and paternal honour killing, and of the ever-present threat of popular insurrection that Painter extracts from Livy, is superseded by a shifting social world that focuses on a cluster of themes concerning interpersonal relations, marriage, and inheritance. But it would be wrong to think that the one is more serious than the other. It is perfectly true that the *Palace* is bulked out with some lighter, fabliau-derived stories, and even jest-book material, but to English readers of the 1560s it would have seemed to offer a kaleidoscope of social possibility for modern life: these are not old histories but 'news', sensational reports of goings on elsewhere.[7] The most extreme example of this aspect of the novella form is provided by the frame of the *Decameron* itself, which was born out of the social catastrophe of the Black Death: beyond the palace and the garden paradise and the elegant, aristocratic narrators lay the traumatized, plague-ridden city of Florence.[8] What was happening there in 1348 might have made anything seem possible, and some sense of this survives, over two centuries later, even in stolid English translation.

There are ten stories from the *Decameron* in Tome 1 of the *Palace*, followed by seven from Bandello and fifteen from Marguerite of Navarre, both of whom were working in the Boccaccian tradition. There is obviously some risk in trying to find a common thread to link the Italianate material with the classical stories, but the subject of fathers and daughters is one fairly obvious point of connection, and it also helps to illustrate both Painter's shift from the political to the social and his refocusing of the collection on the female role. In the stories from Livy the term 'father' has both civic and familial status, as Latin *patres* covers both the patrician class, the senators or 'fathers conscript', and the biological fathers who are so often at the heart of the action. The personal is always framed by the political. In Painter's *Decameron* tales what matters is the father–daughter, not the father–son relationship and how it impacts on her desires and marital destiny.[9] One story that would certainly have appealed to English readers is Novel 34, 'The King of England's Daughter' (*Decameron* 2.3). In this tale, a Florentine financial agent called Alexandro, on his way home from London after his employers have been bankrupted, encounters the newly appointed abbot of one of the finest abbeys in England, who is travelling to Italy with an impressively large retinue. The young abbot is smitten with Alexandro and they are soon on familiar terms, so much so that when they stay overnight at an inn they end up sharing a bed, despite the abbot's elevated status. The reader has probably been anticipating the scene that follows: 'The Abbot laying his arme over him, began to attempte suche amorous toyes, as be accustomed betweene twoo lovers: whereof Alexandro mervayled muche, and doubted that the Abbot being surprysed with [i.e. suddenly seized by] dishonest love, had called him to his bedde of purpose to

---

[7] In fact, this kind of material has already appeared among the classical stories (novel 21 is labelled a 'merie geste', for example). It may be worth noting that the story of the antisocial Timon comes at the end of this section.

[8] It is no coincidence that Boccaccio's young narrators meet at the church of Santa Maria Novella on the edge of Florence.

[9] Fathers and daughters do of course feature in Livy, as we have seen, but the context is rather different from that of the Italianate tales.

prove him' (1: 134). The reader may also have anticipated the next development, which is that the abbot is revealed to be a woman, the King of England's daughter no less, and that she is going to Rome so that the Pope can place her in marriage. But free of her father's control and at large in the world, she is able to gratify her desires with what is, quite literally, passing trade. All is made respectable, nonetheless, as a makeshift betrothal takes place in bed, the Pope later sanctions the marriage, and back in England the King is reconciled to his new son-in-law. This is romance at the far reaches of the preposterous and its excitement for the reader lies in the tantalizing prospect of illicit love mixed with the other unconventional opportunities that it opens up for a daughter on the road between two fathers. A fortunate traveller indeed.

Another independent daughter appears in Novel 38 (*Decameron* 3.9) where Giletta of Narbonne, whose father is a physician, manages after his death to cure the King of France of a fistula and is allowed to take her pick of the young men of the court as a reward. The story is well known as the source of Shakespeare's *All's Well that Ends Well*, so I will not discuss it in detail here. Again, there are two fathers, but their ability to control the daughter is neutralized, one because he is dead and the other (the King) because he is in her debt: ' "Thou hast well deserved a husbande (Giletta) even such a one as thy selfe shalt chose" ', he promises (1: 173). Again, there is the discrepancy of social status, but with the genders reversed: here, it is the woman who is low-born and her obstacle is not the paternal veto, but her prospective husband's disdain for her commonness. Giletta, however, is able to make her own fortune, since she is as skilled in plot contrivance as she is in medicine and her resourcefulness eventually enables her to claim the husband she desires. Stories like this stand at the beginning of a tradition of romantic prose fiction in English, but the promise of fulfilment in the narrative is marked not just by the announcement, 'Reader, I married him', though that happens too, but also by the earlier moment when Giletta is in a position to say, 'Reader, I got to *choose*'.

Both these stories end happily, but the last in the Boccaccio tranche, Novel 39, which concerns Tancredi and Gismonda, does not. The mixing of comedy and tragedy is a characteristic of the *Decameron*, as it was to be of Shakespeare, and the intensity of feeling in this story is sharpened by the outcomes of what has gone before. (In Boccaccio it is the first of the tragic tales of Day 4.) In this story, Gismonda is a young widow, 'lustie, and more wise peradventure than a woman ought to be', who returns to her father Tancredi's house when her husband dies and since her father 'for the love he bare unto her' doesn't want her to remarry, she decides to take a secret lover. The man she chooses, Guiscardo, is one of the servants and is of 'very base birth (but in vertue and honest condicions more noble than the reste)' (1: 180). When Gismonda discovers that her room can be accessed from a cave, the couple are able to pursue their assignations undetected. Tancredi, however, is also in the habit of visiting his daughter in her room and one day, when she is in the garden with her maids, he sits down on a stool by her bed, draws the curtains and falls asleep. Gismonda and Guiscardo then appear and make love on the bed, while Tancredi decides 'to kepe him selfe secrete' so that he can watch them 'privelie', which he does as they make love for 'a great time, as they were wont to do' (1: 183). (The logistics of this are those of sexual fantasy.) Afterwards, he confronts his daughter, but in a way that suggests that the voyeuristic experience has effected a role reversal: '[w]hen hee had spoken those woordes, he kissed her face, weping verie bitterly like a childe that had ben beaten' (1: 184). The mixture of tenderness and chastisement (the kiss is Painter's invention) helps to reinforce the suggestion that Tancredi's private view has been an emasculating experience. This is the moment at which power is transferred from father to daughter. Tancredi's anguished response is to have Guiscardo executed and then to send his heart to Gismonda in a golden chalice, a gesture that acts both as an emblem of revenge and as a perverse love token, as if to say: I offered you my heart, now have his. Unlike her tearful father, however, Gismonda exercises extreme self-control. She pours poison into the chalice, drinks it, and dies while pressing her lover's heart to her own. Tancredi is broken by his daughter's death and allows the two lovers to be buried together.[10]

It is also significant that in a story about a father's desire for a widowed daughter she should choose a man of lower social status as her lover. This is a reiterated theme in the *Palace*, appearing in the stories of Anne of Hungary and the Lady of Burgundy, for example, as well as the Duchess of Malfi. Here, it enables the male relative to conceal his real feelings (perhaps also from himself) beneath a cloak of conventional outrage. But the difference in rank also enables the woman to stake her claims for independent choice, as Gismonda powerfully does in her speech to Tancredi:

> First of all you see, that of one masse of fleshe we have all received flesh, and that one Creatour hath created every lyving creature, with force and puissance equally, and wyth equall vertue: which vertue was the first occasion that made the difference and distinction of us all that were borne, and be borne equall, and they that obtayned the greatest part of vertue, and did the workes of her, were called noble, the rest continuing unnoble. (1: 186)

Gismonda's rhetorical resources are impressive, but it would be futile to argue on the basis of this speech (which follows conventions of its own) that Painter is a social radical. The point is rather that the Italianate tales extend the realm of the possible, in social and sexual terms, despite Painter's efforts to put a moralistic spin on this dangerously suggestive material. In many of these stories, women can be seen to be agents in their own lives, whether fortunately or unfortunately, and the effect of the strong undercurrents of illicit sex, both in the playful homoeroticism in the novel about the King of England's daughter and in the more serious tale of Tancredi's incestuous desire, is to lend some legitimacy to relationships that are illicit only in terms of social difference.

It would be futile, too, to look for much thematic consistency between the classical and the Italianate tales, and my point, anyway, is to argue for a transition from political

---

[10] See also the excellent discussion of this tale by Patrick Kirkpatrick, *English and Italian Literature from Dante to Shakespeare: A Study of Source, Analogue and Divergence* (London: Longman, 1995), 243–6. However, Kirkpatrick emphasizes that Painter translated directly from the Italian (228, 242), but although he knew Ruscelli's edition of the *Decameron* (Venice, 1552), 'he also drew extensively on the translation of Maçon'; Herbert G. Wright, *Boccaccio in England from Chaucer to Tennyson* (London: The Athlone Press, 1957), 157.

to social concerns between the two classes of material. Yet Gismonda's defiant speech on equality certainly resonates with the democratic murmurings of the Livian stories and provides a political frame for the shift of power from father to daughter. That political frame is even more apparent in Giletta's story, which comes immediately before Gismonda's. Here we are told that after marrying the reluctant Beltramo, she returns independently to her husband's country, where 'perceyving that through the Countes absence all thinges were spoiled and out of order, shee like a sage Ladye, with great diligence and care, disposed his things in order againe [and]... restored all the countrie againe to their aunceient liberties' (1: 174). Giletta certainly has an impressive range of recuperative skills and though the genre may allow the heroine to choose her man, we don't really expect her to turn into a humanist prince as well. What's more, the phrase 'aunceient liberties' has a distinctly republican ring about it. It's a Livian touch that has no place in Shakespeare's dramatized version of the story. We might say that this is a point at which 'novel' and 'history' meet, but we might also say that elements of this kind show that prose fiction works in a different way from drama. It suggests how narrative fiction is able to provide the kind of contextual layering for action, and for interpretation of action, that is difficult to convey in the more compressed, speech-based medium of drama.

At this point we need to ask why Painter should have decided to relocate from the city of civility to the palace of pleasure in the first place. The obvious explanation is that for sound commercial reasons he wanted to target a female readership. Redescribing the 'histories' as 'novelles', with their connotations of news and chatter, and then retitling the collection, is consistent with that change of direction and is part of the wider agenda of 'provulgation' and democratization that we have already seen. Indeed, Painter's move is probably the first significant moment in English print culture in which a literary form is reshaped by a publishing decision to reach out to a female audience. It is a moment that is repeated not just in the subsequent history of the novel, which is well documented, but eventually in the publication of 'news' itself, as John Carey has shown in *The Intellectuals and the Masses*. Carey describes how Lord Northcliffe, founder of the *Daily Mail*, introduced a women's section to the paper, started up the women's weeklies, *Forget-Me-Not* and *Home Chat* during the 1890s, and then launched the first tabloid, *The Daily Mirror*, in 1903.[11] While the social conditions of the two periods are obviously very different, there is a parallel in the way in which a masculine form, the newspaper as 'history', is diversified into social and domestic life and broadened from being simply a vehicle for matters of public record to a being medium that could represent itself more intimately as a form of conversation.

If the most striking feature of the composition of Tome 1 of the *Palace* is its sudden change of direction, there is certainly no mistaking Painter's intentions at the opening of Tome 2. In the epistle to his employer at the armoury, Sir George Howard, Painter offers a vigorous defence of the public benefits of translation, and the provulgation agenda is

---

[11] John Carey, *The Intellectuals and the Masses: Pride and Prejudice among the Literary Intelligentsia, 1880–1939* (London: Faber, 1992), 8.

continued in the address to the reader, where he claims to provide profit and delight to all degrees from emperors to 'the rudest vilage girle' (2: 157). Then, reminding readers that the first tome had opened with a contest between six gentlemen, he announces that '[i]n this second parte, in the Forefront, and first Novell of the same, is described the beginninge, continuaunce and ende of a Woman's Commonwealth' (2: 159). The story of the Amazons was obviously designed to appeal to a female audience, but it is also evidence of a greater interest in design itself: Tome 2 has considerably more framing, commentary, and other authorial interventions than the first volume does, and this rudimentary *cornice* suggests another Boccaccian touch. The problem (and this is not very Boccaccian) is that many of these interventions are of an earnestly moralizing kind, and Painter's efforts to appeal to a female readership are continually being compromised by the stubborn set of platitudes he dispenses as he tries to make sense of his rather shocking material. For the modern reader, there are few more depressing examples of this than his conclusion to 'The Duchesse of Malfi': 'You see the miserable discourse of a Princesse love, and of a Gentleman that had forgotten his estate, which ought to serve for a lookinge Glasse to them which bee over hardy in makinge Enterprises' (3: 43). The programme of democratization and popularization represented by the *Palace* may be genuine enough, even if it is driven primarily by commercial interests, but its social and ethical implications are not really within Painter's control.

6.3

This is precisely the opposite of what happens in George Pettie's spin-off from Painter, *The Petite Pallace of Pettie His Pleasure*, published in 1576, the first year of 'The Theater' and the year following the appearance of the two-volume edition of Painter's work. Unlike Painter, Pettie goes to considerable trouble to construct a narrative persona who is very much in control: knowing, mannered, and smooth. But the feminist posturings of the *Petite Pallace* are certainly fake, designed as much for the entertainment of male wits as for the satisfaction of the young gentlewomen to whom they are so assiduously addressed.[12] All this is filtered through the fictional device of the paratexts where the stories are presented not by Pettie himself, but by a friend, one 'R.B.', who explains in his dedication 'to the gentle Gentlewomen Readers' that the tales can't be compared with 'the former Pallaces of Pleasure' because those volumes 'containe Histories, translated out of grave authors & learned writers: and this containeth discourses, devised by a greene youthfull capacitie, and reported in a manner *ex tempore*'. In fact, Painter decided to move beyond history, as we have seen, but where he aimed to rework history

---

[12] On this see Helen Hackett, *Women and Romance Fiction in the English Renaissance* (Cambridge: Cambridge University Press), 48–54, and on Pettie's collection as a whole, R. W. Maslen, *Elizabethan Fictions: Espionage, Counter-Espionage, and the Duplicity of Fiction in Early Elizabethan Prose Narratives* (Oxford: Clarendon Press, 1997), 158–98.

as a novel, Pettie turns it into something else again: discourse. 'Novelles' have oral characteristics too, as I have also suggested, but 'discourses' are more artful than news or chatter. In the 'Letter of G.P. to R.B.' that follows the dedication, Pettie describes the social context of his stories: they are 'Tragicall trifles, whiche you have heard mee in sundrie companies at sundrye times report' (Pettie 1938: 5). But while he wants them to carry an air of effortless spontaneity, he is also ready to acknowledge that they are in fact self-consciously crafted. If anyone objects to 'some wordes and phrases, used contrary to their common custom', he says, then think of these as being like 'new fashions in cutting of beardes, [or] in long wasted doublets' (6). The new fashion that the stories adopt is the rhetorical one that Lyly was to make famous two years later as Euphuism, and it is characterized by repeated alliteration, matching clauses and phrases of equal length, and figures of parallelism and antithesis—doublets in both senses of the term. It is meant to look good and sound good, especially when Pettie gets close to the reader and whispers in her ear. This is a long way from armourer Painter's manly common sense.

It is also a long way from Livy. What Pettie does is to rewrite Livian civility as civil conversation, translating history into style, a move that he went on to substantiate in 1581 with his English version of the first three books of Stephano Guazzo's *Civil Conversation*. (Pettie produced no English Boccaccio, but Bartholomew Yong, who translated the fourth book of Guazzo's work in 1586, published his *Amorous Fiammetta* the following year.) Pettie continues in the direction that Painter followed when he abandoned the city of civility for the palace of pleasure, but in doing so he takes Painter's alternative title a good deal more literally. The civic or political dimensions of civility that reappear even in Painter's Boccaccian tales are completely abandoned here and replaced by a world in which the personal is everything. Turning civility into style, Pettie's 'discourses' are underpinned, in the end, by a philosophy of self-gratification. This is not, it should be stressed, what civil conversation meant to Guazzo, but it is what Pettie reduces it to in the *Petite Pallace*.

The subject matter of Pettie's collection is entirely classical, but it is given a complete Italian makeover, something that is immediately apparent in the Livian stories he takes over from Painter, 'Icilius and Virginia' and 'Curiatius and Horatia'. In the first of these, Icilius is not a young Roman patrician, but 'a courtier of *Italy*' (110), while in the second story Curiatius goes into Rome every day 'to deale with marchants in matters of waight' and on one of these trips spots Horatia 'sittinge at her Fathers dore to take the aire, and to recreate her selfe with the sighte of those that passed by' (167). This sounds much more like fourteenth-century Florence or Naples than ancient Rome. Indeed, it sounds exactly like a *Decameron* tale. What this means is that the Livian stories are reconstructed to foreground the young couples. Where Painter translates Livy, Pettie translates Painter, and when he retitles the story generally known as 'Appius and Virginia' by replacing Appius with Icilius, he removes the legal and political confrontation that was its defining feature in both Livy and Painter. What we get instead is courtship strategy, and the obstacle to fulfilment, at least initially, is not the corrupt magistrate who threatens enslavement and rape, but Icilius's lack of patrimony. Although Appius's scheme is not completely erased, it is pushed towards the end of the narrative so that it becomes merely an impediment to the satisfaction of the young lovers rather than a context and precondition for the story as a whole. The civic aspect of civility disappears. In Pettie's version of the story, the last word goes to Virgilia, who is not mutely slaughtered as she is in Painter, but is allowed to make a grand gesture of self-sacrifice, demanding that her father kills her because 'your power is to weake to wreak the wrong which is offred mee, and your force is to feeble to fence mee from the fury of my foes' (123). So Pettie's final Italianate twist to Livy is to take us back to the territory of parental control and the transfer of power from fathers to daughters. The father holds the knife, but under his daughter's direction.

The second Livian story (Novel 1 in Painter) sets out on a similar course. Much is made of the emotional trials of Curiatius, the young Alban who offers Euphuistic declarations of love to his Roman mistress, only to receive 'waspish' replies in return. Then follows a scene reminiscent of *Romeo and Juliet*, when he attempts to woo Horatia at a masked ball,[13] but Curiatius has less immediate success than Romeo and it is not until he threatens to remove himself to a far country that Horatia relents and they are betrothed. Then comes the civil war which, like the corrupt magistrate motif in the earlier story, is moved to a later point in the narrative so that it can appear simply as a tragic turn of events, rather than as a primary context. Those events are essentially the same as in Painter, but the details are different, as Pettie eyes the female reader. When her brother returns victoriously from the combat, Horatia spots him wearing 'the coate armour of her *Curiatius* which she her selfe with needle work had curiously made' (182). It is a human touch that would have been quite out of place in Painter's Livy, but what is added in the way of fine colouring is a good deal less than what is removed with regard to matters of rather more substance. After Horatia's death, Appius is not put on trial and there is no opportunity for the legal and ethical issues of the events to be debated. With Pettie, we are emphatically not in the city of civility.

So what are we to make of Pettie's translation of Painter? It seems inadequate simply to repeat that the notion of civility has moved from the political to the social, since the social in the *Petite Pallace* is presented merely as surface. What is really extraordinary about Pettie is the faux-moralistic glossing that he uses to finish off his stories, which looks very much like a parody of Painter's earnest struggles to impose order on chaos. The 'moral' Pettie appends to the story of Icilius and Virginia is quite outrageous: young ladies should avoid tyrants, especially if they are older men; indeed, they should avoid older men altogether, because they will not only be jealous but probably impotent into the bargain. Stick to younger men, then:

> And if your parentes in some curious or covetous respecte goe about otherwise to dispose of you, humbly request them that you may chuse where you like, and link where you love, that you may be married to a man rather than mony. (125)

---

[13] Romeo and Juliet are in fact cited as a lesson to oppressive parents at the end of the tale. Painter's version of the story of 'Rhomeo and Iulietta' is at 2.25.

In reducing a story of political oppression and legal corruption, in which a daughter is killed to avoid being raped, to an advertisement for the pleasure principle, counselling that a girl should make sure she gets enough sexual pleasure in marriage, Pettie's tongue is firmly in his cheek. This is a deliberate travesty of the more serious explorations of the woman's right to choose in Painter's Boccaccian tales. And though the 'moral' is ostensibly designed for the enjoyment of Pettie's female readers, the recommendation that they should ignore parental wishes and marry young men with no inheritance on the grounds of their sexual prowess sounds very much as though Pettie is addressing his gentlemen readers, over his shoulder, as it were. That much seems clear from the equally outrageous 'moral' of 'Curiatius and Horatia', which is that the tragedy is all Horatia's fault, because if she hadn't resisted Curiatius for so long, by the time war broke out he would have been a married man and would have been allowed 'to trye his manhood at home with his wife' (183) instead of being conscripted. It is not Horatius's fault, because he would have saved his sister's soul by preventing her probable suicide. And finally, in his summing up, Pettie reaches an almost Wildean level of ironic insouciance: 'to avoyde inconveniences, take time in time... and with *Horatia* hurte not your selves and your friendes with dayntynesse' (184).

To invoke Wilde here is to test the meaning of the 'subversive', because it suggests how the notion of civility might evolve from the matter of government to that of manners while retaining its disruptive edge and, above all, its capacity for questioning both social and literary convention. This is exactly what Pettie is doing in his mockery of tritely moralizing attempts to defuse the explosive potential of the story matter that came into English through Boccaccio and the Boccaccian tradition. And though his immediate target is Painter, Pettie's tales ultimately have the effect of exposing a contradiction in the *Decameron* itself, where women are expected to observe an ideal of sexual propriety and yet not be unresponsive to the ardent passions of young men. Painter had declared that histories are 'like a Mistresse of our life' (2: 150) because they inspire the male reader to behave virtuously. In Pettie's case, the mistress is the reader herself, whose imagined sexual *im*propriety he artfully exploits in order to produce an entirely specious code of conduct in which the real end is the gratification of male desire. That this is subversive is recognized in the third of the prefatory epistles to the *Petite Pallace*, ostensibly from the printer to the reader. Where Painter had thought Boccaccio 'worthy of intire provulgation', the author of the *Petite Pallace*, the author claims, 'was not wylling to have it common, as thinkinge certaine poynts in it to bee to wanton' (8). Pettie was as aware as Ascham that the new Italianate fiction was a Pandora's box and when he went on to translate Guazzo he would also become aware that 'civil conversation' was not just a matter of sweet-talking young ladies, however cleverly this might expose the emptiness of platitudes on correct behaviour, but an ethically grounded ideal of social conduct most fully expressed through the institution of marriage. Recognition of this was to be the next stage in the evolution of the English novella, as we can see from George Whetstone's *Heptameron of Civil Discourses*, published the year after Pettie's translation of Guazzo. But that is another story.

Further Reading

Boccaccio, Giovanni. *Boccaccio in English, 1494–1620*, ed. Guyda Armstrong (London: MHRA, forthcoming).
—— *The Decameron*, trans. G. H. McWilliam, 2nd edn. (London: Penguin, 1995).
Carey, John. *The Intellectuals and the Masses: Pride and Prejudice among the Literary Intelligentsia, 1880–1939* (London: Faber, 1992).
Hackett, Helen. *Women and Romance Fiction in the English Renaissance* (Cambridge: Cambridge University Press, 2000).
Hadfield, Andrew. *Literature, Travel, and Colonial Writing in the English Renaissance, 1545–1625* (Oxford: Clarendon Press, 1998).
Hutson, Lorna. *The Usurer's Daughter: Male Friendship and Fictions of Women in Sixteenth-Century England* (London: Routledge, 1994).
Kirkpatrick, Robin. *English and Italian Literature from Dante to Shakespeare: A Study of Source, Analogue and Divergence* (London: Longman, 1995).
Lewis, C. S. *English Literature in the Sixteenth Century* (Oxford: Clarendon Press, 1954).
Maslen, R. W. *Elizabethan Fictions: Espionage, Counter-Espionage, and the Duplicity of Fiction in Early Elizabethan Prose Narratives* (Oxford: Clarendon Press, 1997).
Painter, William. *The Palace of Pleasure*, ed. Joseph Jacobs, 3 vols. (repr. of 1890 edn.; New York: Dover, 1966).
Pettie, George. *A Petite Pallace of Pettie His Pleasure*, ed. Herbert Hartman (London: Oxford University Press, 1938).
Salzman, Paul. *English Prose Fiction, 1558–1700: A Critical History* (Oxford: Oxford University Press, 1985).
Sidney, Philip. *An Apology for Poetry*, ed. Geoffrey Shepherd, rev. and expanded by R. W. Maslen (Manchester: Manchester University Press, 2002).
Wright, Herbert G. *Boccaccio in England from Chaucer to Tennyson* (London: Athlone Press, 1957).

CHAPTER 7

CLASSICAL TRANSLATION

GORDON BRADEN

In 1601, Philemon Holland, introducing his English version of the elder Pliny's *Natural History*, writes of it as his bid to become part of what already, with time still left on the clock, feels like the institution later known as the Elizabethan age. Translation is a 'third ranke'—after those of noble deeds and original literature—in which one might achieve enduring fame through being part of that moment:

> As for my selfe, since it is neither my hap nor hope to attaine to such perfection, as to bring foorth somewhat of mine owne which may quit the pains of a reader, and much lesse to performe any action that might minister matter to a writer, and yet so farre bound unto my native countrey and the blessed state wherein I have lived, as to render an account of my yeers passed & studies employed, during this long time of peace and tranquilitie, wherein (under the most gratious and happie government of a peerelesse Princesse, assisted with so prudent, politique, and learned Counsell) all good literature hath had free progresse and flourished, in no age so much: me thought I owed this dutie, to leave for my part also (after many others) some small memoriall, that might give testimonie another day what fruits generally this peaceable age of ours hath produced.[1]

Merging his ambition into that of his nation, Holland becomes increasingly fervent about the importance of translation, especially from the ancient classics; critics of his craft are rebuked with the assertion that such translation is itself a warrior's calling, providing the country with a kind of postcolonial payback:

> Certes such *Momi* as these...thinke not so honourably of their native countrey and mother tongue as they ought: who if they were so well affected that way as they should be, would wish rather and endeavour by all means to triumph now over the Romans in subduing their literature under the dent of the English pen, in requitall of the conquest sometime over this Island, atchieved by the edge of their sword.[2]

---

[1] Philemon Holland, trans., *The Historie of the World...of C. Plinius Secundus* (London, 1601), π2ᵛ.
[2] Pliny, *Historie*, π3ᵛ.

The trope is a passing one, but the representation of translation as a patriotic enterprise, already evident in Holland's version of Livy the previous year (where Holland is the sponsor of a deserving immigrant who will bring 'this nation of ours...great fruit and benefit'),[3] is sustained throughout Holland's literary career, which proves to be a long one—centred firmly on the translation of classical prose—and which indeed earns him some measure of the fame he sought. Thomas Fuller, including him in *The Worthies of England*, entitled him 'the *Translator Generall* in his Age', whose 'Books alone of his *Turning* into *English*, will make a *Country Gentleman* a competent library for *Historians*';[4] the collected Holland weighs down a bookshelf in Pope's *Dunciad*. He is the eighth most cited writer in the first edition of the *Oxford English Dictionary*. His prefaces set the tone of F. O. Matthiessen's *Translation: An Elizabethan Art*, and through it of much subsequent discussion of England's early modern translators: 'The translator's work was an act of patriotism. He, too, as well as the voyager and merchant, could do some good for his country: he believed that foreign books were just as important for England's destiny as the discoveries of her seamen, and he brought them into his native speech with all the enthusiasm of a conquest.'[5]

Holland was prompted in his ambition—he acknowledges it more than once—by the example of Sir Thomas North's monumental translation of Plutarch's *Lives* (1579). Holland's Livy and Pliny, as well as later translations of Plutarch's philosophical works (1603, in effect completing North's project), Suetonius (1606), Ammianus Marcellinus (1609), William Camden's *Britannia* (1610), and, rounding out his career in a volume adorned with valedictory encomia, Xenophon's *Cyropaedia* (1632) (Fig. 7.1), are in the same general mould: handsome folio volumes running sometimes over a thousand pages, prestige productions fetching a premium price, though not entirely beyond the means of sufficiently interested general readers (a bound copy of North's first edition retailed for 14s; Holland's Pliny, unbound, went for 13s).[6] Even for someone as industrious as Holland, income from this source was not enough to live on. There is record of his receiving £4 for his Ammianus and £5 for his Camden (on the low side of what a successful London playwright might receive for a single play);[7] during most of his time as a translator he worked at the free school in Coventry and as a practising physician, and despite a small pension from Coventry, he appears to have been in distressed circumstances in his last years. Unsurprisingly, no one else made such a career out of this kind of translating. But the books themselves appear to have sold; they were frequently reprinted, and booksellers kept offering new ones: Josephus and Seneca's philosophical works translated by Thomas Lodge (1602, 1614; the Seneca revised in 1620), Tacitus by

---

[3] Philemon Holland, trans., *The Romane Historie Written by T. Livius* (London, 1600), π5ʳ.

[4] Thomas Fuller, *The Worthies of England* (London, 1662), ³127.

[5] F. O. Matthiessen, *Translation: An Elizabethan Art* (Cambridge, MA: Harvard University Press, 1931), 3.

[6] F. R. Johnson, 'Notes on English Retail Book-Prices, 1550–1640', *The Library*, 5th ser., 5 (1950): 83–112 (108).

[7] H. S. Bennett, *English Books and Readers, 1603 to 1640* (Cambridge: Cambridge University Press, 1970), 229.

FIGURE 7.1 Xenophon, *Cyropaedia*, trans. Philemon Holland (1632), title page

Sir Henry Savile (*Histories* I–IV and *Agricola*, 1591) and Richard Greenwey (*Annals* and *Germany*, 1598), Thucydides by Thomas Hobbes (1629; his first publication), and Augustine's *City of God* by John Healey (1610). There was a recognized market for classics of Latin and Greek prose dressed out (Holland is fond of the clothing metaphor) as classics of English prose.

Most translations of classical prose were not of course given this kind of high-end production. The most widely used circulated in more modest editions; a bound copy of the first issue Nicholas Grimald's version of Cicero's *On Duties* (1556), 'one of the most published secular works of the sixteenth century in England', could be had for 8d.[8] But the expensiveness of the large format translations does not appear to have inhibited their influence. The most famous, indeed, spectacular case of such influence, is the impact of North's Plutarch on Shakespeare, an impact which is extensive and detailed and in more than a few places seems to have involved having North open before him as he wrote.[9] No cheap selection from North's *Lives* was available (none of the big editions had their material remarketed that way) and purchasing a copy would have required careful planning on a playwright's income (which might run £20–30 a year); one way or another, Shakespeare managed. There is trace evidence as well that he worked with Holland's Livy and Plutarch—the latter for the Egyptian lore in *On Isis and Osiris*—and even his Camden.[10] Holland's practice is also sufficiently exemplary of the handling of classical prose by translators throughout the period to justify treating him as a kind of standard.[11]

That handling is closer to a modern standard of fidelity than is generally operative in translations of vernacular prose or of any kind of verse. There are exceptions to this generalization, though they tend to come early. In one freewheeling example, Angel Day publishes the first English version of Longus's pastoral romance *Daphnis and Chloe* (1587) with an interpolated tribute to Queen Elizabeth entitled 'A Shepheards Holidaie' and a title page identifying Day as its author, with in fact no acknowledgement that the rest of the volume is a translation. A shade more discreetly, Alexander Barclay's translation of Sallust's *Jugurtha* (1522, reprinted with revisions by Thomas Paynell in 1557) interleaves the story with emphatic signposting. 'In this warke I purpose to wryte of the batayle/ which the Romayns had and executed agaynst the tyranne Jugurth wrongfully usurpynge

---

[8] Gerald O'Gorman, ed., *Marcus Tullius Ciceroes Thre Bokes of Duties* (Washington, DC: Folger Books, 1990), 15; Johnson, 'Notes on Book-Prices', 99.

[9] The evidence is most accessibly presented in M. W. MacCallum, *Shakespeare's Roman Plays and their Background* (London: Macmillan, 1910); see also my chapter on Shakespeare in Mark Beck, ed., *A Companion to Plutarch* (Oxford: Wiley-Blackwell, forthcoming).

[10] See Geoffrey Bullough, *Narrative and Dramatic Sources of Shakespeare*, vol. 5 (London: Routledge, 1964), 496–505, 551–2; John Adlard, 'Cleopatra as Isis', *Archiv für das Studium der neueren Sprachen und Literatur*, 212 (1975): 324–8. See also Peter Culhane, 'Livy in Early Jacobean Drama', *Translation and Literature*, 14 (2005): 21–44; most of this influence cannot be specifically tied to Holland's translation, but a connection is extremely likely.

[11] Holland has been rightly praised for his superior scholarship; he could, unlike many other translators, work directly from the Greek. But H. B. Lathrop's judgement remains apt: 'we praise him for much the same qualities as his predecessors, and with much the same reservations'; *Translations from the Classics into English from Caxton to Chapman, 1477–1620* (Madison: University of Wisconsin Press, 1932), 304.

the name of a kynge/over the lande of Numydy': 'tyranne' and 'wrongfully usurpynge' are wholesale additions, as the Latin which Barclay prints in the margin clearly shows.[12] The translator elsewhere stated his principles without apology—'some tyme addynge, somtyme detractinge and takinge away suche things [a]s semeth me necessary and superflue'[13]—and others throughout the period casually followed them; but at least in connection with classical prose (and outside the special cases where prose is translated as verse) there is less in this line as we go on. Thomas Heywood's Sallust (1608) is conspicuously more restrained than Barclay's: 'In this Booke, my purpose is, to write the Warre which the Romane people undertooke against *Jugurth* King of *Numidia*.'[14]

We do regularly find intruded glosses, incorporating information that might go into a marginal note or a bracketed insertion within the text—and sometimes does, but also sometimes is wholly assimilated to the translation itself. A wish to anticipate and meet the readers' needs in an unfussy way also animates a pervasive concern often made explicit in the translators' own prefaces. The patriotic mission that Holland claims for translation has a linguistic component, a chauvinism about the English language itself: 'I honour them in my heart, who having of late daies troden the way before me in *Plutarch*, *Tacitus*, and others, have made good proofe, that as the tongue in an English mans head is framed so flexible and obsequent, that it can pronounce naturally any other language; so a pen in his hand is able sufficiently to expresse Greeke, Latine, and Hebrew.'[15] The adjectives 'flexible and obsequent' suggest deference to the way things are done elsewhere, but the message here is really the unique capacity of English; Holland's strong inclination is against 'foreignizing'. The most contentious issue in contemporary polemics about translation is the use of 'inkhorn terms'; Holland is sensitive to the need to import certain kinds of technical language, but sparing in doing so, and sufficiently self-conscious about it to include glossaries 'of such woords of Art...with the explanation thereto annexed, and the same delivered as plainly as I could possibly devise for the capacitie of the meanest'.[16] Holland went so far as to imagine a readership including 'the rude paisant of the countrey' and 'the painefull artizan in town and citie', and in this spirit 'I framed my pen, not to any affected phrase, but to a meane and popular stile. Wherein, if I have called againe into use some old words, let it be attributed to the love of my countrey language: if the sentence be not so concise, couched and knit together, as the originall, loth I was to be obscure and darke: have I not englished everie word aptly?'[17] The emphasis falls on 'englished'; the final criterion is attractive management of the target language.

Other translators are not necessarily as interested in reaching peasants and artisans, but similar principles can be recognized in their work. The practice falls under the

---

[12] Alexander Barclay, trans., *The Famous Cronycle of the Warre/Which the Romayns Had agaynst Jugurth* (London, 1522), 5ᵛ; see further David Womersley, 'Sir Henry Savile's Translation of Tacitus and the Political Interpretation of Elizabethan Texts', *Review of English Studies*, ns 42 (1991): 313–42 (317–18).

[13] Alexander Barclay, trans., *Shyp of Folys of the Worlde* (London, 1509), b4ᵛ.

[14] Thomas Heywood, trans., *The Two Most Worthy and Notable Histories...Both Written by C. C. Salustius* (London, 1608), Bb1ᵛ.

[15] Pliny, *Historie*, π3ᵛ.   [16] Pliny, *Historie*, ²A2ʳ.   [17] Pliny, *Historie*, π3ᵛ; Livy, π4ᵛ–5ʳ.

general model that Massimiliano Morini derives from humanist theory and argues is dominant for this period in England: 'they do not alter the *inventio* and *dispositio* of their sources, but feel free to adapt the *elocutio*, the style, to their and their audience's taste'.[18] As a contemporary puts it: 'retayning the strength and sinew of the Sentence [meaning], I have rendred it as best fitted the property of speech in our owne language'.[19] The usual result is casually expansive, though generally not without perceptible warrants in the original. Individual words are rendered with doublets or triplets, epigrammatic constructions ('concise, couched and knit togither') are rendered paraphrastically, connectives are added to ease the sequence of thought or action, and lighting effects occasionally heighten the moment: 'For fear of this reproch and infamie, see how sinfull lust gat the victory, and conquered constant chastity'; needless to say, 'see' is not in the Latin.[20] Especially long sentences are broken up or recast and—the feature most likely to strike modern readers—a line of what Matthiessen likes to call 'racy' diction runs through almost everything: e.g. 'This unhappie occurrent made us bestirre our stumpes' for 'hoc malo conciti'.[21] To modern ears this is a drop in register, not what you expect in a classic, but neither translators nor their readers seemed to have a problem with it. Much is probably owed to the admirable precedent of North's Plutarch, where the diction offsets but also empassions a stateliness that comes from extraordinarily flexible and obsequent mimicking of the syntax, cadence, and word order of Jacques Amyot's French translation, the text from which North worked; the result manages to sound not French at all:

> it was not the great multitude of shippes, nor the pompe & sumptuous setting out of the same, nor the prowde barbarous showts & songes of victorie that could stande them to purpose, against noble harts & valiant minded souldiers, that durst grapple with them, & come to hands strokes with their enemies: &...they should make no reckoning of all that bravery & bragges, but should sticke to it like men, & laye it on the jacks of them.[22]

The timbre of the prose supplies its own gloss for the obsolete slang at the end; no note is really needed. North found a highly credible voice in which ancient civilization might speak with authority and force in a contemporary environment, and the main line of classical prose translations more or less follows his lead.

It is a voice above all for politics and warfare, but it also has a gift for the fantastical. The most famous passage in North is so because Shakespeare virtually transcribed it in describing Cleopatra's fabulous self-deification on her way to meet Antony: 'she

---

[18] Massimiliano Morini, *Tudor Translation in Theory and Practice* (Aldershot: Ashgate, 2006), 66; for Holland's Livy, see 89–94.
[19] John Sanford, trans., *A Defence of the Catholicke Faith*, by Pierre DuMoulin (London, 1610), A4ᵛ.
[20] Livy, 1.58.5, Holland, 41.
[21] Ammianus Marcellinus, 19.8.12; Philemon Holland, trans., *The Romane Historie* (London, 1609), ¹134.
[22] Plutarch, *Themistocles*, 8.1; Sir Thomas North, trans., *The Lives of the Noble Grecians and Romanes* (London, 1579), 127.

disdained to set forward otherwise, but to take her barge in the river of Cydnus, the poope whereof was of gold, the sailes of purple, and the owers of silver, which kept stroke in rowing after the sounde of the musicke of flutes, howboyes, citherns, violls, and such other instruments…'[23] Shakespeare adds embellishments, but North is already with the programme: Plutarch says nothing about rowers keeping time to the music. The most spacious opportunity for such appreciation turns out to be Holland's Pliny, where the familiar and exotic phenomena of the natural world are the occasion of repeated wonderment: 'As for Cats, marke I pray you how silent they be, how soft they tread when they steale upon the silie birds: how secret lie they in espiall for the poore little Mice to leape upon them.'[24] There is no specific prompting in the Latin for *silie* or *poore* or, most significantly, *marke I pray you*; the English cradles the sense of the original in a kind of heightened attentiveness. Pliny's description of the song of the nightingale calls forth multiple cadenzas from the translator:

> one while, full of her largs, longs, briefes, semibriefes, and minims; another while in her crotchets, quavers, semiquavers, and double semiquavers: for at one time you shall heare her voice full and lowd, another time as low; and anon shrill and on high: thicke and short when she list; drawne out at leisure againe when she is disposed: and then (if shee be so pleased) she riseth & mounteth up aloft, as it were with a wind-organ. Thus she altereth from one to another, and singeth all parts, the Treble, the Meane, and the Base. To conclude, there is not a pipe or instrument againe in the world (devised with all the Art and cunning of man so exquisitely as possibly might be) that can affourd more musicke than this pretie bird doth out of that little throat of hers.[25]

This, about half of a passage conjured from some fifty words of Latin. Pliny's chapter is the source for much of the lore about nightingales in the Renaissance, including those contests in which a particularly competitive bird literally sings itself to death. That legend supplies the conceit for Famiano Strada's neo-Latin poem about a duel between a nightingale and a lutenist (1617), which Richard Crashaw translates into English as 'Musicks Duell' (1646) with rapturous amplifications very much in Holland's spirit and quite possibly suggested by his example.[26] The grounds on which Holland recommends Pliny to his reader are, sensibly, more literary than scientific—'surely it is antiquitie that hath given grace, vigor, & strength to writings; even as age commendeth the most generous and best wines'[27]—and to read through the translation—'almost…a Renaissance phantasmagoria when read at a stretch'—is to encounter time and again information and images that are strewn throughout seventeenth-century English literature and the other arts.[28]

---

[23] Plutarch, *Antony*, 26.1, North, 981.   [24] Pliny, 10.94, Holland, ¹308.
[25] Pliny, 10.43, Holland, ¹286.
[26] Strada's Latin and Crashaw's English are printed *en face*, with the latter's additions clearly visible, in *The Complete Poetry of Richard Crashaw*, ed. George Walton Williams (New York: Doubleday, 1970), 534–43.
[27] Pliny, *Historie*, π3ʳ.
[28] Stuart Gillespie and Robert Cummings, '[Latin] Prose Authors', in Peter France, ed., *The Oxford Guide to Literature in English Translation* (Oxford: Oxford University Press, 2000), 539.

The medium has a homogenizing effect; stylistic differences in the source texts, though recognized (on Ammianus, Holland notes 'the harsh stile of the Author, a Souldior, and who being a Grecian borne, delivered these Hystoricall reports in Latine'[29]), generally are not represented clearly in English. The excesses of Apuleius—'ever the literary fop, conscious of his trappings and assured of a handsome effect'[30]—might have been a natural for uninhibited euphuistic treatment in the new language and William Adlington occasionally gets into the spirit in his *Golden Asse* (1566); but in general, his translation desaturates the original's colour. Latin thieves carouse in hyperbolic high style—'estur ac potatur incondite, pulmentis aceruatim, panibus aggeratim, poculis agminatim ingestis' (something like: 'there was riotous eating and drinking, mountains of meat, heaps of bread, battalions of cupfuls')—while in English 'thei dranke & eate excedingly'; Apuleius's 'ab ipsa Venere septem sauia et unum blandientis adpulsu linguae longe mellitum' ('seven kisses from Venus herself, and one honeyed by the lingering touch of her ingratiating tongue') scale down to 'seven sweete cosses of Venus'.[31] Like North, Adlington is being closely guided by an intervening French translation,[32] though he is also working from the Latin and aware of what he is not bringing over into English. Apuleius 'had written his woorke in so darke and highe a stile, in so strange and absurde woordes, and in such newe invented phrases, as he seemed rather to set it foorth, to show his magnifency of prose, then to participate his dooinges to other'; accordingly,

> I have not so exactly passed thorough the Author, as to pointe every sentence accordinge as it is in Latine, or so absolutely translated every woorde, as it lieth in the prose...considering the same in our vulgar tongue would have appeared very obscure and darke, & thereby consequently, lothsome to the Reader, but nothing erringe as I trust from the given and naturall meaninge of the author, have used more common and familiar woordes...for the plainer setting foorth of the same.[33]

He is not talking only about diction.

The wish to make the work sit comfortably in English more often leads to elaboration and expansion. Beginning in the late sixteenth century, this tendency encounters growing

---

[29] Holland's Ammianus, ¹A2ʳ. Of Ammianus, an appreciative reader of Holland writes, 'A live Porcupine were easilier chewed, then that rough peece, and, I believe, sooner digested'; 'W. R.' in Thomas Lodge, trans., *The Workes of Lucius Annaeus Seneca Newly Inlarged and Corrected* (London, 1620), b3ᵛ.

[30] Charles Whibley, ed., *The Golden Ass of Apuleius, Translated out of Latin by William Adlington* (London: David Nott, 1893), x.

[31] Apuleius, *Metamorphosis*, 4.8, 6.8; William Adlington, trans., *The XI. Bookes of the Goldern Asse* (London, 1566), 36ᵛ, 58ʳ. Adlington is especially consistent in de-escalating descriptions of dawn; see the anthology of examples in Lathrop, *Translations from the Classics*, 160–1.

[32] Now securely identified as that of Jean Louveau (1553) by Robert H. F. Carver, *The Protean Ass: The Metamorphoses of Apuleius from Antiquity to the Renaissance* (Oxford: Oxford University Press, 2007), 300–15.

[33] Adlington, A2ʳ, A3ᵛ.

interest in classical writers valued for commandingly trenchant and difficult styles, riskier business for translators already hypersensitive to the prospect of aggravating their public. Of Seneca, Lodge writes, 'the Author being seriously succinct, and full of *Laconisme*; no wonder if in somthings my omissions may seeme such, as some whose judgement is mounted above the Epicycle of Mercurie, will find matter enough to carpe at'.[34] Important claims have been made for the role of such 'anti-Ciceronian' prose in English intellectual life in the seventeenth century,[35] though translators are uneven in attempting to represent this aspect of the classical works in question. Some scarcely bother; in what might be some kind of joke, Heywood sounds like Polonius when expanding Sallust's *paucis* sixfold: 'wherin, I vow all possible Brevity'.[36] Lodge intermittently tries to keep Seneca's compact phrasing, sometimes with unintelligible results; 'magis quis ueneris quam quo interest' ('it is more important who you are when you travel than where') is mangled into 'It importeth more to know what thou are comming, then when thou arrivest'. Successful attempts typically merge into something more relaxed:

> non est delicata res uiuere. longam uiam ingressus es; et labaris oportet et arietes et cadas et lasseris et exclames 'o mors!', id est mentiaris.
>
> It is no delicate thing to live. Thou art entered into a long way, wherein perforce thou must slip, thou must justle, thou must fall, thou must be wearied, and thou must exclaime, O death! that is, thou liest.

That first phrase hits the target exactly. The rest, without adding anything to the sense, massages the nervously emphatic rhythm of the Latin into a more flowingly 'Ciceronian' cadence.[37]

In a preface to Savile's Tacitus, 'A.B.' calls the original author 'harde' and promises the reader that the translator 'gives thee the same foode, but with a pleasant and easie taste'.[38] But the translation mostly has the confidence of its own ungraciousness, regularly reproducing the choppiness of the Latin and expanding more for clarity than for elegance. 'To take away by maine force, to kill and to spoile, falsely they terme Empire and government: when all is waste as a wildernesse, that they call peace'—Savile more than doubles the word count ('auferre trucidare rapere falsis nominibus imperium, atque ubi

---

[34] Lodge's Seneca (1620), b1r.

[35] Neil Rhodes provides a usefully compact summary, from Morris Croll to Stanley Fish, in his edited collection, *English Renaissance Prose: History, Language, and Politics* (Tempe, AZ: Medieval and Renaissance Texts and Studies, 1997), 8–10.

[36] Sallust, *Catiline*, 4.3, Heywood, B2v.

[37] Seneca, *Epistles*, 28.4, 107.2; Thomas Lodge, trans., *The Workes of Lucius Annaeus Seneca* (London, 1914), 212, 440 (neither passage is revised in 1620). The examples are from Robert Cummings, 'Classical Moralists and Philosophers', in Gordon Braden, Robert Cummings, and Stuart Gillespie, eds., *The Oxford History of Literary Translation in English*, vol. 2 (*OHOLTIE2*; Oxford: Oxford University Press, 2010), 386. On the Ciceronianism of Lodge's prose, see Elaine Cuvelier, *Thomas Lodge, témoin de son temps* (Paris: Didier, 1984), 431–6. The second text here was also translated c.1567 by Queen Elizabeth; see *Elizabeth I: Translations, 1544–1589*, ed. Janel Mueller and Joshua Scodel (Chicago: University of Chicago Press, 2009), 416.

[38] Henry Savile, trans., *The Ende of Nero and Beginning of Galba* (London, 1591), ¶3r.

solitudinem faciunt, pacem appellant'), but does not dull either the analytic sharpness or the venom.[39] So also the assessment of how public perception fatally manoeuvred Servius Sulpicius Galba into a job he could not handle:

> his honorable birth, and the dangerous times covered the matter, entitling that wisedome, which in truth was but slouth: in his flourishing age greatly renowned for service in Germanie: Africke he ruled as Proconsull with great moderation: and growing in yeares, the nearer Spaine uprightly & well: seeming more than a private man, whilest he was private, and by all mens opinions capable of the Empire, had he never bene Emperour.[40]

The translation was much respected; Jonson praised Savile for catching both Tacitus's meaning and style (*Epigrams* 95). Greenwey, though less accomplished, imitated Savile's manner well enough to make for a reasonably uniform collected works.

The non-standard Greek of Thucydides is in some ways even more of a challenge and Hobbes's response goes against the grain celebrated by Matthiessen. An earlier effort, by Thomas Nicolls (1550), openly relied on Lorenzo Valla's Latin version and Claude de Seyssel's French one; Hobbes, proudly able to work directly from the Greek, produced a sturdily straightforward version that is consistently shorter:

> But the woorste that was in this, was that men loste their harte, & hope incontynently, as they feeled themself attaincted. In suche sort, that many, for despaire, holdinge themselves for dead, habandoned & forsoke themself, & made no provisyon nor resistence againste the sickenes. And an other great evill was, that the malady was so contagious, that those, that went for to visitt the sicke, were taken and infected, lyke as the shepe be, one after an other.

> But the greatest misery of all was, the dejection of mind, in such as found themselves beginning to be sicke (for they grew presently desperate, and gave themselves over without making any resistance) as also their dying thus like sheepe, infected by mutuall visitation, for the greatest mortality proceeded that way.[41]

Hobbes's brevity follows from something close to the *uerbum pro uerbo* translating that other translators regularly profess to scorn. Where Nicolls essentially begins again halfway through, Hobbes mimics the continuous sentence structure of the Greek and he avoids the doublets ('harte, & hope', 'habandoned & forsoke', and 'no provisyon nor resistence') and new signposting ('And an other great evill was') that come naturally to his predecessor; he also declines the heightened poignancy that comes with repositioning and prolonging the reference to sheep, but respects Thucydides's characteristic restraint in the use of metaphor.

The overall result has been well characterized by Robin Sowerby: 'despite the occasional high Latinism or homely colloquialism, this is plain, customary (though not

---

[39] Tacitus, *Agricola*, 30.5; Savile, ²255.

[40] Tacitus, *Histories*, 1.49, Savile, ²28; the passage (only partially quoted here) is discussed by Robin Sowerby in 'Ancient History', *OHOLTIE2*, 308–9.

[41] Thucydides, 2.51.4; Thomas Nicolls, trans., *The Hystory Writtone by Thucidides* (London, 1550), 57ᵛ; Thomas Hobbes, trans., *Eight Bookes of The Peloponnesian Warre* (London, 1629), 108.

neat), direct, blunt, analytical expository prose without frills, ambiguities, or tropes that draw attention to themselves'.[42] Hobbes's translation has been called the 'most distinguished of historical translations in the period', but also 'for all his Jacobean credentials...dull'.[43] A certain avoidance of rhetorical and literary effectiveness, though not universal, seems to have been part of the point, consonant with the distrust that both Thucydides and Hobbes felt for figurative language and oratorical skill; in his verse autobiography (1672), Hobbes will remember his motivation for the translation in these terms: 'Hunc ego scriptorem uerti, qui diceret Anglis,/Consultaturi rhetoras ut fugerent' ('I translated this writer to tell the English to flee the rhetoricians they were about to consult').[44] It seems appropriate that Hobbes stumbles at Pericles's summary of the Athenian aesthetic ideal: 'we also give ourselves to bravery, and yet with thrift' for φιλοκαλοῦμεν τε γὰρ μετ' εὐτελείας.[45] Richard Crawley's Victorian translation does not break stride: 'We cultivate refinement without extravagance.'[46] Hobbes's Athenians speak with most conviction when standing for something less genteel: 'at first wee were forced to advance our Dominion to what it is, out of the nature of the thing it selfe; as chiefly for feare, next for honour, and lastly for profit'.[47] The trinity of fear, honour, and profit is already there in Nicolls, though Nicolls passed over the phrase that Hobbes renders 'out of the nature of the thing it selfe': Hobbes's speaker is formulating a scientific law of how it is with human beings and 'Dominion' (ἡγεμονή; the Latin would be *imperium*). A reordered version of this trinity reappears in *Leviathan*: 'in the nature of man, we find three principall causes of quarrell. First, Competition; Secondly, Diffidence; Thirdly, Glory.'[48] Translating Thucydides, Hobbes looks forward to his later career, with its quest for a cold-blooded intellectual austerity both stylistic and substantive.

Most of the examples here have been from history. Most of the texts which Holland chooses to translate are in this category, which dominates among other translators as well; it is in history that they come closest to offering Anglophone readers comprehensive access to what classical writers had to offer. Coverage of the classical canon in general is famously spotty.[49] It was dependent on accidents of individual initiative (Holland the distinguished example), the importunity of friends (often cited by the translators themselves), aristocratic patronage (more often sought than received), and

---

[42] Robin Sowerby, 'Thomas Hobbes's Translation of Thucydides', *Translation and Literature*, 7 (1998): 147–69 (152).

[43] Sowerby, *OHOLTIE2*, 309; Adam Parry, 'Herodotus and Thucydides', in 'Penguin Classics: A Report on Two Decades', *Arion*, 1st ser., 7 (1968): 414.

[44] *T. Hobbes Malmesburiensis Vita*, in Thomas Hobbes, *Metaphysical Writings*, ed. Mary Whiton Chalkins (La Salle, IL: Open Court, 1905), ix.

[45] Thucydides, 2.40.1, Hobbes, 103; see the discussion by Sowerby, 'Thomas Hobbes's Translation of Thucydides', 157–9.

[46] *The Landmark Thucydides*, ed. Robert B. Strassler (New York: Free Press, 1996), 113.

[47] Thucydides, 1.75.3, Hobbes, 41.

[48] *Leviathan*, 1.13; see Richard Schlatter, ed., *Hobbes's Thucydides* (New Brunswick, NJ: Rutgers University Press, 1975), xxi–xxii.

[49] Summarizing the omissions is Lathrop's final topic (*Translations from the Classics*, 307–10).

especially the judgement of booksellers, who commissioned most of the translations, as to what would sell. England had no publisher with the strong humanist allegiances of Aldus Manutius in Venice, the Estiennes in Paris, or Christoph Plantin in Antwerp; the only significant government support for translation concerned the Bible. The great contrast was with France, where royal patronage helped give shape to the whole enterprise.[50] Several French translators—Amyot, Seyssel, Nicolas Oresme (from the fourteenth century, his works printed in the late fifteenth), and Louis Le Roy—sustained careers similar to Holland's, though unlike his, subsidized by positions at court and ecclesiastical appointments. Some of their achievements, especially with Greek writers, paved the way for English successors; Amyot's French Plutarch, specifically commissioned by Francis I, was used by both of the two English translators it took to cover the same ground and was indispensable for one of them (North includes a translation of Amyot's preface). In other cases, the availability of reliable French translations—such as Le Roy's versions of Plato's *Republic*, *Timaeus*, and *Symposium*—may actually have kept English versions of key canonical texts from seeming worth the trouble.

Philosophy is the area with the most conspicuous gaps for English translation.[51] Plato especially: the invisible hand does not find its way to him until after this period, when it has the guidance of Thomas Stanley's *History of Philosophy* (1655–62), itself containing extensive translations from primary texts. Aside from excerpts in anthologies and elsewhere, there is only *Axiochus*, a spurious dialogue of particularly Christian resonance englished by 'Edw. Spenser'—probably Edmund—in 1592 and by an anonymous translator for a collection in 1607. For Aristotle, there are a version of the *Nichomachean Ethics* made from a thirteenth-century Latin abridgement (1547) and John Dee's translation of the *Politics* from Le Roy's French (1598, including Le Roy's own prefatory essay). Epictetus's *Enchiridion* is translated twice (1567, 1610), his *Discourses* not at all; Meric Casaubon's Marcus Aurelius appears in 1634. Holland's Plutarch is preceded by several versions of individual works: 'Plutarch's talent for the brief moral essay, intricately wrought, makes translations from him a perfect gift'[52]—beginning with Sir Thomas Wyatt presenting *The Quyete of Minde* to Catherine of Aragon (1528). Outside of Lodge's folio a few Senecan and pseudo-Senecan works are also translated by others. There are scattered translations of individual works by Cicero, but the closest thing to a general collection is Thomas Newton's gathering of four of them (*On Old Age*, *On Friendship*, *The Dream of Scipio*, and *Paradoxes*) in 1577. The most popular single Ciceronian work in English is Grimald's *On Duties*, not so much a work of philosophy as a primer on Roman civic life. It may be that in philosophy the paganism of antiquity was more of a problem for English readers than elsewhere; translators repeatedly address the issue in ways

---

[50] The contrasting records up to 1600 are displayed visually in R. R. Bolgar, *The Classical Heritage and its Beneficiaries* (Cambridge: Cambridge University Press, 1954), 508–41.

[51] For the details, see Robert Cummings, 'Classical Moralists and Philosophers', *OHOLTIE2*, 371–89.

[52] Cummings, *OHOLTIE2*, 377. One such gift by Thomas Blundeville, dedicated to Queen Elizabeth, consisted of three Plutarchan treatises, two of them translated into verse (1561; see Lathrop, *Translations from the Classics*, 208–10). Several decades later, Elizabeth worked on a verse translation of yet another Plutarchan work; see *Elizabeth I: Translations, 1592–1598*, ed. Mueller and Scodel, 366–447.

meant to be reassuring ('What a Stoicke hath written, Reade thou like a Christian').[53] The most translated philosopher from antiquity, in continuance of a tradition going back to Alfred the Great, is the possibly or almost Christian, Boethius: five complete versions of his *Consolation of Philosophy* during this period, two printed (1556, 1609), three in manuscript (one by Queen Elizabeth), as well as some stand-alone translations from the *metra*. The most passionate public debate about a particular translated text in any genre—with much seen as riding on small verbal differences—involved competing Catholic and Protestant translations of Augustine's *Confessions* (1620, 1631).[54]

Coverage is fairly thorough for imaginative literature from antiquity, though in prose this is a small corpus. The fables of Aesop are Englished repeatedly, in different forms; in accord with the reported practice of Socrates (Plato, *Phaedo* 60D), several of these are in verse.[55] Adlington's Apuleius becomes the first in a series that brings into print English versions of most of the late classical prose romances that survive intact: Heliodorus's *Theagenes and Chariclea* (partial translations in 1567 and 1591, complete ones in 1569 and 1631), Longus's *Daphnis and Chloe* (1587), the anonymous *Apollonius of Tyre* (by way of the thirteenth-century *Gesta Romanorum*, 1594), and even Achilles Tatius's deliberately bizarre *Leucippe and Cleitophon* (1597 and 1638). The influence of these works in Elizabethan literature has been much discussed.[56] Apuleius is the only one of these authors to offer a serious stylistic challenge to translators. Their erotic content sometimes needed muting. Adlington alerts readers of his first edition that he has 'left out certain lines propter honestatem' when his assified narrator copulates with an aroused noblewoman, though it remains clear just what is going on.[57] Day completely excises from *Daphnis and Chloe* the hero's sexual initiation by the helpful young wife of an elderly neighbour; the episode is restored in George Thornley's translation in 1657.

The appetite for the classical historians, however, especially of Rome and its Empire, is deeper and broader. The enterprise of bringing them into English picks up pace as the period goes on; by 1640—after Arthur Grimeston's complete Polybius (1633) succeeds a false start by Christopher Watson (1568)—the one egregious gap remaining is Herodotus, represented only by Barnabe Rich's translation of the first two books.[58] The appetite is not solely literary; it includes practical handbooks of what Captain Fluellen (*Henry V* 3.2.81–2) calls 'the disciplines of the Pristine Warres of the Romans': Frontinus (1539), Vegetius (1572), and Aelian (1616). Translators of fragmentary sources can be enterprising at filling factual lacunae. Holland accompanies his Livy with summaries (misattributed to Florus) of the missing books, as well as a continuous chronology; Savile provides a

---

[53] Lodge's Seneca (1620), b1ʳ.

[54] The controversy surfaces repeatedly in *OHOLTIE2*; see 328–9, 386–7, 422–3.

[55] The complicated record is freshly assessed by Cummings, *OHOLTIE2*, 379–80.

[56] See Samuel Lee Wolff, *The Greek Romances in Elizabethan Prose Fiction* (New York: Columbia University Press, 1912); Carol Gesner, *Shakespeare and the Greek Romance* (Lexington: University of Kentucky Press, 1970); Steve Mentz, *Romance for Sale in Early Modern England* (Aldershot: Ashgate, 2006); Carver, *The Protean Ass*, 327–445.

[57] Adlington, 110ʳ.

[58] See the summary by Sowerby, *OHOLTIE2*, 301–3.

bridge of his own composition to link the end of Tacitus's *Annals* to the start of his *Histories* (translated into Latin, it makes its way into editions of Tacitus). The result is, among other things, to shift classical history from an array of stories about particular people into a larger story of how things went over a long period of time for a particular state. With this shift can be sensed a change in the kind of urgency that the classical sources are felt to manifest. The earlier inclination is to offer them as incentives to general virtue of an upscale sort. Barclay recommends Sallust 'specially to gentylmen/which coveyt to attayne to clere fame and honour: by glorious dedes of chyvalry'; North includes Amyot's praise of history as 'a very lively & sharpe spurre for men of noble corage and gentlemanlike nature, to cause them to adventure upon all maner of noble and great things', while adding on his own that the examples which count the most are of those who 'ventured their persons, cast away their lives, not onely for the honor and safety, but also for the pleasure of their Princes'.[59] Holland shows something of the same spirit when he describes his Livy as 'an english Historie of that C. W. which of all others... affourdeth most plenteous examples of devout zeale in their kind, of wisedome, pollicie, justice, valour, and all vertues whatsoever';[60] but even in doing so he signals that the C. W.—the Commonwealth—is the real protagonist of the history that follows. It is moreover the history of when that commonwealth was a republic; Holland's praise of Elizabeth and her regime may have been entirely sincere, but in the anxious time of her last years the very choice of Livy to translate was a potentially provocative act—especially when the new accessibility of Tacitus made the contrast between Rome's republican and monarchical times particularly disadvantage the latter.[61] Savile's introductory addition to Tacitus includes what is for an Elizabethan a wholly extraordinary judgement on Julius Vindex, who lost his life for conspiring against Nero:

> a man in the course of this action more vertuous than fortunate; who... first entred the lists, chalenging a Prince upholden with thirty legions, rooted in the Empire by fower descents of ancestours, and fourteene yeares continuance of raigne, not upon private dispaire to set in combustion the state, not to revenge disgrace or dishonour, not to establish his owne soveraignety... but to redeeme his cuntrey from tyranny and bondage, which onely respect he regarded so much, that in respect he regarded nothing his owne life or security.[62]

Lightly disguised as an imitation of Tacitus, the passage is a signal to the reader as to how to read the genuinely Tacitean text to follow: monarchical rule such as Nero's, however legitimate, can make rebellion an act of virtue. That is not a lesson Barclay or North or probably even Holland would have countenanced, but it was a text to ponder for those troubled by a rising (and accurate) sense that England was being carried into political waters for which nothing in its own history prepared it.

---

[59] Barclay's Sallust, a5ᵛ; North, *4ʳ, *2ʳ.
[60] Holland's Livy, A5ᵛ.
[61] See Peter Culhane, 'Philemon Holland's Livy: Peritexts and Contexts', *Translation and Literature*, 13 (204): 268–86.
[62] Savile, ¹6; see the analysis in Womersley, 'Sir Henry Savile's Translaton of Tacitus', 318–30.

Hobbes occupied a different place on the political spectrum, but his sense that classical history could be an important source of guidance in dangerous times was even more overt. The partisan topicality of his Thucydides is evident in a preface that argues, with some justification in the text, that the Greek historian—'the most Politique Historiographer that ever writ'—was 'a closet royalist', and in the regular translation of *stasis*, the term for political faction, as 'sedition'.[63] The full scope of that topicality had yet to reveal itself: with cool prescience, Hobbes ventured beyond the focus on Rome to find the great classical history of civil war—far more searching than Caesar's mainly military history of the Roman equivalent—and published his translation of it at the beginning of the reign of Charles I. The *rhetores* against whom he said he wished to warn the English by doing so would of course have been mainly parliamentarian.

Further Reading

Bennett, H. S. *English Books and Readers, 1558 to 1603* (Cambridge: Cambridge University Press, 1965).
—— *English Books and Readers, 1603 to 1640* (Cambridge: Cambridge University Press, 1970).
Braden, Gordon, Robert Cummings, and Stuart Gillespie, eds. *The Oxford History of Literary Translation in English, Volume 2: 1550–1660* (Oxford: Oxford University Press, 2010).
Conley, C. H. *The First English Translators of the Classics* (New Haven, CT: Yale University Press, 1927).
Croll, Morris W. *Style, Rhetoric, and Rhythm: Essays*, ed. J. Max Patrick (Princeton: Princeton University Press, 1966).
Ebel, Julia G. 'A Numerical Study of Elizabethan Translations', *The Library*, 5th ser., 22 (1967): 104–27.
—— 'Translation and Cultural Nationalism in the Age of Elizabeth', *Journal of the History of Ideas*, 30 (1969): 593–602.
Hosington, Brenda, et al. *Renaissance Cultural Crossroads*. http://www.hrionline.ac.uk/rcc.
Lathrop, Henry Burrowes. *Translations from the Classics into English from Caxton to Chapman, 1477–1620* (Madison: University of Wisconsin Press, 1932).
Matthiessen, F. O. *Translation: An Elizabethan Art* (Cambridge, MA: Harvard University Press, 1931).
Morini, Massimiliano. *Tudor Translation in Theory and Practice* (Aldershot: Ashgate, 2006).
Winny, James, ed. *Elizabethan Prose Translation* (Cambridge: Cambridge University Press, 1960).

---

[63] Hobbes, A3ᵛ; Sowerby, 'Thomas Hobbes's Translation of Thucydides', 156, 151.

CHAPTER 8

LAZARILLO DE TORMES AND THE PICARESQUE IN EARLY MODERN ENGLAND

ALEXANDER SAMSON

'Porque consideren los que heredaron nobles estados cuán poco se les debe, pues fortuna fue con ellos parcial, y cuánto más hicieron los que, siéndoles contraria, con fuerza y maña remando, salieron a buen puerto'

> ['those which possess great rents and revenues may understand what small praise is due unto them, seeing that Fortune hath dealt partially with them; and how much commendation they deserve, which in despite of cruel fortune, with force and industry, by rowing out of tempestuous seas, have arrived to fortunate and happy havens' (David Rowlands, 1586)][1]

Lazarillo de Tormes, a book that was subversive, if not blatantly heretical in Spain, came in England to represent its birthplace's corruption, material and spiritual degradation, its plague of rapacious, corrupt clergymen and hypocritical, honour-obsessed *hidalgos*. In Spain, the Inquisitor General, Fernando de Valdés, had placed it on the first Index of prohibited books in 1559, five years after its initial publication. When a 'castigado' [punished] version was published in 1573, it appeared without the fourth and fifth treatises (the Friar of the Order of Mercy and Pardoner episodes), as well as a handful of other piquant moments of anticlerical satire, such as the pastiche of the Sermon on the Mount (St Matthew 5:10—'Blessed are they which are persecuted for righteousness' sake: for theirs is the kingdom of heaven'), exculpating Lazarillo's clearly guilty, thieving father, the miller. The phrase 'padesció persecución por justicia...el Evangelio los llama bienaventurados' [he suffered persecution for justice's sake...the Gospel calls them blessed] is cut along with Lazarillo's invocations of 'el Espiritú Sancto', 'Dios' and 'la hostia consa-

---

[1] Keith Whitlock, ed., *The Life of Lazarillo de Tormes*, trans. David Rowland (Warminster: Aris and Phillips, 2000), 53–5.

grada', and asides such as the unfavourable comparison of the black slave Zaide who steals for love with priests and friars 'uno hurta de los pobres, y el otro de casa para sus devotas' [one steals from the poor and the other from his own monastery for his female devotees].² A text that in Protestant England might have resonated with central ideological concerns about spiritual regeneration, the nature of true piety, and reforming the institutional church, exemplified instead Catholic blindness and its hollowed out, empty spirituality. The first *auto de fe* for Spanish Protestants took place only after Philip II's return from northern Europe in 1559 and personal experience of the Marian burnings. Already by 1590, *Lazarillo* was being cited as an indication of actual economic and social conditions in Spain. *A briefe discourse of the Spanish State* rebuts the assertion that the country abounds with 'fruitfull fields and rich mines... [and] men as haue bene parentes of all good customes', arguing 'let this be tried by *Lazarillo di Tormes*, he being lesse partiall then *Hieronimo Ruscello, Rodirigo di Toledo,* or *Taraphe,* and by the trauellers in *Spaine,* who find nothing in their hosteries but a mat to lye vpon, and a candle to bring them to bed'.³ In another anti-Spanish pamphlet, *A Pageant of Spanish Humours*, from 1599, the figure of the *escudero* from *Lazarillo* is the prototype for its vilification of Spanish *hidalgos* and their social pretensions, lust, and conceitedness: he 'must be soothed and flattered... if there be a Woolfe at the Table, Signior is one... in the streete... Peacocke-like to behold himself... scarce trusted to guard a flocke of *Cabritoes*. And here we will heare the name of a Hidalgo or don.'⁴ This commonplace, stock figure will issue in the composite character of Don Quijote six years later.

Uncertainty about when *Lazarillo* was written compounds the difficulties surrounding its interpretation. Toledan Cortes alluded to at the end could have been those of 1525 or 1538, meaning it might have been penned at any time between 1525 or 1538 and the four printed editions that appeared in 1554; in Burgos, Alcalá de Henares, Medina del Campo, and Antwerp.⁵ The Burgos edition is generally regarded as the *princeps* with

---

² Whitlock, *The Life of Lazarillo de Tormes*, 56–7 and 59. Translations here are my own. Elsewhere they are from Rowland's version ('wherefore he was persecuted... the Gospel doth say, that blessed are such as confess their faults' and 'those which steal from the poor, nor yet at them which convey from the houses they serve') misses the biblical allusion in order to avoid referring to confession and omits the unflattering reference to the priesthood and the anachronistic one to friars. Details of the excisions are in Felix Carrasco's critical edition *La vida de Lazarillo de Tormes y de sus fortunas y adversidades* (New York: Peter Lang, 1997), xciii–xcvii, esp. xcv. On their significance see the discussion by Felipe Ruan, 'Market, Audience and the Fortunes and Adversities of *Lazarillo Castigado* (1573)', *Hispanic Review*, 79 (2011): 189–211.

³ Edward Daunce, *A briefe discourse of the Spanish state with a dialogue annexed intituled Philobasilis* (London: Richard Field, 1590), sig. Eiiiᵛ.

⁴ *A pageant of Spanish humours Wherin are naturally described and liuely portrayed, the kinds and quallities of a signior of Spaine. Translated out of Dutche, By H. w* (London: John Windet for John Wolfe, 1599), sigs. A4ᵛ–B1ᵛ. See also R. O. Jones, ed., *Lazarillo de Tormes* (Manchester: Manchester University Press, 1963), pp. xxiii–xxiv.

⁵ The Medina del Campo edition was discovered only recently, walled up in a house in Extremadura, along with a book in Hebrew, an obscene manuscript, a treatise on chiromancy, and an Erasmian text. For more on this find see Jesús Cañas Murillo, 'Un *Lazarillo* de Medina del Campo: peculiaridades y variantes de una edición desconocida de 1554', *Anuario de estudios filológicos*, 19 (1996): 91–134.

interpolations in the Alcalá edition found also in the Antwerp versions which were published along with a second part, in which Lazarillo is transformed into a tuna fish: 'Adesora senti mudarse mi ser de hombre quiera no me cate, quando me vi hecho pez ni mas ni menos.... luego que en su figura fuy tornado conoci que eran Atunes' [At this inconvenient moment I felt my being change from that of a man, I might wish that it were not tried, when I saw myself transformed into a fish no more no less.... then I realized that I was turned into their shape which was that of tuna fish].[6] This sequel was translated by William Phiston and published in London in 1596.[7] Another new continuation appeared in 1620, written and translated by Juan de Luna.

The genesis of this English translation is complex. At some point after 22 July 1568, the printer Thomas Colwell received permission from the Stationers' Company to print a text entitled 'the meruelus Dedes and the lyf of Lazaro de Tormes'; a title echoing that of an original 1560 French translation *Les feits merveilleux, ensemble la vie du gentil Lazare de Tormes* published at Lyon, then a centre of French Protestant activity. The eventual title of the published English text, *The Pleasaunt Historie of Lazarillo de Tormes a Spaniarde, wherein is conteined his maruelous deedes and life*, echoed both this title, as well as that of the second French edition issued at Paris in 1561, *L'histoire plaisante et facetievse dv Lazare de Tormes*. From this, it is clear that the English translator, David Rowland, had copies of both French translations as well as the early 1554/5 Antwerp Nucio edition. Colwell's permission was sold on to Henry Bynneman on 19 July 1573, a printer with a track record in the market for humorous entertainment. The scholar Gabriel Harvey received a copy of *Lazarillo de Tormes* from his friend Edmund Spenser on 20 December 1578, according to his marginal annotation on a German collection of satirical tales, the *Till Eulenspiegel* by Thomas Murner, dating from the beginning of the century and perhaps published in English around 1528, given to him at the same time:

> This Howletglasse, with Skoggin, Skelton, & Laz[a]rill, given me at London of Mr Spensar XX. Decembris 1[5]78, on condition [I] should bestowe the reading of them over, before the first of January [imme]diatly ensuing; otherwise to forfeit to him my Lucian in fower volumes. Wherupon I was the rather induced to trifle away so many howers, as were idely overpassed in running thorowgh the [foresaid] foolish Bookes: wherin methowgh[t] not all fower togither seemed comparable for s[u]tle & crafty feates with Jon Miller whose witty shiftes, & practises ar reportid amongst Skeltons Tales.[8]

---

[6] *La segunda parte de Lazarillo de Tormes: y de sus fortunas y aduersidades* (Antwerp: Martin Nucio, 1555), sig. A10ʳ. Another edition appeared in Antwerp from the press of Guillermo Simon, also dated 1555. These were followed by Italian editions of both parts at Milan in 1587 (BL 1074.d.1) and 1615. On this bibliography see Manuel Ferrer-Chivite, ed., *La segunda parte de Lazarillo de Tormes: y de sus fortunas y aduersidades (1555)* (Madison: Hispanic Seminary of Medieval Studies, 1993), 203–19.

[7] William Phiston, trans., *The most pleasaunt and delectable historie of Lazarillo de Tormes, a Spanyard and of his maruellous fortunes and aduersities. The second part* (London: Thomas Creede for John Oxenbridge, 1596).

[8] Transcribed in Virginia Stern, *Gabriel Harvey: His Life, Marginalia and Library* (Oxford: Clarendon Press, 1979), 49, see also 207 and 228.

A now lost print edition of *Lazarillo* pre-dated the earliest extant one of 1586, not least because its dedicatee, Sir Thomas Gresham, had died in 1579.[9] It probably dates, in the light of indirect evidence, from 1576.[10] The company Lazarillo keeps is revealing, as is Harvey's description of them all as 'foolish', ranking Skelton above the others for 'witty shiftes, & practises'. Despite its dismissal here, he did perceive the dangers of the picaresque. In his *Four Letters, and Certaine Sonnets* published in 1592, the vice of 'grosse scurility, and impudent calumny' leads 'the Pennilesse Gentleman... to reuiue the pittifull historie of Don Lazarello de Thoemes: to contend with colde, to conuerse with scarcitie: to be laid open to pouertie; to accuse Fortune: to raile on his patrons, to bite his penne, to rend his papers, to rage in all point', while in the *Precursor of Pierce's Supererogation* of 1593 Skelton and Skoggin are innocents to 'Signior Capricio' and his 'sugred baites... [and] poisonous hookes'.[11] Harvey purchased a Spanish grammar in 1578 and by 1590 was using Antonio del Corro's *Spanish Grammer*, where in a marginal list of Spanish books, the title of *Lazarillo* was included.[12] Spenser's poem *Mother Hubberd's Tale* explored the familiar picaresque territory of vagrancy in contemporary England. Although it came out in 1591, it was 'composed in the raw conceipt of my youth' and was almost certainly inspired by his reading of *Lazarillo*. Its description of the counterfeit courtier's bid for favour 'with big words, and with a stately pace' echoes Rowland's squire 'with his accustomed stately pace'.[13] The printer Bynneman was associated with both Spenser and Harvey, whose correspondence he published in 1580.

Similarly, George Turbeville, whose commendatory verses were appended to the end of Rowland's translation, had been published by Bynneman. A *post mortem* inventory following his death in 1583 detailed that the printer possessed 'two hundred bookes of the Spanyardes lyfe', the running header in the 1586 edition, valued at twenty shillings and a further sixty-six copies worth seven shillings.[14] On one level, *Lazarillo* was simply a 'foolish' book, a collection of merry tales, like those found in jest books. Many of the jokes came from a European-wide stock of medieval anticlerical and satirical material: the scene of Lazarillo drinking the blind man's wine surreptitiously through a straw, for example, appeared illustrating a fourteenth-century manuscript of Gregory IX's decretals.[15] The central problem in critical discussions of the text and its translation is the extent to which it was a serious piece of social and religious satire or simply

---

[9] On these issues see the exhaustive study by Julio-César Santoyo, *Ediciones y traducciones inglesas del* Lazarillo de Tormes (Vitoria: Colegio Universitario de Alava, 1978), 17-37.

[10] Notice of this prior now lost edition is derived from Bagford and Hazlitt's bibliographical descriptions.

[11] *The Works of Gabriel Harvey*, ed. Alexander Grosart (London: The Huth Library, 1884), 2 vols., I, 206 and II, 109.

[12] This copy is in the Huntington Library, see sig. S4^v. See Stern, *Gabriel Harvey*, 43.

[13] Edmund Spenser, *Complaints. Containing Sundrie Small Poems of the Worlds Vanitie, London 1591* (Amderstam: Theatrum Orbis Terrarum, facs. edn. 1970) 'Prosopopoia Or Mother Hubberds Tale', sig. O1^r.

[14] Gareth Davies, 'David Rowland's *Lazarillo de Tormes* (1576): The History of Translation', *The National Library of Wales Journal*, 28 (1995), 349-87, esp. 350, 352, 363-4.

[15] Reproduced in Whitlock, *The Life of Lazarillo de Tormes*, 66.

entertainment. From the very outset, lascivious elements of prose fiction were both denounced and emphasized to improve sales. While the humanist Juan Luis Vives, in his 1524 treatise *De institutione foeminae Christianae*, dedicated to Catherine of Aragon so her 'derest doughter Mary shall rede these instructions of myne', proscribed reading 'Celestina the baude mother of noughtynes',[16] the *converso* priest Francisco Delicado four years later, on the title page of his *Retrato de la lozana andaluza* [*Portrait of the Fresh Andalucian Girl*] underlined that it 'contiene munchas mas cosas que la Celestina' [has got even more stuff than *La Celestina*].[17] The narrative crux of the tale, Lazarillo's friends assuring him that 'antes conmigo casase había parido tres veces' [before she was married to me she had two or three children] and his response that 'me hace Dios con ella mil mercedes y más bien que yo merezco; que yo juraré sobre la hostia consagrada que es tan buena mujer como vive dentro de las puertas de Toledo' [by her meanes, God hath done more for me than I haue deserued: and I dare sweare by the holy sacrament, that she is as honest a woman as any that dwelleth within the foure[18] gates of *Toledo*], is the culmination of the ambivalence surrounding whether it is simply a merry book or engaged in more profound social critique.[19] The means of God's aid alluded to have just been fleshed out, where it is clear that the crucial relationship is that between Lázaro and the Archpriest sealed by the marriage. His phrase 'as honest a woman' echoes his assertion in the prologue 'yo no ser más santo que mis vecinos' [I confessing myself to be no holier than my neighbours].[20] Both possible highly ironic assertions are topped by an oath on the sacrament, part of constant Christian invocations that equate God and fortune, from his prayer to the Lord to kill off the sick so he can eat in the second treatise on. Despite his close association with the central ritual of the mass as an altar boy, his praying exemplifies the ignorance and superstition of lay belief in Catholic Europe, with the prohibition on biblical translation and insistence on Latin, something satirized in the episode with the Pardoner, who becomes, in the face of unlettered priests, 'un sancto Tomas', i.e. Thomas Aquinas, burbling for two hours in Latin or what seems like it. The issue as to whether the work is simply Erasmian and humanist or whether it is an example of a soon to be suppressed Spanish Protestantism is still controversial.[21]

This question as to the extent of its Erasmianism overlaps with ultimately sterile debates over authorship. Religious positions apparently rejected in the text (intercession of saints, efficacy of vocal prayer, and indulgences) are used to rule out candidates from the imperial secretary Alfonso de Valdés, to the Jeronimite General Fray Juan de Ortega

---

[16] Juan Luis Vives, *The Instruction of a Christen Woman*, trans. Richard Hyrde, ed. Virginia Beauchamp, Elizabeth Hageman, and Margaret Mikesell (Urbana: University of Illinois Press, 2002), 11 and 25.
[17] Francisco Delicado, *Retrato de la lozana andaluza* (Venice, 1528), title page.
[18] Rowland supplies this information about Toledan topography.
[19] Whitlock, *The Life of Lazarillo de Tormes*, 162–5.
[20] Whitlock, *The Life of Lazarillo de Tormes*, 52–3.
[21] Thomas Hanrahan, '*Lazarillo de Tormes*: Erasmian Satire or Protestant Reform?', *Hispania*, 66 (1983): 333–9 and Terence O'Reilly, 'The Erasmianism of *Lazarillo de Tormes*', in Richard Cardwell, ed., *Essays in Honour of Robert Brian Tate* (Nottingham: University of Nottingham, 1984), 91–100.

or the poet, historian, and Venetian ambassador, Diego Hurtado de Mendoza.[22] A suggestion perhaps insufficiently prominent in the criticism is that 'Vuestra merced' of the frame narrative might have been Juan Tavera, Inquisitor General and Cardinal Archbishop of Toledo, whose synod pronounced against the immorality of the clergy in 1536.[23] The biblicism of *Lazarillo*, with its wealth of pious allusions and the way in which holy writ is wrested deliberately from orthodox interpretations through contextual and intentional distortion on the part of the narrator, is typified in the miserly priest episode with the indirect comparison of his tribulations to the sufferings of Job, with the three days that 'tuve en el vientre de la ballena' [as it were in a whale's belly].[24] God suggests to him the lie that it is mice who have been at the bread in the chest and the sight of the rolls themselves is a 'paraiso panal' [paradise of bread].[25] The message of scripture is consistently perverted through its particular application by Lazarillo to his life. The idealism of evangelical calls for the renewal of the mystical community of Christian believers underlies the satire and critique at the heart of *Lazarillo*.

It has been argued that *Lazarillo de Tormes* was 'a propaganda gift to powers hostile to Spain, like France and England',[26] and that its translations coincided with moments of political tension. Although Rowland had probably produced his translation around 1568, it was published for the first time in 1576, a moment of growing Anglo-Spanish tension, and then reprinted in 1586 in the build-up to the Armada.[27] However, while it is true that translation activity frequently intensified as political tensions did, such a political reading does not account for its massive popularity outside Spain. It was a European-wide bestseller with translations into French (1560, 1561—five different translators had tried their hand at *Lazarillo* before 1678 in France), English (1576?), Dutch (1579), and Italian (1587), then in the seventeenth century into German and Latin. John Minsheu's Spanish–English dictionary of 1599 and John Sanford's Spanish grammar of 1611 were both littered with examples drawn from *Lazarillo* and Rowland's own translation was immensely popular in England with editions in 1576, 1586, 1596, 1624, 1639, 1653, 1655, 1669, and 1677, followed by further translations and new editions. This was in marked contrast to its relative lack of success in Spain after the initial rash of issues in 1554, until the publication of *Guzmán de Alfarache* in 1599, which saw a revival of interest in the original essay into the genre.

Little is known about David Rowland. From Anglesey, he may have studied at St Mary Hall or Corpus Christi College, Oxford, before becoming tutor to Charles Stewart, the son of

---

[22] The former candidate was recently championed by Rosa Navarro Durán in *Alfonso de Valdés, autor del Lazarillo de Tormes* (Madrid: Gredos, 2003). The other two were both alluded to in relation to the book by the early seventeenth century.

[23] Keith Whitlock, 'Review of Anne Cruz, *Discourses of Poverty: Social Reform and the Picaresque Novel in Early Modern Spain* (Toronto: University of Toronto Press, 1999)', *Renaissance Studies*, 14 (2000): 484.

[24] Whitlock, *The Life of Lazarillo de Tormes*, 102–3.

[25] Whitlock, *The Life of Lazarillo de Tormes*, 90–1.

[26] Whitlock, *The Life of Lazarillo de Tormes*, 1.

[27] For an early mention of the Rowland translation, see John Garrett Underhill, *Spanish Literature in the England of the Tudors* (London: Macmillan, 1899), 273–5.

the Earl of Lennox, to whom he dedicated his *Comfortable Ayde for Scholers* in 1568, a collection of English phrases with Latin translations. He travelled in France and Spain and may have worked in the Antwerp office of Sir Thomas Gresham, to whom his translation of *Lazarillo* was dedicated.[28] Gresham was the crown's factor in Antwerp, where at one point he had resided in the house of Charles V's agent, Gasper Schetz. He was responsible for managing the transfer of Mary I's dowry from Seville to England in 1554 and witnessed Charles's abdication in favour of Philip in Brussels in 1556. Rowland's literalization of the text, a refusal to read it as fiction, is apparent in the way the dedication to Gresham is framed:

> Considering that besides much mirth, here is also a true discription of the nature & disposition of sundrie Spaniards. So that by reading hereof, such as haue not trauailed Spain, may as well discerne much of the manners & customs of that countrey, as those that haue there long time continued.[29]

By the time of this second edition in 1586, Spain was the subject of a government ban on travel, so that the book might indeed have offered a substitute for an actual journey to the Iberian peninsula. Gresham was someone who 'for trauaile, dailie conference with diuers nations, and knowledge in all forein matters...is well able to iudge, whether these reports of litle Lazaro be true or not'.[30] George Turbeville's dedicatory verses at the end of the 1586 edition underline this reading: 'Then Lazaro deserves/no blame, but praise to gain,/That plainly pens the Spaniards' pranks/and how they live in Spain'.[31] Rowland's title identifies his protagonist as 'a Spaniard' and the running head 'The Spaniards Life' reinforces its geographical place on every page.

The 1624 and 1639 editions incorporated an illustration opposite the title page, with the verses below: 'Here is Lazarillo's birth and life,/His wily feats and honest wife,/With his seven masters shall you find,/Expressing Spaniards in their kind' (Fig. 8.1). The marginal glosses, twenty out of thirty-four of which were Rowland's, revealed a direct acquaintance with Spain and supplement the text with local knowledge. The phrase 'certain men of honour' is glossed by him in the margin 'They were no Lords, every man is of honour there'.[32] Similarly, as Lazarillo trots after the squire hoping they will stop to buy provisions, Rowland glossed the passage 'There is not such prouision of meate in Spaine'.[33] The verses, although not the translation, offer a reading of one of the crucial questions raised by the text—whether Lazarillo is an adulterer and pimp whose marriage is a sham and cover for an Archpriest's peccadilloes and illegitimate children. The blind man's dress in the illustration suggests gentle origins, that he is in

---

[28] Ross Kennedy, 'Rowland, David', *ODNB* <http://www.oxforddnb.com/view/article/24212> accessed 18 March 2013.

[29] David Rowland, trans., *The Pleasaunt Historie of Lazarillo de Tormes a Spaniarde, wherein is conteined his maruelous deedes and life* (London: Abell Jeffes, 1586), sig. Aii^{r-v}.

[30] *The Pleasaunt Historie*, sig. Aii^v.

[31] *The Pleasaunt Historie*, sig. Hvii^v.

[32] Whitlock, *The Life of Lazarillo de Tormes*, 149 and Davies, 'David Rowland's *Lazarillo de Tormes* (1576)', 373.

[33] Whitlock, *The Life of Lazarillo de Tormes*, p. 107.

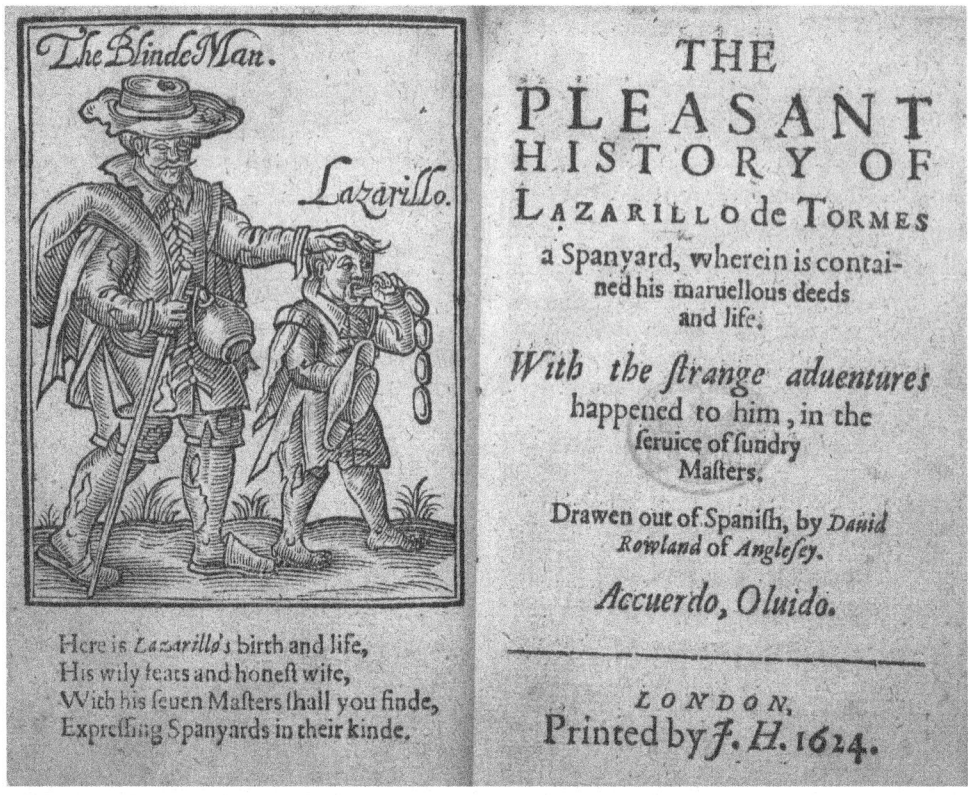

FIGURE 8.1 *The Pleasant History of Lazarillo de Tormes* (London: E. Griffin, 3rd edn., 1639 [1st edn., John Haviland, 1624]), frontispiece and title page. © British Library. C62.aa.18(1)

some way a sturdy beggar, albeit a victim of misfortune. The tag line on the title page 'acuerdo, olvido' [I remember, I forget], echoes the image in the prologue of 'la sepultura del olvido' [the oblivion of the tomb], from which the narrator hopes his publication will rescue 'cosas tan señaladas' [things of such note].[34] It also picks up on the theme of memory and forgetting integral to the narrative structure of fictional autobiography and an extension of the ritual of confession. The dramas of salvation, self-examination, and conscience are the subtext of this incarnation of the picaresque. The gap between what the narrative or narrator reveals and memorializes and what the story suppresses mirrors the recalcitrant sinner's blindness and forgetfulness of salvation and damnation. On the frontispiece of *La Pícara Justina*, the figures sail on the 'Rio del Olvido', the river of forgetfulness, an echo of the classical river, Lethe, crossed in order to reach the underworld. Their ship is topped by Bacchus.

In the dedication of these later editions to Charles Stanhope, the publisher, Thomas Walkley, claimed that beggary was 'A disease, which in respect of the heat of the Climate,

---

[34] R. O. Jones, ed., *La vida de Lazarillo de Tormes* (Manchester: Manchester University Press, 1963), 3.

and the coldnes of charity, is there holden incurable'.[35] Another reissue of the Rowland translation in 1653 saw the editor and translator James Blakeston in his dedication to George, Lord Chandos, Baron of Sudeley, reiterate that this is the 'little History of a Spaniards Life, (for those will mistake it who imagine it a Fiction)'. While in Toledo, Blakeston had endeavoured to 'get a sight of the entyre originall which had not suffered the Inquisitors hand' and the publisher affirmed that Lazarillo 'is always brief, always merry, I might say witty, for right Mirth is never without Wit'.[36] This tendency towards the literal in *Lazarillo*'s reception is related to the genre's origins in confession, an unburdening of conscience and fulfilment of the Pauline injunction *noscete ipsum*. Rowland's translation displays elements of adaptation and appropriation, but the overall strategy is one of exoticization. Five of the marginal notes give currency equivalents, with the translator leaving the original terms 'maravedi' in his translation and calquing other terms like 'blanca' as 'blank', with an annotation explaining 'Two blanks, a maravedi'.[37] His additions to the text are also significant. The 'torreznos y longaniza' or lardons of bacon and a cured sausage, from his time with the blind man, are rendered in translation 'slices of flesh, and sweete carbonados', a phrase used for the first time in England by Gascoigne in his 1575 *The Noble Art of Venerie* published by Bynneman.[38] There is a toning down of the Eucharistic parody in the second treatise with the phrase 'contemplar en aquella cara de Dios, que ansí dicen los niños' [contemplate that face of God], translated 'beholding always that bread as a God'.[39] The friar or priest referred to by way of unfavourable contrast with the thieving black slave Zaide disappears in the translation, the only moment where Rowland follows the Inquisitorial censors,[40] while the repertory of prayers intoned by the blind man in English comes to include 'the life of all the holy saints'.[41] Sectarian divisions influenced the translation as a reading of the text; however, the agenda appears at times ambiguous. On the one hand, the deliberate omission of potentially troubling and controversial issues such as Eucharistic theology or criticisms of the priesthood played down the 'Catholicism' of the text or at least its context. On the other hand, the translation foregrounds this same difference on a national, linguistic, and cultural level, keeping phrases like 'Mantenga Dios a vuestra merced', 'Bésoos, señor las manos', and 'Castilla' from the original in the translation and then offering renderings of the first two, although the suggestion is that there is no precise equivalent of these fine distinctions in etiquette.[42] Despite some archaisms and a few odd cultural transpositions such as 'my sucking years' for 'este oficio le hobiese mamado en la leche' [I had become versed in this office with my mother's milk], 'crow keeper' for 'echacuervos' [swindler,

---

[35] *The Pleasant History of Lazarillo de Tormes* (London: J. H., 1624), sig. A3ᵛ.
[36] *Lazarillo or, The Excellent History of Lazarillo de Tormes, the Witty Spaniard* (London: William Leake, 1653), sigs. A3ʳ⁻ᵛ, A6ᵛ.
[37] Whitlock, *The Life of Lazarillo de Tormes*, 84–5.
[38] Whitlock, *The Life of Lazarillo de Tormes*, 66–7.
[39] Whitlock, *The Life of Lazarillo de Tormes*, 92–3.
[40] Whitlock, *The Life of Lazarillo de Tormes*, 58–9.
[41] Whitlock, *The Life of Lazarillo de Tormes*, 65.
[42] Whitlock, *The Life of Lazarillo de Tormes*, 133, 35, and 141.

mountebank, or quack], Rowland's translation demonstrates a profound, if not infallible, grasp of Spanish with some very difficult phrases elegantly handled and turned into English. For example, the prologue's sentence 'Justó muy ruinmente el señor don Fulano, y dio el sayete de armas al truhán, porque le loaba de haber llevado muy buenas lanzas' becomes 'O how such a knight jousted noughtly, and nowithstanding he hath given his coat of armour to a jester which commended him for running well.'[43] The last phrase is an economic, idiomatic equivalent.

In any discussion of the picaresque in general and *Lazarillo* in particular, a central problem arises in the absence of a generally agreed definition of the genre, despite heroic attempts by a number of critics.[44] There are different approaches to defining the picaresque. One perspective looks at formal aspects of narrative; the fictional autobiography, the temporally displaced narrative voice, episodic structure, and eschewal of idealising epic or romance conventions. The other approach sees the genre in relation to political concerns over poverty, crime, prostitution, vagabondage, social mobility, and aspiration; religious, professional, or other forms of identity, and in Spain, *conversos*; charity and welfare, virtue as the true nobility and the possibility of commoners rising up, as well as an interest in marginal figures. *Lazarillo* is often excluded from the aetiology of the genre because arguably its protagonist has not learnt from his adventures and adversities. Moral degradation is the price of his material rise. The notion of virtue as the true nobility suggested by the prologue's allusion to attaining 'buen puerto', or safe haven, is not borne out by the story, which illustrates instead that it is a virtue simply to rise.[45] A poor youth apparently victimized by society becomes in the increasingly aristocratic milieu of Philip III's reign an irredeemable and dangerous social reprobate. The picaresque's fully-fledged form was only realized with Mateo Alemán's *Guzmán de Alfarache* (Part 1, 1599; Part 2, 1604), which along with Francisco de Quevedo y Villegas's *Historia de la vida del buscón, llamado Don Pablos* (pub. 1626, written c.1604) typified this evolution. No persuasive answer has been offered to the question as to why it took half a century after *Lazarillo* for *Guzmán* to appear or the relative lack of success *Lazarillo* enjoyed in Spain before the latter came to define the genre alongside it.

The immediate context for *Lazarillo*'s appearance in Spain was a public polemic about poor relief begun in 1545 with the Dominican professor of theology at Salamanca, Domingo de Soto's tract *Deliberación en la causa de los pobres* [*Discussion of the Case of the Poor*], which considered the legislative framework for poor relief established at Valladolid in 1523 and Toledo in 1534. He argued that attempts to force vagabonds back to their places of origin (1523) and for cities to appoint magistrates to license legitimate beggars (1534) were misguided because these secular, state-directed forms of poor relief

---

[43] Whitlock, *The Life of Lazarillo de Tormes*, 119 and 149.
[44] The reams of criticism on this subject are ably summarized in Juan Antonio Garrido Ardila, *El género picaresco en la crítica literaria* (Madrid: Biblioteca Nueva, 2008), 20 and *La novela picaresca en Europa, 1554–1753* (Madrid: Visor Libros, 2009), 41–56, esp. 48.
[45] A reading originally suggested by Ron Truman, 'Lázaro de Tormes and the *Homus novus* Tradition', *Modern Language Review*, 64 (1969): 62–7.

took away opportunities for individual charity. Being a beggar 'no solo quiere dezir no tener casa: empero no tener oficio, ni legitima causa, o necessidad de discurrir' [does not only mean being homeless, but also without work or legitimate reason or need for wandering around] and de Soto continued 'los enfermos y viejos y debiles sin molestia los dexen estar en la ciudad' [the sick and old and weak should be left alone to be in the city], although he recognized that 'La mayor cosa que achacan a los pobres para hazer dellos tanta inquisicion es que ingenian artes y fraudes para engañar la republica: haziendose enfermos: inuentado llagas y manquedades falsas para sacar dinero' [the main thing of which they accuse the poor to justify giving them the third degree is that they make up artful ways and frauds to deceive the commonwealth, pretending to be sick, simulating injuries and false limps to make money].[46] A riposte to de Soto's treatise of 30 January was published by the same printer on 20 March. Juan de Medina, abbot of the monastery of San Vicente in Salamanca, proposed a simple solution as his first chapter title stated:

> Que se tenga mucho cuydado que ningun pobre verdadero tenga necessidad de andar publicamente mendigando. Y que para esto se les de lo que han menester en sus estancias vn dia para toda la semana a razon de doce maravedis cada dia para vn hombre. Y diez para vna muger y seys para vn mochacho en caso que no lo puedan ganar con su trabajo.[47]

[that care be taken that no legitimately poor person needs to wander begging publicly. And for this reason they should be given what they need during their stay on a certain day for a week, tuppence for a man, one and half for a woman and a penny for a lad, when they are unable to earn it through their labour]

The debate was not new. The first comprehensive system of poor relief set up in Bruges had been influenced by one of Spain's most illustrious humanists, Juan Luis Vives, in his *De Subventione Pauperum* (1526), written after fourteen years on and off in the city. His radical agenda deplored that at religious festivals 'one has to make one's way into the building between two lines of diseases, vomitings, ulcers or other afflictions' and he counselled that if 'charity had any power over us, she herself would be a law for us (although love needs no law), to hold all things in common'.[48] England's first comprehensive Poor Law had been introduced in 1572, to deal with the huge problem of vagrancy and the sturdy, professional beggars, who it was perceived were plaguing urban environments.[49]

The growing numbers of marginalized urban poor, remarked upon by Juan Luis Vives, created divergent responses. On the one hand, they sparked calls for social reform and poor relief, reflecting the perception of the need for a reinvigorated sense

---

[46] Domingo de Soto, *Deliberación en la causa de los pobres* (Salamanca: Juan de Junta, 1545), sigs. Avi^v, Bii^r, and Cviii^v.

[47] Juan de Medina, *De la orden que en algunos pueblos de España se ha puesto en la limosna: para remedio de los verdaderos pobres [Of the order that in certain Spanish towns has been imposed for alms for the remedy of the true poor]* (Salamanca: Juan de Junta, 1545), sig. A8^r.

[48] See F. R. Salter, ed., *Some Early Tracts on Poor Relief* (London: Methuen and Co. Ltd, 1926), 8 and 10.

[49] See the classic study by A. L. Beier, *Masterless Men: The Vagrancy Problem in England 1560–1640* (London: Methuen, 1985).

of charity and community. On the other hand, picaresque fictions made a spectacle of precisely that degradation, presenting the *demi-monde* of the masterless, mendicant poor as a source of entertainment and humour; looking upon their protagonists with a mixture of fascination and revulsion, mocking their pretensions and veniality while envying their liberty. The genre expressed a fundamental ambivalence. The troubling, subversive evasion of social control, hierarchy, and structure by such outsiders was counterbalanced by the visceral physicality of their punishment within the plot. Paupers could be seen as Christ-like reminders of the universality of God's redeeming grace. However, the sturdy beggar aped aristocratic culture's rejection of *negotium* in their refusal to work and embracing of lesiure, or *otium*. As the fontispiece of *La Pícara Justina* put it (Fig. 8.2), the travellers, poor and happy, were carried along by pleasure 'el gusto me lleva'.

While contemporary debates about the poor certainly shaped *Lazarillo*'s reception in England, it irrupted into a context alongside another newly coined genre: the 'conny-catching' literature instigated by John Awdeley's *The Fraternitye of Vacabondes* (1561?), which in turn influenced Thomas Harman's *A Caveat or Warening for Common Cursetors vulgarely called Vagabones* (1567), reprinted as *The Groundworke of Conny-catching* (1592) at the same time as Robert Greene's pamphlets *A Notable Discovery of Coosenage* (1591), *Greenes Groats-Worth of wit* (1592), and *The Third and Last Part of Conny-Catching* (1592).[50] One of the first criminal biographies in England, of the highwayman James Hind, who was executed in 1652, associated Alemán's fictional *pícaro* with the historical criminal through its title, *The English Gusman; or The History of the Unparallel'd Thief James Hind* (1652), and through another one, *The Pleasant and Delightful History of Captain Hind* (1651), with Lazarillo.[51] In contrast to the criminal exposé and its antecedents, the *pícaro*'s narrative stance is ironic and self-reflexive. The reception of *Lazarillo* in England deliberately collapsed this ironic distance, by reading it through the burgeoning genre of criminal biography. The moralizing end of criminal autobiography depended on its explicit claim to historicity. The picaresque, however, depended on the contrast between spiritual aspiration and 'a materialist epistemology', the impossibility of marrying divine and positive law, the authority of God with that of the magistrate. According to Michael McKeon, the picaresque provided a model for exploring 'the experimental disjunction between unregenerate Character and spiritualizing Narrator'.[52] *Lazarillo*'s originality lies in the way it exploits the divided self of autobiography, the speaking subject that is at the same time the subject of speech; the 'chronological distance between the events and their narration' and a complex configuration of relationships between a 'narrating protagonist and acting protagonist, and of narrator to his

---

[50] Anne Cruz, 'Sonnes of the Rogue: Picaresque Relations in England and Spain', in Giancarlo Maiorino, ed., *The Picaresque: Tradition and Displacement* (London: University of Minnesota Press, 1996), 248–72 (248–9).

[51] Gustav Ungerer, 'English Criminal Biography and Guzmán de Alfarache's Fall from Rogue to Highwayman, Pander and Astrologer', *Bulletin of Hispanic Studies*, 76 (1999): 189–97 (190).

[52] Michael McKeon, *The Origins of the English Novel, 1600–1740* (London: Johns Hopkins University Press, 2002), chap.2, 'From Picaresque to Criminal Biography', 96–100 (96 and 99).

FIGURE 8.2 *Libro de entretenimiento, de la Picara Iustina* (Brussells: Olivero Brunello, 1608), sig. †ir, frontispiece after title page. © British Library. 1074.d.17

former self'.[53] It is a subversion of confession, with the identification of author and narrator fractured and fictionally displaced on to the less certain relationship between protagonist and narrator. The framing device of the 'caso' and 'Vuestra Merced' further blurs the distinction between author, narrator, and subject, as well as bifurcating the reader's response, forcing readers to see the story both from the perspective of its putative addressee, at the same time as reading from the outside the broader implications of the 'case', whatever it may be.

In *Guzmán*, in which the genre attains its canonical form, by contrast the tension between character and narrator is dynamic as it is in spiritual autobiography. In this novel 'the picaro begins to evince a moral standard that is clearly distinguishable from that of his surroundings', something that does feed into the creation of progressive narratives.[54] The protagonists have achieved some kind of self-awareness at the end of both *Guzmán* (with his final conversion) and *La Pícara Justina*, whereas Lázaro's final position is hedged around with irony. Thomas Nashe's *The Unfortunate Traveller* (1594) is the most immediate representative of *Lazarillo*'s 'autodidactic mode' and perhaps the closest to an English picaresque novel from the period. An influx of colonial silver and gold, inflation, and rising prices meant that in Spain distinctions between *hidalgos*, wealthy merchants, and landed peasants were muddied; a process exacerbated by the sale of patents of nobility and the statutes of purity of blood. Economic boom, urbanization, and rising aspirations influenced interest in ameliorating poverty and controlling the poor, sick, and marginal across Europe in this period. Lázaro identifies with the socially aspirant, rather than inherited aristocratic values, with his scathing attack on the *escudero*'s obsession with honour, yet as soon as his own economic circumstances improve, he purchases the clothes and sword that will allow him to dissimulate his own status. If it is a virtue simply to rise, there is no utopian alternative to that which the satire exposes; whereas in other examples of the picaresque, the excluded and disenfranchised are more explicitly incorporated within a moral economy, whose unquestionable authority their journeys lead them to recognize. Mateo Alemán's personal history, his *converso* origins, work as a prison doctor and visiting judge, and the secret report on the workers at the Almadén mercury mines, whose franchise was owned by the Fugger banking family, all fed into his exploration of subjection and status anxiety.

James Mabbe, Stuart England's greatest Spanish translator, was in Madrid when Sebastian de Covarrubias's *Tesoro de la lengua castellana* came out in 1611. He took whole sentences from the dictionary for his Spanish dedication to the translation of *Guzmán de Alfarache*, which he titled *The Rogue* in 1622, as well as numerous phrases, proverbs, and explanatory notes.[55] There were eight editions of this translation and seven of Juan

---

[53] Barry Ife, *Reading and Fiction in Golden-Age Spain: A Platonist Critique and some Picaresque Replies* (Cambridge: Cambridge University Press, 1985), 99.

[54] McKeon, *The Origins of the English Novel*, 238.

[55] For an assessment of his aims in his translation see John Yamamoto-Wilson, 'James Mabbe's Achievement in his Translation of *Guzmán de Alfarache*', *Translation and Literature*, 8 (1999): 137–56.

de Luna's *The Pursuit of the History of Lazarillo de Tormes*, also published in 1622, by the end of the seventeenth century, making them amongst the most popular works of prose fiction in English.[56] A translation of Carlos García's *La desordenada codicia de los bienes agenos* [*Disordered coveting of other people's things*] by William Melvin cashed in on this success, by titling itself *The Sonne of the Rogue, or, The Politicke Theefe* (1638).[57] Guzmán's celebrity within England reached a peak before the Restoration, when he became associated with the royalist cause, which Spain had sought to support through the Treaty of Brussels, concluded in 1657. With Charles II's re-assumption of the throne in 1660, prostitutes returned to the city of London, a fact celebrated in *The Wandring Whore*, a periodical whose pander figure was called Gusman. The 1634 edition of *The Rogue* had appeared with Mabbe's translation of *La Celestina* or *The Spanish Bawd Represented in Celestina*. The 'generic transculturation' of Guzmán continued with his appearance as an astrologer in *Gusmans Ephemeris: or, The Merry Rogues Calendar. Being an Almanack for 1662*.[58]

It is clear that *Lazarillo de Tormes* had a significant impact on the early modern English literary imagination, from Spenser's *Mother Hubberd's Tale* to Thomas Nashe's *Unfortunate Traveller*, Robert Greene's pamphlets, Shakespeare's *Much Ado About Nothing*, and the rash of plays with a character alluded to or named Lazarillo, from Francis Beaumont's *The Woman Hater* (1607) and Thomas Dekker's *Blurt Master-Constable. Or the Spaniards Night-Walke* (1602) to *Match-me in London* (1631). The preface of Thomas Dangerfield's *Don Tomazo* (1680) underlines the moral purpose of picaresque fictions in exposing cheats and cunning contrivances such as those found in *Guzmán* and *Lazarillo*. However, the nature of *Lazarillo*'s influence is more difficult to assess in terms of how it shaped the development and concerns of prose fiction in English. Its English avatars were more often stage characters or allusions in moral treatises. Alemán's *Guzmán*, however, was one of the most popular works of prose fiction in seventeenth-century England and undoubtedly influenced and shaped the great picaresque novels of the eighteenth century: Daniel Defoe's *Moll Flanders* (1722) and *Colonel Jack* (1722), Henry Fielding's *Joseph Andrews* (1742) and *Jonathan Wild* (1743), and Tobias Smollet's *Roderick Random* (1748). The influence on *Moll Flanders*, in particular, has been 'escasamente reconocida por la crítica' [barely registered in criticism], despite it being a 'fiel y nítido ejemplo de la novela picaresca' [faithful and precise example of the picaresque novel].[59] The criminalization of Spain's literary fictions in translation reflected the country's central place in the process of England's national identity formation. English desire to emulate Spain and envy for Spanish imperial power and mercantile success were re-inscribed and demonically inverted in images of tyranny and cruelty, and urban myths of a plague of poverty and bad meat. These stereotypes fed on the recognition

---

[56] Richard Bjornson, *The Picaresque Hero in European Fiction* (Madison: University of Wisconsin Press, 1977), 146–7, n. 15.
[57] Ungerer, 'English Criminal Biography', 189.
[58] Ungerer, 'English Criminal Biography', 191–4.
[59] Juan Antonio Garrido Ardila, 'La tradición picaresca española en Inglaterra' *Bulletin of Hispanic Studies*, 76 (1999): 453–69 (454).

of fundamental homologies between England and Spain. An overly political understanding of the picaresque's reception, however, fails in the face of a humour that was simultaneously at the expense of both Spain and England, mirthful and witty. The picaresque provided a set of devices, structures, and literary resources for the novel that enabled it to grow beyond humanist critiques of its lack of verisimilitude and immorality. The cant and jargon of the urban *demi-monde*, the language of the street, came together with status obsession and anxieties about the base, prurient, and dishonourable, the criminal and marginal. It married a materialist epistemology with the confessional and spiritual journey within the frame of fictional autobiography that placed the subject and subjected at the heart of our troubling obsession with the classes beneath us.

Further Reading

Ardila, Juan Antonio Garrido. *El género picaresco en la crítica literaria* (Madrid: Biblioteca Nueva, 2008).

—— *La novela picaresca en Europa, 1554–1753* (Madrid: Visor Libros, 2009).

—— 'La tradición picaresca española en Inglaterra', *Bulletin of Hispanic Studies*, 76 (1999): 453–69.

Chandler, Frank. *Romances of Roguery: An Episode in the History of the Novel—The Picaresque Novel in Spain* (London: Macmillan, 1899).

Cruz, Anne, *Discourses of Poverty: Social Reform and the Picaresque Novel in Early Modern Spain* (Toronto: University of Toronto Press, 1999).

Guillén, Claudio. *Literature as System: Essays Toward the Theory of Literary History* (Princeton: Princeton University Press, 1971), esp. essays 3 ('Toward a Definition of the Picaresque') and 5 ('Genre and Countergenre: The Discovery of the Picaresque'), 71–106 and 135–58.

Parker, Alexander A. *Literature and the Delinquent: The Picaresque Novel in Spain and Europe, 1599–1753* (Edinburgh: Edinburgh University Press, 1967).

Sánchez Escribano, F. J., ed. *Picaresca Española en Traducción Inglesa* (Zaragoza: University of Zaragoza, 1998).

Santoyo, Julio-César. *Ediciones y traducciones inglesas del* Lazarillo de Tormes (Vitoria: Colegio Universitario de Alava, 1978).

Ungerer, Gustav. 'English Criminal Biography and Guzmán de Alfarache's Fall from Rogue to Highwayman, Pander and Astrologer', *Bulletin of Hispanic Studies*, 76 (1999): 189–97.

Whitlock, Keith, ed. *The Life of Lazarillo de Tormes*, trans. David Rowland (Warminster: Aris and Phillips, 2000).

PART II

PROSE FICTION

CHAPTER 9

WILLIAM BALDWIN'S *BEWARE THE CAT* AND OTHER FOOLISH WRITING

THOMAS BETTERIDGE

William Baldwin was the author of a number of important works of mid-Tudor literature and as editor of the *Mirror for Magistrates* (1563) has long had an important place in accounts of the development of English Renaissance literature. During his lifetime he was probably best known as the writer of the *Treatise of Moral Philosophy* (1547), which went through numerous editions, and as translator of the ribaldry anti-papal work the *Wonderful News of the Death of Paul III* (1552). Baldwin probably died sometime during the autumn of 1563. Although Baldwin's place in literary history is assured due to his role in producing the *Mirror for Magistrates* he is a slightly ambiguous figure. His major works, the *Treatise of Moral Philosophy* and the *Mirror*, are not original compositions, but are rather patchwork texts made up of contributions from other writers as well as Baldwin himself. It is perhaps typical of Baldwin that one text that he probably wrote, *A lyttel treatyse called the Image of Idlenesse, conteynyne certeyne matters moved betwene Walter Wedlock and Bawdin Bachelor. Translated out of the Troyane of Cornyshe tounge into Englyshe, by Olyver Oldwanton, and dedicated to the Lady Lust* (1555), cannot be attributed to him with certainty.[1] This is particularly unfortunate since *A lyttel treatyse* is the first epistolary novel written in English. *Beware the Cat* is the one major prose work over which there is no doubt concerning Baldwin's authorship.

Beware the Cat is strange. It is hard to classify. Is it a history, which is what it claims to be, an interlude, a beast fable, a travelogue, or a parodic humanist treatise? In practice it is all of these and none. Its title page entices the reader by offering 'diverse wounderfull

---

[1] Robert W. Maslen, 'William Baldwin and the Politics of Pseudo-Philosophy in Tudor Prose Fiction', *Studies in Philology*, 97 (2000): 29–60. *A lyttel treatyse called the Image of Idlenesse, conteynyne certeyne matters moved betwene Walter Wedlock and Bawdin Bachelor. Translated out of the Troyane of Cornyshe tounge into Englyshe, by Olyver Oldwanton, and dedicated to the Lady Lust* (1555), ed. Michael Flachmann, *Studies in Philology*, 87 (1990): 1–74.

and incredible matters/Very pleasant and mery to read'. *Beware the Cat* is undoubtedly full of diverse and strange matter. And at times it is pleasant to read, although some of the wonderful stuff it contains is also disgusting and occasionally disturbing. The slipperiness of *Beware the Cat* in a strange way reflects the ambiguous nature of Baldwin's status as a Tudor writer. *Beware the Cat* is an exercise in foolish writing and Baldwin was a fool to write a work that consistently frustrates any and all attempts to fix its meaning. The folly of writing such a slippery feline work is, however, perhaps only exceeded by the foolishness of those who seek to collar *Beware the Cat*, to hang a generic bell onto Baldwin's work in order to warn readers of its approach.

Beware the Cat opens with a dedicatory Epistle and then an Argument. It concludes with an Exhortation. The bulk of the text is made up of the three Orations of Master Streamer, the work's deeply unreliable narrator, during which Streamer seeks to prove that cats can talk and reason as well as humans. The first Oration comprises a series of stories and tales about cats. The second Oration takes a rather different turn since it is mainly concerned with Streamer's preparation of a potion that he hopes will allow him to understanding the language of cats. The third Oration is largely spoken by a female cat, Mouse-slayer, who is heard recounting her life as part of her defence in a feline court of law. All three Orations are presented through Streamer, although often, particularly in the final Oration, other transgressive voices break through—cats, servants, women, and Irish. *Beware the Cat* deliberately evokes Thomas More's *Utopia* both in the way it is presented and in terms of form. It is a dialogue, largely spoken by one person. It was published with a range of textual apparatus which, on the surface, appear designed to elucidate the work's meaning, but in practice simply complicate it further. Streamer is a parodic Hythloday. He is a speaker of nonsense whose authority is based on his ability to travel to strange lands and exotic locales and to report back what he has heard. It is also possible that the name Streamer is intended to mock More—since Streamer is a narrator who streams on and on, creating more and more text.

Beware the Cat was first published in 1570, although it was almost certainly composed in 1553. It may have been produced in 1570 as part of the propaganda campaign occasioned by the Northern Rebellion. It is possible that in 1570 those responsible for publishing *Beware the Cat* assumed its readers would understand Baldwin's cats as representing Catholics in their superstition and bawdiness. This would, however, be a simplistic overtly confessional reading of the text. The concluding Exhortation comments that,

> And that we may take profit by this declaration of Master Streamer, let us so live, both openly and privily that neither our own cat, admitted to all secrets, be able to declare aught of us to the world save what is laudable and honest; nor the Devil's cat, which will we or nill we seeth and writeth all out ill doings, have ought to lay against us afore the face of God, who not only with shame but with everlasting torment will punish sin and wickedness.[2]

If we all have our own cats then clearly to read Baldwin's cats as Catholics is at best reductive and at worst simply wrong. The Exhortation concludes the text by raising more

---

[2] William Baldwin, *Beware the Cat: The First English Novel*, ed. William A. Ringler, Jr. and Michael Flachmann (San Marino, CA: Huntington Library, 1988), 54.

interpretative questions than it solves. What is the difference between 'our cats' and the 'Devil's cat'? Our cats sound like some kind of external conscience, but if this is the case, why does the Devil have one? The cats also seem to have a role in God's punishment of sin. The potential confusion engendered by the Exhortation is, however, entirely appropriate of a work that Baldwin explicitly locates in the fringes of authoritative or establishment culture.

The Argument places the genesis of *Beware the Cat* in a discussion between what appears to be a rather strange collection of men sharing a bedroom while working on the English court's Christmas entertainments. The Argument opens by the narrator, not Streamer, commenting that: 'It chanced that at Christmas last I was at Court with Master Ferrers, then master of the King's Majesty's pastimes, about setting forth certain interludes, which for the King's recreation we had devised and were in learning.'[3] Sharing the room with Ferrers and Baldwin, the narrator of this section of the work, were the former's Astronomer, Master Wilmot, and his Divine, Master Streamer. It would be inappropriate to treat Baldwin's account of the genesis of his work with anything but scepticism, particularly given that one of the text's objects of scorn is people who are too trusting readers. There is, however, a reference in the accounts of the Master of the Revels to a payment being made to a William Baldwin, who appears to have been working as a prop-maker producing a crown of gold paper and buckram for an Irish prince.[4] The Epistle that precedes the Argument provides further details concerning the work's production.[5] In the process, however, it stresses its distance from Streamer's original words and at the same time, in a self-contradictory move, suggests that when Ferrers and Willot read *Beware the Cat* they will 'think they hear Master Streamer speak'.[6] *Beware the Cat* is self-consciously aware of itself as a printed work. This is reflected by the effort that Baldwin makes to stress the oral nature of Streamer's three orations, while at the same time creating a text whose complexity and intertextuality mean that it would be impossible for anyone to actually recount all of the work's matter. Streamer, like Hythloday, is a textual orator—a voluminous, complex speaker who can only exist in print, on a printed page. Having worked through the Epistle and the Argument, the reader finally reaches Streamer's first Oration, where things are not simple.

9.1 'Where fact is lacking, fiction is best'

Streamer opens his first Oration by telling his listeners, in a throw-away comment, that he was lodged at a friend's house that 'hangeth partly upon the town wall that is called Aldersgate'.[7] Streamer's words strongly suggest that he is in the house of the noted

---

[3] Baldwin, *Beware the Cat*, 5.
[4] Albert Feuillerat, ed., *Documents Relating to the Revels at Court in the Time of King Edward VI and Queen Mary* (Louvain: A. Uystpruyst, 1914), 142.
[5] Edward T. Bonahue, '"I know the place and the persons": The Play of Textual Frames in Baldwin's *Beware the Cat*', *Studies in Philology*, 91 (1994): 283–300.
[6] Baldwin, *Beware the Cat*, 3.   [7] Baldwin, *Beware the Cat*, 9.

Protestant printer, John Day. At this point, however, Streamer's narrative takes a wrong turn and becomes an extended digression on how the gates of London got their names. Streamer discusses Aldersgate, Moorgate, Newgate, and Ludgate. He comments that, '…Moorgate took the name of the field without it, which hath been a very moor; or else because it is the most ancient gate of the City, was therof in respect of the other, as Newgate, called the Eldergate'.[8] This comment is accompanied by a gloss in the margin 'Why Moorgate'. This is, however, at best misleading and at worst nonsense. *Beware the Cat* is not the kind of text that requires glosses—although at times it does seek to pass as a source of wisdom and knowledge. Streamer is clearly simply speculating at this point, despite his attempt to buttress his words with historical references. The use Streamer makes of linguistic analysis to explain place names mimics humanist hermeneutics and may be designed to specifically parody the historical work of humanists like John Leland. The opening of *Beware the Cat* mocks the Edwardian vogue for learned and speculative 'commonwealth' works reflected most clearly in the publication in 1551 of the first translation in English of Thomas More's *Utopia*, whose translator and editor, Ralph Robinson, seems not to have realized that More wrote this work with his tongue firmly in his cheek.[9]

Streamer continues his account by telling the reader that while he was sitting by the fire in the print shop he got into a conversation with some of the people working in the printing house concerning the 'wawling' of the cats during the night. He then goes on to report the words of one of the servants, who tells the strange tail of a cat in Staffordshire. This is followed by another catty tale in which a cat speaks Irish. Streamer's first narration is very quickly hijacked by other voices, those of the servants working in the printing house and then the cats who speak in the servants' stories. Terence N. Bowers has suggested that 'Streamer's narrative…is composed of many orally transmitted tales which tend to multiply uncontrollably'.[10] The first servant's story concerns a Staffordshire man who was hailed by a cat as he rode home through Kankwood. Failing to respond when the cat calls his name, he is asked by his feline accoster to 'Commend me unto Tittan Tatton and to Puss thy Catton, and tell her that Grimalkin is dead.'[11] The Staffordshire man returns home and tells his wife and the rest of the household the story in the presence of his cat: 'And when he had told them all the cat's message, his cat, which had harkened unto the tale, looked upon him sadly, and at the last said, "And is Grimalkin dead? Then farewell dame," and therewith went her way and was never seen after.'[12] This brief story is then followed by a much longer one, told by a different man, which is set in Ireland and recounts the death of Grimalkin, who is killed by an Irish kern. This story is far more disturbing than the earlier one. It opens with two kerns stealing some cattle and deciding to hide in a church. While waiting to make their escape the two men cock a

---

[8] Baldwin, *Beware the Cat*, 9.
[9] John Guy, *Thomas More* (London: Routledge, 2000), 93.
[10] Terence N. Bowers, 'The Production and Communication of Knowledge in William Baldwin's *Beware the Cat*: Toward a Typographic Culture', *Criticism*, 33 (1991): 1–29 (10).
[11] Baldwin, *Beware the Cat*, 11.   [12] Baldwin, *Beware the Cat*, 11.

sheep. It is at this point that Grimalkin enters and demands to be fed. The cat then proceeds to eat an entire sheep and an entire cow. The men then decide to flee and in the ensuing chase kill Grimalkin. Although one of the kerns is killed during the fight, the other makes it home and tells his household what had happened:

> When he was come home and had put off his harness... all weary and hungry he set him down by his wife and told her his adventure, which, when a kitling which his wife kept, scarce half a year old, had heard, up she started and said, 'Hast thou killed Grimalkin!' And therewith she plunged in his face, and with her teeth took him by the throat, and ere that she could be plucked away, she had strangled him.[13]

The story of the death of Grimalkin provokes a number of discussions, including on whether or not a cat could eat a sheep and cow at one sitting and on how cats can communicate in secret over long distances. The story of Grimalkin is typical of the oral tales that make up *Beware the Cat*. It is told at fourth hand—the original kern, who has been slain by the kitling, told his wife who told another man who told the servant who told the story to Streamer who tells it to the reader. What is important in this chain is its combination of implausibility and realism. It is inherently unlikely that such a chain of storytelling could produce a true or authoritative story and yet Streamer goes out of his way to provide realistic detail concerning when and where most of the links in the chain of storytelling took place.

Having heard the story of Grimalkin, Streamer and his comrades discuss its truthfulness. For example, when one of the men involved in the debate questions how Grimalkin could have eaten so much at one sitting, one of the other men replies that the Pope, 'all things considered, devoureth more at every meal than did Grimalkin at her last supper'.[14] Streamer, however, disputes this point arguing that, 'although the Pope, by exactions and other baggagical trumpery, have spoiled all people of mighty spoils, ye (as touching his own person) he eateth and weareth as little as any other man...'.[15] This exchange reflects the dangerous nature of the dialogue that Streamer reports as part of his first Oration. The reference to Grimalkin's 'last supper' is clearly potentially blasphemous. At the same time, the use of the example of the Pope to defend Grimalkin's monstrous appetite suggests an inability or a refusal by some of the men in the dialogue to differentiate between different kinds of rhetorical tropes. Streamer is right to suggest that as a man the Pope eats as much or as little as anyone else; however, the Pope as a polemical figure in much of the Protestant propaganda produced during the reign of Edward VI was as monstrous and rapacious as nay mythical giant cat.

The first Oration sets up a pattern that recurs throughout *Beware the Cat* in which the reader is seduced or tricked into believing that they are listening to an authoritative or at least a learned discussion before finding that they are actually reading something very different. As the discussion of Grimalkin continues, a 'well-learned man and one of excellent judgement' comments that 'it doth appear that there is in cats, as in other kinds

---

[13] Baldwin, *Beware the Cat*, 14.   [14] Baldwin, *Beware the Cat*, 15.
[15] Baldwin, *Beware the Cat*, 16.

of beasts, a certain reason and language whereby they understand one another. But, as touching this, Grimalkin I take rather to be an hagat or a witch than a cat.'[16] This does appear to be a relatively sensible comment; however, it then transpires that this well-learned man is called Thomas and had later died of a disease he caught in Newgate prison, 'where he lay long for a suspicion of magic because he had desired a prisoner to promise him his soul after he was hanged'.[17] Thomas is no more reliable as a source of information on cats and witches than Streamer. Or Streamer's naïveté and gullibility is so complete that he does not realize that the reason Thomas is so knowledgeable is that Thomas is himself a witch. Certainly the request of a man's soul does not seem compatible with excellent judgement.

All three Orations contain different voices and discourses. The first is particularly plural in turns of narrative voice. Its one point of relative stability is provided by the fact that they are all being reported by Streamer; however, the reader is constantly reminded by Baldwin that Streamer is a far from trustworthy narrator. *Beware the Cat* could have as its subtitle 'beware the narrator', particularly one who claims learning, wit, and authority. Streamer, like Hythloday, presents himself to the reader, as does Baldwin's prefatory material, as a humanist, a man of letters and learning. By the end of the first Oration he is, however, in the world of Grimalkin, Thomas and Robin Goodfellow. In *Beware the Cat* Baldwin creates an object lesson of the dangers of print, and of print shops, for the learned. In the course of our conversation or a few printed pages one can go from what appears to be an authoritative humanist account of the names of London's gates to a world of cats and witches. And this can happen without the narrator, and therefore if they are not very careful the reader, noticing what has happened.

Streamer's status as an unreliable narrator means that the reader is invited, perhaps even incited, to pay close attention to *Beware the Cat*'s generic status. Baldwin's work is at one level an animal fable which might lead the reader to expect it to have a few relatively straightforward possible meanings; however, as soon as one starts to read Baldwin's work in terms of generic expectations problems arise. To start with, there are a number of possible candidates for the cats. Perhaps the most obvious one is Catholics. R. W. Maslen points out that Baldwin's '...cats exhibit a number of characteristics which Protestant propagandists attributed to the Catholic clergy: they are sexually promiscuous, inordinately greedy...and given to meddling with magic'.[18] However, as I have already suggested, identifying the cats as Catholics is problematic. This is partly because Baldwin's cats look more like *papists* then Catholics. Baldwin's cats have the ability to cross all boundaries and penetrate the secret recesses of the human world. They seem naturally to inhabit the periphery and the hidden. Maslen comments that 'cat culture occupies the spaces left vacant by human society'.[19] This is, however, only partly the case. Cats are at the bottom of a chain of knowledge or wisdom which leads through servants via

---

[16] Baldwin, *Beware the Cat*, 19.   [17] Baldwin, *Beware the Cat*, 19.
[18] Robert W. Maslen, *Elizabethan Fictions: Espionage, Counter-Espionage, and the Duplicity of Fiction in Early Elizabethan Prose Narratives* (Oxford: Clarendon Press, 1997), 79.
[19] Maslen, *Elizabethan Fictions*, 79.

printing and Streamer into the public sphere. There is a sense in which what *Beware the Cat* most consistently demonstrates is the extent to which printed knowledge, indeed by implication all knowledge, has its basis in half-truths and matted catty tales.

9.2 'TO PLAY THE FOOL IN SEASON IS THE HEIGHT OF WISDOM'

Beware the Cat's interest in the relationship between fact and fiction, and wisdom and folly, is focused in Streamer's second Oration upon medicine. This section of Baldwin's work contains a detailed description of the potion that Streamer brews in order to allow him to understand the language of cats. In the process, however, Baldwin reflects on the role of Tudor doctors as potent, potentially rich, tale tellers.

Tudor doctors were constantly in situations that completely outstripped their knowledge. This created a situation in which the role of the doctor became, as much as anything, about finding ways of managing and containing the fear caused by injury or disease. Andrew Wear comments that 'The physician's ability to see into the diseased body and to tell its story created a sense of rationality, of being able to answer the question "why?", which was the hallmark of rational, learned physic.'[20] Being able to narrate a disease, to create a narrative from a patient's symptoms, was an essential skill for a Tudor doctor. And in order to create narrative a doctor needed to be able to name and know the disease that he or she was treating. This emphasis on having to create a logical narrative, to tell a believable story, presented serious problems when the disease could not be fully defined or known, for example, with a new disease like syphilis, which did not appear in classical medicine books. The need to tell a story in order to make a disease understandable had the effect of creating a strange and potentially disturbing link between stories and diseases. Both had beginnings, middles, and ends—finding or discovering the true beginning might help one to fully understand and even predict how the disease/story would end. Wear points out further that 'physicians were concerned with credibility, and in the early modern period stories were still appropriate for conveying the truth, even if the truth was not fully visible. Narrative description could create matters of fact as if they had been seen.'[21] The problem was that creating stories was also what characters like Streamer did. Indeed the Dedication to *Beware the Cat* refers to a work entitled *Cure of the Great Plague* that Streamer is apparently translating out of Arabic. Tudor doctors needed to create narratives in the same way that writers did and this placed their work dangerously close to the emerging form of prose fiction. It is therefore perhaps not surprising to find doctors appearing as characters in some of the earliest printed prose works.

---

[20] Andrew Wear, *Knowledge and Practice in English Medicine, 1550–1680* (Cambridge: Cambridge University Press, 2000), 145.
[21] Wear, *Knowledge and Practice in English Medicine*, 134.

Early modern authors were aware of the medicinal relationship between healing and narrating. Jest books contain numerous stories of trickster doctors. *The Merry jest of a man called Howleglas* (1530) is a collection of stories in which the eponymous 'hero' tricks various people by relying on their greed, stupidity, and general lack of wit. It is a populist version of Erasmus's far more famous *Praise of Folly*. In one of the stories Howleglas makes a very tempting offer to a 'master' of a hospital—for a small fee he will cure everyone in the hospital. The master leaps at this chance to save money and accepts Howleglas's offer:

> Upon the morrow after came Howlegals to [the] hospital with two men after him [and] than he asked the sicke folke, one after the other, what disease they had, and whan he had asked them all, than he made the[m] swere upon a booke/[that] they shold kepe his counsaile what so euer he sayd to the[m]. They answered that they wold. Than sayde Howleglas to them, I haue undertaken[n] to make you all hole, which is unpossible, but I must nedes [burn] one of you all to pouder. And then must I take the pouder of him [and] giue al to the other to drinke therof [with] other medicines [that] I shall minister thereto. And he [that] is the last, wha[n] I shall cal you out of the hospital [and] he that cannot go: shalbe [burned].
>
> Than prepared euer one of [the] sicke folke there crutches [and] gere [that] they wold not be the last. And wha[n] Howleglas was co[m]e to the maisters of [the] hospital: tha[n] called he the[m] [and] tha[n] thei ran out of the hospitall [and] som of them had not ben out of there in x yere before. Than wha[n] the sicke folk wer out of the hospital: than asked he [Howleglas] hys money [and] tha[n] tha master gaue it him [and] than he departed.²²

Howleglas is a parodic doctor, but a very successful one. He clears the hospital and 'cures' all the patients. Indeed, Howleglas makes the cripples walk. One could argue that Howleglas's cure is nothing more than a trick, but in a world in which people were ignorant of the real causes of most diseases there was always the danger that all cures, all medicine, would appear to be nothing more than a jest—and that all doctors were tricksters and conmen.

Tales and quicke answeres, very mery and pleasant to rede (1532) is a collection of jests. It contains numerous stories in which doctors are either the protagonist or the object of ridicule. For example:

> There was a certayn riche man on a tyme, which felle sycke: to the whose curyng came many phisitians (for flyes by heapes will flee to honye). Amonge them all there was one that sayde: that he muste nedes take a glister, if he wolde be holle. Wha[n] the sicke man...harde hym saye so, he sayde in a great furye: Out of doors with those phistians they be madde: For whereas may payne is in my head, they wolde heale me in myne arse.
>
> This fable sheweth that holsom thynges to the[m] that lacke knowledge and experience, seme hurtfull.²³

---

²² *Here beginneth a merye jest of a man that was called Howleglas* (London: William Copland, 1530), C.ii/C.ii (v).

²³ *Tales and quicke answeres, very mery and pleasant to rede* (London? 1532), H.ii (v).

Another jest depicts a surgeon in an even more disreputable light:

> There was an olde woman the which bargained with a surgeon to heal her sore eyes: and whanne he hadde made her eies hole, and that she sawe better she couenaunted that he shulde be payde his moneye, and not before. So he a layde a medycyence to her eyes, that shulde not be taken awaye the space of v dayes. In whiche tyme she might not loke uppe. Euery daye, whan he came to dresse her, he bare awaye somewhat of her householde stouffe, table clothes, candlesticks, and dishes. He lefte no thinge, that he coulde carye clene. So whan her eies were hole, she looked up, and saw that her householde stouffe was caryede awaye, she sayde to the surgeon, that came and required his money for his labour: Syr my promise was to pay you, whan ye made me se better than I did before: That is trouth, quod he. Mary, quod she, but I see worse nowe than I did. Before ye layde medicines to myn eies, I saw moche fayre stouffe in myn house, and now I see nothinge at all.[24]

In this story the surgeon is little more than a thief. The form of *Tales and quick answers* precludes lengthy depictions of doctors narrating diseases. Instead, what the reader is presented with are numerous stories in which doctors and other medical man are represented as being little more than con artists.

Fictions and fictionality hovered around medicine in Tudor England. At the same time, medical books were an important segment of the early English printed book trade. There was, not surprisingly, a large market for self-help books for doctors and works purporting to offer cures, potions, and charms to all manner of ailments. Andrew Borde's *The Breuiary of Helthe* (1547) presents itself as a guide for doctors and learned non-medical readers. It makes the bold claim that 'there is no sickness in man or woman the which may be from the crowne of the heede to the sole of the foote but you shal fynde it in this boke'.[25] At the same time, Borde is keen to warn his readers that:

> every man [and] woman of what degre or estate so euer they be lackynge the speculation of phisiche to beware to minister medicines, although they take nothynge for theyr labour, nor for the medicines, for yf they haue not a doctours learninge, and also knowynge theyr symples howe they shall compounde them, and what operation they be of, and how and whan [and] what tyme they shodle be ministered, such ignorant persons may do great harme.[26]

The *Breuiary* is rather incoherent in terms of its status as an advice book since this warning would seem to pertain only to those who have not read it. Anyone who reads the entire *Breuiary* would clearly be learned in Tudor medicine.

The Antidotarius, published in 1530 by Robert Wyer, focuses specifically on plasters, ointments, oils, and 'wound drinks'. It is difficult to know what to make of the very complex recipes for medicines that this work contains. The following is *The Antidotarius*'s recipe 'To make a good Jews plaster to fresh wounds':

---

[24] *Tales and quicke answeres*, H.iii (v).
[25] Andrew Borde, *The Breuiary of Helthe* (London, 1547), B.ii.
[26] Borde, *The Breuiary of Helthe*, A.iii.

> Take white wax iii ounces, white rosin, Turpentine of each ii ounces, oil of roses, white frankincense of each ii ounces, fresh juices of Roses iii ounces, red wine one measure, and of all these herbs take that ye may get, winter green, syndowe, diapensia, matrisilra, herba serasenica, herba tunici, fumus letre, plantaye great and small, storks bill, herba ruba, of each a like amount till ye have enough, and good wine, strain the herbs and thresh there out the sap and put the wine on the herbs that they may become moist with wine... Then strain it through a cloth, than do the sap and the wine in a kettle [and] therein do the wax, Turpentine, Rosin and oil... than strain it through a cloth and... let it set all together v or vi hours long... and the next day melt it again; and do therein the Maltyke Frankincense and Myre made all in a powder and do it in the kettle and let it set together... and then take it from the fire and let it be cold and ye haue a right Jews plaster that healeth wounds.[27]

What is being described here is a distilling and combining process. Its complexity suggests a desire to make the knowledge contained in *The Antidotarius* radically different to that of popular medicine. The credibility desired by Tudor doctors when they created disease narratives is being transferred in this passage to the process of medicine making.

There is clearly a difference between works like *The Antidotarius* and *The Book of secrets of Albertus Magnus* (1525), which informed its readers that

> The virtue of the hare is showed to be miraculous for the fete if it be joined with a stone or with the head of a black owl, it moveth a man to hardiness, so that he fear not death.
>
> And if it be bounden to his left arm, he may go whether he will and he shall return safe without peril.[28]

This appears to be simple folklore, as does *The Book of secrets*' 'cure' for a wife's lack of sexual desire: 'When a woman desireth not her husband, then let her husband take a little of the tallow of a buck Goat and let him anoint her privy member with it, and do the act of generation she shall love him and shall not do the act of generation afterward with any [other].'[29] It is interesting to note that this advice might even have worked: using lubrication might make a woman 'desire' or at least tolerate her husband more; however, the reason for this cure's efficacy would not be the Tudor one, which is that goats, and male goats in particular, are notoriously lusty and therefore the application of goat grease to a woman's 'privy member' would make her more lustful.

The Second Part of Streamer's Oration opens with Streamer turning to *The Book of secrets* to help him understand the language of cats. And indeed Magnus's work does contain a 'spell' that would have helped Streamer in his quest:

> If thou wilte understande the voices of brydes. Associate with... two felowes in the 28th dayes of October [and] go in to a certayne woode wyth dogges as too hunte, and

---

[27] *The Antidotarius*, (London: Robert Wyer, 1530), B.i (v)/B.ii.
[28] Albertus Magnus, *The Boke of secretes of Albertus Magnus, of the vertues of Herbes, stones and certaine beasts* (London, 1525), E.iiii.
[29] Magnus, *The Boke of secretes*, H.v (v)/H.v (1).

[return] home wyth that beaste, whyche/thou shale fynd fyrst, and prepare it with the hart of a Foxe, [and] thou shalt understand anone the voyce of byrdes or beastes.[30]

Following Magnus's instructions, although far from by the letter, Streamer enters a wood seeking a hedgehog, since he tells that reader 'the flesh thereof [is] by nature full of natural heat—and therefore, the principal parts being eaten, must needs expulse gross matters and subtile the brain....'[31] Streamer searches for a hedgehog because he assumes he needs heat to purge his body of corruption and that once purged, he will be restored to a natural or pure state in which he will be able to hear the entire cosmos. It is the heat of the hedgehog which makes it particularly vital for Streamer, since he knows as a man of learning that heat is essential to the process of purgation.

Having procured the various animals that he needs to perform the charm, Streamer describes in detail the process of preparing the potion he is going to take:

> The flesh I washed clean and put it in a poet, and with white wine, Mellisophillos or Melissa (commonly called blam), rosemary, newt's tongue, four parts of the first and two of the second, I made a broth and set it on a fire and boiled it... in the seething whereof I had a pint of a pottle of wine which I put in the pot. Then, because it was the *solstitium estivale*, and that in confections the hours of the planets must for the better operation be observed, I tarried till ten o'clock before dinner, what time Mercury began his lucky reign.[32]

Streamer's account of the making of the potion that he is going to drink recognizably draws on Tudor medical writing. It could have been copied from the pages of *The Antidotarius*. Streamer gives the reader a detailed description of the preparation to fulfil his earlier promise that 'because you be all my friends that are here I will hide nothing from you, but declare point to point how I behaved myself in both making and taking my philter.'[33] *Beware the Cat*, or at least Streamer's narrative, presents itself to the reader partly as a self-help work. It is intended to be informative and there is therefore a sense in which Streamer's detailed description of the making of his potion is necessary so that others can follow in his footsteps. In these terms, Streamer is a parodic Borde or Hythloday, instructing his listeners (readers) on how to learn from his example.

Streamer's failure as a narrator reflects his failures as a doctor and as a purveyor of advice. Ultimately, he cannot control his text and creates a work whose abundance reflects a trait that Cathy Shrank has argued typifies the work of Andrew Borde.[34] *Beware the Cat* suggests that surrounding Streamer's learned world is one of chaos and noise. Having taken the potion, Streamer finds he can hear everything:

> And one shrewd wife a great way off (I think St Albans) called her husband 'cuckold' so loud and shrilly that I heard that plain; and would fain have heard the rest, but

---

[30] Magnus, *The Boke of secretes*, I.v (3)/I.V (3v).   [31] Baldwin, *Beware the Cat*, 25.
[32] Baldwin, *Beware the Cat*, 27.   [33] Baldwin, *Beware the Cat*, 25.
[34] Cathy Shrank, *Writing the Nation in Reformation England, 1530–1580* (Oxford: Oxford University Press, 2004), 45.

could not be no means for barking of dogs, grunting of hogs, wawling of cats, rumbling of rats, gaggling of geese, humming of bees, rousing of bucks, gaggling of ducks, singing of swans, ringing of pans, crowing of cocks, sewing of socks, cackling of hens, scrabbling of pens, peeping of mice, trulling of dice, curling of frogs, and toads in bogs, chirking of crickets, shutting of wickets, shriking of owls, flittering of fowls, routing of knaves, snorting of slaves, farting of churls, fizzling of girls with many things else...[35]

When Streamer drinks the potion he plunges into a world of language. As the words mount up, the boundaries between different activities and species start to collapse. This passage creates equivalence between 'the trulling of dice' and the 'flittering of fowls'. It also, however, yet again raises questions about Streamer's status as a narrator, since it is impossible to read this passage and think that it is an accurate record of what happened after Streamer had drunk the potion. Does sewing socks make a sound? Is not this item simply in the list to provide a rhyme for 'cocks'? But if this is the case, what is the meaning of this passage? The second Oration at times reads like a work of Tudor medicine, but in passages like this the reader is reminded of the poetic roots of Baldwin's work. Ultimately, Geoffrey Chaucer's *Canterbury Tales* are more important to *Beware the Cat* than *The Antidotarius* or the works of Albertus Magnus.

9.3 'The world is full of fools'

In *Beware the Cat* Baldwin consistently mocks humanist assumptions about human rationality through the specific qualities of prose. Andrew Hadfield comments that '*Beware the Cat* works by never allowing the reader to settle for easy answers and rest assured that the world can be neatly split into sheep and goats.'[36] In Baldwin's hands, the prose of *Beware the Cat*, in its lack of decorum, its refusal to respect any boundaries, spatial, temporal, or generic, and its mixing of fact and fiction, truth and lies, speech and print in a hotchpotch of nonsense, horror, humour, violence, and wisdom, becomes a printed rebuke to humanism. Lorna Hutson has argued that 'For humanists, discourses in which the plot solution emerged from the order of telling were superior to discourses such as chivalric romances in which solutions were reached through the lapse, rather than the ordering, of narrative time.'[37]

Beware the Cat forces together the humanist emphasis on narrative with a number of other discourses to create a text in which narratological ordering simply disguises the chaos at its heart. Or rather, in which the desire of the reader for the order is itself mocked, particularly in the third of Streamer's Orations, which largely comprises the

---

[35] Baldwin, *Beware the Cat*, 32.
[36] Andrew Hadfield, *Literature, Travel, and Colonial Writing in the English Renaissance, 1545–1625* (Oxford: Oxford University Press, 1998), 146.
[37] Lorna Hutson, 'Fortunate Travellers: Reading for the Plot in Sixteenth-Century England', *Representations*, 41 (1993): 83–103 (86).

testimony of a female cat, Mouse-slayer, who tells numerous stories of cat daring-do, most of which involve her exposing human stupidity and culpability. For example, at one stage Mouse-slayer tells the story of how she was once given walnut shell shoes and locked in an attic. The noise of her feet, however, made the superstitious country folk and their ignorant papist priests think the house was haunted and that Mouse-slayer was the Devil. Indeed, when the priests caught sight of her at the top of the ladder they were so scared that complete chaos ensured:

> But when the priest heard me come, and/by a glimpsing had seen me, down he fell upon them that were behind him, and with his chalice hurt one, with his water pot another, and his holy candle fell into another priest's breech (who, while the rest were hawsoning me, was conjuring our maid at the stair foot) and all to-besinged him...the old priest, which was so tumbled among them that his face lay upon a boy's bare arse .. which for fear had beshit himself, had all to-rayed his face, he neither felt not smelt it, nor removed from him.[38]

The failure of the protagonists in this story to properly see and interpret Mouse-slayer is an image of a collective failure of interpretation. Mouse-slayer's stories tell of a world of popular religion and folklore which she, and her human owners, constantly manipulate for their own ends. It is a world without any real moral or ethical code. To seek to interpret—or even worse moralize—Mouse-slayer's world in good humanist fashion would be at best pointless or at worst folly. Mouse-slayer lives and thrives in the world of print, of fiction, of prose; a world in which ultimately what matters is how persuasive one's story is, how clever one's lies are, how powerful one's fictions are.

Beware the Cat at one level echoes Geoffrey Chaucer's *Second Nun's Tale* in its provocative mixing of different genres in the context of a beast fable. But the Canterbury Tale it more directly evokes is *The Canon's Yeoman's Tale*. The central figure in this tale is a Canon who is at once, like Baldwin's cats, at the heart of the story and strangely dispersed or occluded. The Canon's Yeoman opens by telling his readers that

> Ther is a chanoun of religion
> Amonges us, wolde infecte al a toun,
> Though it was greet were as was Nynyvee,
> Rome, Alisaundre, Troye, and othere three.
> His sleights and his infinite falsenesse
> Ther koude no man writen, as I gesse,
> Though that he myghte lyve a thousand yeer.[39]

Given that the *Tale* is going to attempt to expose the Canon, this opening statement is a strangely pre-emptive statement of textual failure. The narrator knows in advance that his words cannot do full justice to the Canon's slights and falseness. The Canon embodies a fictionality that it is beyond Chaucer's fiction to express. Given this opening statement,

---

[38] Baldwin, *Beware the Cat*, 49.
[39] Geoffrey Chaucer, 'The Canon's Yeoman's Prologue and Tale', *The Riverside Chaucer* (Oxford: Oxford University Press, 1987), 270–81 (275).

it is perhaps not at all surprising to find that later in the tale the narrator seems to be in danger of being quite overcome by the Canon's slipperiness: 'It dulleth me whan that I of hym speke,/On his falsehede fayn wolde I me wreke,/If I wiste how, but he is heere and there;/He is so variaunt, he abit nowhere.'[40] The Canon's ability to be here, there, and nowhere is strangely feline and demonically protean. The Canon's Yeoman hates the Canon's falseness, his deceptions, tricks, and lies, and yet cannot draw his eyes away from the fantasy at their heart.

The Canon's Yeoman's Tale is a story about a failed transformation, about the performance, as opposed to the reality, of alchemical change. Matter in Chaucer's tale is not turned to gold. Or rather, the transformation that takes place in this *Tale* is not material so much as graphic. The Canon's Yeoman tells his tale to expose the tricks of his master and in the process transforms the base metal, the empty husks of alchemical discourse, into pleasurable, wondrous fiction: 'Yet forgat I to maken rehersaille/Of waters corosif, and of lymaille,/And of bodies mollificacioun/And also of hire induracioun/Oilles, ablucions, and metal fusible—'.[41] *The Canon's Yeoman's Tale* is poised between the protean quality of the Canon and the graphic specificity of the words of alchemy. The Yeoman's attempts to master the tension between the protean and the specific, literal and metaphorical, reflect the extent to which he represents the trials and pleasures of authorship. Lee Patterson comments that 'Although alchemical study was incapable of making gold, it could produce alchemists: and although it was unable to change the material world, mastering its elaborate theory could change the self-identity of the alchemist. What alchemy provided, in short, was a way to be an intellectual.'[42] *The Canon's Yeoman's Tale* is the story of the emergence of a particular kind of author—one poised between embracing the possibilities offered by texts and textuality, the play of significance, and nostalgia for a world (which of course never actually existed) in which words and meaning were one. Turning the Canon's tricks into a tale at once makes them public and reduces their power—they are made real and at the same moment rendered powerless. This is, of course, what the Canon's Yeoman wanted to achieve, but lurking at the edges of his tale is a desire for alchemy, for real transformation, for a world in which words and meaning are one. *Beware the Cat* is a work of alchemy. It mocks popular wisdom and knowledge, and at the same time expresses a desire to escape the endless textual stream of Streamer's text into an oral world of feline logic—it desires transformation, but ultimately knows that all it can create is alchemists, not gold.

The Third Part of Master Streamer's Oration opens with Streamer waking from a sleep induced by the disgusting potion that he had early brewed. At this point in the story the reader is expecting to hear cat's speak, or rather hear what they are saying, but instead Baldwin mocks us with more Streamer nonsense. The third Oration opens with a lengthy digression on the moon, stars, and sun.

---

[40] Chaucer, 'The Canon's Yeoman's Prologue and Tale', 278.
[41] Chaucer, 'The Canon's Yeoman's Prologue and Tale', 278.
[42] Lee Patterson, 'Perpetual Motion: Alchemy and the Technology of the Self', *Studies in the Age of Chaucer*, 15 (1993): 25–57 (54).

> For you shall understand—chiefly you, Master Willot, that are my lord's astronomer—that all our ancestors have failed in knowledge of natural causes; for it is not the moon that causeth the sea to ebb and flow, neither to neap and spring, but the neaping and springing of the sea is the cause of the moon's waxing and waning. For the moonlight is nothing save the shining of the sun cast into the element by opposition of the sea; as also the stars are nothing else but the sunlight reflected upon the face of rivers and cast upon the crystalline heaven, which because rivers alway keep like course, therefore are the stars alway of one bigness.[43]

Even by Streamer's standards this is nonsense. It is almost as though Baldwin is betting that the reader is now so committed to the story that they will not put the story down even when confronted with a passage like this. Finally, *Beware the Cat* reaches some actual cats and it transpires that what Streamer has been listening to at night is not simply cats talking, but is rather a formal court of cat law with Mouse-slayer defending herself against the charge of breaking cat law by refusing to have sex with a male cat, Catch-rat. Mouse-slayer's defence is to declare her entire like since her 'blind days' of her kitling in order to prove that despite her refusal of Catch-rat's advances she has always been a good cat—in other words, that she has been duplicitous, deceitful, lecherous, and exploitative of her human masters.

The third Oration is Baldwin's ultimately mockery of his readers since, having waited so long to hear a cat speak, the matter of Mouse-slayer's narrative is stories of stories of human stupidity and culpability. Streamer has consumed a disgusting potion and the reader has consumed Streamer's nonsensical words, and Baldwin's foolish text, just to hear an account of human folly. For example, Mouse-slayer tells the cat court about her time as a pet to an 'old bawd' who ran a boarding house frequented by young men. It was this bawd's policy to provide the young men with wenches and to soak them for all they had so that the young men were forced to resort to stealing to get by. Mouse-slayer is very complimentary about the old bawd telling the court that 'And notwithstanding that she used these wicked practices, yet was she very holy and religious. And therefore, although that all images were forbidden, yet kept she one of Our Lady in her coffer.'[44] Despite this, there was one occasion when the old bawd treated Mouse-slayer badly, which was when one of her young men fell in love with a rich merchant's wife. The old bawd befriended the wife and invited her to dinner. Before she arrived, however, the old bawd had fed Mouse-slayer a piece of pudding filled with mustard which made Mouse-slayer cry. When the two women were sitting down, Mouse-slayer came in and sat by the old bawd, prompting the merchant's wife to ask what ailed Mouse-slayer. The old bawd answered that God had punished her daughter, for either her daughter's honesty or cruelty, by turning her into the likeness of a cat, 'wherein she hath been above this two months, continually weeping as you see and lamenting her miserable wretchedness.'[45] Perhaps not surprisingly, the merchant's wife relents and agrees to take the old bawd's young man as a lover. This story is 'borrowed' wholesale by Baldwin, probably from

---

[43] Baldwin, *Beware the Cat*, 35.
[44] Baldwin, *Beware the Cat*, 40.
[45] Baldwin, *Beware the Cat*, 42.

William Caxton's *Fables of Aesop* (1483), where there is a lengthy version of it. The fact that part of Mouse-slayer's testimony is an old tale stolen from another work is parodic. Streamer does not notice the provenance of the story, but then neither does the cat court. The third Oration of *Beware the Cat* presents itself as a piece of sworn testimony, but like the rest of the work it is another patchwork text woven together and made to look whole by the linked transformative powers of print and Streamer's narrative voice.

Mouse-slayer ends her testimony by summing up her defence: 'Thus have I told you, my lords, all things that have been done and happened through me, wherein you perceive my loyalty and obedience to all good laws, and how shamelessly and falsely I am accused for a transgressor.'[46] Of course, this statement begs the question, what are 'good' laws? In the world of cats it is lawful, indeed required, to be greedy, lecherous, and disloyal to one's humans. A good cat is one who uses tricks and lies to get what they want. In Utopia the people are good because the founder, Utopus, has set down laws that mean it is almost impossible not to be virtuous. This, however, suggests that virtue in Utopia, the place, not the book, is largely meaningless. In the world of Mouse-slayer, and in the printed world of Tudor prose, to be virtuous is to lie and trick, to flatter and deceive. It is to use the ability of words to transform things, to make base metals gold and fictions true, simply to satisfy the reader's desire for bawdy tales and merry jests. The 'best' books are those, like *Beware the Cat*, that allow the reader to pretend, to convince themselves that they are reading to gain knowledge, to find out about faraway lands, potent medicines, and hidden secrets—when all that they are reading is folly, foolishness, and the ramblings of fools.

9.4 Conclusion

The Third Part of Streamer's Oration ends on a melancholic note. Streamer promises that he has many more mysteries, far more wondrous to tell, but in the meantime 'I will pray you to help to get me some money to convey me on my journey to Caithness, for I have been going thither these five years and never was able to perform my journey.'[47] One feels that Streamer will never make it to Caithness since he will not be able to keep to the main road or indeed to any recognized route. Instead, he will constantly be going off in different directions, down side alleys and dark lanes. There is, however, a sense that despite all of Streamer's failures as a narrator, the banality of much of Mouse-slayer's discourse, and the ridiculous claims that Streamer makes throughout the course of the text, the reader has been on a genuine journey which is now coming to an end. R. W. Maslen comments that, 'despite his association with hypocrisy, superstition, and manifest folly, Streamer is a vehicle for the truth—an Erasmian mock philosopher.'[48] *Beware*

---

[46] Baldwin, *Beware the Cat*, 51. [47] Baldwin, *Beware the Cat*, 46.

[48] Robert Maslen, 'William Baldwin and the Tudor Imagination', in Mike Pincombe and Cathy Shrank, eds., *The Oxford Handbook of Tudor Literature, 1485–1603* (Oxford: Oxford University Press, 2009), 291–306 (304).

the Cat is a work of alchemy. It turns its readers into consumers of fiction, forges them as intellectuals (if to be an intellectual is to possess Streamer's knowledge and skills), and makes literary critics look wise (since clearly only a fool would treat a work like *Beware the Cat* seriously)—*Beware the Cat* indeed.

Further Reading

Hadfield, Andrew. *Literature, Travel, and Colonial Writing in the English Renaissance, 1545–1625* (Oxford: Oxford University Press, 1998).

Hutson, Lorna. 'Fortunate Travellers: Reading for the Plot in Sixteenth-Century England', *Representations*, 41 (1993): 83–103.

Maslen, Robert W. *Elizabethan Fictions: Espionage, Counter-Espionage, and the Duplicity of Fiction in Early Elizabethan Prose Narratives* (Oxford: Clarendon Press, 1997).

—— 'William Baldwin and the Tudor Imagination', in Mike Pincombe and Cathy Shrank, eds., *The Oxford Handbook of Tudor Literature, 1485–1603* (Oxford: Oxford University Press, 2009), 291–306.

Shrank, Cathy. *Writing the Nation in Reformation England, 1530–1580* (Oxford: Oxford University Press, 2004).

Wear, Andrew. *Knowledge and Practice in English Medicine, 1550–1680* (Cambridge: Cambridge University Press, 2000).

CHAPTER 10

THE ADVENTURES PASSED BY MASTER GEORGE GASCOIGNE: EXPERIMENTS IN PROSE

GILLIAN AUSTEN

UNTIL quite recently, George Gascoigne was the most neglected of the earliest Elizabethan writers, despite being hugely influential in his own time. In the twentieth century, his most successful authorial persona, the Reformed Prodigal, had come to dominate discussion of his work, casting him principally as a moralist and making him extremely unfashionable. But in the last quarter of the sixteenth century, Gascoigne was known as a successful courtly poet and performer, and an important innovator in many literary forms. His most substantial prose works were translations and would have formed a relatively minor part of his literary reputation. Nonetheless, it is his prose work which informs Gascoigne's reputation today.

George Gascoigne's modern reputation rests principally upon four works: the prose fiction *A Discourse of the Adventures passed by Master F.J.*, one of the earliest important texts in the history of the novel in English; his prose play *Supposes*, a source for Shakespeare's *The Taming of the Shrew*; his frequently anthologized poem, 'Gascoignes wodmanship'; and 'Certayne Notes of Instruction concerning the making of verse or ryme in English', the earliest essay on English composition. Three of these works—prose fiction, prose comedy, and poem—belong to just one of his books, *A Hundreth Sundrie Flowres* (1572/3), and the fourth, the essay, was added in its revised edition, *The Posies* (1575).[1] But Gascoigne experimented in many genres, with both medieval, native English forms and avant-garde continental forms. He influenced almost every writer who

---

[1] The authoritative edition is by G. W. Pigman III, *George Gascoigne:, A Hundreth Sundrie Flowres* (Oxford: Oxford University Press, 2000), which incorporates the *Posies*. All subsequent references and quotations from either work are to this volume.

followed him: his medievalizing influenced Spenser, and *Master F.J.* was a source for Sidney's *Arcadia*. He wrote a news pamphlet (*The Spoyle of Antwerpe*), a medieval dream vision (*Complaynte of Phylomene*), and even the earliest English blank verse (*The Steele Glas*), a highly self-conscious pitch at literary fame. Gascoigne also had a crucial role in hybridizing the sonnet: the Italianate form originally imported by Wyatt and developed by Surrey was further developed by Gascoigne before Sidney, Spenser, Shakespeare, and ultimately every other writer of note took it up in the 1590s.[2]

The present essay seeks to consider Gascoigne as a prose writer. Of the four works that usually define his current reputation, three have significant prose elements: *Master F.J.* is partly prose and partly verse; *Supposes* is a prose comedy; and 'Certayne Notes of Instruction' is a prose essay on the art of versification, cast as a letter, one of several fictive letters in Gascoigne's oeuvre. But the sheer range of Gascoigne's prose work—fiction, drama, essays, letters, reportage, moral tracts, and translations from Latin, French, and Italian—is remarkable.

In this period, prose was often as tightly controlled and full of rhetorical devices as any verse form. Gascoigne does not discuss the uses of prose per se in 'Certayne Notes', where one might expect it, nor indeed elsewhere. He only uses the word 'prose' three times in all of *A Hundreth* and, where he does, he is not necessarily making the expected distinction between verse and prose: for example, he twice refers to *A Hundreth* as prose, whereas it is a mixture of prose and verse.[3] Gascoigne contrasts verse and prose only once, in a short poem, '*Gascoignes* Epitaph uppon capitaine Bourcher', where he asks 'Can no man penne in metre nor in prose,/The life, the death, the valiant acts, the fame.../Of such a feere as you in fighte have lost?' (p. 300). On occasion, Gascoigne's choice of prose in itself allowed innovation: for example, he translated Ariosto's *I Suppositi* (using both the prose and verse versions) into the prose *Supposes*. As Lois Potter notes, this allowed him to introduce an improvisational element which belonged at the time to Italian acting, rather than to writing: 'His use of prose enabled him to insert the symbol "&c" at a few points, meaning that the actors were free to improvise, in the Italian manner, if they wished.'[4] The flexibility this introduced was, arguably, a step towards the more natural cadences later captured in iambic pentameter on the English public stage. Given his fearless and often audacious experimentation across all generic boundaries, it seems fair to conclude that Gascoigne would use whatever style or formal element would best suit his poetic invention.

Gascoigne's prose fiction, *A Discourse of the Adventures passed by Master F.J.*, is a hugely significant text and characteristically innovative: only William Baldwin's *Beware the Cat* (1570) pre-dates it as a work of original prose fiction in English. Gascoigne's editor, G. W. Pigman, identifies *Master F.J.* as a 'prosimetrum' (mixing verse and prose), comparing it with Boethius's *De consolatione philosophiae*, Dante's *La vita nuova*, and

---

[2] Gascoigne wrote one of the earliest English sonnet sequences and perhaps the second corona of sonnets (both in the 'Memories', 1565, Pigman, *George Gascoigne: A Hundreth Sundrie Flowres*, 274–83).

[3] Pigman, *George Gascoigne: A Hundreth Sundrie Flowres*, 4, 215.

[4] Norman Sanders et al., *The Revels History of Drama in English* (London: Methuen, 1980), ii. 228.

Sannazaro's *Arcadia*.⁵ Nonetheless, *Master F.J.* is widely recognized as highly innovative and it has inspired the best Gascoigne criticism of recent years. It was published in two versions within two years and its role in each of the collections of work in which it appears adds to the complexity of its status: different sets of prefatory letters in each volume construct two distinct fictions of publication for the work in which this early English prose fiction is published.⁶

Master F.J. was first printed in Gascoigne's anonymous anthology *A Hundreth Sundrie Flowres* (1573), his first publication. Gascoigne had been writing poetry since the early 1560s and cultivated a reputation as a writer and translator at least since his return to Gray's Inn in 1565. But his move into print in 1572/3 was undoubtedly prompted by his persistent financial difficulties and the need to display his many skills in the hope of gaining a new patron. Having deposited much of the material for his book with the printer, Henry Bynneman, Gascoigne left England for a second tour as a mercenary in the Netherlands, serving on this occasion under Sir Humphrey Gilbert.⁷ Gascoigne's absence from London for much of the printing process is very important. Bynneman shared the printing of *A Hundreth* with another printer, Henry Middleton. Adrian Weiss argues that confusion caused by the division of the job between the two printers meant that the volume did not appear in the form Gascoigne intended, with the two plays placed after the letter from the printer and before the prose fiction.⁸ Significantly, Gascoigne was to become a diligent reader of printer's proofs, making him the earliest English author known to check proofs daily.⁹

The disordering of the prefatory matter in the printing of *A Hundreth* is significant in understanding *Master F.J.*, one of its principal items, and helps to explain why the volume was reissued with largely cosmetic revisions just two years later. The three prefatory letters should have been printed together immediately in front of *Master F.J.*, at the front of the volume, and so forming a preface for the entire volume. These letters are ostensibly from the Printer (A.B.), the publisher (H.W.), and the editor/narrator, G.T., supposed friend of F.J. and the rest of the 'sundrie gentlemen'.¹⁰ Arranged in this way, the prefatory material would have introduced a fictive circle of anonymous writers to whom the

---

⁵ Pigman, *George Gascoigne: A Hundreth Sundrie Flowres*, 449–50, note 141.1–2.

⁶ See Gillian Austen, *George Gascoigne*, Studies in Renaissance Literature, 24 (Woodbridge: D. S. Brewer, 2008), 68–74, 84–93, which discusses all of Gascoigne's work and career.

⁷ His first excursion is recorded in 'Gascoignes Voyage into Hollande, *An*. 1575', Pigman, *George Gascoigne: A Hundreth Sundrie Flowres*, 319–28.

⁸ Adrian Weiss, 'Shared Printing, Printer's Copy, and the Text(s) of Gascoigne's *A Hundreth Sundrie Flowres*', *Studies in Bibliography*, 45 (1992): 71–104.

⁹ See *Droomme of doomesday*, pp. 215, 453, in J. W. Cunliffe, ed., *The Complete Works of George Gascoigne*, 2 vols. (Cambridge: Cambridge University Press, 1907, 1910; repr. New York: Greenwood Press, 1969), vol. II. Cunliffe's first volume, *The Posies*, was superseded by Pigman's authoritative edition with commentary in 2000; but his second volume remains the best edition for Gascoigne's other works, apart from the *Steele Glas/Complaynte of Phylomene*, of which there is an annotated edition by William Wallace (see Further Reading); and the *Noble Arte of Venerie*, of which there is no modern edition except the one published as *Turberville's Book of Hunting* (Oxford: Clarendon Press, 1908).

¹⁰ There is a modern spelling edition in Paul Salzman, *An Anthology of Elizabethan Prose Fiction*, World's Classics (Oxford: Oxford University Press, 1987), excluding the letter from the printer, which can be found in the Pigman edition, 3–4.

loosely defined 'Discourse' of *Master F.J.* and the subsequent miscellany of poems, 'The Devises of Sundrie Gentlemen', were attributed. The 'Devises' would then lead into the section attributed to one 'George Gascoigne', the only named author in the volume. It is little surprise that without the supervision of its author the plan failed, for this would have been a superbly witty volume, with a highly sophisticated, self-referential structure, the like of which had never been attempted before.

This sequence of letters, poems, and prose fiction posits a fictive literary circle outside the text, with which its main fictional character, F.J., is associated. The narrator, G.T., who is supposedly F.J.'s friend and confidant, claims to have been given a collection of poems in manuscript, the writings of F.J. and his friends, including 'George Gascoigne'. G.T. has taken it upon himself not only to assume the role of narrator and editor, but then to pass the manuscript to one H.W., an established publisher, to have it printed. Susan C. Staub notes that in *Master F.J.*, G.T. refers to his source, F.J., 'no less than seventy times', a technique which insists on the 'reality' outside the text and is sustained through the volume.[11] This extended fiction of reluctant publication was to become an over-familiar trope for ambitious new authors, but when Gascoigne used it in this witty and structural way it was still thoroughly innovative. It is no surprise that *Master F.J.* was misread as autobiographical: the mixture of reality (Gascoigne as an aspiring author) and fiction (F.J., G.T., and the literary circle, the fictive publisher et al.) was just too sophisticated, especially given the additional confusion caused by the printers' disruption of the sequence.

Three years later, Gascoigne created a similar fiction about the publication of another work, in a prose prefatory epistle for Sir Humphrey Gilbert's *Discourse of a Discoverie for a new passage to Cataia* (March 1576). Gascoigne claims that he had visited Gilbert, his former colonel, at his home in Limehouse that winter, and says he was shown some of Gilbert's writing, including the *Discourse* in manuscript:

> The which...I craved at the saide *S. Humphreys* handes for two or three dayes to read and to peruse. And hee very friendly granted my request, but still seming to doubt that therby the same might, contrarie to his former intention, be Imprinted.
>
> And to be plaine, when I had at good leasure perused it, & therwithall conferred his allegations by the Tables of *Ortelius*, and by sundrie other *Cosmologicall Mappes* and *Charts*, I seemed in my simple judgement not onely to like it singularly, but also thought it very meete (as the present occasion serveth) to give it out in publicke. Wherupon I have (as you see) caused my friends great travaile, and mine owne greater presumption to be registred in print. (Cunliffe, II, p. 564)

Gilbert's *Discourse* was cast as a letter to his brother, but it was in fact a proposal for investors in a mercantile expedition to find the fabled north-west passage to China (Cataia). It was published to promote Martin Frobisher's first expedition in search of the north-west passage in June 1576.[12] This expedition was backed financially by a number of

---

[11] Susan C. Staub, '"According to My Source": Fictionality in *The Adventures of Master F.J.*', *Studies in Philology*, 87 (1990): 101–35.

[12] Cunliffe, *Complete Works*, II, pp. 561–7. See also James McDermott, *Martin Frobisher: Elizabethan Privateer* (New Haven and London: Yale University Press, 2001), 129.

leading courtiers, notably the Earl of Leicester, and it is this connection which explains Gascoigne's involvement in that particular fiction of publication.

Of the two versions of *Master F.J.* the first is generally considered superior. It is a loosely structured story told in letters and poetry, held together by the prose commentary of G.T., a highly opinionated narrator who mediates the reader's understanding and acceptance of the events he is reporting. A young man, F.J., visits a country house in 'the north partes of this Realme' and becomes involved with Elinor, the wife of his host. Elinor already has a lover, her Secretary, who sets up the affair by answering F.J.'s first love letter on her behalf. Shortly after the first letters are exchanged, the Secretary leaves on an extended journey and, during his absence, the young F.J. becomes Elinor's lover, consummating the affair one night in the Gallery of the house. Their relationship has an observer, a jealous unmarried woman called Fraunces, and in the background are Elinor's husband and a number of unnamed courtiers. The inexperienced F.J. celebrates the affair with a sonnet celebrating his success at cuckolding Elinor's husband, but this is an ironic turning point: the Secretary soon returns and F.J. becomes ill through his jealousy (an inset narrative translated from Ariosto). There is a slightly scurrilous literary game led by an older female courtier, Dame Pergo, in which the courtiers exchange stories. When Elinor visits F.J. privately in his room he tells her about his jealousy and suspicion. Elinor reacts angrily and the intimate moment turns quickly into a rape. Following this, Elinor unsurprisingly rejects F.J. and resumes her relationship with the Secretary. The remaining plot revolves around F.J.'s doomed attempts to regain Elinor's favour and Fraunces's rather cruel delight in observing them. The story ends rather inconclusively, when G.T. comments that 'It is time now to make an end of this thriftlesse Historie, wherein although I could wade much further... Yet I will cease, as one that had rather leave it unperfect than make it to plaine' (p. 215).

The lack of distinct boundaries between the fictive framework and the fiction is one of the most effective means by which Gascoigne blends fiction and reality. In his prefatory letter G.T. introduces the fictive literary circle by saying that he obtained 'sundry copies' from F.J. and 'sundry other toward young gentlemen' and that he has 'set in the first places those which Master F.J. did compyle'. At the end of *Master F.J.*, G.T. continues:

> Now henceforwardes I will trouble you no more with such a barbarous style in prose, but will onely recite unto you sundry verses written by sundry gentlemen, adding nothing of myne owne, but onely a tytle to every Poeme, wherby the cause of writing the same maye the more evidently appeare: Neyther can I declare unto you who wrote the greatest part of them, for they are unto me but a posie presented out of sundry gardens, neither have I any other names of the flowers, but such short notes as the aucthors themselves have delivered therby if you can gesse them, it shall no waye offend mee. I will begin with this translation as followeth.' (p. 216)

In this way, the narrative of *Master F.J.* is linked to the next section, 'The Devises of Sundrie Gentlemen', in which G.T. continues to provide the (much briefer) prose links between the poems. One of the most interesting aspects of this first version is the way it is recessed into the controlling fiction by which the present manuscript—all of *A*

Hundreth—has been published by G.T. without the permission of its supposed several authors, the 'sundrie gentlemen'. In this way G.T. sustains the controlling fiction of multiple authorship and characteristically seeks to provoke the reader's curiosity about the identity of the supposed authors of the 'Devises'.[13] His assurance that 'if you can gesse them, it shall no waye offend mee' encourages the reader to 'gesse' and confirms that the game of identifying the author(s)—begun in the prefatory letters—is an important subtextual device in the underlying scheme of *A Hundreth*.

The use of such controlling structures was widespread in Italianate experimental prose fictions: one could cite the storytelling games which unite Chaucer's group of pilgrims, or Boccaccio's and Marguerite de Navarre's parties of nobles. In the same spirit, Gascoigne peoples *A Hundreth* with plausible figures from the nascent world of literary publishing—H.W. as the publisher, G.T. as an aspiring editor and narrator, and F.J. and his circle of friends ('sundrie gentlemen', as well as 'George Gascoigne') as the group of young writers whose work he publishes without their consent. This extended fiction was so successful, and so original, that *Master F.J.* seems to have been read as though it were actually factual and autobiographical. Gascoigne himself mocks (and denies) such credulous readings in the revised edition, whilst conspicuously failing to quash speculation—and even, to some extent, provoking more (the most likely authorial representation is Bartello, a fictional Italian author to whom the tale is ascribed in the revised edition, as we shall see). Later generations, too, have devised a remarkable range of possible biographical readings.[14] The entire 'Discourse' is so dense with literary devices and figures, both familiar and entirely new in 1572/3, that it could almost be an exercise in literary inventiveness. It takes its gossipy narrator and framing fiction (the literary circle) from the Italianate *novelle*; its inset prose narratives are from romance, while the story of F.J.'s Suspicion is a translation of Ariosto's tale of *Sospetto*; and Pergo's exchange of stories is taken from courtly love, as is much of the situation of F.J. and Elinor's affair. But it is easy to see why, when Gascoigne blurs the boundaries between fiction and reality so thoroughly, so many critics have suspected that the tale had some basis in real events.

When Gascoigne returned to England in 1574/5, it seems that he was embarrassed by the state of his first published book and perhaps by some of the conjectures which surrounded it. The entire volume, including a revised version of *Master F.J.*, was published in a revised and extended edition under Gascoigne's own name as his *Posies* (1575). It is in this volume that Gascoigne first fully developed the persona of the 'Reformed Prodigal', although he had used it much earlier, during his days at Gray's Inn.[15] Nonetheless, it is in the *Posies* that Gascoigne first adopted a unified authorial persona, complementing it with what would become his invariable motto in works which bore his name: '*Tam Marti, quam Mercurio*' ['As much for Mars as for Mercury'], which identified him as a soldier-poet, like Turberville, Churchyard, Googe, and Riche.

---

[13] Pigman, *George Gascoigne: A Hundreth Sundrie Flowres*, 566, note 216.10–14.
[14] The range of biographical readings is detailed in Austen, *George Gascoigne*, 74–6.
[15] Gascoigne used the Reformed Prodigal persona as early as 1562 in 'Gascoignes *de Profundis*' (Pigman, *George Gascoigne: A Hundreth Sundrie Flowres*, 290–3).

Essentially the same material is rearranged into '*Floures to comfort, hearbes to cure, and weedes to be avoyded*', but Gascoigne also added substantial new prefatory material. The controlling fiction of the literary circle is abandoned and the whole collection is acknowledged as Gascoigne's. His new prefatory letters group his readers into 'reverend Divines', 'al yong Gentlemen', and 'the readers generally', but these divisions allow him to enact different aspects of his 'Reformed Prodigal' persona and it is unlikely that he expected his readers literally to select and read only the preface which applied to them. Together, these letters defend his publication of *A Hundreth* and set up an alternative extended fiction of publication by which an apparent scandal caused by the contents of *Master F.J.* directly gave rise to the reissue of the volume as the *Posies*:

> I understand that sundrie well disposed mindes have taken offence at certaine wanton wordes and sentences passed in the fable of *Ferdinando Jeronimi*, and the Ladie *Elinora de Valasco*, the which in the first edition was termed The adventures of master F.J. And that also therwith some busie conjectures have presumed to thinke that the same was indeed written to the scandalizing of some worthie personages, whom they woulde seeme therby to know. (pp. 362-3)

If some readers had indeed raised suspicions that *Master F.J.* was based on real events—and we have only Gascoigne's own assertion that this was the case—then it is characteristic that even in this revised edition he seems to provoke speculation at the same time as apparently trying to quash it. For there are other texts in the *Posies* which seem designed to provoke speculation about its relation to reality, including the completed version of 'Dan Bartholmew of Bathe' and the new sequence of poems on the Greene Knight, 'The Fruite of Fetters', which are encoded autobiography and are connected in turn to '*Dulce bellum inexpertis*', which is overtly autobiographical.[16] Clearly, a subtext is being constructed by which the alert reader is led to identify all these personae with Gascoigne himself. But as Bartholmew is the name of one of his personae, then he is most plausibly represented by Bartello, 'he which writeth riding tales': both in the bawdy tales such as *Master F.J.* and the riding tales such as '*Gascoignes* Memories', which he composed while 'riding by the way' (p. 282). And if Gascoigne is indeed Bartello, that does signal both versions of his tale as original prose fiction.

The loss of the Stationers' Register for 1570-5 is a significant disadvantage, as this would have provided the most reliable external evidence of any censorship of, or official action against, the text. In fact, fifty copies of the revised edition, the *Posies*, were seized by Her Majesty's Commissioners on 13 August 1576, when the bookseller Richard Smith returned 'half a hundred of Gascoignes poesies' to the Stationers' Hall.[17] There has been much speculation about the exact level of censorship for these kinds of publication in the period, but if *Master F.J.* had indeed caused some comment, it may (to use Cyndia Clegg's admirable phrase) have been *censured* rather than censored. Certainly, Her Majesty's Commissioners' action against the *Posies* did not impact upon Gascoigne's

---

[16] See Austen, *George Gascoigne*, 93-101.

[17] W. W. Greg and E. Boswell, eds., *Records of the Court of the Stationers' Company, 1576-1602, from Register B* (London: Biographical Society, 1930), 86-7.

other activities, as he published the *Delicate Diet* just three days before the seizure, and just two weeks later he was sent by Lord Burghley secretly to Paris. As Clegg concludes, 'what was censurable in 1573 was revised and became acceptable in 1575, and what was acceptable in 1575 became censorable in 1576... the text changed minimally, but Gascoigne's status and the climate of reception changed substantially'.[18] This remains the most persuasive explanation, highlighting the contingent and pragmatic attitude to authorial control operated by Her Majesty's Commissioners.

The key objection to the notion of a real scandal, apart from the complete lack of any corroborative evidence, is the limited revision which took place, for *Master F.J.* is largely unchanged: if any 'worthy personages' had indeed been scandalized then Gascoigne would not have been suffered to reissue the tale. Of the revisions which were imposed, some changes, most notably losing the gossipy, biased narrator G.T., serve actually to make the story less sympathetic. The tale is relocated to Italy and firmer formal boundaries are imposed, so that it becomes a 'fable' rather than a 'discourse' of 'adventures': this is 'The pleasant Fable of Ferdinando Jeronomi and Leonora de Valasco'. But of course, Italy was by reputation the very home of dissolute living and passionate affairs, so although the change does situate the narrative more firmly in the continental prose tradition, and specifically the Italian *novelle*, this is at best a morally ambivalent relocation. The relationships between characters are more defined than in *Master F.J.*, so that Leonora (Elinor) is married to the 'heyre of Valasco' and Frauncischina (Fraunces) is 'the elder daughter of the lord of Valasco', making the two women sisters-in-law. Gascoigne seems to resist even this nominal relocation by quickly reverting to his characters' original English names. The lord of Valasco has invited Ferdinando (F.J.) to his castle with the particular intention of engineering a match with Frauncischina. Both these changes make Ferdinando's offence against his host a more obvious abuse of his hospitality. The cuckolding sonnet is cut and the rape scene is abbreviated, but little else has been done to ameliorate the moral shortcomings of the tale. Most obviously, Gascoigne's conclusion is hardly typical of a 'fable':

> [Ferdinando] tooke his leave, and (withoute pretence of returne) departed to his house in *Venice*: spending there the rest of his dayes in a dissolute kind of lyfe: and abandoning the worthy lady *Frauncischina*, who (dayly being gauled with the griefe of his great ingratitude) dyd shortlye bring hir selfe into a miserable consumption: whereof (after three yeares languishing) shee dyed: Notwithstanding al which occurrentes the Lady *Elinor* lived long in the continuance of hir acustomed change... (p. 216)

The injustice of this conclusion subverts the overtly moralistic purpose of the fable as a genre: the foolish and dissolute Ferdinando learns nothing and pursues a 'dissolute kind of lyfe'; the apparently virtuous woman Frauncischina falls ill and dies; and the unreformed, promiscuous Leonora continues to enjoy her succession of lovers.

---

[18] Cyndia Clegg, *Press Censorship in Elizabethan England* (Cambridge: Cambridge University Press, 1997), 122.

The ways in which Gascoigne mixed genres and styles and played on and with generic expectations in both *Master F.J.* and the *Fable* influenced many of the important writers of the 1580s, 1590s, and beyond. Robert Maslen and others have argued that *Master F.J.* became a model for Sidney's *Old Arcadia*.[19] Katharine Wilson has explored its influence on Thomas Nashe, Robert Greene, George Whetstone, and John Grange.[20] It also influenced George Pettie and Barnabe Riche, as well as Thomas Deloney, John Lodge, and John Lyly. Nonetheless, Gascoigne's *Master F.J.* would not have formed the most important part of his literary reputation to his contemporaries, and did not do so until the twentieth century, when the dominance of the novel in literary culture threw it into prominence and it became the work upon which his place in modern literary history principally rests.

In 1575, the most significant addition to *The Posies* was 'Certayne Notes of Instruction', an essay which seeks to describe the principles of composition in English. Just as *Master F.J.* influenced Sidney's *Arcadia*, so 'Certayne Notes' influenced Sidney's *Defence of Poesie* (wr. 1579–80) and the subsequent Elizabethan attempts to lay down rules for English composition, both descriptive and legislative. Even James IV of Scotland (the later James I of England) is thought to have been influenced by Gascoigne's essay.[21] Indeed, 'Certayne Notes' is widely recognized as the first critical essay in English. Its rhetorical structure and possible sources have been well studied and its significance was recognized very quickly. As well as Sidney, writers such as Webbe and Puttenham, sensing the flowering of English letters with the enrichment of the language and the increasing number and facility of literary forms, took up the idea of attempting to write down the rules or instructions for English versification. For example, William Webbe acknowledges and quotes from 'thys course of learning to versify in Ryme' (I. 275), in his highly influential *Discourse of English Poetry* (1586).[22]

'Certayne Notes' is cast as a letter to another fictive Italian, Signor Eduardo Donati, and because the essay is cast as a letter it again requires a degree of characterization in the author: '*Signor Edouardo*, since promise is debt, and you (by the lawe of friendship) do burden me with a promise that I shoulde lende you instructions towards the making of English verse or ryme, I will assaye to discharge the same, though not so perfectly as I would, yet as readily as I may...' (p. 454).

Jayne Archer finds support for the general view that Edouardo Donati was a fictive name in the probable allusion to Ælius Donatus, the Roman grammarian and author of the *Ars grammatica*, which would have been extremely familiar to Elizabethan schoolboys.[23]

---

[19] Robert W. Maslen, 'Sidney, Gascoigne, and the "Bastard Poets"', in Constance C. Relihan and Goran V. Stanivukovic, eds., *Prose Fiction and Modern Sexualities in England, 1570–1640* (Basingstoke and New York: Palgrave Macmillan, 2003), 215–34.

[20] Katharine Wilson, *Fictions of Authorship in Late Elizabethan Narratives* (Oxford: Oxford University Press, 2006), 1–51 and *passim*.

[21] Pigman, *George Gascoigne: A Hundreth Sundrie Flowres*, note 454.1, 731.

[22] Austen, *George Gascoigne*, 11–14.

[23] Jayne Archer, '"A notable kinde of rime": The "fine invention" of Gascoigne's *Certayne Notes of Instruction* (1575)', in Gillian Austen, ed., *New Essays on George Gascoigne* (New York: AMS Press, forthcoming).

Gascoigne is even more witty and playful than Sidney, using irony and humour liberally, and quickly subverting the rules he does articulate. For example, he proposes self-contradictory rules such as 'eschew straunge words, or *obsoleta et inusitata*' (p. 458). Even in his fictive framework, Gascoigne subverts the whole notion of laying down 'notes of instruction' with his observation that '*Quot homines, quot Sententiae* [so many men, so many minds], especially in Poetrie' (p. 454). This is not to say that Gascoigne's essay is not serious, or that it does not have a serious purpose. Its very existence indicates Gascoigne's literary ambition: it is a significant step towards elevating English letters to the status of true literature, the classical writers in Latin and Greek. This is the context within which his anti-inkhorn sentiment should be seen. Gascoigne was a very competent Latinist, but he is, typically, slightly ahead of his generation in recognizing the potential for English to become itself a literary language. He was himself a liberal coiner of words, derived from both Latin and native, Anglo-Saxon vocabulary. The *Oxford English Dictionary* lists 173 of Gascoigne's neologisms ('corn-fed', 'indecorum', 'gardening'), as well as 544 existing words which he used in new ways, creating new meanings.[24]

The single most revealing point Gascoigne makes in the 'Certayne Notes' is his very first assertion about the foundation of poetic creativity: 'The first and moste necessarie poynte that ever I founde meete to be considered in making of a delectable poeme is this, to grounde it upon some fine invention' (p. 454). This invention needs to be founded upon what he calls '*aliquid salis*' ['some wit']: 'By this *aliquid salis* I meane some good and fine devise... what Theame so ever you do take in hand, if you do handle it but *tanquem in oratione perpetua*, and never study for some depth of devise in the Invention, and some figures also in the handlyng thereof: it will appear to the skilfull Reader but a tale of a tubbe' (p. 455). Although *inventio* is traditionally the first of the five points of formal rhetoric, Gascoigne's idea of invention extends across the entire content and presentation of his works.[25] It is possible to understand almost all of Gascoigne's work in light of this emphasis on poetic invention: his compulsive experimentation, his range of literary activities and styles, and above all perhaps his attitude to authorship, for Gascoigne habitually developed an authorial persona appropriate to each work, under which he presented it to his readers or audience. Thus in 'Certayne Notes', he adopts the persona of a courtly gentleman, friend of the Italian gentleman with the punning surname, Edouardo Donati; whereas in the *Posies* as a whole, he presents the volume under the persona of the Reformed Prodigal, an ostensibly moralistic persona.

This 'depth of devise', then, extends to the prefatory and in some cases illustrative material which accompanies the literary work, and it may be that the relative neglect in criticism of such apparatus contributed to the more general misreading of Gascoigne's work in the twentieth century. Prefaces and dedications were seen as 'non-literary' and therefore entirely separate, even optional, parts of a work; and yet, in an age of patronage, the circumstances of literary production, and how those circumstances are presented, must

---

[24] The online *OED* is searchable under Gascoigne for examples of his neologizing.
[25] For a contrasting view, see Pigman, *George Gascoigne: A Hundreth Sundrie Flowres*, note 454.13–15, 732.

be significant to the work itself. For if the letters in the *Posies* are read as being literally addressed to the 'Reverence Divines', or 'al yong Gentlemen', rather than as performances of selected aspects of the authorial persona, the Reformed Prodigal, then the entire volume makes less sense: this is not the thoroughly expurgated and moralized edition of *A Hundreth* that it claims to be. Or if the self-portrait in the frontispiece of the *Steele Glas/ Complaynte of Phylomene* (Fig. 10.1) is not recognized as being a self-portrait, it cannot be seen to form a part of the overarching invention of the theme of reflectiveness in that volume: both mirror as metaphor, as figurative tool for estates satire and self-examination, and as the practical means to create a self-portrait.[26] That theme encompasses the *Complaynte of Phylomene*, too, recast as a dream vision, another medieval form for self-examination. Without recognizing the theme of reflectiveness as a witty unifying concept for the volume, it becomes less comprehensible, less accessible, and its achievement is diminished. Gascoigne's 'Certayne Notes', then, articulates the core creative principle of much of his work. In the same way, it is possible to see the extended fiction of the publication of *A Hundreth* as the 'fine Invention' upon which the volume was based.

Shortly after he published the *Posies*, Gascoigne came to the Earl of Leicester's attention when his translation of the *Noble Arte of Venerie* was published. He participated in Leicester's entertainments at Kenilworth Castle and again later on that summer's Progress at Woodstock. Gascoigne rose rapidly in both royal and courtly favour, especially within Leicester's circle of patronage. He was then invited to join in the presentation of gifts to the Queen at New Year 1576, producing the manuscript of *Hemetes the Heremyte*, which he had performed at Woodstock, with its famous frontispiece illustration showing him kneeling before Elizabeth. The prose tale of *Hemetes* is not Gascoigne's: it was most probably written by the host at Woodstock, Sir Henry Lee, as it carries with it several concealed agendas which would benefit Lee and his coterie.[27] What Gascoigne adds to Lee's tale is the prefatory and illustrative material and the three translations, into Latin, French, and Italian. The prose preface reveals Gascoigne's own agenda. He is aiming for courtly preferment and demonstrating his fitness to serve the Queen in whatever capacity she sees fit: 'Yo^r ma^{tie} shall ever finde me wth a penne in my righte hand, and a sharpe sword girt to my left syde...willing to attend yor person in any calling that you shall pleas to appoynt me' (p. 477). Gascoigne's translations demonstrate practical language skills and his facility with French, in particular, would be taken up later in the year by Lord Burghley, who sent him to Paris and on to Antwerp. On his return, he again demonstrated his credentials as a soldier-poet by writing and publishing another important prose work, the official public account of what happened when the Spanish soldiers occupying Antwerp mutinied and ran amok.

Gascoigne's *The Spoyle of Antwerpe* is one of the earliest examples in English of reportage, since the events which it records happened only three weeks before it was printed in

---

[26] See Gillian Austen, 'George Gascoigne and the Transformations of Phylomene', in Sabine Coelsch-Foisner, ed., *Elizabethan Literature and Transformation*, Studies in English and Comparative Literature, 15 (Tübingen: Stauffenberg-Verlag, 1999), 107–19 (108, 115).

[27] See the anonymous edition published by Cadman in 1585, 93.

FIGURE 10.1 George Gascoigne, self-portrait, *The Steele Glas and the Complaynte of Phylomene* (1576), frontispiece

London (including the nine days it took to travel back from Antwerp).[28] The *Spoyle* is far from an impartial account, even though at times Gascoigne is as critical of the complacency of the Dutch as he is of the cruelty of the Spanish. It was, however, an officially sanctioned version of events, published anonymously but 'seene and allowed' and probably issued for its propaganda value. Eleanor Rosenberg, in her study of Leicester's patronage, concludes that Gascoigne's account 'accurately reflects the ambivalence of Elizabeth herself and most of her Privy Council' towards events in the Netherlands, but that it is predominantly anti-Spanish and so 'served their purpose well enough'.[29]

The *Spoyle*, despite Gascoigne's claims that it is a 'true report' (p. 590), reveals a considerable amount of rhetorical structuring and formal organization. It is typical of a 'book of news' in being both factual and exemplary,[30] but its generic register is mixed: Gascoigne incorporates a humorous prose narrative describing his trip on foot through the midst of the fighting, from the English House where he and the English merchants had taken refuge, towards the castle, where the most intense fighting was. He clearly signals this as a change from 'credible report' to eyewitness account: '... let me also say a litle of that which I sawe executed' (p. 594). But what follows is the most obviously structured section of the whole pamphlet: it opens with a set piece dinner at the English House at the height of the battle, during which a report is brought in of a 'hote scarmouche' in progress at the Castle. Gascoigne went up to a high point in the house, from where he could see fires had broken out 'in fower or five places of the towne, towardes the castleyeard', so he took his cloak and sword and ventured outside to see 'the certainty thereof' (p. 594). As he got closer to the Castle, passing over the Bourse, Gascoigne says he saw a 'great trowpe' coming towards him (pp. 594–5) and his description of his excursion quickly degenerates into slapstick as the crowds

> bare me over backwardes, and ran over my belly and my face, long time before I could recover on foote. At last when I was up, I looked on every syde, and seeing them ronne so fast, began thus to bethinke me. What in Gods name doe I heare which have no interest in this action? synce they who came to defend this towne are content to leave it at large, and shift for themselves: And whilest I stoode thus musing, another flock of flyers came so fast that they bare me on my nose, and ran as many over my backe, as erst had marched over my guttes. In fine, I got up like a tall fellow, and wente with them for company: but their haste was such, as I could never overtake the[m] ... (p. 595)

The absolute symmetry of being knocked over first onto his back and then onto his front shows a considerable amount of formal shaping. Gascoigne's physical courage is not, however, in doubt: he actively defended the Governor of the English merchants, Sir Thomas Heton, when the English House was attacked.[31] He turned his experience into

---

[28] See Austen, *George Gascoigne*, 182.
[29] Eleanor Rosenberg, *Leicester, Patron of Letters* (New York: Columbia University Press, 1955), 171–2.
[30] Sandra Clark, *The English Pamphleteers* (Rutherford, NJ: Fairleigh Dickinson University Press, 1983), 89–95.
[31] Heton corroborates Gascoigne's heroism in his report to Lord Burghley, PRO *SP For.*, 70/140, fol. 191, cited in Cunliffe, *Complete Works*, II, p. vi.

this comic episode, another instance where Gascoigne creates an unexpected shift of register in his prose.

The sheer range of Gascoigne's prose work is extraordinary. His longest prose works, however, are all translations. He translated his Gray's Inn play *Supposes* (and the verse *Jocasta*) from Italian in 1566, but he was also fully fluent in Latin and French and published prose translations from all three languages. But it is often his presentation—the prefatory material, the illustrations, or the added poems with which he frames the prose element— which enrich his source most. His anonymous *Noble Arte of Venerie or Hunting* (June 1575) is a translation from the French of a very up-to-date manual of hunting, Jacques du Fouilloux's *La Venerie*.[32] Gascoigne added three original illustrations showing Elizabeth hunting; and poems expressing the point of view of the hunted animal. The *Noble Arte* was produced as one of a pair of volumes by the bookseller Christopher Barker, alongside George Turberville's *Booke of Hauking*, specifically targeted at a courtly readership.[33]

By contrast, Gascoigne's *Droomme of Doomesday* (May 1576), is a very long, dry collection of prose translations of three moralistic Latin tracts for the Earl of Bedford, done primarily to support his Reformed Prodigal persona and to counter his reputation as a profligate. Gascoigne offers Bedford, a well known and devoutly religious literary patron, a conciliatory and penitent 'Gascoigne'. Once again, in his prose dedication, Gascoigne offers a narrative version of how the work came to be written:

> I was (now almost twelve moneths past) pricked and much moved, by the grave and discreete wordes of one right worshipfull and mine approved friend, who (in my presence) hearing my thryftlesse booke of *Poesyes* undeservedly commended, dyd say: That he lyked the smell of those *Poesies* pretely well, but he would lyke the Gardyner much better if he would employe his spade in no worse ground, then eyther Devenitie or morall Philosophie. (Cunliffe, II, pp. 211–20)

There is no more probable candidate for 'one right worshipfull and mine approved friend' than Bedford himself, being no more than polite about the revised *Posies* and actually being critical of Gascoigne's choice of frivolous subjects. In response, in his dedication, Gascoigne offers his least equivocal performance as the Reformed Prodigal: '... I finde my selfe giltie of much time mispent, & of greater curiosite the[n] was convenient, in penning and endyghting sundrie toyes and trifles' (p. 211).

Indeed, the keywords in Gascoigne's dedicatory epistle are authentically Protestant, and include (moral) Reformation, Zeal, Duties, and Profit, as well as authentically courtly, including Desert and Desire.

A similar technique is evident in his much shorter prose translation of another moralistic Latin tract, *A Delicate Diet, for daintiemouthde droonkardes* (August 1576). In both

---

[32] Jean Robertson identified Gascoigne as the translator, in 'George Gascoigne and *The Noble Arte of Venerie and Hunting*', *Modern Language Review*, 37 (1942): 484–5; Charles and Ruth Prouty identified the source text in 'George Gascoigne, *The Noble Arte of Venerie*, and Queen Elizabeth at Kenilworth', in James McManaway, Giles Dawson, and Edwin Willoughby, eds., *Joseph Quincy Adams Memorial Studies* (Washington: Folger Shakespeare Library, 1948), 639–64.

[33] Austen, *George Gascoigne*, 105–15.

the *Droomme* and the *Diet*, Gascoigne created an aptly moralistic authorial persona under which he offered his work to a potential patron. Gascoigne not only produced these prose texts strategically, but marketed them too, making overt connections between his moralistic titles. A reader picking up this slim bundle of papers at the bookseller's stall would be directed to the *Droomme* by Gascoigne's assertion at the beginning of the *Diet* that he came across its original, an epistle by Saint Augustine,[34] as he was working on the *Droomme*: 'Whyles I travayled in Translation, and collection of my *Droomme of Doomes daye*: and was busyed in sorting of the same (for I gathered the whole out of sundry Pamphlets:) I chaunced at passage, to espye one shorte Epistle, written against Dronkennesse' (p. 455). I argue elsewhere that Gascoigne seems to have deliberately produced two distinct portfolios of work: the work he presented under his Reformed Prodigal persona and published under his own name, and the more courtly work which he published anonymously, thus preserving the integrity of this 'George Gascoigne', the Reformed Prodigal. It is one of the primary functions of Gascoigne's prose prefaces and letters that they create a forum for the performance of whichever authorial persona Gascoigne wishes to present his work. In the autumn of 1576, then, while Gascoigne's courtly stock was very high, he also published a series of moralistic titles under his own name using his 'Reformed Prodigal' persona. He was to pursue his courtly success with perhaps his most audacious performance so far when he presented another manuscript work to Elizabeth at New Year 1577.

Whereas Gascoigne had presented the illustrated manuscript of *Hemetes* to Elizabeth in 1576, his manuscript of *The Griefe of Joye* was entirely plain, except for the gold leaf which highlighted every mention of the Queen's name. Every aspect of this work is carefully designed to remind Elizabeth of Gascoigne's successful mission to Antwerp in the summer and in his prose dedication he claims that he is presenting the work: 'that I might make youre Majestie witnesse, how the *Interims* and vacant howres of those daies which I spent this somer in your service have byn bestowed' (p. 514). He even refers specifically to Antwerp in the Second Song, 'The vanities of Bewtie' (2, 32). The underlying invention in the *Griefe of Joy* is that 'the leaves of this pau[m]phlett have passed with mee in all my perilles' (p. 514). Although the fine condition of the manuscript, and the gold leaf highlights, are not the result of being carried inside a man's doublet for three weeks or more, it is designed to look like an unfinished work, breaking off in mid-stanza with a dramatic flourish: '*Lefte unperfect for feare of Horsmen*'.[35] The most striking aspect of the work, though, is how readily Gascoigne casts himself as Elizabeth's own court poet and gives a name to his courtly poet persona. Among the list of courtly ladies in the Second Song is 'Ferenda Natura', linked specifically to 'my banishment to *Bathe*' (2, 23) (referencing his autobiographical poem *Dan Bartholmew*), who addresses Gascoigne's courtly poet persona as 'Bartholmew'. This network of allusions refers the

---

[34] Charles T. Prouty, *George Gascoigne: Elizabethan Courtier, Soldier, and Poet* (New York: Columbia University Press, 1942, repr. 1968), 274.

[35] 'Dan Bartholmew' also breaks in this way in *A Hundreth*; see Pigman, *George Gascoigne: A Hundreth Sundrie Flowres*, 358. See also Prouty, *George Gascoigne*, 97.

reader back to the revised edition of *Master F.J.*, the *Fable*, and illustrates how his witty approach to realism and self-invention runs through his work, both in verse and prose.

On the same date as his manuscript of the *Griefe of Joye*, Gascoigne wrote and illustrated beautiful manuscript letters 'to al my Lordes and goode frendes in Cowrte'.[36] Only his letter to Sir Nicholas Bacon, his relative by marriage, survives. Gascoigne's courtly success was evidently still proving more expensive than remunerative and he was once again in urgent financial need. The letter to Bacon includes an emblematic device of a man about to mount a horse, as well as a self-deprecating verse about how Gascoigne has had to learn to restrain himself, making 'reason' his 'rider'. The emblem and verse complement the prose letter:

> But (my good Lorde) my colltyshe and jadishe trickes have longe sithens broughte me owte of fleashe, as withowte some spedye provysione of good provender I shall never be able to endure a longe jorneye, and therfore am enforcede to neye and braye unto your good Lordship and all other which have the keye of Her Majesties storehowse, beseachinge righte humblie that you will voutchsaffe to reamember me with some extreaordynarye allowaunce when it fallethe.

Gascoigne's prose vividly expresses his conceit: the underlying invention of the starving horse is brought into sharp focus by how consistently it is applied across illustration, verse, and prose. This letter and the *Griefe of Joye* comprise Gascoigne's last known literary works. He died in November that year, a profligate talent in innovative literary forms in both verse and prose.

Further Reading

Austen, Gillian. *George Gascoigne*, Studies in Renaissance Literature, 24 (Woodbridge: D. S. Brewer, 2008).

Cunliffe, J. W., ed. *The Complete Works of George Gascoigne*, 2 vols., vol. II (Cambridge: Cambridge University Press, 1907, 1910; repr. New York: Greenwood Press, 1969).

Heale, Elizabeth. *Autobiography and Authorship in Renaissance Verse: Chronicles of the Self*, Early Modern Literature in History (Basingstoke: Palgrave Macmillan, 2003).

Pigman III, G. W. *George Gascoigne: A Hundreth Sundrie Flowres* (Oxford: Oxford University Press, 2000).

Prouty, Charles T. *George Gascoigne:. Elizabethan Courtier, Soldier, and Poet* (New York: Columbia University Press, 1942, repr. 1968).

Wallace, William L. *George Gascoigne's The Steele Glas and the Complaynte of Phylomene: A Critical Edition with Notes*, Salzburg Studies in English Literature, Elizabethan and Renaissance Studies, 24 (Salzburg: Institut für Englische Sprache und Literatur, University of Salzburg, 1975).

Weiss, Adrian. 'Shared Printing, Printer's Copy, and the Text(s) of Gascoigne's *A Hundreth Sundrie Flowres*', *Studies in Bibliography*, 45 (1992): 71–104.

---

[36] It is reprinted with original spelling in *The Papers of Nathaniel Bacon of Stiffkey*, ed. A. H. Smith and G. M. Baker (Norwich: Norfolk Record Society, 1983), 3–4.

CHAPTER 11

'TURNE YOUR LIBRARY TO A WARDROPE': JOHN LYLY AND EUPHUISM[1]

KATHARINE WILSON

IN 1632, Edward Blount completed an act of literary exhumation. Prefacing his edition of six plays by the Elizabethan author John Lyly, Blount claimed he had 'dig'd up the Graue of a Rare and Excellent Poet', only to discover a forgotten aspect of literary—and social—history: 'All our Ladies were then his Schollers; And that Beautie in Court, which could not Parley *Euphueisme*, was as litle regarded; as shee which now there, speakes not French.'[2] The term 'euphuism' is derived from the eponymous hero of Lyly's two prose fictions, *Euphues. The anatomy of wyt* (1578) and *Euphues and his England* (1580), and is commonly used to describe Lyly's distinctive prose style. However, as Blount suggests, mastering euphuism is a skill which can extend beyond reading alone. Successful imitation is the equivalent of learning another language, and one which gains readers entrance into an elite. It is not as easy as Blount makes it sound. In Peter Hausted's Latin university play, *Senile Odium* (The Hatred of an Old Man), published in 1633, Euphues turns up as a faded celebrity, reduced to a spot of private tutoring. His pupil Gorgonius is laboriously trying to improve his seduction techniques by imitating Lyly's writing. But whenever he embarks on supposedly euphuistic sentences he forgets his words and gets interrupted by scornful rivals. After two attempts to deliver the line, 'O most verdantly vigorous of virgins', he gives up in disgust.[3]

Thankfully, euphuism is far more fluid and dynamic than Gorgonius's painful attempts at rote learning suggest. Rather, it is an evolving mode, which develops in the course of Lyly's own work and in the work of his imitators in order to accommodate the changing

---

[1] I am very grateful to Mike Pincombe for his helpful comments on this essay.
[2] John Lyly, *Six Court Comedies* (London, 1632), A2ᵛ. See also Leah Scragg, 'Edward Blount and the History of Lylian Criticism', *Review of English Studies*, 46.181(1995): 1–10.
[3] Peter Hausted, *Senile Odium*, ed. and trans. Laurens J. Mills (Bloomington: Indiana University Press, 1949), 107. I am grateful to Andy Kesson for this reference.

agendas of those speaking and writing it, and the genres in which it is placed. While it originates in recognizable linguistic markers, the concepts behind Lyly's style become embodied in dramatic and thematic representation. To the inventor of the term (not Lyly), the idea of defining euphuism in academic terms would have been laughable. Fourteen years after the publication of Lyly's first book, his one-time friend and fellow author Gabriel Harvey inveighed against his enemy, the pamphleteer Thomas Nashe, with heavy irony: 'What hee is improued since, excepting his good olde *Flores Poetarum*, and Tarletons surmounting Rhetorique, with a little Euphuisme, and Greenesse inough, which were all prettily stale, before he put hand to penne.'[4] In other words, Nashe's writing is deeply derivative, a patchwork of popular styles which he has tried to inject with the passé literary trends 'euphuism' and 'Greeneness', the latter term referring to Lyly's successor, Robert Greene.

Harvey then refers to the exploitation, and recognition, of a phenomenon rather than to a clearly defined set of rhetorical techniques. As both Blount's court ladies and Hausted's Gorgonius realize, euphuism is a language of opportunism, a guide to how to get on in society. It also requires a calculating discrimination; the most successful euphuists are those who use Lyly's style to ratify their own convictions. Euphuism is primarily a form of intellectual dressing up, and the metaphorical link between clothing and writing resonates throughout his work. One of the courtiers in Lyly's play *Sapho and Phao* (1584) tells his friend to 'turne your library to a wardrope', and the advice might be applied as much to Lyly's readers and imitators as to his personae.[5] As Blount and Hausted suggest, euphuism is a collective mode, which develops beyond the control of its inventor and gives rise to endless imitation. Euphuism is about infinite expansion; a single thought can breed analogies, anecdotes, intellectual choices, and printed pages. It is thus ideally suited to the rapidly developing print culture of the late sixteenth century, as the multitude of texts claiming kinship with Euphues testify. Lyly's style effectively provided the environment in which printed prose fiction was established in the 1580s; euphuism was a new way of dressing up language and writing for fun.

11.1 EUPHUISM ON THE PAGE

Harvey's sneering comment on Nashe was meant to be devastating, but as so often in early modern literature, the last laugh was on Harvey. His criticism reveals the internecine relationships between writers and styles in this period. According to Harvey, Lyly

---

[4] Gabriel Harvey, *Foure Letters and Certaine Sonnets, especially touching Robert Greene* (London, 1592), E2ᵛ.

[5] John Lyly, *Sapho and Phao*, in *The Complete Works of John Lyly* ed. R. Warwick Bond (Oxford: Clarendon Press, 1902), II. 377. All references to Lyly's works are to this edition and are indicated by volume and page number. See also Leah Guenther, 'To Parley Euphuism: Fashioning English as a Linguistic Fad', *Renaissance Studies*, 16.1 (2002): 24–35.

himself had opportunistically deprived his then friend of the fame that should have been his. In publishing the *Anatomy* he had taken credit for the invention of a prose style for which he, Harvey, was partly responsible: 'young Euphues hatched the egges, that his elder freendes laide'.[6] Lyly had rushed his work into print (gaining instant fame), leaving the unrecognized Harvey clucking discontentedly. While Harvey rarely missed a chance of literary self-aggrandizement, he also unwittingly became one of Lyly's most enduring publicists, his insult enshrining 'euphuism' in the popular imagination. His harrumphing suggests quite how widespread and active the practice of what Harvey calls 'euphuing' was before Lyly's work appeared and how impossible it is to trace a single source for it. Lyly's writing has been linked to Cicero, Isocrates, Gorgias, and Guevara among many others, and it can be co-opted to represent different sides in literary debates. Many writers wrote elaborately patterned prose; what Lyly did was effectively to trademark it with some characteristic variations of his own.

Perhaps it is most helpful to view the development of euphuism in the emergent context of printed prose fiction. George Pettie's *A Petite Pallace of Pettie his Pleasure* (1576) was a bestselling collection of short stories supposedly celebrating marriage, but usually detailing its awful consequences. Pettie's prose is peppered with long alliterative speeches, balanced clauses, and rhetorical questions. One example sums up both his manner and matter: 'But see the frailty of our felicity, marke the misery which mortall men are subiect to. A man would have thought this married couple in love so loyall, in estate so high, in all thinges so happy, had bene placed in perpetuity of prosperity. But alas what estate hath fortune ever made so invincible, which vice can not vanquish?'[7]

Equally important is the tone of Pettie's work, which ranges from the apocalyptic to bantering insinuations to women readers. George Gascoigne's 'A Discourse of the Adventures passed by Master F. J.' (1573; revised 1575) is a similarly knowing pseudo-autobiographical tale of a young man, F. J., and his affair with a married woman, which Gascoigne hints is a *roman à clef*. The plot also recalls the tale of Troy, in particular Criseyde's desertion of Troilus. Gascoigne's prose style is unlike that of Pettie or Lyly. The complexity of his work lies primarily in the interlacing of different kinds of writing and literary puzzles apparently designed to enmesh the reader. By his own account, his book earned Gascoigne instant notoriety, and at least one version was censored.

Though Gascoigne's literary celebrity was probably partially self-created, his text undoubtedly changed the Elizabethan literary scene. Lyly, grandson of the celebrated schoolmaster and grammarian William Lily, had graduated from Oxford and failed to gain an academic appointment. His intention appears to have been to imitate Gascoigne, but with caution, to write a more seemingly moral but eye-catching fiction which would cause a stir in influential circles and gain a place in the establishment for its author. Accordingly, in Lyly's first book, *Euphues. The anatomy of wyt*, the complexity of Gascoigne's riddling is matched by the intricacies of Lyly's flashy prose style and by his ambitious claims in the

---

[6] Gabriel Harvey, *Pierces Supererogation or a new prayse of the old asse* (London, 1593), 14^r.

[7] George Pettie, *A Petite Pallace of Pettie his Pleasure* (1576), ed. Herbert Hartman (London: Oxford University Press, 1938), 46. See also J. Swart, 'Lyly and Pettie', *English Studies*, 23 (1941): 9–18.

dedicatory epistle to act as a surgeon dissecting 'wit'. Gascoigne's hero, F. J., is paralleled by Lyly's protagonist Euphues, often identified with Lyly himself. But Euphues also came with a known literary pedigree, featuring as a witty and potentially learned persona in Roger Ascham's educational treatise *The Schoolmaster* (1570). One of the first points to take account of, then, is the multiplicity of connotations which Euphues has, as both text and protagonist. 'Wit' itself is a concept even more fluid than euphuism and as central to its definition. The junk shop of mental images which can be found in the human brain lies behind the extraordinary frame of reference of Lyly's personae.[8]

The multiplicity of interpretation suggested by the title of Lyly's work is equally characteristic of his style. The search for a definitive list of what euphuism is is as misleading as the search for its ultimate origins.[9] Its most characteristic components can, however, be identified by their now less familiar rhetorical names. In brief, Lyly's prose relies heavily on isocolon (clauses of similar syllabic length), parison (clauses with a similar structure), and paramoion (similar sounding words, including figures such as alliteration and assonance). Underlying most of Lyly's comparisons are the concepts of repetition with variance, parallelism, and antithesis, with particular emphasis on the difference between appearance and reality. Many of these structures are contained in monologues in which Lyly's personae debate emotions, ideas, or the merits of different courses of action, often in rhetorical questions.

So for example, when Euphues is considering 'whether beautie or witte moue men most to loue', he reflects:

> How franticke are those louers which are carried away with the gaye glistering of the fine face? the beautie whereof is parched with the Sommers blase, & chipped with the winters blast, which is of so short continuance that it fadeth before one perceiue it florishe, of so small profit that it poysoneth those that possesse it, of so little value with the wyse, that they accompt it a delicate bayte with a deadly hooke, a sweete *Panther* with a deuouring paunch, a sower poison in a siluer potte.[10]

While heavily indebted to Pettie's techniques, Lyly weaves a far more elaborate thread of ideas together. His prose typically shows life as a process of continual change. Here alliterative descriptions of physical perfection mirror each other ('gaye glistering', 'fine face'), and are progressively denuded, first by nature ('parched with the sommers blase, & chipped with the winters blast), and then by a series of clauses stressing transience ('of so short continuance...of so small profit...of so little value'). Beauty turns out to be 'a delicate bayte' and 'a sweete *Panther*', which both conceal danger, and finally 'a sower poison in a siluer potte'. Lyly inverts the word order so that the third comparison gives the dangerous element ('a sower poison') before its attractive container; it is as if readers have just drunk deeply from a silver flagon and realized their mistake too late.

---

[8] For ideas of wit, see R. W. Maslen, *Elizabethan Fictions: Espionage, Counter-Espionage, and the Duplicity of Fiction in Early Elizabethan Prose Narratives* (Oxford: Clarendon Press, 1997), 200–1.

[9] See also G. K. Hunter, *John Lyly: The Humanist as Courtier* (London: Routledge & Kegan Paul, 1962), 265; Jonas Barish, 'The Prose Style of John Lyly', *English Literary History*, 23 (1986): 14–35.

[10] Lyly, *Euphues*, I. 202.

The unexpected appearance of the sweet panther in an otherwise quotidian range of images calls attention to another of Lyly's most characteristic effects. His prose is oriented around the discovery of apparent correspondences and relationships between the human, natural, and classical worlds. Underpinning the dilemmas of his personae is a bizarre collection of analogies and anecdotes. His protagonists support their arguments with references to familiar gods and stories from classical literature, often from the tale of Troy, but also by alluding to a menagerie of extraordinary creatures and their habits, some of which may be found in the pages of writers such as Pliny, author of a famous Latin encyclopaedia of natural history, and others which Lyly appears to have invented. Thus, when Euphues's friend Philautus discovers that Euphues has betrayed him, he exclaims:

> Couldest thou not remember *Philautus* that *Greece* is neuer without some wily *Vlisses*, neuer void of some *Synon*, neuer to seeke of some deceitfull shifter? Why then did his pretended curtesie bewitch thee with such credulytie? Shall my good will bee the cause of his ill wil? bicause I was content to be his friende, thought he mee meete to be made his foole? I see now that as the fish *Scolopidus* in the floud *Araris* at the waxinge of the Moone is as white as the driuen snow, and at the wayning as blacke as the burnt coale, so *Euphues*, which at the first enceasing of our familyaritie, was very zealous, is nowe at the last cast become most faythlesse.[11]

The cast of classical mythology join animals, vegetables, and minerals to form a busy subculture, often undergoing processes of transformation, sometimes revealing their true natures, but often masking them. The story thus takes place on multiple levels, as the tale of Troy is re-enacted in the midst of extreme nature. Euphues is both a shifty Ulysses and a distinctly odd fish.

Lyly's style, so often about deceptive appearances, is intimately and logically tied into his plot. Like Gascoigne, Lyly wrote about betrayal. Euphues deceives his friend Philautus by falling in love with his fiancée Lucilla and starting a secret, but unconsummated, affair with her. She in turn betrays Euphues by discarding him for another lover, Curio. Alliterative words, in particular, gain momentum. There is repeated discussion of trial, trust, and truth, while the concepts of fraud, flattery, friendship, fancy, and fickleness are increasingly interlaced. The book is also deeply contradictory. Lyly's use of parallelism might suggest that he is keen to celebrate balance and harmony and to support his points with academic analogies. Reading one half of a Lylian sentence raises expectations of an antithetical second half; in Philautus's fulmination, 'curtesie' is answered by 'credulytie', 'friende' by 'foole'. The narrative is peppered with arcane examples and seems designed to generate footnotes. But rather than grounding his text in helpful exemples, Lyly's citations allow readers to become engulfed in his own endless creativity. The relevance of the fish Scolopidus's habits to Philautus's situation is left up to readers. As Blount noted, imitating euphuism is like learning another language, but it is also one which readers have to create and evaluate for themselves. Lyly offers his readers entry into a faux elite, his prose a

---

[11] Lyly, *Euphues*, I. 232.

pseudo-academic tissue of images designed to give a veneer of learning, but in fact delivering a very alternative education. Moreover, as readers discover, the natural phenomena to which Lyly refers frequently exhibit contradictory behaviour on different pages, according to the agendas of the personae deploying them. Behind the apparent order, Lyly's natural and rhetorical world runs riot.

The problems of arguing logically from such premises are swiftly exposed in the opening pages of the *Anatomy*. Euphues is a gifted young Athenian who falls into bad company and is subsequently rebuked for wasting his talents by an old man tellingly named Eubulus, or 'good counsel'. Their argument goes to the heart of the text. Eubulus warns Euphues of the corruption with which he is liable to be tainted and the importance of nurture: 'the tender youth of a childe is lyke the temperinge of newe waxe apte to receiue anye forme... as therefore the yron beeinge hotte receyueth any forme with the stroake of the Hammer, and keepeth it beeinge colde for euer, so the tender witte of a childe if with diligence it bee instructed in youth, wyll with industrye vse those qualities in hys age'. Euphues rudely responds with his own set of examples in support of acting according to nature: 'Doe you not knowe... That the stone *Abeston* being once made hotte will neuer be made colde'. It all depends which examples you pick and how you use them, or as Euphues puts it, 'it is ye disposition of the thought yt altereth ye nature of ye thing'.[12] Multiple instances throughout the text confirm Euphues's point of view; examples are cited to prove one point, then recycled to prove the opposite a few pages later. Eubulus's mention of wax is a case in point. While for Eubulus it provided an image of mutability, Lucilla later uses it as proof of genetic inheritance and therefore, stability. Unwittingly echoing Euphues's own thoughts on the power of nature, she observes that, 'as the softe waxe receiueth what soeuer print be in the seale, and sheweth no other impression, so the tender babe being sealed with his fathers giftes representeth his Image most lyuely'.[13] Lyly was always self-conscious about his own praxis and some of his most potent images invoke the idea of printing impressions and their relative permanence.

The only way to operate effectively in Lyly's universe is to choose examples to your own advantage. Now the parallelism underlying euphuism operates beyond the merely linguistic sphere. Euphues finds a friend in Philautus, who he assumes will be 'at all times an other I, in all places ye expresse Image of mine owne person'. Euphues wants to find a parallel, to make himself and Philautus into a walking euphuistic comparison; plot and grammar merge. Euphues confirms his delusions of grandeur when he places himself in a self-selected great tradition of faithful friends: '*Damon* to his *Pythias*... *Titus* to his *Gysippus*... was neuer found more faithfull then *Euphues* will be to his *Philautus*'.[14] The ability to write oneself credibly into a developing literary heritage is an important element of euphuism; Euphues never recognizes the gap between the example and its re-enactment.

The problems come when Lyly's hero encounters a better euphuist than himself. When Euphues meets Philautus's fiancée Lucilla in Naples he is instantly smitten and

---

[12] Lyly, *Euphues*, I. 187, 191, 193.   [13] Lyly, *Euphues*, I. 207.   [14] Lyly, *Euphues*, I, 197–8.

begins flirting with her. And in what for Lyly's successors would become one of the defining characteristics of euphuism, both lovers separately and secretly reflect on their new found attraction to each other in parallel monologues. Now Euphues runs into trouble. While analysing his own situation, he remarks that: 'To true it is that as the Sea Crabbe swimmeth always against the streame, so wit always striueth agaynst wisedome.' A few lines later, this image is gobbled up in an inexorable food chain: 'The filthy Sow when she is sicke, eateth the Sea Crabbe and is immediately recured.' Euphues, however, is less lucky than the filthy sow: 'And can men by no hearb, by no art, by no way procure a remedye for the impatient disease of loue?' Unable to find helpful examples in the natural world, Euphues turns to distorting classical mythology to justify himself: 'Did not *Paris* though he were a welcome guest to *Menelaus* serue his hoste a slippery prancke? If *Philautus* had loued *Lucilla*, he woulde neuer haue suffered *Euphues* to haue seene hir.'[15]

Lucilla meanwhile, like the filthy sow, is an avid consumer and eagerly embraces her status as a negative example. When she retires to her room to consider the ethics of jettisoning Philautus in favour of Euphues, she initially weighs the merits of her lovers in a frequently imitated euphuistic construction: 'I but *Euphues* hath greater perfection. I but *Philautus* hath deeper affection.' She soon begins to refine the concept of value in both the natural and the lapidary sphere: 'For as the Bee that gathereth Honny out of the Weede, when she espyeth the faire flower flyeth to the sweetest... So I although I loued *Philautus* for his good properties, yet seing *Euphues* to excell him, I ought by Nature to like him better... Is not the Dyamonde of more valewe then the Rubie, bicause he is of more vertue?'[16] Throughout his fiction, Lyly uses the example of the bee as an image of creation. Lucilla co-opts it, again echoing Euphues's earlier arguments in favour of the omnipotence of nature. Her assessment of the relative merits of different jewels is equally telling. Lucilla's sound commercial sense in choosing the most valuable lover reflects Lyly's own enterprise in publishing a love story; both ensure that their ventures are profitable.

What is the point of euphuism? The twisted logic Euphues and Lucilla use suggests that the mode is a parody of the abundance of exemplary principles expressed in contemporary conduct books.[17] Any argument can be used on any side of the question. Lyly's unlikely natural phenomena provide no insight into human behaviour. The eccentricities of his language create a screen behind which Lyly can hide his love story; speech takes the place of sex. Parallel monologues in which personae appear to reveal their inward thoughts only point up the distance between them. It is impossible to know what

---

[15] Lyly, *Euphues*, I. 208, 210.

[16] Lyly, *Euphues*, I. 206. See also Joan Pong Linton, 'The Humanist in the Market: Gendering Exchange and Authorship in Lyly's *Euphues* Romances', in Constance C. Relihan, ed., *Framing Elizabethan Fictions: Contemporary Approaches to Early Modern Narrative Prose* (Kent, Ohio: Kent Sate University Press, 1996), 73–97.

[17] See Raymond Stephanson, 'John Lyly's Prose Fiction: Irony, Humor and Anti-Humanism', *English Literary Renaissance*, 11 (1981): 3–21; Judith Rice Henderson, 'Euphues and his Erasmus', *English Literary Renaissance*, 12 (1982): 135–61.

examples the other person has chosen to manipulate. And while Lyly, as narrator, throws in a few moralistic asides, he also goes out of his way to stress his own inability to read his protagonists, often providing readers with a range of alternatives. In the second edition of the text he comments ironically on Euphues's and Philautus's friendship: 'Either *Euphues* and *Philautus* stoode in neede of frindshippe, or were ordained to be friendes: vpon so short warning, to make so soone a conclusion might seeme in mine opinion if it continued myraculous, if shaken off, ridiculous.'[18] Euphuism overwhelms readers with choices—of analogies, examples, and motivations.

The *Anatomy* is less a display of surgical excision than an ongoing process of redescription, with some of the techniques used being apparently designed to mislead. After his betrayal by Lucilla, Euphues turns into an embittered author of tracts and letters, including a misogynistic 'cooling card' addressed to young men in love. Euphues uses the rhetorical figure paradiastole, in this case the redescription of virtue as vice, to dissuade men from believing in female goodness, 'If she be chaste then is she coy,... if a graue Matrone, who can woe hir?'[19] Euphuism presents a universe in which natural phenomena and ethical values are equally vulnerable to incessant metamorphosis. Change is the only viable principle, in both prose and plot. It is thus appropriate that Lucilla, the better euphuist, successfully changes lovers in the course of the text and emerges from the plot with Curio and her father's inheritance, although Lyly later invents a horrible death for her. In the second edition of the text, Lyly stresses that this mutability is also embodied in Euphues himself. He adds an early passage in which Euphues boasts of his Ulyssean flexibility, 'if I be in *Crete*, I can lye, if in *Greece* I can shift, if in *Italy* I can court it'.[20]

Lyly's text thus appears deliberately wayward—a story about swapping sexual partners couched in an absurdist language system devoid of ethics.[21] Yet, the book contains more than fiction. The moralistic tracts with which the book ends are not merely the ravings of Euphues's embittered mind, although there is little sign of his reformation. While they are largely derivative, his letters and miniature essays contain ideas on education which would have been acceptable to Roger Ascham.[22] Euphuism allowed Lyly to reclothe them for a general readership and to suggest a connection, albeit questionable, between Euphues's experience of love and his acquisition of wisdom. The delight in language celebrated by euphuism could be shaped into didactic statements as well as into a love story. The corpus which ends the *Anatomy* turns Lyly's hero into a more improving author; euphuistic fiction becomes the precursor to euphuistic teaching.

---

[18] Lyly, *Euphues*, I. 199.

[19] Lyly, *Euphues*, I. 248. See also Quentin Skinner, 'Paradiastole: Redescribing the Vices as Virtues', in Sylvia Adamson, Gavin Alexander, and Katrin Ettenhuber, eds., *Renaissance Figures of Speech* (Cambridge: Cambridge University Press, 2007), 148–63.

[20] Lyly, *Euphues*, I. 186.

[21] Lyly's 'prodigality' is most fully explored in Richard Helgerson's *The Elizabethan Prodigals* (Berkeley: University of California Press, 1976).

[22] See Fred Schurink, 'The Intimacy of Manuscript and the Pleasure of Print: Literary Culture from *The Schoolmaster* to *Euphues*', in Mike Pincombe and Cathy Shrank, eds., *The Oxford Handbook of Tudor Literature, 1485–1603* (Oxford: Oxford University Press, 2009), 671–86.

But the reading public proved unwilling to be taught. Lyly's transformation of Euphues from lover into priggish moralist was unappreciated by his readers, despite the immediate popularity of his text and style. Lyly duly relaunched his hero into the world of entertaining, but improving, love stories. *Euphues and his England* is a nicely calculated exercise in reader response, equipped with a separate preface for Lyly's previously unacknowledged women readers. Gone are the tracts; moralistic statements are 'sowed...like Strawberies' in a recreational and reformist text.[23] Euphues the moralist and Philautus the would-be lover sail to England, where Philautus eventually chooses an appropriate wife from the English court. The style is broadly similar to that used in the *Anatomy*, though less crammed with comparisons. Drawing on contemporary courtesy books, Lyly presents euphuism as the language of court ladies virtuously discussing questions of love—the image Blount later highlighted. He even inserts a parody of his own earlier text; in one episode Philautus visits Psellus the magician in search of a love potion. After citing many euphuistic examples of the magical properties of the natural world, Psellus readily admits that they are all useless.

Yet Lyly's meditation on the ideas underlying euphuism reaches beyond self-parody. He had packed his first book with *petits récits* involving weird nature and classical gods. In this book the repetition and multiplicity which lie at the heart of euphuism become the main story—or rather stories. *Euphues and his England* is an anthology in which the protagonists and tales often seem to collapse into each other. Posing as parent and painter in the dedicatory epistle, Lyly meditates on the difference between the Euphues of his first and second books. The idea is continued into the first pages of text, a tissue of interweaving narratives of similarly named young men who lead prodigal lives with various outcomes. Euphuism, itself based on repetition and varying, became for Lyly a way of writing a sequel, of creating a text and protagonist which were both the same and different. Lyly's contribution to the book is only part of the story. Euphues, he claims, has only been drawn to the waist. Readers are left to imagine the rest of the 'body' of text and of Euphues; the essentially unfinished and regenerative quality of euphuism is written into the newly reconstituted hero.

Lyly had one very specific reader in mind. His ploy to get noticed had worked. By 1580, he had found a patron in the Earl of Oxford, to whom *Euphues and his England* is dedicated. But Lyly was aiming still higher. Accordingly, the text ends with a tract called 'Euphues Glasse for Europe' in which Euphues praises England, apparently as a prelude to praising its monarch. Yet the Queen had sought to restrict the dissemination of her image; now, paradoxically, the job of the artist was to provide an acceptable mode of non-representation.[24] Lyly's chosen avoidance strategy relies on a further refinement of euphuism, this time the weaving of a skein of anecdotes about ancient art into his plot. Lyly had apologized to his readers for an unfinished Euphues in the prefatory material; by the end of the book he had collected a community of ancient artists refusing to finish

---

[23] Lyly, *Euphues and his England*, II. 8.

[24] See Michael Pincombe, *The Plays of John Lyly: Eros and Eliza* (Manchester: Manchester University Press, 1996), 10–12.

their portraits of authority figures or goddesses. Thus, he recounts how the painter Zeuxis only represented Venus's back. Euphues himself finally breaks off from praise as if overwhelmed by emotion (enacting the rhetorical figure of aposiopesis) and cunningly avoiding describing Elizabeth. Lyly had begun by asking his readers to help him fill in the gaps in his text for seemingly aesthetic reasons. By the end of the book, the euphuistic analogy had become a political strategy.

11.2 Euphuism on stage

This is the last we hear of Euphues from Lyly, although he enjoyed a lively afterlife in the titles of his imitators. But it was only the start of the story of ancient art. By 1583 Lyly had received a commission to write for boy players at the Blackfriars and went on to write eight plays, seven of which are in prose. His first drama, *Campaspe* (1584), marked the expansion of the politicized euphuism which Lyly had begun to explore in *Euphues and his England*. Emerging from the anecdotes which had confined him in the latter book, Apelles takes centre stage, and like Euphues, is an artist obliged to negotiate with unpredictable authority figures. The play features Alexander's supposed love for his captured slave Campaspe and his renunciation of her to his court painter Apelles, who is also in love with her. As ever, Lyly's art is paradoxical, with separate prologues addressed to the court and the Blackfriars stressing the transitory and insubstantial nature of the entertainment. Within the opening speech of the play, however, historical reality intervenes— or at least a version of it. *Campaspe* is set during Alexander's siege of Thebes, when, according to the courtier Clitus, 'Thebes is rased, the people not racked, towers throwne down, bodies not thrust aside, a conquest without conflict, and a cruell warre in a milde peace.'[25] As Lyly's audience was likely to have known, the exact opposite was true. Alexander sacked the city and sold the survivors as slaves. Now euphuism becomes the vehicle for pointing up these disjunctions to the audience. The insertion of 'not' into the clauses disrupts the balance normally contrived in a euphuistic sentence and draws attention to the logical impossibility of war contained in peace.

If euphuism developed through the juxtaposition of odd concepts, in this play the ideas invoked become significantly more alarming. Alexander, Clitus reassures the captive Campaspe, 'drinketh not bloud, but thirsteth after honor'—instantly conjuring up an image of a bloodthirsty tyrant. Alexander's own attempts to present himself as a merciful ruler are equally hard to credit. His peacetime programme relies on contradiction: 'that whilest armes cease, artes may flourish, and ioyning letters with launces, we endeuor to be as good Philosophers as soldiers.'[26] Having just announced that the arts can only thrive in peacetime, Alexander reveals that he has no intention of giving up weapons. Instead,

---

[25] Lyly, *Campaspe*, II. 317. See also Pincombe, *The Plays of John Lyly*, 24–51.
[26] Lyly, *Campaspe*, II. 319.

his alliterative clauses suggest an uncomfortable reading group in which soldiers' books are stuck on spears.

There are fewer of Lyly's odd beasts in *Campaspe*, but plenty of disturbing composites. Language in this play is dissected far more thoroughly than in the *Anatomy*. The contrasts set up are not always between opposites, but between apparently related words. When the courtier Parmenio informs Campaspe's fellow captive Timoclea that Alexander is 'the conquerour' she questions his terminology:

Par. Madame, you neede not doubt, it is *Alexander*, that is the conquerour.
Timo. *Alex.* hath ouercome, not conquered.
Par. To bring al vnder his subiection is to conquer.
Timo. He cannot subdue that wich is diuine.
Par. Thebes was not.
Timo. Vertue is.[27]

'Conquering' is whittled down to 'overcoming', then to 'subjecting' and 'subduing'. But all verbs fail in the face of Timoclea's assertion of an indissoluble core of virtue. Campaspe meanwhile is always attempting to define the balanced way things should be and coins aphoristic euphuisms which reflect on Alexander's lack of decorum: 'In kinges there can be no loue, but to Queenes: for as neere must they meete in maiestie, as they doe in affection.'[28]

The ultimate contrast in the play is between what can and cannot be controlled. Love and virtue remain impossible to subdue, so Alexander gives up his claim to Campaspe. Yet, he seems to regard his desire for her as an exercise in power, rather than emotion, as Lyly shows by his assignment of euphuistic speeches. Look, for example, at his dialogue with his confidant Hephestion, which contains what is effectively Lyly's calling card, a long euphuistic set piece on the dangers of love. The speech showcases many of Lyly's most typical locutions, interlacing Campaspe's charms with their possibly deleterious effect on the martial Alexander: 'Wil you handle the spindle with *Hercules*, when you should shake the speare with *Achilles*?' ... 'I, but she is comly in al parts of the body: yea but she may be crooked in some part of the mind.'[29] However, the speaker is not Alexander, but Hephestion, who seems far better at articulating what a lover should say than his master. Euphuism gives him an acceptable language of love which, as Blount's court ladies later discovered, could be usefully reworked on appropriate occasions.

To analyse such a speech inevitably draws attention to the difference between page and stage, to imagine how boy players would choose to make Alexander's awkwardly threatening euphuisms contrast with Hephestion's slick speech-writing. Lyly himself was always keenly aware of his unspoken contract with both actors and audience. His prologues and epilogues constantly stress his dependence on applause—and willing book buyers. Euphuism had to be translated into theatre, the parallelism of his anecdotes

---

[27] Lyly, *Campaspe*, II. 318.
[28] Lyly, *Campaspe*, II. 349. See also Peter Saccio, *The Court Comedies of John Lyly: A Study in Allegorical Dramaturgy* (Princeton: Princeton University Press, 1969), 40–51.
[29] Lyly, *Campaspe*, II. 329–30.

into plot and subplot.[30] Monologues are exchanged for dialogues, often a run of echoing one-liners. The characteristic balance of a Lylian sentence is frequently varied by a tripartite construction. Thus, Caelia in *Midas* (1590) observes that 'if loue, golde, or authoritie might haue inchaunted me, *Mydas* had obteyned by loue, golde and authoritie'.[31] Characters parallel each other both within the plot and in their own speeches to each other; *Gallathea* (c. 1585), for example, features two young women, both disguised as boys, who echo and vary the words each other uses.

Lyly's prose books allowed him to set up a teasing rapport with his readers by apparently giving them access to a world of arcane knowledge. His plays similarly encourage a comic sense of exclusivity. In *Campaspe* Lyly had given flesh to the ancient stories of Alexander and Apelles; in his next play, *Sapho and Phao*, he tells his audience the truth about love, or rather, the figure of Venus repeatedly invoked in the *Euphues* books. The ferryman Phao, like Euphues and Apelles, has to learn to negotiate his way round a capricious authority figure, in this case Venus, as well as dealing with Sapho the love poet. Venus favours him by making him beautiful, but he still has to try and make money, a contradiction summed up in the relationship between his name and his fortune:

Sapho.	What faire boy is that?
Trachinus.	Phao, the Ferrie man of Syracusa.
Phao.	I neuer saw one more braue: be al Ladies of such maiestie?
Criticus.	No, this is she that al wonder at and worship.
Sapho.	I haue seldome seene a sweeter face. Be all Ferrie men of that fairenesse?
Trachinus.	No Madame, this is he that Venus determined among men to make the fairest. [32]

Phao is a fair ferryman, who earns his living by taking fares, his attributes accumulating in a dialogue in which the speakers mirror each other's syntax.

The euphuism of Lyly's plays is a distinctly aural pleasure and allows for some of his most exuberant puns. Look, for example, at the moment when Sapho asks Phao what will cure lovesickness: '*Phao.* Yew Madame. *Sapho.* Mee? *Phao.* No Madame, yewe of the tree'.[33] Though Lyly's reliance on obscure natural properties gradually decreased, his mockery of elite worlds of language grew more pointed. Both *Gallathea* and *Endimion* (1588) feature pages attempting to ingratiate themselves with ludicrous and fraudulent masters, whom they try to impress by reciting Latin tags and meaningless alchemical terms respectively. Lyly is always conscious of the need for careful linguistic negotiation with unpredictable superiors. As one servant in *Midas* comments, 'if you call a dog a dog, you are vndone'.[34]

---

[30] See Leah Scragg's important work on the links between Lyly's prose and drama, especially '"Any shape one would conceive": From a Prose Style to Lyly's Plays for the First Blackfriars Theatre', in Janet Clare and Roy Eriksen, eds., *Contexts of Renaissance Comedy* (Oslo: Novus, 1984), 61–76; 'Speaking Pictures: Style and Spectacle in Lylian Comedy', *English Studies*, 86.4 (2005): 298–311.

[31] Lyly, *Midas*, III. 124.

[32] Lyly, *Sapho and Phao*, II. 384.

[33] Lyly, *Sapho and Phao*, II. 402.

[34] Lyly, *Midas*, III. 146. See Leah Scragg, 'John Lyly and the Politics of Language', *Essays in Criticism*, 55.1 (2005): 17–38.

Euphuism is always a language of extremes, and of different kinds violently yoked together. In the theatre, this is most strikingly represented by the theatrical transformations Lyly imposes on his characters. Two women in Lyly's plays are turned into talking trees. Euphuism is about change. Resistance to change, especially the changes brought on by love, can seriously alter your state. Yet, those who are too eager for change do not escape either. Most poignantly ridiculous is the case of Haebe in *Gallathea*, due to be sacrificed to a monster who has requested the most beautiful maiden. In what appears to be her final speech, she creatively adapts the standard euphuistic love complaint in a flurry of alliteration: 'Shall it onely be lawfull amongst vs in the prime of youth, and pride of beautie, to destroy both youth and beautie: and what was honoured in fruites and flowres as a vertue, to violate in a virgine as a vice? But, alas! destenie alloweth no dispute; die *Haebe, Haebe* die!'[35] But she doesn't die because she is not beautiful enough. Euphuism is always about superlatives, the fairest and the foulest. Mediocrity is never exemplary.

11.3 PROSE AFTER EUPHUES

To modern readers, such as they are, euphuism may seem like a perverse byway in the history of English literature. Yet, it is hard to overestimate the impact which Lyly's books made on imaginative writing. During the 1580s Euphues the persona became a stalwart of subtitles and paratexts, even when he was of no relevance to the narrative. What is always important about the imitation of Lyly's work is not its accuracy (there are plenty of bad euphuists), but conscious alignment with the cult Lyly had started—Harvey's definition of euphuism. Imitative fiction began as early as 1580, with the publication of Austen Saker's *Narbonus*. But it was not until 1583 that any author effectively replied to the challenges set up by Lyly. Newly graduated from Cambridge, Robert Greene appeared in print with *Mamillia: A Mirrour or looking-glasse for the Ladies of Englande*, which apparently sought to reverse the misogynistic norms of Lyly's first prose book. Lyly wrote about two men who loved one unworthy woman; Greene's story concerns two chaste young women, Mamillia and Publia, who fall victim to the faithless Pharicles.

Greene never mentions Lyly's name. But the shadow of his fiction falls across not just the author, but his personae in the book's many monologues. Euphuism, understood as a distinctly bookish mode, underlies the relationship of Mamillia and Pharicles. They meet when Mamillia is reading (the *Anatomy* perhaps) and establish each other's credentials as competent euphuists by discussing the properties of 'the hearb *Sisimbrium*'. However, euphuistic patterns become more complex when they are used to forecast the likelihood of a suitor's fidelity. Mamillia enjoins herself to 'Choose by the eare, and not by the eye. *Pharicles* is fayre, so was *Paris*, and yet fickle.'[36] Pharicles

---

[35] Lyly, *Gallathea*, II. 465.
[36] Robert Greene, *Mamillia*, in *The Life and Complete Works of Robert Greene*, ed. Alexander B. Grosart (London: Huth Library, 1881–6), II. 23, 25.

embodies the deceptive beauty common to so many euphuistic comparisons. Lying behind the correspondence of 'Pharicles' and 'fayre' lies that of 'Pharicles' and 'Paris'. But though she reads her suitor accurately, Mamillia decides to love him (chastely) anyway.

Mamillia is imbued with a sense of inevitability as much as knowingness. An understanding of euphuism may help to read a situation, but may equally simply provide ballast to existing predilections—which always lead to love. Greene used euphuism as a template for moralistic love stories, with easily identifiable patterns for his readers to recognize. His monologues are accordingly more layered, with sets of similar and usually alliterative clauses piled upon each other. Publia reflects that there is 'no fruit so fine, but the caterpillar wil consume it: no adamant so hard, but wil yield to the file: no metal so strong, but wil bend at the stamp: no maid so free, but loue will bring her to bondage & thraldom'.[37] Greene's repetition of clauses has a cumulative effect; by the end of the speech Publia (like Mamillia) has convinced herself that love is the only option.

Greene spent his career vigorously exploiting Lyly's influence. Parallel pairs of lovers' monologues and emblematic transformations crowd his many fictions even as he, like Lyly, increasingly dropped the habits of odd flora and fauna. By the late 1580s he was busily distancing himself from his predecessor, even though he remained heavily reliant on his tactics. *Menaphon* (1589) includes a parodic recognition scene in which an estranged husband and wife establish their identities by swapping euphuisms. But it would be dangerous to regard Greene's work as evidence of Lyly's unpopularity. In 1589 Greene was able to rely on his readers' familiarity with Lyly's style. Even in the 1630s, when Blount felt Lyly's plays needed to be collected and publicized, Peter Hausted could still make comedy out of Euphues for an academic audience. We may be most familiar with pejorative comments on euphuism, such as Sir Philip Sidney's fury in *A Defence of Poetry* (c. 1579) at 'all stories of beasts, fowls and fishes'.[38] But the amount of space Harvey in 1590 still devoted to ranting about the 'fly-blowne Euphuisme' which had disfigured English literature and made 'no Art, but Euphuistes' suggests quite how thoroughly Lyly's work had permeated literary consciousness.[39]

Euphuism provided a shared cultural reference point, which operated on multiple levels according to context. And if the mode was sometimes ridiculed, it was also recognized. Often used as a shorthand for court life, euphuism was further refined as the preserve of courtly villains and seducers, the stylistic equivalent of mustachio twirling. Look for example at the seduction techniques of Prince Edward in Greene's play *Friar Bacon and Friar Bungay* (c.1592) and Arsadachus in Thomas Lodge's prose fiction *A Margarite of America* (1596). The many linguistic experiments of Shakespeare's Iago include echoes of

---

[37] Greene, *Mamillia*, II. 129.

[38] Sir Philip Sidney, *A Defence of Poetry*, ed. Jan van Dorsten (Oxford: Oxford University Press, 1966; repr. 1988), 71.

[39] Harvey, *Pierces Supererogation*, T4^r. See also Leah Scragg, 'The Victim of Fashion? Rereading the Biography of John Lyly', *Medieval and Renaissance Drama in England*, 19 (2006): 210–26.

euphuism. Predicting Othello's transformations, he observes: 'The food that to him now is as luscious as locusts shall be to him shortly as acerb as coloquintida.'[40] As Vladimir Nabokov's equally florid narrator noted in *Lolita* (1955), 'You can always count on a murderer for a fancy prose style.'[41]

Lyly's texts continued, if sporadically, to be reprinted and retitled, while linguistic parallelism can be traced in authors as diverse as Samuel Johnson and Jane Austen.[42] Lyly's own image remained equally liable to reinterpretation, as Blount's association of euphuism with the French language was more influential than he could have predicted. Lyly's work was aligned with foreign and decadent literature, from which a manly English prose must be reclaimed.[43] It was not until the nineteenth century that euphuism began to be fully debated and reinvented as a forerunner of Victorian aesthetic principles.[44] Walter Pater's nostalgic (and vague) evocation of euphuism in *Marius the Epicurean* (1885) turned it into a blueprint for a new age of style. But it proved to be too good for this world, as Flavian the euphuist poet succumbs to the plague.

A less ethereal euphuist is provided by Sir Walter Scott in the form of the dandified knight Sir Piercie Shafton in *The Monastery* (1820). Shafton's credentials as a euphuist are questionable, and his definition of the mode finely circular: 'that eloquence which no other eloquence is sufficient to praise, that art which, when we call it by its own name of Euphuism, we bestow on it its richest panegyric.'[45] The character was not liked by Scott's readers and, like Euphues, lived on thanks to derogatory references by other writers. Yet Scott's denouement provides a revealing reading of Lyly's first work. The fraudulent Shafton is unmasked as the upstart son of a tailor—the reason behind his delight in fine clothing. For Shafton, library and wardrobe are intimately connected. His literary and sartorial disguises also have a positive result inasmuch as he finds love with a miller's daughter. Opportunistic euphuism then wins out again over two hundred years after its first appearance in print. Perhaps we need to start thinking of Lyly as less a flash in the pan and more as part of the furniture.

Further Reading

Barish, Jonas. 'The Prose Style of John Lyly', *English Literary History*, 23 (1986): 14–35.
Henderson, Judith Rice. 'Euphues and his Erasmus', *English Literary Renaissance*, 12 (1982): 135–61.

---

[40] William Shakespeare, *Othello*, ed. E. A. J. Honigmann (Walton-on-Thames: Thomas Nelson, 1997), 158–9: 1. 3. 349–50.
[41] Vladimir Nabokov, *Lolita* (London: Penguin, 1995), 9.
[42] See Robert B. Heilman, 'Greene's Euphuism and Some Congeneric Styles', in George M. Logan and Gordon Teskey, eds., *Unfolded Tales: Essays on Renaissance Romance* (Ithaca: Cornell University Press, 1989), 49–73.
[43] For Lyly's critical heritage, see Andrew Kesson, *John Lyly and Early Modern Authorship* (Manchester: Manchester University Press, 2013).
[44] See Lene Østermark-Johansen, 'The Death of Euphues: Euphuism and Decadence in Late-Victorian literature', *English Literature in Transition*, 45.1 (2002): 4–25.
[45] Sir Walter Scott, *The Monastery* (Edinburgh: Adam and Charles Black, 1886), 170.

Hunter, G. K. *John Lyly: The Humanist as Courtier* (London: Routledge & Kegan Paul, 1962).

Kesson, Andrew. *John Lyly and Early Modern Authorship* (Manchester: Manchester University Press, 2013).

Lyly, John. *The Complete Works of John Lyly*, ed. R. Warwick Bond, 3 vols. (Oxford: Clarendon Press, 1902).

Maslen, R. W. *Elizabethan Fictions: Espionage, Counter-Espionage, and the Duplicity of Fiction in Early Elizabethan Prose Narratives* (Oxford: Clarendon Press, 1997).

Pincombe, Michael. *The Plays of John Lyly: Eros and Eliza* (Manchester: Manchester University Press, 1996).

Schurink, Fred. 'The Intimacy of Manuscript and the Pleasure Of Print: Literary Culture from *The Schoolmaster* to *Euphues*', in Mike Pincombe and Cathy Shrank, eds., *The Oxford Handbook of Tudor Literature, 1485–1603* (Oxford: Oxford University Press, 2009), 671–86.

Scragg, Leah. '"Any shape one would conceive": From a Prose Style to Lyly's Plays for the First Blackfriars Theatre', in Janet Clare and Roy Eriksen, eds., *Contexts of Renaissance Comedy* (Oslo: Novus, 1984), 61–76.

—— 'John Lyly and the Politics of Language', *Essays in Criticism*, 55.1 (2005): 17–38.

—— 'Speaking Pictures: Style and Spectacle in Lylian Comedy', *English Studies*, 86.4 (2005): 298–311.

Stephanson, Raymond. 'John Lyly's Prose Fiction: Irony, Humor and Anti-Humanism', *English Literary Renaissance*, 11 (1981): 3–21.

CHAPTER 12

ROBERT GREENE

R. W. MASLEN

Robert Greene transformed the face of English prose fiction with the sheer volume, diversity, and inventiveness of his publications. Before he started to write, no English writer had dedicated his entire career to prose fiction, or written so many varieties of it, or demonstrated to the same extent its unparalleled flexibility as a medium, its capacity to function as a vehicle for such an astonishing range of contrasting styles, plots, narrative forms, and points of view. By the time of his death it was possible to imagine oneself as a writer of prose fiction first and foremost; in anachronistic terms, as a professional novelist. And the full implications of this one-man transformation of the English literary scene have only recently begun to be explored with the attention they deserve.[1]

This is partly due to the vagaries of fashion. Greene's style in his romances, long dismissed as grotesquely artificial, is now enjoyed for the qualities that once condemned it: playful experimentation with rhetorical and narrative structure; bold musicality; and the flamboyant display of its own craftsmanship.[2] But his low reputation was also due to a successful smear campaign by his enemies—a campaign to which he was oddly willing to contribute through his presentation of himself, in his later work, as a talented, but feckless hack.[3] And his image was further tarnished by the contempt he expressed for

---

[1] Major recent reassessments include Derek Alwes, *Sons and Authors in Elizabethan England* (Newark, DE: University of Delaware Press, 2004); Steve Mentz, *Romance for Sale in Early Modern England: The Rise of Prose Fiction* (Aldershot: Ashgate 2006); Lori Humphrey Newcomb, *Reading Popular Romance in Early Modern England* (New York: Columbia University Press, 2002); Katharine Wilson, *Fictions of Authorship in Late Elizabethan Narratives* (Oxford: Clarendon Press, 2006); and Kirk Melnikoff and Edward Gieskes, eds., *Writing Robert Greene* (Aldershot: Ashgate, 2008). The last includes an invaluable final chapter listing 'Recent Studies in Robert Greene (1989–2006)', which complements Kevin J. Donovan, 'Recent Studies in Robert Greene (1968–88)', *English Literary Renaissance*, 20.1 (1990): 163–75.

[2] For an account of the changes in Greene's critical fortunes see Kirk Melnikoff and Edward Gieskes, 'Introduction: Re-imagining Robert Greene', in Melnikoff and Gieskes, eds., *Writing Robert Greene*, 1–24.

[3] Brenda Cantar argues that it was largely rival pamphleteers who represented Greene as a hack; see the introduction to her edition of *Menaphon* (Ottawa: Dovehouse Editions, 1996), 20. On Harvey's part in forging his reputation see Sandra Clark, *The Elizabethan Pamphleteers* (Rutherford, NJ: Fairleigh

Shakespeare in a notorious pamphlet written on his deathbed. *Greene's Groatsworth of Wit, Bought With a Million of Repentance* (1592) represents its author as an unscrupulous trickster who repeatedly falls foul of other people's tricks. His pleasure in fooling others takes him from plotting to con his brother out of his inheritance—which ends with his own betrayal by a fellow plotter—to writing for the theatre—which ends with the players abandoning him for a more fashionable writer from among their own ranks (Shakespeare, naturally). It seems appropriate, then, that the terms Greene used to slander Shakespeare—above all the claim that he was 'an upstart Crow, beautified with our feathers' (sig. F1ᵛ), plagiarizing the work of university graduates to make himself look good—have been used to flog the slanderer.[4] Greene has been accused of stealing stories, passages, and phrases from a range of other writers, including himself, since he sometimes repeated parts of his own texts verbatim. In fact, the *Groatsworth* itself may be an act of plagiarism, assembled after Greene's death by Henry Chettle as a means of cashing in on the drama of the famous author's final moments.[5] But whatever proportion of the text is by Greene, it is a highly complex work, as Steve Mentz has shown, which slips easily between literary modes—from romance to erotic *fabliau* to lyric to autobiography to animal fable to confessional missive (it closes with a letter of apology written to his wife)—making the pamphlet a miniature model of his literary career.[6] The *Groatsworth*, in fact, should encourage us not to dismiss, but to look more closely at the strange but fascinating writer whose name it bears.

Greene started out as a nobody.[7] It is not clear, in fact, exactly who he was or what he did in life apart from writing. He came from Norwich, he tells us in his title pages, where his father may have been a saddler or an innkeeper—we don't know which. We don't know what school he attended, though it was probably the Norwich grammar school. We know he graduated from St John's College, Cambridge, like his friend Thomas Nashe (he was later awarded an MA by Oxford too). He may have married a woman named Dorothy, spent her money, and sent her back with a child to her wealthy Lincolnshire family. He may have had a son called Fortunatus with a London hooker. He may have been disinherited by his own father, undergone a deathbed repentance, and written to Dorothy, asking her to pay off his debts. But nearly all these details come either from his quasi-autobiographical fictions, such as the *Groatsworth*, or the pen of his enemy Gabriel Harvey, who made a habit of engaging in literary squabbles with celebrity authors (Lyly and Nashe were among his other targets). Greene's biography as we know it is a

---

Dickinson University Press, 1983), 47. Greene's own part in forging his reputation is discussed in detail by Newcomb, Wilson, and Alwes.

[4] Except where indicated, all quotations from Greene are from the first extant edition as given in *STC*.

[5] For the authorship of the *Groatsworth*, see John Jowett, 'Johannes Factotum: Henry Chettle and Greene's Groatsworth of Wit', *Papers of the Bibliographical Society of America*, 87 (1993): 453–85.

[6] See Steve Mentz, 'Forming Greene: Theorizing the Early Modern Author in the *Groatsworth of Wit*', in Melnikoff and Gieskes, eds., *Writing Robert Greene*, 115–31.

[7] For an elegant discussion of his life see L. H. Newcombe, 'Greene, Robert', *ODNB* <http://www.oxforddnb.com/view/article/11418?docPos=1> accessed 18 March 2013.

commercial fabrication, inseparable from the busy marketplace of print which he dominated in his lifetime—and which continued to draw sustenance from his name after his death, in a series of publications (*The Repentance of Robert Greene* [1592], *Greene's News Both from Heaven and Hell* [1593], and *Greene in Conceit* [1598]) that flaunt it on their title pages.[8] The fictitiousness of his life (and afterlife) is itself a testament to the impact he had on prose fiction, demonstrating as it does the extent to which he made it possible to imagine a nobody as a fitting subject for what has come to be called 'novelistic discourse'.[9]

Greene's career as a writer of prose has been roughly divided by Walter Davis into four distinct phases.[10] From 1580 to 1584, he wrote imitations of John Lyly's celebrated *Euphues* books; from 1585 to 1588, framed collections of short stories; from 1588 to 1589, pastoral romances inspired by ancient Greek romance; and from 1590 to 1592, quasi-autobiographical narratives and stories about London con artists, the celebrated 'cony-catching pamphlets'. Useful though it is as a starting point, this fourfold division is clearly too simplistic. Greene began writing romances based on ancient Greek models as early as 1584; he continued to produce longer romances while writing his framed story collections, autobiographies, and cony-catching pamphlets; and he also wrote books of quite different kinds, such as translations from Italian, French, and Spanish, and the immensely successful satire *A Quip for an Upstart Courtier* (1592). Moreover, there are consistent preoccupations that fuse the different strands of Greene's writing and these can be occluded by any inflexible taxonomy of his works. Above all, Greene resembles his contemporary Marlowe in his obsession with those aspects of human experience that resist categorization or control: with anger, greed, desire, and other emotions; with ageing and other changes that happen over time; with sudden, unexpected events or coincidences that defy all our usual assumptions about cause and effect. He delights in telling stories that reverse the scenarios favoured by the pedagogues of the English educational system, where the old are always wise and youngsters disobedient, where men are intelligent, strong, and responsible and women fickle, foolish, and weak, where rulers are to be respected and their subjects docile. Perhaps his most striking characteristic, in fact, can be summed up in the statement that with Greene's work you can seldom guess what will happen next. This would hardly be true if it could be tidily compartmentalized. In imparting this unpredictable quality to his narratives, Greene built on the achievements of English prose fiction writers of the 1560s and 1570s; and to appreciate his contribution to literary history one has to start with these.[11]

The 1560s saw a major influx of French and Italian short stories into England, in the shape of the hugely influential collections of William Painter and Geoffrey Fenton.

---

[8] The fullest account of Greene's afterlife is given in Newcomb, *Reading Popular Romance*.

[9] The phrase comes from Constance Relihan's *Fashioning Authority: The Development of Elizabethan Novelistic Discourse* (Kent, Ohio: Kent State University Press, 1994).

[10] See Walter R. Davis, *Idea and Act in Elizabethan Fiction* (Princeton: Princeton University Press, 1969), 139. See also Mentz's sevenfold division of his career in 'Forming Greene', 123–5.

[11] The account of the works of Painter, Fenton, Gascoigne, and Lyly that follows draws on my *Elizabethan Fictions: Espionage, Counter-Espionage and the Duplicity of Fiction in Early Elizabethan Prose Narratives* (Oxford: Clarendon Press, 1997).

Greene clearly read Painter's two-part *Palace of Pleasure* (1566–7) very carefully—like many of his contemporaries, including Shakespeare—and transferred its organized eclecticism to his own story collections, such as *Perimedes the Blacksmith* (c.1588) or *Penelope's Web* (1587). Fenton's *Certain Tragical Discourses* (1567) helped bring about the 'feminizing' of English prose fiction in the 1570s, which Greene enthusiastically embraced.[12] Dedicated to Mary Sidney, Philip's mother, the *Tragical Discourses* are a selection of often melodramatic stories derived from the Italian author Matteo Bandello, in which women play a central role. Fenton's insistence that his stories constitute a form of history, articulated in the detailed defence of the historian's craft in his dedication, helped to give English prose fiction its status as a kind of alternative to the chronicles sponsored by governments: a form that acknowledged, as chronicles did not, the crucial parts played by women and desire in the changing fortunes of nations. Greene's two interventions in the quasi-historical matter of Troy—*Penelope's Web* and *Euphues his Censure to Philautus* (1587)—and his cheeky historical romance *Ciceronis Amor* (1589), which describes the love-life of Rome's most celebrated orator, continue Fenton's project of identifying women and desire as the unacknowledged dual motors of European history.

Painter's and Fenton's achievements were built on by the two most influential English writers of the 1570s, George Gascoigne and John Lyly. Gascoigne's only prose fiction, *The Adventures of Master F.J.*, formed part of his miscellany *A Hundreth Sundry Flowers* (1573), revised as *The Posies of George Gascoigne Esquire* in 1575; while Lyly's two *Euphues* books (1578 and 1580) gave their name to an ornately patterned prose style, euphuism, which remained fashionable for at least a decade after their publication. Both Gascoigne and Lyly took devious, witty, feckless young men as their protagonists. In each case these men come as strangers from distant regions to the household of a respected member of society—a Northern English knight in the first version of the *Adventures of Master F.J.*, the Governor of Naples in the first *Euphues* book—and disrupt it by prosecuting an adulterous or quasi-adulterous affair: Master F.J. seduces the knight's wife, Euphues the Governor's daughter, who is betrothed to another man. Both narratives emphasize the complex, stylistically sophisticated repartee between illicit lovers, whose enjoyment of word-play, elegant syntax, and chop-logic masquerading as reason—the verbal counterpart of passionate sex or a skilful card-game—quickly leads them into moral confusion. In each case the women prove more adept at such word-games than the men and are therefore blamed, directly or by implication, for the male protagonist's descent into depravity. Master F.J. ends his adventures as a misogynist, Euphues as a philosopher warning other young men against entangling themselves with women as he did. At the same time, both books adopt an amusingly sardonic view of the kind of counsel dispensed by the reformed Euphues. The recipient of such advice himself, he paid no attention to it when young and there seems little likelihood that his young male readers will be any more influenced than he was by moral instruction—though they will relish, no

---

[12] Another important story-collection from this point of view is George Pettie, *A Petite Pallace of Pettie his Pleasure* (1576), whose author claims to desire only women as readers.

doubt, the artistry of his phrasing, which is so much more attractive when deployed as a weapon in repartee than when trotting out truisms.

Both books, in fact, present themselves as a form of alternative education for their young male readers—much as Fenton's presented itself as an alternative to chronicle history. Euphues before his reformation is a highly talented young man whose training in the art of rhetoric fails to keep him safe in the predatory environment of modern Italy, as represented by the untrained, but mentally acute young woman Lucilla, who first charms and then discards him. Master F.J. too finds his verbal skills, which he devotes to the cut-and-thrust of witty dialogue, more than matched by the native eloquence of his mistress Elinor. Formal humanist education in itself, these narratives insist, leaves its recipients poorly equipped to cope with the quotidian power-games of early modern society. The philosophy of the humanist pedagogues, conveyed to the young in glib sayings, not reasoned treatises, can be exploited by any man or woman witty and unprincipled enough to apply them for private purposes. And the skills involved in deploying these and other verbal tricks persuasively are by no means confined to the educated classes. Male and female con artists, streetwise tricksters, and adolescent truants of all classes are equally capable of picking them up and using them, to the dismay of pedagogues and parents who think to give their children an advantage by providing them with a top-class education.

English prose fiction of the 1570s, then, may be seen not just as an *alternative* form of schooling, but as a form of *anti*-schooling, exposing the flaws in the cherished assumptions of Elizabethan educators. Real life, it implies, operates according to quite different principles than the simplistic formulae promulgated by schoolmasters and tutors; and this can have worrying implications for members of the ruling classes who endeavour to guide their actions by what they have been taught. As often as not, public figures in these books are powerless to regulate either their own lives or those of their inferiors. The social, economic, and philosophical structures of early modern Europe may look stable and well organized, but they are always shifting in response to new pressures, always on the verge of metamorphosis or collapse. The presence in Lyly's and Gascoigne's texts of competing European cultures reinforces this impression. Master F.J. and Elinor introduce French and Italian dances, games, and customs into Northern England, while Euphues is an Athenian in Lucilla's Italian hometown, quickly finding himself Italianated—rendered more devious and subtle than he was already—by her influence. England could easily become a second France and anywhere in Europe could end up as Italy. In addition, the key terms that dominate the two narratives invoke not stability, but improvisation in response to unexpected circumstances. Master F.J.'s 'adventures' are games of chance played for the highest stakes, while the subtitle of the first *Euphues* book—*The Anatomy of Wit*—parades its author's obsession with native, undisciplined intelligence, capable of responding with lightning speed to sudden encounters; his obsession, in fact, with the quickness or 'quick capacity' celebrated by Gascoigne. This is the literary context inherited by Greene and it was in direct response to the challenges these texts threw down that he constructed his scandalous career as a proto-novelist.

In the first of his romances, *Mamillia* (*c.*1580),[13] Greene followed Fenton, Gascoigne, and Lyly in making a passionate and eloquent woman the centre of attention; and although like them he finds her interesting solely in terms of her relationship with men, he differs from his predecessors in refusing to condemn her for her eloquence and passion. Instead, as Derek Alwes has pointed out, he makes her an idealized mother-substitute for her fickle husband, nurturing him and forgiving his infidelities time and again until she has converted him by sheer force of faithfulness into what his culture would have him.[14] There were precedents for such exemplary women in the works of Gascoigne and Lyly: Elinor, F.J.'s mistress, has a well-behaved and intelligent sister called Frances and the second *Euphues* book, *Euphues and his England* (1580), substitutes a clever and courteous Englishwoman, Camilla, for the headstrong Neapolitan Lucilla. But neither of these women could be described as maternal and forgiveness is not their central role; and Greene returns to the forgiving maternal woman so often in his work that she acquires the force of a philosophical idea. By frequently casting women as the imperilled champions of a sexual, social, and religious value system which is always being demolished by men, Greene lays emphasis on the fragility of the humanist pedagogic framework, which needs to be defended or restored by the extemporary verbal acrobatics traditionally gendered as female. Constancy for Greene is a necessarily *active* quality, surviving through constant negotiation with the traitors and humbugs that seek to undermine it. His constant women are always in verbal or physical motion, pursuing, converting, and avenging themselves on the men who assault or betray them. And in doing so they effectively give men a free hand to behave as badly as they like. Thomas Nashe famously called Greene 'the *Homer* of Women' and implied that he praised them in his romances to make himself 'more amiable with [his] friends of the Feminine sexe'.[15] But as Alwes has demonstrated, despite all the prefaces Greene addresses to women, his implied readers in the narrative proper are invariably men and it is men who stand to gain most from subscribing to his ascription of constancy and cultural guardianship to their mothers, sisters, wives, and daughters.[16]

The Adventures of Master F.J. took games of chance or 'adventure' as its theme and *Euphues* was organized around its author's delight in scintillating wit. Greene shares Gascoigne's and Lyly's concern with arranging their work thematically and like them, chooses themes that stress the precarious shiftiness of the world into which his young men and women stray when they leave the parental home (or indeed beforehand, since parents in Greene's work are often untrustworthy), and the ungovernable nature of the mind. He was helped in developing these themes by his passion for the ancient Greek romances that were becoming known in England as he wrote: Longus's *Daphnis and*

---

[13] For the date of *Mamillia* see Wilson, *Fictions of Authorship*, 75.
[14] See Alwes, *Sons and Authors*, 112–26.
[15] *The Works of Thomas Nashe*, ed. R. B. McKerrow, 5 vols. (London: A. H. Bullen, 1904), 1.10.
[16] Alwes, *Sons and Authors*, 112–26. On romances ostensibly addressed to women, but clearly directed at men, see also Lorna Hutson, *The Usurer's Daughter: Male Friendship and Fictions of Women in Sixteenth-Century England* (London: Routledge, 1994), 99, *passim*.

Chloe, Heliodorus's *Aethiopica*, and Achilles Tatius's *Leucippe and Clitophon*, all of which stress the role played by a perverse and unpredictable fortune in the lives of mortals, effecting astonishing coincidences, miraculous resurrections, and unhoped-for reconciliations on the capacious stage of the Mediterranean.[17] Fortune figures largely in Greene's work throughout his life, from the 'injurious fortune' that robs Mamillia of her husband Pharicles in his first romance to the card-games that rob the cony-catchers' victims of their purses in his final pamphlets. But for Greene, fortune is to a great extent an *internal* phenomenon—as Katharine Wilson has shown—whose processes are worked out through the kaleidoscopic changes of the mind and the language it uses.[18] Mamillia would never have lost Pharicles if he had not been unfaithful, or regained him if she had not been eloquent, active, and courageous. The cony-catchers rig all the games of chance by which they fleece their clients. Greene's romances, then, fuse the English writers' fascination with the most ungovernable aspects of human psychology with the generous geographical scale and twisted plotting of the Greeks; and ungovernable minds and devious plotting remained his topic when he turned his attention to the smaller stage of the London underworld at the close of his career.

A series of romances published in 1584 proclaim his preoccupation with themes relating to intractability on their title pages: *Morando: The Tritameron of Love*; *Arbasto: The Anatomy of Fortune*; and *Gwydonius: The Card of Fancy*. The protean forms of irresistible desire, the fluctuations of good and bad luck, and that tricky term fancy, which combines the senses of erotic attraction and of fantasy—a wilful turning away from what is deemed serious, stable, or 'true'—these are Greene's recurrent themes in all the literary forms he made his own. The first of these books, *Morando*, invites its reader to join a houseful of Italian nobles as they debate a series of *questioni d'amore* (questions of love) in imitation of Boccaccio's *Filocolo* and Castiglione's *Book of the Courtier*. But the second and third are more characteristic of Greene's mature romances, in that they expand the topographical and temporal scale of Gascoigne's and Lyly's fictions, inserting romantic attachments between men and women into the context of wars between nations, the twists and turns of whose progress imply the passage of considerable time as each tale unfolds. Time and its effects, indeed, are another abiding preoccupation of Greene's, enshrined in the title of his most popular romance, written in c.1585: *Pandosto: The Triumph of Time*.[19] This stress on time helps to underline the difference between romance and chronicle history. The term 'history' implies the orderly progress of an official narrative, a record committed to paper at the behest of human authorities. 'Time' stresses instead the operation of ungovernable forces that both 'plant and o'erwhelm custom' (to quote the play based on *Pandosto*, Shakespeare's *Winter's Tale*),[20] sweeping aside authority and institutions in

---

[17] For the influence of ancient Greek romance on Greene see Wilson, *Fictions of Authorship*, 85–111 and 124; Davis, *Idea and Act in Elizabethan Fiction*, 138–88; and Arthur F. Kinney, *Humanist Poetics* (Amherst: University of Massachusetts Press, 1986), 181–229.

[18] Wilson, *Fictions of Authorship*, 89–91.

[19] For the date of *Pandosto* see Newcomb, *Reading Popular Romance*, 55–6.

[20] Shakespeare, *The Winter's Tale*, 4.1.9.

favour of biological imperatives or sudden shifts of circumstance, very often brought about by random changes in the moods of individuals or populations. It is hardly surprising, then, to find that monarchs discover themselves subject to the most extreme fluctuations of fortune in Greene's romance. Love, fortune, fancy, and time—none of these can be constrained within the social or geographical boundaries set by government, and the solitary supreme governor—the monarch—is likely to discover this unwelcome fact more swiftly than anyone else. The deposed King of Denmark, Arbasto, alternately weeping and laughing in a hermit's cell before narrating his adventures, sums up the unstable universe of Greene's romances.

But despite the ambitious topography and time-scheme of *Arbasto*, *Gwydonius*, and *Pandosto*, all three are very short—a feature that helps bring out their thematic unity. Brevity was forced on Greene by the market; an Elizabethan author was only paid for a manuscript once, after which the rights to it passed to the printer, so that he found it more profitable to write several short pieces than a single long one, such as Sidney's *Arcadia*.[21] It was also in the author's interest to keep his readers entertained, so that they would keep demanding his work at the local bookstall. Variety as well as brevity was of the essence. Despite their similar themes, *Arbasto* and *Gwydonius* have different outcomes (tragic and comic respectively), while *Pandosto* ends as a tragicomedy, with both marriage and suicide. The three books experiment, too, with stylistic innovations. *Arbasto* is written in the first person—almost uniquely in Elizabethan fiction—while *Gwydonius* and *Pandosto* report dialogue in the manner of a play, dispensing with 'he said' and 'she said' in favour of speech prefixes, or relying on the reader to distinguish between unnamed speakers in successive paragraphs. Greene could be said, in fact, to have brought prose fiction closer to drama than ever before, forging romances, story collections, and pamphlets into a kind of paper playhouse, while making his greatest plays (*Friar Bacon and Friar Bungay* [c.1589] and *The Scottish History of James the Fourth* [c. 1590]) from the stuff of romance. Like a play in production, his prose fiction takes many risks, and its riskiness is both what made it popular and what damned it in the minds of its critics.

Gwydonius offers a fine example of the risks Greene was willing to take.[22] The opening section closely resembles Lyly's first *Euphues* book in plot, pace, and style; but as the narrative unfolds it persistently disrupts the expectations this resemblance might have raised in its first readers. Lyly's *Euphues* books inhabit a world where the older generation is exemplary in its conduct. *Gwydonius* opens instead with the portrait of a despot, Duke Clerophontes, who uses 'such mercilesse crueltie to his forraine enemies, and such modelesse rigour to his native Citizens, that it was doubtfull whether he was more feared of his foes for his crueltie, or hated of his friends for his tyrannie' (sig. B1r). Clerophontes rules part of Sicily, an island synonymous with tyranny in the Renaissance (a reputation

---

[21] For the economics of Greene's career, see Newcomb, *Reading Popular Romance*, 59–70.

[22] See the modern edition ed. by Carmine G. Di Biase, Barnabe Riche Society (Ottawa: Dovehouse, 2003). Andrew Hadfield offers an excellent analysis of *Gwydonius* in *Literature, Travel and Colonial Writing in the English Renaissance, 1545–1625* (Oxford: Clarendon Press, 1998), 180–4.

it owes to the tyrant Dionysius, who featured in the most celebrated English play of the 1560s, Richard Edwards's *Damon and Pythias*).[23] So it comes as no surprise that the Duke's son, too, is 'blemished with detestable qualyties' (sig. B1ᵛ). Where Euphues was an uncharacteristic product of the city of Athens, famous for brilliant statesmen and philosophers, Gwydonius is the spitting image of his despotic father, which lends an ironic flavour to the reams of good advice Clerophontes gives him. Pronounced by a man who is feared by his friends as much as his enemies, the Duke's injunctions to 'Be a friend to all, and a foe to none', to 'trust not without triall, nor commit any secret to a friendlye stranger', and to 'Lend not... a listning eare to the Alarums of love' (sig. B4ᵛ) strike the reader as deeply hypocritical—especially since Clerophontes considers killing his awkward son before deciding to advise him. No surprise, then, that when Gwydonius sets off on his travels, like Euphues before him, he promptly forgets his father's counsel—with predictable consequences: he is arrested in the first country he comes to for financial double-dealing. But he emerges from prison repentant and proceeds to seek employment at the court of an exemplary monarch, the Duke of Alexandria. Clearly, he is no Euphues or F.J., both of whom underwent protracted periods of cheerful prodigality before their downfalls. He has ceased to misbehave within the first few pages of his narrative; and from this point on, Greene's early readers would have had no notion what might happen to him.

The next stage of the narrative is just as unpredictable. In a mirror image of the opening, Duke Orlanio of Alexandria warns his daughter Castania to resist desire; but since Orlanio is as wise as Clerophontes was tyrannical—and since Castania derives her name from the Latin word for chaste (*casta*)—Greene's first readers no doubt assumed she would take heed of his warnings. Sure enough, she begins as a model of self-restraint. When young Valericus attempts to seduce her she rebuffs him in a series of speeches that get steadily blunter the more he persists. But the situation changes. Gwydonius too falls in love with her and she spurns him as she spurned Valericus. Where Valericus's persistence annoyed her, however, she is perversely delighted by Gwydonius's obstinacy. When he refuses to take no for an answer she is impressed by his commitment; and when he chooses to leave Egypt to spare her his unwelcome attentions, she can restrain herself no longer. She sends him a letter that has no equivalent in Lyly or Gascoigne: a declaration of love wholly free from irony or devious mind-games. 'What though the Duke my father be incensed against me, for making (in his minde) so carelesse a choice?' she writes ecstatically,

> What care I for his friendship, so I have thy favour[?] Let him fret, let my friends frowne, let livinges be lost, hap what hap wil, no misling showers of mischance, no boysterous blasts of adversitie, no terrible tempestes of disaster fortune, shall make my constant minde in any respect to move: no torments, no travaile, no care, no calamitie, no penurie, no povertie, no onelie the losse of life shall diminishe my love[:] in liew whereof remain thou but constant, and in pledge of my protested good will, have here my heart and hand, to be thine in duste and ashes. (sigs. M2ᵛ–M3ʳ)

---

[23] See Ros King, ed., *The Works of Richard Edwards* (Manchester: Manchester University Press, 2001).

It is hard to convey the full impact of this extraordinary passage. After Castania's fiercely rational resistance to her suitors, this bold articulation of desire comes as something of a shock even to the modern reader, who has been willing her to confess her love for many pages. But to its early readers it was surely far more shocking. The *Euphues* books lay great stress on the achievement of a moral and philosophical balance in life, an equilibrium that has its counterpart in the balanced clauses of Lyly's prose.[24] Emotion must be tempered with reason, Lyly contends, youthful self-interest with respect for the precepts of your elders, devotion to an individual with devotion to your monarch and country, or respect for the foreign state where you are a guest. The lack of such a balance leads to the humiliation of the prodigal hero in the first *Euphues* book and the achievement of it is what marks out the heroine Camilla in the second as exemplary. But in Greene's passage all balance is lost. Castania's commitment to her lover is absolute and her clauses reflect this in their failure to sustain the elegant dualisms, the succession of neatly paired clauses linked in sound and sense, for which Euphuism was famous. Instead, they build up, in a crescendo constructed from small alliterative units, to a statement of radical *imbalance*, of complete singleness of purpose; and to a final phrase in which alliteration, assonance, and caution are thrown to the winds: 'have here my heart and hand, to be thine in duste and ashes'.

Castania then signs off her letter with a casual blasphemy ('Thine, though the Gods say no', sig. M3ʳ) that might have left Elizabethan readers reeling. Her dismissal of her father's opinion, swiftly followed by a hubristic dismissal of the gods themselves, would in any earlier romance have served as prologue to disaster; and her total reliance on the former libertine Gwydonius ('remain thou but constant') seems to show where disaster will come from. So when Gwydonius's father Clerophontes declares war on Alexandria, the lovers' fate seems sealed. Gwydonius has told neither Castania nor her father that he is Clerophontes's son; to do so now would be fatal; he is therefore trapped in an impossible situation, branded liar and traitor by a twist of fate. The stage is set for a tragic dénouement, which seems all the more likely given the tragic ending of Greene's previous romance, *Arbasto*.

It is the jealous Valericus—Castania's would-be lover—who sets the final act in motion. He makes the double discovery that Castania loves Gwydonius and that Clerophontes is Gwydonius's father; and he gleefully leaks these discoveries to Orlanio, delighted at the chance to humiliate the woman who rejected him. Orlanio responds less like an Egyptian statesman than a Sicilian tyrant, clapping Gwydonius in jail and locking up his daughter, though not before informing her—as every father should—of the reason for her punishment. 'Hath the force of love,' he rants, 'nay rather the furie of lust (vild wretch) so blinded thy understanding, that to accomplish it thou passest not to pervert both humane and divine lawes?' (sig. Q2ʳ). Some of Greene's first readers, no doubt, would have sympathized with the Duke's position; everyone knew, after all, that 'lascivious affection' (sig. Q2ʳ) must be resisted, laws honoured, gods and dukes obeyed. At the same time, they may have found the venom of his language unsettling. And when Orlanio concludes his speech by condemning his daughter to death for a crime she did not commit—a sentence from which she is only saved by the intervention of her brother—it is clear that he is fast becoming a

---

[24] See my *Elizabethan Fictions*, chap. 6.

second Clerophontes. The moral high ground has in fact been lost by this stage in the narrative. The older generation have shown themselves as irascible and impulsive as the young; the counsellors have discarded their own good counsel; and the just ruler seems as capable of breaking the law as his unjust neighbour. All moral direction has gone, and with it any lingering convictions as to where the tale is going.

The ending serves only to compound the early reader's confusion. Gwydonius escapes from prison—again with the help of Castania's brother—and learns that his father has invaded Alexandria. But he also learns that the war has reached an impasse, which the invaders seek to resolve by challenging their enemies to single combat, control of both the dukedoms being the prize. Clerophontes (who is 'huge of stature', sig. R3^v) offers himself as the Sicilian invaders' champion, but the Alexandrians have no champion of equal strength. After a short internal struggle, Gwydonius makes up his mind to accept the challenge on behalf of Alexandria, fighting against his father to defend his lover, betraying his country to display his faith to his future wife. And he expresses this decision in the book's most disturbing passage. 'Is not (fond foole) necessitie above nature?' he soliloquizes. 'Is not the lawe of love above King or Keysar, Father or Friends, God or the Divell? Yes. And so I meane to take it: for either I will valiantly win the conquest and my *Castania*, or lose the victorie, and so by death ende my miseries' (sigs. S3^v–T1^r). There is no attempt here at reasoned argument; this is the language of raw passion, aggravated by treason, prospective parricide, and blasphemy—the latter not even mitigated, this time round, by being directed at the pagan gods. The duel ends in triumph for Gwydonius, an outcome that ensures a reconciliation of the warring nations when he weds Castania. But the moment when he reveals his identity leaves the onlookers baffled; Sicilians and Alexandrians alike stand 'astonished at this strange Tragedie, doubting [...] whether they dreampt of such a rare device, or saw it in effect' (sig. T1^v). And this self-conscious pointing up of the 'rare device' Greene has effected—a plot with all the hallmarks of tragedy, capped with a happy conclusion—indicates his awareness that he has done something new and controversial, a special effect on paper to match the special effects that were dazzling spectators on the London stage. No Elizabethan reader could have predicted such an outcome for the tale Greene had been telling, peopled as it is with rebellious youngsters, erring parents, treason, jealousy, injustice, unprovoked aggression between nations, and the rhetoric of unreason. Neither of the most celebrated literary prodigals of the previous decade—F.J. or Euphues—was permitted to get his girl as Greene's does; and neither of them went so far in their resistance to authority. The ending of *Gwydonius* is designed to be bewildering; as bewildering as the more familiar ending of *Pandosto*, in which a 'comical event', the marriage of Dorastus and Fawnia, is undermined by a 'tragical stratagem' (pp. 224–5), as Fawnia's father, King Pandosto, is seized with remorse for his acts of jealousy, murder, and incest and kills himself in a fit of depression.[25] With these two romances, Greene effectively tore up the script for the kind of moral instruction a writer of fiction was expected to offer his public.

---

[25] All references to *Pandosto* are taken from J. H. P. Pafford, ed., *The Winter's Tale*, The Arden Shakespeare (London: Methuen, 1963), Appendix 4.

The instability of *Gwydonius* can be summed up in the changing connotations of the term 'fancy' in the romance. The subtitle—*The Card of Fancy*—suggests it is a verbal chart or map of the affections, although a 'card' could also be a compass or a component in a card-game.[26] Fancy in Greene's work can only be mapped, its course traced like that of a storm-tossed vessel; it can be won with luck, like a game of cards, but it cannot be shaped, directed, or expunged. At the beginning of the romance it is unequivocally a force to be resisted. Gwydonius, in his prodigal phase, 'follow[s] wilfullye the furie of his owne frantike fancie' (sig. B2^r), though he is warned against it by his father, while Orlanio would have his daughter shun 'the stiffeling stormes of unbridled fancie' (sig. C4^v). For the greater part of the book she obeys his instructions, conscious of fancy's alliterative affinity with frenzy, folly, and fickleness. Valericus's 'fading fancie' (sig. E4^r)—another negative alliteration—seems to prove her right, since it speedily converts itself to 'extreame hate' (sig. F2^v). But fancy that endures is a different matter. Gwydonius's refusal to be put off his 'fixed fancie' (sig. H4^v) by denials soon infects Castania with the same condition ('O lawlesse Love,' she chides herself in a panic, 'O fancie, fraught full of phrensie and furie', sig. I3^r), then convinces her that his feelings are lasting (he shows 'no signes of fleeting fancie, but of firme affection', sig. M1^v). Yet, the lovers' now mutual attachment continues to bear the same name. When Gwydonius is considering whether he should fight his father he describes his love of Castania as 'fancie' (sig. S1^r) and Castania concurs, acknowledging the 'force of fancie' while in prison for Gwydonius's sake (sig. Q4^r). Laden as it has been with negative connotations in the first half of the romance, the term's continued use in the second half is unsettling. Indeed, the frequency with which it is repeated makes one suspect Greene is *trying* to unsettle us; so too does his use of 'fancy', rather than 'love', which has more positive connotations in the romance tradition. What then was Greene's intention in rendering the key term of his book so radically unstable?

Greene's point, it seems, is that time determines meaning.[27] A term used one day will have a different meaning the next, depending on who uses it and under what conditions. This is confirmed by the imprisoned lovers' reliance on *time* to resolve their crises. Gwydonius expresses his certainty that 'the Gods... will *in tract of time* ridde us from blame' (sig. Q3^v), while Castania contends that '*in time* we shall have such happie successe, as the loyaltie of our love, and the cleerenesse of our conscience [...] doo deserve' (sigs. Q4^v–R1^r). It is the length of time he remains loyal that confirms Gwydonius's constancy, and time that ensures that his betrayal of father and country acquires legitimacy—if he had lost the single combat he would have been a traitor, but once it is won he can claim that 'the destinies by my meanes have decreed' that the Dukes and their countries should be reconciled (sig. T1^r). So too the word fancy changes its meaning

---

[26] For 'card' as meaning part of a compass, see Helmut Bonheim, 'Robert Greene's *Gwydonius. The Carde of Fancie*', *Anglia, Zeitschrift für englische Philologie*, 96 (1978): 45–64. For 'card' as map, see 'Card' n. 2 *OED* <http://www.oed.com/view/Entry/27830?rskey=F0VKFT&result=2&isAdvanced=false#eid> accessed 18 March 2013. For the playing card sense, see John Lyly, *Euphues*, ed. Leah Scragg (Manchester: Manchester University Press, 2003), 88.

[27] See my 'Robert Greene and the Uses of Time', *Writing Robert Greene*, 157–88.

according to the moment when it is uttered; there is no single enduring interpretation of a given term and no human agency has any more power to fix a word's meaning than to ensure the outcome of a fight between two evenly-matched contestants. The consistent failures of the legal system in Greene's romances—from Orlanio's summary condemnation of Castania to the King's spontaneous dismissal of the evidence at the trial in *Pandosto*—confirms the impossibility of containing language, even in the interests of legislation. And if language cannot be contained even in the law courts, what hope is there of holding its most powerful users, hereditary monarchs, to account? What hope is there of justice, outside the bounds of a well-executed romance?

Gwydonius's reference to the 'destinies' implies that some supernatural agency may be at work in Greene's universe, ensuring that justice is done in the fullness of time. But the pagan setting of the young man's adventures—the same 'ancient' Mediterranean context Greene uses for *Pandosto*, *Menaphon* (1589), and his story-collections *Penelope's Web*, *Euphues His Censure*, and *Perimedes the Blacksmith*—undermines the characters' conviction that a benevolent destiny, fate, or providence guides their actions. Atrocities are committed—the effective murder of Bellaria in *Pandosto*, the pointless massacres of armies and populations in *Arbasto*, *Gwydonius*, and *Menaphon*—which can hardly be compensated for by an eventual royal marriage. And if the gods may be conveniently questioned in this ancient setting, so too may the mortals they have put in power. The murderous irascibility of Duke Clerophontes is shared by the Kings of Bohemia and Sicily in *Pandosto*, by King Democles in *Menaphon*, and by the King of Denmark in *Arbasto*—which, despite its Northern setting, is clearly set in the pre-Christian world, since it opens with the first-person narrator offering a sacrifice to Astarte in the Phoenician city of Sidon.[28] Time, in fact, is consistently deployed in these romances as an instrument for undermining the power of monarchy—both by implying that all rulers will finally be judged as they deserve once the passing years have robbed them of their crowns and also by demonstrating the extent to which they share their subjects' inability to manipulate history, despite all their efforts to control the narratives of which they form part.

The romance that most insistently stresses this monarchic helplessness is *Pandosto: The Triumph of Time*. Here the term 'time' is repeated as often, and deployed to as many contradictory purposes, as 'fancy' in *Gwydonius*. It is the 'computation of time' (p. 192) that convinces the jealous monarch Pandosto that his wife is pregnant by Egistus—just as it is the 'time of the year' (p. 224) when she was found that eventually helps him identify his long-lost daughter. Pandosto's cupbearer, Franion, disobeys his orders to kill Egistus, certain that his master will forgive his disobedience 'when time should pacify his anger' (p. 189). The opening of the story casts Franion's certainty in doubt by defining jealousy as the only passion impossible to cure 'by tract of time' (p. 184). But such proverbial encapsulations of universal laws have a way of collapsing, in Greene's world, in the face of experience. Despite Pandosto's efforts to pervert the course of justice, his wife

---

[28] The opening is based on Achilles Tatius's *Leucippe and Clitophon*: see Wilson, *Fictions of Authorship*, 89.

is proved innocent, then dies from the stress she has been under; and at this point, time becomes punishment, as Pandosto embarks on an extended programme of contrition, visiting her tomb 'once a day' to mourn her death (p. 199). Later we learn 'how fortune is plumed with time's feathers and how she can minister strange causes to breed strange effects' (p. 178), as Pandosto's lost daughter Fawnia finds her way back to him, preparing the way for the tragicomic ending. The reference to 'strange causes' and 'strange effects' recalls *Gwydonius*'s 'straunge Tragedie' and 'rare device', with their acknowledgement of Greene's gleeful violation of generic expectations. Both romances render themselves strange by demonstrating how far the tragic and the comic are subject to time. If *Pandosto* had ended with Bellaria's death, its tragic status would have been indisputable. If the romance had come to a close with Fawnia's marriage, its ending would have been comic. But by repeatedly carrying through his narrative to the next abrupt change of circumstances, Greene demonstrates the arbitrary nature of generic divisions, and with them the arbitrariness of divisions based on social status, personal reputation, morals, and national identity (nearly all his romances end with a marriage that renegotiates boundaries between nations or city states). Where language itself is arbitrary, as the changing connotations of 'time' and 'fancy' suggest, no human institution can be sure of retaining its identity for long.

It is hardly surprising, then, if Greene should have made his own crisis of identity as an author the subject of his later fictions. His use of a succession of different mottoes on the title pages of his books suggests he was always intensely aware of the image of himself he presented to his readers—and aware too that it was constantly changing.[29] The range of his dedicatees, too, from unknown friends to the highest nobles in the land (*Gwydonius* is dedicated to the Earl of Oxford), demonstrates his willingness to redefine his social position from one book to the next.[30] Then, in about 1590, he started to include his name in the titles of his books, a sign both of his growing commercial success and of his growing interest in weaving his own story into his fictions. And this practice marked a major new stage in his lifetime quest for innovation.

The bulk of his publications with 'Greene' in their titles contain quasi-Chaucerian recantations of his earlier romances. Chaucerian pilgrims feature often, seeking redemption through travel in some unspecified, explicitly non-Catholic way; and in one of them, *Greene's Vision*, Greene even meets the ghost of Chaucer himself, who praises his work.[31] Chaucer renounced his non-religious writings at the end of his life, but Greene's renunciation is far more protracted, lasting from 1590 till his death in 1592. *Greene's Vision* suggests that he gave careful thought to this timing, since he deferred its publication from the year of its writing—1590—till that of his death. Partly no doubt, this deferral occurred

---

[29] On Greene's use of mottoes see Wilson, *Fictions of Authorship*, 166–7.

[30] On Greene's dedications see Melnikoff and Gieskes, eds., *Writing Robert Greene*, 'Introduction', 9–10; and Derek Alwes, 'Robert Greene's Duelling Dedications', *English Literary Renaissance*, 30.3 (2000), 373–95.

[31] A more detailed account of *Greene's Vision* in relation to time is given in my 'Robert Greene and the Uses of Time', *Writing Robert Greene*, 182–7.

because he was not yet ready to turn his talents to theology, as he promises he will in the pamphlet. Perhaps, though, he also deferred because of some deep ambivalence about the need for recantation, making his claims to contrition as double-sided as his representation of himself in the *Groatsworth* as the trickster tricked.

Greene's rejections of romance are nearly all romances, from his lyrical retelling of the story of the Prodigal Son, *Greene's Mourning Garment* (1590), to the story-collection in which he traces the forms of human stupidity, including his own, *Greene's Farewell to Folly* (1591). *Gwydonius* and *Pandosto* show why he felt the need to stage a repudiation of his earlier work, with their scandalous breach of Elizabethan conventions regarding the didactic function of fiction. But they also show how hard it would be for Greene to stage some final repentance, since moods, convictions, affections, even the definition of right and wrong are always changing with the passing time. Perhaps the *only* way to promise reformation, for Greene, was to acknowledge its contingent nature by deferring the moment of that promise's fulfilment till an unspecified moment beyond the limits of the text in which the promise is made.

The supreme statement of the principle of deferral in Greene's writing is the two-part, quasi-autobiographical romance *Greene's Never too Late* (1590). Its title anticipates the risk Greene ran two years later, in the year of his terminal illness: if it is never too late to repent, there is a danger that contrition will be repeatedly put off until the hour of doom, when Greene is represented in the various versions of his deathbed scene scrawling letters to his abandoned wife in which he begs her to pay off his debts—procrastinating payment, in fact, until after the breath has left his body. It might even be said that *Greene's Never too Late* predicts a future scenario for its author very much like this one. At the end of Part One, its protagonist, Francesco, declares his intention to reform himself and go back to his wife, whom he has abandoned just as Greene is said to have abandoned his; and Francesco echoes the narrative's title as he makes this decision: 'remember this… *Nunquam sera est ad bonos mores via*' [it's never too late to take the path of righteousness] (p. 61).[32] But it is not until three-quarters of the way through Part Two that the prodigal husband finally summons up the will to go home to his spouse. And the repentance pamphlets of 1592, which point up the link between Francesco's life and Greene's, imply that even this eventual return was either a fictional or an impermanent one. The *Groatsworth* finds the author back in London, dying in debt to his landlady and as far as ever from his wife. The operation of time in his works precludes the kind of neat Prodigal Son narrative, where a rebellious young man falls on hard times and returns chastened to the path of good conduct, which was the staple of so much Elizabethan fiction and drama.[33] Greene's world is dominated by fortune, not providence; in it, men's minds are subject to fancy and folly, rather than reason; and as a result, no orderly pattern of cause and effect can be guaranteed, no ending certain until the very last page of a romance has been written, the very last heartbeat of a man's life stilled.

---

[32] Quoted from the 1590 edition, *STC* 12253.

[33] The fullest account of the Prodigal Son motif in the period is Richard Helgerson, *The Elizabethan Prodigals* (Berkeley and Los Angeles: University of California Press, 1976).

This is what makes Greene's work so lively and so dramatic. In his celebrated cony-catching pamphlets, the author's bad behaviour in London—the reason for his need for repentance—supplies him with the raw material for a witty exposition of the seamier side of London life; while the very act of exposition puts him in danger of retaliation from the men and women whose crimes he exposes, so that each new cony-catching pamphlet becomes an instalment in a game of cat-and-mouse played out (Greene would have us believe) between the London mafia and the intrepid pamphleteer. Printed paper becomes a performance, implicitly stirring up frantic action in the underworld each time it leaves the press and whipping its audience into frenzied anticipation of the next instalment as each pamphlet ends. We are beginning to learn once again how to appreciate Greene's various performances in his prose. And in doing so, we are learning to read with renewed excitement a forgotten, but vital chapter in the story of the novel.

Further Reading

Alwes, Derek. *Sons and Authors in Elizabethan England* (Newark, DE: University of Delaware Press, 2004).
Barbour, Reid. *Deciphering Elizabethan Fiction* (Newark, DE: University of Delaware Press, 1993).
Clark, Sandra. *The Elizabethan Pamphleteers* (Rutherford, NJ: Fairleigh Dickinson University Press, 1983).
Crupi, Charles. *Robert Greene* (Boston: Twayne Publishers, 1986).
Davis, Walter R. *Idea and Act in Elizabethan Fiction* (Princeton: Princeton University Press, 1969).
Hadfield, Andrew. *Literature, Travel and Colonial Writing in the English Renaissance, 1545–1625* (Oxford: Clarendon Press, 1998).
Helgerson, Richard. *The Elizabethan Prodigals* (Berkeley and Los Angeles: University of California Press, 1976).
Kinney, Arthur F. *Humanist Poetics* (Amherst: University of Massachusetts Press, 1986).
Margolies, David. *Novel and Society in Elizabethan England* (Totowa, NJ: Barnes and Noble, 1985).
Melnikoff, Kirk, and Edward Gieskes, eds. *Writing Robert Greene* (Aldershot: Ashgate, 2008).
Mentz, Steve. *Romance for Sale in Early Modern England: The Rise of Prose Fiction* (Aldershot: Ashgate 2006).
Newcomb, Lori Humphrey. *Reading Popular Romance in Early Modern England* (New York: Columbia University Press, 2002).
Wilson, Katharine. *Fictions of Authorship in Late Elizabethan Narratives* (Oxford: Clarendon Press, 2006).

CHAPTER 13

NASHE'S STUFF

JASON SCOTT-WARREN

> History consists of action; and how unimportant beside this is the question of writing or not writing, how wholly immaterial, beside the fact of doing and making, is the word that describes them.[1]

> Nor is the definition [of material culture] limited only to matter in the solid state. Fountains are liquid examples, as are lily ponds, and material that is partly gas includes hot air balloons and neon signs... Even language is part of material culture, a prime example of it in its gaseous state. Words, after all, are air masses shaped by the speech apparatus according to culturally acquired rules.[2]

On 4 August 1589, a group of radical puritans arrived in Warrington in Lancashire; hidden in their cart were a dismantled printing press, three cases of type, twelve reams of paper, and a supply of ink. They had just completed a six-day journey from Wolston, near Coventry, and were on their way to a new safe house, where they would print the latest in a sequence of spectacularly inflammatory pamphlets designed to shake the foundations of the established church. But as the radicals unloaded their equipment, a case fell on the ground and some type dropped out. The onlookers did not recognize the curious bits of metal and stood 'marvayling what they shold be'. One of the printers, John Hodgkins, thinking on his feet, 'answered they were shott', and was apparently believed. But news of the incident got about and ten days later the insurgents were tracked down to a rented house just outside Manchester. They were taken to London, possibly tortured, and prosecuted for their part in creating the print sensation that was 'Martin Marprelate', who had transformed the terms of engagement by turning

---

[1] Friedrich Ratzel, *The History of Mankind* (1896), 5, quoted in Dan Hicks, 'The Material Culture Turn', in Dan Hicks and Mary C. Beaudry, eds., *The Oxford Handbook of Material Culture Studies* (Oxford: Oxford University Press, 2010), 31.

[2] James Deetz, *In Small Things Forgotten: An Archaeology of Early American Life* (New York: Anchor Books, 1977), 24–5, quoted in Hicks, 'Material Culture Turn', 48.

theological debate into knockabout comedy. 'For jesting is lawful by circumstances, even in the greatest matters.'[3]

Hodgkins's improvised cover story—the disguising of print as shot—is superbly apt to the nature of the violent pamphlet war in which he was engaged. (The printer had apparently spent time working as a 'saltpeterman', a maker of gunpowder; one commentator judged that this made him 'a good printer for such saltpeter and gunnepowder workes').[4] For Martin, laying down a syllogism against the 'petty antichrists, petty popes, proud prelates' was like initiating a bout in a wrestling match, and was best prefaced with a snarl: 'Then have at you'. He delighted in threats of violence, as when he bluntly told the Dean of Salisbury that he would 'shortly...have twenty fists about [his] ears', or (elsewhere) argued him into a noose: 'Thus you see brother Bridges, M. Marprelate...hath proved you to have deserved a caudle of hempseed, and a plaster of neckweed, as well as some of your brethren the papists.'[5] Martin's threats were returned with interest by those writers who were employed by the authorities to answer him in his own vein. The anonymous *Papp with a Hatchet* (1589)—the title of which promises baby food with a lethal cutting-edge—is typical in its fantasies of retribution: 'O here were a notable full point, to leaue *Martin* in the hangmans apron; Nay, he would be glad to scape with hanging, weele first haue him lasht through the Realme with cordes, that when he comes to the gallowes, he may be bleeding newe.'[6] Such lurid imaginings were rendered the more desperate by the fact that nobody knew who or where 'Martin' was—there *was* no body to lash and hang.[7] The anti-Martinists compensated for this by forcing a body on their adversary, bringing him 'attired like an Ape on the stage', so that he could be 'wormd and launced [and]...made a Maygame'.[8] Or they treated Martin's books as his body. In the anonymous *Return of the Renowned Caualiero Pasquill* (1589), Pasquill reports that he has just received a new pamphlet, 'olde *Martins* Protestation in Octauo...I see by the volume, hee languisheth euery day more and more, the pride of his flesh is so much falne, that you may tell euery bone in hys body now' (I 100). The *Protestation* (1589), Martin's last gasp, had been partly typeset by amateurs, and the impending collapse of the Martinist enterprise can be read in the book's disheveled lines of print and in a welter of turned or missing letters. In a period when it was the fate of banned books to be burned by the common hangman, Pasquill's equation between the book and the body made sense.

---

[3] Joseph L. Black, ed., *The Martin Marprelate Tracts: A Modernized and Annotated Edition* (Cambridge: Cambridge University Press, 2008), liv–lv, 115.

[4] Black, ed., *Marprelate Tracts*, liii.

[5] Black, ed., *Marprelate Tracts*, 10, 16, 1, 19.

[6] Anon, *Papp with a Hatchet* (London: T. Orwin, 1589), C4^r.

[7] For the relative shares of the Welsh Presbyterian polemicist John Penry and the Warwickshire gentleman Job Throkmorton in writing the tracts, see Black, ed., *Marprelate Tracts*, xxxvi–xlvi.

[8] *The Works of Thomas Nashe*, ed. R. B. McKerrow, rev. F. P. Wilson, 5 vols (Oxford: Blackwell, 1958), III 354 (subsequent references are supplied parenthetically); Neil Rhodes, *Elizabethan Grotesque* (London: Routledge & Kegan Paul, 1980), 66; Charles Nicholl, *A Cup of News: The Life of Thomas Nashe* (London: Routledge, 1984), 68.

Thomas Nashe cut his teeth on the Marprelate Controversy, to which he contributed at least one pamphlet. His writings are full of echoes of Martin's style, with its unpredictable interplay between the spoken and the written, its mock-politeness and blatant sarcasm, and its running celebration of its own wit and playfulness, as contrasted with the leaden dullness of the enemy. The extent of Nashe's Marprelate-envy is suggested by the name he gave to one of his earliest literary personae, Pierce Penilesse, which borrows Martin's alliteration and his self-conscious plainness (albeit with reference to the rustics of Spenser's *The Shepheardes Calender*, rather than to Luther). As one pamphlet war (the Marprelate Controversy) turned into another (his long-running feud with the Cambridge scholar and civil lawyer Gabriel Harvey), Nashe's name became a byword for textual violence. A Cambridge student comedy, *The Returne from Parnassus*, written around the time of his death in 1601, calls him 'a great schole-boy giuing the world a bloudy nose' and (more flatteringly) says that he 'carryed the deadly Stockado in his pen' (a 'stoccado' was a stab with a pointed weapon).[9] Charles Fitzgeffrey, in a Latin elegy for Nashe published in the same year, wrote that Death had to steal 'the lad's armed tongue and his terrible pen, those twin thunderbolts' before she could attack; otherwise 'Death herself would have feared to die'.[10] Michael Drayton allows Nashe, 'although he but a proser were', a place in the catalogue of poets he included in a verse epistle to Henry Reynolds. 'Sharply *Satirick* was he', judges Drayton, adding that 'Those words shall hardly be set downe with inke;/ Shall scorch and blast, so as his could, where he,/Would inflict vengeance'.[11] Sir William Vaughan, in a medical treatise, recalled how '*Thomas Nash* a scurrilous Pamphleter in *Q. Elizabeths* dayes, vsed to drinke *Aqua vitae with Gun-powder* to inspire his malicious spirit with rayling matter... Which inflaming Potion wrought so eagerly vppon his Braine, that hee would often beate himselfe about the noddle, and scratch the Walls round about him, vntill hee met with some *extrauagant* furious Termes.'[12] Vaughan was only slightly misreporting Nashe's own boast: 'I haue tearmes (if I be vext) laid in steepe in *Aquafortis*, & Gunpowder, that shall rattle through the Skyes, and make an Earthquake in a Pesants eares' (I 195), while Drayton recalls the terms of Nashe's praise of the 'scourge of Princes', Pietro Aretino, whose 'pen was sharp pointed lyke a poinyard; no leafe he wrote on but was lyke a burning glasse to set on fire all his readers' (II 264).[13] More charmingly, Nashe compared his 'sweetly sour and pleasantly sharp' style to the sting of a bee, 'a creature not so bigge as a Wart with thorough hairs on an

---

[9] J. B. Leishman, ed., *The Three Parnassus Plays* (London: Ivor Nicholson & Watson, 1949), 227, 245.

[10] *Caroli Fitzgeofridi Affaniae* (Oxford: Joseph Barnes, 1601), fol. N3r ('Armatum juueni linguam calamumque tremendum/(Fulmina bina) priùs insidiosa rapit'; 'Ipsa quidem metuit mors truculenta mori'); translation by Dana F. Sutton at http://www.philological.bham.ac.uk/affaniae/ceneng.html#29 (accessed 29 January 2011).

[11] Michael Drayton, *The Battaile of Agincourt* (London: William Lee, 1627), fol. 2D1v.

[12] Sir William Vaughan, *The Newlanders Cure* (London: F. Constable, 1630), fol. B2v. Vaughan may have gained his acquaintance with Nashe when writing his study of *The Spirit of Detraction* (London: George Norton, 1611); see fos. P1r–3r for his strictures on railing pamphleteers.

[13] Nashe distances himself from Aretino's atheism at *Works*, I 285. See further Rhodes, *Grotesque*, 26–36.

old wiues chin, yet he is priuiledged, in so much as he is free of Honny lane, to bestir him with his sting as ordinarily as a Sergeant with his mace' (II 185).

All of these comments testify to the overwhelming physicality of Nashe's style. Nashe bites (the pun on 'gnash' was current in his lifetime).[14] His satirical vein is like a sword-thrust, a punch on the nose, a bee-sting; his words are steeped in gunpowder, or inspired by drinking it, as well as by fits of head-banging and wall-scratching. Not coincidentally, his writing has an extraordinary power to evoke the world and the body ('a creature not so bigge as a Wart with thorough hairs on an old wiues chin'). While it is common (in the manner of my first epigraph) to oppose words and deeds and to think of language as a disembodied system that floats above the world of 'brute objects', Nashe's writings invite us to reflect on the extent to which words are deeds and texts are things.

This makes Nashe a useful writer to think with at a moment when early modern studies, and humanities research more generally, is awash with physicality and materiality, with objects of all kinds. The current fascination with material culture has drawn our attention to items of clothing and changes in fashion; to domestic interiors and home furnishings; to the 'face-furniture' of hairstyles and beards; to new technologies and their consequences; and to practices of shopping, collection, and display (among many other subjects). Such studies have opened up a new interdisciplinary space, a ground upon which historians, art historians, anthropologists, archaeologists, literary critics, and museum curators meet. But they have also provoked resistance from literary scholars who complain that the 'thing' is an under-theorized distraction from the core business of textual and historical interpretation. Jonathan Gil Harris worries that the new materialism is merely a new antiquarianism, delivering fetishized, static objects which convey the illusion of touching the past without the need for interpretation. He urges us to recognize that matter is always in motion and that it is only in its mobility, mutability, and transience that it becomes meaningful.[15] For Douglas Bruster, the new materialism is a distraction from the older Marxist tradition 'of materialist criticism concerned with the momentous transition to the modern, proto-capitalist world'. Subjects such as 'class struggle, hegemony, or ideology' are having to make way for 'objects in the world: clothing, crockery, sugar'. The 'critical fetishism' of this turn risks 'replacing large with small and the intangible with what is capable of being touched or held'.[16] Having said that, Bruster goes on to suggest that we should start 'taking sixteenth- and seventeenth-century materialist thought seriously' by attending

---

[14] Harvey asks 'who can tell, what dowty yoonker may next gnash with his teeth?'; *Fovre Letters, and Certaine Sonnets* (London: John Wolfe, 1592), fol. D3ʳ.

[15] Jonathan Gil Harris, 'Shakespeare's Hair: Staging the Object of Material Culture', *Shakespeare Quarterly*, 52 (2001): 479–91 (479–80). See further idem, *Untimely Matter in the Age of Shakespeare* (Philadelphia: University of Pennsylvania Press, 2009).

[16] Douglas Bruster, 'The New Materialism in Early Modern Studies', in *Shakespeare and the Question of Culture* (Basingstoke: Palgrave Macmillan, 2003), 191–206, esp. 192, 194, 204. See also James A. Knapp and Jeffrey Pence, 'Between Thing and Theory', *Poetics Today*, 24.4 (2003): 641–71; and the telling discussion of commoditization and fetishism in Ann Rosalind Jones and Peter Stallybrass, *Renaissance Clothing and the Materials of Memory* (Cambridge: Cambridge University Press, 2000), 7–11.

to figurations and theorizations of materiality in the works of just such writers as Nashe.[17]

This chapter aims to follow up that suggestion and to explore the nature of the 'stuff' purveyed by the author of *Nashes Lenten Stuffe*.[18] But as we begin that investigation, it is worth pausing to reconsider the critiques of Bruster, Gil Harris, and their ilk in the light of arguments elaborated by the anthropologist Daniel Miller in his recent book *Stuff*. For their interventions might well be understood as part of what Miller calls 'a larger denigration of material culture in our own society, where materialism itself is viewed as superficial'.[19] If such things as clothing, appearance, style, and shopping are understood as affairs of the surface, then those who study them might also be tainted with superficiality—hence (until recently) the 'extremely low status' of material culture studies within the discipline of anthropology.[20] As Miller argues, one of the culprits here is the Western intellectual's embrace of a '*depth ontology*', which has it that '*being*—what we truly are—is located deep inside ourselves and is in direct opposition to the surface. A clothes shopper is shallow because a philosopher or a saint—and here we might also include 'a literary/cultural theorist'—'is deep'.[21] A second factor that stokes anxiety about the study of material culture is what Miller calls 'the humility of things', their surprising capacity 'to fade out of focus and remain peripheral to our vision, and yet determinant of our behaviour and identity'.[22] In his analysis, objects furnish defining frames for our behaviour, and to draw attention to them is to provoke an indefinable sense of embarrassment. None of this is to deny that objects require theorization; the process of 'thinking through things' poses numerous conceptual challenges. But recent anthropological work suggests that this process needs also to be material (engaged with the distinctive properties of objects) and visceral.[23]

One way to begin an investigation into Nashe and materiality is to ask what his writing does to conventional ideas of *textual* substance—where the meat of a text is the *res* or thing, the content, which is articulated by means of the words (*verba*). One of the most celebrated and debated critical assessments of Nashe's works is C. S. Lewis's claim that

> though Nashe's pamphlets are commercial literature, they come very close to being, in another way, 'pure' literature: literature which is, as nearly as possible, without a subject. In a certain sense of the verb 'say', if asked what Nashe 'says', we should have to reply, Nothing. He tells no story, expresses no thought, maintains no attitude.

---

[17] Bruster, 'Materialism', 204–5.

[18] For earlier meditations on Nashe's material worlds, see Henry S. Turner, 'Nashe's Red Herring: Epistemologies of the Commodity in Lenten Stuffe (1599)', *English Literary History*, 68 (2001): 529–61; and Julian Yates, *Error Misuse Failure: Object Lessons from the English Renaissance* (Minneapolis: University of Minnesota Press, 2003), chap. 4.

[19] Daniel Miller, *Stuff* (Cambridge: Polity Press, 2010), 22.

[20] Miller, *Stuff*, 51.

[21] Miller, *Stuff*, 16.

[22] Miller, *Stuff*, 50–1.

[23] See especially Nicole Boivin, *Material Cultures, Material Minds: The Role of Things in Human Thought, Society and Evolution* (Cambridge: Cambridge University Press, 2008).

Even his angers seem to be part of his technique rather than real passions. In his exhilarating whirlwind of words we find not thought nor passion but simply images: images of ludicrous and sometimes frightful incoherence boiling up from a dark void.[24]

There is much that one might take issue with here—the idea that there exists something called 'pure' literature, which is without content; the idea that Nashe says nothing (which he might have thought strange, given his clearly enunciated views about hypocritical puritans, miserly patrons, and the children of East Anglian ropemakers). Nonetheless, Lewis's statement testifies to the inescapable suspicion that Nashe's writing inverts the usual relationship between content and style, *res* and *verba*. Where the classical rhetorical tradition insists on the primacy of *res*, and criticizes those who pursue style at the expense of substance, Nashe perversely forces our attention to his 'vaine', a vaine which he insists is utterly original, 'of my owne begetting, and cals no man father in England but my selfe' (I 319). Instead of 'a subject', we are presented with an 'exhilarating whirlwind of words'. Or, to follow the classical tropes, instead of a soul, Nashe gives us a body; instead of a body, he gives us clothing.[25]

But these dichotomies are never simple. When Daniel Miller explores the interlacing of people's identities with their clothing, he reverses the familiar polarities of surface and depth, suggesting that identity is made on the outside, in the interaction between our bodies and objects. Such an interaction is anticipated in the classical rhetorician's understanding of style. Although style and substance, *verba* and *res*, could be separated in theory, in practice they were inextricable; the process by which a soul found its body or a body its clothes was imperceptible. Nor was the surface a matter of trifling ornament. The tropes and schemes of rhetoric provided the *res* with its armour and its weapons. The word 'ornament' derives from the Latin 'ornare', meaning 'to fit out, equip, adorn', often with a militaristic aim.[26] Nashe's invectives, with their 'tearmes...laid in steepe in *Aquafortis*, & Gunpowder', their 'whole artillerie store of eloquence', flex stylistic muscle (I 195, 321). At one delightful moment in his paper-war with Harvey, Nashe magnanimously declares that his enemy 'hath some good words, but he cannot writhe them and tosse them to and fro nimbly, or so bring them about, that hee maye make one streight thrust at his enemies face' (I 282). Here it is a complex interaction of style and meaning (the *point* or *pointedness* of an utterance) that makes polemic deadly (or not).

More generally, throughout his writings, Nashe enjoys confounding the traditional opposition between surface and depth. Amid the hellfire sermonizing of *Christs Teares*

---

[24] C. S. Lewis, *English Literature in the Sixteenth Century Excluding Drama* (Oxford: Clarendon Press, 1954), 416. For divergent responses to Lewis, see Jonathan V. Crewe, *Unredeemed Rhetoric: Thomas Nashe and the Scandal of Authorship* (Baltimore: Johns Hopkins University Press, 1982) and Stephen S. Hilliard, *The Singularity of Thomas Nashe* (Lincoln: University of Nebraska Press, 1986).

[25] Brian Vickers, '"Words and Things"—or "Words, Concepts, and Things"? Rhetorical and Linguistic Categories in the Renaissance', in Eckhard Kessler and Ian Maclean, eds., *Res et Verba in der Renaissance* (Wiesbaden: Harrassowitz Verlag, 2002), 289–335.

[26] Vickers, '"Words"', 290–303, 324; Quentin Skinner, *Reason and Rhetoric in the Philosophy of Hobbes* (Cambridge: Cambridge University Press, 1996), 48–9.

over Jerusalem (1593), he tells the 'Gorgeous Ladies of the Court' that 'it is not the wearing of any costly burnisht apparraile that shall be obiected vnto you for sinne, but the pryde of your harts, which (like the Moath) lyes closely shrouded amongst the thrids of that apparaile. Nothing els is garish apparaile, but Prydes vlcer broken forth' (II 138). The internal sin (pride) is not hidden beneath the externals (clothing), but lurks in their very warp and weft, which in the second sentence turns out itself to be nothing more than the pus-laden bodily extrusion of sin. This is part of a broader Nashean habit of eliding the physical and the spiritual in ways which seem at once bizarrely grotesque and symptomatic of an episteme in which body, mind, and soul were acknowledged to be complexly entangled.[27]

Registering the force of superficies, Nashe is obsessed with the physical, with bodies and clothes as ever-proliferating and often absurdly incoherent assemblages. Nashe's Jack Wilton, turning his back on his early escapades in *The Unfortunate Traveller* (1594), announces himself as 'no common squire, no vndertrodden torch-bearer', launching into an account of his fashionable garb:

> I had my feather in my cap as big as a flag in the fore-top; my French dublet gelte [castrated] in the bellie as though (like a pig readie to be spitted) all my guts had bin pluckt out; a paire of side paned [striped] hose that hung downe like two scales filled with Holland cheeses; my longe stock [stocking] that sate close to my docke [buttocks], and smoothered [concealed] not a scab or a leacherous hairie sinew on the calfe of my legge; my rapier pendant like a round sticke fastned in the tacklings for skippers the better to climbe by; my cape cloake of blacke cloth, ouer-spreading my backe like a thorne-backe [a ray or skate], or an Elephants eare, that hanges on his shoulders like a countrie huswiues banskin [barm-skin, leather apron], which she thirles hir spindle on... (II 227)

What is striking about this blazon is the manic scatter-fire of similes and the repeated recourse to the pointedly homely, downmarket, or bizarre in the choice of vehicles. So we get spitted pigs, Holland cheeses, ships' tackle, elephants' ears (presumably seen in woodcuts, such as those in Gesner's *Historia Animalium*, rather than first-hand), and peasant aprons. It is impossible to put Wilton together from the incommensurable variousness of his comparisons. His description echoes and exacerbates the early modern tendency to see clothing as a complex composite, made up of numerous detachable elements, while the lowly randomness of his object-world looks like a reaction against the Euphuistic style that dominated the prose of the previous generation.[28] Nashe had already travestied the 'old vayne of similitudes' explicitly in the 'scuruy *Prologue*' he provided for his proto-masque of 1592, *Summers Last Will and Testament* (III 234). Wilton eschews laborious classical clichés and far-fetched details of natural history, instead turning his prose into a chaotic inventory of the everyday.[29]

---

[27] Rhodes, *Grotesque*, 11–17, 33–6 and *passim*.
[28] Rosalind Jones and Stallybrass, *Renaissance Clothing*, 22–5.
[29] See Skinner, *Reason*, 188–94, for the rhetoricians' prescription that an orator's images should be far-fetched, but not fanciful or obscure.

However homely the simile, the act of comparison still implies a certain imaginative lavishness. But some of Nashe's most memorable descriptive passages are those in which he is able to collapse the terms of a simile, so that elements of clothing or appearance are not merely *like* other things in the world, they *are* those other things. This is the case with allegorical personifications such as Greediness and his wife Dame Niggardize in *Pierce Penilesse* (1592), the latter dressed 'in a sedge rug kirtle, that had beene a mat time out of minde, a course hempen raile [cloak] about her shoulders, borrowed of the one end of a hop-bag, an apron made of Almanackes out of date (such as stand vpon Screens, or on the backside of a dore in a Chandlers shop), and an old wiues pudding pan on her head, thrumd [ornamented] with the parings of her nailes' (I 167). Something similar happens in *The Unfortunate Traveller*'s description of the anabaptist leader John Leiden and his army of 'base handicrafts, as coblers and curiers and tinkers', issuing forth to battle during the siege of Munster. 'Perchance here and there you might see a fellow that had a canker-eaten scull on his head, which serued him and his ancestors for a chamber pot two hundred yeeres, and another that had bent a couple of yron dripping pans armour-wise, to fence his backe and his belly' (II 232–3). Nashe is sharply attentive to creative recycling—the use of old almanacs to line fire-screens and chandlers' shop doors, the turning of skulls into chamber-pots before they are commandeered again as helmets.[30] Necessity is the mother of invention, for the miser and the anabaptist, but also for the writer.

When Nashe turns explicitly to figure writing we find ourselves in the same world of desperate patchwork. In *The Unfortunate Traveller*, Jack Wilton stops off at Wittenberg to hear university orations that are 'all by patch & by peecemeale stolne out of *Tully*'; these 'stale galymafries' pass for learning in 'many vniuersities at this daie'. 'If of a number of shreds of [Cicero's] sentences [a speaker] can shape an oration, from all the world he carries it awaie, although in truth it be no more than a fooles coat of many colours' (II 246). Nor are these shreds obtained at first-hand. Glancing at one of the most popular Ciceronian cribs, Wilton comments that 'I pitie *Nizolius* that had nothing to do but picke thrids ends out of an olde ouerworne garment' (II 251). *Christs Teares* levels comparable charges at contemporary preachers, who abound in excerpts from scripture, 'but...so vgly daubed, plaistred, and patcht on, so peeuishly speckt & applyde, as if a Botcher (with a number of Satten and Veluette shreddes) should cloute and mend Leather-doublets & Cloth-breeches' (II 123–4). In *Strange Newes* (1593), Nashe picks on an individual preacher, Gabriel Harvey's brother Richard, charging him with recycling his Cambridge sermons in a printed book, the 1590 *Theologicall Discourse of the Lambe of God and his Enemies*. This Nashe describes as 'turning an olde coate (like a Broker)'—a broker being a pawnbroker advancing loans on clothing and household stuff—'and selling it for a new' (II 271).[31] Meanwhile, Harvey's practice in dragging out a pamphlet to the length of *Foure Letters*, when he had initially published only the first two, requires a

---

[30] Rhodes, *Grotesque*, 97.
[31] Jones and Stallybrass, *Renaissance Clothing*, 26–32; David Hawkes, *The Culture of Usury in Renaissance England* (Basingstoke: Palgrave Macmillan, 2010), 31–5.

'sowterly Metaphor', a metaphor fit for a cobbler: 'first contriuing his confutation in a short Pamplet of six leaues, like a paire of summer pumps, afterward (winter growing on) [he] clapt a paire of double soales on it like a good husband [i.e. a thrifty man], added eight sheets more, and prickt those sheets or soales, as full of the hob-nayles of reprehension as they could sticke' (II 263).[32] If texts are clothes, they are usually not new clothes, but clothes broken, clouted, patched, and resold.[33]

The irony of all of these descriptions will not be lost on readers of Nashe, whose books are, without exception, patchwork and piecemeal outfits. Large sections of his first work, *The Anatomie of Absurditie* (1589), and of his later bestseller, *Pierce Penilesse*, are directly translated from Latin sources. The tonal unevenness of *The Unfortunate Traveller*, its cut-and-pasted character, is a key source of its difficulty and its fascination. And his last acknowledged production, *Lenten Stuffe* (1599), is a crazy mixture of mock-chronicle, economic position paper, aetiological fable, and political allegory.[34] The cobbled-together nature of Nashe's writing is partly an inevitable result of his inhabiting a notebook culture. He was able to spot Richard Harvey's recyclings because he found excerpts from *The Lambe of God* in 'a booke of sermons that my Tutor at Cambridge made me gather euery Sunday' and in *Lenten Stuffe* he complained that his writing was hampered by his enforced exile from the capital: 'of my note-books and all books else here in the countrey I am bereaued, whereby I might enamell and hatch ouer this deuice more artificially and masterly...had I my topickes by me...I might haps marshall my termes in better aray' (III 175–6).[35] But Nashe's botching-up of texts is also a deliberate literary artifice. As in his depictions of clothing, so in his textile texts he was repeatedly drawn to the dialectic of poverty and recycling. Although he frequently gives voice to an exalted sense of the possibilities of literary creativity, he continually returns to its fundamental mouldiness—the sense that there is nothing new under the sun, just a lot of more-or-less creative citation. Nashe is the equivalent in the literary sphere of his close contemporary, the inventor Hugh Plat, who found in the famines of the 1590s the inspiration for innumerable 'remedies', many of them based on the ingenious recycling of waste-products.[36] Plat had, appropriately enough, begun his career in print by publishing books of sentences and aphorisms gathered from Seneca, Petrarch, and the Church Fathers.[37]

---

[32] Compare Nashe, *Works*, II 332 ('clapp[ing] a coat ouer a ierkin').

[33] For the recycling of clothes in the period, see Jones and Stallybrass, *Clothing*, 181–93.

[34] See Nashe, *Works*, V 111–14 for McKerrow's assessment of Nashe's heavy reliance on collections of apophthegms, rather than original sources.

[35] On the early modern commonplace book, see most recently Adam Smyth, *Autobiography in Early Modern England* (Cambridge: Cambridge University Press, 2010), chap. 3.

[36] Hugh Plat, *Sundrie New and Artificiall Remedies against Famine* (London: Peter Short, 1596). For Plat as 'dearth scientist', see Ayesha Mukherjee, 'Food and Dearth in Early Modern England: The Writings of Hugh Platt' (unpublished doctoral dissertation, University of Cambridge, 2007). For a brilliant exposition of Nashe's work as an affront to late Tudor ways of marshalling intellectual and material resources, see Lorna Hutson, *Thomas Nashe in Context* (Oxford: Clarendon Press, 1989).

[37] Hugh Plat, *The Floures of Philosophie* (London: Frauncis Coldocke and Henry Bynneman, 1581); *Manuale, sententias aliquot diuinas & morales complectens* (London: Peter Short, 1594).

Nashe's interest in lowly things, substances that are clinging by their fingernails to their objecthood, is, needless to say, intimately connected with his personal lack of that prince among worldly substances, money. For all the 'negative capability', the restless innovation and shiftiness of stance that has been identified in Nashe, there are several constants in his writing, and one is that his writing presents itself as the solution to dire material need.[38] Although he denied that he could be identified with Pierce Penilesse, an impoverished wit forced to plead with Satan for 'delicious gold' (I 165), a slip of the pen suggests their proximity.[39] A year later, in *Christs Teares*, Nashe attributed the 'fantasticall Satirisme' of his skirmishes with Marprelate and Harvey to his need for cash: 'into some spleanatiue vaines of wantonnesse heeretofore haue I foolishlie relapsed, to supply my priuate wants' (II 12–13). *The Unfortunate Traveller*'s Jack Wilton begins life as the embodiment of the cony-catcher or con man; during his subsequent journeys across Europe he dangles from the purse-strings of Henry Howard, Earl of Surrey, 'a right noble Lord, liberalitie it selfe (if in this yron age there were any such creature as liberalitie left on the earth)' (II 242). And the emphasis on literary poverty continues into *Lenten Stuffe*, in which Nashe describes how, fleeing the London authorities in 1597, he was not just parted from his notebooks, but also 'sequestered...from the woonted meanes of my maintenance' and forced to become one of the 'Frier mendicants of our profession'—the Elizabethan equivalent of a pre-Reformation beggar-monk (III 154, 156). From such unpromising beginnings, Nashe's works propose a strong equivalence between copia—the literary fecundity explored by Erasmus in his educational textbook *De duplici copia verborum ac rerum*—and money. Even if writing cannot make you rich, an abundance of words offers a respite from penury and starvation. At one unobtrusive moment in *The Unfortunate Traveller* the Spanish ambassador is welcomed to Rome with a feast, 'where if a poet should spend all his life time in describing a banket, he could not feast his auditors halfe so wel with wordes, as [the Pope] doth his guest with iunkets' (II 317).[40] The comedy of the zeugma barely registers, since this writer regularly entertains the possibility that one might live on words alone.

Predicated on poverty, Nashe's writing feeds on the fantasy that text itself can overcome poverty—not just through its eventual marketability (the fact that it can be turned into pamphlets and sold), but in the very moment of its creation. He is drawn to liars and egregious confabulators, illicit parodists of the arts of rhetoric who use words to create something from nothing. Sir Philip Sidney's *Defence of Poesy* devotes itself to rebutting the charge that poets are liars, but for all that he reverences Sidney, Nashe can blithely denounce a 'libell of leasings' by Martin Marprelate by calling it '*poetica licentia*' or poetic licence (III 347). He attacks Gabriel Harvey for having 'in one booke of tenne

---

[38] For 'negative capability', see Crewe, *Rhetoric*, 33–4; for the absence of stable literary identity, Rhodes, *Grotesque*, 52; for relentless innovation, see Philip Schwyzer, 'Summer Fruit and Autumn Leaves: Thomas Nashe in 1593', *English Literary Renaissance*, 24 (1994): 583–619.

[39] See Nashe, *Works*, I 303 for the denial and compare I 323, where he says that in *Pierce Penilesse* 'I expostulated, why Coblers, Hostlers, and Carmen should be worth so much, and *I*, a scholler and a good-fellow, a begger' (emphasis added).

[40] On the Erasmian connection, see further Hutson, *Nashe*, 38–54.

sheets of paper, ... published aboue two hundred lies', but then goes on to confess that it is not lying per se that is the problem: 'Had they been wittie lies, or merry lies, they would neuer haue greev'd mee: but palpable lies, damned lies, lies as big as one of the Guardes chynes of beefe, who can abide?' (I 269). Even this objection to especially mountainous mendacities would not last. Jack Wilton draws his energy from extempore lies (he brags about the ease with which he coined an 'impregnable excuse to be gone' when he tired of duping a gull, unlike a victim who could only splutter 'lies which he had not yet stampt') and the celebrity-studded narrative of his unfortunate travels is one long shaggy-dog story (II 224–5). *Nashes Lenten Stuffe* is an enormous, exorbitant lie, a red herring of a text in praise of the red herring and of the Utopia of Great Yarmouth. Even as he concludes it, the author knows that this book will be condemned as 'playing with a shettlecocke, or tossing empty bladders in the air' (III 225).

'Empty bladders'—the phrase crystallizes Nashe's paradoxical immaterial materiality, his world of base 'stuff' that does not quite qualify for objecthood because it is too lowly, swollen, and (for all its entertainment-value) ultimately hollow. The *res* that does not quite qualify as *res*—be it Harvey or herring—is his stock-in-trade. In this he resembles that early modern merchant of strange substances, the antiquary. To enter an antiquary's shop is (according to *Pierce Penilesse*) to be confronted with 'a thousand iymiams and toyes', the value of which is pure fantasy: 'They will blow their nose in a box, and say it is the spittle that *Diogenes* spet in ones face.' The antiquary is capable of getting money for old rope, quite literally: 'I know one sold an olde rope with foure knots on it for foure pound, in that he gaue out, it was the length and bredth of Christs Tomb.' Elsewhere, Nashe tells Harvey that he ought not to be ashamed to be called the son of a ropemaker: 'Had I a Ropemaker to my father, & somebody had cast it in my teeth, I would foorthewith haue writ in praise of Ropemakers, & prou'd it by sound sillogistry to be one of the 7. liberal sciences' (I 270). Logic and rhetoric are bellows to inflate any subject, any substance, however lowly. 'Euery man can say Bee to a Battledore, and write in prayse of Vertue and the seuen Liberall Sciences, thresh corne out of the full sheaues and fetch water out of the Thames; but out of drie stubble to make an after haruest, and a plentifull croppe without sowing, and wring iuice out of a flint, thats *Pierce a Gods name*, and the right tricke of a workman' (III 152). To make an inflated discourse out of the thinnest materials is the archetypal Nashean challenge.

This holds true for whole texts and for the extraordinary words that go to make up those texts. Early in his career, Nashe had the temerity to attack Gabriel Harvey for his 'inkehornisme', his tendency to coin or propagate extravagantly unlikely new and strained words and phrases. The list that Nashe compiles is a feast of inflated terms and phrases, many of which proved surprisingly durable; among them are 'conscious mind', 'canicular tales', 'deceitful perfidy', 'notorietie', 'negotiation', 'effectuate', 'this Aretinish mountain of huge exaggerations', 'addicted to Theory'—and, strikingly, 'materiallitie' (I 316).[41] But the assault on Harvey is somewhat blunted when Nashe concludes it by

---

[41] Harvey did not in fact invent 'materiallitie', which (ignoring *OED*, 'materiality, n.', with its ambiguous citation from *c.*1529; see *OED* <http://www.oed.com> accessed 18 March 2013) had been used by several authors in the 1580s.

complaining that 'euerie third line hath some of this ouer-rackt absonisme'—where 'absonisme' is itself plainly a neologism. Here again, this author would come to abandon any scruples he may have had early on, developing a style which was probably more innovative per square yard of patched text than Shakespeare. A search on the online *Oxford English Dictionary*—admittedly a flawed instrument, since its early modern entries are badly in need of updating—currently yields more than seven hundred words (or senses) for which Nashe furnishes the earliest citation.[42]

The list is full of rich coinages, many of which are distilled essence of Nashe. *Christs Teares* condemns those who turn atheists because 'they cannot grosslie palpabrize or feele God with their bodily fingers' (II 115). Here 'palpabrize' is a prickly mouthful of a word that catches the desire of a doubting Thomas to feel before he believes, testing everything on the touchstone of the body.[43] From the same work comes 'multifarious' ('The Scripture thou madest a too-to compounde Cabalisticall substaunce of, by canonizing such a multifarious Genealogie of Comments' [II 80]), a neologism invaluable for a writer who thrives on the evocation of plenitude.[44] When, in his preface to Greene's *Menaphon* (1589), Nashe complains of writers who 'busie themselues with the indeavours of Art, that could scarcely Latinize their neck verse if they should haue neede' (III 315), the freshly-minted 'Latinize' furnishes a word to track the increasing speed of inter-linguistic traffic. Nashe's innovations also enrich the vocabulary of insult ('denunciate', 'ninnyhammer', 'noddyship', 'pish', and 'rampalion'), and of sex ('bona-roba', 'dildo', and 'ingle').[45]

Yet, while some of these coinages are characterful, the principle at work in most of them is very basic: the bigger the better. Nashe seems to have believed that any word could be improved by adding an extra syllable, usually '-ize'; so as well as 'Latinize' and 'palpabrize' we get 'beruffianize', 'chameleonize', 'Christianize', 'documentize', 'encomionize', 'infamize', 'myrmidonize', 'oblivionize', and 'oraculize', 'phlebotomize', and 'superficialize'. Inevitably, in this world of linguistic hyperactivity, some -izes harden into -isms; hence 'Chaucerism', 'Italianism', 'pedantism', and 'thrasonism'. In the letter prefacing the second edition of *Christs Teares*, Nashe explicitly defends his inflationary neologisms, answering 'reprehenders that complain of my boystrous compound wordes, and ending my Italionate coyned verbes all in Ize' by asserting that 'no winde that blowes strong but is boystrous, no speech or wordes of any power or force to confute and perswade but must bee swelling and boystrous' (II 66–7). The claim here is that large words

---

[42] For Nashe's representation in the *OED*, see Jürgen Schäfer, *Documentation in the O.E.D.: Shakespeare and Nashe as Test Cases* (Oxford: Clarendon Press, 1980). It is now possible to antedate many of Nashe's apparent coinages using the EEBO keyword search facility. See also the vocabulary measurements in Louis Ule, *A Concordance to the Works of Thomas Nashe*, 2 vols. (Hildesheim: Olms-Weidmann, 1997).

[43] Rhodes, *Grotesque*, 26

[44] Rhodes, *Grotesque*, 140.

[45] The source for *OED*'s first citation for 'dildo', Florio's *Worlde of Wordes* (1598), likely post-dates its second citation in Nashe's 'Choice of Valentines', which seems to be mentioned by Harvey in 1593; see Charles Nicholl, 'Nashe, Thomas', *ODNB* <http://www.oxforddnb.com/view/article/19790> accessed 18 March 2013.

are especially forceful, as if the extra breath that is required to enunciate them were itself a source of energy, blowing down all before it.[46]

But this defensive passage also casts the value of a long word in economic terms, when Nashe moves on to defend compound words—such terms as 'Saboth-ceased', 'dust-died', 'prayer-prospering', 'fome-painted', and 'mingle-coloured' (to choose a paragraph [II 66–7] more or less at random). In creating such compounds, he imitates rich men 'who, hauing gathered store of white single money together, conuert a number of those small little scutes into great peeces of gold, such as double Pistols and Portugues' (II 184).[47] English abounds in 'the single money of monosyllables, which are the only scandall of it'. So whenever Nashe had several such words to rub together, he took them to the 'compounders... and exchanged them foure into one, and others into more, according to the Greek, French, Spanish, and Italian'. Asserting the virtue of 'carrying much in a small roome' (II 184), Nashe fashions himself as the linguistic equivalent of Marlowe's Jew of Malta, a player in the big league, the international financial/lexical marketplace. At the same time, by claiming that his compounds are a form of legitimate exchange, he defers the obvious charge that his way with language represents a form of illicit coining.[48]

Nonetheless, just as 'double Pistols and Portegues' can always be converted back into paltry 'halfe-pence, three-farthings, and two-pences', so there is frequently a sense that Nashe's 'swelling and boystrous' words are ripe for deflation. It is Nashe who bequeaths us 'impecunious' (when he accuses Harvey of being 'a poore impecunious creature' [III 90]), an orotund Latinate coinage the richness of which is entirely at odds with its meaning ('having no money, penniless; in want of money').[49] In this case, the gold coin turns out to be very little when translated into plain English. 'Protractive' (from the same page of *Haue with You to Saffron-walden* [1596]) is a word that has been stretched on the rack until its sound echoes its sense ('prolonging; extended, lengthy'). But where a straightforward English equivalent exists, extension looks like over-extension, and it is no surprise that the *OED*'s second citation of the word should come from Shakespeare's Agamemnon, rationalizing his failure to conquer Troy with much bombast in *Troilus and Cressida*.[50] Other Nashean novelties such as 'bubbly' and 'balderdash'—brought together in *Lenten Stuffe* as he describes how the sands of the Norfolk coast first separated themselves from the sea, decreeing that they would no more 'haue their heads washt with his *bubbly* spume or Barbers *balderdash*' (III 160)—are revealing in their very frothiness, a momentary boisterousness that gives them only a tenuous claim on substantiality.[51] The *OED* does not trouble to record a fleeting coinage such as 'Gogmagognes',

---

[46] See further the defence of 'huge woords' at *Works*, III 152.
[47] Scutes, Pistols, and Portegues were respectively French, Spanish, and Portuguese coins.
[48] For references to coining, see *Works*, II 237, 258–9.
[49] 'impecunious, adj.', *OED* <http://www.oed.com/view/Entry/92187?redirectedFrom=impecunious#eid> accessed 18 March 2013.
[50] 'protractive, adj. (and adv.)', *OED* <http://www.oed.com/view/Entry/153350?redirectedFrom=protractive#eid> accessed 18 March 2013; William Shakespeare, *The Historie of Troylus and Cresseida* (London: R. Bonian and H. Walley, 1609), fol. B3ʳ.
[51] Nashe had used 'balder-dash' earlier, at *Works*, III 11.

meaning 'greatness' ('great personages...from their high estate and not their high statures propogate the eleuaute titles of their Gogmagognes' [III 186]). Like 'protractive', 'Gogmagognes' expands on expansiveness, but only by reference to the giants conquered by the Ancient Britons, whose claims to a more-than-mythical existence were tenuous indeed. Pricked by the sword of reason, they would deflate like 'an emptie bladder', following Spenser's puffed-up giant Orgoglio.[52]

Nashe's words, then, are among the insubstantial substances with which his universe is replete. He would, I suspect, have been delighted with my second epigraph, in which the materiality of words is found in their gaseousness, in which they sit alongside hot air balloons (objects that are swollen and susceptible to puncturing, but which can take you on extraordinary journeys) and neon signs (objects which turn a gas into the physical words and images that feed the modern commercial marketplace). In his own writings, the windy emptiness of language is registered mainly through an insistent rendering of the physicality of ink and paper. Empty writing prompts immediate thoughts of recycling; thus, Nashe complains that it would have been tolerable had Harvey mauled him in a vendible book, 'but for Chandlers merchandize to be so massacred, for sheets that serue for nothing but to wrappe the excrements of huswiuerie in, *Proh Deum*, what a spite is it' (I 300). Reading Richard Harvey's *Lambe of God*, Nashe reports, 'I could not refrayne, but bequeath it to the Priuie, leafe by leafe as I read it, it was so vgly, dorbellicall, and lamish' (I 198). *The Unfortunate Traveller* begins with detailed instructions as to how it may be recycled in drying and kindling tobacco, or in stopping mustard pots, or for 'anie vse about meat & drinke', or for printers' napkins—whatever they may have been (II 207). Even Nashe's most elaborate tributes to the power of literature cleave close to lowly material. The best he can say for Aretino is that 'if out of so base a thing as ink there may be extracted a spirit, he writ with nought but the spirit of ink, and his style was the spirituality of arts and nothing else' (II 264). Or, to put it another way (praising Surrey): 'The alcumie of his eloquence, out of the incomprehensible drossie matter of cloudes and aire, distilled no more quintescence than would make his *Geraldine* compleat faire' (II 270). The 'base' and 'drossie' never escape from view. In this, as in much else, Nashe's example was formative for Ben Jonson. *The Alchemist*, in particular, plays out the energies of his prose in its portrayal of an imposture which makes dreams of gold the foil for an enchanted engagement with dross.

'Stuff' is, after all, a word for matter which doesn't matter, which is precisely Nashe's matter. (Or it is shorthand for 'stuffing', filling which matters because it is matter, rather than because it is any particular kind of matter.) While much work on early modern material culture has focused on luxury goods and elite consumerism, Nashe creates the feel of the real through his engagement with the failures and the also-rans of the physical realm.[53]

---

[52] Victor I. Scherb, 'Assimilating Giants: The Appropriation of Gog and Magog in Medieval and Early Modern England', *Journal of Medieval and Early Modern Studies*, 32 (2002): 59–84 (73) notes that 'early modern writers increasingly doubted Gogmagog's historicity'. See further Hutson, *Nashe*, 149; Spenser, *Faerie Queene*, I viii 24.

[53] For a recent exception, see Tara Hamling and Catherine Richardson, eds., *Everyday Objects: Medieval and Early Modern Material Culture and its Meanings* (Farnham: Ashgate, 2010).

His love of the insalubrious is legible in the way that his writing career is dogged by fish—from Robert Greene's 'fatall banquet of pickle herring', at which he was allegedly present, to his final magnificent banquet of red herring in *Lenten Stuffe* (I 287–8). The latter text offers a playfully repulsive figuration of Homer as a model ('*Homer* by *Galatæon* was pictured vomiting in a bason…and the rest of the succeeding Poets after him greedily lapping vp what he disgorged' [III 155]), but this presumably covers up the true (and blasphemous) model for Nashe's playful conjurings of something out of nothing, Christ's multiplication of the loaves and fishes. The buried subtext bespeaks Nashe's desire to confect a text that could be simultaneously disgusting and miraculous. More fishy business occurs when, in *The Terrors of the Night* (1594), Nashe wonders why he wanders on to the subject of Iceland: 'A poyson light on it, how come I to digresse to such a dull, Lenten, Northren Clyme, where there is nothing but stock-fish, whetstones, and cods-heads?' But then he acknowledges that his 'Discourse of Apparitions' is one long digression, a dreamy form of mobile stasis akin to angling: 'in a leaden standish I stand fishing all day, but haue none of Saint *Peters* lucke to bring a fish to the hooke that carries anie siluer in the mouth' (I 360–1). 'Fishing in a leaden standish', or inkstand, brilliantly encapsulates the impecunious writer's lot. But perhaps the most revealing of Nashe's fishes surfaces in *Pierce Penilesse*, when he points out that poets, unlike preachers and other retailers of mouldy, second-hand wares, are required to be original. 'Newe Herrings, new, wee must crye, euery time wee make our selues publique, or else we shall bee christened with a hundred newe tytles of Idiotisme' (I 192). Here, in the prose-poetry of the street cry, Nashe finds a voice for his defence of poetry. And it smells of fish.

Further Reading

Black, Joseph L., ed. *The Martin Marprelate Tracts: A Modernized and Annotated Edition* (Cambridge: Cambridge University Press, 2008).

Bruster, Douglas. 'The New Materialism in Early Modern Studies', in *Shakespeare and the Question of Culture* (Basingstoke: Palgrave Macmillan, 2003), 191–206.

Halasz, Alexandra. *The Marketplace of Print: Pamphlets and the Public Sphere in Early Modern England* (Cambridge: Cambridge University Press, 1997).

Harris, Jonathan Gil. *Untimely Matter in the Age of Shakespeare* (Philadelphia: University of Pennsylvania Press, 2009).

Hutson, Lorna. *Thomas Nashe in Context* (Oxford: Clarendon Press, 1989).

Jones, Ann Rosalind, and Peter Stallybrass. *Renaissance Clothing and the Materials of Memory* (Cambridge: Cambridge University Press, 2000).

Miller, Daniel. *Stuff* (Cambridge: Polity Press, 2010).

Nashe, Thomas. *The Works of Thomas Nashe*, ed. R. B. McKerrow and F. P. Wilson, 5 vols. (Oxford: Blackwell, 1958).

Rhodes, Neil. *Elizabethan Grotesque* (London: Routledge & Kegan Paul, 1980).

Turner, Henry S. 'Nashe's Red Herring: Epistemologies of the Commodity in *Lenten Stuffe* (1599)', *English Literary History*, 68 (2001): 529–61.

CHAPTER 14

SIR PHILIP SIDNEY'S *ARCADIA*

GAVIN ALEXANDER

Is not the Prose of *Sir Philip Sidney*, in his sweet Arcadia, the embrodery of finest *Art*, and daintiest Witt?

Gabriel Harvey (1593)

It was an argument that was becoming common in the 1590s: English was now a vehicle for serious literary endeavour able to compete with 'the most-floorishing Languages of Europe'. Having offered Sidney as the benchmark for modern prose, Harvey chooses another friend as the gold standard in verse: 'is not the Verse of M. *Spencer* in his brave Faery Queene, the Virginall of the divinest Muses, and gentlest Graces? Both delicate Writers: always gallant, often brave, continually delectable, somtimes admirable.'[1] Spenser's verse is a keyboard instrument—a virginals—on which the Muses might make music, and music without words at that; Sidney's prose is embroidery, a highly valued visual art. Music and the visual arts were a rich source for analogical thinking about literary writing; in this case, the comparisons emphasize how literary language looks and sounds, rather than what it says. Sidney, Spenser, and Harvey were used to seeing narrative sequences of embroidered tapestries: this visual medium could, like Sidney, tell a story. But embroidery also had the sense of extraneous decoration. The 'embrodery of finest *Art*, and daintiest Witt' may, then, be ornament that does not create or supply sense, but merely embellishes it.

Harvey knew that Sidney preferred the analogy of the visual arts to that of music in his literary theory and practice.[2] Perhaps the best-known instance is when, in *The Defence of*

---

[1] Gabriel Harvey, *A New Letter* (1593), in Martin Garrett, ed., *Sidney: The Critical Heritage* (London: Routledge, 1996), 131.

[2] On Sidney's visual poetics see S. K. Heninger, Jr., *Sidney and Spenser: The Poet as Maker* (University Park: Pennsylvania State University Press, 1989).

Poesy, Sidney discusses not style, but the creation of fictions, and his thoughts turn to embroidery: 'Nature never set forth the earth in so rich tapestry as divers poets have done, neither with so pleasant rivers, fruitful trees, sweet-smelling flowers, nor whatsoever else may make the too-much-loved earth more lovely: her world is brazen, the poets only deliver a golden.'[3] And the analogy is central to his theory of poetry (by which he means fiction-making in prose or verse) as 'an art of imitation, for so Aristotle termeth it in the word *mimēsis*, that is to say, a representing, counterfeiting, or figuring forth—to speak metaphorically, a speaking picture—with this end: to teach and delight' (10). There is something visual, then, about the fictional worlds writers create and about the means by which they entertain and edify us. Speaking pictures are not exactly the same thing as the 'notable images of virtues, vices, or what else' (12), which, according to Sidney, enshrine the writer's moral lessons, but they are close. Both have a tendency, in Sidney's theory, to coincide with individual characters, so that we get 'the portraiture of a just empire...under the name of Cyrus' in Xenophon's account of the upbringing of the Persian king Cyrus the Great, or a 'picture of love in Theagenes and Charikleia' (12) in Heliodorus's *Aethiopika*, a Greek romance from the late classical period. If Sidney's prose in the *Arcadia* is embroidery, is it mere decorative ornamentation of visible lessons such as these, or is it what makes them visible to us in the first place? Sidney was acknowledged by his successors as a revolutionary prose stylist and author of prose fiction, as well as one of the most innovative and influential poets and theorists of the Elizabethan period. In this chapter I shall examine the relationship between the style of his prose and the stories and meanings it delivers.

* * *

Sir Philip Sidney was born in 1554 and died, fighting the Spanish, in 1586. His rich literary output spans less than ten years and is often represented as occupying the margins of what was meant to be—but was failing quite to become—a significant political and military career. When Sidney describes the *Arcadia* it is 'my toyful book' (in a letter to his brother Robert)[4] or 'this idle work of mine' (in the dedicatory epistle in which he offers it to his sister Mary).[5] Working on it, we surmise, between 1577 and 1581, Sidney did much of the writing while staying with his sister at Wilton: 'Your dear self can best witness the manner, being done in loose sheets of paper, most of it in your presence, the rest by sheets sent unto you as fast as they were done' (*OA*, 3). This representation of the writing of what is unquestionably the greatest work of early modern prose fiction as a casual matter is echoed by John Aubrey, with his tale of Sidney scribbling in his notebook while hunting,[6] and by an anecdote attributed (dubiously) to Fulke Greville, which describes

---

[3] In Gavin Alexander, ed., *Sidney's 'The Defence of Poesy' and Selected Renaissance Literary Criticism* (London: Penguin, 2004), 9; subsequent references in parentheses within the text. Hereafter *SRLC*.

[4] Sir Philip Sidney, *The Major Works*, ed. Katherine Duncan-Jones (Oxford: Oxford University Press, 2002), 293.

[5] *The Countess of Pembroke's Arcadia (The Old Arcadia)*, ed. Katherine Duncan-Jones (Oxford: Oxford University Press, 1985), 3. Hereafter *OA*; subsequent references in parentheses within the text.

[6] Michael G. Brennan and Noel J. Kinnamon, *A Sidney Chronology, 1554–1654* (Basingstoke: Palgrave Macmillan, 2003), 75.

Sidney working as he was being dressed: 'he would call for his pages to write, and by reading the last line would remember where he was'.[7]

Did Sidney intend his work for a larger readership? Its title offers the work to the author's sister—it is *The Countess of Pembroke's Arcadia*—and the dedication insists that it is 'only for you, only to you'. The earliest readerly encounters with the *Arcadia* were private affairs. An anecdote finds Sidney himself 'impart[ing] it' to the Earl of Angus in 1581 or 1582.[8] The title of one of the early manuscript copies describes the work as 'A treatis made by Sr Phillip Sydney Knyght of certeyn accidents in Arcadia, made in the yeer 1580 and emparted to some few of his frends. in his lyfe time and to more sence his vnfortunat deceasse'.[9] Sidney's father's secretary, Edmund Molyneux, recalled in 1588 that 'a special dear friend he should be that could have a sight, but much more dear that could once obtain a copy of it'.[10] But these last two representations of the work show us that it was gaining momentum—more copies of the manuscript were being made after Sidney's untimely death in 1586 and Molyneux was choosing to tell us all about it in Holinshed's *Chronicles*. The work already had a reputation. The most important sign that the work was valued, however, was Sidney's own decision to revise it. We have a less clear sense of the dating here, but in around 1583 Sidney moved from some patchwork revision of the later parts of the *Arcadia* to a complete rewrite, going back to its start and revising it page by page. The effect was to decentre the narrative by putting most of the material originally in the narrator's voice into the mouths of his characters, and vastly to enlarge the work by introducing large amounts of new material, as well as by expanding an episode here and a sentence there. It was a job he never finished. The work had been complete in five books (what we now refer to as the 'old' *Arcadia*) and was now unfinished in three (the 'new'), but it was in this expanded and incomplete form that it was first printed—in an edition overseen by Sidney's friend Fulke Greville—in 1590.

Molyneux's account of the *Arcadia* chimes with Sidney's in seeing it as a product of (enforced) leisure; it also emphasizes what might seem the more decorative or artificial aspects of such a work:

> at his vacant and spare times of leisure (for he could endure at no time to be idle and void of action) he made his book which he named *Arcadia*, a work (though a mere fancy, toy and fiction) showing such excellency of spirit, gallant invention, variety of matter, and orderly disposition, and couched in frame of such apt words without superfluity, eloquent phrase and fine conceit with interchange of device, so delightful to the reader, and pleasant to the hearer, as nothing could be taken out to amend it, or added to it that would not impair it...[11]

---

[7] Henry Woudhuysen, *Sir Philip Sidney and the Circulation of Manuscripts, 1558–1640* (Oxford: Oxford University Press, 1996), 305.

[8] Woudhuysen, *Sidney*, 301.

[9] *The Countess of Pembroke's Arcadia (The Old Arcadia)*, ed. Jean Robertson (Oxford: Oxford University Press, 1973), xliii.

[10] Sidney, *Major Works*, 312.

[11] Sidney, *Major Works*, 311–12.

The paradigms of classical rhetoric inform this passage: the stages of composition, from invention and arrangement ('disposition') to style and performance; the need for 'variety' and for decorum ('apt words'); and the intimate and inextricable relationship between thought ('conceit') and expression ('phrase'). Like Molyneux's sentence, rhetorical theory in the sixteenth century tended to devote more time and energy to style than to matter; indeed, many rhetoric books treat only that third stage of composition: they are concerned, that is, not with the seeking out and arranging of the materials of an argument (or a narrative), but only with the setting of them 'in frame of... apt words'. A case in point is *The Arcadian Rhetorike* of Abraham Fraunce, a detailed examination of the rhetorical figures printed in 1588 and taking its English examples exclusively from Sidney. Fraunce's treatise is essentially a translation of a continental rhetoric by Talaeus, the collaborator of the French pedagogue Petrus Ramus, whose schematic reconception of the liberal arts had stripped rhetoric of invention and arrangement and assigned these to logic. These developments contribute to a tendency to admire Sidney's stylistic brilliance in isolation, but we should not be misled into thinking that Sidney's contemporaries could not attend to *what* he said because of their enthralment by *how* he said it.

One of our most important guides here is Sidney's friend and editor Fulke Greville, who, in his account of Sidney's life and writings, emphasizes a moral and political purposiveness to Sidney's tales of shepherds, princes, and princesses in the *Arcadia*:

> in all these creatures of his making his intent and scope was to turn the barren philosophy precepts into pregnant images of life, and in them, first on the monarch's part, lively to represent the growth, state and declination of princes, change of government and laws, vicissitudes of sedition, faction, succession, confederacies, plantations, with all other errors or alterations in public affairs; then again, in the subject's case, the state of favour, disfavour, prosperity, adversity, emulation, quarrel, undertaking, retiring, hospitality, travel and all other moods of private fortunes or misfortunes.[12]

Greville's certainty about how we should read the *Arcadia* has been especially influential on more recent readings of the work, suiting those critics who like their literature to have something to say about the real world, and even to attempt to intervene in it.[13] But it has to some seemed (though this shouldn't necessarily be the case) incompatible with Sidney's representation of the work as written for a private circle of his sister and her female companions. These implied readers are less in evidence in the revised *Arcadia*, which cuts the fairly frequent narratorial asides addressed to the 'fair ladies'. That may be a sign that Sidney was revising not only the work, but his sense of what and whom it was for. Nevertheless, the best way to approach the work is to keep all of its different aspects, priorities, and audiences in play, rather than to choose between them. For the *Arcadia* is

---

[12] Fulke Greville, *A Dedication to Sir Philip Sidney*, in *The Prose Works of Fulke Greville, Lord Brooke*, ed. John Gouws (Oxford: Oxford University Press, 1986), 10–11.

[13] For the best recent reading of the *Arcadia* as concerned with contemporary politics see Blair Worden, *The Sound of Virtue: Philip Sidney's 'Arcadia' and Elizabethan Politics* (New Haven: Yale University Press, 1996). For a survey of this tradition see Annabel Patterson, '"Under...pretty tales": Intention in Sidney's *Arcadia*', in Dennis Kay, ed., *Sir Philip Sidney: An Anthology of Modern Criticism* (Oxford: Oxford University Press, 1987), 265–85.

nothing if not a coming together of many disparate things, as we shall see, and Sidney's earliest readers did not find disunity, but rather showed a determination (misguided perhaps) to find in Sidney's literary practice the perfect embodiment of his literary theory.

* * *

We should consider carefully the possibility that in Sidney's *Defence of Poesy* we might have a precise and apt theoretical model for reading the *Arcadia*. Sidney's 'notable images of virtues, vices, or what else' are exemplary, which is to say that the images of virtue are meant to teach us about virtue and the images of vice will warn us against vice. For Sidney, poetry is able to improve on philosophy by embodying virtues and vices in lifelike people and on history by being able to idealize those people and render them perfect, instead of creating characters who—like the major figures of ancient history—are mixtures of the good and the bad. He was not obliged to take this theoretical turn: Aristotle in the *Poetics* had taught that the tragic hero should be neither wholly good nor wholly bad and Plutarch in an influential essay on how to teach young men to read poetry had stated that poetry represents people as they are in the world, mixtures of the good and the bad. But Sidney, ever the Neoplatonist, chose the idealizing route.

Sidney's students repeated and refined this theory of exemplary characters and a number of early readers read the *Arcadia* in accordance with it. In a section of his *Directions for Speech and Style* (c.1599) devoted to 'Illustracion', John Hoskyns gives us a long list of 'what personages and affeccions are sett forth in *Arcadia*', including 'pleasant idle retirednes in kinge *Basilius*, & the dangerous end of it', 'The mirror of true courage & friendshipp in *Pirocles* & *Musidorus*, miserablenes & ingratitude in *Chremes*... fear & fatall subtiltie in *Clinias*', 'wise courage in *Pamela*, mylde discrecion in *Philoclea*', and so on.[14] Sir William Alexander, who wrote a wonderful bridging passage, first printed in around 1617, suturing the incomplete 'new' *Arcadia* to the last three books of the 'old', describes the *Arcadia* in his brief critical essay *Anacrisis*. For Alexander, Sidney creates characters who are not only beautiful on the outside, but virtuous on the inside:

> affording many exquisite types of perfection for both the sexes, leaving the gifts of nature, whose value doth depend upon the beholders, wanting no virtue whereof a human mind could be capable, as, for men, magnanimity, carriage, courtesy, valour, judgement, discretion, and, in women, modesty, shamefastness, constancy, continency, still accompanied with a tender sense of honour; and his chief persons being eminent for some singular virtue, and yet all virtues being united in every one of them...[15]

In a theory of notable images and speaking pictures, appearances must not be deceptive. Alexander attends to the distinction between mind and body in order to insist that in Sidney what you see *is* what you get, but that very attentiveness is something that the *Arcadia* requires, rewards, and indeed thematizes and problematizes.

---

[14] John Hoskyns, *The Life, Letters, and Writings of John Hoskyns, 1566–1638*, ed. Louise Brown Osborn (New Haven: Yale University Press, 1937), 155–6.

[15] SRLC, 300.

It is, after all, a story about appearance and disguise. Basilius is living among shepherds, and some of those shepherds—Philisides (who represents Sidney), Strephon, Klaius—are well-born men doing the same. Musidorus dresses as a shepherd and his cousin Pyrocles as an Amazon so that the two princes can get near to the two princesses—Pamela and Philoclea—with whom they have fallen in love, in Pyrocles's case after seeing a portrait of Philoclea. Basilius falls in love with the Amazon princess whom Pyrocles is pretending to be (Cleophila in the 'old' *Arcadia*, Zelmane in the 'new') and his wife Gynecia falls in love with the man she perceives beneath the mask. As Pyrocles complains, in one of Sidney's characteristic paradoxical formulations, 'To her whom I would be known to, I live in darkness; and to her am revealed from whom I would be most secret' (*OA*, 85).[16] The job for the two princes is to make their princesses see behind their disguises without directly revealing themselves, so they tell stories about themselves or perform songs and poems that say one thing to everyone else, but carry 'a second meaning' (*OA*, 87) to their beloveds. The princes hide under pseudonyms once they are found out and captured in the 'old' *Arcadia*, as they do in some of the extensive adventures added to the 'new'. And we can understand the narrative more readily when we can unpick the names of its characters—the fire and glory in Pyrocles, the miserliness of Chremes, the ambivalences of Amphialus, and the star-lover (like Sidney's sonneteer avatar Astrophil) in Phili-sides, whose name chimes with its author's. Sound and etymology, then, frame words themselves as matters of surface and substance to be scrutinized rather like the visible surfaces of Sidney's idealized characters.

Disguise and dissimulation are explicitly compared within the work to *poesis*, the poetic making of imitations: indeed, Sidney is forever making comparisons between the activities of his characters and the actions of the poet. When Musidorus pretends to be in love with the shepherdess who attends Pamela, 'he began to *counterfeit* the extremest love towards Mopsa that might be; and as for the love, so *lively* indeed it was in him (although to another subject) that little he needed to *counterfeit* any *notable* demonstration of it' (*OA*, 87, my emphasis; cf., transposed to the first person, *NA*, 129). Poets too, in Sidney's theory, must 'counterfeit' 'notable images' that are 'lively' or lifelike.[17] Again, when Pyrocles has to come up with the bed-trick to end all bed-tricks in order to get both of Philoclea's parents out of the way for a night (each believing they have an assignation with Pyrocles), Sidney loads his description with contemporary terms used to theorize poetic and rhetorical composition: 'invention', 'conceit', 'proportion', 'ground plot', and 'device' (*OA*, 189).

By placing such an emphasis on the importance of creating and seeing behind verbal and visual disguises, Sidney's fiction highlights an important point about notable images and speaking pictures: that they are superficial. When his two heroes think about their disguises, they—like Alexander—draw attention to the inner–outer binary. Pyrocles is spied on by Musidorus (who in the revised *Arcadia* does not know that he is ogling his transvestite cousin) as he sings a sonnet beginning 'Transformed in show, but more transformed in mind' (*OA*, 26; *NA*, 69). When Musidorus then adopts the guise of a

---

[16] Cf. *The Countess of Pembroke's Arcadia (The New Arcadia)*, ed. Victor Skretkowicz (Oxford: Oxford University Press, 1987), 125; hereafter *NA*.

[17] Sidney, *Defence*, e.g. 10, 12, 35.

shepherd he, in turn, sings 'Come, shepherd's weeds, become your master's mind' (*OA*, 36; *NA*, 105). The other side of Sidney's theory of exemplary character requires that we as readers should ourselves be transformed—in mind and then in show, as it were—into living replicas of the virtues of an Aeneas or a Cyrus. That transformation is punningly problematized in Musidorus's words. The imperative 'Come' personifies his shepherd's clothes, both animating them and somehow setting them in motion (*Come here!*), so that when 'Come' moves along the line and turns into 'become' we are more likely to register a transformative movement punning below the surface of the more obvious reading: the clothes should accord with and suit the mind, should be *becoming* (a concern with decorum to which I shall return); but they may also turn *into* that mind, *become* it. Instead of outer expressing inner, inner is now being moulded by outer: the shell forms or turns into the substance. The *Arcadia* is full of such ironic versions (and reversals) of Sidney's model of readerly response, whereby the Platonic idea of a virtue beneath the surface of the character is apprehended by the reader and s/he then becomes a living embodiment of it. Here, a character is in danger of finding that the pleasing surface of his appearance can shape his own identity just as much as it can transform the reader's.

We have, then, seen some play in the space between verbal or visual surfaces and the identities, essences, and meanings that they hide, reveal, or construct. We have seen how the status of Sidney's text as a font of moral or political instruction contrasted to its status as an exemplar of fine literary artifice. I am suggesting that these matters are not unrelated and before I go on to develop this thought it is right to say a little more about Sidney's stylistic achievements.

* * *

My first observation is that Sidney places a premium on mixing and mingling of various kinds and at various levels. This is most obviously the case in the *Arcadia*'s generic affiliations and principal influences, which include Virgilian epic, Greek romance (notably Heliodorus), medieval romance, Italian chivalric romance, the pastoral verse-and-prose fictions of Sannazaro in Italian and Montemayor in Spanish, as well as the work of the ancient and modern historians Sidney loved. Both Hoskyns and Gervase Markham—one of several writers to attempt a continuation of the *Arcadia*—make this observation, noting in particular the influence of Heliodorus, Montemayor, and (in Hoskyns's case) Sannazaro.[18] As Stephen Greenblatt has rightly noted, the *Arcadia* 'is perhaps the supreme Elizabethan example' of this kind of generic fusion, which he terms the 'mixed mode'.[19] The delightful complexity of the *Arcadia*'s plot is one result of this bringing together of different literary kinds and traditions and its romance habit of interlacing plot strands (in the manner of Ariosto) is emblematic of that harmony in variety. Another fundamental mixture is that of verse and prose. The narrative is almost entirely delivered in prose; however, not only do characters frequently use verse to express themselves and advance their

---

[18] Garrett, ed., *Critical Heritage*, 142; Hoskyns, *Life, Letters and Writings*, 155.
[19] Stephen J. Greenblatt, 'Sidney's *Arcadia* and the Mixed Mode', *Studies in Philology*, 70 (1973): 269–78, repr. in Arthur F. Kinney, ed., *Essential Articles for the Study of Sir Philip Sidney* (Hamden, CT: Archon, 1986), 347–56 (347).

causes, but the *Arcadia*'s five books are separated by four extended sequences of pastoral verses, the eclogues. The former use of verse borrows from Montemayor and the latter from Sannazaro, and the effect is to combine pastoral romance with something more like classical (and neoclassical) pastoral, with its formalized representations of shepherds competing and collaborating in verse. Sidney himself draws the connection between these mixtures of genre and of medium in the *Defence*:

> Now in his parts, kinds, or species, as you list to term them, it is to be noted that some poesies have coupled together two or three kinds: as the tragical and comical, whereupon is risen the tragi-comical. Some, in the manner, have mingled prose and verse, as Sannazaro and Boethius. Some have mingled matters heroical and pastoral. But that cometh all to one in this question, for if severed they be good, the conjunction cannot be hurtful. (*Defence*, 25)

English was—as Sidney put it—a 'mingled language', combining Germanic and Romance origins, strong Saxon monosyllables and sinuous Latin polysyllables: 'And why not so much the better, taking the best of both the other?' (*Defence*, 51). This richness was also a strength for Richard Carew, who in a short manuscript essay on 'The Excellency of the English Tongue' (1595–6?) sees the eclecticism of the language and its literary exponents as the driving force in the rapid advancement of English letters: 'looke into our Imitacione of all sortes of verses affoorded by any other Language, and you shall finde that S^r. Phillip Sidney, M^r. Stanihurst, and diuers moe, haue made vse how farre wee are within compasse of a fore imagined impossibility'. Sidney's experimentation with classical and modern European metres and verse forms here parallels an achieved copiousness in literary prose, the product of English's own mixed origins, as well as of the deliberate imitation of classical and continental models. 'Will yow haue all in all for prose and verse?' Carew asks, at the end of a list of those modern English writers who match the achievements of the ancients, 'take the miracle of our age Sir *Philip Sydney*'.[20]

A particular synecdochic badge of English's happy syntheses was the compound noun, a feature of the language highlighted by Sidney in the *Defence*. Sidney's most recently discovered—and most accomplished—student, William Scott, develops this point in his *The Model of Poesy* and ends a list of kinds of compound with these two examples, compounds 'of two particles and a participle, as *never-enough-praised*; and…of the particle and noun, as *between-kingdom*, which Sir Philip Sidney presumes upon after the Latin *interregnum*'.[21] Sidney haunts this discussion, as its source (for Scott is simply elaborating Sidney's remarks in the *Defence*), exemplar (Scott appropriately enough conflates Sidney's coinages 'under-kingdoms' and 'between-times of reigning'),[22] and mascot, for Sidney's coinage 'never-enough-praised' (*NA*, 84) was becoming his own epithet.

The 'never-enough-praised' Sidney was seen as the writer who had moved English forward after a phase when John Lyly's Euphuistic style had been all the rage. Michael Drayton makes this point about prose and—in what is a recognizable feature of discus-

---

[20] G. Gregory Smith, ed., *Elizabethan Critical Essays*, 2 vols. (Oxford: Oxford University Press, 1904), 2.292–3.

[21] British Library, Add. MS 81083, 29v. All quotations from the modernized text of my forthcoming edition.

[22] Sidney, *Defence*, 45; *NA*, 159.

sions of Sidney's prose—links Sidney's innovations here to his achievements as a verse metrician:

> The noble Sidney...
> That heroë for numbers and for prose,
> That throughly paced our language, as to show
> The plenteous English hand in hand might go
> With Greek and Latin, and did first reduce
> Our tongue from Lily's writing, then in use:
> Talking of stones, stars, plants, of fishes, flies,
> Playing with words, and idle similes...[23]

Indeed, the prose-verse analogy may be one of our most useful tools as readers of Sidney's verse-and-prose romance. If we are perplexed by the parallel trajectories of Books I and II, the first interrupted by a near-fatal attack from a lion and a bear, the second by an armed insurrection, we should step back from the precise plot actions and regard the plot shapes, which offer what Franco Marenco calls 'a rhythm on the unfolding of events'.[24] Sidney plots his fiction just as he creates the intricate verse forms for which he was celebrated: there is something, then, of the stanzaic poem about how the *Arcadia* works.

We have already seen how Sidney's sophisticated use of the figures of classical rhetoric made him a sufficient source for the textbooks of Abraham Fraunce and John Hoskyns. Descriptions of the figures from Quintilian to Puttenham think of them as quasi-visible entities, ornaments, and arrangements of matter in space (the implication of the Greek term *scheme* and the Latin *figura*). But rhetoric also attended to the more musical and metrical aspects of the arrangement of words in prose, for the language of prose had also to be properly 'paced', in Drayton's term. The theory of the classical period, with its subdivisions into *cola* and *commata*, recognized the need for units of prose sense to have a pleasing rhythm and shape, drawing meaning out with subclauses (suspended syntax) and describing a circle (the meaning of *period*) with an articulated symmetry of form which is best understood by analogy to musical structure—the balance one finds in any good tune. William Scott finds Sidney exemplary here too, offering an illustration from the scene in the *Arcadia* in which Zelmane begins to reveal to Philoclea that s/he is Pyrocles:

> The incomparable excellencies of yourself (waited on by the greatness of your estate) and the importance of the thing (whereon my life consisteth) doth require both many ceremonies before the beginning and many circumstances in the uttering, both bold and fearful
>
> —there is much art in the contriving this insinuating conceit. Generally that phrase best maintains his dignity that is of somewhat a long return, where there is a kind of dependency of the sentences and clauses, one inferred upon the other and linked one unto the other. I think Sir Philip Sidney hath first attained the perfection of this grave form and I know not if any in any language be more than matchable to him.[25]

---

[23] Michael Drayton, 'To Henry Reynolds, of Poets and Poesy' (1627), in *SRLC*, 293–4.
[24] Franco Marenco, 'Double Plot in Sidney's Old *Arcadia*', *Modern Language Review*, 64 (1969): 248–63, repr. in Kinney, ed., *Essential Articles*, 287–310 (291).
[25] Scott, *Model*, 31^v; quoting *NA*, 230 (cf. *OA*, 119).

At the levels of word, sentence, episode, plot, mode, medium, and genre, then, we see intricate combination and mixture in Sidney's *Arcadia*. What stops this variety from overwhelming the work and its readers is Sidney's care to make the details appropriate, so that—to pick up again on what Molyneux says—we get 'variety of matter, and orderly disposition, and couched in frame of such apt words without superfluity'. The key rhetorical principle of decorum governs the work. Decorum could be a principle of behaviour—morals—as it must have been in Puttenham's lost treatise *De decoro* and as it was in the courtesy manuals of Castiglione and co. But in literature it required the author to take the responsibility for dressing, acting, and speaking appropriately that in real life was an individual's. So Sidney, describing the ugly, splay-footed Miso, wife of the jumped-up shepherd Dametas, in whose charge Pamela is placed: 'Neither inwardly nor outwardly was there anything good in her but that she observed decorum, having in a wretched body a froward [i.e. perverse] mind' (*OA*, 27; cf. *NA*, 18). William Scott terms decorum *proportion* and makes it the key principle of successful poetic composition at all levels: 'The proportionableness of the matter and conceit is two ways...in the agreeableness and conformity of the device with the thing, and in the correspondency of the parts among themselves to the framing of the convenient whole' (19[r]). Put another way, the fiction must be believable, or true to life; and the details of its delivery—character, episode, description, word and phrase—must suit it. Proportion also means self-consistency, says Scott, giving examples from Virgil and Sidney:

> You must make the device continually like itself, the persons one and the same; the describing notes or characters (as after Theophrastus they may be called) of every particular must be constant and answerable to the proposed form: Aeneas always devout, valiant, and wise, his Achates faithful; Pamela in all her behaviour, bearing, state, and majesty in a virtuous resolution, and so commanding an awed love and a reverent respect; Philoclea in all her carriage modestly mild and sweetly virtuous, so, as it were, wooing love and honourable regard; Anaxius proud in all his gestures, swelling in his terms, and evermore behaving himself as one that beholds everything under him. (20[r])

When Scott returns to think about proportion or decorum at the level of style, he again shows that thinking about literary decorum touches on ethics:

> First, then, we require a proportionableness in the style: that is when the words fit the subject...and circumstances, when the style is suitable to the particular kind or poem—as the heroic and tragic is suited with the high style, the comedy and lyric with the mean, the pastoral and satirical with the low or base. Likewise, the persons from whom and to whom, the time and place, as in the conceit so in the uttering and expressing the conceits must be especially regarded. Truth is always the mistress of imitation...We must observe with Tully every motion of the mind to have a proper and peculiar kind of utterance, as anger (saith he) inditeth eagerly, with contention, the phrase cutted and short; sorrow, contrary, hath a lowly, yielding phrase with some amplification and sometimes interrupted (saith he)...Examples of all these easily may be taken out of Virgil and the *Arcadia*, two absolute patterns of decorum. (33[v]–34[r])

This contact between rhetorical poetics and ethics is hard-wired into the Aristotelian tradition (and Aristotle is the *fons et origo* of our paradigms in all three disciplines). Aristotle's *Rhetoric* included detailed treatment of ethics in order that the orator might understand, and simulate, passions, states of mind, and moral positions. Hoskyns credits the *Rhetoric* as one of Sidney's key sources in the representation of human virtues and vices, and—as Scott does with his quietly innovative use of the word 'character'—mentions Aristotle's successor Theophrastus as a model in the description of character types.[26] Sidney, and his text, could so readily be seen as exemplary of morality as well as of style because of the bridge between the two that a basically Aristotelian model of decorum had already created.

* * *

What we find when we start to look more closely at the *Arcadia* is that the analogy between style and morality is explored in ways of fundamental importance to our reading of the work. As I remarked in passing earlier, Sidney thinks about the exemplary plots and characters of fiction in Platonic terms:

> any understanding knoweth the skill of each artificer standeth in that *idea* or foreconceit of the work, and not in the work itself. And that the poet hath that *idea* is manifest by delivering them forth in such excellency as he had imagined them; which delivering forth also is not wholly imaginative, as we are wont to say by them that build castles in the air, but so far substantially it worketh, not only to make a Cyrus, which had been but a particular excellency as nature might have done, but to bestow a Cyrus upon the world to make many Cyruses, if they will learn aright why and how that maker made him. (*Defence*, 9)

Plato's ideas were quasi-geometric forms, which is one reason why the mathematical language of proportion (the word is used by Puttenham as his name for verse form) so readily allows us to recognize analogies between the form of an idealized character and the forms of language which express or surround that character. Sidney, the writer of perfectly balanced periods and the lover of artfully arranged rhetorical schemes, forces us to recognize in his writing a geometric or measured attitude to prose form which can relate the structure of a period to moral and psychological states and to other formal structures (such as plots or political systems or virtues), an attitude, that is to say, which can see an analogy between the parts and wholes of language and the component parts and wholes of other schemes of organization, psychological, societal, moral, and so forth.

Let us examine a period, let us see what 'the embrodery of finest *Art*, and daintiest Witt' looks like. Here, at the opening of Book III of the 'old' *Arcadia*, Sidney describes his two heroes coming together to compare notes:

> There, sitting down among the sweet flowers (whereof that country was very plentiful) under the pleasant shade of a broad-leaved sycamore, they recounted one to another their strange pilgrimage of passions, omitting nothing which the

---

[26] Hoskyns, *Life, Letters and Writings*, 155.

open-hearted friendship is wont to lay forth, where there is cause to communicate both joys and sorrows—for, indeed, there is no sweeter taste of friendship than the coupling of their souls in this mutuality either of condoling or comforting, where the oppressed mind finds itself not altogether miserable, since it is sure of one which is feelingly sorry for his misery; and the joyful spends not his joy either alone or there where it may be envied, but may freely send it to such a well-grounded object, from whence he shall be sure to receive a sweet reflection of the same joy, and (as in a clear mirror of sincere goodwill) see a lively picture of his own gladness. (*OA*, 148)

The balance achieved here comes not only from a control of rhythm, but also from the subject matter—the perfect mutual sympathy of the two cousins. The suspended syntax, with its frequent harmonious subclauses, throws a burden of expectation on the period's conclusion, which delivers us the lifelike, exemplary moral image ('lively picture') that is at the heart of Sidney's literary theory. Looking back on the sentence, we experience its shape and structure as something seen, something substantial: not only do words deliver speaking pictures, but they achieve a solidity of their own in doing so. The sentence is like that, also, because it is about perfected communication: it is expressive because it represents an ideal model of satisfied expression, where something is said that needs saying, and that something is perfectly understood.

So often in Sidney that is not the case. The very tidiness of Gynecia's periods ('For nothing else did my husband take this strange resolution to live so solitary, for nothing else have the winds delivered this strange guest to my country, for nothing else have the destinies reserved my life to this time, but that only I, most wretched I, should become a plague to myself, and a shame to womankind': *OA*, 81, *NA*, 120) is flawed by their failure to meet a basic condition of rhetorical success: for Gynecia is talking to herself and her admissions are hollow. Often, of course, the solitary monologue will be overheard and interrupted and Sidney makes most successful play with those moments where a character can't quite get their words out, where meaning gets stuck between inside and outside and the speaking pictures are mute:

> And here Pyrocles suddenly stopped, like a man unsatisfied in himself, though his wit might well have served to satisfy another. And so, looking with a countenance as though he desired [Musidorus] should know his mind without hearing him speak, and yet desirous to speak to breathe out some part of his inward evil, sending again new blood to his face, he continued in this manner...(*OA*, 14; *NA*, 50–1)
>
> [Musidorus] might see in his countenance some great determination mixed with fear, and might perceive in him store of thoughts rather stirred than digested, his words interrupted continually with sighs which served as a burden to each sentence, and the tenor of his speech (though of his wonted phrase) not knit together to one constant end but rather dissolved in itself, as the vehemency of the inward passion prevailed. (*OA*, 15; *NA*, 51–2)

That last period elegantly describes a failure of periodicity, where the balanced pairs have become fractured paradoxes and the harmonious mixture of elements a dangerous jumble. At this stage, Pyrocles knows that his tale of how he has fallen in love will not be welcome to his cousin, and so he is talking around the issue, and failing to talk. He begins by wishing that his cousin might know his mind and when he speaks his syntax almost lacks a 'constant end' and is 'dissolved in itself'. This way of representing mental torment and breakdown with syntactic disruption is pursued throughout the revised *Arcadia* especially, with its many broken sentences culminating in the unfinished sentence on which the work breaks off.[27] We should note that Sidney at such moments always focuses on the need for understanding and interpretation, and their failure, so that each monologue and dialogue in the *Arcadia* figures the condition of the entire text in relation to its readers, of whom in Sidney's theory so very much is expected.

There are other ways in which what we find in a single period and in the mind that it so successfully stands for will be figured on a larger scale. 'Remember,' counsels Musidorus later in this scene, 'that, if we will be men, the reasonable part of our soul is to have absolute commandment, against which if any sensual weakness arise, we are to yield all our sound forces to the overthrowing of so unnatural a rebellion' (*OA*, 17; *NA*, 70). This landscape of mental rule and rebellion surfaces in the rebellion against Basilius that the princes help to quash in Book II and in a dialogue poem performed in the second eclogues in which—taking the formalized exterior expression of interior states to an extreme—two groups of shepherds speak in the persons of Reason and Passion (*OA*, 119–20): 'Thou rebel vile, come, to thy master yield'—'No tyrant, no; mine, mine shall be the field.' This balletic version of the pattern is given a rather tidy—and specious—ending ('Then let us both to heav'nly rules give place, | Which Passions kill, and Reason do deface.'), and this is an option Sidney always reserves. It is how the 'old' *Arcadia* ends, after all. The two princes have been sentenced to death because Pyrocles has been found in Philoclea's chamber, Musidorus has eloped with Pamela, and Basilius has been found dead. The sentence is confirmed even when it is discovered that their anonymous judge is Euarchus, Pyrocles's father, but is then forgotten as Basilius wakes up magically from a drugged sleep and we get the happy, *deus ex machina*, ending we crave. We find the same pattern, then—the suspiciously tidy resolution of apparently irreconcilable conflict—in a mind, in a poem, in an episode, in a plot.

Sidney draws our attention to the analogy explicitly when he likens narratives to sentences. When Musidorus has forgiven Pyrocles for being in love, he asks for a narrative of events:

> Let me therefore receive a clear understanding, which many times we miss while those things we account small, as a speech or a look, are omitted—like as a whole sentence may fail of his congruity by wanting one particle. (*NA*, 78)

And William Scott develops the point. At the level of plot, he says, we delight in surprising turns of events:

> Such are those *peripeteiae*, as you would say indirect compassings of matters, when the strange, unexpected issue of things falls out otherwise than the direct tenor or purport of that went before and there is something properly and handsomely brought about

[27] See my *Writing After Sidney: The Literary Response to Sir Philip Sidney, 1586–1640* (Oxford: Oxford University Press, 2006), esp. 35–55.

contrary to the bent of the matter or expectation of the reader or beholder, as when friends by some unlooked-for accident fall from one another or enemies are reconciled, which is ordinarily by revealing of something which before was unknown or covered and disguised, as, when the two friends Daiphantus and Palladius combated one another, by the striking of Palladius his helmet from his head Daiphantus knew him to be his entire Musidorus – which accident, so to see friends meet, makes the readers, as they are said thereupon to be, full of wonder and yet fuller of joy than wonder. (22^{r-v})

(An episode in Sidney is of course the best example.) And at the level of sentence or period we appreciate the same thing:

Such are those pretty turnings of your sentences from the apparent bent of your phrase that are, as it were, models of the *peripeteiae*...In all things that discerning judgment of the poet must keep measure and decorum...(23^r)

Again, we see that the theoretical approach which considers each of the levels of poetic creation in terms of measure and proportion is more apt to develop the analogy between those levels, to see how one set of proportions is interestingly like another.

An approach like Scott's has been very successfully pursued by John Carey in a landmark article on 'Structure and Rhetoric in Sidney's *Arcadia*'. 'If we are to understand the work,' Carey states, 'we must regain a sense of its vital rhetorical operation—must see its rhetoric as part of its life': 'the prolific display of figuring in which Sidney's narrative is embodied is not ornate but functional, a linguistic equivalent of a particular and tragic world view'.[28] A 'constant impulse towards deadlock in the rhetoric' (247) is matched to what Carey sees as a mode of plotting derived from Aristotelian tragedy, whereby actions produce the opposite of their intended consequences, and to a 'principle of conflict, of divided loyalties, of tension and struggle within the soul' (250). These 'two basic narrative principles of peripeteia (or reversal) and passion warring against reason' (250) find their figural equivalents in the figures of synoeciosis (expanded oxymoron or paradox) and antimetabole (a conceptual or verbal chiasmus, a-b-b-a). So when Sidney's narrator (to give an example chosen by Carey and Hoskyns) tells us that 'one could not tell whether it were a mourning pleasure or a delightful sorrow' (*NA*, 438), we are not only encountering a pleasing rhetorical decoration, but also a world-view. The peripeteias of Sidney's plots and sentences (and we should note that Carey, in 1984, and William Scott, in 1599, coincide in identifying this Aristotelian term with both) are morally serious and purposive.

When towards the end of Book I the main characters head out to hear that book's and day's eclogues, Basilius stays behind, having 'a sufficient eclogue in his own head betwixt honour...on the one side, and this new assault of Cleophila's beauty on the other side' (*OA*, 41). This 'unquiet contention' (*OA*, 41; cf. *NA*, 111) is interrupted a few lines down by those fleeing the lion and bear who have broken Book I's peace, and as Sidney's narrator backtracks to describe the scene from which they have fled, we find another image of balanced discord and a second 'contention': 'It was, indeed, a place of great delight, for through the midst of it there ran a sweet brook which did both hold the eye open with

---

[28] *Poetica* 18 (1984), 68–81, repr. in Kay, ed., *Sidney: An Anthology*, 245–64 (245).

her beautiful streams and close the eye with the sweet purling noise it made upon the pebble-stones it ran over; the meadow itself yielding so liberally all sorts of flowers that it seemed to nourish a contention betwixt the colour and the smell whether in his kind were the more delightful' (*OA*, 41; cf. *NA*, 111). The sensory overload in this setting, which Sidney goes on to describe metaphorically as both a 'theatre' (the stage for action) and a 'gallery' (a space for exemplary images), seems likely to privilege pleasure over usefulness and we sense in its ability to make us close our eyes that an inattention bred by delight is somehow the cause of the dangerous interruption that follows. Always in Sidney a literary-theoretical model of poetic delight aiding poetic teaching is undermined by representations of delight being pursued for its own sake. We may argue that his rhetorical figuration is purposive and meaningful, but within his fiction he can represent the advantages of ignoring rhetoric, describing an ideal judge, Euarchus, who is able to listen impassively to the eloquent pleadings of the princes, 'letting pass the flowers of rhetoric and only marking whither their reasons tended' (*OA*, 348).

Sometimes all it takes is a pun to get us from one level or discourse to another. Bodily disguise and rhetoric are often yoked. Is it wrong to disguise oneself if one's ends are virtuous? Is eloquence always liable to lead to the deceitful misuse of rhetoric? Philanax ably punctures Pyrocles's eloquent arguments in his own defence in the trial scene of Book V by noting how the man impersonating the woman had lent his outer garment to Gynecia so that she might impersonate him: 'How can you cloak the lending of your cloak unto her?' (*OA*, 337). This example helps us to see that Sidney's *Arcadia* is governed by a condition of metonymic connection between the various discrete and yet related aspects and levels of fictive prose composition, a 'complex network of parallels and analogies through which the author discloses his purpose'.[29] And it is only by being alert to the metonymic dance of Sidney's prose that we see how best to approach the work as interpreters. We should not expect a relation between Sidney's art and his world that is either straightforwardly mimetic (he is telling us about human nature) or straightforwardly allegorical (he is telling us about Elizabethan politics). Rather, the best way to think about the *Arcadia*'s relation to the particular discourses and contexts and literary traditions with which it makes contact is not mimetic or allegorical, but metonymic. This is not to say that you cannot find out something about human nature or Elizabethan politics from the *Arcadia*, but if you wish to do this you will need to disentangle it from the rhetorical and intellectual knot garden in which it is intricated and enwound. And that itself is perhaps the wrong metaphor. Rather, we can only touch (as metonyms do each other) such meanings because they are not separable from the whole complex system that is Sidney's masterwork. There is no ethics without rhetoric, no politics without plot form and generic paradigm, no action without words, no idea without the physical and verbal matter which embodies it.

How, for example, are we to judge the moment in the 'old' *Arcadia* when Musidorus is overcome with desire for the sleeping Pamela and decides to rape her, when it seems to be created by a sequence of metaphors that present the itemized features of her beautiful face as an army first threatening to ambush Musidorus and then seeking a military

[29] Marenco, 'Double Plot', 292.

league with him and against Pamela? Our ethical stance is further confused when Pamela's beauty is described as seeming 'the picture of some excellent artificer' (177), a thing wrought by art, an object of aesthetic response and interpretive enquiry like the text itself. Is Musidorus to blame here, or his author, or the metaphors, which take on a life of their own? Sidney takes pains not to decide such questions, but to make them as involved and enjoyably intractable as possible.

The structures and forms whose metonymic and analogical resemblances are the basis of Sidney's art are all defined by their conclusions. We can only judge the success of a tragic plot or a well-balanced period or a refrain poem when we have reached its end. And Sidney's *Arcadia* has two endings: in its two versions it is perfectly wrapped up (the 'old' *Arcadia*) and fatally imperfect (the 'new'). Sidney's was an ends-oriented literary theory, life, and approach to plot and verse form, but what he knew of life and ethics, of ideas, of words, and of history told him that conclusion should always be provisional, or open-ended. As Greenblatt puts it, 'in the mixed mode, to resolve is to lie',[30] or as Sidney tell us early on in the *Arcadia*, 'there is nothing so certain as our continual uncertainty' (*OA*, 5).

Further Reading

Alexander, Gavin. *Writing After Sidney: The Literary Response to Sir Philip Sidney, 1586–1640* (Oxford: Oxford University Press, 2006).

_____, ed. *Sidney's 'The Defence of Poesy' and Selected Renaissance Literary Criticism* (London: Penguin, 2004).

Duncan-Jones, Katherine. *Sir Philip Sidney, Courtier Poet* (London: Hamish Hamilton, 1991).

Garrett, Martin, ed. *Sidney: The Critical Heritage* (London: Routledge, 1996).

Greville, Fulke. *The Prose Works,* ed. John Gouws (Oxford: Oxford University Press, 1986).

Hamilton, A. C. *Sir Philip Sidney: A Study of his Life and Works* (Cambridge: Cambridge University Press, 1977).

Heninger, S. K., Jr. *Sidney and Spenser: The Poet as Maker* (University Park: Pennsylvania State University Press, 1989).

Hoskyns, John. *The Life, Letters, and Writings of John Hoskyns, 1566–1638*, ed. Louise Brown Osborn (New Haven: Yale University Press, 1937).

Kay, Dennis, ed. *Sir Philip Sidney: An Anthology of Modern Criticism* (Oxford: Oxford University Press, 1987).

Kinney, Arthur F., ed. *Essential Articles for the Study of Sir Philip Sidney* (Hamden, CT: Archon, 1986).

Scott, William. *The Model of Poesy,* ed. Gavin Alexander (Cambridge: Cambridge University Press, 2012).

Sidney, Sir Philip. *The Countess of Pembroke's Arcadia (The Old Arcadia)*, ed. Katherine Duncan-Jones (Oxford: Oxford University Press, 1985).

___ *The Countess of Pembroke's Arcadia (The New Arcadia)*, ed. Victor Skretkowicz (Oxford: Oxford University Press, 1987).

___ *The Major Works*, ed. Katherine Duncan-Jones (Oxford: Oxford University Press, 2002).

---

[30] Greenblatt, 'Mixed Mode', 355.

CHAPTER 15

TOPICALITY IN MARY WROTH'S *COUNTESS OF MONTGOMERY'S URANIA*: PROSE ROMANCE, MASQUE, AND LYRIC

MARY ELLEN LAMB

ALONE in the midst of a 'delicate thick wood', Mary Wroth's primary protagonist, Pamphilia, throws away a book describing a man's inconstancy to a woman who loves him. She exclaims:

> Poore love... how doth all storyes, and every writer use thee at their pleasure, apparrelling thee according to their various fancies? canst thou suffer thy selfe to be thus put in cloathes, nay raggs instead of vertuous habits? punish such Traytors, and cherrish mee thy loyall subject who will not so much as keepe thy injuries neere me.[1]

Since Pamphilia's beloved Amphilanthus will desert her numerous times during this romance, this book is, in a sense, *The Countess of Montgomery's Urania*, and it implicates as well a dense network of creative works—other prose romances, masques, and lyric sequences—which it calls up in other episodes. Pamphilia's blissful lack of awareness of the role she will play in her own narrative of man's inconstancy creates a moment of delicious irony within this text. Her decision to reject a book that does not reflect her experience up to that point in the romance brings to the surface a paradigm for a project underlying this highly self-conscious romance: the intersection of what we today would call 'fiction' and the lived experience of her contemporaries and especially of herself,

---

[1] Mary Wroth, *The First Part of the Countess of Montgomery's Urania*, ed. Josephine A. Roberts (Binghamton, NY: Medieval & Renaissance Texts & Studies, 1995), 317. All citations will be from this edition.

evoked through a persistent and sometimes even blatant topicality that yet resists interpretation. Challenging to modern readers, who tend either to ignore contemporary references or else to use them to make unwarranted assumptions, this topical subtext does not offer dependable biographical fact. But it does offer something else: an underlying sense of lived joy and pain, of a deep and personal engagement in this text creating what Meredith Skura has called, in another context, an 'autobiographical effect'.[2]

The immediate effect of the topicality of Wroth's romance was to scandalize contemporaries; their responses, together with a number of self-referential narratives told by characters about themselves, confirm its presence. Most notably, Sir Edward Denny objected to his alleged representation as a character prevented from stabbing his daughter for adultery only by the physical intervention of her husband.[3] John Chamberlain notes that for 'many others' besides Denny in her romance, Wroth 'makes bold with, and they say she takes great liberty or rather license to traduce whom she pleases, and thinks she dances in a net'.[4] The presence of topicality itself was not unusual by the early seventeenth century. Her uncle Philip Sidney used the letters of his own name for the self-referential figure of the melancholy Philisides in *The Countess of Pembroke's Arcadia*. Published the same year as Wroth's *The Countess of Montgomery's Urania*, Alexander Barclay's romance *Argenis* was explicitly topical and a key interpreting biographical referents was appended to a later edition. But the primary function of Wroth's topical subtext was much more ambitious than the creation of scandal or employing a contemporary literary device. Throughout Wroth's romance, and in particular in the Pamphilia–Amphilanthus narrative and in the three enchantments that structure the portion published in 1621 (here called the *First Part*), Wroth evokes this autobiographical effect to explore the limits of the genre of romance. In the process, as discussed below, she also implicates the kinds of self-reference common to lyrics and masques. The innovative contribution of Wroth's romance to early modern prose fiction is her use of the underlying subtext of topicality to test what we would now call fiction for a form of emotional 'truth'. The result is a sophisticated meditation on the value of fiction, grounded in a profound and personal engagement with the chaotic passions at its core.

In 1621 the first of two parts of Mary Wroth's *The Countess of Montgomery's Urania* appeared in the bookshops of London; the second part was to remain unpublished until 1999. Appearing without the traditional front matter such as a dedicatory epistle from the author, it is not clear whether the 1621 portion of her romance was published without Wroth's approval or if she only wished it to seem so as a mode of self-protection. Taken together, these two parts compose a romance of almost 600,000 words, an immense text even for a genre characterized by long works. Moreover, as the first extant romance written by an Englishwoman, it represents a landmark in the history of English prose. Wroth's romance was only one of several firsts for Mary Wroth. Appended to the printed

---

[2] Meredith Skura, *Tudor Autobiography: Listening for Inwardness* (Chicago: University of Chicago Press, 2008), 27.

[3] Margaret Hannay, *Mary Sidney, Lady Wroth* (Burlington: Ashgate, 2010), 235–7.

[4] John Chamberlain, *Letters*, ed. Norman E. McClure (Philadelphia: American Philosophical Society, 1939), II: 427.

portion of her romance was a sonnet sequence 'Pamphilia to Amphilanthus', the first secular sonnet sequence written by an Englishwoman. First published in 1988, her play *Love's Victory* is the first original play known to be written by an Englishwoman. For these 'firsts' and, even more, for the high quality of her writing, Mary Wroth is now established as a canonical figure from the early modern period; her work is well known to specialists and to students alike.[5]

This rise to visibility is surprisingly recent. Mary Wroth's work was largely inaccessible to most readers until the late 1980s. It was not until 1995 that the first complete edition of her romance printed in 1621 appeared, without the originally appended sonnet sequence, as *The First Part of the Countess of Montgomery's Urania*; her manuscript continuation appeared in 1999 as *The Second Part of the Countess of Pembroke's Urania*.[6] Wroth was one of several early modern women writers whose works surfaced in the 1980s, when an active interest in women's writing caused their texts to be rediscovered and newly valued. Before that, a regrettable tendency to dismiss women's writing was evident in comments by the few critics who read Wroth's romance, however cursorily: it was said to lack underlying meaning; it was described as a derivative imitation of *The Countess of Pembroke's Arcadia*, the romance written by her uncle, Sir Philip Sidney.[7]

In her own time, as well, Wroth's romance met some heavy opposition, in addition to objections to topical references. Writing a romance in the early seventeenth century was a courageous act of female authorship. When Sir Edmund Denny criticized Wroth for writing a work composed of 'lascivious tales and amorous toys' instead of the 'heavenly lays and holy love' written by her aunt, the Countess of Pembroke,[8] he was drawing from a widespread cultural stereotype of the eroticized woman reader of romance imagined as indulging herself in the amorous passions of fictional lovers. While book inventories, as well as allusions by such writers as Shakespeare, demonstrate that men were also avid readers of romance, this fantasy characterized romance and the woman reader alike as frivolous and suspiciously (or delightfully?) sexual.[9] Rather than denying the sexuality of the woman reader (and writer) of romance, Wroth capitalized on it by foregrounding the desires of her primary protagonist, Pamphilia, for her inconstant beloved Amphilanthus. The result was far from frivolous. Through the pain and intermittent

---

[5] Clare R. Kinney, ed., *Ashgate Critical Studies on Women Writers in England, 1550–1700*. Vol. 4:*Mary Wroth* (Burlington: Ashgate, 2009); Paul Salzman, 'Mary Wroth: From Obscurity to Canonization', in *Reading Early Modern Women's Writing* (Oxford: Oxford University Press, 2006), 60–89; Barbara Zimbalist, 'Critical Perspectives on Lady Mary Wroth's *The Countess of Montgomery's Urania*: An Annotated Bibliography', *Sidney Journal*, 24.1 (2006): 45–74; Sheila Cavanagh, *Cherished Torment* (Pittsburgh: Duquesne University Press, 2007); Naomi Miller, *Changing the Subject* (Lexington: University of Kentucky Press, 1996); 'Mary Wroth', *Longman Anthology of British Literature*, Vol. Ib: *The Early Modern Period*, ed. Constance Jordan and Clare Carroll (New York: Longman, 2002), 1668.

[6] Mary Wroth, *The Second Part of the Countess of Montgomery's Urania*, ed. Josephine A. Roberts, completed by Suzanne Gossett and Janel Mueller (Tempe: Arizona Center for Medieval and Renaissance Studies [ACMRS], 1999). All citations will be taken from this edition.

[7] Kinney, 'Introduction', *Ashgate Critical Studies*.

[8] Sir Edward Denny, quoted in Hannay, *Mary Sidney*, 240.

[9] Helen Hackett, *Women and Romance Fiction in the English Renaissance* (Cambridge: Cambridge University Press, 2000), 9–16.

pleasures of Pamphilia's constant love for Amphilanthus, Wroth's romance creates a highly developed portrait of the desiring female subject. Even more audaciously, in what Helen Hackett has called her most 'radical intervention' in the genre of romance, Wroth identified this desiring subject as, in some sense, a version of herself; and scholars have similarly noted that striking parallels between the character Amphilanthus and William Herbert, third Earl of Pembroke, to whom she bore two children, indicate a 'shadowing' or a 'mirror', although not a consistent one-to-one correspondence.[10]

While numerous events cannot be taken as reliably factual, the sense of an underlying and very personal context yet exerts a pressure to recognize Wroth romance as something more than a fiction. But it is not biography, either. Topical referents typically evoke a play of signification open to various possibilities, a shadowy space between fiction and biography that is not quite either one.[11] As Margaret Hannay has pointed out, sometimes an incident presenting reliable topical markers will then veer off into sheer fantasy.[12] Such topical markers include anagrams of names and references to known events. Several characters indicate the presence of topical meanings in their own self-referential narratives. When Pamphilia inadvertently slips into a first-person pronoun, it becomes clear to her listener, Dorolina, that her narrative of Lindamira refers to herself. Some details in Pamphilia's tale also invoke an awareness of Mary Wroth's life. The name of Lindamira's father, Bersindor, is a near-anagram of Wroth's father, Robert Sidney; like Bersindor, Robert Sidney married 'a great heir in little Brittany', or Wroth's mother, the Welsh heiress Barbara Gamage. Details such as these create the 'fierce desire for decoding' that is a deliberate operation of a topical text.[13] But what can be made of Lindamira's fall from the favour of the Queen, angered by rumours of Lindamira's love for her own favourite? No solid evidence exists for such a falling out between Wroth and Queen Anne;[14] it may never have happened, or

---

[10] Hackett, *Women and Romance Fiction*, 163; Roberts, 'Commentary', in Mary Wroth, *First Part*, lxxi–lxxv, lxxxvi–lxxxix; Jennifer Lee Carrell, 'A Pack of Lies in a Looking Glass: Lady Mary Wroth's *Urania* and the Magic Mirror of Romance', *Studies in English Literature*, 34.1 (1994): 79–107; Hannay, *Mary Sidney*, 194–6; Johanna Rickman, *Love, Lust, and License in Early Modern England* (Burlington: Ashgate, 2008), 155–8; Maureen Quilligan, *Incest and Agency in Elizabeth's England* (Philadelphia: University of Pennsylvania Press, 2005), 206–7; Elizabeth Mazzola, *Favorite Sons: The Politics and Poetics of the Sidney Family* (Basingstoke: Palgrave Macmillan, 2003), 77–8; Mary Ellen Lamb, 'Biopolitics of Romance in Mary Wroth's *The Countess of Montgomery's Urania*', *English Literary Renaissance*, 31 (2001): 107–30; Marion Wynne-Davies, '"So much worth": Autobiographical Narratives in the Work of Lady Mary Wroth', in Henk Dragstra, Sheila Ottway, and Helen Wilcox, eds., *Betraying Our Selves: Forms of Self-Representation in Early Modern English Texts* (New York: St. Martin's Press, 2000), 76–93; Louise Schleiner, *Tudor and Stuart Women Writers* (Bloomington: Indiana University Press, 1994), 150–74; Gary Waller, *The Sidney Family Romance* (Detroit: Wayne State University Press, 1993), 253–66; Mary Ellen Lamb, 'Introduction', in Mary Wroth, *The Countess of Montgomery's Urania (Abridged)* (Tempe: ACMRS, 2011).

[11] Carrell, 'A Pack of Lies'.

[12] Hannay, *Mary Sidney*, xii, 234.

[13] Leah Marcus, 'Towards a New Topicality', in *Puzzling Shakespeare* (Berkeley and Los Angeles: University of California Press, 1988), 37.

[14] Barbara Lewalski, *Writing Women in Jacobean England* (Cambridge, MA: Harvard University Press, 1993), 249.

perhaps it was later glossed over. We will never know. Dorolina discreetly withholds comment, yet understands that this tale is 'something more exactly related then a fixion' (*First Part*, 505).

To consider the topical subtext underlying the *Urania*, a brief survey of the lives of Mary Wroth and William Herbert, third Earl of Pembroke, is in order.[15] Around 1587, Mary Sidney (later Wroth) was born to an unusually literary family. Deceased before her birth, her uncle, Philip Sidney, wrote the epic romance, *The Countess of Pembroke's Arcadia*, whose title is echoed by Wroth's *The Countess of Montgomery's Urania*. Her aunt, Mary Sidney Herbert, Countess of Pembroke, to whom she was very close, modelled female authorship in her edition of Philip Sidney's romance and her translations of Psalms and the plays of Robert Garnier. In 1604, at the age of seventeen, Mary Sidney married Sir Robert Wroth. Several indications suggest that the marriage did not begin happily. Ben Jonson observed that 'my Lady Wroth is unworthily married on a jealous husband'.[16] However, by the time of her husband's death in 1614, one month after the birth of their only son James, the couple seem to have reconciled their differences. Mary Wroth was left with an estate burdened by debts, rendered even more burdensome when the death of their son in 1616 caused extensive properties to be transferred to the next male heir, Sir Robert's brother. It was apparently between 1616 and the mid-1620s that Wroth wrote *The Countess of Montgomery's Urania* and her play *Love's Victory*, as well as revising her sonnet sequence, 'Pamphilia to Amphilanthus'. During this time she engaged in a sexual relationship with William Herbert, third Earl of Pembroke, to whom she bore two children, William and Katherine, probably around 1624. Pembroke made no mention of these children, in his will or elsewhere. After Pembroke's death, his brother Philip, however, did take an active interest in promoting the career of young William; and he may have played a role in the advantageous marriages of Wroth's daughter Katherine.[17] Little is known of Mary Wroth's life during the tumultuous time of the Civil War. Mary Wroth died around 1651.

Born in 1580 to Mary Sidney Herbert and her husband Henry, the second Earl of Pembroke, William Herbert would have known his cousin from childhood.[18] Through much of his life, this third Earl of Pembroke attained some notoriety for his amorous relationships. In 1601 he impregnated one of Queen Elizabeth's maids of honour and refused to marry her. His marriage to Lady Mary Talbot, daughter to the wealthy Earl of Shrewsbury, in 1604 was rumoured to be unhappy; the Earl of Clarendon was to remark that Pembroke had 'paid much too dear for his wife's fortune by taking her person into

---

[15] Hannay, *Mary Sidney*; Josephine A. Roberts, 'Life of Mary Wroth', in *Poems of Lady Mary Wroth* (Baton Rouge: Louisiana State University Press, 1983), 3–40; Mary Ellen Lamb, 'Wroth, Mary', *ODNB* <http://www.oxforddnb.com/view/article/30082> accessed 18 March 2013.

[16] Ben Jonson, 'Conversations with Drummond', in *Works*, ed. C. H. Herford and Percy and Evelyn Simpson (Oxford: Clarendon Press, 1947), I: 142.

[17] Hannay, *Mary Sidney*, 295.

[18] Hannay, *Mary Sidney*; Victor Stater, 'Herbert, William', *ODNB* <http://www.oxforddnb.com/view/article/13058?docPos=9> accessed 18 March 2013; Waller, *Sidney Family Romance*, 53–92.

the bargain'.[19] According to Clarendon, Pembroke continued to be attracted to women who displayed 'advantages of the mind as manifested in extraordinary wit and spirit and knowledge, and...great pleasure in conversation'. Like Mary Wroth, he was an accomplished poet. He was an active patron to Ben Jonson; he and his brother Philip were the dedicatees of the first folio of William Shakespeare's plays. Pembroke rose to prominence in the court of King James, who appointed him Lord Chamberlain in 1615. Pembroke was a powerful advocate for the cause of international Protestantism. During the reign of Charles, he served as Lord Steward of the Royal Household, while consolidating powerful connections in Parliament. Following a pleasant dinner at the house of Christiana, Countess of Devonshire, he died in 1630.

Wroth implicates herself and Pembroke in the narrative of the various separations and reunions between Pamphilia and Amphilanthus overarching the formidable array of plots occupying both parts of the *Urania*. When Pamphilia first falls in love with her cousin Amphilanthus, he is involved with her friend Antissia. While as 'the valiantest knight' he joins Pamphilia, as 'the loyalest lady', to resolve the enchantment of the Throne of Love, they only acknowledge their love for each other later, after he reads her poetry. When Pamphilia is enclosed in a second enchantment of the Theater, Amphilanthus recommences a relationship with a former beloved, Musalina, before he, too, is confined in the Theater. He renews his amorous relationship with Pamphilia when he rescues her country from the forces of the King of Celicia. They are parted again when they each believe the other is enclosed in the third enchantment of the Hell of Deceit, to find each other again at the end of the *First Part*. In the *Second Part*, they exchange vows before witnesses in a *de praesenti* marriage, described as 'nott as an absolute mariage' (45). Then, falsely informed by his former tutor, Forsandurus, of a betrothal of Pamphilia to Rodomandro, King of Tartaria, Amphilanthus marries the young princess of Slavonia, who he then sends away. Since Amphilanthus is married, Pamphilia then accepts Rodomandro's proposal. When Forsandurus confesses his treachery on his deathbed, Amphilanthus is reconciled with Pamphilia and also becomes friends with her husband. After restoring order in the countries of Pamphilia and Tartaria, Amphilanthus spends happy time with Pamphilia and Rodomandro in Tartaria. A flash forward reveals that Rodomandro will die, leaving Pamphilia as the mother of a young son, who will also die. Meanwhile, the three friends embark on a journey. They are informed that their adventure, and presumably the narrative itself, cannot continue until Amphilanthus is united with the young knight Fair Design. Named for a cipher on his heart, Fair Design does not know who his father is; the affection Amphilanthus has shown for Fair Design suggests that he will be revealed to be his father. But this revelation does not happen. The text ends mid-sentence after Amphilanthus enquires about the welfare of Fair Design.

The brief flash forward leaving Pamphilia a widow and then the mother of a deceased son provides a parallel to Wroth's life. Various questions rise forcibly to the surface of this narrative. Was there some kind of understanding between them before their

---

[19] Edward Hyde, Earl of Clarendon, *History of the Rebellion and Civil Wars in England*, ed. W. Dunn Macray (Oxford: Clarendon Press, 1888), I: 72; Hannay, *Mary Sidney*, 97.

subsequent marriages to other partners? Specifically, was the *de praesenti* marriage an attempt to suggest, with questionable accuracy, that their offspring were legitimate, as Roberts has proposed?[20] The name of Amphilanthus's tutor, Forsandurus, is an obvious near-anagram for Pembroke's actual former tutor, Hugh Sanford, who was, in fact, the go-between in the marriage negotiations between Pembroke and Mary Talbot. Did Sanford in fact lie to Pembroke about Mary Sidney's betrothal? In the romance, Amphilanthus's marriage occurred before Pamphilia's; while Mary Sidney was married to Robert Wroth shortly before, rather than after Pembroke's marriage. But a more compelling impediment than Sanford's possible duplicity was the unequal status of the respective families at that time.[21] While the Herberts owned vast estates and already wielded influence with James, Robert Sidney had not yet risen to the influence that would create him an earl. Finally, Fair Design's search for Amphilanthus invites interpretation as expressing Wroth's desire for Pembroke to make arrangements for his natural son. Her hopes were dashed in 1626, when Pembroke named his nephew Philip as heir to his lands without any mention of their son William.

Underlying these questions, which are finally unanswerable, is a striking autobiographical effect which permeates much of Wroth's romance: the constant love that Pamphilia, also an inveterate poet, expresses for her very unreliable Amphilanthus circles back to Wroth's construction of herself as an author and as a lover of Pembroke. The actual state of Wroth's emotions is, of course, as indeterminate as the existence of a *de praesenti* marriage. On the level of representation, however, if the psychological pain of a woman's unrequited love for her inconstant beloved is not sufficiently evident in the Pamphilia narrative, it recurs almost obsessively in other narratives, spreading throughout the romance, including Antissia (and her self-referential history of a lady from Great Brittany), Nereana, Alarina, Elyna, Lady Pastora, Silvarina, the Forest Lady, Pelarina, Lisia, the Lady of the Forest Champion, and especially Lindamira and Bellamira, whose narratives resemble Pamphilia's own. Jennifer Carrell describes Wroth's ur-tale in this way: 'a young woman loves a nobleman with whom she has been raised. At court he falls in love with her, but he is unfaithful, sometimes with a queen. Her tears and her poetry prompt him to return to her briefly before leaving her for another woman.'[22] This ur-tale and the constant love it invokes are, of course, in the realm of representation, rather than of sincere self-disclosure. Moreover, the constant love expressed by these women, and the extreme suffering it causes them, is not always portrayed in a positive light. When Pamphilia, for example, descends into a particularly deep depression, her friend Urania, fearful for her life, counsels Pamphilia against constancy as a 'fruitlesse thing' (470). As discussed below, the three enchantments successively complicate the romance's perspective on love, as well as the status of its art in expressing it. Is this love a form of

---

[20] Josephine A. Roberts, '"The Knott Never To Be Untied": The Controversy Regarding Marriage in Mary Wroth's *Urania*', in Naomi Miller and Gary Waller, eds., *Reading Mary Wroth* (Knoxville: University of Tennessee Press, 1991), 109–32 (123).

[21] Hannay, *Mary Sidney*, 94.

[22] Carrell, 'A Pack of Lies', 94.

profound subjectivity or a confining enclosure? The architecture of the structures of the enchantments similarly implicates the art of Wroth's romance in this complex dilemma. The questions that begin with a representation of individual love broaden to reflect forms of subjectivity and of the kinds of fiction through which they are expressed.

The kind of topicality engaged through the Pamphilia plot draws significantly from two other genres, lyric and masque; and both of these provide insights into its operations in this romance. It is as a poet, the author of the sequence 'Pamphilia to Amphilanthus', that Wroth most explicitly identifies herself as, in some sense, her own protagonist. This is not to say that the feelings expressed in sonnets, by Wroth or any poet, are necessarily sincere, any more than their works are autobiographical in a straightforward sense. Love may not always be love; as Arthur Marotti has noted, sometimes it is politics.[23] But the immediate context for many sonnets, as Ilona Bell has also convincingly claimed, often surrounds a relationship, real or imagined. Drawing on the writings of Kenneth Burke, Bell has asked, what kinds of eventfulness may a poem contain? Does it transact an 'amorous courtship'?[24] Does it deflect or enact a romantic or sexual advance? The 'I' of a sonnet creates an autobiographical effect that shifts into the romance as well. In the *First Part*, Pamphilia's verses initiate her first amorous encounter with Amphilanthus. Throughout the romance, numerous relationships are transacted through the exchange of poetry. Even for the vengeful Musalina, being a poet was 'a necessary thing, and as unseparable from a witty lover as love from youth' (498). The poetry written by the abandoned Bellamira was 'an exercise mine undoer taught mee' (386). Pelarina's inconstant beloved responded only to her topical references, turning down the leaves of the pages on which she wrote poems which 'hee thought touched, or came too neere, or I imagine so' (533). Like Wroth, the character Lindamira follows her narrative of unrequited love with a sequence of sonnets and her persona flows seamlessly between prose and poetry.

Masques also engage a form of topicality or self-reference. Aristocratic masquers are not precisely actors; they do not have speaking roles. Their function is instead to perform an idealized version of themselves, an elevation or distillation of the highly theatrical selves they daily perform as courtiers.[25] The degree of personal charisma courtiers were able to infuse into their performances potentially increased their individual status at court.[26] Moving in harmony, courtiers also affirm the social cohesion of their group. In their practised and highly deliberate physical motions, they naturalize their identity, individually and as a group, as aristocrats. Their power to dispel the forces of chaos in the anti-masque—witches, hags, satyrs—proceeds less from what they do than what they are. In Thomas Campion's *Somerset Masque* of 1614, for example, only Bel-Anna

---

[23] Arthur Marotti, '"Love Is Not Love": Elizabethan Sonnet Sequences and the Social Order', *English Literary History*, 49 (1982): 396–428.

[24] Ilona Bell, *Elizabethan Women and the Poetry of Courtship* (Cambridge: Cambridge University Press, 1998), 13.

[25] Stephen Orgel, *Illusion of Power* (Berkeley and Los Angeles: University of California Press, 1975), 38.

[26] Tim Bishop, '"The Gingerbread Host"', in David Bevington and Peter Holbrook, eds., *Politics of the Stuart Court Masque* (Cambridge: Cambridge University Press, 1998), 96.

(played by Queen Anne) can free the knights from a spell; her action is only to pull off a branch from a tree offered to her by Eternity. In Jonson's *Masque of Queenes*, the 'ugly hell, which flaming beneath, smoked unto the top of the roof' disappears suddenly, replaced by the House of Fame, from which descend famous queens from the past; special honour is given to 'Bel-Anna' or Queen Anne.[27] Not only the performers, but the audience is involved in these idealized fictions as well, joining in the final dance that concludes the masque.

As Wroth writes her *Urania*, she is performing not only her role as a constant lover, but also as an aristocratic Sidney, the literary heir of her famous writer-uncle. This identity is made explicit in the cartouche forming the keystone of the triumphal arch on the title page of the *First Part*: 'Daughter to the right Noble Robert Earle of Leicester. And Neece to the ever famous, and renowned Sir Phillips [sic] Sidney knight. And to the most excellent Lady Mary Countesse of Pembroke late deceased'. The aristocratic identity of the author is amply demonstrated in this self-consciously aristocratic work, with its elaborate syntax, the refined sensibilities expressed in its soliloquies and poems, and the sheer numbers of its royal characters. It is suggested on the title page by the elegance of the architecture engraved for the first enchantment of Venus's Throne of Love, which can only be entered by passing through the three towers of Desire, Love, and Constancy. The lovers entrapped in the first two towers will only be freed when 'the valiantest knight' (Amphilanthus) together with 'the loyallest lady' (Pamphilia) enter the tower of Constancy. The Palladian proportions of the three towers and the Throne of Love evoke similarly Palladian sets designed for masques by Inigo Jones,[28] at the same time that the gardens and landscaped paths depict a prosperous country estate. Most remarkably, reader-figures at the bottom of the page, to enter the landscape of the first enchantment, are dressed in extravagant masque costumes: the woman wears a high crown-like headpiece with a descending veil and the man wears buskins, an elaborate hat, and a skirt reaching his knees. How is a reader like a masquer? Like masquers, readers are invited to assume a virtual and very aristocratic identity, whatever their actual location in class might be, entering this landscape of the poem, portrayed under the elaborate cartouche as a Sidney–Herbert estate, to perform the role of celebrated visitor or virtual kin.

The text of the first enchantment invokes the genres both of masque and of lyric. When Pamphilia enters the tower of Constancy, 'Constancy vanished, as metamorphosing herself into her breast' (169). Pamphilia becomes, for a moment, an allegorical figure for Constancy herself.[29] This identification of a masquer, not as playing, but of being an allegorical figure, is very masque-like; and as in a masque, her power is exerted not through difficult actions, but through the mere presence of her person, her charisma. A voice will instruct them to free the prisoners, which they do, and the 'palace and all'

---

[27] Ben Jonson, 'Masque of Queens', in *Complete Masques*, ed. Stephen Orgel (New Haven: Yale University Press, 1969), 123.

[28] Julie Campbell, 'Masque Scenery and the Tradition of Immobilization in the *First Part of the Countess of Montgomery's Urania*', *Renaissance Studies*, 22.2 (2008): 221–39 (232).

[29] Campbell, 'Masque Scenery', 233.

vanishes, much as masque sets suddenly disappear. This enchantment holds up Pamphilia, and through her, with whatever accuracy, a version of the author she shadows as a model to be emulated by lovers. They are free from the psychological trap of a kind of love ruled by Cupid and Venus because their constant love is not affected by the response of a beloved. They are self-sufficient because their unwavering love is not dependent on whether it is reciprocated or not. The narrator explains this enchantment as more than a fiction, as a lived experience shared with the readers, for this 'Throne and punishments are daily built in all humane hearts' (50).

This enchantment before the Throne of Love is not only psychological in nature; it is literary as well. Wroth has invented a new goddess, Constancy, who surpasses Cupid and Venus. This is not to say that the ideal of constant love is original—far from it. But by placing Constancy in a divine pantheon and giving her such surpassing power, Wroth challenges centuries of classical, medieval, and early modern literary traditions that informed the way that love was expressed by actual people. Does the *Urania*, like the first enchantment, offer a way to move outside and beyond these traditions in its elevation of the constancy of its numerous female lovers, and especially of Pamphilia? Does Wroth's romance claim to offer a form of freedom from the tyranny of Venus and Cupid? This claim could be arguably supported by her lyric sequence, 'From Pamphilia to Amphilanthus', appended to the *First Part*. Its first sonnet describes her dream vision, in which Venus placed a flaming heart to her breast, while her son Cupid shuts it inside. The 'I' of the sonnet concludes with 'since: O mee: a lover I have binn'.[30] In the last poem in the 1621 sequence, the narrator instructs herself to 'Leave the discource of Venus, and her sunn/To young beeginers' and to 'now lett your constancy your honor prove' (142). The Folger manuscript version, however, plays with several endings.[31]

In the second enchantment, Constancy is not enough. A critique of the destructive tendency of romances and masques alike to indulge fantasies is levelled in the entrapment of female characters, including Pamphilia, in a magnificent Theater. It is not only a Theater. The letters on its pillars render it also a kind of book; it can be entered only when Pamphilia discovers a key, a term used for topical identifications. Ascending its steps to sit in marble chairs, the women assume the viewing point usually reserved for the king's throne, where the perspective of masque sets was designed to come most into focus. From here, the women imagine their loves 'smiling and joying in them'. This was not, however, an entertainment, but a spell. As Julie Campbell notes, they are immobilized, like figures in a masque, until the arrival of 'the man most loving and most beloved' (Amphilanthus), himself to be enclosed until the arrival of 'the sweetest and loveliest creature that poor habits had disguised greatness in' (Veralinda).[32] This enchantment exposes the risks of indulging fantasies by reading romances, as well as by watching

---

[30] Mary Wroth, *Poems of Mary Wroth*, ed. Josephine A. Roberts (Baton Rouge: Louisiana State University Press, 1983), 85.

[31] Hannay, *Mary Sidney*, 187.

[32] Campbell, 'Masque Scenery'.

masques. Their satisfactions are illusory. While Pamphilia enjoys Amphilanthus's imaginary love, Musalina is actually seducing him; and Pamphilia will have to endure the knowledge of their alliance when Musalina enters the Theater as his partner. Most evocative of masques are the outlandish costumes worn by a number of women attempting the 'poor habits' that had disguised greatness in—as a forest-nymph, as a nun, as a country lass. They are all trapped within the Theater, because their costumes are only assumed. The spell is only resolved with the arrival of Veralinda, whose costume as a shepherdess is not assumed, but 'real': raised by shepherds, she does not yet know that she is a princess. When the enchantment is dissolved (the Theater vanishes), she and Urania both read the 'real' stories of their lives. Is this what we, as reader/masquers, should also be reading instead of romance? Something more 'real'—biography perhaps? Or is this a possible function of the topicality within the *Urania*, to tether itself to 'real' lives, like those read by Veralinda and Urania?

The third enchantment of the Hell of Deceit may refer to the ugly Hell that is the setting of the anti-masque of Jonson's *Masque of Queenes*, but in this case no House of Fame replaces it. This enchantment implicates Wroth's own lyric sequence even more strongly. In two complementary, but different episodes, Pamphilia and Amphilanthus each believe that they see the other entrapped within an enclosure beneath a 'Crowne of mighty stones' (581). Pamphilia believes she sees Musalina and Lucenia about to raze her name from Amphilanthus's exposed heart. Amphilanthus believes he sees Pamphilia with his name written on her exposed heart. This phrase 'Crowne of mighty stones' strongly evokes Wroth's 'crown of sonnets', in which the last line of a sonnet becomes the first line of the next sonnet in her sequence 'Pamphilia to Amphilanthus'. Like the Hell of Deceit, this lyric crown represents enclosure, for its first and last lines describe an entrapping labyrinth ('In this strange labyrinth, how shall I turn?'); and its several references to fire culminate in its penultimate line, 'So though in Love I fervently do burn'. Rather than the wish fulfilment of the second enchantment, the Hell of Deceit is a nightmare. But, remarkably, this enchantment does not really exist. It is only an illusion perpetrated by Musalina's 'devilish art' to separate Pamphilia and Amphilanthus. Neither Pamphilia nor Amphilanthus are 'really' there. Does this enchantment represent Wroth's lyrics, and perhaps a lyric tradition in general, as in some sense unreal, as a destructive fiction?

By the *Second Part*, bizarre incidents that apparently have their genesis in the masque genre foreground the unreality of portions of this romance. Cloud engines portraying masquers as suspended in the air were frequently employed in masque sets designed by Inigo Jones, including the *Masque of Blackness* in which Wroth performed.[33] In what surely represents a parody of masque clouds, the *Second Part* of Wroth's romance features a cloud machine gone berserk. When lost children are recovered from a giant, a cloud inexplicably descends and takes them away for reasons unknown. When the

---

[33] Stephen Orgel and Roy Strong, *Inigo Jones: The Theatre of the Stuart Court*, 2 vols. (Berkeley: University of California Press, 1973), 18; Roberts, 'Commentary', in *First Part*, 723.

young Floristello declares his love for Candiana, a cloud suddenly separates them. A sword, armour, and even a horse descend from a cloud to equip Fair Design as a knight. In an arrangement resembling nothing so much as an elaborate Inigo Jones set, the enchantment of the Inaccessible Rock begins with a structure shooting flames descending from the sky to support an edifice in which Dalinea's tomb is placed unreachably high. These special effects create Wroth's *Second Part* as a bold experiment reflecting on those preposterous elements it shares with masques.

A strong criticism of lyric is also levelled in the *Second Part*. In a friendly social setting, Pamphilia sings a poem by Amphilanthus, attributed to Pembroke, 'Had I loved butt at that rate'. The poem is a masterpiece of psychological manipulation. The male narrator of the poem assumes the blame for his beloved's neglect for, as a woman, she was unable to reciprocate his depth of love. He can blame only himself for her emotional inadequacy: 'Non showld bee prest/Beeyound ther best' (*Second Part* 31). It is a lie on several levels. The introduction to the poem discloses that he had written it 'when hee made a shew of love to Antissia, and had given itt her, though ment to a higher beauty' (30). His claim to love her, presumably understood by Antissia to be sincere, heartlessly led her on, for she did love him. As addressed to a 'higher beauty', presumably Pamphilia, it becomes perhaps even more disturbing. Pamphilia is passionately constant; and it is the 'I' of Amphilanthus that seems unable to return deep love. What does the poem mean when the 'I' is inhabited by Pamphilia? Aspersions against women's inveterate inability to love become deeply ironic. None of this unsettling subtext rises to the surface of this social gathering. Amphilanthus praises her voice and Pamphilia praises his poem. But the falsity and corruption possible to Pembroke's lyric and to the 'I' of his lyric persona has been fully exposed as a 'hell of deceit'.

In addition to masques and lyrics, the *Second Part* also implicates other prose romances. Several scholars have painstakingly traced resonances of several romances in the *Urania*.[34] Of particular importance is Melissea, the author figure of both *Parts*, who determines the narrative by foreseeing the future. In the *Second Part*, Melissea loses her apparent control. Wroth's Melissea draws from other female magicians of romance, and especially from the Lady Felicia of George of Montemayor's *Diana* and of its continuation, Gaspar Gil Polo's *The Enamoured Diana*, both translated into English by Bartholomew Yong in 1598, as well as Ariosto's *Orlando Furioso*, translated by John Harington in 1591.[35] Her evocation of Ariosto's *Orlando Furioso* appears in the name Melissea, a close variant of the name Melissa, Ariosto's female magician; her reference to Ariosto's romance is further supported by her use of his more unusual name Rodomont

---

[34] Roberts, 'Commentary', in *First Part*, xviii–xxxix; Jacqueline Miller, 'Lady Mary Wroth in the House of Busirane', in Patrick Cheney and Lauren Silberman, eds., *Worldmaking Spenser* (Lexington: University Press of Kentucky, 2000), 115–24.

[35] *A Critical Edition of Yong's Translation of George of Montemayor's Diana and Gil Polo's Enamoured Diana*, ed. Judith M. Kennedy (Oxford: Clarendon Press, 1968); Ludovico Ariosto's *Orlando Furioso*, trans. Sir John Harington, ed. Robert McNulty (Oxford: Clarendon Press, 1972); Roberts, 'Commentary', in *First Part*, xxvi–xxviii.

for her Rodomandro, King of Tartaria. Wroth's frequent choice of the adjective 'sage' for her Melissea evokes Montemayor's Felicia, also consistently described as 'sage', and at one point in her manuscript continuation, Wroth even writes 'the sage Felicia' and then crosses out 'Felicia' to write 'Melissea'.[36] Like Wroth's Melissea, Ariosto's Melissa and Montemayor's Felicia are both endowed with foresight into the future and they both use this foresight to further the love relationships of the major protagonists of their respective romances. Their foresight provides a structuring narrative principle; their predictions inevitably come true. But those of Wroth's Melissea increasingly do not. She uses her Melissea figure to expose the limitations of the genre of prose romance as she draws her own to a close.

There are a number of qualities of Ariosto's brilliant *Orlando Furioso* that appear in Wroth's romance, although it is impossible to claim Ariosto as the only source: the sheer number of interlaced tales often interrupting each other; the solicitous and chatty narrator who asks his readers, for example, to forgive Rogero for his inconstancy (as Wroth's narrator requests her readers to forgive Amphilanthus); and the debate over women's constancy, concluding that neither men nor women are capable of it (a central topic although with a different conclusion in the *Urania*). A primary structuring relationship bridging the work is the relationship between Bradamant and Rogero, who are married in the final canto. Melissa's primary function in this romance is to ensure this union in order, the logic of the text pretends, that they may successfully produce the glorious descendants of the d'Este family. Melissa's lengthy list of progeny ends with contemporary personages, most pointedly Ariosto's current patron Hippolito or Cardinal Ippolito d'Este. Melissa intervenes at crucial moments in this romance to promote the welfare of the lovers. Her ring saves Rogero from the magic of the seductive Alcina. She impersonates the Saracen warrior Rodomont in order to break up a dangerous single combat between Rogero and Renaldo. Melissa saves Rogero from dying for grief when Bradamant is betrothed to Leon, who then waives his claim. At the close of the romance, Melissa provides the cloth for their nuptial tent, which foretells the glory of Hippolito (Cardinal Ippolito d'Este). While as one of several magicians, female as well as male, Ariosto's Melissa appears only intermittently, she draws to a successful conclusion a plot that wittily gestures to Ariosto's own hopeful expectations: that the author of a long romance praising the d'Estes, and especially Cardinal Ippolito d'Este, should receive a substantial reward for his artistic efforts. In this hope, he was disappointed.

The closest parallels between Wroth's *Urania* and Montemayor's *Diana*, with its sequel, Gil Polo's *Diana Enamorata*, lie in the many speeches and poems uttered by suffering lovers which, according to the perspectives of these romances, display a nobility—even an innate aristocracy—of soul through the purity of their constant love, freed from the jealousy plaguing baser minds and even from a need for reciprocal devotion. As Montemayor's romance opens, a shepherd mourns the marriage of his beloved shepherdess Diana to the pathologically jealous Delius. Many speeches and songs

---

[36] Wroth, *Second Part*, 61, 424 n. 61.15.

ensue in chains of unmatched lovers, each loving one who does not reciprocate. The sage Felicia brings the primary narratives, except for Diana's, to a successful conclusion. In Gil Polo's sequel, the unhappily married Diana, now desperately in love with the shepherd, journeys with other lovers to the temple of the goddess Diana, where 'sage Lady Felicia makes her abode, whose secret wisedome will minister remedies to our painful passions' (277). Gil Polo's sympathetic development of Diana's unrequited passion for the shepherd who no longer loves her shares with Wroth's romance an interest in the psychological pain of a woman's passion for an unresponsive beloved. Diana's cruel torments, like Pamphilia's, are very productive of verse. Diana's narrative is neatly resolved when her husband Delius dies conveniently of a fit of jealousy. Felicia softens the heart of Diana's shepherd and their marriage takes place immediately. In both the *Diana* and *Diana Enamorata*, Felicia represents a stable narrative centre. Her unfailingly successful remedies supply happy conclusions for the major characters. Yet, it is all a little too neat; as acknowledged in Gil Polo's warning to readers not to base their own lives on these unrealistic fictions of fortunate lovers, 'for one that hath good happe, a thousand there are, whose long and painefull lives with desperate death have been rewarded' (380).

The romances by both Ariosto and Gil Polo run up against the anti-romance of experience: Ariosto cannot praise a different patron; the Cardinal Ippolito is his employer, whatever his low level of generosity. Gil Polo's warning shows his awareness of the discrepancy between his fictions and the probable lived experience of his readers. While in the *First Part* Wroth's Melissea provides successful remedies for love through a Sapphian leap into the sea, in the *Second Part*, her wise-woman is at a loss to reconcile romance and experience. She can only warn Amphilanthus of the treachery of a servant; she is powerless to prevent Forsandurus's betrayal. Unable to obstruct Selarinus's destructive relationship with a fay, Melissea can only provide food and water to save his life after the fay casts him out in a desert. It is surely no accident that topical interpretations rise to the surface of both of these episodes, although without the certainty of biographical fact. As discussed above, the name Forsandurus implicates Hugh Sanford in the prevention of a possible marriage between Pembroke and Wroth (then Mary Sidney), although biographical fact would show that this marriage was never truly feasible. Near the beginning of the *Second Part*, the death of Pamphilia's younger sister Philistella in childbirth clearly calls up the death of Wroth's younger sister Philip in childbirth in 1620. Who then was the dangerous fay? Was she the eighteen-year-old that Philip's widowed husband married five months later, or some other disapproved sexual relationship?[37] However Wroth's romance might manipulate interpretation, the basic events of their lives limit what can happen in her romance: Amphilanthus cannot marry Pamphilia because Pembroke does not marry Mary Sidney (Wroth). Like Philip, Philistella dies and her widowed husband, like Philip's, subsequently engages in a sexual relationship. The

---

[37] Mary Ellen Lamb, 'Topicality and the Interrogation of Wonder in Mary Wroth's *Second Part of The Countess of Montgomery's Urania*', in James Dutcher and Anne Prescott, eds., *Renaissance Historicisms* (Newark: University of Delaware Press, 2008), 258 n. 20.

powers of Melissea as a wise-woman are constrained by events outside the text that are not subject to change.

The same is true of Wroth as an author. Just as a writer of historical fiction can add characters to manipulate opinion but not change the outcome of an actual battle, so the writer of the *Urania* cannot change the outcome of the lives evoked in the topicality of her romance. Her control over these events, and so of her own narrative, is limited. Perhaps this is why Melissea's actions in the *Second Part* become increasingly intrusive and perhaps even desperate. When children of several protagonists are lost to an enchantment, she is able to transport some of them to Lesbos, but others remain captured by giants. This enchantment is, in the words of Clare Kinney, 'frankly incoherent'.[38] Does this relaxation of authorial control suggest that Wroth is writing only for herself, or does it reflect the incoherence of a world gone awry? Melissea announces at least one future event that will not happen in the space of her manuscript. The enchantment of the Inaccessible Rock will only be resolved by a young knight called Fair Design. The exiled King of Denmark also states that only Fair Design can restore him to his kingdom (331). But these tasks must remain unfinished. According to the young Andromarko, Melissea has foretold that further adventures require the reunion of Fair Design and Amphilanthus:

> And Sir, your Faire Designe hath now left all things (beeing certainly informed by severall wisards, especially the sage Melissea), that the great Inchantment will nott bee concluded thes many yeeres; nay, nev[er], if you live nott to assiste in the concluding. For his search is for you, resolving nott to leave you if once found. Till that hapy hower come, and in this Island he is seeking adventur; the best and hapiest, I assure my self, wilbee in finding you.

This is the penultimate sentence of the *Second Part*. The manuscript ends in a sentence fragment: 'Amphilanthus wa[s] extreamly' (418). If, as several critics have claimed, cues in the text gesture to Fair Design as shadowing Pembroke's son by Mary Wroth, then the continuation of this romance is prevented by the intrusion of lived experience.[39] Pembroke's evident estrangement from his natural son precludes the reunion of Amphilanthus and Fair Design in this topical narrative. This 'best and happiest' adventure will never happen and the Fair Design that is simultaneously Wroth's new protagonist, her son, and her highly designed romance, cannot proceed in the anticipated narrative of joyful meeting. In this refusal of the narrative to conclude, the hard facts of lived experience expose and critique the element of wish fulfilment common to the genres of prose romance, masque, and lyric.

---

[38] Clare R. Kinney, '"Beleeve this butt a fiction": Female Authorship, Narrative Undoing, and the Limits of Romance in *The Second Part of the Countess of Montgomery's Urania*', *Spenser Studies*, 17 (2003): 239–50 (245); Cavanagh, *Cherished Torment*, 195–218.

[39] Roberts, 'Commentary', xviii and lxvii; Mueller and Gossett, 'Textual Introduction', xxii–xxiii; Hackett, *Women and Romance Fiction*, 165–6; Lewalski, *Writing Women*, 289, 408 n. 99; Lamb, 'Biopolitics', 121–30.

Further Reading

Cavanagh, Sheila. *Cherished Torment* (Pittsburgh: Duquesne University Press, 2007).
—— 'Endless Love: Narrative Technique in the *Urania*', *Sidney Journal*, 26.2 (2008): 83–100.
Hackett, Helen. *Women and Romance Fiction in the English Renaissance* (Cambridge: Cambridge University Press, 2000).
Hannay, Margaret. *Mary Sidney, Lady Wroth* (Burlington: Ashgate, 2010).
Kinney, Clare R. ed. *Ashgate Critical Studies on Women Writers in England, 1550–1700*. Vol. 4: *Mary Wroth* (Burlington: Ashgate, 2009).
—— '"Beleeve this butt a fiction": Female Authorship, Narrative Undoing, and the Limits of Romance in *The Second Part of the Countess of Montgomery's Urania*', *Spenser Studies*, 17 (2003): 239–50.
Lamb, Mary Ellen. 'The Biopolitics of Romance in Mary Wroth's *The Countess of Montgomery's Urania*', *English Literary Renaissance*, 31.1 (2001): 107–30.
Miller, Jacqueline. 'Lady Mary Wroth in the House of Busirane', in Patrick Cheney and Lauren Silberman, eds., *Worldmaking Spenser* (Lexington: University Press of Kentucky, 2000), 115–24.
Miller, Shannon. 'Constructing the Female Self: Architectural Structures in Mary Wroth's *Urania*', in Patricia Fumerton and Simon Hunt, eds., *Renaissance Culture and the Everyday* (Philadelphia: University of Pennsylvania Press, 1999), 139–61.
Roberts, Josephine A. 'Critical Introduction', in Mary Wroth, *The First Part of the Countess of Montgomery's Urania*, ed. Josephine A. Roberts (Binghamton, NY: Medieval & Renaissance Texts & Studies, 1995).
—— '"The Knott Never To Be Untied": The Controversy Regarding Marriage in Mary Wroth's *Urania*', in Naomi Miller and Gary Waller, eds., *Reading Mary Wroth* (Knoxville: University of Tennessee Press, 1991), 109–32.
Salzman, Paul. 'Mary Wroth: From Obscurity to Canonization', in *Reading Early Modern Women's Writing* (Oxford: Oxford University Press, 2006), 60–89.
Zurcher, Amelia A. 'Ethics and the Politic Agent of Early Seventeenth-Century Prose Romance', *English Literary Renaissance*, 35 (2005): 73–101.

PART III

VARIETIES OF EARLY MODERN PROSE 1: PUBLIC PROSE

CHAPTER 16

UTOPIA AND UTOPIANISM

ROBERT APPELBAUM

'Utopia' is the name of a book, the name of an imaginary island, and the name of an idea. Sir Thomas More (1478–1535) is responsible for the first two and indirectly for the third one as well. In 1516 he published, in Latin, *Libellus vere aureus, nec minus salutaris quam festivus, de optimo rei publicae statu deque nova insula Utopia*, which can be literally translated as *A Truly Golden Little Book, No Less Salubrious than Festive, of the Best State of a Republic, and of the New Island Utopia*. 'Utopia' is Greek for 'No Place', with a pun on the word 'Eutopia', which is Greek for 'Happy Place'. The island does not exist, but it is 'new', or at least new to us, and it comes to our attention in the context of a treatment of 'the best state of a republic'. In fact, the book generally called *Utopia* is divided into two parts; the first part involves a discussion among learned men of 'the best state of a republic'; the second part involves a description of a 'new island' which seems to answer the requirements of a 'best state of a republic', although the narrator of the book (a fictionalized Thomas More) begs to differ. 'I cannot agree and consent to all things' that were said about how the island is run, the narrator says. 'I must needs confess and grant that many things be in the Utopian weal-public which in our cities I may rather wish for than hope after.'[1]

So, going back to 1516, *Utopia* is a book and Utopia is an imaginary island. But by the early seventeenth century, in the words of the *Oxford English Dictionary*, the word came to indicate a pair of complementary ideas: either 'any imaginary, indefinitely-remote region, country, or locality' or else 'a place, state, or condition ideally perfect in respect of politics, laws, customs, and conditions'. The word was generalized, sometimes as a term of praise and sometimes as a term of abuse—for to call an idea or a proposal a 'utopia' could mean that it was ludicrously impractical—and used to indicate the object of either of two kinds, or both kinds at once, of what would still later be called *utopianism*.

Discussions of utopia and utopianism are inescapably complicated by this multiplicity of meanings: a book, an imaginary island, an ideal state, any imaginary island, any

---

[1] Thomas More, *Utopia*, trans. Ralph Robinson (1556), in *Three Early Modern Utopias*, ed. Susan Bruce (Oxford: Oxford University Press, 1999), 123.

ideal state, and any or all of these things in relation to the many-sided impulse that we call 'utopianism'. Discussions will further be complicated by the attitudes we bring to bear upon utopianism. If one imagines that history is progressive, that it is potentially progressive, or that it ought to be progressive, and if one thinks of progress as the achievement, so far as possible, of a 'best state' run according to principles of universal justice, one may well discuss utopia and utopianism as a legacy and a hope. What Thomas More first started (though not without plenty of precedents, as we will see) was a project as yet incomplete and what we learn from studying that project in the documents of the past is, among other things, how to keep the project going. But if one is sceptical about the idea of progress and if one thinks that one ought to study history and texts on their own terms, in view of their immediate circumstances without regard to subsequent developments or one's own political inclination, then there is nothing, in a word, 'utopian' about studying utopia and utopianism. Studying them might well elucidate many things about the period in which they are found to occur and may help one understand how texts work and a certain range of ideas can be developed, but they are not a legacy and they are not a source of hope; they are only what they are.

Total engagement in a project of utopianism, for which More's *Utopia* is a foundational text, or total disengagement from such a project in the name of clarity of intellectual purpose—these are not the only two alternatives available. Surely, there are shades of engagement and disengagement between the two extremes and there are other ways of going about the study of utopia and utopianism entirely. But the two extremes are indicative of the main challenge to interpretative thought that utopia and utopianism present, and not just to us, in the twenty-first century: for the two extremes of engagement and disengagement inherent to the utopian project challenged thinkers of More's own time and for many years to follow; in fact, they are embedded in the construction of the book, *Utopia*, itself.

What follows is a discussion, then, of three things: the sources and intertextualities of *Utopia* and its utopian project, in other words the other texts and historical developments utopia is in dialogue with; the continued development of the utopian framework of thought from 1516 to 1640; and the dialectic of engagement and disengagement that utopianism imposes on people who would respond to it, whether for the sixteenth and early seventeenth centuries or for us.

16.1 Influences, Intertexualities, and Meaning

At least four kinds of sources of influence can be found in the original *Utopia*. Chief among them may be what the original title alludes to when it refers to the 'best state of the republic'. The tradition begins with Plato (c.428–348 BCE) and Aristotle (384–322 BCE), and most especially with Plato's *Republic* (c.380 BCE). This is a tradition, in the first place, of the philosophical dialogue; all of the first part of *Utopia* is a philosophical dialogue in the Platonic mould. But it is a tradition as well of thinking about human community as a *political* society; the original Greek title (not necessarily the title Plato wanted to give it, but the one handed down by tradition) is Πολιτεία, 'Of the City', or more accurately, 'Of the City-State'. Whether in the form of a city-state or some larger entity that can be called a regional or imperial 'state' (in Latin either *civitas* or *respublica*), when society is thought of as a 'state' it is thought of as an entity of more or less consensual association, where the power of making laws and enforcing them is vested in its institutions and appointed officials. Plato and Aristotle both take the existence of the state for granted, but as they enquire into the nature of the state they also enquire into the nature of the 'best state'; indeed, for both philosophers, to enquire into one is to enquire into the other, for to know what a thing like a state *is* requires knowing what a thing like a state *ought to be*. Plato and Aristotle gave various answers to the question of the best state and were in disagreement on many issues, but they both saw that the perfection of the state relied on the state's living up to the principle of universal justice. Aristotle thus underlined the importance of what he called 'distributive justice', the fair distribution of wealth, goods, and social capital among all the citizens of the state. Plato went further and advocated communism.

A second tradition to which More responds is Christian. There seems little question that one of the things More had in mind when he developed his description of the island of Utopia was the prosperous medieval monastery, with its carefully regulated life, its collectivist spirit, its shared labour and meals, its mixed economy, and—for this is a central part of life in Utopia—its piety. Behind the monastic tradition lay the notion of the early Christian communities mentioned in the New Testament. It is said of one of these communities, 'Neither was there any among them that lacked: for as many as were possessors of lands or houses sold them, and brought the prices of the things that were sold, And laid them down at the apostles' feet: and distribution was made unto every man according as he had need.'[2] But the founding of this communist community in the Bible is a spontaneous, voluntary, and collective act. In a monastery, entry to which often involved the renunciation of all one's worldly possessions, communal life was compulsory and (in principle) strictly enforced. So it is in Utopia. Utopia enlists the free will of all its inhabitants; without that free will the utopian project would fall apart. The government of the nation is republican. But Utopia was founded—being similar in this respect to many monastic orders—by a single charismatic and authoritarian leader, Utopus, who established the laws of the new republic, and Utopia is controlled as much by the enforcement of its laws as by the consent of the governed. Many of its laws, when looked at closely, are actually quite restrictive, and offences against the law can lead to forced servitude and even capital punishment.

Much of this serious business of political and economic idealism, and of a strictly enforced legal code, however, is mitigated by way of a third kind of influence that More

---

[2] Acts 4:34-5, *KJV*.

clearly draws upon, the comical or satirical fantasy. When Plato was a young man and the real-life Socrates was holding forth in the marketplace of Athens, there was already a form of writing that made fun of utopianism. It appears most prominently in the comedies of Aristophanes (446–386 BCE); for example, in *The Birds* (414 BCE), where an Athenian, in an absurd response to the political problems of the day, convinces the birds of the area to form their own city in the sky, called Cloudcuckooland. It is hard to establish with certainty what speculative ideas about the city-state Aristophanes was poking fun at, but we can see that by Aristophanes's time a literary tradition was already afloat, where writers at once registered the utopian impulse and mocked it. In the third century BC there flourished in the Greek world a 'cynic' philosopher named Menippus of Gadara who further developed the genres of social satire in a utopian mould. His writings are now lost, but they had a direct influence on the work of Lucian of Samosata (125–180), a favourite of Thomas More and his good friend, the Dutch humanist Desiderius Erasmus (1466–1536). Among Lucian's works was *Menippus*, a dialogue where the cynic philosopher visits the underworld and sees established a new decree to punish men of wealth in the afterlife for having been wealthy, and *A True Story*, a rambunctious narrative involving, among other things, a trip to the moon and a view of the puny and ridiculous earth of men from the point of view of the heavens.

'Menippean Satire', as literary critics are inclined to call it today—a satire of attitudes and ideas, rather than people, articulated through playful narrative, dialogue, or verse, and often openly implausible—was an important part of the humanist project of early modernity. In 1511 Erasmus published *Moriae encomium*, punning on the name of his friend Thomas More, to whom he dedicated the book; or, in English, *The Praise of Folly*. In *The Praise of Folly*, the person Folly herself speaks and argues, foolishly, on behalf of what she stands for, though in the end she makes serious points about religious worship and love, and all along the Folly's praise of herself has important things to say about the human condition. Thomas More's *Utopia* is in some respects a response to *The Praise of Folly*. It is certainly an attempt to experiment with the genre of the Menippean Satire in the wake of what Erasmus had already done with it and to write something that was both foolish and wise, addressing itself, through the ironies of satiric form, to practical and serious business of human society. Critics today are apt to speak of the attitude of works like *The Praise of Folly* and *Utopia* as 'jocoserious', calling attention to the in-betweenness of the discourse, an indefiniteness in attitude and meaning that cannot, and is not supposed to be, ever resolved. *Utopia* is a form of textual *play*. *Utopia* is a *joke*, even if there is much that *Utopia* is serious about. And that is one of the main reasons why it can be said that *Utopia* requires a mixture of engagement and disengagement.

But if *Utopia* comments playfully on the human condition, in the spirit of the wild tales and dialogues of Lucian, it also addresses itself to some important historical developments. London in More's day and age was becoming ever more a thriving urban centre; and his Utopia is a predominantly urban society. England under Henry VIII was aspiring to be a world power and constantly intervening, belligerently, in the affairs on the Continent and Ireland; and so too, Utopia gets involved, with arms, in foreign affairs across the sea. The first stirrings of the Reformation were beginning to be felt; Luther would publicize his Ninety-Five Theses just a year after the publication of *Utopia* and Erasmus himself, though he would never become a Protestant, was an advocate of reform. So too, in an Erasmian spirit, with an emphasis on natural piety, Utopia is religiously experimental. Even more important, it would seem, for the interlocutors in *Utopia* discuss this at some length, there was an economic development to respond to: economic modernization was putting pressure on the old peasantry of More's England and controversies over 'enclosure', the practice of landlords of fencing off parts of their land for their own use, to the detriment of tenant farmers who had traditionally used such lands 'in common', were becoming widespread. Obviously, Utopia has solved such problems by abolishing private property, so that, in principle, absolutely everything, apart from people themselves, are held 'in common'. Utopia is a predominantly urban society which has solved the *agrarian* problem through the state-wide abolition of private property and the republican, egalitarian administration of the common weal.

But there was one development more. All of these historical phenomena—the growth of London and urbanism generally, the new English interest in foreign affairs, religious experimentation and debate on the eve of the Reformation, and the modernization of the English economy at the expense of traditional peasants and the feudal system to which they were accustomed—came at the time of the Age of Discovery. The news of Columbus's first voyage had only arrived in England twenty-three years earlier and the nature of much of the world outside of the Old World still remained, for Europeans, a matter of conjecture. England involved itself in the Age of Discovery on a national level from 1497, when Henry VII sponsored the journey across the Atlantic undertaken by the Italian John Cabot, and though England wasn't very good at taking advantage of discovery or colonization until the seventeenth century, plans for exploration and colonial expansion were always afoot.

More's *Utopia* takes a good deal of its inspiration from Amerigo Vespucci's *Lettera delle isole nuovamente trovate in quattro suoi viaggi* (1504–5), possibly by way of a Latin translation that appeared in 1507. Raphael Hytholday, the traveller in *Utopia*, is said to have been one of the crew members on Amerigo Vespucci's last expedition who were voluntarily left behind in the New World (so that Hythloday had a chance to move about and explore things on his own). The island of Utopia may be 'no place', but it is certainly a part of the New World that was still being explored in More's day. *Utopia* inserts the fictional island into the non-fictional, but still poorly understood, geography of the Americas, in which a crewman of Vespucci might have travelled. And More is clearly responding to an element of Vespucci's letters which make the New World at once attractive and challenging. Parts of the New World, for Vespucci, bring to mind the Golden Age of classical legend, when people were both simpler and more virtuous, and both poverty and wealth were unknown. So the New World can be a place that excites the moral imagination. Its newness can be an innocence. But the New World can also stand as a rebuke to the Old, since its virtue may be held to contrast more than a little favourably with the corrupt life of advanced society in Europe. In a famous essay originally published in 1578, 'Of Cannibals', the Frenchman Michel de Montaigne (1533–92) made this rebuke explicit; the barbarity of the inhabitants of the New World, he asserted, was nothing compared to the barbarity of so-called civilized people, doing what they believe their civility warrants them to do—like persecuting each other because of religious differences. More doesn't go quite that far; but he does explore the possibility that a people of a New World, without the benefit of European civilization, and even without the benefit of revealed religion, might nevertheless live more wholesomely and even more piously than their European counterparts. Although it is a joke, *Utopia* is also a rebuke.

So there are four of the main influences behind the invention of *Utopia*: philosophical speculation about the 'best state'; the communal life of the monastic orders; Menippean Satire with its comic dialogues and fantastic adventures; and the real-world literature of discovery and exploration. Put the four together, along with such ancillary concerns as urbanization, and you have the essential building blocks of *Utopia*. But if you do put the four together, as More has done, you have the makings for what is at once a highly coherent and convincing bipartite exposition—first a philosophical discussion among interlocutors about politics and then a description of the island of Utopia that is intended empirically to prove the main points of the discussion—and a very unstable idea. *Utopia* seems to give hope. With one hand it seems to say, here is a new possibility, a new way of thinking about the world, a new way of imagining collective life, where reason and piety rule rather than convention and passion, and the good of the community rules over the pursuit of private self-interest. Let us renew ourselves. But with the other hand the text seems to say, don't take this new way of thinking terribly seriously. That's not the point. In the final analysis, there is nothing certain about the certainties of the New World and the imaginary paradises with which we would like to populate it.

So the meaning of *Utopia*, in short, inspiring though it may be, is inherently indefinite and unstable. More himself signals this to the reader with his infamous wordplay. Utopia is No Place. Hythloday, the main speaker of the dialogue, is (in Greek) a 'Peddlar of Nonsense'. And there is more to the indefiniteness besides word-play. So far as *Utopia* is meant to entail not a description of a real place, or even a place that is to be 'hoped after', but rather a satirical commentary on real-world Europe, its main meaning would seem to consist in that which it attacks. But it is hard to determine exactly what it is that *Utopia* attacks. As soon as one tries to establish the exact targets of *Utopia*'s satire, one gets caught up in the same back-and-forth of jocoseriousness as the book itself deliberately dallies with. *Utopia* is against private property, but maybe *not really*. *Utopia* is against the Catholic religion as currently practised in the early sixteenth century, but maybe *not really*. *Utopia* is against the modern world of mercantilism, monarchy, urbanism, and High Church Catholicism, but maybe *not really*. More was himself a high-ranking state official, working for a powerful king, and he was both a representative of the rising mercantile class and a devout Catholic. Besides, just look at Utopia itself: it is full of self-contradictions. It is a nation without any laws, but it actually has plenty of laws. It is a nation that has abolished capital punishment; but it actually practises capital punishment. It is a nation where everything and everyone are alike, equal in dignity. But in fact, there are all kinds of inequalities of dignity and even of power and possession in the island. Perhaps Utopia is not so utopian after all...

16.2 Subsequent developments

Utopia was famous from the day of its appearance in print. Some people seem to have been fooled by it, believing that Utopia was an actual island somewhere in the Americas. After all, More had apparently spoken in his own voice in the text; he had made several real people, including himself, the speakers of the dialogue, Raphael Hythloday apart; and he had framed the dialogue by a picture of real events of the day. But eventually, the idea took hold: *Utopia* was jocoserious and there was no such thing as Utopia. What seemed to be important about the text was the utopian idea—a point of view about the real world that was *not* of this world, not confined to its received ideas and dogmatic conventions. And what seemed to be important as well was its utopian jocoseriousness—a way of engaging in literary play, where one both speculated and mocked, where one both asserted and denied. The most famous of all responses to *Utopia* in this respect was *Gargantua and Pantagruel* by the French writer François Rabelais (1494–1553); the First Book of Rabelais's four-volume romp[3] includes a description of the ideal society of the Abbey of Thélème, a place where men and women live together for the sake of pleasure and self-fulfilment, and the guiding principle of life is 'Do What Thou Wilt'. The Second and Third Books contain a number of allusions to the island from Utopia, where the hero Pantagruel is said to have been born, and the Fourth Book tells the tale of a fantastic voyage to islands where the rules of life are vastly different from our own, in a mock-heroic search for what is called the Oracle of the Bottle.

So Rabelais absorbed much of the spirit of *Utopia* and made it much his own. But if meaning is unstable in *Utopia*, in *Gargantua and Pantagruel* it is perhaps even more unstable. Whereas *Utopia* is sometimes mildly humorous, *Gargantua and Pantagruel* openly plays for laughs. Rabelais does not hesitate to sacrifice the seriousness of humanist learning to the requirements of farce. And where More might seem to put forward a programme for collective action, even if only half seriously, Rabelais cannot seem to be doing anything of the kind. He is just expressing a fantasy, *Do What Thou Wilt*, and calling attention to the unpleasant fact that in the modern world one cannot do what one would. It would be better if we could do what we would, Rabelais implies; think of the possibilities. But we can't. And in any case, though there were certainly some readers in England who were familiar with Rabelais's work in French, none of it is was translated into English and published in England until 1653; it would not be until 1694 that the whole of Rabelais's output would be available in English. And, for the most part, writers in England would take a much more cautious approach to the ambiguous jocoseriousness inherent to the humanist utopian project, and a much more cautious approach as well to the politics and social criticism inherent to the utopian project. English writers, generally speaking, wanted to be *engaged* with the utopian project; but at the

---

[3] There is a 'Fifth Book', but many scholars, including this one, doubt that much, if any, of it was written by Rabelais.

same time, they seemed to want to disengage themselves from the radical implications of the project and even, for the most part, from the radical implications of utopian textuality.

A case in point would be the first important work of social thought in England to follow in *Utopia*'s wake, Thomas Elyot's *The Boke Named the Governour* (1531). *The Governour* is a much more conservative document than More's. It begins, indeed, by openly disavowing communism and the notion of the republic that informs More's text, or for that matter Plato's *Republic*, and it ends by promoting a humanist, courtly society, presided over by a powerful monarch and a learned, professional ruling class, a society that is more familiar from Erasmus's (non-satiric) *Enchiridion militis Christiani* (often translated as *The Education of the Christian Prince*: 1503) or Baldassare Castiglione's relatively serious *Il Cortegiano* (*The Courtier*: 1528) than from the Platonic–Morean tradition. *The Governour* makes few jokes; it is not very playful; and instead of challenging the status quo of the social order, though it recommends many reforms, and tries to find a new home for learning and reason in society, it actually apologizes for many aspects of the status quo.

More akin to *Utopia* in form and spirit, though also much more earnest and far less radical, are two political dialogues. The first of these, the *Dialogue Between Cardinal Pole and Thomas Lupset*, by Thomas Starkey, was completed by 1533; it circulated in manuscript only, not being printed until the nineteenth century. The two interlocutors of the dialogue were historical figures, men of Starkey's acquaintance, who played a role in negotiating the relation between church and state in response to reformist impulses both of them shared and to Henry VIII's break from Rome, which Pole (like Thomas More himself) could never fully subscribe to. The main speaker, Pole, is caused to argue in an anti-ecclesiastic mode in favour of an Aristotelian 'mixed monarchy', with a strong Parliament and a weak clerical presence, and to encourage a form of happiness in both individuals and the state where the body and the soul are allowed equally to flourish.

Still more motivated by economic considerations was a second humanist dialogue, Thomas Smith's *Discourse of a Commonweal of this Realm in England*. It was written in 1549, circulating (again) in manuscript, and found its way into print in 1581, four years after Smith's death. Smith's *Discourse* is a dialogue between five different interlocutors, representing different estates and trades, with a knight dominating the conversation. The interlocutors are concerned about a current 'dearth' and troubled by the recent anti-enclosure riots of 1549, which had broken out in several parts of England, climaxing in the protracted Kett's Rebellion in Smith's native East Anglia. The knight leads the interlocutors in analysing the dearth and the discontent to which it has given rise, and the problem, on the one hand, of inflation, and, on the other, of the natural avarice of mankind. His solution is to regulate the economy by governmental policies that exploit the selfish avarice of individuals for the sake of general prosperity and the common good. Like Hythloday in *Utopia*, Smith's interlocutors are indignant over the displacement of small landholders by great landlords seeking to maximize their profits by raising sheep for wool for the export market. But Smith isn't interested in what may be called utopian solutions to the problem. In a later work, *De Republica Anglorum* (written in English, despite its Latin title, and first published in 1583), an analysis of the English constitution, Smith concludes by renouncing the 'vaine imaginations, phantasies of Philosophers', including Plato, Xenophon, and More.[4]

Also in dialogue form, imitating a humanist exercise, but actually something quite different, is *Siuqila: Too Good to Be True*, written by Thomas Lupton and printed in London in 1580. It is the first work in English since *Utopia* to adopt the conceit of an imaginary perfect commonwealth and the first to imitate More's word-play in its use of proper names. *Siuqila* is the name of the main character—Siuqila being the Latin word *aliquis* ('somebody') spelled backwards. He is an Englishman travelling around the world who comes into contact with an individual named Omen—that is *nemo* ('no one'). Omen hails from the country of Mauqsun—that is, *nusquam* ('nowhere'). Siuqila is not allowed entry into Mauqsun; foreigners like him are considered too dangerous an influence. But Omen is glad to spend a long while discussing the 'wonderfull manners' of the people of Nowhere. As Siuqila never enters Mauqsun, the reader never gets to see it in operation, and though Omen tells him a good deal about the laws and the behaviour of the people of Mauqsun, he never actually describes the country. The text gestures mightily in the direction of the genre of *Utopia*, but stops short of one of its most important features, the description of the ideal republic. Yet, that is not the only major difference. Although the dialogue works by pointing out the differences between a very real and troubled England on the one hand and a well-nigh perfect imaginary commonwealth on the other, it does not really stem from a deep humanist understanding of how societies operate. It is, rather, a popular work, made to appeal to certain popular prejudices.

Too Good to Be True may perhaps be described as the first *Puritan* utopia—Puritan (for us) in both an attractive and an unattractive sense. In its attractive aspects, the book embraces Low Church evangelism, personal religion with emphasis on biblical study, universal literacy, moral probity, and, above all, a species of communitarianism, motivated by the rule of charity. As in Puritan leader John Winthrop's famous lay sermon *A Modell of Christian Charity*, delivered aboard the *Arabella* en route from England to Massachusetts (1630), poverty is not so much systematically eradicated in *Too Good to Be True* as energetically mitigated. Almsgiving and charitable works are central to the moral economy of the nation. But more unattractive, from our point of view, and no doubt from the point of view of anti-Puritans of Tudor England as well, is the intolerance of the state of Mauqsun, with its heavy-handed system of justice and its illiberal sanctimony. Mauqsun, we learn, suffers from no crime, from no outbreaks of licentious or immodest behaviour, from no drunkenness or gluttony or irreverence or fornication. No one suffers from the sins of greed, pride, idleness, dishonesty, or irresponsibility. And the reason for such universal purity is that there are very strict, even harrowing laws against all crimes and all sins, with penalties so severe, including capital punishment, that most citizens are cowed into good behaviour, and those who aren't are finally eliminated—mercilessly executed. Simply to fail to educate one's young children, so that

---

[4] Sir Thomas Smith, *De Republica Anglorum: A Discourse on the Commonwealth of England*, ed. L. Alston (Cambridge: Cambridge University Press, 1906), 142.

they cannot recite the Lord's Prayer and Creed, is to expose oneself to very heavy fines; and if one can't pay the fines, one shall then 'recyve twenties stripes, every moneth once, untill he have trayned his children Chrisitianlye and obedientlye'.[5] Meanwhile, to be convicted a second time for the minor crime of usury, or for having borrowed money from a usurer, is punishable by death. A commercial success, *Too Good to Be True* was also accompanied by a sequel, *The Second Part and Knitting Up of the Boke Entitled Too Good to Be True* (1581), which adds a few details but leaves the general picture unchanged. If life were led really as we are encouraged to lead our lives by more earnest church officials and other authorities today, by forces that would come to be associated with the word 'puritanism', life would be 'too good to be true'—only Lupset and his readership clearly 'wish for' and maybe even 'hope after' a life of that kind.

Utopia itself, with its more complex understanding of how nations work and how writing can make a difference in the life of nations, was translated into English in 1551 by Ralph Robinson, a 'citizen and Goldsmythe of London', as he identifies himself, who had been educated at Oxford. Robinson's translation is faulted by modern scholars for its inaccuracies, but Robinson's prose is a good deal livelier than many subsequent efforts and Robinson shows himself to be more than a little capable of appreciating what *Utopia* had achieved. He calls the book *A Fruteful and Plesaunt Worke of the Best State of a Publique Weale, and of the New Yle called Utopia* and in a preface extols it as much for its style and wit as for its content. The translation was reprinted in 1555 and then five times more through 1641. So even if few thinkers of the time would be openly as adventurous as More in thinking about an ideal state, or in engaging in literary play, *Utopia* was available to be read in both Latin and English, and perhaps widely read. In a preface to the translation, Robinson goes to the effort of declaring that More's work belongs to a great new tradition of English letters and that it is only a shame that in subsequent years More refused to take sides with the Reformation, that he was 'so much blinded, rather with obstinacy than with ignorance, that could not or rather would not see the shining light of God's holy truth …'[6]

So the sixteenth century was alive to the new way of thinking and writing that *Utopia* represented, although it could also be apprehensive about it and the legend of the man responsible for it, and it could imagine ways in which utopianism could be developed in the pursuit of more economic parity and even the enforcement of stricter moral codes. Then, as the sixteenth century came to a close, interest in utopian writing leaped forward: engagement and disengagement were equally transformed by a new kind of commitment to the utopian project. On the Continent, most notably, the Dominican monk Tommaso Campanella wrote *La Città del Sole* (1602), which he later translated into Latin and published as *Civitas solis* (1623); another Italian, political philosopher Lodovico Zùccolo published a dialogue called *Il Belluzzi, o vero della città felice* (1615) and another called *La Repubblica d'Evandria* (1625); and the German Lutheran minister Johann Valentin Andreae published *Reipublicae Christianopolitanae descriptio* (1619). All of

---

[5] Thomas Lupton, *Siuqila, Too Good To Be True* (London, 1580), 38.
[6] *Utopia*, trans. Robinson, 146.

these works follow the genre of *Utopia* fairly closely, employing the device of a philosophical dialogue where one of the interlocutors reports on travels to another land. And all of them imagine a republic devoted to the common weal, Campanella in the direction of an authoritarian, but mystical and communist state, Zùccolo in the direction of republican-directed distributive justice, and Andreae in the direction of a meritocratically governed and pious communist state.

Clearly, something was in the air in the early seventeenth century, something which More had anticipated, but which was only just now becoming common currency for political thinkers. In England would come the work of Francis Bacon and Robert Burton. Sir Francis Bacon (1561–1626), one of the great minds of his age, had already written a work from which Andreae had found inspiration, *The Advancement of Learning* (1605), where Bacon called for a wholesale renewal of scientific research and education in England along the lines of empiricism and collective, collegial enterprise. After his death was published the incomplete text, *The New Atlantis*, where Bacon imagines a trip to yet another hitherto unknown island of the Americas, a rational, pious, and generous society devoted to learning. At about the same time, Robert Burton (1577–1640) was writing and rewriting what is conventionally called 'A Utopia of Mine Owne', a section of the preface, 'Democritus Junior to the Reader', to the mammoth *Anatomy of Melancholy* (1621–40). Both Bacon and Burton embrace the Morean principle of literary play, though Bacon does so in a very earnest, un-mocking spirit, while Burton does so humorously and sometimes mischievously. But Bacon and Burton are also thinking quite carefully about the nature of the kind of society they would like to live in. And in this they are akin to other early seventeenth-century utopians. Campanella, Zùccolo, and Andreae were actively involved in the political, religious, and scientific turmoil of their day, each in his own way promoting progressive policies and programmes (the erratic Campanella ended up in jail for most of his adult life as a reward for his efforts). Bacon, by contrast, was an establishment figure, a Member of Parliament and eventually (like Thomas More before him) the Chancellor of England; and Burton was a retiring Oxford don. But all five of these figures are united in wanting to change the world, in wanting to make the world run by more rational principles, in the pursuit of material and spiritual prosperity, more or less collectively, and with a view towards promoting learning and the new science.

In contrast to the work of the previous century, these later utopian works are characterized by the intensity of the commitment of their authors to the utopian project. It is a two-sided commitment, to be sure. On the one hand, these utopias are urgent; the writers want to think past what they take to be the contradictions and limitations of their time; they want to imagine how things might be *done*. On the other hand, the utopias are highly speculative. They are not weighed down by conventions of the present day, as most of the utopias of the sixteenth century could be said to be. They all involve audacious flights of hypothetical fancy. Neither *New Atlantis* nor 'A Utopia of Mine Owne' goes so far as to embrace communism, it is true; the latter in fact openly renounces communism and other apparently impractical ideas in favour of proto-capitalist development and the accumulation of capital. (In some ways, that makes 'A Utopia of Mine

Owne' the most modern of all these works.) But Bacon's and Burton's utopias are nevertheless urgent efforts to rethink the bases of civil society, to repair what Burton thinks of as the 'melancholy' of modern social life, and what Bacon seems to imagine as its disappointing inadequacy. And they are highly imaginative, openly removed from the pressures of the here and now, from popular prejudice and received opinion. Bacon takes his readers to the Island of Bensalem, off the coast of Peru, to view what it would be like, among other things, to live in a society dedicated to acquiring the 'light' of scientific knowledge. Burton keeps his readers at home, but he defies them to imagine a home country transformed into a uniformly prosperous, vibrant, and happy whole.

Somewhat in the same spirit as the work of other utopists of the early seventeenth century, but taking a new tack, comes one last major utopian text: Francis Godwin's *The Man in the Moone* (1638). *The Man in the Moone* is presented not as a dialogue but rather, like *New Atlantis*, as an adventure narrative. This time, however, the destination of the adventurer is not to a better society, where human beings have learned how to organize their lives for the good of the whole, but an otherworldly society, the society of moon people, whose nature is different from that of humans. The tale was written at about the same time as a somewhat similar text by the great astronomer, Johannes Kepler (1571–1630), *Somnium*, published after the astronomer's death in 1634, where another trip to the moon is imagined. But Godwin puts flesh and blood to his story, giving it the tone and trappings of the picaresque novel, a form of writing which originated in the late sixteenth century in Spain. The hero of Godwin's story is one Domingo Gonsales, harnessing the power of high-flying geese, where the protagonist Domingo Gonsales visits a paradisiacal society of giants. It is probably not an exaggeration to credit *The Man in the Moone* (and *not* Kepler's *Somnium*) with being the first work of science fiction ever written, putting into novelistic form a tale which considers the impact of scientific and technological innovation in an imaginary time and place. The technology isn't much; the story is not very sophisticated, either from a scientific or a literary point of view; and the paradisiacal world of the giants, though it answers to some of the commonplaces about the classical Golden Age, doesn't provide the reader, or even the protagonist of the story, with much guidance. But technology, whether earthly or lunar, is the point of the story. The point of the story, that is, is to underscore the promise of technology to compensate humanity for its physical and moral insufficiencies. Unlike *New Atlantis*, *The Man in the Moone* shows us not an ideal society that would be worth imitating if only we could, but a world that we *cannot* imitate because of the limitations of our nature. It asks us instead to look for other kinds of solutions to the problem of the state.

16.3 Engagement and disengagement

One other text that is often mentioned with reference to early modern utopianism is *Mundus Alter et Idem* (1595), written in Latin by English clergyman Joseph Hall, and later loosely (but vividly) translated by John Healey for an edition of 1609, entitled, *The*

Discovery of a New World. Hall's work is a satirical text, more influenced by *Gargantua and Pantagruel*, perhaps, than *Utopia*. In it one Mercurius Brittanicus (the 'British messenger') undertakes a voyage to *Terra Australis Incognita*, a region that the fable locates in the regions of what we now call Antarctica. But what he discovers is no model commonwealth. The *Terra Australis* is a world turned upside down, imagined as a place where the faults and foibles of contemporary English society are ridiculously exaggerated—*alter et idem*, different yet the *same*—the better to point out their inherent absurdity. The book is an extremely negative work, a dystopia rather than a utopia, and so far as it takes aim against the ambitions of free-spirited individuals of contemporary England, holding them up to dystopian ridicule, it anticipates Jonathan Swift's *Gulliver's Travels* (1721), not to mention satires closer to home such as Ben Jonson's comedy, *The Alchemist* (1611).

Whether *Mundus alter et idem* should be counted as a 'utopian' text is debatable. Its negativity would seem to count against it. So too would be the fact that unlike, say, Francis Godwin's Domingo Gonsales, Mercurius Brittanicus has nothing to offer his readers except his story. He learns nothing in his travels; he finds nothing in the 'other world' to admire. But *Mundus alter et idem* would seem then, at the very least, to have something to tell us about the nature of utopian engagement. For in it we see what happens when, for all of the literary power inherent to imaginary voyage, and for all the fun a writer and his readers may have with it, the utopian imagination has nothing to offer but criticism of the present. In it we see what happens, in other words, when the utopian imagination leaves us with nothing either to wish for or hope after.

The production of any utopian fiction would seem to require a measure of *dis*engagement. *Fictionality* seems to demand it. Utopian fiction is inherently ironic precisely because it is fictional. It is inherently about something that is *not*, and very likely *cannot be*. But when that disengagement is carried to an extreme, when it is not also coupled with engagement, though the fiction itself may prosper, the text as a whole may well be, in a word, un-giving. More's *Utopia* may be inherently unstable, but it clearly has something to *give* its readers. So it was in the case of most of More's prominent imitators in the sixteenth and seventeenth centuries, from Thomas Elyot to Francis Godwin. Even Rabelais's silliness (which Rabelais would suggest is actually not so silly) has something to offer. But *Mundus alter et idem* gives us nothing, even if we are willing to be receptive to it. On the other side of its cynicism about the world as it is lies a kind of complacency about the world as it is.

What the counter-example of *Mundus alter et idem* may call our attention to, therefore, is that, if it is to work as *utopian* writing, a utopian fiction will have to couple its disengagement with engagement. But what, then, is the nature of this engagement? Speaking only of work from 1516 to 1640, one is tempted to say that what the writing is engaged with—both in the way it is written and in what, however ironically, it advocates—is what we now call 'modernity'. Utopia is a 'new island' and all the major utopian works of the period attempt to engage with that which is new. This is not newness for its own sake. It is newness for the sake of the betterment of the human condition.

Shortly after the period under consideration, and indeed already percolating in England and the rest of Europe during the 1630s, would come a veritable explosion of utopian writing, with results as varied as the industry-minded *Macaria* by Gabriel Plattes (1641), the radical communist state imagined in *The Law of Freedom in a Platform* by Gerrard Winstanley (1652), and the constitutionalist *Oceana* by James Harrington (1656). In these works the commitment already noticeable in early seventeenth-century utopias is redoubled; it becomes so intense that the boundary between fiction and reality becomes blurred and the ironies of utopian writing come to serve the realities of the utopian project, rather than the other way around.

But how we are to view this transition from the work of people like Bacon and Burton to the work of people like Plattes and Winstanley depends in large part on how we view the development of intellectual history generally. It depends on whether we allow ourselves to see anything like progress in it. It depends as well on how we feel about the project of modernity. And it depends, finally, on whether, as we review the documents and political projects of the past, we allow ourselves to find anything we may still wish for or hope after.

Further Reading

Appelbaum, Robert. *Literature and Utopian Politics in Seventeenth Century England* (Cambridge: Cambridge University Press, 2002).

Bloch, Ernst. *The Principle of Hope*, trans. Neville Plaice, Stephen Plaice. and Paul Knight, 3 vols. (Oxford: Blackwell, 1986).

—— *The Spirit of Utopia*, trans. Anthony Nassar (Stanford: Stanford University Press, 2000).

Boesky, Amy. *Founding Fictions: Utopias in Early Modern England* (Athens, GA: University of Georgia Press, 1996).

Davis, J. C. *Utopia and the Ideal Society: A Study of English Utopian Writing, 1516–1700* (Cambridge: Cambridge University Press, 1983).

Greenblatt, Stephen C. *Renaissance Self-fashioning: From More to Shakespeare* (Chicago: University of Chicago Press, 1980).

Habermas, Jürgen. *The Philosophical Discourse of Modernity*, trans. Frederick Lawrence (Cambridge, MA: MIT Press, 1987).

Hexter, J. H. *More's Utopia: The Biography of an Idea* (Princeton: Princeton University Press, 1952).

Holstun, James. *A Rational Millennium: Puritan Utopias of Seventeenth-Century England and America* (Oxford: Oxford University Press, 1987).

Knapp, Jeffrey. *An Empire Nowhere: England, America, and Literature from 'Utopia' to 'The Tempest'* (Berkeley: University of California Press, 1992).

Manuel, Frank, and Fritzie Manuel. *Utopian Thought in the Western World* (Cambridge, MA: Belknap, 1979).

Marin, Louis. *Utopics: The Semiological Play of Textual Spaces*, trans. Robert A. Vollrath (Atlantic Highlands, NJ: Humanities Press, 1984).

Skinner, Quentin. 'Sir Thomas More's *Utopia* and the Language of Renaissance Humanism', in Anthony Pagden, ed., *The Languages of Political Theory in Early Modern Europe* (Cambridge: Cambridge University Press, 2001), 123–57.

Sylvester, R. S., and G. P. Marc'hadour, eds. *Essential Articles for the Study of Sir Thomas More* (Hamden, CT: Archon, 1977).

CHAPTER 17

ENGLISH SCIENTIFIC PROSE: BACON, BROWNE, BOYLE

CLAIRE PRESTON

'...the *English Tongue*...as it contains a greater stock of *Natural* and *Mechanick Discoveries*, so it is also more inrich'd with beautiful *Conceptions*, and inimitable *Similtudes*, gather'd from...the *Works of Nature*.'[1]

17.1 THE PLACE OF RHETORIC AND POETRY IN SCIENCE

SEVENTEENTH-CENTURY scientific prose is a haunted house. Various remarks by Francis Bacon, if read in isolation from the rest of his opinions, sound inimical to the uses of the imagination, particularly rhetorical tropes and figures, but also literary genres. That his position, and that of the early modern discourse of science as a whole, was anything of the kind has been rehearsed too often by modern critics.[2] But Bacon's pronouncements are undeniably beset by apparent (though not actual) contradiction and inconsistency that, in their turn, have produced the myth of Bacon's call to dismiss rhetoric wholly in favour

---

[1] Thomas Sprat, *The History of the Royal-Society of London*... (1667), 417.
[2] Sprat's hugely influential polemical account of the Royal Society has been adopted wholesale by such modern commentators as Richard Jones ('Science and English Prose Style, 1650–1675' [1951], repr. in Stanley Fish, ed., *Seventeenth-Century Prose: Modern Essays in Criticism* [New York: Oxford University Press, 1971], 53–89), who argued that the Royal Society was categorically hostile to poetry, and Joseph M. Levine, who describes it as denigrating the imagination ('Strife in the Republic of Letters', in Hans Bot and Françoise Waquet, eds., *Commercium Litterarium: Forms of Communication in the Republic of Letters* [Amsterdam and Maarson: APA-Holland University Press, 1994], 306). See Brian

of a plain or somehow de-rhetoricized language of science and scientific expression.³ This misunderstanding of his ideas (and his own literary habits) ignores the elaborate rhetorical practice of his most fervent followers, natural philosophers and historians like Thomas Browne, Robert Boyle, Margaret Cavendish, and Walter Charleton, to name only a few. The traditional account of natural philosophy's 'defeat' of rhetoric by Baconian diktat elides a number of things: it ignores the fact that post-Baconian natural philosophical writing of the seventeenth century has remarkable and unusual rhetorical and imaginative features; and that these were eagerly discussed by the natural philosophers, both in their science and in lay topics; that they all came to science, as Bacon himself did, from the intensely rhetorical humanist training of the grammar schools, universities, and Inns of Court;⁴ and that, as Peter Harrison notes, the traditional structure of a 'natural history' included all the categories of the humanist curriculum, including rhetoric and poetry.⁵ It would, in other words, be *contra naturam* if scientific practitioners themselves were *not* rhetorically adventurous and adept, or if scientific practice, theory, training, and results were not rhetorically dense, imaginatively suggestive, and often formulated in verse, plays, elegies, inscriptions, and utopian essays. There are too many examples of such literary science to require proof; instead, we can attempt to understand the scientific view of the literary by noticing what practising early modern scientists said on the subject.

In 1667 Thomas Sprat paraphrased Francis Bacon on the use of scientific similes: 'The Comparisons which [experiments] may afford will be intelligible to all, becaus they...make the most vigorous impressions on mens *Fancies*.'⁶ Such claims for metaphor and other analogical figures were part of a vigorous debate, largely unresolved, among early modern natural philosophers seeking an appropriate expository style for their experiments, essays, and observations. A presiding need to reform the nature of knowledge according to the directly observable made the choice of scientific expression a peculiarly weighty matter—early modern science had to correct the mistakes of the ancient authorities and to cast off the shackles of scholastic philosophical quibbling, as well as the humanist addiction to the arts of language, all in order to establish the primacy of *res* above *verba*. The vexed problem

---

Vickers's important corrective discussion of this tradition, 'The Royal Society and English Prose Style: A Reassessment', in Brian Vickers and Nancy S. Streuver, eds., *Rhetoric and the Pursuit of Truth: Language Change in the Seventeenth and Eighteenth Centuries* (Los Angeles: UCLA/Clark Library, 1985), 1–76; and John R. R. Christie's vigorous and compelling account of this misrepresentation ('Introduction: Rhetoric and Writing in Early Modern Philosophy and Science') in Andrew E. Benjamin, Geoffrey N. Cantor, and John R. R. Christie, eds., *The Figural and the Literal: Problems of Language in the History of Science and Philosophy* (Manchester: Manchester University Press, 1987), 1–9.

³ Robert M. Schuler, however, argues that Bacon is genuinely ambivalent about the poetic in scientific writing: 'Francis Bacon and Scientific Poetry', *Transactions of the American Philosophical Society*, NS 82.2 (1992): 1–65.

⁴ Jonathan Sawday makes this sensible observation in 'The Transparent Man and the King's Heart', in Claire Jowitt and Diane Watt, eds., *The Arts of Seventeenth-Century Science: Representations of the Natural World in European and North American Culture* (Aldershot: Ashgate, 2002), 12.

⁵ Peter Harrison, '"The Fashioned Image of Poetry or the Regular Instruction of Philosophy?" Truth, Utility, and the Natural Scientist in Early Modern England', in Juliet Cummins and David Burchell, eds., *Science, Literature and Rhetoric in Early Modern England* (Aldershot: Ashgate, 2007), 20.

⁶ Sprat, *History*, 416.

of how to 'do' science was not just an empirical one, but required fresh address to the ways in which the doing of science could be made account of. Even though a rhetorical regimen for early modern science was first discussed in depth by Francis Bacon in *The Advancement of Learning* and the *Parasceve*, and demonstrated by him in *New Atlantis* and *Novum Organum*, there was no default convention or format for presenting matters of fact—natural historians and philosophers published their findings in many genres—and early modern science is marked by a profusion of literary forms and trials. Agreement about which of these might best serve science had not been reached (nor was it even gradually emerging) by the time of Boyle's death in 1691 and the coexistent 'literary technologies' of science available in the seventeenth century are accordingly varied.[7] A striking and universal feature of scientific writing, however, is its interesting and often uneasy relation to rhetorical tropes, narrative structures, and figurative language.

Because Bacon's various remarks seem difficult to reconcile, his supposed hostility to figurative language as an appropriate mode for investigative truth was also poorly understood by some early modern Baconian scientific practitioners, and by their associates, and has been reiterated by the historians of that practice. Thomas Sprat, for example, in his influential, but only marginally authoritative *History of the Royal Society*, asserts that rhetorical ornament is 'a thing fatal to peace and Good Manners' and indicative of civil disorder,[8] apparently extending a proper scientific regard for perspicuous language into an official horror of any sort of eloquence and strategically ignoring Bacon's own utopian fiction of a scientific society in *New Atlantis*. But Bacon's hostility is chimerical: although he had insisted that needlessly elaborate rhetorical ornament is 'a distemper learning',[9] he also judged that 'whatsoever science is not consonant to presuppositions, must pray in aid of similitudes' (in other words, new ideas may require analogies where no appropriate terms exist).[10] And Sprat himself understood this balance perfectly well when he paraphrased Bacon on experiment as a source of fruitful analogy—'experimental comparisons' invigorate the imagination. Other scientific voices seem similarly inconsistent: Robert Boyle claims categorically that rhetoric is an 'obnoxious' art,[11] yet also says that 'proper comparisons do the Imagination almost as much Service, as Microscopes do the Eye', citing not only 'the Illustrious Verulam' as a model and sanctioning authority, but even 'that severe Philosopher Monsieur Des Cartes [who] somewhere says that he scarce

---

[7] I borrow this useful term from Steven Shapin, 'Pump and Circumstance: Robert Boyle's Literary Technology', *Social Studies of Science*, 14 (1984): 481–520.

[8] Sprat, *History*, 111. But, as Catherine Gimelli Martin notes, Sprat himself has been misinterpreted as being wholly anti-rhetorical when in fact he was merely arguing against inane rhetoric ('Rewriting the Revolution: Milton, Bacon, and the Royal Society Rhetoricians', in Cummins and Burchell, eds., *Science, Literature and Rhetoric*, 103).

[9] Francis Bacon, *The Advancement of Learning*, Book 1, Sect. 4.3 in *The Collected Works of Francis Bacon*, ed. James Spedding, R. E. Ellis, and D. D. Heath, 7 vols. (1979) (repr. London: Routledge/Thoemmes Press, 1996), 3, 120. All references to Bacon's works refer to this edition.

[10] Bacon, *De Augmentis*, Book 2, xvii.9 (vol. 3, 137).

[11] Robert Boyle, *An Account of Philaretus During His Minority*, in *Robert Boyle by Himself and His Friends*, ed. Michael Hunter (London: Pickering & Chatto, 1994), 14.

thought, that he understood any thing in Physiques, but what he could declare by some apt Similitude'.[12] William Petty, the statistician and founder-member of the Royal Society, opposed tropes and conceits, but nevertheless produced a dialogue on shipping celebrating his scientifically engineered (and repeatedly unsuccessful) design for a catamaran.[13] Although John Evelyn complained of the neo-Latin jargon of contemporary scientific writing by the *logodædali* ('cunning in words'), he was himself an enthusiastic coiner, the originator of 'coniferous', 'impermeable', 'toxic', and many others.[14] Even the notoriously severe Hobbes was not quite absolute in his repudiation of the ornate: 'reason and eloquence... may stand very well together', he said in *Leviathan*, with the qualification '(though not perhaps in the naturall sciences, yet in the Morall)'.[15] Margaret Cavendish, typically quirky, explains that her atomic poems are presented in verse precisely because '*Poets* Write most *Fiction*, and *Fiction* is not given for *Truth*': her theory of matter, probably erroneous she admits, will better pass in that guise.[16] This was certainly not the reasoning employed by other natural philosophers defending imaginative writing: they tended to argue for *enargeia* (or rhetorical vividness) because it clarified scientific ideas, not because it disguised their doubtfulness. Boyle closely rehearses Philip Sidney's defence of *enargeia* and the poetic images that convey it when he urges 'shining examples', rather than 'precepts or grave discourses', and says, in a close paraphrase of the *Defence*, that 'to condemn Figurative and Indirect ways of conveying ev'n Serious and Sacred matters, is to forget How often Christ himself made use of Parables'.[17] Despite the criticisms of a few particularly splenetic (and non-scientific) critics like Robert South and Robert Crosse, and the exceptional practice of natural philosophers with special interests in the philosophy of language or in mathematics like John Wilkins, Isaac Newton, and John Locke,[18]

---

[12] Robert Boyle, *The Christian Virtuoso* (1690), [A6ʳ]. Subsequent references are given in the text.

[13] William Petty, 'A Dialogue concerning shipping', BL MS Add. 72893, ff. 8–26. Petty and the double-bottom were also the subject of a mock-heroic satire, 'Laudem Navis Geminae' (BL Sloane MS 360, ff. 73ʳ–80ʳ). See Vickers, 'Royal Society', 40.

[14] Also *bibulous, catalysis, emaciate, experimentist, funambule, lampoon, lymphatic, paradigmatic, perennial, reinvigorate*, etc. Perhaps he could excuse *logodædali* as neo-*Greek* and therefore acceptable.

[15] 'A Review and a Conclusion' (Thomas Hobbes, *Leviathan*, ed. Richard Tuck [Cambridge: Cambridge University Press, 1991], 483–4). 'The use of Metaphors, Tropes, and other Rhetoricall figures in stead of words proper... in reckoning, and seeking of truth, such speeches are not to be admitted' (*Leviathan*, I.5.35). Hobbes wrote a Latin verse autobiography. On Hobbes and rhetoric, see David Burchell, '"A Plain Blunt Man": Hobbes, Science, and Rhetoric Revisited', in Cummings and Burchell, eds., *Science, Literature and Rhetoric*, 52–72.

[16] Margaret Cavendish, 'To the Natural Philosophers', in *Poems and Fancies* (1664), [n.p.].

[17] Sprat, *History*, 416; Robert Boyle, *The Second Part of the Martyrdom of Theodora and Didymus* (1687), [A8ᵛ]; and *Occasional Reflections upon Several Subjects, Whereto is Premis'd a Discourse upon such kind of Thoughts* (1665), [b2ᵛ]. Subsequent references are given in the text.

[18] On Wilkins's *Universal Character* see Christie, 'Introduction', 6; Mary Slaughter, *Universal Languages and Scientific Taxonomy in the Seventeenth Century* (Cambridge: Cambridge University Press, 1982); and Rhodri Lewis, *Language, Mind and Nature: Artificial Languages in England from Bacon to Locke* (Cambridge: Cambridge University Press, 2007). And even so, a young protégé of Wilkins sent him his poems with a reference to, 'the generall favour wch all Arts receiv from

the scientific writers of the mid- and late seventeenth century were deeply attentive to the possibilities of rhetoric and of the rhetorically assisted and stimulated imagination as the way to precise and perspicuous expression of matters of experimental and observational fact.

17.2 FRANCIS BACON ON RHETORIC AND THE LITERARY

The long-standing Platonic mistrust of any writing that is rhetorically ornamented or is a species of fiction—that it is a mere imitation of a reality, which is itself no more than a shadowed form of the Ideal; that poetry is thus an imitation of a fake[19]—informed a general uneasiness about the rhetorical and structural artifices of the literary; this uneasiness is apparent everywhere in early modern culture, in the arts, religious practice, and inductively and experimentally produced *scientia*. It is this unease that Philip Sidney was answering in his Aristotelian riposte when he argued in the *Defence of Poetry* that the poetic has the highest capability of expressing universal truth. It is this counter-argument that might be said to undergird the widespread early modern willingness to employ the poetic to express the scientific.

Likewise, it is this unease that prompted Wilkins to propose, in *An Essay towards a Real Character* (1668), that *ignis fatuus* of early modern Neoplatonism, a purely denotative, perfectly conceptual language. This is an extreme and unworkable response to requirements of perspicuity, and far more typical are continuing ruminations by scientists on the use of vernacular rhetoric to convey natural-philosophical fact. Bacon, as Brian Vickers reminds us, 'gave considerable thought to the forms in which he and others should communicate their ideas and discoveries. His concept of language was not monist, a single form of discourse which would always be the same in whatever context.'[20] His pronouncements on language do not, as a result, suggest an a priori disaffection from its powers, but rather the opposite, a just recognition and admiration of its capabilities, and a commensurate concern about its misappropriation or

you' (BL Add MS 18220, 'To the Revd Dr Wilkins Warden of Wadham Coll in Oxford', 118); Newton was the perhaps unwilling subject of a number of poems on astronomy and optics, most notably Edmund Halley's Latin ode to Newton (Newton, *Principia Mathematica* [1687], [A4^{r-v}]); and Locke wrote highly polished familiar letters to Esther and Damaris Masham, whom he styled 'Philoclea' (see Susan Whyman, 'The Correspondence of Esther Masham and John Locke: A Study in Epistolary Silences', *Huntington Library Quarterly*, 66.3/4 [2003]: 275–305; and Sarah Dutton (Sarah Hutton, 'Debating the Faith: Damaris Masham (1658–1702) and religious controversy' in Anne Dunan-Page and Clotilde Prunier, eds., *Debating the Faith: Religion and Letter Writing in Great Britain, 1550–1800* [New York: Springer, 2013]).

[19] See Plato, *Republic* 607b.
[20] Brian Vickers, 'Bacon among the Literati: Science and Language', *Comparative Criticism*, 13 (1991): 249–72 (250).

impropriety.[21] In this, Bacon has a far more liberal view of the imagination and of poetry, imagination's special genre, than has sometimes been recognized by modern commentators, or by the seventeenth-century ones;[22] but he is always careful to insist on a decorum in designating the proper rhetorical mode for specific kinds of scientific writing. In *Parasceve*, his prefatory and preparatory introduction to *Novum Organum*, for example, the third aphorism dismisses *all* ornaments of speech, similitudes, and elegance in general from natural and experimental histories (by which he means works like *Sylva Sylvarum*, of gathered but 'indigested' data on which true natural philosophy is to be based[23]). To admit such elegancies, he concludes in a beautiful similitude, is as much as to organize the tools in a shipbuilder's shop for visual, rather than practical effect.[24] And yet, he also claims in *De Augmentis*, the process of 'inventing' (in its older sense of 'discovering') knowledge must be accomplished by similitude.[25]

Bacon argues that there are rhetorical registers and proprieties to be observed in the writing of science. In a natural 'history', where raw data await construction into axioms by natural philosophers, the rhetorical and the poetic are supererogatory; but in propounding these empirically derived axioms to a wider, less learned, public, tropes allow the abstract to become visible and comprehensible. Bacon's argument here is as much as to say that tropic, illustrative language allows the philosopher, after establishing a general truth from observables, to paint 'the outward beauty of such an axiom'. Thus, when Cowley praises Bacon's programme in his ode 'To the Royal Society', he can commend Bacon's vindication of eloquence and wit from 'all Modern Follies' (merely superfluous eloquence), and in the same stanza describe his 'candid Style like a clean stream', both views compassed within a poem that imagines natural philosophy as a captive prince fed too long on the sweetmeats of scholastic discourse, and Bacon as a Moses leading his people into the promised land of new learning.[26] This complex Baconian amalgam of tropic practice and anti-tropic claims is neither self-consuming nor inconsistent, nor did it ruin or demote poetry in the pre-Enlightenment. It reflects instead Bacon's own measured, and essentially social, sense of linguistic use and propriety across various kinds of natural-philosophical expression, his designation of unfigured and plain style for the gritty, learned work of establishing philosophical truth, and of

---

[21] Vickers, 'Bacon among the Literati', 251. See also John L. Harrison, 'Bacon's View of Rhetoric, Poetry, and the Imagination', *Huntington Library Quarterly*, 20.2 (1957): 107–25; Jeffrey Gore, 'Francis Bacon and the "Desserts of Poetry"', *Prose Studies*, 29.3 (2007): 359–77; and Sean Patrick O'Rourke et al., 'The Most Significant Passage on Rhetoric in the Works of Francis Bacon', *Rhetoric Society Quarterly*, 26.3 (1996): 31–55.

[22] Vickers, 'Bacon among the Literati', 252.

[23] Walter Rawley's preface to *Sylva* apologizes for the 'indigested Heap of Particulars [that] cannot have that lustre, which Bookes cast into Methods have' (*Sylva Sylvarum* [1627], A1[r]). Bacon's distinction of rhetorical registers is discussed by James P. Zappen in O'Rourke et al., 'The Most Significant Passage on Rhetoric', 49–53.

[24] *Parasceve* I.403.

[25] *De Augmentis* III, 218. 'There is no proceeding in invention of knowledge but by similitude.'

[26] Cowley, 'To the Royal Society', 40 (stanzas 2, 9, and 5).

a more poetically free style for the promulgation of that securely established truth to a general audience.

Competing with this Baconian tendency towards rhetorically complex and variously registered natural philosophy was a robust anti-Ciceronian element characterized in England by Hobbes, who partly derived it from the Mersenne circle in which he had moved while in France.[27] Inspired by Tacitus and Sallust, and associated with the Senecan ideal of unadorned and plain language—*quod quae veritati operam dat oratio, inconposita esse debet et simplex* (speech that deals with the truth should be unadorned and plain)[28]—and latterly with Lipsian epistolary precepts of dynamic and rhetorically unhampered expression, it was a style intended to be penetrating and even disconcerting in its directness and perspicuity, quite unlike the regular and shapely elegance of Cicero's periods and rhythms.[29] Bacon's *Essays* might be the most obvious example in English of the anti-Ciceronian; and yet, his theoretical writings advocate a middle way between the plain and the figurative, each mode approved in their proper roles. He himself wrote in both styles. As Stephen Clucas has observed, the Baconian instauration required 'forensic rhetorical investigation of the scientific field of knowledge' and yet, it had to grapple with 'the seemingly insoluble problem of instituting a scientific discourse which did not lay rhetorical claims to authority'.[30] The rhetorical could neither be allowed as the end, or the shaping impulse, of scientific discourse, nor could it be permitted to overwhelm reason in its appeal to the imagination; but its power could be profitably, if carefully, harnessed to promote the power of that discourse. In understanding the range of rhetorical practices and rhetorical philosophies available to the natural philosopher, therefore, we must resist any absolute division between reason and eloquence merely as the *fiat* mainly of later voices; at the time, only Comenius and certain other radical puritans thought of the literary as the absolute antagonist of the scientific or the utilitarian.[31] This Baconian openness issues in a rich tradition in which science is promulgated and discussed (and even satirized) in travel writing, exposition, epistles, dialogues, essays, fables, aphorisms, and verse of all kinds.[32]

---

[27] See Burchell, '"A Plain Blunt Man"', 54. Brian Vickers notes (perhaps contentiously) that Bacon's own habit of rhetorically symmetrical structures style is 'pure English Ciceronian' (*Francis Bacon and Renaissance Prose* [Cambridge: Cambridge University Press, 1968]), 117.

[28] Seneca, *Epistulae Morales*, XL ('On the Proper Style for a Philosopher's Discourse', trans. Richard M. Gunmere [Seneca, 10 vols.] (Cambridge, MA and London: Harvard University Press, 1917; repr. 1989), vol. 4, 264.

[29] David Burchell describes it as 'stylistic terrorism...designed to upset the reader's preconceptions and...complacency' ('"A Plain Blunt Man"', 60). On Lipsius, see E. Catherine Dunn, 'Lipsius and the Art of Letter-Writing', *Studies in the Renaissance*, 3 (1956): 145–56.

[30] Stephen Clucas, 'A Knowledge Broken', in Neil Rhodes, ed., *English Renaissance Prose: History, Language, and Politics* (Tempe, AZ: Medieval and Renaissance Texts and Studies, 1997), 171–2.

[31] Gimelli Martin 'Rewriting the Revolution', 103.

[32] On Bacon's own generic range, see Deborah E. Harkness, 'Francis Bacon's Experimental Writing', in Susannah Brietz Monta and Margaret W. Ferguson, eds., *Teaching Early Modern English Prose* (New York: Modern Language Association of America, 2010), 255.

17.3 THOMAS BROWNE

Even his works of essentially or ultimately spiritual purpose—*Religio Medici, Urne-Buriall* and *The Garden of Cyrus*, and *A Letter to a Friend*—betray Thomas Browne's scientific cast of mind: matters of faith or of morals are very often speculatively investigated, not only as if they were experimental assays, but these thought-experiments are couched in similitudes of the empirically investigated natural world. *Religio Medici* considers resurrection in terms of the behaviour of mercury; *Urne-Buriall* revolves mortuary customs, an apparently anthropological topic, with an eye to sanitary measures and the effect of climate and soil upon decomposing flesh; *The Garden of Cyrus*, often dismissed as a slightly crackpot exercise in arbitrary signification (the figures of five to be found throughout the creation), might also be understood as a botanist's field investigations into plant structure and vegetable germination that turn out to have this unexpected common parameter; and *A Letter to a Friend* adduces meaning from the death of an accomplished young man partly through the evidence of dissection and medical case histories.[33]

In 1649, only three years after the first edition of *Pseudodoxia Epidemica*, the often preposterously florid and Latinate Walter Charleton singled out Browne (with Bacon) as a 'Heroicall Wit' whose English honoured 'the Majesty of our Mother Tongue', whose prose was 'spun as fine and fit a garment, for the most spruce Conceptions of the Minde to appear in publick in, as out of any other in the World', and who disabused the Scholastic claim that 'Latin is the most symphoniacall and Concordant Language of the Rationall Soule'.[34] The symphonic quality of Browne's majestic English we readily recognize in spiritual works like *Religio Medici* and *Urne-Buriall*. The more directly natural-philosophical works, however, show how an equivalent (though adapted) linguistic richness presents in Browne's scientific habits of prose, especially in *Pseudodoxia Epidemica* (1646–72). Unlike Bacon and Boyle, however, Browne never laid out his views of scientific style explicitly and his ideas must be worked out by indirection, through the evidence of his practice.

In discussing authoritative ancient natural historians in *Pseudodoxia*, Browne included the 'elegant [hexameter] lines' of Oppian (*Halieutica* (on fishing) and *Cynegetica* (on hunting) that can be read 'with delight and profit', and he regrets that modern neglect of this writer 'reject[s] one of the best Epick Poets' (*PE* I.viii.51).[35]

---

[33] See, on all these, Reid Barbour, 'Thomas Browne's *A Letter to a Friend* and the Semiotics of Disease', *Renaissance Studies*, 24.3 (2010): 403–19; Claire Preston, *Thomas Browne and the Writing of Early Modern Science* (Cambridge: Cambridge University Press, 2005); and Mary Ann Lund, 'The Christian Physician: Thomas Browne and the Role of Religion in Medical Practice', in Kathryn Murphy and Richard Todd, eds., *A Man Very Well Studyed: New Contexts for Thomas Browne* (Leiden: Brill, 2008), 229–46.

[34] Walter Charleton, 'Epistle Dedicatory', *A Ternary of Paradoxes*, trans. John Baptiste van Helmont (1649), c[1^r]–[c1^v].

[35] By 'epic', Browne means hexameter verse. These two works are now known to be by two different poets called 'Oppianus'. All citations of *Pseudodoxia Epidemica* refer to the edition of Robin Robbins, 2 vols. (Oxford: Clarendon Press, 1982).

He also complains, however, that certain ancient 'Moralists, Rhetoricians, Orators and Poets' relied too much on 'invention', simile, and other illustrative tropes:

> to induce their Enthymemes unto the people, they took up popular conceits, and from traditions unjustifiable or really false, illustrate matters of undeniable truth. Wherein although their intention be sincere,...yet doth it notoriously strengthen common Errors, and authorise Opinions injurious unto truth. (*PE* I.ix.54)

In other words, Browne theoretically approves of the poetic in natural history, but he is compelled to disparage merely rhetorical ('enthymemic') instead of empirical arguments as less true and unfortunately more persuasive. Elsewhere, this careful discrimination allows him to advocate a mixture of literary conventions: the writer should affect a plain and unembellished style, and yet, one which, if not fully Ciceronian, will not offend Ciceronian stylists; he should have little recourse to strange or foreign words, and yet, he is to use esoteric or even homespun (*domi nata*) terms when necessary. He is not to allow mere fluency to overwhelm meaning, but let the language match the subject.[36] These heavily qualified, undogmatic opinions may explain the mixed features of Browne's prose in his mature works, and the nature of his revisions of *Pseudodoxia* over the course of four editions illustrates this ample approach to style. Rarely, in any of his works, does he resort to elaborate conceits, and he was apparently not much interested in the Baconian fable. But as for 'invention' of a more local and contained kind—especially similes and metaphors—some of his most memorable aphoristic formulations are wonderfully tropic: 'heads that are disposed unto schism...do subdivide and mince themselves almost unto atoms' (*RM* I.8); 'to flourish in the state of glory we must first be sown in corruption' (*GC Letter*); and 'the long habit of living indisposeth us for dying' (*UB* 5). As T. W. Westfall, Reid Barbour, and others have noted, Browne adjusted his great encyclopaedic work on error to reflect his growing sense of the power of language to illuminate *and* to distort matters of fact.[37] He is scrupulous, for example, to show how much care must be expended in lexical choice, as when, in a discussion of the flooding of the Nile, he digresses on the foolish use of absolute superlative designations for 'things of eminency in any kinde', designations which are casually made simply to mean 'eminent', rather than 'pre-eminent', but semantically seem to insist on a unique attribute when 'there being but one in every kinde, their attributions are dangerous' (*PE* VI.viii.497). He uses this observation to weave a wide-ranging list of counter-examples from natural and civil history—the relative sizes of the 'greatest' cities, from Rome to Cathay, the relative smallness of the 'smallest' birds from the European wren to the American hummingbird, and the relative height of the 'highest' mountains from Olympus to

---

[36] Thomas Browne, *Amico Opus Arduum Meditanti* ('To a Friend Intending a Difficult Work'), in *The Works of Sir Thomas Browne*, 4 vols., 2nd edn., ed. Geoffrey Keynes (Chicago: University of Chicago Press, 1964), III, 150–5. See also Reid Barbour's discussion of this manuscript fragment in *Thomas Browne: A Life* (Oxford: Oxford University Press, 2013), 296–8.

[37] Barbour, *Thomas Browne*, 298–341; T. M. Westfall, 'Sir Thomas Browne's Revisions in *Pseudodoxia Epidemica*: A Study in the Development of his Mind' (Ph.D. dissertation, Princeton University, 1939).

Cotopaxi (*PE* VI viii.497). And he is willing to extend this history of semantic error into an 'illation' (an inference or a conclusion) of our inability to know God, the true superlative. This is a useful example, not just of Browne's attention to linguistic propriety; it also shows us how in a work apparently so much more strictly ordered than the rhapsodic *Urne-Buriall* or *Garden of Cyrus*, he is willing to let his thinking, like the Nile itself, and like his rhetoric, occasionally o'erflow the measure of his notional subject. For Bacon, the 'problem' of rhetorical choice is that where it can sometimes illustrate it can also distract. For Browne, the very act of attending to the amplitude and variety of language applied to the investigative subject is itself investigative, an enactment of the 'thinking' of science.

Although the fundamental linguistic decision that preceded and governed the choice and execution of style—to write in more inclusive English, rather than in more exclusive Latin[38]—needed justification in the preface, Browne himself promoted Latinate English prose in, among other things, his enormous number of neologisms 'beyond mere English apprehensions' (*PE*, 'To the Reader', 2–3) (more than 800 according to the *OED*; and more than twice that many new uses of existing words). The competing titles of his great work—the official mouthful, *Pseudodoxia Epidemica*, and the rather more homemade *Vulgar Errors*—frame the Anglo-Latinate situation in which Browne and other natural philosophers found themselves, 'mak[ing] claims upon a language which that language [was not] prepared for'.[39] Thus, he recognizes the value of both plainness and of esoteric terms; he denigrates those who are constitutionally incapable of understanding figurative, tropic language; he loves paradox, copious, resonant figures of speech, and, above all, similitudes. In his carefully pliant sense of linguistic propriety, Browne refines and extends the straightforward Baconian antitheses of plainness and eloquence. It is a pliancy he inaugurated in his famous apology for the pirated 1643 edition of *Religio Medici*, in which he asked his readers to understand his work in the 'soft and flexible' tropic sense in which it had been offered.[40] The excuses for *Religio Medici*, a spiritual autobiography, not a scientific work, are unnecessary in *Pseudodoxia*, where the oscillation between Latinity and the vernacular, between the figurative and the unadorned, are unapologetically on display.[41] His revisions of the work show that he was moving towards a more immediate and sometimes sparer style; and it is certainly *different* from the more gorgeous styles of *Religio Medici* and *The Garden of Cyrus*.[42] But in *Pseudodoxia* Browne can write of Satan's

---

[38] *Pseudodoxia* was translated into Dutch, German, and Danish in Browne's lifetime, but Jan Gruter's Latin version never appeared.

[39] Vickers, 'Royal Society', 36. In this essay Vickers oddly takes Browne to task for answering this very insufficiency with 'hard words' because he thinks that *PE* is meant to be purely literary, rather than scientific (33–4).

[40] *Religio Medici*, 'To the Reader' (Keynes I, 10).

[41] Browne's greater linguistic security in *Pseudodoxia* may be owing to advancing years and an established reputation; and partly to the nature of the work as a compendium of fact, rather than of personal opinions (as in *Religio Medici*).

[42] It is not easy to accept Austin Warren's identification of Browne's various registers as high, middle, and low ('The Style of Sir Thomas Browne', *Kenyon Review*, 13 [1951]: 674–87).

attempts to seduce our understanding with falsehoods as 'but Parthian flights, Ambuscado retreats, and elusory tergiversations, whereby to confirme our credulities...' (*PE* I x.64), a sentence in which a glorious Latinate *copia* is to the fore. His aim in the prose of science can hardly be to pare it down to the theoretical denotative quality enjoined by Sprat and Wilkins. As Barbour puts it, 'his pursuit of a more streamlined, less erudite and florid style...did not cancel the beauty or vitality of his prose; rather, various styles interacted with one another in a complex dialogue'.[43] In *Pseudodoxia*, we might say, the rhetoric of science is as extensively, if differently, elaborated as in any of his meditative, rhapsodic works.

In the preface to *Pseudodoxia* Browne asserts 'wee are not Magisteriall in opinions, nor have wee Dictator-like obtruded our Conceptions, but in humility of Enquiries...have only proposed them unto more ocular discerners' (*PE*, 'To the Reader', 4). He criticizes the qualifications of certain ancient authors who 'write dubiously [hesitatingly], even in matters wherein is expected a strict and definitive truth, extenuating their affirmations with *quod aiunt, fortasse, saepe aut numquam*' ('as they say', 'probably', 'often or never', 'sometimes') (*PE*, I.vi.34).[44] But it is a rhetorical gambit he himself constantly uses when he forbears certainty with a conditional phrase ('were there any such species') or states a received idea with *litotes* ('it is not without some question'). Such qualifications are semantic indications of his unmagisterial intentions, themselves arising out of his modesty in the face of the creator ('as his wisdom is infinit, so cannot the due expressions thereof by finite' [*PE*, VI.v.468]). This is not to disagree with Kevin Killeen's characterization of Browne's project in *Pseudodoxia* as 'grand and ambitious',[45] but rather, to frame that grandeur of undertaking in the prose of the lapsarian condition.

This limiting sense of lapsarian understanding is the same that informs Bacon and Boyle's disinclination for treatises and systems ('a great impediment to natural philosophy' [*Proemial*, 3]), says Boyle, who prefers 'the usefulness of Writing Books of Essays' to convey the fragmentary state of knowledge (*Proemial*, 7). The entire structure of *Pseudodoxia* is additionally qualified by Browne's revisions over the four editions during his lifetime and by the way in which he regularly transgresses the boundaries of his own stated topics, as if emphasizing the fluidity of enquiry. This is especially true of what I have elsewhere described as 'establishing' or heuristic essays, ones that lay out evidence *ab initio*, as if for a Baconian natural history, and then proceed to conduct scrutiny of it, rather than setting out to correct an existing error with existing information.[46] A case in point is the chapter 'Of the Cameleon' (an amalgam of the establishing and the corrective essay format), a discussion initiated by the commonplace that the chameleon lives on air alone. This essay is a typical example of the way

---

[43] Barbour, *Thomas Browne*, 307.

[44] This same notification is made by Boyle in *A Proemial Essay...touching Experimental Essays* in *Certain Physiological Essays* (1661), 16. Subsequent references are given in the text.

[45] Kevin Killeen, *Biblical Scholarship, Science and Politics in Early Modern England: Thomas Browne and the Thorny Place of Knowledge* (Aldershot: Ashgate, 2009), 11.

[46] Preston, *Thomas Browne*, 114–17.

Browne moves with ease between classical and modern authorities, between literary and scientific evidence, between data about the designated topic and contingent, but distinct material. His citation of authorities for and against this view refers to the usual suspects in natural history—Aristotle, Pliny, and Solinus for the ancients; Peiresc, Vizzanius, and Bellonius for the moderns—but also to Ovid and Homer. He explains a functional teleology of animal anatomy: chameleons have stomachs, *ergo* they must eat since 'the wisdom of nature abhor[s] superfluities,...effecting nothing in vain' (*PE*, III.xxi.243). He is given to duplicating couplets in which a Latinate hard word is paired with an elucidating (though not always precisely synonymous or more familiar) word—verisimility/probable truth, aggeneration/conversion, incrassation/corpulency, unctuous/full of oyle, pellucid/transparent, jejune/limpid, latitency/hibernation, inspiration/drawing breath, or phlegmatick/cold—a practice that would smack of learned condescension unless it is understood as another kind of qualification, a recognition that expressions in natural philosophy neither dare be complacent or finite nor yet pretend to absolute authority. But *Pseudodoxia* sets out not simply to examine an episodic series of errors, but rather to pursue the 'Encyclopædie and round of knowledge' (*PE*, 'To the Reader', 1), a heroic attempt. Of this intellectual balance between authority and humility, Killeen remarks that it belies 'the common characterisation of Browne in the role of a modest, error-by-error Baconian field-worker, clearing away the undergrowth of nonsense, with a mixture of good sense and empirical competence. Browne's reconstruction of knowledge is grander and more ambitious than it is often taken to be. *Pseudodoxia* scrutinises, or at least skirts, that most burning of issues—the nature of knowledge in a postlapsarian world.'[47]

Another enactment of the infinity of nature is Browne's open-ended, tessellating process of revision, addition, deletion, and adjustment made over a quarter-century, the refining of certain expressions, adding or deleting information as it became available or obsolete, all aimed at a gradual amendment of what Bacon had called 'a knowledge broken'.[48] It is, to use a chemical metaphor, an alembication of knowledge and of style, of refining the image of an emerging order.[49] For example, in 'Of the Cameleon' he adds remarks on the discovery of 'seminall principles' and 'vital atoms of plants and Animals' in rainwater (no doubt based on recent developments in microscopy in the 1660s); he omits passages about lizards and frogs; he restores a correct etymology he had disparaged in the first edition (*PE*, III.xxi.244); and his assumptions about the role of the liver in digestion is finally adjusted in the 1672 edition in the light of his reading of Harvey (*PE*, III.xxi.244).[50]

---

[47] Killeen, *Biblical Scholarship, Science and Politics*, 11.

[48] *Novum Organum*, III.405.

[49] See Claire Preston, 'In the Wilderness of Forms: Ideas and Things in Thomas Browne's Cabinets of Curiosity', in Neil Rhodes and Jonathan Sawday, eds., *The Renaissance Computer: Knowledge Technology in the First Age of Print* (London: Routledge, 2000), 170–83.

[50] Compare the 1672 essay with the 1646 original for a sense of Browne's relatively large-scale revisions.

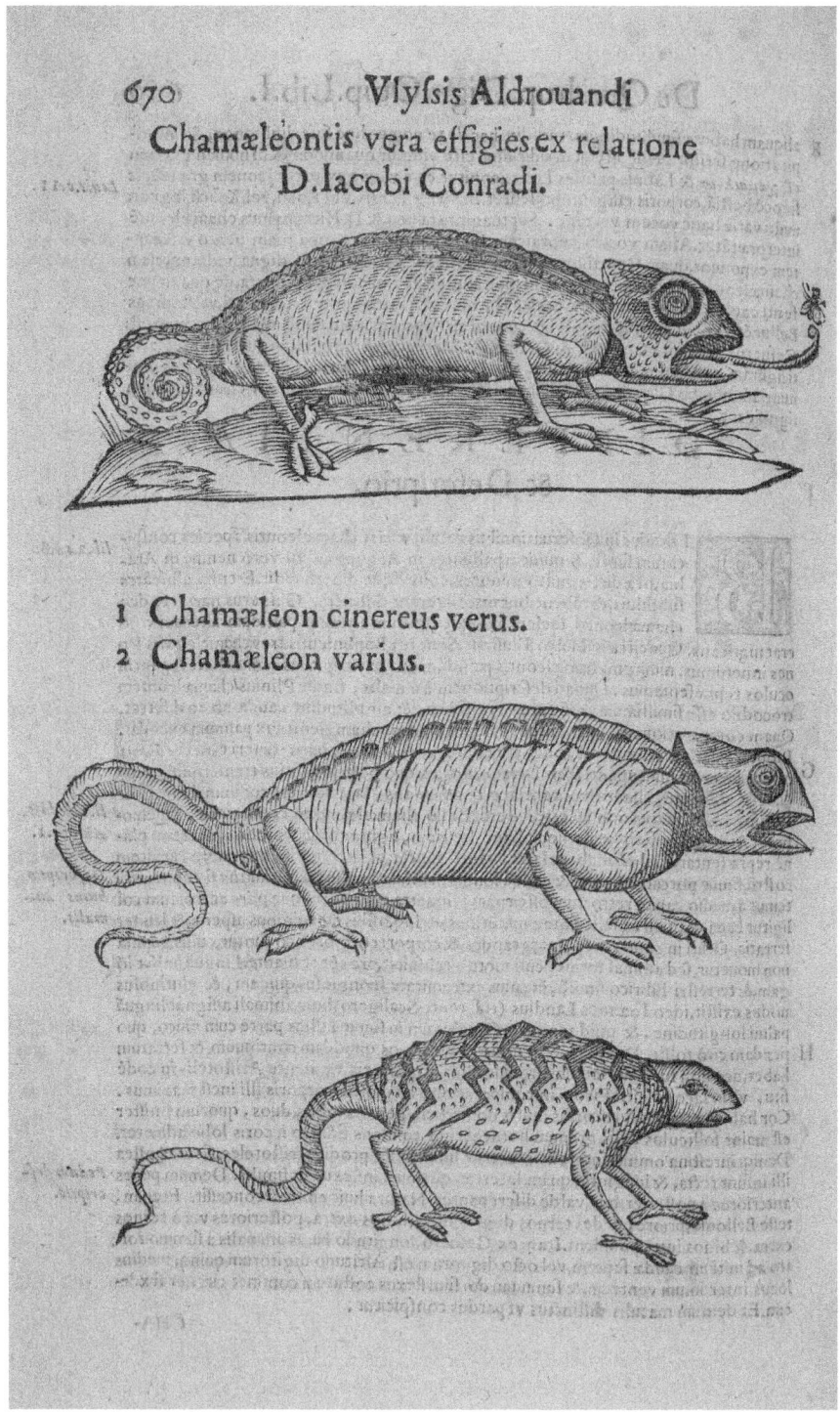

FIGURE 17.1 Chameleon, in Ulisse Aldrovandi, *De Quadrupedibus Digitatis Oviparis* (1637), p. 670

One of the most striking features of the chameleon essay is the substantial digression in the middle of it, which, by the 1672 edition, is very nearly half the length of the whole chapter. This digression, which arises from the consideration of the chameleon's purported air diet, abandons that creature almost entirely to revolve the nature of air and water as aliments, the nature of aliments in the body, how fire uses air, how ignition and flame are caused and sustained, and the presence of micro-organisms in rainwater. All these are significant areas of enquiry that had been experimentally addressed in this period by Harvey, Lower, Boyle, and Hooke, and discussed in recent works by Liceti, Littré, Jorden, Power, Kircher, and others; it is hardly surprising to find Browne clearly *au fait* with recent developments. What is striking is how certain *données* of a traditional reliance on report and authority give way in the course of the chameleon chapter to observable, experimental findings by 'more ocular discerners' who have wholly or in part seen chameleons or investigated digestion and respiration directly. And Browne's purpose in *Pseudodoxia* is precisely that—to move the reader, via an establishing error, into a newer and more immediate world of investigated fact. The digression, which concludes with a few remarks about the nutrition of mythical animals such as the wind-bred mares of Spain and Ariosto's account of Rabican, a horse born from air and flame, gives way to real animals again, but this time with Browne's authoritative evidence from his own observations and experiments. 'We have made a trial' of the sustenance of reptiles, he says; 'we have included' snails in glass to see if they can live without food; 'observations are often made' in winter, when many animals are hibernating, a seasonal variation that affects conclusions about metabolic activity. The final shape of the chameleon essay is, in other words, the shift from the received to the observed, both in his textual references and in his concluding remarks about his own observations and experiments; and from the chameleon—exotic, not exactly mythical, but certainly unavailable in northern latitudes—to the metabolic organization of animals in general; and finally, via a few genuinely mythic instances, back to the chameleon itself (Fig. 17.1).

Unlike Bacon before him or Boyle after him, Browne is not unduly preoccupied with linguistic propriety in science, but only because (we sense that) for him that debate is answered by his own practice and a carefully exercised rhetorical array of English lexis and idioms. Was Browne simply operating at ease on ground smoothed by Bacon and his contemporaries, or does Robert Boyle's return, in the middle of Browne's literary career, to nervous considerations of style represent the actual state of the field?

17.4 ROBERT BOYLE

'Apposite comparisons', said Robert Boyle, are 'a kind of argument' (*CV* [A6ʳ]), and 'wont to be more acceptable than any other to our modern virtuosi' (*CV* [A2ᵛ]). Boyle, even more than Bacon, was obsessed with the propriety of scientific style and was even more voluble than his predecessor on the subject, whom he referred to as 'that great Ornament and Guide of Philosophical Historians of Nature', and whose authority he often claimed when making pronouncements on scientific style.[51] Although he claimed to prefer the 'more reall Parts of Knowledge...hated the study of Bare words', he was temperamentally of a 'poeticke strain',[52] one that prompted a full-blown Christian romance (*The Martyrdom of Theodora and Didymus*) and let him cast a large number of his scientific works as dialogues with distinct, named characters, or as isogogic epistolary essays and familiar letters addressed to the romantically named young men Pyrophilus and Lindamor.[53] Had he not been seduced by natural philosophy in his early twenties and already given to somewhat prim moralizing, Boyle might well have made his mark as a purely imaginative writer like his brother, the romance-writing Earl of Orrery. His early letters betray a powerful, and self-conscious, narrative gift; *Philaretus* itself is a highly shaped romance;[54] 'Accidents of an Ague' has strong generic and thematic similarities to Donne's *Devotions Upon Emergent Occasions*; and *Occasional Reflections* is a series of moralized observations, often of natural phenomena, addressed to 'Sophronia' (his sister, Lady Ranelagh), and very strongly influenced by Bacon's advocacy of fable.[55] He defended what he called 'luxuriant' writing as 'pictures drawn (with Words instead of Colours) for the Imagination' (*OR* a3[r]), especially suited to the young and the unlearned who might not otherwise attend, but also useful to virtuosi; he was careful to excuse 'uneven' writing as a reasonable decorum in casual compositions; and he promoted the dialogue as a fit vehicle for philosophical ideas—his own practice was 'to imagine two or three of my Friends to be present...and to make them discourse as I fancy'd Persons, of their Breeding and tempers, would talk to one another on such an Occasion'(*OR* a1[r]–2[r]).

In an unpublished manuscript of 1647, Boyle employed Sidney's brimstone-and-treacle metaphor of the poetic (i.e. imaginative and/or rhetorical) ornament, so memorably employed in the *Defence*: as Sidney claimed that to read good fictions is to 'see the form of goodness (which seen they cannot but love) ere themselves be aware, as if they took a medicine of cherries',[56] so Boyle renders this quality of moral romance as 'Sugar to the Pill: 'tis no Part of the Pill, but yet 'tis that without which the Pill wud scarce be swallow'd down'.[57] Boyle says that his rhetorical training instilled 'a very cautious & considerate

---

[51] *New Experiments and Observations touching Cold* (1683), B2[r].

[52] *Philaretus*, 10.

[53] Both in fact soubriquets for his nephew Richard Jones.

[54] See Claire Preston, *Writing and Scientific Investigation in Seventeenth-Century England* (forthcoming 2014) on his letter to Lady Ranelagh, and *Philaretus*.

[55] On Bacon's use of fable see Paolo Rossi, *Francis Bacon: From Magic to Science*, trans. Sacha Rabinovitch (Chicago: University of Chicago Press, 1968), 73–134.

[56] Philip Sidney, *A Defence of Poetry*, in *Miscellaneous Prose of Sir Philip Sidney*, ed. Katherine Duncan-Jones and Jan van Dorsten (Oxford: Clarendon Press, 1973), 93.

[57] 'Diurnall Observations, Thoughts, & Collections...April 25th 1647', BP 44, f. 94; quoted in Lawrence W. Principe, 'Virtuous Romance and Romantic Virtuoso: The Shaping of Robert Boyle's Literary Style', *Journal of the History of Ideas*, 56.3 (1998): 377–97 (389). *Greatness of Mind* and *Occasional Reflections* also have further clear echoes of Sidney's *Defence* (also quoted in Principe, 'Virtuous Romance').

way of expressing himselfe',[58] and the persistent tendency to discuss or apologize for style and structure in later works suggests that he remained keenly sensitive to tonal effects and generic propriety, that he was concerned with narrative structure, the status of fictional interventions, and the reception of his work by a very particular audience, whom he hoped to influence in an overtly Sidneian manner by 'rendring Virtue Amiable' to those who are more moved by 'shining examples...than by dry Precepts and grave Discourses'.[59]

Although *Philaretus* is an equivocal conversion narrative (conversion from the imaginative to the devotional in a highly rhetoricized format), it was, significantly, written at the moment when Boyle is said to have undergone a quite different conversion, from the moral to the scientific. This shift, which Michael Hunter, Lawrence Principe, and others have characterized as a 'Great Divide',[60] took Boyle away from the writing of improving works of ethics and devotion (such as *Aretology*, *Theodora*, and the germ of what would become *Seraphick Love*), which he framed in the Sidneian/Horatian mode of inducement 'of well-doing and not of well-knowing only',[61] and towards investigative writing, for which he had largely to invent his own new forms. These forms were not stable over the whole of his literary career and he returned to certain genres (for example, the dialogue) on different occasions, even as he was developing an essentially new narrative style of experimental essay.[62] The variety of these forms, and his willingness to use them at need, suggests a literary sensibility open to the particular strengths of different genres and modes. As well as the dialogue, Boyle wrote familiar epistles, isagogic letters, a romance, autobiography, essays, formal correspondence, and, of course, the full-blown treatise.

In his eulogy of Boyle, Matthew Morgan writes somewhat clumsily of Boyle's reputation as unusually literary: 'He in Philology was profoundly Vers'd,/Poets and Orators fluently rehears'd;/He never them superfluously did quote,/But a new piece of Knowledge to promote...'[63] Boyle was also approved by other scientists for his understanding of 'the true use and signification of words whereby to register and compute...conceptions'.[64] Robert Codrington's Latin ode in praise of Boyle declared him 'not of a more noble genealogy than a literary one'.[65] Indeed, Boyle's style was so

---

[58] *Philaretus*, 11.

[59] *Philaretus*, [A8ᵛ]. See the *paragone* of philosophers and poets in Sidney, *Defence*, 85–7.

[60] Principe, 'Virtuous Romance', 392; see also Michael Hunter, *Robert Boyle: Scrupulosity and Science* (Woodbridge: Boydell, 2000), 42.

[61] Sidney, *Defence*, 83.

[62] Boyle's development of the narrative experimental essay is discussed *inter alia* by Peter Dear, 'Narratives, Anecdotes, and Experiments: Turning Experience into Science in the Seventeenth Century', in Peter Dear, ed., *The Literary Structure of Scientific Argument* (Philadelphia: University of Pennsylvania Press, 1991), 135–63.

[63] Matthew Morgan, 'An Elegy on the Death of the Honorable Mr Robert Boyle' (1692), 13.

[64] William Petty to RB, 15 April 1653, in *The Correspondence of Robert Boyle*, ed. Michael Hunter, Antonio Clericuzio, and Lawrence M. Principe (London: Pickering & Chatto, 2001), I, 142.

[65] Robert Codrington, 'In Honorem Viri Praeclarissimi...Roberti Boyle' [1660], RS Boyle Papers MS 36, 42ᵛ–43ʳ.

distinctive, so civilly mannered (even fussy at times in its careful polite discriminations and literal definitions) that Samuel Butler dubbed it a 'trillo' (an embellishment) and pastiched Boyle's often maddeningly prolix style in an 'occasional reflection' about Walter Charleton trying out ineffectual 'mortiferous unguents' on dogs and kittens before the Royal Society.[66]

Although Boyle moved from moral to natural-philosophical studies in about 1649, he nevertheless maintained a clear hereditary line from Sidney, the primary example of English moral heroic romance, in stating the purposes of the imaginative in scientific writing. In the moral work *Seraphick Love* (partly written in 1648; later completed and eventually published in 1663[67]) he is unequivocal about his fictionalizing of a pious example and frankly intends to claim the freedom of most writers, 'who scruple not in Popular Composures to make Similes and Allusions grounded on Popular Traditions and Perswasions'.[68] The liberal use of simile is one of the most striking features of Boyle's style in *Seraphick Love* and he is particularly inclined to use the processes of the laboratory and the observatory in this way, as when he applies a 'chymical metaphor' of purification in the furnace to the indiscriminate consumption of human life, the virtuous and the vicious together, in public calamities,[69] or when he divides 'seraphic' from 'common' lovers as astronomers are divided from children, the former concerned with what the optic glass reveals in the heavens, the latter diverted merely by the gilded decorations on the outside of the tube.[70] *Seraphick Love*, written just at the juncture of Boyle's literary career as a moralist and as a scientist, is a hybrid of moral purpose kitted out with similitudes of the laboratory and of the practices of observation.

In *Occasional Reflections* (1665) (a work that includes the eponymous essays, the chronologically organized 'Accidents of an Ague' and 'Angling Improv'd to Spiritual Uses') Boyle makes a survey of several key aspects of ornament. Similitudes are 'perhaps no great Vanity' when they provide the natural philosopher with comparisons (*OR* a3[r]), and 'Truths and Notions that are dress'd up in apt Similitudes, pertinently appli'd, are wont to make durable Impressions on [the memory]' (*OR* b2[r]); decorum, he thinks, excuses any style as long as it is maintained (*OR* a[4r]); he judges it wiser to use contemporary examples for guidance on style than ancient ones, since it would be

---

[66] Cited by Marjorie Hope Nicholson, *Pepys' Diary and the New Science* (Charlottesville: University of Virginia Press, 1965), 133. Butler's pastiche of Boyle is 'An Occasionall reflexion upon Dr Charlton's feeling a Dog's Pulse at Gresham-College by R. Boyle Esq.', British Library Additional MS 18220, ff. 98–100 ('Truly, Lindamor, I am of opinion, that a dog is much more proper for the Experiment than the vigorous & vicious Animal co[m]monly styled a Cat, for a Cat, you know is said to have nine lives, eight in reversion & one in possession' (98–9). Swift, of course, took up the parodic cudgel against Boyle in 'Meditation on a Broomstick' (1703). Boyle's prolixity was acknowledged even by his friends and admirers. See also the manuscript fragment 'the Aspiring Naturlist', a dialogue, for an example of Boyle in long-winded form (RS MS 9, ff. 43–4).

[67] Lawrence Principe has noted that the original draft of *Seraphick Love* (1648) is far more 'literary' in its exposition than was previously understood and shows clear signs of Boyle's continental reading during this period ('Virtuous Romance', 379).

[68] *Seraphick Love*, [C1v].   [69] *Seraphick Love*, 38.   [70] *Seraphick Love*, 59.

improper to...have unadvisedly made Shepherds and Nymphs discourse like Philosophers or Doctors of Divinity [even though it is within the writer's ambit to] introduc[e] any whom he represents as intelligent Persons; they may be allow'd[,] ev'n about things ordinary and Mean, to talk like themselves, and employ Expressions that are neither mean, nor ordinary (*OR* a[5ʳ]).

He discusses *protasis* (in rhetoric a proposition, or the first half of a comparison) and notes the perils of over-amplification (*OR* a3[ᵛ]); and he is especially eloquent on the subject of descriptions, '[t]hese being but Pictures drawn (with Words instead of Colours) for the Imagination, the skilful will approve those most that produce in the mind, not the Finest Idaeas, but the Likest...' (*OR* b2[ʳ]). His aim in employing rhetorical, especially those descriptive and prosopopoeical, figures which produce images in the mind, is to 'mak[e] almost the whole World a great *Conclave Mnemonicum*, and a well furnished *Promptuary*, for the service of Piety and Vertue...' (*OR* b2[ʳ]). Eloquent embellishments, he says,

> I will not be forward to condemn...whether they be laid out upon Speculative Notions in Theology, or upon Critical Inquiries into Obsolete Rites, or Disputable Etymologies; or upon Philosophical Disquisitions or Experiments; or upon the florid Embellishments of Language; or (in short) upon some such other thing as seems extrinsical to the Doctrine that is according to Godliness, and seems not to have any direct tendency to the promoting of Piety and the kindling of Devotion. For I consider, that as God hath made man subject to several wants, and hath both given him several allowable appetites, and endowed him with various faculties and abilities to gratifie them; so a man's Pen may be very warrantably and usefully emploi'd, though it be not directly so, to teach a Theological Truth, or incite the Reader's Zeal. (*OR* V, 140–1)

This is the *apodosis* of a reflection whose *protasis* presents syrup of violets as a metaphor of useful eloquence, the colour, smell, and taste of it being grateful to the senses and yet, the concoction itself a purgative whose 'good smell can expel bad humours' (*OR* V, 140). Such remedies are effective in part because they offer 'Allurements to make use of them' (*OR* V, 140). Later in the same reflection he notes, as he did in *Theodora*, that what he calls 'a Nicer sort of Readers...are so far from being likely to be prevailed on by Discourses not tricked up with Flowers of Rhetorick, that they would scarce be drawn so much as to cast their eyes on [serious writing]' (*OR* V, 142). Although he is primarily concerned with pious writings in this passage, the special care he takes to notice that all kinds of writing, including the experimental and natural philosophical, can be rhetorically enhanced deserves notice: even at this early stage, when his concerns have been almost exclusively with moral expression, he is careful to allude to the special linguistic demands of the scientific.

Boyle tells the reader that his reflections are composed according to structure. Each reflection begins with an incident or phenomenon. This *protasis* is, he explains, 'the Ground-work of all the rest' (*OR* [A3ᵛ]), and he uses it to 'ingage an Attention', rather than 'to confine my self to the Magisteriall Dictates of either Antient or Scholasticke Writers' (*OR* [a5ʳ]). A Boylean reflection thus commences with the incident of the title

('Upon my Spaniel's Carefulness not to lose me in a strange place'; 'Looking through a Perspective-Glass upon a Vessel we suspected to give us Chace, and to be a Pyret'; or 'Upon his Paring of a Rare Summer Apple'). Each *protasis* yields its *apodosis*, 'an Application of what was taking notice of in the Subject... some important Moral instruction, or perhaps some Theological Mystery' (*OR* [A6^v]). The paring of an apple yields a reflection on ornament: the gaudy skin of the apple distracts us from the 'true relish' of the sound fruit as figures and tropes 'so often conceal or mis-represent... the true and genuine Nature' of moral discourse (*OR* I, 182). The reflections are moral essays; and yet, the *protasis–apodosis* structure is essentially an inductive one: it moves readerly consideration from the raw datum of the occasion of a spaniel wandering or keeping close to its master's heels to a sublime and more general axiom about our tendency to forget God under distraction until some momentous event occurs to recall us to Him. Often the reflections hover at the edge of Boyle's own experimental investigations. He has a glow-worm in a glass (*protasis*). 'Rare Qualities may sometimes be Prerogatives, without being Advantages...'; 'the light that ennobles him, tempts Inquisitive Men to keep him' (*apodosis*) (*OR* V, 154–5). Elsewhere, his reflections and meditations include metaphors of distillation, perspective and burning glasses, the workings of physic, cloud formations, prisms, the composition of rainwater, magnetism, botany, and cabinets of curiosity. *Occasional Reflections* is a work that incorporates Boyle's axioms of style, his practice of it, and a wealth of similitudes derived from his natural-philosophical studies, the whole work structured like a demonstration of Baconian induction. The structure of the reflections is nowhere explicitly defined that way by Boyle, although he does liken the ability of the reflector to extend large ideas in ethics and divinity from minor matters to the mathematician's art of 'giv[ing] us an exact account of all the Journeys [the sun] performs' from local data (*OR*, 20).

Occasional Reflections shows us a Boyle focused on questions of style, and expressing himself frequently, as Browne did before him, in analogies with experimental practice and scientific theory. If the technologies of observation give him conceits for moral meditations, so too do the subjects of experimental investigation (why rain is not brackish though it originates from the sea; why cheese and vinegar are colonized by microorganisms; or why a prism offers a theory of colours). *Occasional Reflections* complicates his rhetorical theory, too, by revolving the argument for and against rhetorical ornament. Reflection Six in Section II ('Upon the sight of a Looking-glass, with a rich Frame') is a dialogue spoken by three friends. The mirror's frame stands, of course, for rhetorical elaboration of the plain image delivered by the mirror itself. Eugenius approves the elaborate frame because it enforces self-scrutiny by drawing us to the mirror; Lindamor agrees, but believes that ornament will only be rightly understood by the wise; Eusebius thinks it is distracting and deceptive (*OR* II, 199). Elsewhere, Eugenius refers to 'a fancy of your Friend Mr Boyle, who was saying that he had thoughts of making a short Romantick story' in the style of *Utopia* and *New Atlantis* (*OR* II, 199).

Boyle's self-conscious sense of appropriate rhetorical register plays out in *Occasional Reflections*. He worries about 'want of uniformity' of style, regrets that some of the following meditations are 'neglected' or 'luxuriant' (*OR* B1[^v]); he apologizes to the reader in *Angling Improv'd to Spiritual Uses* (Section IV of *Occasional Reflections*) for employing the dialogue, a form which might confuse the fictional and the actual by making the literary vehicle of the discourse seem 'a Story purely Romantick' (*OR* [b4ᵛ]). He excuses stylistic variation and flexibility through the nature of the subject: 'this kind of Composures requires... a loose and Desultory way of writing' (*OR* [B1ʳ]). And yet, in excusing the plainness of some of his experimental writing, he remarks that 'without allowing it any of those advantages that method, style, and decent embellishments, are wont to confer on the composures they are employed to adorn', he will be thought to have failed to present the material properly.[71]

Very many of Boyle's post-1649 scientific writings are cast in established literary formats (notably the dialogue, a form he knew at first-hand from the 'familiar Kind of Conversation' practised in his schoolroom days as a standard humanist genre;[72] and the familiar epistle derived from Seneca). These later works make free with the expressive richness of highly honed humanist rhetoric; and they often dwell on the propriety of the literary in scientific expression. Ultimately, Boyle's many scruples about romance and the value of rhetorical tropes and of the imaginative in general, as expressed in *Philaretus*, *Seraphick Love*, and *Theodora and Didymus*, were at least salved if not borne away entirely by the requirement of these very tools in forging a new language for natural philosophy later in his career.

Brian Vickers observes that '[E]xperiment... is itself a literary genre or rhetorical form'.[73] This is clearly Boyle's thinking and in the *Proemial Essay* he deliberates about an apt, decorous, and utile form for experimental report. As a good Baconian, he is especially critical of 'systems' that pretend to final authority and complete knowledge, and he advocates the essay instead because he requires a fragmentary literary genre for science, one whose style analogically enacts the incompleteness of the experimenter's knowledge and prevents any readerly delusion of completeness.[74] In support of his contention that systems impede natural philosophy, he constructs an elaborate experimental metaphor using an anecdote of a *camera obscura* he saw demonstrated in Leiden. When the aperture is small the picture cast on the wall is clear, but when a larger aperture is allowed to let more light in the chamber, the image disappears. By analogy, systems, when viewed in 'a weak and determinate degree of light', look plausible; however, 'if but a full light of new Experiments and Observations be freely let in upon them, the Beauty of those (delightful, but Phantastical) structures does immediately vanish' (*Proemial*, 8). He tells us that he carefully avoided the 'contamination' of systematic works by Bacon, Gassendi, and Descartes until he felt he had developed his own thinking securely—another

---

[71] John T. Harwood reads this as an admission that the work is not yet polished, rather than a criticism of adornment in natural philosophical writing (*The Early Essays and Ethics of Robert Boyle* [Carbondale: Southern Illinois University Press, 1991], lviii).

[72] *Philaretus*, 12.

[73] Vickers, 'Bacon among the Literati', 268.

[74] On the Baconian bent for the fragmentary, see Clucas ('A Knowledge Broken'), who argues that Bacon's use of aphorism was antithetical to that of Erasmian humanism's totalizing *sententiae* in seeking to prompt the reader towards further investigation, rather than to allow readerly complacency.

instance of his preference for establishing fact *ab initio*, rather than receiving it from 'authority' (*Proemial*, 6). Boyle presents this essay as an isogogic letter (itself a trope) in which he proposes himself to his young friend Pyrophilus as a parabolic or didactic figure, much as he had done in *Philaretus* with its conversion narrative: although he considers that the *Proemial Essay* is written too early in his career, he cannot afford to remain silent on the subject, like the steward who buried his single talent rather than use it.

He is eloquent on the use of parables, and here, as in *Philaretus*, he makes an almost direct quotation of Sidney's *Defence*.[75] This same Boyle, on the other hand, also declares that essays should be written in a philosophical, rather than a 'Rhetorical strain', 'rather clear and significant, than curiously adorn'd. *Ornari res ipsa negat, contenta doceri* [the subject itself needs no ornament; it is enough that it be understood].' Needless rhetorical ornament in scientific writing (or 'too spruce a style'), he goes on to assert, is like painting the lens of a telescope with delightful colours which hinder its correct use. Nevertheless—and here is another Boylean *volte face*—'though it were foolish to colour or enamel upon the glasses of Telescopes, yet to gild or otherwise embellish the Tubes of them, may render them more acceptable to the Users, without at all lessening the Clearness of the Object to be look'd at through them' (*Proemial*, 12). In other words, dull and insipid writing (a style he finds characteristic of many chemical writers) has a tendency to 'disgust' the reader and to work against the conveyance of truth; ornament will draw the reader to the correct apprehension of truth, and the natural-philosophical conceit of the telescope conveys this principle. Yet, in the same essay Boyle can insist its design is 'only to inform Readers, not to delight or Perswade them' (*OR* [a4ʳ]). This apparent renunciation of the Horatian/Sidneian *utile et dulce* (so knowingly paraphrased in *Philaretus*), in comparison with his actual rhetorical practice in the *Proemial Essay*, is, however, hardly definitive: his narratives are structured to place the reader within the occasion of the experiment, 'these being but pictures drawn...for the Imagination' (*OR* [a4ʳ]).

It may be that Boyle's early commitment to moral philosophy and the struggle to find apt styles for it prompted his lifelong attentiveness to the writing of science, and generated the rhetorical diversity of his writings.[76] *The Sceptical Chymist* (1661) exemplifies Boyle's maturing use of literary trope as a tool of scientific discussion and adds the purely fictive account of experimental results to the genuine experimental narrative in which, in the words of James Paradis, 'text became experimental action'.[77] The work is a dialogue between the exponents of a Paracelsian, an Aristotelian, and a sceptic. Boyle's own position is the last one, voiced in the dialogue by Carneades, and his purpose is to show that the two other chemical schools are not founded on evidence. But this is

---

[75] Sidney, *Defence*, 87.

[76] See Harwood, *The Early Essays and Ethics of Robert Boyle* (lviii) on Boyle's many genres, especially in his early writings (1645–55).

[77] James Paradis, 'Montaigne, Boyle, and the Essay of Experience', in George Levine, ed., *One Culture: Essays in Science and Literature* (Madison: University of Wisconsin Press, 1987), 60.

one of many occasions where Boyle's scientific writing could almost be mistaken for a courtesy book. This is not surprising, given the careful explanation he makes of his generic selection: it is, he says, a book designed by a gentleman for gentlemen, 'wherein only Gentlemen are introduc'd as speakers'. Such speakers will therefore speak a language 'more smooth...Expressions more civil[,] than is usual in the more Scholastick way of writing....whence perhaps some Readers will be assisted to discern a Difference betwixt Bluntness of Speech and Strength of reason, and find that a man may be a Champion for the Truth, without being an Enemy to Civility'.[78] With these remarks he can denigrate an older, linguistically obsessed, and disputatious way of writing science that accompanied an outmoded way of doing science (Scholastic philosophy); insist on the social premium enjoyed by properly conducted modern (empirical) science; and do both in the medium of fiction.[79]

The setting of *The Sceptical Chymist* is highly specified, rather than notional, and takes nearly all of the first nine pages to establish—it is 'a relation of what passed a while since at a meeting of persons of several opinions', namely Philiponus (the Paracelsian), Themistus (the Aristotelian), Carneades (the sceptic), and Eleutherius (the neutral party who moderates the discussion). The occasion is detailed: although Boyle had another appointment, to consult with a friend who knows about furnaces, he is persuaded by Eleutherius instead to visit Carneades in his garden on a beautiful summer's day, a vignette in which civility (to meet Carneades) is almost, but not quite overridden by the call of experimental science (to consult about furnaces). They find Carneades already seated in a bower with two other friends and Boyle is reluctant to intrude upon them, but Carneades 'received [Eleutherius] with open looks and armes, and welcoming me also with his wonted freedom and civility, invited us to rest our selves by him...' (*SC* 2–4). An elaborate narrative of civility precedes the dialogue proper—at one point, there are so many apologies and courtesies going back and forth between the various parties that Eleutherius has to remind them that their purpose is to exchange arguments, not compliments (*SC* 14). The purpose of all this, Boyle says at the beginning of the work, is to remind readers not to believe in chemical experiments that are offered 'only by way of Prescriptions, and not of Relations', by which latter term he means accounts by the experimenter of his own processes (*SC* A3[ᵛ]). For Boyle, 'relations' include even such fictional extensions into the social setting of scientific discourse. This is Carneades's position, too—the reason, Boyle says, that so many have been willing to believe in Paracelsian theory is that they have not bothered to try out the experiments themselves or derived credible relations of them from trusted sources (*SC* A3[ᵛ]).[80] Thus, much of the dialogue consists of what Carneades describes as a [Baconian] 'demonstration', rather than a [Scholastic]

---

[78] *The Sceptical Chymist* (1661), A6ʳ. Subsequent references are given in the text.

[79] Boyle has Themistus the Aristotelian insult the Paracelsians as 'sooty Empiricks' (i.e. not gentlemen, probably because they're not Aristotelians). The Boylean Carneades has, as we know from his descriptions of laboratory trials, had sooty hands, too. There seems to be a subtle distinction between gentlemanly toil in the lab, which goes with gentlemanly scepticism and correct judgement, a lower order of the same toil in aid of a misconceived chemical theory, and a mistaken antagonism towards such toil in the form of prescriptive (and also misconceived) Aristotelianism (24).

[80] At certain points in the dialogue, Carneades is actually quoting Boyle verbatim.

'harrangue' (*SC* 25), as when Carneades describes an experiment in which he digested antimony in oil of vitriol and later distilled this by fire to produce sulphur 'of so sulphureous a smell, that upon the unluting of the vessels it infected the Room with a scarce supportable stink' (*SC* 68). The narrative of the process, with the memorable detail of the demotic 'stink', gives a clear sense of an actual event, a demonstration, rather than a precept. It is as if Boyle has realized that his natural gift for narrative and fictional detail is the very tool with which to present the demonstrations, rather than the precepts of natural philosophy.

Near the beginning of the *Proemial Essay*, Boyle describes the usefulness of narrative experimental accounts, even of misinterpreted data. He claims some virtue even in these, since such an essay

> does me no greater injury than *Galileo* upon his first Invention of the Telescope would have done an Astronomer, if he had told him, that he had discover'd in heaven those imaginary new Stars which a late Mathematician has fancy'd himself to have descry'd there, and at the same time had made him a Present of an excellent Telescope, with expectation that thereby the Receiver should be made of the Giver's Opinion; for by the help of his Instrument the Astronomer might not only make divers useful Observations in the Sky, and perhaps detect new Lights there, but discern also his mistake that gave it him. (*Proemial*, 11)

This is a remarkable expression of union between literary and mechanical technologies in science: in this analogy, the telescope and the narrative essay are alike tools of investigation, alike disinterested in conveying fact, even if that fact is open to misunderstanding. That Boyle should express the power of rhetorically fashioned scientific writing in such a striking similitude reminds us exactly how open to the rhetorical early modern science really was. 'Such a way of proposing and elucidating things,' he concluded at the end of his life, 'is...more clear...than any other...' (*CV*, 17–18).

Further Reading

Benjamin, Andrew E., Geoffrey N. Cantor, and John R. R. Christie, eds. *The Figural and the Literal: Problems of Language in the History of Science and Philosophy, 1630–1800* (Manchester: Manchester University Press, 1987).

Boyle, Robert. *An Account of Philaretus During His Minority* in *Robert Boyle by Himself and His Friends*, ed. Michael Hunter (London: Pickering & Chatto, 1994).

Clucas, Stephen. 'A Knowledge Broken', in Neil Rhodes, ed., *English Renaissance Prose: History, Language, and Politics* (Tempe, AZ: Medieval and Renaissance Texts and Studies, 1997), 171–2.

Cummins, Juliet, and David Burchell, eds. *Science, Literature and Rhetoric in Early Modern England* (Aldershot: Ashgate, 2007).

Harkness, Deborah E. 'Francis Bacon's Experimental Writing', in Susannah Brietz Monta and Margaret W. Ferguson, eds., *Teaching Early Modern English Prose* (NY: Modern Language Association of America, 2010), 246–58.

Paradis, James. 'Montaigne, Boyle, and the Essay of Experience', in George Levine, ed., *One Culture: Essays in Science and Literature* (Madison: University of Wisconsin Press, 1987).

Preston, Claire. 'In the Wilderness of Forms: Ideas and Things in Thomas Browne's Cabinets of Curiosity', in Neil Rhodes and Jonathan Sawday, eds., *The Renaissance Computer: Knowledge Technology in the First Age of Print* (London: Routledge, 2000), 170–83.

Principe, Lawrence M. 'Virtuous Romance and Romantic Virtuoso: The Shaping of Robert Boyle's Literary Style', *Journal of the History of Ideas*, 56.3 (1995): 377–97.

Shapin, Steven. 'Pump and Circumstance: Robert Boyle's Literary Technology', *Social Studies of Science*, 14 (1984): 481–520.

Vickers, Brian. 'Bacon among the Literati: Science and Language', *Comparative Criticism*, 13 (1991): 249–72.

—— 'The Royal Society and English Prose Style: A Reassessment', in Brian Vickers and Nancy S. Streuver, eds., *Rhetoric and the Pursuit of Truth: Language Change in the Seventeenth and Eighteenth Centuries* (Los Angeles: UCLA/Clark Library, 1985), 1–76.

CHAPTER 18

RICHARD HAKLUYT

NANDINI DAS

TRAVEL and travel texts have a habit of surfacing everywhere in early modern English writing. Take *Euphues and his England* (1580), John Lyly's sequel to his trend-setting *Euphues: The Anatomy of Wit* (1578), for instance. As the bright and often annoyingly self-satisfied Athenian hero of Lyly's fiction sails towards his destination, he does all that a conscientious traveller could be expected to do. Euphues spends his time reading an account of Britain, plans to write a report of his own observations, and bores his companion with his lengthy discourse. But his long-suffering friend, Philautus, is hardly grateful for the lecture:

> Philautus, not accustomed to these narrow seas, was more ready to tell what wood the ship was made of than to answer to Euphues' discourse; yet, between waking and winking as, one half sick and somewhat sleepy, it came in his brains, answered thus:
> 'In faith, Euphues, thou hast told a long tale. The beginning I have forgotten, the middle I understand not, and the end hangeth not together. Therefore I cannot repeat it as I would, nor delight in it as I ought; yet if at our arrival thou wilt renew thy tale, I will rub my memory. In the mean season, would I were either again in Italy, or now in England. I cannot brook these Seas, which provoke my stomach sore.'[1]

Lyly's quiet joke here is obviously at the expense of Euphues, the seasoned humanist scholar and traveller. The information that he has gleaned so studiously from Caesar's *Gallic Wars*, although not quite the outright lies as travellers' tales were generally reputed to be, is useless for visitors to Elizabethan England. And if the knowledge associated with the reading of travel is in question, the experience of it hardly fares any better. From Jerome Turler's *Traveiler* (1575) to Francis Bacon's essay 'Of Travel' (1612, 1625), the enormous body of travel advice literature that flourished throughout this period might praise the benefits of travel for the individual as well as the state, but Philautus fails to offer a convincing illustration of either. Seasick and sleep-deprived, it is obvious that he likes everything about travel apart from the travelling itself. At the end of Lyly's story he will refuse to follow the example

---

[1] Leah Scragg, ed., *Euphues: The Anatomy of Wit and Euphues and His England by John Lyly* (Manchester: Manchester University Press, 2003), 182.

of Odysseus and return home with the fruits of his experience like all good travellers were advised to do, happily choosing to settle abroad instead.

That travel finds its way into Lyly's prose fiction is not surprising in itself. Travelling and lying went together in popular perception, and travellers' tales were traditionally associated as much with the writing of fiction as with the narratives of facts in history and geography. What is notable here, however, is the way in which Lyly's fiction plays with the disjunction between the experience of travel and the reading of it, and how that encounter with contemporary travel brings with it something that is quite different from the glamour that surrounds a knight's quest or a pilgrim's progress. In its attention to the details of the experience of travel, its emphasis on the gathering of heterogeneous data that threaten to slip out of the grasps of Euphues and Philautus even as they are presented, it introduces something of the everyday and the prosaic, which marks a change both in English fiction and in Lyly's characteristic and instantly recognizable, highly fraught rhetorical style. That moment in *Euphues and his England* offers us an unexpected way into the actual writing of travel in England in the period and into the book that forms the subject of this chapter, *The Principal Navigations, Voyages, Traffiques and Discoveries of the English Nation*, compiled a decade after Lyly's *Euphues* by his fellow Oxford scholar, Richard Hakluyt.[2]

Hakluyt's *Principal Navigations* is the single most significant collection of travel literature ever to be published in English. First printed in 1589, and running to over 1,760,000 words in three folio volumes by the time the second edition is printed in 1598–1600 (Fig. 18.1), it is also one of our largest collections of Renaissance English prose, intimately connected with both its predecessors and successors in the field of travel writing. Admittedly, readers may often find themselves sharing Philautus's confused exhaustion when faced with the seemingly endless assembly of texts in Hakluyt's collection, and those who laugh at Euphues's antiquated travel information may be puzzled equally by the space that Hakluyt affords to ancient documents. At a more fundamental level, however, the understanding of the epistemic gap between the reading and practice of travel that lies at the heart of Lyly's joke also shapes Hakluyt's massive text. The writing of travel, of all the genres of narrative writing in the early modern period, was one of the most problematic when it came to the relationship between theory and practice, text and action. Why does one go about capturing the experience of travel through words, and how? If Philip Sidney, in his *Defence of Poetry*, had claimed that 'it is not *gnosis* but *praxis* must be the fruit' of literature, rhetorically moving the reader from 'well-knowing' to 'well-doing', then what was the status of travel writing, where the novelty and the messiness of the experience of travel demanded written order and therefore invited widespread scepticism about their truth-content, where text constantly threatened to substitute for action, and action undermined the text's efforts to record its essential nature with any degree of accuracy?[3]

---

[2] For biographical information on Hakluyt, see G. B. Parks, *Richard Hakluyt and the English Voyages* (New York: American Geographical Society, 1928), and Peter C. Mancall, *Hakluyt's Promise: An Elizabethan's Obsession for an English America* (New Haven: Yale University Press, 2007).

[3] Katherine Duncan-Jones, ed., *The Defence of Poesy*, in *Sir Philip Sidney: The Major Works* (Oxford: Oxford University Press, 2002), 226.

THE PRINCIPAL NAVIGATIONS, VOYAGES, TRAFFIQVES AND DISCOVEries of the *English Nation*, made by Sea or ouerland, to the remote and fartheſt diſtant quarters of the Earth, at any time within the compaſſe of theſe 1600 yeres:

Diuided into three ſeuerall Volumes, according to the poſitions of the Regions, whereunto they were directed.

The firſt Volume containeth the worthy Diſcoueries, &c. of the *Engliſh* toward the North and Northeaſt by Sea, as of *Lápland, Scrikfinia, Corelia*, the Baie of *S. Nicolas*, the Iſles of *Colgoieue, Vaigatz*, and *Noua Zembla*, toward the great Riuer *Ob*, with the mighty Empire of *Ruſſia*, the *Caſpian* Sea, *Georgia, Armenia, Media, Perſia, Boghar* in *Bactria*, and diuers kingdomes of *Tartaria*:

Together with many notable monuments and teſtimonies of the ancient forren trades, and of the warrelike and other ſhipping of this Realme of *England* in former ages.

VVhereunto is annexed a briefe *Commentary of the true ſtate of* Iſland, and of the Northren Seas and lands ſituate that way: As alſo the memorable defeat of the *Spaniſh* huge *Armada*, Anno 1588.

¶ The ſecond Volume comprehendeth the principall Nauigations, Voyages, Traffiques, and diſcoueries of the *Engliſh* Nation made by Sea or ouer-land, to the South and South-eaſt parts of the World, as well within as without the Streight of *Gibraltar*, at any time within the compaſſe of theſe 1600. yeres: Diuided into two ſeueral parts, &c.

¶By RICHARD HAKLVYT Preacher, and ſometime Student of Chriſt-Church in Oxford.

¶ Imprinted at London by *George Biſhop*, *Ralph Newberie*, and *Robert Barker*. ANNO 1599.

FIGURE 18.1 Richard Hakluyt, *Principal Navigations* (1599), title page.

Hakluyt's attempts to tackle those questions in *The Principal Navigations* would have significant implications both for English travel writing and for English prose itself.

For Hakluyt, the answer to the initial 'why'—the rationale for capturing the *praxis* of travel through words in the first place—is clear. His contribution came in an age when travel and exploration was rapidly changing the visible world, but English participation in that process was belated and disorganized. Italian-born John Cabot, authorized to venture on behalf of the English king Henry VII, had reached Newfoundland in 1498, and there had been other scattered attempts since then. Voyages in search of a northeast passage to China had opened up trade with Russia; others ventured west towards Brazil and the Caribbean, as well as Africa and the Middle East. By the 1580s, England was catching up with countries like Spain and Portugal, thanks to the efforts of people like John Hawkins, Martin Frobisher, Humphrey Gilbert, Francis Drake, and Walter Ralegh. Yet, compared to the explorations and voyages undertaken by their continental rivals, these were unsystematic initiatives, underwritten mostly by individuals or groups of merchants, rather than the product of any concerted English imperial effort. When Hakluyt came to print his very first collection of travel texts, *Divers Voyages Touching the Discoverie of America* (1582), and addressed his dedicatory epistle to Philip Sidney, this is the first thing he mentions. Rather than beginning with the marvels of the New World, as one might have expected him to do, 'I marvaile not a little', he writes, 'that since the first discoverie of America (which is nowe full fourescore and tenne yeeres) after so great conquests and plantings of the Spaniards and Portingales there, that wee of England could never have the grace to set fast footing in such fertile and temperate places, as are left as yet unpossessed of them' (sig. ¶1r). When *The Principal Navigations* is printed in the general wave of English optimism after the defeat of the Spanish Armada seven years later, therefore, his focus on the recording of English travels is both an exhortation and a defence. This time the dedicatory letter to Sidney's father-in-law and Elizabeth I's Principal Secretary, Sir Francis Walsingham, notes how Hakluyt has 'both heard in speech, and read in books other nations miraculously extolled for their discoveries and notable enterprises by sea, but the English of all others for their sluggish security, and continuall neglect of the like attempts [...] either ignominiously reported, or exceedingly condemned'.[4] His response to this 'obloquie of our nation' is to 'speake a word of that just commendation which our nation doe indeed deserve'. '[I]t can not be denied,' he asserts:

> but as in all former ages, they have been men full of activity, stirrers abroad, and searchers of the remote parts of the world, so in this most famous and peerlesse governement of her most excellent Majesty, her subjects through the speciall assistance, and blessing of God, in searching the most opposite corners and quarters of the world, and to speake plainly, in compassing the vaste globe of the earth more th[a]n once, have excelled all the nations and people of the earth. (PN1, sig. *2v)

---

[4] Richard Hakluyt, *The Principal Navigations, Voyages, and Discoveries of the English Nation* (London, 1589), sig. *2r-v. Page references for the two editions of Hakluyt's collection will be subsequently indicated in parentheses as PN1 and PN2.

By the time Hakluyt published the massively expanded second edition of *The Principal Navigations* in 1598–1600, thanks to his editorial enterprise, that claim would be fairly impossible to deny. When the Victorian historian James A. Froude famously called *The Principal Navigations* 'the prose epic of the modern English Nation', it was the pioneering status of this strong nationalistic impetus which his description acknowledged. In subsequent years, Hakluyt's nationalism and the role of *The Principal Navigations* in the construction of the idea of English nationhood have never been in doubt; indeed, they have become the implicit focus of our questioning of Hakluyt's complicity in English projects of colonialism and imperialism.[5]

Over and above that nationalistic drive which provides its rationale, however, the significance of *The Principal Navigations* rests in its response to its second challenge: the 'how' beyond the 'why'. How can a text bridge the gap between the experience and the representation of travel? How does it convince its readers that what they read offers an accurate representation of the experience itself? And what happens to both words and texts in the process? Hakluyt would have known how his predecessors had approached this task. There were those, for instance, whom *The Principal Navigations* describes disparagingly as the makers of 'wearie volumes bearing the titles of universall Cosmographie' (PN1, sig. *3ᵛ). Johann Boemus, whose *Omnium gentium mores* (1520) attempted to provide an all-encompassing account of the cultures of Asia, Africa, and Europe, and was translated in part into English as a *Fardle of Facions* in 1555, would count as one of them. More recently, Sebastian Münster's *Universal Cosmography* had been published in German in 1544 and Latin in 1550, as well as being translated and adapted in countless versions, including in English in 1561 and 1572. And even as Hakluyt was collecting his own material, a so-called 'guerre des cosmographes' had broken out between André Thevet and François de Belleforest, when both published their own volumes of *Cosmographie universelle* in Paris in 1575.[6] Encyclopaedic in scope and heavily influenced by the classical examples of Ptolemy's *Geography* and Pliny's *Natural History*, the focus of the texts produced by writers such as Boemus and Münster was on comprehensiveness. Their descriptions rarely distinguish between ancient and modern authorities, using both instead to synthesize a global model centred on Christian doctrine. That structure is crucial: the time-bound individual voice of contemporary travellers, bringing in new facts and data that so often defy the existing framework, is subsumed within its boundaries.

For Hakluyt, as for the immediate predecessors with whom his links are the closest, such historiographic recastings of the world could never offer an accurate representation of either the *gnosis* or *praxis* of travel. The alternative that he offers, namely that

---

[5] J. A. Froude, 'England's Forgotten Worthies', in J. A. Froude, *Short Studies on Great Subjects* (New York: Charles Scribner and Company, 1868), 361. Originally published in *The Westminster Review*, NS 2 (July, 1582): 32–67. See also David Armitage, *The Ideological Origins of the English Empire* (Cambridge: Cambridge University Press, 2000), chap. 3; Richard Helgerson, *Forms of Nationhood: The Elizabethan Writing of England* (Chicago: University of Chicago Press, 1992), chap. 4; Mary Fuller, *Voyages in Print: English Travel to America, 1576–1624* (Cambridge: Cambridge University Press, 1995), chap. 4.

[6] On this 'war of cosmographers', see Frank Lestringant, *André Thevet* (Geneva: Drozm, 1991), chap. 7; Mancall, *Hakluyt's Promise*, 115–21.

the recording of contemporary history of travel (*peregrinationis historia*) was the only true means to 'certayne and full discoverie of the world' (PN1, sig. *3ᵛ), has its roots in the existing European travel collections of Francanzano da Montalboddo and Giovanni Battista Ramusio. Hakluyt makes multiple references on several occasions to Ramusio's immense three-volume collection of travel accounts, *Delle Navigationi et viaggi* (1550–9), for instance, and would later dedicate his own 1587 Latin edition of Peter Martyr d'Anghiera's *De Orbe Novo Decades* (Alcála, 1516) to Sir Walter Ralegh, in the hope that 'other maritime races, and in particular our own island race, perceiving how the Spaniards began and how they progressed, might be inspired to a like emulation of courage'.[7] Among the English, Hakluyt mentions Richard Eden, whose *Decades of the New World* (1555) consists of translated excerpts and summaries of the travel accounts of a number of continental writers, from Münster to Ramusio, Peter Martyr, Gonzalo Fernández de Oviedo, and Antonio Pigafetta. Along with its much-expanded adaptation by Richard Willes in his *A History of Travayle in the West and East Indies* (1577), Eden's text was the closest predecessor to Hakluyt's *Principal Navigations*, although Hakluyt's emphasis on English voyages would give the latter a distinctive edge over its competitors. Irrespective of their national focus, however, collections of *peregrinationis historia* of this kind depended far more on first-hand accounts (although often through translation and summary), rather than the second-hand redactions of the old cosmographies. More responsive to the rapid expansion of geographical knowledge and alterations in political climate, their form was cumulative and changeable. It was possible for Peter Martyr, for example, to add new reports as the *Decades* were published in multiple editions, as Michael Brennan has shown, while Eden and Hakluyt would both reinterpret its representation of Spanish imperialism in very different ways when preparing their own editions of the *Decades* in the reigns of Mary Tudor and Elizabeth I respectively.[8]

Hakluyt's third group of predecessors were even more sensitive to the demands of time and more clearly aligned with contemporary travel experience. These were the individual travel texts, accounts of recent travels by voyagers and explorers, the eyewitness reports. Their motives and quality of writing are variable, and their writers cover the entire range that William Sherman has identified in his typology of travel writers in this period, from pilgrims, knights, merchants, explorers, and colonizers, to diplomatic and political travellers, captives and castaways, pirates and scientific enquirers.[9]

---

[7] E. G. R. Taylor, ed., 'Epistle dedicatory to Sir Walter Ralegh', in *Original Writings and Correspondence of the Two Richard Hakluyts* (London: Hakluyt Society, 1935), vol. II, 365.

[8] Michael Brennan, 'The Texts of Peter Martyr's *De orbe novo decades* (1504–1628): A Response to Andrew Hadfield', *Connotations*, 6 (1996/7): 277–45. Andrew Hadfield, 'Peter Martyr, Richard Eden and the New World: Reading, Experience and Translation', *Connotations*, 5 (1995/6): 1–22, and *Literature, Travel, and Colonial Writing in the English Renaissance, 1545–1625* (Oxford: Clarendon Press, 1998), chap. 2.

[9] William Sherman, 'Stirrings and Searchings (1500–1720)', in Peter Hulme and Tim Youngs, eds., *The Cambridge Companion to Travel Writing* (Cambridge: Cambridge University Press, 2002), 17–36 (21–30).

A significant number of these were derived from continental sources. In 1580, for example, even as John Lyly's Euphues was reading the antiquated account of Caesar's travels to Britain, Hakluyt asked a possible common acquaintance at Magdalen College, Oxford, the linguist John Florio, to translate the rather more up-to-date accounts of Jacques Cartier's voyages to Canada from Ramusio's collection as *Two Navigations to New France*.[10] Among English initiatives, the first major voyage to be reported in print independently was an account of John Hawkins's third voyage, *A true declaration of the troublesome voyadge of M. J. Haukins to the parties of Guynea and the west Indies in the yeares of our Lord 1567 and 1568* (1569). Others followed, such as the account by Dionyse Settle of Frobisher's second voyage seeking a north-west passage, *A true reporte of the last voyage...by Capteine Frobisher* (1577), and George Best's *True discourse of the late voyages of discoverie for the finding of a passage to Cathaya* (1578). As Thomas Nicolls's description of the Canary Islands, which Hakluyt would later include in his *Principal Navigations*, demonstrates, the authority of such texts lay in their immediacy and closeness to the point of origin of the travel experience. Nicolls begins by opposing his own account based on seven years' travel against the 'great untruthes, in a booke called *The New found world Antarctike*, set out by a French man called Andrew Thevet'. 'It appeareth by the said booke that he had read the works of sundry Philosophers, Astronomers, and Cosmographers, whose opinions he gathered together', he notes, '[b]ut touching his owne travaile which he affirmeth, I referre to the judgement of the experient in our daies, and therefore for mine owne part I write of these Canaria Ilandes, as time hath taught me in manie yeares'.[11] In addition to these printed texts, a large body of documents circulated in private correspondence and in the papers of the trading companies. A storehouse of both foreign and English voices, they consist of texts such as the permit of safe conduct given to Anthony Jenkinson by the Turkish Sultan in 1553, which Hakluyt includes with the note: 'The very originall hereof was delivered me Rich. Hakl. by Master Jenkinson in the Turkish and French tongues' (PN1, 82–3). Richard Staper is thanked profusely in Hakluyt's 1589 epistle to the reader for giving him 'divers things touching the trade of Turkie, and other places in the East', which probably came from the archives of the Levant and Barbary Companies (PN1, sig. *4ᵛ). Others included in Hakluyt's collection, such as the letters describing the first English voyage to India by John Newbery and Ralph Fitch in 1583, form the essential pre-history of the East India Company.

The presentation of these permits and letters in *The Principal Navigations* shows us how intensely Hakluyt's own approach tries to strike a balance between old authority and new experience, the encyclopaedic ambitions of the old cosmographies and the constantly evolving immediacy of the new *peregrinationis historia*. Despite his contempt for the universal cosmographies, the attempt to outline an overarching narrative

---

[10] On Lyly's possible connections with Florio, see Frances Yates, *John Florio: The Life of an Italian in Shakespeare's England* (Cambridge: Cambridge University Press), 53.

[11] Thomas Nichols, *A pleasant description of the fortunate ilandes, called the Ilands of Canaria with their straunge fruits and commodities* (London, 1583), sig. Bi–v.

continues to define the shape of Hakluyt's collection. In the epistle to the reader in the 1598–1600 edition, for instance, he writes eloquently of his self-imposed task to 'incorporate into one body the torne and scattered limmes of our ancient and late Navigations by Sea, our voyages by land, and traffiques of merchandise by both' (PN2, sig. *4ᵛ), and as Matthew Day has shown, for contemporaries like the Oxford scholar Gabriel Harvey too, it was the printing of 'sundry' accounts 'in one volume' that made Hakluyt's text 'a worke of importance'.[12] Accordingly, the 1589 edition follows Ramusio's method of covering the known world. Within its pages, Hakluyt's documents are arranged in chronological and spatial order, starting with the earliest English voyages, focusing on the east and south-east, followed by the northern and western travels. Hakluyt broke with that pattern in the 1598–1600 edition by beginning with the northern voyages, but that rearrangement could be seen to establish yet more firmly what critics like David Harris Sacks have seen as a providential teleology, since now the collection could cover English travels from Geoffrey of Monmouth's account of King Arthur's conquests of Iceland, Denmark, and Norway in 517 AD, to the western successes of Hakluyt's own contemporaries in accounts of the recent English voyages to the West Indies in the 1580s.[13] Hakluyt's professed approach here performs a double duty, providing a narrative alternative to England's undeniable belatedness on the global stage, as well as the means to its correction; historical failure in the actual practice of travel, in Mary Fuller's words, is 'recuperated by rhetoric'.[14] If contemporary English exploration was a fragmented enterprise, reading through the ordered collection of travel reports and ancillary documents in Hakluyt's text at least afforded an overview of progress across time, which could then invite imitation by subsequent travellers.

Yet, even as Hakluyt organizes the immense and disparate collection of material into a single entity, he keeps the contours of individual texts visible. He makes it a point to underline how hard it has been to achieve that overview, presenting the volume undeniably as a conglomeration of disparate accounts, brought together at great cost and 'travail'. As the striking opening passage of the Epistle to the Reader in the second edition exclaims:

> For the bringing of which into this homely and rough-hewen shape, which here thou seest; what restlesse nights, what painefull dayes, what heat, what cold I have indured; how many long & chargeable journeys I have traveiled; how many famous libraries I have searched into; what varietie of ancient and moderne writers I have perused; what a number of old records, patents, privileges, letters, &c. I have redeemed from obscuritie and perishing. (PN2, sig. *4ᵛ)

Hakluyt's editorial approach to the texts in question itself corroborates this understanding, since it has the merit of adopting a concept with which his readers would have been

---

[12] Matthew Day, 'Hakluyt, Harvey, Nashe: The Material Text and Early Modern Nationalism', *Studies in Philology*, 104.3 (2007): 281–305 (290).

[13] David Harris Sacks, 'Richard Hakluyt's Navigations in Time: History, Epic, and Empire', *Modern Language Quarterly*, 67.1 (2006): 31–62.

[14] Fuller, *Voyages in Print*, 12. See also Helgerson, *Forms of Nationhood*, chap. 4.

deeply familiar. The citation of textual authority, as humanist pedagogy habitually taught its students, served to engender trust, enrich one's argument, and display one's scholarly labour. Pedagogues from Erasmus to Roger Ascham and every schoolmaster in between taught their students to draw on the testimony of pre-existing texts to amplify and elaborate their argument, allowing other writers—both ancient and modern—to bear 'witness' to their facts. At its most extreme, it is a habit that generated that classical and Renaissance oddity, the genre of the *cento* compiled almost entirely of quotations and extracts from other writers, which Richard Burton would praise in his *Anatomy of Melancholy* (1621). At its most familiar, its form is that which we saw Thomas Nicolls criticize in André Thevet's habit of subsuming personal experience under 'works of sundry Philosophers, Astronomers, and Cosmographers'. Hakluyt does not deny its power. As with the works of so many of his humanist contemporaries, while the texts he compiles often challenge the knowledge of earlier authorities, it does not preclude them from calling on the supporting voices of the ancients whenever necessary. But Hakluyt's *Principal Navigations*, more than any other travel collection of the period, naturalizes and extends that trope. It makes the citation of witnesses the central narrative principle of his monumental compendium and gives it a unique turn through an overwhelming valorization of the witnessing of *praxis*. Hakluyt's advertised aim, as he declares in his preface, is not only to allow 'those men which were the paynefull and personall travellers [to] reape that good opinion, and just commendation which they have deserved', but also to ascribe to them an unprecedented degree of personal responsibility. '[A]nd further that every man might answere for himselfe, justifie his reports, and stand accountable for his owne doings', Hakluyt asserts, 'I have referred every voyage to his Author, which both in person hath performed, and in writing hath left the same.' 'Whatsoever testimonie I have found in any author of authoritie appertaining to my argument, either stranger or naturall', he notes, 'I have recorded the same word for word, with his particular name and page of booke where it is extant.' And while he promises to 'meddle in this worke with the Navigations onely of our owne nation', he admits that he has occasionally introduced 'some strangers as witnesses of the things done yet are they none but such as either faithfully remember, or sufficiently confirme the travels of our owne people' (PN1, sig. *3ᵛ).

He would have occasion to adapt and elaborate on that editorial principle. As he explains in his dedicatory letter to Walsingham's successor, Sir Robert Cecil, in the final volume of the 1598–1600 edition:

> Now where any country hath bene but seldome hanted, or any extraordinary or chiefe action occureth, if I finde one voyage well written by two severall persons, sometimes I make no difficultie to set downe both those journals, as finding divers things of good moment observed in the one, which are quite omitted in the other. For commonly a souldier observeth one thing, and a mariner another, and as your honour knoweth, *Plus vident oculi, quam oculus* ['several eyes see more than only one']. (PN2, sig. A2ᵛ)

What this means for travel writing in general, and for Hakluyt's readers in particular, is significant. Hakluyt's method brings together textual witnessing and the witnessing of *praxis*, and he makes the conjunction work hard, at multiple levels. He does not claim that subjective records of reality can ever express reality completely through textual means: we know that things observed by one person, after all, are often 'quite omitted' by another, and one man's account may require to be filled in by that of others. It is an assumption emphasized by the organizing principal he adopts, based on the 'double order of time and place' (PN2, sig. A2^v), grouping multiple documents within each geographical section in chronological order. But Hakluyt goes even further, by also listing them in the contents to the volumes under two separate headings: the 'Voyages' themselves, and the 'Ambassages, Treatises, Priviledges, Letters and observations' pertaining to those voyages, which supplement, interrogate, and occasionally contradict the stories told in the narratives that accompany them. In the sections on Anthony Jenkinson's voyages to Russia, for example, that principle of organization opens up lacunae precisely through the sheer abundance of material. For each of the four voyages, Hakluyt gives at least one account from Jenkinson's own ship, as well as supporting documents from other voyagers, both English and foreign, as well as official documentation of their travels. Jenkinson's own account of the first voyage in 1557 is thus juxtaposed with the report of the returning Russian ambassador, Osep Napea, as well as the privileges and charters of the Muscovy Company. Each text fills in the gaps of another: the Muscovy Company documents give us the circumstances of the voyages, but not the details; elements of the journey ignored in Napea's text are covered in Jenkinson's; while the latter's account of the Tsar's displeasure at English lack of respect in the fourth voyage is prefaced by the careful description of Russian diplomatic protocol by the former. By presenting such partial observations in one volume, allowing readers to witness for themselves the imperfections, the fault lines, and the gaps as much as the matter itself, *The Principal Navigations* places itself at the heart of that crucial interchange between the *gnosis* and *praxis* of travel with which we started. The 'travailes' of both Hakluyt and the reader, to use a familiar Elizabethan pun, mingle with the 'travels' of the voyager and the transmission of the scattered pages of his fragile written testimony. In tracing the Jenkinson voyages, as in numerous other instances within Hakluyt's volumes, the act of reading itself turns into a form of *praxis*, a virtual witnessing of those travels newly 'incorporated' into the volume in the reader's hands. That process of active textual observation stimulates 'real' action in its own turn. New knowledge and new witness testimonies are produced in the wake of such action, again to be woven by Hakluyt and his successors into the story of travel.

* * *

Why is that emphasis on witnessing necessary? Commenting on the style of Renaissance English travel writing, William Sherman has noted the 'complex rhetorical strategies' that writers needed to adopt:

> Its authors had to balance the known and the unknown, the traditional imperatives of persuasion and entertainment, and their individual interests with those of their patrons, employers, and monarchs. Given such diverse purposes, early

modern travel writers were often torn between giving pleasure and providing practical guidance, between logging and narrating, between describing what happened and suggesting what could have happened. These rhetorical challenges, along with the novelty of their experiences, left travel writers with acute problems of authenticity and credibility.[15]

What made matters worse, of course, is that fiction often used the same rhetorical strategies to establish the authenticity of its own narratives. From the fantastic voyage at the heart of Lucian's second century *True Story*, to the later narratives at least partially inspired by it, like Thomas More's *Utopia* (1516), the name of whose traveller, Raphael Hythlodaeus, means 'expert in nonsense', Joseph Hall's *Mundus alter et idem* (1605), Francis Bacon's *New Atlantis* (1624, 1627), and Henry Neville's *Isle of Pines* (1668), prose fiction had imitated the testimony of travellers frequently enough for its status to be for ever in doubt.

Despite this, or perhaps because of it, the rhetorical demonstration of personal responsibility remained a standard way of vouchsafing the truth-content of travel accounts. Reporting his journey to China in 1330, in an account which Hakluyt includes both in Latin and in English translation in the 1598–1600 edition, Friar Beatus Odoricus concludes with a sworn statement about the veracity of his narrative:

> I frier Odoricus of Friuli [...] do testifie and beare witnesse unto the reverend father Guidotus minister of the province of S. Anthony, in the marquesate of Treuiso (being by him required upon mine obedience so to doe) that all the premisses above written, either I saw with mine owne eyes, or heard the same reported by credible and substantiall persons. (PN2, II, 66)

Partial vision, as we have seen Hakluyt point out already, is a trade-off that such witnessing has to accept. One man's sight is liable to be subjective and incomplete; as Odoricus confesses, '[m]any other things I have omitted, because I beheld them not with mine owne eyes' (PN2, II, 66). Yet, it is the closest that text can get to the experience of travel, to regenerating the *gnosis* that travel promises its practitioners. Writing a 'discourse on trade' to Michael Lok in 1569, Gaspar Campion asserts, 'I write not this by heare say of other men, but of mine own experience, for I have traded in the countrey above this 30 yeres, and have bene maried in the towne of Chio full 24 yeres, so that you may assure yourselfe that I will write nothing but truth' (PN2, II, 127). Hakluyt himself follows a similar practice in his own writing. The account of Thomas Butts regarding the English voyage to Newfoundland in 1536 is one of the few in *The Principal Navigations* reported by Hakluyt himself, but summing up Butt's journey with the story of a recognition scene that would not have been out of place in the *Odyssey*, Hakluyt hastens to add the stamp of truth to it:

> M. Buts was so changed in the voyage with hunger and miserie, that Sir William his father and my Lady his mother knew him not to be their sonne, untill they found a secret marke which was a wart upon one of his knees, as hee told me Richard Hakluyt

---

[15] Sherman, 'Stirrings and Searchings (1500–1720)', 31.

of Oxford himselfe, to whom I rode 200. miles onely to learne the whole trueth of this voyage from his own mouth, as being the onely man now alive that was in this discoverie. (PN2, III, 131)

Even if the very nature of Hakluyt's collection would seem to make a unified discussion of its prose something of an impossibility, such an emphasis on testimony and witnessing inevitably has both stylistic and social implications for English travel writing. Take style first. In his overview of Tudor travel literature in *The Hakluyt Handbook*, G. B. Parks described Hakluyt's documents as the writings of 'non-professional writers of only accidental skill', but the rhetoric of plainness that they embrace is familiar.[16] It is part of a discursive tradition that we remember Shakespeare's consummate traveller, Othello, adopting when he asserted how his rude speech could only deliver a 'round unvarnish'd tale' (Act I scene iii), or that Montaigne writes about in his essay 'Of Cannibals', when he recommends receiving the news of far-off lands through 'a most sincere Reporter or a man so simple that he may have no invention to build upon and to give a true likelihood unto false devices'.[17] A practical focus on facts and what has been called a functional 'plain' style were recognized ways of establishing the veracity of one's account. Thus, John Davis's records from the 1587 voyage in search of a north-west passage simply notes on 13 August that '[t]his day seeking for our ships that went to fish, we strooke on a rocke, being among many iles, and had a great leake' and follows it with the entry for 14 August, '[t]his day we stopped our leake in a storme': the dry enumeration of facts, date, and circumstance replacing the dramatic and narrative potential of the situation (PN2, III, 118). On other occasions, even in the few literary documents that Hakluyt includes, the plainness of language is brought to the defence of the genre and authorial voice. So praising the writer of the fifteenth-century *Libell of English Pollicie*, a discourse on trade written in verse, Hakluyt explains that 'notwithstanding (as I said) his stile be unpolished, and his phrases somewhat out of use; yet, so neere as the written copies would give me leave, I have most religiously without alteration observed the same: thinking it farre more convenient that himselfe should speake, then that I should bee his spokesman; and that the Readers should enjoy his true verses, then mine or any other mans fained prose' (PN2, *6ᵛ). That advertised 'plainness' and transparency is the counterpart to travel writing's familiar tropes of wonder and inexpressibility. It had existed before Hakluyt, of course: we saw its insistent display of the prosaics of everyday life—the length and the many inconveniences of the journey, details of food, weather, and customs—leaching into Lyly's fiction at the beginning of this chapter, transforming his Euphuistic prose from the inside. But the sheer weight of examples in Hakluyt's *Principal Navigations* would make it the stylistic norm for English travel writing. Perhaps more importantly, however, its use in Hakluyt's volumes introduces English narrative prose to a very specific way of apprehending and communicating reality through text. His insistence on 'plaine' accounts

---

[16] G. B. Parks, 'Tudor Travel Literature: A Brief History', in D. B. Quinn, ed., *The Hakluyt Handbook* (London: Hakluyt Society, 1974), vol. I, 97–132 (102).

[17] Donald M. Frame, trans., *The Complete Essays of Montaigne* (Stanford: Stanford University Press, 1958), 162.

and 'homely stile' focuses on an amalgamation of empirical details, on the apparently objective and transparent recording and precise measurements of facts. But as we have also seen, Hakluyt himself repeatedly reminds us that what the reader receives is partial and imperfect; in fact, that such partial nature and imperfections are what ties the text to the realities of *praxis*, what necessitates the *praxis* of editor and reader alike in its own turn. For numerous writers after Hakluyt, from Thomas Nashe to Lawrence Sterne, that productive tension, between an attempt to reflect reality through text and the use of the inevitable lacunae in such efforts as marks of authenticity in themselves, would become a site of creative engagement.

One consequence of that dependence on linguistic and stylistic transparency, as Stephen Greenblatt has argued, is that authority in early travel writing often derives 'not from an appeal to higher wisdom or social superiority but from a miming, by the elite, of the simple, direct, unfigured language of perception Montaigne and others attribute to servants'.[18] But even the social implications of linguistic plainness aside, Hakluyt's insistence on the plainness of his own editorial 'travails', as well as his tendency to cast the reader in the role of witness to these apparently unmediated voices, effects a different, yet equally destabilizing 'miming' of the travel experience. The sheer range of texts that *The Principal Navigations* harbours is as volatile and as prone to confusing social norms and boundaries as travel and exploration themselves were accused of being by their critics and detractors. If in 1594, Thomas Nashe's *The Unfortunate Traveller* could make his irreverent, acutely pragmatic page-boy hero Jack Wilton a fictional fellow-traveller of the aristocratic Earl of Surrey, then that dissolution of social boundaries is bookended by the 1589 and 1598 editions of Hakluyt. They are volumes dedicated as much to powerful patrons like Francis Walsingham and Robert Cecil as to the ordinary readers who might be inspired actually to turn reading into *praxis*, Sidneian 'well-knowing' into Hakluyt's desired 'well-doing'. Within their pages, the royal letters exchanged between Elizabeth I and the Ottoman Sultans Murad III and Mehmed III share a textual space with instructions prepared by Hakluyt's cousin and mentor, Richard Hakluyt the lawyer, for English merchants in Turkey about 'our Clothing and Dying'; scholarly exchanges between the cartographer Gerald Mercator and Hakluyt himself about the north-east passage are juxtaposed with Hugh Smith's stolidly workmanlike account of the 1580s Pet-Jackman voyage in search of the same. Even the translation of the Latin texts in Hakluyt's collection makes a telling point. As Peter Mancall points out, if Elizabeth and her policy-makers were the only targets of Hakluyt's accounts, he could have simply printed the Latin originals; '[t]he fact of translation itself was proof of Hakluyt's desired audience'.[19]

There is a reason why witnessing takes this curious turn for traveller and reader alike in Hakluyt's collection, shaping both their prose and the nature of the company they keep. Recent historical and literary scholarship has revealed how central the ideas of witnessing and testimony were to a wide range of disciplines in the early modern period,

---

[18] Stephen Greenblatt, *Marvelous Possessions: The Wonder of the New World* (Chicago: University of Chicago Press, 1991), 147.

[19] Mancall, *Hakluyt's Promise*, 98.

and how developments in their conceptualization resonated far beyond their home turf in the practice of law. One prominent aspect of Barbara Shapiro's work on the epistemological status of 'matters of fact', for instance, takes issue with Steven Shapin's claim that the criteria determining the credibility of a witness in the scientific revolution were borrowed from early modern elite codes of honour and civility. As Shapiro has shown, throughout the early modern period, the issue of 'who was deemed trustworthy depended in part on circumstances', not simply on social status or birth.[20] At the same time, English legal practice and the social composition of the English petty jury, which was traditionally charged with determining 'fact' (as opposed to determining 'law', a responsibility assigned to judges), ensured that the assessment of credibility too was gradually freed of its association with the elite. One can see how such a legal perception might have shaped Hakluyt's *Principal Navigations*, where 'plainness', relevance, and immediacy of contact allow merchants to take their place next to monarchs, and seamen's logbooks claim equal importance as scholarly redactions of knowledge.

It also allows us to see some of the most debated features of Hakluyt's collection, like his decision to excise Mandeville's travels from the second edition, in a new light altogether. Andrea Frisch's argument about social changes in early modern France, where the medieval interpretation of testimony as the communal corroboration of the reputation and social standing of disputants slowly begins to lose ground, is equally valid for early modern England.[21] Frisch argues that in circumstances where it was increasingly becoming the practice for witnesses to testify before strangers who could not easily evaluate their moral stance or draw on a communal understanding of their dependability, first-hand accounts and written depositions that recorded experiential knowledge and, in essence, allowed the court to 'observe' a sequence of events or action for themselves, became especially important. The 'epistemic witnessing' of events, in other words, begin to take precedence over the forms of 'ethical' witnessing which formed the cornerstone of medieval legal systems, and the written deposition, capturing and fixing knowledge or *gnosis* and, at the same time, capable of acting as a credible witness of *praxis* for its reader, takes on an epistemological import of its own. For Frisch, the medieval text of Mandeville's incredible *Travels* offer a perfect case study of the earlier form of 'ethical witnessing', with its credibility resting on Mandeville's readers' readiness to believe in his reputation and status as a Christian knight, rather than purely on the style or content of his account. It is no surprise, then, that the document which replaces Mandeville in Hakluyt's 1598–1600 edition is the account of Friar Odoricus, which we have seen before: a document whose evidentiary status, confirmed by the signed and attested statement that accompanies it, we can witness for ourselves.

The written accounts of travels are invested with a unique authority within such a system. While their credibility depends on their links with the actions of individual

---

[20] Barbara J. Shapiro, *A Culture of Fact: England, 1550–1720* (Ithaca: Cornell University Press, 2000), 84. See also Steven Shapin, *A Social History of Truth: Civility and Science in Seventeenth-Century England* (Chicago: University of Chicago Press, 1994).

[21] See Andrea Frisch, *The Invention of the Eyewitness: Witnessing and Testimony in Early Modern France* (Chapel Hill: University of North Carolina Press, 2004).

travellers (allowing every man might 'answere for himselfe'), as written texts, they are, at the same time, clearly separable from their writers. Like the document that Hakluyt reports being found after the capture of the Portuguese ship, the *Madre de Deus*, in 1592, 'enclosed in a case of sweet Cedar wood, and lapped up almost an hundredfold in fine calicut-cloth, as though it had been some incomparable jewel' (PN2, II, sig. *4ʳ), *The Principal Navigations* repeatedly emphasizes the identity of its documents as material objects. They act as evidence as well as testimony, capable of being passed hand to hand, of being exchanged, examined, collected, and valued. If Walter Ralegh's *Discovery of the Large, Rich, and Beautiful Empire of Guiana* in 1596 had begun by apologizing to his investors that his ventures in the New World had failed to return their money and instead 'only returned promises; and nowe for answer of both your adventures, I have sent you a bundle of papers' (sig. A2ʳ⁻ᵛ), Hakluyt's endeavour would turn such bundles of papers into 'treasures', comparable to any of the other material returns of the actual travel itself.

By the time Richard Hakluyt died in 1616, the material he had collected from various sources themselves had become objects to be gathered and valued. By the mid-seventeenth century, *The Principal Navigations* was carried on board as a standard reference by the ships of the East India Company, and Hakluyt's influence would continue to shape the writings of those who followed. Its most notable impact, expectedly, is on the genre of the travel collection itself. The material Hakluyt had continued to accumulate in the intervening years since the publication of *The Principal Navigations* would find its way ultimately into the second great early modern English compendium of travel texts: the four folio volumes of Samuel Purchas's *Hakluytus posthumous or Purchas his pilgrims* (1625). Purchas's handling of these texts has been the subject of much critical attention and his more interventionist editing has led to the characterization of Hakluyt as the ideal editor—discreet, tactful, and restrained—even though Hakluyt, we know, was far from the transparent conduit of textual records of travel that his readers have credited him with being.[22] But both the astounding popularity of Purchas's collections and our continued acknowledgement of *The Principal Navigations*'s place in the construction of England's identity as nation and empire underline Hakluyt's single most significant contribution, his ability to make a virtue of that range of disparate material, of the many different voices that his collection accommodates. It is a lesson which he perhaps learned from the trading companies for whom he worked frequently as a consultant, where financial 'incorporation', the gathering of multiple individual investments into a single entity significantly greater than the sum of its parts, had always provided the basis of the risky new long-distance trading ventures. It is not simply a coincidence, after all, that the most active years of his endeavour coincided with the rapid proliferation of English trading companies and joint-stock ventures, from the Eastland Company, with its interests in

---

[22] See James P. Helfers, 'The Explorer or the Pilgrim? Modern Critical Opinion and the Editorial Methods of Richard Hakluyt and Samuel Purchas' *Studies in Philology*, 94.2 (1997): 160– 86. Fuller, *Voyages in Print*, 149–51. Julia Schleck, ' "Plain Broad Narratives of Substantial Facts": Credibility, Narrative, and Hakluyt's Principall Navigations', *Renaissance Quarterly*, 59.3 (2006): 768–94.

the Baltic trade route in 1579 and the Turkey Company in 1581, to the East India Company in 1600 and the Virginia Company in 1606. What has often been seen as Purchas's more heavy-handed editing of travel texts, as Ralph Bauer has argued, would continue to show a similar sensitivity to the changing face of mercantilism in the seventeenth century under Stuart rule, enfolding both editor and texts within the processes of knowledge and profit production in a new age.[23]

Beyond the travel collection, Hakluyt's engagement with that central disjunction between the experience and representation of travel, and the social and linguistic implications whose traces we have followed throughout this chapter, would continue to develop in travel accounts as different in style and tone as Thomas Coryat's whimsical *Crudities hastily gobbled up in Five Months Travels in France, Italy, &c* (1611) and *Greetings from the Court of the Great Mogul* (1616), and Captain John Smith's *General Historie of Virginia, New England, and the Summer Isles* (1624). The reports that Coryat, the son of a Somersetshire rector, produced of his journeys through Europe, the Middle East, and India offer a relentless collection of the material evidence of individual experience. From incongruously detailed meditations on the size of German beer barrels to self-portraits on the backs of Indian elephants, from reproductions of letters and speeches written, to poems and greetings received, his volumes are in many ways a carnivalization both of that permanent sense of impending slippage between text and experience which drove Hakluyt's collection forward, and of its acute understanding of the granularity of lived experience itself. But they are also examples of that ordinary individual testimony which *The Principal Navigation* had valorized and invited, as is the familiar note with which John Smith begins his *History*, when he asserts at the outset that '[t]his history might and ought to have beene clad in better robes then my rude military hand can cut out in Paper Ornaments', but 'of the most things therein, I am no Compiler by hearsay, but have been a reall Actor'.[24] The truth-content of Smith's account is much debated, but it is undeniable that as a vindication of his actions in the Virginia colony against the alleged opposition of his aristocratic competitors, it significantly opens up a space for a personal, subjective voice in a deeply ideologically and politically inflected arena.

In fiction, too, the 'witnessing' which the *Principal Navigations* had celebrated, and the radically unstable discourse of experience that necessitated it, would leave their mark. Behind the multiplying lists of criminal jargon in Robert Greene's cony-catching pamphlets, for instance, one can see the traces of Hakluyt's word-lists of foreign languages: from Jacque Cartier's Huron vocabulary and John Davis's Eskimo word-list, to the lists of Guinean, Algonquian, and Javanese dialects. There had always been a fascination with the so-called 'canting terms' of the criminal underworld in Elizabethan literature, but the word-lists in Greene's immensely popular 'discoveries' of that alternative society bring something of the strange and the foreign back home to roost in Elizabethan London. If the gaps they open up in one's view of the known, and the tension they con-

---

[23] Ralph Bauer, *The Cultural Geography of Colonial American Literatures: Empire, Travel, Modernity* (Cambridge: Cambridge University Press, 2003), chap. 3.

[24] *The Generall Historie of Virginia, New-England, and the Summer Isles* (London, 1624), sig. [ii]ʳ.

stantly evoke between text and experience, order and fragmentation, identification and estrangement, are early signs of novelistic plurality and the centrifugal pull of lived experience, touches of Bakhtinian *heteroglossia* and 'prosaicism' in early modern prose, then they are shaped implicitly by Hakluyt's compendium. Elsewhere, as Defoe's *Robinson Crusoe* illustrates, the emphasis on 'plainness' and the prosaic, on empirical detail and observation, which Hakluyt's example had also established as an expected narrative turn in travel writing, would continue to be adopted by imaginative fiction as it negotiated its central relationships, both with the individual voice and the world beyond.

Admittedly, such brief examples can show us only glimpses of the inflections that Hakluyt's collection helped to introduce into English travel writing, and of the number of discourses in which it appears both directly and indirectly as participant, interlocutor, and influence. Heterogeneity is their defining feature. The voices of Hakluyt's 'witnesses', as we have seen, are varied and irregular; the picture of early modern English travels that emerges from their pages is an amalgamation of interests, perspectives, and knowledge. Yet, in that very range that it both displays and contains, *The Principal Navigations* stands testimony to the sheer range of early modern English travel writing and the multiplicity of English perspectives on the rapidly expanding world which generated that textual engagement in the first place.

Further Reading

Campbell, M. B. *The Witness and the Other World: Exotic European Travel Writing, 400–1600* (Ithaca, NY: Cornell University Press, 1988).

Carey, Daniel and Claire Jowitt, eds. *Richard Hakluyt and Travel Writing in Early Modern Europe* (Farnham, Surrey, England; Burlington, VT: Ashgate, 2012).

Day, M. 'Hakluyt, Harvey, Nashe: The Material Text and Early Modern Nationalism', *Studies in Philology*, 104.3 (2007): 281–305.

Fuller, Mary. *Voyages in Print: English Travel to America, 1576–1624* (Cambridge: Cambridge University Press, 1995).

Hadfield, Andrew. *Literature, Travel, and Colonial Writing in the English Renaissance, 1545–1625* (Oxford: Clarendon Press, 1998).

Hakluyt, Richard. *The Principall Navigations, Voyages and Discovries of the English Nation, made by Sea or Ouer Land, to the Most Remote and Farthest Distant Quarters of the Earth, at any Time within the Compasse of these 1500 yeres: Divided into Three Severall Parts, According to the Positions of the Regions, whereunto they were Directed* (London, 1589).

—— *The Principal Navigations, Voyages, Traffiques and Discovries of the English Nation, made by Sea or Ouerland, to the Remote and Farthest Distant Quarters of the Earth, at any Time within the Compasse of these 1600 yeres: Divided into Three Severall Volumes, According to the Positions of the Regions, whereunto they were Directed* (London, 1598–1600).

Helgerson, R. *Forms of Nationhood: The Elizabethan Writing of England* (Chicago: University of Chicago Press, 1992).

Maccrossan, Colm. 'New Journeys through Old Voyages: Literary Approaches to Richard Hakluyt and Early Modern Travel Writing', *Literature Compass*, 6.1 (2009): 97–112.

Mancall, Peter C. *Hakluyt's Promise: An Elizabethan's Obsession for an English America* (New Haven: Yale University Press, 2007).

Parker, J. *Books to Build an Empire: A Bibliographical History of English Overseas Interest to 1620* (Amsterdam: N. Israel, 1965).

Parks, G. B. *Richard Hakluyt and the English Voyages* (New York: American Geographical Society, 1928).

Payne, A. *Richard Hakluyt: A Guide to His Books and to Those Associated with Him, 1580–1625* (London: Quaritch, 2008).

Quinn, D. B., ed. *The Hakluyt Handbook* (London: Hakluyt Society, 1974).

Rubiés, Juan-Pau. *Travellers and Cosmographers: Studies in the History of Early Modern Travel and Ethnology* (Aldershot: Ashgate, 2007).

Sherman, William. 'Stirrings and Searchings (1500–1720)', in Peter Hulme and Tim Youngs, eds., *The Cambridge Companion to Travel Writing* (Cambridge: Cambridge University Press, 2002), 17–36.

CHAPTER 19

RAPHAEL HOLINSHED AND HISTORICAL WRITING

BART VAN ES

For modern readers it is self-evident that serious historical writing should be conducted in prose. Today's readers also have a clear sense of what rightly falls under the heading of history: we share a working definition of the subject that involves an account of past events in human affairs with a verifiable basis in truth.[1] These key assumptions, however, were not shared by early modern thinkers. Not only was it commonplace for Renaissance theorists to claim that poets were the word's first historians, there were still many contemporary poets who attempted to maintain this role.[2] History, moreover, was not necessarily human in its focus or restricted to actions that were verifiably true. God's deeds were also historical and, in the human sphere, historians felt at liberty to invent whole speeches and to report stories ranging in subject matter from encounters with giants to monstrous births. Horrible murders (indeed, some straightforward fictions) could comfortably fall under the heading of 'true history'.

Renaissance England might be casual in the way it used the term 'history', but that category could also be more restrictive than it is today. When, for example, the antiquarian William Camden completed his great survey of ancient Britain, the *Britannia*, he made it very clear that he was not writing history, which in this context was a rhetorically and politically elevated form.[3] The *Britannia* set out to reassess the nation's past through research on

---

[1] I here conflate the *Oxford English Dictionary*'s definitions 1–4 for 'history, *n*.' in current usage. See OED <http://www.oed.com> accessed 18 March 2013.

[2] On poets as the first historians see George Puttenham, *Arte of English Poesie*, 196, and Philip Sidney, *Defence of Poesie*, 338–46, in *English Renaissance Criticism*, ed. Brian Vickers (Oxford: Clarendon Press, 1999). On verse historians in the early modern period see Bart van Es, 'Michael Drayton, Literary History, and Historians in Verse', *Review of English Studies*, 59 (2008): 255–69.

[3] D. R. Woolf, *The Idea of History in Early Stuart England: Erudition, Ideology, and 'The Light of Truth' from the Accession of James I to the Civil War* (Toronto: University of Toronto Press, 1990), 21–2; Woolf states that 'if Camden's *Britannia*...makes one thing clear, it is that its author believed he was not a historian' (21).

fragmentary remains such as architectural ruins, coins, original manuscripts, and ancient languages; it might look to modern readers like advanced historiography, but Camden and his contemporaries did not necessarily understand the subject in this way. Certain kinds of writing (such as enquiries into the origins of laws, customs, or institutions) were considered egregiously non-historical. It was for this reason that a sniping rival herald claimed that 'for a mere scholar to be an historian' was 'very unfit and dangerous'.[4] The title 'historical prose' in early modern England is thus a complex and debatable category.

This chapter is headed 'Raphael Holinshed and Historical Writing' and (in this murky field) Holinshed's *Chronicles* do give us certain parameters through which to explore the genres of early modern prose history. Holinshed has become famous above all through the work of William Shakespeare (who used the *Chronicles* extensively as source for his plays). He was not the most prominent or distinguished historian of his era, yet the chronicles that bear his name do provide a usefully inclusive example that gives us a snapshot of the time. The ambitious publisher's original plan had been for a complete world history, but even the treatment of Britain alone that appeared in 1577 was a massive enterprise.[5] The two folio volumes contained separate descriptions and histories of England and Wales; Scotland; and Ireland. In 1587 this became three volumes—a revised and expanded text in which Holinshed (who died around 1580) played no part. Both editions were collaborative efforts: not only were they written by multiple authors, those authors themselves also worked by patching from earlier texts. Within the *Chronicle* there were thus sections of elevated humanist history (in the form, for example, of Sir Thomas More's elegant unfinished monograph on the reign of King Richard III), but these sat alongside less carefully written material including descriptions of pageants, frosts, banquets, plagues, rains, and fires, and details of the punishments meted out to heretics.[6] The book is an extraordinary composite. For this reason, an anatomy of Holinshed's *Chronicles* gives us a good basis for a survey of what counted in the early modern period as 'historical prose'.

19.1 HUMANIST HISTORIOGRAPHY

The intellectual status of Holinshed, which was never high in literary circles, declined steadily over the centuries and has only recently undergone a gradual rise. This low status comes because intellectual historians have conventionally pitched the *Chronicles*

---

[4] Woolf, *Idea of History*, 21. As is the case throughout this essay, I have modernized spelling and letter forms where possible.

[5] On the history and make-up of the chronicle see Steven Booth, *The Book Called Holinshed's Chronicles: An Account of its Inception, Purpose, Contributors, Contents, Publication, Revision and Influence on William Shakespeare* (San Francisco: Book Club of California, 1968) and also Paulina Kewes, Ian W. Archer, and Felicity Heal, eds., *The Oxford Handbook of Holinshed's Chronicles* (Oxford: Oxford University Press, 2012).

[6] On the inclusion of More's text within Grafton's, and subsequently, Holinshed's chronicles see David Womersley, 'Sir Thomas More's *History of King Richard III*: A New Theory of the English Texts', *Renaissance Studies*, 7 (1993): 272–90.

against the rising new form of the period: that of humanist historiography. This mode of writing emerged first in Italy and was based on the rediscovery of the great classical writers on history: most importantly Thucydides, Livy, Sallust, and Tacitus. Humanist historians, such as Niccolò Machiavelli in his *Florentine Histories* (1520–5), working in the light of these Greek and Latin authors, brought a new focus to their study of the past. First, they treated individuals primarily as rational agents, rather than moral subjects of divine judgement and Providence. Second, they selected more circumscribed topics (such as single reigns or rebellions) instead of chronicling a potentially endless series of events. Third and most important, they concentrated on political affairs and excluded material that was not directly relevant to the transfer of power: for this reason humanist historiography was often called 'politic history'.

Taken *en masse*, Holinshed's *Chronicles* clearly lacked this kind of discipline: indeed, F. J. Levy (one of the foremost authorities on the humanist historians) declared that Holinshed 'represented the worst excesses of the old providentialism'.[7] All the same, as Levy acknowledged, there were patches of the chronicle that were more humanist than others, even if this was only because they were copied wholesale from more scholarly hands. For this reason, the starting point of Holinshed still gives us access to what counted to contemporaries as the high end of early modern historical prose.

First amongst humanist histories (and shamelessly reproduced in Holinshed) was Sir Thomas More's *History of King Richard III* (*c.* 1518). Unfinished though it was, More's history remains a high point of English historical writing. In a way that is exceptional in early modern historiography (indeed, in early modern prose generally) it combines tight plotting, incisive characterization, coherent motivation, and unity of subject matter with elegance and variability of style. It is frequently observed that there is cross-fertilization between politic history and drama and More (who knew Roman tragedy as well as history) provides an exemplary case: he is a master of scene setting and the *History*, even incomplete, constitutes a powerful dramatic whole. All of these qualities were readily adopted by Shakespeare, who encountered the *History* by way of Holinshed's chronicles. First amongst many is the character of Richard, crafted by More as a perfect Machiavel:

> Richard the third son, of whom we now entreat, was in wit and courage egall with either of them [his brothers], in body and prowess far under them both, little of stature, ill featured of limbs, crook-backed, his left shoulder much higher then his right, hard favoured of visage, and such as is in states called warly, in other men otherwise. He was malicious, wrathful, envious, and from afore his birth, ever frowarde. [...] No evil captain was he in the war, as to which his disposition was more meetly then for peace. [...] He was close and secrete, a deep dissimuler, lowly of countenance, arrogant of heart, outwardly companionable where he inwardly hated, not letting to kiss whom he thought to kill: dispitious and cruel, not for evil will alway, but other for ambition. [...] Some wise men also weene, that his drift covertly

---

[7] F. J. Levy, 'Hayward, Daniel, and the Beginnings of Politic History in England', *Huntington Library Quarterly*, 50 (1987): 1–34 (3).

conveyed, lacked not in helping forth his brother of Clarence to his death: which he resisted openly, howbeit somewhat (as men deemed) more faintly than he that were heartily minded to his wealth.[8]

In such passages of descriptive analysis More intercuts short and long sentences, uses lists and anecdotes, and employs parallelism to subtle effect. These character sketches combine with set-piece encounters in which More's history brilliantly evokes suspense and terror. One good example is the arrest of Lord Hastings during a meeting in the Tower, where Richard arrives late, languidly apologizes for oversleeping, and asks the Bishop of Ely to send for 'the good strawberries at your garden in Holborn' (47). This courteous, yet imperious request from one who is not yet a king quietly establishes the centre of power. Thus, when Richard suddenly changes his tone to make angry and inexplicable demands the effect is chilling in the extreme:

> With a wonderful sour angry countenance, knitting the brows, frowning and frothing and gnawing on his lips [...] thus he began: 'what were they worthy to have, that compass & imagine the destruction of me, being so near of blood unto the king and protector of his royal person and his realm?' At this question, all the lords sat sore astonied, musing much by whom this question should be meant, of which every man whist himself clear. (More, *Richard III*, 47)

There is a proto-novelistic energy to this writing that is uncharacteristic of the period. More derived much of his approach from Roman accounts of the tyranny of emperors, above all in the *Annals* of Tacitus. In several cases (such as the set-piece scene in which Richard first refuses and then, with feigned reluctance, accepts the throne) he appears to have gone directly to the life of Tiberius, using this (rather than any actual historical records) as the source for his account of the seizure of power.[9]

Although they are generally less dramatic in their reporting of action, other humanist histories share More's willingness to adapt historical narratives, often on classical precedent. One spectacular case is provided by John Hayward's *First Part of the Life and Raigne of King Henrie the IIII* (1599), which landed its author in prison because of the apparent close connections between its account of the deposition of Richard II and the Earl of Essex's rebellion against Queen Elizabeth. The case is an extreme instance of the tendencies of politic history: both because it followed Tacitus particularly closely and because (through its dedication to Essex) it sailed so close to the political wind. When Francis Bacon examined the book as a part of the government's investigation he found Hayward innocent of treason but, he slyly observed, guilty of 'felony' on account of his extensive plagiarism.

Bacon may have disapproved of the undigested classical gobbets and poor political tact of Hayward's history. Yet, he (having also been part of the forward-thinking Essex

---

[8] St. Thomas More, *Richard III*, in *The Complete Works of St. Thomas More*, 12 vols., ed. Richard S. Sylvester (New Haven: Yale University Press, 1963), II, 7–8.

[9] The scholarship here is extensive, but for a coherent overview of More's use of his models see Sylvester's introduction in *Works*, II, pp. lxxi–ciii.

circle) nevertheless shared the essence of this methodology.[10] In the writing of politic history current political experience tended to take priority over any historical research. Bacon's own original composition, *The History of the Reign of King Henry VII* (1622), like More's *History of King Richard III*, thus involved little recourse to the archives. Admittedly, this was in part because Bacon was at this time forbidden to enter London, where the majority of records were kept, but such scholarly delving was in any case not really the providence of the great historian. Such a man, through his experience of great affairs and his reading of earlier learned histories, was primarily responsible for giving pre-existing subject matter moral and intellectual shape. It was his judgement and style, not the accuracy of the minutiae, that were the proper measure of success.

It was for this reason that Bacon and More, like the classical historians, felt at liberty to invent entire speeches and to put these into the mouths of their protagonists.[11] In this respect, More and Bacon matched up to former great historians and men of affairs such as Thucydides, Sallust, and Tacitus.[12] Their practice of imaginative composition (entirely alien to modern readers) shows history to be a rhetorical, moral, and political *art* much more than an indifferent scholarly *discipline*. One example of this within Bacon's *History* is a long oration by Henry VII in which he justifies war with France. The book's Victorian editor puzzled over this passage, not only because in the surviving records there is not even a hint of Henry's presence in parliament, but also because war with France did not in fact occur at this time. The editor speculated that there were perhaps surviving manuscripts, known by Bacon, but not by historians today.[13] This, however, is almost certainly to mistake Bacon's methods, which had more to do with present political lessons than with the precise nature of past events. On inspection, we find that the speech attributed to Henry VII is studded with seventeenth-century vocabulary (words such as 'malcontents', 'impostors', and 'populace' that could not possibly have been used by the first Tudor monarch). These words fit in more with the current situation (which was the threat of war with Spain) than they do with early Tudor policy. Bacon, here, is composing a speech to a present audience, much more than attempting to reconstruct the most likely historical past.

The purpose that drives such imaginative endeavours comes to the fore most clearly in the final stages of the *History*. For as Bacon sums up Henry Tudor's foreign policies the parallels with those of James I become increasingly evident:

> [Henry VII] professed always to love and seek peace; and it was his usual preface in his treaties, that when Christ came into the world peace was sung, and when he

---

[10] On this circle (which did also include Hayward) see Levy, 'Hayward, Daniel'.

[11] See, for example, the speech of Chancellor Morton to parliament in James Spedding, ed., *Works*, 8 vols. (London: Longmans & Co., 1861), VI, 76–81. Spedding, whose assumptions I critique below, does acknowledge this oration as an invention on the model of Thucydides (75n).

[12] Bacon translated Thucydides and forwarded him as the ultimate exemplum; on this translation and the social distinction of the historian see F. J. Levy, 'Afterword', *Huntington Library Quarterly*, 68 (2005): 415–27 (424).

[13] Spedding, *Works*, VI, 117–18n.

went out of the world peace was bequeathed. And this virtue could not proceed out of fear or softness, for he was valiant and active; and therefore no doubt it was truly Christian and moral. Yet he knew the way to peace was not to be desirous to avoid wars. Therefore would he make offers and frames of wars, till he had mended conditions of peace. (238)

Henry's prefaces on the love of peace are no more evident in his treaties than the parliamentary records show a speech of war against France. This closing oration does match closely, however, with the foreign policy vision that James pursued. This, in contrast to Hayward's example, is a successful instance of the application and adaptation of past events to present needs. Bacon's conclusion is a consummate piece of humanist historiography: rhetorically, its neat use of antimetabole and paradox ('peace', 'war', 'war', 'peace') lends his thesis an aphoristic quality that invites reapplication by the reader. That sense of reading history to a present purpose was, as I have argued, a vital part of humanist philosophy.[14] Henry VII (a cautious prince, the first of a new ruling dynasty, and a maintainer of foreign influence through the marriages of his children) provided a fruitful parallel to Bacon's monarch. The continual emphasis on the King's excessive financial extractions perhaps also offered reflection on James's difficulties in this area, which were the root cause of Bacon's loss of office that year.

Humanist history, in spite of the risks, depended upon such parallels. It was a moot point, however, whether this made the form moral, because the lessons of history did not necessarily show reward for good deeds. Thus, though the case of Henry VII might show James I how to pursue a peaceful foreign policy, it might also show him that extortionate taxation could make a monarchy strong. In the same way, the study of tyrants might offer dangerous models: it is often suggested that it was on this logic that Thomas More abandoned his *History of King Richard III*.[15] The idea that humanist history could foster immoral doctrines was certainly recognized in the period, not least because the greatest humanist historian, Niccolò Machiavelli, was also author of the most notorious manual of power: the historiography that he championed was therefore intimately connected to the most cynical theory of governance. Theorists of history, such as Justus Lipsius, attempted to nuance this problem, replacing Machiavelli's morally neutral concept of *virtù* with the warmer notion of prudence in a Christian king.[16] All the same, humanist history remained an uncomfortable if impressive presence. When Prince Henry asked John Hayward (who had survived the reign of Elizabeth) why English historical writing was of such poor quality, the latter replied from bitter experience that

---

[14] On the centrality of this notion for humanist historiographical reading practice see Thomas Blundeville, *The True Order of Wryting and Reading Histories* (London, 1574), F3^b–H4^b; Jean Bodin, *Method for the Easy Comprehension of History*, trans. Beatrice Reynolds (New York: Columbia University Press, 1945), 39–40; and also the seminal article by Lisa Jardine and Anthony Grafton, '"Studied for Action": How Gabriel Harvey Read his Livy', *Past and Present*, 126 (1990): 3–51.

[15] For this and the previously mentioned theories on the *History*'s reception see Sylvester in More's *Works*, II, p. ciii.

[16] See Levy, 'Hayward, Daniel', 7–8. Levy also provides the anecdote about Hayward's conversation with Prince Henry, which I relate below.

'men might safely write of others in manner of a tale, but in manner of a History safely they could not'.[17]

19.2 CHRONICLES

Compared to humanist histories, chronicles had an easier (if less sophisticated) way of proving their moral utility. Conventionally, chroniclers claimed to illustrate God's justice through examples of Providence and divine retribution, and for this purpose, they tended to begin with the earliest days: 'next unto the holy scripture', declared Holinshed, 'chronicles doo carry credit'.[18] Because chronicle (though less perfectly than the Bible) set out to display evidence of God's presence in history, it constituted entirely proper reading, not just for kings and counsellors, but for the common man. Chronicles were thus a popular medium and publishers set out cater for every species of demand. Unlike humanist histories, which were an elite form of literature, chronicles could be very basic productions, both in the quality of their prose and in their physical make-up as printed texts. In the early years of Elizabeth's reign there was fierce commercial rivalry between two compilers of short chronicles, Richard Grafton and John Stow.[19] Grafton's *Abridgement of the Chronicles of England*, which appeared in February 1563, is a pocket-sized book—written in short factual sentences and dominated by an extensive index—that outlines events all the way from the creation of Adam to the reign of Queen Elizabeth I. Grafton's *Abridgement* was rapidly followed by Stow's *Summary* (1563), which in turn sparked Grafton's *Manuel of Chronicles* (1565). The conflict continued across Stow's *Summary of English Chronicles Abridged* (1567) and Grafton's *Chronicle at Large* (1568). In the prefaces to these works the two authors attacked one another's credibility and in the main body of their texts they attracted readers by way of additional tables, almanacs, marginal summaries, running chronologies, and the like. These were lightweight volumes in octavo and duodecimo foldings and thus easy to carry and cheap to buy. Stylistically this was simple prose designed to give access to information, not to describe policy, character, or constitutional change.

As part of their service to readers, popular chronicles generally laid claim to up-to-the-minute topicality. At the same time, as we have seen, they also conventionally began their story from the earliest times. The Christian narrative of creation could admit no notion of the 'prehistoric'.[20] Logically, therefore, a history of the island of Britain should begin with God's separation of the earth from the heavens and the waters, which could

---

[17] John Hayward, *The Lives of the III. Normans, Kings of England* (1613), A2ª–A2ᵇ.
[18] Annabel Patterson, *Reading Holinshed's Chronicles* (Chicago: University of Chicago Press, 1994), vii.
[19] On this quarrel see May McKisack, *Medieval History in the Tudor Age* (Oxford: Clarendon Press, 1971), 110–13.
[20] On the treatment of very early history, including giants, see Arthur B. Ferguson, *Utter Antiquity: Perceptions of Prehistory in Renaissance England* (Durham, NC: Duke University Press, 1993).

be calculated with near-certainty to 3,962 years before the birth of Christ.[21] The physical history of the nation began at that point and commenced with perennial questions about the impact of the Flood, the original name of the landmass, and the origins of the indigenous population of giants.[22] Human history on the island began in 1108 BC with the arrival of Brutus, the supposed grandson of Aeneas, who was bringing his Trojan heroes to a new land.[23] In spite of increased scepticism about these long-established stories, the 1587 *Chronicles* of Holinshed could not avoid this material and even included (from Geoffrey of Monmouth's *Historia Regum Britanniae*) a letter from Brutus to Pandrassus, King of the Greeks.[24]

What such inclusions reflected was not simply credulity about evidence, but a fundamental failure to acknowledge anachronism. The medieval chronicles in which these stories were sourced had a very limited sense of 'pastness': as Peter Burke put it in a now perhaps unfashionably Whiggish study, the Middle Ages lacked a sense of the 'differentness' of history: 'they saw it in terms of the present; they projected themselves back onto the men of the past'.[25] That perspective still stuck firmly even to the Renaissance chronicle, which was in many ways still a medieval form.[26] It was most graphically present in the 1577 version of Holinshed's book through the repeated woodcuts of monarchs. These illustrations were simply recycled across the ages, so that kings hundreds of years apart were depicted as uniform in their armour and dress. This was also true of architecture, with the first construction of London by Brutus (supposedly more than a millennium before the Romans) illustrated with literally the same engraving of an august classical building as was used to depict a castle built by the Saxon King Ella in the sixth century AD.[27] Prose and woodcut alike showed a lack of visual imagination: it was this that made it possible to conceive of the first settler of the island composing learned letters to his fellow monarch in faraway Greece.

The heading 'chronicle' in the early modern period established expectations for this kind of undiscriminating (or open-minded) inclusiveness. There were, in reality, only modest developments on the methodology of late fifteenth-century chroniclers, who

---

[21] This is Grafton's date in his *Chronicle at Large* (1569), 2; calculating by means of the ages and reigns of named individuals in the Hebrew Bible, there was close agreement on this figure between chroniclers.

[22] On the part that the Flood played in the narrative of Britain's early history and the varying accounts of giants and the first human habitation of the island see Stuart Piggott, *Ancient Britons and the Antiquarian Imagination: Ideas from the Renaissance to the Regency* (London: Thames and Hudson, 1989), 43–51.

[23] Grafton, *Chronicle at Large* (1569), 31. Holinshed's *Chronicles* (1587), I, 7, debates Brutus's parentage.

[24] On the way in which Holinshed treats the authority of the letter see McKisack, *Medieval History in the Tudor Age*, 116–19.

[25] Peter Burke, *The Renaissance Sense of the Past* (London: Edward Arnold, 1969), 6.

[26] This is very much the view of F. J. Levy, *Tudor Historical Thought* (San Marino, CA: Huntington Library, 1967), see especially x, 8, 41–2. Recent studies of the chronicle, such as Patterson, *Reading Holinshed's Chronicles*, and David Womersley's *Divinity and State* (Oxford: Oxford University Press, 2010) set out to assess early modern chronicles more dispassionately in their own terms.

[27] Holinshed, *Chronicles* (1577), I, 16 and 140.

(to quote Joseph Levine) 'were usually unwilling and largely unable to make a clear distinction between fact and fiction, either in theory or in practice (though they sometimes attempted it)'.[28] This openness went hand in hand with ambition. The original plan for what came to be called Holinshed's chronicles (set out by the printer and publisher Reyner Wolfe around 1548) had in fact been for 'an universal cosmography of the whole world, and therewith also certain particular histories of every known nation'.[29] And although the scope of Holinshed's *Chronicles* was ultimately more limited, this universal aspect continued to be in evidence in its earlier parts. Comprehensive world history was considered possible because of a presumption of truth in all stories: totalizing accounts such as *Cooper's Chronicle* or Ralegh's *History of the World* included, for example, the labours of Hercules within their narrative. Myths were often rationalized to fit within the bounds of the possible, but they were not understood as a fundamentally different category.[30] For this reason, famous figures such as King Lear or King Arthur continued to appear in chronicles.

This mythic narrative was not the only material found in chronicles that was excluded from humanist politic histories. Thomas Blundeville, author of the only contemporary vernacular treatise on humanist historiography, was very explicit about the limits within which his discipline should direct its attention: 'histories', he observed 'be made of deeds done by a public weal, or against a public weal, and such deeds, be either deeds of war, of peace, or else of sedition and conspiracy'.[31] What Bacon called 'vulgar' (161) deeds were not part of high-level history, but they were readily included in chronicle. As Annabel Patterson has observed, chronicles were essentially a middle-class genre, and they therefore not only addressed, but also depicted the ordinary citizen.[32] It is for this reason that a stage play about a murder, such as the anonymous *Arden of Faversham*, could have its source in Holinshed just as much as a stately tragedy.

The murder of Master Arden, which occurred in the reign of Edward VI, provides a good example of the kind of popular material that made its way into chronicle history. In Holinshed the report takes up many folio pages and (as with accounts of high political action) introduces verbatim reports of the protagonists' words. Here, for example, is the account of how Alice Arden's serving men take on the services of a hired killer, Black Will:

> The serving men knew black Will, and saluting him, demanded of him whither he went. He answered, 'by this blood' (for his use was to swear almost at every word) 'I know not, nor rate not, but set up my staff, and even as it falleth I go'. 'If thou' (quoth they) 'wilt go back again to Gravesend, we will give thee thy supper'. 'By this

---

[28] Joseph M. Levine, *Humanism and History: Origins of Modern English Historiography* (Ithaca, NY: Cornell University Press, 1987), 11.

[29] See Patterson, *Reading Holinshed's Chronicles*, 8.

[30] On the treatment of evidence by 'Cooper's Chronicle' (begun by Thomas Lanquet and continued by the future Bishop of Winchester, Thomas Cooper) see T. D. Kendrick, *British Antiquity* (London: Methuen, 1950), 41–2.

[31] Blundeville, *True Order*, A4ᵇ.

[32] Patterson, *Reading Holinshed's Chronicles*, xii.

blood' (said he) 'I care not, I am content, have with you'. And so he returned again with them.³³

This fairly casual prose gives access to the idiomatic speech and patterns of daily life of less privileged people (we learn, for example, that Master Arden enjoys a breakfast of butter and milk). Popular chroniclers like Holinshed thought such a story worthwhile (although 'it may seem to be but a private matter, and therefore as it were impertinent to this history') simply because the events were extraordinary.

Inclusiveness and direct quotation are Holinshed's hallmarks. This makes its prose highly variable, covering the speeches of condemned criminals, public performances, civic legislation, and genuine transcriptions of historical documents. Only a few pages on from the report of Arden of Faversham's murder, the chronicle thus shifts to a high political register, giving the full text of Queen Mary's letter to the Lords of the Council upon the death of the King (*Chronicles* [1577] I, 1716). The second edition of the chronicles, even more than its predecessor, embraced this notion of inclusivity: in its account of Elizabeth's reign it quotes popular songs, pageants, and even reports on the nature of children's play. The book concludes in a way that exemplifies its status as an encompassing record: the final item is a proclamation concerning the preservation of cereal crops that was issued just months before the *Chronicles* went to press.³⁴

19.3 ANTIQUARIAN LEARNING

Chronicles, I have been stressing, were a radically inclusive mode of prose history. Unlike more elevated humanist works, they reported the deeds of the common people as well as those of monarch. Also unlike those grander histories, they went back to the earliest ages and—as result—reported stories that readers today would consider mythical. Chronicles, though they might sometimes express doubt or offer a series of alternative narratives, tended to offer little discrimination on matters of fact. As D. R. Woolf has stated, history in the Tudor period tended to operate within narrow boundaries, with the orthodox stories (complete with fixed moral judgements) repeated from text to text.³⁵ True, there might be religious conflict between authors and this might produce competing versions, but this was still something different from a coherent investigative mode.³⁶ Neither the inclusive chronicles nor the selective humanist histories set themselves the overarching objective of establishing provable truth.

---

[33] Holinshed, *Chronicles* (1577), I, 1704. As elsewhere, I have modernized spelling and punctuation.

[34] The notion that the Holinshed project was an innovative attempt at creating a kind of national, politically neutral archive is a key argument of Patterson, *Reading Holinshed's Chronicles*.

[35] Woolf, *Idea of History*, xiii, 30–2.

[36] The importance in chronicle of religious dispute (especially the balance of power between church and state) is set out in Womersley's *Divinity and State*. In 'Against Teleology of Technique', *Huntington Library Quarterly*, 68 (2005): 95–108, Womersley argues against an ahistorical search for evolving historical methodology in this period.

There was, however, a different species of prose that was concerned with this business and this was the writing of antiquarians. Leading intellectuals such as William Camden, John Selden, and Robert Cotton were asking new kinds of questions. They were interested in the history of such things as rights, customs, and institutions (researching, for example, the origins of particular taxes or the antiquity of parliament). As evidence, the antiquaries scrutinized such diverse sources as physical documents, coins, and inscriptions; historical developments in language; and archaeological remains. Like many Renaissance developments, the first wave of this thinking had occurred in Italy: in the words of Joseph Levine 'by 1500 the Italian humanists had invented many of the problems and developed most of the skills that were to preoccupy European antiquaries for the next two centuries'.[37] The great poet and intellectual Francesco Petrarca (1304–74) was a pivotal figure in this movement. His successor, Flavio Biondo (1388–1463), had established the model for architectural history in his *Rome Restored* (written 1440–6) and his national historical description *Italy Illustrated* (completed 1453).[38] These works spearheaded a radically new format for the writing of prose history.

Such research was not compatible with the chronicle format. One aspect of Holinshed's book, however, did have a mildly antiquarian bent. This was William Harrison's 'Historical Description of the Island of Britain', which prefaced the narrative history with a geographical and cultural survey of a kind not uncommon in chronicle compilations of the time.[39] In the 'Description' Harrison addressed topics such as the history of migration. He examined changes in the form of government and described the nation through its ancient tribes, local legends, and ruined buildings. As he did so Harrison was, in reality, still very largely dependent on secondary sources, but the questions he was asking inevitably brought new methods to bear. Similar questions were to be asked in the Society of Antiquaries which, by the time of the second (heavily revised) version of Harrison's 'Description', had established a regular pattern of meetings at the Herald's Office in London. In the years between 1590 and 1604, formal presentations were held on an enormous range of topics, including the history of noble titles, court offices, rights of property, land division, funeral customs, parishes, shires, cities, towns, and castles.[40] Speeches in response to specific queries were recorded in manuscript, so these plain, deliberative orations could reasonably be considered a form of prose history.

The dominant prose form that set the Society of Antiquaries in motion, however, was that of William Camden's *Britannia*, published in Latin in 1586 and finally rendered

---

[37] Levine, *Humanism and History*, 78.

[38] See Burke, *Renaissance Sense of the Past*, 20–31.

[39] On the long-standing tradition of geographical-historical descriptions and on Harrison's researches specifically see Arthur B. Ferguson, *Clio Unbound: Perception of the Social and Cultural Past in Renaissance England* (Durham, NC: Duke University Press, 1979), 91–4, and Kendrick, *British Antiquity*, 139–42.

[40] On these meetings, recorded proceedings, and the society in general see Joan Evans, *A History of The Society of Antiquaries* (Oxford: at the University Press by Charles Batey for The Society of Antiquaries, 1956), 11–12, and also Ferguson, *Clio Unbound*, 26–90.

into English twenty-four years later by Philemon Holland (one of the age's greatest translators of classical history). In the same way as Harrison's 'Description' (and, more importantly, Biondo's *Italy Restored*), the *Britannia* adopted a chorographic structure: i.e. it treated land and history at the same time. Chorography is literally 'earth-writing'. In the *Britannia* this involves a systematic survey of the island's landmass that works to uncover all that can be deduced about each region's past. Of course, the same material could be presented through other forms of writing (members of the Society of Antiquaries, for example, also produced annotations and monographs). Yet, chorography offered a more comprehensive way of structuring historical information; as such, it constituted a third important genre of historical prose.

William Lambarde's *Perambulation of Kent* (1576), described as 'containing the description, history and customs of that shire', was the first English antiquarian survey to reach print. The difference between its treatment of the early past and that of Holinshed is remarkable, with Lambarde (in a way comparable to present-day archaeologists) beginning with a picture of the nation divided between Celtic tribes. British history proper, for him, begins with Julius Caesar's account of his expedition to the island. In this, as on all other matters, Lambarde's prose is concerned with the weighing up of historical authority, a process that is aided by the geographic structure of his approach. By following the Kent coastline Lambarde examines the history of Saxon and Norman government in the following way:

> But now I will make toward *Sandwich*, the first of the Ports (as my journey lieth) and by the way speak somewhat of the *Five Ports*, in general.
> *The Cinque Ports*
> I find in the book of the general survey of the realm, which *William* the Conqueror caused to be made in the fourth year of his reign, and to be called *Doomsday*, because (as *Matthew Paris* sayeth) it spared no man (but judged all men indifferently, as the *Lord* in that great day will do) that *Dover, Sandwich,* and *Rumney*, were in the time of King *Edward* the Confessor, discharged almost of all the impositions and burdens (which other towns did bear) in consideration of such service to be done by them upon the Sea, as in their Special titles shall hereafter appear.
> (Lambarde, *Perambulation* [1576], 92–3)

Lambarde is here interested in the history of towns, taxation, and conquest, and considers evidence in the form of charters, place names, chronicles, and physical remains. In a restrained and logical style he eliminates certain sources as unreliable and comes to cautious conclusions on the balance of probability. This deductive methodology is found neither in humanist histories nor in ordinary chronicles: it is the key to a fundamentally innovative perspective on the past.

John Stow, in 1598, took a comparable approach in his *Survey of London*, which is described on the title page as 'Containing the Original, antiquity, increase, modern estate, and description of that city'. Stow's approach is still more directly archaeological than Lambarde's. He is concerned, above all, with the history of buildings and uses direct physical examination over and above the surviving written records. Reporting on the London Bridge Tower, Stow records the following detail:

> This Tower was new begun to be builded in the year, 1426. *John Reynwell* Major of *London*, laid one of the first corner stones, in the foundation of this work, the other three were laid by the Sheriffs, and Bridgemasters, upon every of these four stones was engraved in fair Roman letters, the name of *Jhesus*. And these stones, I have seen laid in the Bridge store house, since they were taken up, when that Tower was of late newly made of timber. This gate and Tower was at the first strongly builded up of stone, and so continued until the year 1577 in the Month of *April*, when the same stone Arched gate, and Tower being decayed was begun to be taken down, and then were the heads of the Traitors removed thence, and set on the Tower over the gate at the bridge foot, towards *Southwark*. (Stowe, *Survey* [1598], 46)

More fully than Lambarde, Stow puts himself into the picture. His personal inspection of ruins and remains is apparent and we have a strong sense of his connection to the great men and institutions of the city. Although there is a folksy element to this involvement with local history, there is also a solid connection to the new antiquarian thinking. Stow can deduce that there is no substance to the old stories of British monarchs because from Tacitus and from the physical remains it is evident that the Celtic tribes did not build walls and '(for the most part)…went naked, painting their bodies, & c. as all the Roman writers have observed' (6).

It is revealing that Stow, who could make such unequivocal antiquarian judgements, should have continued to write chronicles according to the old pattern. This tells us something about the way in which the genres of early modern historical writing (politic history, chronicle, chorography, and others) generally failed to interact. Sophisticated humanist histories still thought little about the nature of their evidence; conversely, forensic antiquarians declined to delve into the realm of court politics. The great collaborative project that goes by the name Holinshed can be thought of as a receptacle of these competing methods. It was in part an old-fashioned chronicle, but it also contained fragments of antiquarianism, Tacitean realpolitik, civic record, news sheet, and church history. Intellectually, this was an unstable combination. Thus, once historians did start to make comparisons across forms of history, the chronicle would be placed under considerable strain. In the seventeenth century, D. R. Woolf has argued, the chronicle did not so much decline as disintegrate into its constituent parts.[41]

Holinshed's reputation declined within a few decades of its publication. It was mocked by self-consciously sophisticated gentlemen, who not only doubted its trustworthiness, but also bristled at its low-church Protestant tendencies. David Womersley has shown the way in which Holinshed generally pushed the record of history in an anti-papal direction. In its defence of the Church of England it had connections with another prose history treated elsewhere in this volume: John Foxe's *Actes and Monuments*. When John Davies scoffed at popular chronicles in his *Epigrammes* he seized on this combination of providential pattern finding and indiscriminate accumulation. Geron, the foolish reader, 'corrects/Old Holinshed our famous chronicler,/with moral rules':

---

[41] D. R. Woolf, 'Genre into Artifact: The Decline of the English Chronicle in the Sixteenth Century', *The Sixteenth Century Journal*, 19 (1988): 321–54 (323).

> The rising in the North, the frost so great
> That cartwheel prints on Thames' face were seen
> The fall of money and the burning of Paul's steeple
> The blazing star and Spaniards' overthrow,
> By these events, notorious to the people,
> He measures times and things forepast doth show.[42]

In this attack, published on the eve of the new century, Davies anticipated a general reaction against chronicle in the Stuart age.

Jacobean Britain would see the appearance of new leaner volumes, better equipped with antiquarian insight and more informed by the methodology of classical historians. In the preface to his *Collection of the Historie of England* (1618) the poet Samuel Daniel fixed upon the neatness and integrity of his book, using a favourite conceit of his that strongly implied a dismissal of Holinshed:

> For mine own part I am so greedy of doing well, as nothing suffices the appetite of my care herein. I had rather be Master of a small piece handsomely contrived, than of vast rooms ill proportioned and unfurnished, and I know many others are of my mind. (Daniel, *Collection* [1618], A3ª)

The controlled, single-voiced shapeliness of Daniel's history was one of its great achievements. In an implicitly antiquarian analogy, he insisted that 'the Reader shall be sure to be paid with no counterfeit coin, but such as shall have the stamp of Antiquity' (A3ᵇ). Daniel was unafraid to dismiss the pre-Roman British history. It was characteristic of nations, he warned, to fabricate mythical origins. In reality, however, states commonly 'rise from springs of poverty, piracy, robbery, and violence, howsoever fabulous writers (to glorify their nations) strive to abuse the credulity of after ages with heroical, or miraculous beginnings' (1Bª). In the *Collection*, Daniel attempted to meld this caution about the historical record with a coherent analytical perspective on the workings of power. The result was a mode of writing quite different from that of sixteenth-century chroniclers. Daniel's prose is complex and judicious, sometimes to the point of obscurity. This, for example, is the opening sentence of his account of the reign of Henry II:

> That short time of peace, before the death of *Stephen*, had so allayed the spirit of contention, and prepared the Kingdom (wearied and defaced with war) to that disposition of quietness: as *Henry Plantagenet* (though a *French-man* borne, and at that time, out of the land: long detained with contrary winds, yet a Prince of so great possessions abroad, as to make him feared, to be too mighty a master at home; or doubtful, where he would set his feet: whether carry *England* thither, or bring those great States to this) was, notwithstanding generally admitted (without any opposition or capitulation, other then the usual oath) to the Crown of *England*: which he received at the hands of *Theobold*, the twentieth day of December, *Anno* 1154, about the three and twentieth year of his age. (Daniel, *Collection* [1618], 67)

---

[42] John Davies, *Epigrammes and Elegies* (1599), Epigram 20, B3ᵇ.

In this opening sentence Daniel pins down one of the great themes of the reign of King Henry: the simultaneous strength and vulnerability of a kingdom that spans the sea. Daniel's account of the reign is consistently concerned with the maintenance of Henry's power: irrelevant material is excluded, quotation is precise and to the purpose, invented speeches are dispensed with, and a consistent (often present tense) narrative is maintained. By the seventeenth century, history had become a university subject: the older, less exclusive understanding of history was being replaced by a concept that was altogether more defined.

I began this essay by stating that, for the early modern reader, history was not necessarily a prose subject. By the middle of the seventeenth century, however, matters had begun to change. The career of Samuel Daniel is itself the most fascinating index of this development. He had begun by writing history as poetry, in his lament *The Complaint of Rosamond* (1592) and in his unfinished historical epic *The Civil Wars* (1596–1609). The failure to complete the latter suggests that Daniel lost faith in the possibility of combining verse and history: his final years were spent on the prose *Collection* and not on the *Civil Wars*. Michael Drayton's famous verdict on Daniel's historical poem ('His rimes were smooth, his meters well did close,/But yet his manner better fitted prose') says something, not just about the poet, but also about the emerging prosaic status of history.[43] Drayton himself suffered under that transition, which likewise affected John Milton in his middle years. Famously, Milton made plans in the late 1630s and 40s for an historical epic, possibly on the reign of Alfred the Great. His decision to write his great poem on a different subject and to write in prose his *History of Britain* is another marker of the new divide.

Between the sixteenth and the seventeenth century, history became, in more than one sense, increasingly prosaic. It is unfashionable to call the intellectual developments of this period 'revolutionary', but undeniably an accommodation of sorts was achieved between humanist politic history on the one hand and antiquarianism on the other.[44] Daniel's 1618 *Collection* (as well as marking the eclipse of verse history and the British legends) involves some kind of union between these historiographic disciplines. Early modern historical prose before that date is a more eclectic category. The two collections of chronicles published under Holinshed's name provide a representative sample of what prose could fall under the heading 'history': the events of the Hebrew Bible, the victories of King Arthur, monstrous births, notable murders, archaeological survey, antipapal invective, and astute political analysis.[45] Historical prose ranged from elevated

---

[43] Michael Drayton, *Works*, ed. William Hebel, 5 vols. (Oxford: Basil Blackwell, 1961), III, ll. 127–8.

[44] On the reaction against F. Smith Fussner's *The Historical Revolution: English Historical Writing and Thought, 1580–1640* (London: Routledge & Kegan Paul, 1962) on this front see Woolf, *Idea of History*, xi–xii; in place of 'revolution' Woolf suggests 'substantial change and growth' (xi).

[45] The victories of King Arthur, which had become notoriously doubtful, were dealt with in a rather circumspect manner in Holinshed. All the same, the court astrologer and historical researcher John Dee continued to submit outlandish accounts of Arthur's conquests to Queen Elizabeth, by whom they were apparently well received. For details on this manuscript history for a political purpose see William H. Sherman, *John Dee: The Politics of Reading and Writing in the English Renaissance* (Amherst, MA: University of Massachusetts Press, 1995), 90–188.

manuscripts addressed to kings to inexpensive popular print. If it is understood to cover all of these categories, then prose history is probably the most widespread secular literature of the Tudor and Stuart age.

Further Reading

Burke, Peter. *The Renaissance Sense of the Past* (London: Edward Arnold, 1969).
Ferguson, Arthur B. *Clio Unbound: Perception of the Social and Cultural Past in Renaissance England* (Durham, NC: Duke University Press, 1979).
—— *Utter Antiquity: Perceptions of Prehistory in Renaissance England* (Durham, NC: Duke University Press, 1993).
Helgerson, Richard. *Forms of Nationhood: The Elizabethan Writing of England* (Chicago: University of Chicago Press, 1992).
Levine, Joseph M. *Humanism and History: Origins of Modern English Historiography* (Ithaca, NY: Cornell University Press, 1987).
Levy, F. J. *Tudor Historical Thought* (San Marino: Huntington Library, 1967).
McKisack, May. *Medieval History in the Tudor Age* (Oxford: Clarendon Press, 1971).
Mendyk, Stan A. E. *'Speculum Britanniae': Regional Study, Antiquarianism, and Science in Britain to 1700* (Toronto: University of Toronto Press, 1989).
Parry, Graham. *The Trophies of Time: English Antiquarians of the Seventeenth Century* (Oxford: Oxford University Press, 1995).
Patterson, Annabel. *Reading Holinshed's Chronicles* (Chicago: University of Chicago Press, 1994).
Woolf, D. R. *The Idea of History in Early Stuart England: Erudition, Ideology, and 'The Light of Truth' from the Accession of James I to the Civil War* (Toronto: University of Toronto Press, 1990)
—— *Reading History in Early Modern England* (Cambridge: Cambridge University Press, 2000).

CHAPTER 20

ASTROLOGY, MAGIC, AND WITCHCRAFT

P. G. MAXWELL-STUART

The Elizabethans and Jacobeans, in company with all their European contemporaries, lived simultaneously in more than one world. The world of physical matter surrounded them and was the one of which they were continuously aware, but realms of super-fine matter inhabited by spirits, angels, demons, and the dead constantly intruded, irregularly and mostly without warning, bringing humans and non-human entities into disturbing and often terrifying contact. So too did the supernatural plane of being where God existed and from which He governed His multifarious creations; and so also did those curious kingdoms and regions so close to Earth, and yet not of it, in which lived fairies, trolls, elves, gnomes, and a great multiplicity of other strange beings—not spirit and yet not matter, either. Humans lived cheek by jowl with all these expressions of different existences, taking them for real, as real as humans themselves, and acutely sensible of their superior powers and abilities which humans bold or foolhardy enough might try to harness or manipulate for their own uses, beneficent or malicious. This is the spiritual, intellectual, psychological, and emotional context to all the occult sciences of the period; and while the geography of the world and of the heavens was changing round about them, people of the sixteenth and early seventeenth centuries, in many important instances, behaved as though these changes were irrelevant and did not impinge upon the realities of their interaction with circumambient Unseens and the entities which existed in them.

20.1 Astrology

Just as the Protestant confessions' rejection of Purgatory made no real difference to popular and indeed, much learned notion about the reality and non-reality, appearance and non-appearance of ghosts, so Galileo's addition of moons to the map of the heavens and Copernicus's earlier removal of Earth from the centre of the cosmos in favour of the sun had little immediate effect on either the techniques or the basic theory of astrology, in spite of the fact that astronomy and astrology were still, at this time, more or less a single science. 'Astrology', however, comprised a number of different, though related, disciplines. *Natural* astrology looked at the sky and weather-signs and drew conclusions therefrom, and also considered the diagnosis and treatment of a patient. *Natal* or *genethliacal* astrology constructed a chart (horoscope) of the heavens as they appeared at a person's birth (or conception) and calculated his or her character and the likely course of that individual's life. *Katarchic* astrology determined from a chart drawn to show the heavens at the moment of a client's question, the best moment to begin a voyage or undertaking of some kind. *Horary* astrology was similar in that it answered a specific question asked of the astrologer and *mundane* astrology sought to answer queries about world events such as earthquakes, outbreaks of plague, or changes of regime. These categories overlapped, and the last four came severally under the general heading *judicial* astrology, and when we find objections to the science—as we do frequently in the literature of the period—it is to the judicial, rather than the natural category that they are directed.

Unease or hostility centred upon the exact functions of the planets and constellations. Were they merely signs, or did they exercise influence upon everything below them? If they influenced, what was the nature of that influence—one which inclined or one which ruled? Pendant upon these were questions about an individual's personal responsibility for sin, and human intrusion upon God's prerogative of complete foreknowledge. Hence Sir Walter Ralegh's careful treading as he writes of 'Fate, and that the Starres haue great influence, and that their operations may diuersly be preuented or furthered'.[1]

No one can doubt, he says, that the stars are more than mere lights in the sky; but when it comes to the extent and character of their influence 'the middle course is to be followed, that as with the Heathen we doe not binde God to his creatures, in this supposed necessity of destinie, so on the contrary we doe not robbe those beautifull creatures of their powers and offices'. The stars and other celestial bodies, he goes on, 'incline the will by mediation of the sensitiue appetite', although they wholly direct minds without reason, meaning those of birds, beasts, and humans who allow themselves to be governed by their passions. But apart from these exceptions, 'howsoeuer we are by the Starres inclined at our birth, yet there are many things both in nature and art, that encounter the same, and weaken their operation'. A good education and Christian upbringing, for example, do much to encourage a favourable planetary inclination and discourage an unfavourable one; and, of course, the immortal soul is quite untouched by any such influence, good or bad, for God 'who hath threatned vnto us the sorrow and torment of offence, could not contrary to his mercifull nature, be so uniust, as to bind vs ineuitably to the destinies, or influences of the Starres, or subiect our soules to any imposed necessitie'.

---

[1] Sir Walter Raleigh, *History of the World* (London: Macmillan, 1971), Book 1, chap. 1, para. 11.

This measured approach, in equally measured, clear, and sinewy prose, however, was far from being the norm. Even when it was allowed that astrology was not altogether beyond the pale, the allowance tended to be grudging or qualified. 'I reject not the prognostications of astronomers [i.e. astrologers], nor the conjectures or forewarnings of physicians, nor yet the interpretations of [natural] philosophers', wrote Reginald Scot in his *Discoverie of Witchcraft* (1584), 'although in respect of the divine prophesies conteined in holie scriptures, they are not to be weighed or regarded.... Whereas these contein onlie the word and will of God, with the other are mingled most horrible lies and cousenages. For although there may be many of them learned and godlie, yet lurke there in corners of the same profession, a great number of counterfeits and couseners.'[2]

Nearly forty years later, Francis Bacon was just as reserved, though less forthright in his expression: 'As for astrology, it is so full of superstition, that scarce anything sound can be discovered in it. Notwithstanding, I would rather have it purified than altogether rejected.... For my part, I admit Astrology as a part of physic, and yet attribute to it nothing more than is allowed by reason and the evidence of things, all fictions and superstitions being set aside.'[3]

The intimate connection between astrology and medicine, to which Bacon refers, provided one of the strong points for anyone who wished to defend the science, and physicians could point to the universities as one of astrology's most potent disseminators; for both Oxford and Cambridge, in company with universities elsewhere in Europe, produced scholars who were excellent astrologers—John Robins of All Souls, for example, and John Fletcher of Caius, among many others—although by the 1570s and 1580s astrology was beginning to fall out of intellectual favour. Nevertheless, as late as 1657 the Quaker Henry Clark could still complain that both universities were turning out large numbers of astrologers to cheat people, as he put it. Richard Forster (c.1546–1616), however, gives us a good example of university-trained, non-cheating medical expertise. A graduate of Oxford, he became a Fellow and then President of the College of Physicians of London, famous not only as a medical practitioner, but also as a mathematician and astrologer. The lengthy title of one of Anthony Asham's books indicates clearly how important the science was to medicine: *A litle herball of the properties of herbes, newly amended & corrected, wyth certayn additions at the end of the boke, declaring what herbes hath influence of certain sterres and constellations, wherby maye be chosen the best and most lucky tymes and dayes of their ministracion, according to the moone beying in the signes of heaven, the which is daily appointed in the almanacke* (1550); and when Leonard Digges dedicated his *Prognostication Everlastinge of Righte Good Effecte* to the Earl of Lincoln in 1576, he illustrated the title page with a version of Zodiac Man, a naked human figure surrounded by the signs of the zodiac, with arrows pointing from them to their areas of special influence in the body, and included, along with sections on natural

---

[2] Reginald Scot, *Discoverie of Witchcraft* (1584), ed. B. Nicholson (London: Elliott Stock, 1886), repr. of 1st edn., Book 9, chap. 4.

[3] Francis Bacon, *De dignitate et augmentis scientiarum* (Norimberg: Riegel & Wiesner, 1829), Book 2, chap. 4.

astrology, such medical observations as, 'The meetest time to take Purgacions etc., is neither in hotte nor colde dayes, that is, from the tenthe of Marche, to the twelfth of June. Further, by rules Astronomical, it must be perfourmed when the Moone is in cold, moist, and watry signes, as Cancer, Scorpius, and Pisces: comforted by Aspectes and radiations of Planets, fortifying the vertue of the body expulsiue' (fol. 20^r).

Forster, Ascham, and a host of others also used astrology as a means of predicting events, interpreting unexpected, but natural phenomena such as comets, and prophesying, although here, of course, they ran the risk of intruding upon religion and politics. In 1583, for example, there took place a conjunction of the planets Jupiter and Saturn at the end of the watery triplicity of Cancer, Scorpio, and Pisces and the beginning of the fiery triplicity of Aries, Leo, and Sagittarius. Richard Harvey immediately published an *Astrologicall Discourse* upon the phenomenon, which set off one of those spats which quite frequently convulsed English astrologers. The question for them was, are we entering the Last Times and approaching the Judgement? 'I am Astrologically induced to this coniecture', wrote Harvey, 'that we are most like to have a new world, by some sodaine, violent, & wonderful strange alteration, which even heretofore hath always hapned, at the ending of one Trigone, & beginning of another.' Robert Tanner (*Prognosticall Iudgement*, 1583) supported him, but Thomas Heath did not and rushed out *A Manifest and Apparent Confutation*, which suggested that Harvey had miscalculated the conjunction and that therefore when it did occur, its effects would be other than Harvey predicted. Richard's brother John then took up cudgels in support of his kinsman—*Astrologicall Addition or Supplement*—but when the brothers' predictions turned out to be wrong, people hostile to astrology seized their chance and used it to condemn the science as a whole.

'So manie as writ of the same', observed the Puritan, Philip Stubbes in his *Anatomie of Abuses* (1583):

> neither iumped togither in one truth, nor yet agreed togither, either of the day, houre, or moneth, when it should be: but in al things shewed themselves like themselves, that is, plaine contradictorie one to another. Insomuchas they writ in defence of their errors, and confutation of the contrarie, one against another, shamefully to behold. By which more than presumptuous audacitie, and rash boldnesse of these, they brought the world into a wonderfull perplexitie and cease, expecting either a woonderfull alteration of states and kingdoms (as these foolish starre tooters promised) or else a finall consummation and overthrowe of all things. Or if not so, yet the strangest things should happen, that ever were heard or seene since the beginning of the world. Wheras, God be thanked, at the verie houre and moment when (as some of them set downe) these woonders and portents should have happened, there was no alteration nor change of any thing seene or heard of, the element being as faire, as bright, as calme, and as pleasant, and everie thing as silent, and in as perfect order and forme, as ever they were since the beginning of the world. By all which apeereth the vanitie and uncerteintie of their curious science.

But if the main thrust of Stubbes's criticism was the inaccuracy of astrological prediction, another puritan, William Perkins (1558–1602), expressed in the clearest and simplest terms one of the principal religious objections to astrology:

> Wee must bee put in minde, not to observe the planetary houres: for men suppose that the hours of the day are ruled by the planets, and hereupon, that some hours are good, and lucky, (as they say) and some unlucky: that men are taken with planets, and borne under unlucky planets. But these are heathenish conceits... We are to feare God, and not to feare the stars... For no man can by learning know the operation of the Starres: because their lights and operations are all mixed together in all places upon earth: and therefore no observation can bee made of this or that starre, more than of this or that herbe, when all herbes are mixed or compounded together... It is a foolishnesse to ascribe the regiment of our affaires to the starres, they being matters contingent, which depend on the will & pleasure of man.[4]

Do the stars incline or rule, and what does one conclusion have to say about human free will and divine omniscience? Perkins was, again, quite clear:

> That part of Astrology, which concerneth the alteration of the ayre, is almost all both false and frivolous; and therefore in a manner all predictions grounded upon that doctrine are meere toyes, by which the silly and ignorant people are notably deluded. As for that other part of Astrologie, concerning Natiuities, revolutions, progressions, and directions of Natiuities, as also that which concerneth election of times, and the finding againe of things lost, it is very wicked; and it is probable, that it is of the same brood with implicite and close Magique.[5]

Perkins was right to link astrology with magic. Many did, such as George Carleton, Bishop of Chichester, whose polemic *Astrologomania* (1623) called it the mate of witchcraft and described it as demonically inspired. 'Mounting from degree to degree, upon the slippery and vncertaine scale of Curiositie', he warned of astrologers, 'they are at last inticed, that where lawfull Artes or Sciences fayles, to satisfie theyr restlesse mindes, euen to seeke to that blacke and vnlawfull Science of Magicke.' A number of other critics also saw a link between medicine and magic. 'There be innumerable charmes of conjurers, bad physicians, lewd surgians, melancholicke witches, and couseners, for all diseases and greefes', grumbled Reginald Scot, 'speciallie for such as bad physicians and surgions knowe not how to cure, and in truth are good stuffe to shadow their ignorance.'[6] Of course, it was not simply inept physicians who supplemented their diagnoses and cures with magic. The skilled and popular, if maverick, Simon Forman not only cast horoscopes for his clients, but wrote (and typically did not finish) hundreds of pages of a manual of astrological physic on which he provided a running commentary to his pupil and fellow physician, Richard Napier, who in his turn wrote *A Treatise touching the Defenc of Astrologie* which, like Forman's work, remained unprinted; and in the early seventeenth century, Nicholas Culpeper (1616–54), like Forman, a physician, astrologer, and fighter of the medical Establishment, produced *The English Physitian, or An astrologo-physical discourse on the vulgar herbs of this nation* (1652) and *Opus astrologicum*

---

[4] William Perkins, *A Commentarie or Exposition upon the Epistle to the Galatians* (Cambridge, 1604), chap. 4.
[5] William Perkins, *A Golden Chaine* (London, 1591), chap. 22.
[6] Scot, *Discoverie of Witchcraft*, Book 12, chap. 14.

(1654), maintaining, however, that 'the astrologer is, or ought to be, very well versed in every part of natural philosophy' and so not entirely reliant upon astrology for his diagnoses.

If it was perhaps via medical consultation that people most frequently came into contact with astrology, almanacs certainly ran it a close second. These were pamphlets or broadsheets containing a variety of information—expected eclipses and conjunctions, the calendar, and a prognostication, that is, an astrological forecast for the coming year. The more elaborate almanacs also contained ephemeredes, tables showing the daily position of the planets and stars throughout the year, which would enable readers to draw up their own horoscopes, genethliacal or horary, so that they would be forewarned of good times or bad for themselves, the church, or the state. Diagrams of 'astrological man', such as Leonard Digges included in his *Prognostication*, also allowed readers to calculate the best times to take medicine or submit to bleeding. Circulating prognostications, however, had its potentially sinister side, as far as a number of English parliaments were concerned and although there was no legislation specifically aimed at astrology—apart, perhaps, from an Act of 1581 forbidding anyone to calculate Elizabeth's nativity—the Tudors, from Henry VIII onwards, tended to treat as felony what they saw as politically motivated predictions, and proclamations, orders from the Privy Council, and bishops' investigations were frequently directed against those who made and published them. Interestingly enough, however, when war broke out between King Charles and parliament in 1642, puritans in the government actually encouraged astrologers and almanac writers to be more open about their work and in 1643 appointed a well-known astrologer and almanac writer, John Booker, to oversee licensing of astrological works on the government's behalf. So the radicalism of puritan MPs coincided with, and encouraged, a radicalization of prognostication which thereby became a potent tool in the hands of authority. William Lilly (1602–81), for example, the most prominent English astrologer in the country, prefaced his almanacs with short essays announcing the downfall of the monarchy and prophesying victory for Cromwell's soldiers, and the title of his three-volume manual, *Christian Astrology* (1647), threw down a challenge to anyone who would argue the contrary.

Lilly, indeed, shows how far the almanac had come. To begin with, most English almanacs were translations of European originals, but as the sixteenth century wore on, more and more were domestic, swelling in numbers until the seventeenth century saw more than 2,000 separate publications appearing in a given year. The size of the market gives a notion of their popularity. Hence, Shakespeare could drop into astrological terminology and even make a joke—'Taurus? That's sides and heart/No, sir: it's legs and thighs'[7]—and expect his audience to follow and appreciate. John Webster, more bold, provided details of a newborn child's nativity—'The lord of the first house, being combust in the ascendant, signifies short life: and Mars being in a human sign, joined to the tail of the Dragon, in the eighth house, doth threaten a violent death.'[8] John Fletcher, bolder still, included

---

[7] William Shakespeare, *Twelfth Night*, Act I, scene 3.
[8] John Webster, *The Duchess of Malfi*, Act II, scene 3.

in his *Bloody Brother* (Act 4, scene 2) a long passage of dialogue (80 verses) almost entirely devoted to technicalities of the science, so much so that one can reconstruct the horoscope being discussed.

Medical consultation, popular literature, and the theatre, then, combined to keep astrology a living and pertinent science in public awareness, even though scholars might wrangle over details and clergymen denounce it from pulpit and the printed page; and those controversies which had produced a spurt of books in the 1580s rose again in the early 1600s. John Chamber (1546–1604), a canon of Windsor, had lectured against astrology at Oxford during the 1570s and now gathered together his thoughts and objections in *A Treatise against Iudicial Astrologie* (1601). These were simple: (1) modern astrologers are embarrassed by their science and therefore confine themselves to writing almanacs; (2) astrology is full of technical flaws; (3) can astrologers solve certain problems such as drawing up a horoscope for eggs in a bird's nest? (4) things happen because of human will or mere chance; (5) only stupid people consult astrologers; and (6) astrology is actually less reliable than other forms of divination. One may note that Chamber confines himself to the judicial forms of astrology—the natural, he leaves alone—and that his arguments vary considerably in force and cogency. They were, however, fun, which is more than can be said for the ponderous reply by Sir Christopher Heydon, *A Defence of Judicial Astrologie* (1603). Its tiresome weight may owe something to his determination to overwhelm Chamber with tidal waves of learning—and no one denied that his book was based on extensive acquaintance with both ancient and modern authorities—just as one of its principal aims, to show that astrology is compatible with Christianity, may owe much to Heydon's collaborator, his chaplain, William Bredon, himself an astrologer.

Liveliness, however, returned in John Melton's *Astrologaster, or The Figure-Caster* (1620), which blisteringly defined astrology as,

> An Art, whereby Cunning Knaves cheat plaine honest Men, that teacheth both the Theory and Practicke of Cousenage, a Science instructing all the Students of it to lye as often as they speake, and to be beleeved no oftener then they hold their Tongues; that tells truth as often as Bawds goe to Church, Witches or Whores say their Prayers, or never but when the English Nones and Greeke Calends meet together [i.e. never]. (pp. 29–30)

When a clergyman, William Foster, charged Dr Robert Fludd, Censor of the College of Physicians, with being a magician, Fludd had no hesitation in coming to his own and astrology's defence in round terms in spite of the fact, clear in his admission of it, that astrology was indeed used for some magical purposes:

> I was, whilst I did sojourn in Rome, acquainted with a very learned and skilful personage, called Master *Gruter*, he was by birth of Switzerland; and for his excellency in the Mathematic, and in the Art of motions and inventions of Machines, he was much esteemed by the Cardinal Saint *George*. The Gentleman taught me the best of my skill in those practices, and amongst the rest, he delivered this magnetical experiment unto me, as a great secret, assuring me that it was tried in his

Country, upon many with good success. When (said he) any one hath a withered and consumed member, as a dried arm, leg, foot, or such like, which Physicians call an Atrophy of the limbs, you must cut from that member, be it foot or arm, the nails, hair or some part of the skin, then you must pierce a willow tree with an Auger or wimble unto the pith, and afterward put into the hole the pared nails and skin, and with a peg made of the same wood, you must stop it closed, observing that in this action the Moon be increasing & the good Planets [be] in such a multiplying Sign as is *Gemini*, and fortunate and powerful over *Saturn* which is a great dryer. The selfsame affect (said he) you shall find in you, take the nails and hair, which is cut off the member, and close them in the root of an hazel tree, and shut up the hole, with the bark of the tree, and after cover it with the earth, and (said he) it hath been tried, that as the tree daily growth and flourisheth, so also by little and little will the patient recover his health. But you must with diligence observe the motion of the heavenly bodies, and especially the places of the Sun and Moon, when this is effected. And to this intent, he did disclose unto me the time and seasons when the preparation unto such a cure should be effected...I boldly affirm, therefore, that all Astrology is not forbidden for as much as there is an especial observation to be had by wise men, of the influence of the stars. And for that purpose, there are hours of election, duly to be observed according unto this or that influence, which is most proper and convenient for our work...[and] that there is no Cacomagical superstition in observing times, days or hours, in which this or that star hath dominion, for the collecting of ingrediences, or preparation and adaption of medicines, or other matters, proper for the cure of man.[9]

Fludd, of course, was a physician and therefore one might expect him to come to astrology's defence. He also had pronounced opinions, defending Paracelsian medicine against the officially approved Galenic, and been well versed in the Christian–Neoplatonic–Hermetic philosophical viewpoint which attended his preferences. In addition to this, he was a practising alchemist; so his profession, his hobby, and his outlook will have combined to make him take astrology with the utmost seriousness.

The tone was thus set for the 1640s and 1650s, during which astrology both flourished under government approval, and yet suffered the usual attacks relating to religious heterodoxy and the charlatanism of its practitioners, arguments (if one may call them such) which echoed those of similar, earlier controversies elsewhere in Europe. English polemicists, in fact, seem to have been highly dependent on other European models to guide them in their hostilities and apologies, the distinguishing feature of their work being its use of the vernacular instead of the Latin which tended to be employed elsewhere. The result of both sides' labours was simple stalemate. Astrology continued to be accepted in medicine, questioned and condemned by religion, and used by everyone. It was a situation familiar to the practitioners and clients of all the occult sciences.

---

[9] Robert Fludd, *Dr. Fludd's Answer*, Second member, chap. 7. Text in W. Huffman, ed., *Robert Fludd* (Berkeley, CA: North Atlantic Books, 2001).

20.2 Magic

Magic, like astrology, was divided into different types. *Natural* magic included what we should call 'conjuring tricks', dependent largely on sleight of hand. *Superstitious* magic relied on the innate power of certain words, phrases, and gestures, usually traditional, to bring about a desired outcome. *Ritual* magic employed elaborate ceremonial and invoked non-human entities, its forms being frequently reminiscent of Catholic ritual and its practitioners of Catholic priests. These requirements, and the use of Latin as well as the vernacular to call up spirits, meant that this category of magic was largely in the hands of learned men. Regardless of which rituals were used, however, invocation followed by evocation remained the fundamental purpose of this type of magic. *Demonic* magic overtly depended on the assistance of an evil spirit to effect its results, whatever their intention, good or bad, and implied the existence of a pact, tacit or overt, between the operator and the demon. Witchcraft can be seen as falling into the categories of 'superstitious' or 'demonic' magic or both, and indeed, magic as a whole should be viewed as a continuum, along which the efforts of humans to manipulate the hidden, preternatural powers of Nature for their own purposes can slide between categories, partaking of the characteristics of any or either according to the nature and intention of the act being performed.[10]

Conjuring tricks tended to be the territory of the juggler. Originally, he was merely someone who amused, but by the sixteenth century we have evidence that he had become a person who used digital dexterity or mechanical devices to produce 'magical' effects and illusions.

'The true art of juggling', wrote Reginald Scot in his *Discoverie of Witchcraft*,

> consisteth in legierdemaine; to wit, the nimble conveiance of the hand, which is especiallie performed three waies. The first and principall consisteth in hiding and conveieng of balles, the second in the alteration of monie, the third in the shuffeling of the cards. He that is expert in these may shew much pleasure, and manie feats, and hath more cunning than all other witches or magicians. All other parts of this art are taught when they are discovered: but this part cannot be taught by any description or instruction, without great exercise and expense of time. And for as much as I professe rather to discover than teach these mysteries, it shall suffice to signifie unto you, that the endevor and drift of jugglers is onelie to abuse mens eies and judgments. (13.22)

He also gives examples of the art of illusion, explains how some of them might be done, and includes diagrams of retractable bodkins to thrust 'through' the tongue, knives to 'slice off' half of one's nose, and an elaborate device to enable the juggler to 'cut off' his head and lay it on a plate, a trick known as 'the decollation of John Baptist' (13.34):

---

[10] Necromancy is not included here because, as the word suggests, it was a form of divination, rather than magic, even though certain magical techniques might be used in summoning up the spirits of the dead.

[The juggler] will shew you a card, or anie other like thing: and will saie further unto you, 'Behold and see what a marke it hath', and then burneth it; and nevertheless fetcheth another like card so marked out of some bodies pocket, or out of some corner where he himselfe before had placed it; to the woonder and astonishment of simple beholders, which conceive not that kind of illusion, but expect miracles and strange works. What woondering and admiration was there at *Brandon* the juggler, who painted on a wall the picture of a dove, and seeing a pigeon sitting on the top of a house, said to the King, 'Lo now your Grace shall see what a juggler can doo, if he be his craftes maister', and then pricked the picture with a knife so hard and so often, and with so effectuall words, as the pigeon fell down from the top of the house stark dead. (13.13)

Some people, however, found it difficult to distinguish between this kind of thing and actual magic, as John Cotta wryly observed in *The Triall of Witch-Craft* (1616): 'Hence as Witches doe strange and supernaturall workes, and truly vnto reason worthy of wonder; so the imposter doth things voide of acceptable reason, in shadow, shew, and seeming onely supernaturall, wondred and admired. And hence it commeth to passe, that with vndiscerning mindes, they are sometimes mistaken and confounded one for another.' One of the major problems which had preoccupied both demonologists and strixologists since the fifteenth century had been how to determine whether a particular act—let us say, flying through the air on a broom to a witches' Sabbat—happened in reality or merely in the individual's imagination. It was a well-established theory, for example, that demons could so interfere with the processes of human sight that they could create an image so realistic that the person who saw it would take it to be genuine. Hence, it was perfectly possible that a witch might wholeheartedly believe she or he was indeed flying to a Sabbat, even though in fact she or he was at home asleep in bed. Therefore 'conjuring tricks' or 'illusions', especially if done with skill, could evoke suspicion either that they were real acts of magic (and so done with demonic help), or that the audience had been hoodwinked by demons into believing that what they were seeing was real and not a trick; and if learned men sometimes had difficulty in discerning truth from falsehood, how much more difficult (said Cotta and others) would it be for the unlettered to separate the genuine from the illusion, or the illusion from the trick?

Amulets, of course, were one of the most frequent evidences of popular recourse to magic. People wore them to ward off evil spirits, disease, and misfortune, either 'consecrating' the amulet themselves or having it done for them by someone who professed skill in magic. William Lilly recalled in his autobiography that when he was secretary and servant to one Gilbert Wright, Wright's wife died in 1624 after a long and painful illness and it was discovered that

she had under her arm-hole a small scarlet bag full of many things, which, one that was there delivered unto me. There was in this bag several sigils, some of Jupiter in Trine, others of the nature of Venus some of iron, and one of gold, of pure angel-gold, of the bigness of a thirty-three shilling piece of King James's coin. In the circumference on one side was engraven, *Vicit Leo de tribu Judae Tetragrammaton* [symbol: cross], within the middle there was engraven a holy lamb. In the other circumference, there was Amraphel and three [symbol: cross]. In the middle, *Sanctus Petrus, Alpha* and *Omega*.[11]

Scot, too, is another useful source for our knowledge of those popular magical practices known as 'superstitions':

> *Against the toothache*: scarifie the gums in the greefe, with the tooth of one that hath beene slaine; *a charme for the headach*: tie a halter about your head, wherewith one hath beene hanged; *a charme to drive awaie spirits that haunt anie house*: hang in everie of the foure corners of your house this sentence written upon virgine parchment, 'Omnis spiritus laudet Dominum, Mosen habent et prophetas, exurgat Deus et dissipentur inimici eius'.[12]

Now, it is true that Scot's work is in part a diatribe against Catholicism, which he sees as a repository of magic and superstitious practices, and anti-Catholicism is a prevailing note, perhaps the prevailing note, in Protestant observations on the role played by the Devil in everyday English life. Thomas Cooper lamented in his *The Mystery of Witch-Craft* (1617) that people continued to seek help from blessers and healers and witches, all of whom he called 'the fitches and onions, yea the garbidge and very deepenesse of Antichrist', since they were nothing less than harbours and hiding-places of secret Catholicism; and likewise, though in cooler terms, Francis Bacon linked superstition with the Catholic church (and aspects of the Anglican establishment) in his essay on the subject: 'The causes of superstition are pleasing and sensual titles and ceremonies; excess of outward and pharisaical holiness; over-great reverence of traditions, which cannot but load the Church; the stratagems of prelates for their own ambition and lucre'. William Ames, however, took a different line in his *Conscience, with the power and cases thereof* (1639), noting the common practice of people to resort to 'Figures, Images, Characters, Charmes, or Writings' to cure diseases, along with 'Herbes and other Medicines, not as they are applyed in a naturall way, but as they be charmed, or as they bee used in some certaine forme and no other'. In such cases, he said, 'the Devill is the author both of the operations, and significations which doe depend on such meanes'. Here he strikes the other dominant note in works on 'popular' magic—that there is, in effect, no difference between superstitions and demonic magic, an opinion with which many other writers concurred. 'By Witches', said William Perkins in 1610, 'we understand not those onely which kill and torment: but all Diviners, Charmers, Juglers, all Wizzards, commonly called wise men and wise women... and in the same number we reckon all good Witches, which doe no hurt, but good, which doe not spoile and destroy, but save and deliver'.[13]

Ritual magic, on the other hand, did not, at least in practice, attract so much vituperation, partly perhaps because it was the provenance of the learned and therefore supposedly almost respectable, partly because those same learned often had influential clients or protectors, and partly because it was much more an affair private to the practitioner.

---

[11] *William Lilly's History of his Life and Times from the Year 1602 to 1681* (Hardpress.net, 2006), 13.
[12] Scot, *Discoverie of Witchcraft*, 12.14.
[13] William Perkins, *A Discourse of the Damned Art of Witchcraft* (London, 1631), 255–6.

John Dee (1527–1608), for example, conducted his conversations with evoked spirits through a series of mediums over several years, but always in the confines of his study; and although he made detailed notes of these scrying sessions, they remained in manuscript and were not made public until after his death. Even so, the very fact that he was a mathematician, alchemist, and astrologer was sufficient to call down troubles upon his head and while his published works deal mainly with mathematics, political geography, and astrology, there was sufficient occult speculation in some of them to rouse suspicions that he might indeed be a magician. His astrology, for example, could serve as an instrument of magic. 'If you were skilled in catoptrics', he wrote in his *Propaedeumata Aphoristica* (1558), 'you would be able, by means of a practical technique, to imprint the rays of any star much more strongly upon any substance exposed to them than Nature does by herself'.[14] This is scarcely different from the astral magic employed by amulet-makers and although Dee regarded it as natural magic, rather than magic of any other kind, to an outside eye the differences might seem to be minimal.

Hence, as early as 1570 he was complaining in his *Preface to Euclid* that he was being called a conjuror, that is, an invoker of spirits, and as late as 1598 he returned to Mortlake from an extended sojourn abroad to find that he had lost much of his library to a mob which, inspired by fear of his 'magical' books and instruments, had broken in and looted them during his absence. Nor did Shakespeare do his reputation much good when he created the figure of Prospero, a ritual magician, since many would have been reminded of Dee whose remarkably wide and diverse learning would thus have been reduced in popular estimation to a single, dubious practice.

20.3 Witchcraft

The fourth general category of magic was that known as 'demonic', and for some time before the sixteenth century witchcraft—the knowledge and skill of those who possessed insights into and control over the hidden powers of Nature and non-human entities—had been assimilated to those forms of magic which were said to rely upon the aid of spirits to achieve their effects. Since these spirits were assumed to be evil, even that exercise of magic which sought to help, rather than hurt, was included in both ecclesiastical and secular condemnation, while divination of any kind, too, was likely to be labelled witchcraft on the grounds that foresight, and hence prediction, was almost bound to be acquired through demonic, rather than divine assistance, and so was equally condemnable.

'Some learned men', says Theophilus in chapter 2 of Henry Holland's dialogue, *A Treatise Against Witchcraft* (1590),

---

[14] John Dee, *Propaedeumata Aphoristica* (1558) (Berkeley, CA: University of California Press, 1978), Aphorism 52.

have distinguished these satanical covenants into their sorts, for some have an open, express and evident league and confederacy with Satan; some a more hid and secret; some a mixed and mean between both. Unto the open and express confederacy belong all manifest conjurations and practices of Pythonists [*diviners*]. Unto the secret kind, all close and secret operations by Satan in divining astrology, palmistry, and the like. Unto the third kind appertain all practices of superstitious magic in all sorceries whatsoever …

Mysodemon: I pray you then, unto which league belong the common sort of our witches, which seem indeed to work by the devil, (so wicked are their lives, so devilish are their inventions, and such dreadful events follow them) and yet have no manifest operation by Satan to their own knowledge, as most of them say in the very hour of their death.

Theophilus: They do belong therefore no doubt to the second and third kind of confederacy, and they work secretly by the devil. (p. 32)

This kind of learned discussion, based on the Bible's various terms for occult practitioners, relied on the rise of Hebrew studies in England during the sixteenth century. Reginald Scot's treatise on witchcraft, published in 1584, had included much the same kind of disquisition at greater length, and on the Continent the Jesuit Martín del Rio would devote similar attention to the Hebrew vocabulary in his *Investigations Into Magic* (1599–1600). By 'the second and third kind' to which Theophilus assigns contemporary English witches, he means diviners and those who work with the help of evil spirits ('familiars'). Here he appears to link two separate types of occult practitioner, the likely reason being that he has in mind the most famous diviner-witch, the so-called 'Witch of Endor' who appears in 1 Samuel 28:7 as *ba'alath 'obh*, a woman with a spirit. The Geneva Bible (and later the King James version) translates this as 'a woman with a familiar spirit', and thus the connection is made between divining and calling up a ghost by the help of a servant-demon and the common English notion of a witch as someone with just such a familiar at her command.

This assumption that most occult sciences were performed only with the help of a demon was both common and widespread. 'Let there be not so few in London as three score women', observed Francis Valleriolus in 1562, 'that occupieth the arte of Phisicke and Chirurgerie. These women, some of them be called Witches, and useth to call upon certaine spirits.'[15] Dr Burcot, if we are to believe Reginald Scot, was introduced to a 'juggler' called Feats, 'who sold maister Doctor a familiar, wherby he thought to have wroughte miracles, or rather to have gained good store of monie'; and even so eminent a man as Adam Squier, Master of Balliol in the 1570s, was accused by Robert Parsons, a Jesuit, of selling some gamblers a familiar spirit to guarantee them success at dice. There were indeed those, of course, as Parsons suggests of Squier, who took advantage of people's credulity and pretended to have a familiar spirit, though they did not. Thus, John Hall exposed a magician called Valentine who 'made the people beleeve, that he could tel all

---

[15] 'The office of a chirurgion', fol. 33ʳ, included in the 1586 edition of Thomas Gale, *The Institucion of Chyrurgerie*.

thinges, present, past, and to come: And the very Thoughtes of men, and theyr diseases, by onlye lokinge in theyr faces.... and otherwhile made them beleve, that he went to aske councel of the devel, by going a little aside, and mumbling to him selfe, and then coming agayne, and would tell them all and more to'.[16]

Nevertheless, the idea that magical operators had power over spirits, whom they used as servants and instruments, had a strong hold over most people's imaginations and convictions, and English witches, in particular, were well known to have spirits attendant upon them to carry out their wishes in return for a drink of their blood, as is famously illustrated in the woodcut which accompanies Matthew Hopkins's *Discovery of Witchcraft* (1647). Therefore, regardless of good intentions—'cunning men, or good witches', said Thomas Ady, 'will undertake to shew the face of a thief in the glass, or of any other that hath done his neighbour wrong privily'[17]—a witch or cunning man or cunning woman or magician, conjuror, diviner, chiromancer, or any other dealing in hidden knowledge and legally forbidden practices was certain to draw down censure from official quarters and condemnation from learned commentators and controversialists.

Interestingly enough, however, the sixteenth century saw relatively few such commentators in England, in comparison with a large number elsewhere in Europe. England preferred, for the edification and entertainment of the crowd, to publish pamphlets purporting to describe the heinous crimes of a witch recently tried and executed. But commentators there were, the best known being Reginald Scot (died 1599), scion of a landed family in Kent, who spent his life as a engineer, collector of subsidies, soldier, and MP for New Romney. His *Discoverie of Witchcraft* seems to have been written partly in reaction to his attendance at witch trials, partly as an English answer to Jean Bodin, a vociferous supporter of the validity of witchcraft, whose dramatic and alarming *Démonomanie des sorciers* had appeared in 1580. Scot makes clear his intentions in the prefatory *Epistle to Readers* (p. xxiii):

> God that knoweth my heart is witnes, and you that read my booke shall see, that my drift and purpose in this enterprise tendeth onelie to these respects. First, that the glorie and power of God be not so abridged and abased, as to be thrust into the hand or lip of a lewd old woman: whereby the worke of the Creator should be attributed to the power of a creature. Secondlie, that the religion of the gospell may be seene to stand without such peevish trumperie. Thirdlie, that lawfull favour and Christian compassion be rather used towards these poore soules, than rigor and extremitie. Bicause they, which are commonlie accused of witchcraft, are the least sufficient of all other persons to speake for themselves; as having the most base and simple education of all others; the extremitie of their age giving them leave to dote, their povertie to beg, their wrongs to chide and threaten (as being void of anie other waie of revenge) their humour melancholicall to be full of imaginations, from whence cheefelie proceedeth the vanitie of their confessions; as that they can transforme

---

[16] Scot, *The Discoverie of Witchcraft*, Book 7, chap. 11. Robert Parsons, *A Briefe Apologie* (Antwerp, 1601), fol. 193b. John Hall, *An Historicall Expostulation against the beastlye abusers, both of Chirurgie, and Physyke, in owre tyme* (London, 1565), sig. Aaa4^r.

[17] Thomas Ady, *A Candle in the Dark* (London, 1656), 40.

themselves and others into apes, owles, asses, dogs, cats, etc: that they can flie in the aire, kill children with charmes, hinder the coming of butter, etc.

He pursues these aims in sixteen Books, each one of which acts as a brick in a very carefully designed structure—Scot was, after all, an engineer—and is designed to further his basic argument, which is not, as many modern writers suggest, a 'rationalist' debunking of the very notion of witchcraft, but a plea that misfortunes should be accepted as divine judgements and decisions of Providence, to be borne with patience and prayer and fasting instead of being seen as the result of demonic activity to be answered by counter-magic which, in his frequently reiterated view, Scot saw as a Catholic and therefore superstitious way of behaving. Most witchcraft accusations, he maintained, were based on dubious theology and mistranslations of scripture. Hence, we find that Books 6–13 of the *Discoverie* are actually extended commentaries on Hebrew words for various kinds of magical operator, filled with illustrative anecdotes drawn from Scot's considerable reading of previous authorities—he cites 200 non-English and 38 English works—these discussions being prefaced by Books on the supposed power of witches and their pact with Satan and followed by others on ritual magic. Scot concludes the whole work by admitting that some forms of natural magic may perhaps have some validity and appends a final section, 'Discourse upon Divels and Spirits', which appears to accept their reality, but, in effect, comes very near to denying it.

No wonder, then, that his book provoked a storm. Henry Holland, William Perkins, and Richard Bernard all criticized it adversely. So too did King James, whose own essay on the subject, *Daemonologie*, appeared in 1597, following his personal brush with treasonous conspiracies on his life, formulated by a near-lethal combination of witches and politicians. But it may be significant that after its first publication, the *Discoverie* remained out of print until 1651, when renewed interest in and fear of witchcraft had been stimulated by the English Civil War and its aftermath. Less controversial were George Gifford's *A Discourse of the Subtill Practices of Devilles by Witches and Sorcerers* (1587) and *A Dialogue of Witches and Witchcraftes* (1593), which see witchcraft as a practical problem for the clergy, rather than a theological exercise for the learned. In them, Gifford warns juries to be on their guard against Satan's trickery and to beware of cunning folk who are just as bad as witches. Whether his work influenced Shakespeare's portrayals of witches, as has been suggested, is, however, open to debate.

Scot and Gifford apart, it is not really until the first two decades of the seventeenth century that we find serious commentary on witchcraft burgeoning in England. There was the usual flurry of pamphlet literature in response to particular events—the demonic possession of fourteen-year-old Mary Glover (1602), for example, and that of Anne Gunter (1605), shown to be a fraud, and the trial of the Pendle Hill witches (1612), written up in a tract by Thomas Potts at the instance of the presiding judges—but with William Perkins, *A Discourse of the Damned Art of Witchcraft* (posthumously published in 1608, six years after his death), Alexander Roberts, *A Treatise of Witchcraft* (1616), John Cotta, *The Triall of Witch-Craft* (1616), and Thomas Cooper, *The Mystery of Witch-Craft* (1617), we have a succession of clergymen (with the exception of Cotta, a physician) vigorously condemning all forms of magic as witchcraft. It may be no coincidence that in 1615–16 London was enthralled by the trial of Frances Howard, Countess of Somerset, who was popularly supposed to have used magic to snare her first husband, the Earl of Essex, and a later lover, Robert Carr, the King's intimate. An anonymous verse-libel likened her to the Classical witch, Canidia:

> She that by spells could make a frozen stone
> Melt and dissolve with soft affection:
> And in an instant strike the factours dead
> That should pay duties to the marriage-bedd:
> Canidia now draws on ...
>
> Whose waxen pictures fram'd by incantation,
> Whose Philters, Potions for loves propagation
> Count Circe but a novice in the trade,
> And scorne all Drugs that Colchos ever made;
> Canidia now draws on.[18]

Between them, then, Perkins, Roberts, and Cooper explored and summarized what were by now the arguments both for accepting the reality of witchcraft, regardless of reservations, and prosecuting anyone whose activities might warrant his or her being called a witch. Cotta, too, while expressing some doubts about some of the methods used to investigate witches, nevertheless maintained that witchcraft was sufficiently real to justify its being probed and investigated by those learned enough to distinguish truth from falsehood; and then in 1627, Richard Bernard, another clergyman, produced his *Guide to Grand-Iury Men*, which one might almost call a summary of these summaries, since, while it continued the strain of caution evident in many earlier English commentaries, it still offered, in the words of its extended title, to advise juries 'what to doe, before they bring in a *billa vera* in cases of witchcraft', and offered its readers a fairly full discussion 'touching witches good and bad, how they may be knowne, evicted [and] condemned'. The book proved popular and was reprinted two years later, a final, conventional flourish before the uneasy lull which preceded another outbreak of similar literature during the English Civil War—like many of its predecessors, sceptical, but not as sceptical as all that.

FURTHER READING

Allen, D. C. *The Star-Crossed Renaissance: The Quarrel about Astrology and its Influence in England* (London: Frank Cass, 1966).
Butterworth, P. *Magic on the Early English Stage* (Cambridge: Cambridge University Press, 2005).
Capp, B. A. *Astrology and the Popular Press* (London and Boston: Faber and Faber, 1979).
Gifford, George. *A Dialogue of Witches and Witchcraftes* (1593) (Brighton: Puckrel Publishing, 2007).

---

[18] BL MS Sloane 1792, fos. 2^v–4^r.

Harkness, Deborah E. *John Dee's Conversations with Angels: Cabala, Alchemy, and the End of Nature* (Cambridge: Cambridge University Press, 1999).

Hill Curth, L. *English Almanacs, Astrology, and Popular Medicine, 1550–1700* (Manchester and New York: Manchester University Press, 2007).

Kassell, L. *Medicine and Magic in Elizabethan London* (Oxford: Clarendon Press, 2005).

Lilly, William. *Christian Astrology* (1647), 2 vols. (Bel Air, MD: Astrology Center of America, 2004).

Perkins, William. *A Discourse of the Damn'd Art of Witchcraft* (1608).

Roberts, Alexander. *A Treatise of Witchcraft* (1616).

Scot, Reginald. *Discoverie of Witchcraft* (1584) (New York: Dover Publications 1972).

Sharpe, J. *Instruments of Darkness: Witchcraft in England, 1550–1750* (London: Hamish Hamilton, 1996).

—— *Witchcraft in Early Modern England* (Harlow: Pearson Education, 2001).

Thomas, K. *Religion and the Decline of Magic* (Harmondsworth: Penguin, 1971).

Woolley, B. *The Queen's Conjuror: The Science and Magic of Dr John Dee* (London: HarperCollins, 2001).

CHAPTER 21

JEST BOOKS

IAN MUNRO AND ANNE LAKE PRESCOTT

WHAT is a 'jest book'? The term was first popularized by nineteenth-century antiquarians as a way of labelling the Tudor and Stuart chapbooks that they were discovering and republishing.[1] The most extensive of such republications was W. Carew Hazlitt's three-volume collection, *Shakespeare Jest-Books: Reprints of the Early and Very Rare Jest-Books Supposed to have been Used by Shakespeare* (1864), which brought together a large number of what might now be considered the 'canonical' English jest books.[2] Hazlitt's title derives from a moment in *Much Ado about Nothing*, where Benedick (apparently) has told a disguised Beatrice that she 'had [her] good wit out of the "Hundred Merry Tales"' (2.1.115).[3] This exchange catalyzed an extensive bibliographic treasure hunt in the early nineteenth century by Samuel Singer and other antiquarians, resulting in the publication of *A C. Mery Talys* (1526) under the title *Shakespeare's Jestbook*.[4] Hazlitt's application of the phrase to his broad collection of comic texts sought to enhance their reputation by drawing them, with little evidence, under the Shakespearean aegis. Seeing the books as something 'used' by a true artist like Shakespeare fits the subsidiary role imagined for the jest book form—an attitude found also in the most important modern collection of jest books, Paul Zall's *A Hundred Merry Tales and other Sixteenth-Century Jestbooks*, which begins by describing them as the 'subsoil for the lush growth of Elizabethan prose fiction and comedy'.[5]

---

[1] The *OED* dates the phrase to 1750, in a letter of Horace Walpole. The most interesting early usage noted by the *OED* is found in William Cowper's *Truth* (1781): 'The Scripture was his jest-book, whence he drew Bons-mots to gall the Christian and the Jew' (*OED*, s.v. 'jestbook', *OED* <http://www.oed.com> accessed 18 March 2013). This suggests that a sense of the jest book as a spur to discourse was already well established.

[2] W. C. Hazlitt, ed., *Shakespeare Jest-Books: Reprints of the Early and Very Rare Jest-Books Supposed to have been Used by Shakespeare* (London: Willis and Sotheran, 1864).

[3] William Shakespeare, *The Arden Shakespeare: Much Ado about Nothing*, ed. A. R. Humphreys (New York: Routledge, 1994).

[4] See Ian Munro, 'Shakespeare's Jestbook: Print, Wit, Performance', *English Literary History*, 71.1 (2004): 89–113.

[5] P. M. Zall, *A Hundred Merry Tales and other Sixteenth-Century Jestbooks* (Lincoln: University of Nebraska Press, 1963), 1.

Modern critical approaches to the English jest book date from Ernst Schulz's 1912 'Die englischen Schwankbücher', which proposed a tripartite classification system: those that present comic short stories; those that are collections of detached individual jests; and those that use a character (real or fictional) to organize their jests or tales biographically.[6] In 1939, F. P. Wilson supplemented Schulz's analysis with a more vigorous and extensive survey, employing the same classifications. For Schulz, and somewhat for Wilson, jest books were less literary 'subsoil' than rudimentary forerunners to the novel, and a corresponding valorizing of the pseudo-biographical texts at the expense of the miscellanies took hold. Although the divisions proposed by Schulz can be useful, it must be emphasized that they are a *post hoc* attempt to rationalize and make orderly a highly disparate group of texts. Something of the difficulty of defining the jest book is shown in the introduction to Wilson's article, which excludes many types of jesting material—single jests, collections in verse, collections that mix comic and serious material, propaganda, and non-narrative humorous forms—and concludes, 'These reservations and exclusions may seem rigorous and sometimes arbitrary, but without them the theme becomes unmanageable.'[7]

Rather than seeing the early modern jest book as a specific and manageable genre, it may make more sense to view it as a manifestation of a broader culture of jesting, laughter, and wit, a culture (as our subsequent discussion will demonstrate) that extends considerably beyond collections of jokes and that involves complex tensions between popular and learned social markings. Tudor joke collections have the appearance of popular literature, and since most were cheap, crudely illustrated if at all, and dealt with topics (doctors, ignorant clergy, slippery lawyers, back-talking wives, fools, apes, the body, verbal gaffes, foreigners, tricksters) in ways that can appear coarse, one can see why they came to seem more suited to semi-literate servants and apprentices than to scholars, lawyers, merchants, and courtiers. Yet while Benedick may scoff that Beatrice has taken her wit from *A C. Mery Talys* he would be startled if she were to take it from Cicero, even though some of the Roman's jokes reappear in Tudor jest books. Indeed, to judge from a phrase or two, Benedick himself has probably been reading *Tales and quicke answeres* (1535), a collection that takes many of its jests from the bookish world of continental humanism.[8] The Tudor jest book has, in fact, an impressive ancestry in written works, if also, presumably, roots in oral tradition going back to caveman days. That ancestry includes classical and Renaissance discussions of the value of jokes (*facetiae*) and wit (*eutrapelia*) to rhetoric, courtiership, conviviality, and political ambition. It includes learned humanist wit and equally learned thoughts on humour's relation to logic, language, food, health, and the body.[9] And it includes theorizing on laughter from

---

[6] E. Schulz, 'Die englischen Schwankbücher bis herab zu *Dobson's Drie Bobs*', *Palaestra*, 117 (1912).

[7] F. P. Wilson, 'The English Jest-Books of the Sixteenth and Early Seventeenth Centuries', in *Shakespearian and Other Studies* (Oxford: Clarendon Press, 1969), 287.

[8] K. P. Chapman, '"Lazarillo de Tormes," a Jest-Book and Benedik', *Modern Language Review*, 55.4 (1960): 565–7.

[9] See C. Holcomb, *Mirth Making: The Rhetorical Discourse on Jesting in Early Modern England* (Columbia: University of South Carolina Press, 2001) on this and much more.

ancient to early modern times. This essay will first lay out this background and then more specifically describe the Tudor jest books themselves.

Benedick's friends would have read in Cicero (and in Quintilian, after his rediscovery by the Italian humanist and jest book writer Poggio Bracciolini) that *facetiae* can usefully affect an audience—fellow senators, for example, or judges in a law court. Cicero devotes a section of his dialogue *De Oratore* to jesting,[10] offering so many examples that, collected, they would make a fine jest book, and indeed his secretary Tiro gathered evidence of his master's wit into volumes now lost.[11] A number of the dialogue's *facetiae* reappear in Renaissance collections, some by way of the second book of Macrobius's fifth-century *Saturnalia*, which imagines a talkative feast for witty guests during Rome's winter festival. There is no space here to list Ciceronian jokes with Tudor progeny, but compare the man who assures a friend standing outside the front door that he is not at home—why will the friend not believe the homeowner himself on the matter?—with Thomas Wilson's version in his *Arte of Rhetorique* (1563).[12] A jest in the same passage about a married man who, hearing that a neighbour's wife has hanged herself on a tree, asks for a slip of that same tree reappears, with a pious allegorical moral appended to it, in the medieval *Gesta Romanorum*.[13]

Cicero's speakers' comments on persuasive laughter would be important to later thinking about the art of being a witty man, a *vir facetus*, as well as about the utility of jests, the inappropriateness of laughing at true wickedness or true wretchedness, the dangers of mere buffoonery, the opportunity for performance, the need for tact, the pleasure of puns, the value of plausibility, and the effectiveness of irony and of unexpected reversals.[14] An example of this last shows how such jests can give us philosophical pause, not just a few laughs: after his loss of the city of Tarentum to Hannibal, Livius has still managed to hold the town's citadel until Fabius recaptures Tarentum itself; Livius then begs Fabius 'to remember that the recapture of Tarentum had been due to his own achievement'. Of course, I remember, replies Fabius, for 'I could never have recaptured the place had you not lost it' (II.lxii.273). The story relates to both psychology and logic, evidence that 'there is no source of laughing-matters from which austere and serious thoughts are not also to be derived' (II.lxi.250). Just as significant for the Tudors are Cicero's distinctions between jests based on *words* and those based on *facts* or *matter* (II.lix.240) and between the snappy one-liner (what we call the 'zinger') and the anecdote ('A funny thing happened on the way to the Forum'). *Tales and quicke answeres* recapitulates this distinction in its title,

---

[10] Marcus Tullius Cicero, *De Oratore*, trans. E. W. Sutton (Cambridge, MA: Harvard University Press, 1968), II.liii.214–II.lxxi.289.

[11] H. Bennett, 'The Wit's Progress: A Study in the Life of Cicero', *The Classical Journal*, 30.4 (1935): 193–202 (194).

[12] Thomas Wilson, *Arte of Rhetorique* (1553), ed. T. Derrick (New York: Garland, 1982), 302.

[13] Cicero, *De Oratore*, II.lxviii.276–lxix.278; Wilson, *Arte of Rhetorique*, 304–5.

[14] B. C. Bowen, 'Ciceronian Wit and Renaissance Rhetoric', *Rhetorica*, 16.4 (1998): 409–29; J. M. Martin, 'Cicero's Jokes at the Court of Henry II of England: Roman Humor and the Princely Ideal', *Modern Language Quarterly*, 51.2 (1990): 144–66; and G. Luck, '*Vir Facetus*: A Renaissance Ideal', *Studies in Philology*, 55 (1958): 107–21.

and indeed includes a version of Cicero's jest: 'Livius that kepte the castell with a garrison, sayde bostynge himselfe/that Fabius had gotte the towne through him and his helpe. you saye trouthe/quod Fabius, for if you had nat loste the towne, I shulde neuer haue gotte it.'[15]

Those who produced Tudor jest books were conversant with theories of laughter that assumed strong the ties between *psyche* (mind/soul) and *soma* (body) that would later be severed by Descartes and then reconnected in our own time. 'Laughter is the best medicine' was thought literally true. A joke is a *Pil to Purge Melancholy*, as one anonymous work called itself in 1599, and in 1628 the title page of *Robin Good-Fellow, His Mad Prankes, and merry Iests* calls itself 'a fit *Medicine for Melancholy*'.[16] Laughter can even pack on the pounds, so the undernourished might try John Taylor's *Laugh, and be Fat* (1612), or if feeling ill could turn to S. R.'s *Doctor Merry-man: Or, Nothing but Mirth* (1619), including its possible play on 'nothing', for the Renaissance enjoyed jokes about no-things and no-bodies.[17] Such titles derive from Galenic medical theory, including that of the medieval 'School of Salerno' summarized in a poem translated by Sir John Harington as *The Englishmans doctor. Or, The schoole of Salerne* (1608). A line in the opening stanza gives the gist: 'Use three Physicians still; first Doctor Quiet,/Next Doctor Merry-man, and Doctor Diet.'[18] Get some rest, eat right, and, so to speak, take a little humour for your humours' sake. Careful, though, for although laughing will help dissolve your brain's black bile, guffaws can cause cardiac arrest or apoplexy.[19] True, there was a certain rich man dying of an intestinal obstruction, unable even to pass gas, who gave up on recovery and prayed for his soul's salvation; his fool chortled that God would hardly grant him Heaven after denying him so small a thing as a fart—and the invalid laughed so hard that the obstruction shook loose.[20] Then there is the dolt who misunderstood his doctor's order to give his sick wife an 'apricot' and gave her an 'ape'—but the ape's antics made her laugh so merrily that she got well.[21]

Apes, like parrots, may figure in Renaissance jests because their disconcerting similarity to ourselves provokes the mixture of pleasure and anxiety that many associated with laughter. Writers on jesting usually recognized its relation to darker forces in society and the psyche, but most important on the mechanics of ambivalence was Laurent Joubert's *Treatise on Laughter*, written in the 1560s but published in 1579; a short English version of his theories is found, for example, in Timothy Bright's *Treatise of Melancholie*

---

[15] Quoted from the 1567 edition, F4ᵛ.

[16] J. Nielson, 'Elizabethan Realisms' (Ph.D. dissertation, McGill University, 1990) offers an edition and lists more such titles.

[17] H. Wilcox, '"Needy Nothing Trimmed in Jollity"', in J. M. Dutcher and A. L. Prescott, eds., *Renaissance Historicisms* (Cranbury: Associated University Presses, 2008), 313–29.

[18] *The Englishmans Doctor*, A6.

[19] V. C. Machline, 'The Contribution of Laurent Joubert's *Traité du Ris* to Sixteenth-Century Physiology of Laughter', in A. G. Debus and M. T. Walton, eds., *Reading the Book of Nature* (Kirksville: Sixteenth Century Journal Publishers, 1998), 251–64.

[20] Thomas Nashe, 'Philopotes', *Quaternio* (1633; 1635 edn., Nn3); cf. *A Banqvet of Jeasts* (1640), 5; William Erwin, '"Physicians are like Kings": Medical Politics and *The Duchess of Malfi*', *English Literary Renaissance*, 28.1 (1998): 95–117, cites Webster's pope who laughs so hard at madmen that his 'imposthume broke' (IV.ii.39–43).

[21] Zall, *A Hundred Merry Tales*, 71–2.

(1586).²² For Joubert, the risible entails a mixture of pain (that poor duke slipping on a puddle of his horse's urine arouses our human pity) and pleasure (what fun to see the high and mighty brought low). Even puns delight but traditionally elicit an 'ouch'. That synergy causes cardiac flutter as the pained heart sucks in restorative blood and the happy heart sends it forth to flush the skin—Joubert wrote before the discovery that blood circulates. This palpitation pulls on the pericardium, making the lungs feel alternate pressure and release so that we laugh, thus aerating the blood and making us more sanguine. Writing with similar assumptions, Richard Mulcaster suggests in his *Positions . . . [concerning] the Training vp of children* (1581) that since students' laughter 'stirreth the hart, and the adjacent partes, then the tickling and panting of those partes themselues' will warm them and move the blood along, curing their colds.²³ Even under Cromwell's hardly festive Commonwealth, *The Academy of Pleasure* (1656), a text on how to be witty at parties, argues that ' 'Tis Mirth that fills the veins with blood/More than wine, or sleep, or food'.²⁴

The role of ambivalence in such theories may be important for understanding both the cruelty of so many jests and the culture's mixed feelings towards deploying humour as a weapon against those 'others' even while helping 'us' to bond, and all the more tightly when jests come with feasting. *A Banqvet of Jeasts* (1630), the great bestselling jest book of the seventeenth century, advertises on the title page that it has not only 'moderne jests' but also 'Witty jeeres' and 'Pleasaunt taunts'.²⁵ Macrobius's *Saturnalia* is the source for the fifteenth-century *Mensa Philosophica*, translated in 1576 as *The Scholemaster, or Teacher of Table Philosophie*, and in 1609 as *The Philosophers Banqvet*. Henry Buttes's *Diets dry dinner* (1599) usefully offers entertaining stories and culinary advice on facing pages. That jests can both entertain a get-together, if only a fancied one at a printed 'banquet', and yet also exclude and mock, is nevertheless a worrisome utility. No wonder that Bishop George Webbe writes in *The Araignment of an Unruly Tongue* (1619) that the tongue can be 'an Arrow framed in the shop of the Scornefull, the feathers of it are Morologie [the art of the Fool] and Eutrapelie [here, witty scoffs] and Jests, it is headed with a desire to disgrace' and sent by the demon Belial.²⁶ Indeed, Sir William Cornwallis, in his *Essayes* (1600), for whom jesting protects 'the wit and the bodie' by letting out 'superfluous humours' much as a sore can do, compares jokes to 'breaking of winde'—to farts.²⁷ Nor did scripture fully clarify matters. In Ephesians 5:4 Paul condemns *eutrapelia*

---

²² Timothy Bright, *Treatise of Melancholie*, trans. G. D. du Rocher (Tuscaloosa: University of Alabama Press, 1980); see also A. L. Prescott, 'The Ambivalent Heart: Thomas More's Merry Tales', *Criticism*, 45.4 (2003): 417–33, and Q. Skinner, 'Why Does Laughter Matter to Philosophy?' The Passmore lecture (December 2000). Available at http://socpol.anu.edu.au/archives/passmore.

²³ *Positions Wherein Those Primitive Circvmstances be Examined, which are Necessarie for the Training vp of Children, either for skill in their booke, or health in their bodie* (1581), H4ᵛ.

²⁴ *The Academy of Pleasure*, E5.

²⁵ See, e.g., M. Jenneret, *Des mets et des mots. Banquets et propos de table à la Renaissance* (Paris: Corti, 1987), trans. J. Whiteley and E. Hugues as *A Feast of Words: Banquets and Table Talk in the Renaissance* (Chicago: University of Chicago Press, 1991).

²⁶ *The Araignment of an Unruly Tongue*, D4.

²⁷ 'Of Iestes, and Iesters', in *Essayes*, I3; Cornwallis also complains, not unlike Benedick twitting Beatrice, of those who memorize jokes and 'robbe books' (I3).

(here meaning mockery), misleadingly translated in the Vulgate as 'scurrility', and yet some Church Fathers had thought laughter both healthy and useful as a weapon against God's enemies: those 'eutrapelie'-feathered arrows had long been used in religious polemic.[28] Understandably, then, the militantly Protestant Geneva Bible (1560) translates *eutrapelia* as 'jesting' but then in a marginal note identifies this as 'ether vaine, or els by example and evil speaking may hurt your neighbour: for other wise there be divers examples in the Scriptures of pleasant talke, which is also godlie' (Ephesians 5:4, note b).

'Godlie' or not, 'pleasant talke' was welcome in Renaissance humanist circles. The art of jesting, whether the inborn ability to shoot witticisms from an inner quiver of wit or retell stories taken from an inner anthology of jests, was vital for rhetoricians striving to amuse, impress, and hence convince. And so the Renaissance jest book, keeping an eye on Cicero and other ancient writers, began in the largely male and Latin-speaking world of papal secretaries and humanist scholars with the *Liber Facetiarum* (A Book of Jests) that Poggio Bracciolini composed in 1451.[29] Some condemned its obscenity, the Council of Trent put it on the Index of forbidden books (for its anticlerical humour?), and modern translators have until recently bowdlerized it, but its jests were hugely popular. Many exploit paradox, logical fallacy, and non sequiturs in ways that would entertain both medieval scholastics and Renaissance humanists. The jests value verbal dexterity and ridicule ignorance, although one would need to choose listeners wisely if retelling stories such as that of the priest who so condemns adultery that he says he would rather make love to ten virgins than to one married woman; the smart replies by women, though, would please those in Thomas More's circle. Poggio, himself of the middle class, wishes to be read by witty men well read in the humanities, although lesser readers are welcome if they do not condemn his wit (89).

Like those of Cicero, Macrobius, Aulus Gellius, and other classical writers, and as the wit of Erasmus or More would also do, Poggio's jests circulated widely, evolving as they went.[30] One tells of a man who dreams a demon gives him a 'ring' that will keep his wife faithful and awakens to find his finger in his wife's vagina (#133, p. 121). Rabelais modifies this into a joke about the jeweller Hans Carvel, and it reappears, as do many other classical and Renaissance jests, in *Tales and quicke answeres* (B1ᵛ). Another example: the actor Gonnella offers, for a fee, to turn a citizen into a diviner, or soothsayer. The two lie in the same bed, into which Gonnella emits a silent fart, then tells the man to sniff the sheets, and when the man says, 'You've farted!' the actor says, 'Pay up, for you have rightly divined' (#165, p. 135; compare *Tales and quicke answeres*, in which smelling a fart becomes inadvertently eating a 'turd' [I1–I1ᵛ]). No wonder that William Caxton put some jests by Poggio at the end of his 1484 edition of Aesop.[31]

---

[28] M. A. Screech, *Laughter at the Foot of the Cross* (London: Penguin, 1997), chap. 33.

[29] 'Selections from the *Facetiae* of Poggio Bracciolini', trans. J. S. Salemi, *Allegorica*, 8.1–2 (1983): 77–178.

[30] One joke, for example, may be found in Macrobius, the late medieval *Mensa Philosophica*, Ottmar Luscinius, A. Barlandus, and *Tales and quicke answeres*: asked why he makes pretty pictures and ugly children, a painter replies that he makes art by day and babies by night (*Tales and quicke answeres*, I1).

[31] Zall, *Hundred Merry Tales*, 39–56.

Educated Englishmen had other Latin jest books to enjoy, published in a number of countries. Heinrich Bebel's *Facetiae* (1508, 1512) was hugely popular, says Barbara C. Bowen in her invaluable catalogue of Renaissance jest books, and it too was a source of later joking in print.[32] Such books must often record jokes heard from servants and in taverns, but many explicitly reject the opinion of 'rustics': 'I joke and play and I have no regard for any judgement passed by uninspired and rustic men', says Bebel, for they do not know that 'such works have been written by the most learned, serious and saintly men'.[33] 'Learned', 'serious', and even 'saintly' Englishmen exploited these jests in part because so many are related to the paradoxes and dilemmas (including the ancient '*insolubilia*') that in the Middle Ages had provoked thought about formal logic and that in the Renaissance, with its shift towards rhetoric, had sometimes been turned from syllogistic aporia into mini-narratives.[34] When pondered, these jokes can disconcert. Some raise questions about null sets: a man agrees to pay forty shillings or 'nothing' for a dagger; when it is time to pay up and the buyer has neither cash nor anything that is 'nothing', the wife hangs up a broken pot and tells the seller the money is in it. Find anything? 'Mary quod he Ryght nought'. Then, she says, you are paid.[35] Zero ('cipher') was still new in the early Renaissance, and there may be nervousness behind the punch line. When a professor, out with a bird catcher, exclaims in English that many birds have settled on the net, the alarmed birds fly off. Please! Silence! The birds return. 'Multae aves adsunt', he now says, and the birds take wing. Again rebuked, the puzzled scholar asks if the birds understand Latin.[36] This is not just a dumb professor joke (an ancient genre) but one on signs and signifiers. A logician would also enjoy a 'convertible': a slugabed youth has a fine answer when told that his brother, up early, has acquired somebody's lost purse. Sure, says the lazy son, and if the owner of the purse had stayed in bed he would not have dropped his money.[37] Over and over one finds in the Tudor jest book, along with many other types of joke, materials appealing to those who had studied or taught the *trivium*. No wonder there is such overlap between the Latin epigrams of More and both English and continental jest books, or that the wit of Erasmus's colloquies can be found in Tudor jokes.

If useful for playing with logic, as the educated (and presumably even those with little Latin and less Greek) also knew, jests serve oral or printed performance, which is why Wilson's *Arte of Rhetorique* devotes a section to them, taking its many examples, for this discussion is in effect a mini-jest book, from Poggio and others, including Cicero, whose categories Wilson adopts and simplifies into narratives and snappy replies. Wilson

---

[32] Reprinted, with other relevant essays, in Barbara C. Bowen, *Humour and Humanism in the Renaissance* (Aldershot: Ashgate, 2004). Bowen describes many humanist jest books ignored here. See also her *One Hundred Renaissance Jokes* (Birmingham: Summa, 1988).

[33] S. Coxon, 'Friendship, Wit and Laughter in Heinrich Bebel's *Facetiae*', *Oxford Berman Studies*, 36.2 (2007): 306–20 (310).

[34] A. L. Prescott, 'Humanism in the Tudor Jestbook', *Moreana*, 24.95–96 (1987): 5–16.

[35] *A C. Mery Talys*, C6.

[36] *Tales and quicke answeres*, I3–I3^v; cf. Poggio, 179.

[37] *A C. Mery Talys*, E5.

claims that jesting helps 'quicken' the 'dulnesse of mannes nature', and that 'the wittie' have 'delitefull saiynges, and quicke sentences' to gain 'good wil'.[38] But rhetoric is also aggressive: aim a joke at somebody and you can 'dashe hym out of countenanunce' (277) and 'make him at his wittes end' (275). 'Pleasaunte sporte' with verbal ambiguities and surprises is also for battle. Some jokes are violent (those who call Christ's words 'this is my body' a mere 'trope' deserve what is left when the t in 'trope' is removed [288]). Some are cruel: Wilson recognizes the 'doggysh' misogyny that energizes the joke about the wife who hangs herself on a tree (305, margin), and he notes smoothly that 'Deformitie of bodye moveth myrthe' (295, margin).

Wit, though, also serves those competing for power and place at a royal or ducal court. The expert on courtly wit was of course Baldassare Castiglione, who may devote the final pages of his *Courtier* (1528) to Platonic love but who gives over some of Book II to the art of the jest, recalling Cicero and anticipating Wilson in creating what is in effect a jest anthology. Those hoping for place at the Tudor or Stuart court would have known of Castiglione, perhaps in the 1561 translation by Thomas Hoby. The context evoked, moreover, is not the homosocial world of Latin-reading scholars or rhetoricians but that of fashion, politics, and witty conversation between the sexes—if also of danger and dissimulation.[39] That world, like those of Cicero, Poggio, and Wilson, thrives on competition and aggression, but its sharp wit is somewhat blunted by courtesy and gallantry even though, inevitably, the jests denigrate the uncourtly and uneducated so as to make us laugh even more securely in our social dominance; the *Courtier*, says the English title page, is for 'yonge gentilmen and gentilwomen abiding in court, palaice, or place'.[40] Adapting Cicero's theory of humour, Castiglione distinguishes between the zinger and the anecdote but adds the practical joke (or reports of practical jokes). The jests themselves are often well known or play with such familiar topics as smartass animals or stupid rustics: we hear of a sassy chess-playing ape, for example, and of an out-of-towner who thinks a trombone player swallows his instrument's movable tube. There are misinterpreted words, oversexed priests, clever women, and, yes, the wife who hangs herself on a tree. English courtiers who repeated these jokes word-for-word might have seemed to lack their own wit, for such jests are made less for adoption than for adaptation. One such English courtier, although he would not comfortably characterize himself as such, was also a Latin-speaking humanist and rhetorically clever lawyer: Thomas More. In all these roles he deployed his ready wit; even his last works, written in the Tower of London while he was awaiting death, are to an astonishing degree enlivened by witty replies and jesting anecdotes.[41] It is significant for the history of the Tudor jest book that it was his

---

[38] Wilson, *Arte of Rhetorique*, 274, 279.

[39] J. Cavallo, 'Joking Matters: Politics and Dissimulation in Castiglione's *Book of the Courtier*', *Renaissance Quarterly*, 53.2 (2000): 402–24; R. Grudin, 'Renaissance Laughter: The Jests in Castiglione's *Il Cortegiano*', *Neophilologus*, 58.2 (1974): 199–204.

[40] Baldassare Castiglione, *The Book of the Courtier*, ed. Virginia Cox, from Thomas Hoby's 1554 translation (London: Everyman, 1994).

[41] So are his polemics; see Prescott, 'The Ambivalent Heart', 422, for a joke from Poggio.

servant Walter Smith who published *XII Mery Iests of the Wyddow Edyth* (1525), his brother-in-law John Rastell who put together *A C. Mery Talys*, and his Latin epigrams that were mined by jest-collectors on the Continent and in England.

Whatever jest books' tumble down the Tudor socio-economic staircase and their exclusion from our own 'literary' canon, joking was once an art claimed for the likes of senators, lawyers, and countesses, although nobody would have denied that jests were also for taverns and playwrights.[42] Nor were jokes found only in jest books, for they enliven collections of epigrams, some emblem books, and such festive works known to the English as Leon Battista Alberti's *Intercenales* ('Dinner Pieces') and Erasmus's 'Convivium Fabulosum', a dialogue in which guests with names such as Eutrapelus and Philogelos ('Laughter Lover') take turns telling funny stories as they dine. And, despite the apparent slide from humanism to *Howleglass* (the English name for the German trickster Til Eulenspiegel, first published in English c.1510), the Restoration would see collections designed to provide gentlemen with anecdotes and clever retorts. Nevertheless, there was a social topple from the analyses and examples given in Book VI.3 of Quintilian's *Institutio oratoria* to collections that even apprentices could afford and that boasted not an Italian courtier or German humanist but, for example, Mother Bunch, who 'was very pleasant and witty, and could tell a tale, let a Fart, drink her draught, scratch her Arse, pay her groat as well as any Chymist of Ale whatsoever'.[43]

Of particular interest, then, is how these latter-day jest books handle jests: with what strategies—narratival, characterological, bibliographical—do they frame their jokes and joking stories? The literary, rhetorical, and philosophical genealogy of jesting and laughter that we have traced rarely has much impact on how English jest books present their material. *Tales and quicke answeres*, discussed above, is drawn mostly from Erasmus and Poggio, but it acknowledges little of its inheritance beyond ascribing a handful of its jests to Plutarch. Classical citation does intermittently ornament this collection, sometimes at considerable length, but it can be difficult to assess the text's seriousness. One version of the ever-popular 'kiss my ass' joke (a woman responds to a man's comment that he cannot kiss her mouth because of her long nose with an invitation to 'kysse me there [i.e. "where"] as I haue nere a nose') moves into a learned moral, full of high sentence, twice as long as the jest itself, while a jest about a dreaming man defecating in his bed prompts a discussion of the truth of dreams that quotes Tibullus, Claudian, and Valerius Maximus, and concludes with a brief discussion of Chaucer's 'Nun's Priest's Tale' and *The House of Fame*.[44] In these cases, it is easy to imagine that the writer is mocking a learned approach to base and vulgar humour, even

---

[42] And, of course, the slide has been halted by our contemporary interest in cultural studies; we even have some brainy booklets on joking and philosophy with such titles as Thomas Cathcart and Daniel Klein's *Plato and a Platypus Walk into a Bar* (New York: Abrams Image, 2006).

[43] Quintilian, *Institutio Oratoria*, ed. and trans. H. E. Butler (Cambridge, MA: Harvard University Press, 1921), II, 439–501 (the analysis of jesting makes a culturally important distinction between sophisticated *urbanitas* and clod-hopping *rusticitas* [446]); *Pasquils Jests: With the Merriments of Mother Bunch* (1632), A3.

[44] *Tales and quicke answeres*, A3–A3^v, C2–C2^v.

though the latter jest has a classical pedigree: in the pseudonymous fourth-century Greek jest book, *Philogelos*, a fig-filled and irritable dreamer cannot avoid defecating in his bed—twice.[45] Towards the end of the period under consideration here, *The Booke of Bvlls* (1636) opens with a pair of dedications, 'To the Blinde Reader' and 'To the Discerning Reader'.[46] Discerning readers are praised for their literary understanding of jest books, aware 'that men excellent among the Greeks, and Latines, have not beene ashamed to Father them', but blind readers are told, 'You cannot dislike them [the jests], unless you are out of love with your own compositions, for out of such simples as you they are certainly compounded as a log is made of a Beetle' (A5^v, A2–A2^v). A jest book imagined as part of a genealogy of wisdom is contrasted to one imagined as formed from collecting and reshaping the composition (or compositions) of the simple (with a pun on 'simple' as a medicinal herb) populace. Less aggressively, the author of *The Cobler of Caunterburie* (1590; see Fig. 21.1) observes, 'Here is a gallimaufre of all sorts, the Gentlemen may finde *Salem*, to sauour their eares with Iestes: and Clownes plaine dunstable dogrell to make them laugh, while their leather buttons flie off.... Thus have I sought to feed all mens Fancies: which if I doe, was it not well done of a Cobler?'[47]

It also seems significant that virtually no English jest books present strong claims of direct authorship. *Wyddow Edyth*, as we noted above, concludes with the words 'by Walter Smith', Thomas More's servant—a statement ironically underscored by the chapters in which Edyth visits More's household and interacts with Smith himself.[48] But such direct authority, however comically inflected, is exceedingly rare. *A Banqvet of Jeasts* does offer an author's address to the reader, but it contains a commonplace argument against the charge of plagiarism: 'I doe not challenge them for mine owne, but gathered from the mouthes of others; and what is stale to me, may be to thee new' (A4^v). Books of jokes seem to be an inherently reproductive genre; in almost all cases, the wit they publish is coded as coming from somewhere else. This is especially true of the collections of longer stories: the jests and songs of *Robin Good-fellow* are told to the narrator by an alehouse hostess on a wet afternoon in Kent; those of *Westward for Smelts* (1620) are related by a group of women that the narrator is ferrying downriver; those of *Tarltons newes out of Purgatorie* (1590, see below) are told by the ghost of Richard Tarlton. In an interesting illustration of the growing power of authorship (and, eventually, the rise of 'Merry England' as a useful marketing tool), *A Banqvet of Jeasts* gradually becomes the work of Archie Armstrong, James I's jester. In the earliest editions of the jest book the address to the reader is signed 'Anonimous' (A5). It is not until 'The sixth Edition, much enlarged for the delight of the Reader' (1640), that the epistle is retitled, 'The Kings Iester to the Reader', although still

---

[45] *The Philogelos or Laughter-Lover*, trans. and ed. B. Baldwin (Amsterdam: Gieben, 1983), no. 243, p. 46. Other jokes concern foolish intellectuals, wives, charlatans, bad breath, astrologers, and more.

[46] *The Booke of Bvlls*, A1, A4.

[47] *The Cobler of Caunterburie*, A3–A3^v.

[48] *XII mery Jests, of the wyddow Edyth* (1573), H3^v. On this jest book, see especially Anne Lake Prescott, 'Crime and Carnival at Chelsea: Widow Edith and Thomas More's Household', in Clare M. Murphy, Henri Gibaud, and Mario A. Di Cesare, eds., *Miscellanea Moreana: Essays for Germain Marc'hadour* (Binghampton, NY: Medieval and Renaissance Texts and Studies, 1989), 247–64.

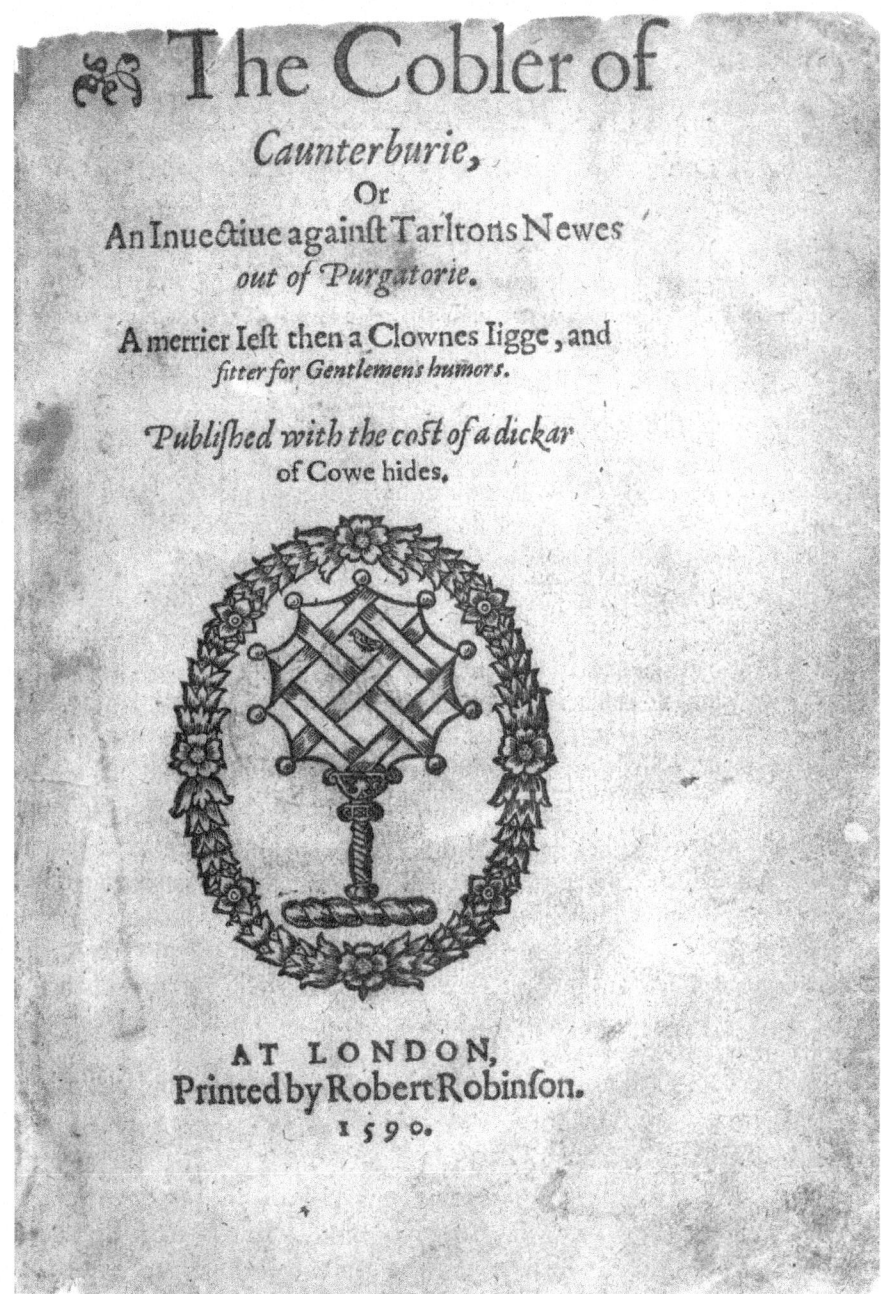

FIGURE 21.1 Anon., *The Cobler of Caunterburie* (1590), title page

signed 'Anonymous'.[49] By 1660 the epistle is signed 'Archee', and the same year saw a related jest book, *A Choice Banquet*, 'Being an Addition to Archee's Jests, taken out of his Closet, but never publisht by him in his life time'.[50] The fact remains, though, that while claims of novelty are commonplace in jest book introductions, this rarely extends to claims of authorial originality; in fact, the authority that the jest book claims typically derives from reproducing something whose origin is unknown or unknowable—witness the frequency with which even quips and puns tend to be framed dramatically, through an invented conversation. In this way, the printing of jests always involves, in complex ways, acts of appropriation. 'Who is speaking?' could be termed a foundational question for jest books. One reason for the relative obscurity of jest books in modern literary criticism is that they require—as do ballads, printed commonplace books, and other miscellanies—theoretical models that are not predicated on concepts of single or even collaborative authorship. In the absence of an authorial 'I', how can we imagine cultural authorization and appropriation functioning through the words on the page?

In English jest books questions of authorship are often elided completely, or are tacitly negotiated through ascribing the book to its nominal celebrity jester—as in *Merie Tales Newly Imprinted and made by Master Skelton Poet Laureat*, in which John Skelton is the dramatic speaker of the jests within the tales but not the maker of the words of the tales themselves. This jest book, which dates from 1567, was part of a surge of jest book publication in mid-century Tudor England, although Skelton had appeared as a comic character in both *A C. Mery Talys* and *Tales and quicke answeres*. The volume concludes with the comment, 'Thus endeth the merry Tales of Master Skelton, very pleasant for the recreation of the mind.'[51] From this perspective, the tales seem to claim primary kinship with the circulatory, anonymous, benign, appropriated, and twice-told narratives that typify jest book discourse. On the other hand, many of the stories name specific people, particularly Cardinal Wolsey (who also appears in *Wyddow Edyth*), and seem to draw on Skelton's personal history. A story in which Skelton refuses to employ his literary talents to authorize Wolsey's posthumous fame ends with the sentence, 'The whyche was verifyed of truthe' (B6). In one of the few moments at which a framing voice appears in the book, the details behind this legitimation are left out (verified by whom? and for whom? and how?), but the desire to use some idea of historical accuracy to validate the tale is apparent.

Religious issues play an important part in framing the *Merie Tales* of Skelton. Published nine years after Elizabeth took the throne, the tales are placed at least four decades earlier, in an England that was still Catholic. By virtue of its reliance on historical authorization—that is, by placing its tales in history through the authority of Skelton—the *Merie Tales* spans the divide of the English Reformation. In other words, in addition to the inherent tensions between oral and print circulation, and between oral and print authority, the *Merie Tales* has a specific historical

---

[49] *A Banqvet of Jeasts* (1640), A3, A5.
[50] *A Banqvet of Jeasts* (1660), A3ᵛ; *A Choice Banquet of Witty Jests, Rare Fancies, and Pleasant Novels* (1660), t.p.
[51] *Merie Tales Newly Imprinted and made by Master Skelton Poet Laureat* (1567), D3ᵛ.

dimension that freights these issues because of the particular forms of cultural legitimation that it employs. The apparent appropriation from oral culture that defines the jest book genre here becomes an act of historical and religious recuperation as well, a way of reframing a Catholic past with a present-day Protestant context. In the *Merie Tales*, religious appropriation has a paradigmatic relation to the appropriation of oral discourse. Indeed, the two are often inextricable, since much of the authority of the church as we see it here is vested in ritual and preaching. The inherent confrontation between the Catholic tales and the Protestant jest book, moreover, necessitates that this dynamic be articulated in the narratives through travesty, parody, and inversion. In the seventh tale, Skelton preaches a sermon to his congregation, which has complained to the Bishop that he keeps a whore and has fathered an illegitimate child. At stake in this tale, clearly, is an issue of appropriate behaviour, as well as of clerical authority. Skelton begins to preach by saying: '*vos estis vos estis*, that is to saye: you be, you be. And what be you?...I saye, that you bee a sorte of knaues, yea, and a man might saye, worse than knaues. And why, I shall show you: you haue complayned of mee to the Byshop' (A8ᵛ–B1). 'Vos estis' is the initial phrase of two well-known expressions from the Vulgate: *vos estis sal terrae* and *vos estis lux mundi*: 'you are the salt of the earth' and 'you are the light of the world', the words Jesus uses in the Sermon on the Mount to address his disciples and define their communal mission. Skelton here appropriates this authorized meaning (itself a particularly appropriate expression of the hierarchical relationship between priest and congregation) and parodically inverts it, transforming a statement of religious and spiritual community into a comic attack on his parishioners. There is a close resemblance, furthermore, between the illegitimate son and the *Merie Tales*, a work whose genealogical connection to its alleged progenitor is murky.

The case of Skelton is exemplary of the popular reception of a number of Renaissance writers, once famous for wit, who later found themselves as the protagonists or even supposed authors of a jest book, a fate that also befell the French poet Clément Marot (perhaps thanks to his self-mockery). In *The Art of English Posie*, George Puttenham confirms the transformation by mocking the 'rimes of *Skelton* (usurping the name of a Poet Laureat) being in deed but a rude rayling rimer and all his doings ridiculous, he used both short distaunces and short measures pleasing onely the popular eare: in our courtly maker we banish them utterly'.[52] On the other hand, Ben Jonson's 1625 masque *The Fortunate Isles* celebrates Skelton. An 'airy spirit...and the intelligence of Jupiter's sphere' named Jophiel comes forth to wish James and the court goodnight and begin the masque; he is interrupted by the entry of Merefool, 'a melancholic student in bare and worn clothes' who has taken up Rosicrucianism and is distressed that he has had no reward for the hunger, thirst, and self-mortification that such mystical travails apparently demand.[53] Intending to have some fun with Merefool, Jophiel tells him that he has

---

[52] George Puttenham, *The Arte of English Poesie*, ed. Hilton Landry (Kent, OH: Kent State University Press, 1970), 96.

[53] *The Fortunate Isles*, in *Ben Jonson: The Complete Masques*, ed. Stephen Orgel (New Haven: Yale University Press, 1969), lines 1–2, line 14.

been sent by the Rosicrucians to serve him, and will summon whatever historical personages Merefool would like to see. Merefool excitedly asks for Zoroaster, Pythagoras, Plato, and so on. Jophiel claims each one is currently unavailable, and offers instead such figures as Howleglass, Skelton, and Scogan (the star of *Scoggins Jests*).[54] Eventually, Merefool is persuaded that Skelton and Scogan should be summoned in place of ancient philosophers. The antimasque proper consists of 'Howleglass, the four knaves, two ruffians (Fitz-Ale and Vapor), Elinor Rumming, Mary Ambree, Long Meg of Westminster, Tom Thumb and Doctor Rat' (lines 277–9). The masque has a particularly English aspect; 'Not content with the wit of his own times', as Jophiel explains to Skelton and Scogan, Merefool 'Is curious to know yours, and what hath been' (lines 205–6). Thus Skelton and Scogan stand as nostalgic symbols, 'in like habits as they lived' (line 193), 'restored to memory of these times' (line 214), representing a popular and vernacular tradition reaching back into English history. Yet if these figures have a nostalgic and nationalist look, they also have a palpable contemporary and commercial aspect from the continued publication of their jest books and poetry. Skelton and the other characters are less static figures that synchronically memorialize a historical moment than mobile entities whose dimensions are diachronic and involve relations within past, present, and future contexts.[55]

Such ghostly mobility also characterizes the emergence of Richard Tarlton, the famous Elizabethan comedian, as a jest book figure.[56] The escapades of *Tarltons Jests* (1611) are replete with specifics designed to contribute local colour. One jest begins, 'At the Bull in Bishops-gate-street, where the Queenes Players oftentime played'.[57] Another describes musicians coming to visit Tarlton 'when he dwelt in Gracious-street at the signe of the Saba, a Tauerne' (B2^v–B3^r). Still, Zall remarks, 'One-quarter [of the jests] seem based on "fact" drawn from such sources as [John] Stow's *Annals* (1592) or from contemporaries who had known Tarlton. The remainder are familiar from conventional jest books.'[58] Whether or not we see *Tarltons Jests* as a genuine relic of Tarlton's wit and jesting, the volume draws its subject (if not its subject matter) from a much earlier volume, *Tarltons newes out of Purgatorie*, first published in 1590 and pseudonymously authored by Robin Goodfellow. Within the frame of the story, a sleeping Robin (having

---

[54] There is some dispute about whether Jonson meant the poet Henry Scogan or John Scogan, who had been Edward IV's jester. In his edition of the masques, Stephen Orgel writes, 'This was a common confusion, but Jonson is not guilty of it' (337). If this is correct, it does nothing to explain why Jonson put Skelton and Scogan together.

[55] See Jonathan Gil Harris, 'Shakespeare's Hair: Staging the Object of Material Culture', *Shakespeare Quarterly*, 52.4 (2001): 479–91.

[56] On Tarlton's celebrity, see especially Alexandra Halasz, '"So beloved that men use his picture for their signs": Richard Tarlton and the Uses of Sixteenth-Century Celebrity', *Shakespeare Studies*, 23 (1995): 19–38. On the exploitation of such figures see also R. W. Maslen, 'The Afterlife of Andrew Borde', *Studies in Philology*, 100.4 (2003): 463–92, who opens with the comment that 'Early modern England had a passion for reviving its dead clowns.'

[57] *Tarltons Jests* (1611), B2.

[58] P. M. Zall, *A Nest of Ninnies and Other English Jestbooks of the Seventeenth Century* (Lincoln: University of Nebraska Press, 1970), 91.

just fled the theatre for its noise and vulgarity) is visited by the ghost of Tarlton, who has been residing in 'a third place that all our great grandmothers haue talkt of, that Dant hath so learnedly writ of, and that is Purgatorie'.[59] Dante-like, Tarlton describes his travels through Purgatory, pausing at the strange torments various figures are enduring; each purgatorial encounter occasions a new merry tale, largely adapted from Italian *novelle* such as Boccaccio's *Decameron*.[60]

In the seventeenth century many jest books show a significant enlargement of the bibliographic apparatus: lengthy and multiple introductions, addresses to patrons, prefatory poems, and other framing material all become ubiquitous. Such expansive introductions do allow a space for the author's voice, but that voice remains typically anonymous and, as we noted earlier, rarely claims ownership of the actual jests. Rather, the space of authorship is used to delineate the complex discursive terrain that jests occupy and to negotiate the varying authorizing forces of oral recreation and printed commodification. *Wit and Mirth*, by John Taylor (first published in 1628), describes its contents as 'Chargeably collected out of Tavernes, Ordinaries, Innes, Bow-ling Greenes, and Allyes, Alehouses, Tobacco shops, Highwaies, and Water-passages./Made vp, and fashioned into Clinches, Bulls, Quirkes, Yerkes, Quips, and Ierkes./Apothegmatically bundled vp and garbled at the request of old Iohn Garrets Ghost'.[61] In one of the most complex authorial positionings of any jest book, Taylor provides three different explanations for the authority of his book. In the first sentence, oral circulation is figured as a chain of lower-class discursive locations, a list that is less an attempt to indicate the jests' provenance than an appeal to the authenticating power of the popular. The jest book becomes an urban network of sites of passage (highways, water-passages) and sites of recreation and mercantile transaction (taverns, tobacco shops). Taylor's role here is that of a field scholar, laboriously gathering the linguistic by-products of translation and exchange—his travels perhaps illustrated by the conical spiral of the sentence down to the exit point of water-passages, a type of location the 'Water Poet' claimed particularly as his own. The second sentence shifts from the oral into the literary, transforming the inventory of urban locations into a taxonomy of verbal wit. In this transformation, the figure of the author shifts from a travelling collector into a compiler and transformer, labelling oral fragments and fashioning them to fit particular literary categories. The project of translation continues in the third sentence, 'Apothegmatically bundled up and garbled at the request of old John Garrets ghost'. Taylor refers to his textual practice in the middle third of the book, where the prose stories suddenly acquire jocular verse tags explaining their moral pith or otherwise commenting on their meaning. In the context of anonymous prose stories, verse becomes an authorial supplement—authorial not only in its explicit craftedness, but also as part of the process of mediation and transla-

---

[59] *Tarltons newes out of Purgatorie* (1590), B2.

[60] Cf. Tarlton's other ghostly appearance in 1590, in *Almond for a Parrat*, one of the later anti-Martin Marprelate pamphlets. The epistle is dedicated to Will Kemp, 'Iestmonger and Vice-gerent [i.e., regent] generall to the Ghost of Dicke Tarlton' (A2).

[61] *Wit and Mirth* (1628), t.p.

tion, with Taylor offering his own readings of the jests as a guide to his readers' interpretations.

The presence of 'old John Garrets ghost' is the strangest authorizing presence in *Wit and Mirth*. Before the jests begin, Taylor gives us a verse dream vision in which the ghost of John Garret, a popular Elizabethan court wit or jester, appears 'to rouse thy dull and lazy Muse from idleness', commanding him to write a book of jests (A4ᵛ). In contrast to the ghost of Tarlton, who relates his own news, Garret merely motivates the jests that follow. This is a marvellously multivalent image. It effects a strategic substitution of the one for the many: instead of the overwhelming polyvocality implied by the first sentence of the title page, we are given the single voice of a singular jester who tells of his ambitious climb to the pinnacle of courtly wit, where, he says, 'my purse received what my wit did plow' (A5). The ghost is also obviously a figure for Taylor to emulate, a model of the social and financial gains available to a person of wit: a double, then, or perhaps a father. Indeed, the scene has a smack of *Hamlet* to it, although what Taylor records in his tables are exactly the trivial fond records that Hamlet erases. Through the supplement of the ghost the generic quality of Taylor's jest book, its implicit position in a genealogy of printed jests, is transformed into a familial genealogy, through a paternal voice of commandment and blessing. A paternal voice, moreover, that seeks to incorporate itself into Taylor's *corpus*, for the ghost complains that Taylor's previous works have neglected him. Driven on by this dream vision, the author becomes what Marjorie Garber might call a ghost-writer, fashioning his gathered material under the uncanny influence and mediating presence of past wit and mirth.[62]

The jest book's trip down from elite Latin to popularity and cheap print (if that is indeed 'down') took place during the period covered by this essay. The early vernacular Tudor jest books such as *A C. Mery Talys* and *Tales and quicke answeres* have sources deep in Roman and continental humanist jesting, but because they are in English, not Latin, their links to antiquity and to Renaissance humanism are easily forgotten. It is wise to remember, then, when reading Tudor jest books, that the earlier ones, however much they star members of the lower orders such as the dumb, dumber, and dumbest men of Gotham or such lowborn crooks as the protagonist of *Wyddow Edyth*, were not at first, or not admittedly, taken from the 'folk'. No matter how many versions of these jests were in fact told over an ale by peasants and apprentices—or no matter how often very ancient versions must have been told for millennia to relieve the tedium of hunting and gathering or to bond over a fire in front of the cave—in early modern Europe the printed versions had begun, at least in theory, as a revival of elite classical wit. We still bond over jokes, and now they circulate electronically in such numbers that we can each make and store collections of our own. It is time, looking back from the electronic age, to do the Tudor jest book more justice as an energetic and clever contribution to its own print and even oral culture, one that must have entertained readers of all classes, even the likes of Beatrice and Benedick.

---

[62] See Marjorie Garber, *Shakespeare's Ghost Writers: Literature as Uncanny Causality* (New York: Methuen, 1987).

Further Reading

Brown, Pamela. *Better a Shrew than a Sheep: Women, Drama, and the Culture of Jest in Early Modern England* (Ithaca: Cornell University Press, 2003).

Bowen, Barbara C. *Enter Rabelais Laughing* (Nashville: Vanderbilt University Press, 1998).

—— *Humour and Humanism in the Renaissance* (Aldershot: Ashgate, 2004).

Holcomb, Chris. *Mirth Making: The Rhetorical Discourse on Jesting in Early Modern England* (Columbia: University of South Carolina Press, 2001).

Kahrl, Stanley J. 'The Medieval Origins of the Sixteenth-Century English Jest-Books', *Studies in the Renaissance*, 13 (1966): 166–83.

Lipking, Joanna B. 'Traditions of the Facetiae and Their Influence in Tudor England' (unpublished dissertation, Columbia University, 1971).

Munro, Ian. '*A womans answer is neuer to seke*': Early Modern Jestbooks, 1526–1635 (Aldershot: Ashgate, 2007).

Prescott, Anne Lake. 'The Ambivalent Heart: Thomas More's Merry Tales', *Criticism*, 45.4 (2003): 417–33.

—— 'Humanism in the Tudor Jestbook', *Moreana*, 24.95–96 (1987): 5–16.

Thomas, Keith. 'The Place of Laughter in Tudor and Stuart England', *Times Literary Supplement* (21 January 1977): 77–81.

Woodbridge, Linda. *Vagrancy, Homelessness, and English Renaissance Culture* (Urbana: University of Illinois Press, 2001).

CHAPTER 22

POLITICAL PROSE

NICHOLAS MCDOWELL

More than in other literary forms, political argument and change are registered and initiated in prose: in any history of prose, the representation of political theory and communication of political argument must be to the fore. But it would be hard, and potentially misleading, to argue for 'political prose' as a satisfactory genre in its own right in the 1500–1640 period; rather, the political is a category which ranges across the modes of historical, philosophical, religious, and fictional writing and is to be found in such prose genres as the utopia, the dialogue, and travel writing, as well as works which have a more obviously polemical or theoretical political purpose. As has been recently pointed out, 'one of the problems with the concept of "political thought" is that it has tended to limit the number of places in which historians of early modern England have looked to find contemporaries thinking about politics' to those canonical texts which look most like modern, secular conceptions of a political treatise—although literary scholars over the last two decades have been more inclined than historians (and probably at times over-inclined) to hear the political resonance of every textual form.[1] My discussion below, which of course is necessarily highly selective, consequently encompasses several prose writers, prose works, and kinds of prose writing which are treated from other perspectives elsewhere in this volume.

This is not to say that educated early moderns did not have a concept of politics as a crucial branch of human behaviour and a distinct category of knowledge. In the humanist curriculum undertaken by every Elizabethan and Jacobean grammar-school boy, civil science (*scientia civilis*) was, as a subset of moral philosophy, part of the fifth and culminating element of the *studia humanitatis*. Some commentators argued that in the Aristotelian tripartite division of Renaissance moral philosophy into ethics, œconomics, and politics, the superior discipline was politics because it concerned the good of the state, which was a higher good than the individual or the family. Hence, Thomas Hobbes

---

[1] Peter Lake, 'Puritanism, (Monarchical) Republicanism, and Monarchy', *Journal of Medieval and Early Modern Studies*, 40.3 (2010): 463–97 (463).

felt justified in declaring in *De Cive* (1642) that in writing about civil science he was making a contribution to the most valuable of all of the sciences.[2] In *The Advancement of Learning* (1605), Francis Bacon concludes his anatomy of knowledge with 'Civil Knowledge', declaring, with a flourish, that 'with civil knowledge [I] have concluded Human Philosophy'. Later, in the *Novum Organum* (1619), he refers to 'natural philosophy [and] the other sciences, logic, ethics, and politics'. If politics hardly seems to equate with logic as the kind of science on which one might compose a textbook—it is, says Bacon in the *Advancement*, the 'subject which of all others is most immersed in matter, and hardliest reduced to axiom'—Bacon sought to develop something like a handbook to political behaviour in his *Essays, or Counsels, Civill and Morall* (1597, 1612, 1625), one of the best places to quarry for trenchant remarks on early modern English (elite) culture.[3] The *Essays*, in their initial 1597 incarnation, have aptly been described as 'an analysis of the language of politics' in the last decade of Elizabeth's reign; and, as we shall see, the aphoristic style of the *Essays* should remind us that, if the political did not habitually take any particular mode of prose, prose style was understood to imply particular political perspectives.[4]

Several further preliminary points should be made. The idea of 'English' political prose from 1500–1640 needs to be qualified firstly by the fact that several of the works discussed below, such as those by Thomas More and George Buchanan, were composed in Latin, the language of international scholarship and diplomacy, and later translated into English, and through translation found a more 'popular' (or at least literate) audience; and secondly, that several of the most influential political prose writers of the period were not English, such as the Scotsmen John Knox, Buchanan, and James VI and I. Finally, any discussion of political languages and ideas in Britain before 1640 is faced with the temptation of reading backwards from the political ferment of the Civil Wars of the 1640s and the constitutional innovations of the 1650s—two decades which are perhaps the great age of political prose in English—and so runs the risk of creating a falsely linear (or 'Whiggish') narrative of inevitable progress towards ideas and arguments that can look more like modernity. There has been a particularly lively debate over the last decade about the extent to which republican and anti-monarchical political thought existed before the execution of Charles I in 1649, in poetry and drama, as well as prose.[5] I seek here to side-step some of the pitfalls of anachronism, while preserving the outlines

---

[2] Jill Kraye, 'Moral Philosophy', in Charles B. Schmitt and Quentin Skinner, eds., *The Cambridge History of Renaissance Philosophy* (Cambridge: Cambridge University Press, 1988), 303–86 (305); Quentin Skinner, 'Hobbes's Changing Conception of Civil Science', in *Visions of Politics. Volume III: Hobbes and Civil Science* (Cambridge: Cambridge University Press, 2002), 66–86 (66).

[3] Francis Bacon, *Major Works*, ed. Brian Vickers (Oxford: Oxford University Press, 2002), 265, 288; *Works of Francis Bacon*, ed. J. S. Spedding, R. L. Ellis, and D. D. Heath, 14 vols. (London, 1857–74), IV, 112.

[4] F. J. Levy, 'Francis Bacon and the Style of Politics', in Arthur F. Kinney and Dan S. Collins, eds., *Renaissance Historicism* (Amherst, MA: University of Massachusetts Press, 1987), 146–67 (166).

[5] See, e.g., Andrew Hadfield, *Shakespeare and Republicanism* (Cambridge: Cambridge University Press, 2005); and the (sceptical) account in Blair Worden, 'Republicanism, Regicide and Republic: The English Experience', in Martin Van Gelderen and Quentin Skinner, eds., *Republicanism: A Shared European Heritage*, 2 vols. (Cambridge: Cambridge University Press, 2002), I, 307–28.

of the historical narrative—it is unquestionable, for example, that John Milton's apology for the regicide, *The Tenure of Kings and Magistrates* (1649), engages deeply and explicitly with the Calvinist resistance theory developed by Knox and Buchanan in the mid-sixteenth century—by focusing less on ideas of kingless government than on representations of the *abuse* of kingship.

I am particularly concerned with the impact of the two great movements of this period, the Renaissance and the Reformation, on perceptions of tyrants and definitions of tyranny in English prose. The first section of the essay sketches the influence of the Roman historian Tacitus on representations of kings, courts, and tyrants from the second decade of the sixteenth century to the third decade of the seventeenth; the second section explores the rise of, and reaction to, theories of resistance and tyrannicide that emerged from mid-sixteenth-century religious conflict, but were nonetheless indebted to classical thought. One conclusion that may be taken from the essay is the need for some qualification, in the British context at least, of Richard Tuck's powerful argument that the ideal of a life of active and virtuous public service that animated early and mid-sixteenth-century European political writing, largely derived from the Roman moralist Cicero, gave way after around 1580 to a 'reason of state' mentality, influenced by Tacitus, which was characterized by scepticism and flexible morality, and which could buttress absolutism as much as it could justify, in the context of the English revolution, political innovation.[6] This narrative of the development of political thought is interestingly comparable to once dominant and now much qualified arguments in the sphere of English prose style about a shift in late Elizabethan England from Ciceronian to Senecan and Tacitist styles. What we shall find, rather, is that Tacitist and Ciceronian political languages cohabited in English writing as early as Thomas More and the very beginning of the Henrician age. It should be emphasized, finally, that the prose works discussed below have been selected as far as possible both for their intellectual force and innovation *and* for their literary interest.

22.1 Tacitism and tyranny from More to Bacon

Within four years of the accession of Henry VIII to the throne in 1509, Thomas More (c.1478–1535) began to compose a history, apparently first in English and then in Latin, of the ascent of Richard III to power in the aftermath of the death of Edward IV in 1483. Both versions remained unfinished: More seems to have left them aside soon after he entered the King's service and became a Privy Councillor in 1517.[7] The vernacular *History of King Richard the Third* first appeared in several of the Tudor chronicle histories

---

[6] Richard Tuck, *Philosophy and Government, 1572–1651* (Cambridge: Cambridge University Press, 1993).

[7] The most recent discussion of the composition of the work is George M. Logan, 'More on Tyranny: The *History of King Richard the Third*', in Logan, ed., *The Cambridge Companion to Thomas More* (Cambridge: Cambridge University Press, 2011), 168–90.

published by Richard Grafton, before William Rastell published the text from More's own manuscript in his 1557 edition of More's works. (The reign of Mary I meant it was no longer potentially dangerous to advertise the name of More the Catholic martyr.) Thereafter, Rastell's text was incorporated into the Elizabethan chronicle histories of Holinshed (where Shakespeare read More and found inspiration for his *Richard III* [1592–3]) and Stow, with the result that its distinctiveness as a finely crafted prose narrative was to an extent submerged: its literary form, with invented orations given to characters in the narrative and an emphasis on the role of individual psychology in historical action and political behaviour, did not find a worthy vernacular imitation until Francis Bacon's *History of the Reign of Henry VII* (1622), which is similarly an important work of political thought, as well as historical and literary prose.

More's *History* is a highly sophisticated piece of historical writing which shows his humanist immersion in the techniques of classical history, particularly the ancient Roman historians Sallust, who charted the decline of the Roman republic into imperial tyranny; Tacitus, who recounted the tyrannical excesses of the early Roman emperors; and Suetonius, who wrote the lives of the 'Twelve Caesars'. Aristotle, in both the *Politics* and the *Nicomachean Ethics*, is very clear on the distinction between a king and a tyrant. As Milton explains in *The Tenure of Kings and Magistrates*: 'Aristotle and the best of Political writers have defin'd a King, him who governs to the good and profit of his People, and not for his own ends.'[8] Or, as More himself puts it in one of the 280 Latin epigrams that he composed in the first two decades of the sixteenth century, which were published in the 1518 edition of his *Utopia* (first pub. 1516), a tyrant 'feels that the people were created for him so that, of course, he may have subjects to rule'.[9] The tyrant treats all other people, whether civil subjects in the public sphere or friends and family members in the private, as purely instrumental in his pursuit or maintenance of power. The character of a tyrant as someone who is not bound by normative human bonds of affection and trust is exemplified in the famous character sketch of Richard at the beginning of the *History*, which also illustrates the influence on More of Tacitus's account of the emperors Tiberius and Nero as masters of dissimulation:

> Hee was close and secrete, a deepe dissimuler, lowlye of counteynaunce, arrogant of heart, outwardly coumpinable where he inwardely hated, not letting to kisse whome hee thoughte to kyll: dispitious and cruell, not for euill will alway, but after for ambicion, and either for the suretie or encrease of his estate. Frende and foo was muche what indifferent, where his advauntage grew, he spared no man deathe, whose life withstoode his purpose.[10]

---

[8] John Milton, *Political Writings*, ed. Martin Dzelzainis (Cambridge: Cambridge University Press, 1991), 10–11; see n. 36.

[9] See epigram no. 198, 'What is the best form of government' ('Quis optimus reipub.[lica] status'), in *Complete Works of St Thomas More. Volume 3, part 1: The Latin Poems*, ed. Clarence H. Miller et al. (New Haven and London: Yale University Press, 1984), 228–31.

[10] *Complete Works of St Thomas More. Volume 2: The History of King Richard III*, ed. Richard S. Sylvester (New Haven and London: Yale University Press, 1963), 8. All references to the *History* are to this edition.

The powerfully evocative phrase 'not letting to kisse whom he thought to kyll' is derived from the account in Tacitus, *Annals* 14.56 describing Nero's behaviour after he refuses to let his former tutor Seneca leave the court: Nero 'added to his words an embrace and kisses, [for] he was made by nature and trained by habit to veil his hatred with treacherous caresses' ('his adicit complexum et oscula, factus natura et consuetudine exercitus velare odium fallacibus blanditiis').[11] As Dermot Fenlon has observed, More's Richard 'thrusts his way forward from the pages of Suetonius and Tacitus to assume power in Renaissance England [as] a classical tyrant in a Christian setting'.[12]

Richard's most outrageous violation of natural bonds and boundaries is, of course, the murder of his two young nephews, the princes in the Tower, an act which 'al the bandes broken that binden manne and manne together, withoute anye respecte of Godde or the worlde' (p. 6). Nero's treatment of Seneca is pointedly recalled when Richard welcomes the second nephew out of the sanctuary of Westminster, with More extracting grim irony from Richard's title of 'Protector': 'The protector toke him in his armes & kissed him with these wordes: Now welcome my lord even with al my hart' (p. 42). Although Richard does not actually violate the church's law of sanctuary, he does force the Queen and her children out through intimidation, and More gives Richard's co-conspirator, Buckingham, a brilliant speech of rhetorical redescription or *paradiastole*, condemning sanctuary as a convention which preserves criminals from the law (pp. 30–2). Here we see how the tyrant makes even language and meaning subject to his will. For More, the abuse of the divine law of sanctuary also exemplifies the way in which tyranny subordinates God's law to the will of the tyrant; and the point is placed in the mouth of Queen Elizabeth: 'was there never tyrant yet so devilish, that durst presume to break [the right of sanctuary]' (pp. 37–8). The sacrament of marriage is then also violated by Richard when, with the connivance of self-interested clerics and lawyers, he works to secure his own legitimacy by having the marriage of Edward and Elizabeth declared retrospectively invalid. The tyrant's abuse of the marriage sacrament in More's *History*, of course, assumes ironic resonance in the light of More's later personal history, specifically his execution in 1535 by Henry VIII for refusing to accept his king's break from Rome in the pursuit of a divorce. Given that the *History* seems to have been composed before More entered Henry's service, if we want to relate it to Henry's rule we should probably treat it as a work of counsel to the new King, rather than a criticism of him—a warning of how good government, by which a king properly acts as a father to his people and which is exemplified in More's text by the rule of Edward IV, can rapidly fall into tyrannous conditions in which all human, natural, and divine law is violated and people are treated as slaves. Reginald Pole, once a scholar patronized by Henry and a man doubtless familiar with More's *History*, would later compare Henry both to Nero and to Richard III as one of the great tyrants of history.[13]

---

[11] Michele Valerie Ronnick, 'A Note Concerning Elements of Tacitus's Depiction of Nero in Thomas More's *Historia Richardi Regis Angliae*', *Moreana*, 36 (December, 1999): 64–5.

[12] Dermot Fenlon, 'Thomas More and Tyranny', *Journal of Ecclesiastical History*, 32 (1981): 453–76 (456). See also Logan, 'More on Tyranny'.

[13] Greg Walker, *Writing Under Tyranny: English Literature and the Henrician Reformation* (Oxford: Oxford University Press, 2005), 6.

In writing a Tacitist analysis of historical power politics, More anticipated, by well over half a century, the interest in later Elizabethan England in the depiction of tyranny, court corruption, and statecraft by the Roman historians, and in particular Tacitus. The interest was shaped by the so-called 'new humanism' of late sixteenth-century Europe, which was characterized, in the aftermath of the Florentine Niccolò Machiavelli's notorious separation of politics from morality in *The Prince* (c. 1513), by 'efforts to reconcile a pragmatic and analytical approach to politics with an underlying commitment to fundamental religious and ethical norms'.[14] Tacitus appealed to the pre-eminent 'new humanists' such as Montaigne and the great Flemish scholar Justus Lipsius because they saw analogies between life under the absolutist monarchies of their time and the tyrannies of imperial Rome; and also because Tacitus exposed the dissimulation and immorality that purchased success in political life but, unlike Machiavelli, he did not advocate the behaviour he described. There are glimpses of the fascination of More's historical style for those who were adapting Tactitus in England at this time. Tacitus was the principal source for Ben Jonson's tragic drama *Sejanus His Fall* (c. 1603), which depicts the suppression of liberty and virtue under Tiberius and his notorious favourite, Sejanus, and which powerfully conveys Jonson's sense, as Blair Worden puts it, of the Tiberian 'extravagance of servility and flattery' in the final years of Elizabeth's reign. Around the time he was writing *Sejanus His Fall* in 1602, Jonson accepted an advance for 'a book called Richard Crookback', presumably a play about Richard III. The work was never written, or has not survived, but Jonson's close annotation of his copy of More's Latin version of the *History* indicates that More would have been his principal source for 'Richard Crookback': there are over 1,600 annotations in 3,000 lines of print (whereas Jonson's copy of More's more famous exploration of politics and society, *Utopia*, is 'nearly unmarked').[15]

The first English translations of Tacitus's *Agricola* and *Histories*, by the Oxford scholar Henry Saville, appeared in 1591 and Richard Grenewey's rendering of the *Annals* followed in 1598: they inaugurated a vogue for Tacitist prose style, as well as political analysis.[16] The argument of Morris Croll, in his seminal articles, for a shift in English prose style at the end of the sixteenth century, from imitation of Ciceronian eloquence to a preference for the sharper, aphoristic, paradoxical style of Tacitus and the Stoic philosopher Seneca, was over-schematic and has since been much modified. Moreover, it has been shown that 'the relation between style and ideology' in England is more 'fluent and

---

[14] Malcom Smuts, 'Court-Centred Politics and the Uses of Roman Historians, c. 1590–1630', in Peter Lake and Kevin Sharpe, eds., *Culture and Politics in Early Stuart England* (Basingstoke: Macmillan, 1994), 21–44 (25). See more generally Peter Burke, 'Tacitism, Scepticism, and Reason of State', in J. H. Burns and Mark Goldie, eds., *The Cambridge History of Political Thought, 1450–1700* (Cambridge: Cambridge University Press, 1991), 479–98; Tuck, *Philosophy and Government*, passim.

[15] Blair Worden, 'Ben Jonson Among the Historians', in Lake and Sharpe, eds., *Culture and Politics in Early Stuart England*, 67–90 (77); Robert C. Evans, *Habits of Mind: Evidence and Effects of Ben Jonson's Reading* (Lewisburg: Bucknell University Press, 1995), 162, 168.

[16] On these translations and their influence, see Marku Peltonen, *Classical Humanism and Republicanism in English Political Thought, 1570–1640* (Cambridge: Cambridge University Press, 1995), 124–35.

provisional' than Croll maintained in his arguments that an 'Attic', anti-Ciceronian style expressed 'the disillusion of the modern intellectual under the absolutist regimes of the seventeenth century'.[17] Nonetheless, the heterodox political character of late Elizabethan English Tacitism is apparent in the association of several of its foremost exponents with the circle around the Earl of Essex, who led a failed insurrection against Elizabeth in February 1601, at a time when the anxiety about the succession to Elizabeth, which characterizes the 1590s, had reached a pitch. Saville, a known intimate of Essex, had written for his rendering of the *Histories* his own introductory account of the fall of Nero in the style of Tacitus: in this account deposition and resistance are viewed as morally indifferent political acts performed by men possessed both of classical virtue and Machiavellian *virtù*.[18] Saville's translation and original Tacitist work were very closely imitated by Sir John Hayward in his *The First Part of the Life and Raigne of King Henrie IIII* (1599), which depicts the deposition of a weak Richard II and the accession of Henry IV. The work was dedicated to Essex and Hayward was immediately suspected by Elizabeth herself of having had seditious intent in his history—of drawing implicit analogies between the weak Richard and Elizabeth, and between the virile Bolingbroke and Essex. Hayward was arrested and interrogated by Francis Bacon and Edward Coke, among others. Hayward was eventually released, but the attraction of his history to the supporters of Essex is suggested by their apparent arrangement of a dramatic adaptation of Hayward's work in the days before the rebellion, presumably to remind the audience of the historical precedent for the deposition of a monarch.[19]

Hayward, like More, invents speeches for his characters and adopts a semi-dramatic mode of prose—his work comes, of course, after a decade of history plays on the English stage—as he sets about exposing the 'politic history' of courts, according to which specific historical episodes reveal universal laws of human behaviour and motivation, applicable to all times.[20] But Hayward is also writing after Machiavelli and his history is Machiavellian in its morally neutral exploration of dark political arts and the psychology of political actors, expressed in aphoristic style. So Hayward has the Archbishop of Canterbury (supposedly the representative of Christian ethics) tell Bolingbroke that it is too late to step away from conflict over the throne because Bolingbroke is popularly spoken of as a contender: 'even good princes are nice in points of soveraignty & beare a nimble eare to the touch of that string' (p. 66). The aphorism is, in fact, taken straight from

---

[17] See, e.g., Morris Croll, 'Attic Prose: Lipsius, Montaigne, Bacon', in Stanley Fish, ed., *Seventeenth-Century Prose: Modern Essays in Criticism* (New York: Oxford University Press, 1971), 3–25; Deborah Shuger, 'Conceptions of Style', in Glynn P. Norton, ed., *The Cambridge History of Literary Criticism. Volume III: The Renaissance* (Cambridge: Cambridge University Press, 1999; pbk. edn., 2006), 176–86 (178, 185).

[18] David Womersley, 'Sir Henry Saville's Translation of Tacitus and the Political Interpretation of Elizabethan Texts', *Review of English Studies*, NS, 42 (1991): 313–42.

[19] The conventional assumption that the play was Shakespeare's *Richard II* is shown to be wrong by Blair Worden, if not quite conclusively, in 'Which Play was Performed at the Globe on 7 February 1601?', *London Review of Books*, 23.13 (10 July 2003): 22–4.

[20] F. J. Levy, 'Hayward, Daniel and the Beginnings of Politic History', *Huntington Library Quarterly*, 50 (1987): 1–34.

Savile's own effort at Tacitist history, 'The Ende of Nero and Beginning of Galba', when Titus Vinius tells his friend Galba that he has no choice but to proceed with rebellion against Nero: 'Even good princes are jelous of soveraine points, and that string being touched, have a quicke eare.'[21] Elizabeth's reaction to Hayward's 'politic history' made the Tacitist (and Machiavellian) point that had caught Hayward's eye in Savile.

Although Francis Bacon had been called in to comment on the seditious implications of Hayward's book, in the context of its dedication to Essex, Bacon had himself been a client of Essex until 1597 and his writing of that period exhibits a considerable Tacitist influence. In the first edition of the *Essays*, which appeared in that year, each essay consists essentially of a series of separated aphorisms, in which, as elsewhere in his work, Bacon sets about 'constructing a system [of knowledge] using an anti-systematic form', so that the structure of the argument becomes 'cellular', rather than sequential, clustering aphorisms which develop various perspectives on a theme.[22] The 1597 *Essays* are characterized by a dispassionate Machiavellian political realism, as Bacon offers a conduct book for the courtier which emphasizes the place of dissimulation in court life and political action: 'If you dissemble sometimes your knowledge of that you are thought to know, you shall be thought another time to know that you know not' ('Of Discourse').[23] The *Essays* may reflect the disillusionment that Bacon felt about his own efforts to follow the path in the 1590s of 'the ethical courtier, one who sought patronage as a means to approach the seat of power in order to influence the monarch to govern well'—a path set out in works such as *The Book Named the Governor* (1531), in which Thomas Elyot assures his readers that the 'end of all doctrine and study is good counsel...wherein virtue may be found'.[24] The Ciceronian model of counsel and service proposed in *The Book Named the Governor*, according to which rhetorical eloquence naturally persuades kings, courtiers, and patrons to virtue, was found wanting by Elyot himself, as his opposition to Henry's first divorce left him increasingly isolated and disillusioned.[25] In the three editions of his *Essays*, Bacon blends this Ciceronian tradition of humanist counsel (discussed in more detail below) with a cynical 'new humanist' realism in what amounts to a conduct or advice book for a man like Essex about how to master the vicissitudes of a life in politics and advance a career in the court.

By the third edition of the *Essays* of 1625, Bacon had himself experienced a rise to high office, acting as James I's Attorney General and Lord Chancellor, and an abrupt fall from grace, having lost his status and been imprisoned in the aftermath of charges of corruption in 1621. By dedicating the 1625 *Essays* to the Duke of Buckingham, the controversial

---

[21] Savile quoted in David Womersley, 'Sir John Hayward's Tacitism', *Renaissance Studies*, 6 (1992): 46–59 (54).

[22] Brian Vickers, *Francis Bacon and Renaissance Prose* (Cambridge: Cambridge University Press, 1968), 82.

[23] Bacon, *Major Works*, 82. All references to Bacon's *Essays* are to this edition.

[24] Levy, 'Francis Bacon and the Style of Politics', 166; Elyot quoted in John Guy, 'The Henrician Age', in J. G. A. Pocock, ed., *The Varieties of British Political Thought, 1500–1800* (Cambridge: Cambridge University Press, 1993), 13–46 (14).

[25] See the lengthy exposition in Walker, *Writing Under Tyranny*, 123–278.

favourite of James I whose influence persisted under Charles I, Bacon would seem to have been making a new bid for preferment through a display of his Machiavellian knowledge of courts. There are many more essays in the 1625 edition and the original 1597 essays have been expanded, their spiky aphoristic structure smoothed out into more continuous prose. Nonetheless, the argumentative progression of each essay retains the provocative and unsettling effect of the aphorism. One might expect 'Of Simulation and Dissimulation', given the title, to present a Machiavellian account of the need for deceit in court politics. But in fact, Bacon opens his essay by declaring that dissimulation is the habitual practice of 'weaker' politicians: 'Dissimulation is but a faint kind of policy or wisdom; for it asketh a strong wit and a strong heart to know when to tell truth, and to do it. Therefore it is the weaker sort of politiques that are the great dissemblers' (p. 349). But this is not a Ciceronian rejection of dissimulation either, for Tacitus is then quoted to distinguish between dissimulation as the practice of a tyrant and the 'arts or policy' of successful rule:

> Tacitus saith, 'Livia sorted well wit the arts of her husband and dissimulation of her son'; attributing arts or policy to Augustus, and dissumulation to Tiberius... For if a man have that penetration of judgement as he can discern what things are to be laid open, and what to be secreted, and what to be shewed at half lights, and to whom and when (which indeed are the arts of life, as Tacitus well calleth them), to him a habit of dissimulation is a hindrance and poorness. (p. 349)

As we continue our progress through the essay, it becomes apparent that openness is, in fact, a particularly subtle form of dissimulation used by those who are masters of 'arts or policy'.[26] Yet, habitual dissimulation is both 'more culpable, and less politic': though Bacon incorporates Tacitus to advise courtiers and rulers on how to flourish in a world of power politics, Bacon also ascribes habitual dissimulation to the tyrant (p. 351). Rulers who are regarded as tyrannical are morally reprehensible, but also poor politicians. Christian ethics are never quite simply detached from pagan politics in the *Essays* or elsewhere in his writing.

In his *History of the Reign of King Henry VII*, published in 1622, the year after his disgrace and expulsion from the Jacobean court, Bacon adopts Tacitus's annalistic model, as well as More's semi-dramatic form of historical prose narrative, to present a generally positive portrait of a man who was, as Bacon says in dedicating the book to the Prince of Wales, the future Charles I, 'ancestor to the king your father and yourself'. And yet, Bacon's psychological analysis of Henry VII also encompasses characteristics of a ruler that were associated by the classical writers with tyranny, in particular, the constant fear of enemies and suspicion of everyone around him—More dwells on the awful insecurity of the tyrant in his Latin epigrams and in the portrait of Richard III, who 'never hadde quiet in his mind, he never thought himselfe sure' (p. 88). Bacon's Henry VII is 'a dark

---

[26] See the patient close reading by Martin Dzelzainis, 'Bacon, "Of Simulation and Dissimulation"', in Michael Hattaway, ed., *A Companion to Renaissance Literature and Culture* (Oxford: Blackwell, 2000), 233–40.

prince, and infinitely suspicious', 'full of apprehensions and suspicions', who 'did suck in sometimes causeless suspicions which few else knew'. (The point about Henry is echoed in the general maxims of 'Of Simulation and Dissimulation': 'For if a man be thought secret, it inviteth discovery; as the more close air sucketh in the more open' [p. 350].) This paranoia makes Henry occasionally act tyrannically, as when he has 'divers great men' publicly cursed as the 'King's enemies' on the strength of 'intelligence [from] confessors and chaplains'.[27] It is hard not to suspect that Bacon is here making a point about the way that Henry's descendant James had behaved in hanging Bacon out to dry on slim evidence.

Henry is also characterized by a material avarice which rides roughshod over law: he was of a 'disposition [which] nourished and whet on by bad counsellors and ministers, proved the blot of his times: which was the course he took to crush treasure out of his subjects' purses by forfeitures upon penal laws' (pp. 116–17). As More tells us in his epigrams, the tyrant is defined by, among other things, his suppression of his subjects and disregard for laws.[28] The charge that Charles I had allowed himself to be misled by 'evil counsellors' into violating English law and custom was voiced in the later 1620s in parliament by men such as Sir John Elliot, who would die in prison in 1632, and it would become central to parliamentarian apology for civil war in the 1640s.[29] In 1626 Buckingham, who would be assassinated three years later, was compared in detail to Tacitus's Sejanus by Elliot, who was immediately sent to the Tower. Charles is supposed to have observed, in a comment which recalls Elizabeth I's reaction to Haywayd's *Henry IIII* a quarter of a century earlier: 'If the Duke is Sejanus, I must be Tiberius.'[30] In Bacon's 1625 *Essays* and 1622 *History* we can see how in early Stuart England Tacitism could be thought to offer both lessons in how to gain or maintain positions of courtly power *and* a language of protest against court corruption and tyrannical abuse. If a Tacitist rhetoric against tyranny developed under James I, primarily in the context of 'court-centred' politics, then in the later 1620s it contributed to the tensions between crown and parliament which gathered increasing force in that decade and culminated in Charles's Personal Rule from 1629. The remarkable puritan cleric Thomas Scott published, while a minister in Utrecht, a series of ferocious polemics against peace negotiations with Spain in the mid-1620s, at the same time as he translated the Italian satirist Trajano Boccalini's playful and heavily Tacitist accounts of the character of tyranny and court corruption, such as *Ragguagli di Parnasso* (1612/13) or, in Scott's version, *News from Parnassus* (1622). By the early 1650s, indeed, the Tacitist account of tyranny had been assimilated into a context of popular political polemic (or 'public sphere') beyond

---

[27] Francis Bacon, *The History of the Reign of King Henry VII*, ed. Brian Vickers (Cambridge: Cambridge University Press, 1998), 34, 106, 202.

[28] See no. 109, 'The difference between a tyrant and a king', in *Complete Works of St Thomas More. Volume 3, part 1: The Latin Poems*, 163.

[29] See, e.g., Derek Hirst, *England in Conflict, 1603–1660* (London: Arnold, 1999), 128–9, 169–70.

[30] Smuts, 'Court-Centred Politics', 40–2; Curtis Perry, *Literature and Favouritism in Early Modern England* (Cambridge: Cambridge University Press, 2006), 229.

court and university: the printer, former soldier, and republican John Streater turned to Tacitus to show Oliver Cromwell to be a latter-day Nero.[31] When, in 1649, Milton came to attack the recently executed Charles I as a Machiavellian 'deep dissembler' in *Eikonoklastes*, he set about doing so by accusing the King of having learned his lessons in politic statecraft from Shakespeare's *Richard III*. If we believe Milton, Thomas More's Tacitist history had indirectly, through Shakespeare, provided a tyrant with lessons in how to tyrannize; but by reading Shakespeare's play, Milton advises, the English people might also discover how tyranny works.[32]

22.2 Counsel and resistance from More to Filmer

There is a striking moment in More's *History of King Richard the Third* in which More imagines the reaction of the common people to Richard's usurpation of the English crown: 'And so they said that these matters be kings' games, as it were, stage plays, and for the more part played upon scaffolds, in which poor men be but the lookers-on. And they that wise will be meddle no farther. For they that sometime step up and play with them, when they cannot plays their parts, they disorder the play and do themself no good' (p. 81). Those who involve themselves in the drama of kings and courts are more likely to find themselves swinging from the scaffold than performing on it. Should men then do nothing in the face of tyranny? Book I of More's *Utopia*, a work that advertises itself as 'concerned with the best state of a commonwealth' ('libellus uere aureus de optimo reipublicae statu'), engages explicitly with the issue of whether tyrannous rule can be prevented or softened through counsel in the dialogue between the characters of 'More' and Raphael Hythloday. The issue had famously been a topic of debate in Plato's *Republic* and it was part of the archetypal humanist debate in northern Europe about the relative merits of public service (the *vita activa*) versus scholarly retreat (the *vita contemplativa*). Hythloday adopts the Platonic position that the learned man who seeks to counsel kings will end up seduced by tyrannous ways or thrown to wolves. The character of More, however, argues that the virtuous counsellor must 'not leave and forsake the commonwealth. You must not forsake the ship in a tempest because you cannot rule and keep down the winds.' Rather, he must employ all his craft and wit to shape policy; 'and that which you cannot turn to good, so to order it that it be not very bad. For it is not possible for all things to be well unless all men were good, which I think will not be yet

---

[31] On Boccalini, see Tuck, *Philosophy and Government*, 101–3; on Scott, see Peltonen, *Classical Humanism*, 229–70; [Streater], *A Further Continuance of the Grand Politick Informer* (31 October 1653), 42–3.

[32] See Nicholas McDowell, 'Milton's Regicide Tracts and the Uses of Shakespeare', in Nicholas McDowell and Nigel Smith, eds., *The Oxford Handbook of Milton* (Oxford: Oxford University Press, 2009), 252–71.

this good many years.'³³ In a fallen world men must use their cunning to deflect as best they can the naturally tyrannical tendencies of princes. The figure of More defends the principles propagated by the moralists of republican Rome, pre-eminently Cicero in works, such as *De officiis*, that became standard humanist textbooks, by maintaining that public service in the pursuit of virtue is the noblest way of life. The recognition and reward of virtuous service or *virtus* is also the best way to establish a free commonwealth. The people of Utopia live 'in a state of perfect liberty, free from the threat of internal tyranny as well as external conquest, in consequence of being governed in the interests of all its citizens'; rather than, as in contemporary European monarchies, in the material interests of ruling elites secured by hereditary succession and the dispensation of patronage.³⁴ The Utopians have attained this state because their society is built around the encouragement of *virtus* and a system of representation and consultation which ensures the rule of the wise: in short, '*Utopia* is found to endorse a full-blooded Ciceronian republicanism.'³⁵

Of course Utopia is not, by definition, the real world: the work is not a political treatise, but a fiction in the Erasmian 'folly' tradition, in which deadly serious issues are treated with ironic wit and arguments filtered through inversion and paradox. In the real and fallen world men have 'so to order it that it be not very bad'. More himself followed the path of the *vita activa* by entering Henry VIII's service—only to end up on the scaffold. In Utopia the *principem* or first official (not 'prince', as Ralph Robinson in 1551 and some modern translators have it) is elected for life 'unless he be deposed or put down for suspicion of tyranny' (p. 62). Moreover, the Utopians had in the past freed some of their neighbours from tyranny and despite the Utopian abhorrence of war, they are ready to take up arms 'to deliver from the yoke and bondage of tyranny some people that be therewith oppressed' (p. 107). But More never, it would seem, countenanced the idea of resistance to his own king: his final 'response to tyranny [under Henry VIII] was martyrdom, not holy war'.³⁶ Even the most radical constitutional speculations of the Henrician age were framed in terms of the vital political and moral role of 'good counsel'. Thomas Starkey's *A Dialogue between Pole and Lupset* (c. 1529–35), which remained unpublished until the nineteenth century, opens with another rehearsal of the 'dialogue of counsel', in which Starkey's interlocutors debate the merits of the *vita activa*. Starkey, indeed, seems to have intended that his *Dialogue* be presented to Henry VIII in a bid for court preferment; but one wonders what Henry would have made of a work in which the figure of 'Pole'—representing Reginald Pole, the prominent Henrician cleric and later Catholic cardinal to whom Starkey had acted as secretary in Padua in the 1520s and

---

³³ Thomas More, *Utopia*, ed. Richard Marius (London: J. M. Dent, 1994), 48. This edition reprints the 1551 translation by Ralph Robinson.
³⁴ See Quentin Skinner, 'Political Philosophy', in Schmitt and Skinner, eds., *The Cambridge History of Renaissance Philosophy*, 389–452 (448).
³⁵ Brendan Bradshaw, 'Transalpine Humanism', in Burns and Goldie, eds., *The Cambridge History of Political Thought*, 95–131 (119).
³⁶ Fenlon, 'Thomas More and Tyranny', 470.

who refused to support Henry's divorce, bringing down terrible retribution on his family—repeatedly attacks the idea of hereditary monarchy as a corrupting influence on a country:

> Po[le]. wel, master lup[sett]....yet remember our purpos wel...to fynd out the best ordur that by prudent pollycy may be stablysched in our rea[l]me <& cuntry>...what ys more repugnant to nature, than a whole natycon to be governyd by the wyl of a prynce, wych ever followyth hys frayle <fantasy> & unruled affectys, what is more contrary to reason then al the hole pepul to be rulyd by hym...loke to the romanys, whose commyn weale may be exampul to al other, whych lyke as theyr consullys so lyke wyse theyr kyngys chose ever of the best & most excellent in vertue...thys successyon of pryncys by inherytance & blode was broght in by tyrannys & barbarous pryncys[.][37]

As well as the historical example of the Roman republic, Pole cites the contemporary example of Venice, where there is 'no grete ambysyouse desyne to be ther duke, because hye ys restrynyd to gud ordur & polytyke' (p. 123). Pole suggests that the English monarch should similarly become a type of Venetian doge within a 'mixed state' constitution, his power restrained by a system of checks and balances in which Parliament would elect a 'Council of Fourteen' composed of a combination of the wise: citizens, bishops, judges, and lords. The argument that England would be best served by a 'mixed' constitutional form would become a standard feature of works, such as Sir Thomas Smith's *De Republica Anglorum: A Discourse of the Commonweal of England* (c. 1565; pub. 1583), which loom large in Patrick Collinson's influential argument that Elizabethan England was regarded as a 'monarchical republic' by urban intellectuals who conceived of themselves as Ciceronian 'citizens', as well as subjects of the crown, and who maintained their constitutional right to counsel monarchs on the legal limits of their actions.[38] But Starkey's remarkable work goes further in pressing the claims of elective over hereditary monarchy and implying that Henry should sacrifice his power to secure the stability and liberty of his country. Starkey's ideas are shaped by a combination of Ciceronian republicanism and modern Venetian example: the *Dialogue* may have been influenced by Gaspar Contarini's *De Magistratibus et Republica Venetorum*, written in the 1520s and published in 1543, which had some impact in England when it was translated as *The Commonwealth and Government of Venice* by Lewis Lewkenor in 1599.[39] Starkey was to align himself with Henry and against his mentor Pole over the break from Rome and it would be anachronistic to categorize the *Dialogue* as straightforwardly oppositional to Henrician 'tyranny': as with *Utopia* and many pieces of sixteenth-century political prose, including Edmund Spenser's much-discussed *A View of the State of Ireland*, written

---

[37] Thomas Starkey, *A Dialogue between Pole and Lupset*, ed. T. F. Mayer (London: Royal Historical Society, 1989), pp. 71–2. A new, modernized edition of this work is much needed.

[38] See John F. McDiarmid, ed., *The Monarchical Republic of Early Modern England: Essays in Response to Patrick Collinson* (Aldershot: Ashgate, 2007).

[39] See Andrew Hadfield, *Literature, Travel, and Colonial Writing in the English Renaissance, 1545–1625* (Oxford: Oxford University Press, 1998), 22–3, 47–58.

Dialogue-wise (1598; pub. 1633), the work takes the literary form of a dialogue, a playful form beloved of humanists and reflecting the importance attached by Cicero to the role of conversation and rhetoric in shaping a virtuous civil society.[40] So we cannot simply ascribe the views of characters in the dialogue either to the author or to those real people, such as Reginald Pole, represented as interlocutors. Nor do we find even in a work as radically speculative as Starkey's *Dialogue* any notion of the legitimacy of active resistance to a ruler who has turned tyrannical.

Starkey's *Dialogue* is a notably secular discussion of political organization. It was to be mid-sixteenth-century religious conflict which provoked the development of explicit theories of resistance and tyrannicide. The English and Scottish clerics who chose exile in Geneva, Strasbourg, and Frankfurt over martyrdom after Mary I restored Catholicism to England in 1553 became 'pioneers and innovators in subversive political thinking'.[41] The theories of resistance that were developed by the Marian exiles had roots in Lutheran constitutional discussion, but also took vital inspiration from the concluding chapter of Calvin's *Institutio religionis Christianae*, first published in 1536, and its discussion of a mixed monarchy in which the 'magistrates of the people appointed to moderate the licence of kings' might be said 'to have a duty to intervene against the ferocious licence of such kings' in the name of the liberty of the people.[42] John Ponet's *A Short Treatise of Politike Power, and of the true obedience which subjects owe to kynges* was published anonymously in Strasbourg in 1556 and deals explicitly with the question of 'Whether it be lawful to depose an evil governor and kill a tyrant', invoking a series of examples of depositions and assassinations from biblical, classical, and English history (including that of Richard II). Although Ponet, formerly bishop of Winchester, does not actually mention Mary Tudor at any point, and is more obviously concerned with the tyranny of the Catholic bishops, his arguments nonetheless assume clear political significance as he elaborates, in a manner at times reminiscent of Starkey, on the idea of a mixed constitution, which he describes as 'the best sort of all' (sig. Av^r):

> For as...among the Romaynes, the *Tribunes* were ordayned to defende and mayntene the libertie of the people from the pride and iniurie of the nobles: so in all Christian realmes and dominiones God ordayned meanes, that the heads the princes and gouernours should not oppresse the poore people after their lustes, and make

---

[40] See the insightful discussion of humanist conversation in Jennifer Richards, *Rhetoric and Courtliness in Early Modern Literature* (Cambridge: Cambridge University Press, 2003). See further Andrew Hadfield's account, evidently relevant to my argument here, of the way in which dialogues concerned with how to best manage the crisis in Ireland in the 1590s, such as Spenser's *A View* and Richard Beacon's *Solon His Follie* (1594), employ a Ciceronian form, while in fact pursuing a sceptical Tacitean analysis which questions conventional Ciceronian assumptions about the moral basis and function of government ('Cicero, Tacitus and the Reform of Ireland in the 1590s', in *Shakespeare, Spenser and the Matter of Britain* [Basingstoke: Palgrave Macmillan, 2004], 90–104).

[41] Donald R. Kelley, 'Elizabethan Political Thought', in Pocock, ed., *Varieties of British Political Thought*, 47–79 (53).

[42] Calvin quoted and translated in Skinner, 'Political Philosophy', 446. See also Quentin Skinner, *The Foundations of Modern Political Thought*, 2 vols. (Cambridge: Cambridge University Press, 1978), II, 189–348.

their willes their lawes. As in Germanye betwene the emperour and the people, a Counsail or diet: in Fraunce and Englande, parliamentes, wherin ther mette and assembled of all sortes of people, and nothing could be done without the knowlage and consent of all. (sig. Avii^{r-v})

A key distinction for continental Lutheran and Calvinist theorists of resistance was between 'inferior magistrates' and private persons: while resistance to tyrannical rule was lawful for the former, it was never legitimate for the latter to take political action. This distinction was maintained, for instance, by the Huguenots who wrote in the aftermath of the St Bartholomew's massacres in France in 1572, such as the anonymous author of *Vindiciae contra tyrannos* (1579), which was partially translated into English in 1588 as *A Short Apologie for Christian Soldiers*—and which, Blair Worden has argued, shaped the (disillusioned) imaginative exploration of the state of Elizabethan politics in Sir Philip Sidney's romance *Arcadia* (c. 1580).[43] Ponet accepts the distinction, but then immediately cites the exception of those individuals who are directly commanded by God to act; and then goes on to render that qualification of divine inspiration itself somewhat irrelevant by appealing to the sanction of 'common autoritie upon juste occasion':

I thinke it can not be maintained by Goddes worde, that any private man maie kill, except (wher execucion of juste punishement upon tirannes, idolaters, and traiterous governours is either by the hole state utterly neglected, or the prince with the nobilitie and counsail conspire the subversion or alteracion of their contrey and people) any private man have som special inwarde commaundement or surely proved mocion of God: as Moses had to kill the Egipcian, Phinees the Lecherours, and Ahud king Eglon, with suche like: or be otherwise commaunded or permitted by common autoritie upon juste occasion and common necessitie to kill. (sig. Iviii^{r-v})

Nonetheless, private persons, even inspired ones, can only act, according to Ponet, when the punishment of tyrants is neglected by 'the hole state'. His fellow exile, Christopher Goodman, takes the same position in *How Superior Powers Ought to be Obeyed* (Geneva, 1558), a political work which, typically of the Marian exiles, derives from a sermon. When magistrates 'cease to do their dutie', as was the case in Catholic England, then God gives 'the sworde in to the peoples hands, and he him self is become immediately their head' (pp. 179–80). John Knox, who would return to Scotland after Mary's death to play a leading role in the Reformation, also argued from Geneva in 1558 that since in Catholic states 'no ordinary justice can be executed', the punishment of idolatrous—which for Knox is equated with tyrannous—rulers 'must be reserved to God and unto such means as He shall appoint':

In such places, I say, it is not only lawful to punish to death such as labour to subvert the true religion, but the magistrates and people are bound so to do unless they will provoke the wrath of God against themselves. And therefore I fear not to affirm that

---

[43] Blair Worden, *The Sound of Virtue: Philip Sidney's Arcadia and Elizabethan Politics* (New Haven and London: Yale University Press, 1996), chap. 16.

it had been the duty of the nobility, judges, rulers and people of England not only to have resisted and againstanded Mary that Jezebel whom they call their queen, but also to have punished her to the death, with all the sort of her idolatrous priests[.][44]

Knox's style is that of the prophetic preacher—exhortatory, declamatory, and zealous. Although Knox uses legal, classical, and patristic authorities, the Bible is the only source of precedents that he truly values: 'when Knox identified himself with Jeremiah, or Mary Tudor with Jezebel, he was doing much more than invoking scriptural parallels or paradigms. He was appealing to biblical "case law" to establish precedents which were universally binding because they revealed to man the immutable laws of God.'[45] As the reference here to 'Mary that Jezebel' indicates, Knox is relentlessly *ad hominem* in his polemic against Mary as a woman, as well as a Catholic. His *First Blast of the Trumpet against the Monstrous Regiment of Woman*, again published in Geneva in 1558, caused Knox some embarrassment when Elizabeth I, who recognized that the arguments about women could be applied to her equally as well as Mary, ascended the throne at the end of that year. Knox equates a female ruler with a tyrant because both are idols, which Knox defines as 'that which hath the form and appearance but lacketh the virtue and strength which the name and proportion do resemble and promise...such, I say, is every realm and nation where a woman beareth dominion'.[46]

Knox and the Scottish Protestants faced the whole problem again when the Catholic Mary Stuart returned to Scotland in 1561 to claim her right to rule. By 1567 Mary was deposed and expelled to England, to the outrage of Catholic Europe. The Scottish humanist George Buchanan, whose previous pupils as a tutor in France had included figures such as Montaigne, became the formidable propagandist of the new Scottish Protestant state. In his Latin dialogue *De jure regni apud Scotos*, written in 1567–8, but first published in 1579 (and not translated into English in the early modern period), Buchanan dispenses with the terminology of 'inferior magistrates' and private persons to state simply that obedience is not due to tyrants, who ought to be put to death by any means by any person; nor does Buchanan in any way qualify his insistence on the authority of the individual citizen to kill a tyrant by locating that authority in divine inspiration. The crucial biblical text with which any resistance theorist had to engage was Romans 13 ('Let every soul be subject unto the higher powers'); those who cite this text in support of obedience to tyrants, says Buchanan, will 'immediately have to face the objection that Ahab was killed at God's command'.[47] It has been persuasively argued that the great classical scholar Buchanan—who refers in one of his Latin poems to the 'pious daggers' of Brutus, murderer of Julius Caesar—was influenced in his reductive interpretation of the Calvinist argument for tyrannicide by the Ciceronian definition, outlined in *De officiis*, of the

---

[44] *The Appellation to the Nobility and Estates* (1558), in John Knox, *On Rebellion*, ed. Roger A. Mason (Cambridge: Cambridge University Press, 1994), 103–4.

[45] Knox, *On Rebellion*, pp. x–xi.

[46] Knox, *On Rebellion*, 23.

[47] George Buchanan, *A Dialogue on the Law of Kingship among the Scots*, ed. Roger A. Mason and Martin S. Smith (Aldershot: Ashgate, 2004), 125.

tyrant. For Cicero, the tyrant is the enemy of all mankind—and it is always lawful to kill an enemy with whom you are at war. John Milton, who would add to the second edition of *The Tenure of Kings and Magistrates* a list of citations from Reformation authorities, including Goodman and Knox, to defend his argument for regicide, makes the same, Ciceronian argument: a 'just King' is 'the public father of his Countrie', but a tyrant is 'the common enemie' against whom the people may lawfully proceed 'as against a common pest, and destroyer of mankinde'.[48] The Calvinist resistance theorists had no wish to introduce republican government such as that in Venice, which they associated with the subordination of clerical authority. Rather, they 'wished to limit and contain their monarch'.[49] Nonetheless, and as the example of Milton suggests, their arguments would become part of the polemical and intellectual context of the English Revolution. If the Circeronian theory of tyrannicide shaped the apology of Buchanan for the deposition of Mary Stuart and of Milton for the execution of Charles Stuart some seventy years later, then we may again need to qualify the claim that it was above all the Tacitist thinking of the 'new humanism' which facilitated the more radical political thinking of the 1640s and 1650s.[50]

Buchanan's arguments created scandal around Europe and his *De jure regni apud Scotos* was banned even by the Scottish parliament in 1584. In Elizabethan and early Stuart Britain the appeal of the Calvinist resistance theorists to biblical precedent for popular revolt against tyrannical rulers became polemically associated with the alleged campaign of Presbyterian and 'puritan' activists to stir up popular political ferment. In John Whitgift's polemical responses to the Presbyterian divine Thomas Cartwright in the early 1570s, we can see how the opponents of Presbyterian church government associated its self-governing structures, not without some reason, with the urban republican values and systems of the city-states of Switzerland and Germany in which it had developed.[51] The most impressive prose work to emerge from this anti-Presbyterian reaction in later Elizabethan England is Richard Hooker's *Of the Laws of Ecclesiastical Polity*, the first four books of which appeared in 1593 and the fifth in 1597; the books most explicitly concerned with the relationship between ecclesiastical organization and political power did not appear, however, until 1648 (the sixth and eighth books) and 1661 (the seventh book). Against what he regards as the dangerous individualism of puritan biblical fundamentalism and (alleged) claims to supra-rational inspiration, Hooker defends the Elizabethan church settlement as ensuring the national unity secured by an interdependent church and state: his concern is very much with locating national structures of government in their particular historical context against both Catholic and Calvinist visions of a supra-national church government that could and should be applied in the

---

[48] George Buchanan, *The Political Poetry*, ed. Paul J. McGinnis and Arthur H. Williamson (Edinburgh: Lothian Print, 1995), 86; Martin Dzelzainis, 'The Ciceronian Theory of Tyrannicide from Buchanan to Milton', in Roger A. Mason and Caroline Erskine, eds., *George Buchanan: Political Thought in Early Modern Britain and Europe* (Aldershot: Ashgate, 2012), 173–88; Milton, *Political Writings*, 16–17.

[49] Tuck, *Philosophy and Government*, 233.

[50] Tuck, *Philosophy and Government*, 202–78.

[51] See the stimulating discussion in Lake, 'Puritanism, (Monarchical) Republicanism, and Monarchy'.

same manner everywhere.⁵² So Hooker's defence of episcopacy in England, against the importing of a Calvinist church polity from Geneva, rests on appeals to history, tradition, and reason, as well as scripture. It is important to remember that the appeal here to 'natural' reason is always partly polemical, constructed in opposition to the supposed insanity of those who claim private inspiration; but the invocation of reason also suffuses Hooker's prose, impressively turning style into an embodiment of argument as 'the complex sentence [becomes] the reflection of rational process'.⁵³

Hooker's optimistic valuation of man's rational capacity against a Calvinist emphasis on man's innate depravity appealed to later anti-Calvinist, tolerationist radicals who were resolutely opposed to a compulsory state church, such as the Leveller William Walwyn.⁵⁴ At the same time, Hooker's conception of the universe, as operating according to universal rational laws, leads him to outline a theory of the origin of government, as dependent on the rational consent of the people, which bears some comparison with the later political philosophy of contract developed by John Locke and others: 'To take away all such mutual grievances, injuries, and wrongs, there was no way, but only by growing unto composition and agreement among themselves, by ordaining some kind of government public, and by yielding themselves thereunto, that unto whom they granted authority to rule and govern, by them the peace, tranquillity, and happy estate of the rest might be procured.'⁵⁵ But Hooker's myth of political origins becomes notably more proto-Hobbesian than proto-Lockean in the eighth book of the *Laws*, significantly first published in the months before the execution of Charles I. If monarchical power derives from the consent of the people, that does not make the monarch subject to control by the people: 'as there could be in natural bodies no motion of any thing unless there were some which moveth all things and continueth unmovable, even so in politic societies there must be some unpunishable or else no man shall suffer punishment... *Kings* therefore no man can have lawfully power and authority to judge... on earth they are not accountable to any.'⁵⁶

Hooker's theory of consent leads him to distinguish explicitly between the domestic power of a father and the political power of a king. But the patriarchal analogy was a central theme and rhetorical motif of *The Trew Law of Free Monarchies* (Edinburgh, 1598) composed by James VI as King of Scotland in response to the arguments for resistance advanced by Buchanan and also the Catholic polemicist Robert Parsons. James, probably the most learned of British monarchs (thanks in great part to Buchanan, who had acted as his tutor) and a considerable prose writer, makes some ringing declarations of the divine right of kings to absolute power: 'Kings are called Gods by the prophetical King David, because they sit

---

⁵² See Richard Helgerson, *Forms of Nationhood: The Elizabethan Writing of England* (Chicago and London: University of Chicago Press, 1992), 269–83.

⁵³ George Edelen, 'Hooker's Style', in W. Speed Hill, ed., *Studies in Hooker* (Cleveland: Press at Case Western Reserve University, 1972), 244.

⁵⁴ Nicholas McDowell, *The English Radical Imagination: Culture, Religion, and Revolution, 1630–1660* (Oxford: Clarendon Press, 2003), 84–7.

⁵⁵ Richard Hooker, *Of the Laws of Ecclesiastical Polity*, ed. Arthur Stephen McGrade (Cambridge: Cambridge University Press, 1989), 89 (I.x.4).

⁵⁶ Hooker, *Laws*, 219–20 (VIII.ix.2).

upon God his throne in the earth, and have the count of their administration to give unto him.' A king is the father of his people and the rule of the father over his children is not derived from the consent of his children. Indeed, a king has the power of life and death over his subjects as a father has over his children. In 1610 James, now King of England, told Parliament that: 'As for the father of a family, they had of old under the Law of Nature *patriam potestatem* [fatherly power], which was *potestatem vitae et necis* [the power of life and death], over their children or family, (I mean such fathers of families whereof kings did originally come).' James accepted that a king may behave tyrannically; but a tyrannical king would be held accountable only by God and his actions could never license uprising. A good king, James accepts, will behave according to the law, of which he is the author; yet, 'he is not bound thereto but of his good will, and for example-giving to his subjects'.[57]

Patriarchalism was, as J. P. Somerville observes, 'at once an account of the origins of government and a description of the nature of political power. It served to show that men had not originally been free, but were born into civil subjection.'[58] As an ideology it became increasingly prominent during Charles I's 'Personal Rule' in the 1630s and found its most powerful expression in Robert Filmer's *Patriarchia*, composed c. 1628–32, but not published until 1680, after several revisions. For Filmer, the power of kings originated in the power God granted Adam over his children: 'I see not then how the children of Adam, or of any man else, can be free from subjection to their parents. And this subjection of children is the only fountain of all regal authority, by the ordination of God himself.' He goes on to make many of the points that James had made in *The Trew Law of Free Monarchies*, but Filmer is even more rhetorically forceful and locates his political theory squarely within the current disputes between Charles and parliament which would eventually lead to civil war: 'the prerogative of a king is to be above all laws, for the good only of them that are under the laws, and to defend the people's liberties—as his majesty graciously affirmed in his speech after his last answer to the Petition of Right.'[59] *Patriarchia* might look to modern democratically minded readers as the apogee of absolutist hubris in a Caroline England which would soon be consumed by civil war; but it is worth noting that Filmer would prove to be the shrewdest critic of Milton's awkward claims in the *Tenure* and the *Defensio pro populo Anglicano* (1651) that the unpopular act of regicide was performed on behalf of the 'better' part of the people of England: 'Nay J. M. will not allow the major part of the Representors to be the people, but "the sounder and better part only" of them... If "the sounder, the better, and the uprighter" part have the power of the people, how shall we know, or who shall judge who they be?'[60]

---

[57] James VI, *The True Law of Free Monarchies*, and 'Speech to Parliament, 21 March 1610', in *Political Writings of James I and VI*, ed. J. P. Somerville (Cambridge: Cambridge University Press, 1994), 64, 182, 75. The most recent discussions of James's political thought can be found in Ralph Houlbrooke, ed., *James I and VI: Ideas, Authority and Government* (Aldershot: Ashgate, 2006).

[58] J. P. Somerville, *Politics and Ideology in England, 1603–1640* (Harlow: Longman, 1986), 30.

[59] Robert Filmer, *Patriarcha and Other Writings*, ed. J. P. Somerville (Cambridge: Cambridge University Press, 1991), 7, 44.

[60] Robert Filmer, *Observations Concerning the Originall of Government* (1652), in Filmer, *Patriarchia and Other Writings*, 199.

Further Reading

Bacon, Francis. *Essays* (1597 & 1625), in *Francis Bacon: The Major Works*, ed. Brian Vickers (Oxford: Oxford University Press, 2002).
Filmer, Robert. *Patriarcha and Other Writings*, ed. J. P. Somerville (Cambridge: Cambridge University Press, 1991).
Hooker, Richard. *Of the Laws of Ecclesiastical Polity*, ed. Arthur Stephen McGrade (Cambridge: Cambridge University Press, 1989).
James I and VI. *Political Writings of James I and VI*, ed. J. P. Somerville (Cambridge: Cambridge University Press, 1994).
Knox, John. *On Rebellion*, ed. Roger A. Mason (Cambridge: Cambridge University Press, 1994).
Lake, Peter, and Kevin Sharpe, eds. *Culture and Politics in Early Stuart England* (Basingstoke: Macmillan, 1994).
More, Thomas. *The History of King Richard III*, in *Complete Works of St Thomas More, Volume 2*, ed. Richard S. Sylvester (New Haven and London: Yale University Press, 1963).
Peltonnen, Marku. *Classical Humanism and Republicanism in English Political Thought, 1570–1640* (Cambridge: Cambridge University Press, 1995).
Pocock, J. G. A., ed. *The Varieties of British Political Thought, 1500–1800* (Cambridge: Cambridge University Press, 1993).
Somerville, J. P. *Politics and Ideology in England, 1603–1640* (Harlow: Longman, 1986).
Starkey, Thomas. *A Dialogue between Pole and Lupset*, ed. T. F. Mayer (London: Royal Historical Society, 1989).
Tuck, Richard. *Philosophy and Government, 1572–1651* (Cambridge: Cambridge University Press, 1993).

CHAPTER 23

MODES OF SATIRE

DERMOT CAVANAGH

SIX years after the death of the great Elizabethan satirist, Thomas Nashe, a contemporary writer, Thomas Dekker, imagined his tormented afterlife: 'still haunted with the sharpe and *Satyricall spirit* that followd him heere upon *earth*'.[1] What kind of '*Satyricall spirit*' stalked Nashe even after the grave? For Dekker, it issued from a sense of personal rancour at the fatal neglect of his talent. The refusal of philistine and miserly patrons to offer support meant that this gifted writer subsisted on an impoverished diet of pickled herrings that shortened his days. This mordant reflection offers a broader insight into the period's understanding of satire and some of the perils that attended it. Dekker suggests that the undoubted forcefulness of the mode issues from perceived slights and iniquities. On this view, the satirist's anger derives from despair at the obtuseness of the world, its culpable failure to recognize what is truly valuable. As Nashe's unhappy fate shows, the world is unlikely to reward this exposure of its failings.

That satire should be abrasive and attack poor judgement, corruption, and delusion was certainly perceived as its essential quality in early modern culture. The mode was understood to be unconstrained either by the deference accorded to privileged individuals or institutions or by the decorum expected when addressing sensitive experiences. This was reinforced by a misunderstanding of the term's etymology. It descends from 'satura', meaning a mixture or medley of different things, but it was long thought to derive from the satyr play of classical theatre. In this mode of performance, the actors imitated satyrs, half-men and half-goats, and, with the extensive licence accorded by this role, they assailed the moral failings of the society around them.[2] As George Puttenham explained in *The Arte of English Poesie* (1589), poets committed to this form

---

[1] Thomas Dekker, 'A Knight's Conjuring' (1607). Quoted in Ann Rosalind Jones, 'Inside the Outsider: Nashe's *Unfortunate Traveller* and Bakhtin's Polyphonic Novel', *English Literary History*, 50 (1983): 61–81 (62).

[2] Alvin Kernan, *The Cankered Muse: Satire of the English Renaissance* (New Haven: Yale University Press, 1959), 62–3.

also 'intended to taxe the common abuses and vices of the people in rough and bitter speeches, and their invectives were called *Satyres*'.³

In many instances, therefore, early modern satire easily accommodates the tendency towards polarized thinking that, according to Stuart Clark, pervaded the period.⁴ Satire was a powerful medium for polemical attack. By excoriating individuals, practices, and beliefs that obstructed those principles which should govern social and spiritual life it answered to the needs of authors 'with a sense of moral vocation and with a concern for the public interest'.⁵ In this form of polemical satire, the reprobate was distinguished from the responsible and widespread deficiencies in prevailing moral standards were identified.

Yet, this was not the only path that prose satire followed. Indeed, the intentions of some instances of the form remain debatable rather than clear-cut. Satire was also a compelling medium for those who sought to question, rather than reinforce, sectarian boundaries and moral oppositions. Indeed, in its more experimental forms, such polarized thinking itself becomes the object of satirical inquiry and this suited writers of a more sceptical temperament, allowing them to query those habits of thought that underpinned moral discrimination. This technique also called into question the author's own relationship to their satirical material, as well as their authority to pass judgement.

In this chapter, these distinct potentialities of prose satire will be examined in three phases. In the first section, Erasmus's *Praise of Folly* will be shown to revive the sceptical quality of Menippean satirical form to cultivate toleration and to inhibit oppositional thinking. In the second part, the undoubted utility of satire for the much more single-minded purpose of polemic will be considered in Stephen Gosson's *The School of Abuse*. Finally, the chapter will return to Nashe, the pre-eminent satirist of the period, and consider how the significance of his work derives from its undoubted polemical forcefulness, as noted by Dekker, but also its double-sidedness. A key aim of this account is to question two critical assumptions concerning early modern satire. First, is its consideration as primarily significant for poetic composition and as a shaping influence upon later sixteenth-century theatre.⁶ Second, and more recent, is an emphasis on its prominence during the seventeenth century, when it helped to consolidate political divisions. The latter view has tended to set aside earlier instances of satire as deriving from a period where an 'orthodox Tudor commitment to consensus and harmony' existed, in contrast to the much more disputatious culture of Stuart England.⁷ In contrast, this chapter will consider the radical potential of earlier instances of prose satire in the spirit of Lorna Hutson's observation that 'prose is more capable than poetry

---

³ George Puttenham, *The Arte of English Poesie* (1589), 20.
⁴ Stuart Clark, *Thinking With Demons: The Idea of Witchcraft in Early Modern Europe* (Oxford: Clarendon Press, 1997), chap. 4.
⁵ Ruben Quintero, 'Introduction: Understanding Satire', in Ruben Quintero, ed., *A Companion to Satire: Ancient to Modern* (Oxford: Blackwell, 2007), 1–11 (1).
⁶ See, for example, Kernan, *The Cankered Muse*, 141–246.
⁷ Andrew McRae, *Literature, Satire and the Early Stuart State* (Cambridge: Cambridge University Press, 2004), 1.

of accommodating and objectifying the various accents and forms of contemporary discourse'.[8] The capacity to scrutinize contemporary values is a crucial quality of sixteenth-century satire, which also allowed it to question 'dominant cultural assumptions about the relation between morality and power' with a remarkable degree of energy and flexibility.[9]

23.1 SATIRE AND SCEPTICISM: ERASMUS

'[I]n all humaine thynges, there is so great darkenesse and diversnesse, as nothyng maie be clerely knowne', observes Folly in Erasmus's great mock encomium, the *Praise of Folly* (1509; printed 1511), translated into English by Thomas Chaloner in 1549. This viewpoint, which Folly claims for her own, was also: 'affirmed by my *Academicall philosophers* [i.e. classical sceptical thinkers], the lest arrogant amonges all theyr *Sectes*'.[10] In the *Praise of Folly*, Erasmus revived the classical legacy of satire as a medium for scepticism and this had crucial implications for the mode. Folly believes that laughter is the best response to the absurdity of the world, although this does not inhibit anger at abuses of power. Her commitment to sceptical reflection resonates strongly with Erasmus's broader intellectual and moral attitudes. In particular, it reinforces his commendation of a simple Christian piety, along with the imperative to suspend judgement on all matters that did not conflict directly with the decrees of the Church. Over a decade later, in his response to Luther in *De Libero Arbitrio* ('The Freedom of the Will' [1524]), Erasmus attacked the presumption of securing absolute certainty in matters of theological judgement and the intolerance this promoted.[11] Erasmus concedes that the teaching of the Church might not be comprehensible on all questions. However, it preserves an enduring wisdom that it would be foolhardy to challenge on the basis of one's own limited intellectual powers. Yet, as we'll now see, Erasmus did not exempt the Church or even himself from his strictures regarding human vanity and corruption; far from it. His satire advances a devastating and wide-ranging critique of the illusions and misjudgements that distort understanding of the world and that damage the lives we lead within it.

To reveal how drastically we misconstrue our own experience, Erasmus's satire sets out to challenge acceptance of what is self-evident, along with what distinguishes the serious from the absurd. Folly finds an analogy for this approach in the Silenus, a small carved wooden figure with a repugnant exterior, but which could be opened to display something uniquely precious such as the beautiful features of a God. What provokes Erasmus's

---

[8] Lorna Hutson, *Thomas Nashe in Context* (Oxford: Clarendon Press, 1989), 133.
[9] McRae, *Literature, Satire and the Early Stuart State*, 6.
[10] Erasmus, *The Praise of Folie* (1549), trans. Thomas Chaloner, sig. I3ʳ. All quotations to this edition are in parentheses in the text.
[11] See Richard H. Popkin, *The History of Scepticism from Erasmus to Descartes* (New York: Harper & Row, 1964), esp. 4–7; Joseph Lecler, *Toleration and the Reformation*, trans. T. L. Westow, 2 vols. (London: Longman, 1960), I, 114–33.

satire is the continuous failure to grasp the wisdom embodied in this object. Human life and affairs, Folly proposes, can be considered as Silenus-like because all that is regarded as pleasing and imposing is, with a switch of perspective, grotesque and what appears to be degraded is beautiful. The inability to realize this is all too common and Erasmus's text exposes a world characterized by drastic forms of misrecognition. The Silenus reminds us that our habitual understanding of what is truly desirable and repellent is founded poorly and this example has an obvious correspondence with satire because it too can be said 'to represent or portray varieties of ugliness by assuming their external shape', yet the alert reader 'will be able to uncover the rare quality of imaginative wisdom within'.[12] However ridiculous Folly may appear, she possesses more insight than we suspect.

The principal aim of Erasmus's satire, therefore, is to inhibit polarized thinking, to break down the habitual patterns by which we judge the world around us. For example, the forms of authority that shape our social and spiritual lives possess enormous power and elicit a striking degree of consent, but to what purpose? Folly describes how the commonly accepted hierarchies that stratify the Renaissance world are, in fact, absurd. Vast disparities in status and resources are secured in ways that are merely the result of theatrical imposture. The principle of the Silenus helps with this as it reveals the widespread misapprehension of values, notably with regard to temporal power. A king may be acclaimed and showered with honours even though 'so meane and poore a caitive as he is, [is] least deseruyng them, as not seldome the veriest tirannes that ever reigned, have natheles with publike ceremonies been cannonised into the noumbre of the gods' (sig. E2^r). An aristocrat may flaunt pride in his ancestry, but he should rather be called 'a villaine, and a bastarde, because he is so many discentes disalied from vertue, whiche is the onely roote of true nobilitee' (sig. E4^r). Everywhere, falsehood is taken for reality. Those worldly figures who are revered as being worthy of emulation are, in fact, atrocious: 'evin this great prince, whom all men honor as their god and soveraigne, deserveth skarce to be called man, seyng like the brute beastes, he is trained by affections, and is none other than a servaunt of the basest sort' (sigs. E3^v–E4^r). Laughter helps to free us from delusions like this: the more we laugh at the world, the more its deceits and iniquities are revealed.

Yet, the form of authority most responsible for exposing such follies only compounds them. The satirical asperity of the *Praise of Folly* is acute when it documents the failure of the Catholic Church. The latter was divinely instituted to act as the custodian of God's word and to shape the lives of the faithful towards salvation. Yet, it now advances forms of superstition and delusion that are wildly remote from the simplicity and force of Christ's teaching. Indeed, as Erasmus observed elsewhere, the whole conception of 'the Church' had become distorted. Its most exalted members—priests, bishops, and popes— 'are in truth nothing but the Church's servants' and the privileges accorded to them invert a true sense of Christian hierarchy because 'it is Christian people who are the Church, whom Christ himself calls "greater", in the sense that bishops ought to serve them'.[13] The

---

[12] Michael Seidel, *Satiric Inheritance: Rabelais to Sterne* (Princeton: Princeton University Press, 1979), 71.

[13] Erasmus, 'Adages 'II vii 1 to III iii 100', in *The Collected Works of Erasmus*, trans. and annotated by R. A. B. Mynors (Toronto, Buffalo, and London: University of Toronto Press, 1992), Vol. 34, III iii 1, 271.

loss of this perspective means the spiritual life, which should proceed under the awareness of death and God's judgement, has become indistinguishable from a life of ambition and material gratification. In Folly's account, the seeming reality of the world is best regarded as a theatrical performance and 'the human attachment to illusions' is perceived 'as a constitutive feature of human desire itself'.[14] Yet, under Folly's satirical gaze, religious hierarchies and practices are not revealed to be ridiculous and fraudulent simply because of a general human propensity towards credulity, but because they help to maintain worldly advantages. Folly denounces the Church's practice of selling indulgences, whereby the remission of sins could be purchased, rather than atoned for in Purgatory. She observes how 'some usurer, or man of warre, or corrupte judge' will be so chronically deceived and self-deceived that he will expend 'one halfpenie of all his evill gotten goods' and 'straight thynke that the whole hoorde of his former mislife, is at ones forgevin hym' (sig. H3^v). Most heinously, the Church has squandered its religious authority because its material interests are best served by promoting illusions. Anyone who questions this wild distortion of Christian virtue brings down upon his or her head the wrath of the Church's claque of loyal theologians who will readily denounce any perceived threat to their interests as heresy: '[F]or that is the thunderbolt, wherwithall they threten suche, as stande not best in theyr favour' (sig. L4^v).

In its outrage at corruption the *Praise of Folly* fulfils a traditional purpose of satire. Yet, Erasmus had written at length elsewhere on the Silenus in his *Adages* as part of an equally excoriating attack on the failings of the Church.[15] Much of this material also appears in the mouth of Folly. However, there is a crucial difference in the contexts in which these sentiments appear that is crucial to understanding the satiric practice of the *Praise of Folly*. In his commentary on the Silenus in the *Adages*, Erasmus shows that we are deceived by appearances and prefer illusion to reality. The solution is to reverse our normal habits of perception and to concentrate on interior essences. In contrast, in the *Praise of Folly*, such clarity of vision is much harder to sustain. Erasmus adopts a set of satirical techniques that are far more intricate and self-qualifying than simply expressing indignation. In short, the most ferocious sentiments are embedded in a work that destabilizes assurance over its wider purposes and it is in this respect that the work's sceptical commitment becomes most pronounced. The *Praise of Folly* does not simply observe the world as theatrical or play-like, it is an instance of 'serious play' itself.

This particular form of satire, as a number of commentators have shown, was adopted both by Erasmus and by his great friend, Thomas More, in his *Utopia*.[16] In this respect, both writers were attempting to revive the serio-comic art of satire developed by the Greek writer Menippus. His writings were lost, but they shaped profoundly the practice of his successor, Lucian, whose works were translated and greatly admired by More and

---

[14] W. Scott Blanchard, *Scholars' Bedlam: Menippean Satire in the Renaissance* (London and Toronto: Associated University Presses, 1995), 123.

[15] See, Erasmus, 'Adages', III iii 1, 271.

[16] See, for example, Douglas Duncan, *Ben Jonson and the Lucianic Tradition* (Cambridge: Cambridge University Press, 1979), 9–76; Blanchard, *Scholars' Bedlam*.

Erasmus. Lucian's conception of satire stressed its ludic or playful capacities by mixing serious points with the absurd and by provoking laughter whilst revealing the truth. The intention was that 'the writer not only displays his own wit but also tests and invigorates the wit of his readers' by making the distinction between the true and the false difficult to identify.[17] The speakers of these satires were usually foolish or unreliable and they viewed the world 'upside-down', questioning common-sense assumptions and exposing the contingent quality of the conventions that structure our social lives. In particular, this mode allowed satirists to become 'critical investigators of authority and its constitution in both ancient texts and contemporary institutions'.[18] In this conception of its function, satire is highly mobile and highly sceptical. It will not settle into a uniform pattern or allow a systematic identification of a higher form of truth; indeed, it undermines the possibility of certain judgement itself.

The most obvious of these destabilizing techniques is the simple fact that the work is not directly attributable to Erasmus's own views, but to Folly, who busily condemns folly. This means that the text is constantly beset by contradictions and uncertainty over its coherence because Folly's voice is so prone to wild fluctuations of register and perspective. Her tone shifts from ribald humour, sympathetic accommodation of human weakness, outrage at inequity, and anguish at corruption to spiritual rapture. Consequently, the reader's attitude to her is equally fluctuating and playful. For example, in her outpouring of anger at the papacy, she stresses its propensity to act like an acquisitive territorial prince. The papacy seeks constantly to expand its worldly influence by augmenting its possessions through statecraft, violence, and ultimately war, which is 'so cruell and despiteous a thing, as rather it becometh wilde beasts, than men' (sig. P2^v). So far, so clear. Yet earlier, Folly had praised 'warre, the verie head and springe of all great enterprises' (sig. D3^r) as part of her attack on bloodless and impractical humanists like Erasmus, whose company one would do well to avoid: 'For bidde ones one of these sages to diner, and either with his silent glommyng, or his darke and elvisshe problemes he will trouble all the bourde' (sig. E1^r). The world needs a healthy quotient of self-love, Folly argues, to produce sociability, courage, industry, prudence, and other virtues. If one did not have a healthy amount of self-regard, it would be impossible to achieve any purposeful goal. Who would go to war if they did not wish for fame and reputation? Who would fight if they were hampered by scruples and cavils over the justice of the cause? What use would a philosopher be in war: 'who soked vp with longe studie, leane, and colde of bloudde, maie scantly draw theyr wynde? Naie than must fatte and lustie bloudds doe the feate' (sig. D3^r).

In these frequent moments of reversal and self-contradiction we learn that Folly is both the exponent and target of the work's satire. The adoption of her voice as the narrator (or perhaps performer) of the work makes it metamorphic in conception.[19] The

---

[17] Duncan, *Ben Jonson*, 25.
[18] Blanchard, *Scholars' Bedlam*, 12.
[19] See Wayne A. Rebhorn, 'The Metamorphosis of Moria: Structure and Meaning in *The Praise of Folly*', *PMLA*, 89 (1974): 463–76.

ironies in the work are multi-layered. Folly does acquire a kind of authority as we begin to see the truth and power of her propositions about the theatricality of our social lives, for example, and the necessity to perpetuate illusions to maintain this. However, the satirical spirit of the work is mercurial and its mockery soon bends against her as we also learn that she too is implicated in what she satirizes. In this respect, Folly's inconsistent attitudes and tonal registers are typical of Menippean satire. The different sections of the *Praise of Folly* complement and qualify each other, and this further intensifies its riddling and paradoxical qualities.

This technique also affects Erasmus's authority as a satirist who passes judgement upon the world. Given that his beliefs are also ridiculed as a further instance of folly, we cannot appeal to an author outside the text as a stable point of reference that will help us adjudicate the confusions and uncertainties we encounter. His vocation as a humanist would be negated by the Christian simplicity commended by Folly at the conclusion, a simplicity that would also disable the composition of the work we have just read. Throughout, the *Praise of Folly* suggests not only 'that good and evil are inextricably mixed in this life', but that we should acknowledge that truth can be found even in those contrary features of ourselves or others that we would wish to reject or deny.[20] Significantly, this resistance to polemical self-assurance was identified by its first translator into English, the diplomat and humanist, Thomas Chaloner. In his prefatory address 'To the reader', Chaloner acknowledges how adroitly Erasmus moves 'betweene game and ernest' (sig. A3ʳ) and this reveals how folly is commingled amongst all our thought and activities:

> how so ever a certaine secte of faulte finders condemne all things, that fully square not with theyr owne rules, yea twyce blinde in this, that amongst the commen errours and infyrmitees of mortall men, they will beare nothyng with their bretherne, as who saieth, they were demigodds, and not more than one or two waies lynked in folies bands. (sig. A2ʳ)

Satire in this mode embraces a sceptical recognition of shared human limitation without surrendering the capacity to think critically about the world. Chaloner recognizes fully the work's large-minded resistance to oppositional thinking because we all share qualities with what we condemn.

23.2 Satire and polemic: Stephen Gosson

In *The Schoole of Abuse* (1579), Stephen Gosson shares Erasmus's indignation at the follies of the world and he also recognizes the possibility, at least, of possessing something in common with behaviour that should rightfully appal us. He does so from a radically

---

[20] Thomas O. Sloane, *Donne, Milton and the End of Humanist Rhetoric* (Berkeley: University of California Press, 1985), 80.

different perspective, however, that explores the potential of satire in a distinct way. Lorna Huston has illuminated how Gosson's text shares the concern with reforming social morality and reviving indigenous economic enterprise that dominated similar mid-sixteenth-century works.[21] These satires targeted decadent habits of consumption that threatened not only personal, but national well-being. They sought to impress on the reader that apparently incidental or marginal indulgences have potentially drastic repercussions. *The Schoole of Abuse* warns that in 'those thinges, that we least mistrust, the greatest daunger doth often lurke' and that there is more threat from 'undermining than plaine assaulting; in friendes than foes'.[22]

The great utility of satirical writing for Gosson was its capacity to reveal these submerged dangers both to the individual and to the body politic. *The Schoole of Abuse* is not purely satirical, of course, and it is dominated by a didactic concern to reform unregenerate habits of indulgence and consumption. Yet, as Alvin Kernan has noted, the vividness and realism of Gosson's writing makes it one of the major examples of prose satire prior to the emergence of Thomas Nashe.[23] One strain of antipathy in Gosson's text is directed towards the idea of play itself and to the delight that derives from game-playing, recreation, and imaginative exercise. This is the principle, of course, upon which Erasmus's protean mode of satire depends. In contrast, *The Schoole of Abuse* argues that all the multiple and alluring forms of play present a drastic risk to integrity. For instance, succumbing to a taste for poetry and drama is to invite, as Gosson puts it, liberty to loosen the reins and to initiate a process of moral degeneration: 'from Pyping to playing, from play to pleasure, from pleasure to sloth, from sloth too sleepe, from sleepe to sinne, from sinne to death, from death to the devill' (sig. B3ʳ). This hostility is most notable in the work's notoriously strident anti-theatricality, but also in the mode of satirical writing that Gosson adopts. The latter possesses its own rhetorical artfulness but it is dedicated to very different ends to those of Erasmus. The latter loved to qualify oppositions and undermine moral certainty. Gosson's text reminds us that satire could also be militantly partisan. As Jesse M. Lander has demonstrated, polemical and controversial compositions were at the centre of the period's literary culture in the wake of the Reformation. Such texts are, in many respects, antithetical to the dialogic literary writing that has come to be valued most in the study of the period's canonical works. In contrast, polemical literature conceived of itself 'as a weapon, wielded by one camp against another in an effort to defend and solidify a collective identity'.[24] Satire was a significant medium for writers who sought to create and sustain oppositions, rather than break them down. Gosson certainly recognized its power for those, like himself, who were determined to advance the godly values of the Reformation. Satire provided a way to establish the

---

[21] Hutson, *Thomas Nashe in Context*, 23–6.
[22] Stephen Gosson, *The Schoole of Abuse* (1587), sig. C8ʳ. All quotations to this edition of the work in parentheses in the text.
[23] Kernan, *The Cankered Muse*, 49–50.
[24] Jesse M. Lander, *Inventing Polemic: Religion, Print, and Literary Culture in Early Modern England* (Cambridge: Cambridge University Press, 2006), 11.

writer's authority as he revealed 'the world as a battlefield between a definite, clearly understood good, which he represents, and an equally clear-cut evil'.[25]

In this respect, Gosson used his experience as an example of the dangers that play could present. *The Schoole of Abuse* acknowledges his shameful error of judgement in becoming a playwright. This leads him to concede, embarrassingly, that his plays are still performed. Such admissions lend considerable rhetorical power to the work as it resorts continually to a confessional mode, an authorial 'I' who testifies to his own lapses and delusions. Gosson wonders how can 'I take upon mee to drive you from Playes, when mine owne workes are daily to bee seene upon stages, as sufficient witnesses of mine own folly' (sig. A4^v). The answer is simple: he has reformed and is now able to see his experience whole and with the clarity of one who 'hath beene shooke with a fierce ague' and who can now 'giveth good counsell to his friends when he is wel' (sig. A3^r). This constitutes the basis of his authority to mobilize satire at the expense of those who remain immersed in the illusory world of play.

Gosson's attack on the latter is predicated on a reversal of the Silenus principle inasmuch as it is the beautiful and alluring surfaces of the aesthetic that distracts us from its contaminating interior. Poets exploit and refine their techniques 'as ornamentes to beautife their workes, and sette their trumperie to sale without suspect' (sig. A6^v). Their compositions undoubtedly enthral us: they can excite desires and make vivid a range of experiences. However, in neither of these respects is there any necessary concern with the moral character or effects of their productions. For example, Virgil presents compellingly the 'lust of Dido' and Ovid instructs us bewitchingly in 'the Craft of Love' (sigs. A6^{r-v}). Consequently, writers are 'enimies to vertue' because they indulge and 'effeminate the minde' (sigs. A7^r; B7^r), dilating, rather than regulating, its imaginative scope. Literary and theatrical compositions attempt to satisfy the appetite for sensation, rather than seeking to 'procure amendement of manners, as spurres to vertue' (sig. B7^r). Satire has real value because it can distinguish what is truly serious from the unruly incitements of play. Gosson's text aims to provide a rhetorical 'school' in which the author's own understanding of what a disciplined and virtuous life consists of can be experienced. At the same time, others can be taught how to diagnose and purge themselves of the symptoms that once afflicted the author.

As this phrasing indicates, Gosson is fond of medical metaphors, but he is equally drawn to dietary analogies. Indeed, it is as if he has understood the true etymology of the term satire as a medley and its frequent association with a variety of dishes. As Arthur Kinney notes, *The Schoole of Abuse* explores a wide spectrum of rhetorical modes and techniques with a subtle and shifting use of personae and registers.[26] However, Gosson wishes to introduce a strict principle of selectivity and discrimination into our habits of consumption. Consequently, he commends the 'wisedome, which in banqueting feedes most upon that, that doth nourish best' (sig. A6^r). *The Schoole of Abuse* laments the decline of 'the olde

---

[25] Kernan, *The Cankered Muse*, 22.
[26] Arthur Kinney, 'Stephen Gosson's Art of Argumentation in *The Schoole of Abuse*', *Studies in English Literature, 1500-1900*, 7 (1967): 41-54 (50-2).

discipline of Englande' marked by the hardiness of the country's ancestors who 'fed uppon rootes and barkes of trees' and who, from necessity, consumed resources sparingly to draw the maximum of nourishment from them: 'if they had taken but the quantitie of a beane...they did neither gape after meate, nor long for the cuppe, a great while after' (sigs. C4^{r-v}). This admirably austere quality of life is contrasted with Gosson's pungent mockery of contemporary excess: 'the exercise that is nowe amonge us...banqueting playing, pipyng, and dauncing, and all such delightes as may win us to pleasure, or rocke us a sleepe' (sig. C4^v). Theatre-going itself is a form of surfeiting on spectacle and sensation, but it carries an additional and mortal risk because an audience who have 'nigh burst their gutts with over feeding' can at least resort to a purge: 'but the surfite of the soule is hardly cured' (sigs. B8^v–C1^r).

Gosson's text shows the reader how easily one becomes addicted to pleasures that glut the body and overcharge the soul. Its anger is directed towards the many audience-pleasing forms of composition and performance that pervade the world. These show no concern to sift health-giving from adulterated content for the benefit of the reader or audience: '[T]he Corne which they sell, is full of Cockle,' observes Gosson of playmakers, 'and the drinke they draw, uttercharged with dregges' (sig. C8^r). Theatre is a cardinal example of the dangers of play because it indulges an unrestricted range of tastes which are intended only to please the sensual appetite: 'There set they abroche straunge consortes of melody, to tickle the eare: costly apparell, to flatter the sight: effeminate gesture, to ravishe the sense: and wantone speache, to whet desire too inordinate lust' (sig. C2^v). Playmakers are more insidious than indulgent cooks who only desire to please the tongue, rather than nourish the whole body, because theatre is able to breach our outward senses and contaminate our most inward faculties: 'But these by the privy entries of the eare, slip downe into the hart, and with gunshotte of affection gaule the minde, where reason and virtue should rule the roste' (sig. C3^r). In a series of sketches of the audience behaviour he had witnessed, *The Schoole of Abuse* exposes how the contagion of 'bawdrie' spread during theatrical performances, presenting a particular threat to the moral continence of women: 'Such ticking, such toying, such smiling, such winking, and such manning them [i.e. women] home' (sig. C5^v).

Gosson understands his responsibility to preserve the health of society from those forces that threaten it. Once the appetite of the citizenry has become well-regulated, the sober members of a reformed commonwealth will be enabled to resist decadent and, ultimately, enervating forms of indulgence. *The Schoole of Abuse* recounts with delight the instructive tale of Mithecus, the outstanding cook of classical Greece, whose talents met with incomprehension when he travelled to Sparta: 'thinking there for his cunning to be accounted a God, the good lawes of Licurgus and custome of the country were to hot for his diet' (sig. A8^v). Gosson aspires to instil a similarly Spartan distaste for pleasure by creating a text that is rhetorically compelling, but edifying as well: '*Plutarch* likeneth the recreation that is gotte by conference, too a pleasaunt banquet: the sweet pappe of the one sustaineth the body, the savery doctrine of the other doth norish the minde: and as in banquetting, the wayter standes ready to fill the Cuppe' (sig. C2^r). Good composition, like the text we are reading, has this instructive and satisfying function: it elicits our fascination with the phenomena it excoriates, but then shows how we can move beyond this prurient interest towards more responsible concerns.

It is easy to contrast Gosson in invidious terms to the principled tolerance represented by Erasmus and to characterize the satirical venom of *The Schoole of Abuse* in negative terms. However, it is equally important to remember that controversial works produce 'arguments and identities: early modern polemic is not only polarizing but also pluralizing'.[27] The other side of Gosson's argument derives from his passionate concern for the well-being of the commonwealth. His argument acclaims 'The politike Lawes, in well governed common wealthes, that treade downe the proude, and upholde the meeke' (sig. B4^v). For Gosson, the real vocation of the citizen should be the fashioning of a virtuous and godly society; this is the most rewarding field within which to exercise creative energy and to refine one's power of judgement. The satirical technique of *The Schoole of Abuse* can appear to be grounded on a simplistic contrast between a vanished age of disciplined achievement and a degraded present. His work certainly acclaims the 'Trophes and Triumphes of our auncestours, which pursued vertue at the harde heeles, and shunned vyce as a rocke for feare of shipwracke' (sig. B4^v). Yet, this example is cited to confront the task that now faces English society: to build a more just and fulfilling commonwealth. Past glories 'are excellent maisters to shewe you that this is right Musicke, this perfecte harmony' (sig. B4^v), rather than being distracted by the clamour of commercial theatrical entertainment. Admittedly, Gosson's understanding of the commonwealth is strongly hierarchical. It centres on the rightful obligations that should bind the distinct social ranks and estates to each other and hold them all within their appropriate place (see sig. E5^r). Yet, it is also marked by an emotive appeal to those in authority, including the Queen, to uphold the principles of justice that should apply to and govern the conduct of all members of the body politic, or else we 'lye wallowing like Lubbers in the Ship of the common wealth, crying Lord, Lord, when wee see the vessel toyle, but joyntly lay our handes and heades, and helpes together, to avoyd the danger, and save that which must be the suretie of us all' (sigs. E4^v–E5^r). At a time of such peril, when crucial choices need to be made about the character and destiny of the commonwealth, scepticism is another form of luxury that satire cannot afford to indulge.

23.3 Thomas Nashe and the resources of satire

Gosson's text stands on the cusp of a major new movement in satire initiated primarily by the controversial Marprelate pamphlets of 1588–9.[28] These unlicensed texts attacked episcopacy and advanced puritan ideas with an outrageous degree of scurrility. They

---

[27] Lander, *Inventing Polemic*, 34.
[28] See *The Martin Marprelate Tracts: A Modernized and Annotated Edition*, ed. Joseph L. Black (Cambridge: Cambridge University Press, 2008), xv–cxii.

provoked, in turn, equally forceful counterblasts and this facilitated the rise of the 'satirical journalism' of the 1590s, which absorbed readily 'the imagery and idioms of everyday life, along with its more sordid aspects' and embraced 'a new and dazzling kind of speed in colloquial prose'.[29] At the pinnacle of this movement was the satirist Thomas Nashe, who intervened energetically against the Marprelate tracts and wrote in a cornucopian variety of idioms primarily, but not exclusively, in prose.

Despite his forceful attacks on Marprelate, Nashe's viewpoint is notoriously difficult to identify. The texts he composed display a bewildering variety of registers and perspectives. For example, the author's anti-puritanism stands in an odd relationship to his forbiddingly penitential work, *Christs Teares over Jerusalem* (1594).[30] The latter outdoes Gosson in its rigorous forswearing of worldly indulgences. This includes even the cherished mode of satire which Nashe renounces, it seems, with some regret: 'A hundred unfortunate farewels to fantasticall Satirisme. In those vaines heere-to-fore have I misspent my spirite, and prodigally conspir'd against good houres.'[31] Yet, his contemporaneous work of prose fiction, *The Unfortunate Traveller* (1594), is written in a very different spirit. From the outset, Nashe makes clear that this work will be dedicated to the art of play: 'Gallant Squires, have amongst you', he begins, in an attempt to distract his readers from their card and dice games. Instead, he will now present the sensational account of Jack Wilton's travels and adventures, a text he claims to have recovered from a discarded bundle of 'wast paper'.[32] As the work proceeds, its implications also involve a form of 'serious play', although not quite as envisaged by Erasmus. Indeed, *The Unfortunate Traveller* includes a hostile caricature of the latter that reveals much of its unstable temper, as well as the manner in which Nashe explored the potential of satire.

When he arrives in Rotterdam in the service of the Earl of Surrey, Nashe's amoral protagonist and narrator, the wily page Jack Wilton, meets both Thomas More and 'aged learnings chief ornament, that abundant and superingenious Clarke, *Erasmus*'. After this barbed compliment, Jack deems it 'superfluous' to record any of the conversations he enjoyed with these illustrious humanists, but he deciphers the motivations that underlay the *Praise of Folly*: '*Erasmus* in all his speeches seemed so much to mislike the indiscretion of Princes in preferring of parasites and fooles, that he decreed with himselfe to swim with the stream, and write a booke forthwith in commendation of follie' (245). Subsequently, Jack observes Erasmus's own credulity. When the latter meets Cornelius Agrippa, portrayed as a conjuror, he requests the recreation of a famous episode from the life of the great Roman rhetorician and statesman Cicero: his defence of the alleged parricide Sextus Roscius.[33] Erasmus affirms 'that til in person he beheld his

---

[29] Neil Rhodes, *Elizabethan Grotesque* (London: Routledge & Kegan Paul, 1980), 21.

[30] See Philip Schwyzer, 'Summer Fruit and Autumn Leaves: Thomas Nashe in 1593', *English Literary Renaissance*, 24 (1994): 583–619.

[31] Quoted in Schwyzer, 'Summer Fruit and Autumn Leaves', 609.

[32] 'The Unfortunate Traveller', in *The Works of Thomas Nashe*, ed. Ronald B. McKerrow, rev. F. P. Wilson, 5 vols. (Oxford: Basil Blackwell, 1958), II, 207. All quotations to this edition are in parentheses in the text.

[33] On the equivocal representation of Agrippa, see Jonathan V. Crewe, *Unredeemed Rhetoric: Thomas Nashe and the Scandal of Authorship* (Baltimore: Johns Hopkins University Press, 1982), 77–8.

importunitie of pleading, hee woulde in no wise bee perswaded that anie man coulde carrie awaye a manifest case with rhetorike so strangely'. Agrippa then purports to resurrect Cicero in the act of making his great oration and this spectacle is so convincing 'that all his auditours were readie to install his guiltie client for a God' (252).

This is one of many instances where *The Unfortunate Traveller* exposes the self-interest and obtuseness of its protagonists. In that sense, the satirical temper of the work is polemical as Jack's travels reveal pompous humanists, Italianate villainy, and the massacre of the deluded and defenceless Anabaptists at Munster. Closer to home, Jack encounters ludicrous aristocrats like the Earl of Surrey and the time-serving camp-followers that populate Henry VIII's army in its largely pointless campaign in France. The work reveals a world where social status has no relationship to virtue and reality is theatrical, a matter of play and imposture. The sinister powers that dominate this context are revealed as cruel and absurd. As an aspiring mercenary in the imperial wars that devastate Europe, Jack witnesses the clash between 'the King of *France* and the *Switzers*' that leaves the French soldiers 'sprawling and turning on the stained grasse, like a Roach new taken out of the streame'. The identities of these warring soldiers soon becomes blurred; they are simply the dead, or worse, the half-dead, like the 'bundell of bodies fettered together in their owne bowells' that remind Jack, in a classical parallel, of the punishments inflicted by tyrannical Roman emperors who tied the living bodies of the condemned to corpses: 'so were the halfe living here mixt with squeazed caracases long putrifide' (231).

Yet, these powerful observations, with their strong current of moral outrage, do not derive from a stable commitment to the interests of the commonwealth like Gosson's. Jack Wilton is, to put it mildly, an unreliable narrator. This functions in a very different sense to Erasmus's Folly who is, by her nature, implicated in the absurdities she exposes, but innocent of any attempt to manipulate others, including the reader, to her own advantage. However, the reader's relationship to Jack is much more wary: the narrator's motivations in *The Unfortunate Traveller* are called into question because he is compromised so deeply by the world he also reveals. For example, in his derogatory sketch of Erasmus's prince-pleasing career (and also Cicero's audacious handling of a 'manifest case'), Jack notes how the art of rhetorical eloquence serves the interests of its exponents, rather than the truth of the case. Yet, Cicero's defence of Sextus Roscius was a famous example of how unjust accusations could be overturned and powerful interests defied. Nashe's protagonist shows himself, in contrast, to be a highly skilled manipulator of language for his own specious purposes.

At the beginning of his scandalous account of his travels, Jack is a 'certain kind of an appendix or page' attached to Henry VIII's encampment at Tournai and Térouanne in 1513 (209). There he dedicates himself to a career of trickery and deception at the expense of a variety of authority figures who hold a position in the hierarchy of the camp, but without, in his eyes, any entitlement to respect. Jack singles out the cider merchant for his first attempt at a 'lewd monilesse device' and proves to be a virtuoso in the art of linguistic deceit. Jack convinces this 'old servitor, a cavelier of an ancient house' of the esteem in which he holds him: 'partly for the high descent and linage from whence hee sprong, and partly for the tender care and provident respect he had of pore souldiers' (210; 211). Once he has ensnared his sympathy with this disarming use of the language of compliment and social deference, Jack insinuates that the victualler is in great danger and that his case has been discussed by the King's council. The conviction of this 'dronken Lord', that Jack's status as a page means he has access to counsels of, drives him into a paroxysm of 'unspeakable tormenting uncertaintie' (213), which he resolves by bribing Jack to disclose all he knows. The latter convinces the cider merchant that he is suspected of being an enemy agent and is on the verge of denunciation and death: 'the King saies flatly you are a myser and a snudge [skinflint]' (215). There is only one way to redeem his reputation, of course, which is to distribute his cider freely amid the soldiers of the camp. The 'welbeloved Baron of double beere' also resigns his estate to the King, which leads to the latter's discovery and punishment of Jack's trickery (216).

Described in this way, it is tempting to perceive Nashe's protagonist as an anti-hero whose carnivalesque exploits retaliate upon the unjust privileges and exclusions imposed by an oppressively hierarchical society. There is certainly much in his behaviour that conforms to this picture and, on occasion, Jack sees himself in this way. As he plots his revenge upon the clerks responsible for the camp's finances he exclaims 'I thinke confidently I was ordained Gods scourge from above for their daintie finicalitie' (226). Yet, only moments later, he confesses how energetically he preserved the hierarchy of the English court on his return to it by acting as a kind of physical censor who stamped approval on the bodies of any 'stranger or out-dweller' who sought admission to the precincts of the King's Great Chamber: 'we set a red marke on their eares, and so let them walke as authenticall' (228). Jack's presence as a satirist within the work allows him, on the one hand, to debunk the conventions by which status and authority are maintained; on the other, he demonstrates a chilling facility to inhabit the idioms and roles that he disparages. Equally troubling, is the growing awareness that the playful energy of the text also involves a shaping of others to one's will that is both demeaned and relished by it. In this sense, Margaret Ferguson is surely correct to suggest that *The Unfortunate Traveller* 'creates a space of play in which the human artist's power can be exercised and analyzed at once'.[34]

For example, Jack deploys the arts of language in a way that both satirizes their artificiality and that allows him to exploit their utility in instrumental ways. For all his disdain for Erasmus, Jack's rhetorical fluency involves the dexterous use of the copiousness that the former commended to help expand and vary the figurative use of language. This involved reformulating the same expression in a plurality of ways. 'I have wepte so immoderatly and lavishly', Jack confesses as he describes to the cider merchant his immoderate grief at the suspicions that threaten the latter's life: 'that I thought verily my palat had bin turned to pissing Conduit in *London*. My eyes have bin dronke, outragiously dronke, wyth giving but ordinarie entercourse through their sea-circled Islands

---

[34] Margaret Ferguson, 'Nashe's *The Unfortunate Traveller*: The "Newes of the Maker" Game', *English Literary Renaissance*, 11 (1981): 165–82 (165).

to my distilling dreriment' (213). Later, we see him persuading his gull to disburse his wares freely with another rhetorical device, a preposterous exemplary proof drawn from nature: 'The hunter pursuing the Beaver for his stones, hee bites them off, and leaves them behinde for him to gather up' (215). In his private reflections on the imbecility of his prey we are left in no doubt as to Jack's growing awareness of his talent for eloquence and how words can establish identities, shape expectations, and confirm beliefs. This is one of the central effects of the satire Nashe develops throughout *The Unfortunate Traveller*, as the narrator learns the full extent of the theatrical imposture that passes for reality in the world around him and that sustains the appearance of authority.

In one respect, therefore, Nashe's work demonstrates the tremendous polemical force satire could command and that we have considered in this chapter. Jack skewers the crimes, follies, and pretensions of those around him who play deceptive or self-deceiving roles. Yet, *The Unfortunate Traveller* is equally adept in exploring the duality of the mode. Nashe understood the Menippean tradition as thoroughly as Erasmus, especially its capacity to break down fixed moral and political oppositions.[35] The Earl of Surrey worships his Italian mistress as extravagantly as any member of the idolatrous Catholic faith that he and Jack encounter in Italy and the violent punishments and executions that conclude the text are as grotesque as the crimes they punish. It is not possible to take a 'side' in *The Unfortunate Traveller* or to adopt a uniform perspective. Furthermore, Nashe destabilizes his narrator's moral authority in a much more disturbing way than Erasmus: Jack's own interests and motivations are increasingly shown to be complicit with the world he both debunks and exploits.

Appropriately enough, the legacy of Nashe's work is itself a divided one that demonstrates the openness and volatility of satire. As Graham Roebuck points out, Nashe's use of the term 'cavalier' as a heroic epithet for those brave and patriotic spirits who defied the puritan sedition of the Marprelate pamphlets added lustre to its usage in royalist discourse in the seventeenth century.[36] Yet, Nashe's work was also claimed by alternative traditions. As was noted above, the term 'cavalier' appears in *The Unfortunate Traveller* to capture the decrepit boorishness of the cider merchant and it has similarly derogatory implications elsewhere (220). This semantic legacy was also recollected and explored in puritan satirical works such as John Goodwin's *Anti-Cavalierism* (1642).[37] Nashe's legacy was as complex and divided as his own exploration of the resources of satire.

---

[35] On Nashe's indebtedness to Menippean satire, see Blanchard, *Scholars' Bedlam*, 108–34; Hutson, *Thomas Nashe in Context*, 127–51. See also Howard D. Weinbrot, *Menippean Satire Reconsidered: From Antiquity to the Eighteenth Century* (Baltimore: Johns Hopkins University Press, 2005).

[36] See Graham Roebuck, 'Cavalier', in Claude J. Summers and Ted-Larry Pebworth, eds., *The English Civil Wars in the Literary Imagination* (Columbia and London: University of Missouri Press, 1999), 9–26, esp. 23–5. For an example of Nashe's anti-Marprelate writing in this mode see 'The Returne of the renowned Cavaliero Pasquil of England' (1589), in *The Works of Thomas Nashe*, I.

[37] See Roebuck, 'Cavalier', 24–5.

Further Reading

Connery, Brian A., and Kirk Combe, eds. *Theorizing Satire: Essays in Literary Criticism* (Basingstoke: Macmillan, 1995).
Elliott, R. C. *The Power of Satire: Magic, Ritual, Art* (Princeton: Princeton University Press, 1960).
Gilmore, John. *Satire* (London: Routledge, 2011).
Kernan, Alvin. *The Cankered Muse: Satire of the English Renaissance* (New Haven: Yale University Press, 1959).
Kinney, Arthur. *Markets of Bawdrie: The Dramatic Criticism of Stephen Gosson* (Salzburg: Salzburg Studies in English Literature, 1974).
McConica, James. *Erasmus* (Oxford: Oxford University Press), 1991.
McRae, Andrew. *Literature, Satire and the Early Stuart State* (Cambridge: Cambridge University Press, 2004).
Peter, J. D. *Complaint and Satire in Early English Literature* (Oxford: Clarendon Press, 1956).
Quintero, Ruben, ed. *A Companion to Satire* (Oxford: Blackwell, 2007).
Rummel, Erika. *Erasmus* (London: Continuum, 2004).
Scott-Warren, Jason. *Early Modern English Literature* (Cambridge: Polity Press, 2005), esp. chap. 3.
Smet, Ingrid A. R. de. *Menippean Satire and the Republic of Letters, 1581–1655* (Geneva: Droz, 1996).

CHAPTER 24

NEWS WRITING

JOAD RAYMOND

24.1 INTRODUCTION

THE anonymous printed pamphlet, entitled, *Hereafter ensue the trewe encountre or batayle lately don betwene. Englande and: Scotland* (?1513), has some claim to be the earliest extant English news pamphlet. As such, it marks the convergence between a number of pressures and conventions and opportunities that would shape British news culture, and hence the book trade, and, ultimately, the literary and political culture of the archipelago. It describes the battle of Flodden Field between the forces of Henry VIII and those of James IV, King of Scotland. The latter was slain at the battle. From the very start, news print was involved with propaganda and the death of kings.

Yet, it is an unimposing and, at first glance, uninspired object (and there survive only a handful of copies), though the organization of the text was to set a pattern for thousands of future pamphlets. The title page, with its meandering title, incorporates a woodcut of the Earl of Surrey approaching James IV in front of the assembled Scottish forces. No author was named on the title page: most early news publications were anonymous. Pages two and three of the single, folded sheet have a narrative, in blackletter type, describing the negotiations before battle, of the lie of the land, and of the battle, before listing the English noblemen slain. After the narrative concludes on the fourth and final page, there is a list of the slain English noblemen and then a colophon: 'Emprynted by me. Richarde. Faques dwllyng In poulys churche yerde.' The prose is factual, but has none of the complex rhetoric of proof and demonstration, of eyewitnessing and impartiality that would characterize later reports:

> In this batayle the scottes hadde many great Auauntagies, that is to witte the hyghe. Hylles and mountains a great wynde with them and sodayne rayne all contrary to oug bowes and Archers
>
> It is nat to be douthted but the scottes fought manly and were determyned outher to wynne ye felde or to dye[.] They were also as well apoynted as was possyble at all poyntes with Armoure & harneys so that fewe of them were slayne with arrows

Howbeit the bylles dyd bete and hewe them downe woth some payne and daunger to Englysshemen.[1]

The pamphlet dwells on the treating between the two kings and on James's proud defiance, exhibited in his herald's approach to the Earl of Surrey. The complex decorum of this encounter would have bypassed all but the most informed and attentive reader. However, the significance is expanded in a contemporaneous publication that serves as a partner to the news pamphlet: *A ballade of the Scottyshshe kynge* (no place or date, but probably issued by the same printer-publisher, Richard Faques, in 1513). This small folio ballad, attributed to John Skelton, illustrated with a woodcut of the battle, mocks King James for his arrogance: 'In your somnynge ye were to malaperte/ And your harolde no thynge expert/ Ye thought ye dyde it full valyauntolye/ But not worth thre skppes of a pye'. His pride and his inexperience point to his illegitimacy, and the fatal outcome is providential. In contrast, Henry 'is our noble Champyon. | A kynge anointed and ye be non' ([¶]ᵛ). As a news report the ballad is uninformative/it relies on prior knowledge of the event. Its purpose is, rather, to gloss the event with a celebratory, nationalist perspective, complementing the news in *The trewe encountre*.

By 1640 this was very familiar material: perhaps the greatest shift over these decades was in readers' acclimatization to this kind of news report. There would be significant developments in 1618–22, but the seismic change in the quantity and nature of news would take place in the 1640s. While there is no indication that *Trewe encountre* is an official publication, and the imprint suggests a commercial publication, including an indication of where the item could be purchased, it must have been tolerated by some means, and can therefore be regarded as something like propaganda, though it might be misleading to infer that it had much in common with modern forms of publicity assigned that name. Moreover, its very difference from *A ballade of the Scottyshshe kynge* indicates that its intent was to inform, rather than persuade. The desire of some element of Henry's government to publicize the military victory over the Scots is only one of the forces that brought this nascent form into existence. The commercial potential inherent in printed news was another, which itself depended on an audience of literate consumers and a means of distribution (both of these certainly restricted at this point). To these can be added an apparatus by which news that was traditionally disseminated orally could be translated into written form—which is to say, a shared news rhetoric; and also writers of news and suppliers of news. The quantity of news pamphlets that appeared over the following seven decades suggests that these factors were only intermittently present: if Tudor news is turned into a narrative, it is one that doesn't really get moving until the 1580s.

This may be the consequence of developments after 1513 that inhibited the evolution of the press, as well as of the limitations imposed by literacy and commercial infrastructure. These developments include, above all, legal restrictions. Two years later, Pope Leo X would issue a decree requiring all cities under his influence to prevent

---

[1] *Hereafter ensue the trewe encountre* (?1513), [A2ʳ].

the printing of any book without a licence granted by Rome or a local bishop. He reasoned thus:

> Complaints from many persons, however, have reached our ears and those of the apostolic see. In fact, some printers have the boldness to print and sell to the public, in different parts of the world, books—some translated into Latin from Greek, Hebrew, Arabic and Chaldean as well as some issued directly in Latin or a vernacular language—containing errors opposed to the faith as well as pernicious views contrary to the Christian religion and to the reputation of prominent persons of rank. The readers are not edified. Indeed, they lapse into very great errors not only in the realm of faith but also in that of life and morals. This has often given rise to various scandals, as experience has taught, and there is daily the fear that even greater scandals are developing.[2]

Two years after this, Luther posted his 95 theses, polemic about the reformation of the church grew more acute, and anxiety increased about the pernicious influence of printed debate. Henry VIII became the first European ruler to prohibit a specific list of books (the *index librorum prohibitorum*) in a proclamation of 1529; Pope Paul IV issued the first papal Index three decades later, in 1559. Print was dangerous because it was public, because it risked the spread of debate, and because readers could be influenced outside of traditional institutional structures of authority. And news—it would gradually be learned—was dangerous because it encouraged discussion of matters of state, it encouraged 'lavish discourse', gossip and rumour, and uncontrolled and uncontrollable speech and opinion.[3] For this reason, printed news would become the object of increasing suspicion—yet, there would be such a close affinity between news and printing that printed news would appear in one form or another, with varying intensity and frequency, until the development, at the end of our period, of something very much like the modern newspaper.

24.2 WHAT IS NEWS, AND WHY DID IT MATTER?

News—the noun: it was also in Stuart times a verb, to *news* it about—has two aspects. First: it is an event that is communicated: news of a king's death, a battle, a monstrous birth, or a strange fish washed up on a shore. News events, according to sociological research on modern news media, become newsworthy because of their possession to some degree of some of twelve characteristics: frequency (it has to fit into a cycle), scale, unambiguity (its implications have to be finite and identifiable), meaningfulness (primarily relevance to your circumscribed cultural context), predictability (we want or predict that it should happen),

---

[2] *Decrees of the Ecumenical Councils*, Vol. 1: *Nicaea I—Vatican II*, ed. Norman P. Tanner (Georgetown: Georgetown University Press, 1990), online text at <http://www.ewtn.com/library/COUNCILS/LATERAN5.HTM> accessed 5 May 2011.

[3] Fritz Levy, 'The Decorum of News', in Joad Raymond, ed., *News, Newspapers and Society in Early Modern Britain* (London: Frank Cass, 1999), 12–38.

unpredictability (because rare events are newsworthy), continuity with earlier news, and composition (i.e. they fit expectations of balance or interest). In addition, news events in the modern, Western world, according to the same sociologists, prioritize elite nations, elite people, personify news, and focus on bad news.[4] News is thus a commodity, but it is also a currency, something defined by, and itself defining, relationships between communicators. It can take one of many forms—a conversation in the street or in bed, a newsletter, a pamphlet, or a television programme—but these forms also participate in a common pattern of communication. What is communicated within this pattern, whether true or false, old or new, interesting or tedious, is constitutively defined as news through its transmission.

In oral exchange, news could be a social pleasantry. Diaries and libel cases record neighbours and travellers encountering each other and asking 'what news?'[5] It is both a means of commencing or affirming a relationship and a sensuous human need, a material fact of our existence as social beings. The evidence we have of these conversations derives from where they went wrong—and news turned into scandal, slander, or sedition,[6] conversations that violated norms and hence left a legal record—or when they were exceptional and literate individuals, such as Thomas Cotton, John Rous, and Nehemiah Wallington, wrote them down in diaries. As most people in this period were illiterate, it is not possible to recover any but the broadest contours of this oral news culture. Where historians have been able to be more specific, and to explore the content of conversations, it has usually been through its contact with written and printed culture. As Adam Fox and others have shown, oral exchanges fed off the enhancement in the supply of news by the invention of the printed periodical; news and rumour moved freely between printed and manuscript exchange; writing reinvented oral traditions. Indeed, the very idea of an oral culture is one that was, and could only be, formulated after the appearance of print (writing was too obviously exclusively elite before then). Early sixteenth-century England was not simply an oral society; seventeenth-century England was not simply a text-based society; and though the relationships between modes of communication shifted in the period, this cannot be reduced to one displacing another.[7]

News that was written down presents a richer and more complex resource. It includes familiar communications, newsletters, commercially produced newsletters, and scribal separates of news. What had been an informal mode of communication was

---

[4] Johann Galtung and Mari Ruge, 'Structuring and Selecting News', in Stanley Cohen and Jock Young, eds., *The Manufacture of News: Social Problems, Deviance, and the Mass Media* (London: Constable, 1973), 62–72. See also Roger Fowler, *Language in the News: Discourse and Ideology in the Press* (London and New York: Routledge, 1991); Stuart Hall, 'The Social Production of News', in Hall et al., eds., *Policing the Crisis: Mugging, the State, and Law and Order* (Basingstoke: Macmillan, 1978).

[5] Joad Raymond, *The Invention of the Newspaper: English Newsbooks, 1641–1649* (1996; Oxford: Clarendon Press, 2005), 1 and the sources cited there; Adam Fox, *Oral and Literate Culture in England 1500–1700* (Oxford: Clarendon Press, 2000), 349–51.

[6] David Cressy, *Dangerous Talk: Scandalous, Seditious, and Treasonable Speech in Pre-Modern England* (Oxford: Oxford University Press, 2010).

[7] Fox, *Oral and Literate Culture*; Adam Fox and Daniel Woolf, eds., *The Spoken Word: Oral Culture in Britain, 1500–1850* (Manchester: Manchester University Press, 2002); Peter Burke, *The Art of Conversation* (Cambridge: Polity Press, 1993).

commercialized through the emergence in the early sixteenth century, across Europe, though initially in Venice and Rome, of *avvisi*. These serial news sheets, produced in scribal workshops, compiled stories of news from various sources—including overseas, gathered from the wisps of mercantile trade routes—and were sold to the educated elite, providing them with political and commercial information, facilitating their engagement in public life, as well as enriching their everyday conversation.[8] The most celebrated commercial manuscript newsletter consumers included the Fuggers family, proprietors of an Augsburg financial house, who collected, from 1568 onwards, regular newsletters that were distributed widely across Europe.[9] In England, and on a more modest scale, there were John Pory, John Chamberlain, Samuel Pecke, and, perhaps, Joseph Meade (who is discussed further below)—all early seventeenth-century writers, suggesting that England lagged behind Europe in this respect.[10] Prior to this, individuals wrote regular newsletters, but did so in semi-formal arrangements, not as professionals with multiple recipients.

Nonetheless, written news had a different character from oral—and, subsequently, printed news, though printed news throughout its early history was little more than printed manuscript news. Ben Jonson, who was interested in and perhaps inspired by the peculiar nature of print, its capacities to reach an audience, to preserve the letter, and to detract from the spirit of written words, returned to satire of printed news. In his masque, *News from the New World* (1620), a writer of manuscript newsletters claims to write a thousand or more newsletters a week, to all parts of the country and to all ranks of persons, tailoring his news to the religious disposition of his recipient. This archetypal newsletter writer disputes with an exemplary printer about the value of their trade: for the former, printing makes news common, and therefore no longer news, while written news, though it may be untrue, is still news; for the printer, the truth is also altogether irrelevant, but the very printing indicates the truth of news to a vulgar audience, 'who will indeed believe nothing but what's in Print. For those I doe keep my Presses, and so many Pens going to bring forth wholesome relations, which once in halfe a score yeares (as the age growes forgetfull) I Print over againe with a new date.'[11] Print therefore has a fraught relationship with the truth and with the appetites of a

---

[8] Mario Infelise, *Prima dei giornali. Alle origini della pubblica informazione* (Rome: Laterza, 2002); Filippo De Vivo, *Information & Communication in Venice: Rethinking Early Modern Politics* (Oxford: Oxford University Press, 2007); on these workshops in Britain, see Harold Love, *The Culture and Commerce of Texts: Scribal Publication in Seventeenth-Century England* (1993; Amherst: University of Massachusetts Press, 1998), 90–137 and *passim*.

[9] V. von Klaswill, ed., *The Fugger News-Letters* (London: John Lane, 1924).

[10] Thomas Birch, ed., *The Court and Times of Charles I*, 2 vols. (1848); William S. Powell, *John Pory 1572–1636: The Life and Letters of a Man of Many Parts* (Chapel Hill, NC: University of North Carolina Press, 1977); *The Letters of John Chamberlain*, ed. Norman Egbert McClure, 2 vols. (Philadelphia: American Philosophical Society, 1939); Richard Cust, 'News and Politics in Early Seventeenth-Century England', *Past & Present*, 112 (1986): 60–90; Ian Atherton, '"The Itch Grown a Disease": Manuscript Transmission of News in the Seventeenth Century', in Raymond, ed., *News, Newspapers and Society*, 39–65; David Randall, 'Joseph Mead, Novellante: News, Sociability and Credibility in Early Stuart England', *Journal of British Studies*, 54 (2006): 293–312.

[11] C. H. Herford and Percy and Evelyn Simpson, eds., *Ben Jonson*, 10 vols. (Oxford: Oxford University Press, 1925-50), 7: 515.

credulous public. Jonson's chosen form is a masque and the commerce in and culture of news represents his principle of disorder, from which an ideal of order must be rescued. He would proceed to explore the same matrix of relationships—news, truth, print, commerce, credibility, and publicity—in his play *The Staple of News* (1626, 1631): some aspect of printed news threatened to upstage him, or even the dramatic form itself.[12]

Printed news was regarded with scepticism: from its very earliest days it was associated with falsehood and deception. The very fact of its commonality, its relative lack of social prestige, and its non-exclusivity (more a hypothetical characteristic than a reality because of low levels of literacy) resulted in its denigration—yet, that was precisely the quality that also gave it a distinctive power and therefore authority. Printed news encouraged discussion of matters of state; it could make public things that should possibly be the province of a well-informed and well-educated few. Print affirmed that rumours were true; but it also disseminated untruths. Printed news was thus characterized by a potent ambivalence, one that perhaps more clearly articulates the social tensions around the possession and communication of the news than it does the actual truthfulness of the medium.

24.3 ANTWERP, 1576

How did you know news was true? Over the first two centuries of printed books, there rapidly developed a range of verbal and paratextual means of demonstrating that a news report was truthful and accurate, and even impartial. Central to these was the notion of testimony and eyewitnessing. News close to the source was privileged, which is one of the particular qualities of the epistolary form. One early and sophisticated news pamphlet shows some of these qualities in play: *The spoyle of Antwerp* (1576) by George Gascoigne (who is not identified as the author in the text: he merely refers to himself as 'a true English man, who was present'). This is atypical of Tudor news pamphlets in some respects: it has a literary merit deriving from a careful and reflective prose style; its realization of events is vivid; it is not translated, but written in English; and it is a detailed account of a particular event. In other respects it is typical: it concerns war, and conflict between Protestants and Catholics.

Gascoigne had complained in April 1576, in a preface to another's book, that he was obliged to 'march amongst the Muses for lacke of exercise in martiall employes'. Later that year, he was writing news to Lord Burghley, Secretary to State, from Paris and then Antwerp, apparently in an official capacity. Hence, he was in Antwerp in October and

---

[12] Joad Raymond, *Pamphlets and Pamphleteering in Early Modern Britain* (Cambridge: Cambridge University Press, 2003), 140–4; D. F. McKenzie, '*The Staple of News* and the Late Plays', in W. Blissett, J. Patrick, and R. W. Van Fossen, eds., *A Celebration of Ben Jonson* (Toronto: University of Toronto Press, 1973), 83–128; Mark Z. Muggli, 'Ben Jonson and the Business of News', *Studies in English Literature*, 32 (1992): 323–340; Marcus Nevitt, 'Ben Jonson and the Serial Publication of News', in Joad Raymond, ed., *News Networks in Seventeenth Century Britain and Europe* (London: Routledge, 2006), 51–66.

November 1576 to witness the sacking of the city by Spanish forces.[13] Soon after, he wrote the pamphlet, beginning 'Since my hap was to bee present...' The emphasis on eyewitnessing serves the convention of proof, but it more evidently colours this personal report than most other instances. Yet, Gascoigne also dwells at unusual length on his conscientiousness and his strategy of reporting. His pamphlet, he writes, will 'answer all honest expectations with a meane truthe, set downe between thextreme surmises of sundry doubtfull mindes: And encreased by the manyfolde light tales which haue been engendred by fearful or affectionate rehersals' (Aii^r). In an age of confessional conflict, the notion that the truth needed to be presented in a non-emotional way was far from universal. He proceeds to argue for moderation:

> let these my few woordes become a forewarnynge on bothe handes: and let them stande as a Lanterne of light between two perilous Rockes... To that ende, all stories and Chronicles are written: and to that ende I presume to publishe this Pamphlet: protestyng that neither mallice to the one syde, nor partiall affection to the other, shall make my pen to swarve any iote from truth of that which I will set down & saw executed: For if I were dispose to write maliciously agaynst the vanquishers: their former barbarous cruelty, insolences, Rapes, spoyles, Incests, and Sacriledges, committed in sundrie other places, might yeeld mee sufficiente matter without the lawful remembrance of this their late stratagemne... But as I sayd before, mine onely entent is to set downe a plaine truthe, for the satisfiynge of sutche as have hetherto beene caried aboute with doubtfull reportes: and for a profitable example unto all sutche as beeyng subiect to like imperfections, might fall thereby into the like calamities. (sigs. Aii–Aiii^v)

The 'plaine truth' is a rhetorical commonplace, but that should not lessen the significance of what Gascoigne is undertaking in applying his understanding of the plain style, *captatio benevolentiæ*, and *narratio* to a bloody event of pan-European significance he has days before witnessed. He does, however, assume that his readers already know the contents of the false news reports, which makes his corrections harder to penetrate at times. Rather than describing, as an historian might, he sets about clarifying the context of Spanish antagonism to the city, though, like a sophisticated historian, and unlike most early modern news writers, he includes the question of *why* in his analysis.[14]

In setting the scene, he establishes both his credibility (though he is perhaps a little disingenuous about his reason for being there—he may have been spying) and the tense mood in the city: 'At this time and xii. dayes beefore I was in the sayde towne of *Antwerpe* vpon certeine priuate affaires of myne owne: so that I was enforced to become an eyed witnes of their entry and all that they did. As also afterwards (for all ye gates were kept first shut + I could not departe) to beeholde the pitiful stratageme which folowed' (Avii^r). He is trapped within the city and finds himself a victim, as well as a witness, when he is

---

[13] Humfrey Gilbert, *A Discourse of a Dicouerie for a new Passage to Cataia* (1576), sig. ¶¶¶i^r; *ODNB*, 'Gascoigne, George'.

[14] Nicholas Brownlees, *The Language of Periodical News in Seventeenth-Century England* (Newcastle upon Tyne: Cambridge Scholars Publishing, 2011), 46–51.

trampled underfoot by fleeing Walloon forces at one point. He nonetheless diligently states what he cannot affirm: 'Their order of entry into ye Castle yeard, and of their approch to the trenches, I did not see, for I could not get out of the town... yet as I heard it rehearsed by sundry of them selues, I wil also here rehearce it for a truth' (Bi^r). His writing balances a judicious presentation of facts with a sense of the drama of events. The horror of the piles of dead bodies he frames in an orderly way: 'Now I haue set downe the order of their entry, approch, charge, and assaulte: together with their proceeding in victory: and that by credible report, both of the Spanyerdes themselues, and of others who serued in their company: let me also say a little of that which I sawe executed' (Biii^v), and he proceeds to describe the fighting he sees when he leaves the English house, as well as the bullet that narrowly misses him. While he does not hesitate to accuse the Spaniards of 'barbarous cruelty' (Bvii^v), this accusation will be levelled through the lens of a clear narrative, nor will he be impartial: 'And now to keep promise, and to speake without parciality: I must needs confesse, that it was the greatest victory, and the roundlyest executed, that hath bene seene, red, or heard of, in our age' (Bvi^v). Only after admitting this can it be seen how ungodly their slaughter is, conducted after the signs of God's favour shown in their victory. Gascoigne performs a remarkably inventive display of balance and reserved emotion, such as are associated with modern, objective reporting.[15]

Gascoigne is an unusually *literary* news writer and it is perhaps this self-consciousness that assists him in forging a journalistic style that anticipates later developments in reportage. Perhaps most startling is this painterly reference: 'I forbeare also to recount the huge numbers, drowned in ye new Toune: where a man might behold as many sundry shapes and formes of mans motion at time of death: as euer *Mighel Angelo* dyd portray in his tables of Doomes day' (Ci^r). If we were to view the history of news writing in the period 1500–1640 as a narrative, however, Gascoigne is an interesting anomaly: his attention to detail in the techniques of news reporting was not picked up again until Thomas Gainsford was writing between 1622 and 1624. Most of the narrative has to be seen in terms of the development of practicalities, rather than style, and these were driven by the terms of book-commerce, government regulation, and the circumstances of international politics.

24.4 SENSATION

Not all domestic news was subject to these restrictions. In fact, a significant proportion of press output was newsy: providential pamphlets on strange and miraculous phenomena, crimes and punishments, and witchcraft.[16] Such publications, judging by official censures on the news press, were assigned to a different category from

---

[15] Teun A. van Dijk, *News as Discourse* (Hillsdale, NJ: Lawrence Erlbaum, 1988).
[16] Alexandra Walsham, *Providence in Early Modern England* (Oxford: Oxford University Press, 1999); Julie Crawford, *Marvelous Protestantism: Monstrous Births in Post-Reformation England*

military and parliamentary news. While timeliness was essential to political news, this kind of news fitted longer cycles, and these materials were seldom as precisely dated, and were occasionally recycled. By turns prurient and titillating, they mixed sensation with moral instruction and shaped their narratives with reformed providential and soteriological reflection. Proselytizing preachers, like Henry Goodcole and Thomas Cooper, often with a zealous or puritan agenda, found the news pamphlet, despite its gossipy and even immoral associations, a useful vehicle for exploring elements of Calvinist theology. While political news was circumscribed by social norms and censorship practices, Protestant soteriology was well suited to the forms of cheap print.

Two examples of different approaches to this mixing of news and instruction will be sufficient. The first, *A most horrible & detestable Murther committed by a bloudie minded man vpon his owne Wife: and most strangely Reuealed by his Childe that was vnder fiue yeares of age* (1595), begins with a two-page address 'To the Christian Reader' with the most direct kind of moralizing: 'How many most execrable murthers haue there beene done of late time, which hath bin published for our example to the world, thereby to put vs inminde of our duties to God, & withhold vs from like trespasses, by viewing their shamefull ends, whom deservedly the Law cuts off for such offences. But so rageth the enemie of mankinds, day and night restlessly with his temptations, that he ceaseth not to vrge vs all to mischeife' (sig. A2^r). The devil is frequently an important character in these pamphlets—so much so that they may be said to express a culture of 'popular Manicheanism'.[17] The purpose is expressly didactic: 'And that the falls of others may make vs to leaue those sinnes so deeply ingrafted in our harts, that in the last daye we may reape the reward of our charitie and other good deedes to our needie Brethren extended ...' (A2^v). The anonymous author is not proposing that the pamphlet will suppress the uxoricidal urges of its readers; rather, the murder is used as a more general lesson in the nature of salvation. The narration does not reveal a motive, but describes how Raph Meaphon returned from labouring and, 'comming home, his wife with her sonne or fiue yeares, or scarse so much, beeing a bed, he knocked, and was let in, where he fel to rayling and chiding with her: and in the end, whether it were a matter pretended, or otherwise, but lead thereunto by the Diuel, the ancient enemie of our saluation, which doubtless prouoked him therevnto, he drew out hys knife and cut her throate, and so leauing her weltring in her owne goare' (A3^r), he went on to fire the house. By a providential turn, the child is saved and acts as a (truth-speaking and innocent) witness against the father, who is

---

(Baltimore, MD: Johns Hopkins University Press, 2005); Peter Lake with Michael Questier, *The Antichrist's Lewd Hat: Protestants, Papists and Players in Post-Reformation England* (New Haven: Yale University Press, 2002); David Cressy, *Travesties and Transgressions in Tudor and Stuart England* (Oxford: Oxford University Press, 2000).

[17] Peter Lake, 'Deeds against Nature: Cheap Print, Protestantism and Murder in Early Seventeenth-Century England', in Kevin Sharpe and Peter Lake, eds., *Culture and Politics in Early Stuart England* (Basingstoke: Macmillan, 1994), 257–83, esp. 277.

duly executed—still without confessing the fact, further truth of his reprobation. The pamphlet concludes with a further moral counsel on the certain revelation of sins, 'how the fowles of the ayre, yea the stones in the wall shall declare such horrible sinnes, that the punishment due for the same may be worthely rewarded, as we see by this and many others' (A4^v).

A sharp contrast can be found in *A Detection of damnable driftes, practized by three Witches arraigned at Chelmisford in Essex* (1579). The anonymous author begins with a protest: 'Accept this pamphlet (Christian Reader) view and peruse it with discretion, and hedefulnesse. No trifles are therin conteined worthy to be contemned, nor pernicious fantazies deseruyng to bee condemned' (Aii^r). Indeed, there are not: the text of the pamphlet consists of the confession of the witches and the evidence submitted against them, expressed in the formal language of court record ('Item, the saied Mother Staunton...'). Some details are nonetheless titillating: 'Besides the sonne of this Mother Smith, confessed that his mother did keepe three Spirites, whereof the one called by her greate Dick, was enclosed in a wicker Bottle: The seconde names Little Bicke, was putte into a Leather Bottle: And the third termed Willet, she kepte in a Wolle Packe. And thereupon the house was commaunded to bee searched. The Bottles and packe were found, but the Spirites were vanished awaie' (Avi^v). Despite such particularity, the pamphlet provides no substantial context for the events—not even the sentences—and either relies on the reader already possessing such context, or, more likely, pushes the reader away from gossip towards a more abstract, theological interpretation. The court depositions are framed as an essay in the character of election and reprobation:

> in this pretie plot may holsome hearbes of admonitions for the vnwarie, and carelesse, and soote flowers to recreate the wearied senses, be gathered. For on thone side the cleare sight maie espie the ambushmentes, whiche Sathan the secrete woorkemaister of wicked driftes, hath placed in moste partes of this realme, either by craftie conueighaunces, to creepe into the conceiptes of the simple, or by apparaunt treacherie to undermine and spoile the states of such as God permitteth him to haue power ouer. And on the other side the eye that is wimpled, may hereby be aduertised of the darkenesse, wherewith his vnderstanding is ouercast, and puttyng of the veile of vanitie, maie reclaime his concept, and esteeme of the impietie of the offendours and vilanie of their actes, according to the woorde of God, and waightinesse of the case. (Aii^{r-v})

There is a manifest disjuncture between the merely illustrative and unedifying detail of the vanishing spirits and the Manichean moral categories with which the reader is instructed to approach the text. This very heterogeneity is typical of news publications and reminds us that readers may not have approached the matter with the moral earnestness that clerical authors recommended.[18]

---

[18] On moralizing and providential pamphlets, see Sandra Clark, *The Elizabethan Pamphleteers: Popular Moralistic Pamphlets, 1580–1640* (London: Continuum, 1983); Walsham, *Providence*; Lake, *Antichrist's Lewd Hat*.

24.5 NEWS IN TRANSLATION, 1589–1640

In part because of the appetite for overseas news, in part because of apprehensiveness about the dangers of publishing 'domestic' or British news, much news publishing in Britain involved translation of foreign-language news pamphlets. While there were various occasional publications—ballads and pamphlets on the rebellion of the northern earls in 1569–70, for example; and sensational publications on witches and monstrous births—the first glut of news publications appeared in 1589. The Marprelate Controversy was raging, one of the earliest pamphlet wars in English, exposing and satirizing Anglican bishops, and showing the power of the press to reach and influence a broad reading public. Meanwhile, the Protestant Henri of Navarre ascended to the French throne. This dramatic injection of confessional interest into the French Wars of Religion increased English readers' appetite for news—or, at least, publishers' estimation of that appetite. Over the next four years, dozens of news pamphlets appeared, directly translated from the French (with little adjustment for the English audience), a glut that ended with the King's reconversion to Protestantism in 1593.[19]

During this period, the printer-bookseller John Wolfe, something of a specialist in cheap news pamphlets, as well as illicit printing (until he became a beadle of the Stationers's Company—the trade guild with a monopoly over printing and publishing, which preserved order in the book trade—in 1587), effectively invented the news serial. His pamphlet *Newes out of France on the First of this moneth of March* (1592) was conceived as part of a series, which continued with *The Chiefe Occurrences of Both the Armies* (1592), *The Continual Following of the French King* (1592), *A Discourse of That Which is Past, Since the Kings Departure from Gouy* (1592), *A True Relation of the French Kinge His Good Successe… With Other Intelligences Given by Other Letters Since the Second of May* (1592), and *A Journall, Wherein is Truly Sette Downe from Day to Day, what was Doone… from the Coming of the Duke of Parma into Fraunce, Untill the Eighteenth of May 1592* (1592). It is possible that his earlier *Newes Lately come on the last day of Februarie 1591, from diuers partes of France, Sauoy, and Tripoli in Soria* (1591) was also intended as part of this series. Wolfe was not only specializing in publishing news ('Truely translated', as the title page of the last item claimed, 'out of the French and Italian Copies, as they were sent to right Honourable persons'), but also experimenting with new means of publishing it. A serial publication offered the opportunity to secure an ongoing, loyal audience (and thus stable profits—news was a 'steady-seller', though it generally only sold in single editions). Wolfe had perhaps taken the idea from another serial news publication, the weekly *Bills of Mortality*, which had first appeared in 1581. These government publications documented the deaths in London by parish and cause, constituting a print record of the city's demographic that was also read as news,

---

[19] Raymond, *Pamphlets*, 103–8; Paul J. Voss, *Elizabethan News Pamphlets: Shakespeare, Spenser, Marlowe and the Birth of Journalism* (Pittsburgh, PA: Duquesne University Press, 2001); Lisa Ferrarou Parmalee, *Good Newes from Fraunce: French Anti-League Propaganda in Late Elizabethan England* (Rochester, NY: University of Rochester Press, 1996).

provoking fear in readers as plague crept towards them.[20] They furnished the idea of serial, periodical news if anyone was able to seize it: and Wolfe appears to have done so.

With the end of the French Wars of Religion the production of news pamphlets abated; with the outbreak of the Thirty Years War in 1618 there was another efflorescence and a more sustained development of the serial press. London booksellers began to produce translations of Dutch and German news sheets. A more developed news-periodical business existed in mainland Europe at this time: weekly vernacular newspapers appeared in Strasbourg and Antwerp in 1605, Basel in 1610, Paris in 1613, Frankfurt and Vienna by 1615, and Amsterdam in 1618, all of which had superseded *Mercurius Gallobelgicus*, a semi-annual, Latin news publication that first appeared in 1592. From 1618 through 1620 London publishers—generally those specializing in inexpensive print—translated foreign pamphlets. Among these titles we can find *A Catalogve of the Depvties of the High and Mightie States Generall of the Vnited Prouinces* (1618), *The true description of the execution of iustice, done in the Grauenhage, by the counsell of the Generall States holden for the same purpose, vpon Sir Iohn van Olden Barnauelt Against whom the said States purposely thereunto appointed, did worthily pronounce sentence of death according to his deserts; which was executed vpon the third day of May, 1619. stilo nouo. at ten of the clocke in the morning* (1619), and *A most true relation of the late proceedings in Bohemia, Germany, and Hungaria Dated the 1. the 10. and 13. of Iuly, this present yeere 1620* (1620). These publications, though they have been removed from the histories by subsequent historians, are identical to later 'corantos' in every respect except seriality: they are occasional publications. At some point in late 1620 (the earliest surviving issue is unlikely to have been the first) a Dutch publisher issues, for distribution in Britain, an English translation of a Dutch news sheet. This followed the original in its folio format, irregular periodicity, and plainness of style:

> *From Crakow in Poland. Iuly* 4.
> The Polonians haue begun to warre with the Turks, and the new Generall *Kothwits* is gone with the whole armie to Podolia: the report goeth, that they haue had an hot skirmish with the Turkes.[21]

In 1621 English stationers—especially Thomas Archer, Nathaniel Butter, and Nicholas Bourne—displaced the imports with London-printed translations. These initially imitated the Dutch in assuming folio format, but then reverted to the quarto format of 1618, which was traditional for English-printed pamphlets. In this form the serial publications—they never achieved the fixed periodicity that would enable them to be called periodicals in the strict meaning of the word—known as 'corantos' survived until their suppression in 1632. After a brief revival in late 1638 they would continue until they were displaced by the weekly newsbooks, containing news of Britain, that began to appear in November 1641.[22]

---

[20] Mark Jenner, 'London', in Joad Raymond, ed., *Oxford History of Popular Print Culture*, vol. 1: *Cheap Print in Britain and Ireland to 1660* (Oxford, 2011), 297–300, and references cited there.

[21] *Newes from the Low Countries, or a Courant out of Bohemia, Poland, Germanie, &c.* (Amsterdam, 9 August 1621), recto.

[22] For the history of corantos condensed in this paragraph, see Folke Dahl, *Dutch Corantos 1618–1650: A Bibliography* (The Hague: Koninklijke, 1946); F. Dahl, *A Bibliography of English Corantos and Periodical*

The language of the corantos in the 1620s is largely factual. It sketches events, usually under locatives and with specific dates—both lending an air of credibility to reports and serving as typographical divisions before the invention of headlines—in unemotive language. Glossing is absent, prefatory remarks and transitions are kept to a minimum. This is the consequence of a literalist approach to translation, but also, perhaps, a sign of nervousness about the dangers of publishing news. It was indeed a risky business, as Joseph Meade indicated in one newsletter dated 22 September 1621: 'My Corrantoer Archer was layd by the heeles for making or adding to Corrantoes &c. as they say: But now there is another who hath gott license to print them & sell them honestly translated out of Dutch.'[23] Meade suggests that it was precisely a more creative approach to the translation of Dutch corantos that landed Archer in trouble, and his successor had promised to be more 'honest', that is to say, literal.

To obtain more news, and more diverse news, one could turn to manuscript newsletters such as those Meade supplied, as part of a patron–client relationship, rather than a narrowly commercial one, to Sir Martin Stuteville. Meade's newsletters conveniently overlapped with the early corantos, which he was able to incorporate with his own reporting in various ways. He articulated clearly the distinction between news sources: 'domestick', 'merely forraine', and 'mixt', which last involved news of embassies at home and overseas.[24] With his foreign news he tended to indicate his sources, the letters he learned it from; with domestic news he related it as fact, without any such frame, though as a Cambridge don he cannot have witnessed much of the court news first hand. He was aware, however, that the value of his service lay in the heterogeneity of his news content and the inclusion of domestic news that was not available in printed sources. This does not mean he did not have to be careful: though there was not normally a direct form of censorship affecting correspondence, written communication was nonetheless subject to the laws governing libel and the more general risks of irritating those in power. The following is a typical example of the privileged news, reported in a mildly anodyne, positive tone:

> On munday His Matie went to Parliament, then most graciously signified his acceptance of their loves vnto him, which was more then he expected; & also approved of their doings, which he acknowledged to be wisely and temperately done. And that now he studied how & wherein to give them all the content he could; and therefore, that there was not any intendment of his whatsoever, not any affection which beare to any person, how great soeuer, but that if they should fine it prejudiciall to state and commonwealth, he would decline from the same; yea though it extended to his son Charles...[25]

Newsbooks 1620–1642 (London: Bibliographical Society, 1952); Joseph Frank, *The Beginnings of the English Newspaper, 1620–1660* (Cambridge, MA: Harvard University Press, 1961); Michael Colin Frearson, 'The English Corantos of the 1620s', Ph.D. thesis, University of Cambridge (1993); Nicholas Brownlees, *Corantos and Newsbooks: Language and Discourse in the First English Newspapers (1620–1641)* (Pisa: ETS, 1999) and *Language of Periodical News*; Raymond, *Pamphlets*, chap. 4.

[23] BL: Harl. MS 289, fol. 122^r.
[24] BL: Harl. MS 289, fol. 129^v. On Meade as a newsletter writer, see Randall, 'Joseph Mead, Novellante'.
[25] BL: Harl. MS 289, fol. 43^r.

The language of Meade's reporting parallels the indirect phrasing of this delicate negotiation between parliamentary supply and monarchical prerogative. This is precisely the kind of news that was unavailable in print until 1641. Much of Meade's foreign news was transcribed from printed corantos, which he evidently regarded as sufficiently reliable. At times (this example is from March 1623) he could go so far as to declare: 'I haue no more newes to send you at this present then what I enclose & you shall find in the book I send.'[26] However, there were respects in which corantos seemed to him unsatisfactory. When he included them with his newsletters to Stuteville he would annotate them with minor corrections and glosses. For example, in a copy of *Corante, or, Newes From Italy* (Amsterdam, 9 July 1621) that he sent to Stuteville, Meade corrected the printed sentence: 'In Morauia, there are more principall Lords and Burgers committed to prison, whose expectation, as also in Prague of the prisoners shall this weeke be done…' He deleted 'expectation' and inserted 'execution', probably based on inference.[27] Elsewhere, he corrected linguistic errors, he identified where obscure towns were, and more generally, he supplied glosses and explanations where the reader (in this case, specifically Stuteville) would benefit from more context. Hence, where one coranto had the phrase 'The Turkes day at Regensburg…', Meade corrected 'Turkes day' to 'Reicks day' and then glossed it in the margin: 'so they call the day of the Imperiall Diet'.[28] As literal translations from texts initially produced for readers in the United Provinces, the corantos may have needed some clarification for most British readers. However, the publishers may have been concerned that by taking the liberty of 'adding to' the originals, as Archer had, they risked a spell in prison.

The exception to the convention of avoiding editorial comment on printed news is Thomas Gainsford, who edited the corantos of the syndicate of news publishers (Butter and Bourne, plus Thomas Archer, Bartholomew Downes, and William Sheffard) between 1622 and 1624. Gainsford had a political vision: he was a champion of the Protestant cause in Bohemia, a critic of James's appeasement of the Spanish, and an advocate of a more active involvement in Europe.[29] He also adopted a more interventionist approach to editing the news, digesting fragmentary reports into a continuous narrative, and gently steers the interpretation thereof. This introduction to an unnumbered coranto, *Good Newes for the King of Bohemia* (April 1622) is probably his work:

Gentle Reader;
Because I see, that the generall *Currantos* coming weekely ouer, haue rather stifled their owne credites, then giuen satisfaction vnto the world; and that yet men throng as fast to heare Newes, as they beyond the Seas throng ouer, and huddle together all manner of things to please the people, both here and else-where; I could not chuse but take pitty of their longings and desires, that are truly affectionate to Religion, and the Cause of the *Palatinate*, and so expose vnto thee, whosoeuer thou art, this Relation of credite, which came to my hands the twelfth of Aprill, wherein

---

[26] BL: Harl. MS 289, fol. 294. [27] BL: Harl. MS 289, fol. 84.
[28] BL: Harl. MS 289, fos. 79, 82; *Corante* (Amsterdam, 25 June 1621).
[29] Raymond, *Pamphlets*, 135–7 and references there.

you shall see a modest declaration of the affaires of *Germany*, and the tumultuous proceedings of such *Princes*, as either wish well to the King of *Bohemia*, or suppose themselues wronged by the Emperours imperiousnesse, and *Bauariaes* ambitious hastinesse to vsurpe anothers inheritance, and so I fall to the matter, as I finde it thus written.[30]

The note distinguishes the sympathetic reader, and the distinction is not between Protestant and Catholic alone: the specification of those who are *truly* affectionate puts the zealous (the puritan) against the lukewarm and implies that these correspond to positions on foreign policy. What follows is not a plain translation, but a careful narrative with embedded value judgements. In a gesture that anticipates the fierce, contestatory journalism of the 1640s, the editor dismisses and discredits other news sources ('poore Papististicall Newes-mongers', A3ᵛ). He provides not only detail as to time and place—which is central to reporting in the corantos—but analyses cause and motivation, which is uncommon. His dramatizations of circumstance—'When the Duke of *Brunswicke* heard of this, he forthwith bestirred himselfe…' (B1ᵛ)—move silently beyond the testimony of an eyewitness and engage the reader at the cost of the objective tone that underpins the journalistic authority. However, the colour of the writing paves the way for the influence of news pamphlets on fictional narrative prose that would define the novel: a process that is effectively anatomized in Defoe's *Memoirs of a Cavalier* (1720), an early novel based on 1620s corantos.

After Gainsford's death, the corantos reverted to the plainer style, with largely factual statements, supplied without context, relying on very active interpretation by the reader:

> From *Vienna the 22. of October*
> Some fiue dayes agoe departed hence the Count of Alethyn going towards Offen about the treatie of Peace with the Grand Seignior.[31]

This is an extreme case—most reports have more colour and context than this—but it illustrates how the reader is required to situate the news in relation to previous reports (about conflict with the Turks), and how one report might stimulate interest in future news, for which it is little more than a trailer. Even this, however, was regarded as risking incursion upon *arcana imperii* by both James and Charles, and corantos were tolerated provided they caused no offence, and, it seems, provided they did not report domestic news. In 1627 Charles I's Secretary of State wrote to the Master and Wardens of the Stationers's Company stating that the king had noted 'the vnfitting liberties which some of your Companie doe take in printing Weekely for their owne privat gaine, diuers false and scandalous papers vnder the titles of Advises and Courantoes which being gathered out of false advertisements or framed here by some idle persons, doe abuse the people, and often times raise disadvantageous and scandalous reports vpon the proceedings and successes of his Maiesties frends and allies'. The concern is not

---

[30] *Good Newes for the King of Bohemia* (April 1622), sig. A3ʳ.
[31] *A Continvation of all the Principall Occurrences which hath happened to the Leaguers* (1625), 6.

about the misrepresentation of the King—which by unspoken consent is beyond the pale—but about misrepresentation of foreign powers; the letter imposes a licenser specifically for printed news.³²

Interest in the news in the 1620s itself came to be associated with opposition politics.³³ Charles's resistance to using the news as a means of harnessing the sympathy of his subjects may be regarded as all the more surprising, given that his friend the Duke of Buckingham, with whom he had undertaken the Spanish Match escapade, sought to cultivate 'popularity' through a serial, published in the same year, 1627, describing his Île de Ré expedition. The bookseller Thomas Walkley's *Continued Iournall of All the Proceedings* (six issues in August through November 1627) sought to exploit the publicity potential of the serial form, turning its (presumed) patron the Duke into a military hero, much as the Swedish King Gustavus Adolphus would be (without Walkeley's support) in 1631–2.³⁴

Charles decided to ban corantos in 1632, through a Star Chamber decree:

> Upon Considerac[i]on had at the Board of the greate abuse in the printing & publishing of the ordenary Gazetts and Pamphletts of newes from forraigne p[ar]t[e]s, And upon significa[ti]on of his ma[jes]t[ie]s expresse pleasure and Com[m]aund for the p[re]sent suppressing of the same, It was thought fitt and hereby ordered that all printing and publishing of the same be accordingly suppresst and inhibited. And that as well Nathaniell Butter & Nicholas Bourne Booke Sellers, under whose names the said Gazetts have beene usually published, as all other Stationers, Printers and Booke Sellers, p[re]sume not from henceforth to print publish or sell any of the said Pamphletts, &c, as they will answer the Contrary at theire p[e]rills. And Mr Secr[etary]e Windebanke is lykewise prayed to send for the said Butter and Bourne, and to lay a strict Com[m]aund upon them on that behalfe.³⁵

The proscription, it was rumoured, had been at the petitioning of the Spanish ambassador, supported by a faction of English noblemen. The championing of the cause of Gustavus Adolphus in the corantos, and the implicit criticism of Charles's refusal to support him, had made the publishers vulnerable. The ensuing silence may have provided a breeding ground for opposition politics and rumour. Perhaps aware of this tide of opinion, in December 1638 Charles granted a patent to Butter and Bourne, allowing them exclusive rights 'for the imprinting & publishing of all matter of History or News of any forraine place or Kingdome since the first beginning of the late German warres to this present'.³⁶ The ensuing monopoly corantos, with an irregular name and a highly irregular

---

³² Geoff Kemp and Jason McElligott, eds., *Censorship and the Press, 1580–1720*, 4 vols. (London: Pickering & Chatto, 2009), 1: 285.

³³ Thomas Cogswell, 'The Politics of Propaganda: Charles I and the People in the 1620s', *Journal of British Studies*, 29 (1990): 187–215; Cust, 'News and Politics'; Kevin Sharpe, *The Personal Rule of Charles I* (New Haven and London: Yale University Press, 1992), 644–730.

³⁴ Thomas Cogswell, '"Published by Authoritie": Newsbooks and the Duke of Buckinghams's Expedition to the Île de Ré', *Huntington Library Quarterly*, 67 (2004): 1–25.

³⁵ Folke Dahl, 'Amsterdam: Cradle of English Newspapers', The Library, 5th series, 4 (1949), 166–78 (173–4); Kemp and McElligott, eds., *Censorship and the Press*, 1: 290.

³⁶ Dahl, 'Amsterdam—Cradle of English Newspapers', 173–4; Sharpe, *Personal Rule*, 653.

periodicity, appeared until September 1641 (a handful, not properly a serial, appeared in 1642) in much the same format as the earlier series. In January 1641 Butter expressed an intention to make them weekly, to 'keepe a constant Day every week' (in the same editorial stating that he had almost given up because of a zealous licenser, who '(out of partiall affection) would not oftentimes let passe apparent truth'), but his translated news would within the year be displaced by a weekly newsbook containing news of the English parliament, which proved to be a runaway commercial success.[37]

Butter's condemnation of the licenser—and the title page of this issue advertised: 'Examined and Licenced by a better and more Impartiall hand then heretofore'—is striking for its boldness. The irritating licenser had been replaced, but Butter's comments indicate that the news content was actively censored and that this was not sensational news to his readers. The development of the news periodical between 1500 and 1640 was certainly shaped by press controls, though the influence may have been complicated and indirect. Historians have long assumed that the print publication of domestic news was interdicted. There was, in fact, no such outright proscription (though one may have been written into the Ordinances of the Stationers's Company in the now-lost 'red book'); instead, norms and mores were sufficient to regulate the production of domestic news. Repeated royal proclamations, ad hoc legislation, such as the ban on preventing publications reporting the assassination of Henri IV of France (not an Act or Ordinance, but a direction issued to the Stationers's Company by the Lord Treasurer), and frequent harassment of individual stationers by parliament and other institutions, kept publishers, printers, and news writers on their toes. The abolition of the Courts of Star Chamber and High Commission in July 1641 facilitated the appearance of the weekly newsbook of domestic news in 1641, but the precipitants were more the ideological conflict between king and parliament and the fracture in the body politic that left stationers freer to become involved in politics. After 1640 news publications would become a particular focus for press controls; prior to that, the influence of censorship on news printing was no less real for having been unspoken.

24.6 SMILING PICKTHANKS AND BASE NEWSMONGERS[38]

News is barely definable, it is a context-specific piece of information, a commodity, a currency, and a social activity. Yet, its nature came into sharper focus, and was beginning to be subject to reflective analysis, during the century and a half leading up to 1640. This was, in part, because of the greater dissemination of written and printed forms, but also because of the growth of a secular textual culture that had a part to play in the shift towards a market economy and the formation of a centralized state. News was

---

[37] For Butter's comments, Dahl, *Bibliography*, 251; Raymond, *Invention*, chap. 2.
[38] *1 Henry IV*, III.ii.25.

disseminated by oral exchange, writing, and printing; the latter, which has generally been taken as the central focus in histories of news, growing out of the former two, but shaping them in turn. All three were interdependent. But in symbolic terms, printed news acquired a particular force, and it was to prove, in a later period, a powerful component in the shaping of democracy. As it acquired social and political influence it developed a prominence in literary culture—symbolizing commerce, mendacity, addictiveness, the shape of time, and the power of communication. Yet, it also influenced the writing of history, as a way of thinking about evidence and testimony.[39]

While early printed news was firmly rooted in the epistolary tradition, and relied on the plain style of that tradition to communicate reliability and veracity, with time the personal nature of the epistle disappeared and simultaneously, editorial opinion was introduced and experimented with—the Stuart newspaper was shaped by the interaction of domestic and foreign news, editorial intervention, and advertising. Writing about news was rooted in English vernacular traditions and adapted to the commercial printing practices and transport networks particular to Britain. Yet, developments in news writing also need to be seen as one instantiation of a set of profound shifts—perhaps a revolution—occurring more or less simultaneously across Europe. It is partly because of the emergence of European news networks, owing to war and commerce and, perhaps, interest in transnational communities and civic engagement, that there was sufficient demand for foreign news in Britain to justify the development of a news business.[40] And it is the intersection between the local culture, and the extension of a European network into the archipelago, that gives news writing in English its heterogeneous and frequently cosmopolitan character.

FURTHER READING

Brownlees, Nicholas. *The Language of Periodical News in Seventeenth-Century England* (Newcastle upon Tyne: Cambridge Scholars Publishing, 2011).
Cust, Richard. 'News and Politics in Early Seventeenth-Century England', *Past & Present*, 112 (1986): 60–90.
Dooley, Brendan, and Sabrina Baron, eds. *The Politics of Information in Early Modern Europe* (London and New York: Routledge, 2001).
Fox, Adam. *Oral and Literate Culture in England, 1500–1700* (Oxford: Clarendon Press, 2000).
Lake, Peter, with Michael Questier. *The Antichrist's Lewd Hat: Protestants, Papists and Players in Post-Reformation England* (New Haven: Yale University Press, 2002).

---

[39] Raymond, *Invention*, chap. 6; J. Paul Hunter, *Before Novels: The Cultural Contexts of Eighteenth-Century English Fiction* (New York: W. W. Norton, 1990).

[40] Brendan Dooley and Sabrina Baron, eds., *The Politics of Information in Early Modern Europe* (London and New York: Routledge, 2001); Raymond, ed., *News Networks*; Roger Chartier and Carmen Espejo, eds., *La aparición del periodismo en Europa: Comunicación y propaganda en el Barroco* (Madrid: Marcial Pons Historia, 2012).

Parmalee, Lisa Ferrarou. *Good Newes from Fraunce: French Anti-League Propaganda in Late Elizabethan England* (Rochester, NY: University of Rochester Press, 1996).

Randall, David. 'Joseph Mead, Novellante: News, Sociability and Credibility in Early Stuart England', *Journal of British Studies*, 45 (2006): 293–312.

Raymond, Joad. *The Invention of the Newspaper: English Newsbooks, 1641–1649* (1996; Oxford: Clarendon Press, 2005).

—— ed. *News, Newspapers and Society in Early Modern Britain* (London: Frank Cass, 1999).

—— *Pamphlets and Pamphleteering in Early Modern Britain* (Cambridge: Cambridge University Press, 2003).

Voss, Paul J. *Elizabethan News Pamphlets: Shakespeare, Spenser, Marlowe and the Birth of Journalism* (Pittsburgh, PA: Duquesne University Press, 2001).

Walsham, Alexandra. *Providence in Early Modern England* (Oxford: Oxford University Press, 1999).

PART IV

VARIETIES OF EARLY MODERN PROSE 2: PRIVATE PROSE

PART IV

VARIETIES OF EARLY MODERN PROSE 2: PRIVATE PROSE

CHAPTER 25

LETTERS

ALAN STEWART

The letter was the most important textual form of the early modern period. After face-to-face conversation, it served as the second form of communication between people, and was therefore the principal means of contact between parties at any distance.[1] Information was passed on, trade facilitated, orders given, and ties maintained through the exchange of letters. As such, surviving letters from the period—both 'state papers' and those surviving in family archives—now serve as an invaluable resource for social historians and biographers alike, as they attempt to reconstruct the cultural worlds of the early modern period.[2] But early modern letters are by no means a transparent medium. They were composed and written according to—and sometimes in contravention of—protocols that became increasingly highly elaborated. And they were never without their creative or imaginative or even duplicitous elements, which during the early seventeenth century started to develop into what would become one of the leading literary genres in English, the epistolary novel.

25.1 A HISTORY OF LETTERS

To consider English letters between 1500 and 1640 necessarily means starting the story *in medias res*. Many of the most notable models of the letter tradition were already long in place by the turn of the sixteenth century—from Paul's epistles to Ovid's laments in his *Heroides* (verse letters that lie beyond the scope of this chapter). Despite this, the Renaissance conception of the letter was markedly different from what had gone immediately before. In the later medieval period, letters were written according to the *ars*

---

[1] For a general survey with multiple illustrations, see Alan Stewart and Heather Wolfe, *Letterwriting in Renaissance England* (Washington, DC: Folger Shakespeare Library, 2004).

[2] See, for example, James Daybell, *Women Letter-Writers in Tudor England* (Oxford: Oxford University Press, 2006).

dictaminis, whose origins have been traced to the late eleventh-century writings of Alberic of Monte Casino. The *ars dictaminis* treated letter-writing as a rhetorical art and elaborated a protocol which prescribed forms and formulae for writing.[3] The rise of humanism in trecento Italy, however, tempered those protocols through a revival of interest in the classical period's *epistolae familiares* (familiar letters), sparked by Francesco Petrarca's 1345 rediscovery in Verona's cathedral library of a manuscript of Cicero's familiar letters to Atticus, Quintus, and Brutus, a revelation that famously moved the poet to tears. Petrarch was inspired by Cicero to develop a new critical theory of letter-writing and to write and collect his own prose letters, a habit that became popular with such prominent Florentine humanists as Giovanni Boccaccio, Coluccio Salutati, Leonardi Bruni, and Poggio Bracciolini, the last two of whom edited and published (in manuscript) collections of their own letters. By the time the printing press appeared in Europe, letter-writing was a fashionable academic movement, ripe for development, and in 1495 Marsilio Ficino became the first living writer to disseminate his personal correspondence in print.

It was the Dutch humanist, Desiderius Erasmus of Rotterdam, who most fully realized the possibilities of the letter form, and who had the most influence on the direction of English letters.[4] He not only published many of his letters, but used them to create the image, and subsequently the reality, of a pan-European network of like-minded humanist scholarly men, whose printed letters not only promulgated their ideas, but also promoted their careers. Erasmus forged his lasting reputation through a manipulation of the familiar letter in print, simultaneously ensuring that letters were central to his pedagogical programme.[5] He dictated that any edition of his works 'that concern literature and education' should contain four key works, of which the first was *De conscribendis epistolis*, his most sustained meditation on letter-writing, on which he worked for several years. *De conscribendis* developed from a study aid for some of Erasmus's pupils in Paris, through various drafts, until it reached its final form as a full-scale textbook in

---

[3] James J. Murphy, '*Ars dictaminis*: The Art of Letter-Writing', in *Rhetoric in the Middle Ages: A History of Rhetorical Theory from Saint Augustine to the Renaissance* (Berkeley: University of California Press, 1974), 194–268; Lee Perelman, 'The Medieval Art of Letter Writing: Rhetoric as Institutional Expression', in Charles Bazerman and James Paradis, eds., *The Textual Dynamics of the Professions* (Madison: University of Wisconsin Press, 1991), 97–119; Malcolm Richardson, 'The *ars dictaminis*, the Formulary, and Medieval Epistolary Practice', in Carol Poster and Linda C. Mitchell, eds., *Letter-Writing Manuals and Instruction from Antiquity to the Present: Historical and Bibliographical Studies* (Columbia, SC: University of South Carolina Press, 2007), 52–66.

[4] See, for example, Judith Rice Henderson, 'Erasmus on the Art of Letter-Writing', in James J. Murphy, ed., *Renaissance Eloquence: Studies in the Theory and Practice of Renaissance Rhetoric* (Berkeley: University of California Press, 1983), 331–55; Erika Rummel, 'Erasmus' Manual of Letter-Writing: Tradition and Innovation', *Renaissance and Reformation*, ns 13 (1989), 299–312; Gideon Burton, 'From *ars dictaminis* to *ars conscribendi epistolis*: Renaissance Letter-Writing Manuals in the Context of Humanism', in Poster and Mitchell, eds., *Letter-Writing Manuals*, 88–101.

[5] Lisa Jardine, *Erasmus, Man of Letters: The Construction of Charisma in Print* (Princeton: Princeton University Press, 1993); Judith Rice Henderson, 'Humanism and the Humanities in Erasmus's *Opus de conscribendis epistolis* in Sixteenth-Century Schools', in Poster and Mitchell, eds., *Letter-Writing Manuals*, 141–77.

1522. It was a runaway success and soon established itself as a set text in both Lutheran and Catholic schools across Europe.[6] Erasmus's lead was followed by other major continental scholars of the sixteenth century. The Spanish humanist Juan Luis Vives, for example, published his own *De conscribendis epistolis* in 1534, a work more interested in exploring the classical history of the mechanics of letter-writing, especially from the Roman period. Other popular Latin discourses, often published together, include Aurelio Lippo Brandolino's *De ratione scribendi libri tres* (1498), Christoph Hegendorph's *Methodus epistolis conscribendi* (1526), Konrad Celtis's *Methodus conficiendarum epistolarum* (1537), and Georgius Macropedius's *Methodus de conscribendis epistolis* (1543), while towards the end of the century, the Low Countries scholar Justus Lipsius produced his *Epistolica institutio* (1590).[7]

Erasmus's exemplars and techniques constantly draw on the languages of letter-writing: in his *De copia*, to give only the most prominent example, the first practical demonstration Erasmus gives of copious writing is on the phrase 'tuae litterae me magnopere delectarunt' ('your letter pleased me mightily'), in which he copiously produces some two hundred variants.[8] In this way, Erasmus promulgated his definition of the letter (sometimes citing as authority the Greek sophist Libanius, sometimes Terence's contemporary Turpilius):

> The letter is variously defined by Latin writers, but with essentially the same meaning. The Greek sophist Libanius defines the letter in this way: 'A letter is a conversation between two absent persons.' He further defines conversation to mean familiar speech, to have us understand that the letter differs hardly at all from the ordinary speech of everyday conversation. He cautions that it is a great error to use tragic grandiloquence in the composition of letters and to expend all one's intellectual energies in the pursuit of brilliance, profuseness of style, and ostentatious display where there is least need of it. For the style of a letter should be simple and even a bit careless, in the sense of a studied carelessness.[9]

Erasmus understood that, at its best, the familiar letter was a tremendously affecting genre, one that seemed to provide an insight for the reader into the relationship between writer and recipient, and which could be used to influence readers.

Erasmus's educational programme served as the model for several major English grammar schools in the sixteenth century, where the study of letters by classical authors

---

[6] Desiderius Erasmus, *De conscribendis epistolis*, in *Collected Works of Erasmus*, vol. 25, *Literary and Educational Writings*, 3, *De conscribendis epistolis, Formula, De civilitate*, ed. J. K. Sowards (Toronto: University of Toronto Press, 1985).

[7] Lawrence D. Green, 'Dictamen in England, 1500–1700', in Poster and Mitchell, eds., *Letter-Writing Manuals*, 102–26.

[8] Desiderius Erasmus, *Copia: Foundations of the Abundant Style (De duplici copia verborum ac rerum commentarii duo)*, trans. and ed. Betty I. Knott, in *Collected Works of Erasmus*, vol. 24, *Literary and Educational Writings*, 2, *De copia/De ratione studii* (Toronto: University of Toronto Press, 1978), 348–54.

[9] Desiderius Erasmus, *A Formula for the Composition of Letters (Conficiendarum epistolarum formula)*, trans. and ed. Charles Fantazzi, in *Collected Works*, vol. 25, 258–67 (258).

was a key part of the curriculum, as was the imitation of those letters. The statutes of Rivington School, for example, prescribe for the upper forms

> to be exercised in devising and writing sundry epistles to sundry persons, of sundry matters, as of chiding, exhorting, comforting, counseling, praying, lamenting, some to friends, some to foes, some to strangers; of weighty matters or merry, as shooting, hunting, etc.; of adversity, of prosperity, of war and peace, divine and profane, of all sciences and occupations, some long and some short.[10]

This kind of 'devising and writing' worked through the imitation of classical letters. A letter would be taken as an example; an imitative letter would transpose the letter to a different recipient and occasion, repeating the form and much of the vocabulary; another version would then replicate the letter's form with a very much changed vocabulary. William Kempe's *The education of children in learning* (1588) gives as its example 'the first Epistle of the first booke' of Johann Sturm's schoolboy edition of Cicero's epistles (in which the letters were arranged starting with the easiest), a letter from Cicero to his wife Terentia: 'if you be in health, it is well: I am in health. I haue long looked for your Messengers. When they shall come, I shalbe more certaine what I am to do; and then I will forthwith certifie you of all things. See that you looke very carefully to your health. Farewell. The Calends of September.'[11] Kempe then suggests that the student should write 'an Epistle in English of the like sentence, which he shall expresse in Latin with *Ciceroes* phrase'. So whereas '*Cicero* writeth to his wife, let vs imagin the Father to write to his Sonnes: he writeth of her messengers, of certaintie what to do, of care for her health: let the father write to their letters, of certaintie what to looke for, of care for their learning, in this wise':

> *Peter Cole to Iohn and Charles his sonnes, sendeth greeting.*
> *If ye be in good health, it is well. I my selfe am in good health. Oftentimes I finde lack of your letters, the which being brought, verely I shall be more certayne what I am to looke for, and will certifie you thereof forthwith. Apply your Studye diligently. Farewell. The Ides of December* (sig. G1^{r-v}).

The student then translates this letter back into Latin.

Kempe's model certainly demonstrates the strong pull of humanist teaching ideals, but there is a practical problem here: the English letter produced by this exercise looks nothing like a sixteenth-century English letter. It follows the Roman form of dating, pretty much obsolete by 1588. Its superscription ('Peter Cole to Iohn and Charles his sonnes, sendeth greeting') follows a Latin formula, not recognizable to an English letter-writer. The letter's valediction has no signature, which in an English letter would be considered odd and invalid, if not downright rude. In short, this strategy may help a student's Latin, but would hardly teach useful letter-writing skills in English. It was a dilemma that John Brinsley, master of Ashby School in Leicestershire, acknowledged in his 1612

---

[10] Cited in Stewart and Wolfe, *Letterwriting in Renaissance England*, 22.
[11] William Kempe, *The education of children in learning* (London: John Potter and Thomas Gubbin, 1588), sig. G1^{r}.

pedagogical manual, *Ludus literarius*, in the voice of the schoolmaster Philoponus: 'As for inditing Letters in English, I haue not exercised my schollars in them at all; neyther haue I knowne them to be vsed in Schooles: although they cannot but bee exceeding necessary for scholars; being of perpetvall vse in all our whole life, and of very great commendation, when they are so performed.'[12]

Thus, while it is impossible to deny Erasmus's influence on generations of English schoolboys and university undergraduates, it might be fairly objected that Erasmus had less direct influence on the writing of everyday correspondence. Even if a good number of young Englishmen came away from their education with Erasmus's letter-writing precepts etched in their memories, there is still quite a leap to be made from these Latin models to their possible application in a vernacular English setting. To fill the gap a series of letter-writing manuals (or epistolographies) in English began to appear.[13]

25.2 THE ENGLISH SECRETARIES

The first letter-writing manual in English was William Fulwood's *The enimie of idlenesse*, which first appeared in 1568 and went through ten editions by 1621. While its dedication to a prominent London merchant, 'Master Anthony Ratcliffe, Master of the worshipfull Companie of the Merchant Tailors of London',[14] suggests it is embedded in the commercial concerns of England's capital, the book is in essence a translation, with a few amendments, of a recent edition of a French manual entitled *Le stile et maniere de composer, dicter et escrire toute sorte d'epistre, ou lettres missiues, tant par reponse, que autrement* (1553), itself drawn from two earlier works, *Prothocolle des secretaires* (1534) and Pierre Fabri's *Le grant et vray art de pleine rhetorique* (1521).[15] (The debt owed by English epistolographies to their French predecessors has been routinely occluded by scholars.)[16] *The enimie of idlenesse* is divided into four books. The first sets forth 'the necessarie precepts, which belong to the well composing and indicting of Epistles and Letters' with some examples, while the second prints English translations of letters by scholars drawn from the Florentine scholar Angelo Poliziano's *Illustrium virorum epistolae*, one of Erasmus's preferred sources for examples. The third book examines 'the manner and forme how to write by answer', matching a letter of a particular kind with

---

[12] John Brinsley, *Lvdvs literarivs: or, the grammar schoole* (London: Thomas Man, 1612), sigs. Y3^v–Y4^r.
[13] W. Webster Newbold, 'Letter Writing and Vernacular Literacy in Sixteenth-Century England', in Poster and Mitchell, eds., *Letter-Writing Manuals*, 127–40.
[14] William Fulwood, *The enimie of idlenesse* (London: Leonard Maylard, 1568), sig. A2^r.
[15] As established by Claude La Charité, '*Le stile et maniere de composer, dicter et escrire toutes sortes d'epistres, ou lettres missives* (1553): de la *disposition* tripartite de Pierre Fabri au poulpe épistolaire', in Catherine Magnien, ed., *L'épistolaire au XVIe siècle* (Paris: Éditions de Rue d'Ulm, 2001), 17–32.
[16] On French letter-writing see Magnien, ed., *L'épistolaire au XVIe siècle*; Luc Vaillancourt, *La lettre familière au XVIe siècle: rhétorique humaniste de l'épistolaire* (Paris: Champion, 2003); Guy Gueudet, *L'art de la lettre humaniste* (Paris: Honoré Champion, 2004).

its proper response; and the fourth and final book contains some love letters and a few English verses not found in its French original. Aside from these verses, there is little original matter in Fulwood's volume.

Fulwood's 'necessarie precepts' include detailed instructions on how a letter should be addressed, in 'three necessary points', namely: the 'salutation of recommendation' (in effect, the greeting with which the letter opens), the subscription (corresponding to the modern valediction and signature), and the superscription (the modern address). These last two speak to the physical appearance of the letter. As these manuals reveal, there evolved complex protocols dictating the material aspects of the manuscript letter.[17] A letter usually comprised a single piece of paper: if the writer could afford it, a large bifolium sheet (a folium folded in half). The text would be written on the 'front' page of this folded sheet and continued inside, if necessary. The 'back' page, however, had to be kept blank: when the text was completed, the letter was folded up, with the 'back' page now forming the outside of the letter. The loose flaps were then held in position with some melted wax (and sometimes thread or ribbon) and stamped with a seal. Letter-writers corresponding with their social betters should not skimp on paper: to use a scrap of paper was considered insulting to the recipient, so that surviving letters written on less than half a sheet invariably comment on and apologize for the fact. In practical terms, the writer had to remember to leave enough of the paper blank to ensure that the folding and sealing processes did not obscure the written text. But there were further, detailed protocols about the use of blank space. The subscription, as Fulwood notes, 'must be don according to the estate of the writer, and the qualitie of the person to whome we write: for to our superiors we must write at the right syde in the nether ende of the paper, saying: By your most humble and obedient sonne, or seruant, &c. And to our equalles we may write towards the midst of the paper saying: By your faithfull frende for euer: &c. To our inferiors we may write on high at the left hand saying: By yours &c.' (sigs. a7^r–a8^r).

Abraham Fleming's 1576 volume *A panoplie of epistles, or, a looking glasse for the vnlearned* is less concerned with everyday life. Although its title page bolsters its appeal to the 'vnlearned' by boasting that it contains 'a perfect plattforme of inditing letters of all sorts, to persons of al estates and degrees, as well our superiors, as also our equals and inferiours', it betrays that its sources are 'the best and the eloquentest Rhetoricians that haue liued in all ages, and haue beene famous in that facultie. Gathered and translated out of Latine into English.'[18] And indeed, the only English names included among the Greek, Latin, and continental authors are two sixteenth-century scholars, Roger Ascham and Walter Haddon, whose contributions are of letters originally written in Latin.

---

[17] Jonathan Gibson, 'Significant Space in Manuscript Letters', *The Seventeenth Century*, 12 (1997): 1–9; Stewart and Wolfe, *Letterwriting in Renaissance England*, 35–54; Alan Stewart, *Shakespeare's Letters* (Oxford: Oxford University Press, 2008), 39–74; James Daybell, 'Material Meanings and the Social Signs of Manuscript Letters in Early Modern England', *Literature Compass*, 6.3 (2009): 647–67; idem., *The Material Letter in Early Modern England* (Basingstoke: Palgrave Macmillan, 2012).

[18] Abraham Fleming, *A panoplie of epistles* (London: Ralph Newberie, 1576), title page.

Perhaps the most influential English epistolography was Angel Day's *The English secretarie*, first published in 1586.[19] As its title suggests, this manual aims to be more 'English' than its predecessors, despite being modelled clearly on Erasmus. Its focus is on instruction, rather than merely on example, and it pushes the reader to understand the function of the principal rhetorical parts of a letter: the 'exordium' ('a beginning or induction to the matter to be written'); the 'narratio or propositio' ('wherein is declared or proponed, in the one by plaine tearmes, in the other by inference, or comparison, the verie substance of the matter whatsoeuer to be handled'); the 'confirmatio' ('wherein are amplified or suggested many reasons, for the aggrauating or proof of any matter in qustion [sic]'); and the 'peroratio' ('in which after a briefe recapitulation of that which hath beene vrged, the occasions thereof are immediatelie concluded').

The English secretarie also outlines the four generic distinctions of letters—demonstrative, deliberative, judicidal, and familiar—and the subdivisions within, hinting at the myriad purposes that letters necessarily served. For example, demonstrative letters can be 'descriptorie', 'laudatorie', or 'vituperatorie', deliberative letters can be 'hortatorie and dehortatorie', 'swasorie and disswasorie', 'conciliatorie and reconciliatorie', 'petitorie', 'commendatorie', 'consolatorie', 'monitorie', 'reprehensorie', or 'amatorie', and judicial letters can be 'accusatorie', 'excusatorie', 'expostulatorie', 'purgatorie', 'defensorie', 'exprobatorie', 'deprecatorie', or 'inuectiue'. Familiar letters are broken down into eight subdivisions: 'narratorie', 'nunciatorie', 'gratulatorie', 'remuneratorie', 'iocatorie', 'obiurgatorie', 'mandatorie', and 'responsorie'. Later editions included not only examples and explanations of these four divisions, but also specialized sections dealing with descriptions of figures, schemes, and tropes, and a discourse on the parts and offices of a secretary—the male servant whose main function was to pen letters.[20]

While Day, like his predecessors, implies that letter-writing is an expertise that should be common to all educated men, the late sixteenth and seventeenth centuries saw the rise of more utilitarian manuals. *The marchants avizo* by 'I B [John Browne] merchant' first appeared in 1589 and went through four editions by 1640, making it one of the most popular of all such manuals. Browne was a prominent figure in the Bristol Society of Merchant Venturers and his book reeks of Bristol mercantile and maritime life. Dedicated to 'Maister Thomas Aldworth Marchant of the Citie of Bristow and to all the Worshipfull companie of the Marchants of the saide Citie',[21] *The marchants avizo*, as its title page suggests, is designed for merchants trading with the Iberian peninsula, or rather, for those working for them there: it is 'Very necessarie for their sonnes and seruants, when they first send them beyond the seas, as to Spaine and Portingale or other

---

[19] Angel Day, *The English secretarie* (London: Richard Jones, 1586). See also Lynne Magnusson, *Shakespeare and Social Dialogue: Dramatic Language and Elizabethan Letters* (Cambridge: Cambridge University Press, 1999), 61–90.

[20] For the major changes see Angel Day, *The English secretorie* (London: Richard Jones, 1592); idem, *The English secretary* (London: P. S[hort] for C. Burbie, 1599).

[21] I[ohn] B[rowne], *The marchants avizo very necessarie for their sonnes and servants, when they first send them ... to Spaine and Portingale* (London: William Norton, 1589), sig. A2^r. See also Magnusson, *Shakespeare and Social Dialogue*, 114–37.

countreyes'. The letters are part of a package of information including the wares to be dealt in, the 'weights, measures and values of money' in foreign countries, and Spanish models of contract documents. The types of sample letters give a sense of the eventualities that the factor might expect in transmitting news and arranging deals: 'A Letter written to your Master, if your ship be forced by weather into any place, before you come to your Port of discharge' (sig. B.iiij.ᵛ); 'A Letter to be written to your Master presently upon arriuall at your Port' (sig. Cʳ); 'A Letter to be written to your Maister, or some other man that is of worship, next after your first letter' (sig. Cᵛ); 'A Letter to be sent in that ship where you haue laden goods for any Marchant' (sig. C.iij.ʳ); and so on.

Following Day's success, the subgenre of the 'secretary' emerged, a manual aimed at training budding secretaries, or others with occasional secretarial or letter-writing duties, how to write and act according to the dignity of their position: Thomas Gainsford's *The secretaries studie containing new familiar epistles* (1616) was an early example.[22] However, this wide-ranging genre soon became more tailored to entertainment than practical training, its content often more akin to the stuff of prose romances. From the archives of the Stationers's Company, it seems that in 1636 a volume was planned, entitled, 'Loues Secretary or a Cabinett of choice and Curious Letters Complementall and occasionall &c.', though no copy survives.[23] Over the following decades, however, French models of book secretaries were to dominate the English print market, among the first of which were Jean Puget de la Serre's *La secretarie de la cour* (1628), which provided some of the raw materials for *The academy of complements* by 'Philomusus'; and his *Le secrétaire à la mode* (1640), which was promptly translated by John Massinger as *The secretary in fashion*.[24]

25.3 REAL LETTERS

The journey of most early modern letters ended when they reached their recipient: they were either destroyed or kept among a family's papers. A good number of family collections have come to light in subsequent centuries, and are now available to readers in libraries and local record offices, but in the period they remained private. Some letters, however—largely those relating to state affairs, diplomatic business, or contemporary scandals—circulated in the period quite widely, sometimes as manuscript 'separates' (individual copies, perhaps prepared professionally by scribes), and sometimes copied

---

[22] Thomas Gainsford, *The secretaries studie containing new familiar epistles* (London: Roger Jackson, 1616). See Linda C. Mitchell, 'Letter-Writing Instruction Manuals in Seventeenth-Century and Eighteenth-Century England', in Poster and Mitchell, eds., *Letter-Writing Manuals*, 178–99.

[23] Stationers's Register entry for 31 May 1636. Edward Arber, ed., *A transcript of the registers of the Company of Stationers of London; 1554–1640 A.D.*, 4 vols. (London: privately printed, 1877), 4: 338.

[24] Philomusus, *The academy of complements* (London H. Mostley, 1640); John Massinger, *The secretary in fashion* (London: Godfrey Emerson, 1640).

into individuals' personal miscellanies. For much of the period to 1640, however, these personal letters did not enter into print.

One epistolary genre that took early advantage of print was the newsletter. As early as 1518, news was being peddled in letter form: printing in Antwerp, 'John of Dousborowe' gave England *The copye of the letter folowynge whiche specifyeth of ye greatest and meruelous uisyoned batayle that euer was sene or herde of and also of the letter yt was sent frome the great Turke vnto our holy fad[er] ye pope of Rome*.[25] Virtually every major news event from then on merited its own letter—the form vouchsafing that the news came from a personal source, located at the heart of the action. Here, Erasmus's idea of 'a conversation between friends' became a device to authenticate the news being conveyed. During the English campaign in Normandy (1589–92) such newsletters, published by John Wolfe, developed into something approaching a series;[26] by the Thirty Years War three decades later, the newsletter had become recognizably the forerunner of the newspaper.

However, these newsletters were usually anonymous or pseudonymous. Indeed, while continental figures like Ficino and Erasmus printed their Latin letters in print, Englishmen seem to have been less willing, or had fewer opportunities, to make the move under their own names. True, the letters of the sixteenth-century humanist scholar Roger Ascham were posthumously published,[27] but these (like Erasmus's) were the product of a Latinate European humanist culture, rather than of English prose. Among the first writers to explore the specifically *English* print possibilities of letters were Edmund Spenser, fresh from his 1579 *Shepheardes calender*, in which the poet was identified only as 'Immerito', and his long-time friend Gabriel Harvey, a fellow of Pembroke Hall, Cambridge. In their *Three proper, and wittie, familiar letters: lately passed betweene two vniuersitie men* (1580),[28] a sequence of letters allows Harvey, in particular, to present to a print readership his ideas on a series of issues as expressed to 'Immerito'—ostensibly 'the earthquake in Aprill last', but more importantly, 'Immerito's' poetry and the question of quantitative verse in 'our English refourmed versifying'. The volume includes other genres, notably Latin verse, but it is the epistolary exchange, supposedly a private one made public by a mutual friend ('a wellwiller to them both'), that allows 'G.H.' and 'Immerito' into the economy that would later be called the Republic of Letters, as they nonchalantly register their familiarity with court figures (Philip Sidney and Edward Dyer) and locations (Leicester House, where Spenser was employed as a secretary).

---

[25] *The copye of the letter folowynge whiche specifyeth of ye greatest and meruelous uisyoned batayle that euer was sene or herde of and also of the letter yt was sent frome the great Turke vnto our holy fad[er] ye pope of Rome*, (Antwerp: 'John of Dousborowe', 1518).

[26] Joad Raymond, *Pamphlets and Pamphleteering in Early Modern Britain* (Cambridge: Cambridge University Press, 2003), 98–160.

[27] Roger Ascham, *Familiarium epistolarum libri tres*, ed. Edward Grant (London: Francis Coldock, 1576).

[28] [Gabriel Harvey and Edmund Spenser], *Three proper, and wittie, familiar letters: lately passed betvveene tvvo vniuersitie men: touching the earthquake in Aprill last, and our English refourmed versifying With the preface of a wellwiller to them both* (London: H. Bynneman, 1580).

The Spenser–Harvey experiment was in some ways half-hearted, Spenser appearing under a pseudonym, and Harvey under his initials. English writers remained wary of publishing their letters in print for the next century. An intriguing exception is the controversialist (and eventual bishop of Norwich) Joseph Hall, who in 1608 published the first two 'decades' (groups of ten) of his *Epistles*, which, as Gary Schneider notes, 'marks the first lengthy single-author epistolary document published by a living, native Englishman designated by the rubric "letter" or "epistle".'[29] Dedicating the first volume to Prince Henry, Hall noted that English was falling behind its competitors, remarking that 'your Grace shall herein perceiue a new fashion of discourse by Epistles; new to our language, vsuall to all others: and (as Noueltie is neuer without some plea of vse) more free, more familiar. Thus, we do but talke to our friends by our pen, and expresse our selues no whit lesse easilie; some-what more digestedlie.'[30] Every letter is written to a named, and often public, figure, among them the Lord Denny, the Lord Hay, the Earl of Essex, and various intimates of Prince Henry's circle, such as Sir Thomas Chaloner and Sir David Murray. A few epistles are very closely tied to contingent circumstances: the opening letter, for example, is to Jacob Wadsworth 'Lately reuolted in Spaine' (Wadsworth had converted to Catholicism while serving on an embassy to Spain) and is described as 'Expostulating for his departure, and perswading his returne'. But all the letters are undated and most are less precisely fixed, primarily providing an opportunity for Hall to expatiate on various topics—'Of the contempt of the world', 'Of true honour', and 'Concerning the Miracles of our time'—in a style that owes more to the essay form (recently popularized by Francis Bacon, and John Florio's translation of Montaigne) than to the possibilities of the epistolary genre. Hall's *Epistles* eventually ran to six decades in three volumes[31] and he remained the only English author to print his correspondence in English until James Howell first published his collection *Epistolae Ho-Elianae. Familiar letters domestic and forren* in 1645.[32]

In the intervening years, the lead was taken, as often happened in the sixteenth and seventeenth centuries, by French writers.[33] The foremost French letter-writer of the early seventeenth century was Jean-Luis Guez, sieur de Balzac, who authored some twenty-seven letter collections. Balzac's letters were first published in France in 1624 and proved so popular as an import that in 1632 Richard Whitaker produced an edition (in French) in London—provoking the Court of High Commission to order both the Paris and London editions to be burned.[34] Two years later, William Tirwhyt produced a translation of *The*

---

[29] Gary Schneider, *The Culture of Epistolarity: Vernacular Letters and Letter Writing in Early Modern England, 1500–1700* (Newark, DE: University of Delaware Press, 2005), 237.

[30] Joseph Hall, *Epistles, the first volume: conteining two decads* (London: Eleazar Edgar & Samuel Macham, 1608), sig. A4ᵛ.

[31] Joseph Hall, *Epistles, the second volume: conteining two decads* (London: Eleazar Edgar & Samuel Macham, 1608); idem, *Epistles. containing two decades… The third and last volume* (London: E. Edgar, and A. Garbrand, 1611).

[32] James Howell, *Epistolae Ho-Elianae. Familiar letters domestic and forren; divided into six sections, partly historicall, politicall, philosophicall, upon emergent occasions* (London: Humphrey Moseley, 1645).

[33] Laurent Versini, *Le roman épistolaire* (Paris: Presses Universitaires de France, 1979).

[34] For details, see the account in *STC* 12455.5.

letters of mounsieur de Balzac and three more volumes followed (volumes 2 and 3 at least translated by Sir Richard Baker) in 1638–9.[35] Although Balzac's letters were much commented upon for their style, much of the interest in them no doubt derived from the fact that these were letters to such political luminaries as Cardinal Richelieu, Cardinal de la Valete, and the duc d'Espernon.

But it would be the decades immediately after the period covered by this volume that would see the greatest advances in the dissemination of letters in English, both real and fictional. Collections, edited anonymously, drew on the correspondences of leading Elizabethan politicians such as William Cecil, Lord Burghley, Robert Dudley, Earl of Leicester, Sir Thomas Smith, and others, and highlighted their status as *arcana imperii* through their titles: *Cabala, mysteries of state, in letters of the great ministers of K. James and K. Charles* (1654); *Cabala, sive, Scrinia sacra mysteries of state & government: in letters of illustrious persons, and great agents* (1654); *Scrinia Ceciliana, mysteries of state & government in letters* (1663), and so on.[36] In addition, publishers put out the diplomatic correspondence of Francis Walsingham, collected by Dudley Digges (*The compleat ambassador*, 1655); the letters of Francis Bacon (*Remaines*, 1648; *Resuscitatio*, 1657); and of those of the well-connected (and recently deceased) Tobie Matthew (1659).[37] Authorized—although whether tacitly or explicitly is unclear—by the new political order of the Interregnum, publishers thus started to make public in print for the first time the kind of letters and state papers that had previously circulated only amongst restricted coteries in manuscript copies.

---

[35] W.T. (trans.), *The letters of Mounsieur de Balzac. Translated into English, according to the last edition* (London: Richard Clotterbuck, 1634); *New epistles of Mounsieur de Balzac. Translated out of French into English, by Sr. Richard Baker Knight. Being the second and third volumes* (London: Fra. Eglesfield, Iohn Crooke, and Rich. Serger, 1638); *A collection of some modern epistles of Monsieur de Balzac. Carefully translated out of French. Being the fourth and last volume* (Oxford: Francis Bowman, 1639).

[36] *Cabala, mysteries of state in letters of the great ministers of K. James and K. Charles, wherein much of the publique manage of affaires is related/faithfully collected by a noble hand* (London: M.M., G. Bedell and T. Collins, 1654); *Cabala, sive, Scrinia sacra mysteries of state & government: in letters of illustrious persons, and great agents, in the reigns of Henry the Eighth, Queen Elizabeth, K. James, and the late King Charl[e]s* (London: G. Bedell and T. Collins, 1654); *Scrinia Ceciliana, mysteries of state & government in letters of the late famous Lord Burghley, and other grand ministers of state, in the reigns of Queen Elizabeth, and King James, being a further additional supplement of the Cabala* (London: G. Bedell and T. Collins, 1663).

[37] Dudley Digges, *The compleat ambassador, or, Two treaties of the intended marriage of Qu. Elizabeth of glorious memory comprised in letters of negotiation of Sir Francis Walsingham, her resident in France: together with the answers of the Lord Burleigh, the Earl of Leicester, Sir Tho. Smith, and others* (London: Tho. Newcomb for Gabriel Bedell and Thomas Collins, 1655); Francis Bacon, *The remaines of the Right Honorable Francis, Lord Verulam, Viscount of St. Albanes, sometimes Lord Chancellour of England being essayes and severall letters to severall great personages, and other pieces of various and high concernment not heretofore published* (London: B. Alsop for Lawrence Chapman, 1648); idem, *Resuscitatio, or, Bringing into publick light severall pieces of the works, civil, historical, philosophical, & theological*, ed. William Rawley (London: Sarah Griffin for William Lee, 1657); Tobie Matthew, *A collection of letters, made by Sr Tobie Mathews Kt.... To which are added many letters of his own, to severall persons of honour, who were contemporary with him* (London: Henry Herringman, 1659).

25.4 LETTERS IN FICTION

Letters had long been a stock device of fiction, especially in such genres as the romance and the novella. In each of these genres, English authors lagged well behind their counterparts in Spain, Italy, and France, and many of the English-language examples of the sixteenth century were translations or adaptations of existing Continental works.[38] So, typically, Diego de San Pedro's *Cárcel de amor*, which dates from around 1485, did not make it into print in English until 1548 when John Bourchier, Lord Berners's translation *The castell of loue* was published.[39] The letters in *Castell of loue* are used in a manner analogous to that of the sustained speech: the narrative (headed by the word 'auctor') stops and a communication is signalled, whether that be a speech or a letter. *The castell of loue* does, however, distinguish its letters in one respect: they are given a solid material form, which lends them to being torn up in passion, and, on one memorable occasion, being drunk. A similar manoeuvre can be seen in translations of the popular prose narrative of Eurialus and Lucretia by Enea Silvio Piccolomini (later Pope Pius II), which saw multiple editions in English from 1515;[40] and Jorge de Montemayor's bestselling Spanish romance, *Diana* (whose translation into English by Bartholomew Yong appeared in 1598).[41] In England, the same techniques were appropriated by George Gascoigne in his 'The aduentures of Master F.I.' (1573); John Lyly's *Euphues. The anatomy of wyt* (1578), and Robert Greene's *Philomela* (1592).[42]

Certain English writers did, however, start to play more inventively with the possibilities of the genre. As is well known, many printed books of all genres were prefaced by what are now known as a 'dedicatory epistle', a printed 'letter' usually from the author (sometimes the editor, printer, or publisher) to a patron, existing or potential; this was sometimes replaced by, or complemented with, a piece 'To the reader', which also took the form of a quasi-letter. Exploiting and parodying this tradition, George Gascoigne's (supposedly) anonymous 1573 collection, *A hundreth sundrie flowres*, is prefaced by a series of letters that describe the process by which the sequence published as 'The aduentures of Master F.I.' came to press.[43] In a letter to his friend H.W., G.T. describes how he had taken 'a number of *Sonets*, lates, letters, Ballades, Rondlets, verlayes and verses, the

---

[38] Versini, *Le roman épistolaire*.

[39] John Bourchier, Lord Berners (trans.), *The castell of loue, translated out of Spanishe into Englyshe* (London: [R. Field for] Iohan Turke, 1548).

[40] See, for example [Enea Silvio Piccolomini], *The goodli history of the moste noble and beautyfull ladye Lucres of Scene in Tuskane* ([London]: John Day, 1553).

[41] Jorge de Montemayor, *Diana of George of Montemayor: translated out of Spanish into English*, trans. Bartholomew Yong (London: Edm. Bollifant for G[eorge] B[ishop], 1598).

[42] [George Gascoigne], *A hundreth sundrie flowres bounde vp in one small poesie* (London: Richard Smith, 1573); John Lyly, *Euphues. The anatomy of wyt* (London: [T. East] for Gabriel Cawood, 1578); Robert Greene, *Philomela The Lady Fitzvvaters nightingale* (London: R. B[ourne and E. Allde] for Edward White, 1592).

[43] [Gascoigne], *Hundreth sundrie flowres*.

workes of your friend and myne Master *F.I.* and diuers others' and had 'with long trauayle confusedly gathered [them] together' and 'reduce[d] them into some good order... in this written Booke' (sig. Aij^v). G.T. then passed the resulting 'written Booke' (a manuscript volume) to H.W. and 'charged' H.W. that he 'should vse them onely for mine owne partiuler commoditie, and eftsones safely deliuer the original copie to him againe'. But rather than reserving it for private use, H.W. 'entreated my friend *A.B.* to emprint' it, '[a]nd further haue presumed of my selfe to christen it by the name of *A hundredth sundrie Flowres*' (sig. Ai^r). So here a sequence of prefatory letters is used to explain the progress of a pile of papers into the finished printed book—and then G.T. continues to act as a self-appointed editor for F.J.'s papers, describing the occasion that prompted each piece of writing, an editorial intervention that soon slips into a full-blown narrative.[44]

Other writers explored the possibilities of the letter form within the narrative with increasing subtlety. Philip Sidney, for example, more fully develops the fictional possibilities of the *female* letter-writer. In book V of his *Arcadia* (the hybrid version published in 1593), two letters written by women are printed, but in ways that play with, and comment on, the narrative. At this point, King Basilius is apparently dead and his wife Gynecia and the princes Musidorus and Pyrocles are on trial for his murder, with Basilius's counsellor Euarchus serving as judge. Philanax makes the case against the three and then Pyrocles defends himself. As Pyrocles finishes his speech—and we, as readers, await the verdict—the narration draws our attention elsewhere: '*Philanax* like a watchfull aduersary curiously marked all that [Pyrocles] saide, sauing that in the beginning he was interrupted by two Letters were brought him from the Princess *Pamela* and the Lady *Philoclea*:... each wrate in this sort for him in whome their liues ioys consisted.'[45] Each letter, first Philoclea's, then Pamela's, is then printed in its entirety. The letters are impassioned, but almost incoherent. Philoclea opens: 'My Lords, what you will determine of me is to me uncertain; but what I have determined of myself I am most certain, which is no longer to enjoy my life than I may enjoy him for my husband whom the heavens for my highest glory have bestowed upon me. Those that judge him, let them execute me...' (sig. 2R3^r), whereas Pamela's opening gambit is: 'In such a state, my Lords, you have placed me as I can neither write nor be silent. For how can I be silent, since you have left me nothing but my solitary words to testify my misery? And how should I write... who neither can resolve what to write, nor to whom to write?' (sig. 2R3^r). The fragmented syntax of the letters is not simply a sign of the female inability to control rhetoric (a trope with which Sidney plays variously throughout the *Arcadia*); it is also a symptom of the difficult process by which the letters had been penned: 'Many blots had the tears of these sweet ladies made in

---

[44] Alan Stewart, 'Gelding Gascoigne', in Constance C. Relihan and Goran V. Stanivukovic, eds., *Prose Fiction and Early Modern Sexualities in England, 1570–1640* (Basingstoke: Palgrave Macmillan, 2003), 147–70.

[45] Philip Sidney, *The Countesse of Pembrokes Arcadia... Now since the first edition augmented and ended* (London: [John Windet] for William Ponsonbie, 1593), 2R2^v–3^r.

their letters, which many times they had altered, many times torn, and written anew, ever thinking something either wanted or were too much, or would offend, or (which was worst) would breed denial' (sig. 2R3ᵛ). The papers are blotted by the mixture of tears and ink, the expressed emotion of the women compromising the content of their letters, producing 'blots'. The blots are permanent, but writing is shown not to be: the women change their minds, revise, and occasionally rip the paper to shreds, forcing themselves to start again. In reality, this should result in final 'clean' drafts, rid of their blots and obliterations, but the muddled syntax still conveys the multiple material layers of the letters' composition.

Then we are told how the letters found their way to Philanax. The princesses, in prison, asked one of their guards to present the letters 'to the principall Noblemen and Gentlemen together'. But, the guard was 'trustie to *Philanax*, who had placed him here' and so he

> deliuered them both to him, (what time *Pyrocles* began to speake) which he sodaynly opened, and seing to what they tended, by the first words, was so farre from publishing them... that he wee would not himselfe reede them ouer, doubting his owne hart might be mollified, so bent vpon reuenge. Therefore vtterly suppressing them, he lent a spitefull eare to *Pyrocles*... (sigs. 2R3ᵛ–4ʳ)

These letters thus operate within the narrative in a very particular manner. They are quoted in full, so the reader reads them immediately after Pyrocles's speech. But they are not of course written then, a product of that moment—they are written and revised over a period of time, in a different location. Nor, indeed, are they *read* at that moment: although Philanax receives and opens the letters, he does not read beyond 'their first words'. We are told what is contained in these unread letters, not at the moment when he fails to read then—just after Pyrocles starts his oration—but at the point just after Pyrocles has finished speaking, and when Philanax has long since disregarded the letters. And in plot terms, the letters simply do not register. As Pyrocles starts his speech, Philanax, presumably sitting to one side, is approached by a gaoler who hands over two letters and withdraws. Philanax opens them, glances at the opening words, then reads no further. He then 'suppress[es]' them—perhaps stuffs them up his sleeve, in his pocket. The letters disappear from the hearing, and from the plot. But the narrative gives a life to these letters, belying their supposed suppression. And it uses the material production of the letters to let us into the mental state of the letter-writers, Philoclea and Pamela, and to expose the dubious workings of the unintended recipient, Philanax. Sidney's sophisticated use of letters in the *Arcadia* is decades ahead of his time, but it points the way towards later advances in epistolary fiction.

From the occasional use of letters in narrative works, it would appear an inevitable step that prose works would come to be entirely in letter form, and indeed, there are two early sixteenth-century examples: Juan de Segura's *Processo de cartas de amores* (1548), which contains 44 letters, but which ends with the romance of Luzindaro and Medusina (an enclosure in the final letter); and Alvise Pasqualigo's *Lettere amorose* (1563), an altogether more substantial work of some 557 letters in two books.[46] However, neither of these works had an afterlife in, or even any perceptible influence on, English vernacular literature. The first English epistolary fiction in prose seems to have been the work of the vigorously prolific Nicholas Breton: a 1602 pamphlet, entitled, *A poste with a madde packet of letters*.[47] With the exception of its title page and table of contents, the entire book is comprised of letters. Breton's letter 'To the Reader' tells of how the book came into being: 'you shal vnderstand, that I know not when, there came a Post I know not whence, was going I know not whither, and carryed I knowe not what: But in his way I knowe not how, it was his happe with lacke of heed, to let fall a Packet of Idle Papers.' The packet bore the superscription (i.e. was addressed) 'to him that findes it', and since it was Breton's 'fortune to light on it', he opened 'the enclosure, in which I founde diuers Letters written, to whom, or from whom, I could not learne'. Leaving any further comment to the reader, Breton suggests that, if these find favour, 'when I meet next with the Poste, it may be I will cast about with him for more of them'. The reader is thus allowed to catch sight of 'A Letter of comfortable aduise to a friend, and his answere', 'A Letter of aduise to a yong Courtier, and his answere', and so on. Each pair of letters provides the opportunity for a vignette, as Breton sketches a (usually quite conventional) situation. Later editions of Breton's bestseller would augment the collection, including among the new additions 'Letters of loue betwixt *Rinaldo* and *Lorina*', a sequence of four letters back and forth between the lovers. Although it is never explained how the answers came to be in the same dropped packet as the original letters—a major lapse of plausibility—Breton's publication of intercepted correspondence proved a bestseller, with at least sixteen editions by 1685.

The possibilities of this kind of sustained fictional correspondence were further exploited by the 1638 translation by Jerome Hainhofer of Jacques du Bosc's *Nouveau receuil de lettres des dames de ce temps: auec leurs responses* (1635) as *The secretarie of ladies*.[48] Subtitled 'A new collection of Letters and Answers, composed by Moderne Ladies and Gentwomen', *The secretarie of ladies* aimed 'to vindicate the honour of dames, and to make it appeare that Letters are not the peculiar heritage of one sexe'. The Reader is advised that 'if there bee any who cannot yet consent that Gentlewomen should write, I assure my selfe this book will convert them; where they shall finde so many things of worth, they shall bee compeld to renounce their ignorance or envy'. Rather than provide models for composition, these letters animate a conversation between two women, one socially superior to the other. Pairs of letters are matched on given topics—so the first letter, 'She prayes her to returne to Paris, and bring her in dislike with the Country', is paired with one that 'Answers, that besides the losse of their

---

[46] Charles E. Kany, *The Beginnings of the Epistolary Novel in France, Italy, and Spain*, University of California Publications in Modern Philology 21:1 (Berkeley, CA: University of California Press, 1937), 71–3.

[47] Nicholas Breton, *A poste with a madde packet of letters* (London: [Thomas Creede] for Iohn Smethicke, 1602).

[48] Du Bosc, trans. I[erome] H[ainhofer], *The secretary of ladies. Or, A new collection of letters and answers, composed by moderne ladies and gentlewomen* (London: Tho. Cotes, for William Hope, 1638).

conversation, she is vext with that of the Country: and that she will never made vew of solitude while she can hope the honour of their company'. As the two women work their way through common topics of conversation—life in Paris versus courtly life, men and their inconstancy, love, marriage, and social etiquette—there emerges an intense, and perhaps inappropriate relationship between them, where the socially superior woman rebukes the other for her overly ardent expressions of love.

Hainhofer's translation seems to be as far as the English-language epistolary novel develops by 1640. But a real watershed may already have occurred. In 1635, Charles I issued a proclamation that permitted his subjects to use the royal post for private mail, perhaps as a way to raise funds. The long-time viability of the service was assured by Oliver Cromwell's 1657 Act 'for settling the Postage of England, Scotland and Ireland' and Charles II's 1660 Act 'for erecting and establishing a Post Office'; in 1661, postmarks were introduced to help accountability and in 1680 cut-price intra-London and Westminster correspondence became possible, thanks to William Dockwra's penny post.[49] And with this new, cheap, relatively reliable and impersonal mail system came new possibilities for literary letters. As Ian Watt famously insisted, the development of the epistolary novel, culminating in the eighteenth-century masterpieces of Henry Fielding and Samuel Richardson, was 'materially assisted by a very great improvement of postal facilities', starting with the establishment of the penny post. As a result, 'Their drama unrolls in a flow of letters from one lonely closet to another', producing the effect that he names 'private experience'.[50] Such an experience was not possible before 1640: hence, the highly personalized, messily material, and intermittently experimental examples that characterize the genre of letters in Tudor and early Stuart prose.

Further Reading

Barnes, Diana G. *Epistolary Community in Print, 1580–1664* (Farnham: Ashgate, 2013).
Daybell, James. *The Material Letter in Early Modern England* (Basingstoke: Palgrave Macmillan, 2012).
—— 'Material Meanings and the Social Signs of Manuscript Letters in Early Modern England', *Literature Compass*, 6.3 (2009): 647–67.
—— *Women Letter-Writers in Tudor England* (Oxford: Oxford University Press, 2006).
Gibson, Jonathan. 'Significant Space in Manuscript Letters', *The Seventeenth Century*, 12 (1997): 1–9.
Kany, Charles E. *The Beginnings of the Epistolary Novel in France, Italy, and Spain*, University of California Publications in Modern Philology 21:1 (Berkeley, CA: University of California Press, 1937).

---

[49] Stewart and Wolfe, *Letterwriting in Renaissance England*, 121–4.
[50] Ian Watt, *The Rise of the Novel: Studies in Defoe, Richardson and Fielding* (Berkeley: University of California Press, 1957), 189; for the influence of Watt's dictum, see James How, *Epistolary Spaces: English Letter Writing from the Foundation of the Post Office to Richardson's Clarissa* (Aldershot: Ashgate, 2003). See also the influential study by Janet Gurkin Altman: *Epistolarity: Approaches to a Form* (Columbus, OH: Ohio State University Press, 1982).

Magnusson, Lynne. *Shakespeare and Social Dialogue: Dramatic Language and Elizabethan Letters* (Cambridge: Cambridge University Press, 1999).

Poster, Carol, and Linda C. Mitchell, eds. *Letter-Writing Manuals and Instruction from Antiquity to the Present: Historical and Bibliographical Studies* (Columbia, SC: University of South Carolina Press, 2007).

Robertson, Jean. *The Art of Letter Writing: An Essay on the Handbooks Published in England During the Sixteenth and Seventeenth Centuries* (Liverpool: Liverpool University Press, 1943).

Schneider, Gary. *The Culture of Epistolarity: Vernacular Letters and Letter Writing in Early Modern England, 1500–1700* (Newark, DE: University of Delaware Press, 2005).

Stewart, Alan. *Shakespeare's Letters* (Oxford: Oxford University Press, 2008).

—— and Heather Wolfe. *Letterwriting in Renaissance England* (Washington, DC: Folger Shakespeare Library, 2004)

CHAPTER 26

....

DIARIES

....

ADAM SMYTH

In the early modern period the term 'diary' lacked the generic stability it would later acquire, and this chapter will consider a range of texts (including chronicles, spiritual autobiographies, financial accounts, and annotated almanacs), all of which need to be seen as relating in some way to the category of the diary. Alongside this recognition of an interlinked network of life writing texts, this chapter will also stress how modern expectations of the diary as a form linked with intimacy, candour, and self-revelation are only fitfully present in this period, and are only gradually emerging across the sixteenth and seventeenth centuries: most early modern diaries were texts as much linked with the recording of actions in the world and public events as they were registers of any kind of inner life. As a consequence, the diary reminds us to pause in scepticism at many of the claims for cultural modernity implicit in the period marker 'early modern'. The diary of Lady Margaret Hoby (1571–1633) of Hackness, Yorkshire, is a useful place to start because it raises then confounds many of these modern expectations of diaries, privacy, and subjectivity, and so illustrates how the diary was not yet the form we know today.

Describing her activities on Thursday 23 August 1599, Margaret Hoby wrote the following:

> In the morninge I praied: then I took order for things about the house tell I went to breakfast, and sonne after I took my Coach and went to linton wher, after I had salluted my mother, I praied, and then, walkinge a litle and readinge of the bible in my Chamber went to supper: after which I hard the Lector [reading of biblical text] and sonne after that went to bed.[1]

The term 'diary', from the Latin *diarium* (daily allowance), was in circulation from the 1580s, if not before, and Hoby's text, composed between 1599 and 1605, seems to satisfy many of our expectations of the form. Hoby presents a first-person prose account, organized as daily entries, written close to the time of the events described (so lacking the lens of retrospection), recording the largely first-hand experiences of the writer. In other ways,

---

[1] *The Private Life of an Elizabethan Lady: The Diary of Lady Margaret Hoby, 1599–1605*, ed. Joanna Moody (Stroud: Sutton, 1998), 9. Hoby's manuscript is British Library MS Egerton 2614.

however, Hoby's text seems more distant: if we anticipate a diarist reflecting back on her own self, producing an anguished introspection and that sense of 'the single and peculiar life' (to use Rosencrantz's lonely words) that contemporary culture equates with selfhood, then Hoby's text resists our modern expectations. Hoby does note moments of reflection—'I betook me to priuat praier and examenation'[2]—but the specific nature of that contemplation is rarely explored. Hoby's diary is less a path to inwardness and more a logbook of actions across several spheres: she manages the manor and parsonage of Hackness in her husband's absence; pays and supervises servants; works in the garden; plays music; reads and writes (annotating the margins of her Bible); offers medical advice to local residents; and helps at births. Julie Crawford has argued that Hoby's diary is not the document of private retreat and introspection we might expect, but rather, a record of the puritan Hoby's religious and political activism in recusant Yorkshire.[3] Hoby's diary is certainly dominated by religion: her textual life is a record of puritan spiritual industry, an account of prayers and religious exercises, often led by Hoby's chaplain Richard Rhodes, and it conveys a sense that many events, including quotidian occurrences like mild illness, are products of God's interventions: Hoby's 'febelnis of stomack', the week before, is a 'Iust punishment' from God, 'to corricte my sinnes'.[4] While Hoby's final 'and sonne after that went to bed' anticipates Samuel Pepys's famous 'And so to bed', in most respects Hoby's diary seems very different from Pepys's descriptions of a 1660s life of secular pleasure—descriptions which are often regarded as paradigmatic of the form.

It would be a mistake, however, to think of Hoby's diary as a resistant, unyielding text. The lack of inwardness is not a lack at all: for Hoby, the diary was not a space in which to describe interiority, but rather, a site for the recording of actions, prayers, and God's role in shaping events. Many early modern diaries begin with, and remain preoccupied by, public events: the diary of Edward VI, perhaps unsurprisingly, records his official duties and royal travels;[5] Walter Yonge's diary opens with '5 November 1605. This daye there was an horrible treason intended to bee put in practise against the Kinge James the first';[6] William Whiteway of Dorchester started his diary after the appearance of 'a Blazing Star in the South East' and the 1618 execution of Walter Ralegh;[7] and a sharpened sense of history, induced by events such as plague, Civil War, or royal successions, encouraged many to record the world around them[8]—like John Rous, whose 1625–42 diary opens

---

[2] *Hoby*, ed. Moody, 6.

[3] Julie Crawford, 'Reconsidering Early Modern Women's Reading, or, How Margaret Hoby Read her de Mornay', *Huntington Library Quarterly*, 73.2 (2010): 193–223.

[4] *Hoby*, ed. Moody, 7.

[5] Jonathan North, ed., *England's Boy King: The Diary of Edward VI, 1547–1553* (Welwyn Garden City: Ravenhall, 2005).

[6] BL Add MS 28032, f. 3.

[7] BL MS Egerton 784, f. 5. Elizabeth Clarke, 'Diaries', in Michael Hattaway, ed., *A New Companion to English Renaissance Literature and Culture* (Oxford: Wiley-Blackwell, 2010), volume 1, 447–52 (448). David Underdown, ed., *William Whiteway of Dorchester: His Diary, 1618–1635* (Dorset: Dorset Record Society, 1991).

[8] Sharon Cadman Seelig, *Autobiography and Gender in Early Modern Literature: Reading Women's Lives, 1600–1680* (Cambridge: Cambridge University Press, 2006), 4.

with the note that Charles I's 'coming to the crowne was very joyous to the well-affected, but to Papists not very welcome'.[9] Modern expectations of intimacy and personal revelation are often not met. The 1550–63 diary or 'chronicle' of Londoner Henry Machyn is a largely non-narrative record of public events in London, particularly funerals (Machyn was a clothier and often provided the trappings), and also news of crimes, executions, government proclamations, and ceremonies such as the lord mayor's show.[10] Machyn's text is heavily informed by chronicles like Edward Hall's *The Union of the Two Noble Families of Lancaster and York* (1548)[11]—revealing how diaries might be motivated by an impulse to record public history before they became personal documents of self-accounting. Something similar is apparent in the diary of Charles Wriothesley (1508–62), who, as Windsor Herald, witnessed and recorded many major political events: his first sustained account is a detailed description of Anne Boleyn's coronation ('The great hall at Westminster was rytchlie hanged with rych cloath of Arras, and a table sett at the upper end of the hall...where the Queene dyned').[12] Wriothesley seems to have conceived of his chronicle as a largely celebratory record of the monarchs he served and he provides a positive account of Henry VIII's religious reforms. Henry Machyn's text also owes much to parish registers. Machyn was parish clerk of Holy Trinity-the-Less, where he maintained the parish register, and its skeleton runs through his 'diary' ('The seventeenth day of November was buried the old Countess of Derby buried at Colham, Sir Edward Hastings being her executor').[13] Indeed, records of burials remain the central, unifying subject of the text, and the format and rhetoric of the parish register informs many entries.

The regularity of Hoby's entries and her starkly functional prose suggests not an absence of drama or imagination, but a commitment to a stable form of writing. Indeed, as Sharon Cadman Seelig notes, the very point of Hoby's diary was to record and aid regular spiritual discipline: '[w]hat may strike the modern reader as...tedious, [or] repetitious...is in fact a sign of order, stability, and meaning in Margaret Hoby's life'.[14] The repetitious records, which seem to rob the text of a sense of Hoby's agency and personality, in fact record her 'self-determination and self-control'.[15] Similarly, the muted textual presence of Hoby's husband Thomas expresses not, necessarily, a loveless life, but rather, Hoby's sense of the genre in which she was writing. It is dangerous to read diaries as

---

[9] *Diary of John Rous*, ed. Mary Anne Everett Green (London: Camden Society, 1856), 1.

[10] 'A London provisioner's chronicle, 1550–1563, by Henry Machyn: manuscript, transcription, and modernization', ed. Richard W. Bailey, Marilyn Miller, and Colette Moore, <quod.lib.umich.edu/m/machyn>.

[11] Ian Mortimer, 'Tudor Chronicler or Sixteenth-Century Diarist? Henry Machyn and the Nature of His Manuscript', *Sixteenth-Century Journal*, 33 (2002): 981–98.

[12] *A Chronicle of England during the reigns of the Tudors, from A.D. 1485 to 1559, by Charles Wriothesley, Windsor Herald*, ed. William Douglas Hamilton (London: Royal Historical Society, 1875 and 1877), Camden New Series, XI and XX, vol. 1, 20–1.

[13] 'A London provisioner's chronicle', entry number six, modernized text.

[14] Seelig, *Autobiography*, 22.

[15] Seelig, *Autobiography*, 33.

sources for data without attending to genre's mediations: the reader relying on Hoby's diary would be surprised at her dramatic married life. At the time of writing, she was three years into her third marriage, to Sir Thomas Hoby; her first husband was Walter Devereux, brother to the Earl of Essex (executed for treason in 1601); and her second was Thomas Sidney, brother to the poets Philip and Mary. In those passages when Hoby draws on the cadences and sentences of the Bible and the Book of Common Prayer—using an established register to describe her own actions—the diary suggests not the erasure of Hoby's personality, but rather, the articulation of a sense of self through the use of available, biblical scripts. This writing of individuality through the adoption of shared, public templates invokes the dual meaning of identity as both sameness and uniqueness, and recalls that apparent combination of liberty and constraint in Catherine Belsey's note that to 'be a subject is to have access to signifying practice, to identify with the "I" who speaks', while necessarily also being 'held in place in a specific discourse, a specific knowledge, by the meanings available there'.[16] That this perhaps seems a paradoxical practice has much to do with post-Romantic conceptions of identity as detached, introspective, and interiorized. But the idea of identity generated in Hoby's text is different.

As Hoby's text suggests, religion, and in particular puritanism, was an important catalyst in the production of early modern diaries. The Calvinist *Thirty-Nine Articles* (1563) decreed that each individual was infected with original sin; that only faith, and not good works, could save the sinner; and that double predestination meant God had chosen the 'elect' to be saved and the 'reprobate' to be damned. Many responded to predestination not with the passivity we might expect, but rather, with a desire to find evidence of God's grace, and their election, in the smallest of actions.[17] Protestant guides to spiritual well-being advised readers to construct records of their actions as a means to discern their sin and God's graceful interventions, and out of these accounts of self-scrutiny, diaries sometimes emerged. In *A Fountaine of Teares* (Amsterdam, 1646), John Featley stressed that in order to 'see my God with joy', the Christian's sins 'must be seene by mee, and be bewayled by mee; *in sadnesse* they must'. To this end, 'I will therefore sitt downe, and...examine my selfe how I have spent the day.'[18] Featley lists thirty-eight questions—'At what time, in the morning, did I arise from my bed?'; 'What first did I?'; 'What sighes, and groanes have I sent to heaven for pardon for it?'—which, once answered, will yield 'mine account', a textual record of little actions that, accumulatively, constitutes an account of one's days.[19] In his *Journal or Diary of a Thankful Christian* (1656), John Beadle outlined how to keep spiritual accounts and imagined a broader, proto-secular diary growing out of the process of spiritual self-accounting he urged on Christians: while the diary would begin as a record of 'all Gods gracious dealings with us', it might soon expand to include 'the severall occurrenes of the Times we meet with, as they have

---

[16] Catherine Belsey, *The Subject of Tragedy: Identity and Difference in Renaissance Drama* (London and New York: Methuen, 1985), 5.
[17] Jason Scott-Warren, *Early Modern Literature* (Cambridge: Polity Press, 2005), 238–40.
[18] John Featley, A *Fountaine of Teares* (Amsterdam, 1646), 89.
[19] Featley, *Teares*, 89–91.

reference to the Countrey and Nation we live in. It is good to keep an History, a Register, a Diary, an Annales, not onely of the places in which we have lived, but of the mercies that have been bestowed on us, continued to all our dayes.'[20] Versions of this prescription are evident in many diaries. In the words of Alice Thornton (1627–1706), who composed 'A Book of Remembrances' of her life: 'it is the dutie of every true Christian to remember and take notice of Allmighty God our Heavenly Father's gracious acts of Providence over them...even from the wombe, untill the grave bury them in silence'.[21] The young Samuel Ward (1572–1643)—future Master of Sidney Sussex College, Cambridge—used his diary to catalogue his manifold sins: 'Thy little affection in hearing Master chattertons good sermon upon the 34 vs. of the 25 of Math. Thy adulterous thoughts, that Day. Thy backwardnes in calling to mynd the sermons that day...Thy anger, agaynst M.N. for his long prayers.'[22] Ralph Josselin—vicar of Earls Colne in Essex—titled his manuscript 'A thankfull observacion of divine providence and goodnes towards mee and a summary view of my life'[23] and his record for 4 November 1640 reads: 'came safe to Cranham. returning I thought of my thoughts at Huntingdon Bridge, and god had brought me back, increased with wife goods and parts, lo this was the Lords doing it was marvellous towards me'.[24] The paradoxical idea of agency at work here—actions performed by Josselin are, more fundamentally, actions performed by God—is a feature of many diaries.

Scholars often link this process of spiritual self-examination with an emerging interiority and indeed, this might sometimes be the case. A 1618 spiritual guide advised readers to 'descend into your owne soules, and well...prosecute the examination of your owne estates; whether you be as yet regenerated or no'.[25] If a language of introspection and a preoccupation with self did develop out of these religions examinations, it was inflected by a lexicon of sin, grace, repentance, guilt, corruption, and longed-for forgiveness, creating a particular vocabulary of inwardness. But spiritual self-reflection need not only lead inwards. While a narrative of puritan-induced interiority has dominated histories of the diary, spiritual accounting might in fact prompt a recording of external actions. We see this with Hoby, and in those spiritual memoirs which include detailed

---

[20] John Beadle, *Journal or Diary of a Thankful Christian* (1656), 10–11. Featley and Beadle are discussed in Sara Heller Mendelson, 'Stuart Women's Diaries and Occasional Memoirs', in Mary Prior, ed., *Women in English Society, 1500–1800* (London and New York: Methuen, 1985), 181–210.

[21] Mendelson, 'Stuart Women's Diaries', 187; Alice Thornton, *The Autobiography of Mrs Alice Thornton*, ed. C. Jackson, Surtees Society 62 (1875), 1.

[22] *Two Elizabethan Puritan Diaries, by Richard Rogers and Samuel Ward*, ed. M. M. Knappen (Chicago: American Society of Church History, 1933). Discussed in Scott-Warren, *Early Modern Literature*, 238.

[23] *The Diary of Ralph Josselin, 1616–1683*, ed. Alan Macfarlane (Oxford: Oxford University Press, 1991), 1. Quoted in *An Astrological Diary of the Seventeenth Century: Samuel Jeake of Rye, 1652–1699*, ed. Michael Hunter and Annabel Gregory (Oxford: Clarendon Press, 1988), 8.

[24] 'Diary of Ralph Josselin', <http://linux02.lib.cam.ac.uk/earlscolne/diary>. See also *Josselin*, ed. Macfarlane.

[25] Quoted in *The Notebooks of Nehemiah Wallington, 1618–1654: A Selection*, ed. David Booy (Aldershot: Ashgate, 2007), 16.

records of domestic routine, reading habits, social visits, or health, such as the autobiographical meditations of Lady Grace Mildmay (1552?–1620), Elizabeth Walker (1623–90), or Lady Elizabeth Delaval (b. 1649). We see it, too, in the diary of Samuel Jeake (1652–99), a nonconformist merchant and astrologer from Rye who used his diary to record a torrent of detail as he attempted to discern God's presence in his life:

> Towards evening returned home: and by the way about 6h 30' p.m. in a dark lane riding cross a descent made by a Rivulet of water the Girth being Loose, my Saddle for want of a Cruppier ran forward on the horse's neck; & I was twice like to be thrown off into the water where being alone in the night, I might either have been drowned or trod underfoot by my horse, or at least have been all wet. But the good hand of God directed me to stop & retire before I was quite off, & the horse being very gentle did not impede it.[26]

In fact, Jeake's ideas about God's agency are complicated by his simultaneous emphasis on astrology as an explanatory framework for life's occurrences. Jeake draws detailed horoscopes throughout his diary, particularly when dealing with money: he cast a sequence of horoscopes on 20 April 1694 when he bought tickets for the Million Adventure state lottery. But both Jeake's attention to God's minute interventions, and his interest in astrology's capacity to shape all events, illustrate how the diary became a form preoccupied with quotidian particularity.

Wood-turner and shopkeeper Nehemiah Wallington (1598–1658), who lived and worked in the City of London, showed a similar conception of his writing as predominantly a record of God's interventions. Wallington was a compulsive chronicler, compiling no less than fifty notebooks, of which seven survive today—despite frequently emphasizing the difficulty of writing ('oh now, now...with the leafe I must...turne my dulsome pen with my shaking hand to wright other matter')[27] and the potential sin of pride in his efforts. These extant notebooks include sustained autobiographical reflections, alongside other forms of writing: letters, prayers, and passages excised from sermons, news books, or the Bible. This mingling of genres, and a consequent sense of the 'diary' as a permeable form which bled, untroubled, into other kinds of writing, is also more broadly characteristic: modern criticism which too anxiously aims to set up a rigid conception of genre, and 'to clear the air by imposing limits on autobiographical emissions',[28] betrays this spirit of generic unfixity and experimentation. Many diaries were prefaced with a retrospective autobiography that covered the life up until the point of writing. There were often overlaps between the diary or autobiography and the commonplace book—a text in which aphorisms, plucked from reading or conversation, were arranged under thematic headings to provide the compiler with a store-house of pieces of eloquence—as can be seen in the written life of the parliamentary general Sir

---

[26] *Jeake*, ed. Hunter and Gregory, 226–7.
[27] *Wallington*, ed. Booy, 9. Paul Seaver, *Wallington's World: A Puritan Artisan in Seventeenth-Century London* (London: Methuen, 1985).
[28] Paul Delaney, *British Autobiography in the Seventeenth Century* (London: Routledge & Kegan Paul, 1969), 1.

William Waller (1598?–1668). In a bid to represent the 'stormy sea' of his life, Waller organized his account under thematic headings informed by commonplace books: headings such as 'In Prisons Frequent', 'By Great Sicknesses', and 'By Hassards of War', under which Waller distributed his experiences, cut up into aphoristic parcels, and designed, among other things, to demonstrate God's protecting providence.[29]

Wallington hoped that his writings would 'bring glory to God',[30] and his notebooks record his attempts to overcome sin ('I have offen prayed unto God to lay some logge or blocke in my way when I am temted to sinne') and express thanks to God for his interventions ('And heere I did see Gods grat merci to me: that when I tempted one to comit sinne with me in jesting and daliance: but shee resisted me: and I was glad of it').[31] Events are significant in Wallington's world as a means to uncover this divine purpose. Wallington also hoped his notebooks would be read by future readers (he wrote his first notebook 'in Roman hand that others mite benifet by it as well as I'),[32] and in this sense, his remarkable writings are also representative: early modern diaries were frequently public, or semi-public records, written in part to aid the spiritual and moral education of family and community. Diaries were thus often in some ways exemplary, which complicates assumptions about accuracy, candour, and privacy. In 1593, Devonshire yeoman Robert Furse constructed a diary that aimed to assure future generations of the virtues and achievements of Furse's family, and to bolster their legal claims to land: Furse sought to 'sette furthe what our progenytors have bynne of them selves and spessyally those that have bynne wythyn this seven score yeres', and hoped that 'hys heres [heirs] … [and] there sequele … [enjoy] longe lyfe and prosperytye'.[33] And while no diaries were printed in the period, manuscript copies might circulate widely within communities: Ralph Josselin read, and was encouraged to write by, other people's journals,[34] and royalist Sir John Gibson (1606–65), imprisoned in Durham Castle in the 1650s, sent his written life out to other readers. His manuscript contains valedictions, modelled on Ovid's *Tristia*, beginning 'Poor little Booke, thou must to Welburne goe' and 'Thou must from Durham, unto Elston goe.'[35]

Puritanism was, however, only one catalyst for the production of diaries: the popularity of self-writing in, for example, Catholic Italy indicates other causes were at work. Money is a second powerful diary prompt. In fact, religion and finance often overlap, as spiritual guides deploy a discourse drawn from financial bookkeeping: '[i]n thy selfe, for the helping forward of Repentance, keep a continuall audit, and take account of thy selfe

---

[29] Hannah Cowley, *The Poetry of Anna Matilda* (1788), 97–139 (103).

[30] *Wallington*, ed. Booy, 10.

[31] *Wallington*, ed. Booy, 45.

[32] *Wallington*, ed. Booy, 10.

[33] H. J. Carpenter, 'Furse of Moreshead: A Family Record of the Sixteenth Century', in *Reports and Transactions of the Devonshire Association for the Advancement of Science, Literature and Art*, 26 (1894): 168–84 (169).

[34] Clarke, 'Diaries', 449.

[35] BL Add MS 37719, ff. 113ᵛ, 208. For Gibson's manuscript, see Adam Smyth, ' "Rend and teare in peeces": Textual Fragmentation in Seventeenth-Century England', *The Seventeenth Century*, 19 (2004): 36–52.

and estate'.[36] The instruction to 'cast up your accounts', as a metaphor for spiritual self-examination—'cast up also all your wants, and see what at present you stand in need of'[37]—is extremely common. The portion of the 1656–78 spiritual diary of Elizabeth, Viscountess Mordaunt, covering 1657, is organized into columns headed 'To returne thanks for' and 'To ask perden for'—in effect, spiritual debts and credits.[38] Under 'To ask perden for', Mordaunt offers exacting confessions such as 'I haue sayd one or to things that wer not exactely true.'

The early modern period was not only the time of Shakespeare, Donne, and Sidney: it was also the golden age of financial accounting, a period in which printed guides to inventorying money were popular and formative. The financial record was often an early stage in the generation of later diaries: a foundation on which the narrative diary was built. Samuel Pepys's apparently impulsive prose seems to have begun life as a list of expenses which was gradually worked up into fluent prose: at two points in the diary from the first half of 1668, these earlier drafts survive in an unrevised form.[39] Here, from 10 to 19 April, and 5 to 17 June 1668, Pepys neglected to revise into narrative the sparse notes and financial accounts which provided the skeleton for his subsequent prose entries: in these moments, the earlier records, normally effaced, become visible, bound into the volume next to blank pages. Thus, for Friday 5 June:

At Barnet for milk	00. 00. 06
On the highway to menders of the highway	00. 00. 06
Dinner at Stevenage	00. 05. 06

And for Monday 8 June:

Father's servants (father having in the garden told me bad stories of my wife's ill words)	00. 14. 00
One that helped at the horses	00. 01. 00
Menders of the highway	00. 02. 00
Pleasant country to Bedfd. where while they stay I rode through the town and a good country town and there drinking	00. 01. 00
we on to Newport	
and there light and I and WH to the church and there give the boy	

---

[36] Thomas Taylor, *The Practice of Repentance* (1629), 299. Quoted and discussed in Barbara Lewalski, *Protestant Poetics and the Seventeenth-Century Religious Lyric* (Princeton: Princeton University Press, 1979), 158–9.

[37] Beadle, *Journal*, 105.

[38] *The Private Diarie of Elizabeth, Viscountess Mordaunt*, ed. Robert Jocelyn (Duncairn: Privately printed, 1856), 225–39.

[39] *The Diary of Samuel Pepys*, ed. Robert Latham and William Matthews, 11 vols. (Berkeley and Los Angeles: University of California Press, 1970–83), vol. IX, 160–8 (10–19 April 1668) and 224–43 (5–17 June 1668). Mark S. Dawson, 'Histories and Texts: Refiguring the Diary of Samuel Pepys', *The Historical Journal*, 43.2 (2000): 407–31.

These early notes reveal the beginnings of Pepys's famous text as a series of financial accounts, subsequently reworked into the supposedly 'spontaneous' prose we know today. (In fact, there is a broader, more complicated process of textual traffic beneath the smooth surface of Pepys's text, involving many kinds of texts: but financial accounts are central.) The prominence Pepys gives to his finances throughout the diary registers the presence of these early notes as a kind of foundation under the later text, although, in general, Pepys effaces the process of drafting and reworking. But these skeleton entries let that process be glimpsed. The centrality of money as a topic in many other early modern diaries suggests a similar writing process was often at work: the 1616–19 diary of Lady Anne Clifford (1590–1676) is organized not as continuous prose, but in two columns—a more personal narrative at the centre, with public and social events on the left—which duplicates the layout of her financial accounts.[40] The popular perception of Pepys as someone who, in his diary, offers unmediated plunges at life—whose diary was written, in the words of one critic, 'frankly and swiftly to get down what had stirred [Pepys'] mind each day'[41]—breaks down in the light of this evidence. Pepys's famously impulsive prose was not immediate, 'unconscious', or unreserved, but was, in fact, the product of distinct and careful stages of revision.[42] Pepys's diary represents not spontaneity, but the artful construction of spontaneity.

The kind of subjectivity conveyed in diaries informed by financial accounts might also differ from a modern idea of inwardness. Pepys certainly writes about interiority, but many diaries informed by finance construct a sense of identity through objects and possessions, and so generate a subjectivity that is less about interiority and detachment, and more about things in the world. This recalls that Renaissance homonym, lost—as Margreta de Grazia has noted—to modern pronunciation: what *one* is depends on what one *owns*.[43] The word 'personality' has an etymological link with 'personalty', or 'personal property':[44] it might be a subjectivity, not of depths, but of accumulated things—as if Hamlet's identity was not 'that within which passeth show', but his cloak and his tables. Such an alternative to that better-known story of alienation and depth is one reminder of the virtues of exploring a Renaissance that is not always and only proto-modern.

Financial records also influenced diary writing by encouraging a particular idea of truthfulness in accounting: assumptions about how to create a reliable record often

---

[40] Adam Smyth, *Autobiography in Early Modern England* (Cambridge: Cambridge University Press, 2010), 90.

[41] Percival Hunt, *Pepys in the Diary* (Pittsburgh: University of Pittsburgh Press, 1959), 175. Quoted in Dawson, 'Histories and Texts', 416.

[42] *The Diary of Samuel Pepys*, ed. Latham and Matthews, vol. I, xli–lxvii. See also Dawson, 'Histories and Texts'. For transcripts of Pepys's earlier notes that were never written up into his finished diary, and which therefore show one early stage in his ongoing process of revising, see *Diary*, vol. IX, 160–8 (10–19 April 1668) and 224–43 (5–17 June 1668).

[43] Margreta de Grazia, 'The Ideology of Superfluous Things', in Margreta de Grazia, Maureen Quilligan, and Peter Stallybrass, eds., *Subject and Object in Renaissance Culture* (Cambridge: Cambridge University Press, 1996), 17–42 (34).

[44] Rebecca Elisabeth Connor, *Women, Accounting, and Narrative: Keeping Books in Eighteenth-Century England* (London and New York: Routledge, 2004), 131–2.

migrated from financial accounting to diary writing. Hugh Oldcastle's *A Briefe Instruction and Maner How to Keepe Bookes of Accompts After the Order of Debitor and Creditor* (now lost, but reissued by John Mellis in 1588)—a translation of Luca Paccioli's *Summa de Arithmetica, Geometria, Proportioni et Proportionalita* (Venice, 1494)—first popularized double-entry bookkeeping for an English readership, and a flood of other printed guides followed, including James Peele's *The Pathwaye to Perfectnes* (1569) and John Carpenter's *A Most Excellent Instruction* (1632). These guides forged a powerful connection between certain regularized ways of ordering financial accounts and connotations of honesty, clarity, balance, virtue, and truth, and these methods for constructing good records became common traits of diaries.

The accountant must 'bee prompt and readdy' in his recording of every single transaction, no matter how small. A 'marchant may be applied unto Argus', Mellis writes, 'which as Poetes shewe, had a hundreth eyes'[45]—just as diaries became associated with quotidian detail. While some kinds of financial record might be collaboratively written, the financial 'journal' was to be the work of only one hand. '[N]o man is to write, but hee that keepth the Accounts',[46] 'for in times of controversie he can best answer for his own postings'.[47] Guides to accounting thus encouraged a connection between the individual compiler, the privacy of records, and a reliable journal of events. In order to generate the impression of truthfulness, entries in financial accounts should adhere to particular rhetorical templates, such as 'In the name of God, AMEN...The Inventory of me A.B. Citizen and Mercer of *London*, containing my whole estate generall, in Lands, Rents, Goods, ready money, Debts and Creditors which I have in this present world, at this present day'.[48] Diary entries are rhetorically regular, and this regularity is linked to connotations of order and trust. The pages of the financial account were to be full, with no space, since blanks suggest records might be added later on, perhaps duplicitously. This connection between spatial fullness and truth found its narrative equivalent in diaries that strained for the effect of having conveyed the whole day—from 'Waking in the morning', until 'and so to bed'. Perhaps most importantly of all, guides stressed that good accounting is based around the construction of multiple, interconnected notebooks, and that records should be shunted from book to book, and revised in the process. John Mellis urged compilers to create an initial inventory of possessions and debts; a second book, called the 'Memoriall or Remembrance' or waste book, to note down business transactions as they occur; a journal, into which, every five or six days, the compiler should transfer this information, producing a leaner narrative; and finally, the ledger, or 'great booke of accompte'.[49] This process of transmission and revision produces, in

[45] John Mellis, *A Briefe Instruction and Maner How to Keepe Bookes of Accompts After the Order of Debitor and Creditor* (1588), sig. B3.
[46] John Carpenter, *A Most Excellent Instruction For The Exact And Perfect Keeping Merchants Bookes of Accounts* (1632), 6.
[47] Richard Dafforne, *The Merchant's Mirrour, or, Directions for the Perfect Ordering and Keeping of his Accounts* (1684), 8.
[48] Carpenter, *Excellent Instruction*, 92.
[49] Mellis, *Briefe Instruction*, sig. H8.

theory, increasingly regular records whose system and clarity means the accountant can tell 'at *all times*, and in *every respect*, how *his Estate standith*',[50] and so demonstrate his honesty, virtue, godliness, diligence, skill, and social credit.[51] By compiling his accounts, an individual 'in an Instant can see (as he doeth his Person in a mirror) his whole estate and in what posture it is in at the time'.[52]

The practice of constructing reliable records through a process of transmission and rewriting lies behind many diaries: perhaps the biggest misconception about diary writing is that it was immediate and artless. We see this process at work in John Evelyn's diaries for the 1630s. Evelyn began his diary writing by setting down notes in almanacs, 'in imitation', he wrote, 'of what I had seen my father do',[53] and these notes formed the first, preparatory stage of his later diary writing.[54] This can be seen below: on the left, Evelyn's almanac annotation for 2 July 1637, entered close to this date; on the right, the entry for this day in the diary, composed some time after 1660.

[July 2] A oxfor I first Receued the holy communion being yn in Bal Coll Chap Mr Cooper preacht[55]	Upon the 2d of July, being the first of the Moneth, I first received the B: Sacrament of the Lords Supper in the Colledge Chapell, one Mr Cooper, a fellow of the house preaching; and at this tyme was the Church of England in her greatest splendor, all things decent, and becoming the peace, and the Persons that govern'd. The most of the following Weeke I spent in visiting the Colleges, and several rarities of the University, which do very much affect young comers; but I do not find any memoranda's of what I saw.[56]

Only two of Evelyn's annotated almanacs survive—a third disappeared after a Sotheby's sale in 1925—so it is not possible to anatomize the whole diary in this way. But even these brief instances suggest a compositional practice that has important implications for how we think about autobiographical texts: most fundamentally, that the production of Evelyn's diary was less the direct transcription of lived experience, and more the result of successive revisions of prior texts.[57] Lady Anne Clifford constructed a series of closely

---

[50] Richard Dafforne, *The Apprentices Time-Entertainer Accomptantly* (1640), sig. B.

[51] Ceri Sullivan, *The Rhetoric of Credit: Merchants in Early Modern Writing* (London: Associated University Press, 2002).

[52] Robert Colinson, *Idea Rationaria, or The Perfect Accomptant* (1683), 2.

[53] *The Diary of John Evelyn*, ed. E. S. De Beer, 6 vols. (Oxford: Clarendon Press, 1955), vol. II, 10.

[54] Frances Harris, *Transformations of Love: The Friendship of John Evelyn and Margaret Godolphin* (Oxford: Oxford University Press, 2002), 16 n. 2: 'Evelyn made his original diary entries in printed almanacs, which he had bound and interleaved with blank sheets (BL Add MS 78407: bookseller's bill, 24 July 1661). Some retain the *aide-mémoire* style imposed by the limited space.'

[55] Annotations in Thomas Langley, *Langley 1637 a new almanack and prognostication* (1637) (now in Balliol College, Oxford).

[56] *Diary of John Evelyn*, ed. De Beer, vol. I, 19–20.

[57] Nussbaum notes that John Wesley 'kept diaries that were little more than lists of activities he assigned to a precise hour, but he later expanded them into a more discursive narrative journal'. Felicity Nussbaum, 'Toward Conceptualizing Diary', in James Olney, ed., *Studies in Autobiography* (Oxford: Oxford University Press, 1988), 128–40 (130).

related autobiographical texts which chronicle her lifelong, and ultimately successful, battle for the inheritance of her family estates in Westmorland and Yorkshire.[58] These texts constitute 'the longest surviving autobiographical record of the early modern era'[59] and include an autobiography, a chronicle, and a diary, as well as financial accounts. Each of these first-person accounts is, it seems, linked through a chain of transmission and revision: the financial accounts fed into the diaries, which supplied the chronicles, which informed the autobiography. If there is a tendency in contemporary culture, perhaps even a craving, to associate diary writing with immediacy, candour, and 'guileless disclosure',[60] and if, as Laura Marcus notes, the presence in life writing of spontaneity's perceived opposites—artfulness and literary craft—is read as a kind of falseness,[61] the accumulative, ongoing, deliberate practice of early modern diary writing suggests that these assumptions need rethinking. To put that more aphoristically: early modern life writing was as much about writing as it was about life.

Evelyn's use of printed almanacs as sites in which early proto-diaries were logged, before being revised into fuller narrative, was typical of his time: the almanac was a crucial text lying beneath many early modern diaries. Printed almanacs were staggeringly popular: Thomas Nashe said selling them was 'readier money than ale and cakes',[62] and these cheap, diminutive, portable books provided readers with monthly calendars; astrological and meteorological prognostications; details of fairs and journeys between markets; notes of what were deemed canonical historical events; political chronologies; medical tips; discussions of the planets' influence on the well-being of the body; and more. Almanacs were often interleaved with blank pages, on which readers added notes of their activities: their journeys; illnesses; financial dealings; and the births, deaths, and marriages of their family's life. This is what Evelyn did—his bookbinder's bill from June 1662 makes reference to an 'Almanacke bound with pages Extraord[inary]'[63]—and so did many others from a wide social spectrum: farmers counting their herd; elite women such as Lady Isabella Twysden (1605–57) of Roydon Hall, Kent; non-elite women such as Sarah Sale (*fl.* 1680), who entered detailed notes about money and agriculture after the death of her husband ('I find in my Husbands Acomt money pd. for hay which I knew not before the money dew to me for hay is 5–0 the money for pease is—4 10');[64] the tireless Warwickshire antiquarian Sir William Dugdale (1605–86), whose fifty heavily annotated volumes fed into many writing projects, including his

---

[58] Katherine O. Acheson, ed., *The Memoir of 1603 and The Diary of 1616–1619* (Ontario: Broadview, 2007); D. J. H. Clifford, ed., *The Diaries of Lady Anne Clifford* (Stroud: Sutton, 2003).

[59] Acheson, ed., *Memoir*, 9.

[60] Roger Cardinal, 'Unlocking the Diary', *Comparative Criticism*, 12 (1990): 71–87 (78).

[61] Laura Marcus, *Auto/biographical Discourses: Theory, Criticism, Practice* (Manchester: Manchester University Press, 1994), 6.

[62] Thomas Nashe, *Have With You To Saffron Walden* (1596). Quoted in Bernard Capp, *English Almanacs, 1500–1800: Astrology and the Popular Press* (Ithaca and New York: Cornell University Press, 1979), 44.

[63] BL Add MS 78638.

[64] Cardanus Rider, *British Merlin* (1680), Folger A2254.5.

autobiography;[65] and John Dee (1527–1608), occultist, astrologer, mathematician, and adviser to Queen Elizabeth, who kept a diary through almanac annotations between 1577 and 1601.[66] The owner of a 1613 copy of Arthur Hopton's *New Almanacke* (possibly a puritan minister called Matthew Page) added the following notes to the page for January:

> I wen$_\wedge^t$ to Canterbury wth. T.K.
> This day Anthony was taken blinde: & his eyes
> continued sore & swolne
> this night one of my greate teethe fell out by y^e fireside
> Goodwife Paine tooke Anth: to nurse
> Anthonye departed this life about eyght
> of y^e clocke in y^e morning 17
> 19 I went to Lenham to Markes Haule for
> my wife hir breasts.[67]

Many extant almanacs contain similar annotations: a series of staccato entries which don't quite cohere into a narrative, as criticism generally deploys that term: as a representation of temporality which, in Hayden White's words, 'strains for the effect of having filled in all the gaps', and which lends to events a moral significance.[68] One connection between these annotated texts and diary writing is textual transmission. Materials added to almanacs were frequently transferred to other texts: diarists often generated a life through a process of shifting material from text to text, starting with an almanac, expanding records with each movement. Many attributes of diaries are due to the later-effaced presence of the almanac as an early text in an ongoing process of rewriting: this founding compositional moment shaped the contents and form of later diaries. Almanac annotations often picked up on topics raised by the printed text: notes of political events; the weather; journey distances; and, in particular, records about health. The prominence of these topics in later diaries reflects in part a flow of influence from printed almanac to manuscript annotations to later diaries. In other ways, the dynamic between print and manuscript was more complicated. Early printed almanacs seem not to have envisaged readers adding annotations. The first printed almanacs to signal an awareness of this mode of consumption—Thomas Purfoote's *A blanke and perpetuall Almanacke* (1566) ('a memoriall... for any... that will make & keepe notes of any actes... Worthy of memory, to be registered') and Thomas Hill's *An almanack... in forme of a booke of memorie necessary for all such, as haue occasion daylie to note sundry affayres, eyther for receytes, payments, or such lyke* (1571)—came some time after the

---

[65] The originals are kept at the Dugdale home at Merevale; microfilm copies are available at Warwick Record Office MI 318. See also *The Life, Diary, and Correspondence of Sir William Dugdale*, ed. William Hamper (London: Harding, Lepard and Co., 1827).

[66] *The Diaries of John Dee*, ed. Edward Fenton (Charlbury: Day Books, 1998).

[67] Arthur Hopton, *A new almanacke and prognostication for the yeare of our Lord God 1613* (1613), Bodleian Ash. 66.

[68] Hayden White, *The Content of the Form: Narrative Discourse and Historical Representation* (Baltimore and London: Johns Hopkins University Press, 1987), 5 and 11.

practice of annotating seems to have become established. Purfoote's and Hill's texts, which included blanks and encouraged readers to 'make & keepe notes', were responding to, and reinforcing, but not initiating this practice. Publishers had thus reorganized the almanac's material form in response to new modes of reading, and had thus described a loop of influence: printed texts received readers' annotations, which catalysed the reworking of those printed texts.

If religion and finance, therefore, were two powerful forces behind the emergence of diary writing, the willingness of readers to improvise in largely unforeseen ways with cheap printed books was another spark. More generally, the eagerness with which readers added notes of their lives to printed books reflects the fact that early modern life was increasingly organized around official written records: at the parish level, citizens would have been conscious of their lives being tracked in documents such as parish registers, introduced by Thomas Cromwell in 1538 with the radical aim of recording the birth, death, and marriage of almost every individual, no matter what rank. Rising literacy rates meant individuals might appropriate this culture of record-keeping to produce their own written accounts. If the administrative movement some historians call a Tudor revolution in government—the extension of a newly consistent level of bureaucracy to the process of rule—encouraged a sense of England as a record-keeping society, a culture committed to the production of textual traces, then the proliferation of improvised diaries and other life writing forms reflects the trickling down of this culture of accounting.

The archival turn within literary studies of the last twenty years has yielded many new texts, and has made it clear that an earlier story of the diary's development, organized around elite male writers (Pepys and Evelyn) producing texts that seem recognizable to us, and that produce 'a sense of the times in which it was lived',[69] needs to be rewritten to include—at the very least—a much greater generic diversity and, as a result, a much wider social spectrum of writers.[70] Previous assumptions that diary writing was limited to the middle and upper classes, and that lower socio-economic groups lacked the necessary money, literacy, free time, and solitary space,[71] need revising if we recognize the overlaps between diaries and hugely popular texts like annotated almanacs. The

---

[69] Seelig, *Autobiography*, 5.

[70] For work that has examined other forms, see Ronald Bedford, Lloyd Davis, and Philippa Kelly, eds., *Early Modern Autobiography: Theories, Genres, Practices* (Ann Arbor: University of Michigan Press, 2006); James S. Amelang, *The Flight of Icarus: Artisan Autobiography in Early Modern Europe* (Stanford: Stanford University Press, 1998), 28–41. For anthologies of autobiographical texts that give a sampling of some of these forms, see Elspeth Graham et al., eds., *Her Own Life: Autobiographical Writings by Seventeenth-Century Englishwomen* (London and New York: Routledge, 1989); David Booy, *Autobiographical Writings by Early Quaker Women* (Aldershot: Ashgate, 2004); David Booy, *Personal Disclosures: An Anthology of Self-Writings from the Seventeenth Century* (Aldershot: Ashgate, 2002); and Helen Ostovich and Elizabeth Sauer, eds., *Reading Early Modern Women: An Anthology of Texts in Manuscript and Print, 1550–1700* (London and New York: Routledge, 2004), 241–315.

[71] Effie Botonaki, *Seventeenth-Century English Women's Autobiographical Writings: Disclosing Enclosures* (Lampeter: Edwin Mellen Press, 2004), 4–6.

point where, for example, a financial account ends and a diary begins, is often not clear, and it would be anachronistic to insist on a rigid distinction. Indeed, since manuscripts originating outside of aristocratic circles have a low survival rate, our sense of the social range of diary writers is still probably too narrow.[72]

Of course, this laudable emphasis on *ad fontes* raises problems of its own, not least in terms of access: the stress on the archives—prompted, in part, by a desire to modify the corpus of literary studies—means that those who can't travel to these libraries, local archives, or aristocratic houses enjoy little of that celebrated sense of the canon opening up. Digital editions can offer a substitute, such as the online transcription of Elizabeth Isham's writings—a vade mecum (1608–48) and a recently uncovered autobiographical 'Booke of Rememberance' (*c*. 1639)[73]—or the 1550–63 'chronicle' of Londoner Henry Machyn.[74] But it is an irony of current work in early modern studies—and in literary studies more generally—that an emphasis on the materiality of texts and the fetishizing of the archival real runs parallel with an enthusiasm for digitization projects which replace the real with the virtual. Indeed, a broader question which still needs thinking through is what, exactly, materiality means in the culture of the digital.

Why have scholars paid little attention to the diary as a genre of writing? In part, this is because diary writing often appears plain, unadorned, and non-literary, if by 'literary' we mean language that strives for something more than the instrumental. Diaries seem to lack the edges and gaps and obvious artifice on which criticism typically gains purchase. But even apparently functional prose has its generic debts, conventions, and rhetorical preferences, just as anti-rhetorical plain-speaking is an identifiable rhetorical mode. The neglect of genre is also due to the fact that scholars have tended to excise facts and vignettes, while paying little attention to the larger whole. This is certainly a tempting methodology: partly because excerpts can be so arresting (like Dr Simon Forman, on seeing *Macbeth* at the Globe in 1611: 'obserue Also howe Mackbetes quen did Rise in the night in her slepe & walke and talked'),[75] and partly because the generic heterogeneity of many diaries seems to invite a crumbling into parts. Thus, the 1602–3 diary of Inns of Court lawyer John Manningham might be read for its aphorisms ('a wicked king is like a crazed ship'), sermon notes, epigrams, jokes (including one about Shakespeare's sexual conquests), medical recipes (for 'the windines in the stomach'), or its notes on a Middle Temple performance of *Twelfth Night*: the diary almost rattles with the many different pieces of life that came at this young lawyer.[76] The problem with excising is not only that highlights reflect the scholar's priorities, not the diarist's, and thus tend to

---

[72] Clarke, 'Diaries', 612.

[73] Isham's texts are being studied by a team at the University of Warwick led by Elizabeth Clarke and Erica Longfellow: <www2.warwick.ac.uk/fac/arts/ren/projects/isham>.

[74] 'A London provisioner's chronicle', <quod.lib.umich.edu/m/machyn>.

[75] *The Autobiography and Personal Diary of Dr Simon Forman, 1552 to 1602*, ed. J. O. Halliwell (Oxford: Oxford University Press, 1849); excerpts included in G. Blakemore Evans, ed., *The Riverside Shakespeare* (Chicago: Houghton Mifflin Harcourt, 1997), volume 1, 1966–7.

[76] *The Diary of John Manningham of the Middle Temple, 1602–1603*, ed. Robert Parker Sorlien (Hanover: University Press of New England, 1976).

affirm, rather than challenge preconceptions; but also that excising suggests that the diary is an unmediated 'source' that neutrally conveys facts—leaving the diary *qua* writing unexplored. With similar consequences, much diary scholarship has, perhaps unsurprisingly, organized itself around the authors of these texts, plotting (or at least implying) a direct path from the writing to the life. By emphasizing the writerly aspects of the diary (its rhetorical forms; its discourses; and its generic debts), and the sustained processes of transmission and redrafting that often lay beneath these apparently artless texts, we can gain a richer and more historically sensitive appreciation of that interaction between an urge to record the contemporary world and the necessity of following literary and conceptual precedents.

What role does gender have in diary writing? The puritan catalyst for diary writing was certainly seen as applicable to both women and men, and, as a result, women produced many spiritual diaries, as can be seen with texts by Lady Anne Harcourt; Lady Frances Pelham; Mary Roberts; Mary Rich, Countess of Warwick; and many others.[77] Scholarship has been aware of this tradition, but this awareness was part of the reason why early to mid-twentieth-century scholarship paid less attention to the spiritual diary as a form. In a familiar circular argument, scholars convinced by a male-dominated literary canon, faced with evidence of women's writing, relegated those forms in which women's agency was apparent (spiritual diaries; translations; and religious verse) to bolster that existing canon. An awareness of a devotional diary tradition has also sometimes created a too-rigid sense of the kinds of texts women might write: women's diaries need not always be texts of inwardness and privacy, but might also record political events (as Isabella Twysden's did), or social mobility and visibility (as Margaret Hoby's did). If it is broadly true that, as Sara Heller Mendelson has argued, women's diaries tend to be organized around the household, in contrast to men's diaries, which focus on public life,[78] this was not always the case: Isabella Twysden's annotations include 'the 11 of Sep 1645 princ rupert delivered up bristoll on treaty to Sr Tho: farfax'. There is a danger that scholarship recycles early modern prescriptions about female behaviour. Recent work has demonstrated how women left representations of themselves across a range of written forms, including diaries, financial accounts, letters, fictional romances, annotated printed texts, and even recipe books, and there is a strong case for using the inclusive term 'life writing' as a way to highlight the connection between these various genres and to throw off unhelpfully static assumptions about restriction, privacy, and decorum.[79]

The rise of diary writing is often linked with the supposed 'birth' of early modern subjectivity. Ever since Jacob Burckhardt's *Die Kultur der Renaissance in Italien* (1860), the Renaissance has been formulated as the moment in which a discernibly modern sense of

---

[77] *The Harcourt Papers*, ed. Edward H. Harcourt (Oxford, 1880), vol. 1, 169–96; University of Nottingham MS Portland PwV 89; East Sussex Record Office DUN/52/10/3.

[78] Mendelson, 'Stuart Women's Diaries', 199.

[79] Julie A. Eckerle and Michelle M. Dowd, eds., *Genre and Women's Life Writing in Early Modern England* (Aldershot: Ashgate, 2007).

self was born—when individuals began to conceive of themselves as self-reflective, detached, and interiorized.[80] Often Shakespeare, and, in particular, *Hamlet*, stand as epitomes of this 'modern depth'.[81] '[A]ll of us', writes Harold Bloom, with a characteristic level of understatement, 'were to a shocking degree, pragmatically reinvented by Shakespeare'.[82]

One problem with this entrenched narrative is its unhelpful sense of medieval culture. Later periods are often made radical by scholars homogenizing what went before, and, as David Aers has noted, the supposed novelty of early modern subjectivity depends upon a misleadingly unified medieval culture, free from economic instabilities, class conflicts, and ideological contests, 'a static homogenous collective...in which there could not be any self-conscious concern with individual identity or subjectivity'.[83] The Burkhardtian narrative has also led to an almost exclusive prioritizing of one model of subjectivity, based around modern ideas of difference, individuality, and alienation. But early modern diarists also constructed selfhood through a process of identifying, even overlapping, with other figures, narratives, and events. This is evident when diary writers recycle biblical sentences to articulate their own life, or represent their life as a rearticulation of former experiences: as royalist prisoner John Gibson did, in his commonplace book/diary, by invoking a coterie of individuals who represented the tribulations of the good man: Charles I, Charles II, Archbishop William Laud, John the Baptist, Ovid, Ulysses, and St John Chrysostome. All of these figures endured various forms of suffering and exile, and Gibson conceived of his life as a retelling of their stories.

If subjectivity was not necessarily a novel aspect of early modern culture, what does seem newly characteristic is a fascination with attempts to *represent* that sense of self: in portrait, lyric, financial account, soliloquy, in the 'burgeoning...language of reflexivity',[84] in annotations added to printed books, in appropriated documents of bureaucracy such as parish registers, and, of course, in the diary. It is this culture of self-writing that resonates in Shakespeare's plays, which feature many characters preoccupied with, and tormented by, finding ways of registering a life: 'I am a scribbled form', says the collapsing King John, 'drawn with a pen/Upon a parchment, and against this fire/Do I shrink up'.[85] In this slippage between person and text, characters are characters in that double sense: both personalities and written letters. This is what Claudius puns on, as he frets over Hamlet's letter telling of his 'sudden and more strange return'. 'Know you the hand?' says Laertes. ''Tis Hamlet's character', Claudius replies.[86]

---

[80] Burckhardt wrote that in the Middle Ages, 'man was conscious of himself only as a member of a race, people, party, family or corporation'; it was only in the Renaissance that 'man became a spiritual *individual*, and recognized himself as such'. Jacob Burckhardt, *The Civilization of the Renaissance* (Oxford: Phaidon Press, 1944), 81.

[81] Francis Barker, *The Tremulous Private Body: Essays on Subjection* (Ann Arbor: University of Michigan Press, 1995), 31.

[82] Harold Bloom, *Shakespeare: The Invention of the Human* (New York: Riverhead Books, 1998), 17.

[83] David Aers, 'A Whisper in the Ear of Early Modernists; or, Reflections on Literary Critics Writing the "History of the Subject"', in David Aers, ed., *Culture and History 1350–1600: Essays on English Communities, Identities and Writing* (New York and London: Harvester Wheatsheaf, 1992), 177–202 (187).

[84] Scott-Warren, *Early Modern Literature*, 226.

[85] *2 Henry IV*, 1.1.60–1; *Macbeth*, 1.5.61–2; *King John*, 5.7.32–4. [86] *Hamlet*, 4.7.49.

Further Reading

Aers, David. 'A Whisper in the Ear of Early Modernists; or, Reflections on Literary Critics Writing the "History of the Subject"', in David Aers, ed., *Culture and History, 1350–1600: Essays on English Communities, Identities and Writing* (New York and London: Harvester Wheatsheaf, 1992), 177–202.

Amelang, James S. *The Flight of Icarus: Artisan Autobiography in Early Modern Europe* (Stanford: Stanford University Press, 1998).

Bedford, Ronald, Lloyd Davis, and Philippa Kelly, eds. *Early Modern Autobiography: Theories, Genres, Practices* (Ann Arbor: University of Michigan Press, 2006).

Connor, Rebecca Elisabeth. *Women, Accounting, and Narrative: Keeping Books in Eighteenth-Century England* (London and New York: Routledge, 2004).

Crawford, Julie. 'Reconsidering Early Modern Women's Reading, or, How Margaret Hoby Read her de Mornay', *Huntington Library Quarterly*, 73.2 (2010): 193–223.

Dawson, Mark S. 'Histories and Texts: Refiguring the Diary of Samuel Pepys', *The Historical Journal*, 43.2 (2000): 407–31.

Eckerle, Julie A., and Michelle M. Dowd, eds. *Genre and Women's Life Writing in Early Modern England* (Aldershot: Ashgate, 2007).

Marcus, Laura. *Auto/biographical Discourses: Theory, Criticism, Practice* (Manchester: Manchester University Press, 1994).

Nussbaum, Felicity. 'Toward Conceptualizing Diary', in James Olney, ed., *Studies in Autobiography* (Oxford: Oxford University Press, 1988), 128–40.

Seelig, Sharon Cadman. *Autobiography and Gender in Early Modern Literature: Reading Women's Lives, 1600–1680* (Cambridge: Cambridge University Press, 2006).

Smyth, Adam. *Autobiography in Early Modern England* (Cambridge: Cambridge University Press, 2010).

CHAPTER 27

LIFE WRITING

DANIELLE CLARKE

AMIDST the myriad definitions and descriptions that have come to the fore in recent years as critics and historians have become more and more interested in the discursive and narrative constructions of early modern lives, one thing is certain. 'Life writing', at least in any of the forms familiar to a modern readership, did not exist in 1550, but manifests in multiple and plural ways by 1700. It is not, of course, the case that writers prior to the seventeenth century did not draw on their own experiences, nor that they did not playfully insert their own personas into textual artefacts, but it can reasonably be said that there are few—if any—forms *specifically* devoted to the exploration of individual lives. As Meredith Skura argues

> older writing about oneself appeared only in scattered passages and was incidental to other purposes; or it was allegorical; or it presented the author's life as moral exemplar rather than individual experience; or it did not talk about the development of personality.[1]

'[T]he author's [or subject's] life as moral exemplar' is a key generic development in this period, and what is notable is the gradual broadening of the social base of who may count as exemplary. The exemplary does not therefore require to be placed outside the generic parameters of what counts as life writing, rather, it needs to be more thoroughly investigated as a rich source of relevant materials. The guises in which 'life writing' appear are themselves the products of complex events, generic evolution, and the hybridization of forms and traditions, but it might reasonably be claimed that 'life writing' (as a diverse, yet loosely affiliated body of materials) constitutes the first truly vernacular and properly demotic mode of written expression of the early modern period. However, it is important to note that 'life writing' was, by definition, only accessible to a relatively small proportion of the population and that exclusion from written forms of discursive 'self-construction' does not equate simply with a lack of selfhood or

---

[1] Meredith Skura, '*A Mirror for Magistrates* and the Beginnings of English Autobiography', *English Literary Renaissance*, 36 (2006): 26–56 (26).

subjectivity.² In other words, contrary to what most criticism assumes, the self may well be constructed in discourse, but it does not follow that this discourse is necessarily, or even primarily, written. This chapter seeks first, to outline some critical and definitional issues; second, to examine the origins, practices, and uses of what later might be called 'biography'; and finally, to explore some examples of what Elspeth Graham calls 'self-writing', asking, in particular, why women found the business of writing lives (both their own and those of individuals to whom they were closely linked) so amenable and in what ways life writing enabled (or disabled) female agency.

It is useful from the start to displace some modern assumptions about what a life is, how it might be written, and the uses to which that written life might be put. Adam Smyth rightly makes the point that 'the craving of modern readers for narrative' tends to obscure the more complex, coded, and fragmented ways in which self-identity might be recorded and circulated in this period.³ Equally, the inevitable dependence of literate selfhood on inherited models and paradigms creates a tricky paradox in relation to both biography and autobiography in the period (and I suggest that the two modes of life writing are closely related, and that one is the logical outcome of the other), namely, the tension between the idea of the exceptional individual (the modern conception, at least until the latter part of the twentieth century, of the kind of life 'worthy' of being written) and the conventions governing the form in which that individual might articulate him or herself, or be articulated. As Peter Burke argues '[t]oday it may seem odd or even contradictory that the biography or autobiography of the unique individual should follow a pattern, but for readers and writers of the Renaissance, who were taught to model themselves on the exemplary figures of antiquity, there was no paradox'.⁴ Rather than an exclusive focus on the specificity of the individual, early modern life writing tends to the conventional and the typological, with certain constants remaining in place even under the pressures of ideological factionalism and political contestation.⁵ As the editors of *Her Own Life* (a seminal work in defining the field) note, autobiographies are 'public documents with a social purpose' as much as they are personalized accounts of interior selves.⁶ Inherited models, primarily from

---

² Elaine McKay, 'English Diarists: Gender, Geography and Occupation, 1500–1700', *History*, 90 (2005): 191–212, usefully surveys the social, regional, and gender bias of the existing evidence. The phrases are Burke's in 'Representations of the Self from Petrarch to Descartes', in Roy Porter, ed., *Rewriting the Self: Histories from the Renaissance to the Present* (London: Routledge, 1997), 17–28.

³ Adam Smyth, 'Almanacs, Annotators and Life-Writing in Early Modern England', *English Literary Renaissance*, 38 (2008): 200–44 (218).

⁴ Burke, 'Representations of the Self', 23. Gordon Braden makes much the same point in 'Biography', in Gordon Braden, Robert Cummings, and Stuart Gillespie, eds., *The Oxford History of Literary Translation in English*, vol. 2, *1550–1660* (Oxford: Oxford University Press, 2010), 322–30: 'the lives of the saintly bear a systematic disability...holiness has a way of blurring into uniformity' (327).

⁵ See E. Pearlman, 'Typological Autobiography in Seventeenth-Century England', *Biography*, 8 (1985): 95–118.

⁶ Elspeth Graham et al., eds., *Her Own Life: Autobiographical Writings by Seventeenth-Century Englishwomen* (London: Routledge, 1989), 3.

antiquity (Plutarch pre-eminently) and from religious writings, suggest the parameters for articulating the self, a series of categories that run the risk of reducing very different lives to some degree of conformity, as the commonality between, for example, the seven ages of man speech in Shakespeare's *As You Like It* and the Unton portrait suggests. The pictorial representation of Sir Henry Unton's life, by an unknown artist, depicts spatially what life writings express through linear (although not unilinear) narrative, with the key point being that the various events of Henry's life are presented to the viewer simultaneously, without any obvious pattern of causation linking the events depicted. The events of Sir Henry Unton's life selected for the portrait are divided into three main categories: education and career; death and burial; and interests and accomplishments. The figure of the 'subject' is present in many, but not all of the panels, and in the majority of them, he is dead. The figure of the deceased is understood primarily through categories that precede the life, to which the 'subject' is subordinated; the subject does not in any emphatic way determine or influence the categories that communicate the contours of the self to the viewer. Questions of topography are vital (a gesture perhaps at classical notions of the relationship between environment and character) and the life is envisaged as a journey, a set of transitions between different places (home, Oxford, travel in Italy, the Netherlands, France, and home), albeit one that is not depicted in a linear fashion (see the tangle of paths in the top right of the portrait).[7] The Unton portrait is instructive, not least because it draws attention to the formal aspects of the depiction of lives in this period and renders them static, memorial, and exemplary in character; it also suggests the ways in which early modern lives are orientated in relation to quite specific parameters—the picture is presided over by the distinctly allegorical Petrarchan figures of Death and Fame.[8] For all its charm and historical interest, the Unton portrait, like Jacques's speech, focuses on externals, on surfaces, and fails to disclose the inner subject; the subject here is self-evidently performative, a cultural construction.

It is perhaps the writing *process* itself that brings the key parameters of selfhood into play, as autobiography, in particular, '*raises* questions about "self", writing, "experience", and literary convention with particular intensity'.[9] Or, to put this slightly differently, it is in writing that we can see evidence of these processes in formation. Equally, it is important to recognize the degree to which such conventions are historically determined, as Michael Mascuch eloquently explains:

> discourse, broadly conceived to include all types of instances of signification...is the locus of the sense of individuality. And because instances of discourse are themselves discrete events, mediated by local circumstances, it follows that the concept of

---

[7] The image (NPG 710) can be viewed at <http://www.npg.org.uk/collections/search/portrait.php?search = ap&npgno = 710>, accessed 2 March 2011.
[8] These figures come, of course, from Petrarch's *Trionfi* and have a vibrant afterlife in the iconography of Elizabethan England. See, for example, D. G. Rees, 'Petrarch's "Trionfo Della Morte" in English', *Italian Studies*, 7 (1952): 82–96.
[9] Graham et al., eds., *Her Own Life*, 21.

individuality is historically and culturally contingent. The prevailing cultural and historical conditions determine the limits of what it is appropriate or possible to feel and state about personal identities in a given situation.[10]

As numerous critics assert, what is at stake is not simply the status of the individual subject of a life, but his or her capacity to exhibit behaviours and ideals that reinforce, rather than undermine, the status quo: 'self-description... referred to understandings of oneself *within* a wider frame, and more often than not individuality was marked less by how one stood *out* than by how effectively one fitted *in*'.[11] Thus, writing a life is often a way of ensuring that selfhood is seen to take socially acceptable forms and that ideologies are reinforced, rather than undermined by individuals. The place of subjectivity within culture will depend heavily upon what we believe about the nature of the self, namely, whether the self is thought of (in the post-Enlightenment construction) as autonomous, or whether it is understood to be a rhetorical effect, the product of discourse (and here the Renaissance shares some ground with the post-modern). A focus on one conceptualization of the self by no means ensures or guarantees the non-existence of the other, as Catherine Belsey's formulation suggests: 'to be a *subject* is to have access to signifying practice, to identify with the "I" who speaks'.[12] The point is that the self, whether communicated in written discourse or not, is not in any sense a simple construction, and that the form of the 'I' in which it might be written or spoken is not itself a unique articulation, rather it is a shared, communal one: 'In discourse, the 'I' upon which so much our sense of self is based appears as a grammatical form rather than as an elementary phenomenological unit.'[13]

The paradox that the self might be *felt* to be unique at the same time as it is *expressed* in terms that are anything but would seem to be a feature of self-writing in all periods, but perhaps has particular force in a period that comprehends the self through so many different frameworks, not all of them compatible. So, for example, many of the exemplary lives that we read from the later sixteenth and seventeenth centuries derive their material from Protestant practices of self-examination and self-scrutiny, yet frequently comprehend the results of such processes within larger narratives of fall, salvation, despair, and transformation.[14] As Elspeth Graham notes, 'Calvinist writing is characterised by the presentation of a deeply interiorised, spiritual notion of self, constructed in complex relation to a watchful, interpreting self', although as Peter Burke

---

[10] Michael Mascuch, *Origins of the Individualist Self: Autobiography and Self-Identity in England, 1591–1791* (Stanford: Stanford University Press, 1997), 16.

[11] Ronald Bedford, Lloyd David, and Philippa Kelly, eds., *Early Modern Autobiography: Theories, Genres, Practices* (Michigan: University of Michigan Press, 2006), 14.

[12] *The Subject of Tragedy*, quoted in Smyth, 'Almanacs', 239.

[13] Mascuch, *Origins*, 15. Mascuch usefully quotes Benveniste's *Problems in General Linguistics*: 'In some way language puts forth "empty" forms which each speaker, in the exercise of discourse, appropriates to himself and which he relates to his "person", at the same time defining himself as *I* and his partner as *you*', quoted 15.

[14] For accounts of this process in relation to Lady Margaret Hoby, see Sharon Cadman Seelig, *Autobiography and Gender in Early Modern Literature: Reading Women's Lives, 1600–1680* (Cambridge: Cambridge University Press, 2006), 15–33.

points out, this is not specific to Protestant writing in the period.[15] To be exemplary then, points in two directions at once; it is perhaps to be seen to embody attributes that are universally desirable within a particular community to an exceptional degree, rather than to deviate from those norms. As Ronald Bedford and his colleagues state, the idea of the autonomous self may be anachronistic for the early modern period, but is 'but one effect of numerous discourses and institutions that construct subjectivity as a nexus...a volatile intersection of identities, roles, actions, and beliefs'.[16] One could justifiably argue that the issue is more to do with the relative status and authority given to different conceptions of the self, rather than that one notion gives way in historical sequence to another: for the Renaissance, however, the self was, to an extent, determined by its public and communal orientation. As Peter Burke puts it, self-identity might more usefully be seen in this period as 'a tool for negotiation within the web of the world'.[17]

The ways in which these two conceptions of the self are inextricably intertwined is revealed by thinking about the key category for investigating (and creating) character that the Renaissance inherited from classical rhetoric: *ethos*. And it is this category, albeit in modified and domesticated form, that underlies the assumptions and structures of both biography and autobiography in the period. When individuals sat down and wrote narratives about their lives and their experiences, they rarely did it on the assumption that their inner lives were, per se, interesting to others; rather, they did it because they felt that there was something to be learned from their experiences. In the case of autobiography, particularly those authored by women, this process of articulation may well have been coextensive with the inauguration of the self, the identification of subjectivity through the process of engaging with precedents, models, and questions of authority. In turn, the value of those experiences to a reader or audience (as I suggest below, the funeral sermon was one site where life writing is found in the period) was predicated on the idea of the individual's good character, his or her personal credit—in short, *ethos*. *Ethos* is 'the means whereby a speaker or writer projects a self-image', the cultivation of a specific persona designed to convince an audience (or readership).[18] But *ethos* is not necessarily an authentic self, rather, it is a self narratively constructed with the authenticity *effect*, for it is this that renders the subsequent narrative convincing. In this way, then, selfhood is a consequence of *ethos*, not vice versa: 'The writer/speaker must therefore have a sense of various character types and know which of these to assume to appeal to this or that

---

[15] Elspeth Graham, 'Women's Writing and the Self', in Helen Wilcox, ed., *Women and Literature in Britain, 1500–1700* (Cambridge: Cambridge University Press, 1996), 209–33 (214). See also Burke, 'Representations of the Self': 'introspection and self-examination were not Protestant monopolies at this period...these practices were part of the preparation for confession' (27).

[16] Ronald Bedford, Lloyd David, and Philippa Kelly, eds., *Early Modern English Lives: Autobiography and Self-Representation, 1500–1660* (Aldershot: Ashgate, 2007), 6.

[17] Burke, 'Representations of the Self', 21.

[18] Thomas O. Sloane, 'Rhetorical Selfhood in Erasmus and Milton', in Walter Jost and Wendy Olmstead, eds., *A Companion to Rhetoric and Rhetorical Criticism* (Oxford: Blackwell Publishing, 2006), 112–27 (113).

audience in this or that situation.'¹⁹ *Ethos* is less a set of qualities than the development of a relationship between speaker and audience (or author and reader), and depends less on inner qualities than on the capacity of the speaker to make himself or herself credible, capable of being believed. *Ethos* actively encourages the production of *personae*, or the enunciation of the self in terms of already accepted roles: women writers venturing into autobiography frequently negotiate their authority by recourse to these socially accepted positions: for example, piety (Stubbes, Rich, and Thornton), martyrdom, the loving and loyal wife (Hutchinson), and the mother (Stubbes and Brettergh). The importance of this quality (for Aristotle it is 'trustworthiness') perhaps explains the sometimes formulaic nature of early modern writings about the self—their tendency to apologize for their presumption, or to explain away self-revelation—and, in particular, provides a rationale for the tendency of early modern self-writers to draw heavily upon authorizing frameworks that are *social* in origin: conversion narratives, saints' lives, deathbed professions, and their roles as wives or mothers. The rhetorical category of *ethos* also bequeaths more obviously structural frameworks for the presentation of a life (and in this respect at least, 'life writing' might be clearly distinguished from diaries and letters, although in some cases these forms of creating records are drawn on for the writing of lives), as a glance at Aristotle's *Art of Rhetoric* will demonstrate. In Section 7, 'Character', Aristotle reveals the parameters by which a speaker might attempt to persuade an audience of the credibility of a given character (or perhaps, more precisely, a persona): 'Let us after this go through the *characters* of men in regard to their emotions, habits, ages and fortunes.'²⁰ These categories are still highly relevant in the description of character in the Renaissance, as writers seek to establish the 'social and hierarchical structures within which [self-representations]... were understood and expressed'.²¹ Such frameworks are largely formal, and conventional, but 'formality of style does not necessarily mean impersonality... impersonality does not mean lack of personhood'.²² But *ethos* for the Renaissance exceeds the formal dimensions of character, it becomes a mode of self-presentation, the zone of interaction between selfhood and external perception of that selfhood; it has little to do with factual or historical truth, but concerns itself with the cultural and social positioning of an individual in relation to others. It is rhetorical in every sense; a motivated form of self-representation (or representation by another) ultimately intended to be persuasive, if not didactic in character. Thus, Lucy Hutchinson's *Life* of her husband is not only intended to rehabilitate him as a man of integrity, honour, and virtue, but to provide a careful, if evasive, *apologia* for her own politics. Accounts of individual lives, certainly in the pre-Civil War

---

¹⁹ Sloane, 'Rhetorical Selfhood', 113. See also Wendy Olmert, *Rhetoric: An Historical Introduction* (Oxford: Blackwell Publishing, 2006), chaps. 4 and 5, and Jennifer Richards, *Rhetoric*, New Critical Idiom (London: Routledge, 2008).
²⁰ *The Art of Rhetoric*, trans. Hugh Lawson-Tancred (Harmondsworth: Penguin Classics, 1991; 2004), 172–3.
²¹ Bedford et al., eds., *Early Modern Autobiography*, 6.
²² Bedford et al., eds., *Early Modern Autobiography*, 4.

period, tend to adopt, implicitly or explicitly, some kind of ideological or didactic frame; the life is intended to symbolize something beyond itself and its subject: piety, good conduct, and political or ideological allegiance.

John Aubrey's 'life' of the poet Michael Drayton provides a useful starting point, and an instructive contrast, for thinking about the differences between modern and early modern conceptions of how to write a life:

> MICHAEL DRAYTON ESQ natus in Warwickshire at Atherston upon Stower: quaere Thomas Mariett.
>
> He was a butcher's sonne; was Squire viz. one of the Esquires to Sir Walter Aston Knight of the Bath, to whom he dedicated his Poeme. Sir J Brawne of... was a great Patron of his.
>
> He lived at the bay-windowe house next the East-end of St Dunstan's church in Fleet-street. Sepultus in north cross [aisle] of Westminster abbey. The Countesse of Dorset (Clifford) gave his Monument. This Mr Marshall (the stone-cutter) who made it, told me so.
>
> Sir Edward Bissh Clarencieux [King-of-Arms] told me, he asked Mr Selden once (jestingly) whether he wrote the commentary to his *Polyolbion* and *Epistles*, or Mr Drayton made those verses to his Notes.[23]

Aubrey's text, admittedly, is in note form, rather than in continuous, finished prose, yet, it shares various characteristics with more obviously 'finished' pieces of life writing and arguably represents one of many variations within the form. The first key feature that will strike the reader is the focus on practical detail: place of birth, social status, place of residence, burial place (this last a direct consequence of Aubrey's own antiquarian interests), and the almost total absence of focus on what we might now call the inner life. This relative lack of what one might call emotional intensity is a marked feature of much early modern life writing, at least in comparison with modern interest in emotion and feeling.[24] The second key feature is the dependence on oral testimony—not solely what was written or recorded about a life, but what was said and exchanged. Thus, the validity, and the value, of a life narrative might depend as much on the 'credit' of the speaker. So, on the one hand, Aubrey's *Lives* roughly appropriate a set of inherited structures and categories for sorting and categorizing identity, whilst on the other, relying on reputation and personal credit. This direct connection of many written lives—whether biography or autobiography—with the communities that produced them, and, in turn, consumed them, is a key feature of many early modern lives, certainly of those that fall outside of the category of highly born and exemplary figures.[25] Place, in its extended sense of both social position and geo-cultural location, is powerfully deterministic in the early modern period. This contrasts markedly with what a modern reader might expect from a

---

[23] John Aubrey, *Brief Lives*, ed. John Buchanan-Brown (Harmondsworth: Penguin, 2000), 115–16.

[24] See Seelig, *Autobiography and Gender*: 'a number of these texts are both strangely recalcitrant as a source of information and persistently intriguing' (9).

[25] See, for one example, John Collinges, *The Excellent Woman: Discoursed more privately from Proverbs 31.29, 20, 31* (London, 1669).

written 'life'; to be sure, concrete details about birth, domicile, work, and so on, but in addition an objectively verified account of an individual's interests, proclivities, and concerns, based upon written evidence, along with more speculative interest in responses, motivations, and patterns. Early modern lives do exhibit these qualities, but in powerfully different ways, often seeing the events of early childhood through the lens of later achievements, as in the *Life* of Elizabeth Cary, where her later conversion to Catholicism is presented as having been proleptically present throughout her life.

There is little to discern in Aubrey's account of Drayton the man, much less Drayton the poet, and Aubrey's seemingly arbitrary musings about tomb inscriptions and the like seem to have little bearing on the kinds of things that a modern reader might want to know about Drayton. Yet, the *form* of Aubrey's sketch merits a little more attention. Like other lives written in the period that present contemporary, as opposed to historical or classical, figures, Aubrey depends heavily upon testimony and anecdote. Likewise, a figure such as Fulke Greville, writing his *Life of the Renowned Sir Philip Sidney*, derives a good deal of his own writerly authority from his personal proximity to Sidney, the idea that he has had privileged access to the individual concerned. The value of the life lies in the character of its subject, which clearly includes 'blood' and lineage:[26]

> not only the Endowments of Nature, but even the Enoblements of the Mind, and Genius, are many times inherent in the Bloud and Linage. Some Families are privileg'd from Heaven in Excellencies, which now and then in particular Branches, like new Stars, appear and beautifie the sphere they shine in.[27]

Like Aubrey, Greville relies not only on what a modern reader would consider to be 'evidence' (books, letters, and documents), but on an already determined idea of Sidney's *ethos* that is then presented by means of unsubstantiated evidence of his credit with his contemporaries:

> Here I am still enforced to bring pregnant evidence from the dead: amongst whom I have found far more liberall contribution to the honor of true worth, than among those which now live; and in the market of selfnesse, traffique new interest by the discredit of old friends.[28]

Greville's reliance on personal recall and reminiscence usefully reminds us of the didactic roots of what later comes to be called biography, where the individual's *ethos* trumps all other considerations, including that of evidence. Indeed, stretching credulity, particularly where matters of the soul are concerned, helps to offset the necessarily conformist nature of many of these accounts. Not coincidentally, perhaps, the proximity to the subject that Greville repeatedly asserts serves to enhance his own reputation—and this credit by association is a feature of many examples of life writing in the period. Greville, in particular, is strongly motivated by his own self-representation as he writes his life of

---

[26] Burke, 'Representations of the Self', 24, notes the importance of physical appearance as an expression of the inner self; again, the classical model is in evidence.
[27] Sir Fulke Greville, *The Life of the Renowned Sir Philip Sidney* (London, 1651), sig. A3^r.
[28] Greville, *Life*, 22.

Sidney (although it was not published until after his death). Greville repeatedly uses the 'I' persona as he explains to the reader what he has selected and why: 'An outward passage of inward greatness', he writes, 'which in a popular Estate I thought worth the observing'; 'This Narration I adventure of, to shew the clearness, and readiness of this Gentlemans judgement, in all degrees, and offices of life'; 'For proof wherof, I will pass from the testimonie of brave mens words, to his own deeds'.[29] Whilst Greville's presence in his encomiastic text is unusual in degree, it is certainly not unusual in kind, and the representation of a relationship between the writer and the individual written about is a decidedly new feature of early modern life writing, quite different in character from the *modus operandi* of the inherited models (although saints' lives depend quite heavily on proximate testimony and witness accounts). The credibility of the account is enhanced, not called into question, by the personal motivation and investment of the recorder or reporter.

That this differs markedly from the classical models can be seen by taking a brief look at perhaps the most influential set of lives known to early modern readers, Plutarch's *Lives of Noble Grecians and Romans*, translated by Thomas North. Once again, the lines of classification are not altogether clear, as one of the many forms that narrative history takes in the period is that of the life. As René Weiss notes: 'For him the writing of biography and of comparative lives is writing history and, specifically, the history of the two cultures which most obviously shaped his own identity.'[30] Historical writing in the period very frequently overlaps with what we might now designate life writing or biography: chronicle histories often included extended portraits of royal or noble individuals which became the prism through which historical events were refracted and narrated. Once again, historical writings were influenced by classical models—and these frequently adopted the model of exploring the *gestae* of a great man as a way of touching on broader political issues, as John Hayward's *Life and Raigne of King Henrie IIII* indicates.[31] Thus, even at its inception, life writing was an elastic category that created deliberate and self-conscious ligatures between private and public, often as part of a larger ideological, political, or theological trend or agenda. This is undoubtedly the case with the kinds of models of biography that were available to early modern readers (and, in turn, writers), many of which derived more or less directly from either the classical model, or used a historically distant subject in order to draw parallels and analogies with current crises and dilemmas, or drew on a long history of hagiographical writing which proved surprisingly durable in the face of profound religious change. As Gordon Braden outlines, the early modern period saw a

---

[29] Greville, *Life*, 25, 33, 48. The last quotation here alludes quite specifically to the elements of a man's character and actions that combine to create *ethos*. See Quintilian, *Institutio Oratoria*, trans. H. E. Butler, 4 vols. (Cambridge, MA: Harvard University Press, 1920), Book 6.1.15–25 (2, 393–9).

[30] René Weiss, 'Was There a Real Shakespeare?' *Textual Practice*, 23.2 (2009): 215–28 (217).

[31] John Hayward, *Life and Raigne of King Henrie IIII*, ed. John J. Manning, Camden Society, 4th series, 42 (London: Camden Society, 1991). See Danielle Clarke, '"The sovereign's vice begets the subjects error": The Duke of Buckingham, "Sodomy" and Narratives of Edward II, 1622–28', in Tom Betteridge, ed., *Sodomy in Early Modern Europe* (Manchester: Manchester University Press, 2002), 46–64.

large number of translations of biographical texts, loosely defined, and these, in turn, spawned a series of imitations.[32] He makes the important point, however, that 'the early modern biographies and autobiographies that now count most did not attract English translators during this period', citing texts such as Vasari.[33] English taste, at least as measured by demand for appropriate texts in English, seems to have run more towards the exemplary, the typological, and the analogical than towards the exploratory. Beyond the great collections of classical lives translated into English (Plutarch, Suetonius's *Lives of the Caesars*, translated by Philemon Holland in 1606, and Xenophon's *Cyropaedia*, published in 1632), there were a number of life stories of monarchs, particularly of Henri IV, perhaps because his narrative touched on so many topics relevant to English concerns.

Plutarch's *Lives* is perhaps the best known of classical biographical texts, primarily because of its deep influence upon Shakespeare, and his political and stylistic indebtedness to Sir Thomas North's translation, itself based on Amyot's French translation. As Weiss asserts, Shakespeare's interest in Plutarch is driven by a shared perception of 'the relationship between life and history', and this tendency to use the framework of a life almost metonymically to explore other concerns is a feature of almost all early modern life writing.[34] In other words, it is not usually the case until the end of the period that the *life* per se is the primary focus of interest, rather, its exemplary potential is what matters. This is made manifest in North's preface to Plutarch's *Lives*, and its publication in 1579 suggests its role in providing bolstering authority to Elizabeth's reign, despite the potentially troublesome parallels posed by at least some of the lives.[35] Elizabeth herself is presented as embodying, as well as fulfilling, the various qualities of the figures delineated by Plutarch, a particularly interesting gambit on North's part, as Elizabeth moves into a period of her reign where her gendered body natural is increasingly subordinated to her body politic, at least iconographically. North writes

> who is fitter to give countenance to so many great states, than such an high and mighty Princess? who is fitter to revive the dead memory of their fame, than she that beareth the lively image of their vertues? who is fitter to authorise a work of so great learning and wisedom, than she whom all do honour as the Muse of the world?[36]

Although Elizabeth is posited as the primary reader, North's preface makes it clear that the purpose of the *Lives* is the edification of the reader through example:

> I hope the common sort of your subjects, shall not only profit themselves hereby, but also be animated to the better service of your Majesty. For among all the profane books, that are in reputation at this day, there is none ... that teacheth so much honour, love, obedience, reverence, zeal, and devotion to Princes, as these lives of Plutarch do.[37]

---

[32] Braden, 'Biography', 322–30.   [33] Braden, 'Biography', 324.
[34] Wiess, 'Real Shakespeare?' 217.   [35] The Life of Antony, for example.
[36] *Plutarch's Lives Englished by Sir Thomas North*, 10 vols. (London: J. M. Dent, 1910), I, 1.
[37] Plutarch, *Lives*, I, 2.

The Life of Pericles provides a useful example of what the Elizabethans might have found instructive in their Plutarch, aided and guided by the marginal commentary. The Life opens with an illustrative anecdote, a narrative that provides the exemplary frame for the life to follow. As rhetorical treatises suggest, Plutarch then provides detail about Pericles's birth and background (including the detail of his mother's dream of giving birth to a lion). The Life proceeds through Pericles's education, his manners, his character, exploits, key sayings, and so on. What is important about this largely conventional account, however, is its heavy investment in presenting Pericles as the embodiment of a certain kind of virtuous man modelled on a rhetorical, as well as a political, ideal:

> he grew not only to have a great mind and an eloquent tongue, without any affectation, or gross country terms: but to a certain modest countenance that scantly smiled, very sober in his gait, having a kind of sound in his voice that he never lost or altered, and was of very honest behaviour, never troubled in his talk for anything that crossed him, and many other such like things, as all that saw them in him, and considered them, could but wonder at him.[38]

Many of the manoeuvres here are fairly typical, not only of classical lives, but of early modern ones too: the stress on bearing and speech, the idea of constancy in character, and the interpellation of the audience into an admiring role. Also typical is the passage that follows this, where this narrative embodiment of *ethos* is enlivened (and given external authority) by the inclusion of an anecdote—Pericles's patience in the face of public attack by 'a naughty busy fellow'.[39] Certainly, Plutarch attempts to establish the credibility of his account by the inclusion of divergent views, but the rhetorical effect of these is simply to enhance and augment Pericles's reputation; they are raised only in order to be dismissed. As North's paratextual frame suggests, however, the purpose of the life is less to describe the inner self of Pericles than to exemplify qualities that chime with Elizabethan conceptions of monarchy by analogy:

> And that most hated power, which in his life time they called monarchy, did then most plainly appear unto them, to have been the manifest ramper and bulwark of the safety of their whole state and common weal: such corruption and vice in government did then spring up immediately after his death, which when he was alive, he did ever suppress and keep under in such sort, that either it did not appear at all, or at the least it came not to that head and liberty, that such faults were committed, as were unpossible to be remedied.[40]

Thus, the exemplary individual embodies not only the ideal state, but an entire political ideology.

Just as classical texts bequeathed the Renaissance a set of easily recognizable types of virtue and vice, biblical texts were also mined for examples of conduct, morality, and behaviour. In the case of female examples, these were mostly neatly arrayed on either side of a binary split between morality and immorality, and were deployed in a spirit of familiar exchange of example and counter-example. Figures such as Deborah, Judith,

---

[38] Plutarch, *Lives*, II, 128. [39] Plutarch, *Lives*, II, 128–9. [40] Plutarch, *Lives*, II, 185.

Esther, Susannah, and Jael were used in various ways to provide precedents for female courage, leadership, constancy, and capacity to rule. Of equal importance for the consideration of the influence of textual traditions and models on early modern conceptualizations of women's language are the non-specific textual cruxes of the Bible—the Pauline epistles in particular—where moral issues relating to the place of women's speech are played out, with arguably real effects in real households and communities.[41] Questions surrounding scriptural exemplarity are, in principle, similar to those arising from the classical tradition—certainly, many of the key hermeneutic methods of selection, commentary, and application are analogous—but there are also significant differences. In the first instance, the authority of the text is not in dispute, but its interpretation often is—and the grounds of the debate are often concerned not so much with textual authority, but with issues relating to historical or cultural context; the points at issue are concerned with the *application* of the text. Secondly, modes of transmission, with their explicit emphasis on the relationship of the individual to the word, often overtly include women as part of the target audience, whether through her reading a commentary or sermon, hearing them read, or via the husband's role as moral and spiritual head of the household. Thirdly, the tradition of scriptural commentary, based around exemplary figures and key textual passages, hybridizes with a range of other textual forms to produce a generically diverse body of material that has as its end the translation of scriptural example into moral action in the world, even where this 'action' might properly be defined as inaction in the face of apparent temptation or provocation. Unsurprisingly, such examples focus on the woman's role in the family and in the household, and stress the importance of proper conduct and the correct use of language and speech.

Exemplarity, of course, is an acknowledged feature of the dominant form of life writing in the early modern period. The lineaments of such narratives are surprisingly similar in many ways to the classical models, but with a number of crucial differences, as Bedford et al. note: 'the texts in question are often underwritten by a patchwork of formalized spiritual and secular commonplaces that remark on the *non*-uniqueness of the individual's sensation or experience'.[42] There is a good deal of crossover and hybridization between different kinds of religious life writing, with some expanded lives tracing their origins to key texts like Foxe's *Book of Martyrs*, and others having a double life as single sermons or texts, and being incorporated in important compendia such as Samuel Clarke's *Lives of Ten Eminent Divines* (1662). Once again, however, the life itself is a narrative framework through which to accomplish other kinds of cultural and textual work. One notable development in life writing through the period is the identification of relatively ordinary individuals as being somehow exemplary, their very ordinariness often enhancing their spiritual commitment. One textual form where this kind of life writing appears is in encomiastic funeral sermons. They are heavily invested in turning the

---

[41] A telling early example of the real effects of such proscriptions—and the ways in which they might be read against the grain—can be found in the case of Anne Askew; see *The Examinations of Anne Askew*, ed. Elaine V. Beilin (Oxford: Oxford University Press, 1996), 29–30.

[42] Bedford et al., eds., *Early Modern Autobiography*, 6.

well-lived spiritual life to rhetorical account, not only from the pulpit, but also through print circulation.[43] The increasing use of contemporary figures as one modality of exemplarity suggests a particular kind of response to a perceived 'crisis'; the need to enlarge upon the established authorities and figures by extending the illustration of virtues into the realm of the experiential—by and large, that many of these sermons, in the first instance, address a community that would have known the deceased personally. This is not to imply that the 'living exemplar' does not have a purchase well before this—texts like Foxe's *Book of Martyrs* played a key part in the construction and circulation of types of virtuous Protestant resistance and piety. The figure of Lady Jane Grey, for example, was explicitly packaged to this exemplary end in *The Life, Death and Actions of... Lady JANE GRAY* (1615), her writings revealing the 'never enough to be imitated virtues of that most admirable, wise, learned, and religious lady' (Sig. A2r). What is particularly engaging about the exemplary women commemorated in sermons is that they are praised for the proper exercise of reading and writing; they are held up for emulation not purely and simply in terms of their virtue, charity, and piety, but the exercise of these as manifested in, and symbolized by, their use of literacy both in the home and in the parish and community.

Examples like these, linking biblical *topoi*—often, although by no means universally, derived from the Book of Proverbs—with the literate practice of an exemplar whose authority is augmented by the fact that she exists in the collective memory of family, parish, and community, abound in seventeenth-century writing, not solely in the rather predictable form of the funeral sermon, but in other emergent forms, forms that might loosely be grouped under the anachronistic heading of 'life writing'—diaries, collections of exemplary lives, and mothers' advice manuals. Samuel Clarke's *Lives of ten Eminent Divines* (1662) includes the lives of several middle-ranking women renowned for their pious virtue; Mrs Margaret Corbet is eulogized for her reading, her catechizing, and her charity, and these good works are framed by references to the Book of Proverbs, 31:29 in particular (507), along with other scriptural texts and biblical figures. As with many of these sermons, the exemplary function of the text is enhanced by the inclusion of a brief account of the deceased's life and character. As Michael Mascuch notes in his account of Stubbes's *Christal Glasse for Christian Women* (1591), very little specific detail is included of Katherine Stubbes's life, yet the text is notable for the inclusion of an extended first-person narrative. He claims that she is 'one of the first ordinary people to have been (albeit posthumously, and at her husband's initiative) identified by a voice individualized through an extended narrative performance'.[44] His analysis contains the key points, namely, that this 'self-writing' is *produced* for a very particular purpose; the text's multiple editions and popularity attest to the effectiveness of the use of the 'authentic' first person. This fascinating text also illustrates the proximity of biography and autobiography in the period, as the first-person narrative is incorporated and mediated by the

---

[43] For a full discussion, see Eric Carlson, 'English Funeral Sermons as Sources: The Example of Piety in Pre-1640 Sermons', *Albion*, 32 (2000): 567–97.

[44] Mascuch, *Origins*, 55.

framework that Philip Stubbes dictates. Many biographies in the period are simultaneously forms of self-writing—Hutchinson on Colonel Hutchinson, Greville on Sidney, and Walton on Donne, Herbert, Hooker, and Wotton.[45] More traditional accounts stress this very continuity between forms, but recent criticism has tended to bifurcate them more starkly, as accounts of autobiography have been increasingly interested in the relationship between gender and this form of writing. There is not room in this piece to do this burgeoning area of scholarship justice, but a few remarks seem pertinent.[46] One is that many of these texts share key characteristics with male-authored biographies and autobiographies, although the emphasis is often more squarely on private virtue and familial roles. As Wray notes, many of these texts have their origins in religious exercises and reveal 'the continual documenting of spiritual business'.[47] The category of 'self-writing', as practised by early modern women, is a notoriously elastic one and encompasses not one, but a wide range of forms. Graham, for example, refers to 'the clear lack of any stable form of self-writing, which relates to a wider unfixity of genres in the period'.[48] What this suggests, however, is that women are hybridizing different forms, using models that are proximate, at hand, and permitted, with emergent rhetorics for the self, and producing innovative and demotic texts. Without fixed, 'high' forms for self-writing to hand, women appear to exploit the fluidity of the discourses of the self in order to fashion subjectivities strongly rooted in the private world, whilst reflecting on and affecting the public one. This negotiation is all the more loaded and pointed for women attempting to contest the notion that the space of the household is merely private, and perhaps goes some way to explaining why autobiography held such interest for them. As Graham argues: 'The exploration and exploitation of a variety of forms, rather than adherence to a recognized format for articulating the self, is the crucial characteristic of self-writing, and in particular of women's self-writing, of the period.'[49]

In order to try and put some shape on the burgeoning and hybrid nature of 'life writing' in the early modern period, it is instructive to return to Aubrey's intriguing sketches of key early modern individuals. The *Lives* is a fascinating text for the student of life writing in the period, partly because it marks a key transition between evolving forms. Whilst the *Lives* undoubtedly focus on individuals, rather than 'exemplary or cautionary narratives', pulling together broadly evidence-based facts and snippets about these individuals, it lacks either the overarching narrative and teleological frameworks that characterize proto-biography in the period (hagiography, for example), or the focus on

---

[45] See essays in Kevin Sharpe and Steven Zwicker, eds., *Writing Lives: Biography and Textuality, Identity and Representation in Early Modern England* (Oxford: Oxford University Press, 2008).

[46] For a survey of recent work in the field, see Michelle M. Dowd and Julie A. Eckerle, 'Recent Studies in Early Modern English Life Writing', *English Literary Renaissance*, 40.1 (2010): 132–62, and their collection of essays, *Genre and Women's Life Writing in Early Modern England* (Aldershot: Ashgate, 2007).

[47] Ramona Wray, 'Autobiography', in Laura Lunger Knoppers, ed., *The Cambridge Companion to Early Modern Women's Writing* (Cambridge: Cambridge University Press, 2009), 194–207 (196).

[48] Graham, 'Women's Writing and the Self', 209–10.

[49] Graham, 'Women's Writing and the Self', 213.

a continuous, interiorized self that might be said to be the salient feature of modern biography.[50] The chaotic plurality of Aubrey's text(s), with their propensity to run seemingly unrelated details together, or to juxtapose fact with anecdote, provides us with a salutary lesson in thwarted biographical expectations that might usefully be extrapolated to the unwieldy and undefined category of life writing in the early modern period. It seems important to put some parameters in place as a prompt to further reflections. The term 'life writing' has been used here to denote exactly that: any form of writing that attempts the conscious representation of a life, whether written from the external or the internal point of view. The key terms, I suggest, 'life' and 'writing', are both in the process of formation during this period, and their relationship is unstable and at times opaque, yet, this does not in any sense mean that the early modern period does not have a sense that lives might be written, and of the multiple ways in which this might be done. As Meredith Skura argues

> Instead of starting with modern expectations that predetermine the origins of autobiography by predefining its nature, newer studies have begun to explore various examples of a more loosely defined 'life writing', that is, any kind of writing in which the narrator is writing about her or himself. The question is not, 'When was the first modern autobiography written?' but rather, 'How did people write about themselves before the formal requirements of autobiography were encoded?'[51]

This approach might also usefully be applied to the process of writing the lives of others, as both narrative types have their origins in the same kinds of texts, and similar humanist assumptions about the capacity of the literate encounter with the example to build character and boost morality. Both types of writing are closely related, each drawing to some extent on the rhetorical tradition of *res gestae* (as Skura herself implies in her arguments about the importance of the *Mirror for Magistrates*' modelling or staging of first-person narratives) and incorporating generic elements from a range of other texts and traditions. Not all life writing appears in the form of prose—as a range of critical attempts to address questions of identity and self-writing in Shakespeare's Sonnets suggest—and many early modern poetic texts are interested in complex games of secrecy and self-revelation (Spenser). Neither is it necessarily the case that life writing turns up in predictable forms; it is emphatically not a genre, nor is it unequivocally allied with the factual, as opposed to the fictive (so apparently lifelike accounts of the virtuous deaths and confessions of figures like Brettergh or Stubbes stretch credulity and subordinate it to the didactic function of the account). As work by Adam Smyth, and others, has demonstrated, auto/biography often appears on the margins or in the interstices of other forms, and may in fact be, in some instances, characterized by its embrace of the quotidian, the seeming arbitrariness of juxtaposition, and its lack of emotional depth as it apparently fails to distinguish between events that to modern readers seem hardly equivalent in impact. Such judgements, however, fail to consider the material aspects of keeping records (paper and books) or their function. Agency and subjectivity are subtly

---

[50] Braden, 'Biography', 322. [51] Skura, '*A Mirror for Magistrates*', 27.

manifest in such accounts, but do not present textually in forms that are familiar to us: the task is to decode the conventions that structured the presentation of the self. Much as the poetic or narrative 'I' is as likely to be performative as authentic in this period (or at least to play with these possibilities in ways that frustrate attempts to map speaker onto writer), so too the terms in which individual lives are recorded are frequently heavily indebted to social and cultural norms and expectations, and their narrative impact is frequently understood (and justified) by their potential moral and didactic impact. The task for the reader, therefore, is to understand the complexities of textual representations of subjectivity, in all their historical complexity and specificity.

FURTHER READING

Bedford, Ronald, Lloyd David, and Philippa Kelly, eds. *Early Modern Autobiography: Theories, Genres, Practices* (Michigan: University of Michigan Press, 2006).

—— —— —— *Early Modern English Lives: Autobiography and Self-Representation, 1500–1660* (Aldershot: Ashgate, 2007).

Braden, Gordon. 'Biography', in Gordon Braden, Robert Cummings, and Stuart Gillespie, eds., *The Oxford History of Literary Translation in English*, vol. 2, *1550–1660* (Oxford: Oxford University Press, 2010), 322–30.

Burke, Peter. 'Representations of the Self from Petrarch to Descartes', in Roy Porter, ed., *Rewriting the Self: Histories from the Renaissance to the Present* (London: Routledge, 1997), 17–28.

Dowd, Michelle M., and Julie A. Eckerle, eds. *Genre and Women's Life Writing in Early Modern England* (Aldershot: Ashgate, 2007).

—— —— 'Recent Studies in Early Modern English Life Writing', *English Literary Renaissance*, 40.1 (2010): 132–62.

Graham, Elspeth, et al., eds. *Her Own Life: Autobiographical Writings by Seventeenth-Century Englishwomen* (London: Routledge, 1989).

Mascuch, Michael. *Origins of the Individualist Self: Autobiography and Self-Identity in England, 1591–1791* (Stanford: Stanford University Press, 1997).

Seelig, Sharon Cadman. *Autobiography and Gender in Early Modern Literature: Reading Women's Lives, 1600–1680* (Cambridge: Cambridge University Press, 2006).

Sharpe, Kevin, and Stephen Zwicker, eds. *Writing Lives: Biography and Textuality, Identity and Representation in Early Modern England* (Oxford: Oxford University Press, 2008).

Skura, Meredith. '*A Mirror for Magistrates* and the Beginnings of English Autobiography', *English Literary Renaissance*, 36 (2006): 26–56.

CHAPTER 28

ESSAYS

PAUL SALZMAN

IN a period of considerable generic experimentation, the essay stands out as a vehicle for early modern reading and writing practices. Francis Bacon, the most visible English exponent of the form, offers a typically concise summary of the nexus between reading, conversation, and reflection that is characteristic of the rationale for the early modern essay: 'Reading maketh a full man; conference a readye man; And writing an exacte man' (1597: 1).[1] The early modern essay is the perfect example of self-conscious intertextuality, in part fuelled by its connections with the commonplace book. So it is not long before Bacon refers to the most famous of all Renaissance essayists: 'And therefore Mountaigny saith prettily...' (1625: 5). Montaigne balanced the essay's reliance on commonplace knowledge with self-examination and introspection: 'I am one of those that feele a very great conflict and power of imagination' (i.40).[2] Montaigne's style of personal revelation leads him to offer a witty and ironic reflection on the way that, for him, the essay is less a repository, more a self-analysis: 'These are but my fantasies, by which I endevour not to make things knowen, but my selfe... And if I be a man of some reading, yet I am a man of no remembring' (ii.236).

Montaigne generates the feeling that his essays convey a kind of mediated autobiography, while Bacon typifies the English essayist who is assembling and negotiating a series of commonplaces, where the impression of an individual response is conveyed more through prose style than through personal revelation. In his searching and original analysis of the early modern essay, Scott Black stresses the nexus between a method of reading, and a method of writing, in which essays are 'the tools with which readers negotiate a print culture composed of numerous other negotiations and negotiators' (11).[3] But

---

[1] References to Francis Bacon, *Essays* (1597); and Francis Bacon, *The Essays, Or Counsels* (1625); See also the authoritative edition by Michael Kiernan (Oxford: Clarendon Press, 2000).

[2] References to Michel Montaigne, *Essays*, trans. John Florio (1603), 3 vols. (repr. New York: AMS Press, 1963).

[3] References to Scott Black, *Of Essays and Reading in Early Modern Britain* (New York: Palgrave Macmillan, 2006).

within what might sound like a rather claustrophobic space, these negotiations produced works that are often striking in their aphoristic immediacy. When we read Bacon's essays, we don't feel that we 'know' him the way that we feel we know Montaigne, but we do feel that we have some access to Bacon's distillation of his reading and thought, where reading, writing, and thought, in Scott Black's terms, are inseparable.

But if we begin with Bacon as the major, canonical example of the early modern English essay, we have to take into account the way his approach to the genre changed as he tinkered with his work over a period of some thirty years. This process was in part a shift from the brief, clipped, elliptical essays published in 1597, which clearly show their connections with the commonplace book, and the essays as they appeared in their 1625 printing, where they have not only increased dramatically in number (from ten to fifty-eight), but also each one has grown, and Bacon's style breathes more easily and has become more self-reflective. While the essays in the 1597 volume seem to be purely occasional pieces, by 1625 they become a cumulative glimpse into Bacon's cogitations, during which he does not simply incorporate past wisdom into his essays, but mingles his own wisdom with that of the ancients. This is most appropriate for an adherent to the cause of humanist notions of progress and advancement, and for the author of *The Advancement of Learning*. Bacon also used the essay form to distil the political experience he garnered during his slow rise to eventually become Lord Chancellor, and his rapid fall in 1621. The tiny 1597 volume was entitled *Essayes. Religious Meditations. Places of perswasion and disswasion*. In 1625, the title emphasizes the political wisdom being dispensed: *The Essayes or Covnsels, Civill and Morall* (Fig. 28.1). The essays that are 'counsels' provide not only a careful analysis of realpolitik, but also a glimpse into the nature of a man experienced in negotiating the slippery path to advancement, who provides a view from the top, and also from the bottom.

A good example is the essay that was entitled 'Of Sutes' in 1597. When the 1597 volume was published, Bacon was an ambitious, frustrated thirty-six-year-old, who had gained little from the efforts of his patron, the Earl of Essex, despite offering ample evidence of his legal and philosophical ability. In particular, Bacon had failed twice in suits to become attorney general, so it is scarcely surprising that 'Of Sutes' has a cynical tone throughout. The opening of the essay is a good example of how Bacon's curt, aphoristic style arrests the reader's attention: 'Manie ill matters are vndertaken, and many good matters with ill mindes. Some embrace Suites which neuer meane to deal effectually in them. But if they see there may be life in the matter by some other meane, they will be content to winne a thanke or take a second reward' (6). Some of this essay may read like a manual of instruction for suitors, but the penultimate sentence seems to reflect Bacon's own experience of ill-judged timing: 'But tyming of the Sutes is the principall, tyming I saye not onely in respect of the person that shoulde graunt it, but in respect of those which are like to crosse it' (7).

By the time of the 1625 volume, where the title becomes 'Of Sutours' (as it was in the contents and running head for 1597), Bacon could look back on the success of his suits to King James (as opposed to Elizabeth), which led to him finally becoming attorney general in 1613, then lord chancellor in 1618, but losing everything following his

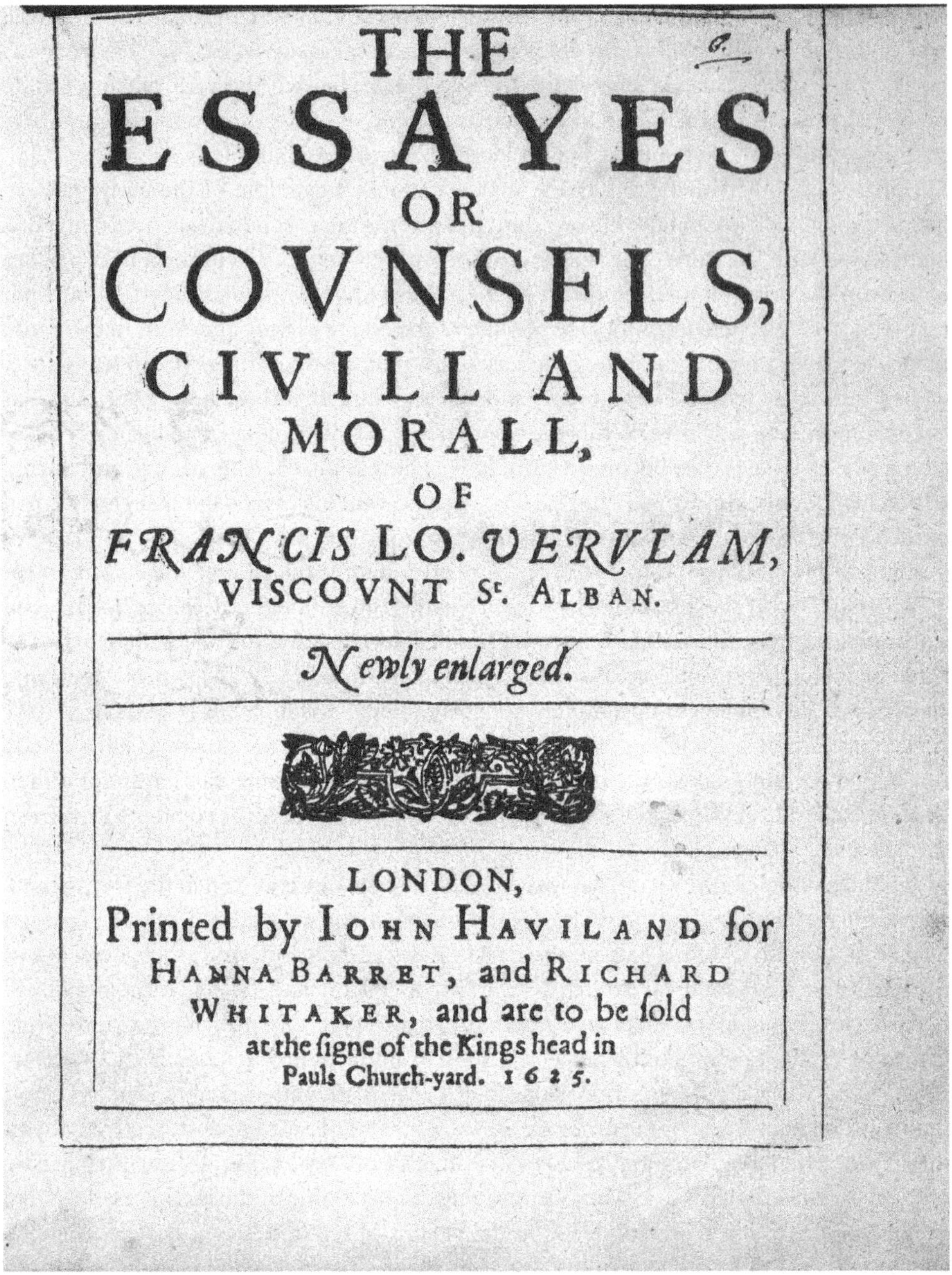

THE ESSAYES OR COVNSELS, CIVILL AND MORALL,

OF *FRANCIS LO. VERVLAM*, VISCOVNT S^t. ALBAN.

Newly enlarged.

LONDON,
Printed by IOHN HAVILAND for HANNA BARRET, and RICHARD WHITAKER, and are to be sold at the signe of the Kings head in Pauls Church-yard. 1 6 2 5.

FIGURE 28.1 Francis Bacon, *Essays* (1625), title page

impeachment in 1621. The reworked opening of the essay in 1625 offers a remark directed at public policy, rather than a reflection of private experience, and at the cost of losing the punchiness of the previous opening sentence with its balanced 'ill matters'/'ill mindes': 'Many ill Matters and projects are vndertaken; And Priuate *Sutes* doe Putrifie the Publique Good' (288). The bitter tone is further enhanced by the stylistic avoidance of any balance at all ('ill' is replaced by 'bad'): 'Many Good Matters are vndertaken with Bad Mindes; I meane not only Corrupt Mindes, but Craftie Mindes, that intend not Performance' (288). Given the considerable popularity of Bacon's essays—they circulated in manuscript, as well as going through twelve editions (in various formats) prior to 1625—pronouncements about public policy and political expediency must have been read against the background of Bacon's personal experiences, and the 1625 reflection on suits would have struck an ironic note with many. The 1597 essay ended with a wry reflection on how it must have felt to have pursued men of influence: 'Nothing is thought so easie a request to a great person as his letter, and yet if it bee not in a good cause, it is so much out of his reputation' (7). The 1625 version ends with a more expansive view expressed by someone who had by now moved from suitor to recipient of many suits, some of which were his undoing: 'There are no worse Instruments, then these Generall Contriuers of *Sutes*: For they are but a Kinde of Poyson and Infection to Publique Proceedings' (291).

The expanded collection contains many essays that could be classified as broadly political, covering topics such as 'great place', 'seditions and troubles', and 'the true Greatnesse of Kingedoms and Estates'. Given that Bacon's essays were so popular, these kinds of topics were taken up by other essayists, and the comparatively abstract political or social essay of reflection remained influential through to eighteenth-century essayists like Samuel Johnson. Bacon's style may have expanded in the manner discussed above, but even the later style remains aphoristic and eminently quotable, sticking in people's minds even today: '*What is Truth;* said jesting *Pilate*; And would not stay for an Answer'; 'Men feare *Death*, as Children feare to goe in the darke'; '*Revenge* is a kinde of Wilde Justice'. This reflects the interconnection between essay and commonplace book, and it illustrates how Bacon's essays were political counsels and also, in Stanley Fish's apt phrase, a 'continuous attempt to make sense of things'.[4] Yet, the Montaigne side of the essay equation has also crept into Bacon's later volume, with a number of more personal reflections on subjects that, if not entirely apolitical, are not exactly connected to public policy or individual political action. The most famous of these is the essay on gardens, which appeared for the first time in the 1625 volume. The opening of this essay neatly illustrates Bacon's use of a more relaxed style: 'God *Almightie* first Planted a *Garden*. And indeed, it is the Purest of Humane pleasures. It is the Greatest Refreshment to the Spirits of Man; Without which, *Buildings* and *Pallaces* are but Grosse Handy-works' (266).

'Of Gardens' is not simply a philosophical musing, as it reflects Bacon's long-standing, practical interest in gardening and garden design. The detailed advice about, not merely

---

[4] Stanley Fish, *Self-Consuming Artefacts* (Berkeley: University of California Press, 1972), 81.

design, but also planting, serves in the end to increase the reader's sense of Bacon's engagement and personality. Pleasure is taken in the very naming of the plants:

> I like also little Heaps, in the nature of Mole-hils, (such as are in Wild Heaths) to be set, some with Wilde Thyme; Some with Pincks; Some with Germander, that gives a good Flower to the Eye; Some with Periwinckle; Some with Violets; Some with Strawberries; Some with Couslips; Some with Daisies; Some with Red-Roses; Some with Lilium Convallium; Some with Sweet-Williams Red; Some with Beares-Foot; And the like Low Flowers, being withal Sweet, and Sightly. (276)

The delight in specificity spills over into a cajoling tone quite unlike the curt, politic advice of the 'counsels': 'For as for *Shade*, I would have you rest, upon the *Alleys* of the *Side Grounds*, there to walke, if you be Disposed, in the heat of the yeare, or day' (278). The essay is carefully composed to induce the repose reflecting a well-planned garden, as Bacon moves from the general structure to the variety of plantings, to the use, showing that nothing compares 'to the true Pleasure of a *Garden*' (145). The self-reflexive and, at times, almost whimsical tone of this essay perhaps indicates Montaigne's influence, but the careful structure and the attention to detail is characteristic of Bacon and what might already be called an English essay style.

Bacon also wrote essays which move between cynical (or knowing) counsel and more expansive reflection.[5] Two interrelated essays move in this characteristic way between apparent autobiography and political counsel: 'Of Parents and Children' and 'Of Marriage and Single Life'. In the first of these two essays, the childless Bacon seems especially self-revealing when he writes 'the Noblest workes, and Foundations, haue proceeded from *Childlesse Men*; which haue sought to express the Images of their Minds; where those of their Bodies haue failed' (32). Bacon goes on to consider the discord created by distinctions between siblings: 'A Man shall see, where there is a House full of *Children*, one or two, of the Eldest, respected, and the Youngest made wantons; But in the middest, some that are, as it were forgotten, who, many times, neuerthelesse, proue the best' (33). Bacon himself had an older brother, Anthony, three older half-brothers, and five sisters. Anthony was in some respects Francis's shadowy friend, rival, and alter-ego, let down in the end by illness, which allowed Francis to secure some of Anthony's political credit with the incoming King James.[6] The essay concludes with a self-satisfied aside: '*Younger Brothers* are commonly Fortunate' (35).

Francis Bacon did not marry until 1606 (he had courted Elizabeth Hatton unsuccessfully a decade earlier) and his views on marriage begin with an often-cited aphorism: 'He that hath *Wife* and *Children*, hath giuen Hostages to Fortune, For they are Impediments, to great Enterprises' (36). In this essay, Bacon seems to be having a dialogue with himself about the consequences of marriage and the relationship between great enterprise, and being unencumbered: 'the best workes, and of greatest Merit for the Publike, haue proceeded from the *vnmarried*, or *Childlesse Men*' (36). Once again, it

---

[5] In Fish's view, a characteristic of Bacon's method is the accommodation of 'disparate and contradictory visions', Fish, *Self-Consuming Artefacts*, 119.

[6] See Markku Peltonen, 'Bacon, Francis', *ODNB* <http://www.oxforddnb.com/view/article/990?docPos=1> accessed 18 March 2013.

is tempting to see some self-aggrandizement here. Yet, at the same time, Bacon muses that unmarried men may be 'best Masters', but they are not always best subjects because 'they are light to runne away'. This essay, in particular, unfolds more as a meditation than as a series of commonplaces and it balances counter-arguments about personal versus state responsibility.

When most people today think of the early modern English essay (or perhaps one should say 'if' they do), Bacon is the only writer who comes to mind, but the popularity of the genre is attested to by numerous examples, many of which were extremely popular as printed books in the seventeenth century, and many of which circulated in manuscript. Indeed, the popularity of the printed essay collection in particular provoked a grumpy reflection from Ben Jonson on the 'undigested' nature of essays. Jonson finds fault with the idea that the essay collection inflected by the commonplace book was worthy of public display; in his view, the essay was an example of a genre that made sense as a private study aid, rather than a public utterance (he makes this remark in his own commonplace/miniature essay collection, *Timber, or Discoveries*, which was, of course, only published posthumously, in 1641):

> *Some* that turne over all bookes, and are equally searching in all papers, that write out of what they presently find or meet, without choice; by which meanes it happens, that what they have discredited, and impugned in one worke, they have before, or after extolled the same in another. Such are all *Essayists*, even their Master *Mountaigne*. These in all they write, confesse still what bookes they have read last; and therein their owne folly, so much, that they bring it to the *Stake* raw, and undigested: not that the place did need it neither; but that they thought themselves furnished, and would vent it.[7]

It is true that many early modern essay collections were reflections of a fad and were not especially well digested. We would certainly now demur at the idea that Montaigne adds nothing to what he has read, but Jonson's notion that the essay shades into a mere recapitulation hints at Scott Black's analysis of the genre as being to do with *how* to read and the intertextuality of early modern thought in general. For Bacon, as we have seen, there was, in fact, an elaborate process of digestion that is reflected in the constant revision of his essays, and is evident in their increasingly crafted nature. One can contrast Bacon with William Cornwallis, an essayist who is now comparatively obscure, but who might be seen as matched only by Bacon in his fascination with the way a commonplace could metamorphose into an essay. Indeed, Don Cameron Allen has argued that Cornwallis, rather than Bacon, was a pioneer of the essay form in England; he first published his collection in 1600 and it was very successful, if not quite as popular as Bacon's, running to nine editions by 1632.[8] Cornwallis is a less intellectual, but also less studied, essayist than

---

[7] Ben Jonson, *Timber or Discoveries* (1641), N4.
[8] Don Cameron Allen, ed., *Essayes by Sir William Cornwallis the Younger* (Baltimore: Johns Hopkins University Press, 1946), ix; Allen suggests that Bacon's 1597 volume is of aphorisms, rather than essays, but that seems to me to be splitting hairs, and one can give Bacon credit as first essayist but see Cornwallis as similarly pioneering, especially prior to Bacon's revised 1612 collection. References are to this edition of Cornwallis.

Bacon; his casual style is more attuned to Montaigne, and the sense of autobiographical musing that seems immediate and attractive to us would have horrified Jonson.[9] Like Montaigne (though less expansively), Cornwallis offers glimpses of an attractive personality musing about commonplace ideas in a less than entirely commonplace way. If you read through his essays consecutively you get a clear sense of Cornwallis's personal history. Cornwallis also comments on broadly political or social ideas from the perspective of a comparatively modest gentleman, rather than being a political 'player' like Bacon. One can scarcely imagine Bacon frequenting an alehouse, let alone writing an essay on one as Cornwallis did. At the same time, Cornwallis shared a number of topics with Bacon, notably counsel, vainglory, fame, ambition, love, and friendship.

Cornwallis's attractive personal tone is evident from the first essay in his collection, 'Of Resolution', which balances between a certain stoicism and a disarming admission of his humanity: 'Me thinkes I am strong and able to encounter any affection; but hardly haue my thoughts made an ende of this gallant discourse, but in comes a wife or a friend, at whose sight my Armour of defence is broken, and I could weepe with them or be content to laugh at their triuiall sports' (5). Even when Cornwallis offers a conventional account of the nature of his studies, he injects a personal note:

> My steps are the steps of mortality, and I do stumble and stagger for company and crawle rather then goe; yet I desire to get further and to discouer the Land of light. To this end I reade and write, and by them would faine catch an vnderstanding more then I brought with me before decrepitenesse and death catch me. (34)

The search for enlightenment through study is made literal, and as we build up a picture of Cornwallis's personality through the essays we see him as a modest and often self-deprecating man—again, this is in contrast to Bacon, who is not only an (impressively intelligent) egotist, but whose essays remain separate instances of contemplation and often of proselytizing for the cause of the author. In 'Of Affection', Cornwallis disarmingly argues himself towards a fairly typical stoical position, but on the way offers some poignant evocations of babies and parental engagement: 'Euen that honest harmelesse Affection which possesseth parents towards their children, mee thinkes, whilst they are yet but lumpes of flesh and things without all merit should not be so ardent and vehement. Pitty and commiseration fittes them better then loue, of which they are no way worthy' (81). And yet, he goes on, how fortunate it is that logic does not prevail in this area: 'But it is well that Nature hath cast the extremities of this disease vpon mothers' (81). Cornwallis is, like all essayists, drawn to moral maxims and sage generalizations, but he tends to inject a personal note that moves his argument obliquely. Bacon and Cornwallis's essays on vainglory further this comparison. Bacon begins with a maxim, leading to a confident assertion:

> It was prettily Deuised of *Aesope; The Fly sate vpon the Axle-tree of the Chariot wheele, and said, What a Dust doe I raise?* So are there some *Vaine Persons*, that whatsoeuer goeth alone, or moueth vpon greater Means, if they haue neuer so little

---

[9] In Essay 12, 'Of Censuring', Cornwallis praises Montaigne, but says that he has not read him in French, but rather, in an English translation (though apparently not Florio's), 42; and see Allen's note.

a Hand in it, they thinke it is they that carry it. They that are *Glorious*, must needs be *Factious*; For all Brauery stands vpon Comparisons. (1625: 308)

Bacon's essay unfolds in this way through to a stern conclusion: '*Glorious* Men are the Scorne of Wise Men; the Admiration of Fooles; the Idols of Parasites; And the Slaues of their own Vaunts' (311). As in most of Bacon's 'moral' essays, memorable phrases are marshalled in order to offer general conclusions about human nature. Cornwallis veers between this style and something more idiosyncratic, or even eccentric. For Cornwallis, vainglory migrates from soldiers and statesmen to everyone, including the author: 'Let vs thinke then of vaine-glory as it deserueth (and not of the name but nature) not with a disallowance in generall but particularly applying it, disallow so much of our selfe as is infected with it' (186). Cornwallis always thinks of his essays as provisional in this way. As he notes in his essay on essays, unlike other 'short writings', even Montaigne's, 'mine are Essayes, who am but newly bound Prentise to the inquisition of knowledge and vse these papers as a painter's boy a board, that is trying to bring his hand and his fancie acquainted' (190). Cornwallis is devoted to the idea of the assay/essay that meanders: 'Nor if they stray, doe I seeke to amende them; for I professe not method, neither will I chaine my selfe to the head of my Chapter' (202). And yet, as with all such tropes, Cornwallis in fact exercises careful control over his supposed wanderings and tends to structure his essays through a combination of vivid image and self-reflection, as indeed the essay from which I have been quoting concludes:

> If there be any yet so ignorant as may profit by them, I am content; if vnderstandings of a higher reach dispise them, not discontent; for I moderate thinges pleasing vpon that condition, not to be touched with thinges displeasing. Who accounts them darke and obscure, let them not blame mee, for perhaps they goe about to reade them in darknesse without a light, and then the fault is not mine but the dimnesse of their owne vnderstanding. If there be any such, let them snuffe their light and looke where the fault of their failing restes. (202)

One of Cornwallis's more endearing moments, for a modern reader, which for an early modern reader may well have been part of his persona as eccentric, is his defence of female education. This occurs in a wonderful essay on fear, which begins with a quirky dismantling of male self-confidence:

> We heare from our nurses and olde women tales of Hobgoblins & deluding spirits that abuse trauellers and carry them out of their way. We heare this when wee are children and laugh at it when we are men, but that we laugh at it when wee are men, makes vs not men; for I see few men. Wee delight not perhaps in Iigges, but in as ridiculous thinges wee liue. (108)

Cornwallis segues into an analysis of why women might be fearful and decides that education will enable women to overcome any physical weakness: 'wee leaue our women ignorant and so leaue them fearefull' (108). Cornwallis stresses that all women lack is opportunity: 'I do not think women are much more faultie in Nature's abilities then men, but they faile in education; they are kept ignorant and so fearefull' (109). He concludes that he 'would haue them learned and experienced' (109), and this will give them an equality with men that will counter fear and also enable women to participate in a wider range of experiences.

In his more fanciful vein, Cornwallis, as noted above, is able to produce a wonderful jeu d'esprit such as his essay on alehouses. This is, in part, another piece of self-deprecation, evident in the lively opening sentences:

> I Write this in an Alehouse, into which I am driuen by night, which would not giue me leaue to finde out an honester harbour. I am without any company but Inke & Paper, & them I vse in stead of talking to my selfe. My Hoste hath already giuen me his knowledge, but I am little bettered; I am now trying whether my selfe be his better in discretion. (67)

Cornwallis then turns to a favourite theme: hypocrisy and degree. He notes that 'every one speaks well & means naughtily'. This applies to all levels of society from 'drunken Cobler' to 'hawking Gentleman'. Cornwallis is able to tie this neatly to his location, thereby moving from the clichéd notion of commonality to a more vivid and personalized meditation on degree:

> I haue thus been seeking differences; and to distinguish of places, I am faine to fly to the signe of an Ale-house and to the stately coming in of greater houses. For Men, Titles and Clothes, not their liues and Actions, helpe me. So were they all naked and banished from the Herald's books, they are without any euidence of preheminence, and their soules cannot defend them from Community. (67)

This attraction to paradox led Cornwallis to publish a specific collection of essays demonstrating his wit and tapping into a growing interest in the intersection between paradox and satire. The enlarged edition, titled *Essays of Certain Paradoxes*, was published in 1617 and contains six paradoxical essays on topics such as 'Good to be in debt' and 'The praise of Richard III'. These kinds of essay are in part influenced by the rhetorical dexterity practised through exercises that formed part of the repertoire of anyone with a grammar school education, but as written by Cornwallis, or Donne (who will be discussed below) the exercise becomes far more original and multi-faceted. Four unpublished paradoxes by Cornwallis exist, preserved in a single manuscript source (a commonplace book belonging to Sir Stephen Powle—a source which again underlines the link between essay and commonplace).[10] The major published piece, on Richard III, is perhaps more of historical than literary interest, and lacks Cornwallis's usual verve as he enumerates Richard's 'negative' qualities and actions and justifies them.[11] Indeed, Cornwallis may be aiming for paradox, but his defence of Richard's legislative record anticipates modern assessments. The technique of recounting Richard's dark deeds and then claiming they were politic or sensible or moral becomes rather repetitive after a while. The problem lies with the serious nature of the subject, and Cornwallis is more

---

[10] R. E. Bennett, 'Four Paradoxes by Sir William Cornwallis the Younger', *Harvard Studies and Notes in Philology and Literature*, 13 (1931): 219–40; references are to this edition.

[11] *Essayes of certaine Paradoxes* (1617).

impressive tackling 'The Praise of the French Pockes', which is a free translation of an essay by the Spanish writer Gaspar Hidalgo, first published in 1605.[12] In this essay, Cornwallis offers a witty narrative of overturned expectations, whereby 'the noble and illustrious disease of the French Pockes' is held to be in 'reuerend estimation'. In part, Cornwallis opines, this is because the pox is a visible sign of transgression and therefore holy: 'what greater token of holiness can there be in a man, then to haue a sense and feeling of his sinnes' (D4^v). The pox is also admired for being so well travelled and for choosing out those of a high social rank. Here Cornwallis does offer some social satire, but it is done with a light touch. The final essay in this brief volume is 'That it is Good to be in Debt'. Here Cornwallis veers between amusing examples of the sensible nature of financial indebtedness and a rather more serious notion of indebtedness in the natural world (for example, the sun lends the stars light) and spiritual indebtedness. The essay, and accordingly the volume, concludes on a more sombre note than one might have expected from the earlier spirited witticisms: 'I must resolue to liue in debt: in debt to GOD, for my being; in debt to CHRIST, for my well-being; in debt to Gods sanctifying SPIRIT, for my new being' (F4^v).

The four paradoxes that survive in manuscript are generally more light-hearted, but an earlier version of the debt paradox: 'That it is a happiness to be in debt', has a similarly spiritual and serious conclusion. It is difficult to determine their exact status, but stylistically these manuscript essays are not nearly as polished as those that Cornwallis published. The opening essay is the most comic: 'That a great redd nose is an ornament to the face'. This includes the apercu 'to haue a great Red nose is the true marke of a good witt' (224). The other essays are in a similar vein: 'That miserie is true Faelicity' and 'That Inconstancy is more commendable then Constancie'.

Paradoxical essays like Cornwallis's were modish exercises and this is evident in those produced by John Donne. As Helen Peters notes, 'Paradoxes were a fashionable feature of the Inns of Court Revels' and this was part of the influence behind Donne, as well as the long Classical tradition of paradox that had its most famous Renaissance manifestation in Erasmus's mock encomium *Praise of Folly* (*Morae encomium*, 1511, translated into English 1549).[13] Donne's ten paradoxes (and a number wrongly assigned to him) circulated quite widely in manuscript before their posthumous publication. They are generally shorter, and wittier, than Cornwallis's, as one might expect from Donne. Donne makes little attempt to explore a potential argument, however paradoxical, but rather throws out as many twists as his imagination can encompass, with the resulting paradox taking on something of the style of an early Bacon essay. For example, in 'That only Cowards dare dye', Donne writes: 'Truly this life is a tempest, and a warfare; and he that dares dye to escape the anguishes of it, seemes to me but so valiant, as he which dares hang himselfe, least he be prest to the warres' (10).[14] As one might expect, two of Donne's

---

[12] See Bennett, 'Four Paradoxes', 220; Cornwallis's father was the ambassador to Spain from 1604 to 1609.

[13] John Donne, *Paradoxes and Problems*, ed. Helen Peters (Oxford: Clarendon Press: 1980), xx.

[14] References to *Paradoxes and Problems*.

paradoxes are directed at women: 'That women ought to paint themselves', which is reasonably benign, and 'That it is possible to find some vertue in some women', which reinforces a standard misogyny: 'Necessity makes even bad things good, and prevayles also for them' (22). Donne's problems belong to an associated genre, which is aphoristic and again, traditionally a display of wit. A good example is 'Why dye none for love now?', which is brief enough to be quoted in full so that the sting in the tail might be enjoyed (and it provides yet another example of a misogyny taken for granted by gentlemen of wit at the time): 'Because woemen are become easyer? Or because these later times have provided mankind of more new meanes for the destroying themselves and one another: Poxe, Gunpowder, young marriages and Controversyes in Religion? Or is there in truth no precedent or example of it? Or perchance some doe dye, but are therefore not worthy the remembering or speaking of' (26). While the paradoxes and problems reflect Donne's fashionable engagement with what we might call Inns of Court literary display, Donne's engagement with religion, leading to his career in the church, also produced variations on the essay form. The two main examples of this are the posthumously published *Essays in Divinity* and the considerably more famous *Devotions Upon Emergent Occasions*, first published in 1624 and reprinted a number of times during Donne's lifetime. In the former volume, Donne has a series of short essays taking as his starting point the first verse of Genesis for Book One and the first verse of Exodus for Book Two. The verse from Exodus, 'Now these are the names of the Children of Israel which came into Egypt, &c.', provokes a series of reflections on the diversity of God's creation, and it includes a moving statement of trust in the potential for a unified Christian faith: 'Synagogue and Church is the same thing, and of the Church, *Roman* and *Reformed*, and all other distinctions of place, Discipline, or Person, but one Church, journeying to one *Hierusalem*, and directed by one guide, Christ Jesus.'[15] The *Devotions* are specifically offered as meditations, rather than essays, but the two genres are related. The twenty-three devotions trace Donne's experience of illness and accordingly offer a kind of autobiographical spiritual reflection. As a whole, the sections offer a series of essayistic exercises, each also including a prayer and an expostulation. But there is a drama created by the sudden onset, duration, ebb and flow of illness, exemplified in the arresting opening: 'Variable, and therefore miserable condition of Man, this minute I was well, and am ill, this minute.'

Devotions is famous for the passage that is one of literature's most quoted reflections; in context, it is part of Donne's meditations on faith at a time of crisis, and in its provisional move from the individual to the world at large, as it connects one person with all people through a concentration on mortality, it resembles the idea of the essay as exploratory: 'No Man is an *Iland*, intire of it selfe; euery man is a peece of the *Continent*, a part of the *maine*; if a *Clod* be washed away by the *Sea*, *Europe* is the lesse, as well as if a *Promontorie* were, as well as if a *Mannor* of thy *friends*, or of *thine owne* were; Any Mans *death* diminishes *me*, because I am inuolued in *Mankinde*; And therefore neuer send to

---

[15] John Donne, *Essays in Divinity*, ed. Evelyn M. Simpson (Oxford: Clarendon Press, 1951), 51.

know for whom the *bell* tolls; It tolls for *thee*.'[16] If Donne blurs the distinction between meditation, spiritual advice, and the essay, this is also evident in a number of other early modern writers, and the very blurring reminds us that most early modern genres are, in Rosalie Colie's terms, 'mixed', and Colie herself noted that the essay was both a 'new' early modern genre and a particularly amorphous one.[17] A good example is the collection of 'resolves', essays by Owen Felltham which, like Bacon's essays, were a kind of public commonplace book that Felltham expanded from first publication in 1623, when he was only twenty-one, until the 1661 edition, which, handsomely published in folio, represents Felltham's mature thoughts.[18] Felltham's essays were popular in all their versions and capture exactly the combination of didacticism and wit that carries on the renaissance ideal of *sprezzatura* (sprightly stylishness without pretension) that we have seen in Cornwallis, although Felltham is far more sober and spiritual in tone and subject matter than Cornwallis. In the 1623 volume (which I discuss here, given that Felltham's final revised volume is well outside the boundary dates of this *Companion*) we see versions of the aphoristic style driven by a (perhaps precocious) Christian stoicism.[19] For example, Felltham has a pithy account of the necessity to dwell upon mortality: 'He that dyes dayly, seldome dyes dijectedly' (20).[20] The hundred 'resolves' can veer towards the cliché at times, but generally Felltham's urbane tone carries the reader past any dull patches. Indeed, the evenness of tone makes *Resolves* a more coherent whole than many early modern essay collections—an effect enhanced by the fact that the individual essays are numbered, rather than named. Even on secular subjects like friendship, Felltham's advice tends to be cautious and even somewhat dampening:

> Euen between two faithfull friends, I thinke it not conuenient that all secrets be imparted; neither is it the part of a friend, to fish out that, which were better concealed. Yet I obserue some, of such insinuating dispositions, that there is nothing in their friends heart, that they would not themselues know with him; and this, if I may speake freely, I count as a fault. (111)

Felltham's subtitle, 'divine, moral, political', points to the serious and often spiritual nature of his book, and it also echoes an earlier mixed genre text that, Kate Lilley has argued, indicates how women, so often excluded from canonical genres like the essay, were in fact also engaged with this fashionable form.[21] Lilley specifically notes how the

---

[16] *Devotions Upon Emergent Occasions* (1624), 415–16.

[17] Rosalie Colie, *The Resources of Kind: Genre Theory in the Renaissance* (Berkeley: University of California Press, 1973).

[18] For an account of the changing nature of the volume see McCrea Hazlett, '"New Frame and Various Composition": Development in the Form of Owen Felltham's "Resolves"', *Modern Philology*, 51 (1953): 93–101.

[19] On this see Ted Larry Pebworth, '"Real English Evidence": Stoicism and the English Essay Tradition', *PMLA*, 87 (1972): 101–2.

[20] References to Owen Felltham, *Resolves* (1623).

[21] Kate Lilley, 'Dedicated Thought: Montaigne, Bacon, and the English Renaissance Essay', in Susannah Brietz Monta and Margaret W. Ferguson, eds., *Teaching Early Modern Prose* (New York: MLA, 2010), 95–112.

structure of Elizabeth Grymeston's advice book, *Miscelanea. Meditations. Memoratives* (1604) 'is modelled in style and structure on essay collections'.[22] Grymeston's advice is indeed decidedly essayistic, and relies on a series of commonplaces to guide her son towards a godly life: 'What is the life of man but a continuall battel, and defiance with God? What haue our eies and eares beene, but open gates to send in loades of sinne into our minde?' (C4). The volume as a whole is indeed miscellaneous, containing prayers and meditations, as well as essays of advice, in poetry and prose, and ends, as Lilley notes, with a series of aphoristic miniatures not unlike Bacon's earliest essays, albeit even shorter.

There are many further examples of the essay blurring into other genres, and the essay as a form encouraged experimentation of all kinds. It stretched especially in the direction of biography and mock biography on the one hand, and in the direction of autobiography on the other. As potentially a form of biography, the essay has some links with the Character. The description of character 'types' has a long history, but in the early seventeenth century the collection of 'Characters' became extremely popular, beginning with the rather bland and didactic *Characters of Virtues and Vices* (1608) by the clergyman Joseph Hall, but fuelled by the publication of a series of Characters purportedly (but not actually) written by Thomas Overbury. Overbury had written a poem entitled 'A Wife', but after his scandalous death in the Tower in 1613 (this complicated situation involved the marriage of King James's favourite Robert Carr to Frances Howard against the advice of Overbury, and, after the eclipse of Carr, an eventual charge of poisoning directed at Howard) the name of Overbury was enough to entice the publisher Lawrence Lisle to commission a series of prose characters which he published as being by Overbury.[23] This volume, entitled *A Wife Now the Widow of Sir Thomas Overbury* (1614), contained twenty-two characters and was a runaway success, leading to successive expanded editions. The 'Overbury' Characters share some features with the essay, notably the witty, epigrammatic style and the aphoristic summing up of, in this case, the qualities of character types.

The scandal of the Carr/Howard marriage seems reflected in the three Characters that follow Overbury's idealizing 'A Wife' poem: 'A good Woman', 'A very very Woman', and 'Her next part'. This sequence begins with further idealized qualities inherent in a good wife, with such succinct and stylish sentences as 'She hath a content of her owne, and so seekes not a husband, but finds him' (D2^v).[24] This is contrasted by the negative portrait of 'a very very woman', who embodies all the clichés of vanity: 'She reads ouer her face euery morning, and sometimes blots out pale & writes red' (D2^v). Like many essays, these Characters are structured through accumulating observations, rather than a gathering argument, although they often reach a neat conclusion: 'Her chiefe commendation

---

[22] 'Dedicated Thought', 109.

[23] For the literary and political responses to the scandal see especially Alastair Bellany, *The Politics of Court Scandal in Early Modern England: News Culture and the Overbury Affair* (Cambridge: Cambridge University Press, 2002).

[24] References to *A Wife now the Widow of Sir Thomas Overbury* (1614, the fifth impression).

is, shee brings a man to repentance' (D3). The final Character in this trilogy continues the misogynistic theme: 'Her Deuotion is good clothes, they carrie her to Church, expresse their stuffe and fashion, and are silent' (D3ᵛ).

This sequence is followed by a collection of witty dissections of Jacobean types; for example: '*A Puritane.* Is a diseas'd peece of *Apocrypha*, binde him to the Bible, and hee corrupts the whole text' (F). Virtually all of the Characters are satirical, though as well as scorned figures like 'A Dissembler', 'A Flatterer', 'A Whore', and 'An ignorant glory-hunter' there are 'A Wise-man' and 'A Noble Spirit', but the real verve lies in the satire.

John Earle's collection of Characters, *Microcosmographie* (1628), was equally famous in its time and went through even more editions in the seventeenth and eighteenth centuries than Overbury's. Earle's collection is more varied than the Overbury Characters and is less consistently satirical. Earle begins with the benign character of a child and it illustrates his urbane tone, which helps to move his Characters rather closer to the style of the essay. Earle's many memorably phrased aphorisms build up a picture of the personality of the writer, rather than just delivering a series of quips to type-cast a character:

> *A Childe*
> Is a Man in a small Letter, yet the best Copie of *Adam* before hee tasted of *Eve*, or the Apple; and hee is happy whose small practice in the World can only write this Character.... His Soule is yet a white paper vnscribled with obseruations of the world, wherewith at length it becomes a blurr'd note booke.... Wee laugh at his foolish sports, but his game is our earnest: and his drums, rattles and hobby-horses, but the Emblems, & mocking of mans businesse. (B1–2)[25]

Earle is capable of sharp wit, but his generalized targets mean that the effect is usually benign, as with, for example, the clever opening sentence of '*A selfe-conceited Man*': 'Is one that knowes himselfe so well, that he does not know himselfe' (C3ᵛ). Perhaps inspired by Cornwallis's essay on an alehouse, Earle includes the Character of a tavern, which is 'a degree, or (if you will) a paire of stayres aboue an Alehouse' (C4ᵛ). Earle's Character is less personal than Cornwallis's essay, but is nevertheless quirky and individual: '"Tis the best Theater of natures, where they are truly acted, not plaid' (D). The essayistic nature of Earl's volume is also enhanced by its range, as it covers some ingenious social types with reflections upon them; for example, a shark (that is, someone who sponges off people), a blunt man, a critic, a reserved man, and a vulgar-spirited man 'That comes to London to see it, and the pretty things in it, and the chiefe cause of his journey the beares' (J3ᵛ), as well as a number of places ('Paul's walk', 'a bowl-alley').

It is perhaps this concrete particularity as a ground for wit that in the end marks out the Character as different to the essay. This can be illustrated by Nicholas Breton's attempt to cash in on the popularity of both genres with *Characters Upon Essays Moral and Divine* (1615). Breton's rather abject dedication to Bacon places him amongst those

---

[25] References to John Earle, *Microcosmographie* (1628). Earle's autograph manuscript is held in the Bodleian Library (Eng. Misc. f. 89) and is also available in facsimile (Leeds: Scolar Press, 1966); quotations have been checked against it.

who followed Bacon's lead, but the idea of 'charactering' the essays is both a glance at fashion and also a description of how the abstract topics of the essays are turned into something like a Character. Breton's essays do, however, remain fairly abstract, lacking in general the detail of the true Character; this is evident from their topics: wisdom, learning, knowledge, practice, patience, love, peace, war, valour, resolution, honour, truth, time, death, faith, and fear. Indeed, Breton's volume is really a fairly conventional essay collection that gestures towards the Character, presumably in order to increase sales. Breton's rather abstract essays contrast nicely with a clever volume from a similarly prolific and popular author, Richard Brathwait. Brathwait's *Essays Upon the Five Senses* (1620) neatly covers seeing, hearing, touching, tasting, and smelling. Brathwait's tone is essentially moralizing and tends to undercut the more adventurous possibilities that might have arisen from the notion of each sense as an occasion for reflection. There is a considerable amount of sermonizing, so that taste evokes Eve and sin, rather than sensuality: 'No tempting delight shall feede my *appetite*.'[26]

Where the Character might point to the essay as biography, the essay as autobiography reaches perhaps its apogee in Henry Peacham's *The Truth of Our Times: revealed out of one man's experience by way of essay* (1638). Peacham combines his general reflections—essays on such issues as schooling (he was himself a schoolmaster), opinion, or fashion—with a kind of discontinuous autobiographical narrative. In the section 'Of making and publishing Bookes', for example, Peacham offers a heartfelt account of the trials and tribulations of authors, noting 'I have (I confesse) published things of mine owne heretofore, but I never gained one halfepenny by any Dedication that ever I made, save *splendida promissa*' (39).[27] Within a fairly conventional discussion of travel, Peacham enlivens his account with some anecdotes from his knowledge of the Netherlands and Germany. Similarly, when explaining why it is important to know one's homeland as well as countries abroad, Peacham typically moves from the general to the particular (and personal): 'here are many rarities in *England*, and our coast townes are worthy the view and the knowing, if it were but onely to satisfie strangers, who are many times inquisitive of the state of *England*, yea, and many times know it better than most of our home-borne gentlemen: herein Sir *Robert Carr* of *Sleford* in *Lincoln-shire*, a noble gentleman, and my worthy friend was much to be commended' (144). Peacham's whimsical reflections anticipate the style and tone of the Augustan essayists like Addison, and might in some ways be seen as marking the bridge between the early modern essay and the second golden age of the genre in the early eighteenth century. Indeed, as with so many genres of early modern prose, the essay as practised by writers like Bacon, or Cornwallis, or numerous others, was new and experimental, and also formative.

In a fascinating discussion, Helen Deutsch traces the way that the essay dealt with the issue of disability, beginning with Montaigne's 'On Cripples' and Bacon's 'On Deformity',

---

[26] Richard Brathwait, *Essays Upon the Five Senses* (1620), 51; Brathwait is another example of the dual popularity of Essay and Character, as he includes the Character of a Shrew and a sequence of resolves in this volume.

[27] References to Henry Peacham's *The Truth of Our Times* (1638).

moving through William Hay's 1754 essay exploring the connection between his own disability and subjectivity, to an early twentieth-century essay by Randolph Bourne.[28] Deutsch is especially interested in the shifting nature of how a disability might be characterized, but she singles out the essay as a genre which, starting in the early seventeenth century, facilitates the combination of flickering self-examination with exemplarity. Bacon's chameleon tone is illustrated by the careful placement in his 1625 volume of 'Of Deformity' after 'Of Beauty'. 'Of Beauty' concludes somewhat darkly that 'for the most part it makes a dissolute *Youth*, and an *Age* a little out of countenance: But yet certainly againe, if it light well, it maketh Vertues shine, and Vices blush' (153). 'Of Deformity' moves from the balanced near paradox of its opening sentence—'*Deformed Persons* are commonly euen with Nature: For as Nature hath done ill by them; So doe they by Nature' (154)—to a conclusion that consists of a roll-call of admirable examples culminating in Socrates.

After a period of neglect, we seem now to be experiencing a revival of interest in the essay as a vital literary genre, with contemporary practitioners being associated with a concurrent vogue for imaginative and experimental non-fiction writing of various kinds. The modern essay from Virginia Woolf through to Joan Didion or P. J. O'Rourke is a revitalized form that has gathered momentum and attention from the early twentieth century to the present day, when essay collections (along with short stories) have become viable again for publishers. From this perspective we are in a position to rescue the early modern essay from a period of, if not neglect, then under-appreciation.

Further Reading

Black, Scott. *Of Essays and Reading in Early Modern Britain* (New York: Palgrave Macmillan, 2006).

Fish, Stanley. *Self-Consuming Artefacts* (Berkeley: University of California Press, 1972).

Hall, Michael. 'The Emergence of the Essay and the Idea of Discovery', in Alexander J. Butrym, ed., *Essays on the Essay* (Athens, GA: University of Georgia Press, 1989), 73–91.

Lilley, Kate. 'Dedicated Thought: Montaigne, Bacon, and the English Renaissance Essay', in Susannah Brietz Monta and Margaret W. Ferguson, eds., *Teaching Early Modern Prose* (New York: Modern Language Association, 2010), 95–112.

O'Neill, John. *Essaying Montaigne: A Study of the Renaissance Institution of Writing and Reading* (London: Routledge, 1982).

Pebworth, Ted Larry. '"Real English Evidence": Stoicism and the English Essay Tradition', *PMLA*, 87 (1972): 101–2.

Vickers, Brian. *Francis Bacon and Renaissance Prose* (Cambridge: Cambridge University Press, 1968).

---

[28] Helen Deutsch, 'The Body's Moments', *Prose Studies*, 27 (2005): 11–26.

CHAPTER 29

DOMESTIC MANUALS AND THE POWER OF PROSE

CATHERINE RICHARDSON

DOMESTIC manuals were produced in large numbers in early modern England, and for that reason, they can be seen as an influential genre of prose writing—we can presume that many people read them or heard them read, or at least had access to a copy. And yet, there is not a great deal of direct evidence for their ownership: we know, for instance, that a copy of Lewis Bayly's *The Practice of Pietie* was bought for Anne Newdigate at the cost of 2s in 1621, and that Nehemiah Wallington, the seventeenth-century puritan and London artisan, bought William Gouge's *Of Domestical Duties*. Such anecdotal examples give us valuable information about ownership, but Wallington is almost unique in offering an insight into the way these volumes were used. He helpfully records that, having purchased his copy, he subsequently drew up a list of '31 articles for my family for the reforming of our lives', to which his household set their hands.[1] We cannot know how representative Wallington's 'active' reading of his Gouge was, however, as it is an exceptional account. This essay therefore comes at the question of use from a different angle, studying how the manuals work internally—what their prose form might be able to tell us about the way they were used and their potential impact on their early modern readers. In doing so, it addresses the way these prose writers explore the connections between individuals within a household and investigates their methods for forging links between theory and practice.

I focus in what follows on texts about domestic behaviour, as opposed to volumes on household work and on husbandry. The former are more conceptual, laying out ideals of conduct based largely on biblical principle, whereas the latter treat the practical tasks of

---

[1] Vivienne Larminie, *Wealth, Kinship and Culture: The Seventeenth Century Newdigates of Arbury and Their World* (Woodbridge: Boydell & Brewer for Royal Historical Society, 1995), 199; Paul Seaver, *Wallington's World: A Puritan Artisan in Seventeenth-Century London* (London: Methuen, 1985), 79. As Arnold Hunt argues with reference to early modern sermons, 'We know all too little about the ways in which [they] may have influenced popular action and opinion'; Arnold Hunt, *The Art of Hearing: English Preachers and their Audiences, 1590–1640* (Cambridge: Cambridge University Press, 2010), 5.

domestic labour—the preparation of food or the types of medicine which the housewife might need to administer, and the tilling of the soil and the successful cultivation of various crops and animals.[2] It is for these behavioural texts that the connections between theory and practice are most complex and most urgent.

The behavioural texts are in many ways strikingly similar to one another in their style and content. They advise on the nature of the relationships of which the household was comprised—husband and wife, parents and children, masters and servants—in order to achieve a peaceful and harmonious domestic life. As William Whately ambitiously states, 'So shall your loves be sure, your hearts comfortable, your example commendable, your houses peaceable, your selves joyfull, your lives chearefull, your deaths blessed, and your memories happie for ever.'[3] To this end, they deal with two major issues—the division of roles between the heads of the family (the husband and wife) and the negotiation of power relations between the household's various combinations of superior and inferior. With regards to the former, William Gouge maintains that the husband should 'meddle with the great and weightie affaires of the family (as performing Gods worship, appointing and setling good orders, providing convenient house-roome, and other necessaries for the family: keeping children when they grow great, or waxe stubborne, in awe: ruling men servants, with the like)' and the wife with 'some lesse, but very needfull matters, as nourishing and instructing children when they are young, adorning the house, ordering the provision brought into the house, ruling maid servants.'[4] Theories of social order are repeatedly reiterated. The patriarchal division of household authority is underpinned by acceptance of the inherent human need for authority and subjection, and the logic of the following statement from Robert Cleaver was to be taken as self-evident: 'For as in a citie, there is nothing more unequall, then that every man should bee like equall: so it is not convenient, that in one house every man shuld be like and equall together. There is no equality in that citie, where the private man is equal with the Magistrate...but rather a confusion of all offices and authoritie.'[5] Avoiding confusion entailed accepting hierarchy—in the majority of cases then, tolerating domestic inferiority.

The writer's authority to speak on these matters is a significant factor in our understanding of the relationship between theories and practices of domestic life: Natasha Glaisyer and Sara Pennell point out the importance of 'a conception of the authors [of didactic texts]...as equipped with the expertise to dispense appropriate knowledge' and the text's consequent status as 'a substitute for oral, face-to-face educative

---

[2] The divisions between such texts were not always clear-cut and they altered across the period. Lynette Hunter sees this as a symptom of wider changes in the market for popular print as their appeal broadened, Lynette Hunter, 'Books for Daily Life: Household, Husbandry, Behaviour', in John Barnard and D. F. McKenzie, eds., *The Cambridge History of the Book in Britain, Volume IV, 1557–1695* (Cambridge: Cambridge University Press, 2002), 521.

[3] Willam Whately, *A Bride-Bush or, A Direction for Married Persons. Plainely Describing the Duties common to both, and peculiar to each of them* (Felix Kingston for Thomas Man, 1619), 220.

[4] William Gouge, *Of Domesticall Duties Eight Treatises* (London: John Haviland for William Bladen, 1622), 259.

[5] Robert Cleaver, *A godlie forme of hovseholde government* (Felix Kingston for Thomas Man, 1598), 170.

relationships'.[6] Many of the most popular of these books were written by Protestant preachers on the fringes of orthodoxy. Henry Smith, also known as 'Silver-Tongued Smith', began his career as a radical preacher, but was eventually elected lecturer at St Clement Danes without Temple Bar in 1587, where he was famous for his very popular and affecting sermons. William Whateley was known as the 'Roaring Boy of Banbury' for his preaching in Oxfordshire, and William Gouge, minister of St Ann's Blackfriars, preached twice every Sunday and gave a celebrated Wednesday lecture for thirty-five years.[7] They were clearly influential and persuasive speakers, and some of them were also married men—a part of that most significantly new type of post-Reformation family, the married clergy.[8] As writers of didactic literature then, their claim to expertise lay partly in their own experience as family men, but largely in that gained by ministering to their flocks. The title pages of Whately's and Gataker's texts, for instance, foreground their authors' role as 'Minister and Preacher of Gods Word in Banburie in Oxfordshire' and 'Pastor of Rotherhith' respectively. Not unrelated to their sermons (which several of them also published), their profession gave their texts a weight of spiritual authority which encouraged Wallington, and presumably others like him, to change their behaviour according to the precepts contained within them.

Several treatises maintain a residue of their spoken contexts as marriage sermons, an integral part of the celebrations. Henry Smith's *A Preparative to Marriage*, for instance, begins 'You are come hither to be contracted in the Lord', and other authors discuss a process of event-based beginnings for their texts followed by revision and expansion, an issue of pressing time often hovering in the background. Gataker refers to the 'happy conjunction' at which 'some part of it was preached, the residue through streits of time being for that time suppressed', and Whately argues that 'as a Wedding dinner, so a Wedding Sermon, may not be taxed for a little more than ordinary length and varietie, for why should any reasonable creature bee lesse willing to feed his mind than his belly?'[9] The lively and potentially interactive nature of such a basis in performance occasionally comes across in the printed texts too: Whately anticipates disagreement with the words 'But here perhaps some weake spirited man may interrupt me, and say...'.[10]

---

[6] Natasha Glaisyer and Sara Pennell, eds., *Didactic Literature in England 1500–1800* (Aldershot: Ashgate, 2003), 9.

[7] Gary W. Jenkins, 'Smith, Henry', *ODNB* <http://www.oxforddnb.com/view/article/25811?docPos=3> accessed 18 March 2013; Brett Usher, 'Gouge, William', *ODNB* <http://www.oxforddnb.com/view/article/11133?docPos=1> accessed 18 March 2013.

[8] Kathleen Davies argued, against earlier certainties, that most of the attitudes to family life which the conduct books express are peculiar to Protestantism, but can be found in pre-Reformation works too. And what differences there were—she points to a rejection of the connection between voluntary sexual abstinence in marriage and the obtaining of grace and the possibility of divorce and remarriage in a limited range of circumstances—in fact, they showed an altered understanding of the sacraments on which such advice was based, rather than the practice of marriage. Kathleen M. Davies, 'Continuity and Change in Literary Advice on Marriage', in R. B. Outhwaite, ed., *Marriage and Society* (London: Europa, 1981), 78.

[9] Henrie Smith, *A Preparative to Mariage* (London: R. Field for Thomas Man, 1591), 1; Thomas Gataker, *A good vvife Gods gift and, a vvife indeed. Tvvo mariage sermons* (London: Iohn Hauiland for Fulke Clifton, 1623), Epistle dedicatory; Whately, *Bride-Bush*, 2.

[10] Whately, *Bride-Bush*, 99.

The dedication of several of these texts to exemplary individuals gives them a further platform of authority from which to engage the new and wider audience which print allows. William Lowth's *The Christian Mans Closet*, for instance, is dedicated to 'the right worshipfull and his singular good friends, M. Thomas Darcie and M. Brian Darcie Esquiers' because 'your worships are Fathers of many children (which I am perswaded are dearly beloved unto you) and maisters of great families'. Authority is shared in domestic manuals, then, between author and dedicatee: it is the combination of the theological knowledge and pastoral experience of the clerical author and the exemplary status of the elevated patron that underwrites their advice.[11] Although based on ancient biblical exemplar, they insist upon their relevance to contemporary family dynamics.

And we might imagine the way they intervened in those contemporary domestic situations. Art historian Tara Hamling, analysing how the decoration of household interiors might have been used by their inhabitants, utilizes information from these manuals to reconstruct domestic pious practice. She finds direct connections in 'the transmission of imagery from the title pages of Protestant advice manuals to the walls and ceilings of houses', which shows how central these texts were to household life. But she also suggests less obvious associations: for instance, that 'the godly patriarch could invoke a higher authority' if his walls were decorated with visual and verbal examples of God's judgements. This enables us to imagine a potential scenario for the reading out of domestic prose within the household, one in which it interacts with other cultural forms. We have a sense of what we might call the 'event' of a prose text—the moment at which it is interpreted, understood, and consumed.[12]

Such scenarios comment interestingly on the position of this chapter in a section on 'private prose'. Domestic manuals are specifically addressed to households as a whole, either in the sense that their sections speak to different members of those households in turn, or that their messages are intended to be disseminated from the domestic head to his subordinates, or both. They are not, in other words, written for individuals, but for those who find themselves part of a specific community; and their subject is the relationship between individuals and communal life. This makes them potentially very different types of work to the diary or the letter, the focus of other essays in this section, but nevertheless concerned with life within the household, albeit in a time at which 'private' life had very different meanings.

---

[11] Gouge's dedication is rather different, his text offered '*TO THE RIGHT HONOVRABLE, RIGHT VVorshipfull, and other my* beloued Parishioners, Inhabitants of the Precinct of *Black-friers LONDON*', saying 'I make you all as one Patron.' Here, the parish takes on the identity of the godly household which legitimates the publication of the text.

[12] Tara Hamling, *Decorating the 'Godly' Household* (New Haven: Yale University Press, 2010), 115–17. Hunt argues that 'A sermon on the printed page was arguably not a sermon at all: it could not save souls, because it lacked the converting power of the spoken voice' and this provides a useful analogy to the domestic manuals; Hunt, *The Art of Hearing*, 10. See, however, Henry Smith, who insists in his preface that his reader, presumably the lone male head of the family, 'Reade, pray, and meditate; thy profite shall be little in any booke, vnlesse thou reade *alone*, and vnlesse thou reade all and record after' (my italics), *Preparative*, 'To the reader'.

As was suggested in Robert Cleaver's statement above about the 'city of confusion', the early modern household was seen as central to the maintenance of social order. It was the smallest and most intense of a series of interlocking spheres which formed a model of governance which was structurally utterly convincing, if rather harder to put into practice. The monarch ruled his or her realm, giving protection in exchange for subjects' loyalty; the mayor and magistrates ruled the town and ensured the good behaviour of its citizens. In a similar way, the husband ruled his household: his family in the widest sense of wife, children, servants, and apprentices obeyed him as a representative of God, because the model for these potentially diverse forms of authority was the nature and quality of Christ's relationship with his church—that of a loving father whose sacrifice compelled the willing obedience of his flock. This is a further element of the priest's authority to write on domestic matters, given his analogous role in relation to his congregation.[13]

Because these spheres of authority fitted within one another like a series of identically painted Russian dolls, the smallest, indivisible 'doll' of the household was, in theory, the simplest because it was the most direct and straightforward manifestation of a species of social relationship. It is first in historical terms, as Perkins points out: 'Among al the Societies & States, wherof the whole world of mankinde from the first calling of *Adam* in Paradise, unto this day, hath consisted, the first and most ancient is the Familie.' But it is also placed at the beginning of life—the sphere in which men must practise for their public roles, and in which their competency can be tested: 'And look as the Superiour that faileth in his private charge, will prove uncapable of publike employment; so the Inferiour, who is not framed to a course of Oeconomicall subjection, will hardly undergoe the yoke of civill obedience.'[14] Success in the smaller sphere should guarantee the realization of the larger. As Gouge puts it, 'What excellent seminaries would families be to Church and Commonwealth' if 'the head and severall members of a family would be perswaded every of them to be conscionable in performing their owne particular duties'?[15] Domestic practice is the very stuff of political theory and the extra-domestic significance of these texts, then, lies in the very high stakes which this political view of the household gives to successful family life. Only seeing the relationship between daily activity and such ideals can guarantee the kingdom's stability.

The rhetorical style which the manuals adopt in many ways foregrounds a learned, rather than a practical knowledge, one which generates an educated and theologically sophisticated authorial authority. They disseminate and make material the order of which they write through a number of typographical features. Very careful

---

[13] Helen Moore points out the philosophical connections: 'Self-government (or ethics) and the government of the state (politics) are two branches of moral philosophy: the third is "oeconomics", or the government of the household.' Helen Moore, 'Of Marriage, Morals and Civility', in Jennifer Richards, ed., *Early Modern Civil Discourses* (Basingstoke: Palgrave Macmillan, 2003), 36.

[14] William Perkins, *Christian oeconomie: or, A short survey of the right manner of erecting and ordering a familie according to the scriptures*, trans. Tho. Pickering Bachelar of Diuinitie, London, 1609, Epistle dedicatory.

[15] Gouge, *Domesticall Duties*, Epistle dedicatory.

division—often lengthy tables of contents, chapters with subheadings, and marginal notes about shifts in argument—is used by authors to impose an order intended to increase understanding. Listing six parts to his work, William Lowth says 'I thinke it meete to divide the argument unto you that be here present, to the ende that an order being observed, all thinges may the more easily be understood.'[16] Gouge underlines the connections between his sections: 'For by method sundry and severall points appertaining to one matter are drawne forth, as in a chaine one linke draweth up another... As method is an helpe to Invention, so also to retention. It is as the thread or wier whereon pearles are put, which keepeth them from scattering.'[17] Whately states conversationally, 'Now then, that we may not loose ourselves for want of order, I must needs ranke these duties into their severall kinds and heads, for the better helpe of mine owne and your memories', and a marginal note marks that division so that it may be returned to easily.[18] Typographical order generates social order.

The clear division into sections is mirrored by the analytical distinctions which are made between the contents themselves, in a run of subtle differentiations which attempt to impose an order of sameness by dividing human relationships and behaviours into similar but discrete groups: 'Next unto parents and children wherby the family is increased,' says Perkins, 'is a second sort of couples, which are helpes therunto. And they are Masters and servants.'[19] The interlinked responsibilities of household members and the connections between their different types of authority and subjection are echoed in the careful divisions of the text.

In rhetorical terms too, these are self-consciously learned works. Many writers make extensive use of contraries in their explanations of central concepts. Gouge offers the most extended defence of the technique: 'And because contraries laid together doe much set forth each other in their lively colours, I have to every duty annexed the contrary fault, and aberration from it. For many that heare the duties thinke all well enough, till they heare also the contrary vices, whereby in their consciences they are most convinced.'[20] Gataker echoes the dichotomies of behaviour in pleasing verbal forms: 'And if she be so that performeth not the *Office* of a *Wife*; what is she then that doth the contrary? Who when she should be an *Helper*, prooveth *an Hinderer*.'[21] The function of these techniques is the additional clarity and the variety of approach which will further the authors' didactic aims. The shape of their works is in the service of familial salvation, national order, and, no doubt, an authorial pride achieved through use of scholarly rhetorical form.

The most obvious example of the transfer of these preachers' learning and professional skills to the pages of the pamphlets is their biblical exegesis. Robert Cleaver and Thomas Gataker both take Genesis as their subject: from '*Let us make Adam a helper like*

---

[16] William Lowth, *The Christian mans Closet* (London, 1581), fol. 3ᵛ.
[17] Gouge, *Domesticall Duties*, Epistle dedicatory.
[18] Whately, *Bride-Bush*, 2.
[19] Perkins, *Christian oeconomie*, 152.
[20] Gouge, *Domesticall Duties*, Epistle dedicatory.
[21] Thomas Gataker, *A good wife Gods gift and, a wife indeed. Two marriage sermons* (1623), 7.

unto himselfe.' Cleaver concludes that 'By the *Helper*, is signified the utilitie and profit of the service, and by the similitude and likenesse, is signified love' and goes on to explore the relationship between the two: 'But as wee would that the man when he loveth should remember his maiestie, so we would that when he ruleth, he forget not his love.'[22] Gataker's assessment of Adam's state is thought-provokingly simple: '*Adam in Paradise*, though he were *truly happie*, yet was he *not fully Happie*: his *Happinesse* was not compleat; he was nothing so well yet as he might be, while he was yet *without a Mate*.'[23] Such a distinction, between 'true' and 'full' happiness, shows the complexity of the thinking which lies behind the clear divisions of these writers' prose. They are thought-provoking sentences in the sense that they encourage meditation on similarity and dissimilarity, and therefore on the theoretical distinctions between states.

There are points in these texts, however, at which such unshakable and authoritative pronouncements weaken and a hesitancy and equivocation creeps into the prose. Such points are most prominent in the writing of Gouge and Whately, two sermonizers who had had to cope with direct responses from their audiences in the past. Gouge's statements on the difficulties of communicating hard lessons are well known. 'I remember that when these *Domesticall Duties* were first uttered out of the pulpit', he says, 'much exception was taken against the application of a wives subjection to the restraining of her from disposing the common goods of the family without, or against her husbands consent.' Print, in this context, becomes a form of defence, a way of pointing up the parts of complex arguments which are lost in the initial rush of audience response to a spoken thesis: 'But surely they that made those exceptions did not well thinke of the *Cautions* and *Limitations* which were then delivered, and are now againe expresly noted.' Given such a chance to set the record straight, Gouge also makes an explicit connection between the form of his prose, his typography, and his meaning:

> Now that in all those places where a wives yoke may seeme most to pinch, I might give some ease, I have to every head of wives duties made a reference, in the margin over against it, to the duties of husbands answerable thereunto, and noted the reference with this marke *, that it might the more readily be turned unto. Yea I have further parallel'd, and laid even one against another in one view, the heads of husbands and wives duties, as they answer each other.[24]

He also adds a table of contents which runs to twelve pages to aid in this task. The complexities of marriage and the pains of patriarchal subservience are to be mitigated by the forms of the printed manual.

This openness to the idea that patriarchal subjection is arduous and likely to provoke resentment if poorly managed is striking. Whately handles his section on the wife's subjection to her husband rather differently to the rest of his text, using a distinct mode of address and anticipating problems from the start. 'This duty had so much more neede to bee pressed, because, though it be so plane, as it cannot be denied, yet it is withal so hard,

---

[22] Cleaver, *A godlie forme*, 155.   [23] Gataker, *Two marriage sermons*, 28.
[24] Gouge, *Domesticall Duties*, Epistle dedicatory.

that it can hardly bee yeelded unto' he states honestly—the duty is logical (plain) but very testing—the movement from its theory to its practice is inherently fraught with problems.[25] This ready admittance that such demands are extremely hard to fulfil points to the endless processes of negotiation between writer and initial audience and between readers and their families which lie behind the distances that these texts imagine between theory and practice. Whately even suggests a kind of censorship by public opinion: 'I was verily afraid to deliver my mind as concerning the lawfulnesse of an husbands using such a medicine [violence]. But I confessed, that wee must not conceale a needful truth, for feare of inconveniences.'[26] In addition to showing very clearly the contested nature of the central elements of patriarchy, these quotes demonstrate the vibrancy of everyday debates on the subject which must underlie so many early modern plays' engagements with the contests around male authority.

The careful rhetorical division into sections and the distinctions made between concepts are challenged by domestic practice then, and the former is often explicitly an attempt to contain and control the latter. The manuals are full of injunctions, especially to wives, to consider the theory when faced with the practice. Gouge suggests with his usual succinctness that 'Though an husband in regard of evill qualities may carrie the Image of the devill, yet in regard of his place and office he beareth the image of God.' In other words, the material qualities of reality are consistently to be trumped and overridden by the ideals of spiritual perception. Gataker's reminder that '*Circumcision is accounted* no other than *Uncircumcision, if a man be not a keeper of the Law*' makes this painfully clear.[27] As a husband, modelling one's behaviour on the magistrate did not perhaps require too much imagination, and some of these men may have been, or assumed that they would one day be, fulfilling both roles. Thinking through one's role within the household in terms of the relationship between Christ and his church, however, was a different matter. Perkins shows the move from experience to metaphor clearly in his exposition of the three fruits of the marriage bed: 'I. The having of a blessed seed...II. The preservation of the bodie in cleannesse...III. The holy estate of marriage is a lively type of Christ and his Church, and this communion of married persons, is also a figure of the conjunction that is between him, and the faithfull.'[28] The first two are recognizable aspects of human behaviour, however hard to control, but the third is altogether different. The Russian dolls of analogy, then, are in fact made of very different stuff; the faces which they give to early modern authority are less solidly human as they increase in size—less clearly connected with everyday practice—and seeing their familial likeness to one another often means moving from recognizing the

---

[25] Whately, *Bride-Bush*, 192. Gouge anticipates a related question about his organization of his material: 'Why should inferiours duties be more fully expressed, and placed in the first ranke?', to which he provides the answer 'Surely because for the most part inferiours are most unwilling to undergoe the duties of their place. Who is not more ready to rule, than to be subject?', *Domesticall Duties*, 22.

[26] Whately, *Bride-Bush*, 169.

[27] Gouge, *Domesticall Duties*, 273; Gataker, *Two marriage sermons*, 12.

[28] Perkins, *Christian oeconomie*, 116.

parity of particular actions in the exercise of authority, to appreciating similarity in the quality, rather than the character, of actions, to recognizing a sophisticated set of metaphorical parallels centred on mutual responsibility occasioned by different kinds of loving sacrifice. The manuals offer a version of this shift writ large: a dizzying movement from the bodies of ordinary men and women to the sacred and resonant body of Christ. It is upon these distinctions between similitude and disparity that the project of early modern patriarchal authority rests, and they get to the heart of the wonderful tension between prose style and content which makes the manuals so endlessly interesting, if frustrating, to read.

It was, of course, a central function of both the priest's role and the role of these texts to make connections between theological concepts and daily practice. Gouge makes this very clear as he examines the relationship between the general and the particular: 'The life and power of Gods word consisteth in this particular application thereof unto our selves'—the Bible only has power if the faithful live it out as practice, rather than reading it as text.[29] To this end, he uses a simile to clarify the relationships between the spheres of analogy: 'The glorious and bright Sunne in the firmament, and a dimme candle in an house, have a kinde of fellowship, and the same office, which is to give light: yet there is no equality betwixt them.'[30] The separation between fellowship in office and equality of nature and effect is shown neatly, efficiently, and in a way which lingers in the mind's eye. Gouge is not alone in his use of such explicatory techniques, and it is here that we get to the heart of the connection between prose style and the relationship between texts and audiences. It is these writers' use of simile which bears the theologically significant weight of scaling up or down the concepts of authority and of connecting the spiritual and material worlds to one another, as the remainder of this essay aims to demonstrate.

Authors offer a rich variety of comparisons in order to elucidate the kinds of behaviour they are advocating, and that variety links their seriousness of message and their lightness of delivery as prose texts. The vast majority of the images fall into the following categories: there are figures of husbandry and interaction with animals, images from manufacturing and professional practices, similes of the body and medicine, of domestic activity (including the use of different kinds of vessel and culinary conceits), and of buildings. Moving outside the household, there are military similes, ones around educative processes and those surrounding the purity and controllability of water. In other words, these similes are not unfamiliar ones from other types of early modern prose, but their referents are by and large quotidian ones, grounded in the practices of everyday life, rather than the flights of poetic fancy. Exploring the way this range of images employs its readers' knowledge of other areas of life in the service of domestic harmony demonstrates what is perhaps the most obvious and distinctive formal strategy used to bridge the gap between theory and practice. Some writers use far more of them than others: Lowth, for instance, employs very few indeed, Cleaver and Smith draw on comparatively

---

[29] Gouge, *Domesticall Duties*, 129.   [30] Gouge, *Domesticall Duties*, 344.

few given the length of their texts, and Whately, Gataker, and Gouge use them in the largest numbers. Images of buildings, domestic practice, animals, husbandry, manufacture, and the body are by far the most popular, used by the majority of writers even if they only employ them once or twice. I focus on a few of the most common categories here, in order to show how simile is used by authors in addressing the difficult issue of the joining of human beings into productive and peaceable relationships.[31]

The most popular images of husbandry are those which employ the processes of cultivation. Gataker and Gouge use the idea of grafting productively, Gataker in respect of the relationship between parents and children:

> Children are as branches shooting out of one stem, divided and severed either from other, or as grifts and siences cut off, or boughes and branches slipped off from their native stocke, and either planted or engraffed else-where. Man and Wife are as the stocke and sience, the one ingraffed into the other, and so fastned together, that they cannot againe be sundred.

The extension of the image to treat the subject fully is striking. Gouge uses the same idea to express the relationship between Christ and his people: 'Christ laying hold on us by his spirit, and we on him by faith, we come to be incorporated into him, and made one body, as the science and stocke one tree.'[32] The process is natural and productive, and yet, it involves a significant amount of husbandry.

In addition, there are images of the tending of plants: the instruction to 'water...the tender buds of thrift, dutifulnesse, and other graces which begin to bud forth, and to appear a little above ground', or Lowth's focus on moderation: 'Plantes when they are moderately watered, grown and increase the better, but with overmuch, they are choked.'[33] The need for an active spirituality comes across clearly in all of these images, and the labour which those who work on the land put into the production of their crops provides a useful analogy for the relationship between natural gifts and cultivated abundance. Work, they insist, has an essential place in spiritual development. The manuring of the land is also well used: in Whately's colloquial term it must 'be goodded (according to the country phrase), as well as plowed and harrowed, else it will bring forth very little but weeds'. For Lowth, the potential barrenness of 'a field albeit it be very fertile, without culture, diligent dressing and manuring' is instructive, and similarly for Gataker, the image of '*a cursed soile*, yeelded nothing, though never so well manured and managed, but *thornes and thistles*, but *briers and brambles*, but *hemlocke and henbane*, and the like *noisome weeds*'.[34] The knowledge which is called on here is not abstract or abstruse, but rather, a kind of wisdom passed almost silently between generations and amongst communities.

---

[31] In past writing on the manuals, a couple of groups of images have often been considered out of context, and this tends to skew our sense of their overall effect on a reader. See, for instance, Sid Ray, '"Those Whom God Hath Joined Together": Bondage Metaphors and Marital Advice in Early Modern England', in Kari Boyd McBride, ed., *Domestic Arrangements in Early Modern England* (Pittsburgh, PA: Duquesne University Press), 15–47.

[32] Gataker, *Two marriage sermons*, 5; Gouge, *Domesticall Duties*, 98.

[33] Whately, *Bride-Bush*, 129; Lowth, *Closet*, fol. 14ʳ.

[34] Whately, *Bride-Bush*, 125; Lowth, *Closet*, fol. 9ᵛ; Gataker, *Two marriage sermons*, 52.

Linked to these powerful images of growth and decay, which gain their potency from seasonal cycles of production and consumption, are those of animal husbandry and the controlling of beasts. The behaviour of animals is used as a way of exploring the godly community, either in positive or negative terms. Gataker identifies man's desire to work together by analogy to the animal kingdom: '*Man* being a *Creature* of the kinde, not of those that love only to flocke, and feed, and bide, and live together, as *Dawes* and *Stares* doe; but of those that desire to combine, and worke and labour also together, as the Bee and the *Pismire*; hee stood in need, as of *Societie*, so of *Assistance*.' Similarly, Gouge sees the family as 'a Bee-hive, in which is the stocke, and out of which are sent many swarmes of Bees: for...out of families are they sent into the Church and common-wealth'. The images join the two levels of the analogy and show how the texts aim at the creation of both ideal communities and perfect households. For Perkins, families in which God is served 'are, as it were, little Churches, yea even a kind of paradise upon earth', but their opposite can be 'compared to an heard of swine, which are alwaies feeding upon the maste with greedinesse, but never looke up to the hand that beateth it downe, nor to the tree from whence it falleth'. The appropriate response to God's word is suggested by an image of its opposite, as the reader simultaneously holds in their mind the churchly paradise and the wood of swine.

Many of these images, then, are given the considerable status of trying to separate out the behaviour of Christian families from that of reasonless animals—for instance, Whately asks rhetorically of the effects of whoredom, 'Doth it not transforme men into the savage rudenesse of the bruit creatures, where no young almost can know his sire?' and questions whether or not 'it were a bruitish profanenesse for any man, to sit him downe to his table, as an horse to the manger, and cram himselfe with viands without craving the licence and blessing of God first'.[35] This imagery is therefore at the heart of one of the manuals' crucial distinctions, as it vividly represents the differences between those who are able to exercise the power of the mind over the lusts of the body and those who are not. Obvious here is an imagined godly reader already secure in their status as the former.

The majority of animal husbandry images, therefore, centre around the ubiquitous and enormously important early modern parallel between the bridling of the emotions and the controlling of horses. 'The way to maintain authoritie in this societie, is not to use violence, but skill', Whately insists, and the skills which are explored are characterizing in social, as well as moral, terms: gained by those of middling status upwards in the management of valuable early modern beasts.[36] These images are sometimes residual, cropping up in passing references to 'unbridled passion', but are often considerably

[35] Gataker, *Two marriage sermons*, 29; Gouge, *Domesticall Duties*, 17; Perkins, *Christian oeconomie*, 8; Whately, *Bride-Bush*, 3, 16.

[36] Whately, *Bride-Bush*, 100. These skills in animal management are a source of obvious pride: 'Men that ride horses, have a wand and a spurre both: but they chuse rather to set forward the horse, with the sound or touch of a little whiske, than with the sharpenesse of the iron spurre' (163). For more on the significance of horses in early modern society see Erica Fudge, *Renaissance Beasts: Of Animals, Humans and Other Wonderful Creatures* (Champaign, IL: University of Illinois Press, 2004).

extended. For instance, knowing how to deal with one's wife means applying skills in distinction, 'Even as he that is to ride an horse, must make his bridle fit for the mouth of the poore beast, a snaffle for one, a bit for another, an hard and heavy bit for one, a lesser and lighter for another, for every bridle will not agree to the mouth of every beast.' Cleaver applies the idea to the contract of marriage, 'First therefore, it serveth as a strong bridle to pull backe the force and headines of carnall, naturall, and brutish lust', and Perkins to children, who 'are to bee restrained by the bridle of discipline'.[37] In other words, the notion of bridling is associated with all unruly behaviour which is not governed by the mind, and it works against natural human tendencies, imagined entirely pejoratively. Although the modern reader tends to find such images offensive, largely because the relationship between superior rider and inferior horse is so often an explicitly gendered one, they were clearly an important part of the explication of control through skill. Lowth applies the analogy to wit: 'No horse willingly obeyeth his rider except he be first made tame & gentle by the diligent and wise handling of his breaker, so is their no wit, but yt it wil prove fierce, cruel, & outrageous except it be tamed brideled & subdued by wholsom precepts & good education.' He separates a reader and his or her wit from one another, seeing the latter as something in need of control if the former is to grow to fulfil their potential. Individuals were to apply such lessons not only to others, but also to themselves, each 'whole' (family; husband and wife; mind and body) being made up of superior and subservient parts.

Whately uses a run of images of manufacture in a similar way, connecting the pride felt about good working practice to domestic skills: 'He never yet learnt to worke well in any worke, that would cast his eye more upon his neighbours fingers than his owne'; showing bad practice as a source of shame, pointing out both that 'The skilfullest Carpenter, or other Artificer that is, shall yet bungle and worke very unskilfully, if when his head is light and wefty with drinke, hee take his axe or plane, or other tooles in his hand', and also the effect which this might have on expensive raw materials: 'A good worke may be marred (you know) by an ill manner of doing it: as good stuffe may be soiled by the bungerly making.'[38] Whately appeals to the expertise of the craftsman and his proficiency in making the kind of material distinctions which are analogous to both the horseman's dexterity and the scholar's expertise in dividing the elements of an argument: 'experience teacheth al men to know the proper qualities of those things that are much under their hands', he points out and, as 'Those also that deale in metals, give not the same heate to everie metal', so 'The husband must diligently observe by his wives actions, whether she be Leade, or Tinne, or Iron, or Steele, or of what mettall she is made.'[39] This very material imagistic process has the effect of denaturing women by setting them alongside objects and processes. Seeing it in this explicatory context, however, also situates it as a part of the strange way in which prose brings together the dissimilar to draw out surprising connections—a series of formal, rather than categorical

---

[37] Whately, *Bride-Bush*, 6, 130; Lowth, *Closet*, fol. 10; Cleaver, *A godlie forme*, 138; Perkins, *Christian oeconomie*, 42.
[38] Whately, *Bride-Bush*, 135, 208, 218.
[39] Whately, *Bride-Bush*, 131.

associations. The materiality of these ideas and the notion that sensory skills are analogous to 'interpersonal' ones makes human relationships appear logical and capable of being learned, and takes the irrational heat out of actual domestic situations. Such ideas encourage the transfer of skills between occupational and affective relationships, and they aim at a confidence-building sense of coherence in the range of different contexts in which men have authority over their world.

The other ubiquitous husbandry image is the yoking of animals together at the plough, and again, this has wider connotations of human obedience. Whately takes the idea back to Eden in order to point out its connections to fundamental elements of human nature, saying that obedience 'is a yoake laid upon them in their creation, which also since their fall, hath been made cumbersome, and so they are ever loath to beare it': it is not the yoke of obedience itself, but rather, mankind's altered, disobedient nature which is cumbersome. But the image is more often used as a way of exploring mutuality. Gouge uses it in relation to the problems which occur in marriage, when the couple: 'by their discontent make the burden much more heavy then otherwise it would be: even as when two oxen are in one yoke, and the one holdeth backe, the draught is made much harder to the other'. Later in his work, however, it takes on its most familiar form, as a way of pointing up both the equalities and the inequalities of marriage simultaneously: the husband and wife 'are yoak-fellowes in mutuall familiaritie, not in equall authoritie'.[40] The value of such images lies, then, in an accessibility—a point of meditation on things which must have been seen by readers on a regular basis. They are stable (widely shared and consistent) mental images, whose meanings can therefore be bifurcated—divided into their similarities to and differences from the other half of their 'simile pair'. In the process, the everyday is elevated as a way of thinking about human connections.

In the wide range of domestic images too, writers appeal to a knowledge of best practice—perhaps not so much to a pride in skill, but rather, to a common-sense idea of what works and what does not. On temperance, for instance, Whately says 'it is easie to put out the fier by with drawing fewell, at least to keep ye flame within the chimney, by laying on no more matter, than will sere the turne'; or his advice that whores are best avoided: the reader is to 'consider, that even cold water will become hot, if it bee set too neare the fier'. Gouge's assertion 'that husbands and wives should endevour to helpe forward the growth of grace in each other, because we are all so prone to fall away and wax cold, even as water if the fire goe out, and more fewell be not put under' seems to fall into the same category of appeals to common sense.[41] Clearly, then, these images are not simply aimed at women or servants as the most regular providers of fuel to fires, but rather, appeal to a baseline of domestic practice which is especially apt for the subject matter under consideration—the material practices of the household offering an analogy to its social relations.

Like the dichotomy between reason and the senses which is explored through the management of beasts, household images offer writers an opportunity to investigate the

---

[40] Whately, *Bride-Bush*, 209; Gouge, *Domesticall Duties*, 246, 303.
[41] Whately, *Bride-Bush*, 10, 12; Gouge, *Domesticall Duties*, 243.

connections between the physical and human, earthly and spiritual elements of the household. This is the other key binary on which the arguments of the manuals turn because they aim at a holistic view of domestic issues in order to ensure that sufficient weight is given to the spiritual over the material. Gataker's run of images on the subject is instructive here. He begins with the commonplace that 'surely if any outward thing may helpe to grace a *Man*, apparell, jewels, plate, hangings, house-furniture, attendants, followers, retinue, revenew, issue, &c. then *a worthie Wife* as much as, yea much more than any such'. The fact that houses contain people and goods, Christian practice and the things of the world, necessitates both connections between the two and a hierarchizing of both elements of the metaphor. Again, there is to our eyes a troubling setting of objects against people in the process of comparison—a wife or one's hangings. Gataker continues by moving from the physical to the textual, with an allusion to the biblical comparison of spiritual and material worth: 'She is *a greater blessing* than either *House* or *Inheritance*: and *her price is above Pearles.*' However, having begun to think about pearls, he immediately pursues the metaphor back to the mundane to draw out the absurdity of any other kind of prioritization: 'And if there be so much *seeking* generally on all hands after the one, much more may there justly be as much after the other.'[42] The very visceral connections which the household makes between people and things, as the location which puts them into a close conjunction, not only of use and production, but also of the expression of social status, invites this kind of investigation of human relationships through the quotidian experience of material culture. Individuals and objects are linked through the times and places in which the manuals are likely to have been read, as explored above, but also to instinctive practices and common-sense solutions which might not, without similes, immediately come to mind in the search for salvation.

But the house also offers a way of talking about the body, in a series of metaphors which speaks directly to the concept of the body politic. The biblical idea that the husband is head of the wife's body is central and striking enough to encourage a great deal of thought about the connections between wholes and parts. This close connection between the two should be the essential grounds for a kind of communication envisaged as internal to a perfectly coherent body: as Gouge puts it, 'our particular places and callings are those bonds whereby persons are firmly and fitly knit together, as the members of a naturall body by nerves, arteries, sinewes, veines, and the like, by which life, sense and motion is communicated from one to another'. As the husband resembles Christ in his headship, so this model is also one by which body and fully developed spirit are connected: 'by this meanes is Christ made more fit to doe good to the Church, as an head to the body, and the Church is made more capable of receiving good from Christ, as a body from the head, being knit to it by the soule, and by veines, sinewes, nerves, arteries, and other like ligaments'.[43] True perfection is therefore to be found not as an individual, but as an inextricable part of a larger, nourishing whole, and the image makes it clear that

---

[42] Gataker, *Two marriage sermons*, 38, 57–8.   [43] Gouge, *Domesticall Duties*, 16, 98.

these two central relationships, with Christ and one's wife, are the only source of bodily wholeness, of being fully human.

More often than not, however, the 'body of the household' is a monstrous travesty of such perfection. Gataker again has a run of arresting similes on the subject. He begins with another inspirational biblical passage which doubles body parts and subjection, suggesting that woman 'was at first *taken out of man*; and is therefore by *Creation as a limbe reast from him*. And the[n] was afterward joyned againe in Mariage with Man, that by *Nuptiall coniunction* becomming *one flesh* with him, she might be as a *limbe restored* now and *fastned* againe *to him*.' This positive coming together in marriage of things previously separated in creation—a re-creation—is contrasted against the '*Woman* that beareth the *Name*, and standeth in the *roome of a Wife*, but doth not the *office* and *dutie* of *a Wife*' who is compared to '*an eye of glasse*, or a *silver nose*, or a *an ivorie tooth*, or *an iron hand*, or *a woodden leg*, that... beareth the *Name* of *a limbe* or *a member*, but is not truly or properly any *part* of that *bodie* whereunto it is fastned'. As a useless appendage that does not fulfil her role, 'she may therefore be compared rather to... a *wolfe*, or *a cancer*, that consumeth the flesh, wasteth the vitall parts, and eateth even to the verie heart', and it is only in this sense that she may be considered a part of her husband, parasitic like gangrene. Weaving positive and negative images of the relationship between appendages and bodies together, Gataker creates a discursive field within which the broader concept of connection can be explored.[44] The rhetorical use of body parts, it has been argued, offers 'a remarkable density of implication'—they concentrate the attention of the reader and draw meaning into themselves, broadening thought processes, rather than narrowing them. Common to all in a more fundamental sense than the yoke, the body is similarly, but more richly, susceptible to emblematization in the mind's eye. A fundamentally 'lively' image, its meanings are reiterated with the subject's every movement. The particular cluster of ideas writers extend in this context are those around different kinds of joining: the appendages' 'status as "part" implies by definition a relation'.[45] Gataker's use of a wide range of linked images offers a rhetorical model of this exact process of linking, echoing in his prose style the relationships between parts and wholes which his images explore.

When presented negatively, however, these images of body parts aim to normalize approved behaviour by presenting its comically awkward and/or disgustingly arresting opposite. Cleaver offers the whole and 'perfect bodie', achieved when one marriage partner endeavours 'to supplie the others wants... they both helping and doing their

---

[44] Gataker, *Two marriage sermons*, 9–10. Work on the body has suggested that such images of parts and wholes were central to understanding social systems, and for mediating between sacred and secular meanings. David Hillman and Carla Mazzio argue that 'the spatially imagined body was perhaps the most common vehicle for the making of social and cosmic metaphors in early modern Europe' and that 'The relations between bodily and cognitive systems of organization are in many ways most powerfully encoded by the symbolics of any given part'; David Hillman and Carla Mazzio, eds., *The Body in Parts: Fantasies of Corporeality in Early Modern Europe* (New York and London: Routledge, 1997), xiii, xii.

[45] Hillman and Mazzio, eds., *Body in Parts*, xii, xv.

best together' against which the contorted and distinctly un-classical body of the domestically incompetent is imagined. Whately states, 'That house is a misshapen house, and (if we may use that terme) a cramp-shouldered, or hutch-backe house', using the rhetorical weight of the absurdity of the image as a way of changing behaviour through the analogy it sets up with ridiculous domestic actions. Gouge uses the language of monstrosity:

> Goe therefore, O wives, unto the schoole of nature, looke upon the outward parts and members of your bodies. Doe they desire to be above the head? are they loth to be subject unto the head? Let your soule then learne of your body. Were it not monstrous for the *side* to be advanced above the *head*? If the body should not be subject to the head, would not destruction follow upon head, body, and all the parts thereof?

Whately is doing a similar thing when he presents the idea that 'the head is not always actually stooping unto the foote: for then the body would grow crooked and ill shapen', when the husband is 'putting his hand to every little matter'.[46] These images mock behaviour, inducing ridicule by giving it a harsh and judgemental visual form. They offer a distorted mirror which reflects back at the reader a monstrous image, as opposed to the likeness of their public form on which their status is based. In doing so, they offer a degrading mockery, a rhetorical jeering which is akin to *charivari*, to the rough derision through which early modern communities policed themselves.[47]

Images of medicinal remedies and surgical procedures, obviously closely linked to ideas of the healthy, as opposed to the ailing body, share some of these effects. Like domestic images, some of them are also intended to have the effect of making spiritual matters take on the urgency and generate the common-sense response of practical ones. 'Wouldest thou suffer thine husband to poison himself', Whately asks, 'for feare of enduring his anger, if thou shouldest snatch the poison out of his hand?' Clearly, the answer here is 'no', and thinking about one's behaviour in terms of an immediate effect on the body is similarly instructive: 'Who ever kept a bitter thing for any other purpose, than to make a medicine? and is not that a bad husband, that is good for little, but to be his wives purgation?... If he be gaule and aloes in her mouth, is it any wonder, though she strive to spit him out?' But the lowness of being spat out of the mouth of one's wife again mocks unsuitable behaviour, offering an image which challenges the pretensions of a husband whose status must be maintained by a series of carefully controlled gestures.

---

[46] Cleaver, *A godlie forme*, 231; Whately, *Bride-Bush*, 98, 148b; Gouge, *Domesticall Duties*, 335.

[47] This suggests the consonances between the manuals' focus on domestic behaviour and the wider range of writing on conduct in the period. It demonstrates how they might have been seen to engage with the developing concepts of civility in manners explored in Anna Bryson's work, where she identifies 'the social superiority of the "civil" gentleman whose self-control and capacity to navigate "civil society" elevated him above the brutish multitude'. Anna Bryson, *From Courtesy to Civility* (Oxford: Clarendon Press, 1998), 278.

In addition, images which aim to encourage private chastisement employ the boundaries of domestic modesty on which notions of potential shaming play. Whately offers a rather shocking figure of display which sets a householder up as a kind of cheap entertainment: 'Many a man would be willing to open his griefe to a Physician, and to have a Chirurgion see his sore, which yet would be loath to have it opened at the market place, and shewed to all his neighbours.'[48] The household emerges from such opposing images of restorative privacy and undignified exposure as the perfect location for censure—it is within doors that familial issues should be worked out—and the images themselves simultaneously foreground and create a particular kind of domestic context within which they are to be consumed.

So many of the images—from husbandry, animal and household practice—are about the joining of individuals within the household. But there are also, in the context of the bond between husband and wife, more explicit considerations of the way human relationships work. Gouge goes back to first principles and examines the Biblical language very closely: 'To set forth the firmnesse of the mariage bond he [St Paul in Ephesians 5] addeth this Emphaticall phrase, *shall be joyned*, (or as the word properly, according to the naturall notation thereof signifieth, *shall be glued*) to his wife.' This gluing he expounds as follows:

> Things well glued together are as fast, firme, and close as if they were one intire peece. Yea we observe by experience that a table will oft times cleave in the whole wood, before it will part asunder where it is glued: so as an husband ought to be as firme to his wife as to himselfe: and she to him.

All writers address the topic: even the metaphorically sparse Perkins gives the parenthetical explanation that man must '*cleave unto his wife*, (as two boords are joyned together with glue)'. Gataker states that 'It is easier glewing againe of boards together, that have beene unglewed, than healing up the flesh that is gashed and divided: and the reason is, because there was but an artificiall connexion before in the one, there was a naturall conjunction in the other', and in doing so, he links these images to those of the body.[49] But far from sticking to the translation of joining as gluing, the authors also offer figures of knitting, of cementing, of knotting, of plastering, of soldering, and of joining, in the technical sense of the carpenter's trade. Read *en masse* like this, they provide a discursive field within which relationships are explored in various fully material terms—the weight of worldly joinings brought to bear for the common-sense light they shed on this shadier area of human affairs.

Seeing the whole range of images employed on the topic in these manuals helps us to understand how highly variety was valued in the effort to explore practice in relation to biblical models of behaviour. Some authors offer such a process in microcosm: runs of different images in the service of the same explanation: 'Wherefore now, as thou lookest, that every other thing should be fit to receive the things, that thou wouldst put into them,

---

[48] Whately, *Bride-Bush*, 65, 79, 102.
[49] Gouge, *Domesticall Duties*, 111–12; Perkins, *Christian oeconomie*, 10; Gataker, *Two marriage sermons*, 4.

the vessel the liquor, the ground the seede, the chest the clothes, the house the guest, and other like, so take care that thy wives heart be fit to entertaine thy directions...' says Whately; 'as theeves steale in when the house is emptie; like a Turtle, which hath lost his mate, like one legge when the other is cut off, like one wing when the other is clipt, so had the man been if the woman had not been joyned to him' Smith explains.[50] Both men aim to give their reader the greatest possible chance of understanding the point by analogy, in the process flashing a bizarre set of images in their mind's eye like an eclectic prose equivalent of an early moving picture.

And these different rhetorical joinings of concepts and images show how complexly people might think about domestic life through reading this kind of prose, and how they were being encouraged to make connections between practice and theory, between everyday life and theological engagement. They imbue the everyday with weight and moment as they make these connections. The onslaught of diverse comparisons, which insists that the reader imagine various images and scenarios either in quick succession, as in the examples above, or within a wide discursive field of diverse similes set up across the text as a whole, can seem like a prosaic chaos in which meaning becomes elusive. But it is the focus on joinings, on interconnectedness and relationality, which brings ideas, images, and people together under the umbrella of the text as a whole. The strict arrangement of the manuals contains the variety of their images, just as the structures of house and family enclose and control human behaviour. Gouge's choice of images of joining involves the contrast between two textile processes, tailoring and knitting. Exploring the nearness of coming 'into one flesh' he argues: 'This is somewhat more then to be *of Christs flesh*. That shewes we are as it were cut out of Christ: this shewes that we are againe knit to him.'[51] The image shows a deeply material way of imagining the connection between the individual and their God, one rooted in familiarity with craft skills on the one hand and generated by biblical language on the other, the whole giving a shape to the consonance between the everyday and the spiritual which is at once quotidian and miraculous. It offers suggestions about the way the texts might have operated within an early modern house, which was itself a repository for a family's knitted, cemented, knotted, plastered, soldered, and joined objects.

Further Reading

Davies, Kathleen M. 'Continuity and Change in Literary Advice on Marriage', in R. B. Outhwaite, ed., *Marriage and Society* (London: Europa, 1981), 58–80.
Glaisyer, Natasha, and Sara Pennell, eds. *Didactic Literature in England, 1500–1800: Expertise Constructed* (Aldershot: Ashgate, 2003).
Hamling, Tara. *Decorating the 'Godly' Household* (New Haven: Yale University Press, 2010).
Hunter, Lynette. 'Books for Daily Life: Household, Husbandry, Behaviour', in John Barnard and D. F. McKenzie, eds., *The Cambridge History of the Book in Britain, Volume IV, 1557–1695* (Cambridge: Cambridge University Press, 2002), 514–32.

---

[50] Whately, *Bride-Bush*, 143; Smith, *Preparative*, 19.   [51] Gouge, *Domesticall Duties*, 123.

Moore, Helen. 'Of Marriage, Morals and Civility', in Jennifer Richards, ed., *Early Modern Civil Discourses* (Basingstoke: Palgrave Macmillan, 2003), 35–50.

Orlin, Lena Cowen. *Private Matters and Public Culture in Post-Reformation England* (Ithaca: Cornell University Press, 1994).

Richardson, Catherine. *Domestic Life and Domestic Tragedy in Early Modern England: The Material Life of the Household* (Manchester: Manchester University Press, 2006).

Wall, Wendy. 'Literacy and the Domestic Arts', *Huntington Library Quarterly*, 73.3 (2010): 383–412.

—— *Staging Domesticity: Household Work and English Identity in Early Modern Drama* (Cambridge: Cambridge University Press, 2002).

PART V
RELIGIOUS PROSE

CHAPTER 30

IMMETHODICAL, INCOHERENT, UNADORNED: STYLE AND THE EARLY MODERN BIBLE

KEVIN KILLEEN

Theophilus Wodenote, writing what he terms 'a sequestered divine his aphorisms' in 1654, extols in rhapsodic terms both the pith of biblical idiom and its adaptability as a language of analysis:

> How ragged are mens expressions? How poor the pithiness of their discourses? In sight of the sacred Scriptures, their most accomplished Treatises are not so much as the light of a candle to the glorious brightness of the Sun in his chiefest splendour: In Gods book every particle hath his poise, every tittle is useful; every syllable is sententious; every word is wonderful.[1]

The biblical Word attracted a degree of astonishment that it penetrated so accurately, so astutely through time to refract the present. Its diamond edge and ability to cut to the quick did not necessarily indicate, however, an unalloyed appreciation of its eloquence. The English Bible was not deemed a work of consummate style. Indeed, comment was often made on the rough edges of the text, the discordance between books, its difficulty and internal contradictions, and, according to seventeenth-century standards, its stylistic crudity: rather than a polished gem, it was a whetstone for its readers. Robert Boyle sums up the complaints: 'For some of them are pleased to say that Book is too obscure, others, that 'tis immethodical, others, that it is contradictory to it self, others, that the neighbouring parts of it are incoherent, others, that 'tis unadorned, others, that it is flat and unaffecting, others, that it abounds with things that are either trivial or impertinent,

---

[1] Theophilus Wodenote, *Eremicus theologus, or, A sequestred divine his aphorisms* (1654), 9–10.

and also with useless Repetitions.'² Where subsequent centuries have found in the Bible, or at least the 1611 Authorized Version (Fig. 30.1), the quintessence of English prose, its contemporaries were more ambivalent, and a certain embarrassment about the quality of writing in the scriptures is evident throughout the era.

Thomas Wilson, writing one of the numerous aids to biblical reading that poured from the early modern press, cautions: 'We may not be offended with the simplicity and plainness of stile and matter, which wee find in scripture.'³ Other texts similarly worry over or seek to mitigate the plainness: 'although we find not in sacred scriptures the idle or delicate itch of Words, that external sweetness or allurement', says Benjamn Keach, we find instead 'a Grave and Masculine Eloquence'. Such readers explained that the Bible needed to be accommodated to the varying capacities of both its original and modern-day audience: 'Because the multitude of readers is promiscuous, it was needful that it should be understood by all.'⁴ The unfortunately comprehensive remit of the Bible—needing to descend to the meanest capacities—had, it was plain, obliged the Holy Spirit to compromise stylistically, to resist the Ciceronian, Attic, or Asiatic eloquence and indeed the sophistication of thought it might otherwise have tended to. Among the many who voiced this as an unfortunate and primal instance of dumbing down, James Fergusson in 1659 notes of the penmen of scriptures that, perhaps with some reluctance, they 'would affect great plainnesse of speech, dimitting themselves, so far as is possible, unto the capacity of the meanest'.⁵ John Wilson, some years after, similarly concludes, 'they are Written for all sorts and ranks of Men to make use of... therefore they are for the most part drawn in a vulgar condescending style'.⁶ In part, this is the product of the Bible's own rough-hewn theatrics, when, for instance, 'the Lord sayd to Hosea, Goe, take unto thee a wife of whoredomes and children of whoredoms: for the land hath committed great whoredom, departing from the Lord'. The God who enjoins his prophet to marry a prostitute and threatens then to strip naked and thrash Israel is not the God of delicate sensibility, nor was the prosody that rendered these warnings, with its crudity and repetitious vigour, deemed decorous or intrinsically literary to early modern tastes.⁷

Even amongst those who thought the Bible perfectly pitched to its task, few saw that task as involving an aesthetic experience. Edward Lane, a colonel in the New Model Army, thought that the political subject matter of the text precluded civility as unsuitable to God's exasperation with the recalcitrance of the nation, that this was a prose and theatre of God's Word, which, by any standards of decorum, demanded rigour and roughness. He noted in 1654 how the prophets of the Bible were not only conspicuously

---

² Robert Boyle, *Considerations touching the Style of the Holy Scriptures* (1661), in Michael Hunter and Edward B. Davis, eds., *The Works of Robert Boyle*, 14 vols. (London: Pickering & Chatto, 2000), vol. 2, 394.

³ Thomas Wilson, *Theological Rules, To Guide Us in Understanding and Practice of Holy Scripture* (1625), 6.

⁴ Benjamin Keach and Thomas Delaune, *Tropologica: A Key to Open Scripture-Metaphors* (1682), sig. A2ᵛ, citing the stylistic authority of Matthias Flacius Illyricus, *Clavis Scripurae Sacrae* (1562).

⁵ James Fergusson, *A brief exposition of the Epistles of Paul to the Galatians and Ephesians* (1659), 182.

⁶ John Wilson, *The Scriptures genuine interpreter asserted* (1678), 183–4.

⁷ Hosea 1:2.

FIGURE 30.1 *King James Bible* (1611), title page

theatrical, but necessarily disrespectful in forcing their attentions upon a polity who would rather not listen:

> An Isaiah must go naked, an Ezekiel must pourtray a city on a tyle, raise forts against it, lay siege to it, lie on his side and eat dung; a Hosea must take a common harlot to wife; an Amos must be call'd from among the herds-men, gathering sycamore-fruit: others much be taken from their Publicans seat (in the Custom-house) and fishing trade. And the Truth must be delivered in a dark uncouth maner.[8]

The Bible's uncouth truth, so to speak, its blunt manner and exposure of social hypocrisy, was a touchstone for its more radical deployment: 'For if there come unto your assembly', as the Epistle of James has it, 'a man with a gold ring in goodly apparel and there come in also a poore man, in vile raiment, and ye have respect to him that weareth the gay clothing, and say unto him, sit thou here in a good place and say to the poore, stand thou there', then, as James goes on bluntly, 'if ye have respect to persons, ye commit sinne'.[9] The prose that bore such stark and unadorned matter was unlikely to receive much attention on the grounds of its parallelism and syncresis—indeed, the reader doing so might be missing the point, though we could note also that frankness was itself a literary trope. David Colclough, writing on the trope of *parrhesia*—blunt outspokenness—in biblical rhetoric, notes the early modern admiration of bold style against the mincing subterfuges of compromised everyday speech, taking Jesus's as a rhetorical exemplar of the fearless, if inelegant, Word.[10]

This essay will explore both the embarrassment at the text that runs through the era and the countervailing argument that the Bible did indeed measure up a set of responses, the bulk of which appeared in the Restoration period, which attempted to laud a biblical aesthetic and to characterize it in terms of the sublime or majestic vehemence. However, noting such aesthetic responses, the many instances in which the Bible was acclaimed or carped at, risks at least a kind of anachronism. The Bible was less often assessed for its style than for its efficacy, its personal and political turning of men and women to God's providential purposes. While the pen-men of scripture, from its poets to its gruff prophets, might be more or less able to turn a phrase neatly, and while in ineffable manner they might be the prophetic channel for the Holy Spirit, they remained human and their texts remained ephemeral, material, and subject to decay and tampering. Theophilus Wodenote, quoted earlier, might enthuse how 'In Gods book every particle hath his poise'; however, the opposite of finding the Bible to be the beautiful and replete Word of God was not for everybody an aesthetic ranking of the scriptures in relation to the behemoths of classical style. Rather, to see the human flaws in the text, its breakages in

---

[8] Edward Lane, *An image of our reforming times: or, Jehu in his proper colours* (1654), sig. A4^r.
[9] Epistle of James, 2:2–3, 2:9, referred to regularly enough in comment on judicial equity, for example, Enoch Grey, *Vox coeli, containing maxims of pious policy* (1649), 15; Gerard Winstanley, *A letter to the Lord Fairfax* (1649), 12.
[10] David Colclough, *Freedom of Speech in Early Stuart England* (Cambridge: Cambridge University Press, 2005), 77–119. See, for example, John Prideaux, *Sacred eloquence: or, the art of rhetorick, as it is layd down in Scripture* (1659) for one of the many systemic biblical rhetorics, in which an arsenal of tropes are laid out with biblical examples.

transmission, and its dependence on the meagre resources of human language, led in a curious, but long-running, tradition to an almost outright anti-biblicism, in which the reader was required to filter the prose away, to be left with its wordless core. This is not, by any means, a step towards philosophical scepticism and secularism, though it was usually temperamentally sceptical and often anticlerical. On the contrary, it constituted one of major strands of radical Protestant thought on the nature of grace and spirit. To ask whether the style of the Bible was reckoned fine in the seventeenth century, in the way it so evidently was in the eighteenth and nineteenth centuries, is to interpose an aesthetic question which, while no doubt present, was not in the period divorced from the issue of how prose worked the soul up to the state of grace it was seen to promise. Thus, the latter half, of the essay, the antiphon to the discussion of biblical prose presented in the first half, is a series of texts that seek to make the language of the Bible fade to transparency. This, it seems to me, is an important and neglected aspect of the subject of biblical prose that has tended to see its major vectors in the discussion of 'influence' of the Bible (in subsequent centuries) and assessment of the often told story of the English translation.[11] These two issues—influence and translation—demand prefatory attention, but neither is quite the central matter they have seemed to be.

There is much early modern prose—from the luxurious and learned to the relatively plain—that incorporates biblical phrasing into its fibre. The half-reference and the implied citation were, in an era that knew its Bible so thoroughly, a deeply rooted verbal habit. However, the flow and prosody of early modern literature, if we can generalize such a thing, bears surprisingly little resemblance to any biblical style. Sermon literature, for example, a field that produced some of the most brilliant prose of the era, owed many stylistic debts—to classical oratorical traditions, to Ramist habits of explication, and to traditions of moral exhortation—but it rarely aims to mimic the measure and rhythms of scriptural prose. Characterized in rhetorical terms, most notably by Debora Shuger, the English sermon, florid and ornate, lofty or plain, bore only a peripheral resemblance to its source material.[12] Moreover, when writers produced 'defences' of biblical style—against the usually unspecific and whispered attacks on its eloquence—they tended to focus on its rich use of tropes and figures. But this is hardly what we mean by prosody, the texture and feel of a piece of writing, which can only be hinted at by an analysis of rhetorical ornament: early modern humanist habits of prose do not, in general, absorb the rhythms or copy the grain of the biblical.

---

[11] The influence of the Bible receives entertaining treatment in the impressively jaundiced view of C. S. Lewis, *The Literary Impact of the Authorised Version* (London: Athlone Press, 1950); a thorough treatment of the Bible as literature is David Norton, *A History of the Bible as Literature*, 2 vols. (Cambridge: Cambridge University Press, 1993); see too Hannibal Hamlin and Norman W. Jones, eds., *The King James Bible after Four Hundred Years: Literary, Linguistic, and Cultural Influences* (Cambridge: Cambridge University Press, 2011); and Harold Boom, *The Shadow of a Great Rock: A Literary Appreciation of the King James Bible* (New Haven: Yale University Press, 2011).

[12] Debora Shuger, *Sacred Rhetoric: The Christian Grand Style in the English Renaissance* (Princeton: Princeton University Press, 1986); see also Peter McCullough, Hugh Adlington, and Emma Rhatigan, eds., *The Oxford Handbook of the Early Modern Sermon* (Oxford: Oxford University Press, 2011).

Neither is the issue of translation a defining one in ascertaining the reception of biblical prose. While translation is of course important in other respects—battles raged over fidelity to and nuance of meaning, over the way doctrine was rendered, or how custom and culture might be seen as the context for action—comment is not frequently made on the scriptures being stylistically superior in the original. The Bible, as much in Hebrew or Greek as in its English rendering, was seen as an unprepossessing document and the English Bible was by no means thought of as stylistically detached from its origins. The desideratum that the Bible be read in the original tongues did not mean that it was considered any more elegant in those languages, even if it was closer to the primal Word. Complaints over translations tended to centre on theological and ecclesiastical, rather than aesthetic issues. And while a barbarous Latin, or Anglicization of Latin, might irk and rouse the inner pedant in the most mild-mannered humanist, in relation to the Bible, fidelity to the text, rather than aesthetics, was always the governing principle of translation. Accurate and scholarly rendering of phrase, rather than eloquence, was the chief criterion in the translation of the Bible.[13]

A further caveat to any discussion of biblical style is that there is, in fact, no such thing, there being no single biblical language, and the Bible being a hotchpotch of books. But early modern responses—while recognizing this—did have a sense of there being a typical Hebrew prose metre, which was identifiable still in translation. Francis Roberts, whose *Clavis Bibliorum* (1648) comments on and compares the styles of various biblical books, considers Luke as the most scholarly of the gospel writers: 'By the very stile, which seems notably to indigitate Luke unto us, partly it being compleat and polished Greek becomming Luke an accurate Grecian.' Nevertheless, there was, in Roberts's view, a definite seepage of Hebrew style into Luke's narrative: 'it being replenished with Hebraismes, suitable to Luke's native Genius, being by country a Syrian of Antioch, (the Syrian language being one of the Hebrew dialects)'.[14] Robert Boyle notes similarly, 'though the New Testament be not written in Hebrew, yet its Writers being Hebrews, have chiefly conform'd themselves to the Style of the Translators of the Old Testament'.[15] This sense of a text that was both generically diverse and yet thematically unified is pervasive and the stylistic dynamics of the Hebraic idiom were deemed to be still at work when it came to the English reading experience. Naomi Tadmor has noted Tyndale's working on the supposition that the Hebraic idiom transposed neatly into English and how English developed, in a complex reciprocity with its understanding of scriptural terms, over the seventeenth century.[16]

---

[13] Alister McGrath, *In the Beginning: The Story of the King James Bible* (London: Hodder & Stoughton, 2001), 254–6; Gordon Campbell, *Bible: The Story of the King James Version, 1611–2011* (Oxford: Oxford University Press, 2010), 79–81.

[14] Francis Roberts, *Clavis Bibliorum, The key of the Bible, unlocking the richest treasury of the Holy Scriptures* (1648), 170.

[15] Boyle, *Style of the Holy Scriptures*, 450.

[16] Naomi Tadmor, *The Social Universe of the English Bible: Scripture, Society and Culture in Early Modern England* (Cambridge: Cambridge University Press, 2010). Much has been written on the translation of the Bible. See, for instance, David Daniell, *The Bible in English* (New Haven: Yale

30.1 'FETCH'D FROM THE FISHERY AND THE SHEEPFOLD'

The existence of the Bible in English, for all that it was the rallying cry of the Reformation, remained something of a sop to the unlearned. Nathaniel Ingelo in 1658 offered a somewhat backhanded comment on the English scriptures, arguing that as a prince is content to engage in diplomacy that must travel via interpreters, so those short of the requisite Hebrew and Aramaic should be satisfied that they do in fact receive 'the same mind of God' as the educated:

> And herein God shewed his care of the unlearned, who are the greater part of the world; for though they cannot read the Originall; yet having a Translation, which, in that it is a Translation, agrees with the Original, they receive the same mind of God that the Learned do. Why should any man be unsatisfied with this way of delivery, whereas Princes and States, in matters which they esteem the greatest, receive the Proposals of Ambassadours by an Interpreter?[17]

This is not an entirely ringing endorsement of the ability of the vernacular to act as conduit of the Word of God, but it is typical of the ambivalence about the scriptures, a text that indulged such dubious genres as parables, and whose status in classical rhetoric was particularly low, bordering on the Aesopian and childish. It was also, however, the form in which Jesus frequently spoke to his disciples, to the not infrequent embarrassment of expositors. Ingelo ventures the idea in 1658 that plainness in the Bible is itself a veil, a stylistic distraction, though he concedes that attempts to discover the complex pith were not always successful: 'many that pretended to be great enquirers into profound mysteries, could not perceive any wisdome in them [parables]...nor discern truth, unlesse it were hid a little more under Philosophical shadowes'.[18] John Lightfoot explains that this was a Jewish cultural matter, evident (if not entirely excusable, aesthetically speaking) across their sacred, profane, and exegetical writings: 'Christs speaking of

---

University Press, 2003); Gerald Hammond, *The Making of the English Bible* (Manchester: Carcanet Press, 1988); Gerald Bray, *Translating the Bible: From William Tyndale to King James* (London: Latimer Trust, 2010); S. L. Greenslade, 'English Versions of the Bible, 1525–1611', in Stephen Greenslade, ed., *The Cambridge History of the Bible*, vol. 3 (Cambridge: Cambridge University Press, 1963); Richard Griffiths, ed., *The Bible in the Renaissance: Essays on Biblical Commentary and Translation in the Fifteenth and Sixteenth Centuries* (Aldershot: Ashgate, 2001); Lynne Long, *Translating the Bible: From the 7th to the 17th Century* (Aldershot: Ashgate, 2001); other important work, though the list is far from exhaustive, includes David S. Katz, *God's Last Words: Reading the English Bible from the Reformation to Fundamentalism* (New Haven: Yale University Press, 2004); Lori Anne Ferrell, *The Bible and the People* (New Haven: Yale University Press, 2009); James Simpson, *Burning to Read: English Fundamentalism and Its Reformation Opponents* (Cambridge, MA: Harvard University Press, 2007); David Norton, *A Textual History of the King James Bible* (Cambridge: Cambridge University Press, 2005).

[17] Nathaniel Ingelo, *The perfection, authority, and credibility of the Holy Scriptures* (1658), 69–70.
[18] Ingelo, *Perfection...of the Holy Scriptures* (1658), 2.

Parables, which he doth so exceeding much through the Gospel, was according to the stile and manner of that Nation, which were exceedingly accustomed to this manner of Rhetorick. The Talmuds are abundantly full of this kinde of oratory, and so are generally all their ancient writers.'[19]

The Bible's multi-generic composition served, usefully enough, as a way of excusing and mitigating the parts deemed unsophisticated. Indeed, it allowed them to play their part in the spiritual and aesthetic crescendos of the encyclopaedic whole. However, praise of scriptural variety often sought to deny that it was prompted by any such concerns. John Barton's *The Art of Rhetorick* (1634), 'fitted to the capacities of such as have had a smatch of learning', aims to laud the rhetorical breadth of the Bible, while insisting it barely deigns to notice such matters. The Bible must be seen as 'altogether eschewing, and utterly condemning the impertinent use of frothie criticismes', but was nevertheless written 'in beautifull varietie, majesticall style, and gracefull order, infinitely and incomparably transcend[ing] the most pithie and pleasing strains of humane Eloquence'.[20] In such accounts, the encyclopaedic range of the Bible was part of its quality, and the stylistic mish-mash became, in itself, an aspect of scriptural eloquence. The prose of the Old Testament prophets may have little in common with the narrative impulses and prosody of the New. Yet, however much their styles differ, there was a presumption that they formed a coherent whole, a hermeneutic unity, which created in its wake a sense of at least incipient stylistic integrity. Jeremy Taylor, in his *Antiquitates christianae*, argues that the dictating spirit conceived a conscious variation in prosody to embody the shift by which the Old Testament was enfolded into the new: 'with a new style, with a quill taken from the wings of the holy Dove; the Spirit of God was to be the great Engraver and the Scribe of the New Covenant'.[21]

Characterizing the styles of individual books served to explain, in part, their purpose and utility. Francis Roberts in 1648 notes of Revelation that its idiom, though obscure, is by its sheer stylistic resonance able to pierce through even the most resolute ambivalence or stupidity: 'The stile is stately and sublime, and may wonderfully take the highest notion; The expressions quick, piercing and patheticall, and may pleasingly penetrate the dullest affection.'[22] Indeed, this capacity to go where other prose could not reach was the most characteristic defence of the scriptural aesthetic, that its adoption of rough and smooth, plain and majestic, served purposes of spiritual alchemy difficult to characterize, but evident in effect and, moreover, efficacious across a span of audience; 'Whether we read David, Isaiah, or others whose stile is more sweet, pleasant and rhetorical', explains Edward Leigh in 1654 'or Amos, Zachary and Jeremiah, whose stile is more rude, every where the Majesty of the Spirit is apparent'.[23]

---

[19] John Lightfoot, *The harmony, chronicle and order of the New Testament* (1655), 31.
[20] John Barton, *The art of rhetorick concisely and compleatly handled exemplified out of holy writ* (1634), sig. A3ʳ.
[21] Jeremy Taylor, *Antiquitates christianae* (1675), Xiv.
[22] Roberts, *Clavis Bibliorum*, 312.
[23] Edward Leigh, *A systeme or body of divinity consisting of ten books* (1654), 9.

There was general agreement that the different books of the Bible worked on different kinds of intellect. John Williams, in a sermon preached late in the seventeenth century, sums up a set of class-conscious distinctions that existed widely around the rude and unlearned status of many biblical writers: 'But now though all the Parts of Scripture are not equally alike, but like the Inspired Writers themselves, of whom some were bred up in the Nurseries of Learning, and others fetch'd from the Fishery and the Sheepfold; yet are they all plain in the same essential Doctrine, and in which the Salvation of Mankind is concerned.'[24] The social origins of the pen-men of scripture run deep in their assessment of and rumbling embarrassment at the nature of biblical rhetoric, with the proviso that the scriptures, seen in the round, approach the encyclopaedic, and what they lack in finesse, they make up for in the universality of their design:

> He makes use of the Poetical Vein in David, the Oratory of an Isaiah, the Rusticity of an Amos, the Elegancy of a Luke, the Plainness of a Peter, the Profoundness of a Paul, to serve the common Design of instructing Mankind in the knowledge of God, and their Duty to him, without that Artificial Method which the Learned Part of the World expect to find, and think fit to observe.[25]

This deeply embedded presumption, that the Bible was coarse and troublingly plebeian, might also prompt a more bullish insistence that its rhetoric was unparalleled. Henry Lukin in 1669 argues that, in Isaiah at least, the nature of scriptural rhetoric trumps its classical correlates: 'although there is nothing Pedantick in it, there is such a mixture of loftiness and gravity...that the flower and master-piece of Grecian Oratory is not to be compared with Eloquence of the Prophet Isaiah'.[26] James Ussher insists it is written with 'great simplicity of words, and plainnesse and easinesse of style, which neverthelesse more affected the hearts of the hearers, then all the painted eloquence and lofty style of Rhetoricians and Oratours'.[27] Annotating the 'poetic' books—Job, Psalms, Proverbs, Ecclesiastes, and the Song of Solomon—Arthur Jackson notes their inclination to mystery and complexity, a style that is intrinsically enwrought and filigree: 'the stile and expressions of these Poeticall Books are farre more dark and difficult, and fuller of many knotty intricacies'.[28]

Such analysis often ascribed to the scriptures a set of qualities around its splendour, majesty, and, in particular, its sublimity, that it was a writing suited to the enormity of its subject matter, its sweep, and all-encompassing encyclopaedism of time, government, and spirit. The primary point of reference in such defences was Dionysius Longinus, the first-century Greek theorist of the sublime, who made passing reference to the 'law-giver

---

[24] John Williams, *The divine authority of the scriptures a sermon preached at St. Martins in the Fields, September 2. 1695* (1696), 29.

[25] Williams, *The divine authority of the scriptures*, 26.

[26] Henry Lukin, *An introduction to the Holy Scripture* (1669), 9.

[27] James Ussher, *A body of divinitie, or, The summe and substance of Christian religion catechistically propounded* (1645), 14, 10.

[28] Arthur Jackson, *Annotations upon the five books immediately following the historicall part of the Old Testament* (1658), sig. A2[v–r].

of the Jews', Moses, as supposed author of the Pentateuch, whose account of the creation in Genesis was set in admiring contrast to the inadequacies of Homer and Hesiod.[29] Sublimity works for Longinus by a rhetoric that does not so much persuade, as transport its audience by its emotional heft, an explanation that might easily be wrought to how the Bible worked its spiritual effects on readers, less by logic than by an irresistible magnetism. A related and much-quoted classical salve to the inferiority complex of a culture that felt itself bound more closely to the biblical, though more admiring of the Greek and Roman legacy, was Amelius the Platonist, a contributor to a third-century Neoplatonic revival around Plotinus, who attributed the 'Wisdom of a Philosopher' to St John, while still describing him as a Barbarian.[30]

Embarrassment with biblical style crescendos in the Restoration period, not coincidentally alongside the various 'Augustinian' redefinitions of taste that the period underwent. One of the most formative and extensive biblical defences did not, however, come from a dedicated literary or biblical theorist, but rather, from the natural philosopher Robert Boyle, whose *Some Considerations touching the Style of the Holy Scriptures* (1661) was both admired and influential.[31] Boyle addresses a set of 'cavillers', whom he describes as 'divers witty men who freely acknowledge the Authority of the Scripture [but] take exceptions at its Style ... giving men injurious and irreverent thoughts of it'.[32] While their complaints seemed to have floated widely in the intellectual and aesthetic aether, these cavillers have anonymity as almost a defining trait and (like the elusive early modern atheist) tended to make it into print only in refutation form. Boyle takes it upon himself to collect and dismiss a range of such criticisms, noting, for example, objections to the triviality of the Bible, exemplified in Jesus's habit of answering different questions from those he was asked. Such intriguing complaints, be they Boyle's own internal dialogue or part of some more ill-defined conversation, receive an answer, but rarely any attribution: 'His oratory took a shorter Way than Ours can follow it in', his parables designed to pass straight into hearers' hearts, bypassing the need for reasoned dialogue.[33]

Among his defence strategies, Boyle throws rich metaphors back at the cavillers and 'querulous readers', noting, for example, that one 'should remember that our Saviour

---

[29] Longinus, *Peri hypsous, or Dionysius Longinus of the height of eloquence. Rendred out of the originall by John Hall* (1652), XVII. See, for example, Meric Casaubon, *A treatise concerning enthusiasme* (1655), 142.

[30] William Cave, *Antiquitates apostolicae* (1676), 160; Williams, *The divine authority of the scriptures*, 29; Richard Burthogge, *Causa dei, or, An apology for God* (1675), 260; Ralph Cudworth, *The true intellectual system of the Universe* (1678), 305–6; Henry Hammond, *A paraphrase and annotations* (1659), 187; Nathaniel Hardy, *The first general epistle of St. John* (1656), 37. Knowledge about Amelius came into widespread circulation largely though Augustine, *Of the Citie of God, with the learned comments of Jo. Lod. Vives, trans J.H.* (1610), 319.

[31] On the impulses underlying discussion of biblical style, in particular, in Robert Boyle's writing, see Robert Markley, *Fallen Languages: Crises of Representation in Newtonian England, 1660–1740* (Princeton: Princeton University Press, 1993), 34–62; see also Roger Pooley, *English Prose of the Seventeenth Century, 1590–1700* (London: Longman, 1992), 93–102.

[32] Boyle, *Considerations*, 393. This is cited and explored by, for example, Thomas Pierce, *A decad of caveats to the people of England* (1679), 380.

[33] Boyle, *Considerations*, 425.

could successfully imploy even clay and spittle to illuminate blind eyes', in which analogy, the clay and spittle of biblical style, might not be gentile medicine, but nevertheless work upon the congenital human blindness.[34] Answering the objection that the Bible was a work exhibiting a 'disjoynted Method'—that it was, generically, rhetorically, or methodologically incoherent—Boyle answers with an analogy of a treasure banked in small coins, not being worth less, for being in such unsorted currency: 'sure we should Judge that Man a very Captious Creature, that should take Exceptions at a Profer'd sum, onely because the Half Crowns, Shillings and Six pences, were not sorted in Distinct Heaps, but huddled into One'.[35] Such a reply no doubt comes very close to conceding the disjointedness it seeks to defend against, and such concessions are very much a part of the strategy he adopts.

Addressing the stylistic deficit from another angle, Boyle notes that large portions of scripture have quite functional purposes, such as the delivery of the law, and that clarity at such moments demands that the work abstain from cloudiness and rhetorical dressing:

> It will not be thought necessary that such parts of Scripture should be eloquently written, that the Supreme Legislator of the World, who reckons the greatest Kings amongst his Subjects, should in giving Lawes tye himself to those of Rhetoric, the scrupulous observation of which would much derogate from those two qualities so considerable in Lawes, Clearness and Majesty.[36]

There is in such a response exasperation that critics of the text would task God with more ornament. Boyle goes on to note that in our quotidian reading of 'human' works with similarly particularized functions—not only the law, but chemistry too—we do not ask for such embellishment:

> How many of us can dwell on Lawyers, Physicians and Chymists Books, though oftentimes written in Terms as harsh and as uncourtly, as if those Rudenesses were their Design? And yet we can Neglect and scorn the Scripture, because in some Passages we there find the Mysteries and other Matters of Religion, deliver'd in a Proper and Theological style.[37]

He includes a quasi-anthropological account of stylistic deficiency, 'that as to many passages of Scripture accus'd of not appearing Eloquent to European Judges, it might be justly represented, That the Eastern Eloquence differs widely from the Western' with their 'Dark and Involved Sentences... their Abrupt and Maimed way of expressing themselves'.[38] Similar defences, tracing shifts in aesthetic styles across time, are not encountered too frequently, in a culture very much attuned to its own fine taste, but are met on occasion, as for instance in the controversial writing of Robert Ferguson in 1675, who likewise admits that what appeals to the seventeenth century may be relative:

---

[34] Boyle, *Considerations*, 411, John 9:6.   [35] Boyle, *Considerations*, 412–13.
[36] Boyle, *Considerations*, 401.   [37] Boyle, *Considerations*, 449.
[38] Boyle, *Considerations*, 451.

If that which even among our selves is accounted Eloquence in one Age, ceaseth to be held so in another, why might not the Scripture stile have admirably suited the Genius of those times it was first calculated for, though it do not accord to our western Rules of Oratory? And who knows but that our Europaean Stile may be as little relished by the Asiaticks, as theirs is by us.[39]

30.2 SCENT AND DISSENT: SMELLING THE PROSE OF GOD

Robert Ferguson, paired here with Boyle, appears initially to be another in a queue of defences of scriptural style, but he is, in fact, defending something different—the dissenter's relationship to the Bible. This relationship was often deemed to be half-hearted, at best, and there was a rich and ambivalent tradition which viewed the Bible in its all too human prose as being simultaneously conduit to and obstacle to the spirit. Dissenters, separatists, and nonconformists are not noted for their engagement with aesthetics, which tends rather to be a response to classicisms, but such radicals, of various hues, do offer alternative and, at times, startling understandings of biblical prose, and it is to these responses that the last section of this essay turns. They do not (with Ferguson as the exception) attend to stylistic criticism of the Bible as such, but are nevertheless very much part of what the early modern period considered the problem of biblical prose.

Ferguson engages conspicuously with scriptural aesthetics, insisting that the Bible exhibited an enviable and inimitable pairing of form and function: 'The Stile of the Scripture doth plainly breath of God. With what Brevity without Darkness; with what Simplicity without Corruption; with what Gravity without Affectation; with what Eloquence without Meretricious Ornaments; with what Plainness without Flatness or Sordidness; with what Condescensions to our Capacities, without Unsuitableness to the Subject Matter, is the Scripture written?'[40] Occasionally, he concedes, the meaning may not be clear, but that, in turn, is either down to the subject matter being beyond our capacities or, in effect, the lack of good footnotes:

If there be at any time Obscurity in the Scripture-Stile, it is either from the Sublimity of the Matter declared, which no Words though never so easie in themselves, can help us to adequate Notions of: Or it is from some Reference to ancient Customs and Stories, which made the Expressions easie to the Age and Persons first concerned in them, though they may be Dark to us.[41]

---

[39] Robert Ferguson, *The interest of reason in religion with the import & use of scripture-metaphors* (1675) 95.
[40] Ferguson, *The interest of reason*, 92.
[41] Ferguson, *The interest of reason*, 92–3.

Obscurity in an ancient text might demand that scholarship rectify the gaps in context, but it should not be deemed an intrinsic flaw. Ferguson insists that a reconfigured taste is necessary to appreciate the scriptures: 'The pretence of want of Eloquence in the stile of the Scripture is a groundless, as well as a false calumny. And it ariseth first from a mistake of the Nature of True Eloquence, as supposing it to consist in a flourish of painted Words, or a smooth structure of periods.'[42]

In one regard, Ferguson could hardly be more measured in his defence of biblical style, but, nonconformist and occasional conspirator that he was, his writing attracted fierce attacks from some who saw it as a mere camouflage of orthodoxy, covering up the dissenters' putative disdain for reason as a tool of religious belief.[43] Ferguson does not intend to avoid entirely the nonconformist position that grace precedes understanding, that reading, even of the scriptures, does not offer a conduit to knowledge, so much as a reformulation into words of an ineffable spiritual infusion: 'Grace both helps us to use Reason aright for the discovering the true meaning of Scripture Enunciations; and furnisheth us with a holy Sagacity of smelling out, what is right and true, and what is false and perverse.'[44] Such a habit of smelling out the intricate meanings of the Word adds a curious, but perhaps still aesthetic, element to encounters with the Bible, as part of a hermeneutic arsenal that revels in the multi-dimensionality of the scriptural experience he expects:

> There are no empty frigid phraseologies in the Bible, but where the expressions are most splendid, and lofty, there are Notions and things enough to fill them out. God did not design to endite the Scripture in a pompous tumid stile, to amuse our fancies, or meerly strike to our Imaginations with the greater force, but to instruct us in a calm and sedate way; and therefore under the most stately dress of words, there always lyes a richer quarry of things and Truths, Words being invented to express natural things and humane thoughts, the utmost signification they can possibly bear, proves but scanty and narrow, when they are apply'd to the manifesting Spiritual and celestial Objects.[45]

There is, in such a formulation, a disparity between what words—though in most stately dress—can express and the corresponding 'spiritual and celestial Objects'. In such apparently inoffensive claims, that words were weak and might push only so far, to 'the utmost signification they can possibly bear', Ferguson was, in the estimation of his opponents, revealing his true anti-scriptural colours, part of a long-running dispute over the degree to which the human hand in the scriptures was grounds for suspicion.

The Holy Ghost, as is appropriate, employed ghost-writers—illustrious, inspired, occasionally stylish, but still human. They were not 'authors' in the emergent senses that were current in early modern understandings of the role. They were more routinely

---

[42] Ferguson, *The interest of reason*, 92–3; Roger L'Estrange, *The Observer*, no. 398, 5 September 1683.

[43] See, for example, William Sherlock's appendix to Joseph Glanvill's *An Account of Mr Ferguson, his Common-Place-Book* (1675).

[44] Ferguson, *The interest of reason*, 153.   [45] Ferguson, *The interest of reason*, 160.

described as 'pen-men' of the text. These were, in some sense, scribes or conduits of the Word, but it seemed clear to early modern thinkers that their human roles, social status, and professions had a role in the texts they produced. If, in the writers cited earlier, this was a cue for discussing the literary qualities of their texts, for others it was evidence that the Bible itself had its ephemeral, or non-divine, aspects. The Independent, John Goodwin, in a late 1640s dispute with William Jenkin, argued that the human variables in penman, translator, and material production were such that a work liable to mutability, which could be torn and rent and mistranslated, could not be the immutable Word of God, nor even the foundation of religion: 'every Bible, in what language soever, whether printed, or transcribed, whether consisting of paper, parchment, or other like materiall, was built and form'd, and made into a book by men. There is no point, letter, syllable, or word, in any of them, but is the workmanship of some mans hand, or other', adding that he might defer to him if he could produce an angelic Bible, that if Jenkin had 'a Bible that fell out of heaven, written, or printed without hands, he is desired to produce it for the accommodation of the world'.[46] The Word of God is a wordless matter, according to Goodwin, not subject to the vicissitudes of Ink and Paper, but rather, the more impalpable workings of spirit. This argument involves distinguishing between a matter and substance that are substantially different from style: 'though I willingly acknowledge... that the manner of the phrase and style of the Scriptures, is a rich character of their Divinity', the Word subsists independently of any 'gracious and super-added advantage of any thing in the Scriptures'.[47]

Such a claim is intricate, to put it kindly. The Bible, in phrase and style, contains something of the character of Divinity, he argues—it is, after a fashion, the diffusion of God on earth, but it remains an object like other objects, subject to the same decay. For some, its grandeur made it all the more liable to idolatry. This is an aspect of dissenting thought that runs deep, that reading the prose that contained the Word of God might be a distraction from the Word. In a trick by which the Bible was made to disappear, a strand of seventeenth-century thinking held that the biblical only served its purpose when it had become entirely transparent, a prose that had turned to scent and retained none of its material distraction.

The best example of such thought comes earlier in the seventeenth century when a dispute arose between Henry Ainsworth, who would become a formidable biblical commentator, and John Smyth, fellow separatists in the exile community in Holland.[48] They engaged in a wrangle over whether 'reading', including reading the Bible during prayer, was a practice that might itself be sacrilegious. The argument centred on whether the Word, holy though it may be, might induce an idolatrous adoration of the book as object

---

[46] John Goodwin, *Neophytopresbyteros, or, The yongling elder, or, novice-presbyter* (1648), 34. See John Coffey, *John Goodwin and the Puritan Revolution: Religion and Intellectual Change in Seventeenth-Century England* (Woodbridge: Boydell Press, 2008), 131–67.

[47] Goodwin, *Neophytopresbyteros*, 39–40.

[48] On the importance of these Dutch exiled communities, see Keith L. Sprunger, *Dutch Puritanism: A History of English and Scottish Churches of the Netherlands in the Sixteenth and Seventeenth Centuries* (Leiden: Brill, 1982).

and whether this, in turn, might be as pernicious as image worship. Smyth issues a series of 'objections for bookworship', suggesting that the allure of the book was a will-o'-the-wisp. In treating the book reverentially, the reader was likely, he asserts, to misplace their spiritual focus from God to object, in the same way that gazing at a stained glass window, the beholder was liable to idolatry, in the opinion of many early modern Protestants. Translations, constituting a form of commentary, are no more than 'apocrapha' and have no sacred status. Smyth objects, moreover, to the ways in which the act of reading is itself a kind of ceremony—along with such hated acts as genuflecting before crucifixes: 'books or writings are in the nature of pictures or images, and therfore in the nature of ceremonies, and so by consequent reading in a book is ceremonial'.[49] This is a remarkable claim for a Protestant, seemingly rejecting the central reformation axiom that the Bible constituted the central focus of reformed religion and should be available in the vulgar tongue of the people.

Smyth's idiosyncratic, if not unfathomable, argument aims, on the authority of the Bible, to keep the Bible away from any act of 'spiritual worship'. He argues that the New Testament abolition of the law is supported by a precise set of injunctions *against* reading. When, for example, it is said of Christ in the temple that 'he closed the book and he handed it to the minister and sat down' (Luke 4:20), for Smyth, in this action, reading itself, 'the ceremonie of book worship or the Ministerie of the letter', is abolished. The apostles, we discover, had no books between Pentecost and the writing of the books of the New Testament, '7, 10 or 20 yeeres after Christs death'.[50] Among his reasons, he states sarcastically, we must suppose 'Bicause upon the day of Pentecost fyerie cloven tongs did appeare, not fiery cloven books.'[51] Ainsworth, answering Smyth, defends the scriptures by collating the instances from the Bible in which reading is depicted positively, such as Moses's command for a seven-yearly recitation of the law before the people. For Ainsworth, Smyth's laudable concern to avoid idolatry has preposterous consequences: 'so all reading must be abolished out of the Church; and that would the Divil faine bring to pass'.[52]

There is something wonderfully involved in a scriptural argument against reading the scriptures, though many of Smyth's arguments are sophisticated enough, centring on the instability of human languages in translation. For Smyth, it is not the sanctity of the original languages per se that is at stake, but rather, the need for a prophetic revivification of the gospel in any act of prayer and a sense that the Bible as object intrudes on this process, inhibiting the ethereal channels of prayer. The book itself, in the ideal reading act, would have to be a transparent medium of communication with God, with a catalytic purity, and this, for Smyth, can never be the case. With the merest psychological slippage of attention, idolatry—worship of an object other than God—was liable to occur.

---

[49] John Smyth, the Se-Baptist, *The differences of the Churches of the Separation* (1608), 4.
[50] Smyth, *Differences of the Churches*, 11.
[51] Smyth, *Differences of the Churches*, 6–7.
[52] Henry Ainsworth, *Defence of the Holy Scriptures* (1609), 31. Deuteronomy 31:10.

At times, what seems to be a fierce anti-biblical rhetoric can be a hermeneutic manoeuvre, insisting on one or other mode of interpretation as being faulty or partisan, this being particularly the case when discussion of enthusiasm or idolatry comes into play. Jacob Bauthumley, shoemaker and Ranter, seems at points to be undermining any biblical foundations to religiosity with his insistence in *The light and dark sides of God* (1650) that the biblical text is no different from any other writing, going so far as to claim that 'I must not build my Faith upon it.' However, the fuller context of such statements is not anti-scriptural, but embodies the not infrequent inversion whereby the spirit infuses the Word with God's meaning, rather than the Word itself—bare, empty, and carnal until awoken with spirit—being primary:

> for take Scripture as it is in the History, it hath no more power in the inward man, then any other writings of good men, nor is it in that sense a discerner of the secrets…I must not build my Faith upon it or any saying of it, because such and such men writ or speak so and so, but from that divine manifestation of my own spirit…I do not go to the letter of Scripture, to know the mind of God, but I having the mind of God within, I am able to see it witnessed and made out in the Letter.[53]

Bauthumley's rather beautiful text earned him fierce censure and punishment—he had his tongue burnt through with a hot iron—and is part of a longer strain of radicalism suspicious of the scriptures not in themselves, but insofar as they were liable to be turned into an idol: 'neither is the fault in the Book, but in mens carnall conception of it; and seeing men make an Idoll out of it', says Bauthumley:

> and yet this is no detracting from the glory or authority of Scripture; because the Scripture is within and spirituall, and the Law being writ in my spirit, I care not much for beholding it in the Letter…that is the true Bible, the other is but a shadow or counterpart of it.[54]

We might not customarily suppose such writing to belong to the realm of aesthetics or that it has much to do with the history of prose. But such an idea—that the Word that turns to shadow upon being read properly—is not a great distance from the sublime language which, rather than persuade, manages to transport its readers out of themselves, and produces its vehement emotion by a strange aesthetic alchemy. The effect that the English of the Bible had on the literature of the seventeenth century is incalculable, intangible, and vast, and occurs almost despite itself. Neither the measure of the biblical sentence with its idiosyncratic cadences—as they were rendered in English—nor the hypnotic throb of its formulae and repetitions, nor indeed the archaic, oracular echo in its voice, were particularly amenable to seventeenth-century tastes and understanding of eloquence. Nevertheless, it was an era that theorized the emotional and affective workings of the Bible extensively, and whose grappling with scriptural prose tells us a good deal about its wider aesthetic conceptions.

---

[53] Jacob Bauthumley, *The light and dark sides of God or A plain and brief discourse of the light side (God, Heaven and angels.) The dark side (Devill, sin, and Hell.)* (1650), 72.

[54] Bauthumley, *The light and dark sides of* God, 75–6. See Nigel Smith, 'Bothumley, Jacob', *ODNB* <http://www.oxforddnb.com/view/article/37163> accessed 18 March 2013.

FURTHER READING

Campbell, Gordon. *Bible: The Story of the King James Version, 1611–2011* (Oxford: Oxford University Press, 2010).

Daniell, David. *The Bible in English* (New Haven: Yale University Press, 2003).

Hamlin, Hannibal, and Norman W. Jones, eds. *The King James Bible after Four Hundred Years: Literary, Linguistic, and Cultural Influences* (Cambridge: Cambridge University Press, 2011).

Hessayon, Ariel, and Nicholas Keene, eds. *Scripture and Scholarship in Early Modern England* (Aldershot: Ashgate, 2006).

Hill, Christopher. *The English Bible and the Seventeenth-Century Revolution* (London: Penguin 1993).

McCullough, Peter, Hugh Adlington, and Emma Rhatigan, eds. *The Oxford Handbook of the Early Modern Sermon* (Oxford: Oxford University Press, 2011).

Norton, David. *A History of the Bible as Literature*, 2 vols. (Cambridge: Cambridge University Press, 1993).

Shuger, Deborah. *The Renaissance Bible: Scholarship, Sacrifice and Subjectivity* (Berkeley: University of California Press, 1994).

—— *Sacred Rhetoric: The Christian Grand Style in the English Renaissance* (Princeton: Princeton University Press, 1986).

Tadmor, Naomi. *The Social Universe of the English Bible: Scripture, Society and Culture in Early Modern England* (Cambridge: Cambridge University Press, 2010).

CHAPTER 31

THE STYLE OF AUTHORSHIP IN JOHN FOXE'S *ACTS AND MONUMENTS*

THOMAS S. FREEMAN AND
SUSANNAH BRIETZ MONTA

ANY study of the prose of John Foxe's *Acts and Monuments* faces a number of challenges, not least the fact that Foxe did not write much of his book. Contemporaries were well aware that the *Acts and Monuments (A&M)* consists to a large extent of extracts from other works, often reprinted verbatim.[1] Indeed, as with Foxe's incorporation of Marian martyrs' letters previously edited by Henry Bull, Foxe sometimes repeated not only the text, but also the marginal notes of earlier works.[2] Not surprisingly, any discussion of the style and authorship of the 'Book of Martyrs' is necessarily and vastly complicated by its textual and generic multiplicities.[3] Nevertheless, John Foxe's book made him an instant *literary* celebrity. By 1570, a handful of English writers, notably Geoffrey Chaucer, William

---

[1] When presenting previously unpublished material, as with eyewitness narratives of events that were woven into his text, Foxe often carefully repeated the account which had been sent to him. See Thomas S. Freeman, 'Notes on a Source for John Foxe's Account of the Marian Persecution in Kent and Sussex', *Historical Research*, 67 (1994): 203–11. Also compare John Marbeck's lengthy account of his ordeals under Henry VIII, which he sent to Foxe (BL, Lansdowne MS 389, fos. 240ʳ–276ʳ), with the version Foxe printed (*A&M* [1570], 1386–99).

[2] See Elizabeth Evenden and Thomas S. Freeman, *Religion and the Book in Early Modern England: The Making of John Foxe's 'Book of Martyrs'* (Cambridge: Cambridge University Press, 2011), 133–4 (hereafter cited as *R&B*).

[3] Daniel Woolf, 'The Rhetoric of Martyrdom: Generic Contradictions and Narrative Strategy in John Foxe's *Acts and Monuments*', in Thomas F. Mayer and D. R. Woolf, eds., *The Rhetorics of Life Writing in Early Modern Europe: Forms of Biography from Cassandra Fedele to Louis XIV* (Ann Arbor, MI: University of Michigan Press, 1995), 243–82. On the multiple voices (of martyrs, interrogators, etc.) in the book's pages see Evelyn Tribble, 'The Peopled Page: Polemic, Confutation, and Foxe's Book of Martyrs', in George Bornstein and Theresa Tinkle, eds., *The Iconic Page in Manuscript, Print, and Digital Culture* (Ann Arbor, MI: University of Michigan Press, 1998), 109–22.

Langland, and Thomas More, had gained fame for their writings. Yet, none of these figures attained the immediate and widespread popular acclaim that Foxe did as author of the 'Book of Martyrs'. Although Foxe was a prolific author who wrote many works, including a highly regarded and influential commentary on Revelation, his other literary achievements were completely overshadowed by the *Acts and Monuments*. He became instantly identified with the 'Book of Martyrs' and his reputation utterly intertwined with it. As Patrick Collinson observed, 'There are few instances in English literary history of a more complete fusion of author and text.'[4]

This situation is profoundly paradoxical since by most modern understandings of the term, Foxe was not an 'author' at all. Today, an author is popularly understood to be the person who composes a particular work; an author's discourse is commonly valued for its originality, its reflections of its author's particularities. By contrast, in the early modern period imitation of classical models, or *imitatio*, was highly regarded. While *imitatio* may encompass an admittedly wide spectrum of practices, ranging from what we might today consider loose translation to freely ranging transformations of one's originals, it remains generally true that a writer's claim to the status of 'author' was often built upon his or her imitation of authoritative texts such as Virgil's *Aeneid*.[5] Given the high esteem in which *imitatio* was held, originality—especially in matters pertaining to religion—was often suspect. Thus, the Catholic polemicist Robert Parsons criticized Foxe for questioning ancient authors and traditional authorities.[6] In such a culture, the function of the author's name is much more complicated than an indication of single, original authorship, as Marcy North's work has shown.[7] A name may authorize (in the sense of ratify or empower) a particular text; it may indicate strong and mutually beneficial associations between author and text; it may (as in the case of the popular editions of pseudo-Augustinian prayers published by Foxe's printer, John Day) suggest traditional, but spurious, or even simply hopeful, linkages. The name of the early modern author, then, signifies in a number of ways other than a simple, straightforward claim to original composition.

Problems attendant upon the study of conceptualizations of authorship and stylistic imitation in the period are present *a fortiori* in the case of Foxe's book. In a text that essentially deconstructs itself, it is not easy to discuss authorship, and it is futile to do so on the basis of prose style. But a study of the prose in the *A&M* may nevertheless shed light both on the work itself and on the early modern period's complex understandings of authorship. Despite the fact that contemporaries knew Foxe had not originated much

---

[4] Patrick Collinson, 'John Foxe and National Consciousness', in Christopher Highley and John N. King, eds., *John Foxe and his World* (Aldershot: Ashgate, 2002), 16.

[5] The classic work on Renaissance *imitatio* remains Thomas M. Greene's *The Light in Troy: Imitation and Discovery in Renaissance Poetry* (New Haven: Yale University Press, 1982); on the religious dimensions of *imitatio* see Nandra Perry, 'Imitatio and Identity: Thomas Rogers, Philip Sidney, and the Protestant Self', *English Literary Renaissance*, 35.3 (2005): 365–406.

[6] Robert Parsons, *Treatise of Three Conversions* (St Omer, 1603–4), vol. 1, 81–8.

[7] Marcy North, *The Anonymous Renaissance: Cultures of Discretion in Tudor-Stuart England* (Chicago: University of Chicago Press, 2003), esp. chap. 1.

of his book's material, beginning with the second edition of the 'Book of Martyrs', published in 1570, the title page proclaimed that the book was the work of 'the Author Ihon Foxe'.[8] This claim was reiterated in all subsequent unabridged editions of the *A&M*, occasionally emphasized in rubricated letters or large type. Traditionally, scholars have also stressed Foxe's authorship of the *A&M*. Indeed, the standard biography of Foxe (in a striking demonstration of how closely its subject is identified with the 'Book of Martyrs') is titled *John Foxe and his Book*.[9] In recent years, however, as appreciation for the work's textual complexity has increased, the pendulum has swung in the opposite direction and scholars are muting or minimizing assertions of Foxe's authorship. But such approaches may inadvertently suppress the extent to which Foxe exerted editorial control over his materials. Throughout his recent monograph on Foxe, for example, John King refers to him, not as the author of the *A&M*, but as its 'author-compiler' or 'compiler'.[10] There is much to be said for this terminology, particularly since King is careful to state that Foxe 'stood at the center' of the project which created the 'Book of Martyrs' and that he 'shaped the collection through the provision of prefaces, introductions to particular sections, transitions, marginal glosses, and varied forms of commentary and paratext'.[11] Still, characterizing Foxe as a compiler runs the risk of circumscribing his role and obscuring our understanding of how the *A&M* was written.

King's assertion that 'we may best think of Foxe as an "author-compiler" in the manner of Raphael Holinshed' epitomizes this danger, for the comparison is both instructive and misleading.[12] The second of the two editions of Holinshed's *Chronicles* was printed after Holinshed's death and extensively revised by Abraham Fleming, a forward Protestant. But even in the first edition, Holinshed had to accommodate the editorial views of contributors such as John Stow, a religious conservative. As a result, Holinshed's *Chronicles* are characterized by a pronounced multivocality, not least on religious topics and English church history.[13] In contrast—despite factual inconsistencies, often chaotic chronology, and organizational lapses—all unabridged editions of the *A&M* speak with a single editorial voice, particularly on religious topics, that admits no doubts or qualifications. That editorial voice belongs to John Foxe. The legitimacy of his claim to authorize the 'Book of Martyrs' rests on the fact that the millions of words in it, despite their being written by authors across the centuries and the religious spectrum, support his viewpoint.

In what follows, we examine Foxe's own bids for authority as articulated in the prefaces he wrote for the *Acts and Monuments*. We also consider the complexities of early

---

[8] Significantly in the first edition of the *Acts and Monuments*, published in 1563, the claim is merely that the material in the book was 'Gathered and collected...by John Foxe'.

[9] J. F. Mozley, *John Foxe and his Book* (London: SPCK, 1940).

[10] John N. King, *Foxe's 'Book of Martyrs' and Early Modern Print Culture* (Cambridge: Cambridge University Press, 2006), *passim*.

[11] King, *Print Culture*, 58 and 68.

[12] King, *Print Culture*, 23.

[13] This multivocality is discussed in chapters by Susan Doran, Peter Marshall, Alexandra Walsham, and the authors of this essay in Ian Archer, Felicity Heal, and Paulina Kewes, eds., *The Oxford Handbook to Holinshed* (Oxford: Oxford University Press, 2012).

modern authorship in a case such as that of Foxe's book, so much of which was not written by him, but which nevertheless reflects his religious viewpoints quite precisely. Indeed, religious polemical purposes drive the prefaces' assertions of a deferred and collective authority, as well as Foxe's meticulous editorial labours. Throughout his book, the hand of a careful rhetorician is at work, a rhetorician who in early modern terms could claim the quite flexible label of 'Author'.

31.1 Deferred, collective authority: the rhetoric of Foxe's prefaces

Foxe's prefaces to the *A&M* establish the book's polemical, historical, and rhetorical goals. They also contain Foxe's most explicit discussions of authorship. Perhaps the most apparent feature of these prefaces is simply their bulk. The *A&M* is announced with tremendous fanfare. Its multiple prefatory addresses resemble the 'extensive supplemental material' published in humanist editions of classical Latin texts.[14] Foxe carefully revised, rearranged, added, and excised prefaces over each of the four editions published during his lifetime (in 1563, 1570, 1576, and 1583). His careful attention to this material bespeaks its importance to him. Like early modern prefaces more generally, Foxe's prefaces stake claims to authority both for Foxe and for his book.[15] In his prefaces, Foxe exercises careful rhetorical control and gives extended attention to writerly concerns such as the status of rhetoric, the importance of decorum (suiting style to matter), and the dangers of sophistry. He also makes precise use of rhetorical figures and tropes both to structure and to illustrate his work's claims. Finally, the prefaces reveal Foxe's concern with authorship, conceived primarily *not* as the origination of discourse, but as the *rhetorical* ability to present the matter at hand in the most effective and affecting way. As Foxe articulates and justifies the purposes behind his book, he is concerned with questions of style and specifically with decorum: how ought martyrs to be honoured in his printed work? How may their stories be set forth to godly purposes? Foxe's English prefaces wrestle with the proper uses of rhetoric in ecclesiastical history and labour to establish a deferred and collective form of authorship, one in which Foxe himself is meant to recede behind the authority of the various materials and voices he presents, even as that recession itself is a carefully managed rhetorical feat.[16]

---

[14] North, *Anonymous Renaissance*, 20.

[15] On the Renaissance preface see Kevin Dunn, *Pretexts of Authority: The Rhetoric of Authorship in the Renaissance Preface* (Stanford: Stanford University Press, 1994).

[16] Foxe's work also features prefatory material in Latin ('Ad Doctum Lectorem' and 'Ad Dominum Jesum Christum Servatorem Clementissimum', for example), as well as prefatory material not written by Foxe (such as Latin poems written in praise of Foxe's work). Here, we discuss only English-language material written by Foxe.

Foxe's preface, titled in 1563, 'A declaration concerning the utilitie and profite of thys history', and in 1583, simply 'The utilitie of this story', has been discussed with respect to the shifting genres Foxe imagines for his book.[17] But it is also important to note the rhetorical categories in the preface's shifting titles. Foxe's preface claims authority for his work on the basis of its utility and profit; eloquence emerges as a secondary matter—not a matter of secondary importance, but one that follows and derives from the importance of the material being discussed. The preface's stance on style shares some similarities with that in the fourth book of Augustine's *De Doctrina Christiana*. There, Augustine classifies the styles of particular biblical passages and selections from patristic figures according to the purpose a passage seems to have—whether it be teaching (plain style), praising or blaming (middle), and exhortation (grand)—and not according to stylistic features primarily. For Augustine, purpose and function are primary concerns; while for Cicero, the grand style is the queen of styles, for Augustine, the plain style often takes pride of place because of its teaching purpose. Similarly, the widely influential reformer Philip Melanchthon defended appropriate eloquence while insisting that style should be firmly in the service of clear instruction.[18]

Foxe's preface, too, insists that style should emerge from, be subordinate to, and work in harmony with instructional purposes. The many revisions he makes to this preface between 1563 and 1570, often stylistic improvements on the original, indicate that its discussion of style, eloquence, and decorum was important to Foxe. In the 1563 and 1570 prefaces, Foxe begins in a style heavily reliant on pairs, balanced phrases, and careful qualifications. These features resemble both those of classical Latin's middle style and William Tyndale's heavy use of binarisms in his translations of scripture.[19] For example, in 1563 Foxe writes that he fears he may seem to have in hand matter 'superfluous and needeles', and that given the contemporary glut of printed books, 'manye good men doo both perceive, and inwardlye bewayle this insatiable gredines of wryting and printing'.[20] The preface then claims that 'ornaments of wyt and eloquence' ought to be applied to the worthiest subjects—martyrs for the true faith.[21] By the preface's end, Foxe's style approaches the grand style of the peroratio, the rousing climax to a classical oration. The preface thus both considers and models different stylistic registers, establishing Foxe's

---

[17] The title changes dramatically over the four editions published during Foxe's lifetime. The 1570 title may bear witness to the Catholic assault on the 1563 text: '**To the true Christian Reader**, what utilitie is to be taken by readyng of these Historyes' (emphasis ours).

[18] See Peter Mack, *A History of Renaissance Rhetoric, 1380–1620* (Oxford: Oxford University Press, 2011), 109–20; and Randall Zachman, 'Calvin and Melanchthon on the Office of the Evangelical Teacher', in *John Calvin as Teacher, Pastor, and Theologian* (Grand Rapids: Baker Academic, 2006), 37–9.

[19] Janel Mueller, *The Native Tongue and the Word* (Chicago: Chicago University Press, 1984): Tyndale's Pauline style depends on 'the binary linkage of sentences (or verb phrases) in an antithetical, correlative, or comparative relation' (193).

[20] *A&M* (London, 1563), Bv^v. The 1570 preface's language differs slightly: 'many do both perceive ...' and 'gredines' is replaced with 'boldnes' (*A&M* 1570, iii^r).

[21] *A&M* (1563), Bvi^r.

firm preference that style follow function while endorsing and demonstrating appropriate eloquence.

Foxe's preface begins by worrying over the excessive number of books in the world. His opening is an ethical bid, a *captatio benevolentiae* (capture of the readers' good will): he, like 'manye good men' (1570: 'many') perceives and regrets the excesses of print. The burden of authorship seems heavy, as he worries over how he might be censured for presuming to take on the persona of a 'writer'. Here is the 1563 text:

> I perceyved well how learned this age of ours was, and I could not tell what the secrete and close judgementes of the Readers would determine, if sodaynly one should prease in with other, taking upon hym the person of a wryter in the syght of al men, which were not sufficiently furnished with such ornamentes and graces as are requisite to the accomplishing of so waighty an endevour, which could not utter some matter excellent and synguler, and joyning things together not onely great, but also necessarye for the condition of the tyme with lyke gift of utterance satisfie and encrease the industry of the learners, the utility of the studious, and the delight of the learned. Which vertues the more I perceived to be wanting in me, the lesse I durst be bold to become a writer.[22]

The role of 'writer' is imagined as a 'person', a persona one may inhabit, or be inadequate to take up, as the case may be. In an instance of the humility *topos*, a common feature of Renaissance prefaces, Foxe writes that he lacks what is needed for such a role: the ability to teach *and* delight, to suit eloquent 'utterance' to the 'matter' at hand. In the 1570 preface, his humility is asserted more strongly *and* with more style in carefully balanced phrasing: 'neither could I tell what the secrete judgementes of readers wold conceave, to see so weake a thing, to set upon such a weyghty enterprise'.[23] This humble beginning is itself what Cicero advises in *De inventione* for the openings of speeches: the orator should claim authority through apparent modesty and seemingly spontaneous eloquence (as exhibited in the 1570 preface's figure of parison: the use of corresponding structures in a series of phrases or clauses). The preface will go on to justify Foxe's act of writing explicitly, using the utility and profit of reading about martyrs to embolden authorship.

Foxe defends his work's promulgation using religious and rhetorical arguments. Specifically, Foxe slightly modifies classical rhetoric's understanding of the functions of the plain, middle, and grand styles. For Cicero, and for the author of the *Rhetorica ad Herennium*, the three classical styles were generally associated with three purposes: to teach (plain style), to delight (middle style), and to move (grand style).[24] In Foxe's 1563 list of purposes for his work (to satisfy and increase learners' industry, the utility of the

---

[22] *A&M* (1563), sigs. Bv^v–Bvi^v.

[23] *A&M* (1570), *iii.

[24] The most commonly studied classical rhetorical texts in the Renaissance were the anonymous *Rhetorica ad Herennium* and Cicero's *De Inventione* (Mack, *History of Renaissance Rhetoric*, 3–4); Renaissance rhetoricians were generally interested in adapting and revising classical rhetoric's three-style system (Mack, *History of Renaissance Rhetoric*, *passim*), as we argue Foxe is in the preface under discussion.

studious, and the delight of the learned), teaching occupies two spots in the list and delight only one. He tips the balance towards the instructional (plain), downplays the delightful (middle), and seemingly omits anything that would correspond to the grand style. In the 1570 edition, Foxe combines the first two instructional purposes: he feels he is insufficient 'to serve the utility of the studious, and the delight of the learned'.[25] His beautifully balanced revision states that he lacks the literary skills for either teaching (plain style) or delight (middle).

The grand style is not without place, however, nor is Foxe's purported humility entirely ingenuous. In the 1570 preface, Foxe inserts a phrase lamenting his inadequacy to the *matter* at hand: he is 'not sufficiently furnished with such ornamentes able to satisfie the perfection of so great a story'.[26] Foxe will build towards the highest rhetorical goal—that of moving the listener or reader to virtue, or to right judgement or decision—within the next page, after teaching has been firmly established as the basis of all he does, and after the 'perfection of so great a story' has been shown to merit eloquent treatment. What seems to overcome Foxe's stated fear is the profit and utility of the *matter* discussed. In 1563, Foxe writes that if we are willing to 'decke, trym, and set ... out with the ornamentes of wyt and eloquence' worldly or secular affairs, how much more should we 'accept and embrace' the lives and doings of martyrs; in 1570, acceptance and embracing give way to conserving 'in remembrance'.[27] Martyrs' words and actions don't 'delight the eare' so much as 'garnish the lyfe' (1563 and 1570); they give examples and instruction, beyond mere literary pleasure.[28] Foxe's preface reorients rhetorical goals: delight, the motive often associated with the middle style, is defined, not as merely stylistic delight, but as moral reform, even moral beauty. What is most appropriately decked, trimmed, or garnished is the reader's 'lyfe' itself, not just the writer's style. The 1570 preface stresses the martyrs' affective power even more strongly: rather than the ability to 'enstruct' (1563) men in godliness, for example, stories of martyrs 'encourage' men to godliness.[29] The grand style's function of moving the reader appears in this revision, as does a hint of Foxe's affinity for what Janel Mueller has called a Tyndalian affective rhetoric. Simply writing history (for Foxe) or translating scripture (for Tyndale) is not enough: a translator's or author's style must also inspire affective readerly responses.[30]

For Foxe, eloquence has a place, provided that the subjects upon which it is lavished are deserving. Foxe finds precedent for his work in the hymns and songs of Prudentius and St Gregory of Nazianzene, superior in Foxe's judgement to Pindar's odes precisely because of their sacred matter. Similarly, in 1563 Foxe insists upon the eloquence of ancient orations on martyrs: 'What availeth here to make rehersal of the eloquent orations of the most eloquent men, Ciprian, Chrisostome, Ambrose, and Hierome, and

---

[25] *A&M* (1570), *iii.   [26] *A&M* (1570), *iii.
[27] *A&M* (1563), Bvi^r; *A&M* (1570), *iii. The 1570 preface makes another slight change: men 'bestow all their ornamentes of wyt and eloquence in garnishyng' worldly affairs.
[28] *A&M* (1563), Bvi^r; *A&M* (1570), *iii.
[29] *A&M* (1570), *iii.
[30] Mueller, *The Native Tongue and the Word*. See also the preface to the 1560 Geneva Bible, which stresses the power of scripture to shape the 'affections of the heart'.

never more eloquent, then when they fell into the commendations of the godly Martyrs?'³¹ Anderson has recently discussed this preface's worry over the inundation of books in the context of the work's anxiety over print, arguing that the work uses print against itself, to give the illusion of unmediated access to archival materials.³² What is striking in this preface, however, is that Foxe's ostensible anxieties about print are resolved through a turn to orality: Foxe likens his work to that of classical rhetorical orations and adapts classical rhetorical purposes to suit his own—namely, to move people towards godliness through the *exempla* of the martyrs. Foxe will himself embrace the eloquence he praises in patristic orations by the preface's end, where the elevation of his style articulates a call to imitation, collective remembrance, and the publishing of martyrs' lives. This is grand-style exhortation (*movere*—that is, to move) in Foxean terms.

Over the course of this preface, Foxe establishes his subject's worthiness and moves from ostensible fear over assuming a writer's 'persona' towards a cooperative form of authorship, or at least a call for the reader to begin a cooperative effort with the 'writer', garnishing his/her life so that martyrology may yield the proper fruit. Fittingly, the first-person singular pronoun of the preface's opening expands to a first-person plural in a passage that remains stable from 1563 to 1570: 'let us not faile then in publishing and setting fourth their doinges, least in that point we seme more unkinde to them, then the writers of the primitive church were unto theirs'.³³ By the preface's end, Foxe reveals the fruit and utility to be taken from the martyrs' stories as he urges his readers, along with himself ('us'), to learn from their examples to suffer patiently, forgive, behave charitably, neglect worldly things, and be willing to suffer should we be called to do so. Here, then, is the 'utility and fruit to be taken of this history' that justify the name of 'writer' for Foxe himself, the matter that both deserves all the ornamentation eloquence can offer and subordinates the mere 'delight' of eloquence to godly profit.

In Foxe's other prefaces, he maintains something of this first-person plural, so to speak, as he claims authority for his text in ways that deflect attention from Foxe himself. That is, Foxe presents his work as authoritative precisely because it is *not* original. Two prefaces added to the 1570 edition, for example, list 'The Names of the Authors alleged in this Booke, besides many and sondry other Authors whose names are unknowen, and also besides divers Recordes of Parliament, and also other matters found out in Registers of sondry Byshops of this Realme', as well as 'The names of the Martyrs in this booke conteined', from the time of John the Baptist to the present. These lists were added after Foxe's 1563 edition had come under fire from Catholic polemicists such as Thomas

---

³¹ *A&M* (1563), Bvi^r. His triple use of 'eloquent' within one sentence—emphatic, if inelegant—was revised in 1570: he praises the 'learned Orations of eloquent Cyprian, Chrysostome, Ambrose, & Hierome, who never shewed their eloquence more, then when they fell into the commendations of the godly Martyrs' (*iii).

³² Benedict Anderson, 'Neither Acts Nor Monuments', *English Literary Renaissance*, 41:1 (2011): 3–30.

³³ *A&M* (1563), Bvi^v; *A&M* (1570), *iii^v. The 1570 preface inserts small statements that emphasize the importance of reader response for Foxe. For example, in the preface's second paragraph, Foxe writes that he felt compelled to write, not only for the martyrs 'wel deserving' (as in 1563), but also because of the 'benefites by them received' for 'our partes'.

Stapleton and Nicholas Harpsfield for what they deemed heretical departures from the true church's history and authoritative teachings; Foxe counters that his book speaks with and for 'Authors' and martyrs whose historically continuous testimony is to be trusted, claiming collective authorship under the sign of his name.[34]

Because Foxe's work labours to disclose divine patterns behind history's particularities, one of his greatest authorizing claims is historical precedent: that the martyrs whom he commemorates are early Christian martyrs' worthy successors. In the 1563 preface 'A declaration concerning the utilitie and profite of thys history', Foxe uses anaphora (the beginning of successive sentences or phrases with similar or identical words or phrases) to mark this continuity:

> Those standing in the foreward of the battell, did receive the first encountre and violence of their enemies, and taught us by that meanes to overcome such tiranny. But these as spedely, lyke olde beaten soldiours did winne the field in the reward of the battaile. Those did, like famous husband men of the world, sow the fields of the church, that first lay unmanured and waste. And these with the fatnes of their bloude did cause it to battell and fructifie.[35]

Here, and in the lists of 'Authors' and 'martyrs' whose voices are added to Foxe's own, lies evidence of Foxe's fundamental conservatism: Protestants represent continuity with ancient Christian tradition, while Catholics innovate and presume upon the idiosyncrasies of particular episcopal authorities. Consider, for example, Foxe's criticism of Innocent III's papal reign in his preface 'To the true and faithfull congregation of Christes universall Church': 'Whatsoever the Byshop of Rome denounced, that stode for an oracle, of all men to be received without opposition or contradiction: whatsoever was contrary *ipso facto* it was heresy.'[36] Foxe's deferral of authority has rhetorical purpose: it is to move him out of centre stage, to eliminate the perception of originality, and to gain authority precisely from his deference to other authorities.

The greatest textual authority for Foxe's culture was, of course, the Bible. For Foxe, as for John Bale, scripture, and especially the Book of Revelation, illuminates history.[37] Indeed, the *A&M* may be read as an extended commentary on the Bible and on Revelation in particular, an ecclesiastical historical companion to and development of Bale's *The Image of Two Churches* (Fig. 31.1). Foxe's prefaces make clear his indebtedness

---

[34] *A&M* (1570), Ci^v and Cii^r–Ciii^r. On sixteenth-century rhetorical handbooks' assertion of *martyria/testatio* as an 'artless' proof, an important means to win credit (*fides*) for rhetoricians' arguments, see R. W. Serjeantson, 'Testimony: The Artless Proof', in Sylvia Adamson, Gavin Alexander, and Katrin Ettenbruner, eds., *Renaissance Figures of Speech* (Cambridge: Cambridge University Press, 2008), 183–4. An argument could be made that the 'Kalendar' of martyrs from the 1563 edition served a similar function; that 'Kalendar' provoked controversy from both reformers and Catholics, such that the 1570 edition's much fuller list of martyrs, whose testimony was included in the book, would seem to be both a less provocative and a more rhetorically substantive move.

[35] *A&M* (1563), Bvi^r. Foxe's 1570 revision sharpens the anaphora to 'They... so these... They... These... They... these'.

[36] *A&M* (1570), *iii^v.

[37] See Bale's preface to *The Image of Both Churches*, in *The Select Works of John Bale*, ed. Henry Christmas for the Parker Society (Cambridge, 1849), 253.

FIGURE 31.1 John Foxe, *Actes and Monuments of the Christian Church* (1570), title page. The title page of the *A&M* pictures and contrasts the True and the False Churches, illustrating Foxe's indebtedness to John Bale's *The Image of Two Churches*.

to the Bible, as well as his belief that his book is an historical dilation upon biblical themes. Like a medieval commentator, Foxe's authority in the preface, entitled, 'To all the professed frendes and folowers of the Popes procedynges: Foure Questions propounded' (added in 1570), stems from that of the sacred text upon which his preface expands. The preface links Foxe's book to scriptural authority, as each of its four questions is derived from a particular biblical passage. For example, Foxe's first question, whether the church of Rome is like Mount Sion, is clearly to be answered negatively. For Foxe, the Roman church has none of Mount Sion's qualities, as outlined in Isaiah 11: 'The wolfe shall dwell with the Lambe, and the Leopard with the Kid: The calfe, the Lyon, and the Sheepe shall feede together, and a young child shall rule them. The Cow also and the Beare shall abyde together, with their young ones, and the Lyon shall eate chaffe and foder lyke the Oxe.'[38] Foxe argues that Rome is not this church with a sentence whose content *and* structure shape the biblical passage's relevance to the history he narrates: 'in the sayd Church of Rome is, & hath bene now so many yeares such killyng and slaying, such crueltie & tyranny shewed, such burnyng and spoylyng of Christen bloud, such malice and mischeif wrought, as in readyng these histories may to all the world appeare'.[39] In place of Isaiah's *discordia concors*, its pairs of reconciled opposites—wolves and lambs, leopards and kids—Foxe uses pairs that merely iterate discord: killing and slaying, and burning and spoiling. Foxe's history is presented as if it acted neutrally, without any one person's explicit design, as in the last clause, which curiously lacks an explicit agent: 'as in readyng these histories may to all the world appeare'. Yet, his rhetorical knowledge and care are everywhere present and indeed, often flaunted. In a preface added in 1570, 'To the True and Faithfull Congregation of Christes universall Church', Foxe intertwines biblical language with rhetorical precedent, the Reformation with the Renaissance, so to speak, as he protests against adversaries like Harpsfield: 'such accusers must beware they play not the dogge, of whom Cicero in his Oration speaketh, which beyng set in *Capitolio* to fray away theeves by night, left the theeves and fell to barke at true men walkyng in the day...to carpe where no cause is...to swallow camels, and to strayne gnattes: to oppresse truth with lyes, and to set up lyes for truth'.[40] Foxe uses the resources of classical rhetoric (Cicero's oration) and biblical allusion (Matthew 23:24: 'Ye blind guides, which straine out a gnat, and swallowe a camell') to defend his book with the most authoritative works he can muster.

In his preface to the Queen, which undergoes radical changes between the 1563 and 1570 printings, Foxe's rhetoric again indicates both his care in shaping his claims to authority and his boldness in asserting his book's place just beneath that of scripture. In 1563, the preface develops elaborate parallels between Constantine, the first Christian emperor and patron of the ecclesiastical historian Eusebius, and Elizabeth I, the new Protestant Queen of England and dedicatee of the ecclesiastical historian John Foxe. Foxe uses corresponding verbal structures (parison) to create order and pattern both within the historical example of Constantine and Eusebius's relationship and between Constantinian days and his own. Surveying Constantine's era, for example,

---

[38] A&M (1570), *iiii^r. [39] A&M (1570), *iiii^r. [40] A&M (1570), ii^r.

Foxe writes that he does not know whom to praise the most, 'the good Emperour, or the godly Byshoppe: the one for his Princely proferre, the other for his godly and sincere praise to God for the marvelous workes and syncere peticion. The Emperour for his rare and syngular affection in favouring and furtherynge the Lordes churche, or the Byshoppe in zealyng the publique business of the Lorde.'[41] Similarly, Foxe uses parison to draw Elizabeth and Constantine together: 'I could not enter mention of the one [Constantine], but must nedes wryte of the other [Elizabeth].'[42] Foxe's rhetoric performs his desire 'to compare tyme with tyme, and place with place', and not, incidentally, to hint that his history ought to be accepted and honoured as were Eusebius's labours.

The 1570 preface's rhetoric proclaims its very different purpose. Gone are the carefully balanced sentences, gone the heavy use of parison. Instead, cumulative sentences pile phrases upon phrases, mimicking and (Foxe hopes) exposing the furious assaults his work has suffered. Notoriously, the ornamental 'C' at the preface's opening no longer begins the word 'Constantine', but rather, 'Christ', whose precepts Foxe hopes Elizabeth will follow a bit more energetically than she has to date (Fig. 31.2). Foxe's attitude towards rhetoric, like his attitude towards his queen, seems to have darkened slightly. Foxe heatedly accuses Catholics of using sophistry and tries to separate proper rhetoric from sophistry. His Catholic detractors have spared 'no cost of hyperbolicall phrases', attacking his book with

> the like sort of impudencie as sophisters use somtymes in their sophismes to do (and some times is used also in Rhethoricke) that when an Argument commeth against them which they can not well resolve in dede, they have a rule to shift of the matter with stout words and tragicall admiration, wherby to dash the opponent out of countenaunce, bearing the hearers in hand, the same to be the weakest and slendrest argument that ever was heard, not worthy to be aunswered, but utterly to be hissed out of the scholes.[43]

In danger of overlapping sophistry and rhetoric ('sometimes is used also in Rhethoricke'), Foxe's sentence, by the end, dismisses sophistry from learned consideration ('hissed out of the scholes') in balanced verbal phrases ('not worthy to be aunswered, but utterly to be hissed').

Still, parison dominates only at the preface's end, and in a way that both indicates Foxe's recovered balance and pushes his godly agenda. Foxe offers a sideways rebuke of Elizabeth, writing that he has heard of Elizabeth's 'zeale' to 'furnish all quarters and countreyes of this your Realme with the voyce of Christes Gospell, and faithfull preachyng of his word'. But he notes in parentheses—'(speedely I trust)'—that her reputed zeal has not yet produced much fruit. Foxe reintroduces parallel structure in order to present his work as driving the dissemination of the gospel he so desires: 'like as by the one [scripture] the people may learne the rules and preceptes of doctrine: so by the other [the 'Book of Martyrs'] they may have examples of Gods mighty working in his church,

---

[41] A&M (1563), Bi^{r-v}. [42] A&M (1563), Bi^v. [43] A&M (1570), *i^v.

FIGURE 31.2 John Foxe, *Actes and Monuments of the Christian Church* (1570), image of Elizabeth as Constantine (p. 1). This famous woodcut displays an enthroned Elizabeth within an ornate capital 'C'. In the first edition of the *A&M*, this was the beginning of the word 'Constantine', in the preface to the Queen, and linked the two sovereigns together. In the second edition, the capital 'C' was retained at the beginning of the preface, but now it began the word 'Christ', as Foxe had quietly discarded the comparison of Elizabeth to the first Christian emperor.

to the confirmation of their faith, and the edification of Christian life'.[44] Foxe's work—the second part of the parison—complements Elizabeth's stated aims, but given the qualification Foxe inserts just prior ('speedely I trust'), the logic of the sentence is driven by the parison's second half: the dissemination of martyrs' examples is to push the Queen to disseminate the gospel.

The preface's penultimate sentence uses structured repetition in the form of a chiasmus to similar ends. The two examples of chiasmus (a figure that takes the shape of an

---

[44] *A&M* (1570), *ii*.

'x': A:B, B:A) are highlighted below. Foxe writes that 'observing and notyng' the 'excellent workes of the Lord' in 'historyes, minister[s] to the readers thereof wholesome admonitions of lyfe, with experience and wisedome, **bothe to knowe God in his woorkes, and to worke the thyng that is godly**: especially *to seke unto the sonne of God for their salvation, and in his fayth onely to finde that they seeke for*, and in no other meanes'.[45] Foxe's theology is carefully woven into his prose: human knowledge and action are drawn to and circumscribed by God. Faith in Christ is the fulcrum of the second, looser, chiasmus, framed by a seeking whose target and origin is the centre of the chiasm (itself a Christic figure, by virtue of its 'x' or cross shape). The order of the chiastic figures may also be significant: through studying Foxe's ecclesiastical history, readers will know God in his (historical) work, and thereby learn the heart of the gospel: to seek salvation *sola fide*. Whether Elizabeth's zeal ever manifests itself as it should, Foxe's history will push towards godly evangelization.

Given the function of these chiastic figures—which both proclaim Foxe's rhetorical skill and defer authority to Christ, upon whom the second chiasmus turns—the slight revision of the 1583 title page's proclamation of Foxe's authorship is fitting. The 1583 title page claims that the book is revised and augmented 'by the Authour (through the helpe of Christ our Lord) John Foxe, which desireth thee good Reader to helpe him with thy Prayer'. The parenthetical assertion offers a deferral of authority that seems characteristic of the assertions made in Foxe's prefatory material: Foxe is ostensibly the author, but importantly, not the originator of the history he structures and presents. The bid for collectivity—'good Reader... helpe him with thy Prayer'—also reflects the claims Foxe's prefaces have staked: he does not stand alone, a solitary originator of discourse, but instead, as a 'writer' authorized by the truths he perceives in the histories he shapes.

31.2 The Author as Editor? Shaping the *Acts and Monuments*

We also see Foxe the rhetorician in his careful construction of the work, whose ideological and intellectual uniformity was achieved through close editing. Foxe frequently emended texts before incorporating them in his book, a proclivity manifested in his Latin martyrologies, precursors of the *A&M*. For example, when Foxe reprinted, in his *Commentarii*, a list of John Wiclif's responses to questions from Richard II and his councillors, he deleted passages in which Wiclif declared his belief in purgatory.[46] Foxe employed a similar discretion throughout the first edition of the 'Book of Martyrs', as when one Lollard's denial of Christ's Resurrection and another's denial of his Incarnation

---

[45] *A&M* (1570), *ii[v]*.
[46] Cf. John Foxe, *Commentarii in ecclesia gestarum rerum* (Wendelin Rihel, 1554), fos. 34[v]–37[v] with Foxe's source, Bodleian Library, Bodley MS e Museo 86, fos. 66[v]–68[r].

were both airbrushed out of Foxe's version of their interrogations.[47] Foxe occasionally rewrote unguarded utterances of those whom he regarded as proto-Protestants. Margery Baxter's claim, made in 1429, that the Lollard leader William White was a great saint in heaven and a most holy doctor, was altered to the assertion that he was 'a good and holye man'.[48] Foxe also modified Thomas Butler's declaration, in 1488, that Christ's death saved all sinners from eternal punishment to read instead that 'no *faithfull* man should abide any payne after the death of Christ for any sinne because Christ died for our sinnes'.[49] From the start, Foxe not only compiled documents, but also closely read them and shaped them to suit his purposes.

This close editing was greatly intensified in the second edition, whose title page, significantly, was the first to identify Foxe as the work's author. Catholic writers' attacks upon the first edition prompted Foxe's almost obsessively painstaking editorial oversight.[50] Perhaps surprisingly, Foxe was stunned and (less surprisingly) bitter about the vehemence and ubiquity of these criticisms. He mordantly commented in the second edition's dedication that

> A man would have thought Christ to have bene new borne agayne and that Herode with all the Citie of Jerusalem had bene in uproare. Such blustering and styrring was then against that poor book through all the quarters of England, even to the gates of Louvaine: so that no English papist in all the Realm thought him selfe a perfect Catholike unlesse he had cast out some word or other to give that book a blow.[51]

Foxe took these attacks both personally and seriously. Considerable sections of the second edition were devoted to direct rebuttals of his Catholic critics.[52] Researchers were pressed into service to supply Foxe with manuscript evidence to counter attacks on his work.[53] As the ramparts were being extended, vulnerable points were fortified and cracks in the walls filled. Material reprinted from the first edition or introduced to the second was rigorously edited to remove errors.

Foxe went to considerable lengths to correct factual mistakes. For instance, the text of the second edition stated that the villages of Merindol and Cabrieres, where terrible massacres of Waldensians had taken place, were in 'the valley of Angrone'. Someone had conflated the sites of different atrocities inflicted on separate groups of Waldensians: Merindol and Cabrieres are in Provence, while the Angrogna valley is in Piedmont.

---

[47] Cf. *A&M* [1563], 373 and 1740 with London Guildhall Library MS 9531/9, fol. 4[r-v] and Lichfield Public Record Office MS B/A/1/12, fol. 168[v].

[48] Cf. *A&M* [1563], 356 with Westminster Diocesan Archives MS B.2.8, fol. 61[r].

[49] Cf. *A&M* [1563], 1739 (my emphasis) with Lichfield Record Office MS B/A/1/12, fol. 166[v].

[50] On these attacks see *R&B*, 137–8.

[51] *A&M* [1570], sig. *1[r].

[52] E.g., compare *A&M* [1570], 676–700, 761–2, 830–2, 936–9, and 2130–4 with Nicholas Harpsfield, *Dialogi sex contra summi pontificatus, monasticae vitae, sanctorum, sacrarum imaginum oppugnatores et pseudomartyres* (Christopher Plantin, 1566), 830–2, 847–50, and 953–4 and Thomas Harding, *A reiondre to M. Iewels replie against the sacrifice of the Masse* (John Fowler, 1567), fos. 184[r]–185[v].

[53] Thomas S. Freeman, 'John Bale's Book of Martyrs? The Account of King John in *Acts and Monuments*', *Reformation*, 3 (1998): 206–10.

However, Foxe soon noticed the mistake. The erroneous words 'in the valley of Angrone' were crossed out with a pen-stroke *in every copy* of the second edition.⁵⁴ Moreover, eleven pages later, Foxe mentioned the earlier mistake and assured readers that it had been 'rased out with pen'.⁵⁵ This incident underscores Foxe's determination to eliminate demonstrable inaccuracies. It also reveals how closely he proofread the 1570 edition's text. In order to catch the mistake within eleven pages of its first having been printed, Foxe must have been reading the copy soon after it came off the press. (As a rough calculation, a single press could print about two pages of a book a day; since three presses were used simultaneously to print the second edition, the mistake was detected and corrected within, at most, a week, and very probably, a few days.⁵⁶)

Foxe's editorial zeal meant that material reprinted from the first edition was finecombed for mistakes. In 1563 a compositor apparently had problems reading a transcription of the examinations of John Fortune, a Marian martyr. In the first edition, Fortune is quoted as saying (in reference to the Great Schism) that the popes were '*spiritual* men for in *xvi days* ther wer thre popes'. In the second edition, this passage was silently corrected: the popes were '*spitefull* men for in *xvii monethes* there were three popes'.⁵⁷ At times, these corrections were minute enough to border on the pedantic. The first edition records that the Marian martyr Robert Ferrar was burned in the city of Carmarthen; the second edition states that Ferrar was burned in the *town* of Carmarthen.⁵⁸

This meticulous editing was not driven by an abstract desire for accuracy and exactitude, but by polemical exigencies, primarily the need to appear completely accurate and thus deprive confessional opponents of any foothold when they attacked the book's veracity. In the *A&M* accuracy is the servant of confessional polemic and Foxe's painstaking emendations are often intended to conceal inconvenient facts. As we have seen, this was Foxe's practice in the Latin martyrologies and in his first edition. But in the second edition, in response to the confessional attacks on his first edition, Foxe's 'corrections' were far more thorough.

The examinations of the Marian martyr John Careless provide an excellent example. Foxe printed them in his first edition, but their frequent references to doctrinal disputes among Marian Protestants validated Catholic charges of Protestant divisiveness. In the second edition, after informing the reader that he was omitting 'nedeless matter', Foxe cut over three pages describing the disputes among Marian Protestants over predestination.⁵⁹ All told, Foxe's strategic omissions reduced the original examination's six pages to two.⁶⁰ Foxe's emendations also operated at a more detailed level. Repeating an account printed in his first edition of a book burning that took place in 1557, Foxe, in his second edition,

---

⁵⁴ *A&M* [1570], 1075. ⁵⁵ *A&M* [1570], 1086. ⁵⁶ *R&B*, 19, 163, and 183.
⁵⁷ *A&M* [1563], 1636 and *A&M* [1570], 2100 (our emphases).
⁵⁸ *A&M* [1563], 1100 and *A&M* [1570], 1724.
⁵⁹ Cf. *A&M* [1563], 1529–32 with *A&M* [1570], 2101. In the second edition, Foxe made a number of cuts to documents that he had already printed in the first edition. For example, compare the articles charged against Joan Baker in *A&M* [1563], 373 with *A&M* [1570], 927. The original document is London Guildhall MS 9531/9, fol. 25ᵛ.
⁶⁰ Cf. *A&M* [1563], 1529–35 with *A&M* [1570], 2101–2.

omitted a passage in which Marian authorities compared their actions to the orthodox emperors Theodosius and Valentinian burning heretical books.[61]

Foxe was particularly concerned about some of the material that had been translated from Latin for his first edition. These translations were not Foxe's, but the work of anonymous translators; sometimes, perhaps because of the haste with which the first edition was printed, they contained careless errors that demanded correction. Misled by the same verbal similarity that inspired Gregory the Great's famous pun, one translator rendered the phrase 'potestate angelus altiori' as a 'higher power unto England'. In the second edition, this was corrected to 'a power higher than aungels'.[62] Often, the earlier Latin translations were emended to remove passages that Catholic critics could use against Foxe. For example, the translation of Aeneas Sylvius Piccolomini's account of the Council of Basel in the first edition was, if anything, too faithful to the original to suit Foxe, who wanted to present the council's anti-papal faction in the best possible light. Thus, St Augustine's famous dictum, that he did not believe what was in scripture unless it was vouched for by the authority of the church, was quoted by the anti-papalists at the Council in support of their arguments. This embarrassing text—a favourite among Counter-Reformation Catholics—was included in the first edition, but unobtrusively dropped from the second.[63] The translator had been alert enough to omit Piccolomini's description of Louis d'Aleman, Archbishop of Arles (the leader of the anti-papal faction), collecting relics of saints and bringing them to the Council in a moment of crisis. In the second edition, Foxe added a sentence stating that d'Aleman ordered members of the Council to pray; he simply did not mention that they were praying to the saints for their intercession.[64] Foxe's meticulous, almost finicky, attention to detail ensured that his role in the volume went beyond that of a mere compiler.

Foxe's precise editing extended beyond deleting passages to rewriting them. The second of three articles charged against the Lollard William Taylor stated that he believed that 'Christ must not be worshipped because of his humanity.'[65] Foxe retained the passage, but tendentiously changed it to 'No humaine person is to be worshipped by reason of his humanity.'[66] This rewriting could be done systematically, yet unobtrusively, as Foxe carefully altered key passages within a text he reprinted.[67] Sometimes, however, Foxe's rewriting of a text transformed it almost beyond recognition. For

---

[61] Cf. A&M [1563], 1545 with A&M [1570], 2147. The passage originally appeared in Conrad Hubert, *A briefe treatise concerning the burning of Bucer and Phagius at Cambridge*, trans. Arthur Golding (Thomas Marsh, 1562), sig. F1ʳ.

[62] Cf. A&M [1563], 237 with A&M [1570], 600.

[63] Cf. Aeneas Silvius Piccolomini, *De Gestis Concilii Basiliensis Commentariorum libri II*, ed. and trans. Denys Hay and W. K. Smith (Oxford: Clarendon Press, 1967), 90 and A&M [1563], 297 and A&M [1570], 802.

[64] Cf. Piccolomini, *De Gestis Concilii Basiliensis*, 179 and A&M [1563], 319 and A&M [1570], 815.

[65] 'Chistus non est exorandus racione humanitatis' (*The Register of Henry Chichele, Archbishop of Canterbury, 1414–43*, ed. E. F. Jacob, 4 vols. [Oxford: Oxford University Press, 1937–47], III, 160).

[66] A&M [1570], 780.

[67] See, for example, Thomas S. Freeman, 'Offending God: John Foxe and English Protestant Reactions to the Cult of the Virgin Mary', in Robert N. Swanson, ed., *The Church and Mary*, Studies in Church History 39 (Woodbridge: Boydell & Brewer, 2004), 230–2.

example, when Foxe reprinted *Patrick's Places*, a translation of the Scottish evangelical Patrick Hamilton's *Loci communes*, first printed in 1531, the original text underwent a sea change. Foxe made the work more explicitly predestinarian. He also recast much of the text into syllogisms, giving the theological arguments a more formal structure. Above all, Foxe inserted his own commentary—as long as the original text itself—into the version which appeared in the 'Book of Martyrs'.[68] Readers of the *A&M* may have thought that they were reading a piece by Patrick Hamilton, but Foxe was as much the author of the version of *Patrick's Places* that appeared in the 'Book of Martyrs' as the Scottish evangelical had been.

Many of Foxe's revisions paid as much attention to style as content. His oversight of material translated from his Latin martyrologies sometimes involved detailed changes in wording to express the same essential thought in more felicitous language. In the *Rerum*, Thomas Cromwell, who would become one of the *A&M*'s heroes, was described as 'vir obscuro loco natus'. In the first edition, this was rather harshly translated as 'a man but of base stock and house'. The second edition transforms the statement into 'of simple parentage and house obscure'.[69] Foxe also cast an eagle eye over material sent to him by informants. Although Foxe frequently seems to have passed material to the printing house verbatim, his pen always hovered over the arriving texts. An account of a Marian persecutor's sudden death—John Williams, the chancellor of the diocese of Gloucester— was sent to Foxe, headed 'The straunge and hasty death of Doctour Wyllyams'. Foxe passed it along to the printers, only pausing—in order to heighten the sense that this death was God's judgement—to replace the word 'hasty' with 'fearful'.[70]

While the second edition was being printed, Foxe was particularly concerned to moderate some of the caustic language used against Catholics in his first edition. Paradoxically, this was also a response to the Catholic barrage against his work. Foxe was aware that polemic, like revenge, is best served cold: in order to rebut these attacks successfully, he needed to maintain the appearance of calm, dispassionate accuracy. To this end, Foxe systematically toned down passages that were egregiously inflammatory or abusive. Thus, the first edition's disparaging of Bishop Bonner's 'doggs eloquence' became a criticism merely of his 'rhetoricall repetition'.[71] Similarly, a description of Bonner bearing 'great envy and malice' towards Cranmer was amended to his bearing 'no great good will' towards the archbishop.[72] And a declaration that some Marian martyrs were 'brought unto the bloudy seate of the Consistorye' was changed to 'brought to the open Consistory'.[73]

These changes not only demonstrate Foxe's thorough, indeed, microscopically close, editing, but also his sensitivity to prose style. The most extreme examples of this sensitivity are passages that were inventions of Foxe and others. Such inventions were

---

[68] See *R&B*, 242–3.   [69] See *Rerum*, 154, *A&M* [1563], 598 [recto 589] and *A&M* [1570], 1346.
[70] Cf. BL, Harley MS 425, fol. 135ᵛ with *A&M* [1583], 1911.
[71] Cf. *A&M* [1563], 1491 with *A&M* [1570], 2095.
[72] Cf. *A&M* [1563], 1491 with *A&M* [1570], 2054.
[73] Cf. *A&M* [1563], 1506 with *A&M* [1570], 2076.

infrequent and more likely to occur in Foxe's Latin martyrologies than in the *A&M*. One startling example is Foxe's claim, first made in his first Latin martyrology, but repeated in all editions of the *A&M*, that Reginald Pecock, a prominent anti-Lollard writer, declared that Christ's body was not present in the sacrament. All of the evidence suggests that this surprising statement is entirely Foxe's invention.[74] Foxe also composed a speech for the martyr William Gardiner to deliver to the King of Portugal, justifying his iconoclasm.[75] In these cases, it is clear that the passages were Foxe's invention. In other cases, where demonstrably fictitious material was presented—such as Latimer's celebrated last words, the last words of the martyr James Bainham, and even an account of a shipwreck putatively suffered by William Tyndale—biblical and hagiographical tropes were borrowed and adapted to glorify Protestant martyrs.[76] Whether Foxe invented these incidents or simply repeated, with willing credulity, what others told him is uncertain.

Rewriting passages was the most obvious way Foxe shaped the 'Book of Martyrs', but it was not the only one. Foxe wrote the marginal notes for the *A&M* himself, providing direct commentary on the text.[77] Thus, Foxe's book was mediated for its readers through several interpretative levels involving both direct commentary and unobtrusive emendation. The number of marginal notes vastly increased between the first and second editions as Foxe responded to his critics. For instance, seven marginal notes accompanied the story of William Tyndale in the first edition; in the second edition there were 102.[78] Foxe's account of John Hooper required only twelve marginal notes in the first edition; in the second edition it had 114.[79] And the life and martyrdom of Thomas Cranmer was garnished with eighty-five marginal notes in the first edition; seven years later, there were 380 marginal notes.[80]

Perhaps the most important, yet least obvious, way in which Foxe shaped the 'Book of Martyrs' was through his arrangement of its contents. The first edition has a truly chaotic structure resulting, in large part, from the disruption of its chronological narrative by the insertion of material that arrived while the book was being printed.[81] In the second edition, relative order was imposed on the book's contents, but it was not a strictly

---

[74] See the discussion of this in *R&B*, 46–7.

[75] See Thomas S. Freeman and Marcello J. Borges, '"A grave and heinous incident against our holy Catholic Faith": Two Accounts of William Gardiner's Desecration of the Portuguese Royal Chapel in 1552', *Historical Research*, 69 (1996): 1–17 (7–8).

[76] See respectively Thomas S. Freeman, 'Texts, Lies and Microfilm: Reading and Misreading Foxe's "Book of Martyrs"', *Sixteenth Century Journal*, 30 (1999): 23–46 (42–5); Thomas S. Freeman, 'The Importance of Dying Earnestly: The Metamorphosis of the Account of James Bainham in Foxe's *Book of Martyrs*', in R. N. Swanson, ed., *The Church Retrospective* (Woodbridge: Boydell & Brewer, 1997), 278–9; and David Daniell, 'Tyndale and Foxe', in David Loades, ed., *John Foxe: An Historical Perspective* (Aldershot: Ashgate, 1999), 24–8.

[77] For Foxe writing the *A&M*'s marginal notes see *R&B*, 169–70.

[78] Cf. *A&M* [1563], 513–22 with *A&M* [1570], 1224–32.

[79] Cf. *A&M* [1563], 1049–64 with *A&M* [1570], 1674–84.

[80] Cf. *A&M* [1563], 1470–1503 with *A&M* [1570], 2031–67.

[81] See *R&B*, 117–24.

chronological one. Instead, Foxe follows a loose chronological format, but rearranges stories and episodes for a variety of reasons. One of these was to make the *A&M* more readable by interposing episodes of comic relief amidst the grim tales of suffering and death. For example, in the first edition, Foxe introduces a story of a panic created by a false alarm of fire in a crowded building: 'Hitherto gentle Reader, we have remembered a great number of lamentable and bloody tragedies of such as have been slayne through extreme crueltie. Nowe I will here set before thee againe a mery and comycal spectacle, wherat thou mayest now lawgh and refresh thy selfe.'[82] Similarly, Foxe prefaced a story of Bishop Bonner losing his temper during an episcopal visitation with the explanation that he included it 'although it touch no matter of religion' because 'it may refresh the reader weried percase with other dolefull storyes'.[83]

Foxe organized his book's material for thematic, as well as stylistic, reasons. As a case in point, the lives of the popes were often constructed so that a particular pope would personify particular vices or crimes. In his second edition, Foxe carefully arranged anecdotes about Sixtus IV to present a pattern in which pimping and prostitution progressed to the sale of indulgences (in Foxe's eyes, spiritual prostitution), and then, with a story about Sixtus granting an indulgence absolving sodomy, Foxe intertwined the twin themes.[84] We might also consider Foxe's treatment of the final years of Henry VIII's reign. In the first edition, the rather chaotic arrangement of this material reflected both haste and the haphazard acquisition of information. In the second edition, this material was presented out of chronological sequence, but carefully arranged nonetheless, in order to highlight the themes of unjust persecution, evil counsellors, and royal failure to reform the church.[85]

These examples of Foxe's editing are taken from the first two editions, and largely from the second because Foxe exercised the tightest editorial control over the second edition. Foxe was only minimally involved in preparing the third edition, which essentially reprinted the second edition's text without change.[86] Foxe participated more extensively in editing the fourth edition; although the haste with which it was prepared meant that he could not edit it as closely as he had the second, Foxe did closely supervise the material he added to the fourth edition.[87] The fourth edition, printed in 1583, was the last printed during Foxe's lifetime. There would be a further five unabridged editions printed until the ninth edition was printed in 1684. Additions were made to these editions, but the core text, so painstakingly edited by Foxe, remained unchanged throughout.

As we have seen, Foxe's editing of this core text was so thorough and systematic that his role is much closer to that of an author—understood as one who shapes and disseminates

---

[82] *A&M* [1563], 621.   [83] *A&M* [1563], 1692.
[84] Cf. *A&M* [1563], 38 with *A&M* [1570], 860.
[85] Thomas S. Freeman, 'Hands Defiled with Blood: The Account of Henry VIII in Foxe's "Book of Martyrs"', in Tom Betteridge and Thomas S. Freeman, eds., *Henry VIII in History* (Farnham: Ashgate, 2012).
[86] A few relatively minor changes were made to the text of the third edition and new preliminary materials and a new index were added (*R&B*, 262–71).
[87] See *R&B*, 296–305 and 308–12.

a body of text—than a compiler—one who assembles texts mostly by simple accretion. Perhaps the analogy which best describes Foxe's relationship to the text of the 'Book of Martyrs' would be that of a conductor who also arranges and orchestrates the work of the composers he is conducting. While not the creator of the score, he dictates the ways in which it is heard.

There is no single prose style in the 'Book of Martyrs'. Not only is the text of the work written by scores, if not hundreds, of people, but, more fundamentally, the writings incorporated into the martyrology came from a wide variety of genres. Nevertheless, we believe that it is valid to discuss both the authorship and the prose of the 'Book of Martyrs'. Revisions within the *Acts and Monuments* were not haphazard; instead, from the second edition onward, the work was carefully arranged and edited for the purposes of edifying readers, countering polemical opponents, and even, on occasion, entertaining those who perused its pages. A gifted rhetorician, Foxe was alert both to the importance of style and to the varied ways in which multiple concepts of authorship might signify in the early modern period, as his prefaces clearly demonstrate. Taking pains to shape the prose content of the 'Book of Martyrs' to serve his didactic and polemical purposes, Foxe emended the texts he gathered or acquired with remarkable attention to detail, with the result that a huge compilation was, nevertheless, astonishingly uniform and unambiguous in the messages it presented to generations of readers. Foxe certainly did not work alone, but drew on the research of a battalion of collaborators and writings of an army of sources. Still, the themes of the book and the vision of the church and its history that it presented came from the mind of John Foxe. In this crucial sense, it was, without question, *Foxe's* book of martyrs.

Further Reading

Adamson, Sylvia, Gavin Alexander, and Katrin Ettenbruner, eds. *Renaissance Figures of Speech* (Cambridge: Cambridge University Press, 2007).

Anderson, Benedict. 'Neither Acts Nor Monuments', *English Literary Renaissance*, 41 (2011): 3–30.

Evenden, Elizabeth, and Thomas S. Freeman. *Religion and the Book in Early Modern England: The Making of John Foxe's 'Book of Martyrs'* (Cambridge: Cambridge University Press, 2011).

King, John N. *Foxe's 'Book of Martyrs' and Early Modern Print Culture* (Cambridge: Cambridge University Press, 2006).

Knott, John R. *Discourses of Martyrdom in English Literature, 1563–1694* (Cambridge: Cambridge University Press, 1993).

Lander, Jesse M. *Inventing Polemic: Religion, Print and Literary Culture in Early Modern England* (Cambridge: Cambridge University Press, 2006).

Mack, Peter. *A History of Renaissance Rhetoric, 1380–1620* (Oxford: Oxford University Press, 2011).

——— *Elizabethan Rhetoric: Theory and Practice* (Cambridge: Cambridge University Press, 2004).

Monta, Susannah B. *Martyrdom and Literature in Early Modern England* (Cambridge: Cambridge University Press, 2005).

Mueller, Janel. *The Native Tongue and the Word: Developments in English Prose Style, 1380–1580* (Chicago: University of Chicago Press, 1984).

North, Marcy. *The Anonymous Renaissance: Cultures of Discretion in Tudor-Stuart England* (Chicago: University of Chicago Press, 2003).

Shuger, Debora. *Sacred Rhetoric: The Christian Grand Style in the English Renaissance* (Princeton: Princeton University Press, 1988).

Woolf, Daniel R. 'The Rhetoric of Martyrdom: Generic Contradiction and Narrative Strategy in John Foxe's *Acts and Monements*', in Thomas F. Mayer and Daniel R. Woolf, eds., *Rhetorics of Life-Writing in Early Modern Europe: Forms of Biography from Cassandra Fedele to Louis XIV* (Ann Arbor, MI: University of Michigan Press, 1995), 243–82.

CHAPTER 32

THE MARPRELATE CONTROVERSY

JOSEPH L. BLACK

'AND hold my cloak there somebody, that I may go roundly to work. For I'se so bumfeg the Cooper, as he had been better to have hooped half the tubs in Winchester than write against my worship's pistles.'[1] Tossing his cloak aside and cracking his knuckles confidently in anticipation of the fight to come, this swashbuckling speaker sounds like the sort of habitual tavern brawler Mercutio describes in *Romeo and Juliet*, 'one of those fellows that, when he enters the confines of a tavern, claps me his sword upon the table and says "God send me no need of thee!"' (3.1.5–8). But the source of this quarrel was not one that even the inventive Mercutio could anticipate. The unfortunate Cooper is Thomas Cooper, the elderly and distinguished Bishop of Winchester, and the fighting words he is being challenged to defend here in the spring of 1589 are his belief that the offices of bishops and archbishops were lawfully established in church and state, and not to be replaced by any new form of church government. At the time, Cooper (born *c.* 1517) could draw on memories of church quarrels that reached back to the reign of King Henry VIII. Fifty years of religious polemic had passed through his hands, yet, the pamphlets that introduced this particular voice to the ongoing fray of ecclesiological dispute struck him as disturbingly novel, the writing unlike anything he had seen before in print or manuscript. 'I think the like was never committed to presse or paper, no not against the vilest sort of men, that have lived upon the earth', he exclaimed, bewildered by the style, language, and polemical mode that now confronted him.[2] But by the time his opponent had retrieved his cloak and walked away from the bishops, he had quite thoroughly bumfegged,[3]

This essay draws on the Introduction to Joseph L. Black, ed., *The Martin Marprelate Tracts* (Cambridge: Cambridge University Press, 2008). All citations from the tracts refer to this edition.

[1] *Hay any Work for Cooper* (1589), in *Marprelate Tracts*, 109.

[2] Cooper, *Admonition to the People of England* (1589), 35.

[3] The *OED* defines 'bumfeg' as to flog or thrash. As this is the first recorded usage, however, the definition arises primarily out of the context in which Marprelate uses it.

he had not only sparked the most famous pamphlet war in Renaissance England, but had also given writers of the period a sharpened sense of the resources offered by English prose and a broadened repertoire of strategies for its use. His name was Martin Marprelate.

The Martin Marprelate tracts are a series of six pamphlets and a broadsheet printed on a secret press between October 1588 and September 1589 and distributed with the help of well-organized 'puritan' social networks. They attack the Elizabethan church, particularly church government by bishops (hence the pseudonym, Mar-prelate), and argue on behalf of an alternative, Presbyterian system. Their author was almost certainly the Warwickshire gentleman Job Throkmorton, probably assisted by the Welsh cleric John Penry, who also managed the press.[4] More than two dozen others are known to have been involved in the tracts' production and distribution; all risked charges of treason. The novelty Cooper noted did not lie in the substance of Martin's arguments: the reform agenda he proposed had been honed over almost two decades of Presbyterian opposition. Instead, what seemed unprecedented was Martin's method of presentation. With his conversational prose, ironic modes of argument, fluid shifts among narrative voices, swaggering persona, playful experiments with the conventions of print controversy, and willingness to tell unflattering personal stories about named opponents, Martin shattered conventions of decorum that had governed debates about the church since the accession of Queen Elizabeth. Cooper was exaggerating to some extent: many elements of Martinist style had roots in the vehement polemic of the earlier Reformation, as Cooper himself likely recognized. Even with these models in mind, however, nobody in England had read anything quite like these publications. The tracts sparked a nationwide manhunt, accompanied by a multimedia campaign in which church and state joined forces to counter the influence of what Martin and his opponents both termed 'Martinism'. Martinism and anti-Martinism would proceed to engage one another in a complex and mutually informing dialogue. To talk about the literary, cultural, or stylistic impact of the Marprelate Controversy is to talk about the combined effects of the Marprelate tracts and this anti-Martinist campaign.

At the time, and down the centuries, most commentators on the Marprelate Controversy joined Thomas Cooper in denouncing the tracts as base, scurrilous invective. Beginning in the later nineteenth century, however, pioneering research by scholars such as Edward Arber, J. Dover Wilson, R. B. McKerrow, and William Pierce won the tracts a new reputation as some of the finest Elizabethan prose satires, worthy of their own chapter in the literary history of the sixteenth century. Martinist style remains the focus of many studies, particularly the influence of Martin's wittily colloquial prose on the literature of the Elizabethan Golden Age of the 1590s. But more recent accounts of the Marprelate Controversy have also begun to address a broad range of interconnected literary, historical, religious, legal, and social issues. The tracts are increasingly recognized as playing a key role in the history of Renaissance English pamphlet warfare.

---

[4] For debates over the authorship of the tracts and the evidence for the roles of Throkmorton and Penry, see Black, ed., *Marprelate Tracts*, xxxiv–xlvi.

The Marprelate tracts urged the necessity of public debate on controverted subjects, and sought to create a popularizing polemic that modelled the sound of that debate. Outraged contemporaries responded in ways that crystallize contemporary anxieties concerning satire, libel, and the social uses of print. In addition, Martin's constructions of polemical genealogy helped create a tradition of oppositional writing that would eventually extend from the early Reformation through the civil wars of the 1640s and into the Restoration. In response, church and state reframed this oppositional tradition as treason, reformulated the foundations for conformity to the established church, and crafted counter-arguments that would become standard weapons for decades to come against religious and political opposition. Finally, the Marprelate Controversy generated unparalleled evidence for the histories of authorship and collaboration, surreptitious book production, and underground reading. Legal and other records detail how the tracts were printed on the run against a backdrop of informers, disguises, and code-names, with manuscripts left surreptitiously under hedges and plans made in guarded conversations held in open fields; they were sold out of back doors by sympathetic local officials, read aloud by servants to their fellows, discussed in locked rooms, and handed down for decades in village communities. Documenting the intersections of popular and learned readerships, and print, manuscript, and oral cultures, this important archive illuminates Renaissance reading practices and Renaissance beliefs in the powers, and dangers, of effective prose.

The essence of Martinism—the reason why the tracts had the impact they did, and why they continue to be read—is Martin Marprelate's distinctive voice. Some background is needed to explain why that voice was created and what Throkmorton and the others involved in the Marprelate project hoped to achieve.

* * *

The primary subject of Elizabethan debates between the established church and its Protestant critics was not religion per se, but polity. How should the church be structured and governed? What elements of worship and ceremony accorded best with scripture? On these questions, Martin Marprelate makes no original contributions. The tracts faithfully lay out the mainstream puritan or Presbyterian platform first presented in England in the early 1570s and fine-tuned in numerous publications, petitions to parliament, and other forms of public persuasion. Martin argues for the elimination of clerical hierarchy and its replacement with a fourfold system of governance by pastor, doctor, elder, and deacon. He urges the necessity of purging various elements of church practice, including the use of clerical vestments, the reading of homilies instead of preaching, and the presence of Apocryphal texts in the Book of Common Prayer. Like other Presbyterians, he also allies himself with reform traditions that went back to the Lollards and medieval estates satire by supplementing anti-episcopal arguments with the perennial tropes of anticlerical complaint, denouncing non-residency, pluralism, and simony, and accusing the higher clergy of pride, ambition, greed, lordliness, and misuses of spiritual and secular power. These arguments and accusations appear throughout the tracts, at times, in passages that could be lifted from any number of reform-minded publications of previous decades. A central motive of the Marprelate project, however, was the belief that polemic of this kind had ceased to be effective: the 'most part of men', Martin observes, 'could not be gotten to read anything written in the defence of the one and against the other'.[5] Something new was needed to get a public surfeited to the point of inattention by years of printed debate to heed once more the urgent message of reform.

A jaded reading public was not the only problem. By 1588, reformers also confronted official constraints that had over the previous half-decade made it increasingly difficult for them to publicize their platform. The troubles began for Presbyterians when long-time opponent John Whitgift was named Archbishop of Canterbury in 1583. A decade earlier, Whitgift had engaged in extended polemical battle with Thomas Cartwright, a founding father of English Presbyterianism; as archbishop, Whitgift now had the opportunity, not just to argue for, but to implement conformity. He initiated sweeping efforts to clamp down on dissent, impose uniformity within the church, and block reformers from gaining access to channels of influence. His efforts to restrict parliamentary debate were particularly consequential for the Marprelate project. Throkmorton and Penry both played a role in the 1586–7 parliament, the high-water mark of Elizabethan Presbyterianism as a movement with a political voice on the national scene. Penry wrote *A Treatise Containing the Aequity of an Humble Supplication* (Oxford, 1587) to urge the need for ministers in his native Wales. The pamphlet, printed openly by a licensed printer, was presented in support of a revolutionary 'bill and book' that sought to abolish the legal and liturgical structure of the established church and replace it with a Presbyterian form of worship. Whitgift ordered the entire edition confiscated and had Penry arrested, examined before the court of high commission, and sentenced to prison.[6]

Throkmorton, who sat in parliament as a burgess for Warwick, ran into trouble during the same debate. He had already managed to create an international diplomatic incident with a speech calling for the execution of Mary Queen of Scots, whom he denounced with eloquent vituperation. Threatened with imprisonment in the Tower for offending her son King James, Throkmorton managed one parting shot before fleeing the city. Protesting attacks that dismissed the bill under discussion as 'puritan', Throkmorton revealed his religio-political sympathies, as well as his gift for expression:

> To bewayle the distresses of God's children, it is puritanisme. To finde faulte with corruptions of our Church, it is puritanisme. To reprove a man for swearing, it is puritanisme. To banishe an adulterer out of the house, it is puritanisme. To make humble sute to her Majestie and the High Courte of Parleament for a learned ministery, it is puritanisme. Yea, and I feare me we shall come shortly to this, that to doe God and her Majestie good service shalbe coumpted puritanisme, and thease are of the cunning sleightes of Sathan and his instrumentes in this age.[7]

---

[5] *Hay any Work*, in *Marprelate Tracts*, 115.

[6] Penry describes these events in *Th' Appellation of John Penri* (La Rochelle, 1589), 3–5, 39–43. Martin dramatizes his examination in *Epistle* (1588), in *Marprelate Tracts*, 28.

[7] *Proceedings in the Parliaments of Elizabeth I*, ed. T. E. Hartley, 3 vols. (Leicester: Leicester University Press, 1981–95), 2:314. The order of clauses in the last sentence has been corrected in accordance with the text's manuscript source, Pierpont Morgan Library MS MA 276.

In addition to the characteristically colloquial and yet rhythmically controlled language, Throkmorton's concern for the polemical uses of calumny and the rewriting of reformist language would become central features of the Marprelate tracts. As 'Martin Senior' would explain to his brother 'Martin Junior',[8] understanding the case against reform required an understanding of 'bishops' English', the speakers of which 'wrest our language in such sort, as they will draw a meaning out of our English words, which the nature of the tongue can by no means bear'. The list of examples that follows culminates in a close echo of Throkmorton's parliamentary speech: 'to entreat her Majesty and the parliament that the miseries of the church may be redressed, in the prelates' language is, to seek the overthrow of the state and the disquietness of her subjects'.[9]

Frustrated by the collapse of Presbyterian plans to enact reform through legislation, Penry and Throkmorton began to explore other means of publicizing the cause. They were joined by the printer Robert Waldegrave, who had courted legal troubles throughout the 1580s for printing puritan books. By April 1588, church officials finally lost their patience: Waldegrave's shop was raided and his printing materials destroyed.[10] Penry arranged for the purchase of a press (possibly acting as Throkmorton's agent) and by May, the project was established in the house of Mrs Elizabeth Crane in East Molesey, Surrey. Over the next few months Waldegrave printed works by Penry, by John Udall, a popular preacher removed from the ministry for his views, and, by about the middle of October, the first Marprelate tract, *The Epistle*.[11]

The chain of published attack and counter-attack that preceded the *Epistle* recapitulated the clash between reform demands for public debate and the insistence by defenders of the church that any such debate was both unnecessary and politically dangerous. To Presbyterians such as Throkmorton, Penry, and Udall, open debate mirrored the egalitarian ideals of their congregational practice, in which 'there bee much searching of the trueth by sufficient reasoning without all by matters, quarrels, evasions and colours whatsoever' and 'the judgement of al shalbe sufficiently heard, without stopping of free & sufficient answere, without Lordly carrying away of the matter'.[12] In 1587, Presbyterian requests for plain style and non-magisterial argument elicited a magisterially dismissive 1,400-page rebuttal from John Bridges, Dean of Salisbury, entitled, *A Defence of the Government Established in the Church of Englande*. Developing objections Whitgift had made in his exchanges with Cartwright in the 1570s and anticipating positions advanced subsequently by Richard Hooker, Bridges saw no need to debate those who so obdurately refused to acknowledge the validity of the status quo. To Bridges, the central issue

---

[8] The fifth Marprelate tract, *Theses Martinianae* (1589), purports to be written by Marprelate's son Martin Junior, and the sixth, *The Just Censure and Reproof of Martin Junior* (1589), by his son Martin Senior. Despite the new pseudonyms, both tracts are clearly the work of the same pen that voiced Martin Marprelate: see Black, ed., *Marprelate Tracts*, xliv–xlv.

[9] *Just Censure*, in *Marprelate Tracts*, 183–4.

[10] Martin discusses the destruction of Waldegrave's press in *Epistle*, in *Marprelate Tracts*, 23–4.

[11] For the movements of the press and the other households involved, see Black, ed., *Marprelate Tracts*, l–lvi.

[12] John Field (attrib.), 'Praeface to the Christian Reader', in William Fulke (attrib.), *Briefe and Plaine Declaration* (1584), sig. A3ʳ.

was the question of interpretative authority, as Hooker would later suggest when he wondered if reformers would ever be content 'to referre your cause to any other higher judgement then your owne'.[13]

Bridges' *Defence* generated conventional responses by Presbyterian stalwarts Dudley Fenner and Walter Travers.[14] Both condemned his casual colloquialisms and habit of interspersing brief quotations from his opponents' texts into lengthy, often playful sentences. Not only was the church determined to turn its back on the model divinely provided for its organization, they argued, but it appeared also to be thumbing its nose at reformers as it did so. Martin Marprelate added his voice to this chorus of complaint. Like his predecessors, Martin advocates a syllogistic manner of disputation and rebukes the church for refusing to take seriously the debate over reform. The difficulty lay in crafting an appeal to a public that had apparently lost its taste for traditional polemic, while still honouring the call for scholarly discussion 'without all by matters, quarrels, evasions and colours whatsoever'. The resulting tension between means and ends informs the entire Marprelate project: Martin advocates an embattled disputational ideal in a polemic that defiantly flouts that ideal. The same ambivalence would be replicated in texts produced by the anti-Martinist campaign, where it would, in turn, provoke debates throughout the 1590s on issues of appropriate style, the relation of writer to textual personae, and the social responsibilities of authorship.

The first two Marprelate tracts mount sustained critiques of the brick-sized *Defence*—'a portable book, if your horse be not too weak', as Martin remarks.[15] The adjective 'long-winded', in the modern sense of 'tedious lengthiness', makes its first recorded appearance in Martin's assault on Bridges' logical, exegetical, grammatical, and rhetorical laxity.[16] 'His style is as smooth as a crabtree cudgel' and his verbosity, Martin gleefully argues, compelled the stationer Thomas Chard to seek legal protection against action for the debt incurred to print the *Defence*, 'for men will give no money for your book, unless it be to stop mustard pots'.[17] These attacks on an opponent's syntax, grammar, and even marketability might seem frivolous, but Martin argues that form reflects substance. While 'honest and godly causes' could be defended by 'good proofs and a clear style', Bridges had 'defended our church government which is full of corruptions, and therefore the style and the proofs must be of the same nature that the cause is'.[18] That is, a defence of the indefensible could be founded only on specious logic and slippery language. Fenner and Travers had accused Bridges of playing, rather than arguing; Martin asserts that a senseless book deserves a foolish response, and so adopts the voices of the episcopal dunce, stage clown, and rustic simpleton to represent the opponents such jesting deserved. He had no choice,

---

[13] Richard Hooker, *Folger Library Edition of the Works of Richard Hooker*, gen. ed. W. Speed Hill, 7 vols. in 8 (Cambridge, MA: Harvard University Press, 1977–98), 1:29.

[14] Dudley Fenner, *Defence of the Godlie Ministers, against the Slaunders of D. Bridges* (Middelburg, 1587); Walter Travers, *Defence of the Ecclesiastical Discipline* (Middelburg, 1588).

[15] *Epitome* (1588), in *Marprelate Tracts*, 56.

[16] *Hay any Work*, in *Marprelate Tracts*, 139.

[17] *Epitome* and *Epistle*, in *Marprelate Tracts*, 56, 14.

[18] *Epitome*, in *Marprelate Tracts*, 57.

Martin claims with an air of naïve scrupulousness: 'otherwise dealing with Master Doctor's book, I cannot keep *decorum personæ*'.[19] With characteristic irony, Martin, on his opening page, simultaneously distances himself from outrages of polemical manner by blaming them on his opponent, and establishes a sophisticated narrative voice that exploits his own refusal to play by the polemical rules.

This doubleness and fluidity characterize the Martinist voice throughout the tracts. 'Martin Marprelate' is both an opponent of the bishops and a fellow primate as foolish as his episcopal brethren, the 'proud, popish, presumptuous, profane, paltry, pestilent and pernicious prelates'.[20] Repeatedly shifting perspective, he is both person and stance, Martin and *a* Martin. The name itself is multivalent, playing ironically with contemporary senses of 'Martin' as monkey, bird, ass, dupe, or rustic clown. As anti-Martinist writers would frequently note, 'Martin' was a name associated generally with foolery or madness. Confident and direct, the voice models spoken discourse and soon becomes an almost physical presence at the reader's side. We hear Martin's laughter ('py hy hy hy. I cannot but laugh, py hy hy hy') and see him struggling to catch his breath after quoting one of Bridges' lengthy sentences ('Do you not see how I pant?').[21] We watch with complicit amusement as he conjures up opponents, then responds to onlookers trying to butt into the conversation from their seats in the (textual) margins. When a voice relegated to a side note points out that Marprelate has, as a result of one rhetorical flourish, 'put more than the question in the conclusion of your syllogism', Martin interrupts his own narrative to reply: 'This is a pretty matter, that standers-by must be so busy in other men's games: why sauceboxes must you be prattling? You are as mannerly as bishops, in meddling with that you have nothing to do, as they do in taking upon them civil offices.'[22] Speakers and addressees walk in and out of Martin's pages, like actors making their entrances and exits. Opponents deliver their own set-piece speeches, instructing the anti-Martinist troops.[23] Indirect address slides mid-sentence into direct address. In a letter to his brother Martin Junior, Martin Senior wonders what might happen 'if a man should go and ask thine uncle Canterbury' a certain question. But the fictive frame suddenly shifts when Martin Senior parenthetically addresses Martin Junior as if his brother, hasty and literal minded, were actually in his presence: '(but stay boy, I mean not that thou shouldest go and demand the question of him)'.[24] Text and dialogue, conventions of print and conventions of orality, repeatedly blur: the Marprelate tracts are fundamentally performative.

Francis Bacon would speak for many when he condemned the theatrical turn Martin had apparently initiated: 'matters of religion', he notes, were now being 'handled in the

---

[19] *Epistle*, in *Marprelate Tracts*, 7.
[20] *Epistle*, in *Marprelate Tracts*, 10.
[21] *Hay any Work* and *Epitome*, in *Marprelate Tracts*, 66, 103.
[22] *Epistle*, in *Marprelate Tracts*, 10.
[23] *Just Censure* offers speeches in the voices of John Whitgift and John Aylmer, Bishop of London (*Marprelate Tracts*, 171–5, 185–6).
[24] *Just Censure*, in *Marprelate Tracts*, 184.

style of the stage'.²⁵ In a letter of advice that Richard Hooker would incorporate into his *Lawes of Ecclesiastical Politie* (1593), George Cranmer observed that whereas respectable reformers such as Thomas Cartwright had 'set out the [Presbyterian] discipline as a Queen, and as the daughter of God', Martin 'to make her more acceptable to the people, brought her forth as a vice upon the stage'.²⁶ Others invoked the recently deceased comic actor Richard Tarleton or the jest-book fool John Scoggin: as John Lyly rhymed the charge, 'These tinkers termes, and barbers jestes first *Tarleton* on the stage,/Then *Martin* in his bookes of lies, hath put in every page'.²⁷ The family resemblance among Martin, Vice, and clown was clear to contemporaries confronted with such shared characteristics as direct address, racy insinuations, quarrelsomeness, personal taunts, and use of dialect, personae, and word-play. The identification with Tarleton, a performer famous for his ability to improvise, registers contemporary uneasiness with Martin's extemporizing fluidity. Clowns were furthermore associated with the jig, a form of stand-up routine comprising jokes and bawdy stories. With their narrative economy in scene-setting and characterization, the jig and its print counterpart, the jest book, offer formal and tonal analogues for Martin's one-liners and pointed *ad hominem* anecdotes.

Additional sources of the Martinist mode include manuscript satire and other vehicles of coterie or popular culture, such as orally circulated story or song. In his bumfegging of Thomas Cooper, for example, Martin draws on verses originating in Oxford in the 1560s that circulated sexual rumours about Amy Cooper, Cooper's wife.²⁸ The provocative (apparent) suggestion of homoerotic intimacy between John Whitgift and Andrew Perne, the Dean of Ely and Master of Peterhouse, might have made its way into manuscript libel; only Martin Marprelate would dare make the accusation in print.²⁹ To contemporary readers, these personal attacks on church officials were Martin's most shocking innovation. While reform polemicists had inveighed against episcopacy for years, they had, on the whole, denounced the office, rather than the individuals who occupied it. Restraint had been the recent convention on this issue: according to Bacon, 'all indirect or direct glances or levels at men's persons' were 'ever in these cases disallowed'.³⁰ But as Cooper complained, the Martinists were 'not contented to lay downe great crimes generally, as some other have done, but with very undecent tearmes, charge some particular Bishops with particular faultes'.³¹ These 'faultes' ranged from stupidity to bigamy, closet Catholicism to contented cuckoldry, swearing, gambling, and Sabbath-day bowling to theft, corruption, and public brawling. By naming names, Martin rewrote

---

²⁵ 'An Advertisement Touching the Controversies of the Church of England', in Brian Vickers, ed., *Francis Bacon* (Oxford: Oxford University Press, 1996), 3.

²⁶ In Hooker, *Works*, 6:43. For Hooker's use of Cranmer's letter, see *Works*, 6:44–51.

²⁷ John Lyly (attrib.), *Mar-Martine* (1589), in *Complete Works of John Lyly*, ed. R. Warwick Bond, 3 vols. (Oxford: Clarendon Press, 1902), 3:426. For the reference to Scoggin and an additional reference to Tarleton, see Lyly (attrib.), *Whip for an Ape* (1589), in *Works*, 3:419.

²⁸ For Martin's gibes about Amy Cooper, see *Certain Mineral and Metaphysical Schoolpoints* (1589) and *Hay any Work*, in *Marprelate Tracts*, 93, 102, 112 (and notes).

²⁹ See *Epistle* and *Just Censure*, in *Marprelate Tracts*, 29, 180 (and notes).

³⁰ 'Advertisement', in Vickers, ed., *Francis Bacon*, 19.

³¹ Cooper, *Admonition*, 36–7.

traditional ecclesiological polemic for the popular culture of ballad, jig, and libel. Scriptural exegesis and chains of syllogistic reasoning had proved a hard sell, but scandalous stories circulated quickly: with every retelling, Martin could secure broader attention to his scrutiny of episcopal claims to spiritual and secular authority. Martinist display, to use his own repeated term, demonstrated to the community at large not only the invalidity of an office, but also the unworthiness of the individuals who occupied it.[32]

Martin likely found much of his polemical ammunition in the archive compiled over the years by John Field, the administrative heart of Elizabeth Presbyterianism. With help from sympathizers throughout the country, Field had gathered grievances, transcripts of trials and interrogations, stories of badly behaving clerics, and other information related to the repression of reform.[33] Patrick Collinson suggests that Field learned the propaganda value of such material from John Foxe; in essence, this register imitated Foxe's attempt to present the history of a movement through the lives of those persecuted on its behalf.[34] Martin implicitly refers to Field's compilation midway through the *Epistle*, when he warns the bishops that they should note 'what a perilous fellow M. Marprelate is: he understands of all your knavery, and it may be he keeps a register of them: unless you amend, they shall all come into the light one day'.[35] Scandal-prone church officials are therefore not the only people Martin names. Throughout the tracts, Martin humanizes the cause of reform by setting his stories of autocratic clerics against the stories of those who suffered at their hands. Martin furthermore justifies his course by contrasting his open examinations supported by evidence with the closed procedures the bishops employed. 'My book shall come with a witness before the high commission', he remarks, after providing the names and addresses of several men victimized by John Aylmer, Bishop of London. In contrast, 'what is the seat of justice they commonly use in these cases, but only some close chamber at Lambeth, or some obscure gallery in London palace? Where, according to the true nature of an evil conscience, that flyeth and feareth the light, they may juggle and foist in what they list without controlment.'[36] Denied trial by formal debate, Martin shifted the venue to print and mounted a trial of the Elizabethan episcopate in the court of public opinion.

While drawing strategies and content from theatre, coterie satire, and legal documents, the Marprelate tracts also experiment with the conventions governing print publication. Martin's critique of episcopacy extends into all available textual space: his mockingly discursive titles, facetious imprints, chatty marginal notes, inventive running heads, coy subscriptions, and even irreverent errata all become sites for polemical

---

[32] For Martinism as display, see *Theses Martinianae* and *Protestation of Martin Marprelate* (1589), in *Marprelate Tracts*, 161, 198.

[33] A portion of this material was published in *A Parte of a Register* (Middelburg, 1593?). The rest remained in manuscript and eventually ended up in Dr Williams's Library, London; it is calendared in *The Seconde Parte of a Register*, ed. Albert Peel, 2 vols. (Cambridge: Cambridge University Press, 1915).

[34] See Patrick Collinson, 'John Field and Elizabethan Puritanism', in S. T. Bindoff, J. Hurstfield, and C. H. Williams, eds., *Elizabethan Government and Society: Essays Presented to Sir John Neale* (London: Athlone, 1961), 127–62 (145–7).

[35] *Epistle*, in *Marprelate Tracts*, 33.

[36] *Epistle* and *Protestation*, in *Marprelate Tracts*, 13, 203.

point-scoring.[37] The tracts also play with expectations of genre. Five of the seven experiment with the fictive possibilities of the personal letter. The *Epistle* gestures ironically at the rhetoric of petitions, contrasting the colloquial confidence of Martin's charges with the self-abasing feebleness of the language of supplication. Several of the tracts similarly undermine the quotation–response form of the animadversion, the traditional mode of printed debate, by juxtaposing Martin's conversational responses with his opponents' formal language. The *Just Censure* rewrites to Presbyterian ends John Whitgift's own articles of examination, concluding with the mock-legalistic vow 'I, Martin Senior, Gentleman, do here protest, affirm, propound, and defend, that if John Canterbury will needs have a fool in his house, wearing a wooden dagger and a cockscomb, that none is so fit for that place as his brother John a Bridges, dean of Sarum.'[38] The broadsheet *Schoolpoints* likewise packages scandalous charges against named bishops in the formal wording of theological or university disputation, creating an ironic contrast between the genre and the indefensible resolutions he invites the church to defend—that a bishop may have two wives at once, for example (Marmaduke Middleton, Bishop of St David's, defendant).

Of course, Martin Marprelate was not the first English polemicist to employ such popularizing means as colloquial prose, irreverent abuse, dialogue, ironic personae, or linguistic and textual play. Pamphlet wars throughout the earlier stages of the Reformation had produced numerous analogues for all these devices, and the Marprelate tracts draw repeated attention to their own polemical genealogy. Most obviously, Martin positions himself as the latest champion of Presbyterian protest, citing such writers as Cartwright, Field, Fenner, Travers, Udall, Penry, and Anthony Gilby. But he also anchors these writings in a tradition of reformist challenge that included writers of the previous generation such as William Tyndale, John Frith, Robert Barnes, John Hooper, James Pilkington, and John Foxe. Other publications associated with the Marprelate project extend this family tree. The preface of a *c.* 1588 reprint of a ploughman text first published around 1550, *O Read me, for I am of Great Antiquitie. I Plaine Piers which can not Flatter*, figures Martin Marprelate as the grandson of Piers Ploughman, and may have been intended to play a role in the Marprelate project. A 1592 Presbyterian petition attributed to Throkmorton defends Marprelate by allying him with an oppositional culture that reached back through Tyndale, Barnes, Hooper, and Hugh Latimer to John Wyclif, *Piers Ploughman*, and the pseudo-Chaucerian *Ploughman's Tale*.[39] Because anticlerical and anti-Catholic arguments were easily repackaged for anti-episcopal purposes, these alliances with the heroes of the English Reformation and with an extended tradition of proto-Protestant complaint helped legitimate the cause of reform and rebut the charge of introducing innovations.

---

[37] For running heads, see *Marprelate Tracts*, 209–10; for subscriptions and errata, *Epistle, Epitome*, and *Protestation*, in *Marprelate Tracts*, 45, 85–6, 207; for marginalia, *Epistle, Epitome*, and *Just Censure* (throughout) and *Hay any Work* (occasionally).

[38] *Just Censure*, in *Marprelate Tracts*, 181.

[39] *Petition Directed to Her Most Excellent Majestie* (Middelburg, 1592), esp. 34–8.

Writings of the earlier Reformation also offered Martin Marprelate possible models of style, language, and polemical approach. Martin was clearly familiar with Tyndale's colloquial directness and linguistically inventive abuse, as attested by his extensive citations from Tyndale's work in *Theses Martinianae*. Martin also knew the work of writers such as John Bale and William Turner: he mentions Turner, draws on works by Bale, and gestures towards some of their more famous anticlerical publications.[40] Bale, in particular, seems a likely source for such Martinist strategies as pseudonyms and personae, irreverent puns on opponents' names, and even dialogic marginalia. The preface and ironic apparatus of Bale's translation of Stephen Gardiner's *De vera obediencia an oration* (1553), for example, has a strongly Martinist feel, as do several of his other works. Other possible influences include Luke Shepherd, Simon Fish, William Baldwin, Robert Crowley, and Thomas Becon. But while these writers all share elements of Martinist style, few offer anything like Martin's sustained narrative sophistication and self-reflexive play with textuality. Whatever his sources, Martin did something new with them, and in the process introduced late Elizabethan writers to the possibilities offered by the vernacular vigour and linguistic inventiveness of earlier sixteenth-century prose.

* * *

A nationwide hunt for Martin and his accomplices began in November 1588, about the time the second tract was published. With officials searching cellars and questioning the usual suspects, church and state also launched a parallel publicity campaign designed to counter the Martinist challenge in the public sphere. At first, they employed traditional means to disseminate official condemnation. In the early months of 1589, Thomas Cooper published his collection of point-by-point rebuttals; rising clerical star Richard Bancroft delivered an anti-Martinist sermon, soon published, at Paul's Cross, the outdoor pulpit that served to publicize the official line on political and religious issues; a previously unpublished sermon on obedience John Whitgift had preached in 1583 was dug out of a desk drawer and supplied with a freshly written preface that denounced Martin's 'lewd and shameles libels'; and the Queen issued a proclamation that required all copies of the tracts to be turned in so they could be 'utterly defaced', and warned anyone with knowledge of their 'Authours, Writers, Printers, or dispersers' to report to the authorities.[41] These responses all emphasize the dangers Martinist style posed to political, religious, social, and even economic order. To challenge one element of hierarchy, they argued, was to challenge all forms of hierarchy—a slippery slope argument King James would later summarize succinctly as 'no Bishop, no King'.[42]

---

[40] Martin mentions Turner in *Epistle* (*Marprelate Tracts*, 38), draws on Bale's *Pageant of Popes* (1574) for historical information, and probably refers to works such as Turner's *The Huntying & Fyndyng out of the Romishe Fox* (Bonn, 1543; Antwerp, 1544?) and Bale's *Yet a Course at the Romyshe Foxe* (Antwerp, 1543) when he employs the language of fox-hunting in his own attacks (e.g. *Epistle*, in *Marprelate Tracts*, 19).

[41] Richard Bancroft, *Sermon Preached at Paules Crosse* (1589); John Whitgift, *Most Godly and Learned Sermon* (1589), sig. A2^v; *Proclamation against Certaine Seditious and Schismatical Bookes and Libels* (1589).

[42] Reported in William Barlow, *The Summe and Substance of the Conference...at Hampton Court* (1604), 36.

As if to mock these efforts of suppression, two more Marprelate tracts appeared before the end of March 1589. With the investigation dragging on and no end in sight to Martinist provocation, new strategies seemed to be required. On the advice of Richard Bancroft, a future archbishop, the church decided to launch an unusual counter-offensive: they would sponsor hired pens to defend the embattled bishops with writings that deployed Martin's own stylistic weapons against him. These officially encouraged publications likely comprise two collections of satirical verse, *Mar-Martine* (1589) and *A Whip for an Ape: or Martin Displaied* (1589), and six prose satires: *Martins Months Minde* (1589), *Pappe with an Hatchet* (1589), *An Almond for a Parrat* (1590), and three tracts by 'Pasquill', *A Countercuffe given to Martin Junior* (1589), *The Returne of the Renowned Cavaliero Pasquill of England* (1589), and *The First Parte of Pasquils Apologie* (1590). John Lyly and Thomas Nashe were almost certainly involved in this campaign, with Lyly probably responsible for *Mar-Martine* and *Pappe with an Hatchet*, Nashe for *Almond for a Parrat*, and the two collaborating on *Whip for an Ape*. Nashe and sometimes Robert Greene have been associated with the other four, but in general, the authorship of these, like that of many satirical pamphlets of the period, remains unclear. Notably, Lyly, Nashe, and Greene were all either practising or soon-to-be practising playwrights: Bancroft recognized that for his strategy to be effective these commissioned publications needed to address the same popular audience Martin had targeted. Anti-Martinist theatre, however, seems likely to have been independent of the official campaign, a product more of theatrical enterprise than episcopal propaganda. These interludes drew on the conventions of such traditional genres as the beast fable and morality play, returning, like Martin himself, to the resources offered by earlier Reformation modes of polemical engagement.[43]

On the whole, the prevailing mode of this anti-Martinist prose is exuberant one-upmanship, as if these polemical mercenaries were competing not only with Martin, but also with one another to devise the most imaginative insults and witty comparisons. Many readers consider *Almond for a Parrat* the most successful appropriation of Martin's style and voice. The most polemically effective is probably *Martins Months Minde*, which makes good use of a fictive frame built around the narrative of Martin's last days, with his speeches of repentance, autopsy results, funeral, last will, and epitaphs. But while stylistically and linguistically interesting, these pamphlets can also be densely allusive and learnedly satirical. Too often, their rhetorical virtuosity seems an end in itself, and their imagined audience one of fellow university wits, rather than provincial alehouse grumblers concerned about the powers of the local church courts. Ultimately, Bancroft's anti-Martinist campaign confirmed contemporary anxieties about the power of print and helped popularize among an emerging class of professional writers the very elements of Martinist style it had set out to condemn.

Opposition to the campaign would become a recurring trope among the numerous conventional responses to the Marprelate tracts. Lyly himself registered uneasiness

---

[43] Descriptions only remain of these performances and they are collected in E. K. Chambers, *The Elizabethan Stage*, 4 vols. (1923; repr. Oxford: Clarendon Press, 1967), 4:229–33.

about claiming the moral high ground on issues of decorum while deploying rhetorical strategies identical to those he denounced. Recognizing that readers might disapprove of his borrowed style, he invites them to blame Martin for any 'bad tearmes' they find in *Pappe with an Hatchet*.[44] But Lyly was not the only one with reservations. *A Myrror for Martinists* (1590), for example, criticizes both 'the late *Martine* libellers' and their 'repliers, who notwithstanding they have chosen the better part, yet handle it not so charitably and modestly as it requireth'.[45] The objection is characteristic: what unites the works of these commentators is disapproval, not of church government by bishops, but of the tactics the hierarchy had adopted in its defence. In a work written in 1589, but not published until 1593, Gabriel Harvey offers a sustained consideration of anti-Martinist discourse. Attacking Lyly as the author of *Pappe with an Hatchet*, he argues that it were better to confute levity with gravity, 'ridiculous Martin with reverend Cooper', than enlist in the defence of the church this 'professed jester, a Hick-scorner, a scoff-maister, a playmunger, an Interluder; once the soile of Oxford, now the stale of London, and ever the Apesclogg of the presse'. Harvey's argument appeals to more than decorum. In both the *Advertisement for Pap-hatchet, and Martin Mar-prelate* and *Pierces Supererogation* (1593), the attack on Thomas Nashe, in which he published the *Advertisement*, Harvey sets anti-Martinist prose against a range of recent English and continental publication, contrasting his opponents' railing wit with their contemporaries' more substantial literary, scholarly, scientific, and devotional achievements. The critique is partly the insider's refusal to be impressed by the efforts of a fellow stylist: the 'finest wittes', he remarks, 'preferre the loosest period in M. Ascham, or Sir Philip Sidney, before the tricksiest page in Euphues, or Pap-hatchet'. But Harvey also argues that the appropriation of Marprelate's disorderly language threatened to displace not only quality prose, but also the fundamentals of civil discourse on which society rested. 'If the world should applaude to such roisterdoisterly Vanity', he warns, 'what good could grow of it, but to make every man madbrayned, and desperate; but a generall contempt of all good order, in Saying, or Dooing; but an Universal Topsy-turvey?' As for Martin, Harvey takes his own advice and offers a scholarly rebuttal of what he saw as the weaknesses of the Presbyterian cause: given a monarchical framework, he concludes, there could be no further reformation in England without 'an Upsy-downe' in political structure.[46]

Attacks on Thomas Nashe by both Harvey brothers (Richard, as well as Gabriel) spiralled eventually into the Harvey–Nashe quarrel, a complex exchange that continued the debate generated by the Marprelate Controversy concerning the social uses of print. The Harveys, arguing for the role of print culture in promoting good learning and proper behaviour, accused Nashe of taking 'uppon him in civill learning, as *Martin* doth in religion, peremptorily censuring his betters at pleasure'.[47] But the most

---

[44] *Pappe with an Hatchet*, in Lyly, *Works*, 3:396.
[45] T. T., *Myrror for Martinists* (1590), 1.
[46] Harvey, *Advertisement*, published in *Pierces Supererogation* (1593), 74–5, 84, 137.
[47] Richard Harvey, *Theologicall Discourse of the Lamb of God* (1590), sig. a2ᵛ. This opening Epistle is not found in all copies.

sophisticated contemporary analysis of the Marprelate Controversy is Francis Bacon's 'An Advertisement', a government brief written in 1589 for manuscript circulation. While Bacon deplores Martin's willingness 'to turn religion into a comedy or satire', he finds the strategy of lowering the response to Martin's level equally misguided. Like Gabriel Harvey, Bacon seems less concerned with the validity of the arguments offered by either side than with stability and social harmony. His emphasis is on the politics of style and his message to the state is that the freeing up of polemical language, this 'strange abuse of antics and pasquils', represented a danger the state's own campaign was helping to legitimate, rather than suppress. The style of both Marprelate and the anti-Martinists reached out to a more broadly constituted audience than had been the norm for printed debate, and Bacon had no faith in the wisdom of crowds: 'whatsoever be pretended, the people is no meet judge nor arbitrator, but rather the quiet, moderate, and private assemblies and conferences of the learned'.[48]

Bacon and the Harveys, however, were on the losing side of this quarrel. While the Marprelate project failed in its campaign to topple episcopacy (and probably contributed to the collapse of organized Presbyterianism in the early 1590s), most scholars agree that the tracts and the controversy they generated did influence late Elizabethan literature and culture. Admittedly, this influence is easier to intuit than to document. But the effectiveness of Martin's strategies for reaching a popular audience probably encouraged the transition in prose style from rhetorical formality to extemporizing colloquialism, contributing to the development of English comic fiction. Martin's *ad hominem* attacks and the equally personal anti-Martinist response probably popularized the satiric and ironic modes that would characterize much literary production in the decade after their publication. Finally, Martin's success in getting himself heard over the many other voices competing in print probably caught the attention of other writers, including those who had been hired to denounce Martin's polemical strategies. Thomas Nashe's post-Martin prose is often discussed as exemplifying the influence of Martinism, particularly with respect to his performative manner and self-reflexive play with ironic personae. Nashe, in turn, is increasingly recognized as a major influence on the literature of the 1590s, making him an important conduit for the transmission of Martinist style. A case can also be made for the controversy's influence on Robert Greene, another writer increasingly seen as an influential presence in the literary culture of the 1590s, particularly with respect to his experiments with personae and cultivation of authorial celebrity.

Prohibitions against onstage reference to topical political and religious subjects mean that controversy is largely an implicit presence in late Elizabethan drama, a matter more of echo and parallel than direct allusion. But arguments can be made for lines of connection here as well. Like verse and prose fiction, drama of the 1590s built on turn-of-the-decade developments in colloquial language, comic prose, satirical modes, and ironic self-presentation. More generally, playwrights, like writers in other genres, could draw on newly resonant tropes developed by the anti-Martinist campaign. These lines of response were in some degree traditional, in that they had been used in England against

[48] 'Advertisement', in Vickers, ed., *Francis Bacon*, 3, 19.

reformers long before Martin appeared on the scene. But to meet the challenge of what contemporaries recognized as a radical culmination of reformist rhetoric, these countering measures were given formulations that would retain cultural currency for years after the Marprelate press had been silenced. Martin was figured repeatedly as the emblematic bad subject, his irreverent populist appeal redefined as a treasonous refusal to recognize any authority other than selfish individual desires. The attack on church hierarchy was branded an exercise in economic redistribution, with reformers accused of seeking episcopal revenues for themselves. Recurrent attacks on Presbyterian scholarship asserted that the desire for reform was founded on wilful ignorance. More generally, *the* Martin became *a* Martin quite early in the Marprelate Controversy, a name for any figure who embodied attributes inimical to the smooth workings of social order. 'Martinism' came to signify culturally as pride, self-love, or unmerited self-conceit. Martin's name got attached to troublemakers of any sort: the noisy, the irreverent, the challenging, the railing, the libellous, and the scheming. In print controversy, to be a Martin was to be a bad reader or a bad interpreter, anybody who crossed the accepted boundaries of rhetorical practice.[49]

Once the social meanings of the Martinist persona were established, they became available for literary or polemical appropriation. Any figure characterized by social or political opposition, self-love, inappropriate self-confidence, unruliness, greed, envy, propensities to satirical attack, or self-serving interpretative practices could acquire Martinist valences. Counter-discourses on the meaning of Martinism also appeared: some appropriations deploy the Martinist voice and persona in ways that signify cleverness, wit, satirical truth-telling, or plain-speaking opposition to abuses of power. The most famous of these positive deployments would appear fifty years after the initial controversy, when Martin Marprelate was resurrected by oppositional writers in the 1640s like Richard Overton.[50] Overall, what Martin Marprelate did better than almost any other writer of his period was to create a voice that got noticed. Contemporaries responded to Martin, usually angrily, occasionally admiringly (for technique, if not for content), often with baffled consternation. But they did respond, and Martin would retain his reputation as a dangerous writer whose polemical style threatened all forms of authority for almost a century after he first appeared. And perhaps Martin would consider that reputation a sign of success. For in his view, the main goal was to get talked about, because in the marketplace of ideas, God's (Presbyterian) truth would eventually emerge the winner.

Further Reading

Anselment, Raymond A. *'Betwixt Jest and Earnest': Marprelate, Milton, Marvell, Swift, and the Decorum of Religious Ridicule* (Toronto: University of Toronto Press, 1979).

---

[49] For a detailed discussion of anti-Martinist tropes, see Black, ed., *Marprelate Tracts*, lxv–lxxxiii.
[50] See Black, ed., *Marprelate Tracts*, lxxxv–xc.

Arber, Edward. *An Introductory Sketch to the Martin Marprelate Controversy, 1588–1590* (1879; repr. London: Archibald Constable, 1895).

Carlson, Leland H. *Martin Marprelate, Gentleman: Master Job Throkmorton Laid Open in His Colors* (San Marino, CA: Huntington Library, 1981).

Collinson, Patrick. *The Elizabethan Puritan Movement* (London: Jonathan Cape, 1967).

Halasz, Alexandra. *The Marketplace of Print: Pamphlets and the Public Sphere in Early Modern England* (Cambridge: Cambridge University Press, 1997).

Kendall, Ritchie. *Drama of Dissent: The Radical Poetics of Nonconformity, 1380–1590* (Chapel Hill: University of North Carolina Press, 1986).

King, John N. *English Reformation Literature: The Tudor Origins of the Protestant Tradition* (Princeton: Princeton University Press, 1982).

Lake, Peter. *Anglicans and Puritans? Presbyterianism and English Conformist Thought from Whitgift to Hooker* (London: Unwin Hyman, 1988).

Lander, Jesse. *Inventing Polemic: Religion, Print, and Literary Culture in Early Modern England* (Cambridge: Cambridge University Press, 2006).

Marprelate, Martin. *The Martin Marprelate Tracts*, ed. Joseph L. Black (Cambridge: Cambridge University Press, 2008).

Pierce, William. *An Historical Introduction to the Marprelate Tracts* (London: Archibald Constable, 1908).

Raymond, Joad. *Pamphlets and Pamphleteering in Early Modern Britain* (Cambridge: Cambridge University Press, 2003).

——ed. *The Oxford History of Popular Print Culture, Volume 1: Cheap Print in Britain and Ireland to 1660* (Oxford: Oxford University Press, 2011).

CHAPTER 33

SERMONS

PETER MCCULLOUGH

WITH the possible exception of the Bible in English and the Book of Common Prayer, no prose works were more widely encountered across all classes of English speakers in the early modern period than sermons. Unlike prose genres composed for consumption in written or printed form—letters, romances, essays, characters, histories, and religious polemic—the sermon did not, in its primary oral form of delivery, depend upon literacy for its exemplification and dissemination of the variety and power of English prose. And the sheer number of sermons preached anywhere in Britain, especially from the late Elizabethan decades and after, outstripped literally by miles the accessibility of the only competing genre of performed prose—drama—which, for experience of it, required proximity to London theatres or the chance appearance of a travelling troupe in a provincial town or city. Given their popularity and prominence, sermons also contributed to religious books being the largest percentage of titles printed in English before the outbreak of the Civil War: 1,200 sermons appeared during the reign of Elizabeth alone, and almost twice that number between her death in 1603 and 1640.[1] But in spite of this prominence in the period, the modern critical history of sermons—particularly the formal study of sermons as prose—has been comparatively limited. Perhaps the best introduction to sermons in a volume such as this, then, is a critical survey which traces the two dominant disciplinary approaches—the literary and the historical—hitherto pursued quite independently of each other, but the integration of which probably offers the best scope for future study.

Early modern prose and the sermon grew up together, from the first stirrings of Tudor humanism to the 'rational age' of the Royal Society. The centrality of religion to early modern culture, and the sermon as that culture's hallmark, means that no genre provides so many and so varied specimens of English prose across the whole chronological range of the period, and early twentieth-century critics, in particular, went to considerable

---

[1] James Rigney, 'Sermons into Print', in Peter McCullough, Hugh Adlington, and Emma Rhatigan, eds., *The Oxford Handbook of the Early Modern Sermon* (Oxford: Oxford University Press, 2011), 198–212 (204); Arnold Hunt, *The Art of Hearing: English Preachers and their Audiences* (Cambridge: Cambridge University Press, 2011), 125–7.

lengths to construct taxonomies of those styles. Morris W. Croll's magisterial case for 'Senecan', 'Attic', 'Baroque'—or otherwise 'anti-Ciceronian'—prose style as the antecedent of modern English prose was, of course, their only begetter.[2] Although Croll himself made only passing reference to preachers such as Andrewes and Donne (and for the latter, Croll's gestures are towards his poetry), others were quick to mine the rich vein of sermons for stylistic analysis. The best of these mid-century studies was George Williamson's refinement and extension of Croll's thesis, *The Senecan Amble*. Its eighth chapter, 'Scheme and Point in Pulpit Oratory', still offers some of the best insights into the distinctive 'pointed' style of Lancelot Andrewes, and its dying fate through the seventeenth century to the Restoration divines Gilbert Burnet and John Tillotson.[3]

But Williamson's healthy aversion to overgeneralizations about style within a single author's work, as well as across authors and periods, also registered the hazards of assigning definitive stylistic labels to sermon prose. Perhaps only Andrewes was a practitioner of anything like 'pure' Senecanism: 'a virtuoso in the short sentence', 'addicted to far-fetched metaphor or catachresis; wit or formal ingenuities... and minute divisions of the text' (238, 239). In other preachers, Williamson found shadings or sudden eruptions of Senecanism: Donne 'moves between the schematic and the modulated loose period' (245); in Hall 'a basic terseness emerges from time to time' (247); while Tillotson is 'no less devoted to the short sentence than Andrewes, but without the trimmings' (272). The slipperiness of the stylistic category which Williamson tried so valiantly to grasp is well summed-up in his summary assessment of the stylistically transitional, mid-century sermon theorist John Wilkins: 'if Wilkins's programme is Senecan, it points to the style of Hall and South rather than that of Andrewes and Donne, though both may be called Senecan' (250). Those who have compared even a single paragraph each by Donne and Andrewes—much less Hall and South—may be baffled by how Williamson could posit them as practitioners of the same stylistic 'programme', and his attempt to do so highlights the risks of using generalizing labels for sermon prose.

The problem of forced labels is even more acute in what were until very recently the standard monographs on the early modern sermon: W. F. Mitchell's *English Pulpit Oratory from Andrewes to Tillotson* (1932), J. W. Blench's *Preaching in England in the late Fifteenth and Sixteenth Centuries* (1964), and Horton Davies's *Like Angels from a Cloud: English Metaphysical Preachers 1588–1645* (1986). Although separated by three decades, they all pursue the categorizing impulse of Croll and Williamson, though they use even less useful labels. Williamson's 'Senecan' and 'anti-Ciceronian' were at least literary-historical terms, or at any rate had Roman models, which early moderns, beginning with Erasmus, knew and used in their own conscious revival of a Classical debate over prose style (1–30). Mitchell, though, moved away from Roman styles to combine anachronistic literary and religious descriptors like 'metaphysical' and 'Anglo-Catholic' for stylistic

---

[2] Morris W. Croll, *Style, Rhetoric, and Rhythm: Essays by Morris W. Croll* (Princeton: Princeton University Press, 1966).

[3] George Williamson, *The Senecan Amble: Prose Form from Bacon to Collier* (Chicago: University of Chicago Press, 1951), 231–2, 237–41.

categories which obliterated very real differences, not just in style, but also in churchmanship and theology. Blench chose to carve-up a century of preaching into regnal chunks ('Henrician', 'Elizabethan', etc.), and further subdivided those with the questionable stylistic brands of 'plain', 'colloquial', and 'ornate'. And as late as 1986, Davies tried to keep alive the notion of 'metaphysical' preaching 'to describe dozens of preachers... who shared little more than their grammar school education, conformity to the Church of England, and Davies's own estimation of their "eloquence" '.[4] The Achilles' heel of all these approaches was their attempt to force the hundreds of early modern sermon authors into stylistic, period, and religious categories which could never accommodate them without overgeneralization and anachronism. Over the same period, the most lasting and useful sermon criticism focused on individual authors. These included T. S. Eliot's trenchant 1926 comparison of Andrewes and Donne as preachers, and Evelyn M. Simpson's mostly biographical and bibliographical account of Donne's sermons. And soon the first scholarly editions of sermons by Andrewes and Donne put them more firmly on a canonical footing.[5]

Two questions which early stylistic surveys of sermons failed sufficiently to ask were, 'What did early modern preachers think that sermons were, generically?', and 'What did they think they were for, functionally?' I will venture more detailed answers to those questions later in the chapter, but I must say here that preachers were not usually—as one might begin to think from Williamson, for example—engaged in self-conscious attempts at being stylish, or aligning themselves with any particular style for its own sake. Style study alone, with its focus upon local effects such as sentence length, parallelism, cadence, and rhetorical tropes and figures, fails in the first instance to attend sufficiently to genre— that is, to the larger structural parts which make a sermon a sermon, rather than simply a sample of prose. Secondly, and even more important, it fails to attend sufficiently to purpose and function—to the 'why' and 'to what purpose' the preacher deploys form and technique. To date, the best application of Crollian style study to the form and function of early modern preaching remains the sustained analysis of Donne's sermons, which makes up the majority of Joan Webber's study of Donne's prose style.[6] Loosed from the period-survey's need to generalize and categorize across many authors in a large period, Webber can confidently, and correctly, assert how both the 'Senecan' and 'Ciceronian' cohabit in Donne's rich prose (22–4), assess the full range of his rhetorical and grammatical devices

---

[4] Lori Anne Ferrell and Peter McCullough, eds., *The English Sermon Revised: Religion, Literature and History, 1600–1750* (Manchester: Manchester University Press, 2000), 3–6.

[5] T. S. Eliot, 'Lancelot Andrewes', *TLS*, 1286 (23 September 1926), 621–2; repr. in *Selected Essays of T. S. Eliot* (New York: Harcourt, Brace & World, 1960), 299–310; Evelyn M. Simpson, *A Study of the Prose Works of John Donne*, 2nd edn. (Oxford: Clarendon Press, 1948), 255–90; G. M. Story, ed., *Lancelot Andrewes: Sermons* (Oxford: Clarendon Press: 1967); George R. Potter and Evelyn M. Simpson, eds., *The Sermons of John Donne*, 10 vols. (Berkeley and Los Angeles: University of California Press: 1953–62); Janel Mueller, ed., *Donne's Prebend Sermons* (Cambridge, MA: Harvard University Press, 1971).

[6] Joan Webber, *Contrary Music: The Prose Style of John Donne* (Madison: University of Wisconsin Press, 1963), 21–182.

(31–70), his metaphor and imagery (71–89), and attend to sermons as coherent wholes (143–82), as well as to the crucial components of authorial personality and performance (90–122). From other critics in this period, only Brian Vickers's lapidary (and regrettably short) introductions to Andrewes and Donne surpass Webber's combination of formal analysis with sensitivity to the generic functions of the sermon; and Richard McCabe skilfully traced the generic influences of satire and meditation on the sermons of Donne and Andrewes's critically neglected contemporary, Joseph Hall.[7]

Webber's work, though, does show signs of its age. Her borrowing of the term 'Baroque' from Croll to describe Donne's prose, for example, may no longer be viewed as helpful or even valid for literary analysis. Yet, Webber's contribution still stands out, if only because it was a signpost in sermon studies that was not followed for some fifty years. But it may now point the way for renewed study of sermons as prose after a long, but very productive, detour. And that detour was history. The revolution in British ecclesiastical history sparked by the work of Patrick Collinson, and furthered by scholars such as Peter Lake, Nicholas Tyacke, and Kenneth Fincham, ushered the sermon centre-stage as historical evidence for a completely new understanding of English religion from the reign of Elizabeth to the Civil War.[8] Anachronisms like 'Anglican', 'Puritan', and 'Anglo-Catholic' were swept aside and replaced by a far more nuanced understanding of the shadings of theology and churchmanship within English Protestantism. And this was shown primarily by close historical readings of sermons.

But the sermon emerged in the new ecclesiastical history not only as a key source of historical evidence. It was also identified as a focal point of conflict between a dominant preaching-centred Calvinist consensus and an emergent 'high' churchmanship that was anxious, from at least the 1590s, about the dilatory effects of the cult of the sermon upon liturgical and sacramental worship.[9] A new study of the Jacobean bishops even showed that commitment to preaching constituted 'the preaching pastor' as a distinct brand of episcopacy.[10] These divisions cut so completely across the alignments between prose

---

[7] Brian Vickers, ed., *Seventeenth Century Prose* (London: Longmans, Green and Co., 1969), 70–5, 93–7; Richard A. McCabe, *Joseph Hall: A Study in Satire and Meditation* (Oxford: Clarendon Press, 1982), chap. 6.

[8] Patrick Collinson, *The Elizabethan Puritan Movement* (London: Jonathan Cape, 1967; repr. Oxford: Clarendon Press, 1990); Collinson, *The Religion of Protestants* (Oxford: Clarendon Press, 1982); Peter Lake, 'Lancelot Andrewes, John Buckeridge, and Avant-Garde Conformity at the Court of James I', in Linda Levy Peck, ed., *The Mental World of the Jacobean Court* (Cambridge: Cambridge University Press, 1991), 113–33; Nicholas Tyacke, *Anti-Calvinists. The Rise of English Arminianism, c.1590–1640* (Oxford: Clarendon Press, 1987); Tyacke, 'Lancelot Andrewes and the Myth of Anglicanism', in Peter Lake and Michael Questier, eds., *Conformity and Orthodoxy in the English Church, c.1560–1660* (Woodbridge: Boydell Press, 2000), 5–33; Kenneth Fincham, *Prelate as Pastor: The Episcopate of James I* (Oxford: Clarendon Press, 1990).

[9] Lake, 'Lancelot Andrewes'; Eric Carlson, 'The Boring of the Ear: Shaping the Pastoral Vision of Preaching in England, 1540–1640', in Larissa Taylor, ed., *Preachers and People in the Reformations and Early Modern Period*, (Leiden: Brill, 2001), 249–96; Peter McCullough, *Sermons at Court: Politics and Religion in Elizabethan and Jacobean Preaching* (Cambridge: Cambridge University Press, 1998), 155–67; Mary Morrissey, 'Scripture, Style and Persuasion in Seventeenth-Century English Theories of Preaching', *Journal of Ecclesiastical History*, 53.4 (2002): 686–706 (698–9).

[10] Fincham, *Prelate as Pastor*, 250–76.

style and churchmanship posited by Blench, Mitchell, and Davies that historians did not even pause to notice them. No longer could 'metaphysical wit', or the use of patristic exempla and Classical learning, or a delight in patterned syntactical structures be used to group together preachers as doctrinally and politically different as Thomas Playfere, Donne, and Andrewes. Indeed, only perhaps at the extremities of nonconformist preaching and the *sui generis* sermons of Andrewes can one find reliable congruity between doctrinal or ecclesiological views and prose style. And Andrewes himself, a preacher long held in high literary regard, emerged (largely on the evidence of his court sermons) as one of the most important, even revolutionary, ecclesiastical figures of his age. But it was Andrewes's content, not his style, which received scrutiny.[11] Conversely, John Donne's sermons, which among those of Andrewes's contemporaries loom so large in both quantity and quality, were left largely unremarked upon because his theology and politics, so carefully couched or even elided by rhetorical strategies of caution and discretion, refuse to fit neatly onto the new map of ecclesiastical history.[12] The lesson to be learned here, or one that at least seems to be emerging as different critical approaches take turns working with sermons, is that they resist not only stylistic categories and schemes, but historiographical ones also.

Inspired by the new ecclesiastical history—rather than New Historicism with its bias against religious texts and culture—work in the two decades which spanned the turn of the last century has produced an unprecedented flourishing of sermon studies. Scholars from literature departments joined colleagues from history and politics to assess sermons' influential engagement with the wider public sphere generally, as well as with highly specific social and historical contexts.[13] The recognition of how specifically tailored sermons were to occasion and place of preaching, and how they both reflected and shaped public debate, prompted two book-length institutional histories (both with 'politics' firmly in their titles) of London's most prominent pulpits, the royal court and Paul's Cross.[14] And Lori Anne Ferrell traced the most compelling politico-religious debates of the English reign of James VI & I through the sermons preached by that King's own chaplains.[15] This work has, however, focused mostly upon the very elite minority of English preaching encountered in the metropolis and at court. Parochial and provincial preaching has begun to attract the social historical attention it deserves in the work of Ian Green, and in Arnold Hunt's seminal study of sermon reception by both listeners and readers.[16]

---

[11] Lake, 'Lancelot Andrewes'; Tyacke, 'Lancelot Andrewes'.

[12] Jeanne Shami, 'Donne and Discretion', *English Literary History*, 47.1 (1980): 48–66.

[13] Ferrell and McCullough, eds., *English Sermon*; McCullough, Adlington, and Rhatigan, eds., *Handbook*.

[14] McCullough, *Sermons at Court*; Mary Morrissey, *Politics and the Paul's Cross Sermons, 1558–1642* (Oxford: Oxford University Press, 2011); see also Matt Jenkinson, 'Preaching at the Court of Charles II: Court Sermons and the Restoration Chapel Royal', in McCullough, Adlington, and Rhatigan, eds., *Handbook*, 442–59.

[15] Lori Anne Ferrell, *Government by Polemic: James I, the King's Preachers, and the Rhetorics of Conformity, 1603–1625* (Stanford: Stanford University Press, 1999).

[16] Ian Green, 'Preaching in the Parishes', in McCullough, Adlington, and Rhatigan, eds., *Handbook*, 137–54; Hunt, *Art of Hearing*.

Far less well-represented, and therefore ripe for new work, is study of the sermon under the rubric of this volume—that is, literally, as prose. There have been some moves in this direction, following a revived scholarly interest in rhetoric. Most invaluable is Peter Mack's lucid analysis of how preachers and authors of religious controversy deployed the grammar school and university arts of rhetoric and logic.[17] Sophie Read's essay on Andrewes's misunderstood and often maligned strategies of punning ('or more accurately the rhetorical figures of syllepsis, antanaclasis and paronomasia'), shows the theological and linguistic seriousness of his word-play.[18] Janel Mueller demonstrates, more economically than Webber had done, how Donne managed 'to pursue periodic composition while introducing aphoristic high points' in a style which heeds Bacon's call for striking clarity without sacrificing expansive Ciceronian structures of parallel comparison and proportion.[19] And specific kinds of sermons, whose authors can be found consciously adapting classical political rhetoric, Old Testament prophetic forms, legal rhetoric, and competing Classical and Protestant modes of consolation and piety, have been essayed respectively for Virginia Company sermons, Paul's Cross 'jeremiads', assize sermons, and funeral sermons.[20] The need for better scholarly texts of sermons, not just reliably edited for textual accuracy, but also annotated sufficiently to address matters of historical content, context, and sources, is addressed in a new annotated edition of selected sermons by Andrewes and a wholly new edition of the complete sermons of Donne.[21]

Because of their variety—as specimens of English prose or otherwise—the most productive critical approaches to date have attended closely either to individual preachers' prose strategies, detailed institutional or political contexts and content of sermons, or narrower subgenres. What common ground is there, then, between such a diverse number of authors whose prose styles and contexts for preaching vary so radically? And what critical approach can join the best aspects of the hitherto parallel critical traditions of style and history? The answer seems to me to be what in the period was called

---

[17] Peter Mack, *Elizabethan Rhetoric: Theory and Practice* (Cambridge: Cambridge University Press, 2002), 253–92.

[18] Sophie Read, 'Puns: Serious Wordplay', in Sylvia Adamson, Gavin Alexander, and Katrin Ettenhuber, eds., *Renaissance Figures of Speech* (Cambridge: Cambridge University Press, 2007), 81–96 (94).

[19] Janel Mueller, 'Periodos: Squaring the Circle', in Adamson, Alexander, and Ettenhuber, eds., *Figures of Speech*, 61–80 (72).

[20] Andrew Fitzmaurice, '"Every man, that prints, adventures": The Rhetoric of the Virginia Company Sermons', in Ferrell and McCullough, eds., *English Sermon*, 25–42; Mary Morrissey, 'Elect Nations and Prophetic Preaching: *Types* and *Examples* in the Paul's Cross Jeremiad', in Ferrell and McCullough, eds., *English Sermon*, 43–58; Hugh Adlington, 'Restoration, Religion, and Law: Assize Sermons, 1660–1685', in McCullough, Adlington, and Rhatigan, eds., *Handbook*, 423–41; Hunt, *Art of Hearing*, 306–20 (for assize sermons); Eric Carlson, 'English Funeral Sermons as Sources: The Example of Female Piety in pre-1640 Sermons', *Albion*, 32.4 (2000): 567–97; Frederic B. Tromly, ' "According to sounde religion": The Elizabethan Controversy over the Funeral Sermon', *Journal of Medieval and Renaissance Studies*, 13 (1983): 293–312; Mack, *Elizabethan Rhetoric*, 279–82 (for funeral sermons).

[21] Peter McCullough, ed., *Lancelot Andrewes: Selected Sermons and Lectures* (Oxford: Oxford University Press, 2005); Peter McCullough (gen. ed.), *The Oxford Edition of the Sermons of John Donne*, 16 vols. (Oxford: Oxford University Press, forthcoming, 2012–).

'delivery', and in ours might be called 'performance'. For it is in imagining these prose works delivered to a listening audience that we meet every sermon author on the terms which he and his audience would have shared and understood. And that is also where prose style, of whatever label or description which we might assign to it, had a functional existence, an historical context, a *raison d' être*—to exhort and persuade.

What exactly, though, is a sermon? Taking the long view through the history of Christianity, preaching had its roots in the declamations of the Christian scripture's Old Testament prophets (cf. Is. 61:1). In the New Testament, Jesus endorsed it in no uncertain terms ('Goe yee into all the world, and preach the Gospel to every creature', Mark 16:15), and then exemplified it in the 'Sermon on the Mount' (Matt. 5–7). In the infancy of the new church, it was confirmed by the apostles, chief among them Peter and Paul (Acts 3, 13), as a defining function of chosen ministers. In that apostolic age, preaching had as its primary function the conversion of non-Christians. But within only a few centuries, and certainly after the conversion of the Roman emperor Constantine (313 CE?), preaching was increasingly directed at Christians themselves, to confirm their faith, doctrine, and morals. Augustine's *On Christian Doctrine* (c.396–427) was the first and most influential of many handbooks which theorized how to preach. Augustine's legacy of *ars praedicandi* ('the art of preaching') flourished throughout the Middle Ages. In varying degrees, all preachers' manuals followed Augustine's lead in endorsing the employment by the preacher of the whole arsenal of Classical rhetoric to compose and deliver persuasive, and often highly artful, interpretations of scripture. Theories of preaching were further refined and extended by Erasmian humanism and, in Protestant countries, reformed according to the ideals of its intensified scripturalism.[22]

In the most basic early modern English terms, a sermon was a discourse upon a text from the Bible delivered to a congregation or auditory by an authorized minister.[23] The sermon's function, again very basically, was to deliver some combination of three things: explication, application, and exhortation.[24] That is, the 'explication' (interpretation) of the chosen scripture in doctrinal or moral terms; the 'application' of those doctrines or morals to the lives of those listening; and, finally, the 'exhortation' (encouragement) to the listeners that they accept and act upon the lessons of the first two. Crucial in all early modern preaching, regardless of style or theology, was the large role played by the emotions, which in most preachers' practice put an especially high premium on exhortation, even at the expense of explication or application. Arnold Hunt has firmly shown that, far from being intellectually arid or overly dialectical, 'the "stirring up of godly emotions" was central to the puritan understanding of preaching'.[25] Donne has always been recognized as a particular master of pulpit emotion, but he was by no means unusual. Eliot's condemnation of Donne in the pulpit as 'a little of the religious spellbinder, the Reverend

---

[22] Greg Kneidel, '*Ars Prædicandi*: Theories and Practice', in McCullough, Adlington, and Rhatigan, eds., *Handbook*, 3–20.

[23] For regulations governing preaching in the period, see McCullough, Adlington, and Rhatigan, eds., *Handbook*, Appendix III.

[24] Morrissey, 'Theories of Preaching', 693.

[25] Hunt, *Art of Hearing*, 82.

Billy Sunday of his time, the flesh-creeper, the sorcerer of emotional orgy' reveals less about Donne than Eliot himself, including perhaps how few sermons by other preachers of the period he had read. Eliot's hero, by contrast, was Andrewes, who he found 'purely contemplative' and 'his emotions wholly contained in and explained by its object'.[26] But Andrewes, not Donne, was the exception for his time. Although his sermons hardly lack emotion, they appeal to feeling, not in bursts of emotive imagery like Donne's, but in an incremental accretion of pointed, aphoristic argument, which often builds toward indignation directed at minds lesser than his—which is to say, he was in both temperament and literary style rather like Eliot.

Donne, however, gives us a very clear, and widely applicable, statement of what sermons were supposed to do, by way of contrasting them with more academic theology ('divinity') lectures:

> a Sermon intends *Exhortation* principally and *Edification*, and a holy stirring of religious affections, and then *matters of Doctrine*, and points of *Divinity*, occasionally, secondarily, as the words of the text may invite them; But *Lectures* intend principally *Doctrinall points*, and matter of *Divinity*, and matter of *Exhortation* but *occasionally*, and as in a *second* place.[27]

'Matter of *Exhortation*' is where genre and style come into play, for it was verbal structures and style which were necessary for raising emotions. So here the inherited strategies of Classical rhetoric for persuasion—the larger structures of the sermon derived from the Classical oration, as well as the whole panoply of tropes and figures, each of which carried a defined expressive function—met the Christian imperative for exhortation.[28]

But there were, of course, acute anxieties about keeping the 'stirring of religious affections' within the bounds which Donne called 'holy'. George Herbert made the same point about the preaching of his ideal country parson: 'The character of his Sermon is Holiness; he is not witty, or learned, or eloquent, but Holy.'[29] In an important intervention in sermon study, Mary Morrissey wisely cautions against reducing early modern sermons to nothing more than Classical orations dressed in a surplice, instead of a toga. Although her distinction that early modern sermons *used* rhetoric, rather than constituted a recognized *branch* of rhetoric, may seem a fine point, it is a crucial one. For even in matters of exhortation, all preachers were guided by an overriding desire for didactic clarity to which the arts of rhetoric, logic, and grammar were subjugated. 'Plainness', then, was an ideal for all preachers, and not just 'puritans'. This pedagogical directness that was a stated aim for all preachers—from advanced Protestants like William Perkins to high-churchmen like Andrewes, with Donne somewhere in between—was mistaken

---

[26] Eliot, 'Lancelot Andrewes', 302, 308–9.

[27] Donne, *Sermons*, VIII, 95.

[28] For the Classical oration, see Peter McCullough, 'Donne as Preacher', in Achsah Guibbory, ed., *The Cambridge Companion to John Donne* (Cambridge: Cambridge University Press, 2006), 167–81 (169–80); Webber, *Contrary Music*, 143–4; and Kneidel, '*Ars Prædicandi*', 11–13; for tropes and figures, see McCullough, 'Donne as Preacher', 171; and Brian Vickers, *In Defense of Rhetoric* (Oxford: Oxford University Press, 1988), 294–339.

[29] F. E. Hutchinson, ed., *The Works of George Herbert* (Oxford: Clarendon Press, 1941), 233.

by earlier critics as the forerunner of 'plain style' in the Royal Society, Restoration sense.[30] But 'plainness' in the early modern sense was a deeply relative term governed by the decorums of context (place and auditory). So, plain and direct preaching at court, for example, was usually far more sophisticated in form and content than that in a country parish, as a function of the different expectations and abilities of the two auditories. On this point Herbert is again instructive, even extending it to the preacher's need to respond to differences of ability within a single congregation, 'with particularizing of his speech now to the younger sort, then to the elder, now to the poor, and now to the rich'. By implication too, Herbert's famous criticism of preachers who prefer 'crumbling a text into small parts, as, the Person speaking, or spoken to, the subject, and object, and the like' is very probably not (as sometimes assumed) an indictment of Andrewes's court style. At court and the universities, the division of the scriptural text according to the rules of grammatical analysis (as in Herbert's complaint), or according to Aristotelian categories of logic, was a routine feature of sermons.[31] Herbert, writing of 'the country parson', is more likely articulating the style he judged inappropriate for 'Countrey people; which are thick, and heavy'.[32]

Preaching theorists, even those for humbler auditories like the Jacobean Richard Bernard, advised the use of 'engines of that Arte and grace of speaking'.[33] And while Herbert disdained the 'witty, or learned, or eloquent', he also said that the same ideal country preacher 'procures attention by all possible art', preaches on 'moving and ravishing texts, whereof the Scriptures are full', deploys tropes like 'Apostrophes to God', as well as significant gestures (the Classical orator's *actio*) like the 'busy cast of his eye on his auditors' and the manifestation in his own body and voice the emotions he intended to raise in his listeners: 'cordially expressing all that we say; so that the auditors may plainly perceive that every word is hart-deep'.[34] Equally misled is the assumption that preachers of a more godly stripe placed a strict ban on *exempla* from patristic or Classical authors, or quotations in Latin, Greek, and Hebrew. As Morrissey argues, and as Noam Reisner has shown even more fully, protestations against 'human' learning in sermons were again carefully guided by decorum and kept more in the breach than the observance.[35]

By convention, sermons were usually preached after—not during—prayer book services, a separation unfamiliar today, but in the period marked by the ringing of a separate 'sermon bell' to summon those who came to listen, rather than to pray. Also surprising by modern standards is the fact that early modern sermons were expected to last one hour, and were vividly timed by an hourglass fixed to or near the pulpit.[36] The primary

---

[30] Morrissey, 'Theories of Preaching', 694.
[31] Mack, *Elizabethan Rhetoric*, 261–79.
[32] Hutchinson, ed., *Works of George Herbert*, 233, 235.
[33] Quoted in Morrissey, 'Theories of Preaching', 694.
[34] Hutchinson, ed., *Works of George Herbert*, 232–3.
[35] Morrissey, 'Theories of Preaching', 695–6; Noam Reisner, 'The Preacher and Profane Learning', in McCullough, Adlington, and Rhatigan, eds., *Handbook*, 72–86; see also Donne, *Sermons*, X, 146–9.
[36] Emma Rhatigan, 'Preaching Venues: Architecture and Auditories', in McCullough, Adlington, and Rhatigan, eds., *Handbook*, 87–119 (93–5); John Craig, 'Sermon Reception', in McCullough, Adlington, and Rhatigan, eds., *Handbook*, 178–97 (185, 187).

venue for early modern preaching was of course the parish church. Although in the early Elizabethan decades some isolated or poor parishes were lucky to have a sermon once a quarter, by the reign of James I, monthly sermons had become a statutory minimum, and in most parishes a weekly sermon was common. In cities and towns, especially London, enthusiasm for the word preached could extend to supplementary sermons, sometimes called 'lectures', on weekdays and Sunday afternoons. And in the largest regional centres, such as Norwich, Hereford, and London, outdoor pulpits in use since the Middle Ages continued as vibrant, and politically prominent, sites for sermons as major civic events. Finally, of course, institutions such as the court, cathedrals, Inns of Court, universities, colleges, and guilds were important sponsors of frequent and prominent preaching.[37]

The sermon, then, was a largely free-standing event, with the preacher and his prose the sole focus of attention for an entire hour (or two, if at an outdoor pulpit). The first words from the preacher's mouth, though, were not his own, but the chosen text from the Bible which would be his line and compass for the whole sermon. The scriptural text—chosen to fit the occasion and the auditory, but not necessarily a reading appointed for the day in the Book of Common Prayer—could be obvious, or witty, or even shocking.[38] But the rhetorical and spiritual challenge of arresting the audience's attention always started here. Most preachers followed the declamation of their chosen text with a feature borrowed from the Classical oration—an 'exordium', sometimes called the 'sum' or 'summary'—which did the crucial work of applying the chosen text to the day, liturgical season, or occasion. A typically curt opening from Andrewes's sermon at court on Easter Day 1620 jolted his auditory into a dramatic conflation of the historical time of his text (John 10:11–17, Christ's resurrection appearance to Mary Magdalen in the garden) and the present time of his sermon: 'It is Easter day abroad: And it is so in the text.'[39] This is breathtakingly economical 'application' of text to auditory, with only two short clauses anticipating the whole sermon's dramatization of how the listener could meet Christ just as immediately at the Easter sermon and communion as Mary Magdalen met Christ outside the empty tomb. It also captures the sheer intensity of Andrewes's scripturalism, and his sense of liturgical time, where scripture, historical event, and present feast day are inseparable from the outset. Donne was a master of striking, highly metaphorical exordiums which often held audience attention by first veering away from the most obvious applications of the text, only to further intensify audience engagement with it and him by resolving the exordium on a surprising or unexpected appropriateness of the text to the occasion.[40]

Joseph Hall's 1623 sermon before the masters and students of law at Gray's Inn on Jeremiah 17:9 ('*The heart is deceitfull aboue all things*') combined a frank, almost

---

[37] Rhatigan, 'Preaching Venues', 103–16.
[38] McCullough, 'Donne as Preacher', 177; Peter McCullough, 'Preaching and Context: John Donne's Sermon at the Funerals of Sir William Cokayne', in McCullough, Adlington, and Rhatigan, eds., *Handbook*, 213–67 (231–3).
[39] McCullough, ed., *Lancelot Andrewes*, 224.
[40] McCullough, 'Donne as Preacher', 177–8; McCullough, 'Preaching and Context', 233–6.

confrontational acknowledgement of his listeners' profession with his abilities as a character writer, and just a hint of the dramatist in an exordium which, especially if imagined with the grand flourish of oral delivery, sounds like a prologue to a play:

> I know where I am; in one of the famous Phrontisteries of Law, and Iustice: wherefore serves Law and Iustice, but for the preuention or punishment of fraud and wickednesse? Giue me leaue therefore to bring before you, Students, Masters, Fathers, Oracles of Law and Iustice, the greatest Cheator and Malefactor in the world, our owne Heart.[41]

The first sentence combines self-assertion with ostensible compliment. 'I know where I am' was a conventional humility topos for preachers before grand auditories, but Hall's forceful placement of it at the opening of his exordium carries perhaps more self-assertion than deference. The epithet for Gray's Inn as one of the 'Phrontisteries of Law' demonstrates the linguistic inventiveness of many of the better sermons of the period, for here we have what, according to the *OED*, is the first usage of this anglicized form of the Greek 'phrontisterion', meaning 'a school, college, or other educational institution'. But both Hall and his listeners would have been alert not only to its less grand literal sense ('a thinking shop'), but also its origin—'applied by Aristophanes in ridicule to the school of Socrates' (*OED*, 'phrontesterion')—and hence, its ironic, as well as complimentary, potential. The ensuing rhetorical question, of course, by design allows answering 'yes' or 'no'. Just the right amount ironic edge in delivery of these opening lines would establish a position of moral authority for Hall and leave his listening lawyers asking whether they lived up to their own calling—which is to say, Hall had them exactly where he wanted them. But before pushing his oblique criticism too far, Hall then takes cover in a formulaic humble request for permission to continue. And here we see in small one of the great accomplishments of sermon prose which can be lost from view without imagining performance, and that is the importance of *timing*. Hall builds towards a climax with the hierarchical ascent in address from 'Students, Masters, Fathers' to the hyperbole 'Oracles of Law and Iustice'. The object he proposes continues the build-up by promising, again hyperbolically, 'the greatest Cheator and Malefactor in the world'. But then (presumably after a pause to intensify expectation) comes the deflating shock of pulling back the curtain to reveal the tragic villain: 'our owne Heart'. Not only does a presumed external threat become suddenly internal and personal, but also by Hall's simple shift from singular first person ('*I* know...Giue *me* leaue') to plural first person ('*our* owne Heart'), he increases surprise and furthers audience sympathy and trust by binding his preaching self to his listening auditors.

The Bible exerts a sustained influence on the form, style, and content of sermon prose because 'the preacher's task was to explain the words of the text and apply them to the circumstances of the sermon'. Or, as Donne put it, the parts of the sermon were to proceed only 'as the words of the text may invite them'.[42] After the declamation of the text, and the usual exordium, this was first done in a generic part common to all sermons in

---

[41] Joseph Hall, *The Great Imposter, laid open in a sermon at Grayes Inne, Febrary 2. 1623* (London: J. Haviland for H. Fetherstone, 1623), 1–2.

[42] Morrissey, 'Theories of Preaching', 693; Donne, *Sermons*, VIII, 95.

the period, the 'division' of the text into the parts of it that would be addressed. This could be done according to a host of methods, ranging from the extremely elaborate to the directly simple, based either on chosen words, themes, or metaphors extracted from the text, or on categories from grammar (usually parts of speech) or logic (such as definitions, relationship, circumstances, syllogisms, or fallacies). Preaching on Ecclesiastes 12:1 ('*Remember now thy Creatour in the dayes of thy youth*') at court in 1626, Henry King (Donne's younger friend and literary executor) omitted any introductory summary or exordium, opting instead for a direct opening statement of his division, here a sequence of moral lessons drawn from single words or phrases from the verse and their grammatical relationships:

My Division is plainly thus:

1 A *Monition* to quicken the Memory, *Remember*.
2 The *Object* presented to it, the *Creatour*.
3 The *Application* of that Object, *Thy Creatour*.
4 The *Distance* at which wee must take him, *Youth*.
5 The *Light* by which we best may view this Obiect, *In the daies of thy youth*.
6 The *Time* which hastes to bring us home and set us neere unto God, *Now*.[43]

Without the customary exordium, King's blunt declaration ('My division is plainly thus') would have had an even more surprising force in delivery. And the swift, simple enumeration of his proposed points not only signalled a kind of frankness suitable for Lent, but also likely provided this young preacher with an easy outline to follow from memory, as well as for his auditors to follow and perhaps later note down or even reconstruct, in a common practice known as 'repetition'.[44]

Andrewes's divisions could be highly elaborate, with some of his multiplied refining subdivisions of logical and grammatical 'heads', 'parts', and 'points' taking up a full folio page in print, as in his division of the 1609 Christmas sermon text (Gal. 4:4–5), '*When the fulnesse of time was come, God sent his Sonne ... that we might receive the Adoption of sonnes*'.[45] But they could also be startlingly brief, as with the grammatical despatch afforded Zachariah 12:10 ('Respicient in Me, quem transfixerunt. *And they shall looke upon Me, whom they have pierced*') on Good Friday 1597:

The principall words are but two, and set downe unto us, in two points. ¹The *sight* it self, that is, the thing *to be seene*: ²and the *sight* of it; that is, the act of *seeing* or looking. *Quem transfixerunt* is the Object, or spectacle propounded. *Respicient in Eum*, is the Act, or duety enjoined.[46]

These two divisions by Andrewes well illustrate the pitfall of using labels like 'elaborate' or 'metaphysical' to describe even a single preacher's method and style. Even more

---

[43] Mary Hobbs, ed., *The Sermons of Henry King (1592–1669), Bishop of Chichester* (Aldershot: Scolar Press, 1992), 115.
[44] Hunt, *Art of Hearing*, 72–81.
[45] McCullough, ed., *Lancelot Andrewes*, xxxii, 162–3; see also Mack, *Elizabethan Rhetoric*, 272–3.
[46] McCullough, ed., *Lancelot Andrewes*, 123.

important, they illustrate how prose elaboration, or its opposite, was dictated by the preacher's text and his chosen exposition of it, and not the reverse. The fulsome division of the 1609 Christmas text replicated, before the sermon was even fully underway, both a key word in the text ('*fulnesse*') and a key concept in Andrewes's exegesis: 'In that of *Gods*, every point is *full*... And this is *Our fulnesse*' (163). The brevity of the Good Friday division, by contrast, flirts with mimesis in its deliberately sharp focus on the spectacle of the crucified Christ ('*Quem transfixerunt*') on which the auditory, through the preacher's words, is to fix its gaze ('*Respicient in Eum*'). It is even tempting to see further mimetic effects in a possible pun on 'points' and in the lexis studded with sharp t's, hard c's, and the pun-laden syllable '*fix*'. Everything in this prose about crucifixion—imagery, diction, sound, and theme—is, it must be said, nailed down.

The bulk of the preacher's hour, though, was given over to his elaboration of the parts announced in his division. And it is at this point where surveying what preachers did with their prose in their hours becomes most difficult. Their strategies for holding an auditory's attention were as numerous and varied as the number of sermons themselves. As many of the earlier critics discussed above have shown, sermons are a happy hunting ground for every rhetorical trope and figure known to prose. Closer attention to the use preachers made of these to convey meaning and emotion, though, treats sermons with more generic and literary respect than as so many handbooks of literary terms. Hall uses paranomasia (punning) not for a verbal joke, but as a striking and efficient way to do the serious work of dividing his text: 'See then, I beseech you, the *Impostor*, and the *Imposture*; the Imposter himselfe, *The heart of man*; The Imposture, *Deceitfull aboue all things*' (4). Colloquialism keeps his prose vivid and his arguments sharp: 'It is not for me to be a stickler betwixt the Hebrewes, and the Greeke Philosophers' (6). Apostrophe and a catalogue of grammatically parallel epithets express contempt: 'Oh poore blind Pagans, halfe-sighted Turkes, bleare-eied Iewes, blind-folded Papists, Squint-eyed Schismaticks, purblind ignorants, how well doe they finde themselues pleased with their devotion' (12). Anecdotal simile creates moments of surprising, even uncomfortable, recognition for the listener: 'like some false strumpet, that entertaines her husband with her eyes, and in the meane time treads vpon the toe of an Adulterer vnder the board' (20). Catalogues of antitheses do the work of expanding (*copia*) a sharp moral point, here clinched by moving strategically from recognizable contemporary exempla to climactic biblical ones: 'now euery one of natures birds is a Swan; Pride is handsomnesse[;] desperate fury, valour; lauishnesse is noble munificence, drunkennesse ciuility, flattery complement, murderous reuenge, justice... *Absolom* will goe pay his vowes, *Herod* will worship the Babe' (33). And prosopopoeia allows an enlivening variation of the preacher's voice and persona: 'the heart... thinkes to goe beyond the deuill himselfe: I can (thinks it) swallow his bait, and yet auoid his hooke; I can sinne, and liue; I can repent of sinning, and defeat my punishment by repenting... I can put my selfe vnder the protection of a Sauiour and escape the arrest.' But then that same figure allows greater force to the preacher's own voice when it responds in judgement: 'Oh the world of soules that perish by this fraud, fondly beguiling themselues, whiles they would beguile the Tempter' (39–40). To be sure, most sermons are not entirely composed of tropes and figures, but preachers knew how to deploy them selectively, and because of that, with great effect.[47]

A local effect relating to diction which deserves further study is early modern preachers' use of Latin, Greek, and Hebrew. Not least, it is a vital part of the texture, or lexis, of sermons preached to elite auditories. There are cases—usually with Hebrew, which very few auditors in even elite congregations would have understood—where a simple display of learning is no doubt the motive. Although there is still no scholarly consensus about the extent of Donne's knowledge of Hebrew in the original, his rich response to the metaphorical and interpretative possibilities of Hebrew texts, especially the Targums ('Chaldee paraphrases') and rabbinical commentaries, has been well shown.[48] Donne was most alert to the beneficial effects of well-deployed Latin tags or quotations in English prose. Since these were almost always followed by English translations, the most obvious advantage is repetition of an important point while simultaneously diversifying the lexical range. So the phrases '*Inter tot millia millium*, amongst so many thousand thousands' double the sense of multiplication Donne desires and also give the aural advantages of the Latin's homoioptoton ('*millia millium*') and polyptoton in English ('thousand thousands'). The onomatopoeic potential in Pliny's description of how painters could capture the thunder of a disturbed soul is exploited by declaiming it before a free English translation: '*Tonitrua, perturbationes animæ*; they would paint thunder which was not to be seen, but heard'. And in the same sermon, Latin tags are used to title the parts of Donne's division, in an exploitation of the tiny distinction a single letter can make in a Latin declension: '*sis aliquid*' (be something), '*hoc age*' (do something), and '*sis aliquis*' (be like someone).[49] But it is Andrewes who carries the palm for sermon prose which can almost be described as multilingual. This is prominent from the outset of all of his sermons, when he declaimed his text, first in Latin (sometimes, but not always, from the Vulgate), and then English. The two then travelled together throughout each sermon, with Andrewes enriching, rather than merely decorating, his exegesis with the expanded etymological senses and multiple forms of key words in at least two languages, often with significant polemical and doctrinal import.[50]

More work needs to be done, though, which considers sermons as wholes, rather than hunting either for snippets which contain historical evidence or, alternatively, exemplary tropes and figures or quotable set-pieces. Again, keeping delivery or performance in mind helps here, and a potentially useful model is dramaturgical analysis, which attends to what Emrys Jones called Shakespeare's 'scenic form', that is, how, why, and in what order the dramatist organized the parts (acts and scenes) of a whole play.[51] Andrewes's Christmas 1609 treatment of the '*fulnesse of time*', for example, when considered structurally

---

[47] Mack, *Elizabethan Rhetoric*, 279.

[48] Chanita Goodblatt, *The Christian Hebraism of John Donne* (Pittsburgh: Duquesne University Press, 2010).

[49] Donne, *Sermons*, VIII, 186, 178, 175.

[50] See examples discussed in McCullough, ed., *Lancelot Andrewes*, 354, 367, 406, 433–4.

[51] Emrys Jones, *Scenic Form in Shakespeare* (Oxford: Clarendon Press, 1971).

'is relentlessly symmetrical, proceeding in a minute exegetical *gradatio* through the component parts of the biblical text and revealing only incrementally a sum of parts that is greater than the whole'. The 1620 Easter sermon on Mary Magdalen combines three interlocking structures—the narrative progression, verse by verse, of Mary's encounter with Christ; three fully realized dramatic characters (Mary, angels, and Christ); and ten abstract 'characters' of love—as well as a climactic 'recognition scene', which have been compared both to complex Shakespearean plotting and to medieval mystery plays.[52]

If Andrewes works in tight, highly calibrated structures of argumentative progression, though, Donne is the master of larger-scale shifts and contrasts. A common technique is the deployment of a rhetorically heightened passage early in the sermon, often in the division's first part, as if Donne were keen to grab and hold attention early on. A fine example is the vast period of some forty lines which extends and suspends, in a series of parallel 'as if' clauses, the ironic question of whether God had 'done so much more for thee... for nothing'. Clearly pleased with its power, Donne incorporated the same passage verbatim into two sermons. Another well-known example, from the 'second prebend sermon' of 1626, is the terrifying picture of separation from God which opens, 'Let me wither and weare out mine age in a discomfortable, in an unwholesome, in a penurious prison.' Also situated in the division's first part, this incredible passage unites imagery and parallel syntax to replicate, almost to recreate, the inconceivable weight of spiritual despair which finally resolves in the brachylogia of being 'swallowed up, irreparably, irrevocably, irrecoverably, irremediably'—or what Vickers calls 'those last four terrible adverbs'. Set-piece though this undoubtedly is, it does not stand alone. Rather, it is deliberately heightened not just to hold the attention, but also to enforce the moral point Donne makes in the ensuing paragraph. There, the proliferated tropes, figures, and parallel syntax of the preceding paragraph disappear to make room for the simple rhetorical question, 'But was this *Davids* case? was he fallen thus farre, into a diffidence in God?' which Donne answers—and thereby throws off both the form and sense of oppression he had previously built up—with a single syllable: 'No'. The consolation which follows is only intensified by the prose picture of despair which came before.[53]

So in both its local rhetorical effects, and in its larger generic structures, the best sermon prose works by the careful combination of argument and rhetorical elaboration, which exploits contrast and variety strategically. That is, it has an aim not unlike the Horation ideal of 'teaching and delighting', but with a spiritual, moral, and social imperative more intense than that afforded by many early moderns to any poetry or drama. It is also best understood and studied now with an imagination which is not only sympathetic to the early modern Christian goals of exhortation and edification, but also alive to how its rhetorical strategies were deployed as parts of complex wholes, and very much meant to be seen and heard.

---

[52] McCullough, ed., *Lancelot Andrewes*, 404, 448.
[53] Donne, *Sermons*, IV, 148–9 and VIII, 176–7; VII, 156–7; Vickers, ed., *Prose*, 96.

FURTHER READING

Ferrell, Lori Anne. *Government by Polemic: James I, the King's Preachers, and the Rhetorics of Conformity, 1603–1625* (Stanford: Stanford University Press, 1999).

—— and Peter McCullough, eds. *The English Sermon Revised: Religion, Literature and History, 1600–1750* (Manchester: Manchester University Press, 2000).

Hunt, Arnold. *The Art of Hearing: English Preachers and their Audiences* (Cambridge: Cambridge University Press, 2011).

McCabe, Richard A. *Joseph Hall: A Study in Satire and Meditation* (Oxford: Clarendon Press, 1982).

McCullough, Peter, ed. *Lancelot Andrewes: Selected Sermons and Lectures* (Oxford: Oxford University Press, 2005).

—— *Sermons at Court: Politics and Religion in Elizabethan and Jacobean Preaching* (Cambridge: Cambridge University Press, 1998).

—— Hugh Adlington, and Emma Rhatigan, eds. *The Oxford Handbook of the Early Modern Sermon* (Oxford: Oxford University Press, 2011).

Mack, Peter. *Elizabethan Rhetoric: Theory and Practice* (Cambridge: Cambridge University Press, 2002).

Morrissey, Mary. *Politics and the Paul's Cross Sermons, 1558–1642* (Oxford: Oxford University Press, 2011).

—— 'Scripture, Style and Persuasion in Seventeenth-Century English Theories of Preaching', *Journal of Ecclesiastical History*, 53.4 (2002): 686–706.

Potter, George R., and Evelyn M. Simpson, eds. *The Sermons of John Donne*, 10 vols. (Berkeley and Los Angeles. University of California Press, 1953–62).

Read, Sophie. 'Puns: Serious Wordplay', in Sylvia Adamson, Gavin Alexander, and Katrin Ettenhuber, eds., *Renaissance Figures of Speech* (Cambridge: Cambridge University Press, 2007), 81–96.

Webber, Joan. *Contrary Music: The Prose Style of John Donne* (Madison: University of Wisconsin Press, 1963).

Williamson, George. *The Senecan Amble: Prose Form from Bacon to Collier* (Chicago: University of Chicago Press, 1951).

CHAPTER 34

THE BOOK OF COMMON PRAYER

DANIEL SWIFT

On 9 February 1588, Richard Bancroft preached a history lesson. Bancroft was a canon of Westminster, later Archbishop of Canterbury, and his sermon that day defended the episcopal hierarchy of the Church of England against the recent attacks published in the mocking Martin Marprelate tracts. St Paul's Cross, where he stood, was the principal pulpit of the Elizabethan church, and this was the first Sunday of the parliamentary year. Due to the date, location, and subject, this sermon may be considered close to an official pronouncement of the doctrine of the late Elizabethan church, but instead of simply scolding the church's opponents and reaffirming the official orthodoxy, Bancroft recounted the textual history of the Book of Common Prayer.

Bancroft begins by acknowledging dissent. 'As touching the Communion booke, you knowe what quarrels are picked against it', he allows, and continues: 'although for myne owne opinion there is not the like this day extant in Christendome'. This is praise for the prayer book, yet hedged with caution, and strikes the pragmatic tone that carries Bancroft through his brief account. As he relates,

> In the beginning of King *Edwards* raigne, notwithstanding it was then carefully compiled and confirmed by a synode: yet by and by after (that I may use Master *Foxes* words) *Through the obstinate and dissembling malice of manie*, it was impugned. Thereupon it was againe reviewed, and after published with such approbation, as that it was accounted the Worke of God. But yet not long after there were againe, who affirming the same to resemble the Masse booke, *Divisiones occasionem arripiebant*: Did greedily hunt, (as *Alesius* saith) for occasion of division.[1]

The 1549 Book of Common Prayer, which Bancroft is here describing, was the first edition of the standard liturgical scheme for the Edwardian English church, but its textual

---

[1] Richard Bancroft, *A Sermon preached at Paules Crosse the 9. Of Februarie being the first Sunday in the Parlement, Anno. 1588* (London, 1588), 53.

history was deeply tangled. Those opponents who held that it did 'resemble the Masse booke'—that is, traditional Catholic primers—were categorically correct. In his biography of Thomas Cranmer, the main author of the prayer book, Diarmaid MacCulloch has traced Cranmer's sources: the 1549 Book of Common Prayer was partly based upon Cranmer's 1538 Latin breviary, which prescribed 'the daily recitation of prayer, praise, and readings of scripture'. This 1538 breviary, in turn, took as a major source a 1535 'revised breviary by the Spanish Cardinal Francisco de Quinones, commissioned by Henry VIII's bitter enemy Pope Paul III as a pilot scheme for reforming and standardizing the Church's worship'.[2] Inside this apparently single book—the 1549 Book of Common Prayer—lies a tangle of compromising sources, revisions, and criticism. As Bancroft's sermon stresses, not only was this convoluted textual history popularly known; the English church authorities, in reviewing the liturgy, took seriously critical opposition to the prayer book and attempted to revise it accordingly.

Bancroft's history of liturgical controversy and textual emendation continues. As he recounts, following the popular objection to the 1549 prayer book, Cranmer sent a copy to Martin Bucer, who concurred with the need for further revision. 'Some things indeed there are, saith he', relates Bancroft, 'which except a man do charitably interpret, may seeme not sufficiently to agree with the Word of God'. These criticisms were incorporated into the second version of the *Book of Common Prayer*, which was published in 1552: 'Upon this occasion the booke was againe carefully survaied and almost in every point (which then was so cavilled and wrested) corrected and amended' (54). Bancroft ends his textual history here: preaching in 1588, he is part of a church whose central liturgy was prescribed by the 1559 Book of Common Prayer, which was largely based upon the 1552 version. Yet, his defence, even here, is cautious: that the liturgy was 'almost in every point...corrected' suggests the possibility of not only further opposition, but also further revision. Nowhere does this sermon claim that a perfect prayer book exists, or might one day be reached. Instead, as Bancroft declares, 'for myne owne opinion' the one they have is preferable to a range of other possibilities.

Bancroft's surprisingly open account of the fluid textual status of the Book of Common Prayer reveals two simple points. The early modern prayer book was a work in progress—not only revised but revisable—and this was publicly known and popularly discussed. The modern republication of early modern books belies the complex origins and textual states of those works. The standard modern scholarly edition of the early modern prayer book is that published by the Folger Library in 1976 and based upon the 1559 version.[3] Its cover declares that this is 'The Elizabethan Prayer Book', and while this is technically true, it obscures the convoluted history that Bancroft's sermon

---

[2] Diarmaid MacCulloch, *Thomas Cranmer: A Life* (New Haven: Yale University Press, 1996), 222.

[3] John E. Booty, ed., *The Book of Common Prayer 1559* (Washington, DC Folger Shakespeare Library, 1976). I will quote from this as the control edition throughout, although also referring to variations in the 1549 and 1552 editions of the prayer book, published in modern editions as *The First Prayer-Book of Edward VI* and *The Second Prayer-Book of King Edward VI* (London: The Ancient and Modern Library of Theological Literature, n.d.).

raises. This may have been the orthodox liturgy for the Elizabethan church, but that is not to say that it was accepted by all Elizabethans. Those who questioned it did so because they believed it was unfinished; and those who defended it too saw the possibility of further revision.

The Book of Common Prayer was the central devotional text of early modern England. Judith Maltby has detailed the widespread popular attachment to the prayer book, while Ian Green has traced its extravagantly successful printing history. As Green shows, the three most frequently published books in early modern England were Sternhold and Hopkins's version of the psalms, a popular catechism called *The ABC with Catechism*, and the prayer book, and he goes on to observe that the *ABC with Catechism* was heavily based upon the prayer book liturgy. The Book of Common Prayer went through 290 editions between 1549 and 1642; it was revised and reissued in 1549, 1552, 1559, and 1604, in folio, quarto, octavo, and even smaller versions; in black print and Roman type, with one column or two. Its liturgy and devotions were reprinted in special forms of prayer and thanksgiving: in 1572, following the St Bartholomew Day Massacre; in 1599, marking the departure of troops to Ireland; in 1604, commemorating the entry of James into England; and in times of plague, drought, and the threat of Spanish invasion. The Book of Common Prayer was a flexible textual project. In 1605, for example, a special edition was issued to give thanks for the deliverance of the King from the Gunpowder plotters. At 46 pages, this quarto version incorporates lengthy prayers written specifically for the occasion into the order of the standard service.[4]

Even outside its printed versions, the language of the prayer book further circulated in the great flood of popular devotional books that dominated early modern publishing. It is worth quoting Green at length on this unseen second generation diffusion:

> What also strikes one forcibly looking at printed prayers from the 1540s to the 1730s as a whole is the extent to which the characteristics of what might be called Prayer Book devotion—the doctrines implicit in the prayers and collects in Cranmer's original *Book of Common Prayer*, and the balance there between exposition, thanksgiving, confession, and petition—can be found in a high proportion of the texts of the majority of the collections of prayers in our sample. In terms not only of the number of copies of the Prayer Book that were printed in the two centuries after 1549, but also of the central thrust of so many of the collections of supplementary prayers that sold well enough in the same period to qualify for our sample, the *Book of Common Prayer* became the benchmark for early modern Protestant devotion. No other vision of prayer came near to having the same degree of penetration in the country at large, and among Protestants of all levels.[5]

In the eyes of some, the English church was focused on the prayer book to an unhealthily exclusive degree. The Puritan Henry Barrow, writing from exile in the Netherlands in

---

[4] See, for example, *A Fourme of Common Prayer to be used...necessarie for the present tyme and state* (London, 1572); *A Prayer for the good successe of her Majesties forces in Ireland* (London, 1599); *Prayers and Thenksgiving to be used by all the Kings Majesties loving servants for the Happy Deliverance of his Majestie...from the most traitorous and bloody intended Massacre by Gunpowder* (London, 1605).

[5] Ian Green, *Print and Protestantism in Early Modern England* (Oxford: Oxford University Press, 2000), 277.

1590, found in the Book of Common Prayer a synecdoche of all that was wrong with the Elizabethan church. As he insisted,

> By this Book are the Priests to administer their sacraments, by this Book to church their women, by this Book to burie their dead, by this Book to keep their *Rogation*, to say certaine Psalmes and praiers over the earthe and grasse, certayne gospels at crosswaies &c. This Book is good at all assaies; yt is the only Booke of the world.[6]

Thinly veiled under Barrow's repetitions is the charge of idolatry, but his greatest condemnations are reserved for the unoriginality, not of English worshippers, but the object of their worship. The Book of Common Prayer is, he insists, his syntax tripping over his disgust, 'a stinking patcherie divised apocrypha *Leiturgie*': that is, it was not only fake, it was also derivative. For Barrow, the problem is that the prayer book has insufficiently escaped its source. 'For the thing yt selfe', he mocks, 'yt is evident to be abstracted out of the Popes blasphemous MASSE-BOOK' (I4^r).

This history of the Book of Common Prayer is a history of passionately contested ongoing revision. As Judith Maltby, the prayer book's most sensitive historian, has written, 'there was probably no other single aspect of the Reformation in England which touched more directly and fundamentally the religious consciousness, or lack of it, of ordinary clergy and laity, than did the reform of rituals and liturgy'.[7] The architecture of the Book of Common Prayer was imprecisely finished and its enormous political and cultural importance in early modern England was a function precisely of its malleability: of the possibility that it could, once more, be rewritten. In the spring of 1604, not long after the arrival of a new king to the English throne and the issue of a lightly revised new version of the prayer book, a group of London ministers published their *Survey of the Booke of Comon prayer, By way of 197 Quares grounded upon 58 places*. In opening their list of liturgical criticisms, the petitioning priests addressed the King. 'Vouchsafe to examine the book of Common Prayer', they plead, 'which is, as it were, the Helena of Greece, and cause of all these controversies' (B^r). Helen of Troy was the most beautiful woman in the world, and the cause of great wars, and in reaching for her image this group of dissenting ministers suggest something of the extraordinary power of the early modern prayer book. The Book of Common Prayer was not only the devotional centrepiece of an age that was passionately religious; it was also the best-known literary text in an extravagantly literary culture; and its transient state is both an index and a product of its cultural centrality.

* * *

The Book of Common Prayer is 'the ripe fruit of centuries of worship', wrote C. S. Lewis, who was one of its great admirers.[8] 'The word "liturgy" derives from two Greek words:

---

[6] Henry Barrow, *A Brief Discoverie of the False Church* (Dort, 1590), 14^r.

[7] Judith Maltby, *Prayer Book and People in Elizabethan and early Stuart England* (Cambridge: Cambridge University Press, 1998), 4.

[8] C. S. Lewis, *English Literature in the Sixteenth Century Excluding Drama* (Oxford: Oxford University Press, 1954), 215.

"leitos", public; and "ergon", work', notes the liturgical historian Stanley Morison, and liturgy is by definition public: a liturgy is not the work of a single author, but a common text, created in committee and informed by a long history of shared devotional practice. Morison observes that 'the earliest reference to the existence of the Christian religion in Britain occurs in Tertullian', writing in about 208, and Christianity was spread through Britain by missionaries from Gaul using Latin service books. The central service book was the 'Sarcramentarium' or 'Liber Sacramentorum', which contained the Rite of the Mass and the sacraments: this, he explains, 'rarely came into the hands of the people. It was, by its nature, the priests' book.'[9] This is one way to see the origins of the Book of Common Prayer, as part of a long history stretching back to the Latin service books brought to Britain by missionaries, but another starting-point might be 1534 and the Act of Supremacy. The Act of Supremacy placed the single royal, national, and ecclesiastical institution of the church under the direct jurisdiction of King Henry VIII. By the early sixteenth century, the English church endorsed many local variations upon the Roman Rite. These local uses—'ad usum Sarum', 'ad usum Herefordensem', and many others— commemorated locally famous saints and days, but the English church under Henry was marked by a tendency towards centralization, and therefore required a standard liturgical form. The prayer book was to be, in the phrase of Timothy Rosendale, 'the Church of England's textual establishment'.[10]

In 1541, Edward Whitchurch in London printed the two-volume *Portiforium, Secundum usum Sarum noviter impressus*. 'The original liturgical book of the English Rite was a breviary in Latin' notes Morison, and the form, language, and content of this book were all traditional: it was most radical in its removal of any mention of the Pope (10). In 1542, Cranmer began to reform service books through Convocation, and in 1544 he issued a liturgy in English, followed by a volume of *Devout Prayers and Collects* in 1547. On 28 January 1547, Edward VI succeeded to the throne, and on 11 April Compline was sung in English for the first time in the Royal Chapel. By November, English was being introduced into the Mass. In March 1548, Richard Grafton published 'The order of Communion', a Quarto text of Communion in English. The Act of Uniformity was passed in January 1549, and on 7 March of that year Edward Whitchurch published the first edition of the Book of Common Prayer. It was cheap. 'The kings maiestie', read a promulgation issued soon after publication, 'strictly chargeth and commandeth that no maner of person do sell the present booke unbounde above the price of ii shyllinge and ii pence the piece'.

The first prayer book was a careful blend of the novel and the traditional. The editor John Booty describes:

> Its major source was the Sarum use, the traditional worship of the Western Church as formulated at the See of Salisbury, but it was influenced by the liturgical reforms

---

[9] Stanley Morison, *English Prayer Books: An Introduction to the Literature of Christian Public Worship* (Cambridge: Cambridge University Press, 1945), 5, 8–10.

[10] Timothy Rosendale, *Liturgy and Literature in the Making of Protestant England* (Cambridge: Cambridge University Press, 2007), 40.

of Cardinal Quinones with respect to the Breviary, by Lutheran Church Orders—mainly in terms of didactic and hortatory content—by the Great Bible of 1539, and to a lesser extent by Cranmer's study of Eastern liturgies, particularly that of St. John Chrysostom. (341)

The content was a blend of theologians and movements, but the form, Booty goes on to note, was conventional. 'Cranmer's concern to preserve continuity can be detected in the very structure of the Prayer Book, which seems to be patterned after the medieval liturgical library in its divisions', he writes (367), for the prayer book follows the traditional division of Breviary (for Morning and Evening Prayer), Missal (for the Collects, Epistles, Gospels, and Communion), Processional (for the Litany), and Manual (for the other rites). 'It preserved the basic pattern of parochial worship, matins, Mass, and evensong' notes Eamon Duffy, but he goes on to stress the new prayer book's radical doctrinal agenda: 'it set itself to transform lay experience of the Mass, and in the process eliminated almost everything that had till then been central to lay Eucharistic piety. The parish procession, the elevation at the sacring, the pax, the sharing of holy bread, were all swept away.'[11] There were, nonetheless, popular riots in Devon and Cornwall of those who objected to the new English use.

Revision began immediately. The first prayer book of March 1549 was followed by a new pontifical—the form for consecrating archbishops and bishops—later in the same month, and in 1550 *The Book of Common Prayer, noted* by John Merbecke was published, setting out the sung portions. On 1 November 1552, a second prayer book became the official one in use. This presented a liturgy more clearly marked by the reforming tendencies of the Edwardian church, and to pre-empt resistance, it was accompanied by a second Act of Uniformity which noted 'a great number of people in divers parts of this realm following their own sensuality', and enforced use of this book on pain of punishment. The 1552 prayer book remained in use until the death of Edward on 6 July 1553. As Stanley Morison notes, 'His funeral was conducted by Cranmer according to its provisions', but following the accession of Mary 'Gardiner, of Winchester, celebrated for Edward VI a Latin requiem Mass according to the Sarum rite' (51). In the autumn, the new Queen repealed all new liturgical uses, and at the start of the new year an injunction returned divine service to Latin.

The history of the prayer book is a history of struggles such as these: between rival forms and uses, between languages and revisions. It is also tied deeply to the shifting occupancy of the English throne. Publication of the prayer book ceased during the reign of Mary, but following her death and the accession of Elizabeth to the throne in November 1558, the prayer book returned to the English church. In 1559, her version was issued; it followed closely the forms of the 1552 edition, and was, as ever, made standard by a new Act of Uniformity. When James acceded to the English throne in 1603 he, too, sought to mark the prayer book. He called the Hampton Court Conference—a conference now chiefly recalled as the origin of the King James Version of the Bible—and

---

[11] Eamon Duffy, *The Stripping of the Altars: Traditional Religion in England, 1400–1580* (New Haven: Yale University Press, 1992), 464.

issued a new version of the Book of Common Prayer in January 1604, although one which again largely followed its predecessor. The 1604 prayer book remained in use in the English church during the reign of James's son Charles. Following the outbreak of war in August 1642, the King's army carried copies of the *Soldiers Prayer Book*, a manual of prayers based upon the prayer book; in 1644, however, the Westminster Assembly authorized the use of an alternative form, the *Directory of Public Worship of God*, and public use of the Book of Common Prayer was made illegal on 4 January 1645.

Although the early modern history of the Book of Common Prayer has no definitive starting point, it has a clear end: with the 'Ordinance for taking away the Book of Common Prayer, and for establishing and putting in execution of the Directory for the publique worship of God'. The Ordinance begins:

> The Lords and Commons assembled in Parliament, taking into serious consideration the manifold inconveniencies that have arisen by the Book of Common-prayer in the Kingdome, and resolving, according to their Covenant, to reform Religion according to the Word of God, and the Example of the best Reformed Churches, have consulted with the Reverend, Pious, and Learned Divines called together to that purpose; and do judge it necessary, that the said Book of Common Prayer be abolished.[12]

The law is striking for its turn of phrase, and how this moment casts light back over the whole history of the prayer book in English. For this law seeks to 'abolish' the prayer book, but this must mean not the material object itself, but rather, the network of practices which spread out from it. The 'Ordinance', that is, seeks to end the prayer book's role, rather than its existence, and in doing so, emphasizes the degree to which the Book of Common Prayer is not most meaningfully a book. Rather, it is a use, or a practice, and this is what the law stresses when it continues: 'the said Book of Common Prayer, shall not remain, or be from henceforth used in any Church, Chappell, or place of publique worship'.

The history of the Book of Common Prayer is a history of use. What the traditional narrative of dates and editions obscures is that it is not quite correct to see these as successive versions. Rather, this is a book in flux, always in multiple forms: and it exists in order to instruct a set of practices which take place outside itself. The entire rationale of the Book of Common Prayer exists only in how it considers the ways in which others will use it, and this rationale is made explicit in the passage which begins the 1549 version. 'The Preface' opens by noting that this new work replaces a previous form which had fallen into corruption: 'these many yeeres passed this Godly and decent ordre of the auncient fathers, hath bene so altered, broken, and neglected by planting in certaine stories, Legendes, Despondes, Verses, vaine repeticions, Commemoraciones and Synodalles' (3). Previous liturgical forms, it begins, are not simply incorrect, but have been made so in misuse. The Book of Common Prayer does not present itself as a break with the past, but rather, establishes its authority upon the continuity with a tradition of previous practices which have themselves become deformed by repeated enactment.

---

[12] C. H. Firth and R. S. Rait, eds., *Acts and Ordinances of the Interregnum, 1642–1660* (London: HMSO, 1911), 582.

There is, however, tension in the word 'use': for it may refer both to the form of a ceremony as it is set out on the page and also the performance of that ceremony. That is, it refers to both the book and the ritual: it is both verb and noun, and the prayer book presents the word in both these senses. Here is the triumphant claim from the preface: 'Where heretofore, there hath been great diversitie in saying and synging in churches within this realm: some folowyng Salisbury use, some Herford use, some the use of Bangor, some of Yorke, & some of Lincolne: Now from henceforth, all the whole realm shall have but one use' (4). And here is the key command from the Act of Uniformity, as added to copies of the prayer book in 1552 and extended in 1559:

> all and singular ministers in any cathedral or parish church or other place within this realm of England, Wales, and the marches of the same, or other the Queen's dominions shall, from and after the Feast of the Nativity of Saint John Baptist next coming, be bounden to say and use the matins, evensong, celebration of the Lord's Supper, and administration of each of the sacraments, and all their common and open prayer, in such order and form as is mentioned in the said book. (6)

The keyword 'use' describes both object and process, both script and performance, for the Book of Common Prayer exists most powerfully, not as a publication, but as a project.

* * *

The prayer book is a literary project, and the slight changes of phrase and emphasis through its successive editions reveal its shifting ambitions. It presents itself as a work of careful balance. The 1549 version ended with a brief self-justificatory essay, called 'Of Ceremonies, why some be abolished and some retayned', but following popular resistance to this first prayer book, the essay was moved to the front, where it sits in all successive versions. It is a subtle piece of writing, aimed simultaneously at those who would object to the prayer book's retention of traditional elements and also those who would dislike its novelty:

> whereas in this our time the minds of men are so diverse that some think it a great matter of conscience to depart from a piece of the least of their ceremonies, they be so addicted to their old customs, and again on the other side, some be so newfangled that they would innovate all thing, and so do despise the old, that nothing can like them but that is new, it was thought expedient not so much to have respect how to please and satisfy either of these parties, as how to please God and profit them both. (19)

While ostensibly presenting liturgical controversy as a minor quibble to be risen above, the preface actually responds to both charges. Against those who find the prayer book traditional are balanced those who find it too novel; and to each, the prayer book suggests an offer of salvation. The Book of Common Prayer is designed to contain the various minds of its worshippers in corporate forms of devotion; it is a work, therefore, premised upon agreement, but one deeply aware of the possibility of disagreement. It is worth looking at a series of key moments from the prayer book to see these projects at work: the balance of inclusion and exclusion, the formation of common worship from a divided community, and the arrangement of a human life into a devotional structure.

Following the prefatory matter is the calendar of set readings—this is present from 1549, and 1552 adds, while subsequent versions retain, additional charts and an almanac—but prayer book service, like the day, begins with Morning Prayer. In 1549, this is called 'Matins', and opens simply with the priest saying the Lord's Prayer, but 1552 changes the name to 'Morning Prayer' and expands the service into a dense literary event; 1559 follows this. The priest 'with a loud voice' reads at the opening a quotation from scripture: the prayer book includes a dozen of these, all upon the theme of contrition: 'I do know mine own wickedness', from the Psalms, and 'Correct us, O Lord', from Jeremiah, among others. This is then followed by a brief explication of those scriptural quotations. 'Dearly beloved brethren, the Scripture moveth us in sundry places, to acknowledge and confess our mainfold sins and wickedness', the priest explains, and asks the congregation 'to accompany me with a pure heart and humble voice' in saying the General Confession.

Each movement of the service builds upon the one previous: the opening emphasis upon the priest's voice in turn informs his instruction to the congregation that their voices should be 'humble', and where one voice has been speaking on behalf of the group, now all those present follow him in saying aloud, together:

> Almighty and most merciful Father, we have erred and strayed from thy ways, like lost sheep. We have followed too much the devices and desires of our own hearts. We have offended against thy holy laws. We have left undone those things which we ought to have done, and we have done those things which we ought not to have done, and there is no health in us. (50)

This moment establishes many of the rhetorical habits of the prayer book. The General Confession, which was added by Cranmer to the 1552 version, opens with two pairs of hendiadys—'Almighty and most merciful' and 'erred and strayed from thy ways', with its internal rhyme—but builds to a simple simile: 'like lost sheep'. This is followed by three sentences, each beginning 'We have', which move the congregation through the stages of confession. The first of these, which includes another hendiadys, explains our distraction. The second shifts the subject to 'thy holy laws', and this is rhetorically the simplest sentence of the Confession: a sentence about simplicity which itself includes no flourishes, as if to shy away from the distraction which has earlier led us to sin. But the third of these sentences opens out onto two longer and parallel phrases which form, in turn, a chiasmus, and from there leap to the third clause, 'and there is no health in us', which returns the subject to 'us' just in time for the second half of the Confession, which begins: 'O Lord, have mercy upon us miserable sinners'.

The sentences of the General Confession flow into one another, and their characteristic hendiadys, in turn, echoes their movement of identities collapsing into a single voice. The rhetorical and theological meanings, that is, are perfectly parallel. From here, the priest pronounces the Absolution to the congregation, and apart from replying 'Amen', their voices are quiet again, and then, in turn, the priest declares the Lord's Prayer 'with a loud voice'. The prayer book's repeated stress on the sounds of voice reveals how deeply the service is intended to be also an aural experience, and the act of speaking is here given weight: following the Lord's Prayer, the priest instructs, 'O Lord open thou our lips', and the congregation respond: 'And our mouth shall show forth thy praise'.

This is a key moment for the prayer book, not only because it embodies the larger project of corporate worship, but it was also revised between the 1549 and later versions. Ramie Targoff's *Common Prayer* argues that the reformed liturgy 'collapsed the differences between personal and liturgical worship by introducing a single paradigm for devotional language' which, in turn, fostered a single devotional community: this process is exemplified in the prayer book's contrasting 1549 and 1552 versions of this moment of confession.[13] Where the earlier book instructs the priest to lead prayer as an individual—'O Lorde, open thou my lippes'—the latter version emends the pronoun: 'O Lord, open thou our lyppes'. The replies by the congregation correspond: in 1549, 'And my mouthe shal shewe forth thy prayse'; in 1552, 'And our mouth shal shewe forth thy prayse'. 'Comparison of the 1552 text with its 1549 predecessor reveals Cranmer's rapidly evolving commitment both to dismantling the divisions between clerical and lay worship, and to creating an increasingly collective model of public prayer', argues Targoff, who concludes: 'the 1549 Prayer Book tentatively begins what the 1552 edition more fully achieves: the transformation of the liturgy from one based on private reading and silent prayers to a practice built upon shared or responsive texts read aloud by minister and congregation' (28, 35).

The formation of a single community of worshippers is the great ambition of the Book of Common Prayer: it seeks to align the disparate voices of a group within a single chorus. The instructions for Evening Prayer follow those for Morning Prayer; from 1552 onwards, these are, in turn, followed by the Litany, and then the set readings for each day of the liturgical year. These include a collect, an epistle, and a section from the gospels, and these set readings dominate the prayer book as a whole, filling half its pages. Only towards the end of the book are given the instructions for church rites: for Holy Communion, Baptism, Confirmation, Matrimony, Visitation and Communion of the Sick, Burial, and the Thanksgiving of Women after Childbirth. These were inevitably the most controversial, and most frequently revised, elements of the prayer book: and they articulate most clearly the central theme of community formation, both as an ambition and a challenge.

The order for Communion opens in all editions with the possibility of exclusion: with an instruction to the priest that if there is among the congregation 'an open and notorious evil liver, so that the congregation by him is offended', then he must exhort this failed worshipper to repent and forbid him from the service 'until he have openly declared himself to have truly repented and amended his former naughty life'. All must be 'persuaded to a godly unity', for Communion is both the performance and guarantee of the unity of the English church, and precisely because of this emphasis upon social formation, this rite was the most contested of all elements of the prayer book (247). Its revisions reveal the evolution of English theology, as well as the challenges to the project of the prayer book as a whole.

---

[13] Ramie Targoff, *Common Prayer: The Language of Public Devotion in Early Modern England* (Chicago: University of Chicago Press, 2001), 4.

In the 1549 version, the rite is 'The Supper of the Lorde and Holy Communion, Commonly Called the Masse' and the priest stands before 'the Altar'; from 1552 onwards, it is no longer referred to as 'the Masse' and the priest stands before 'the Table'. In each of these elements, the tension of doctrinal struggle is played out: from a traditional vision in 1549 to a more strictly reformed understanding in 1552, and then an attempted reconciliation of the two in 1559 (the 1604 prayer book follows the form given in 1559). In 1549, the priest recites a psalm at the start of the service; in 1552 and after, this is replaced by the Ten Commandments, as part of the greater emphasis throughout the second book upon teaching and learning. In 1552, the congregation are exhorted 'to remember the poor' and those who appear unwilling to receive Communion are at length encouraged to do so; in each of these cases, the 1559 version follows its predecessor in the emphasis upon worldly community and the reciprocal network of duty that binds the congregation.

The moment of administration itself is different in all three books and this reveals most clearly their doctrinal intentions. In 1549, the priest offers 'The bodye of our Lorde Jesus Christe which was geven for thee, preserve thy bodye and soule unto everlasting lyfe' and 'The bloud of our Lorde Jesus Christe which was shed for thee, preserve thy body and soule unto everlastyng lyfe'. While there is no mention of transformation, the actual materials of the real presence—the body and the blood—are named at the moment of administration itself. In 1552, this hint at transubstantiation vanishes and the materials now have a strictly memorial role. 'Take and eate this, remembraunce that Christ dyed for thee, and feede on him in they hearte by faythe, with thankesgeving', the priest instructs, and: 'Drinke this in remembraunce that Christ's bloude was shed for thee, and be thankefull'.

These would appear to be neatly opposed theologies, but the prayer book's larger project, as embodied in the Communion rite, is to reconcile distinction into a single form. The 1559 book therefore—and followed in 1604—reconciles the two theological positions by simply placing them next to each other. At the moment of administration the priest now says both: 'The body of our Lord Jesus Christ which was given for thee, preserve thy body and soul into everlasting life: and take and eat this, in remembrance that Christ died for thee, and feed on him in they heart by faith' and 'The blood of our Lord Jesus Christ, which was shed for thee, preserve thy body and soul into everlasting life: and drink this in remembrance that Christ's blood was shed for thee, and be thankful' (264). The contradiction remains. What defines the prayer book is the attempt at reconciliation, rather than its achievement.

The rites which follow Communion in the prayer book are determined by this same pattern: the 1549 version implies an often traditional theological understanding, which is revised in 1552 to conform more closely to a reformed conception of sacramental process; the 1559 book chiefly follows its immediate predecessor, while erasing the more extreme elements, and is, in turn, followed by the 1604 version. Each of these rites is marked by the tensions within early modern English theology: if at times the prayer book appears contradictory or half-finished, this is because it is most coherently viewed as an ongoing project of revision and reconciliation between doctrinal positions. To give one further example: the 1549 version of the rite for public baptism includes an exorcism.

The priest says, 'I commaunde thee, uncleane spirite, in the name of the father, of the sonne, and of the holy ghost, that thou come out, and departe' (1549: 219). But central to English Calvinist thought is a more metaphorical conception of sin and its agents than this literal presence of the devil, so in the 1552 version of the prayer book, the exorcism is removed. This does not mean, however, that the devil disappears, for later in the rite, in the interrogation of godparents, the priest asks, 'Doest thou forsake the devyl and al his workes?' (1552: 175). The presence remains, in a turn of phrase, and implies the apparently abandoned older theology.

The rite for the ministration of baptism in church is the first of the cycle of church rites which conclude the prayer book; it is followed by that for baptism in private houses, and the promises of each of these two are then affirmed in the following rite, for Confirmation. Confirmation completes the process of baptism, but stresses the capacity of the child to reflect and answer; the church rite is dominated by the Catechism, which enacts the child's comprehension. Just as Confirmation is the completion of Baptism, so, too, is the form of solemnization of Matrimony in the prayer book the fulfilment of a pre-existing contract. The couple to be wed must have already published their banns prior to the service, and the church rite itself exists to make public the private expression of consent.

The rites form an order which is also a narrative. Communion is first, as the transcendent sacrament; but the rites which follow are arranged in the stages of a proper Christian life: baptism, confirmation, matrimony, the sicknesses of age, and then death. Sitting awkwardly at the end of this series is the rite for the churching of women, but logically the Order for the Burial of the Dead should come last, and this has perhaps the most evocative poetry of the prayer book: a poetry, as before, made from a patchwork of scripture, chiefly from the book of Job and the Psalms. 'Man that is born from woman hath but a short time to live, and is full of misery', says the priest by the graveside, and then, as the body is lowered: 'earth to earth, ashes to ashes, dust to dust', which is the most extreme example of the doubling liturgical habit that defines the language of the Book of Common Prayer.

David Cressy's study *Birth, Marriage, and Death* highlights the cultural importance of the church rites of baptism, marriage, and funerals. 'These rites of passage', he argues, 'gave cultural meaning to natural processes, and constructed a social and religious framework to biological events.'[14] Human experience, that is, was, for the worshippers of early modern England, ordered by the liturgy prescribed in the Book of Common Prayer. Historians have long noted one apparent curiosity of the Order for the Burial of the Dead: that it withholds mention of the one who died. 'It is not too much to say that the oddest feature of the 1552 burial rite is the disappearance of the corpse from it', notes Eamon Duffy in *The Stripping of the Altars* (475). The reason for this is simple: the logical conclusion of reformed, specifically Calvinist, theological understandings of death is that the living may not affect the dead, and nor should they mourn for them. But it is

---

[14] David Cressy, *Birth, Marriage, and Death: Ritual, Religion, and the Life Cycle in Tudor and Stuart England* (Oxford: Oxford University Press, 1997), 2.

only fitting that the dead should be absent from the Book of Common Prayer: for it is a book for the living, for their handling and their use, the product of worldly debate and argument.

* * *

How, then, did early modern worshippers use their prayer books? The Book of Common Prayer was the set text for early modern English church worship, and therefore central to each ecclesiastical service; its set forms dictated the proper performance of the rites that mark the lifespan of all English worshippers. This orthodox practice is, however, only the first generation of prayer book use, and the small size and ready availability of the prayer book meant that it was taken also as the centre of private forms of devotion.

Prayer book annotation was a common enough activity in the early modern period to be the punch-line of a joke in Philip Sidney's *Arcadia*: the foolish Mopsa writes a poem about Cupid in her prayer book and is mocked for her sentimentality. Of the hundreds of sixteenth- and seventeenth-century prayer books now preserved in archives in England and America, many contain manuscript annotations: emendations, notes, lists, and handwriting exercises. These annotations fall loosely into three groups. First, worshippers inscribed their prayer books and the psalters with which they were bound with simple, repetitive handwriting exercises, dates, and notes. Robert Bird, of Corfe Castle in Dorset, wrote his name and initials repeatedly into his 1597 folio prayer book and psalter; the annotations are dated 1611, and also include the alphabet and single letters scattered at random through the pages.[15] In 1631, someone began a love letter to Elizabeth Lettisham on the frontispiece of her prayer book. 'Sweet hart and better come read me this letter', it begins, but the remaining lines have been crossed out. On the next page, Timothy Levett had a math lesson. 'In the bible are 1100 60 14 chapters', he wrote, and noted small crosses next to each book counted.[16]

These annotations are possessive: they mark the specific copy of the prayer book as the personal property of a single individual. Such rough jottings—love letters or spelling exercises—suggest that the people of early modern England approached their prayer books with lightness, but other notes have greater weight. Many early modern devotional works are inscribed with rough genealogies, such as the folio 1549 prayer book now in the Bodleian, which includes the births, deaths, and marriages in the family of William and Anne Priest of Cambridge between 1591 and 1654, and the 1571 psalter now in the British Library, whose front and back covers are covered with the dates of deaths and marriages in the Knollys and Saunders families between 1617 and 1659.[17]

Second, the liturgy was often emended to reflect contemporary events. Most commonly, the litany's invocation of the monarch is updated. The litany dates from the 1552 prayer book, where it reads: 'That it maye please thee to kepe Edward the sixth, thy servaunt, our King and governour'.[18] In subsequent editions, the name and gender of the

---

[15] BL C108.f.10. [16] NYPL *KC 1606 (BCP).
[17] CUL Sel.3.218; BL C.18.a.9. [18] BCP (1552), 42.

monarch is altered; but worshippers also emended their personal copies by hand. A Bodleian copy of the 1552 prayer book was therefore emended to include the name of Elizabeth, 'our queen', in the litany; in a 1596 folio prayer book now in the British Library, 'O Lord save the Queene' is carefully altered to 'King'.[19] Other volumes are updated according to a more zealous monarchism. The 1604 prayer book, updated after the Hampton Court Conference, asks 'That it may please thee to blesse and preserve our gracious Queene Anne, prince Henry and the rest of the kings and queens royall issue'.

Manuscript additions to a 1599 prayer book in the British Library insert this prayer into the Elizabethan litany; in a 1606 quarto prayer book in the Bodleian, Henry's name is crossed out and replaced with 'Charles', indicating that it was written sometime between the death of Henry in 1612 and the death of Anne in 1618.[20] These emendations gesture towards a commonly held sense, among early modern worshippers, that their personal prayer books must be contemporary. The Book of Common Prayer was not, in its material form, held sacred; rather, it required attention when it faltered or fell into anachronism. Although it may now appear paradoxical, this second category of prayer book additions gestures towards the enormously high cultural value placed upon the precise phrasing of the liturgy and simultaneously, the popular understanding that this cultural value was a product of the malleability, rather than the stasis, of the liturgical text.

The third type of manuscript annotations personalize the prayer book's devotional structures. Robert Bird drew simple devotional lessons from his reading of liturgy. Under the reading for Good Friday in his 1597 prayer book, he noted 'The dayes and ours passe away so doth the life of man.' This simple Christian lesson is not a conventional exegesis of the reading for the day, which is the description of the final meeting between Pontius Pilate and Christ from the gospel of John; rather, it is Bird's personal moral drawn from his reading of the liturgical text. Later, under the reading for the 19th Sunday after Trinity, he summarizes 'Learning without profit': the warning against such sterile knowledge is a fair gloss on Ephesians 4:17, which is the set text for the day. This particular moral clearly had resonance for Bird: he later begins, but does not complete, the phrase.[21] A 1586 Book of Common Prayer now in the Huntington Library is heavily annotated with broad devotional lessons such as 'The Whole Life of a Christian is nothinge else but a Contyewall tryall of his constancy in his Continuall warfare' and 'It is faith which must make us Cheerefull in Aflications/It is faith which must make us patient in Tryalls'; in the left margin is a list of extra-liturgical scriptural references to what were, for this worshipper, key texts.[22] A 1600 octavo prayer book now in the New York Public Library was bound with seventy extra blank pages which are covered with meditations, copies of the psalms, and scriptural quotations. The manuscript additions here outweigh the set liturgy, which was taken as an inspiration for the flights of personal devotion, rather than the formal limit of worship.[23]

---

[19] BOD C.P. 1552 d.6, sig. B.v.r; BL 1609/4817, sig. A2r.
[20] BL C.175.dd.1, sigs. A.vi.r, B.ii.v; BOD Douce C.P.e.1606, sigs. D3r, D5v. The same emendation appears in NYPL *KC 1615.
[21] BL C108.f.10.   [22] Huntington Library 438000:7.   [23] NYPL *KC + 1600.

Other early modern readers more explicitly personalize the prayer book's teachings according to individual devotional taste. During Elizabeth's reign, an anonymous worshipper annotated his prayer book along lines which suggest a tentatively traditional faith. In this 1552 folio, manuscript marginalia translate a small number of the English verses back into Latin; the Holy Ghost, excluded from the reformed Collect, is reinserted in the margin; and a short prayer is added to the instruction for the administration of communion. The new prayer, which hopes that 'The bodie of our Lorde/The bloode of our Lorde...bringes my bodie and soule into everlasting lyfe', returns a traditional presence and efficacy to the reformed version of the Mass.[24]

Annotations of this third category personalize the communal worship of the reformed prayer book. In a 1559 folio edition, a set of annotations added between 1612 and 1618 revise the scriptural translations to apply them directly to the individual reader. The plea, in the Morning Prayer—'Turn thy face away from our sinnes, O Lord'—is rephrased in a marginal note: 'Hide thy face from my sins'. By rewriting the prayer, this worshipper addresses God directly; by replacing the prayer book's communal 'our sinnes' with an individual 'my sins', he relocates the liturgical community inside the structure of his own sin and salvation. Again, later in Morning Prayer, 'correct us' is underlined and glossed as 'correct me'.[25] For this early Stuart believer, the prayer book was a rough guideline to personal devotion, rather than a set of communal instructions.

Early modern readers personalized their prayer books: by inscribing them, emending them, and even using them as scrap paper on which to scribble, they insisted that the prayer book was a personal possession. More than that: by rewriting prayers to make them personally applicable, they showed that early modern faith meant the gentle negotiation between set forms and personal belief, rather than a passive acceptance of a liturgy imposed from above. During the reign of Queen Mary, Francis Muscott attempted to update his Edwardian prayer book. This is a fairly eccentric project: the 1552 prayer book which he held in his hands was specifically premised upon an anti-Catholic sacramental theology, and Mary herself simply banned it as soon as she acceded to the throne. Muscott nonetheless added marginalia to the communion service—'By Body and Blode unto everlasting lyfe'—which introduced a Marian sacramentalism to the reformed rite, and in the litany he altered Edward's name to Mary's.[26] For Muscott, as for all of these early modern worshippers, there was no simple doctrinal binary between Catholic and Protestant or traditional and reformed liturgies.

In a recent essay on the medieval liturgies from which the Book of Common Prayer descended, Bruce Holsinger argues that 'liturgy more often functions as provocation to new cultural production than a conservative hindrance to aesthetic and stylistic creativity'.[27] In revising and annotating their copies of the Book of Common Prayer, the worshippers

---

[24] BOD C.P. 1552 d.6, sigs. C.ii.r, p.i.v.
[25] BL C.175.dd.1, sigs. A.r, A.v.
[26] CUL Sel.3.220, sigs. P.i.v, B.v.r.
[27] Bruce Holsinger, 'Liturgy', in Paul Strohm, ed., *Middle English*, Oxford Twenty-First Century Approaches to Literature (Oxford: Oxford University Press, 2007), 305.

of early modern England took liturgy as the prompt for personal devotion and personal creativity; but they also again stress how the prayer book is a shifting work, never limited by the strict text of its formal contents.

Further Reading

A Survey of the Booke of Comon prayer, By way of 197 Quares grounded upon 58 places (London, 1610).
Bancroft, Richard. *A Sermon preached at Paules Crosse the 9. of Februarie being the first Sunday in the Parlement, Anno. 1588* (London, 1588).
Barrow, Henry. *A Brief Discoverie of the False Church* (Dort, 1590).
Booty, John E. *The Book of Common Prayer 1559: The Elizabethan Prayer Book* (Washington, DC: Folger Shakespeare Library, 1976).
Cressy, David. *Birth, Marriage, and Death: Ritual, Religion, and the Life-Cycle in Tudor and Stuart England* (Oxford: Oxford University Press, 1997).
Cummings, Brian. *The Book of Common Prayer: The Texts of 1549, 1559, and 1662* (Oxford: Oxford University Press, 2011).
Duffy, Eamon. *The Stripping of the Altars: Traditional Religion in England, 1400–1580* (New Haven: Yale University Press, 1992).
Green, Ian. *Print and Protestantism in Early Modern England* (Oxford: Oxford University Press, 2000).
Holsinger, Bruce. 'Liturgy', in Paul Strohm, ed., *Middle English*, Oxford Twenty-First Century Approaches to Literature (Oxford: Oxford University Press, 2007), 295–314.
Lewis, C. S. *English Literature in the Sixteenth Century Excluding Drama* (Oxford: Oxford University Press, 1954).
MacCulloch, Diarmaid. *Thomas Cranmer: A Life* (New Haven: Yale University Press, 1996).
Maltby, Judith. *Prayer Book and People in Elizabethan and Early Stuart England* (Cambridge: Cambridge University Press, 1998).
Morison, Stanley. *English Prayer Books: An Introduction to the Literature of Christian Public Worship* (Cambridge: Cambridge University Press, 1945).
Rosendale, Timothy. *Liturgy and Literature in the Making of Protestant England* (Cambridge: Cambridge University Press, 2007).
Targoff, Ramie. *Common Prayer: The Language of Public Devotion in Early Modern England* (Chicago: University of Chicago Press, 2001).

CHAPTER 35

RICHARD HOOKER'S *OF THE LAWES OF ECCLESIASTICALL POLITIE*

RUDOLPH P. ALMASY

The latest validation of Richard Hooker's importance as a writer of prose comes with the decision to include Hooker in the 2010 MLA publication *Teaching Early Modern Prose*. In the chapter devoted to Hooker, Paul Stanwood suggests how Hooker's prose can and should be taught to undergraduates as he underscores Hooker's contributions as a thinker, as well as a prose stylist. Hooker is known not only as the writer of what many regard as the major prose work of the sixteenth century—*Of the Lawes of Ecclesiasticall Politie*—but even as the person who 'invented prose in English'.[1] Whether one regards this claim as exaggeration, Hooker remains an extraordinary writer for a variety of reasons. The *Politie*, a unique genre, continues to be read and studied; and scholars of religious thought, literature, history, and rhetoric have especially in the last forty years explored Hooker's achievement.[2] Whether one views Richard Hooker as a philosopher, theologian, ecclesiastic, political theorist, controversialist, logician, or even pastor, his work is lively, cogent, complex—and inviting.

Since Hooker would have thought of his task as a description of the basis of the sixteenth-century Church of England, it is important not to shorten the title to *Lawes of Ecclesiasticall Politie*. Such a shortening gives the impression that Hooker is

---

[1] Susanna Brietz Monta and Margaret W. Ferguson, eds., *Teaching Early Modern English Prose* (New York: The Modern Language Association of America, 2010), 214.

[2] Work on the modern edition of Hooker's complete writings began over 40 years ago. The project not only produced two volumes of essays, one at the beginning and the other at the end of the project, but also extraordinarily valuable introductions, commentaries, supplements, and appendices. *The Folger Library Edition of The Works of Richard Hooker*, ed. W. Speed Hill et al. 7 vols. (Cambridge, MA: Belknap Press of Harvard University Press, 1977–98). All citations will be to this edition with volume and page number in parenthesis. Another indication of the importance of the *Politie*, especially for students, is the decision of Oxford University Press to work with A. S. McGrade on a new, more accessible edition of the work.

establishing the 'laws' of the Elizabethan church. Hooker's description works best when the reader approaches the text, not in search of church laws, but in search of an understanding of the basis of changeable 'lawes' which inform church government, indeed, inform members about living 'as it were the life of God' (I.112). I believe that Hooker too would not have countenanced shortening the title since he needs to suggest that the church is not a matter of private construction, even by someone as talented as himself, nor an idiosyncratic construction based on a probable reading of scripture. Rather, the established church reflects God's creation in all its variety, the insights of rational thought throughout the ages, and the wisdom brought to the state by embracing the history and continuity of Christianity as a local church—the reformed Church of England in this case—is part of that continuity. Hooker, as a public voice, whether official or not, is not legislating a static entity, but identifying how the needs of the Kingdom of God can be realized in a changing world.

One ought not to approach the *Politie* without knowing the controversialist environment that produced it and how Hooker responded to that environment.[3] One also needs a sense of Hooker's relationship with John Whitgift. From the moment the Elizabethan church settlement went into effect in 1560, there were voices dissatisfied with the arrangement. These voices sought to rid the church of all Church of Rome abuses. The campaign to 'purify' Elizabeth's church further went on for over a decade, and then in 1572 *An Admonition to the Parliament* appeared. This tract sought parliamentary action to change worship and church government along the lines of John Calvin's church in Geneva. John Whitgift, then Master of Trinity College, Cambridge, was commissioned by Archbishop Parker to respond, and his *Answer against the Admonition* produced a 'reply' from Thomas Cartwright, England's leading Presbyterian at the time. As was not unusual, Whitgift answered with his *Defence of the Answer* (1573), which was composed of twenty-three 'tractates' covering what was always, it seemed, an expanding number of topics required by answering the opponent's new material. The polemic proceeds piecemeal, as Cartwright's text is broken up into divisions, with passages of Cartwright's text appearing and being refuted. Predictably, Cartwright responded, with his *Second replie* (in two parts: 1575 and 1577) using the same form to attack Whitgift. In such an arena it was imperative to have the last word and so be perceived as the victor of a specialized academic disputation, the nuances of which were available only to a small scholarly community. A question to explore is Hooker's relationship with John Whitgift; whether he is defending Whitgift, who becomes Archbishop in 1583, whether he is moving in different theological directions than his Archbishop, and why he deliberately used materials from Cartwright's two replies, fifteen years old, in a work which duplicated some of the opponent's words in

---

[3] A good introduction to this environment is W. B. Patterson's 'Elizabethan Theological Polemics', in Torrance Kirby, ed., *A Companion to Richard Hooker* (Leiden: Brill, 2008), 89–119. For brevity's sake, I will use the word *Politie*, rather than the more usual *Lawes*, since the work is not a compilation of laws, but rather, Hooker's testament to the achievement he would have felt was the established church.

new ways. In a sense, Hooker's *Politie*, coming twenty years after the *Admonition*, is a hybrid, as it searches for a new way to do polemics.

The Whitgift–Cartwright exchange was only one of many following the first *Admonition*. Peter Milward's *Religious Controversies of the Elizabethan Age: A Survey of Printed Sources* (1977) is helpful in seeing how much polemical literature (all now online) was produced during Elizabeth's reign. This output provides a necessary context for not only what Hooker said, but how he said it. Many of these tracts, as tedious and predictable as they are, are worth exploring to gauge, on the one hand, how different Hooker's work is, and on the other, how Hooker's hope for a united, interdependent worshiping community of English citizens intent on living 'as it were the life of God' might be reflected in the work of so many others. With this in mind, one of the issues in Hookerian studies is to gauge how much of Hooker's performance and the performance of others like Whitgift, Bridges, and Cooper, all within the polemical and political environment of the late 1580s and 90s, either excludes or attempts to include all in a worshiping community. Does the discursive strategy, as well as the voice and language of the polemicist, invite in or marginalize?

Hooker's biography does suggest that he was cast into this controversialist arena. Born in 1554 and dying in 1600, Hooker knew only the Church of England under Elizabeth, a church perceived as a stable state arrangement having existed a number of years longer—and without serious modification—than the Edwardian or Marian arrangements. At a young age, Hooker became connected to that church through important officials. Bishop Jewel was his patron as he enrolled in Corpus Christi, Oxford and proceeded to a BA and MA at the same time that Whitgift was battling with Cartwright. A talented fellow intellectually, he was appointed deputy to the Professor of Hebrew. But his connections did not stop with Jewel. He was the nephew of John Hooker, a scholar with ties to Peter Martyr Vermigli. Three of Hooker's pupils had their own connections and would prove indispensable when the *Politie* was ready to be published in the early 1590s. There was Edwin Sandys, son of the Archbishop of York, George Cranmer, great nephew of Archbishop Cranmer, and future brother-in-law William Churchman, son of John Churchman, prominent in London's Merchant Taylor's Company. Sandys and Cranmer were involved with the *Politie* project that was probably written in the home (and with the financial support) of John Churchman, Hooker's future father-in-law. Perhaps because of his intellectual talents and his skill in argumentation, Hooker caught the eye of church leaders, was asked to preach at Paul's Cross in 1581 (possibly on predestination), and, through Archbishop Sandys's influence, was appointed by Archbishop Whitgift in 1584 Master of the Temple congregation; that is, the congregation's chief minister and administrator.

But by the 1580s, a new generation of puritans continued relentless in their call for further reformation. They embraced a Presbyterian polity more enthusiastically than before, even organizing along Presbyterian synodic lines. And they seemed to have influence within parliament for a serious challenge to Elizabeth's recalcitrance over change. It was in the midst of this environment, in the midst of the politics of London, and in that institution where England's future lawyers were being trained that Hooker was assigned to his battle station. And battle station it was, for as soon as he came to claim his mastership, another leading Presbyterian, Walter Travers, a cousin of Hooker, urged him to accept a nascent Presbyterianism in the Temple congregation. Travers, a friend to Cartwright, was a popular preacher, had hoped to be appointed master, and had earlier written a handbook on Presbyterian polity. In the *Politie*, Hooker refers to Travers's *De Disciplina Ecclesiastica*, translated in 1574 by Cartwright as *A Full and Plaine Declaration of Ecclesiastical Discipline out of the word of God and of the declining of the Church of England from the same*. The first of many conflicts happened immediately when Travers asked Hooker to wait until he was 'called' by the congregation. Hooker knew that in the Church of England pastors were not called, but rather, appointed. Such confrontation with Travers would inform the *Politie*, which would reflect the contrast between an episcopal hierarchy and the authority of the congregation, the link between church and state which Hooker celebrates, and the potentially personal dimension of Hooker's work.

The relationship between Hooker, the superior, and Travers was intense and personal, with Travers seizing opportunities to expose his cousin's theological errors, attacking what he preached, and sending out 'angry informations…daylie' (V.228). The situation became so difficult that Whitgift removed Travers in 1586; Travers appealed to the Privy Council, condemning the unsound matter in Hooker's preaching on predestination, grace, justification, and the Church of Rome. Hooker responded to Whitgift with *The answere of Master Richard Hooker to a supplication preferred by Master Walter Travers*. Hooker's complaint against Travers had to do with his behaviour, public behaviour which challenged a superior, the public accusation by an inferior that Hooker caused disturbance.

Although Travers's work is not cited much in the *Politie*, this confrontation, as well as Travers's disregard for 'the established order of the churche' (V.248) and his attack on a superior, had to affect Hooker's approach to writing. That approach considered whether serious thought could occur in the midst of anger and whether surmises were all that were needed to find the truth. And it took into account the danger to church and state when 'all men mighte think what the liste and speak openly what they thinke' (V.247). Hooker understood the need to find time and opportunity to compose his thoughts about fundamental theological issues, all the time worrying deeply about destructive behaviour in the heat of debate that resulted in getting people riled up and encouraged the private few to believe they could prevail. Surely, Hooker must have felt the need for a new type of writing which, as it entered the public sphere, had to be less focused on the personal and the petty, and would not duplicate 'some unquiet kinde of proceedinges' (V 229).

Travers's accusations no doubt troubled Hooker, who was portrayed as sinister and conspiratorial, tongue and pen not interested in peace. And Travers openly complained about Hooker's manner of teaching. But it may have been Travers's insistence that his cousin was not theologically knowledgeable that got Hooker's goat. For we see in *The answere* and in the *Politie* that Hooker, as he was to become a representative of his church and state, took pains to portray himself as a man of peace and intelligence capable of the intellectual work required to settle the debate once and for all. And in his intellectual superiority, Hooker complains about the 'other': don't proclaim unless the issues are completely understood; understanding only comes from long and thorough study, from careful thinking and considered articulation; 'many talke of the truth, which never sounded the depth from whence it springeth' (I.56)—meaning the Presbyterian opponents like cousin Travers.

Truth in the *Politie* comes from the 'certainty of evidence' contrasted with faith's 'certainty of adherence', concepts Hooker explores in his *Learned Sermon of the Nature of Pride*. These concepts helped Hooker articulate the difference between matters of faith and matters of polity. For the Presbyterians, of course, faith included embracing a divinely designed New Testament church structure. The Church of England rejected such an article. As Hooker states, 'what was used in the Apostles time, the scripture fullie declareth not' (I.23). Polity is not a matter of 'certainty of adherence', an adherence that embraces God's promise of salvation and offer of grace. Rather, polity has to do with the 'evidence' which one assembles through learning and an understanding of the past. When one searches for the certainty of evidence to support, for example, the historical development of polity in a local church like England's, one needs an aggressive intellect which will find the evidence and then present the explanation. But the human mind easily confuses things. The objective controversialist needs right understanding, particularly for 'controversies of disputation', which Hooker admits he is pursuing. One must be led logically by a good teacher, led to understand the 'evidence' that the teacher, Richard Hooker in this case, marshals. Convinced that he possessed understanding and intellect, Hooker would have been insulted when Travers said publicly that his cousin was a poor scholar. The source of right understanding—and Hooker is always critical of his opponents on this measure—is the maturity of one's judgement. Only an informed mind could understand the social, ecclesiastical, and political world which Hooker would say the *Politie* explains so lucidly. Travers and his like simply didn't know enough to criticize Hooker and the church, and they failed to remain silent in their ignorance.

Hooker would also have been disturbed that Travers misrepresented his appeal to reason in understanding theological concepts. As the *Politie* makes plain, especially in its first book, human reason is necessary in forging the 'certainty of evidence' for specific ecclesiastical polity. But the English Presbyterians had a problem with reason, and the scepticism about reason, as well as human judgement, can be traced to Cartwright's exchange with Whitgift. For Hooker, as the Holy Spirit leads one to truth through scripture, so the Spirit can also lead through reason, that is, through 'sounde divyne reason'(V.255). The *Politie* does celebrate reason and Hooker is known for elevating the power of reason. But we have to recall that it is reason used in 'controversies of disputation'—in that search for the 'certainty of evidence'—that determines the consensus upon which truth is built, rather than private judgement and slight surmises which, for Hooker, characterize the Presbyterian case. In *The answere* and in the

Politie, Hooker's embrace of reason, a reason informed by grace and understood as a divine gift to the human and the corporate, is 'the moste sure and sauff waie whereby to resolve thinges doubted of in matters apperteyninge to faith and christian religion' (V. 255).[4]

In approaching the *Politie*, one has to be careful not to assume that Hooker's authorities are in competition. Grace and nature go together, as do reason and scripture. As many have noted, Hooker had a gift for syncretism. Scripture's purpose is to reveal the means to salvation. Reason's value is in discovering and articulating what is and ought to be in the 'state of men in this world'. To be in this world, even 'to live as it were the life of God', is to be in a political and social environment which depends on human intellect to understand the operations of law and to discover what is appropriate for one's particular time 'in this world', especially by focusing attention on first principles, which is the work of Book I.[5] Matters like orderly governance and the *adiaphora* of worship are devised by reason, relying on consensus, goodwill, legislation, and the voices from the past: 'the generall and perpetuall voyce of men is as the sentence of God him selfe' (I.83). Hooker carves out a site of human effort appropriate and necessary for Christ's earthly church. Tracing how Hooker uses this site, often in remarkable ways, can be a fascinating exercise. And it can also reveal Hooker's differences with both his Presbyterian, as well as his conformist, brethren.

We are not sure why Hooker began a comprehensive response to the Presbyterian challenge. That response, fundamentally political, is cast as a forensic proposition. Here are the opening words of Hooker's preface:

> Surely the present forme of Church government which the lawes of this land have established, is such, as no lawe of God, nor reason of man hath hitherto bene alleaged of force sufficient to prove they do ill, who to the uttermost of their power withstand the alteration thereof. Contrariwise, The other which in stead of it we are required to accept, is only by error and misconcepit named the ordinance of Jesus Christ, no one proofe as yet brought forth whereby it may cleerely appeare to be so in very deede. (I. 2)

There is a great deal in these opening sentences: a 'present forme' changeable in the future, judged acceptable because it does no 'ill' and much good; a 'present forme' established by law, consistent with the law of God and the reason of man. Hooker's opponents 'withstand' or resist the law of the land. They offer English citizens a polity built not on law and reason, but rather, on erroneous thinking. Although these opening sentences suggest the forensic nature of a public disputation, the form Hooker invents is a far

---

[4] David Neelands explores how Hooker saw the relationship between reason and scripture in 'Hooker on Scripture, Reason, and "Tradition"', in Arthur Stephen McGrade, ed., *Richard Hooker and the Construction of Christian Community* (Tempe, AZ: Medieval and Renaissance Texts and Studies, 1997), 75–94.

[5] Torrance Kirby tackles Hooker's extraordinary use of law—from 'the highest metaphysical principle to the most concrete institutional issues of a particular time and place'—in 'Reason and Law', in *Companion*, 251–71.

different public utterance than typical polemic. For Hooker is not only defensive in answering the Presbyterians but, more importantly, constructive in explaining the achievement which is the Elizabethan church.[6] Polemical disputation, as waged by Whitgift, Bridges, Cooper, and others, was a form of prose investigation that had become static, unable to develop further as discourse. Thus, to be more than defensive and damning, Hooker dared to try a more philosophical form. Such an attempt was needed when we note how the *Politie* served the needs of the state as prose debate entered the public sphere to imagine a worshipping community. Traditional polemic proved a confining school exercise. Something other had to be invented to give the definitive sentence on the controversy. And so, Hooker's prose strategy searches for new ways to invite in citizen-worshippers as they embrace a more universal and extensive representation of the Church of England.

For that representation, Hooker sensed what needed to be covered and how. The preface announces that there will be eight essays or 'bookes of discourse' (I.34). The first will 'declare therein what lawe is, how different kinds of lawes there are, and what force they are of according unto each kind' (I.35). 'If men had beene willing to learne how many lawes their actions in this life are subject unto, and what the true force of ech law is, all these controversies might have dyed the very day they were first brought forth' (I.139). Book II 'sifts' the 'chiefest principle' in the debate that 'scripture ought to be the only rule of all our actions'. Book III follows by refuting the notion that scripture describes an ecclesiastical structure 'the lawes whereof admit not any kinde of alteration'. The fourth book counters the accusation that since the Church of England retains popish rites, such ceremonies must be excised.

Many agree that Hooker made a brilliant decision to begin Book I with the notion that the Church of England was founded on law, and that different kinds of law inform every aspect of political, social, and ecclesiastical experience. Professor McGrade praises Hooker's notion of law as the 'single master idea in his work'.[7] Professor Kirby labels it 'a radical, foundational proposal'.[8] The great variety of law—eternal, celestial, natural, rational, human, and positive—invites awe and humility, as each citizen participates in a world defined by law: 'That little thereof which we darkly apprehend, we admire, the rest with religious ignorance we humbly and meekly adore' (I.62). Although there is disagreement in the scholarly community over Hooker's precise meanings, sources, and

---

[6] McGrade in the introduction to his edited version of the *Politie* for the Cambridge Texts in the History of Political Thought (1989) argues, especially in his discussion of Book V, that Hooker undertook 'a solidly constructive project' that presented 'a distinctively public devotional theology' (xix). McGrade continues this praise in his foreword to *Construction*: 'The *Lawes*, continuing the pastoral emphasis of Hooker's sermons, is arguably what it professes to be, an effort to satisfy the desire for Christian community which was so widely professed at the end of the sixteenth century, but Hooker serves this desire with extraordinary alertness to the fact that community is never simply given. *Construction*—construing, reconstructing, shoring up, new building—is constantly needed' (xiv).

[7] A. S. McGrade and Brian Vickers, eds., *Richard Hooker, 'Of the Laws of Ecclesiastical Polity': An Abridged Edition* (New York: St. Martin's Press, 1975), 16.

[8] Kirby, 'Reason and Law', 251.

modifications, the concept of law did provide him with a frame to emphasize order and harmony, concepts popular throughout the century, and the wisdom of the hierarchy and the public, as well as intellectual differentiation among citizens. It also enabled him to appropriate a variety of authorities which determine the affairs of humankind, to indicate how scripture and its interpretation (surely the crux of the debate) was only one authority, and how law, whether permanent or positive, defined church, state, and citizenship. Hooker says that Book I, 'concerning lawes, and their severall kindes in generall', has laid a new foundation on which to build 'hereunto that which commeth in the next place' (I.110). But this new foundation also directs the reading, Hooker controlling, unlike Whitgift, the disputational materials, seizing control of the discourse, and constructing himself as above the controversy, vastly more rational, knowledgeable, and tolerant than his church's adversaries.

Four books remain in the *Politie* 'and are bestowed about the specialities of that cause which lyeth in controversie' (I.35). Book V defends the Elizabethan church's 'publique duties' and its ministry. Books VI and VII concern ecclesiastical jurisdiction—the power of the lay eldership and the power of the bishop. The final book argues for the ecclesiastical dominion of 'the Prince or Soveraigne commaunder over the whole bodie politique' (I.36).

There is much that is not known about why *Of the Lawes of Ecclesiasticall Politie* came into existence. Hooker could have undertaken the project to satisfy his own intellectual curiosity and defend the church he admired. Perhaps he wrote to put Walter Travers and his fellow troublemakers in their place. Or perhaps there was something more official, more public, behind the project. He does say he is writing 'for mens information' (I.1). And Hooker does seem to be responding to the unanswered *Second replie* and so completing Whigift's defence, surely with Whitgift's knowledge, and perhaps, approval.

We do know that Hooker remained at his post in the Temple until 1591. During these years the nonconformists continued to agitate for substantial changes, indeed, for the overthrow of the episcopal system. The attack was enhanced by the appearance of the Marprelate tracts, seven of them between 1588 and 1589, precisely when Hooker would have started on his project. Perhaps because of these tracts, Hooker determined not to engage in ridicule, sarcasm, and *ad hominem*. In Hooker's mind, Marprelate did not promote harmony and peace, as he viciously satirized the bishops; indeed, he angered and divided. Hooker sensed the need for another type of prose, one that would promote rational thinking, humility, and peace. His prose needed to be energetic, assertive, and inclusive, displayed with confidence and authority, reflecting how the church and state needed to be represented.[9] But one of the tracts especially may have encouraged him to start writing. *Oh Read over D. John Bridges: The Epistle to the Terrible Priests for the Convocation House* speaks of polity. Marprelate writes to Dean Bridges: 'I would advise you, learn this of me: that the Church government is a substantial point of religion, and

---

[9] One of the best descriptions of Hooker's style is found in Brian Vickers 'Introduction 2' to the McGrade and Vickers *Abridged Edition*, 41–59.

therefore of the substance of the building...his Grace [Whitgift] shall one day answer me this point'.[10] It wasn't Whitgift who answered; it was Richard Hooker.

Might he have been answering on behalf of his Archbishop? During these years, Whitgift did pursue an aggressive campaign to silence opposition, assigning projects to Richard Bancroft, Bishop of London, and to Thomas Cooper, Bishop of Winchester. But was the *Politie* another such project? There is no evidence that Whitgift officially commissioned Hooker to write an *apologia* for the Church of England. However, the Archbishop surely would have known what Hooker and his friends were working on, and it does appear, regardless of the differences between Whitgift and Hooker, that Whitgift helped with the project. He may have seen Hooker's future book as one more weapon in his arsenal to attack and silence. Perhaps he felt that a work such as Hooker's could speak to all of Christendom about the Church of England as legitimate, reformed, even apostolic, as Jewel's *Apology* had done thirty years earlier. We know that from 1591 to 1595 Hooker was working on his writing in London, supported by absentee livings which Whitgift probably arranged, residing at the Churchman house with influential friends like Edwin Sandys, Member of Parliament.

Hooker shared his writings with Sandys and George Cranmer, another well-connected former student. Books I–IV, plus an enlarged preface, were in print by 1593, allegedly in time to be used by Sandys in parliament against all nonconformists. It is the preface which announces 'The matter conteyned in these eyght bookes' (I.34). The entry for the Stationers's Register also indicates eight books, although only four appeared in 1593. And Hooker's 'advertisement to the Reader' at the end of Book IV explains: 'I have for some causes...thought it at this time more fit to let goe these first four bookes by themselves, then to stay both them and the rest, till the whole might together be published' (I.345). To many, this statement indicates that all eight books were finished or nearly finished, each following an identical pattern of composition. It would not be until 1597, however, when Book V, the defence of the Book of Common Prayer, would appear, and it would be lengthier than the first four books combined.

We cannot be sure what was happening. There is evidence that his lay collaborators had some influence over the project. We assume it was their doing that Hooker added chapters 8 and 9 to his preface. These additions directly blame the Presbyterians for the separatists. The long chapter 8 stresses political dangers: the world will be 'cleane turned upside downe' (I.42), Hooker warns, should the discipline be 'received'. Citizens need 'to feare the manifold dangerous events likely to ensue upon this intended reformation, if it did take place' (I.36). For many, Hooker seems uncharacteristically alarmist in this chapter, although throughout the *Politie* he frequently cites the dangers of this kind of change to the good order of state and church.

Regardless of additions, the preface does shape the reader's attitude towards John Calvin, his Geneva, and his polity, towards the English Presbyterians, the 'learneder

---

[10] The passage is quoted in Diarmaid MacCulloch, *The Reformation: A History* (New York: Viking, 2003), 376.

sort', and the not so learned. Hooker urges his opponents 'to call your deedes past to a newe reckoning, to reexamine the cause yee have taken in hand and to trie it even point by point... to search the truth... [to] sift unpartiallie youre owne hearts' (I.51). After Hooker's explanation, they should be able to accept the Church of England with clear consciences, and so cease causing trouble. The preface does identify earnest Presbyterians as one of the principal audiences Hooker had in mind. At the same time, there is always the 'other' who is politically dangerous. Some readers are merely intellectually unsound, dealing as they do with 'meere probabilities' (I.33). Note too the well-meaning, obedient English citizens who could be troubled by puritan accusations and seduced into the 'snares of glosinge speech' (II.30). Faced with a variety of readers, Hooker constructs himself as tolerant and sympathetic, and above all intellectually sound, promising that important 'certainty of evidence' to those who would listen. On the one hand, he has developed a 'briefe' for his church, presented before the Presbyterians, but also before potential Presbyterian sympathizers and conformists alike, even before the whole world. Hooker offers the 'intier bodie' of the case so all can 'find ech particular controversies resting place, and the coherence it hath with those things, either on which it dependeth, or which depend on it' (I.36). But the preface goes one step further, as Richard Hooker portrays himself as the universal judicial voice who has tried all things and presents his 'finall resolute persuasion' (I.2). The judge finds in favour of the 'present forme of Church government', with a judicial proclamation which, for Tudor England, expected silence. His is 'the sentence of judiciall and finall decision' discussed in chapter 6 as the only force to end contentions. Whether or not Hooker started with these constructions in the earlier books before adding a preface, it is a different reading experience to start immediately with Book I and ignore the preface, at least for a while. Indeed, because of that influential preface, one should ask how can the *Politie* be read?

Knowledge of the publishing history should help us in this reading. Apparently, Hooker had difficulties in finding a publisher. That his Archbishop does not appear to have helped launch the enterprise could suggest a lack of enthusiasm. As many have remarked, there is an independence of thought in Hooker's work.[11] Edwin Sandys agreed to finance the printing so that the first books, at least, would be out in time for the 1593 parliament. Since it took Hooker four more years to complete the comprehensive Book V and since Sandys and Cranmer did comment on a draft of Book VI, it is assumed lay collaborators had some influence in encouraging Hooker to revise and expand the remaining books. Hooker supposedly was to follow exhortations to emphasize the political dangers of innovation, to show how attacks on the church were attacks on the state, to condemn the innovation of the lay eldership, to attend to the particulars of the controversy, and to satisfy both the learned and the simple. To my mind, these are not exhortations Hooker would have particularly needed, exhortations which would have led to significant and lengthy revisions. Speculation abounds on the success of the collaborators

---

[11] See Peter Lake, *Anglicans and Puritans? English Conformist Thought from Whitgift to Hooker* (London: Unwin Hyman, 1988) for an analysis of how Hooker departs from Whitgift's more conventional conformist positions.

in influencing Hooker to change what he had originally conceived or initially written. Perhaps the length of Book V is their doing. It appeared as a separate volume in 1597, probably because the last three books, for whatever reasons, were not ready or too massive to publish along with Book V. At the end of Book V, Hooker asks readers to 'have patience with me for a small time, and by the helpe of Almightie God I will pay the whole'. 'For a small time' suggests that Books VI, VII, and VIII were on their way to being finished. But they did not appear in 'a small time'.

John E. Booty, in his Introduction to Book V in the Folger Edition, speculates which chapters would have been in a first version of Book V and then how revision would have enlarged the composition. Whether Booty's speculations are correct, the alleged additions to Book V would have still reflected Hooker's announced interest in the particulars of the controversy and in responding to passages from opponents. Things are not really different—just more, in my opinion. And the 'more' has made Book V a complete, enthusiastic defence and celebration of the worship and ministry within the established church. Characteristically Elizabethan, Hooker treats many of the details as *adiaphora*, acceptable because a church has the power to enact its own ceremonies. As Hooker remarks in the opening of Book V, 'Lawes touching matter of order are changeable, by the power of the Church: articles concerninge doctrine not so' (II.38), and worship is not doctrine. Yet, God still approves because the church's judgement is based on 'stronge and invincible remonstrances of sound reason' (II.47). For Hooker, the Book of Common Prayer manifests the value of corporate worship in which all citizens participate and so are absorbed into the public experience of worship, an experience centred on prayer and priest, reading and preaching, the scriptures rightly understood, the sacraments rightly administered. Such public worship, characterized by individual and corporate thanksgiving, helps English citizens 'to live as it were the life of God'. The goal, as Professor McGrade writes, is an 'intelligently guided, socially effective communal piety'.[12] As Hooker suggests then that worship folds the private into the corporate, the individual citizen into the worshipping community, his work goes beyond mere defence to indicate how the established church was in the world serving the needs of both the individual and Elizabethan society. The interdependent worshipping communion fulfils that divine law which unites 'all into one bodie, a lawe which bindeth them each to serve unto others good, and all to preferre the good of the whole before whatsoever their owne particular' (I.69). This is, indeed, to do the will of God.

But the issue of 'more' in the *Politie*, as a result of revision, needs to be dealt with in confronting Book VI, which answers 'whether all Congregations or Parishes ought to have laie Elders invested with power of Jurisdiction in Spirituall causes' (III.1). The original Book VI can be reconstructed from the notes Sandys and Cranmer made.[13] This reconstruction indicates that Hooker's strategy was not significantly different from that used in the books published in 1593: an opening, a review, and enlargement of the topics

---

[12] McGrade and Vickers, eds., *Abridged Edition*, 36.
[13] Rudolph P. Almasy, 'Richard Hooker's Book VI: A Reconstruction', *The Huntington Library Quarterly*, 42.2 (Spring 1979): 117–39.

of the debate (more than likely covered by Whitgift), and then Hooker's new contribution which would bring closure. For Book VI, that contribution would have been a review of Old Testament civil and judicial arrangements as the alleged basis for the eldership. Unfortunately, however, the text which exists is not a complete Book VI. We find two chapters that might have been original, but then a piece of writing, atypical of Hooker's strategy in the other parts of the *Politie*, which by some has been labelled a 'tract on penance', with Catholic writers the principal opponents. These 'chapters', 3 through 6, have been printed in the Folger Edition as part of Book VI, based on the argument that Hooker thought it wise, perhaps influenced by his friends, to revise the four unpublished last books. Not only did Book V expand significantly, but Book VI would have expanded too as Hooker reviewed spiritual jurisdiction and English ecclesiastical law in order to provide context for the eldership debate.[14]

Whatever was happening in Hooker's life, now assigned a living at Bishopsbourne in 1595, none of the last books appeared before his death in 1600. Books VI and VIII appeared in 1648, and Book VII in 1662.[15] Was the delay the result of revision and expansion? Or were the last three books finished in the early 1590s, but for some reason withheld, perhaps for financial reasons? Were there possible printer concerns since the earlier books had not sold well? Were new pastoral responsibilities or ill health interfering? Or was Hooker growing weary of a project that now seemed superfluous since the Presbyterians had quieted by the mid-1590s. Was Archbishop Whitgift dissatisfied with a project less Calvinistic for his taste? And was the ecclesiastical climate changing in ways that affected Hooker, for example, on the issue of the *jure divino* basis of episcopacy, which Hooker did not seem ready to embrace? Were there atrophy and disinterest as the nation waited for a new, younger monarch? As the country neared a time of change, were the anxieties reflected in the last books overwhelming to Hooker, books covering what Hooker felt were the weightiest matters? It may be the case that Hooker's alarm about civil unrest, about lay power, about bitter disrespect for bishops, and about the responsibilities of the monarch was his way of dealing with the anxieties of the 1590s, anxieties he could not quite resolve in his discourse. Finally, perhaps Hooker was less suited to investigating the particulars of the debate, preferring instead the more general, philosophical problems he tackled so well in the earlier books. We simply don't know.

What we do know is that a great deal of political activity was happening in the late 1580s and 90s, and Hooker's work should be related to what was happening and who else was writing. We have been alerted to this need particularly through the work of Torrance Kirby and Peter Lake, as well as others, who are determining Hooker's relationship to Calvin and Whitgift and other predecessors, to the notion of a magisterial reformation,

---

[14] Some believe that the tract on penance is no part of the *Politie*. See, for example, W. Speed Hill's statement in chapter 3, 'Works and Edition II', *Companion*, 41–9. Others disagree. For example, Lee W. Gibbs, 'Book VI of Hooker's *Lawes* Revisited: The Calvin Connection', in W. J. Torrance Kirby, ed., *Richard Hooker and the English Reformation* (Dordrecht: Kluwer Academic Publishers, 2003), 243–61.

[15] See C. J. Sisson, *The Judicious Marriage of Mr Hooker and the Birth of 'The Laws of Ecclesiastical Polity'* (Cambridge: Cambridge University Press, 1940) which explores some details of Hooker's biography, the state of the last three books, and the story behind the disposition of his manuscripts.

and to the Anglicanism of the seventeenth century. Firmly grounded in a reformist orientation, as Professor Kirby argued, Hooker may still have been advancing beyond Calvinism, becoming innovative as he followed where his thoughts led. Through these textual negotiations Hooker is not only practising a new prose strategy, but developing his own identity as someone other than a typical polemicist. He is also developing or constructing the identity of a religious establishment that later came to be called 'Anglican'. Professor Lake, for example, stresses how Hooker created 'a distinctive and novel vision of what English protestant religion was or rather ought to be'.[16] That is, as Hooker engaged the controversy at a particular time in Elizabeth's reign and through a new type of discourse, he did not simply repeat the conformist answers, but rather, began to look afresh at scripturalism and authority, human potential and religious understanding, and worship and polity.[17]

There are several ways, then, of reading the *Politie*. Anyone who peruses the contents of any book will see Hooker engaged in a controversy which can be traced back several years to the *Admonition*. Second, there surely is the influence of the personal, revealed especially in the language reserved for his 'opposites'. So often Hooker's text—as constructive or irenic as some want to see it—characterizes the Presbyterian opponents as either plagued by misjudgement or by psychological disorder. They follow 'the law of private reason, where the law of publique should take place' (I.140). In an age 'full of tongue and weake of braine', many 'preferreth rest in ignorance before wearisome labour to knowe' (I.81). But not all, for as he adjusted to the polemical arena, Hooker played with the notion of multiple readers with different skills. But there were only a few like Hooker who thrived on 'wearisome labour', for he had 'more sharpnes of witt, more intricate circuitions of discorse, more industrie and depth of judgment then common habilitie doth yeeld' (II.43). In differentiating among readers, Hooker is very much directing the reading and the reader of the treatise. Of course, Hooker's work has to be read in relationship to the ecclesiastical and political atmosphere of the late 1580s and early 90s, especially in the wake of the Marprelate tracts. Finally, the *Politie* should not be seen as the product of a retiring intellectual writing in the privacy of his study. Rather, readers need to be alert to traces of corporate authorship in a work that has a polemically constructed ideology. And closely related to this sense of corporate authorship is the question of revision. But to look for revision is first to understand the architecture of the *Politie* and its individual books.

Scholars continue to explore the challenges the *Politie* offers. Is it a discourse which holds together? Is there coherence in Hooker's book and thought? Does Book I's insistence on the primacy of law in fact provide the foundation for subsequent 'meditations'? Is there agreement on what Hooker understood as natural law or predestination or grace,

[16] Lake, *Anglicans and Puritans?*, 146.
[17] This is not to suggest that as Hooker was looking with new eyes at fundamental issues he was pursuing a *via media* sense of the Elizabethan church as somehow the result of a negotiation or compromise between Rome and Geneva. Both 'Anglican' and *via media* are anachronisms and should not be used to characterize Hooker's understanding of the 'moderate kind' (I.342–3) of reformation the Church of England pursued in the sixteenth century.

reason or the sacraments, ecclesiastical jurisdiction or ministry? Exploring such challenges, tracing ideas to intellectual and theological predecessors and determining Hooker's adjustments and deviations, as well as looking forward to those who used—or exploited Hooker—in the seventeenth century, has been the principal work of contemporary scholars.[18] This is especially true since the appearance of the Folger Edition, which has attracted the attention of scholars of religion, history, politics, literature, and rhetoric. Indeed, Hooker's contributions to European intellectual life have been celebrated in a recent, comprehensive volume in Brill's Companions to the Christian Tradition series, the 2008 *A Companion to Richard Hooker*. Among the volume's topics, there are chapters on sin, grace, predestination, faith, assurance, reason, hermeneutics, prayer, the sacraments, ministry, and episcopacy. Such work also has elevated Hooker's reputation within the Reformation as a serious thinker, independent, adventurous, and yet, for many, orthodox. It may not be possible to find consensus on what Hooker really thought about matters that informed the work of theologians during the Reformation. It is not so much that this or that label can be easily applied (generalizations about Hooker now so suspect), but rather, how much and for what reasons he used, say, Aristotle, Augustine, Aquinas, or Calvin, and what he was doing rhetorically within the discourse. These issues will continue to fascinate scholars and perhaps frustrate them, for Hooker may not have set out to write philosophy or theology for the sake of philosophy and theology. For as eloquent and substantial as Hooker can be, his was a practical enterprise with a straightforward goal: to persuade those who were either not conformists or only lukewarm conformists to embrace the established church's government, mode of worship, and limited scripturalism and to 'resolve the conscience, and...shewe...what in this controversie the hart is to thinke' (I.34). If not resolve and accept, at least obey.

In this respect, Hooker would have understood his work as dialectics. But at the same time, he knew his rhetoric. He did seek to move his readers—to move them to admire the sixteenth-century Church of England, as well as to fear the potential for disruption by the Presbyterian system. The play between Hooker's dialectic and rhetoric should be further explored, especially in Hooker's multiple constructions of himself, in how he defined the 'good' which the Ciceronian orator sought, in how he used praise to elevate the established church, and in how his various readers were to be affected by his prose.[19] But even as Hooker plays at being the good orator fighting for order and against disruption, the *Politie* cannot be called a *summa*. Even when Hooker began to think more deeply on matters like grace and free will, and the sacraments and predestination, his writings are reactive. Let me explain.

Only one response to Hooker's *Politie* appeared in his lifetime, the anonymous *A Christian Letter* in 1599. The *Letter* criticized Hooker's characterization of Calvin and

---

[18] For Hooker's reputation see Diarmaid MacCulloch, 'Richard Hooker's Reputation', in *Companion*, 563–610, as well as Michael A. Brydon, *The Evolving Reputation of Richard Hooker: An Examination of Responses, 1600–1714* (Oxford: Oxford University Press, 2006).

[19] For example, see Brian Vickers, 'Public and Private Rhetoric in Hooker's *Lawes*' in *Construction*, 95–145.

accused him of teachings contrary to the articles of the Church of England. Hooker countered sections of the letter with notes that would have been part of a formal reply (we are back to the importance of having the last word). He also began writing more sustained and thoughtful responses on certain topics raised in the *Letter*, responses which have come down to us as fragments in a Trinity College, Dublin manuscript. But the *Christian Letter* also criticizes Hooker's style of writing, preferring the more typical arrangement of material which John Whitgift used. In Whitgift's book, so describes the writer, 'wee finde the question judicially sett downe, his aunswere to the matter in question sensible, his reasons eyther from holy scripture, from Fathers or new writers, without all circumferences and crooked windings, directly applied' (IV.73). Clearly, there was little appreciation for the new type of prose Hooker was doing. The writer complains of 'swelling wordes of vanitie, and cunningly framed sentences [which] blind and intangle the simple', of Hooker's 'metaphisicall and crupticall method to bring men into a maze' (IV.72). To read Richard Hooker is to 'walke as in a labyrinth, and [be] suddenlie overwhelmed as in the deepe sea' (IV.73).

What this Presbyterian took for a labyrinth is for Professor Stanwood a monumental achievement, a new type of writing, 'incomparably the best that ever was written in our Church'—so says William Covell, who wrote the first defence of the *Politie* in 1604. The massive project, so well conceptualized and informed by a sense of classical rhetoric, holds together quite well, Hooker in control of his *dispositio*. Each book is clearly organized and emphatically designed from opening *exodium* to *confutatio* and *confirmatio* to the *conclusio*. Indeed, Hooker demonstrates that sustained philosophical writing, with themes integrated and divergent material assembled, could be done in English. While others stuck with merely duplicating the words of the opponent, Hooker risked a discourse that performs as judicial judgement. As such, it does at least three things: leads the reader to embrace that judgement, puts the opponent in his place, and serves the political needs of church and state. As Hooker's material and methodology separated him from his fellow polemicists, perhaps elevating him in some manner, he may very well have wanted his project to 'overwhelm'.

Considering the reading practices of the time, Hooker demands more than usual from his readers. The *Politie* is a call to understand, to obey, to surrender, to embrace, to celebrate the church 'being both a societie and a societie supernaturall' (I.131) which includes all English citizens. But the polyvalent invitation assumes a hierarchy of abilities and temperaments. Some should merely obey; some might understand and yet be stubborn; some may see the truth after Hooker's exposition and embrace it; others might be too lazy even to try. Hooker might be able to educate some towards that 'certainty of evidence'. Others who are disordered, shrouded by that 'mist of passionate affection', may be converted only by prayer. And so, with multiple purposes and readers, Hooker also constructs his different voices—as partisan polemicist, as brotherly teacher, even pastor, as authoritarian schoolmaster, as judge. Obsessed with mature and wise judgement (and not timid in exposing the many who are foolish), Hooker speaks as a public voice representing not only the corporate identity of church and state, but the order, the coherence, the stability, and the variety of the very universe which is described in Book I.

And so, Hooker, as he helps shape the identity of the established church (as well as his own multiple identities), is also insisting that the identity of his readers be informed by the public order and public responsibilities of church and state. Hooker writes with a hope, surely naïve, to end an ecclesiastical controversy which had the potential to pull apart Elizabethan society—and we certainly know what happened in the seventeenth century. The desire of the discourse is, to use Speed Hill's wonderful word, 'repose'.[20] That is, the work itself and often Hooker's personae (but not always) perform, we might say, tranquillity: they hope to mould readers—partisan, non-partisan, and everyone in between—into tranquil, well-ordered individuals who would rehearse those Elizabethan ideals of security, harmony, humility, and peace. Perhaps this hope is realized as an individual's inner experience of union with God, which Deborah Shuger explores in *Habits of Thoughts in the English Renaissance*. However, could it be that Hooker's goal was to encourage or create a human and social community of citizen-worshippers who could indeed 'live as it were the life of God'?

Further Reading

A Celebration of Richard Hooker (on the 400th Anniversary of Hooker's *Of The Laws of Ecclesiastical Polity*), *Sewanee Theological Review*, 36.2 (1993).

Anglican Theological Review, 84.4 (2002), an issue focusing extensively on Richard Hooker.

Armentrout, Donald, ed. *This Sacred History: Anglican Reflections for John Booty* (Cambridge, MA: Cowley Publications, 1990).

Atkinson, Nigel. *Richard Hooker and the Authority of Scripture, Tradition, and Reason* (Carlisle, CA: Paternoster Press, 1997).

Brydon, Michael A. *The Evolving Reputation of Richard Hooker: An Examination of Responses, 1600-1714* (Oxford: Oxford University Press, 2006).

Gibbs, Lee. 'Theology, Logic, and Rhetoric in the Temple Controversy between Richard Hooker and Walter Travers', *Anglican Theological Review*, 65.1 (1983): 177–88.

Hill, W. Speed. 'The Authority of Hooker's Style', *Studies in Philology*, 67.3 (July 1970): 328–38.

—— 'The Problem of the "Three Last Books"', *Huntington Library Quarterly*, 34.4 (1971): 317–36.

—— ed. *Studies in Richard Hooker: Essays Preliminary to an Edition of His Works* (Cleveland: The Press of Case Western Reserve University, 1972).

Hooker, Richard. *The Folger Library Edition of The Works of Richard Hooker*, ed. W. Speed Hill et al., 7 vols. (Cambridge, MA: Belknap Press of Harvard University Press, 1977–98).

Kirby, Torrance, ed. *A Companion to Richard Hooker* (Leiden: Brill, 2008).

—— ed. *Richard Hooker and the English Reformation* (Dordrecht: Kluwer Academic Publishers, 2003).

—— *The Theology of Richard Hooker in the Context of the Magisterial Reformation* (Princeton: Princeton Theological Seminary, 2000).

Lake, Peter. *Anglican and Puritan? English Conformist Thought from Whitgift to Hooker* (London: Unwin Hyman, 1988).

---

[20] W. Speed Hill, 'The Authority of Hooker's Style', *Studies in Philology*, 67.3 (July 1970): 337.

McGrade, Arthur S. 'The Coherence of Hooker's *Polity*: The Books on Power', *Journal of the History of Ideas*, 24.2 (1963): 163–182.

—— ed. *Richard Hooker and the Construction of Christian Community* (Tempe, AZ: Medieval and Renaissance Texts and Studies, 1997).

Secor, Philip. *Richard Hooker: Prophet of Anglicanism* (Toronto: The Anglican Book Centre, 1999).

Shuger, Debora Kuller. *Habits of Thought in the English Renaissance: Religion, Politics, and the Dominant Culture* (Berkeley: University of California Press, 1990).

Sisson, C. J. *The Judicious Marriage of Mr Hooker and the Birth of 'The Laws of Ecclesiastical Polity'* (Cambridge: Cambridge University Press, 1940).

Voak, Nigel. *Richard Hooker and Reformed Theology: A Study of Reason, Will, and Grace* (Oxford: Oxford University Press, 2003).

PART VI
MAJOR PROSE WRITERS

CHAPTER 36

GABRIEL HARVEY

H. R. WOUDHUYSEN

36.1

Here is a trivial, everyday incident, a family quarrel: 'My father began to chyde and square with me at y̅e̅ Table: I præsently, & doing my duty, ryse from y̅e̅ bowrd, saying only: I pray you good Father, pray for me and I will pray for you.'[1] We have to imagine a tall and handsome young man with black hair and a dark complexion who has something of the look of an Italian.[2] He may, at this point, sport a moustache and almost certainly has a taste for fine clothes. Throughout his life, he seeks to rise early, at five o'clock, and to eat little and to drink less. This is Gabriel Harvey: his father, John, is a prominent citizen and landowner in the town of Walden (now better known as Saffron Walden) in Essex; the father also has a rope-making business. The family, John and his wife Alice, and their children, of whom Gabriel is the eldest, four boys and three girls, live in a substantial house in the centre of the town. They are not grand, but claim kinship with another local citizen, Queen Elizabeth's Secretary of State, Sir Thomas Smith, that 'bladder, full of Branes', as Gabriel Harvey called him.[3] Smith was Harvey's patron and hero: when he died in 1577, the young scholar produced a volume of Latin poems commemorating him under the evocative title *Smithus*.

The man who recorded his quarrel with his father remembered in his own words 'to leaue some memorials behinde him',[4] and the memorials have not entirely perished. He published Latin lectures and poems; the private letters he exchanged with Edmund Spenser, and which were printed in 1580, are amusing; the pamphlet war with Thomas

---

[1] *Gabriel Harvey's Marginalia*, ed. G. C. Moore Smith (Stratford-upon-Avon: Shakespeare Head Press, 1913), 143.
[2] Virginia F. Stern, *Gabriel Harvey: His Life, Marginalia and Library* (Oxford: Oxford University Press, 1979), 16 n.15, 42 n.32.
[3] Harvey, *Marginalia*, 139.
[4] Harvey, *Marginalia*, 233.

Nashe helped establish how to be rude in print. Yet, it is in Harvey's handwritten works, his manuscripts and the marginalia he so carefully and beautifully wrote in his printed books, that he appears most fully and willingly to have memorialized himself: 'giue me entrance, & lett me alone... giue me footing, & I will finde elbow roome', he wrote in his copy of Erasmus.[5] As a scholarly academic he can be brilliant in print, but only in Latin. When he writes for publication in English, he is diffuse and over-elaborate: something always seems to go wrong. Print, in his view, was the perfect medium for self-advertisement but, as he found to his cost, it could also be confining, not affording him sufficient elbow-room. He can only fully become himself in what is handwritten. Blank pieces of paper, leaves, sheets, gatherings, notebooks, commonplace books, letter-books, the endpapers of printed books, their gutters and margins, even between the lines of print: these alone seemed to give him the space he needed in which to express his self.

Hence, it has often been said it is possible to get closer to Gabriel Harvey than to almost any other Englishman of the Renaissance.[6] His manuscripts, especially his marginalia, present him, it would appear, as he really was: his mind, his hopes, and his thoughts, his very mental processes appear to be laid open.[7] Harvey's own interest in using manuscript, as opposed to print, provides a context in which to examine an account in his Letter-Book of the attempted seduction of his sister by a nobleman.

36.2

For Harvey, the books he owned were storehouses of useful material, the means to an end, not an end in themselves. The titles of just over 150 of his books are known, of which around 130 can now be located: the books and their annotations bear eloquent witness to his interest in law, history, politics, rhetoric, medicine, and contemporary literature. Harvey's marginalia have probably become his best-known prose writings: his comments on recent writing (including *Hamlet*) in his copy of Speght's 1598 edition of Chaucer are read more frequently and with more pleasure than, say, *Pierces supererogation*.

Harvey cultivated a version of the distinctive italic hand so highly prized in Tudor Cambridge; Nashe referred sneeringly to it as his 'faire capitall Romane hand'.[8] Some

---

[5] Harvey, *Marginalia*, 137.

[6] *Letter-Book of Gabriel Harvey, A.D. 1573–1580*, ed. Edward John Long Scott, Camden Society, NS 33 (1884), p. v; quotations from it incorporate corrections printed in G. C. Moore Smith, 'Gabriel Harvey's Letter-Book', *Notes and Queries*, 11.3 (1911): 261–3, and those taken from the manuscript, British Library MS Sloane 93. Cf. Harvey, *Marginalia*, 51.

[7] Cf. Caroline Ruutz-Rees, 'Some Notes of Gabriel Harvey's in Hoby's Translation of Castiglione's *Courtier* (1561)', *Publications of the Modern Language Association*, 25 (1910): 608–39, cited by James Nielson, 'Reading Between the Lines: Manuscript Personality and Gabriel Harvey's Drafts', *Studies in English Literature*, 33 (1993): 43–82 (76).

[8] *The Works of Thomas Nashe*, ed. R. B. McKerrow, rev. F. P. Wilson, 5 vols. (Oxford: Basil Blackwell, 1958), 3.60.

books are scarcely touched by Harvey's pen beyond a signature or his initials. In others, almost every inch of paper has been covered. Moore Smith believed that the notes were 'written only for his own eye',[9] but reading in the Renaissance was by no means always an exclusively solitary activity. Books were often social instruments to be read in company, as Harvey read Livy with (on different occasions) Philip Sidney, Thomas Smith's son, and Thomas Preston. In a less high-minded way, he could snigger over copies (bound together) of Scoggin, Skelton, *Lazarillo de Tormes*, and *Howleglas* with Spenser in London. Books were also to be read with his pupils and passed around among family and friends as gifts or purchases: they might be inscribed 'gabrielis harveij et amicorum'.[10] Harvey's library and his attachment to the notes he wrote in the books were sufficiently well known to be joked about in the Cambridge Latin comedy *Pedantius*, acted at Trinity College in 1581 and later to be referred to in his dispute with Nashe.[11]

In books from his library, the potent mixture of manuscript and print, of reading and writing, suggests that Harvey was involved in an extensive and interminable conversation with himself and others.[12] He makes the speaker in one of his poems say, 'I reade, and I reade, till I needes must cease,/And insteade of drye studdy, fall to gentle chatt' (*Letter-Book*, p. 134), as if the one naturally went with the other. The marginalia have a semi-public status, providing what has been called a 'manuscript personality', but it is of Harvey's own making. This may account, in part, for his characteristic boasting: 'I redd ouer this Ciceronianus twise in twoo dayes, being then Sophister in Christes College', he noted in a book by Ramus, or in a French-language manual, 'Apt & reddy pronunciation of the Alphabet, one weeks exercise', or in his copy of Foorth's *Synopsis Politica*, 'This synopsis filled the weight of scarcely three hours: at the third I was an expert at it.'[13] It is quite probable that Harvey had some of his printed books open in front of him when he lectured and that he taught using their marginalia.[14]

Those marginalia were also quarried as a source for books both written and unwritten: they served as manuscript miscellanies, and like such miscellanies, they had a relatively public character. As might be expected, Harvey is well aware of the distinction that can be drawn between what has been printed and what is manuscript. For example, he bets Spenser 'al the Books and writings in my study, which you know, I esteeme of greater value, than al the golde and siluer in my purse, or chest' that the poet will not be sent abroad in the near future.[15] Similarly, in a work by Ramus (1570) he notes 'This whole booke, written & printed, of continual & perpetual use'. Yet, the distinction is not an

---

[9] Harvey, *Marginalia*, 54.

[10] Stern, *Gabriel Harvey*, 125 n.143, 199, 204, 208, 211, 214, 216, 223, 229, 236, 239.

[11] Stern, *Gabriel Harvey*, 249, 252; H. S. Wilson, 'The Cambridge Comedy *Pedantius* and Gabriel Harvey's *Ciceronianus*', *Studies in Philology*, 45 (1948): 578–91 (581).

[12] William H. Sherman, *John Dee: The Politics of Reading and Writing in the English Renaissance* (Amherst, MA: University of Massachusetts Press, 1995), 15.

[13] Stern, *Gabriel Harvey*, 211, 214, 232. Some of Stern's transcriptions have been silently corrected.

[14] Cf. Sherman, *John Dee*, 70–3.

[15] *The Poetical Works of Edmund Spenser*, ed. J. C. Smith and E. De Selincourt (Oxford: Oxford University Press, 1912), 641.

absolute or simple one: Harvey's marginalia raise the question of whether the print or the handwritten annotation is the text, whether what appears literally to be marginal is not in fact central: 'the glosse oftentymes marreth the Text', as he noted in his copy of Erasmus's *Parabolae*, but what if the gloss is the text?[16] Perhaps this is what he meant when he wrote 'The Glosse,/Is grosse:/The Texte/Is nexte' (*Letter-Book*, p. 125).

Printed books circulate, but Harvey's manuscripts (apart from presentation copies for patrons) tend towards the private and secret. Where he mentions manuscripts, he usually does so in terms suggesting private knowledge to be kept to oneself. For Harvey, manuscripts do not circulate, are not published, or made available for multiple copying. Some knowledge was not to be shared, but to be stored in what he almost always referred to as a paper-book, a book of blank paper in which to write. His enemy Nashe had a 'great Paper-boke' of commonplaces, but his heroes also tended to keep their most valuable ideas and information in these sorts of compilations: 'Erasmus three cheefist Paper bookes' were 'His Similes', 'His prouerbes', and 'His Apothegges'.[17] Elsewhere, Harvey notes:

> Doctor Dale—the great pragmatic, and the most judicious ambassador I have known—used to say 'Give me no. 1' when he wanted Justinian; 'Give me no. 2' when he wanted his Speculum iuris; 'Give me no. 3' when he wanted Livy. For he made more of these three authors than of all the rest, and he supplied himself with a manuscript notebook of secrets.[18]

The key word here is perhaps 'secrets', as in the second item of a collection of manuscripts Harvey owned: 'This torne booke was found amongst the paper bookes, & secret writings of Doctor Caius.'[19] The professional's knowledge is cheapened if it is made public. In 1589, Harvey noted of a physician and surgeon who practised in Leicester, 'The best instructions [for treating disease are] in Mr Leas paperbooke. which he commonly called his boosum-booke: sumtime his Vade mecum.'[20] Elsewhere, Harvey referred to the alchemist and medical man John Hester's 'Chymical Epistle' as 'An other Vade mecum';[21] no known printed work by Hester quite fits this title, and the term 'vade mecum' seems here to signify a medical manuscript. Doctors do not publish their hard-earned skills since doing so would put them out of a job.

Some of Harvey's obsession with paper-books and secret knowledge can be traced to his distinctive paranoia; part of it also comes from an early and determining incident in his career. At Sir Thomas Smith's funeral in 1577, Harvey quarrelled with the Vice-Chancellor of Cambridge University, Andrew Perne, another keen book collector. The

---

[16] Harvey, *Marginalia*, 146, 136.

[17] *Pierces supererogation* (1593), sig. K2^r; Harvey, *Marginalia*, 141.

[18] Lisa Jardine and Anthony Grafton, '"Studied for Action": How Gabriel Harvey Read his Livy', *Past and Present*, 129 (1990): 30–78 (64).

[19] British Library Add MS 36674, fol. 23^r; Harvey, *Marginalia*, 214. In one of his printed works, Harvey's younger brother John talks about old English prophecies found 'in the secret paper-bookes of certaine English Antiquaries' (John Harvey, *A discoursive probleme concerning prophesies* [1588], sig. H4^v).

[20] Harvey, *Marginalia*, 127–8; this antedates *OED* vade mecum, its earliest citation being from 1629. See *OED* <http://www.oed.com> accessed 18 March 2013.

[21] Eleanor Relle, 'Some New Marginalia and Poems of Gabriel Harvey', *Review of English Studies*, NS 23 (1972): 401–16 (415).

dispute was over 'certaine rare manuscript bookes' of Smith's which his widow and co-executors wished Harvey to have, and which Perne was after for himself or for the university.[22] There was no sense in which the 'rare manuscript bookes' could be copied and shared: they were for their owner's eyes only. Smith's manuscripts were like Dale's paper-books, private collections of secrets and laboriously acquired knowledge. In a passage in his Letter-Book, Harvey refers to his having 'on suer frende', which he calls 'my Familiar'; then, assuming an editorial role, he adds, 'by his familiar, it is most likely he menith his Paperbooke' (*Letter-Book*, pp. 72–3). The definition is not exclusive: in one of his most heavily annotated printed books (Demosthenes's *Gnomologiae*), he writes of how he does not miss other Greek authors as long as he has this book, calling it 'One of mie pockettings; & familiar spirits'.[23] The paper-book and the heavily annotated printed book are where secrets are hidden from public view and where ideas and dreams can be privately explored. Although he undoubtedly had other personal notebooks,[24] the manuscript known as his Letter-Book, now in the British Library, is stuffed with autograph material illustrating these dual purposes.

The manuscript measures about 6 by 8 inches and consists now of just over 100 leaves. Harvey began it as a place for keeping fair copies of letters relating to his academic troubles over his MA in 1573. The first page has two poignant Stoic epigraphs, the first in Greek, which can be translated as 'My sufferings have been my lessons', and the second in Greek and Latin: 'It is better to be wronged than to do wrong'. At the end of the book he also copied several letters of an academic and personal nature from the early 1570s. The bulk of the volume is taken up by various literary pieces, including verses on the death of the poet George Gascoigne, letters and compositions which may have been intended in some form for publication, a Skeltonical poem, 'The Schollers Looue', and the story of his sister's seduction by an unnamed nobleman. These literary pieces are full of false datings, the invocation of various friends in their proposed publication, 'distancing frameworks', ruses, and shifts.[25] For example, he claims to have found two of the letters copied in the Letter-Book by chance 'amongst A number of myne oulde scatterid Papers', when he can be caught almost in the act of composing them there (*Letter-Book*, p. 77). Among the publication plans is one for 'Certayne younge Conceytes, and Poeticall deuises' that have been 'copied owt of A schollars Paperbooke' and published by a gentleman friend who had borrowed them 'as once his priuate exercises of pleasure, at idle howers'. The paper-book is explicitly where the scholar indulges in his 'priuate exercises of pleasure'

---

[22] Stern, *Gabriel Harvey*, 38; Patrick Collinson, 'Andrew Perne and his Times', in Patrick Collinson et al., eds., *Andrew Perne: Quatercentenary Studies*. Cambridge Bibliographical Society Monograph 11 (1991), 1–34 (21–5).

[23] Stern, *Gabriel Harvey*, 208; this antedates *OED* pocketing *n.*¹, its earliest citation being from 1638, *OED* <http://www.oed.com/view/Entry/238680?rskey=xzj5gQ&result=1&isAdvanced=false#eid> accessed 18 March 2013. For another 'familiar Spirit' belonging to Mr Goring, see Ruutz-Rees, 'Some Notes of Gabriel Harvey's', 630.

[24] He valued the Commonplace Book (British Library, Add MS 32494) at a hundred pounds. In one marginalium (Peter Whitehorne, *Certeine wayes* [1573], sig. F3ᵛ) he refers to 'my booke of Mechanical Experiments'.

[25] Josephine W. Bennett, 'Spenser and Gabriel Harvey's *Letter-Book*', *Modern Philology*, 29 (1931): 163–86; Nielson, 'Reading Between the Lines', 74.

(*Letter-Book*, p. 143): nothing can be printed from it without the fair copying and revision which Harvey once called 'transcripting and reforming'.[26]

36.3

If Harvey's reading was only a means to an end, at worst a distraction from the real business of humanist life, writing was also largely a waste of time, a displacement activity. In his Commonplace Book, he notes 'Auoyde all writing, but necessary: wch consumith unreasonable much tyme, before you ar aware: you haue alreddy plaguid yourselfe this way: Two Arts lernid, whilest two sheetes in writing.'[27] More strikingly, he cites two of his heroes who did not write. 'This vulgar bad habit of writing', he noted, 'often makes readers dilatory and usually makes actors cowardly. The followers of Socrates were wiser: they preferred teachings that were unwritten, spoken, preserved by memorization. "Take your hand from the picture", runs the old saying. "Take the pen from your hand", so runs my saying now.'[28] Christ did not write his gospels: he charged people not to write, but to preach. 'Don't sit around and write'. Elsewhere, he records a story of Apollonius Tyaneus, who, when asked 'why he writt nothing, being so excellently hable: answered, It was not his dessigne, To sitt still.' Harvey preserves his own command: 'Throw your pen away and sharpen your tongue.' As he puts it, 'All writing layd abedd, as tædious, & needles. All is now, jn bowld Courtly speaking, and bowld Industrious dooing.'[29]

The contempt for writing takes a distinctive form. In a richly annotated volume of Guicciardini's writings, Harvey records a remark made to him by John Young, Bishop of Rochester, 'Leaue scribling… & now in deed to the purpose'.[30] 'Scribling', the Juvenalian *insanabile scribendi cacoēthes*, is another word like 'secrets' that seems to acquire a significance for Harvey all of its own: 'Read as much as you can every day as quickly as you can', but the results should be kept in the mind, not expressed through the pen, for the itch to write, the incurable passion for scribbling, is a waste of time. 'There is nothing more vain than being in the habit of writing with a passion for scribbling.'[31] Books and manuscripts are not enough in themselves: Harvey despises 'Bookewormes: & Scriblers: pen & inkhorn men: paperbook men, men in their bookes or papers: not in their heds, or harts'.[32] Modern writers, 'this scribling generation', who are no good, can be dismissed as 'scribling paltryes'; his foe Robert Greene and the ballad-maker William Elderton are

---

[26] Harvey, *Marginalia*, 74; for 'idle howers', see this volume, p. 619.
[27] Harvey, *Marginalia*, 89.
[28] Jardine and Grafton, ' "Studied for Action" ', 77.
[29] Harvey, *Marginalia*, 144 ('Abijce pennam, et Linguam acue'), 144–5, 148 ('non sedete, et scribite'), 153.
[30] Stern, *Gabriel Harvey*, 188.
[31] Harvey, *Marginalia*, 125, 143 ('Nihil uanius vsitato scribendi Cacöethe').
[32] Stern, *Gabriel Harvey*, 187.

'the very ringleaders of the riming, and scribbling crew'; Greene himself was the one with 'the running Head, and the scribling Hand'. The psychology of Harvey's opposition to scribbling goes deeper: when he wants to excuse himself, as over the publication of letters to Spenser, he argues that it was unfortunate 'to imprint in earnest, that was scribled in iest'.[33] Likewise, his 'Answer to A Millers vayne Letter' in the Letter-Book is said to have been 'scriblid longe since', and 'The Schollers Looue' was 'scribled at the first in a hurlewind of conceit' (*Letter-Book*, pp. 90, 102).

Perhaps all writing, even of marginalia, is scribbling: 'No more scribling', he wrote in a heavily annotated volume, 'but enjoy the excellent, & divine notes, which you have alreddi written'.[34] After one reading of Livy, undertaken with Thomas Preston, Master of Trinity Hall, in around 1584, Harvey noted how: 'Owr special notes & particular obseruations, both moral, politique, militarie, stratagematical, & other of anie worth or importance, wee committed to writing.'[35] Books have to be read, and what is of value has to be written down, yet the fact remains that for Harvey, reading and writing are only means to a larger end.

36.4

Harvey commits nothing to paper without a purpose of some kind: the Letter-Book provides a place—between marginalia and print—for his own designs and compositions. Most attention has been focused on the central part of the manuscript, in which Harvey wrote and rewrote the compositions which would eventually emerge in print in 1580 as the letters he exchanged with Spenser. The process of transforming these 'Patcheries, and fragments' from manuscript into print is complicated, involving false starts, rewritings, and changes of mind:[36] it is important because of the flickering light it sheds on Spenser's life, the making of *The shepheardes calender*, and on the links he may have had with Sidney and his friends. Uniquely, Harvey's drafts allow the process of composition to be charted from manuscript to print and back again to manuscript, since his own copy of the 1580 letters survives with his corrections and revisions.[37]

The Letter-Book drafts combine Harvey's characteristic play of the literary composition and the autobiographical fragment; as Nielson has put it, 'what gives Harvey's drafts in manuscript their unique air of authenticity is more than anything else how inauthentic we can see him being'.[38] The pattern is one that Harvey seems unable to resist. He claimed that his first significant publication, the *Ode Natalitia* of 1575, was written during

---

[33] *Pierces supererogation*, sigs. A3^r, G1^v; *Foure letters, and certaine sonnets* (1592), sigs. A4^v (cf. sig. G2^r), D1^r, C2^v.
[34] Stern, *Gabriel Harvey*, 182 n.96.
[35] Jardine and Grafton, '"Studied for Action"', 43.
[36] Spenser, *Poetical Works*, 632.
[37] David McKitterick, review of Stern, *Gabriel Harvey*, *Library*, 6.3 (1981): 348–53.
[38] Nielson, 'Reading Between the Lines', 68.

the morning and afternoon of St Stephen's Day (26 December 1574: the date is significant), pouring forth, as it were, extempore in a few hours before and after lunch.[39] In the prefatory letter to the *Ciceronianus*, he tells William Lewin that the work is just what 'I was able to throw together in about five days'.[40] This sort of public boasting in print is like his more private declarations of how long it took him to read and master the books he annotated.

Harvey's public persona combines with what Moore Smith coolly called 'a certain inclination to finesse or trickery in Harvey's character'.[41] It is as if his boasting can be offset or mitigated by a degree of mystification: if Harvey is part of a hidden, secret world of which the reader is only allowed hints or glimpses, then perhaps he really does have something special to boast about. Mystification is particularly useful in relation to names: identities can be hidden and disguised, rendered in the shorthand of first names or initials, or referred to in a riddling, unspecific way. The special few will understand who is intended. This is what has made Spenser's *The shepheardes calender* (1579) such a happy hunting-ground for allegorists, allusion-seekers, and other conspiracy theorists.

Connected to this sort of mystification was an admiration for tricks and ruses: in the copy of *Howleglas* that Spenser gave him, Harvey referred to 'subtle & crafty feates' and to 'witty shiftes, & practises'.[42] He warmed to these sorts of things: like the commonplaces and proverbs to which he was addicted, they mixed the high and the low, presenting a paradoxical view of the world. Low or common wisdom might be worth more than book-learning, just as native cunning might outwit aristocratic or courtly brilliance. There was something else about merry jests to which he responded: the circumstantial detail on which they rely. Harvey is one of the few people of the period who can be seen in various interiors—'at the table' with his father, in his galleried study at Trinity Hall, or 'by ye fierside in his pore chamber' (*Letter-Book*, p. 182). The letters in the first part of the Letter-Book are full of similar sorts of details: 'the bel began to ring', 'This was after eiht A clock in the forenoon', 'We had talk not long sinc in M. Nuces chamber', 'I hauing bene veri sore sick, and at the self same time waring A charcher, feeling mi hed sumwhat could, (for it was in the deadist time of winter)', and 'we had now bene at it from immediatly after dinnar til thre A clock'.[43] Circumstantial details mattered to Harvey and helped to establish authenticity, the truthfulness of his story, or to make a point. One of the accusations made against him during the matter of his MA in 1573 was that 'I wuld needs in al hast be A studdiing in Christmas, when other were A plaiing, and was then whottist at mi book, when the rest were hardist at there cards.' This seems to have stung, and in one of the letters to Spenser, dated 7 April 1580, the setting

---

[39] Warren B. Austin, 'Gabriel Harvey's "Lost" *Ode* on Ramus', *Modern Language Notes*, 61 (1946): 242–7.

[40] H. S. Wilson, 'Gabriel Harvey's Orations on Rhetoric', *English Literary History*, 12 (1945): 167–82 (168).

[41] Harvey, *Marginalia*, 26.

[42] Stern, *Gabriel Harvey*, 49.

[43] Harvey, *Letter-Book*, 2, 3, 7, 12 (a 'charcher' is a kercher, as in handkerchief), 13.

for his discourse on earthquakes is 'a Gentlemans house, here in *Essex*', where he was 'well occupied...at Cardes, (which I dare saye I scarcely handled a whole twelue-moonth before)'.[44]

Describing the setting and adding such extraneous details shows what has been called Harvey's 'amazing sensitivity to factors of time, place, weather and other circumambient conditions'.[45] It can be linked to his interest in proverbs and colloquial speech, but it also comes out of the courtly fiction and courtesy literature that he so much enjoyed and admired. It would be wrong to underestimate Harvey's debt to Castiglione, della Casa, Guazzo, and especially George Gascoigne. He took enormous pleasure in his much-mourned friend Gascoigne's *Posies* of 1575, noting he bought his copy on 1 September 1577, and inscribing the title page with the word 'Aftermeales'. By the revised version of *The Adventures of Master F.J.*, he wrote 'The wanton discourse of A. C. at idle howers'.[46] A. C. was presumably Arthur Capel; the choice of 'discourse' is characteristic, but the precise sense of 'wanton' is hard to tie down, since it can stretch from the condemnatory to the merely amorous. Before Shakespeare had used it in the dedication to *Venus and Adonis*, 'idle howers' was a favourite phrase of Harvey's.[47]

36.5

Harvey's earliest surviving attempt to write in this 'wanton' vein appears to be his account in the Letter-Book of the attempted seduction of his sister by a nobleman.[48] It combines hidden identities, circumstantial detail, vivid speech, the erotic narrative, and merry jests, the high and the low in a remarkable way. One of the story's most striking features is the relative tightness of its telling. Despite several lacunae, the narrative and exposition are reasonably clear and form a contrast with Harvey's often incomprehensible rants and 'clever' writing in the 1590s, where he seems determined to obscure what he is saying. The pieces against Lyly and Nashe deter readers by their lack of organization and sprawling, mannered prose, yet the seduction story is deftly and neatly told in just over 5,000 words.

---

[44] Harvey, *Letter-Book*, 14; Spenser, *Poetical Works*, 613; cf. Kendrick W. Prewitt, 'Gabriel Harvey and the Practice of Method', *Studies in English Literature*, 39 (1999): 19–39 (26), and Gerard Passannante, 'The Art of Reading Earthquakes: On Harvey's Wit, Ramus's Method, and the Renaissance of Lucretius', *Renaissance Quarterly*, 61 (2008): 792–832 (793), who connect the detail with Castiglione.

[45] Margaret Schlauch, *Antecedents of the English Novel, 1400–1600: From Chaucer to Deloney* (Warsaw: PWN and London, Oxford University Press, 1963), 226.

[46] Harvey, *Marginalia*, 165.

[47] His collected poems are to be presented as 'his private exercises of pleasure at idle howers', just as 'The Schollers Looue' is 'A few idles howers of A young Master of Art' (Harvey, *Letter-Book*, 143, 102), and later (post-1598) he can refer to his poems '& discourses, as at idle howers, or at flowing fitts he hath compiled' (Harvey, *Marginalia*, 233).

[48] Harvey, *Letter-Book*, 143–58; British Library, Sloane MS 93, fos. 71ʳ–84ʳ.

It starts with a six-point summary of what is to come. On the next page, a heading announces that this is 'A Noble Mans Sute to A Cuntrie Maid'. The nobleman has a servant called P., who initiates the attempted seduction by inviting the maid to a Sunday supper of rabbits at Mr S.'s in an unnamed town. The summary calls for a first meeting on Monday week, at which the unspecified 'matter' is indirectly moved, but 'without offer of anie thing': this meeting is not described elsewhere. The second meeting has P. armed with malmsey (a sweet wine) and shortcakes. He watches the maid, accompanied by a poor woman, go milking; the food and drink are consumed in a wood. While the woman gathers sticks, P. carefully begins his master's suit to discover the maid's mind. She finds the approach hard to accept since she can't believe the nobleman knows her and because he has 'so goodlie A ladie of his owne'. It turns out that the nobleman has seen the maid and fancies her more than his own lady. The maid protests her own lowly status ('that she was but A milkmaide') and ordinary looks and, when P. gives her a silk girdle and a pair of gloves from the nobleman who intends to look after her generously, the maid 'kept aloofe', suspecting that P., not the nobleman, is the real suitor. According to the summary, P.'s next gift comes three or four days later 'at I. R.' or, in the narrative, a day or two later at an unspecified place. It consists of an enamelled ring, with the inscription '"Don IAMYE"', on a ribbon of orange tawny; P. swears the nobleman took the ring from his own hat, where it had been sewn by his aunt 'mieladie of W'.[49]

Uncertain what to do, the maid thanks her suitor 'for his loouing tokens', but says she cannot let him have his wicked way with her. P. professes to be astonished by her behaviour, saying he would advise his own sister to yield: he uses 'whot and ernest wordes' about how foolish she is being. The maid does not know how to respond but refuses again to yield. Changing his tack, P. now wants the maid to name a place where the nobleman can meet her. In the end, she agrees that the nobleman and P. can come 'ouer to her fathers howse in sutch A streat, vppon sutch A daye towards ye eueninge'. The following Wednesday, on 'A maruelous foggie mistie eveninge' at about 5 p.m., the two men go up the street, but the maid is not there. Instead, one of her brothers is in the house, and in the malthouse P. finds the maid's mother, sister, and two servants. Disappointed and fed up by their wasted journey on the 'mistiest and foggiest night, that was that winter', they leave 'well mirid and weried'. A day or two later, P. tells the maid about how disappointed his master was not to find her at home. She said she was not mocking him by her absence and would send him a letter in a day or two. P. is pleased at this news, 'for then he thought her deade suer'.

The narrative now alters to an epistolary exchange and the initial summary begins to fade out. Before doing so, it records that P. had 'manie A shrode wettie iorney' always in the evening, and that he only spoke to the maid 'thurrough A pale', never entering her

---

[49] The posy should perhaps read 'Don Damy' (French for 'The gift of a friend'); this motto is recorded on other contemporary rings, see Joan Evans, *English Posies and Posy Rings* (London: Oxford University Press, 1931), 33, and Robert Day, 'Posey Rings', *Journal of the Royal Historical and Archaeological Association of Ireland*, 4.6 (1883): 61–4, no. 93.

father's house. The next section begins with the narrator's statement that 'P. cummes me the next night for her letter', which P. can only collect after two further visits. The first letter allows the maid to apologize for not being able to speak to the nobleman when he visited; it reveals he is 'Milord A S.'. She still refuses to yield to his desires and asks him to destroy her letter. The nobleman writes a flattering reply, protesting his genuine love for her, and, agreeing with P.'s suspicion that the maid 'had her secretarye', wants an answer the next day. Two days later, the maid replies, protesting her chastity and begging the nobleman to take his affections elsewhere: she rejects his claims of her cruelty and his unhappiness in his 'long letters'—of which only one has so far been provided. Again, she asks him to destroy her letter. The following night, the nobleman replies to her second letter, but what he says is not given. With it came 'a small gould ring from his owne fingar' or, according to the summary, 'A prettie bowed goulden ring, wch P. swore Milord tooke from his owen fingar'.

On the next page there is another letter, headed 'The Maides farewell', and signed 'cruell M.'. In this, her third letter, the maid's resistance shows some signs of weakening; she refers to the failed 'mistie foggie euening' visit and to the nobleman's two 'larg and louing letters'. However, she still protests her social inferiority and that a liaison would ruin her: she bids him farewell, assuring him that his secret is safe with her. Just as the nobleman's second letter is not given, so his 'fresh Reiointer' to the maid's third letter is omitted. Having decided not to write any more, the maid is sufficiently moved by his 'so loouing A letter' that she wants 'to make an ende' with a 'fewe lines', some in verse, signed 'pore M.'. She is not going to change her mind: she is not cruel, but wary; he is not unhappy, but unsatisfied. 'Vnhappie am I rather, that, but there A strawe.'

Two days before Christmas Day in 1574, the nobleman sends P. to talk to the maid, who agrees to speak to her suitor 'at sutch A neighbours howse' and to meet him on St Stephen's Day (26 December). When they meet at night, he is semi-undressed; he kisses her and tries to get her on to the bed, but she resists. The 'good wife of ye howse' gathers how things are going and puts an agreed plan into action, leaving the house by a side door, knocking 'at her owne dore', and saying that M.'s mother is asking for her. The nobleman is furious, swears, orders her to yield, demands another meeting, says he will be true only to her and to his wife, and tells her she can have anything she wants, using 'him as familiarly and bowldly at any time, as her owne brother'. He makes her take the cash he extracts from his pocket. She goes, taking the money (it was only thirteen shillings, in shillings and sixpences), and promises to meet him on St Stephen's Day (the chronology seems a little muddled at this point). The day was 'marvelous wet' and the falling rain and snow cause flooding. Despite this, before six o'clock, the maid walks seven miles in the morning to avoid seeing the nobleman. P. goes to the place appointed for the meeting, to be told the maid has gone into the country to see a friend, but that she is expected back around the New Year.

On 30 December, 'hauing no other new yeares gift, but this sillie sheete of paper', 'by counsell of on, she trustid well', she sent verses to the nobleman, explaining that her father had wanted her to go to a 'kinsman' a few miles away and that she had to obey him. She continues in prose: P. has told her that the nobleman has been asking after his old letters; he may send new letters 'by P. to ye pore womans you wot of'. On the morning of 'friday next' (presumably 7 January 1575), she will ask 'on, that can not reade himself' to go to the poor woman's and find a letter that she will say she wrote to be sent to her brother 'the day before he cam downe of his owne accord vnsentfor'. The nobleman must therefore seal his letter and write on 'ye backside, in a small raggid secretary hand' the address: 'To mie louing brother Mr G. H., on of ye fellowes of Pembrook hall in Cambridg'. If the illiterate servant gives her the nobleman's disguised letter 'before cumpany' she can say: 'it was A letter I had writt to be sent my brother Gabriell at sutch time as he cam home to mie fathers; and so kept it still; and by chaunce left it in sutch A place; and therefore sent now for it; being loth it should cum in any others hands'. The nobleman is so taken with this ruse or so keen to correspond with the maid that he makes the bearer wait while he answers her, addressing the letter to 'my louing brother | m^r Gabriell Haruey'.

As before, with his other communications, the contents of the nobleman's letter are not given, but it is intercepted and an unsigned letter is sent to the nobleman. The writer, who is at Walden, explains that on New Year's Eve, as he was riding towards Cambridge, he met 'A cuntrie fellowe' he had often seen 'at mie fathers here in Walden'. The countryman explains that he has a letter that should have been sent to the writer in Cambridge, 'but that I [the writer] cam home to miefathers that verie time, it should haue bene sent me'. The letter is from his sister Mercy and the writer asks to see it. Although it is addressed to the writer, the countryman at first refuses to let him see it, but when he gives it to him and the writer opens it, he claims to have been 'sumdeale abasshid' and 'astonied' by it. The greeting was: 'Mine owne sweet Mercy, as if it had bene addressid to mie sister from sum loouer of hers, and not scriblid from mie sister to A brother of hers', and the subscription signed by 'Phil'. This was familiar enough, but what presumably shocks the writer—so that he had much ado 'to dissemble mie suddain fansies, and comprimitt mie jnward passions'—was the reference in the nobleman's letter to 'ye possessing of her according to prommis'.[50] The writer and the countryman engage in some banter over 'A faier Inglish crowne' in a 'prettie paper' accompanying the letter; the writer eventually claiming the money as his own. However, the countryman persuades the writer to return the letter and the crown, so that he may deliver them to the sister, from whom the writer can retrieve them. The writer adds his own 'tokin, will her in mie name, to looke, ere she leape. She maie pick out ye Inglish of it herself.'

Having told this story of the meeting with the countryman, the writer conveys to the nobleman his puzzlement about 'sutch A letter, and tokin, sent, not from you, as I take it, but in your L. name, from I knowe not whome, to A sister of mine'. He wonders who 'this lustie suter should be' and what the signature and the address signify, saying he means to get to the bottom of it all with his sister. However, circumstances stop him from doing this, and he says that he intends to 'huddle up A word, or twoe to mi sister by sum of y^e Markit folkes'.

---

[50] *OED* comprimit *v.* 3b, meaning to settle or allay, its first citation, *OED* <http://www.oed.com/view/Entry/37913?rskey=dxPxZP&result=2&isAdvanced=false#eid> accessed 18 March 2013.

36.6

The narrative has attracted a certain amount of attention as being 'compelling reading', a 'distorted fancy', and 'a literary hoax', but also as showing 'marks of individual genius far beyond the ordinary'.[51] Despite its relatively simple and familiar narrative, the issues it raises are complex. They include questions about its setting in the Letter-Book and hence, its relation to Harvey's other writings and to contemporary writings, and, above all, its truthfulness.

Its position and state in the Letter-Book point in different directions. Compared to many of the other compositions in the manuscript, the handwriting of the narrative is neat, suggesting that it is a fair copy. Yet, it is not included in Harvey's publication plans (*Letter-Book*, pp. 77–8, 89; fos. 42^r, 48^v), and if he is transcribing, rather than composing or thinking about what he wants to say, there are some peculiar lacunae in the narrative. The initial summary is written in a looser and smaller hand than the following narrative and they do not match each other exactly. Blank space is left for the first and the third of the lord's three missing letters, but there is scarcely sufficient room for the second of them (*Letter-Book*, pp. 149, 150–1, 156; fos. 76^v, 77^v, 82^r).[52] There is also Harvey's rather unexpected use of the ampersand. After the unsuccessful meeting at the maid's home, P. tells her that 'Milord did half suspect she mockid him. &c.'; in the next paragraph, the maid explains her difficulties, adding that 'if she had bine there, there had bene no speaking with Milord at that time. &c.' (*Letter-Book*, pp. 146–7; fol. 74^r). Later and more conventionally, when the lord is disappointed during their erotic encounter, he is made to expostulate 'god confounde me, if thowe wantes, while I haue. &c.' (*Letter-Book*, p. 152; fol. 79^r). Perhaps there was more to come or Harvey was signalling that it did not need to be spelled out, as he may be doing when he uses the ampersand in a similar way elsewhere (*Letter-Book*, pp. 64–5, 88, 100–1, 182). Various deletions and corrections that Harvey makes to the narrative may result from simple errors of transcription, but some of his interlineations and marginal additions, as well as attempts at rearrangement, suggest his revising hand.

The narrative may be incomplete because Harvey did not have the original materials with which to finish it, or because his imagination failed him, or because he meant to return to it and produce a final version later. Readers have increasingly taken the view that the attempted seduction is founded on fact, but that the narrative itself is essentially

---

[51] Nielson, 'Reading Between the Lines', 61; Muriel C. Bradbrook, 'No Room at the Top: Spenser's Pursuit of Fame', in J. R. Brown, ed., *Elizabethan Poetry*, Stratford-Upon-Avon Studies, 2 (1960), 91–109 (109 n. 7); Katherine Wilson, 'Revenge of the Angel Gabriel: Harvey's "A Nobleman's Suit to a Country Maid"', in Mike Pincombe, ed., *The Anatomy of Tudor Literature: Proceedings of the First International Conference of the Tudor Symposium* (Aldershot: Ashgate, 1998), 79–89 (84); Schlauch, *Antecedents of the English Novel*, 224.

[52] The absence of the second letter may possibly be explained by the loss of one or two leaves after fol. 76.

invented.[53] If this is right, then Harvey's skill lies in his ability to create a sense of veracity through attention to circumstantial detail and in the story's ambiguous sense of morality.

Although its time scheme is not entirely clear, it does have a distinct chronology of years, months, days, and dates, even of times ('fiue A clock in ye eueining', 'in ye morning before six A clocke'). A running element in the seduction narrative of that winter of 1574–5 is the weather: it takes place during 'A marvelous foggie mistie eueninge', on 'sutch A mistie night', involving 'manie A shrode wettie iorney', 'the mistiest and foggiest night, that was that winter', and 'A marvelous wet day', with flooding caused by 'raine, and snowe', when 'The raine continued ye whole day'. The setting is in and around Walden, with journeys to and from Cambridge, where Pembroke Hall is named. There is a wood, a place where the maid goes milking a mile from Walden, streets in the town, a wooden fence around the father's house, which has a parlour and a malthouse near it, a neighbour's house with its 'litle parlour' and a useful side door, and the 'pore womans' house where letters are to be left. The people in the story are variously named, P., Mr S. (of the rabbit supper), J. R. (at whose property the ring is delivered—if he is a person and not a place), the nobleman 'Milord A S.' or 'Phil.', his aunt 'miladie of W.', the object of his desires 'cruell M.', 'pore M.', or Mercy, and her brother 'Mr G. H.', 'Gabriell', or 'm^r Gabriell Haruey'. Besides them there are various unnamed characters: 'ye Maides mother, her sister, and two of her fathers servants: and in ye Parlour on of her bretheren', the 'pore woman' who gathers sticks and who is presumably the owner of the house where letters are to be left, and the 'on, that can not reade himself', who may also be the witty 'cuntrie fellowe' Harvey meets on the road to Cambridge.

The country fellow refers to 'ye best coate to mie back', which highlights the aristocratic nature of the lord's dress, his hat with the posy ring in it, and his undress, while waiting for the maid 'in his dublet, and his hose, his points vntrust, and his shirt lying out round about him'. This state is Hamlet-like, with the ties between his doublet and hose undone and with his shirt extending all around him. Later on, poor P., on the other hand, 'was fajnt to cum on pattins, bycause of ye great wett'.

The country setting is further established by activities such as the family's working in the malthouse ('sum turning ye mault, sum steaping, sum looking on'), the maid's hat blowing off while she is bowling, and the gathering of sticks in the wood for winter fires, the rabbits, and the malmsey and cakes. Proverbial language and country wit run through the narrative with, for example, the maid's reluctance to be 'cast up for hawks meate'. Two sorts of gifts are exchanged in the story, the letters which pass between the maid and the nobleman and the nobleman's expensive presents to the maid. The letters are represented by their contents and their physical constituents, 'this sillie sheete of paper',[54] 'this prettie paper', the 'inke, and paper' that will not satisfy the lord, the pen that she might 'put up', and the seal, superscription, and subscription of the lord's intercepted

---

[53] Cf. Stern, *Gabriel Harvey*, 38 n.16 with Nielson, 'Reading Between the Lines', Wilson, 'Revenge of the Angel Gabriel', and Jason Scott-Warren, 'Harvey, Gabriel', *ODNB* <http://www.oxforddnb.com/view/article/12517> accessed 1 April 2011.

[54] The same phrase occurs in a letter to Sir Thomas Smith, Harvey, *Letter-Book*, 178.

letter. Harvey actually writes the lord's false address to him in the secretary hand the narrative calls for.

The lord's gifts consist of fancy clothing (the 'good faier sylk girdell, and A hansum paier of glooues') and jewellery, the enamelled ring on a ribbon 'of urring tanye', and the 'prettie bowed goulden ring... from his owen fingar'. The bowed or bent ring can be connected to the 'twoe or thre crackd grotes, and bowd testerns' that the country fellow retains for the maid, which, in turn, relate to the 'crackd grote in ye opening' that Harvey expects to find in the package. Wilson is right to detect a sexual innuendo here, since the adjective had a contemporary moral sense (*OED* 4); she also links the discussion to the countryman's hope of finding 'an ould Angell', perhaps punning on Harvey's Christian name; instead, there is 'A faier Inglish crowne', 'A crowne of gould'.[55] This contrasts with the 'half A score ould aungels' the lord might have sent the maid instead of the posy ring and the women of 'fiue hundrid powndes A yeare' who would be easier to seduce than the maid. The angels may have been old, but they would have been worth ten shillings each, so giving her five pounds, as opposed to the measly '13^s in testers, and shilli*ngs*', the lord extracts from his pocket.

The narrative owes much to Chaucer, as well as to Gascoigne, and has been called a 'Chaucerian fabliau' in which the lord is the clear loser.[56] Yet, as with Chaucer, the story is not as straightforward as it at first appears. The lord's reported reference to 'ye possessing of her according to prommis' is easy to miss, but hard to forget; Mercy answers his letters and accepts his gifts. The substitutions of the servant P. for the lord as his proxy wooer, of the milkmaid for the lord's lady, of brother for sister (the lord asks the maid to 'vse him as familiarly and bowldly at any time, as her owne brother'), and of letters suggest a world turned upside down. A combination of country wit (Walden) and academic brilliance (Cambridge) defeat wealthy aristocratic desire. The narrative contrasts interestingly with another contained in the paper-book of an Oxford contemporary of Harvey's, William Withie, who was also an admirer of Gascoigne.[57] Where Withie fantasizes about town and gown relations in a merry story of an inn-keeper's wife and her rings, Harvey produces a much more elaborate and elaborately structured story, inverting social relations. The story enacts what Eutrapelus, one of his alter egos, is able to do 'to convert great matters into small ones, small into great ones. This is Eutrapelus's secret metamorphosis: serious matters of others being converted into jests, your own jests into serious discussions.'[58] If Harvey doesn't quite manage to spell out the exact nature of the serious matters (besides his sister's attempted seduction) in the narrative, it is because he lacks the literary ability. He is perhaps too close to the story to disentangle its personal meaning from his own desire to produce a masterpiece and to display his skill as a letter writer:

---

[55] Wilson, 'Revenge of the Angel Gabriel', 87.
[56] Wilson, 'Revenge of the Angel Gabriel', 85.
[57] Warren B. Austin, 'William Withie's Notebook: Lampoons on John Lyly and Gabriel Harvey', *Review of English Studies*, 23 (1947): 297–309.
[58] 'Magna in parva mutat Eutrapelus: parva in magna. Arcana metamorphosis Eutrapeli. Aliorum seria, in iocos convertenda: tui ipsius Ioci in seria', Stern, *Gabriel Harvey*, 160–1, 177; Passannante, 'The Art of Reading Earthquakes', 810.

the narrative flaw by which he appears to know that 'Phil.' is the lord is perhaps part of this. Harvey's own role, introduced by 'P. cummes me the next night for her letter', hints that the sister's letters are, in fact, his own work; this would justify the lord's suspicion that she has 'her secretarye', while edging his sister out of the story, which ends with his plans to reprove her.

Harvey's presence in his sister's story allows him to elaborate on its personal significance in ways which may have amused him. For example, the erotic encounter between the nobleman and the maid takes place on St Stephen's Day 1574, the day on which Harvey reports that he wrote the *Ode Natalitia*. The coincidence seems happily manufactured and is part of the piece's genuine allusiveness. The maid's letters are far more expressive than the single, rather brief example of the lord's epistolary skill, even to the extent of her rather moving aposiopesis or breaking off in her third letter, signifying her sense of worthlessness: 'Vnhappie am I rather, that, but there A strawe.'[59] The only time Harvey reproduces the lord's own words, it is with a strong element of mockery with his swearing at his sexual disappointment: 'Heare was good M. good M. and A great deale more. god confounde me, god confounde me, if thowe wantes, while I haue. &c.' His strong oaths and suggestive rage (what she wants and what he has done or what he possesses) belong to a different world from the clever dialogue of Harvey and the countryman. What gives the story a Richardsonian colouring is the mixture of 'curious minuteness' with the sister's 'somewhat ambiguous' conduct.[60]

36.7

Whether all the details of the story are true or not, there is some external corroboration for it. Harvey had a sister called Mercy, who was born in about 1556;[61] 'Milord A S.' or 'Phil.' can be identified with Philip Howard, who was entitled to be called Earl of Arundel and Surrey and whose aunt, 'miladie of W.' was Jane, the wife of Charles Neville, Earl of Westmorland. Philip Howard was born at Arundel House in London in June 1557; his father was Thomas Howard, Duke of Norfolk, and his maternal grandfather was the Earl of Arundel. Following his wife's death, the Duke of Norfolk married the daughter of Thomas Audley, Baron Audley of Walden. At the time of the attempted seduction, Philip Howard, then seventeen and a half, and his wife Anne, daughter of Thomas, Lord Dacre of Gilsland, to whom he was married when they were both twelve in 1569 (the marriage was solemnized in 1571 when the couple were fourteen), were living at Audley House. He was a student at St John's College, Cambridge, gaining his MA in 1576. His dissolute life in London eventually came to an end and, following his wife, he converted to Roman

---

[59] Harvey uses the same expression at the end of one of his letters to Spenser, *Poetical Works*, 632.
[60] Harvey, *Marginalia*, 16.
[61] Harvey, *Marginalia*, 6; Walter G. Colman, review of Stern, *Gabriel Harvey*, *English Studies*, 64 (1983): 169–74 (170) shows that Stern's belief that she was the same person as Mary is wrong.

Catholicism, was arrested for treason, and died in 1595 in the Tower of London. In 1886, he was named Venerable Philip Howard, was beatified in 1929, and canonized in 1970.[62]

The piety surrounding St Philip Howard has, perhaps, obscured the episode with Mercy Harvey. An early Jesuit biography explicitly states that his dissolute life and neglect of his wife began after his coming to court in about 1576.[63] More surprisingly, given the publication of the *Letter-Book* and Moore Smith's identification of the lord in *Notes and Queries*, there is no reference to the attempted seduction in the Catholic Record Society's volume devoted to him. The *Oxford Dictionary of National Biography* does not touch on the part Mercy Harvey may have played in his life. However, there are some traces that tend to suggest a factual background to the narrative. High on a list of family and servants 'appoynted to remove to Walden' in or around October 1571, is the household's Clerk Comptroller, Edward Pecocke, who had his own servant: Pecocke might have been the P. who assisted the lord in the seduction.[64] In the marginalia in his copy of Erasmus's *Parabolae* (1565), by a passage he marked about how great riches bring no pleasure to a fool while a wise man enjoys life even in humble circumstances, Harvey wrote: 'You knowe, who vsed to write: Vnhappy Philip'. He cross-referred this passage to another one later on in which a servant, asked what his master was doing, replies that he is seeking bad things to do when he has good at hand: by this Harvey wrote 'Vnhappie Philip'. The formula, suggesting both ill-fortune and unluckiness, as well as being miserable and wretched, seems to have been a favourite of Harvey's and, as late as 15 February 1585, he signed a letter to Burghley about his wish to become Master of Trinity Hall 'Vnhappy Haruey'.[65]

If there was a story about Harvey's sister, it would not have been something Nashe could or would pass over. In *Have with you to Saffron Walden* (1596), he says that Harvey's 'nere neighbors' have 'whispred to me of his Sister, and how shee is as good a fellow as euer turnd belly to belly; for which she is not to be blam'd, but I rather pitie her and thinke she cannot doo withall, hauing no other dowrie to marie her'. This 'baudy sister' is not named, but in *The Unfortunate Traveller* (1594), the narrator insists that he is 'by nature inclined to *Mercie* (for in deede I knewe two or three good wenches of that name)'.[66] There is one further small piece of evidence about the affair. In his copy of Henry Howard, Earl of Northampton's *A defensatiue against the poyson of supposed prophesaies* (1583), which was a reply to Richard Harvey's *An astrological discourse upon the conjunction of Saturne & Jupiter* (1583), Gabriel Harvey wrote that 'it is not the Astrological Discourse, but a more secret mark, whereat he shootith', adding his own comment, after quoting from

---

[62] See Moore Smith, 'Gabriel Harvey's Letter-Book', 261; John Hungerford Pollen, SJ, and William MacMahon, SJ, eds., *The Ven. Philip Howard, Earl of Arundel, 1557–1595*, English Martyrs, 2, Catholic Record Society 21 (1919); J. G. Elzinga, 'Philip Howard, [St Philip Howard], Thirteenth Earl of Arundel', *ODNB* <http://www.oxforddnb.com/view/article/13929?docPos=1> accessed 18 March 2013.

[63] *The Lives of Philip Howard, Earl of Arundel, and of Anne Dacres, his Wife*, ed. H. G. Fitzalan-Howard (London: Hurst and Blackett, 1857), 12–17, 178–81.

[64] Hungerford and Pollen, *Philip Howard, Earl of Arundel*, 18.

[65] Harvey, *Marginalia*, 137, 48.

[66] Nashe, *Works*, 3.129, 2.213: McKerrow (*Works of Thomas Nashe*, 4.258) was sceptical that the latter referred to the sister.

Virgil's *Eclogues* 3, 'Latet anguis in herba: et per me latebit, etiam adhuc' ('A snake lurks in the grass: and it will remain concealed even by me').[67] There were academic, as well as intellectual differences between Harvey and Howard, but the 'more secret mark' and the snake in the grass hint at something personal. Henry Howard was living at Audley House with his nephew Philip at the time of the attempted seduction.

The Letter-Book itself may also contain further traces of the affair. Harvey had three sisters: Alice, who married in 1570, Mercy, and Mary, who was not baptized until 1567. When Harvey records that, in the spring of 1573, a fellow of Pembroke 'riding thurrouh Walden calid in at mi fathers hous, and tould on of mi sisters, that I wuld be at Walden that niht' (*Letter-Book*, p. 27), it may well have been Mercy. In the seduction narrative, when P. looks into the malthouse, Mercy's sister is there: presumably, this is Mary, aged seven and a half. It seems reasonable, as Moore Smith suggested,[68] to connect the Mercy narrative with a letter Harvey wrote to Sir Thomas Smith's wife, Philippa, from Pembroke Hall on 29 March in an unnoted year. He seeks to 'to mooue an ernest sute...in the behalf of A pore sistar of mine: wch for sundri good causis...is maruelous desirous to do you seruice' (*Letter-Book*, pp. 170–1). In the narrative, Mercy repeatedly calls herself a 'pore wench' and signs three of her letters 'pore M.'. Harvey's 'bould request', his 'ouer sawci petition', must have been written before 1577, since Sir Thomas was still evidently alive. In the letter, he reports that he repaired to Smith 'about A litle busines I had of his' seven or eight years ago. Smith helped Harvey in his earliest years as an undergraduate at Christ's College, where he matriculated in 1566.[69] If Harvey repaired to him towards the end of his first year or during his second year as an undergraduate, this could place the letter in March 1575, just after the seduction. Harvey tells Lady Smith that he has 'A special regard, and brotherli consideration of mi sisters welfare' and that he is moved to seek a post 'thurrouh A certain inward affection of mine own'. If Lady Smith does take Mercy into her service, he goes on, he promises her she shall have 'A diligent, and trusti, and tractable maiden of hir, besides sutch seruice as she is able to do in sowing, and the like qualities requisite in a maid'.

36.8

The first piece in the second series of Virginia Woolf's *The Common Reader* (1932) is an essay on 'The Strange Elizabethans', in which she examined the seduction narrative. She says of the maid's letters that 'she bears herself with a grace and expresses herself with a resonance that would have done credit to a woman of birth and literary training', adding that 'Words chime and ring in her ears, as if she positively enjoyed the act of writing.' Her

---

[67] Stern, *Gabriel Harvey*, 72; cf. D. C. Andersson, *Lord Henry Howard (1540–1614): An Elizabethan Life*, Studies in Renaissance Literature 27 (Cambridge: D. S. Brewer, 2009), 102.

[68] Harvey, *Marginalia*, 16.

[69] Harvey, *Marginalia*, 9–10; Stern, *Gabriel Harvey*, 13.

style is 'natural and noble...incapable of vulgarity, and equally incapable of intimacy'. Woolf's argument is that in the end 'we know very little about Mercy Harvey, the milkmaid, who wrote so well': finally, she concludes that 'The background of Elizabethan life eludes us'.[70] The essay does not concern itself with the truth of the narrative, but with its elusive nature. She captures the richness and immediacy of the story and of its language, but at the same time, suggests the unknowableness of the truth about it and of the people swept up in it.

Virginia Woolf is right that the Elizabethan prose-writers do not generally 'solidify the splendid world of Elizabethan poetry'.[71] Harvey is not a Spenser or a Sidney in prose, but in his narrative he appears to take the reader closer to the fabric of everyday life than might be expected—as long as the reader remembers that, like an episode from *The Faerie Queene*, it is no more than an appearance.

Further Reading

Bennett, Josephine W. 'Spenser and Gabriel Harvey's *Letter-Book*', *Modern Philology*, 29 (1931): 163–86.
Harvey, Gabriel. *Gabriel Harvey's Marginalia*, ed. G. C. Moore Smith (Stratford-upon-Avon: Shakespeare Head Press, 1913).
——— *Letter-Book of Gabriel Harvey, A.D. 1573–1580*, ed. Edward John Long Scott, Camden Society, NS 33 (1884).
Jardine, Lisa, and Anthony Grafton. '"Studied for Action": How Gabriel Harvey Read his Livy', *Past and Present*, 129 (1990): 30–78.
Kintgen, Eugene R. *Reading in Tudor England* (Pittsburgh, PA: University of Pittsburgh Press, 1996).
Nashe, Thomas. *The Works of Thomas Nashe*, ed. R. B. McKerrow, rev. F. P. Wilson, 5 vols. (Oxford: Basil Blackwell, 1958).
Nielson, James. 'Reading Between the Lines: Manuscript Personality and Gabriel Harvey's Drafts', *Studies in English Literature*, 33 (1993): 43–82.
Passannante, Gerard. 'The Art of Reading Earthquakes: On Harvey's Wit, Ramus's Method, and the Renaissance of Lucretius', *Renaissance Quarterly*, 61 (2008): 792–832.
Popper, Nicholas. 'The English Polydaedali: How Gabriel Harvey Read Late Tudor London', *Journal of the History of Ideas*, 66 (2005): 351–81.
Prewitt, Kendrick W. 'Gabriel Harvey and the Practice of Method', *Studies in English Literature*, 39 (1999): 19–39.
Relle, Eleanor. 'Some New Marginalia and Poems of Gabriel Harvey', *Review of English Studies*, NS 23 (1972): 401–16.
Scott-Warren, Jason. 'Harvey, Gabriel', *Oxford Dictionary of National Biography*, <http://www.oxforddnb.com/view/article/12517>, accessed 1 April 2011.
Sherman, William H. *John Dee: The Politics of Reading and Writing in the English Renaissance* (Amherst, MA: University of Massachusetts Press, 1995).

---

[70] *The Essays of Virginia Woolf*, ed. Andrew McNeillie and Stuart N. Clarke, 6 vols. (London: Hogarth Press, 1986–2011), 5.338, 339.
[71] Woolf, *Essays*, 5.335.

Smith, G. C. Moore. 'Gabriel Harvey's Letter-Book', *Notes and Queries*, 11.3 (1911): 261–3.
Spenser, Edmund. *The Poetical Works of Edmund Spenser*, ed. J. C. Smith and E. De Selincourt (Oxford: Oxford University Press, 1912).
Stern, Virginia F. *Gabriel Harvey: His Life, Marginalia and Library* (Oxford: Oxford University Press, 1979).
Wilson, Katherine. 'Revenge of the Angel *Gabriel*: Harvey's "A Nobleman's Suit to a Country Maid"', in Mike Pincombe, ed., *The Anatomy of Tudor Literature: Proceedings of the First International Conference of the Tudor Symposium* (Aldershot: Ashgate, 1998), 79–89.
Wolfe, Jessica. *Humanism, Machinery, and Renaissance Literature* (Cambridge: Cambridge University Press, 2004).

Both Knox and Buchanan were prolific authors of prose, and what follows will consider the variety of forms and purposes to which they turned their pens. Political and controversial works, often published in the heat of national and dynastic dramas, helped to shape the radical reputations that would come to mark John Knox and George Buchanan as major voices of the Scottish Reformation. Among these are Knox's *First Blast of the Trumpet against the Monstrous Regiment of Women*, his strident denunciation of female rule of 1558; Buchanan's *Ane Detectioun of the duinges of Marie Quene of Scottes*, published in a variety of forms in Scots, English, and Latin in the early 1570s; and his *De Iure Regni apud Scotos* of 1579, a work of political theory justifying the deposition of Mary and defending the legitimacy of violent action against tyrannical rulers.

Knox and Buchanan are also well known as Scotland's first Protestant historians, as the former's *History of the Reformation in Scotland* and the latter's *Rerum Scoticarum Historia* have become foundation texts in Scottish Protestant identity, and, indeed, Scottish national identity. In addition, Knox's devotional writings and personal letters offer rich insight into the Calvinist mind and form of expression in the mid-sixteenth century.

The observant reader may well question why two Scottish authors are discussed in a volume about English prose. A cursory glance at some of the titles listed so far may summon the impression—and rightly so—that the vast majority of Buchanan's output was in the Latin language, augmented by a smattering of Scots. In the case of Knox, the question is even more vexed, as his contemporary and his more recent critics have challenged the authenticity of his Scots tongue, and viewed his writings—and the church and education system that his Reformation brought forth—as vehicles of Anglicization, detrimental to Scots language and culture. The implications of nationality and language will be drawn out in the final section of this chapter, but for now, it may suffice to emphasize that the Scotsmen Knox and Buchanan strode the historical and literary stage in a fundamentally British moment. The Scottish Reformation of 1560 had been shaped by English aid, and a developing amity with England and concurrent rejection of the auld French alliance. And the monarch whom Knox and Buchanan served, and then rejected, Mary Queen of Scots, was driven by her claim to the English throne. Knox and Buchanan were the most international of Calvinists, and England, it will be emphasized, loomed heavily on their horizons.

37.1 CONTROVERSIAL AND POLITICAL WRITING

It was in 1558, during his spell of exile in Geneva, that Knox wrote and published the three tracts that reveal his Calvinist voice at its most urgent and desperate. In *The First Blast of the Trumpet against the Monstrous Regiment of Women* Knox thundered against the rule of Mary Tudor in England on the grounds of her Catholic faith, her Spanish marriage, her persecution of Protestants, but most of all, her gender. And in *The Appellation to the Nobility and Estates of Scotland* and *The Letter to the Commonalty*,

CHAPTER 37

JOHN KNOX, GEORGE BUCHANAN, AND SCOTS PROSE

CAROLINE ERSKINE

JOHN Knox and George Buchanan were contemporaries and knew one another well, but they were very different men, very different Protestants, and very different writers. Both studied under John Mair at St Andrews in the 1520s, but thereafter, their paths diverged. Knox was ordained as a priest, but turned against the Catholic faith in the 1540s and spent the next twenty years moving in Protestant circles in Scotland, England, France, Germany, and Switzerland, including almost two years spent as a galley slave following the French capture of St Andrews Castle in 1547. He returned to Scotland in the summer of 1559 hoping to advance the cause of Reformation, and his sermon in Perth, which provoked an iconoclastic riot, is indicative of the mark he made. With the Reformation achieved in the summer of 1560, Knox was significant in systematizing the message of the Protestant Kirk as co-author of the *Confession of Faith* and the *First Book of Discipline*, and thereafter, he acted, as minister at St Giles Cathedral in Edinburgh, as a key mouthpiece of Protestantism.

Buchanan, in contrast, although he flirted with Protestantism as early as the 1530s, spent the early part of his career travelling extensively in Catholic Europe, in France, Portugal (where he again faced accusations of heresy and was imprisoned by the Inquisition), and Italy. By the time of his return to Scotland after the Reformation, and already a prolific author of poetry and drama, Buchanan had become a Protestant. He spent the years after 1561 at the court of Mary Queen of Scots as her occasional tutor, before the murder of her second husband Darnley and her swift marriage to the Earl of Bothwell turned him against her. He went on to serve as Moderator of the General Assembly of the Church of Scotland in 1567, the summer in which Mary was deposed, and thereafter, he actively sought to destroy her reputation and prevent her restoration to the Scottish throne.

Knox demanded that the Regent Mary of Guise cease the persecution of Protestants and implement Reformation. Should she neglect to perform this duty, it was the obligation of the nobility, as duly constituted powers within the Kingdom of Scotland, to bypass the crown and implement proper forms of worship. At this juncture, the sequence of dynastic shifts in the Tudor, Stuart, and Valois families that would accelerate the possibility of Reformation in Scotland remained in the future, and Knox existed in a state of partial suspension: contented and settled in his adopted home, while simultaneously jittery and impatient, awaiting news from Scotland and England.

Yet, while the 1558 tracts are conventionally regarded as a canon-within-a-canon in Knox's corpus of prose writing,[1] it is worth observing that they represent not so much a moment of crystallization in Knox's thinking and rhetoric, but rather, a culmination in his reactions to exile that had been building at least since the accession of Mary Tudor to the English throne in 1553. The reader finds an early taste of this in the 1554 tract *A Faithful Admonition to the Professors of God's Truth in England*, in which Knox, as minister to an English congregation in Frankfurt, heatedly condemned the Catholic powers of Europe, which England was in danger of joining:

> But, O Englande, Englande! yf thou obstinately wilt returne into Egypt; that is, yf thou contracte marriage, confederacy, or league, with such princes as do mayntayne and advance ydolatrye, (such as the Emperoure, which is no lesse enemy unto Christe than ever was Nero;) yf for the pleasure and frendshippe (I saye) of such princes, thou returne to thyne olde abhominations, before used under the Papistrie, then assuredly, O England! thou shalte be brought to desolation, by the meanes of those who favours thou sekest, and by whome thou arte procured to fall from Christ, and to serve Antichrist.[2]

This example reveals many of the defining features of Knox's prose. On the one hand, the reader encounters the deeply Old Testament concern of kingdoms or nations covenanting with God and the question of whether England would be an Israel or an Egypt. On the other hand, is the more immediate post-Reformation concern with 'Papistrie', idolatry, and Antichrist. And finally, the fearless, even reckless meddling with contemporary politics—the comparison of the Holy Roman Emperor with the tyrant Nero was dynamite in both Frankfurt and in England, given that the Emperor Charles V had become the father-in-law of Mary Tudor through her marriage to Philip of Spain. As a consequence of this publication, the Frankfurt English congregation, in league with the nervous municipal authorities, ejected Knox from the city in 1555.

The tone and content of the 1558 tracts suggest that Knox was not bowed by his experiences in Frankfurt. Collectively, these tracts are, as Roger Mason has put it, 'less systematic political treatises than religious polemics couched in the language of Old Testament

---

[1] Roger A. Mason, ed., *John Knox: On Rebellion* (Cambridge: Cambridge University Press, 1994).
[2] John Knox, *A Faithful Admonition to the Professors of God's Truth in England*, in *The Works of John Knox*, ed. David Laing (Edinburgh: Wodrow Society, 1854), vol. III, 308–9.

prophecy'.³ As Susan Felch emphasizes, in structural terms, *The First Blast* is 'a textbook example of a public classical oration', rigidly conventional in its engagement with scriptural and patristic sources.⁴ Knox believed that Old Testament law was still applicable in his own time. He quoted Deuteronomy on the Jewish law for the election of kings, which excluded foreigners and women, and argued that this law did not merely appertain to the Jews, but had remained in force ever since.⁵ And he mined the Old Testament for positive and negative examples of female rule. On the one hand, the paragon of female virtue, Deborah, a ruler whom God raised up 'to be a mother and deliverer to His oppressed people', and on the other hand, Jezebel and Athaliah, wanton tyrants and deserving casualties of God's vengeance.⁶ It is, in part, this distinction—Knox's acknowledgement that female rule could be both approved by God and beneficial for a kingdom—that has led Felch to argue against a simple reading of Knox as a misogynist.⁷ Knox's impassioned rhetoric, which appeared to roundly denounce female capabilities, may have clouded an argument that was considerably more nuanced. Further evidence of the subtlety and complexity of Knox's relationship to womankind, and to particular women, can be sought elsewhere, in his *History of the Reformation* and in his personal letters.

Related to Knox's Old Testament style was his strong preoccupation with covenant ideas, and it is here, again, that the centrality of England to his ideas is once again apparent. In Knox's conception, England was in danger of backsliding precisely because that kingdom had already experienced Protestant Reformation under Edward VI, but had declined with the succession of his Catholic sister. England was covenanted with God on Old Testament terms: 'I fear not to affirm that the Gentiles (I mean every city, realm, province or nation amongst the Gentiles embracing Christ Jesus and His true religion) be bound to the same league and covenant that God made with His people Israel.'⁸ Consequently, England was under a greater expectation—from God and from Knox—to oppose the forces of Catholic tyranny. In contrast, because in 1558 Scotland had not yet implemented Reformation, no such covenant existed.⁹

The jeremiad form—an exhortation to maintain the high standards of Protestant worship or to suffer divine punishment for backsliding—is one that George Buchanan adopted as well, if uncharacteristically, and in a very different context. While a large portion of Knox's corpus of writing preceded the Scottish watersheds of the 1560 Reformation and the 1567 deposition of Mary Queen of Scots, the bulk of Buchanan's prose output was produced afterwards, and in response to these events. His *Ane Admonitioun to the trew Lordis maintenaris of Justice, and obedience to the Kingis Grace,*

---

³ Roger A. Mason, *Kingship and the Commonweal: Political Thought in Renaissance and Reformation Scotland* (East Linton: Tuckwell, 1998), 139.

⁴ Susan M. Felch, 'The Rhetoric of Biblical Authority: John Knox and the Question of Women', *Sixteenth-Century Journal*, 26 (1995): 805–21 (811).

⁵ John Knox, *First Blast of the Trumpet*, in Mason, ed., *On Rebellion*, 28.

⁶ Knox, *First Blast of the Trumpet*, 34.

⁷ Felch, 'Rhetoric of Biblical Authority', 813–20.

⁸ John Knox, *Appellation*, in Mason, ed., *On Rebellion*, 103.

⁹ Mason, *Kingship and the Commonweal*, 156–9.

published in 1571, adopted a style reminiscent of Knox's *Appellations* to press the Scottish nobility to maintain their fight against the party of the exiled Mary Queen of Scots, urging them to 'considder how godlie is ye action that 3e haif tane on hand to writ'.[10] Buchanan took on a sermonic tone to assert that God was on the side of the reformers and the King's party:

> Think it na les providence of 3our hevinlie fader than gif he had send 3ow ane legioun of angellis to 3our defence. And remember yat he schew him self neuir mair freindfull and succurabill to na people yan he hes done to 3ow and traist weill gif 3e will pseveir in obedience and recognosce his manifold graces he will multiply his benefites to 3ow and 3our posteritie and sall neuir leave 3ow until 3e for3et him first.[11]

This covenantal language of God's expectations of His people was highly unusual for Buchanan. Indeed, it is tempting to speculate that Buchanan was here adopting Knox's style, using the conventions of his appellations, which must have been familiar and well established in Scotland by the 1570s. To explain this, the context is central. The *Admonitioun* was written in the immediate aftermath of the assassination of the Earl of Moray, early in 1570. The killing of the regent not only left Scotland leaderless in a crucial stage of the struggle against the Queen's party, but was also a crushing personal blow to Buchanan, who had been a friend and client of Moray. This was a desperate period for Buchanan in which he all but gave up his Latin writing.

The *Admonitioun* is therefore one of the only instances in which Buchanan unreservedly adopted the Calvinist language strongly associated with Knox and the Scottish Reformation. In general, it was humanism, more so than Calvinism, that marked Buchanan's intellect and morality, and imprinted itself upon his writings in a style that privileged classical rhetoric over Christian exegesis, and that is therefore surprisingly secular for the sixteenth century.

The spare elegance of Buchanan's Latin style is best illustrated in his short, but explosive, tract of political theory, *De Iure Regni apud Scotos*. Written in 1567 in defence of the deposition of Mary Queen of Scots, and published in 1579, the *De Iure Regni* advocated a radical theory of resistance that went some way beyond the noble-led action against Mary to admit the possibility that private individuals—would-be assassins—could legitimately act against tyrants. The tract takes the form of a dialogue between the wise master Buchanan and the naïve pupil Thomas Maitland. Maitland was a diplomat and his inclusion in Buchanan's schemes was much against his own will, and the will of his family—William Maitland of Lethington was a loyal supporter of Mary Queen of Scots and the target of another of Buchanan's polemics, the *Chamaeleon*, written around 1570.

The dialogue form allowed Buchanan to place words in the mouths of his 'characters', and it was this tactic that facilitated a degree of distance from the biblical exegesis

---

[10] George Buchanan, *Ane Admonitioun to the trew Lordis*, in P. Hume Brown, ed., *Vernacular Writings of George Buchanan* (Edinburgh: William Blackwood & Sons, 1892), 22.

[11] Buchanan, *Admonitioun*, 36.

beloved of Knox. It was Maitland who raised Old Testament examples, such as the order by the prophet Jeremiah that the Jews obey the tyrannical king of the Assyrians, so that Buchanan could then relativize them, in this case, with the argument that single scriptural examples should not be treated as precedents: 'The prophet does not command the Jews to obey all tyrants but only the king of the Assyrians. If you wish to infer a legal principle from what is ordained in one particular case, first, you know very well—for dialectic has taught you—how absurdly you would be proceeding.'[12] Buchanan even went so far as to scorn the jeremiad style beloved of Knox, ridiculing the claim that God set tyrants over peoples as a punishment and insisting that only royal sycophants and flatterers would claim such a thing. 'If anyone maintains that even bad princes are ordained by God, beware of the sophistry of such talk.'[13]

The flexibility of Buchanan's writing, his apparently effortless shift between multiple languages, genres, and registers, is also illustrated by the tract that is effectively a companion piece to the *De Iure Regni*, written at around the same time, but with a considerably more immediate and scurrilous purpose. The *De Maria Scotorum Regina*, published in 1571, was originally produced in response to the demands of Elizabeth's government for evidence against Mary Queen of Scots, following her flight to England in 1568. The evidence compiled by Buchanan, among others, included the controversial Casket Letters, which purported to offer proof, in the Queen's own hand, of her complicity in an adulterous affair with Bothwell and the murder of Darnley. While the English government had been at first reluctant to judge Mary's case, the exposure of the Ridolfi Plot of 1571 made an attack on her character expedient and Buchanan's text, which is better known by its translated title of *Ane Detectioun of the duinges of Marie Quene of Scottes*, was seized upon for publication. Jenny Wormald has aptly described Buchanan's polemic as 'copy for the *Sun* in the style of *The Times*', as it perpetrated a series of insinuations and falsehoods against Mary.[14] One would not wish to make an enemy of Buchanan. In one passage that illustrates the boldness of his attack, Buchanan added planned infanticide to the charges of adultery and mariticide. He claimed insight into a meeting with her advisers where, having fallen out of love with Darnley and come to actively despise him, Mary raised the possibility of divorce:

> Here someone voiced the objection that if that were done their son would be made a bastard, since he had been born out of wedlock... She thought over that suggestion for a little, and realised that it was true; and as she dared not at that time reveal her plan to make away with her son, she gave over the idea of divorce. Yet, from that day onward she never left her intention of destroying the king, as may well be perceived from what followed.[15]

---

[12] George Buchanan, *A Dialogue on the Law of Kingship among the Scots: A Critical Edition and Translation of George Buchanan's* De Iure Regni apud Scotos Dialogus, ed. and trans. Roger A. Mason and Martin S. Smith (Aldershot: Ashgate, 2004), 117.

[13] Buchanan, *Law of Kingship*, 115.

[14] Jenny Wormald, *Mary Queen of Scots: A Study in Failure* (London: Collins & Brown, 1991), 14.

[15] George Buchanan, *A Detection of Mary Queen of Scots*, in W. A. Gatherer, ed., *The Tyrannous Reign of Mary Stewart: George Buchanan's Account* (Edinburgh: Edinburgh University Press, 1958), 170.

To discuss the published translation of 1571 would be to depart from Buchanan's literary production and enter into the intrigues of the translator and his political masters, but it is worth observing that yet again, the issue of Anglo-Scottish relations was central to the production and reception of the *Detectioun*. The English translator, working at the behest of Elizabeth's minister, William Cecil, converted Buchanan's Latin into what is best described as 'pseudo-Scots', in an effort to disguise the involvement and interest of the Elizabethan regime.[16]

37.2 HISTORICAL WRITING

For both John Knox and George Buchanan, the writing of history was a gargantuan task that resulted in the largest single pieces of work of their respective canons. As such, Knox's *History of the Reformation in Scotland* and Buchanan's *Rerum Scoticarum Historia* are deserving of considerable attention. What follows will consider, firstly, the differences of scope, style, and priorities between Knox and Buchanan; and, secondly, the ways in which key figures of the period are portrayed, in particular, Knox himself, and Mary Queen of Scots. The question of how the histories produced by Knox and Buchanan have contributed to the shaping of Scottish Protestant and national identity will be considered in the final section.

Very different as Knox and Buchanan were as historians, we may readily grasp their intentions in undertaking to write in this genre. History could serve as a conduit for the broad sweep of their ideas, and provide opportunities to give life and speech to abstract political and theological ideas. The writing of history was the most immediate way to convey the passions and ideas of their own time, while presenting complex theories in an accessible and personalized style. Beyond these general observations, however, it is possible to discern individual interests and priorities behind these two historical projects.

Knox had conceived his project of writing the *History of the Reformation* before the Scottish Reformation itself was completed in 1560. The material in Book II, which charted the burgeoning of the Protestant movement and the developing resistance against Mary of Guise down to 1559, was originally intended as a polemical justification of the reformers' position, an urgent contribution to a live debate. He stated in the preface that his original intent had been to narrate the period from 1558–61, but he then realized the value of extending the coverage backwards to narrate the lives and sufferings of those who had been martyred for the Protestant cause.[17] With the Reformation completed in 1560, Knox widened the scope of his project again, projecting backwards to the

---

[16] George Buchanan, *Ane detectioun of the duinges of Marie Quene of Scottes* (London: John Day, 1571); James E. Phillips, *Images of a Queen: Mary Stuart in Sixteenth-Century Literature* (Berkeley: University of California Press, 1964), 62–3.

[17] John Knox, *History of the Reformation*, in Laing, ed., *Works of John Knox* (1846), I, 4.

fifteenth century and forwards to the personal reign of Mary Queen of Scots. Knox occasionally digressed from his historical narrative to allude to the time of its composition, for example, in mentioning Mary Queen of Scots 'that now myschevouslie regnes', or in commenting approvingly, and at considerable length, on the murder of Mary's servant David Riccio in 1566.[18]

Buchanan, in contrast, wrote not simply a history of the Scottish Reformation, but a history of Scotland from the earliest times to his own. The *Historia* began with the (mythical) founding of the Scottish monarchy in 330 BC and included the lives, and the often-gruesome deaths, of the early kings of Scots. The pattern that Buchanan began with these mythical kings continued throughout the *Historia*, with the narrating of regular acts of resistance against tyrannical monarchs, down to the recent examples of the regicide of James III, and the depositions of Mary of Guise and Mary Queen of Scots. He sought to demonstrate that the political disruptions of 1559–60 and 1567 were consistent with practices in Scottish history in the long term. By terminating with the death of the Regent Mar in 1572, and thereby giving an account of the deposition of Mary in 1567, Buchanan's coverage extended beyond that of Knox. Significantly, the organizing principle of Buchanan's account was not the developing Reformation, but was, rather, the Scottish monarchy and acts of resistance against it.

Further comparisons between Knox and Buchanan can be drawn based on their respective conceptions of history. For Knox, Calvinist theology led inescapably to the conclusion that God's providence was an irresistible and total force behind the shaping of history. Thus, the *History of the Reformation* is replete with statements that deny human agency in human action and intention. For example, 'God so blessed the laubouris of his weak servandis, that na small parte of the Baronis of this Realme began to abhorre the tyranny of the Bischoppes: God did so oppin thare eyis by the light of his woord, that thei could clearelie decerne betuix idolatrie and the trew honouring of God.'[19] This was a world-view that left little room for independent human agency or contingency, although, as a historical method, it was not as lacking in sophistication as this description may suggest. As Richard Kyle explains, 'Knox was no fool in this regard for he also recognized that events has secondary causes (i.e. human beings), and he knew the importance of worldly considerations to these weak instruments of the Lord.'[20]

By contrast, although Buchanan's Calvinism gave some colouring to the content of his *Historia*, his general conception of history owed more to humanism.[21] As a humanist exercise, the study of history was designed to encourage morality and good citizenship in its elite readers, as preparation for their lives of public service. Correspondingly, Buchanan's *Historia*, following the fashion of Guicciardini and Machiavelli, is filled with

---

[18] Knox, *History of the Reformation*, I, 173, 235.

[19] Knox, *History of the Reformation*, I, 298.

[20] Richard Kyle, 'John Knox's Concept of Divine Providence and its Influence on his Thought', *Albion: A Quarterly Journal Concerned with British Studies*, 18 (1986): 395–410 (403).

[21] Caroline Erskine, 'Humanism and Calvinism in George Buchanan's *Rerum Scoticarum Historia*', *Records of the Scottish Church History Society*, 35 (2005): 90–118.

stirring motivational speeches in political, judicial, military, and ecclesiastical contexts, all carefully crafted examples of the art of rhetoric.

Both Knox and Buchanan, writing in their respective styles, created heroes and villains to embody the values of their histories, and on one thing they were agreed: Mary Queen of Scots was to be portrayed in the most negative possible terms, as a wife, as a mother, as a Catholic, and as a queen. In Buchanan's account, the tone was much the same as in the *Detectioun*: pretended insight into Mary's plans and motives. Thus, as Bothwell and Mary's conspiracy against Darnley was planned, Mary pretended reconciliation with him to divert suspicion when the house was blown up—but her haste to avoid the destruction of a fine piece of furniture betrayed her involvement. 'The bed in which the queen had lain for some nights, was removed from its place, and a worse one substituted in its stead; amid such prodigality of character, such was their care for a little money.'[22]

In contrast to Buchanan's status as a judgemental narrator prying into Mary's secrets, Knox's treatment of the Queen recounted real events, as he had several audiences with her in the early 1560s. The standard pattern for these meetings was established quickly: Knox would reduce Mary to tears by hectoring her on the errors of her Catholic faith. On one occasion, Knox told the Queen, 'When it shall please God to deliver you fra that bondage of darknes and errour in the which ye have been nurisshed, for the lack of trew doctrin, your Majestie will fynd the libertie of my toung nothing offensive.'[23] These accounts have made a considerable contribution to fixing the reputations of the overbearing, intolerant Knox and the weak and melodramatic Mary. But are they fact or fiction, narration or creation? Tellingly, a recent compilation of sources has placed one of these accounts under the heading of 'Early Modern Literature', emphasizing the tension between Knox's recollections of actual conversations and the imposed ideological thrust of his narrative, which was, of course, highly critical both of Catholicism and female rule.[24]

The portrayal of Knox himself also offers an opportunity to compare the historical styles and methods of our two historians. The difficulty of reckoning Knox's contribution to the making of the Scottish Reformation is compounded by the fact that he played a significant role in recording and narrating the details of it, and therefore may have had the power to construct—and overemphasize—his own place in history. Knox could hardly have avoided covering his own part in events and referred to himself regularly, in the third person, beginning in 1546, as he accompanied George Wishart in the period leading up to his mentor's execution for heresy, through to 1564 and the termination of the narrative. Jenny Wormald has suggested that his 'towering place in the history of the Scottish Reformation' may owe something to the significance of his *History of the*

---

[22] George Buchanan, *The History of Scotland Translated from the Latin of George Buchanan*, ed. and trans. James Aikman (Glasgow: Blackie, Fullarton & Co., 1827), II, 493.

[23] Knox, *History of the Reformation*, II, 387.

[24] Caroline Erskine, Alan R. MacDonald, and Michael Penman, eds., *Scotland: The Making and Unmaking of the Nation* (Dundee: Dundee University Press, 2007), V, 282–4.

Reformation and his self-promotion within the text.[25] J. H. Burns agrees, commenting that Knox was 'no mean self-publicist'.[26] In contrast, James Kirk argues that Knox's account of his actions in bringing about the Reformation was not self-aggrandizing or exaggerated: 'He might be ever-ready to blow his Master's trumpet, as he put it, but he was remarkably reticent in much of his *History* about blowing his own.'[27] To go some way to reconciling these views, it might be argued that while Knox did not exaggerate his own contribution to the shaping of the Reformation, his chosen emphasis on reformers and martyrs downplayed the role of the Scottish aristocracy, with their manifold kin interests and conflicts, and international diplomacy, in its consolidation.

More subtle coverage of these varied historical causes is to be found in Buchanan's *Historia*, a narrative that gave Knox a role, but not the starring role. Gordon Donaldson's statement that Knox was not mentioned in the *Historia* until as late as the coronation of James VI in 1567 is inaccurate.[28] Knox made his first appearance in Buchanan's narrative, albeit without introduction or the inclusion of any background or biographical detail, at the siege of St Andrews in 1546. He reappeared in Perth in 1559, giving a provocative sermon that inspired an iconoclastic riot, and was last taken note of for his sermon at the coronation of James VI in 1567.[29] Knox's death in 1572 was not recorded in Buchanan's *Historia*, although it took place only one month after Buchanan's chosen termination point, the death of the Regent Mar and the handover of power to Morton. It is surprising (or perhaps telling) that Buchanan should forgo the opportunity to eulogize the influential reformer. Put simply, Buchanan's humanist priorities required a different sort of Protestant hero than the firebrand providentialist Knox.

37.3 PERSONAL AND RELIGIOUS WRITING

While the discussion of controversial and historical writing has largely covered George Buchanan's prose output, in the case of John Knox there is much more to be said, with his personal correspondence and his devotional writing (and the extensive overlap between these two forms) worthy of consideration. Before moving on to these areas, however, it is worth pausing to consider Knox's association—or lack thereof—with some of the founding texts of the English and Scottish Reformations. It needs to be emphasized that the *Confession of Faith* and the *First Book of Discipline* which institutionalized and defined Scottish Protestantism in the aftermath of the Reformation Parliament of 1560 were the work of a committee of which Knox was only one member. Similarly,

---

[25] Jenny Wormald, 'Godly Reformer, Godless Monarch: John Knox and Mary Queen of Scots', in Roger Mason, ed., *John Knox and the British Reformations* (Aldershot: Ashgate, 1998), 239.

[26] J. H. Burns, *The True Law of Kingship: Concepts of Monarchy in Early Modern Scotland* (Oxford: Clarendon Press, 1996), 122.

[27] James Kirk, 'Knox and the Historians', in Mason, ed., *John Knox and the British Reformations*, 15.

[28] Gordon Donaldson, *Scottish Church History* (Edinburgh: Scottish Academic Press, 1985), 91.

[29] Buchanan, *History of Scotland*, II, 362, 404, 527.

although Knox's name has been heavily associated with the Geneva Bible of 1560, laboriously translated into English in the second half of the 1550s by exiles in Geneva who were Knox's friends and colleagues, recent research has demonstrated that Knox's own contribution to the project was slight.[30]

As the foregoing examples of Knox's controversial and historical writings will have illustrated, the great reformer was not necessarily a great theologian: quite simply, his strengths did not lie in this area. He was the author of a number of religious treatises, most notably his *On Predestination* of 1560, a defence of Calvin's theology in which Knox could not resist resorting to polemic to attack those with whom he disagreed. While the text is populated by 'pestilent and perverse' papists, Knox reserved most of his ire for Anabaptists, those who 'wolde have all things in common, contrary to the ordre of nature and policie'.[31]

For a more human and, we might say, humane understanding of Knox's beliefs and his writing style, we would do well to consider his personal correspondence. As Kenneth Farrow has noticed, there is a strong connection between Knox's personal letters and his *History of the Reformation*, as he often gave narratives of events to his correspondents, events that were later re-narrated in the *History*.[32] For example, in a letter to Anne Locke of 1559, Knox told the story of a recent iconoclastic riot in Perth:

> After complaint and appellatioun frome such a deceitfull sentence, they putt to their hands to reformatioun in Sanct Johnstoun, where the places of idolatrie of Gray and Blacke Friers, and of Charter-house monkes, were made equall with the ground; all monuments of idolatrie, that could be apprehended, consumed with fire; and preests commanded, under paine of death, to desist frome their blasphemous masse.[33]

The style here is recognizably similar to that of the *History of the Reformation*. However, Knox has not been entirely honest with his correspondent. The riot was, in fact, inspired by one of his own sermons, but he has neglected to mention this. This example may serve to illustrate some of Knox's aims in writing a very long letter—presumably, the long sections of narrative were intended for a wider readership than the recipient alone.[34]

Of greater interest to many critics are the letters in which Knox apparently reveals his true personality and his true voice. Susan Felch has emphasized the value of Knox's letters to female correspondents, including the above-mentioned Anne Locke, the wife of a London merchant who hosted Knox when in London, and corresponded with him between 1556 and 1562. Also of significance is Knox's correspondence with Elizabeth

---

[30] Dale Warden Johnson, 'Marginal at Best: John Knox's Contribution to the Geneva Bible, 1560', in Mack P. Holt, ed., *Adaptations of Calvinism in Reformation Europe: Essays in Honour of Brian G. Armstrong* (Aldershot: Ashgate, 2007), 241–8.

[31] John Knox, *On Predestination*, in Laing, ed., *Works* (1856), V, 73, 211.

[32] Kenneth D. Farrow, *John Knox: Reformation Rhetoric and the Traditions of Scots Prose, 1490–1570* (Bern: Peter Lang, 2004), 145.

[33] *John Knox to Mrs Anna Locke*, in Laing, ed., *Works* (1864), VI, 23.

[34] Felch, 'Rhetoric of Biblical Authority', 812.

Bowes, the mother of the woman he later married, Marjory. In these letters we encounter a Knox with a significantly different voice from the confident interpreter of God's Word and providence that resounds from his published works. For example, in his first letter to Mrs Bowes of 1553, the reader encounters a meeker Knox, one lacking in confidence about his calling, and his fitness to guide and lead others:

> Albeit I never lack the presence and plane image of my awn wreachit infirmitie, yit seing syn sa manifestlie abound in al estaitis, I am compellit to thounder out the threattnyngis of God aganis obstinat rebellaris; in doing whairof (albeit as God knaweth I am no malicious nor obstinat sinner) I sumtymes am woundit, knowing my self criminall and giltie in many, yea in all, (malicious obstinacie laid asyd,) thingis that in utheris I reprehend.[35]

For Susan Felch, then, study of Knox's correspondence with his female network militates against any simple equation of Knox as a misogynist, whatever his dealings with Mary Tudor and Mary Queen of Scots. She finds him to be a warm and sensitive writer with a deep regard for the spiritual development of his friends and concludes: 'It is primarily idolatry rather than misogyny which motivates Knox. The regiment of women is a subset of idolatry; it is monstrous not because females are inherently monstrous, but because such rule is against the word of God.'[36]

37.4 THE POLITICS OF LANGUAGE AND NATIONALITY

In sum, the significance of the writings of Knox and Buchanan lies in their status as founding texts for a new Scotland—a Protestant Scotland. Their historical writings, in particular, have been seen as formative of new national identities. As Crawford Gribben has written of Knox, 'His history was to be a history of the Reformation in Scotland, and his writing of the Reformation would self-consciously parallel the writing of the nation itself. But in writing of the nation, Knox would be fashioning himself, sculpting a personality that would haunt the Scottish imagination.'[37] Profoundly shaped by his experiences as an exile, his choice of history as a project, and the tone of what he wrote, echoed the choices made by his friends: John Foxe, Knox's supporter in the Frankfurt controversy of 1554–5, authored his *Acts and Monuments* with much the same aims for England as Knox had for Scotland.

Roger Mason has explored these questions with reference to both of our historians and argues that it was Buchanan's account, rather than Knox's, that had the greater

---

[35] *John Knox to Mrs Bowes*, in Laing, ed., *Works* (1854), III, 338.
[36] Felch, 'Rhetoric of Biblical Authority', 813.
[37] Crawford Gribben, 'John Knox, Reformation History and National Self-Fashioning', *Reformation and Renaissance Review*, 8 (2006): 48–66 (54).

potential to serve the Protestant cause. One issue was that, while Buchanan's *Historia* came before the reading public in print in 1582, Knox's *History of the Reformation* remained inaccessible, with the first edition of 1587 suppressed by the Elizabethan authorities, and another full edition published only as late as 1644. A second issue was that, for Knox, the writing of history was not the priority in a career that had engaged with many forms and genres of writing, and encompassed preaching and politicking as well. Or, as R. D. S. Jack has concisely put it, 'Knox wrote a lot and not always well.'[38] In contrast, Buchanan's broader scope and more elegant style provided Protestant Scotland 'with the historical legitimacy it required but which Knox had failed to provide'.[39]

The greatest controversy over Knox's contribution to the shaping of national identity, however, has been one of language, rather than history. A succession of scholars have viewed the Reformation in Scotland, and Knox as its embodiment, as a force for Anglicization, with the closer relationship with England, and, in particular, reliance on the English Geneva Bible in the absence of a Scots translation, as contributing to a decline in the Scots language. The arguments of commentators like Billy Kay have a long pedigree, as even Knox's contemporary opponents ribbed him for his mixed Scots and English forms. In particular, Ninian Winzet, a Catholic controversialist living in exile on the Continent, wrote against Knox in Latin 'for I am nocht acquyntit with 3our Southeroun'.[40] It must be emphasized, however, that Knox's Catholic opponents used their Scots language as only one of a rich variety of rhetorical strategies aimed at discrediting Knox and the Reformation he represented. A reading of the controversial writings of Winzet and his fellow Scottish Catholics in exile reveals the inventiveness and viciousness of their polemic—with allegations against Knox ranging from incest to witchcraft.[41] That they chose to attack Knox as a Scot, and as a writer of Scots, is hardly surprising.

A comparison of Knox's language with that of a contemporary historian of Scotland will be instructive. Described as 'Scotland's first vernacular prose historian'—a designation that suggests that Knox was not a vernacular historian—Robert Lindsay of Pitscottie lived through the Scottish Reformation in Fife and wrote his account of it shortly afterwards.[42] In these passages, each historian narrates the events immediately following the murder of Cardinal Beaton, and the opening of the siege of St Andrews Castle, in 1546.

Knox, *History of the Reformation*
And so was he brought to the East blockhouse head, and schawen dead ower the wall to the faithless multitude, which wold not believe befoir it saw: How miserably

---

[38] Ronald S. Jack, *Scottish Prose, 1550–1700* (London: Calder & Boyars, 1971), 45.

[39] Mason, *Kingship and the Commonweal*, 181.

[40] Ninian Winzet, *Niniane Winzet's Works*, ed. J. King Hewison (Edinburgh: Blackwood, 1888), I, 138; Billy Kay, *Scots: The Mither Tongue* (London: Grafton, 1988), 69.

[41] Thomas Graves Law, ed., *Catholic Tractates of the Sixteenth Century, 1573–1600* (Edinburgh: Scottish Text Society, 1901).

[42] Crawford Gribben, 'Introduction', in Crawford Gribben and David George Mullan, eds., *Literature and the Scottish Reformation* (Aldershot: Ashgate, 2009), 10.

lay David Betoun, cairfull Cardinall. And so thei departed, without *Requiem aeternam*, and *Requiscant in pace*, song for his saule. Now, becaus the wether was hote, (for it was in Maij, as ye have heard,) and his funerallis could not suddandly be prepared, it was thowght best, to keap him frome styncking, to geve him great salt ynewcht, a cope of lead, and a nuk in the boddome of the Sea-toore, (a place where many of Goddis children had bein empreasoned befoir,) to await what exqueis his brethren the Bischoppes wold prepare for him.[43]

Lindsay of Pitscottie, *Historie and Cronicles of Scotland*
Then the cry raise into the toun and said the cardinall was slaine; then they that favorit him gat ledderis to leder the wall, trowand that he had bene on lyfe to haue helpit him. Bot the men of war thairin persaiffit thame, and to that effect brocht him done in ane pair of scheitis and laid him on the wall heid, that all might sie him deid that they might mak no defence for his lyfe. And in the mean tyme quhene he was lyand on the wall deid as I haue schawin to zow, ane callit Guthrie loussit done his ballope point and pischit in his mouth that all the peill might sie; bot it was ane misnurtartnes deid and he was bot ane knaif that did it, and thraif never the better efterwart bot dieit ane sudden deid ffor he could not gett lessur to say god help him and so endit money of thaim that had put hand in him. And than quhen they had done quhat they pleisit to him thay tuik him and saltit him and pat him in ane keist and eirdit him schamefullie in ane midding quhair he lay the space of sevin monethis or evir he was eirdit in kirk or queir.[44]

To compare the two styles is to notice the apparently more authentic Scots orthography of Lindsay of Pitscottie, with the use of the yogh (although excised by a modern editor), the <quh> form, and the <-is> and <-it> suffixes for plural nouns and verbs. However, recent scholarship has argued that the view of Knox's Anglicized language requires further interrogation. We might note the presence of more obviously Scots forms in Knox's letter to Mrs Bowes, quoted above. This analysis can also be extended to Knox's more explicitly public writings. Building on a suggestion of R. J. Lyall, and by taking his analysis back to manuscripts of Knox's writings—of which few were written in his own hand—Kenneth Farrow has painstakingly demonstrated that multiple interventions by scribes, editors, and publishers may have created an impression of Anglicized language that was neither Knox's intention, nor his natural authorial voice.[45] In short, Knox wrote in a wide variety of forms and styles, always seeking to tailor the medium and the message to ensure maximum impact upon his intended readership. Scholarship of the 1558 tracts, as discussed above, has emphasized the subtlety of the distinction he made between Scotland and England in their respective relationships to God. We should not be surprised to find Knox engaging with the languages of Scotland and England on multiple levels as well, and we need not conclude that this was a compromise or betrayal of authentic Scottish values.

---

[43] Knox, *History of the Reformation*, I, 178–9.
[44] Robert Lindsay of Pitscottie, *The historie and chronicles of Scotland*, ed. A. J. G. Mackay (Edinburgh: Blackwood, 1911), 83–4.
[45] R. J. Lyall, 'Vernacular Prose before the Reformation', in R. D. S. Jack, ed., *The History of Scottish Literature* (Aberdeen: Aberdeen University Press, 1988), 163–82 (178); Farrow, *John Knox*, 14–22.

To conclude, Knox's reputation has long been controversial, and literary judgements, in particular, have tended to be negative. Maurice Lindsay, for example, has displayed a dismissive attitude to most of his output, with only slightly less derision for the *History of the Reformation*, but heaped praise upon the apparently more authentic Scots of Lindsay of Pitscottie's *Historie and Cronicles of Scotland*.[46] However, a new wave of research is challenging the old assumptions about Calvinist misery and Anglicization dampening Scottish distinctiveness. The new scholarly edition of Buchanan's *De Iure Regni* is indicative of renewed interest in this polymath as a writer whose importance extends beyond the geographical confines of Scottish history to the broader fields of British and continental Renaissance and Reformation studies. Scholarship on John Knox is also developing in more positive and subtle directions. The final word will go to Kenneth Farrow: 'Not only is John Knox's *The Historie of the Reformatioun* the finest literary prose work of the times to which it belongs so inseparably, it is one of the very greatest works of prose in the *whole of Scottish literature*.'[47]

Further Reading

Buchanan, George. *A Dialogue on the Law of Kingship among the Scots: A Critical Edition and Translation of George Buchanan's* De Iure Regni apud Scotos, ed. and trans. Roger A. Mason and Martin S. Smith, (Aldershot: Ashgate, 2004).

Dawson, Jane E. A. *Scotland Re-Formed, 1488–1587* (Edinburgh: Edinburgh University Press, 2007).

Farrow, Kenneth D. *John Knox: Reformation Rhetoric and the Traditions of Scots Prose, 1490–1570* (Bern: Peter Lang, 2004).

Felch, Susan M. 'The Rhetoric of Biblical Authority: John Knox and the Question of Women', *Sixteenth-Century Journal*, 26 (1995): 805–21.

Gribben, Crawford. 'John Knox, Reformation History and National Self-Fashioning', *Reformation and Renaissance Review*, 8 (2006): 48–66.

—— and David George Mullan, eds. *Literature and the Scottish Reformation* (Aldershot: Ashgate, 2009).

Knox, John. *On Rebellion*, ed. Roger A. Mason (Cambridge: Cambridge University Press, 1994).

Mason, Roger A. ed. *John Knox and the British Reformations* (Aldershot: Ashgate, 1998).

—— *Kingship and the Commonweal: Political Thought in Renaissance and Reformation Scotland* (East Linton: Tuckwell, 1998).

Warnicke, Retha M. *Mary Queen of Scots* (Abingdon: Routledge, 2006).

---

[46] Maurice Lindsay, *The History of Scottish Literature* (London: Robert Hale, 1992), 118–23.

[47] Farrow, *John Knox*, 319–20.

CHAPTER 38

ROBERT BURTON AND *THE ANATOMY OF MELANCHOLY*

ANGUS GOWLAND

FEW works of literature from the English Renaissance have posed problems of interpretation to modern readers in such acute form as Robert Burton's *The Anatomy of Melancholy* (first edition, 1621). In the later twentieth century, since Northrop Frye's influential classification of the *Anatomy* as a type of 'Menippean satire' in his *Anatomy of Criticism* (1957), and especially since Stanley Fish's reader-response analysis in *Self-Consuming Artifacts* (1972), Burton studies have been haunted by the question of how to approach its apparently extraordinary prose.[1] In a sense, this is nothing new. As a work that presents a huge quantity of heterogeneous textual content and blends serious and humorous modes, the *Anatomy* has been read in many different ways since its publication.[2] But when Frye identified Burton's book as a satirical 'anatomy' within a Menippean tradition that culminated with Swift and Sterne, and when Fish portrayed his experience of being offered 'a series of false promises' by a work which systematically undermined the reader's confidence 'in himself and everything else', it came to be seen as virtually the model of a text in which all was intentionally not what it seemed.[3] Literary studies since Frye and Fish have wrestled with a range of questions about the work—its quotational method, its organization, and its employment of satire and irony alongside scholarly discourse—many of which reflect a prevailing confusion about Burton's authorial status. Is he a serious writer of relatively modest ambition, whose fundamental purpose is to communicate a more or less coherent body of useful knowledge to his readers?

---

[1] Northrop Frye, *The Anatomy of Criticism: Four Essays* (Princeton: Princeton University Press, 1957), 311–12; Stanley Fish, *Self-Consuming Artifacts: The Experience of Seventeenth-Century Literature* (Berkeley: University of California Press, 1972), 303–52.

[2] On the early reception of the *Anatomy*, see Mary Ann Lund, *Melancholy, Medicine and Religion in Early Modern England: Reading 'The Anatomy of Melancholy'* (Cambridge: Cambridge University Press, 2010), 196–203; Angus Gowland, *The Worlds of Renaissance Melancholy: Robert Burton in Context* (Cambridge: Cambridge University Press, 2006), 295–9.

[3] Frye, *Anatomy of Criticism*, 301–2; Fish, *Self-Consuming Artifacts*, 303–4; Rosalie Colie, *Paradoxia Epidemica: The Renaissance Tradition of Paradox* (Princeton: Princeton University Press, 1966), 430–60.

Or is he given to irony and sophisticated trickery, interleaving the serious parts of his work with clues indicating a deeper layer of meaning that undercuts or adds to its literal sense, introduces ambiguity or incoherence, and is accessible only to readers who are prepared to do the work?[4] After a brief biographical sketch, in the first part of what follows I shall outline the principal interpretative problems posed by the *Anatomy* to modern readers, offering some suggestions about how these can be approached and possibly resolved. In the second part, I shall draw attention to some of the key features of the book—particularly the relationship between its medical psychology and literary rhetoric—as Burton himself conceived them. No single study will ever be able to provide an exhaustive account of the contents of this lengthy and complex work, but as I hope to show, the author's own remarks about his enterprise, and its intended effects on its readership, do help us to anchor our reading of a text that sometimes seems to have been designed to beguile and confuse, just as it informs and entertains.

Robert Burton was born on 8 February 1577 in the village of Lindley, Leicestershire, into the ranks of the landed gentry, and attended grammar schools in Sutton Coldfield and Nuneaton before proceeding to Brasenose College in Oxford in 1593. As he tells us in the *Anatomy* ('Democritus Junior to the Reader', vol. 1, p. 3),[5] he spent most of his life as a scholar in Oxford at Christ Church, where in 1599 he was elected to a Studentship—subsequently receiving his BA in 1602, his MA in 1605, and his BD in 1614—and where, from 1624 until his death in January 1640, he acted as librarian. As well as serving for three years as clerk of the Oxford Market, in 1616 his career as a divine proceeded with his appointment to the benefice of St Thomas in Oxford, a position that was supplemented in 1624 by the Rectorship of Walesby in Lincolnshire. He resigned this position in 1631, but in 1633 (or possibly 1634), thanks to the patronage of the dedicatee of the *Anatomy*, Lord Berkeley of Seagrave, he received the Rectorship of Seagrave in Leicestershire.

---

[4] For the former approach, see, for example, Lawrence A. Babb, *Sanity in Bedlam: A Study of Robert Burton's 'The Anatomy of Melancholy'* (Ann Arbor: Michigan State University Press, 1959); Judith Kegan Gardiner, 'Elizabethan Psychology and Burton's *Anatomy of Melancholy*', *Journal of the History of Ideas*, 38 (1977): 373–88; Michael MacDonald, *Mystical Bedlam: Madness, Anxiety and Healing in Seventeenth-Century England* (Cambridge: Cambridge University Press, 1981); J. B. Bamborough, 'Introduction', in Robert Burton, *The Anatomy of Melancholy*, ed. Rhonda Blair, Thomas Faulkner, and Nicolas Kiessling, introd. and comm. J. B. Bamborough, 6 vols. (Oxford: Clarendon Press, 1989–2000). For some examples of the latter, which are far more numerous, see Jean Starobinski, 'La Mélancolie de l'Anatomiste', *Tel Quel*, 10 (1962): 21–9; Ruth A. Fox, *The Tangled Chain: The Structure of Disorder in 'The Anatomy of Melancholy'* (Berkeley and London: University of California Press, 1976); W. Scott Blanchard, *Scholars' Bedlam: Menippean Satire in the Renaissance* (Lewisburg, PA: Bucknell University Press), 135–61; Devon L. Hodges, *Renaissance Fictions of Anatomy* (Amherst: University of Massachusetts Press, 1985), 107–23; Martin Heusser, *The Gilded Pill: A Study of the Reader-Writer Relationship in 'The Anatomy of Melancholy'* (Tübingen: Stauffenburg Verlag, 1987); R. Grant Williams, 'Disfiguring the Body of Knowledge: Anatomical Discourse and Robert Burton's *The Anatomy of Melancholy*', *English Literary History* 68, (2001): 593–613.

[5] Henceforth, I shall be referring to the text of the *Anatomy* by Partition, Section, Member, and Subsection (although references to the preface ['Democritus Junior to the Reader'] will be indicated by 'DJR'), and then (unless specified otherwise) to the volume and page numbers in *The Anatomy of Melancholy*, ed. Blair, Faulkner, and Kiessling.

Burton's literary career seems to have had an inauspicious beginning in August 1605, when his Latin pastoral comedy *Alba*—performed before James I at Christ Church—was described by an observer as 'very tedious' and boring to the King.[6] In the following year, he composed a comedy satirizing false philosophy and pseudo-scholarship, *Philosophaster*, a work now usually treated as a minor precursor of the *Anatomy*, but which has now begun to attract serious interpretations in its own right.[7] By the time *Philosophaster* was performed in February 1618, however, Burton had almost certainly begun his composition of the work which would dominate the remainder of his writing life and by which he would become famous, *The Anatomy of Melancholy*. This appeared in its first edition in 1621; but he continued to expand and modify the book in versions issued in 1624, 1628, 1632, and 1638. A final edition with the last set of additions and corrections from the author's hand was published posthumously in 1651. By this time, the book was almost one and a half times its original size, a considerable expansion for a work which was over 350,000 words in length when it first appeared in print.

Unfortunately, we know little about Burton's life in Oxford—there is perhaps some truth in his claim to have 'liv'd a silent, sedentary, solitary, private life...penned up most part in my study' (DJR, vol. 1, p. 3)—but we do at least have ample information about his scholarly activities and preferences. Burton bequeathed a total of around 1,700 titles from his large personal library to the Bodleian and Christ Church, and the surviving contents of this library now not only give us valuable insight into the authors and subjects which interested him, but also reveal his reading habits in the form of copious annotations and marginalia.[8] Most importantly, however, Burton's library confirms the most striking first impression about the author gleaned from the *Anatomy* by generations of readers: he was a scholar with truly encyclopaedic interests, not only well-versed in medicine and theology (the two disciplines then most obviously related to the subject of melancholy), but fascinated by works of history, politics, geography, astronomy, astrology, mathematics, agriculture, law, poetry, and other forms of popular literature, as well as by contemporary news pamphlets. This 'roving humor', as Burton refers to his eclectic interests, is attested by nearly every page of the work, where he conducts his discussions 'like a ranging Spaniell, that barkes at every bird he sees' (DJR, vol. 1, p. 4).

Before proceeding to the text, we should note one unmistakable characteristic of its intellectual complexion. The *Anatomy* is a product of the humanism of late Renaissance Europe, and one of Burton's aims was undoubtedly to make the fruits of this movement

---

[6] See Richard L. Nochimson, 'Studies in the Life of Robert Burton', *Yearbook of English Studies*, 4 (1974): 85–11 (98).

[7] Kathryn Murphy, 'Jesuits and Philosophasters: Robert Burton's Response to the Gunpowder Plot', *Journal of the Northern Renaissance*, 1 (2009): 109–28, where the play is presented as an attack on Roman Catholic scholasticism and Jesuitism.

[8] See Nicolas Kiessling, *The Library of Robert Burton* (Oxford: Oxford Bibliographical Society, 1988).

available to an English audience in the vernacular.⁹ He had no time for puritans who thought that 'nothing must be read but Scriptures' and who therefore rejected classical learning (3.4.1.4, vol. 3, p. 391, n. k), and the prominent role of ancient Greek and Roman authors in the work is very difficult to miss.¹⁰ Most studies of the *Anatomy* have noted the way in which Burton has 'mingled *Sacra prophanis*' and quoted both 'Neotericks' and 'Antients' (DJR, vol. 1, p. 19) in a '*Maceronicon*' that mixes English with (mainly) scholarly Latin (DJR, vol. 1, p. 11). There has also been some discussion of his redeployment of the traditional humanist polemics about the futility and obscurity of scholasticism.¹¹

Yet, if Burton's humanistic credentials are clear, it must be admitted that our grasp of the intellectual setting of his work is currently very far from complete. In England in the early decades of the seventeenth century, Galenism continued to dominate orthodox learned medicine, but the intellectual environment generally was highly eclectic and fluctuating. In late humanist scholarship, where the disciplines of moral philosophy, rhetoric, philology, history, and poetry retained their traditional priority, the forms of learning and discursive production rooted in the university arts course contended with the more pragmatic strains of 'vernacular' humanism; in philosophy, persisting and revived elements of scholastic Aristotelianism and Neoplatonism rubbed up against, and sometimes blended with, theological currents that were becoming increasingly contentious and diversified after the Reformation; and all these systems of thought were increasingly being confronted by challenges posed by new forms of scepticism and the nascent 'new science'.¹² It does not seem unreasonable to make it a minimal requirement of interpretations alleging the incoherence (or otherwise) of the *Anatomy* that they should be based in a reasonably solid grasp of this intellectual environment—which unfortunately has not always been the case.¹³ However, it is not easy to situate Burton precisely in this complex world, and indeed, it is often difficult to identify his opinion in

---

⁹ His claims that '[i]t was not mine intent to prostitute my Muse in *English*, or to divulge *secreta Minervæ*, but to have exposed this more contract in *Latin*', but was forced to write in the vernacular by 'our mercentary Stationers', should probably be treated with suspicion, especially given his 'chiefe motives' in writing: 'The generalitie of the Disease, the necessitie of the Cure, and the commodity or common good that will arise to all men by the knowledge of it' (DJR, vol. 1, 16, 23).

¹⁰ Nevertheless, the *Anatomy* is described as an 'antihumanist' satire in Blanchard, *Scholars' Bedlam*, 135.

¹¹ Gowland, *Worlds of Renaissance Melancholy*, 19–22, 26–8, 98–138, 178, 197–203. See also Murphy, 'Jesuits and Philosophasters'.

¹² On medical thought in this era see Ian Maclean, *Logic, Signs and Nature in the Renaissance: The Case of Learned Medicine* (Cambridge: Cambridge University Press, 2002) and *Le monde et les hommes selon les médécins de la Renaissance* (Paris: CNRS Editions, 2006). For useful summaries of the contemporary intellectual environment in Europe generally, see Richard Tuck, 'The Institutional Setting' and Stephen Menn, 'The Intellectual Setting', both in Daniel Garber and Michael Ayers, eds., *The Cambridge History of Seventeenth-Century Philosophy* (Cambridge: Cambridge University Press, 1998), 9–32, 33–86. On late Elizabethan England in particular, see the case-study in D. C. Andersson, *Lord Henry Howard (1540–1614): An Elizabethan Life* (Woodbridge: Boydell & Brewer, 2009), especially the comments at 4–8.

¹³ A significant strand of recent scholarship has tended to agree with the judgement of Gardiner, 'Elizabethan Psychology and Burton's *Anatomy of Melancholy*', that the intellectual framework of the *Anatomy* is fundamentally coherent; see, for instance, Christopher Tilmouth, 'Burton's "Turning

his detailed dissections of scholarly controversies. The proliferation of diverse and often starkly contradictory authorities found throughout the *Anatomy* stands as an eloquent, if sometimes chaotic, testament to an intellectual world in extreme ferment.

38.1 APPROACHING THE TEXT

Criticism of the *Anatomy* in recent years has tended to be polarized between interpretations that emphasize its literary aspects—leading to a view of the work as quintessentially playful, ironic, satirical, and perhaps parodic—and those focusing on its intellectual content—in which case, it is presented as fundamentally a learned encyclopaedia of doctrines about melancholy. There are legitimate grounds to both approaches, and the most interesting studies have fully acknowledged that it is a work of scholarship that implements the Horatian goals printed on the illustrated title page from the third edition onwards: *Omne tulit punctum qui miscuit utile dulci*—it is designed to entertain, as well as inform its readership. It has been a long-running problem, however, to separate the genuinely satirical, ironic, or parodic elements in the text from those which reflect conventional practice in the world of contemporary humanist scholarship.

At the centre of this difficulty lie Burton's compositional methods. The classification of the *Anatomy* as a Menippean satire, or, at least, as something more than a straightforwardly serious work of medical and philosophical learning, has usually depended at least partially upon an interpretation of his methods as being categorically different from those employed by contemporary scholars writing about the same or similar subjects, whether they be learned physicians, philosophers, or theologians. Here we can usefully distinguish three aspects of the *Anatomy* that are illustrative of Burton's methods and also reveal some of the playful literary elements of the text: its presentation and organization; the relationship between the explicitly satirical introduction, 'Democritus Junior to the Reader', and the main body of the *Anatomy*; and finally, the quotational form of Burton's prose throughout.

To start, then, with the arrangement of the work. The *Anatomy* is a large and, to some eyes, unwieldy book, and although Burton is always directly or indirectly concerned with the subject of melancholy, a significant body of scholarship has emphasized the ways in which its varied content and occasional digressions create the impression of an intentionally disorganized and even chaotic text. For modern readers, this impression is created perhaps most strikingly by the synoptic tables which Burton inserted before the beginning of each of the three Partitions of the *Anatomy*. For some critics, who find that the elaborate structure and detail of the tables hinder, rather than assist, the reader's passage through the book, they are a deliberate representation of the labyrinthine character of the *Anatomy*—and perhaps playful, ironic indications of the disorderly discourse that

Picture": Argument and Anxiety in *The Anatomy of Melancholy*', *Review of English Studies*, 56 (2005): 524–49. But cf., for example, the reading in Williams, 'Disfiguring the Body of Knowledge'.

follows.[14] The tables have also been seen more specifically as late, 'somewhat decayed' examples of the dichotomizing method espoused by Petrus Ramus and his followers, promising clarity and structure, but delivering a fair amount of obscurity and confusion.[15]

Now that we are used to different presentational techniques, it is a legitimate question whether they remain as useful now as they were in the 1620s, but when viewed alongside contemporary examples there is no reason to think that they were intended by Burton to be anything other than helpful guides through a long and complex book. Even if their occasionally excessive detail reflects Burton's predilection for copious prose, the tables are accurate summaries of the structure and content of the three Partitions, and any perception that they are poorly organized dissipates when they are compared with contemporary examples (for example, the tables in Theodor Zwinger's *Methodus Apodemica* [1594]). The notion that Burton's tables are Ramist, moreover, is hard to maintain in the light of the fact that synoptic tables of the kind found in the *Anatomy* had been used by humanists for many decades before Ramus, at least, from the beginning of the sixteenth century, and were commonplace in contemporary medical texts.[16] A similar point holds for Burton's Index (first appearing in the second edition), which can look peculiarly unhelpful now, but which is very similar to the indexes used by other late humanist encyclopaedists.[17]

Nevertheless, there are significant elements of the presentation and structure of the *Anatomy* that mark it as something more than a purely pedagogical or scholarly work and clearly indicate Burton's desire to provoke the imagination of his readership. The first hints of this can be found in the full title of the book, which refers to the procedures of dissection (*'Medicinally, Historically, Philosophically Opened and Cut up'*). And the same goes for the names of the different parts of the main text. It is not difficult to find works of medical *practica* following the traditional Hippocratic sequence of kinds, causes, symptoms, prognostics, and cures, or Renaissance texts organized into parts and sections; but Burton's terms of 'Partition', 'Section', 'Member', and 'Subsection'

---

[14] See, for example, Jean Robert Simon, *Robert Burton et 'l'Anatomie de la mélancolie'* (Paris: Didier, 1964), 422; Fox, *Tangled Chain*, 22–7.

[15] David Renaker, 'Robert Burton and Ramist Method', *Renaissance Quarterly*, 24 (1971) : 210–20 (212–13); see also K. J. Höltgen, 'Robert Burtons *Anatomy of Melancholy*: Struktur und Gattungsproblematik im Licht der Ramistischen Logik', *Anglia*, 94 (1976) : 388–403 (396, 402–3); and Jonathan Sawday, 'Shapeless Elegance: Robert Burton's Anatomy of Knowledge', in Neil Rhodes, ed., *English Renaissance Prose: History, Language and Politics* (Tempe, AZ: Medieval & Renaissance Texts & Studies, 1997), 173–202 (199–202). On Ramist method see Walter Ong, *Ramus, Method, and the Decay of Dialogue* (Cambridge, MA: Harvard University Press, 1958) and Neal Gilbert, *Renaissance Concepts of Method* (New York: Columbia University Press), 129–44.

[16] For a more detailed discussion see Angus Gowland, 'Rhetorical Structure and Function in *The Anatomy of Melancholy*', *Rhetorica*, 19 (2001): 1–48 (21–7).

[17] Cf. Fox, *Tangled Chain*, 31, interpreting the 'wholly illogical' elements of the index. On the relatively undeveloped character of the humanist index at this time see Ann Moss, *Printed Commonplace Books and the Structuring of Renaissance Thought* (Oxford: Oxford University Press, 1996), 235.

suggest elegantly that the structure of the book has been produced by the 'cutting' method of an anatomist.

Second, and quite apart from the substantial satirical introduction (to which I shall come shortly), there are several prefatory parerga—some of which were added in the third and fourth editions—which announce the key themes of the main text and make suggestions about how it should be approached by its readers. From the first edition onwards, the Latin poem 'Lectori male feriato' acts as a bridge between the satirical preface and the first Partition, warning the 'idle and frivolous Reader' not to find fault with the work or its author, and threatening that 'Democritus Junior' will, like the Greek philosopher whose tale is told in the preface, return such treatment with interest by demonstrating the folly and madness of his accusers.[18] The third edition of 1628 brandished the famous illustrated frontispiece to the *Anatomy*, engraved by Christof Le Blon the elder, with ten sections containing personified representations of (and a host of symbols relating to) the different species of melancholy, as well as images of Burton and the Greek philosopher Democritus. And from 1632, the illustrated title page was accompanied by an explanatory poem, 'The Argument of the Frontispiece', with stanzas glossing and decoding the imagery of each section ('Ten distinct Squares heere seene apart/Joyned in one by Cutters art').[19]

The fourth edition also included three more parergic texts. The first of these, 'Democritus Iunior ad Libruum Suum', is another Latin poem. It opens by bidding the book to 'express the genius' of its author, and goes on to expand the theme of 'Lectori male feriato' with a little more humility, anticipating the diverse responses to the *Anatomy* by different kinds of reader, and drawing attention to the mixture of useful learning and pleasurable stories and jokes found inside it.[20] The second parergon new to the fourth edition was 'The Authors Abstract of Melancholy διαλογικῶς', a poetic composition delivered (one assumes) in the author's own voice; it expresses the twofold

---

[18] Robert Burton, *The Anatomy of Melancholy. What it is, with all the kindes, causes, symptomes, prognostickes, and severall cures of it. In three maine partitions with their severall sections, members, and subsections. Philosophically, medicinally, historically, opened and cut up. By Democritus Junior* (Oxford: Henry Cripps, 1621), 72. The first edition ended with 'The Conclusion of the Author *to the Reader*' (sigs. D d d^r–D d d 3^v); this did not appear in later editions, but much of its content was subsequently relocated to the beginning of the satirical preface. Burton's pre-emptive criticisms of hostile readers belong to a humanist tradition extending at least as far back as Erasmus's letter to Maarten van Dorp (Desiderius Erasmus, *Praise of Folly and Letter to Maarten Van Dorp*, trans. Betty Radice and ed. A. H. T. Levi [London: Penguin Classics, rev. edn. 1993] 148–60), and More's prefatory letter to Peter Giles in *Utopia* (Thomas More, *Utopia*, ed. George M. Logan and Robert M. Adams [Cambridge: Cambridge University Press, 1989], 6–7).

[19] On the imagery of the frontispiece, see Margery Corbett and Ronald Lightbown, *The Comely Frontispiece: The Emblematic Title-page in England, 1550–1660* (London, Henley, and Boston: Routledge & Kegan Paul, 1979), 190–200; E. Patricia Vicari, *The View from Minerva's Tower: Learning and Imagination in 'The Anatomy of Melancholy'* (Toronto: University of Toronto Press, 1996), 209–212; William R. Mueller, 'Robert Burton's Frontispiece', *Publications of the Modern Language Association of America*, 64 (1949): 1074–88.

[20] There has been little sustained discussion of these parergic elements in the *Anatomy*, but see now Lund, *Melancholy, Medicine and Religion*, 24–50.

nature of melancholic experience ('Naught so sweet as Melancholy...Naught so sad as Melancholy...'), incorporating some of the symptomatology discussed in the main treatise, and may well have been an influence on Milton's 'L' Allegro' and 'Il Penseroso'.[21] Finally, in this edition Burton also inserted another brief Latin poem, this time immediately before the beginning of the first Partition, 'Heraclite fleas, misero sic convenit ævo'. This recapitulates the main theme of the satirical preface: that the world is mad and so requires the tears of Heraclitus and the laughter of Democritus.

By drawing attention to the heterogeneous materials found in the *Anatomy* (humorous and serious, learned and popular), to its potentially controversial or even offensive content, and to the curiously aggressive character of its melancholic author, each element of the parergic apparatus reiterates or expands upon themes found in 'Democritus Junior to the Reader'. In short, they reinforce the significance of the preface for understanding the book as a whole. There have been many interpretations of this introductory satire (sometimes it is the only part of the book that is read closely), and only a schematic summary of its principal features is possible here, but it is very clear that Burton considered this very substantial introduction to be an indispensable guide to reading the rest of the *Anatomy*. On the frontispiece, it is described as 'a Satyricall Preface Conducing to the following Discourse', and in the most basic terms, its explanation of the author's *persona*, his choice of subject, and the manner in which he presents his materials—taken together—provide us with a number of important thematic and interpretative guidelines for making sense of some of the ostensibly puzzling or obscure features of the main treatise.

38.1.1 'Democritus Junior to the Reader'

When the first edition of the *Anatomy* appeared in 1621, its title page identified the author as 'Democritus *Iunior*', but his real name was revealed at the end of the conclusion (Fig. 38.1).[22] Rather than reflecting a desire for anonymity, then,[23] Burton's adoption of this pseudonym indicates a penchant for playing with his audience's expectations—the preface opens by planting the question, 'Gentle Reader, I presume thou wilt by very inquisitive to know what Anticke or Personate Actor this is...arrogating another mans name...' (DJR, p. 1)—but more importantly, as he goes on to explain, it is the first step by which the reader is led to interpret the *Anatomy* within a moralized, satirical framework that is fully appropriate to its subject matter. The significance of Burton's *persona*, we are told, relates neither to Democritean atomism nor to popular kinds of 'Pasquill, or Satyre' (DJR, p. 1), but to the account of Democritus as the 'laughing philosopher'

---

[21] See, most recently, Harold C. Hurley, *The Sources and Traditions of Milton's 'L' Allegro' and 'Il Penseroso'* (Lewiston, NY: Edwin Mellen Press, 1999), chap. 3.

[22] Burton, *The Anatomy of Melancholy* [1621], sig. D d d 3ᵛ.

[23] The second edition omitted his name entirely, but referred to his birthplace and family home in Leicestershire (2.2.3.1, vol. 2, 224), with all subsequent versions presenting his portrait and family arms on the frontispiece.

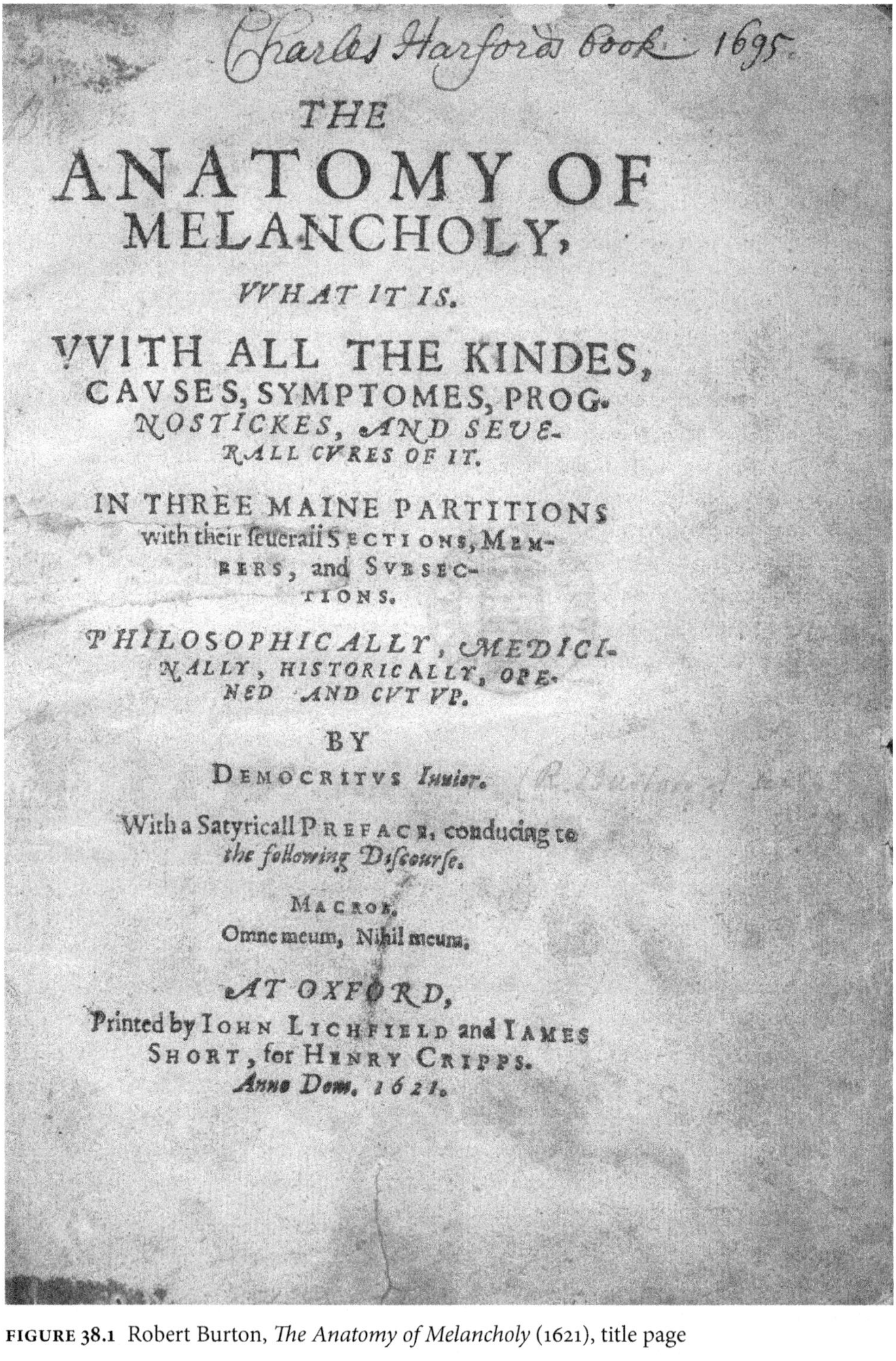

Charles Harford's book 1695

THE

ANATOMY OF

MELANCHOLY,

VVHAT IT IS.

VVITH ALL THE KINDES,

CAVSES, SYMPTOMES, PROG-

NOSTICKES, AND SEVE-

RALL CVRES OF IT.

IN THREE MAINE PARTITIONS

with their seuerall SECTIONS, MEM-

BERS, and SVBSEC-

TIONS.

PHILOSOPHICALLY, MEDICI-

NALLY, HISTORICALLY, OPE-

NED AND CVT VP.

BY

DEMOCRITVS Iunior.

With a Satyricall PREFACE, conducing to

the following Discourse.

MACROB.

Omne meum, Nihil meum.

AT OXFORD,

Printed by IOHN LICHFIELD and IAMES

SHORT, for HENRY CRIPPS.

Anno Dom. 1621.

FIGURE 38.1 Robert Burton, *The Anatomy of Melancholy* (1621), title page given by the pseudo-Hippocratic *Letter to Damagetes*. This text had long been the subject of humanistic literary and philosophical interest, and Burton reproduced it '*verbatim* almost' (DJR, p. 33) within his own preface.[24]

Burton's adaptation of the *Letter to Damagetes* is an exercise in humanistic *imitatio* and a literary-satirical tour de force. According to 'Democritus Junior', his namesake's investigation of madness ('to find out the seat of this *atra bilis or* Melancholy' [DJR, p. 6]), and equally importantly, his demonstration and ridicule of the madness of humanity, was required even more urgently by 'this life of ours' than it was by 'the World in his time' (DJR, p. 37). The moral message of the *Letter*, rooted in a mixture of Stoic, Cynic, and Epicurean themes distancing the philosophical sage from the irrational and absurd passions of the rest of humanity, is reshaped by Burton to become the vehicle for the diagnosis and satirical condemnation of the melancholy of the contemporary world. His relentless analysis of the varied forms of the prevailing melancholic madness—invariably construed in Stoic terms as a form of passionate foolishness—has a universal application: 'For indeed who is not a Foole, Melancholy, Mad?... Who is not sick, or ill disposed, in whom doth not passion, anger, envie, discontent, feare & sorrow raigne? Who labours not of this disease? Give me but a little leave, and you shall see by what testimonies, confessions, arguments I will evince it' (DJR, p. 25); only '*Nicholas nemo*, or Mounsieur *no-body*' is excepted (DJR, p. 107). Burton's preface fluctuates between deadly vituperation and light-hearted mockery (even self-mockery), but the moral seriousness appropriate to classical humanist satire persists throughout.

Much can and has been said about the style and content of 'Democritus Junior to the Reader'—particularly about its intriguing utopian interlude[25]—but fundamentally, its principal task of 'conducing' to the main treatise is accomplished by its identification of melancholy as a condition that in a real moral and spiritual sense, at least potentially and to some extent, afflicts everyone, including the author himself (DJR, I, p. 7: 'I was not a little offended with this maladie...'). If the Renaissance was, in some sense, the 'golden age' of melancholy—and its prominence in the dramatic and spiritual, as well as medical, works of this era is well known[26]—then the preface to the *Anatomy* offers its own account

---

[24] See Jean Jehasse, 'Démocrite et la renaissance de la critique', *Etudes seizièmistes offertes à Monsieur le Professeur V.-L. Saulnier*, ed. R. Aulotte et al. (Geneva: Droz, 1980); Thomas Rütten, *Demokrit— Lachender Philosoph und Sanguinischer Melancholiker: Eine pseudohippokratische Geschichte* (Leiden: Brill, 1992); Cathy Curtis, 'From Sir Thomas More to Robert Burton: The Laughing Philosopher in the Early Modern Period', in Ian Hunter, Stephen Gaukroger, and Conal Condren, eds., *The Persona of the Philosopher in Early Modern Europe* (Cambridge: Cambridge University Press, 2006), 90–112. On the associations of Democritus with atomistic natural philosophy see Christoph Lüthy, 'The Fourfold Democritus on the Stage of Early Modern Science', *Isis*, 91 (2000): 443–79.

[25] See J. Max Patrick, 'Robert Burton's Utopianism', *Philological Quarterly*, 27 (1948): 345–58; J. C. Davis, *Utopia and the Ideal Society: A Study of English Utopian Writing, 1516–1700* (Cambridge: Cambridge University Press, 1981), 85–104; Jean Starobinski, '"Démocrite parle": L'utopie mélancolique de Robert Burton', *Le Débat*, 29 (1984): 49–72; Robert Applebaum, *Literature and Utopian Politics in Seventeenth-Century England* (Cambridge: Cambridge University Press, 2002), 81–7; and Gowland, *Worlds of Renaissance Melancholy*, 205–94, esp. 261–5.

[26] See, for instance, Jean Delumeau, 'L' âge d'or de la mélancolie', *L'histoire*, 42 (1982): 28–37; Angus Gowland, 'The Problem of Early Modern Melancholy', *Past & Present*, 191 (2006): 77–120. The classic

of this phenomenon. To paraphrase the central argument: we are all afflicted by passions; passions are irrational diseases of the soul; and such irrational diseases of the soul, as he explains many times in the book, are both causes and symptoms of melancholic madness. This is his explanation for the 'Epidemicall' proportions of the disease, which has motivated him to perform the 'generall service' of 'prescib[ing] means how to prevent and cure so universall a malady' (DJR, I, p. 110). As Burton knows and admits, although this moral-psychological conception of melancholy is grounded in his reading of ancient philosophy and scripture, it does not neatly coincide with the more restricted understanding of the disease found in the learned medical works of the Renaissance.[27] Nevertheless, it enables him to elaborate an expansive analysis of the condition in its multifarious—indeed, as he says, practically infinite—forms, whilst plausibly maintaining their common moral-psychological basis, and therefore, their relevance to his general readership.

By establishing the character of melancholy in these terms as a widespread psychological, as well as bodily, disease, then, 'Democritus Junior to the Reader' provides an explanation for Burton's choice of subject whilst preparing his readership for the amalgamation of (principally) medical, moral, and spiritual material that will be encountered in the rest of the book. But, moving from the explicitly satirical preface to the three Partitions of the main treatise, how are we to adjust our expectations of the manner in which Burton will be handling his materials? Here we come to the most significant fissure in modern Burton studies: is the main treatise mainly 'straightforward and factual', being devoted to a 'serious, "scientific" consideration' of melancholy,[28] or is the work satirical or parodic all the way through?[29] Once again, the best guide is Burton himself; and he is deliberately ambiguous. On the one hand, in the closing passages of the preface, 'Democritus Junior' is presented as waking 'as it were out of a dreame', having had 'a raving fit', and 'now being recovered, and perceiving mine errour, cry with *Orlando, Solvite me,* pardon *(o boni)* that which is past, and I will make you amends in that which is to come; I promise you a more sober discourse in my following Treatise' (DJR, I, p. 112). On the other hand, however, almost immediately he invites us to doubt his ability—or

---

study of Renaissance medical theories of melancholy is Raymond Klibanksy, Erwin Panofsky, and Fritz Saxl, *Saturn and Melancholy: Studies in the History of Natural Philosophy, Religion and Art* (London: Thomas Nelson, 1964), but see also Winfried Schleiner, *Melancholy, Genius and Utopia in the Renaissance* (Wiesbaden: Harrassowitz, 1991), and Noel Brann, *The Debate over the Origin of Genius during the Italian Renaissance: The Theories of Supernatural Frenzy and Natural Melancholy in Accord and in Conflict on the Threshold of the Scientific Revolution* (Leiden: Brill, 2002).

[27] See Burton's generally accurate discussion at 1.1.3.1–3, I, pp. 162–8, where it is precisely defined as a disease of the imagination, materially caused by black bile, and typically yielding the symptoms of groundless fear and sorrow.

[28] The view of J. B. Bamborough, expressed in his introduction to the Clarendon edition (I, xxxiii), and his commentary at IV, 51—broadly following Sir William Osler's description of the work as 'a medical treatise': 'Robert Burton: The Man, his Book, his Library', in *A Way of Life and Other Selected Writings of Sir William Osler* (New York: Dover Books, 1958), 90.

[29] See, for instance, the views in Fish, *Self-Consuming Artifacts*, 332–50; Colie, *Paradoxia Epidemica*, 430–60; and Williams, 'Disfiguring the Body of Knowledge'.

perhaps more accurately, his willingness—to keep this promise. Apologizing in advance, if when 'anatomizing this surly humor...I launce too deep' and 'make it smart', he explains that ''tis a most difficult thing to keepe an even tone, a perpetuall tenor, and not sometimes to lash out', and he indicates that sometimes, the combination of his subject matter and his own melancholic condition will give him no choice but to adopt a Juvenalian mode: '*difficile est Satyram non scribere*, there be so many objects to divert, inwards perturbations to molest' (DJR, I, p. 113).[30] His readers are thereby prepared for a 'serious' discourse punctuated by substantial satirical interludes, but also for discursive modes that will be varied throughout. The dichotomy between viewing the main treatise as either 'scientific' and serious or satirical is a false one: 'one may speake in jest, and yet speake truth' (DJR, I, p. 111). The *Anatomy*, in this sense, is the 'playing labor' (DJR, I, p. 7)—Burton's reworking of 'serious play' (*serio ludere*)—of an author whose scholarly-philosophical and literary-satirical purposes are inextricable.

The preface also throws important light upon Burton's choice of compositional method: 'it is a *Cento* collected from others' (DJR, I, p. 110), an assemblage of quotations stitched together with authorial glosses, comments, and asides. Quotations and citations of authority are ubiquitous in humanistic philosophy and literature, and are also important in contemporary Galenic medical texts, and in this respect, the *Anatomy* simply accentuates a feature of the learned discourse of the author's environment. But at the same time, his method is distinct from other forms of learning, since as a *cento* it is almost exclusively comprised by argumentation from authority and Burton's own glosses upon his sources, enabling the presentation of a vast body of scholarship accompanied by a detached, idiosyncratic commentary.

In an extended section defending the book against imagined critics (which in later editions incorporated material from the 'Conclusion' of 1621 [DJR, I, pp. 8–20]),[31] Burton gives guidance for those who, like many of the *Anatomy*'s modern readers, find themselves perplexed by the appearance of the text. His book, he says, is yet another symptom of a 'scribling age' in which vainglorious writers recycle the work of their predecessors ('No newes here, that which I have is stolne from others...As Apothecaries we make new mixtures every day, poure out of one Vessell into another...as I have done' [DJR, I, pp. 8–9]). But the *Anatomy* also presents itself as a commentary upon that chaos and confusion, and upon the learned procedure by which 'wee skim off the Creame of other mens Wits' and 'lard [our] leane bookes with the fat of others Workes' (DJR, I, pp. 9, 11). This is precisely what happens when an author composes a *cento*, a quotational method which Burton here claims is to be commended for its honesty—it does not claim spurious originality—but also as the most appropriate means of expressing his humanistic authorial *persona*.

> I have only this of *Macrobius* to say for my selfe, *Omne meum, nihil meum*, 'tis all mine and none mine. As a good hous-wife out of divers fleexes weaves one peece of Cloathe, a Bee gathers Wax and Hony out of many Flowers, and makes a new bundle of all,

---

[30] The quotation is from Juvenal, *Satura* I.30.
[31] Burton, *The Anatomy of Melancholy* [1621], sigs. D d d I^r–D d d 3^v.

> *Floriferis ut apes in saltibus omnia libant,*
> I have laboriously collected this *Cento* out of divers Writers, and that *sine injuria*, I have wronged no Authors, but given every man his owne...I cite & quote mine Authors, (which howsoever some illiterate scriblers accompy pedanticall, as a cloake of ignorance, and opposite to their affected fine stile, I must & will use)...I can say of my selfe, whom have I injured? The matter is theirs most part, and yet mine, *apparet unde sumptum sit* (which *Seneca* approves) *aliud tamen quam unde sumptum sit apparet,* which nature doth with the aliment of our bodies, incorporate, digest, assimulate, I doe *conquoquere quod hausi,* dispose of what I take. I make them pay tribute, to set out this my *Maceronicon,* the method onely is myne owne, I must usurpe that of *Wecker è Terentio, nihil dictum quod non dictu priùs, methodus sola artificem ostendit,* we can say nothing but what hath beene said, the composition and method is ours onely, and shewes a Schollar. (DJR, I, p. 11)

Although the book is stuffed with material from other books, Burton's readers (particularly those who have been prepared by the parergic instructions to be attentive) are thereby prompted to notice the author's rhetorical *dispositio* of his material and his creative 'digestion' of his quotations,[32] showing this 'Schollar' at work. We are, in other words, guided to be sensitive to a layer of meaning that may supervene upon the learned assemblage of texts in the main treatise, a layer that may well be ironic. After all, even this discussion of quotations is conducted through quotations.

In this respect, Burton's most important predecessors were the humanists Justus Lipsius and Michel de Montaigne, both of whom practised and reflected upon the paradoxical activity of writing a *cento*, and presented it as a form of self-expressive ventriloquism: in selecting, presenting, and commenting on the words of others, the author reveals not only his erudition, but also his personal judgements. As Lipsius had written in his own famous *cento*—the *Politicorum sive Civilis Doctrinae libri sex* (1589)—'everything is mine, and nothing...'; but, he continues, 'I have not in fact given bare or scattered maxims', and so 'to prevent them from flowing around and being *mortar without limestone*..., he has used the 'cement' of his own words, connecting his quotations 'fittingly' and making 'definitions, distinctions, and selections'. As such, the *cento* is peculiarly demanding of its readers. They should not only take care to 'observe the distinctions between my words and those of others', but should also remember that in this form of writing 'departures from the original meaning' of the texts being quoted are 'always allowed and even praised'.[33] Burton's readers are given similar instructions, as he not only claims to be making 'a new bundle' from his 'divers fleeces' in which he 'may likely adde, alter, and see farther then my Predecessors'

---

[32] An important humanistic locus for the creative 'digestion' of commonplaces is found in Erasmus's *Dialogus Ciceronianus* (1528): see Desiderius Erasmus, 'The Ciceronian: A Dialogue on the Ideal Latin Style', trans. Betty I. Knott in *Collected Works of Erasmus, Vol. 28: Literary and Educational Writings 6*, ed. A. H. T. Levi (Toronto, Buffalo, and London: University of Toronto Press, 1986), 402, 442.

[33] Justus Lipsius, *Politica: Six Books of Politics or Political Instruction*, ed. and trans. Jan Waszink (Assen: Royal Van Gorcum, 2004), 233–9. See also Michel de Montaigne, *The Complete Essays*, ed. and trans. M. A. Screech (London: Penguin Books, 1991), III.12, 1197.

(DJR, I, p. 11), but also jokes that 'it is a *Cento* collected from others, not I, but they that say it' (DJR, I, p. 110).

At the same time, we are prompted to detect the ways in which Burton has gone further than the great Flemish humanist and followed in the steps of Montaigne ('I only quote others the better to quote myself') by accentuating the stylistic expressivity of the *cento*.[34] If some find the *Anatomy* to be not to their taste, this is precisely because 'I have assay'd, put my selfe upon the Stage'; and one consequence of this is that 'I must abide the censure, I may not escape it. It is most true, *stylus virum arguit*, our stile bewaies us, and as Hunters find their game by the trace, so is a mans *Genius* descried by his workes... I have layd my selfe open (I know it) in this Treatise, turned mine inside outward' (DJR, I, p. 13). Even if many of Burton's words are taken from the works of others, the prose of the *Anatomy* bears the indelible imprint of his personality.[35] This, at least, partly explains the enduring appeal of a book written 'in an extemporean stile... with as small deliberation as I doe ordinarily speake'—a rhetorical contrivance not to be taken at face value.[36]

More specifically, we are encouraged to see the text as the literary expression of the author's own melancholic '*malus Genius*' (DJR, I, pp. 7, 17). Burton's announced intention to 'expresse my selfe readily & plainely' without embellishments can be taken as an indication that the fluctuating, wide-ranging, and digressive style is deliberately constructed to create the impression of a textual effusion of its author's melancholy, mirroring the vast, variegated complexity of the disease itself (1.3.1.4, I, p. 407).[37] In his own words, 'as a River runnes sometimes precipitate and swift, then dull and slow; now direct, then *per ambages*; now deepe, then shallow; now muddy, then cleare; now broad, then narrow; doth my stile flow: now serious, then light; now Comicall, then Satyricall; now more elaborate, then remisse'. Such modulations are determined by the *decorum*, not only of the matter in hand, 'as the present subject required', but also of the writer's own unpredictable moods, 'as at that time I was affected' (DJR, I, p. 18). We are thereby led to wonder whether the 'confused lumpe' of the *Anatomy* is somehow to be taken as a figuration (or 'evacuation') of the melancholic 'Impostume', of which Burton says he 'was very desirous to be unladen' (DJR, I, pp. 7, 17).

---

[34] Montaigne, *Essays*, I.25, 166; also III.12, 1196. According to Montaigne, the erudition of Lipsius's *Politica*, as well as Lelio Capilupi's *Centones ex Virgilio* (1555), was itself revelatory of their authors' 'wits' (I.26, 166). But cf. the critical thrust of the discussion of quotation at III.12, 1196–7 and III.13, 1212. See Francis Goyet, 'A propos de "Ces pastissages de lieux communs" (Le rôle des notes de lecture dans la genèse des *Essais*'), *Bulletin de la Société des Amis de Montaigne*, 5–6 (1986): 11–26 and 7–8 (1987): 9–30.

[35] See the classic readings in Joan Webber, *The Eloquent 'I': Style and Self in Seventeenth-Century Prose* (Madison: University of Wisconsin Press, 1968), 80–114; and Bridget Gellert Lyons, *Voices of Melancholy: Studies in Literary Treatments of Melancholy in Renaissance England* (London: Routledge & Kegan Paul, 1971), 113–48.

[36] See Gowland, 'Rhetorical Structure and Function', 2, 47.

[37] See also Burton's reference to 'my melancholy spaniels quest' in the 'Digression of Ayre' (2.2.3.1, II, 58), indicating that here, at least, his writing is to be taken as the expression of his melancholic imagination.

38.2 READING THE MAIN TREATISE

The main treatise is divided into three Partitions, the first two principally discussing the kinds, causes, symptoms, prognostics, and therapies of the principal forms of melancholy (of the head, whole body, and hypochondrium), and the third covering the two subspecies of love melancholy—erotic and religious—following the same medical-analytical sequence. A detailed account of their extremely diverse contents is obviously not possible here.[38] Instead, I shall now offer a condensed account of some of the key features of the Galenic medical psychology found in the main treatise, before relating them to the literary-rhetorical dimension of the *Anatomy*. This will lead to some suggestions about Burton's intentions with regard to his readership.

38.3 MELANCHOLY AND THE IMAGINATION

According to Burton—who here, as usual, follows the majority of his learned medical contemporaries—melancholy is fundamentally a disease of the imagination. Considering whether the affected part in the disease is the brain or heart (a question raised frequently in Galenic accounts), he opts for both: the brain is affected, because 'being a kinde of *Dotage*, it cannot otherwise bee'; the heart is also disturbed, because its principal symptoms of 'feare and Sorrow', which are passions, 'be seated in the Heart'. But referring to a number of eminent physicians (including Eliano Montalto, Girolamo Capo di Vacca, and Girolamo Mercuriale), he explains further that 'the *Braine* must needs primarily be misaffected, as the seat of *Reason*, and then [secondarily] the *Heart*, as the seat of *Affection*'. More specifically, this is because the psychic source of the melancholic disease is to be found in the brain, namely, in the power of imagination: 'for as much as this malady is caused by precedent *Imagination,* with the *Appetite,* to whom spirits obey', the affection is 'communicated to the *Heart,* and other inferior parts, which sympathize and are much troubled' (1.1.3.2, I, pp. 163–4). In Burton's definition of melancholy, then, which appeals to the *communis opinio doctorum*, it is the imagination that is primarily 'hurt and misaffected', with the consequence that, in many cases, the rational powers of understanding are also affected. In other words, the psychological pathology of melancholy originates in what Burton and his contemporaries termed *prava* or *laesa imaginatio*

---

[38] For some more or less comprehensive studies see Babb, *Sanity in Bedlam*; Vicari, *The View from Minvera's Tower*; and Gowland, *The Worlds of Renaissance Melancholy*. There has been a recent revival of interest in the political, and religious-political, aspects of the work: see, for example, Douglas Trevor, *The Poetics of Melancholy in Early Modern England* (Cambridge: Cambridge University Press, 2004), 116–49; Adam Kitzes, *The Politics of Melancholy from Spenser to Milton* (London: Routledge, 2006), 123–50; Jeremy Schmidt, *Melancholy and the Care of the Soul: Religion, Moral Philosophy, and Madness in Early Modern England* (Aldershot: Ashgate, 2007), 47–102; and Lund, *Melancholy, Medicine and Religion*, 51–76.

('depraved' or 'damaged' imagination), with any dysfunctions of reason being secondary or accidental.

What does the condition of melancholic *prava imaginatio* entail in this account? In the 'Digression of Anatomy', Burton provides a clear discussion of the powers of the soul which shows his general adherence to the Aristotelian faculty psychology that had usually been incorporated within medieval and Renaissance Galenic theories of melancholy. The part of his account that is most relevant here concerns the manner in which the 'inner senses' of the soul analyse and process perceptual data from the external senses of sight, hearing, taste, touch, and smell. In the front ventricle of the brain, the common sense receives data in the form of sensory *species* and 'discerne[s] all differences of objects' in terms of their sound, colour, and so on. The common sense passes on the sensory species it has processed in the form of phantasms, communicated through the medium of animal spirits, to the imagination, or 'phantasie', in the middle ventricle of the brain, which 'more fully examine[s]' the species, 'and keepes them longer, recalling them to mind againe, or making new [species] of his owne'. The power of the imagination to create its own new sense-species—either from the species received from the common sense or from those stored in the memory in the posterior ventricle—is important, as it explains the role of the imagination in producing hallucinations: '[i]n *Melancholy* men this faculty is most Powerfull and strong, and often hurts, producing many monstrous and prodigious things, especially if it be stirred up by some terrible object, presented to it from common sense, or memory'. The human imagination, he says, 'is subject and governed by *Reason*, or at least should be; but in Brutes it hath no superior...' (1.1.2.7, I, p. 152).

How does the imagination become depraved in melancholy, and with what consequences? It can be subject to interference by demonic spirits which are attracted to the imagination by the superabundant, corrupt black bile in the melancholic body and its darkened animal spirits, which they manipulate to 'alter' and disturb 'the minde' of the sufferer (1.2.1.2, I, p. 193). But more commonly, the imagination is depraved naturally by the black bile, whose qualities and vaporous emanations cause a variety of mental dysfunctions. The key source here, cited by Burton and discussed at length by contemporary learned physicians, is Galen's *De symptomatum causis* II.7.2: 'For *Galen*' here, Burton writes, 'imputeth all to the cold that is blacke, and thinkes that the spirits being darkned, and the substance of the Braine cloudy and darke, all the objects thereof appeare terrible, and the *minde* it selfe, by those darke obscure, grosse fumes, ascending from black humours, is in continuall darknesse, feare & sorrow, divers terrible monstrous fictions in a thousand shapes & apparitions occurre, with violent passions, by which the braine and Phantasie are troubled and eclipsed' (1.3.3.1, I, pp. 418–19). More specifically, he explains that the imagination depraved in this way is 'the first steppe and fountaine' of the diversity of mental perturbations that are simultaneously causes and symptoms of melancholy. By 'mis-conceaving or amplifying' the sensory species received from the common sense or memory, the imagination produces distorted or disturbing phantasms, which are communicated by means of the spirits to the heart, 'the seat of affections', which responds, in turn, by generating emotional perturbations and a corresponding flood of melancholic spirits and humours (1.2.3.1, I, p. 249).

This emphasis on the centrality of the depraved imagination is marked in the *Anatomy*, not just by Burton's insistence that '[so] great is the force of Imagination [that] much more ought the cause of Melancholy to be ascribed to this alone, then to the distemperature of the body' (1.2.3.1, I, p. 249), but also by his composition of a digression 'Of the Force of Imagination' (1.2.3.2, pp. 250–5).[39] Imaginative depravation often triggers the corruption of the powers of the intellect, such as opinion, discourse, and ratiocination (1.1.3.2), and this predicament becomes all the more serious when it is considered that after the Fall the other rational power of soul, the will, is weakened and depraved in all men, leading us to 'give so much way to our *Appetite*, and follow our inclination, like so many beasts' (1.1.2.11, p. 161). Little wonder, then, that 'imagination' is, in effect, 'the rudder of this our ship, which reason should steire, but overborne by phantasie, cannot manage, and so suffers it selfe and this whole vessell of ours to be overruled, and often overturned' (1.2.3.2, I, p. 254).

38.4 Imagination, rhetoric, and therapy

There is little in Burton's account of the role of the imagination in melancholy that cannot be found in contemporary learned medical sources. Arguably, however, one of the main functions of the Galenic medical psychology here—and perhaps in the work as a whole—is to provide the theoretical skeleton for a body of humanistic moral philosophy and practical spiritual guidance. This brings us to the core of Burton's project in the *Anatomy*, as we see when we turn to the role of the imagination in his discussion of the therapy of melancholy. 'As some are so molested by Phantasie', he writes, 'so some againe by Fancy alone, and a good conceit, are as easily recovered', since the imagination affects the motions of the humours, spirits and blood, and thereby 'imperiously commande[s] our bodies' (1.2.3.2, I, pp. 253–4).

Because the imagination acts as a hinge between melancholic perturbations and the bodily humours and spirits, it is possible to ameliorate or even cure the condition by purely psychological means. The imaginative disturbances of the disease, Burton urges, should in the first place be resisted by rational measures applied by the force of will: 'let [the melancholic] oppose, fortify, or prepare himselfe against them, by premeditation,

---

[39] Here his description of the 'wonderfull effects and power' of this faculty remains—just—within the province of the Aristotelian psychology he has elaborated earlier in the book, although his catalogue of the ways in which the imagination is responsible for incubus, ecstatic derangement, visions, demonic illusions, lycanthropy, bewitchment, a host of vices, and even death draws upon a heterogeneous range of sources and asserts that such phenomena involve occult and supernatural forces that supervene upon the internal physiological processes typically prioritized by learned Galenists (see also 1.3.3.1, 424–7).

reason, or as we doe by a crooked staff, bend himselfe another way' (2.2.6.1, II, p. 101). In principle, it should be possible for us to 'frame our selves as wee will... whatsoever the Will desires, shee may command: no such cruell affections, but by discipline they may bee tamed' (2.2.6.1, II, pp. 103–4). We are here in the domain of the ancient moral-philosophical *cultura animi*—and, more specifically, of consolation—but it is not hard to see that Burton's insistence upon the power of the depraved imagination and the perversity of the will requires the melancholic to have some form of external assistance: ''tis not so easily performed. Wee know this to be true, we are led captives by passion, appetite, wee should moderate our selves, but we are furiously carried, we cannot make use of such precepts... you may as well bid him that is diseased, not to feele pain, as a melancholy man not to feare, not to be sad: 'tis within his blood, his braines, his whole temperature, it cannot be removed' (2.2.6.1, II, p. 103). For postlapsarian melancholics with depraved judgement and feeble reason, he concludes, 'the best way for ease is to impart our misery to some friend . . .', who can address it by 'counsell... wisdome, perswasion, advise', and 'good meanes, which we could not otherwise apply unto our selves' (2.2.6.1, II, p. 104).

This position has support from Galenic medical authority, scripture, and ancient moral philosophy (2.2.6.2, II, p. 109). But most revealing of the therapeutic dimension of the literary-philosophical enterprise of the *Anatomy*, I would suggest, is his mobilization here of Cicero to establish the curative potential of rhetoric: 'Assuredly a wise and well spoken man may doe what he will in such a case', Burton writes, and 'a good Orator alone, as *Tully* holds, can alter affections by power of his eloquence, *comfort such as are afflicted, erect such as are depressed, expell and mitigate feare, lust, anger, &c.*' (2.2.6.2, II, p. 110). This has immediate implications for what follows in the book—a lengthy 'Consolatory Digression', supplemented from the second edition onwards with a concluding discourse of spiritual comfort—where we see the clearest instances of Burton implementing his conception of the power of language, in the form of philosophical and spiritual philosophical precepts, to remedy melancholy.[40] As these parts of the *Anatomy* show, his view is that for such precepts to be effective, they ought to conform to reason or theological rectitude, but in some cases it may be appropriate to employ manipulative or deceptive linguistic-cognitive strategies. In any case, he argues, it is imperative to 'divert' the melancholic from his or her troubling thoughts and counteract the effects of the depraved imagination: 'prosperity' must be 'set... against adversity', the mind must be 'recreate[d]... by some contrary object' (2.2.6.1, pp. 101–2); the melancholic's 'cogitations' must be distracted and their 'continuall meditations' diverted 'another way' (2.2.4.1, p. 68), 'for his phantasie is so restlesse, operative and quicke, that if it be not in perpetuall action, ever employed, it will worke upon it selfe, melancholize, and be carried away instantly, with some feare, jealousie, discontent, suspition, some vaine conceipt or other' (2.2.6.2, p. 107). And in some situations, the only remedy will be to induce a contrary passion in the melancholic, which is tantamount to

---

[40] See also the discussion at 2.2.4.1, II, 90–1.

'driv[ing] out one disease with another', or 'by some fained lye, strange newes, witty device, artificiall invention, it is not amisse to deceive them'—as in the medical case-history of a 'melancholy King, that thought his head was off', who was cured 'by putting a leaden cap thereon, the weight made him perceave it, and freed him of his fond imagination' (2.2.6.2, II, pp. 111–12).

As we shall soon see, these therapeutic principles have a direct relationship with Burton's conception of the capabilities of the text of the *Anatomy*, for, as many readers have noticed, he claims that the work is concerned not only with presenting knowledge about melancholy, but also with implementing its therapy. It is practical philosophical writing of the most direct kind, whose effects are to be registered on both the author and his readership. In the preface, we are told that Burton is following Democritus in seeking 'to better cure [melancholy] in himselfe, by...writings and observations', as well as to 'teach others how to prevent & avoid it' (DJR, p. 6). However, the thought here is not simply that learning about melancholy will provide the author and his readers with a body of useful doctrine, but that the activity of writing and reading will themselves have concrete effects upon their souls and bodies. For his own part, Burton describes his book as the product of his experiential *'melancholizing'*—a term he uses to describe the restless melancholic imagination 'work[ing] upon it selfe' (2.2.6.2, p. 107); and the process of writing it, as we have already noted, as both a 'playing labor' to offset his propensity to idleness and the 'evacuation' of a melancholic 'Impostume' (DJR, p. 7). As for his readers, Burton is also clear that he is writing, conventionally enough, 'for the common good of all' (DJR, p. 8), and he presents himself more specifically as a 'Melancholy Divine' offering 'an absolute cure' of body and soul, the 'Spirituall' therapy of *corpus per animam*, as well as the 'Corporall' therapy of *animam per corpus* (DJR, pp. 22–3). Yet, it is not just that 'all men' will benefit from 'the knowledge' of melancholy (DJR, p. 23), but that 'these following lines' in the book, 'when they shall be recited, or hereafter read, will drive away Melancholy (though I be gone)' (DJR, p. 24). This therapeutic capacity is underlined in the miniature preface to the third Partition on love melancholy, where—in a figure made famous within humanistic literary circles by Erasmus in his letter to Maarten van Dorp—Burton deploys the Lucretian notion of a harsh philosophical discourse with a sweet literary coating. Here, he expresses the hope that his 'writings...shall take like guilded pilles, which are so composed as well to tempt the appetite, and deceave the pallat, as to helpe and medicinally worke upon the whole body, my lines shall not onely recreate, but rectifie the minde' (3.1.1.1, p. 5).[41]

The *Anatomy* can be interpreted as an intentionally therapeutic text in several different ways. For instance, as many critics have emphasized, to read the *Anatomy* is to be guided through the world of Renaissance knowledge, and it is hard to miss Burton's ironic and doubtful attitude towards many of his quotations. Like Montaigne, he revels

---

[41] Erasmus, *Praise of Folly and Letter to Maarten Van Dorp*, 141. At DJR, I, 111, Burton quotes from Erasmus's letter, as well as the Horatian dictum ('Quamvis ridentem dicere verum quid vetat?') which immediately precedes the Lucretian passage in question.

in distancing himself from his sources by using terms such as 'perhaps', 'somewhat', 'some', 'they say', 'I think', and so on, in order to 'soften and tone down' his propositions, and his habit of leaving contradictions between authorities glaringly unresolved is well known.[42] Here we might detect not just a traditional humanistic distrust of speculative philosophy (and a corresponding emphasis on the priority of practical ethics), but also an inclination towards some kind of informal scepticism as a means of attaining tranquillity.[43] In a sense, an ironic attitude seems to be intrinsic to the project of the *Anatomy*, since as a *cento* it portrays Burton adopting a detached pose, sifting through and commenting on the Renaissance encyclopaedia in search of useful material. But in his discussion of 'that tyannising care' of curiosity as a cause of melancholy, his opposition of the 'trouble' and 'torment' of fruitless philosophical enterprises to the simple ignorance of 'those barbarous *Indians*' (1.2.4.1, pp. 363–4) suggests that, for Burton, the adoption of a sceptical position with regard to the limits of human understanding has some practical utility for alleviating psychic discomfort.

As I have already suggested, however, perhaps the most important aspect of the therapeutic enterprise of the *Anatomy* is its rhetorical character, and this has rarely been appreciated or analysed. Leaving aside the proliferation of particular figures and tropes throughout the book, Burton makes it clear that his aim is to conjoin philosophical and spiritual wisdom with literary-poetic eloquence—hence, the Horatian maxim on the frontispiece and the 'earnest intent' he expresses that his writing will 'profit', as well as 'please', its readers (3.1.1.1, p. 5)—in a manner that drew, in part, upon a conventional classical understanding of rhetoric as the art of arousing or overcoming the passions. When delivered with eloquence, the wisdom of the *Anatomy* provides pleasurable means of addressing melancholic perturbations, and, more generally, of assisting readers in search of a healthy moral-psychological equilibrium. In the 'Consolatory Digression', where this aspect of the work becomes paramount, Burton states that his aim is to 'give some content and comfort' to the 'distressed', but also to bring those who are happy 'to a moderation, and make them reflect and knowe themselves, by seeing the unconstancy of humane felicity, others misery' (2.3.1.1, p. 125). The digression accomplishes this by presenting an eclectic collection of '[p]hilosophicall and Divine precepts' in prose and poetry, interspersed with vivid rhetorical 'examples' of happiness and misery, all gathered together in order to 'balance our hearts', 'counterpoise those irregular motions' of vices 'with their opposite vertues', and 'then to pacifie our selves by reason', or else 'to divert by some other object, contrary passion, or premeditation'— just 'as Mariners when they goe to Sea, provide all things necessary to resist a tempest' (2.3.6.1, p. 187).

---

[42] Montaigne, *Essays* III.11, 1165. In the *Anatomy*, see especially the terminology employed in the generally sceptical 'Digression of the Ayre' (2.2.3.1, II, 33–58) and the conclusion to the discussion of chemical preparatives at 2.5.1.3, II, 243–4.

[43] As is emphasized in Richard Tuck, *Philosophy and Government, 1572–1671* (Cambridge: Cambridge University Press, 1993), xiii, Renaissance scepticism was fundamentally psychological, rather than epistemological.

It should also be clear now that this therapeutic rhetoric also has a more specific function with regard to the disease of melancholy, one that is directly tailored to the depraved imagination at the root of psychic disturbances. 'As Imagination, feare, griefe, cause such passions, so conceipts alone', Burton writes, 'rectified by good hope, counsell, &c. are able againe to helpe' (2.2.6.2, p. 110). A discourse that rectifies melancholic passions thereby employs philosophical, spiritual, and even medical doctrine in a persuasive fashion, effectively substituting *recta ratio* (or spiritual truth) for the misleading phantasms of the melancholic imagination. It is true that reading and thinking, as he makes clear in the digression 'Of the Misery of Schollers', can cause or worsen the disease by upsetting the body's physiological balance and aggravating the damaged imagination of the melancholic (1.2.3.15, pp. 303–4, 308).[44] But these activities may also be forms of rational and imaginative therapy, fortifying the soul with rational precepts, and displacing the painful or disturbing 'conceipts' of the depraved imagination by means of pleasurable and healthy ones. The right kind of book, in other words, can help to 'expell Idleness and melancholy'—so long as it distracts the melancholic from disturbing thoughts (2.2.4.1, pp. 68, 84), is pleasurable, rather than vexatious, and '[p]rovided alwaies that his malady proceede not from overmuch study' (p. 90).

In this sense, the *Anatomy* is built upon a conception of the power of language to affect the working of the imagination, specifically in its production of healthy or unhealthy 'conceipts'. Therapeutic words which deliver harsh rational precepts with eloquence (Burton's 'gilded pilles') can enable the understanding and the will to check or rectify the mistaken sense-images of the diseased imagination, or, more directly, may substitute its pathogenic species for healthy ones. In effect, that is what Burton seeks to do when he is 'diverting' himself and his readers with 'pleasurable' or amusing imagery to induce 'contrary passions', when he entertains or 'diverts' them with his digressions, or when, in his 'Democritean' satirical mode, he seeks to provoke laughter (see 2.2.6.4, II, p. 117). From this point of view, of course, the fusion of literary and philosophical elements in the work can be explained as the medium for a fairly straightforward therapeutic conjunction of wisdom and eloquence. But it is also tempting to see here not just a standard humanistic conception of rhetoric, with a Quintilianic emphasis on the power of imagery to move the passions,[45] but something akin to the more precise formulation of the goals of rhetoric in Bacon's *Advancement of Learning* (1605)—namely, to 'practise and win the Imagination from the Affection's part, and contract a confederacy between the Reason and Imagination against the Affections', or, more concisely, 'to apply Reason to Imagination for the better moving of the will'.[46]

---

[44] See also the discussions of idleness at 1.2.2.6, 243 and the dangers of reading at 2.2.6.2, 107–8 and 3.4.2.3, 414.

[45] See Quentin Skinner, *Reason and Rhetoric in the Philosophy of Hobbes* (Cambridge: Cambridge University Press, 1996), 182–8.

[46] Brian Vickers, ed., *Francis Bacon: A Critical Edition of the Major Works* (Oxford and New York: Oxford University Press, 1996), II, 238–9.

We might expect that the *Anatomy* is consistently tailored to implement such a therapeutic enterprise, and indeed, this seems to be the most common interpretation of the work at present.[47] But whilst Burton undoubtedly has benevolent intentions towards his readership, his work does not consistently perform a curative role. In a revealing passage added in the third edition of the work issued in 1628, which illustrates the particular role of literary rhetoric—and its limitations—in the work, he acknowledged that there were substantial parts of the book that were dangerous for melancholics to read:

> Yet one Caution let mee give by the way to my present or future Reader, who is actually Melancholy, that hee read not the Symptomes or prognostickes in this following Tract, least by applying that which hee reads to himselfe, aggravating, appropriating things generally spoken, to his owne person (as Melancholy men for the most part doe) hee trouble or hurt himself, and get in conclusion more harme then good. I advise them warily to peruse that Tract, *Lapides loquitur* (so said *Agrippa de occ. Phil.*) *& caveant Lectores ne cerebrum iis excutiat*. (DJR, p. 24)[48]

Here he is referring to the tendency of the melancholic to 'melancholize', for his imagination to 'worke upon it selfe' in an erroneous and destructive fashion. And what this passage also shows is an awareness that when he is discussing domains of knowledge where the therapeutic literary-rhetorical 'gilding' of the doctrinal 'pill' is either inappropriate or ineffective—the most distressing areas of symptomatology and prognostics—the depraved imagination of the melancholic reader may no longer be worked upon or reined in. Put simply, there are some harsh and bitter truths about melancholy that no amount of eloquence can disguise.

Further Reading

Babb, Lawrence A. *Sanity in Bedlam: A Study of Robert Burton's 'The Anatomy of Melancholy'* (Ann Arbor: Michigan State University Press, 1959).
Fish, Stanley. *Self-Consuming Artifacts: The Experience of Seventeenth-Century Literature* (Berkeley: University of California Press, 1972).
Gowland, Angus. *The Worlds of Renaissance Melancholy: Robert Burton in Context* (Cambridge: Cambridge University Press, 2006).
Klibansky, Raymond, Panofsky, Erwin, and Saxl, Fritz. *Saturn and Melancholy: Studies in the History of Natural Philosophy, Religion and Art* (London: Thomas Nelson, 1964).
Lund, Mary Ann. *Melancholy, Medicine and Religion in Early Modern England: Reading 'The Anatomy of Melancholy'* (Cambridge: Cambridge University Press, 2010).

---

[47] Vicari, *The View from Minerva's Tower*; John Miller, 'Plotting a Cure: The Reader in Robert Burton's *Anatomy of Melancholy*', *Prose Studies*, 20 (1997): 97–101; Lund, *Melancholy, Medicine and Religion*.

[48] 'He speaks stones, and readers should beware in case he bashes their brains out with them': Cornelius Agrippa, *De occulta philosophia libri tres* (Köln, 1533), sig. aa iir, itself an adaptation (as noted by the editor in Robert Burton, *The Anatomy of Melancholy*, ed. A. R. Shilleto [London and New York: George Bell & Sons, 1893]), of Plautus, *Aulularia* II. l–2.

Lyons, Bridget Gellert. *Voices of Melancholy: Studies in Literary Treatments of Melancholy in Renaissance England* (London: Routledge & Kegan Paul, 1971).

O'Connell, Michael. *Robert Burton* (Boston: Twayne Publishers, 1986).

Simon, Jean Robert. *Robert Burton et 'l'Anatomie de la mélancolie'* (Paris: Didier, 1964).

Tilmouth, Christopher. 'Burton's "Turning Picture": Argument and Anxiety in *The Anatomy of Melancholy*', *Review of English Studies*, 56 (2005): 524–49.

Vicari, E. Patricia. *The View from Minerva's Tower: Learning and Imagination in 'The Anatomy of Melancholy'* (Toronto: University of Toronto Press, 1996).

Webber, Joan. *The Eloquent 'I': Style and Self in Seventeenth-Century Prose* (Madison: University of Wisconsin Press, 1968).

CHAPTER 39

'WHEN ALL THINGS SHALL CONFESSE THEIR ASHES': SCIENCE AND SOUL IN THOMAS BROWNE

KEVIN KILLEEN

WRITING his haughty and occasionally blistering review of Thomas Browne's *Religio Medici*, the philosopher Kenelm Digby weighs up its amorphous subject matter: 'This gentlemans intended Theame; as I conceive', he concludes, is 'the scope and finall period of True religion', by way of which, Browne goes 'wading so deep in sciences' that he finds himself lost in digressive circles on the science of the soul, of resurrection and revivification, the 'abstracted subtilties' of eternity and flux.[1] Digby considers, with not a little snobbery, that a physician 'whose hands are inured to the cutting up & eies to the inspection of anatomized bodyes' is not naturally suited to the contemplation of 'a Separated and unbodyed Soule'. This is not, however, too rigorous a separation: although practical anatomy may dim the mind to such matters, knowledge of the soul and its fate in eternity still requires 'a totall Survey of the whole science of Bodyes'.[2] That the 'whole science of Bodyes' happened also to be the subject of Digby's forthcoming *magnus opus* has made Browne scholars deeply suspicious. It has been treated, by and large, as a criticism designed to protect Digby's own intellectual turf, if not a grandiose piece of self-puffery.[3] That there was a physics (as well as a theology) of resurrection, however, would be neither

---

[1] Kenelm Digby, *Observations Upon* Religio Medici, 2nd edn. (1644), 75, 99, 116.
[2] Digby, *Observations*, 9–11.
[3] Kenelm Digby, *Two treatises in the one of which the nature of bodies, in the other, the nature of mans soule is looked into in way of discovery of the immortality of reasonable soules* (1644); James N. Wise, *Sir Thomas Browne's 'Religio Medici' and Two Seventeenth-Century Critics* (Columbia: University of Missouri Press, 1973); Ronald Huebert, 'The Private Opinions of Sir Thomas Browne', *Studies in English Literature, 1500–1900*, 45.1 (2005): 117–34 (118).

alien nor anathema to Browne, whose conception of religion was wholly imbricated with his understanding of natural philosophy. Indeed, Digby's comment might be seen as a proper entry point upon a work which, though a labyrinthine mixture of the personal, the theological, and the scientific, deals continually and capaciously with the soul and its philosophical relation to the 'elemental composition' of body, 'these walls of flesh, wherein the soul doth seem to be immured before the resurrection'.[4] From the bodies of angels, to the predestinate soul, to the fate of material atoms in the resurrection, *Religio Medici* brushes close to the theological materialism that so preoccupies early modern philosophy. Browne made rapid pre-publication peace with Digby, in part by implying his own work was the mere hackery of his youth, dashed off as Digby's reply so evidently was, and the two texts went forth as awkward conjoined twins over subsequent decades, prompting Samuel Johnson's acerbic comment: 'The reciprocal civility of authors is one of the most risible scenes in the farce of life.'[5]

Religio Medici remains a perplexing amalgam, with its wandering subject matter and its rhetorical silkiness. Its uppermost level is a meditation on religion, though even within such a category, it is a slippery entity, at one moment confessional and irenic, capaciously tolerant and gentle on heresies, while the next it is fastidious and captious about the radical presence in England. It is by turns a rhapsody on Laudian ceremony, a miscellany of scriptural *curiosa* troubling the categories of faith and reason, and a disquisition on spirit, soul, and body.[6] Rhetorically and perhaps philosophically, this is a full-scale lecture on indirection. Quite often, in recent decades at least, it has been treated as an autobiography, again, perhaps, following Digby, who comments: 'What should I say of his making so particular a narration of personall things, and privat thoughts of his owne, the knowledge whereof can not much conduce to any mans betterment (which I make account is the chiefe end of his writing this discourse)?' Oscillating between admiration and exasperation, as so many of Browne's subsequent readers have done, Digby heaps praise upon him 'our authors æquanimity and...magnanimity...the owner of a solid head and of a strong generous heart', though he tempers that praise too. He is, Digby puts it with winning pomposity: 'a very fine ingenious Gentleman: but for how deepe a Scholler, I leave unto them to judge, that are abler than I'.[7] If *Religio Medici* does qualify as autobiography, it is not because there is any great quantity of personal Browne-life in the text, but rather, because, through its delirious range of topics, the work revels in its own authorial tone, shifting between a conversational diffidence—whose modesty would concede each point it makes upon the proffering of any better argument—and full oratorical grandeur. It is, or it might seem to be, tone, rather

---

[4] Thomas Browne, *Religio Medici* (1643) 1.37.

[5] Samuel Johnson's 'Life of Sir Thomas Browne', in Browne, *Christian Morals* (1756), i–lxi, at ix.

[6] The religious politics of *Religio Medici* receives interesting treatment in Debora Shuger, 'The Laudian Idiot', in Reid Barbour and Claire Preston, eds., *Sir Thomas Browne: The World Proposed* (Oxford: Oxford University Press, 2009), 36–62.

[7] Digby, *Observations*, 29, 38–9, 75. Among recent works on *Religio Medici* as autobiography, see Ladina Bezzola Lambert, 'Moving in Circles: The Dialectics of Selfhood in Religio Medici', *Renaissance Studies*, 19.3 (2005): 364–79.

than substance, that is the unifying centre of the work, that the personal is identifiably present in the voice and the stylistic singularity. This inimitable prose strategy will be central to the ensuing discussion of *Religio Medici*, but it is also an important proviso that, for his contemporaries, the work was 'about' something—it was philosophically and theologically engaged, and the second half of the essay returns to Browne's extensive poetics of the embodied and the unembodied soul.

39.1 PROSE AND IDIOM: CHARACTERIZING STYLE IN *RELIGIO MEDICI*

The distinctive prose idiom of *Religio Medici* has been the basis of Browne's enduring reputation. It is one of the few works of prose from the seventeenth century that has rarely, if ever, been out of print and it has attracted consistent critical attention. Lionized by an impressive line-up of writers, from Charles Lamb to Coleridge, from Poe, Emerson, and Melville to, more curiously, Bram Stoker in preparing *Dracula*, Browne has an illustrious history of admirers.[8] Borges and Sebald have responded to the lost and labyrinthine qualities of his writing, while Tony Kushner reconstitutes a misanthropic miserly Browne for the stage, characterizing his prose as an 'ornate jewelled swooniness'.[9] A heady twentieth-century effort went into identifying the quality of the prosody, its metre, cadence, and scansion, or attempting to locate its essential pulse, whether in its 'Hebraic symmetry', its relentlessly duplet-phrasing, or its putative relations to Baroque, Asiatic, Ciceronian, or Senecan characteristics.[10] 'Is Browne among the cadenced?' asks Austen Warren, in terms that might as easily be asking whether he is among the predestinate and the elect.[11]

Prose as a disembodied subject of analysis, divorced from the thick histories and context in which texts might be seen, has or had fallen out of literary favour, though the tide may be turning. But it is not returning unchanged. This chapter makes the probably uncontentious case that prose style is tightly wound up in its subject matter, though this

---

[8] Claire Preston tells the story of the discovery of Bram Stoker's notes for *Dracula*, as well as providing an account of the afterlife and reception of *Religio Medici*. *Thomas Browne and the Writing of Early Modern Science* (Cambridge: Cambridge University Press, 2005), 4–9.

[9] Tony Kushner, *Hydiotaphia, or The Death of Dr Browne: An Epic Farce about Death and Private Capital Accumulation*, in *Death and Taxes, Hydriotphia & Other Plays* (New York: Theatre Communications Group, 2000), 34.

[10] Norton Tempest, 'Rhythm in the Prose of Sir Thomas Browne', *Review of English Studies*, 3 (1927): 308–18; William Whallon, 'Hebraic Synonymy in Sir Thomas Browne', *English Literary History*, 28 (1961): 335–52; see, in particular, the articles of Morris Croll in Stanley Fish, ed., *Seventeenth-Century Prose: Modern Essays in Criticism* (New York: Oxford University Press, 1971); Morris Croll, *Style, Rhetoric, and Rhythm* (Princeton: Princeton University Press, 1966); and Daniela Havenstein, *Democratizing Sir Thomas Browne: Religio Medici and its Imitators* (Oxford: Clarendon Press, 1999).

[11] Austin Warren, 'The Style of Sir Thomas Browne', *Kenyon Review*, 13 (1951): 674–87 (680).

is not to say that there is any deterministic relationship between what is said and how, particularly in a work whose subject is quite so indeterminable. If English Literature has largely forgone analysis of prose over the past few decades, however, the history of science has taken up the subject with some gusto. Much has been written, for example, on the rhetorical strategies by which scientific communities formed and authorized themselves, the idioms of 'gentlemanly' address by which the natural philosopher distinguished himself from the artisan gatherer of knowledge. Scientific discourse was unambiguous in the importance it placed on rhetorical courtesy and frumperies, rarely enough allowing mere expertise to trump refined manners.[12] This recent history of reading prose rhetoric as a part of the social fabric in which texts are enfolded is not the same, of course, as reading for the stylistic panache that Browne demonstrates. Although he was reckoned and recognized as a natural philosopher, Browne's prose is quite distinct from his scientific contemporaries, and usefully complicates any attempt to define what scientific prose looked like. It is further complicated by the amalgam of subject matter that constitutes *Religio Medici*. The same idiom that explores Laudian ceremony also engages the ontology of angels, baffles itself in scriptural minutiae, and asks what chemical processes might be at play in the bodily resurrection of the apocalypse.

Browne's writing responds to a broad set of philosophical and religious contexts, scientific and political upheavals, while maintaining, it might be said, its idiosyncratic distance as well. *Religio Medici* appeared in 1642/3 (Fig. 39.1), a time of unparalleled upheaval, and his subsequent body of writing—*Pseudodoxia Epidemica* in 1646, *Hydriotaphia, or Urn Burial*, and *The Garden of Cyrus* in 1658—appeared over the era of the Civil War, regicide, and interregnum, with its turmoil and displacement. A number of posthumous tracts, a large volume of letters from after 1660, and a collection of working notes and experimental *problemata* make for a more hefty corpus, however. If there is a defining tone that characterizes Browne across his works, it is what has been described by Claire Preston as a contingent, provisional, and uncertain habit of statement, a willingness to hold competing explanations in play without resolution.[13] And yet, this provisionality and reticence is delivered with such booming oratorical panache as to admit no objection. Browne's statements of belief or his investigations of fact generally allow that he might be wrong, that he is not at all to be taken as authoritative, and yet, to dispute mere fact, in the presence of a voice so rotund, so intoned and homiletic, is to appear sniping and picky. The fate of readers who pick thus—from Alexander Ross, Browne's contemporary and stock pedant of early modern England, to Stanley Fish, the critical theorist who, in the 1970s, made a set of sometimes bizarre moral-poetic accusations against *Religio Medici*—is to be counted a reader who cannot hear the oceanic in

---

[12] Peter Dear, ed., *The Literary Structure of Scientific Argument: Historical Studies* (Philadephia: University of Pennsylvania Press, 1991), 137; Margaret J. Osler, ed., *Rethinking the Scientific Revolution* (Cambridge: Cambridge University Press, 2000), preface; Steven Shapin, *A Social History of Truth: Civility and Science in Seventeenth-Century England* (Chicago: University of Chicago Press, 1994).

[13] Preston, *Thomas Browne and the Writing of Early Modern Science*, passim.

FIGURE 39.1 Thomas Browne, *Religio Medici* (1642)

Browne's writing, the greater swell of his rhetoric.[14] This is Browne's wonderful rhetorical trick, to insist on his openness to contradiction in a voice whose majestic torrent brooks no interruption, that is softly and flexibly incontrovertible, a voice that has, at times, perhaps naïvely, been seen as an irenic and tolerant disposition, but which is both fastidious and relentlessly creedal.

Religio Medici is all about what Browne does not know, plumbing fabulous depths of ignorance. This begins as the lulling, if not the confounding of reason, although it does not end there. He quotes Tertullian's dictum from *De Carne Christi* on the incarnation and bodily resurrection 'Certum est quia impossibile est'—'It is certain because impossible'.[15] What is provable remains mundane; 'ordinary and visible objects' yield 'not faith but perswasion'. Browne will have his paradoxes run rings around ocular proof as much as reason. He is, he tells us, 'thankfull that I lived not in the dayes of miracles, that I never saw Christ nor his Disciples'. A Christian who denies he would have willingly seen Christ may border on paradox, but underlies an epistemology that revels in its insufficiencies. To know is one thing, but *Religio Medici* is more interested in the faulty tools of knowing, the fractures in reason, and how such a flawed instrument forces us to recalibrate the limits of knowledge: 'acquainting our reason how unable it is to display the visible and obvious effect of nature'.[16] 'It is impossible', he explains, that 'to the weaknesse of our apprehensions, there should not appear irregularities, contradictions and antinomies'.[17] The work employs a sometimes Pauline, sometimes Platonic attempt to comprehend the invisible—which is the real object of knowledge, be it form or faith—through a transposition of the visible, 'that universall and public Manuscript that lies expans'd unto the eyes of all', in which the 'common Hieroglyphicks' of nature, the signatory presence of God in creation, may be discerned.[18] This rhapsodic supposition that the natural world will yield its dividend of theology may, of course, cover a degree of tension, described by Brook Conti as less a marriage of faith and reason, than an amicable 'divorce settlement' in which 'each faculty gets custody of the issues proper to it'.[19] This is, however, a very messy divorce. If Browne seeks an obfuscation and humbling of reason, it is less often to elevate doctrine, than for the almost sensual pleasure of bafflement.

Time is a topic whose paradoxes Browne indulges in fully; and though time may present its puzzles, he insists that it remains within the remit of ordinary philosophy, a mere bagatelle of a mystery in comparison with eternity, which is more exquisitely opaque: 'Time we may comprehend, 'tis but five days elder then our selves and hath the

---

[14] Alexander Ross, *Medicus Medicatus* (1645); Stanley Fish, *Self-Consuming Artifacts: The Experience of Seventeenth-Century Literature* (Berkeley: University of California Press, 1972).

[15] Tertullian, *De Carne Christi* 5.4 in *Ante-Nicene Fathers*, ed. Alexander Roberts, vol. 3 (Edinburgh: T. & T. Clark, 1885); *Religio Medici* 1.9.

[16] *Religio Medici* 1.10.

[17] *Religio Medici* 1.21.

[18] *Religio Medici* 1.16.

[19] Brooke Conti, '*Religio Medici*'s Profession of Faith', in Barbour and Preston, eds., *The World Proposed*, 149–67 (157).

same Horoscope with the world.' From the panache of this claim, that time, created on the first day, is hardly older than humanity created on the sixth, he asserts that eternity constitutes an altogether more delightful 'extasie' to 'confound my understanding':

> but in eternity there is no distinction of tenses, and therefore that terrible terme Predestination, which hath troubled so many weake heads to conceive, and the wisest to explaine, is in respect to God no prescious determination of our estates to come, but a definitive blast of his will already fulfilled, and at the instant that he first decreed it.[20]

Browne's plunging himself into obfuscation is the major rhetorical dynamic of *Religio Medici*, but there is another keynote at play here. In one of his many rhetorical swivels, he sallies out with what seems a forthright attack on 'that terrible terme' Predestination, with all its political freight, but pulls back from the brink of controversy. Though it seems initially blunt and unequivocal, predestination—still doctrinally orthodox into the 1630s—emerges relatively unscathed: the 'definitive blast' of God's will remains in place, but outside of time and, more significantly, beyond the realm of the knowable. It turns out only to be an attack on the 'weake heads' of his political adversaries, an ill-defined non-Arminian wing of the church.[21] While Browne appears at times irenic, and while he depicts himself as above theological hair-splitting, he rarely fails to make it plain which side of the split hair he is on.

William Hazlitt, writing in 1820, describes Browne's insistent pushing towards 'the utmost verge of conjecture' and that any topic is considered only to 'bewilder his understanding in the universality of its nature and the inscrutableness of its origin'. It is a prose constructed in 'the intricate folds and swelling drapery of dark sayings and impenetrable riddles'.[22] Hazlitt suggests—and it is the experience of many of Browne's readers—that the philosophical content of such arguments is enwrought in its prose form, that the 'swelling drapery of dark sayings' constitutes its mystery and theology. Not every reader, however, responds so effusively to the idiosyncratic prose. Noah Webster, the dictionary compiler, complained that his lexographic predecessor, Samuel Johnson, had paid far too much attention to seventeenth-century writers who 'had neither taste nor a correct knowledge of English', in particular, Browne, of whom Webster says, 'the style of Sir Thomas Browne is not English'. It was, he supposed, 'astonishing that a man attempting to give the world a standard of the English language should have ever mentioned his name, but with a reprobation of his style and use of words', chiding, in particular, Browne's Latinate vocabulary and giving examples of the mangled syntactical forms that Browne so routinely intrudes into his prose.[23] Hazlitt and Webster are closer in their

---

[20] *Religio Medici*, 1.11.
[21] This element of *Relgio Medici*, its relationship to Laudian ecclesiastical politics, has received a large amount of attention and I will not discuss it here. It occupies only a relatively small, if important, part of the text.
[22] William Hazlitt, *Complete Works*, 21 vols. (London: Dent, 1931), VI, 333, 335.
[23] Noah Webster, 'Letter to Dr David Ramsay' (Oct. 1807), in James Boulton, ed., *Samuel Johnson: The Critical Heritage* (London: Routledge, 1971), 129.

estimation than might appear. Both suppose that unintelligibility is not incidental, but the very signature tune of Browne.

Reason crumples in its effort to encompass the enormity and complexity of nature, itself providing only a mere glimmer of the ineffable beyond. Philosophy or theology can offer only a shadowy engagement with the real. Browne, however, performs a sleight of hand, in rendering this incomprehensibility, producing his own version of that collapse of reason in the marrow of his prose. *Religio Medici* skews its syntax as an object lesson in abasement and humility in the face of the inexplicable. 'To difference my self nearer, & draw into a lesser circle, There is no Church whose every part so squares unto my conscience', he tells us, early on.[24] Aside from his deft squaring of a circle in the course of the phrase, aside too from his noun, where a verb should be, the ostensible meaning is to clarify or to particularize his position, which he does first by 'differencing' himself, which should imply moving apart, rather than moving 'neerer'. In both local phrase and wider theme, Browne has his grammar work at the outer parameters of coherence. He manages to profound as a verb, meaning to drill down and plumb mysteries: 'There is no danger to profound these mysteries, no *Sanctum sanctorum* in Philosophy.'[25]

The apocalypse, for Browne, is the moment 'when all things shall confesse their ashes', making the word 'confess' do things it has surely never before or since had to do—the expected collocation of confessing sins or crimes is wrought into the entirely more demanding instance of every object admitting the general dissolution of the self in death and handing back its ashes.[26] The context here is ostensibly the perishability of books, of the 'leaves of Solomon', of burnt libraries and laws—only the scriptures being 'a worke too hard for the teeth of time'.[27] The ashes of the eschaton in *Religio Medici* belongs to a philosophic-theology that I will return to. At issue, here, is the conscious and continual collapse of grammar; a syntax awry and frequently a semi-tone off-key; collocations that are only fleetingly and poetically logical; a carefully wrought imprecision in, as Tony Kushner has put it, a 'style of such voluptuous baroquosity it melts the straight lines and tight angles of the Euclidean universe'.[28] This is most evident in the subterranean effects of Browne's sentence structures, the length and weighting of which, with their balanced or ill-balanced clausal swell, produces an unfathomable polyphony.[29] Brownean single-sentence paragraphs perform an elaborate tracery of ideas, though editing sometimes obscures this intricacy.

Early modern prose is, it might be said, quite proud of the labyrinthine dimensions of its pauseless sentences, its rhetorical theory consummately aware of both the architecture of texts and the interior design of its sentences. If Browne disobeys every rule of *inventio*, the process of selecting, unfolding, and sticking to one's topic—his is a fireworks display of subject matter, rather than a single explosion—he

---

[24] *Religio Medici* 1.5.   [25] *Religio Medici* 1.13.   [26] *Religio Medici* 1.23.
[27] *Religio Medici* 1.23–4.   [28] Kushner, *Hydiotaphia*, 34.
[29] A recent and excellent essay on this topic is Sharon Cadman Seelig, ' "Speake that I may see thee": The Styles of Sir Thomas Browne', in Barbour and Preston, eds., *Sir Thomas Browne*, 13–35.

might be following the very prototype of the individual 'period' given in a 1665 work, *The mysterie of rhetorique unveil'd*, in which John Smith assessed the aesthetic design and balance of sentences:

> That period is the most excellent, which is performed with two Colons (and sometimes Commas) or four parts of a sentence, as that which suspends the mind, and satisfies the ears... Herein beware that the Period be not shorter then the ear expects, nor longer then the strength and breath of the Speaker or Reader may bear, and that it finish its course in a handsome and full comprehension.[30]

This describes, though dryly, something of the style of *Religio Medici* and yet, we are right to suppose that Browne does more than follow the (not-yet-written) manual. Such analysis may describe the scaffold of a sentence, but not what it does once it becomes live and independent. For Browne, the individual sentence, in its complexity, works to replicate the disjointedness of the world.

If *Religio Medici* revels in the unintelligible nature of nature, the crumple of reason that the mind experiences as it tries to comprehend the infinite, it is particularly adamant that the processes of nature should not be ascribed to nature itself—it being a kind of intellectual hubris to suppose that 'nature' is thus independent. To do so is 'to devolve the honor of the principall agent upon the instrument', to nature instead of God: 'Then let our hammers rise up and boast they have built our houses, and our pens receive the honour of our writings.' Such a rebellion of the tools is, for Browne, an unthinkable arrogating of the honour that belongs properly to the divine. Being mildly jealous of his creation, God will not, however, allow too great a degree of presumption, and though his practice may be to transcribe the world in perfect circles of natural regularity, according to the 'forelaid principles of his art', occasionally too he will include sheer oddities, 'hee doth sometimes pervert, to acquaint the world with his prerogative, lest the arrogancy of our reason should question his power, and conclude he could not'.[31] God, it seems, launches prevenient strikes against regularity, lest we suppose our minds sufficient to grasp the enormities of scale on which nature is etched. Irregularity in the world, as in grammar, serves to baffle our certainties and presumptions about its workings.

It would be wrongly formulating the issue, however, to suppose that *Religio Medici* is in any straightforward way about reason and faith. Browne is interested in the essential unintelligibility of the world, not because he has abnegated reason and passed the buck to faith, if by that we were to mean accepting theological truths cordoned off from philosophical or scientific investigation. On the contrary, Browne announces his rigorous intention to marry science to his contemplation of God. In fact, nature will have to do so entirely, God being otherwise unknowable, 'for we behold him but asquint upon reflex or shadow; our understanding is dimmer than Moses eye, we are ignorant of the backparts, or lower side of his divinity', he explains, with passing reference to God's jaunty

---

[30] John Smith, *The mysterie of rhetorique unveil'd* (1665), 136.
[31] *Religio Medici* 1.16.

refusal in Exodus to allow Moses to see his enigmatic backparts.[32] The point is more that when we look, as Paul has it, through a glass darkly, the very distortion of paradox acts as a corrective to our naturally skewed perspectives.[33] Whether it is the soul in man or the heaven beyond the outer crystalline sphere that we aim to discern, 'we must suspend the rules of our philosophy, and make all good by a more absolute piece of opticks'.[34] Paradox depends on momentarily assenting to what cannot, more logically, be true, a comprehension that functions only asquint, with reason rectified by a 'more absolute piece of opticks'.

39.2 THE PHYSICS OF RESURRECTION

Browne is aware, he tells us, that he spends his time, 'raking into the bowells of the deceased' and that the 'continuall sight of anatomies, skeletons, or cadaverous reliques' might make us suppose him insensitive to death, or, as Digby suggests, insensitive to soul.[35] But this, he argues, makes him all the more aware of the delicate conditionality of the self at the cusp of life, before, during, and after, which he terms our 'being and life in three distinct worlds'. The first world has the not-yet-born child apparently biding time, yet to encounter enough objects to have formed itself into full being: 'in that obscure world and wombe of our mother, our time is short, computed by the moone; yet longer than the dayes of many creatures that behold the sunne, our selves being not yet without life, sense, and reason, though for the manifestation of its actions, it awaits the opportunity of objects'.[36] The unborn child patiently waits for the stimulation of objects, to prompt 'sense and reason' into life, less a Lacanian moment than a child greedy for toys or an ambitious courtier waiting for a place. Browne's midwifery gives way, however, to theology, and just as a new-born will leave behind it the 'secondine' or afterbirth, so at death the body becomes the disposable portion of the self: 'till we have once more cast our secondine, that is, this slough of flesh, and are delivered into the last world, that is, that ineffable place of *Paul*, that proper *ubi* of spirits'.[37]

Though momentarily seeming so, this is no ascetic repudiation of body, which, in all its physicality, is the crucial, though fragile, conduit to knowledge of the soul. '[I] have examined the parts of man', Browne explains, 'and know upon what tender filaments that fabric hangs...considering the thousand doors that lead to death'.[38] This is the physician of the title speaking, a figure who has often been lost in critical discussion of *Religio Medici*, focused on the politics of Laudianism and ceremony that occupy the

---

[32] *Religio Medici* 1.12; Exodus 33:23.   [33] 1 Corinthians 13:12.
[34] *Religio Medici* 1.49.   [35] *Religio Medici* 1.38.
[36] *Religio Medici* 1.39.   [37] *Religio Medici* 1.39.
[38] *Religio Medici* 1.44.

opening parts of the work.[39] But fully half of the first part of *Religio Medici* deals in one way or another with spirit and soul and their relation to body, first, how angels might be said to subsist as material beings, together with the nature of Platonic and diabolic spirits (29–36), the subject of so much early modern speculation.[40] Browne the vivisectionist seems to emerge, momentarily, in his discussion of an imagined quasi-chemical process of spiritual liposuction: 'Do but extract from the corpulency of bodies, or resolve things beyond their first matter and you discover the habitation of angels.'[41] When one syringes away all the material of angels, in the nothing and the no-place (or the ubiquity) that is left, we can discover their native habitat. Though this may be a rhetorical, rather than a laboratory experiment, the same cannot be said of his efforts to locate the soul in humans. If it is too early for him to be responding to Descartes's positioning of the soul in the pineal gland, via a process of anatomical observation and haphazard elimination, Browne nevertheless probes the material body for signs of the soul, worrying that there is no organ where it might be located: every 'crany' of the brain seems to be the same in beasts: 'this is a sensible and no inconsiderable argument of the inorganity of the soule.'[42] From here on to the end of first book, death is the chief topic of *Religio Medici*, from its encompassing Adamic legacy to fear of, or as Browne will have it, embarrassment at death (37–45), moving on to his treatment of the last judgement, the afterlife, and the constitution of hell and, most oddly, the physics or, at times, the chemistry of resurrection, it being hard to say to what modern science we should attribute the natural philosophy of the soul in the apocalypse (47–60).

'How shall the dead arise?' Browne asks, but this is not a theological question. The tools that address this are philosophical and the analogies by which such a resurrection can be comprehended are scientific—the action of mercury and the experimental palingenesis of plants. The oddness in this is the supposition that such a central theological tenet—the rising of the dead—might and must be understood in terms of its physics. The Browne who seemed to insist on the productive unintelligibility of the world, who revels in what is unknowable, chooses to think out the mechanisms by which the dispersed self might return to its proper shape. It is important to *Religio Medici*, rhetorically

---

[39] See, however, Mary Ann Lund, 'The Christian Physician: Thomas Browne and the Role of Religion in Medical Practice', in Kathryn Murphy and Richard Todd, eds., '*A man very well studyed*': *New Contexts for Thomas Browne* (Leiden: Brill, 2009), 229–46, and Andrew Cunningham, 'Sir Thomas Browne and his *Religio Medici*: Reason, Nature and Religion', in Ole Peter Grell and Andrew Cunningham, eds., *Religio Medici, Medicine and Religion in Seventeenth Century England* (Aldershot: Scolar Press, 1996), 12–61.

[40] Much of the scholarship around this has centred on Milton; see, in particular, two excellent recent works: Joad Raymond, *Milton's Angels: The Early-Modern Imagination* (Oxford: Oxford University Press, 2010); and N. K. Sugimura, '*Matter of glorious trial*': *Spiritual and Material Substance in* Paradise Lost (New Haven: Yale University Press, 2009).

[41] *Religio Medici* 1.35.

[42] *Religio Medici* 1.36. Descartes's location of the soul in the pineal gland occurs in print in *The Passions of the Soul* (1649), though the idea was mooted earlier in an unpublished *Treatise on Man* (c.1637, published 1662) and in letters. See René Descartes, *Selected Philosophical Writings*, ed. and trans. John Cottingham (Cambridge: Cambridge University Press, 1988), 230.

and structurally, that even at such quasi-scientific moments, it is attended by creedal statements, that even while the text wrestles with a set of physical processes, the motion of matter on the last day, its rhetorical form is one of abnegating the need for explanation: 'I beleeve that our estranged and divided ashes shall unite againe, that our separated dust after so many pilgrimages and transformations into the parts of mineralls, plants, animals, elements, shall at the voyce of God returne into their primitive shapes; and joyne againe to make up their primary and predestinate forms.'[43] In the whirlwind of the eschaton, the dust out of which we were formed will remember its origin and return to its proper owner. Browne imagines the course of the world, from creation to apocalypse, as an exhalation of matter into its distinct and individual forms and its further individuation over time, till at the apocalypse, they will retreat through all their processes of dissolution and return to their pristine condition:

> As at the creation of the world, all the distinct species that we behold, lay involved in one masse, till the fruitfull voyce of God separated this united multitude into its severall species: so at the last day, when these corrupted reliques shall be scattered in the wildernesse of formes, and seeme to have forgot their proper habits, God by a powerfull voyce shall command them backe into their proper shapes, and call them out by their single individuals.[44]

In what borders on the philosophically comic, Browne parallels the dissolution of matter that occurs in death and decay with the sperm of Adam dividing and subdividing into the entire human race: 'Then shall appeare the fertilitie of Adam, and the magicke of that sperme that hath dilated into so many millions.' But any such dispersal of matter will be rectified and reversed, just as mercury does on the laboratory table: in its silvery liquidity being perhaps the most incongruous model of resurrection to be found: 'I have often beheld as a miracle, that artificiall resurrection and revivification of Mercury, how being mortified into thousand shapes, it assumes againe its owne, and returns into its numericall selfe.'[45] Just as quicksilver can miraculously revivify itself in 'artificiall resurrection', plants too are models of the reconstitution of the body at the apocalypse. Explaining the process of palingenesis, bringing a plant back to life from its burnt and ashy leaves, Browne insists that he is wearing the garb of a philosopher, though no scholastic or 'schoole philosopher'. Rather, he characterizes himself as 'a sensible artist', meaning an artist of experience and the sensible or bodily realm, in order to figure forth what God will accomplish, not metaphorically, but in 'ocular' fashion. This is a passage worth quoting at some length, for its rhetorical panache and disciplinary breadth:

> Let us speake naturally, and like philosophers, the formes of alterable bodies in these sensible corruptions perish not; nor, as we imagine, wholly quit their mansions, but retire and contract themselves into their secret and unaccessible parts, where they may best protect themselves from the action of their antagonist. A plant or vegetable consumed to ashes, to a contemplative and schoole philosopher seemes utterly

[43] *Religio Medici* 1.48.   [44] *Religio Medici* 1.48.   [45] *Religio Medici* 1.48.

destroyed, and the forme to have taken his leave for ever: but to a sensible artist the formes are not perished, but withdrawne into their incombustible part, where they lie secure from the action of that devouring element. This is made good by experience, which can from the ashes of a plant revive the plant, and from its cinders recall it into its stalk and leaves againe. What the art of man can doe in these inferiour pieces, what blasphemy is it to affirme the finger of God cannot doe in these more perfect and sensible structures? This is that mysticall philosophy, from whence no true scholler becomes an atheist, but from the visible effects of nature, growes up a reall divine, and beholds not in a dreame, as Ezekiel, but in an ocular and visible object the types of his resurrection.[46]

The pulverized matter and dust of being, in such an account, does not altogether forget its origin or 'wholly quit' its mansion, but rather, contracted into its 'secret and unaccessible' atomic or Platonic form, awaits a revivification. Burning does not destroy, but only rehouses the form and memory of its original, 'withdrawne into their incombustible part'.[47] Thomas Bartholin, the Danish physician, writing in his anatomy on the qualities of teeth, how their hardness gives them the ability to withstand fire, notes that Tertullian supposed they might, on these grounds, be the durable seedling of the self, 'that in them is the Seed of our future Resurrection'.[48] Matter, it seems, contains an innate homing instinct. At one moment philosophical, the next mystical, Browne incorporates both experiment and patristics, until he shifts to an insistence that the resurrection, as conducted by the finger of God, must have its 'types' and models in nature, and these be the ocular and experimental correlates he finds in his science.

Browne's is only a brush with natural philosophy, it might be said, as, earlier on, it was only a brush with Laudian ceremony—this is his essayistic strategy and not necessarily any penetrating contribution to early modern science. But seventeenth-century Europe was thoroughly wrapped up in just such questions of theological materialism, the nature of body, its relation to soul, and the curious memory of matter. Joseph Glanville, in the *Vanity of Dogmatizing* (1661), explores the tendency of matter, the leaf of a herb in this instance, to leave its tracery intact in its surrounding environment, the frosted water of a winter's night being imprinted with the memory of leaves that had lodged there earlier. Glanville comments:

> Now these airy Vegetables are presumed to have been made, by the reliques of these plantal emissions whose avolation was prevented by the condensed inclosure. And therefore playing up and down for a while within their liquid prison, they at last settle together in their natural order, and the Atomes of each part finding out their proper place, at length rest in their methodical Situation.[49]

---

[46] *Religio Medici* 1.48.

[47] A related report of such an experiment occurs in *Transactions of the Royal Society*, 3 November 1674.

[48] Thomas Bartholin, *Bartholinus anatomy* (1668), 347. The patristic sources are widespread, but include Augustine, *City of God*, 20.20; Tertullian, *Contra Marcion*, 5.9–10; and *On the Resurrection of the Flesh*, 35, the latter being Bartholin's source on teeth.

[49] Joseph Glanvill, *The vanity of dogmatizing* (1661), 46–7.

Atoms here are almost wilful and animate in the resumption of their form, Glanville going on to address this in terms of palingenesis directly, 'the artificial resurrection of Plants from their ashes, which Chymists are so well acquainted with'.

Robert Boyle, perhaps the foremost proponent of experimental and mechanical philosophy, is still closer to Browne, discussing the body in the resurrection by reference to alteration and physical identity, how water turned into ice retains the same corporeal identity, how the leaven of bread permits of change within stability, noting too 'those Chymical Experiment by which Kircherus... and others, are affirmed to have by a gentle heat been able to reproduce in well-closed Vials the perfect Idea's of Plants destroyed by the fire'. He notes also his own experience of some 'alcalisate ashes' of burnt poppy revivifying 'which seems to argue, that in the saline and earthy, i.e. the fix'd Particle of a Vegetable, that has been dissipated and destroyed by the violence of the fire, there may remain a Plastick Power inabling them to contrive disposed Matter, so as to reproduce such a Body as was formerly destroyed'.[50] Such plastic power is, he posits, the animating mechanism for deriving Eve from Adam's rib and the raising of Ezekiel's valley of dry bones.[51]

If the chemistry of resurrection is a viable subject, this does not, of course, obviate theological controversy. Guy Holland, writing his attack on mortalist ideas that the soul dies with the body, engages *Religio Medici* as an authority on the soul, though less to condemn Browne's recounting of his brief flirtation with 'the Arabian Heresy', than to enlist Browne in proving the indestructibility of matter, despite the continual mutation it may be subject to:

> Naturall and materiall forms themselves also do not perish at their parting from their matters, but onely are dissolved and dissipated, lying after that separation in their scatted atomes within the bosome of nature... so that the entity of their form remains still unperished after corruption, though not in the essence and formality of a form, or totally and compleatly. Thus teacheth the learned Authour of *Religio Medici*.[52]

Holland, a Jesuit, will not entirely have Browne as an ally, but as he proves useful, will borrow from him. Peter Heylyn, discussing the nature of resurrection in *Theologia veterum* (1654), similarly supposes that the coming together of dispersed pieces of dissolved and attenuated matter speaks to theological questions: 'For it is found by those who do trade in Chymistry, that the forms of things are kept invisibly in store, though the materials of the same be altered from what first they were', reporting on the experiment of reproducing a plant from its macerated atoms and the ashy salt extracted from a vigorous pummelling of its parts, remarking how 'The ingenuous Author of the Book called Religio

---

[50] Robert Boyle, *Some Physico-Theological Considerations about the Possibility of the Resurrection* (c.1675), in *The Works of Robert Boyle*, ed. Michael Hunter and Edward B. Davis, 12 vols. (London: Pickering & Chatto, 2000), VIII, 295–313 (302–3). Kircher's demonstration was performed to Queen Christina of Sweden in 1656.

[51] Ezekiel 37:7–10.

[52] Guy Holland, *Grand Prerogative of Humane Nature* (1653), 6–7.

Medici, doth also touch upon this rarity.'[53] Heylyn, it is true, is no scientist, but Robert Boyle, Henry Power, Kenelm Digby, and Henry More all provide impressive attempts to have physical phenomena yield eschatological conclusions, all supposing that physics, experimental and philosophical, should naturally lead to theology.

There were also exasperated responses to such physico-theology. Writing his critique of Henry More's millennial physics, *An explanation of the grand mystery of godliness* (1660), Joseph Beaumont takes the philosopher to task for his providing an account of the mechanisms by which the resurrected body with its 'Terrestrial consistency of Flesh and Blood' might find the celestial spheres too 'subtile' and incongruous an element to subsist in. 'Could Dr More forget', asks Beaumont, 'that both the Resurrection, and Ascension and residence of Bodies in Heaven, are not atchieved by any natural ways or means, but solely by the supernatural Power of God?'[54] It is perhaps strange that Browne, so insistent that he revels in things beyond the human ken, should not agree. Of all the mysteries and theological *arcana* that might provide juice for paradox, bodily translation to heaven in the apocalypse might seem high on the list. Yet, Browne insists that this is an area for the natural, rather than the contemplative, philosopher to take over.

Browne's chemical resurrection cannot entirely be rescued from itself by reference to the history of ideas, that that was how they thought back then. On the contrary, it was very much a cutting-edge concatenation of disciplines, and if few enough (if eminent) scientists had engaged in such topics, fewer still did so in the luscious language out of which Browne sculpts his concoctions of physico-theology. Having Boyle for a colleague in ideas on the material action of the last day may be some mitigation, but Browne is not Boyle, by any stretch of the mechanical imagination; Browne's is a poetics of the physics of the resurrection (bringing a third incompatible term to the table). We should not shy away too much from the implication that it is a 'poetics' of the topic insofar as it is incoherent and incomplete as either a piece of natural philosophy or as a piece of theology. But this is an incoherence with (almost) a theological basis. *Religio Medici* toys with and is content with the beautiful half-theory, and the mere glimpse of the world's inner workings, because the world is endued with the character and unknowability of God: science magnifies one's capacity for ignorance. Nature, down to its most microcosmic and microscopic miniature forms, even when studied, anatomized, and searched as far as it will go, always results in metaphor. It tells us something only obliquely and aslant about God. When Browne considers again the chemistry of last things, his theology in the laboratory prompts him to note that things burnt to their utmost vitrify, or turn glaseous:

> Philosophers that opinioned the worlds destruction by fire, did never dream of annihilation, which is beyond the power of sublunary causes; for the last and proper action of that element is but vitrification or a reduction of a body into glasse; and

---

[53] Peter Heylyn, *Theologia veterum, or, The summe of Christian theologie* (1654), 471.
[54] Joseph Beaumont, *Some observations upon the apologie of Dr. Henry More for his mystery of godliness* (1665), 10; Henry More, *An explanation of the grand mystery of godliness* (1660).

> therefore some of our chymicks facetiously affirm, that at the last fire all shall be crystallized and reverberated into glasse, which is the utmost action of that element.[55]

Few moments in the history of eschatology can surpass the poetics of this, when Browne suggests that the final conflagration would not lead to the destruction of the world, as such, because fire does not ultimately annihilate. Rather, the last stage of firing 'vitrifies', or renders the material glass. Thus, the world, in its final burning, may turn into a glass model globe of itself. This is a beautiful apocalypse. Browne shifts, with little sense of discordance, from the quotidian action of the laboratory to the divine action of the eschaton, and though attached to the sometimes pejorative 'chymicks', the word 'facetiously' may here bear the sense of polished and 'elegantly', rather than flippant or jokingly. The idea works for Browne, not because he is a card-carrying and committed member of the glass-apocalypse school of physics, but because it permits a passingly lovely glimpse of how to square divine benevolence with divine wrath. Who the philosophers and chymics are, I have yet to discover, though the royalist soldier, James Howell, suggests it to have a certain currency. Considering his sight of the Venetian glass-works, he writes in a letter to his brother, in a work published in 1645: 'Surely, that grand Universal-fire, which shall happen at the day of judgment, may by its violent-ardor vitrifie and turn to one lump of Crystal, the whole Body of the Earth', adding 'nor am I the first that fell upon this conceit'.[56]

Browne has shifted from the quasi-embodied soul of angels, through to the resurrection of the individual body and on, finally, to the apocalypse. If the dissolved individual can be saved, there is no such biblical promise of the preservation of nature, but Browne dismisses the possibility of absolute annihilation, by, it might be said, another sleight of hand. If one individual survives, who, in their microcosm, reiterates the entirety of the cosmos, then the whole world survives with them: 'Nor need we fear this term "annihilation" or wonder that God will destroy the workes of his creation: for man subsisting, who is, and will then truely appeare a microcosme, the world cannot bee said to be destroyed.'[57] He continues with a passage in which resurrected bodies will be able to see the totality of the world in, as William Blake might have it, a grain of sand, to discern a microcosm in the seed of a plant:

> For the eyes of God, and perhaps also of our glorified selves, shall as really behold and contemplate the world in its epitome or contracted essence, as now it doth at large and in its dilated substance. In the seed of a plant to the eyes of God, and to the understanding of man, there exists, though in an invisible way, the perfect leaves, flowers, and fruit thereof: (for things that are in *posse* to the sense, are actually existent to the understanding.) Thus God beholds all things, who contemplates as fully his workes in their epitome, as in their full volume, and beheld as amply the whole

---

[55] *Religio Medici*, 1.48.
[56] James Howell, *Epistolæ Ho-Elianæ: familiar letters domestic and forren* (1645), 55.
[57] *Religio Medici*, 1.50.

world in that little compendium of the sixth day, as in the scattered and dilated pieces of those five before.[58]

Religio Medici, in its butterfly way, does not settle for very long on any topic, from its opening doctrinal tease to his innocent brushes with heresy and on to his labyrinthine dealings with nature and the borderlands of science. The work occupies a perplexing terrain, with its admixture of the personal, the theological, and the scientific. Its style continually overwhelms, if indeed it does not become, its subject matter. It is prose which, in its rhetorical curvature, in what may be its theology of language, dazzles like few other writers, a prose which is rich, thick, and clogs the arteries.

Further Reading

Barbour, Reid, and Claire Preston, eds. *Sir Thomas Browne: The World Proposed* (Oxford: Oxford University Press, 2009).

Croll, Morris. *Style, Rhetoric, and Rhythm* (Princeton: Princeton University Press, 1966).

Cunningham, Andrew. 'Sir Thomas Browne and his *Religio Medici*: Reason, Nature and Religion', in Ole Peter Grell and Andrew Cunningham, eds., *Religio Medici, Medicine and Religion in Seventeenth Century England* (Aldershot: Scolar Press, 1996).

Dear, Peter, ed. *The Literary Structure of Scientific Argument: Historical Studies* (Philadephia: University of Pennsylvania Press, 1991).

Fish, Stanley. *Self-Consuming Artifacts: The Experience of Seventeenth-Century Literature* (Berkeley: University of California Press, 1972).

Killeen, Kevin. *Biblical Scholarship, Science and Politics in Early Modern England: Thomas Browne and the Thorny Place of Knowledge* (Aldershot: Ashgate, 2009).

Murphy, Kathryn, and Richard Todd, eds. *'A man very well studyed': New Contexts for Thomas Browne* (Leiden: Brill, 2009).

Osler, Margaret J., ed. *Rethinking the Scientific Revolution* (Cambridge: Cambridge University Press, 2000).

Preston, Claire. *Thomas Browne and the Writing of Early Modern Science* (Cambridge: Cambridge University Press, 2005).

Shapin, Steven. *A Social History of Truth: Civility and Science in Seventeenth-Century England* (Chicago: University of Chicago Press, 1994).

[58] *Religio Medici*, 1.50.

Bibliography

Primary Sources

Anon., *A Choice Banquet of Witty Jests, Rare Fancies, and Pleasant Novels* (London: printed by T.J. to be sold by Peter Dring, 1660).

Anon., *A collection of some modern epistles of Monsieur de Balzac. Carefully translated out of French. Being the fourth and last volume* (Oxford: Francis Bowman, 1639).

Anon., *A Commentarie or Exposition upon the Epistle to the Galatians* (Cambridge, 1604).

Anon., *A Continvation of all the Principall Occurrences which hath happened to the Leaguers* (1625).

Anon., *A Delicate Diet, for daintie mouthde droonkardes* (1576).

Anon., *A Detection of damnable driftes, practized by three Witches arraigned at Chelmisford in Essex* (1579).

Anon., *A dialogue between a doctor and his disciple, in which several passages of Holy Scripture are illustrated, and various points of Christian doctrine and practice explained*, BL Add MS 14,537 (7th–8th century).

Anon., *A Discourse of the Damned Art of Witchcraft* (London, 1631).

Anon., *A Fourme of Common Prayer to be used...necessarie for the present tyme and state* (London, 1572).

Anon., *A Fruteful and Plesaunt Worke of the Best State of a Publique Weale, and of the New Yle called Utopia* (London, 1555).

Anon., *A Golden Chaine* (London, 1591).

Anon., *A Hundreth Sundry Flowers* (London, 1573).

Anon., *A lyttel treatyse called the Image of Idlenesse, conteynyne certeyne matters moved betwene Walter Wedlock and Bawdin Bachelor*, trans. Olyver Oldwanton (London, 1555).

Anon., *A lyttel treatyse called the Image of Idlenesse, conteynyne certeyne matters moved betwene Walter Wedlock and Bawdin Bachelor. Translated out of the Troyane of Cornyshe tounge into Englyshe, by Olyver Oldwanton, and dedicated to the Lady Lust* (London, 1555), ed. Michael Flachmann, *Studies in Philology*, 87 (1990): 1–74.

Anon., *A most horrible & detestable Murther committed by a bloudie minded man vpon his owne Wife: and most strangely Reuealed by his Childe that was vnder fiue yeares of age* (1595).

Anon., *A Pageant of Spanish Humours* (London, 1599).

Anon., *A Parte of a Register* (Middelburg, 1593).

Anon., *A pleasant dialogue betweene the cap and the head* (London, 1564).

Anon., *A pleasaunt dialogue or disputation betweene the cap, and the head* (London, 1564).

Anon., *A Prayer for the good successe of her Majesties forces in Ireland* (London, 1599).

Anon., *A Quip for an Upstart Courtier* (London, 1592).

Anon., *A Treatise against Iudicial Astrologie* (London, 1601).
Anon., *A true declaration of the troublesome voyadge of M. J. Haukins to the parties of Guynea and the west Indies in the yeares of our Lord 1567 and 1568* (London, 1569).
Anon., *A Wife now the Widow of Sir Thomas Overbury* (London, 1614).
Anon. *Merie Tales Newly Imprinted and made by Master Skelton Poet Laureat* (1567).
Anon. *Mirror for Magistrates* (London: Iohn Charlewood, 1563).
Adlington, William, trans. *The XI. Bookes of the Goldern Asse* (London, 1566).
Ady, Thomas. *A Candle in the Dark* (London, 1656).
Agrippa, Cornelius. *De occulta philosophia libri tres* (Köln, 1533).
Alemán, Mateo. *The Life of Guzmán de Alfarache*, 2 vols. (London, 1599–1604).
Alexander, Gavin, ed. *Sidney's 'The Defence of Poesy' and Selected Renaissance Literary Criticism* (London: Penguin, 2004).
Andrewes, Lancelot. *Lancelot Andrewes: Selected Sermons and Lectures*, ed. Peter McCullough (Oxford: Oxford University Press, 2005).
—— *Lancelot Andrewes: Sermons*, ed. G. M. Story (Oxford: Clarendon Press, 1967).
Arber, Edward, ed. *A Transcript of the Registers of the Company of Stationers of London; 1554–1640 A.D.*, 4 vols. (London: privately printed, 1877).
Aristotle, *On Rhetoric: A Theory of Civic Discourse*, ed. and trans. George A. Kennedy (Oxford: Oxford University Press, 1991).
—— *The Art of Rhetoric*, trans. Hugh Lawson-Tancred (Harmondsworth: Penguin Classics, 1991).
Ascham, Roger. *English Works*, ed. William Aldis Wright (Cambridge: Cambridge University Press, 1904).
—— *Familiarium epistolarum libri tres*, ed. Edward Grant (London: Francis Coldock, 1576).
—— *The Scholemaster* (London, 1570).
—— *Toxophilus: The Schole of Shoting* (London, 1545).
Awdeley, John. *The Fraternitye of Vacabondes* (London, 1561).
Bacon, Francis. *Major Works*, ed. Brian Vickers (Oxford: Oxford University Press, 2002).
—— *Resuscitatio, or, Bringing into publick light severall pieces of the works, civil, historical, philosophical, and theological*, ed. William Rawley (London: Sarah Griffin for William Lee, 1657).
—— *The Advancement of Learning* (London: Henrie Tomes, 1605).
—— *The Essayes*, ed. M. Kiernan (Oxford: Oxford University Press, 1985).
—— *The remains of the Right Honorable Francis, Lord Verulam, Viscount of St. Albanes, sometimes Lord Chancellour of England being essayes and severall letters to severall great personages, and other pieces of various and high concernment not heretofore published* (London: B. Alsop for Lawrence Chapman, 1648).
—— *Works of Francis Bacon*, ed. J. S. Spedding, R. L. Ellis, and D. D. Heath, 14 vols. (London: 1857–74).
Baldwin, William. *A marvelous hystory intitulede, beware the cat* (London, 1584).
—— *A Treatise of Morall Philosophie by William Baldwin. Enlarged by Thomas Palfreyman. A Facsimile Reproduction of the Edition of 1620*, ed. Robert Hood Bowers (Gainesville, FL: Scholars Facsimiles and Reprints, 1967).
—— *A Treatise of Morall Phylosophie, contaynyng the sayinges of the wyse* (London, 1547).
—— *Beware the Cat: The First English Novel*, ed. William A. Ringler, Jr. and Michael Flachmann (San Marino, CA: Huntington Library, 1988).

Baldwin, William. *The Tretise of Morall Phylosophy...Newly perused, and augmented by William Baldwyn* (London, 1556).
—— *Wonderful News of the Death of Paul III* (London, 1552).
Bale, John. *The Image of Both Churches*, in *The Select Works of John Bale*, ed. Henry Christmas for the Parker Society (Cambridge: Cambridge University Press, 1849).
Bancroft, Richard. *A Sermon preached at Paules Crosse the 9. Of Februarie being the first Sunday in the Parlement, Anno. 1588* (London, 1588).
—— *Sermon Preached at Paules Crosse* (London, 1589).
Barclay, John. *Argenis* (London, 1621).
—— *Argenis*, ed. Mark Riley and Dorothy Pritchard Huber, Bibliotheca Latinitatis Novae/Medieval and Renaissance Texts and Studies, 273, 2 vols. (Assen: Royal van Gorcum and Tempe, AZ: Arizona Center for Medieval and Renaissance Studies, 2004).
—— *Barclay his Argenis: or, the Loves of Poliarchus and Argenis*, ed. Kingsmill Long (London, 1625).
—— *John Barclay his Argenis*, trans. Robert Le Grys (London, 1628).
Barlow, William. *The Summe and Substance of the Conference at Hampton Court* (London, 1604).
Barnaud, Nicholas. *Le Reveille-Matin des Francois, et de Leur Voisines* (Geneva, 1574), British Library MS Stowe 159.
Barret, Robert. *The Theorike and practike of moderne warres* (London, 1598).
Barrow, Henry. *A Brief Discoverie of the False Church* (Dort, 1590).
Bartholin, Thomas. *Bartholinus anatomy* (London, 1668).
Beadle, John. *Journal or Diary of a Thankful Christian* (London, 1656).
Beaumont, Francis. *The Woman Hater* (London, 1607).
Beaumont, Joseph. *Some observations upon the apologie of Dr Henry More for his mystery of godliness* (London, 1665).
Blundeville, Thomas. *The True Order and Methode of writing and reading Hystories* (London, 1574).
—— *The True Order of Wryting and Reading Histories* (London, 1574).
Booty, John E., ed. *The Book of Common Prayer 1559* (Washington, DC: Folger Shakespeare Library, 1976).
—— ed. *The First Prayer-Book of Edward VI* (London: The Ancient and Modern Library of Theological Literature, n.d.).
—— ed. *The Second Prayer-Book of King Edward VI* (London: The Ancient and Modern Library of Theological Literature, n.d.).
Booy, David, ed. *The Notebooks of Nehemiah Wallington, 1618–1654: A Selection* (Aldershot: Ashgate, 2007).
Borde, Andrew. *The Breuiary of Helthe* (London, 1547).
Bourchier, John, trans. *The castell of loue, translated out of Spanishe into Englyshe* (London: [R. Field for] Iohan Turke, 1548).
Boyle, Robert. *A Proemial Essay touching Experimental Essays*, in *Certain Physiological Essays* (London, 1661).
—— *An Account of Philaretus During His Minority*, in *Robert Boyle by Himself and His Friends*, ed. Michael Hunter (London: William Pickering, 1994).
—— *Some Physico-Theological Considerations about the Possibility of the Resurrection* (c. 1675), in *The Works of Robert Boyle*, ed. Michael Hunter and Edward B. Davis, 12 vols. (London: Pickering & Chatto, 2000), Vol. 8, 295–313.
—— *The Christian Virtuoso* (London, 1690).
—— *The Correspondence of Robert Boyle*, ed. Michael Hunter, Antonio Clericuzio, and Lawrence M. Principe (London: Pickering & Chatto, 2001).

—— *The Second Part of the Martyrdom of Theodora and Didymus* (London, 1687).
Brathwait, Richard. *Essays Upon the Five Senses* (London, 1620).
Breton, Nicholas. *A poste with a madde packet of letters* (London: [Thomas Creede] for Iohn Smethicke, 1602).
Brinsley, John. *Lvdvs literarivs: or, the grammar schoole* (London: Thomas Man, 1612).
B[rowne], I[ohn]. *The marchants avizo very necessarie for their sonnes and servants, when they first send them... to Spaine and Portingale* (London: William Norton, 1589).
Browne, Thomas. *Amico Opus Arduum Meditanti* ('To a Friend Intending a Difficult Work'), in *The Works of Sir Thomas Browne*, ed. Geoffrey Keynes, 4 vols., 2nd edn. (Chicago: University of Chicago Press, 1964).
—— *Religio Medici* (London: Printed for Andrew Crooke, 1642).
Buchanan, George. 'A Detection of Mary Queen of Scots', in *The Tyrannous Reign of Mary Stewart: George Buchanan's Account*, ed. W. A. Gatherer (Edinburgh: Edinburgh University Press, 1958).
—— *A Dialogue on the Law of Kingship among the Scots: A Critical Edition and Translation of George Buchanan's* De Iure Regni apud Scotos Dialogus, ed. and trans. Roger A. Mason and Martin S. Smith (Aldershot: Ashgate, 2004).
—— *Ane Admonitioun to the trew Lordis* in *Vernacular Writings of George Buchanan*, ed. P. Hume Brown (Edinburgh: William Blackwood & Sons, 1892).
—— *Ane detectioun of the duinges of Marie Quene of Scottes* (London: John Day, 1571).
—— *The History of Scotland Translated from the Latin of George Buchanan*, ed. and trans. James Aikman (Glasgow: Blackie, Fullarton & Co., 1827).
—— *The Political Poetry*, ed. Paul J. McGinnis and Arthur H. Williamson (Edinburgh: Lothian Print, 1995).
Bullein, William. *A Dialogue against the Fever Pestilence* (London, 1564).
—— *A dialogue both pleasant and piety-full, against the fever pestilence* (London, 1564).
—— *The governement of healthe* (London, 1558).
Burton, Robert. *The Anatomy of Melancholy*, ed. A. R. Shilleto (London and New York: George Bell & Sons, 1893).
—— *The Anatomy of Melancholy*, ed. Thomas C. Falulkner, Nicholas K. Kiessling, and Rhonda L. Blair, 6 vols. (Oxford: Clarendon Press, 1989–2000).
Cabala, mysteries of state in letters of the great ministers of K. James and K. Charles, wherein much of the publique manage of affaires is related/faithfully collected by a noble hand (London: M. M., G. Bedell, and T. Collins, 1654).
Carleton, George. *Astrologomania* (London, 1623).
Caroli Fitzgeofridi Affaniae (Oxford: Joseph Barnes, 1601).
Carpenter, John. *A Most Excellent Instruction For The Exact And Perfect Keeping Merchants Bookes of Accounts* (London, 1632).
Cartier, Jacques. *Navigations to Newe Fraunce*, trans. John Florio (London: H. Bynneman, 1580).
Castiglione, Baldassare. *Il Cortegiano* (London, 1528).
—— *The Book of the Courtier*, ed. Virginia Cox (London: Everyman, 1994).
Cavendish, Margaret. 'To the Natural Philosophers', in *Poems and Fancies* (London, 1664).
Caxton, William. *Fables of Aesop* (London, 1483).
Chamberlain, John. *Letters*, ed. Norman E. McClure (Philadelphia: American Philosophical Society, 1939).
Charité, Claude La. *Le stile et maniere de composer, dicter et escrire toutes sortes d'epistres, ou lettres missives* (London, 1553).

Chaucer, Geoffrey. 'The Canon's Yeoman's Prologue and Tale', in *The Riverside Chaucer*, ed. Larry D. Benson et al. (Oxford: Oxford University Press, 1987), 270–81.

Cicero, Marcus Tullius. *De Inventione*, trans. H. M. Hubbell (Cambridge, MA: Harvard University Press, 1968).

—— *De Oratore*, trans. E. W. Sutton (Cambridge, MA: Harvard University Press, 1968).

—— *Marcus Tullius Ciceroes Thre Bokes of Duties*, ed. Gerald O'Gorman (Washington, DC: Folger Books, 1990).

Cleaver, Robert. *A godlie forme of hovseholde government* (London: Felix Kingston for Thomas Man, 1598).

Cleland, James. *Institution of a Young Nobleman* (London, 1605).

Clere-Ville, Bartholomé de. *The copye of the letter folowynge whiche specifyeth of ye greatest and meruelous uisyoned batayle that euer was sene or herde of and also of the letter yt was sent frome the great Turke vnto our holy fad[er] ye pope of Rome* (Antwerp: John of Dousborowe, 1518).

Clifford, Anne. *The Diaries of Lady Anne Clifford*, ed. D. J. H. Clifford (Stroud: Sutton, 2003).

—— *The Memoir of 1603 and The Diary of 1616–1619*, ed. Katherine O. Acheson (Ontario: Broadview, 2007).

Codrington, Robert. 'In Honorem Viri Praeclarissim' [1660], RS Boyle Papers MS 36.

Coëffeteau, Nicolas. *Histoire de Poliarque et d'Argenis* (Paris, 1628).

Coke, John. *The debate betwene the heraldes of Englande and Fraunce* (London, 1550).

Colinson, Robert. *Idea Rationaria, or The Perfect Accomptant* (London, 1683).

Collinges, John. *The Excellent Woman: Discoursed more privately from Proverbs 31.29, 20, 31* (London, 1669).

Commonplace Book. British Library, Add. MS 32494.

Contarini, Gaspar. *De Magistratibus et Republica Venetorum* (London, 1543).

Copland, William. *Here beginneth a merye jest of a man that was called Howleglas* (London, 1530).

Corante, or News from Italy, Germany, Hungaria, Bohemia, Spaine and Dutchland (Amsterdam: Printed by Boyer Johnson, 1621).

Cornwallis, Sir William. *Essayes by Sir William Cornwallis the Younger*, ed. Don Cameron Allen (Baltimore: Johns Hopkins University Press, 1946).

Covarrubias. *Tesoro de la lengua castellana* (London, 1611).

Cowley, Hannah. *The Poetry of Anna Matilda* (London, 1788).

Cox, Leonard. *The Arte or Crafte of Rhetoryke* (London, 1532).

Culpeper, Nicholas. *Opus astrologicum, or, An astrological work left to posterity* (London: printed by J. Cottrel for Ri. Moone and Steph. Chatfield, 1654).

—— *The English Physitian, or An astrologo-physical discourse on the vulgar herbs of this nation* (London: George Thomason, 1652).

Dafforne, Richard. *The Apprentices Time-Entertainer Accomptantly* (London, 1640).

—— *The Merchant's Mirrour, or, Directions for the Perfect Ordering and Keeping of his Accounts* (London, 1684).

Dangerfield, Thomas. *Don Tomazo* (London, 1680).

Daniel, Samuel. *The Complaint of Rosamond* (London, 1592).

—— *The Defence of Ryme* (London: Edward Blount, 1603).

—— *The Queen's Arcadia* (London, 1605).

Daunce, Edward. *A briefe discourse of the Spanish state with a dialogue annexed intituled Philobasilis* (London: Richard Field, 1590).

Day, Angel. *The English secretarie* (London: Richard Jones, 1586).

Day, John. *The English secretary* (London: P. S[hort] for C. Burbie, 1599).

—— *The English secretorie* (London: Richard Jones, 1592).
Dee, John. *The Diaries of John Dee*, ed. Edward Fenton (Charlbury: Day Books, 1998).
Dekker, Thomas. 'A Knight's Conjuring' (London, 1607).
—— *Blurt Master-Constable. Or the Spaniards Night-Walke* (London, 1602).
—— *Match-me in London* (London, 1631).
Delicado, Francisco. *Retrato de la lozana andaluza* (Venice, 1528).
de Mediolano, Joannes. *The Englishmans doctor; or, The schoole of Salerne*, trans. John Harrington (London: John Helme and John Busby, 1608).
Dialogue between Rogerius and Jurisprudentia on tit.xiv of lib. i of the Codex, BL MS Royal 11.B.XIV (13th century).
Dickenson, John. *Greene in Conceit* (London: Richard Bradocke for William Jones, 1598).
Digby, Kenelm. *Observations Upon Religio Medici*, 2nd edn. (London, 1644).
—— *Two treatises in the one of which the nature of bodies, in the other, the nature of mans soule is looked into in way of discovery of the immortality of reasonable soules* (London, 1644).
Digges, Dudley. *The compleat ambassador, or, Two treaties of the intended marriage of Qu. Elizabeth of glorious memory comprised in letters of negotiation of Sir Francis Walsingham, her resident in France: together with the answers of the Lord Burleigh, the Earl of Leicester, Sir Tho. Smith, and others* (London: Tho. Newcomb for Gabriel Bedell and Thomas Collins, 1655).
Donne, John. *Devotions Upon Emergent Occasions* (London: printed by A. M. for Thomas Jones, 1624).
—— *Essays in Divinity*, ed. Evelyn M Simpson (Oxford: Clarendon Press, 1951).
—— *Paradoxes and Problems*, ed. Helen Peters (Oxford: Clarendon Press, 1980).
—— *The Oxford Edition of the Sermons of John Donne*, ed. Peter McCullough, 16 vols. (Oxford: Oxford University Press, forthcoming, 2013–).
—— *The Sermons of John Donne*, ed. George R. Potter and Evelyn M. Simpson, 10 vols. (Berkeley and Los Angeles: University of California Press, 1953–62).
Drayton, Michael. *The Battaile of Agincourt* (London: William Lee, 1627).
Du Bosc, I[erome] H[ainhofer], trans. *The secretary of ladies. Or, A new collection of letters and answers, composed by moderne ladies and gentlewomen* (London: Tho. Cotes for William Hope, 1638).
Dugdale, William. *The Life, Diary, and Correspondence of Sir William Dugdale*, ed. William Hamper (London: Harding, Lepard and Co., 1827).
DuMoulin, Pierre. *A Defence of the Catholicke Faith*, trans. John Sanford (London, 1610).
Elyot, Thomas. *Of the knowledge which maketh a wise man* (London, 1533).
—— *Pasquil the Playn* (London, 1533).
—— *The Bankette of Sapience* (London, 1539).
—— *The Boke named the Governour* (London, 1531).
Erasmus, Desiderius. *A formula for the composition of letters (Conficiendarum epistolarum formula)*, in *Collected Works of Erasmus*, trans. and ed. Charles Fantazzi (Toronto: University of Toronto Press, 1978).
—— 'Adages II vii 1 to III iii 100', in *The Collected Works of Erasmus*, trans. and annot. R. A. B. Mynors (Toronto: University of Toronto Press, 1992), Vol. 34, III iii 271.
—— *Collected Works of Erasmus: Literary and Educational Writings 2, De Copia/De Ratione Studii*, trans. Betty I. Knott, ed. Craig R. Thomson (Toronto: University of Toronto Press, 1978).
—— *Copia: foundations of the abundant style (De duplici copia verborum ac rerum commentarii duo)*, in *Collected works of Erasmus*, trans. and ed. Barry J. Knott (Toronto: University of Toronto Press, 1978), Vol. 24, 348–54.

Erasmus, Desiderius. *De conscribendis epistolis*, trans. Charles Fantazzi (Toronto: University of Toronto Press, 1985).
—— *De ratione studii* and *De copia* (London, 1512).
—— *Dialogus Ciceronianus* (London, 1528).
—— *Education of a Christian Prince* (London, 1516).
—— *Parabolae, sive similtudines* (London, 1587).
—— *Parallels Parabolae sive similia*, trans. R. A. B. Mynors, in *Collected Works of Erasmus*, ed. Craig R. Thompson (Toronto: University of Toronto Press, 1978).
—— *Praise of Folly and Letter to Maarten Van Dorp*, trans. Betty Radice and ed. A. H. T. Levi (London: Penguin Classics, 1993).
—— *The Ciceronian: A Dialogue on the Ideal Latin Style*, trans. Berry I. Knott, in *Collected Works of Erasmus, Vol. 28: Literary and Educational Writings 6*, ed. A. H. T. Levi (Toronto: University of Toronto Press, 1986).
—— *The Praise of Folie*, trans. Thomas Chaloner (London, 1549).
Evelyn, John. *The Diary of John Evelyn*, ed. E. S. de Beer, 6 vols. (Oxford: Clarendon Press, 1955).
F., T. *Newes from the North* (London, 1578).
Featley, John. *A Fountaine of Teares* (Amsterdam, 1646).
Fenner, John. *Defence of the Godlie Ministers, against the Slaunders of D. Bridges* (Middelburg, 1587).
Fenton, Geoffrey. *Certain Tragicall Discourses* (London, 1567).
Ferrer-Chivite, Manuel, ed. *La segunda parte de Lazarillo de Tormes: y de sus fortunas y aduersidades (1555)* (Madison: Hispanic Seminary of Medieval Studies, 1993).
Fidge, George. *The English Gusman; or The History of the Unparallel'd Thief James Hind* (London: T. N. for Humphrey, 1652).
Filmer, Robert. *Observations Concerning the Originall of Government* (London: R. Royston, 1652).
—— *Patriarcha and Other Writings*, ed. J. P. Somerville (Cambridge: Cambridge University Press, 1991).
Fleming, Abraham. *A panoplie of epistles, or, a looking glasse for the vnlearned* (London: Ralph Newberie, 1576).
Forman, Simon. *The Autobiography and Personal Diary of Dr. Simon Forman, 1552 to 1602*, ed. J. O. Halliwell (Oxford: Oxford University Press, 1849).
Foxe, John. *Actes and Monuments* (London: John Day, 1563).
—— *Comentarii in ecclesia gestarum rerum* (Wendelin Rihel, 1554).
Fulke, William. *Briefe and Plaine Declaration* (1584).
Fuller, Thomas. *The Worthies of England* (London, 1662).
Fulwood, William. *The enimie of idlenesse* (London: Leonard Maylard, 1568).
Gainsford, Thomas. *The secretaries studie containing new familiar epistles* (London: Roger Jackson, 1616).
Gale, Thomas. *The Institucion of Chyrurgerie* (London, 1586).
García, Carlos. *La desordenada codicia de los bienes agenos* [*Disordered coveting of other people's things*] (Paris, 1619).
Gascoigne, George. *A Hundreth Sundrie Flowres*, ed. G. W. Pigman III (Oxford: Oxford University Press, 2000).
—— *A hundreth sundrie flowres bounde vp in one small poesie* (London: Richard Smith, 1573).
—— 'Certayne Notes of Instruction Concerning the Making of Verse or Ryme in English', in *Ancient Critical Essays Upon English Poets and Poesy*, ed. Joseph Haslewood (London: Robert Triphook, 1815), Vol. 2.

—— *Droomme of Doomesday* (1576).

—— *Hundreth Sundrie Flowres* (London, 1572/3).

—— *Noble Arte of Venerie or Hunting* (London: Henry Bynneman for Christopher Barker, 1575).

—— *Voyage into Hollande* (London, 1575).

Gataker, Thomas. *A good vvife Gods gift and, a vvife indeed. Tvvo mariage sermons* (London: Iohn Hauiland for Fulke Clifton, 1623).

Gifford, George. *A Dialogue of Witches and Witchcraftes* (London, 1593).

—— *A Discourse of the Subtill Practices of Devilles by Witches and Sorcerers* (1587).

Gilbert, Humfrey. *A Discourse of a Dicouerie for a new Passage to Cataia* (London, 1576).

Gill, Alexander. *Logonomia Anglica* (London: John Beale, 1619).

Glanvill, Joseph. *The vanity of dogmatizing* (London, 1661).

Good Newes of the King of Bohemia (London, 1622).

Gosson, Stephen. *The Schoole of Abuse* (London, 1587).

Gouge, William. *Of Domesticall Duties Eight Treatises* (London: John Haviland for William Bladen, 1622).

Grafton, Richard. *Chronicle at Large and Meere History of the Affayres of Englande* (London: H. Denham for R. Tottle and H. Toye, 1569).

Green, Mary Anne Everett, ed. *Diary of John Rous* (London: Camden Society, 1856).

Greene, Robert. *A Notable Discovery of Coosenage* (London, 1591).

—— *Greenes Groats-Worth of wit* (London, 1592).

—— *Mamillia*, in *The Life and Complete Works of Robert Greene*, ed. Alexander B. Grosart (London: Huth Library, 1881–6).

—— *Morando: The Tritameron of Love* (London, 1584).

—— *Pandosto: The Triumph of Time* (London: John Wolfe, 1588).

—— *Penelope's Web* (London, 1587).

—— *Philomela The Lady Fitzvvaters nightingale* (London: R. B[ourne and E. Allde] for Edward White, 1592).

—— *The Honorable Historie of Friar Bacon and Friar Bungay* (London: Elizabeth Allde, 1630).

—— *The Third and Last Part of Conny-Catching* (London, 1592).

Greville, Fulke. *A Dedication to Sir Philip Sidney*, in *The Prose Works of Fulke Greville, Lord Brooke*, ed. John Gouws (Oxford: Oxford University Press, 1986), 10–11.

—— *The Life of the Renowned Sir Philip Sidney* (London, 1651).

Grymeston, Elizabeth. *Miscelanea. Meditations. Memoratives* (London, 1604).

Guazzo, Stefano. *La Civil Conversation* (London: T. Dawson for Richard Watkins, 1581).

—— *The civile conversation of M. Steeven Guazzo*, trans. George Pettie (London: Richard Watkins, 1581).

—— *The civile conversation of M. Stephen Guazzo, written first in Italian, diuided into foure bookes, the first three translated out of French by G[eorge] pettie* (London, 1586).

Guevara, Antonio de. *The golden boke of Marcus Aurelius emperour and eloquente orator* (London: Thomas Berthelet, 1535).

Guicciardini, Lodovico. *Hore di Ricreatione*, trans. into English in James Sanford', *The Garden of Pleasure* (London, 1573).

Gusmans Ephemeris: or, The Merry Rogues Calendar. Being an Almanack for 1662 (London, 1663).

Hakluyt, Richard. 'Epistle Dedicatory to Sir Walter Ralegh', in *Original Writings and Correspondence of the Two Richard Hakluyts*, ed. E. G. R. Taylor (London: Hakluyt Society, 1935).
—— *The Principal Navigations, Voyages, and Discoveries of the English Nation* (London, 1589).
Hall, Joseph. *An Historicall Expostulation against the beastlye abusers, both of Chirurgie, and Physyke, in owre tyme* (London, 1565).
—— *Epistles, the first volume: conteining two decads* (London: Eleazar Edgar & Samuel Macham, 1608).
—— *Epistles. containing two decades... The third and last volume* (London: E. Edgar, and A. Garbrand, 1611).
—— *The Great Imposter, laid open in a sermon at Grayes Inne, Febr. 2. 1623* (London: J. Haviland for H. Fetherstone, 1623).
Harcourt, Edward H., ed. *The Harcourt Papers* (Oxford, 1880), Vol. 1. University of Nottingham MS Portland PwV 89; East Sussex Record Office DUN/52/10/3.
Harding, Thomas. *A reiondre to M. Iewels relie against the sacrifice of the Masse* (London: John Fowler, 1567).
Harman, Thomas. *A Caveat or Warening for Common Cursetors vulgarely called Vagabones* (1567).
Harpsfield, Nicholas. *Dialogi sex contra summi pontificatus, monasticae vitae, sanctorum, sacrarum imaginum oppugnatores et pseudomartyres* (Christopher Plantin, 1566).
Harrison, William. 'The Description and Historie of England', in *The first and second volume of Chronicles*, ed. Raphael Holinshed (London, 1587; 2nd edn.).
Harvey, Gabriel. *A New Letter* (London, 1593).
—— *Fovre Letters, and Certaine Sonnets* (London: John Wolfe, 1592).
—— *Foure Letters and Certaine Sonnets, especially touching Robert Greene* (London, 1592).
—— *Letter-Book*. British Library, Sloane MS 93.
—— *Letter-Book of Gabriel Harvey, A.D. 1573–1580*, ed. Edward John Long Scott, Camden Society, NS 33 (1884).
—— *Pierces Supererogation or a new prayse of the old asse* (London, 1593).
—— *The Works of Gabriel Harvey*, ed. Alexander Grosart (London: The Huth Library, 1884).
—— and Edmund Spenser. *Three proper, and wittie, familiar letters: lately passed betvveene tvvo vniuersitie men: touching the earthquake in Aprill last, and our English refourmed versifying With the preface of a wellwiller to them both* (London: H. Bynneman, 1580).
Harvey, John. *A discoursive probleme concerning prophesies* (London, 1588).
Harvey, Richard. *An astrological discourse upon the conjunction of Saturne & Jupiter* (London, 1583).
—— *Lambe of God* (London: J. Windet for W. P[onsonby], 1590).
—— *Theologicall Discourse of the Lamb of God* (London, 1590).
Hayward, John. *Life and Raigne of King Henrie IIII*, ed. John J. Manning, Camden Society, 4th series, 42 (London: Camden Society, 1991).
—— *The First Part of the Life and Raigne of King Henrie IIII* (London, 1599).
—— *The Lives of the III. Normans, Kings of England* (London, 1613).
Herbert, George. *The Works of George Herbert*, ed. F. E. Hitchinson (Oxford: Clarendon Press, 1941).
Hereafter ensue the trewe encountre or batayle lately don betwene. Englande and: Scotland (London, 1513).

Heylyn, Peter. *Theologiaveterum, or, The summe of Christian theologie* (London, 1654).
Hill, Thomas. *An almanack... in forme of a booke of memorie necessary for all such, as haue occasion daylie to note sundry affayres, eyther for receytes, payments, or such lyke* (London, 1571).
Hobbes, Thomas, trans. *Eight Bookes of The Peloponnesian Warre* (London, 1629).
Hoby, Margaret. *The Private Life of an Elizabethan Lady: The Diary of Lady Margaret Hoby 1599–1605*, ed. Joanna Moody (Stroud: Sutton, 1998).
Holinshed, Raphael. *Chronicles of England, Scotland and Ireland* (London: Reginald Wolfe, 1577).
Holland, Guy. *Grand Prerogative of Humane Nature* (London, 1653).
Holland, Henry. *A Treatise Against Witchcraft* (London, 1590).
Hooker, Richard. *Folger Library Edition of the Works of Richard Hooker*, gen. ed. W. Speed Hill, 7 vols. (Cambridge, MA: Harvard University Press, 1977–98).
—— *Of the Laws of Ecclesiastical Polity*, ed. Arthur Stephen McGrade (Cambridge: Cambridge University Press, 1989).
Hopton, Arthur. *A new almanacke and prognostication for the yeare of our Lord God 1613* (1613), Bodleian Ash. 66.
Hoskyns, John. *The Life, Letters, and Writings of John Hoskyns, 1566–1638*, ed. Louise Brown Osborn (New Haven: Yale University Press, 1937).
Howard, Henry. *A defensatiue against the poyson of supposed prophesaies* (London, 1583).
Howell, James. *Epistolae Ho-Elianae. Familiar letters domestic and forren; divided into six sections, partly historicall, politicall, philosophicall, upon emergent occasions* (London: Humphrey Moseley, 1645).
Hubert, Conrad. *A briefe treatise concerning the burning of Bucer and Phagius at Cambridge*, trans. Arthur Golding (London: Thomas Marsh, 1562).
Hyde, Edward, Earl of Clarendon. *History of the Rebellion and Civil Wars in England*, ed. W. Dunn Macray (Oxford: Clarendon Press, 1888).
James VI. *The True Law of Free Monarchies*, and 'Speech to Parliament, 21 March 1610', in *Political Writings of James I and VI*, ed. J. P. Somerville (Cambridge: Cambridge University Press, 1994).
Jocelyn, Robert, ed. *The Private Diarie of Elizabeth, Viscountess Mordaunt* (Duncairn: privately printed, 1856).
Jonson, Ben. 'Conversations with Drummond', in *Works of Ben Jonson*, ed. C. H. Herford and Percy and Evelyn Simpson (Oxford: Clarendon Press, 1947).
—— 'Masque of Queens', in *Ben Jonson: The Complete Masques*, ed. Stephen Orgel (New Haven: Yale University Press, 1969).
—— *The Fortunate Isles*, in *Ben Jonson: The Complete Masques*, ed. Stephen Orgel (New Haven: Yale University Press, 1969).
—— *The Works of Ben Jonson*, ed. C. H. Herford, and Percy and Evelyn Simpson, 11 vols. (Oxford: Clarendon Press, 1925–52).
—— *Timber or Discoveries* (London, 1641).
Kempe, William. *The education of children in learning* (London: John Potter and Thomas Gubbin, 1588).
Kinde Kit, of Kingstone. *Westward for Smelts* (London, 1620).
Knox, John. *A Faithful Admonition to the Professors of God's Truth in England*, in *The Works of John Knox*, ed. David Laing (Edinburgh: Wodrow Society, 1854).
—— *History of the Reformation*, in *The Works of John Knox*, ed. David Laing (Edinburgh: Wodrow Society, 1854).

Knox, John. *On Rebellion*, ed. Roger A. Mason (Cambridge: Cambridge University Press, 1994).
La segunda parte de Lazarillo de Tormes: y de sus fortunas y aduersidades (Antwerp: Martin Nucio, 1555).
Lambarde, William. *Perambulation of Kent* (London, 1576).
Langley, Thomas. *Langley 1637 a new almanack and prognostication* (London, 1637).
Les feits merveilleux, ensemble la vie du gentil Lazare de Tormes (Lyon, 1560)
Lever, Ralph. *The Arte of Reason, rightly termed Witcraft* (London: H. Bynneman, 1573).
Lindsay, Robert of Pitscottie. *The Historie and Chronicles of Scotland*, ed. A. J. G. Mackay (Edinburgh: Blackwood, 1911).
Lipsius, Justus. *Politica: Six Books of Politics or Political Instruction*, ed. and trans. Jan Waszink (Assen: Royal Van Gorcum, 2004).
Lowth, William. *The Christian mans Closet* (London, 1581).
Luna, Juna de. *The Pursuit of the History of Lazarillo de Tormes* (London, 1622).
Lupton, Thomas. *Siuqila, Too Good To Be True* (London, 1580).
Lyly, John. *Euphues. The anatomy of wyt* (London: [T. East] for Gabriel Cawood, 1578).
—— *Euphues: The Anatomy of Wit and Euphues and His England by John Lyly*, ed. Leah Scragg (Manchester: Manchester University Press, 2003).
—— *Papp with a Hatchet* (London, 1589).
—— *Sapho and Phao*, in *The Complete Works of John Lyly* ed. R. Warwick Bond (Oxford: Clarendon Press, 1902).
—— *Sixe Court Comedies* (London, 1632).
—— *The Plays of John Lyly: Eros and Eliza*, ed. Michael Pincombe (Manchester: Manchester University Press, 1996).
Lynne, Walter. *A Watch-word for wilfull women* (London, 1581).
Magnus, Albertus. *The Boke of secretes of Albertus Magnus, of the vertues of Herbes, stones and certaine beasts* (London, 1525).
—— *The Book of the secrets of Albertus Magnus* (London, 1525).
Man, Judith. *An Epitome of the History of Faire Argenis and Polyarchus* (London, 1640).
Manningham, John. *The Diary of John Manningham of the Middle Temple, 1602–1603*, ed. Robert Parker (Hanover: University Press of New England, 1976).
Manuale, sententias aliquot diuinas & morales complectens (London: Peter Short, 1594).
Marcellinus, Ammianus. *The Romane Historie*, trans. Philemon Holland (London, 1609).
Massinger, John. *The secretary in fashion* (London: Godfrey Emerson, 1640).
Matthew, Tobie. *A collection of letters, made by Sr Tobie Mathews Kt To which are added many letters of his own, to severall persons of honour, who were contemporary with him* (London: Henry Herringman, 1659).
Medina, Juan de. *De la orden que en algunos pueblos de España se ha puesto en la limosna: para remedio de los verdaderos pobres* [*Of the order that in certain Spanish towns has been imposed for alms for the remedy of the true poor*] (Salamanca: Juan de Junta, 1545).
Mellis, John. *A Briefe Instruction and Maner How to Keepe Bookes of Accompts After the Order of Debitor and Creditor* (London, 1588).
Melvin, William. *The Sonne of the Rogue, or, The Politicke Theefe* (London, 1638).
Meres, Francis. *Witt's Academy: A Treasurie of Goulden Sentences, Similes and Examples* (London, 1636).
Milton, John. *John Milton: Political Writings*, ed. Martin Dzelzainis (Cambridge: Cambridge University Press, 1991).

Montaigne, Michel de. *Les Essais*, ed. J. Balsamo, M. Magnien, and C. Magnien-Simonet (Paris: Gallimard, 2007).

—— *The Complete Essays*, ed. and trans. M. A. Screech (Harmondsworth: Penguin Books, 1991).

—— *The Complete Essays of Montaigne*, trans. Donald M. Frame (Stanford: Stanford University Press, 1958).

Montemayor, Jorge de. *Diana of George of Montemayor: translated out of Spanish into English*, trans. Bartholomew Yong (London: Edm. Bollifant for G[eorge] B[ishop], 1598).

More, Henry. *An explanation of the grand mystery of godliness* (London, 1660).

More, Sir Thomas. *A dyaloge of syr Thomas More, knyght* (London, 1529).

—— *A fruteful, and pleasaunt worke of the beste state of a publyque weale, and of the newe yle called Utopia*, trans. Ralph Robinson (London, 1551).

—— *History of King Richard III* (London, 1518).

—— *Libellus vere aureus, nec minus salutaris quam festivus, de optimo reipublicae statu deque nova insula Utopia* (London, 1516).

—— *Richard III*, in *The Complete Works of St. Thomas More*, ed. Richard S. Sylvester, 12 vols. (New Haven: Yale University Press, 1963).

—— *Utopia*, ed. Richard Marius (London: J. M. Dent, 1994).

Morgan, Matthew. 'An Elegy on the Death of the Honorable Mr Robert Boyle' (1692).

Morley, Thomas. *A plaine and easie introduction to practicall musicke* (1597).

Munday, Anthony. *Amadis de Gaule*, ed. Helen Moore (Aldershot: Ashgate, 2004).

Nabokov, Vladimir. *Lolita* (London: Penguin, 1995).

Nashe, Thomas. *Have With You to Saffron-Walden* (London: John Danter, 1596).

—— *The Anatomie of Absurditie* (London: Charles Whittingham, 1589).

—— *The Return of the Renowned Caualiero Pasquill* (London: John Charlewood, 1589).

—— *The Unfortunate Traveller*, in *The Unfortunate Traveller and Other Works*, ed. J. B. Steane (New York: Penguin Books, 1973).

—— *The Works of Thomas Nashe*, ed. R. B. McKerrow, rev. F. P. Wilson, 5 vols. ([1904] Oxford: Basil Blackwell, 1958).

New epistles of Mounsieur de Balzac, trans. Sr. Richard Baker Knight, 3 vols. (London: Fra. Eglesfield, Iohn Crooke, and Rich. Serger, 1638).

Newes from the Low Countries, or a Courant out of Bohemia, Poland, Germanie, &c. (Amsterdam, 1621).

Newton, Isaac. *Principia Mathematica* (London, 1687).

Nichols, Thomas. *A pleasant description of the fortunate ilandes, called the Ilands of Canaria with their straunge fruits and commodities* (London, 1583).

—— trans. *The Hystory Writtone by Thucidides* (London, 1550).

Occasional Reflections upon Several Subjects, Whereto is Premis'd a Discourse upon such kind of Thoughts (London, 1665).

Oldcastle, Hugh. *A Briefe Instruction and Maner How to Keepe Bookes of Accompts After the Order of Debitor and Creditor* (now lost, but reissued by John Mellis in 1588).

Painter, William. *The Palace of Pleasure*, ed. Joseph Jacobs, 3 vols. (New York: Dover, 1966).

Palfreyman, Thomas. *A Treatyce of Morall Philosophy* (London, 1557).

—— *Morall Phylosophie* (London, 1610).

Papp with a Hatchet (London: T. Orwin, 1589).

Peacham, Henry. *The Truth of Our Times* (London, 1638).

Penry, John. *A Treatise Containing the Aequity of an Humble Supplication* (Oxford: Joseph Barnes, 1587).

Pepys, Samuel. *The Diary of Samuel Pepys*, ed. Robert Latham and William Matthews, 11 vols. (Berkeley and Los Angeles: University of California Press, 1970–83).
Perkins, William. *Christian oeconomie: or, A short survey of the right manner of erecting and ordering a familie according to the scriptures*, trans. Tho. Pickering Bachelar of Diuinitie (London, 1609).
Petition Directed to Her Most Excellent Majestie (Middelburg, 1592).
Pettie, George. *A Petite Palace of Pettie His Pleasure* (London, 1576).
—— *A Petite Pallace of Pettie His Pleasure*, ed. Herbert Hartman (London: Oxford University Press, 1938).
Petty, William. 'A Dialogue concerning shipping', BL Add MS 72893.
—— 'Laudem Navis Geminae', BL Sloane MS 360, fos. 73^r–80^r.
Philomusus, *The academy of complements* (London: H. Mostley, 1640).
Phiston, William, trans. *The most pleasaunt and delectable historie of Lazarillo de Tormes, a Spanyard and of his maruellous fortunes and aduersities. The second part* (London: Thomas Creede for John Oxenbridge, 1596).
Piccolomini, Aeneas Silvius. *De Gestis Concilii Basiliensis Commentariorum*, ed. and trans. Denys Hay and W. K. Smith (Oxford: Clarendon Press, 1967).
—— *The goodli history of the moste noble and beautyfull ladye Lucres of Scene in Tuskane* (London: John Day, 1553).
Plat, Hugh. *The Floures of Philosophie* (London: Frauncis Coldocke and Henry Bynneman, 1581).
Plat, Neil. *Sundrie New and Artificiall Remedies against Famine* (London: Peter Short, 1596).
Plutarch. *Plutarch's Lives Englished by Sir Thomas North*, 10 vols. (London: J. M. Dent, 1910).
—— *The Philosophie, commonlie called, the Morals*, trans. Philemon Holland (London: Dent, 1911).
Positions Wherein Those Primitive Circvumstances be Examined, which are Necessarie for the Training vp of Children, either for skill in their booke, or health in their bodie (London, 1581).
Prayers and Thenkesgiving to be used by all the Kings Majesties loving servants for the Happy Deliverance of his Majestie…from the most traitorous and bloody intended Massacre by Gunpowder (London, 1605).
Proclamation against Certaine Seditious and Schismatical Bookes and Libels (London, 1589).
Purchas, Samuel. *Hakluytus posthumous or Purchas his pilgrims* (London, 1625).
—— *Purchas His Pilgrimage* (London, 1613).
Purfoote, Thomas. *A blanke and perpetuall Almanacke* (London, 1566).
Puttenham, George. *The Arte of English Poesie* (London, 1589).
Quevedo, Francisco de. *Historia de la vida del buscón, llamado Don Pablos* (London, 1626).
Quintilian. *Institutio Oratoria*, trans. Donald Russell, 4 vols. (Cambridge, MA: Harvard University Press, 2001).
—— *Pasquils Jests: With the Merriments of Mother Bunch* (London, 1632).
Ralegh, Walter. *Dialogue betweene a Counsellor of State and a Justice of the Peace* (London, 1614).
—— *The prerogative of parliaments in England* (London, 1628).
Rastell, John. *New boke of Purgatory* (London, 1530).
Ratzel, Friedrich. *The History of Mankind* (London, 1896).
Rawley, Walter. *Sylva Sylvarum* (London, 1627).
Rider, Cardanus. *British Merlin* (1680), Folger A2254.5.
Ross, Alexander. *Medicus Medicatus* (London, 1645).
Rowland, David. *The Pleasant History of Lazarillo de Tormes*, ed. Gareth Alban Davies and Frank Martin (Newtown: Gwasg Gregynog, 1991).

────── trans. *The Pleasaunt Historie of Lazarillo de Tormes a Spaniarde, wherein is conteined his maruelous deedes and life* (London: Abell Jeffes, 1586).

Roy, William. *A proper dyaloge betwene a gentillman and an husbandman* (London, 1529).

Salicetus, Nicolas. *The Antidotarius* (Robert Wyer: London, 1530).

Sallust. *Here begynneth the famous cronycle of the warre, which the romayns had against Iugurth vsurper of the kyngdome of Numidy*, trans. Alexander Barclay (London, 1522).

Samuel, William. *The arte of angling* (London, 1577).

Savile, Henry, trans. *The Ende of Nero and Beginning of Galba* (London, 1591).

Scot, Reginald. *The Discoverie of Witchcraft* (London: William Brome, 1584).

Scrinia Ceciliana, mysteries of state & government in letters of the late famous Lord Burghley, and other grand ministers of state, in the reigns of Queen Elizabeth, and King James, being a further additional supplement of the Cabala (London: G. Bedell and T. Collins, 1663).

Seneca. *Epistulae Morales*, trans. Richard M. Gunmere, 10 vols. (Cambridge, MA and London: Harvard University Press, 1917).

────── *The Workes of Lucius Annaeus Seneca Newly Inlarged and Corrected*, ed. Thomas Lodge (London, 1620).

Shakespeare, William. *Much Ado about Nothing*, ed. A. R. Humphreys, The Arden Shakespeare (New York: Routledge, 1994).

────── *Othello*, ed. E. A. J. Honigmann, The Arden Shakespeare (Walton-on-Thames: Nelson, 1997).

────── *The Historie of Troylus and Cresseida* (London: R. Bonian and H. Walley, 1609).

────── *The Riverside Shakespeare*, ed. G. Blakemore Evans (Chicago: Houghton Mifflin Harcourt, 1997).

────── *The Winter's Tale*, ed. J. H. P. Pafford, The Arden Shakespeare (London: Methuen, 1963).

Sherry, Richard. *A Treatise of Schemes and Tropes* (London, 1550).

Shyp of Folys of the Worlde, trans. John Barclay (London, 1509).

Sidney, Sir Philip. *A Defence of Poetry* (London: Printed for William Ponsonby, 1595).

────── *A Defence of Poetry*, ed. Jan van Dorsten (Oxford: Oxford University Press, 1966).

────── *A Defence of Poetry*, in Brian Vickers, ed., *English Renaissance Literary Criticism* (Oxford: Clarendon Press, 1999), 336–91.

────── *An Apology for Poetry*, ed. Geoffrey Shepherd, rev. and expanded by R. W. Maslen (Manchester: Manchester University Press, 2002).

────── *The Countesse of Pembrokes Arcadia... Now since the first edition augmented and ended* (London: [John Windet] for William Ponsonbie, 1593).

────── *The Defence of Poesy*, in *Sir Philip Sidney: The Major Works*, ed. Katherine Duncan-Jones (Oxford: Oxford University Press, 2002).

────── *The Major Works*, ed. Katherine Duncan-Jones (Oxford: Oxford University Press, 2002).

Smith, A. H., and G. M. Barker, eds. *The Papers of Nathaniel Bacon of Stiffkey* (Norwich: Norfolk Record Society, 1983).

Smith, Henrie. *A Preparative to Mariage* (London: R. Field for Thomas Man, 1591).

Smith, John. *The Generall Historie of Virginia, New-England, and the Summer Isles* (London, 1624).

────── *The mysterie of rhetorique unveil'd* (London, 1665).

Smith, Thomas. *A Discourse of the Commonweal* (London, 1549).

────── *A letter sent by I.B. Gentleman* (London, 1572).

────── *Communicacion*, BL Add MS 4,149, BL Add MS 48,047.

────── *Communicacon of the Quenes Highnes Mariage* (London, 1561).

Smith, Thomas. *De recta et emendata anglicae scriptione* (London, 1568).
—— *De Republica Anglorum*, printed as *The common-welth of England* (London, 1589).
—— *De Republica Anglorum: A Discourse on the Commonwealth of England*, ed. L. Alston (Cambridge: Cambridge University Press, 1906).
Soto, Domingo de. *Deliberación en la causa de los pobres* (Salamanca: Juan de Junta, 1545).
Spenser, Edmund. *Complaints. Containing Sundrie Small Poems of the Worlds Vanitie, London 1591* (Amderstam: Theatrum Orbis Terrarum, facs. edn. 1970).
—— *The Poetical Works of Edmund Spenser*, ed. J. Smith and E. de Selincourt (Oxford: Oxford University Press, 1912).
Sprat, Thomas. *The History of the Royal-Society of London* (London, 1667).
Stafford, William. *A compendious or briefe examination of certayne ordinary complaints of divers of our country men in these our days* (London, 1581).
Stanley, Thomas. *History of Philosophy*, 4 vols. (London, 1655–62).
Starkey, Thomas. *A Dialogue between Pole and Lupset*, ed. T. F. Mayer (London: Royal Historical Society, 1989).
Streater, J. *A Further Continuance of the Grand Politick Informer* (London, 1653).
T., W., trans. *The letters of Mounsieur de Balzac. Translated into English, according to the last edition* (London: Richard Clotterbuck, 1634).
Tales and quicke answeres, very mery and pleasant to rede (London, 1532).
Tarlton, Richard. *Tarltons newes out of Purgatorie* (London, 1590).
Taylor, Thomas. *The Practice of Repentance* (London, 1629).
Tertullian, *De Carne Christi* 5.4, in *Ante-Nicene Fathers*, ed. Alexander Roberts, vol. 3 (Edinburgh: T. & T. Clark, 1885).
Travers, Walter. *Defence of the Ecclesiastical Discipline* (Middelburg: Richard Schilders, 1588).
Vaughan, Sir William. *The Newlanders Cure* (London: F. Constable, 1630).
—— *The Spirit of Detraction* (London: George Norton, 1611).
Vives, Juan Luis. *De institutione foeminae Christianae* (London, 1524).
—— *De Subventione Pauperum* (London, 1526).
—— *Education of a Christian Woman* (London, 1524).
—— *The Instruction of a Christen Woman*, trans. Richard Hyrde, ed. Virginia Beauchamp, Elizabeth Hageman, and Margaret Mikesell (Urbana: University of Illinois Press, 2002).
W., H., trans. *A pageant of Spanish humours Wherin are naturally described and liuely portrayed, the kinds and quallities of a signior of Spaine* (London: John Windet for John Wolfe, 1599).
Whately, William. *A Bride-Bush or, A Direction for Married Persons. Plainely Describing the Duties common to both, and peculiar to each of them* (London: Felix Kingston for Thomas Man, 1619).
Whibley, Charles, ed. *The Golden Ass of Apuleius*, trans. William Adlington (London: David Nott, 1893).
Whitehorne, Peter. *Certeine wayes* (London, 1573).
Whitgift, John. *Most Godly and Learned Sermon* (London: Thomas Orwin for Thomas Chard, 1589).
Willes, Richard. *A History of Travayle in the West and East Indies* (London, 1577).
Wilson, Thomas, *A discourse uppon usurye* (London, 1572).
—— *The Arte of Rhetorique* (London: Richard Grafton, 1553).

—— *The Rule of Reason* (London, 1561).
Wroth, Mary. *Poems of Mary Wroth*, ed. Josephine A. Roberts (Baton Rouge: Louisiana State University Press, 1983).
—— *The First Part of the Countess of Montgomery's Urania*, ed. Josephine A. Roberts (Binghamton, NY: Medieval & Renaissance Texts & Studies, 1995).
—— *The Second Part of the Countess of Montgomery's Urania*, ed. Josephine A. Roberts (Binghamton, NY: Medieval & Renaissance Texts & Studies, 1995).
Wyatt, Thomas. *The Quyete of Minde* (London, 1528).
Xenophon. *The Bookes of Xenophon contayning the discipline, schole and education of Cyrusthe noble Kyng of Persie*, trans. William Barker (London, 1552).
—— *The Education of Cyrus*, trans. Wayne Ambler (Ithaca, NY and London: Cornell University Press, 2001).
Younge, Richard. *Drunkard's Character* (London, 1638).

Secondary Sources

Adlard, John. 'Cleopatra as Isis', *Archiv für das Studium der neueren Sprachen und Literatur*, 212 (1975): 324–8.
Aers, David. 'A Whisper in the Ear of Early Modernists; or, Reflections on Literary Critics Writing the "History of the Subject"', in David Aers, ed., *Culture and History 1350–1600: Essays on English Communities, Identities and Writing* (New York and London: Harvester Wheatsheaf, 1992), 177–202.
Alexander, Gavin. *Writing After Sidney: The Literary Response to Sir Philip Sidney, 1586–1640* (Oxford: Oxford University Press, 2006).
Almasy, Rudolph P. 'Richard Hooker's Book VI: A Reconstruction', *The Huntington Library Quarterly*, 42.2 (Spring 1979): 117–39.
Altman, Janet Gurkin. *Epistolarity: Approaches to a Form* (Columbus, OH: Ohio State University Press, 1982).
Alwes, Derek. 'Robert Greene's Duelling Dedications', *English Literary Renaissance*, 30.3 (2000): 373–95.
—— *Sons and Authors in Elizabethan England* (Newark: University of Delaware Press, 2004).
Amelang, James S. *The Flight of Icarus: Artisan Autobiography in Early Modern Europe* (Stanford: Stanford University Press, 1998).
Anderson, Benedict. 'Neither Acts Nor Monuments', *English Literary Renaissance*, 41:1 (2011): 3–30.
Andersson, D. C. *Lord Henry Howard (1540–1614): An Elizabethan Life* (Woodbridge: Boydell & Brewer, 2009).
Archer, Ian, Felicity Heal and Paulina Kewes, eds. *The Oxford Handbook to Holinshed* (Oxford: Oxford University Press, 2012).
Archer, Jayne. '"A notable kinde of rime": The "fine invention" of Gascoigne's *Certayne Notes of Instruction* (1575)', in Gillian Austen, ed., *New Essays on George Gascoigne* (New York: AMS Press, forthcoming).
Ardila, Juan Antonio Garrido. *El género picaresco en la crítica literaria* (Madrid: Biblioteca Nueva, 2008).
—— 'La tradición picaresca española en Inglaterra', *Bulletin of Hispanic Studies*, 76 (1999): 453–69.

Ariosto, Ludovico. *Orlando Furioso*, trans. Sir John Harington, ed. Robert McNulty (Oxford: Clarendon Press, 1972).
Armitage, David. *The Ideological Origins of the English Empire* (Cambridge: Cambridge University Press, 2000).
Atherton, Ian. '"The Itch Grown a Disease": Manuscript Transmission of News in the Seventeenth Century', in Joad Raymond, ed., *News, Newspapers and Society in Early Modern Britain* (London and Portland, OR: Frank Cass, 1999), 39–65.
Aubrey, John. *Brief Lives*, ed. John Buchanan-Brown (Harmondsworth: Penguin, 2000).
Augustine, *De Doctrina Christiana*, ed. and trans. R. P. H. Green (Oxford: Clarendon Press, 1995).
Austen, Gillian. *George Gascoigne*, Studies in Renaissance Literature 24 (Woodbridge: D. S. Brewer, 2008).
—— 'George Gascoigne and the Transformations of Phylomene', in Sabine Coelsch-Foisner, ed., *Elizabethan Literature and Transformation*, Studies in English and Comparative Literature 15 (Tübingen: Stauffenberg-Verlag, 1999), 107–19.
Austin, Warren B. 'Gabriel Harvey's "Lost" Ode on Ramus', *Modern Language Notes*, 61 (1946): 242–7.
—— 'William Withie's Notebook: Lampoons on John Lyly and Gabriel Harvey', *Review of English Studies*, 23 (1947): 297–309.
Babb, Lawrence A. *Sanity in Bedlam: A Study of Robert Burton's 'The Anatomy of Melancholy'* (Ann Arbor: Michigan State University Press, 1959).
Bakewell, Sarah. *How to Live: A Life of Montaigne* (London: Chatto & Windus, 2010).
Baldwin, B., ed. and trans. *The Philogelos or Laughter-Lover* (Amsterdam: Gieben, 1983).
Baldwin, C. S. *Renaissance Literary Theory and Practice: Classicism in the Rhetoric and Poetic of Italy, France and England, 1400–1600*, ed. Donald L. Clark (New York: Columbia University Press, 1939).
Bamborough, J. B. 'Introduction', in Robert Burton, *The Anatomy of Melancholy*, ed. Rhonda Blair, Thomas Faulkner, and Nicolas Kiessling, 6 vols. (Oxford: Clarendon Press, 1989–2000).
Barbour, Reid. *Deciphering Elizabethan Fiction* (Newark: University of Delaware Press, 1993).
—— *Thomas Browne: A Life in Full* (forthcoming).
—— 'Thomas Browne's *A Letter to a Friend* and the Semiotics of Disease', *Renaissance Studies*, 24:3 (2010): 403–19.
—— and Claire Preston, eds. *Sir Thomas Browne: The World Proposed* (Oxford: Oxford University Press, 2009).
Barish, Jonas. 'The Prose Style of John Lyly', *English Literary History*, 23 (1986): 14–35.
Barker, Francis. *The Tremulous Private Body: Essays on Subjection* (Ann Arbor: University of Michigan Press, 1995).
Barnard, John, and D. F. McKenzie, eds. *The Cambridge History of the Book in Britain, Volume IV: 1557–1695* (Cambridge: Cambridge University Press, 2002).
Bauer, Ralph. *The Cultural Geography of Colonial American Literatures: Empire, Travel, Modernity* (Cambridge: Cambridge University Press, 2003).
Beck, Mark, ed. *A Companion to Plutarch* (Oxford: Wiley-Blackwell, forthcoming).
Bedford, Ronald, Lloyd Davis, and Philippa Kelly, eds. *Early Modern Autobiography: Theories, Genres, Practices* (Ann Arbor: University of Michigan Press, 2006).
—— —— —— *Early Modern English Lives: Autobiography and Self-Representation, 1500–1660* (Aldershot: Ashgate, 2007).

Beier, A. L. *Masterless Men: The Vagrancy Problem in England, 1560–1640* (London: Methuen, 1985).

Beilin, Elaine V., ed. *The Examinations of Anne Askew* (Oxford: Oxford University Press, 1996).

Bell, Ilona. *Elizabethan Women and the Poetry of Courtship* (Cambridge: Cambridge University Press, 1998).

Bellany, Alastair. *The Politics of Court Scandal in Early Modern England: News Culture and the Overbury Affair* (Cambridge: Cambridge University Press, 2002).

Belsey, Catherine. *The Subject of Tragedy: Identity and Difference in Renaissance Drama* (London and New York: Methuen, 1985).

Benjamin, Andrew E., ed. *The Figural and the Literal: Problems of Language in the History of Science and Philosophy* (Manchester: Manchester University Press, 1987).

Bennett, H. *English Books and Readers, 1603–1640* (Cambridge: Cambridge University Press, 1970).

—— 'The Wit's Progress: A Study in the Life of Cicero', *The Classical Journal*, 30.4 (1935): 193–202.

Bennett, Josephine W. 'Spenser and Gabriel Harvey's *Letter-Book*', *Modern Philology*, 29 (1931): 163–86.

Bennett, R. E. 'Four Paradoxes by Sir William Cornwallis the Younger', *Harvard Studies and Notes in Philology and Literature*, 13 (1931): 219–40.

Birch, Thomas., ed. *The Court and Times of Charles I*, 2 vols. (1848).

Bishop, Tim. 'The Gingerbread Host: Tradition and Novelty in the Jacobean Masque', in David Bevington and Peter Holbrook, eds., *The Politics of the Stuart Court Masque* (Cambridge: Cambridge University Press, 1998), 88–120.

Bjornson, Richard. *The Picaresque Hero in European Fiction* (Madison: University of Wisonsin Press, 1977).

Black, Jack L., ed. *The Martin Marprelate Tracts: A Modernized and Annotated Edition* (Cambridge: Cambridge University Press, 2008).

Black, Scott. *Of Essays and Reading in Early Modern Britain* (New York: Palgrave Macmillan, 2006).

Blair, Ann. 'Reading Strategies for Coping with Information Overload ca. 1500–1700', *Journal of the History of Ideas*, 64.1 (2003): 11–28.

Blanchard, W. Scott. *Scholars' Bedlam: Menippean Satire in the Renaissance* (London and Toronto: Associated University Presses, 1995).

Blank, Paula. *Broken English: Dialects and the Politics of Language in Renaissance Writings* (New York: Routledge, 1996).

Bloom, Harold. *Shakespeare: The Invention of the Human* (New York: Riverhead Books, 1998).

Boccaccio, Giovanni. *Boccaccio in English, 1494–1620*, ed. Guyda Armstrong (London: Modern Humanities Research Association, 2011).

—— *The Decameron*, trans. G. H. McWilliam, 2nd edn. (London: Penguin, 1995).

Bodin, Jean. *Method for the Easy Comprehension of History*, trans. Beatrice Reynolds (New York: Columbia University Press, 1945).

Boivin, Nicole. *Material Cultures, Material Minds: The Role of Things in Human Thought, Society and Evolution* (Cambridge: Cambridge University Press, 2008).

Bolgar, R. R. *The Classical Heritage and its Beneficiaries* (Cambridge: Cambridge University Press, 1954).

Bonahue, Edward T. '"I know the place and the persons": The Play of Textual Frames in Baldwin's *Beware the Cat*', *Studies in Philology*, 91 (1994): 283–300.

Bonheim, Helmut. 'Robert Greene's *Gwydonius. The Carde of Fancie*', *Anglia, Zeitschrift für englische Philologie*, 96 (1978): 45–64.

Booth, Steven. *The Book Called Holinshed's Chronicles: An Account of its Inception, Purpose, Contributors, Contents, Publication, Revision and Influence on William Shakespeare* (San Francisco: Book Club of California, 1968).

Booy, David. *Autobiographical Writings by Early Quaker Women* (Aldershot: Ashgate, 2004).

—— *Personal Disclosures: An Anthology of Self-Writings from the Seventeenth Century* (Aldershot: Ashgate, 2002).

Botonaki, Effie. *Seventeenth-Century English Women's Autobiographical Writings: Disclosing Enclosures* (Lampeter: Edwin Mellen Press, 2004).

Boulton, James, ed. *Samuel Johnson: The Critical Heritage* (London: Routledge, 1971).

Boutcher, W. 'Marginal Commentaries: The Cultural Transmission of Montaigne's *Essais* in Shakespeare's England', in P. Kapitaniak and J.-M. Maguin, eds., *Shakespeare et Montaigne* (Montpellier: Société Française Shakespeare, 2004), 13–27.

Bowen, B. C. 'Ciceronian Wit and Renaissance Rhetoric', *Rhetorica*, 16.4 (1998): 409–29.

—— *Humour and Humanism in the Renaissance* (Aldershot: Ashgate, 2004).

—— *One Hundred Renaissance Jokes* (Birmingham: Summa, 1988).

Bowers, Terence N. 'The Production and Communication of Knowledge in William Baldwin's *Beware the Cat*: Toward a Typographic Culture', *Criticism*, 33 (1991): 1–29.

Bradbrook, Muriel C. 'No Room at the Top: Spenser's Pursuit of Fame', in J. R. Brown, ed., *Elizabethan Poetry*, Stratford-Upon-Avon Studies 2 (London: Edward Arnold, 1960): 91–109.

Braden, Gordon. 'Biography', in Gordon Braden, Robert Cummings, and Stuart Gillespie, eds., *The Oxford History of Literary Translation in English*, Vol. 2, 1550–1660 (Oxford: Oxford University Press, 2010), 322–30.

Bradshaw, Brendan. 'Transalpine Humanism', in J. H. Burns and Mark Goldie, eds., *The Cambridge History of Political Thought, 1450–1700* (Camrbidge: Cambridge University Press, 1994), 95–131.

Brennan, Michael. 'The Texts of Peter Martyr's *De orbe novo decades* (1504–1628): A Response to Andrew Hadfield', *Connotations*, 6 (1996/7): 277–45.

—— and Noel J. Kinnamon, *A Sidney Chronology, 1554–1654* (Basingstoke: Palgrave Macmillan, 2003).

Brownlees, Nicholas. *Corantos and Newsbooks: Language and Discourse in the First English Newspapers (1620–1641)* (Pisa: Edizioni ETS, 1999).

—— *The Language of Periodical News in Seventeenth-Century England* (Newcastle upon Tyne: Cambridge Scholars Publishing, 2011).

Bruster, Douglas. 'The New Materialism in Early Modern Studies', in *Shakespeare and the Question of Culture* (Basingstoke: Palgrave Macmillan, 2003), 191–206.

Brydon, Michael A. *The Evolving Reputation of Richard Hooker: An Examination of Responses, 1600–1714* (Oxford: Oxford University Press, 2006).

Bühler, Curt C. 'A Survival from the Middle Ages: William Baldwin's Use of the *Dictes and Sayings*', *Speculum*, 23 (1948): 76–80.

Bullough, Geoffrey. *Narrative and Dramatic Sources of Shakespeare*, Vol. 5 (London: Routledge, 1964).

Burckhardt, Jacob. *The Civilization of the Renaissance* (Oxford: Phaidon Press, 1944).

Burke, Peter. 'Representations of the Self from Petrarch to Descartes', in Roy Porter, ed., *Rewriting the Self: Histories from the Renaissance to the Present* (London: Routledge, 1997), 17–28.

—— 'Tacitism, Scepticism, and Reason of State', in J. H. Burns and Mark Goldie, eds., *The Cambridge History of Political Thought, 1450–1700* (Cambridge: Cambridge University Press, 1991), 479–98.

—— *The Art of Conversation* (Cambridge: Cambridge University Press, 1993).

—— *The Renaissance Sense of the Past* (London: Edward Arnold, 1969).

Burns, J. H. *The True Law of Kingship: Concepts of Monarchy in Early Modern Scotland* (Oxford: Clarendon Press, 1996).

Cala, Carmen Espejo, ed. *Barroco y comunicación* (Seville: University of Seville, 2011).

Campbell, Julie. 'Masque Scenery and the Tradition of Immobilization in the *First Part of the Countess of Montgomery's Urania*', *Renaissance Studies*, 22.2 (2008): 221–39.

Cantar, Brenda. *Menaphon* (Ottawa: Dovehouse Editions, 1996).

Capp, Bernard. *English Almanacs, 1500–1800: Astrology and the Popular Press* (Ithaca and New York: Cornell University Press, 1979).

Cardinal, Roger. 'Unlocking the Diary', *Comparative Criticism*, 12 (1990): 71–87.

Carey, John. *The Intellectuals and the Masses: Pride and Prejudice among the Literary Intelligentsia, 1880–1939* (London: Faber, 1999).

Carlson, Eric. 'English Funeral Sermons as Sources: The Example of Piety in Pre-1640 Sermons', *Albion*, 32 (2000): 567–97.

—— 'The Boring of the Ear: Shaping the Pastoral Vision of Preaching in England, 1540–1640', in Larissa Taylor, ed., *Preachers and People in the Reformations and Early Modern Period* (Leiden: Brill, 2001), 249–96.

Carpenter, H. J. 'Furse of Moreshead: A Family Record of the Sixteenth Century', *Reports and Transactions of the Devonshire Association for the Advancement of Science, Literature and Art*, 26 (1894): 168–84.

Carver, Robert H. F. *The Protean Ass: The Metamorphoses of Apuleius from Antiquity to the Renaissance* (Oxford: Oxford University Press, 2007).

Cavallo, J. 'Joking Matters: Politics and Dissimulation in Castiglione's *Book of the Courtier*', *Renaissance Quarterly*, 53.2 (2000): 402–24.

Cavanagh, Shelia. *Cherished Torment: The Emotional Geography of Lady Mary Wroth's 'Urania'* (Pittsburgh: Duquesne University Press, 2007).

Cave, Terrence. *How to Read Montaigne* (London: Granta, 2007).

—— *The Cornucopian Text: Problems of Writing in the French Renaissance* (Oxford: Oxford University Press, 1979).

Chambers, E. K. *The Elizabethan Stage*, 4 vols. (Oxford: Clarendon Press, 1967).

Chapman, K. P. '"Lazarillo de Tormes", a Jest-Book and Benedik', *Modern Language Review*, 55.4 (1960): 565–7.

Chastel, André. *The Palace of Apolidon*, The Zaharoff Lecture for 1984–5 (Oxford: Clarendon Press, 1986).

Clark, Sandra. *The Elizabethan Pamphleteers* (Rutherford, NJ: Fairleigh Dickinson University Press, 1983).

—— *Thinking With Demons: The Idea of Witchcraft in Early Modern Europe* (Oxford: Clarendon Press, 1997).

Clarke, Danielle. *The Politics of Early Modern Women's Writing* (Harlow: Pearson Education, 2001).

Clarke, Danielle. '"The sovereign's vice begets the subjects error": The Duke of Buckingham, "Sodomy" and Narratives of Edward II, 1622-28', in Tom Bettridge, ed., *Sodomy in Early Modern Europe* (Manchester: Manchester University Press, 2002), 46-64.

Clarke, Elizabeth. 'Diaries', in Michael Hattaway, ed., *A New Companion to English Renaissance Literature and Culture* (Oxford: Wiley-Blackwell, 2010), Vol. 1, 447-52.

Clegg, Cyndia. *Press Censorship in Elizabethan England* (Cambridge: Cambridge University Press, 1997).

Cogswell, Thomas. '"Published by Authoritie": Newsbooks and the Duke of Buckinghams's Expedition to the Île de Ré', *Huntington Library Quarterly*, 67 (2004): 1-25.

—— 'The Politics of Propaganda: Charles I and the People in the 1620s', *Journal of British Studies*, 29 (1990): 187-215.

Colclough, David. '*Parrhesia*: The Rhetoric of Free Speech in Early Modern England', *Rhetorica*, 17 (1999): 177-212.

Colie, Rosalie. *Paradoxia Epidemica: The Renaissance Tradition of Paradox* (Princeton: Princeton University Press, 1966).

—— *The Resources of Kind: Genre Theory in the Renaissance* (Berkeley: University of California Press, 1973).

Collinson, Patrick. 'Andrew Perne and his Times', in Patrick Collinson, ed., *Andrew Perne: Quatercentenary Studies*, Cambridge Bibliographical Society, Monograph 11 (1991), 1-34.

—— 'John Field and Elizabethan Puritanism', in T. Bindoff, J. Hurstfield, and C.H. Williams, eds., *Elizabethan Government and Society: Essays Presented to Sir John Neale* (London: Athlone, 1961), S127-S162.

—— 'John Foxe and National Conciousness', in Christopher Highley and John N. King, eds., *John Foxe and his World* (Aldershot: Ashgate, 2002), 10-34.

—— *The Elizabethan Puritan Movement* (London: Jonathan Cape, 1967; repr. Oxford: Clarendon Press, 1990).

—— *The Religion of Protestants* (Oxford: Clarendon Press, 1982).

Connor, Rebecca Elisabeth. *Women, Accounting, and Narrative: Keeping Books in Eighteenth-Century England* (London and New York: Routledge, 2004).

Conti, Brooke. '*Religio Medici*'s Profession of Faith', in Reid Barbour and Clair Preston, eds., *Sir Thomas Browne: The World Proposed* (Oxford: Oxford University Press, 2008), 149-67.

Cooper, Helen. *The English Romance in Time: Transforming Motifs from Geoffrey of Monmouth to the Death of Shakespeare* (Oxford: Oxford University Press, 2004).

Corbett, Margery, and Ronald Lightbown. *The Comely Frontispiece: The Emblematic Title-page in England, 1550-1660* (London: Routledge & Kegan Paul, 1979).

Cox, Virginia. *The Renaissance Dialogue: Literary Dialogue in its Social and Political Contexts, Castiglione to Galileo* (Cambridge: Cambridge University Press, 1992).

Coxon, S. 'Friendship, Wit and Laughter in Heinrich Bebel's *Facetiae*', *Oxford Berman Studies*, 36.2 (2007): 306-20.

Crane, Mary Thomas. *Framing Authority: Sayings, Self, and Society in Sixteenth-Century England* (Princeton: Princeton University Press, 1993).

Crawford, Julie. *Marvelous Protestantism: Monstrous Births in Post-Reformation England* (Baltimore: Johns Hopkins University Press, 2005).

—— 'Reconsidering Early Modern Women's Reading, or, How Margaret Hoby Read her de Mornay', *Huntington Library Quarterly*, 73.2 (2010): 193-223.

Cressy, David. *Birth, Marriage, and Death: Ritual, Religion, and the Life Cycle in Tudor and Stuart England* (Oxford: Oxford University Press, 1997).

—— *Dangerous Talk: Scandalous, Seditious, and Treasonable Speech in Pre-Modern England* (Oxford: Oxford University Press, 2010).

—— *Travesties and Transgressions in Tudor and Stuart England* (Oxford: Oxford University Press, 2000).

Crewe, Jonathan V. *Unredeemed Rhetoric: Thomas Nashe and the Scandal of Authorship* (Baltimore: Johns Hopkins University Press, 1982).

Croll, Morris W. 'Attic Prose: Lipsius, Montaigne, Bacon', in Stanley Fish, ed., *Seventeenth-Century Prose: Modern Essays in Criticism* (New York: Oxford University Press, 1971), 3–25.

—— *Style, Rhetoric, and Rhythm: Essays by Morris W. Croll* (Princeton: Princeton University Press, 1966).

Cruz, Anne. 'Sonnes of the Rogue: Picaresque Relations in England and Spain', in Giancarlo Maiorino, ed., *The Picaresque: Tradition and Displacement* (London: University of Minnesota Press, 1996), 248–72.

Culhane, Peter. 'Livy in Early Jacobean Drama', *Translation and Literature*, 14 (2005): 21–44.

—— 'Philemon Holland's Livy: Peritexts and Contexts', *Translation and Literature*, 13 (2004): 268–86.

Culpeper, Jonathan, and Merja Kytö. *Early Modern English Dialogues: Spoken Interaction as Writing* (Cambridge: Cambridge University Press, 2010).

Cummings, Robert. 'Mirrors for Policy', in Gordon Braden, Robert Cummings, and Stuart Gillespie, eds., *The Oxford History of Literary Translation in English, Vol. 2, 1550–1660* (Oxford: Oxford University Press, 2010), 408–17.

Cunningham, Andrew. 'Sir Thomas Browne and his *Religio Medici*: Reason, Nature and Religion', in Ole Peter Grell and Andrew Cunningham, eds., *Religio Medici, Medicine and Religion in Seventeenth Century England* (Aldershot: Scolar Press, 1996), 12–61.

Curtis, Cathy. 'From Sir Thomas More to Robert Burton: The Laughing Philosopher in the Early Modern Period', in Ian Hunter, Stephen Gaukroger, and Conal Condren, eds., *The Persona of the Philosopher in Early Modern Europe* (Cambridge: Cambridge University Press, 2006), 90–112.

Cust, Richard. 'News and Politics in Early Seventeenth-Century England', *Past & Present*, 112 (1986): 60–90.

Dahl, Folke. *A Bibliography of English Corantos and Periodical Newsbooks, 1620–1642* (London: Language Arts & Disciplines, 1952).

—— *Dutch Corantos, 1618–1650: A Bibliography* (The Hague: Koninklijke, 1946).

Daniell, David. 'Tyndale and Foxe', in David Loades, ed., *John Foxe: An Historical Perspective* (Aldershot: Ashgate, 1999), 24–8.

Davies, Gareth. 'David Rowland's *Lazarillo de Tormes* (1576): The History of Translation', *The National Library of Wales Journal*, 28 (1995): 349–87.

Davies, Kathleen M. 'Continuity and Change in Literary Advice on Marriage', in R. B. Outhwaite, ed., *Marriage and Society* (London: Europa Publications, 1981), 58–80.

Davis, Walter R. *Idea and Act in Elizabethan Fiction* (Princeton: Princeton University Press, 1969).

Day, Matthew. 'Hakluyt, Harvey, Nashe: The Material Text and Early Modern Nationalism', *Studies in Philology*, 104.3 (2007): 281–305.

Day, Robert. 'Posey Rings', *Journal of the Royal Historical and Archaeological Association of Ireland*, 4:6 (1883): 61–4.

Daybell, James. 'Material Meanings and the Social Signs of Manuscript Letters in Early Modern England', *Literature Compass*, 6.3 (2009), 647–67.
—— *Women Letter-Writers in Tudor England* (Oxford: Oxford University Press, 2006).
Deakins, Roger. 'The Tudor Prose Dialogue: Genre and Anti-Genre', *Studies in English Literature*, 20 (1980): 5–23.
Dear, Peter. 'Narratives, Anecdotes, and Experiments: Turning Experience into Science in the Seventeenth Century', in Peter Dear, ed., *The Literary Structure of Scientific Argument* (Philadelphia: University of Pennsylvania Press, 1991), 135–63.
—— ed. *The Literary Structure of Scientific Argument: Historical Studies* (Philadelphia: University of Pennsylvania Press, 1991).
Deetz, James. *In Small Things Forgotten: An Archaeology of Early American Life* (New York: Anchor Books, 1977).
Delaney, Paul. *British Autobiography in the Seventeenth Century* (London: Routledge & Kegan Paul, 1969).
Dent, R. W. *John Webster's Borrowing* (Berkeley: University of California Press, 1960).
Desan, Philippe, ed. *Dictionnaire de Michel de Montaigne*, 2nd edn. (Paris: Champion, 2007).
Descartes, René. *Selected Philosophical Writings*, ed. and trans. John Cottingham (Cambridge: Cambridge University Press, 1988).
Deutsch, Helen. 'The Body's Moments', *Prose Studies*, 27 (2005): 11–26.
Dewar, Mary. 'The Authorship of the "Discourse of the Commonweal"', *Economic History Review*, 2nd ser., 19 (1966): 388–400.
Donaldson, Gordon. *Scottish Church History* (Edinburgh: Scottish Academic Press, 1985).
Donovan, Kevin J. 'Recent Studies in Robert Greene (1968–88)', *English Literary Renaissance*, 20.1 (1990): 163–75.
Dooley, Brendan, and Sabrina Baron, eds. *The Politics of Information in Early Modern Europe* (London and New York: Routledge, 2001).
Dowd, Michelle M. 'Recent Studies in Early Modern English Life Writing', *English Literary Renaissance*, 40.1 (2010): 132–62.
—— and Julie A. Eckerle, eds. *Genre and Women's Life Writing in Early Modern England* (Aldershot: Ashgate, 2007).
Duffy, Eaon. *The Stripping of the Altars: Traditional Religion in England, 1400–1580* (New Haven: Yale University Press, 1992).
Duncan, Douglas. *Ben Jonson and the Lucianic Tradition* (Cambridge: Cambridge University Press, 1979).
Dunn, Kevin. *Pretexts of Authority: The Rhetoric of Authorship in the Renaissance Preface* (Stanford: Stanford University Press, 1994).
Dzelzainis, Martin. 'Bacon, "Of Simulation and Dissimulation"', in Michael Hattaway, ed., *A Companion to Renaissance Literature and Culture* (Oxford: Blackwell, 2000), 233–40.
—— 'The Ciceronian Theory of Tyrannicide from Buchanan to Milton', in Roger A. Mason and Caroline Erskine, eds., *George Buchanan: Political Thought in Early Modern Britain and Europe* (Aldershot: Ashgate, 2012).
Edelen, George. 'Hooker's Style', in W. Speed Hill, ed., *Studies in Hooker* (Cleveland: Press of Case Western University, 1972), 241–77.
Eisenberg, Daniel. *Romances of Chivalry in the Spanish Golden Age* (Delaware: Juan de la Cuesta, 1982).

Erskine, Caroline. 'Humanism and Calvinism in George Buchanan's *Rerum Scoticarum Historia*', *Records of the Scottish Church History Society*, 35 (2005): 90–118.

—— Alan R. MacDonald, and Michael Penman, eds. *Scotland: The Making and Unmaking of the Nation* (Dundee: Dundee University Press, 2007).

Erwin, William. '"Physicians are like Kings": Medical Politics and *The Duchess of Malfi*', *English Literary Renaissance*, 28.1 (1998): 95–117.

Es, Bart van. 'Michael Drayton, Literary History, and Historians in Verse', *Review of English Studies*, 59 (2008): 255–69.

Evans, Joan. *A History of The Society of Antiquaries* (Oxford: At the University Press by Charles Batey for The Society of Antiquaries, 1956).

—— *English Posies and Posy Rings* (London: Oxford University Press, 1931).

Evans, Robert C. *Habits of Mind: Evidence and Effects of Ben Jonson's Reading* (Lewisburg: Bucknell University Press, 1995).

Evenden, Elizabeth, and Thomas S. Freeman, *Religion and the Book in Early Modern England: The Making of John Foxe's 'Book of Martyrs'* (Cambridge: Cambridge University Press, 2011).

Fabri, Pierre. 'Au poulpe épistolaire', in Catherine Magnien, ed., *L'épistolaire au XVIe siècle* (Paris: Éditions de Rue d'Ulm, 2001), 17–32.

Farrow, Kenneth D. *John Knox: Reformation Rhetoric and the Traditions of Scots Prose, 1490–1570* (Bern: Peter Lang, 2004).

Felch, Susan M. 'The Rhetoric of Biblical Authority: John Knox and the Question of Women', *Sixteenth-Century Journal*, 26 (1995): 805–21.

Ferguson, Arthur B. *Clio Unbound: Perception of the Social and Cultural Past in Renaissance England* (Durham, NC: Duke University Press, 1979).

—— *Utter Antiquity: Perceptions of Prehistory in Renaissance England* (Durham, NC: Duke University Press, 1993).

Ferguson, Margaret. 'Nashe's *The Unfortunate Traveller*: The "Newes of the Maker" Game', *English Literary Renaissance*, 11 (1981): 165–82.

Ferrell, Lori Anne. *Government by Polemic: James I, the King's Preachers, and the Rhetorics of Conformity, 1603–1625* (Stanford: Stanford University Press, 1999).

—— and Peter McCullough, eds. *The English Sermon Revised: Religion, Literature and History, 1600–1750* (Manchester: Manchester University Press, 2000).

Fincham, Kenneth. *Prelate as Pastor: The Episcopate of James I* (Oxford: Clarendon Press, 1990).

Firth, C. H., and R. S. Rait, eds. *Acts and Ordinances of the Interregnum, 1642–1660* (London: HMSO, 1911).

Fish, Stanley. *Self-Consuming Artifacts: The Experience of Seventeenth Century Literature* (Berkeley: University of California Press, 1972)

—— ed. *Seventeenth-Century Prose: Modern Essays in Criticism* (New York: Oxford University Press, 1971).

Fitzalan-Howard, H. G. *The Lives of Philip Howard, Earl of Arundel, and of Anne Dacres, his Wife* (London: Hurst and Blackett, 1857).

Fowler, Elizabeth, and Roland Greene, eds. *The Project of Prose in Early Modern Europe and the New World* (Cambridge: Cambridge University Press, 1997).

Fowler, Roger. *Language in the News: Discourse and Ideology in the Press* (London and New York: Routledge, 1991).

Fox, Adam. *Oral and Literate Culture in England, 1500–1700* (Oxford: Oxford University Press, 2000).

Fox, Adam and Daniel Woolf, eds. *The Spoken Word: Oral Culture in Britain, 1500–1850* (Manchester: Manchester University Press, 2002).

Fox, Ruth A. *The Tangled Chain: The Structure of Disorder in 'The Anatomy of Melancholy'* (Berkeley and London: University of California Press, 1976).

Frame, Donald M. *Montaigne: A Biography* (London: Hamish Hamilton, 1965).

France, Peter, ed. *The Oxford Guide to Literature in English Translation* (Oxford: Oxford University Press, 2000).

Frank, Joseph. *The Beginnings of the English Newspaper, 1620–1660* (Cambridge, MA: Harvard University Press, 1961).

Frearson, Michael Colin. 'The English Corantos of the 1620s', Ph.D. thesis, University of Cambridge (1993).

Freeman, Thomas S. 'Hands Defiled with Blood: The Account of Henry VIII in Foxe's "Book of Martyrs"', in Tom Betteridge and Thomas S. Freeman, eds., *Henry VIII in History* (Aldershot: Ashgate, forthcoming).

—— 'John Bale's Book of Martyrs: The Account of King John in *Acts and Monuments*', *Reformation*, 3 (1998): 206–10.

—— 'Notes on a Source for John Foxe's Account of the Marian Persecution in Kent and Sussex', *Historical Research*, 67 (1004): 203–11.

—— 'Offending God: John Foxe and English Protestant Reactions to the Cult of the Virgin Mary', in Robert N. Swanson, ed., *The Church and Mary*, Studies in Church History 39 (Woodbridge: Boydell & Brewer, 2004), 230–2.

—— 'Texts, Lies and Microfilm: Reading and Misreading Foxe's "Book of Martyrs"', *Sixteenth Century Journal*, 30 (1999): 42–5.

—— 'The Importance of Dying Earnestly: The Metamorphosis of the Account of James Bainham in Foxe's *Book of Martyrs*', in R. N. Swanson, ed., *The Church Retrospective* (Woodbridge: Boydell & Brewer, 1997), 278–9.

—— and Marcello J. Borges. '"A Grave and Heinous Incident against our holy Catholic Faith": Two Acounts of William Gardiner's Desecration of the Portugueese Royal Chapel in 1552', *Historical Research*, 69 (1996): 7–8.

Friedrich, H. *Montaigne* (Berkeley: University of California Press, 1991).

Frisch, Andrea. *The Invention of the Eyewitness: Witnessing and Testimony in Early Modern France* (Chapel Hill: University of North Carolina Press, 2004).

Froude, J. A. 'England's Forgotten Worthies', in J. A. Froude, ed., *Short Studies on Great Subjects* (New York: Charles Scribner and Company, 1868).

Frye, Northrop. *The Anatomy of Criticism: Four Essays* (Princeton: Princeton University Press, 1957).

Fudge, Erica. *Renaissance Beasts: Of Animals, Humans and Other Wonderful Creatures* (Chicago: University of Illinois Press, 2004).

Fuller, Mary. *Voyages in Print: English Travel to America, 1576–1624* (Cambridge: Cambridge University Press, 1995).

Fussner, F. Smith. *The Historical Revolution: English Historical Writing and Thought, 1580–1640* (London: Routledge & Kegan Paul, 1962).

Galtung, Johann, and Mari Ruge, 'Structuring and Selecting News', in Stanley Cohen and Jock Young, eds., *The Manufacture of News: Social Problems, Deviance, and the Mass Media* (London: Constable, 1973), 62–72.

Garber, Marjorie. *Shakespeare's Ghost Writers: Literature as Uncanny Causality* (New York: Methuen, 1987).

Gardiner, Judith Kegan. 'Elizabethan Psychology and Burton's *Anatomy of Melancholy*', *Journal of the History of Ideas*, 38 (1977): 373–88.
Gesner, Carol. *Shakespeare and the Greek Romance* (Lexington: University of Kentucky Press, 1970).
Gibson, Jonathan. 'Significant Space in Manuscript Letters', *The Seventeenth Century*, 12 (1997): 1–9.
Gilbert, Neal. *Renaissance Concepts of Method* (New York: Columbia University Press).
Glaisyer, Natasha, and Sara Pennell, eds. *Didactic Literature in England, 1500–1800* (Aldershot: Ashgate, 2003).
Goodblatt, Chanita. *The Christian Hebraism of John Donne* (Pittsburgh: Duquesne University Press, 2010).
Gore, Jeffrey. 'Francis Bacon and the "Desserts of Poetry"', *Prose Studies*, 29.3 (2007): 359–77.
Gowland, Angus. 'Rhetorical Structure and Function in *The Anatomy of Melancholy*', *Rhetorica*, 19 (2001): 1–48.
—— *The Worlds of Renaissance Melancholy: Robert Burton in Context* (Cambridge: Cambridge University Press, 2006).
Graham, Elspeth, Hilary Hinds, Elaine Hobby, and Helen Wilcox, eds. *Her Own Life: Autobiographical Writings by Seventeenth-Century Englishwomen* (London: Routledge, 1989).
Grazia, Margreta de. 'The Ideology of Superfluous Things', in Margreta de Grazia, Maureen Quilligan, and Peter Stallybrass, eds., *Subject and Object in Renaissance Culture* (Cambridge: Cambridge University Press, 1996), 17–42.
Green, Ian. *Print and Protestantism in Early Modern England* (Oxford: Oxford University Press, 2000).
Green, Lawrence D. 'Dictamen in England, 1500–1700', in Carol Poster and Linda C. Mitchell, eds., *Letter-Writing Manuals and Instruction from Antiquity to the Present: Historical and Bibliographic Studies* (Columbia, SC: University of South Carolina Press, 2007), 102–26.
Greenblatt, Stephen. *Marvelous Possessions: The Wonder of the New World* (Chicago: University of Chicago Press, 1991).
—— 'Sidney's *Arcadia* and the Mixed Mode', *Studies in Philology*, 70 (1973): 269–78.
Greene, Thomas M. *The Light in Troy: Imitation and Discovery in Renaissance Poetry* (New Haven: Yale University Press, 1982).
Greg, W. W., and E. Boswell, eds. *Records of the Court of the Stationers' Company, 1576–1602, from Register B* (London: Bibliographical Society, 1930).
Gribben, Crawford. 'Introduction', in Crawford Gribben and David George Mullan, eds., *Literature and the Scottish Reformation* (Aldershot: Ashgate, 2009), 1–18.
—— 'John Knox, Reformation History and National Self-Fashioning', *Reformation and Renaissance Review*, 8 (2006): 48–66.
Grudin, R. 'Renaissance Laughter: The Jests in Castiglione's *Il Cortegiano*', *Neophilologus*, 58.2 (1974): 199–204.
Guenther, Leah. 'To Parley Euphuism: Fashioning English as a Linguistic Fad', *Renaissance Studies*, 16.1 (March 2002): 24–35.
Gueudet, Guy. *L'art de la lettre humaniste* (Paris: Honoré Champion, 2004).
Guillerm, Luce. *Sujet de l'écriture et traduction autour de 1540* (Paris: Aux Amateurs des Livres, 1988).
Guy, John. 'The Henrician Age', in J. G. A. Pocock, ed., *The Varieties of British Political Thought, 1500–1800* (Cambridge: Cambridge University Press, 1993), 13–46.

Guy, John. *Thomas More* (London: Hodder, 2000).
Hackel, Heidi Brayman. *Reading Material in Early Modern England: Print, Gender, Literacy* (Cambridge: Cambridge University Press, 2005).
Hackett, Helen. *Women and Romance Fiction in the English Renaissance* (Cambridge: Cambridge University Press, 2000).
Hadfield, Andrew. *Literature, Travel, and Colonial Writing in the English Renaissance, 1545–1625* (Oxford: Clarendon Press, 1998).
—— 'Peter Martyr, Richard Eden and the New World: Reading, Experience and Translation', *Connotations*, 5 (1995/6): 1–22.
—— *Shakespeare and Republicanism* (Cambridge: Cambridge University Press, 2005).
—— *Shakespeare, Spenser and the Matter of Britain* (Basingstoke: Palgrave Macmillan, 2004).
Halasz, Alexandra. '"So beloved that men use his picture for their signs": Richard Tarlton and the Uses of Sixteenth-Century Celebrity', *Shakespeare Studies*, 23 (1995): 19–38.
Hall, Stuart. 'The Social Production of News', in Chas Critcher Hall et al., eds., *Policing the Crisis: Mugging, the State, and Law and Order* (Basingstoke: Macmillan, 1978), 53–80.
Hamlin, W. H. 'Florio's Montaigne and the Tyranny of "Custome": Appropriation, Ideology and Early English Readership of the *Essayes*', *Renaissance Quarterly*, 63 (2010): 491–544.
—— '*Montagne's Moral Maxims*: Seventeenth-Century English Aphorisms Derived from the *Essayes* of Montaigne', *Montaigne Studies*, 21 (2009): 209–24.
Hamling, Tara. *Decorating the 'Godly' Household* (New Haven: Yale University Press, 2010).
—— and Catherine Richardson, eds. *Everyday Objects: Medieval and Early Modern Material Culture and its Meanings* (Farnham: Ashgate, 2010).
Hammond, Paul. 'The Play of Quotation and Commonplace in *King Lear*', in Lynette Hunter, ed., *Toward a Definition of Topos: Approaches to Analogical Reasoning* (Basingstoke: Macmillan, 1991), 78–129.
Hannay, Margaret. *Mary Sidney, Lady Wroth* (Burlington: Ashgate, 2010).
Hanrahan, Thomas. '*Lazarillo de Tormes*: Erasmian Satire or Protestant Reform?', *Hispania*, 66 (1983): 333–9.
Harkness, Deborah E. 'Francis Bacon's Experimental Writing', in Susannah Brietz Monta and Margaret W. Ferguson, eds., *Teaching Early Modern English Prose* (New York: Modern Language Association of America, 2010).
Harris, Frances. *Transformations of Love: The Friendship of John Evelyn and Margaret Godolphin* (Oxford: Oxford University Press, 2002).
Harris, Jonathan Gil. 'Shakespeare's Hair: Staging the Object of Material Culture', *Shakespeare Quarterly*, 52 (2001): 479–91.
—— *Untimely Matter in the Age of Shakespeare* (Philadelphia: University of Pennsylvania Press, 2009).
Harrison, John L. 'Bacon's View of Rhetoric, Poetry, and the Imagination', *Huntington Library Quarterly*, 20:2 (1957): 107–25.
Harrison, Peter. '"The Fashioned Image of Poetry or the Regular Instruction of Philosophy?" Truth, Utility, and the Natural Scientist in Early-Modern England', in Juliet Cummins and David Burchell, eds., *Science, Literature, and Rhetoric in Early-Modern England* (Aldershot: Ashgate, 2007), 15–36.
Hartley, T. E., ed. *Proceedings in the Parliaments of Elizabeth I, 1558–1581* (Leicester: Leicester University Press, 1981).

Harwood, John T. *The Early Essays and Ethics of Robert Boyle* (Carbondale: Southern Illinois University Press, 1991).

Hausted, Peter. *Senile Odium*, ed. and trans. Laurens J. Mills (Bloomington: Indiana University, 1949).

Havenstein, Daniela. *Democratizing Sir Thomas Browne:* Religio Medici *and its Imitators* (Oxford: Clarendon Press, 1999).

Hazlett, McCrea. ' "New Frame and Various Composition": Development in the Form of Owen Felltham's "Resolves" ', *Modern Philology*, 51 (1953): 93–101.

Heilman, Robert B. 'Greene's Euphuism and Some Congeneric Styles', in George M. Logan and Gordon Teskey, eds., *Unfolded Tales: Essays on Renaissance Romance* (Ithaca: Cornell University Press, 1989), 49–73.

Helgerson, Richard. *Forms of Nationhood: The Elizabethan Writing of England* (Chicago: University of Chicago Press, 1992).

—— *The Elizabethan Prodigals* (Berkeley and Los Angeles: University of California Press, 1976).

Henderson, Judith Rice. 'Erasmus on the Art of Letter-Writing', in James J. Murphy, ed., *Renaissance Eloquence: Studies in the Theory and Practice of Renaissance Rhetoric* (Berkeley: University of California Press, 1983), 331–55.

—— 'Euphues and his Erasmus', *English Literary Renaissance*, 12 (1982): 135–61.

Heninger, S. K., Jr. *Sidney and Spenser: The Poet as Maker* (University Park: Pennsylvania State University Press, 1989).

Heusser, Martin. *The Gilded Pill: A Study of the Reader–Writer Relationship in 'The Anatomy of Melancholy'* (Tübingen: Stauffenburg Verlag, 1987).

Hexter, J. H. *More's Utopia: The Biography of an Idea* (Princeton: Princeton University Press, 1952).

Hicks, Dan. 'The Material Cultural Turn: Event and Effect', in Dan Hicks and Mary C. Beaudry, eds., *The Oxford Handbook of Material Culture Studies* (Oxford: Oxford University Press, 2010), 25–98.

Hill, W. Speed. 'The Authority of Hooker's Style', *Studies in Philology*, 67.3 (July 1970): 328–38.

Hilliard, Stephen S. *The Singularity of Thomas Nashe* (Lincoln: University of Nebraska Press, 1986).

Hirst, Derek. *England in Conflict, 1603–1660* (London: Arnold, 1999).

Hobbs, Mary, ed. *The Sermons of Henry King (1592–1669): Bishop of Chichester* (Aldershot: Scolar Press, 1992).

Hodges, Devon L. *Renaissance Fictions of Anatomy* (Amherst: University of Massachusetts Press, 1985).

Hoffmann, G. *Montaigne's Career* (Oxford: Oxford University Press, 1998).

Holcomb, C. *Mirth Making: The Rhetorical Discourse on Jesting in Early Modern England* (Columbia: University of South Carolina Press, 2001).

Holsinger, Bruce. 'Liturgy', in Paul Strohm, ed., *Middle English*, Oxford Twenty-First Century Approaches to Literature (Oxford: Oxford University Press, 2007), 295–314.

Höltgen, K. J. 'Robert Burtons *Anatomy of Melancholy*: Struktur und Gattungs problematik im Licht der Ramistischen Logik', *Anglia*, 94 (1976): 388–403.

Houlbrooke, Ralph, ed. *James I and VI: Ideas, Authority and Government* (Aldershot: Ashgate, 2006).

How, James. *Epistolary Spaces: English Letter Writing from the Foundation of the Post Office to Richardson's 'Clarissa'* (Aldershot: Ashgate, 2003).

Huchon, Mireille. '*Amadis*, "Parfaicte idée de nostre langue françoise"', in Nicole Cazauran and Michel Bideaux, eds., *Les Amadis en France au XVIe siècle* (Paris: Éditions Rue d'Ulm—Presses de l'École normale supérieure, 2000), 183–200.

Huebert, Ronald. 'The Private Opinions of Sir Thomas Browne', *Studies in English Literature, 1500–1900*, 45.1 (2005): 117–34.

Huffman, W., ed. *Robert Fludd* (Berkeley, CA: North Atlantic Books, 2001).

Hulme, Peter, and Tim Youngs, eds. *The Cambridge Companion to Travel Writing* (Cambridge: Cambridge University Press, 2002).

Hunt, Arnold. *The Art of Hearing: English Preachers and their Audiences* (Cambridge: Cambridge University Press, 2011).

Hunt, Percival. *Pepys in the Diary* (Pittsburgh: University of Pittsburgh Press, 1959).

Hunter, G. K. *John Lyly: The Humanist as Courtier* (London: Routledge & Kegan Paul, 1962).

Hunter, Matthew, and Annabel Gregory, eds. *An Astrological Diary of the Seventeenth Century: Samuel Jeake of Rye, 1652–1699* (Oxford: Clarendon Press, 1988).

Hunter, Michael. *Robert Boyle: Scrupulosity and Science* (Woodbridge: Boydell, 2000).

Hunter, Paul. *Before Novels: The Cultural Contexts of Eighteenth-Century English Fiction* (New York: W. W. Norton, 1990).

Hurley, Harold C. *The Sources and Traditions of Milton's 'L'Allegro' and 'Il Penseroso'* (Lewiston, NY: Edwin Mellen Press, 1999).

Hutson, Lorna. 'Fortunate Travellers: Reading for the Plot in Sixteenth-Century England', *Representations*, 41 (1993): 83–103.

—— *The Usurer's Daughter: Male Friendship and Fictions of Women in Sixteenth-Century England* (London: Routledge, 1994).

—— *Thomas Nashe in Context* (Oxford: Clarendon Press, 1989).

Iemma, P. *Les Repentirs de l'Exemplaire de Bordeaux* (Paris: Champion, 2004).

Ife, Barry. *Reading and Fiction in Golden-Age Spain: A Platonist Critque and Some Picaresque Replies* (Cambridge: Cambridge University Press, 1985).

Ijsewijn, Jozef. *Companion to Neo-Latin Studies Part I: History and Diffusion of Neo-Latin Literature*, 2nd edn. (Louvain: Leuven University Press and Peeters Press, 1990).

Infelise, Mario. *Prima dei giornali: Alle origini della pubblica informazione* (Rome: Laterza, 2002).

Jack, Ronald S. *Scottish Prose, 1550–1700* (London: Calder & Boyars, 1971).

Jacob, E. F., ed. *The Register of Henry Chichele, Archbishop of Canterbury, 1414–43*, 4 vols. (Oxford: Oxford University Press, 1937–47).

Jardine, Lisa. *Erasmus, Man Of Letters: The Construction Of Charisma in Print* (Princeton: Princeton University Press, 1993).

—— and Anthony Grafton, '"Studied for Action": How Gabriel Harvey Read his Livy', *Past and Present*, 129 (1990): 30–78.

Jenkinson, Matt. 'Preaching at the Court of Charles II: Court Sermons and the Restoration Chapel Royal', in Peter McCullough, Hugh Adlington, and Emma Rhatigan, eds., *The Oxford Handbook of the Early Modern Sermon* (Oxford: Oxford University Press, 2011), 442–59.

Jenneret, M. *Des mets et des mots. Banquets et propos de table à la Renaissance* (Paris: Corti, 1987), trans. J. Whiteley and E. Hugues as *A Feast of Words: Banquets and Table Talk in the Renaissance* (Chicago: Chicago University Press, 1991).

Johnson, Dale Warden. 'Marginal at Best: John Knox's Contribution to the Geneva Bible, 1560', in Mack P. Holt, ed., *Adaptations of Calvinism in Reformation Europe: Essays in Honour of Brian G. Armstrong* (Aldershot: Ashgate, 2007), 241–8.

Johnson, F. R. 'Notes on English Retail Book-prices, 1550–1640', *The Library*, 5th ser., 5 (1950): 83–112.

Jones, Ann Rosalind. 'Inside the Outsider: Nashe's *Unfortunate Traveller* and Bakhtin's Polyphonic Novel', *English Literary History*, 50 (1983): 61–81.

—— and Peter Stallybrass, *Renaissance Clothing and the Materials of Memory* (Cambridge: Cambridge University Press, 2000).

Jones, Emrys. *Scenic Form in Shakespeare* (Oxford: Clarendon Press, 1971).

Jones, R. O., ed. *La vida de Lazarillo de Tormes* (Manchester: Manchester University Press, 1963).

Jones, Richard Foster. *The Triumph of the English Language* (Palo Alto, CA: Stanford University Press, 1953).

Jowett, John. 'Johannes Factotum: Henry Chettle and Greene's Groatsworth of Wit', *Papers of the Bibliographical Society of America*, 87 (1993): 453–85.

Kany, Charles E. *The Beginnings of the Epistolary Novel in France, Italy, and Spain*, University of California Publications in Modern Philology (Berkeley: University of California Press, 1937).

Kay, Billy. *Scots: The Mither Tongue* (London: Grafton, 1988).

Kay, Dennis, ed. *Sir Philip Sidney: An Anthology of Modern Criticism* (Oxford: Oxford University Press, 1987).

Kelley, Donald R. 'Elizabethan Political Thought', in J. G. A. Pocock, ed., *Varieties of British Political Thought* (Cambridge: Cambridge University Press, 1996), 47–79.

Kelly, Douglas. 'Interlace and the Cyclic Imagination', in Carol Dover, ed., *A Companion to the Lancelot-Grail Cycle* (Cambridge: D. S. Brewer, 2003), 55–64.

Kemp, Geoff, and Jason McElligott, eds. *Censorship and the Press, 1580–1720*, 4 vols. (London: Pickering & Chatto, 2009).

Kendrick, T. D. *British Antiquity* (London: Methuen, 1950).

Kennedy, Judith M. *A Critical Edition of Yong's Translation of George of Montemayor's* Diana *and Gil Polo's* Enamoured Diana (Oxford: Clarendon Press, 1968).

Kernan, Alvin. *The Cankered Muse: Satire of the English Renaissance* (New Haven: Yale University Press, 1959).

Kesson, Andrew. *John Lyly and Early Modern Authorship* (Manchester: Manchester University Press, 2013).

Kiessling, Nicolas. *The Library of Robert Burton* (Oxford: Oxford Bibliographical Society, 1988).

Killeen, Kevin. *Biblical Scholarship, Science and Politics in Early-Modern England: Thomas Browne and the Thorny Place of Knowledge* (Alderhsot: Ashgate, 2009).

King, John N. *Foxe's 'Book of Martyrs' and Early Modern Print Culture* (Cambridge: Cambridge University Press, 2006).

King, Ros, ed. *The Works of Richard Edwards* (Manchester: Manchester University Press, 2001).

Kinney, Arthur. *Humanist Poetics* (Amherst: University of Massachusetts Press, 1986).

—— 'Stephen Gosson's Art of Argumentation in *The Schoole of Abuse*', *Studies in English Literature, 1500–1900*, 7 (1967): 41–54.

Kinney, Clare R., ed. *Ashgate Critical Studies on Women Writers in England, 1550–1700*. Vol. 4: *Mary Wroth* (Burlington: Ashgate, 2009).

Kirby, W. J. Torrance, ed. *Richard Hooker and the English Reformation* (Dordrecht: Kluwer Academic Publishers, 2003).

Kirkpatrick, Robin K. *English and Italian Literature from Dante to Shakespeare: A Study of Source, Analogue and Divergence* (London: Longman, 1995).

Kitzes, Adam. *The Politics of Melancholy from Spenser to Milton* (London: Routledge, 2006).

Klein, Daniel. *Plato and a Platypus Walk into a Bar* (New York: Abrams Image, 2006).

Knapp, James A., and Jeffrey Pence. 'Between Thing and Theory', *Poetics Today*, 24:4 (2003): 641–71.

Knappen, M. M. *Two Elizabethan Puritan Diaries, by Richard Rogers and Samuel Ward* (Chicago: American Society of Church History, 1933).

Kraye, Jill. 'Moral Philosophy', in Charles B. Schmitt and Quentin Skinner, eds., *The Cambridge History of Renaissance Philosophy* (Cambridge: Cambridge University Press, 1988), 303–86.

Kushner, Tony. *Hydiotaphia, or The Death of Dr Browne: An Epic Farce about Death and Private Capital Accumulation*, in *Death and Taxes, Hydriotphia and Other Plays* (New York: Theatre Communications Group, 2000).

Kyle, Richard. 'John Knox's Concept of Divine Providence and its Influence on his Thought', *Albion: A Quarterly Journal Concerned with British Studies*, 18 (1986): 395–410.

Lake, Peter. *Anglicans and Puritans? English Conformist Thought from Whitgift to Hooker* (London: Unwin Hyman, 1988).

—— 'Deeds against Nature: Cheap Print, Protestantism and Murder in Early Seventeenth-Century England', in Kevin Sharpe and Peter Lake, eds., *Culture and Politics in Early Stuart England* (Basingstoke: Macmillan, 1994), 257–83.

—— 'Lancelot Andrewes, John Buckeridge, and Avant-Garde Conformity at the Court of James I', in Linda Levy Peck, ed., *The Mental World of the Jacobean Court* (Cambridge: Cambridge University Press, 1991), 113–33.

—— 'Puritanism, (Monarchical) Republicanism, and Monarchy', *Journal of Medieval and Early Modern Studies*, 40.3 (2010): 463–97.

—— with Michael Questier. *The Antichrist's Lewd Hat: Protestants, Papists and Players in Post-Reformation England* (New Haven: Yale University Press, 2002).

Lamb, Mary Ellen. 'The Biopolitics of Romance in Mary Wroth's *Urania*', *English Literary Renaissance*, 31 (2001): 107–30.

—— 'Topicality and the Interrogation of Wonder in Mary Wroth's *Second Part of The Countess of Montgomery's Urania*', in James Dutcher and Anne Prescott, eds., *Renaissance Historicisms* (Newark: University of Delaware Press, 2008), 247–58.

Lander, Jesse L. *Inventing Polemic: Religion, Print, and Literary Culture in Early Modern England* (Cambridge: Cambridge University Press, 2006).

Langer, U., ed. *The Cambridge Companion to Montaigne* (Cambridge: Cambridge University Press, 2005).

Larminie, Vivienne. *Wealth, Kinship and Culture: The Seventeenth Century Newdigates of Arbury and Their World* (Cambridge: Boydell & Brewer for the Royal Historical Society, 1995).

Lathrop, H. B. *Translations from the Classics into English from Caxton to Chapman, 1477–1620* (Madison: University of Wisconsin Press, 1932).

Law, Thomas Graves, ed. *Catholic Tractates of the Sixteenth Century, 1573–1600* (Edinburgh: Scottish Text Society, 1901).

Lecler, Joseph. *Toleration and the Reformation*, trans. T. L. Westow, 2 vols. (London: Longman, 1960).

Leishman, J. B., ed. *The Three Parnassus Plays* (London: Ivor Nicholson & Watson, 1949).

Lestringant, Frank. *André Thevet* (Geneva: Drozm 1991).

Levine, Joseph M. *Humanism and History: Origins of Modern English Historiography* (Ithaca: Cornell University Press, 1987).
Levy, F. J. 'Francis Bacon and the Style of Politics', in Arthur F. Kinney and Dan S. Collins, eds., *Renaissance Historicism* (Amherst, MA: University of Massachusetts Press, 1987), 146–67.
—— 'Hayward, Daniel and the Beginnings of Politic History in England', *Huntington Library Quarterly*, 50 (1987): 1–34.
—— *Tudor Historical Thought* (San Marino, CA: Huntington Library, 1967).
Levy, Fritz. 'The Decorum of News', in Joad Raymond, ed., *News, Newspapers and Society in Early Modern Britain* (London and Portland, OR: Frank Cass, 1999), 12–38.
Lewalski, Barbara. *Protestant Poetics and the Seventeenth-Century Religious Lyric* (Princeton: Princeton University Press, 1979).
—— *Writing Women in Jacobean England* (Cambridge, MA: Harvard University Press, 1993).
Lewis, C. S. *English Literature in the Sixteenth Century Excluding Drama* (Oxford: Clarendon Press, 1954).
Lewis, Rhodri. *Language, Mind and Nature: Artifical Languages in England from Bacon to Locke* (Cambridge: Cambridge University Press, 2007).
Lilley, Kate. 'Dedicated Thought: Montaigne, Bacon, and the English Renaissance Esssay', in Susannah Brietz Monta and Margaret W. Ferguson, eds., *Teaching Early Modern English Prose* (New York: Modern Language Association, 2010), 95–112.
Lindsay, Maurice. *The History of Scottish Literature* (London: Robert Hale, 1992).
Logan, George M. 'More on Tyranny: The *History of King Richard the Third*', in George M. Logan, ed., *The Cambridge Companion to Thomas More* (Cambridge: Cambridge University Press, 2011), 168–90.
Love, Harold. *The Culture and Commerce of Texts: Scribal Publication in Seventeenth-Century England* (Amherst: University of Massachusetts Press, 1998).
Luck, G. '*Vir Facetus*: A Renaissance Ideal', *Studies in Philology*, 55 (1958): 107–21.
Lund, Mary Ann. *Melancholy, Medicine and Religion in Early Modern England: Reading 'The Anatomy of Melancholy'* (Cambridge University Press, 2010).
—— 'The Christian Physician: Thomas Browne and the Role of Religion in Medical Practice', in Kathryn Murphy and Richard Todd, eds., *'A man very well studyed': New Contexts for Thomas Browne* (Leiden: Brill, 2009), 229–46.
Lüthy, Christoph. 'The Fourfold Democritus on the Stage of Early Modern Science', *Isis*, 91 (2000): 443–79.
Lyall, R. J. 'Vernacular Prose before the Reformation', in R. D. S. Jack, ed., *The History of Scottish Literature* (Aberdeen: Aberdeen University Press, 1988), 163–82.
Lyons, Bridget Gellert. *Voices of Melancholy: Studies in Literary Treatments of Melancholy in Renaissance England* (London: Routledge & Kegan Paul, 1971).
McCabe, Richard A. *Joseph Hall: A Study in Satire and Meditation* (Oxford: Clarendon Press, 1982).
MacCallum, M. W. *Shakespeare's Roman Plays and their Background* (London: Macmillan, 1910).
McClure, Norman Egbert, ed. *The Letters of John Chamberlain*, 2 vols. (Philadelphia: The American Philosophical Society, 1939).
McCrae, Andrew. *Literature, Satire and the Early Stuart State* (Cambridge: Cambridge University Press, 2004).
MacCulloch, Diarmaid. *The Reformation: A History* (New York: Viking, 2003).
—— *Thomas Cranmer: A Life* (New Haven: Yale University Press, 1996).

McCullough, Peter. 'Donne as Preacher', in Achsah Guibbory, ed., *The Cambridge Companion to John Donne* (Cambridge: Cambridge University Press, 2006), 167–81.

—— 'Preaching and Context: John Donne's Sermon at the Funerals of Sir William Cokayne', in Peter McCullough, Hugh Adlington, and Emma Rhatigan, eds., *The Oxford Handbook of the Early Modern Sermon* (Oxford: Oxford University Press, 2011), 213–67.

—— *Sermons at Court: Politics and Religion in Elizabethan and Jacobean Preaching* (Cambridge: Cambridge University Press, 1998).

McDermott, James. *Martin Frobisher, Elizabethan Privateer* (New Haven and London: Yale University Press, 2001).

McDiarmid, John F., ed. *The Monarchical Republic of Early Modern England: Essays in Response to Patrick Collinson* (Aldershot: Ashgate, 2007).

MacDonald, Michael. *Mystical Bedlam: Madness, Anxiety and Healing in Seventeenth-Century England* (Cambridge: Cambridge University Press, 1981).

McDowell, Nicholas. 'Milton's Regicide Tracts and the Uses of Shakespeare', in Nicholas McDowell and Nigel Smith, eds., *The Oxford Handbook of Milton* (Oxford: Oxford University Press, 2009), 252–71.

—— *The English Radical Imagination: Culture, Religion, and Revolution, 1630-1660* (Oxford: Clarendon Press, 2003).

Macfarlane, Alan. *The Diary of Ralph Josselin, 1616-1683* (Oxford: Oxford University Press, 1991).

McGrade, A. S., and Brian Vickers, eds. *Richard Hooker's 'Of the Laws of Ecclesiastical Polity': An Abridged Edition* (New York: St. Martin's Press, 1975).

Machline, V. C. 'The Contribution of Laurent Joubert's *Traité du Ris* to Sixteenth-Century Physiology of Laughter', in G. Debus and M. T. Walton, eds., *Reading the Book of Nature* (Kirksville: Sixteenth Century Journal Publishers, 1998), 251–64.

Mack, Peter. *A History of Renaissance Rhetoric, 1380-1620* (Oxford: Oxford University Press, 2011).

—— *Elizabethan Rhetoric: Theory and Practice* (Cambridge: Cambridge University Press, 2002).

—— 'Montaigne and Shakespeare: Source, Parallel or Comparison?', *Montaigne Studies*, 23 (2011): 151–80.

—— *Reading and Rhetoric in Montaigne and Shakespeare* (London: Bloomsbury, 2010).

—— 'Rhetoric, Ethics, and Reading in the Renaissance', *Renaissance Studies*, 19 (2005): 1–21.

McKay, Elaine. 'English Diarists: Gender, Geography and Occupation, 1500–1700', *History*, 90 (2005): 191–212.

McKenzie, D. F. '*The Staple of News* and the Late Plays', in W. Blissett, J. Patrick, and R. W. Van Fossen, eds., *A Celebration of Ben Jonson* (Toronto: University of Toronto Press, 1973), 83–128.

McKeon, Michael. *The Origins of the English Novel, 1600-1740* (London: Johns Hopkins University Press, 2002).

McKisack, May. *Medieval History in the Tudor Age* (Oxford: Clarendon Press, 1971).

McKitterick, David. 'Review of Stern, *Gabriel Harvey*', *Library*, 6.3 (1981): 348–53.

Maclean, Ian. *Le monde et les hommes selon les médécins de la Renaissance* (Paris: CNRS Editions, 2006).

—— *Logic, Signs and Nature in the Renaissance: The Case of Learned Medicine* (Cambridge: Cambridge University Press, 2002).

McNeillie, Andrew, and Stuart N. Clarke, eds. *The Essays of Virginia Woolf*, 6 vols. (London: Hogarth Press, 1986–2011).

McRae, Andrew. *Literature, Satire and the Early Stuart State* (Cambridge: Cambridge University Press, 2004).

Magnusson, Lynne. *Shakespeare and Social Dialogue: Dramatic Language and Elizabethan Letters* (Cambridge: Cambridge University Press, 1999).

Maltby, Judith. *Prayer Book and People in Elizabethan and Early Stuart England* (Cambridge: Cambridge University Press, 1998).

Mancall, Peter C. *Hakluyt's Promise: An Elizabethan's Obsession for an English America* (New Haven: Yale University Press, 2007).

Mander, Jenny, ed. *Remapping the Rise of the European Novel* (Oxford: Voltaire Foundation, 2007).

Marcus, Laura. *Auto/biographical Discourses: Theory, Criticism, Practice* (Manchester: Manchester University Press, 1994).

Marcus, Leah. 'Toward a New Topicality', in *Puzzling Shakespeare: Local Reading and its Discontents* (Berkeley and Los Angeles: University of California Press, 1988), 32–42.

Marenco, Franco. 'Double Plot in Sidney's Old *Arcadia*', *Modern Language Review*, 64 (1969): 248–63.

Marotti, Arthur. '"Love Is Not Love": Elizabethan Sonnet Sequences and the Social Order', *English Literary History*, 49 (1982): 396–428.

Mascuch, Michael. *Origins of the Individualist Self: Autobiography and Self-Identity in England, 1591–1791* (Stanford: Stanford University Press, 1997).

Maskell, D. 'Quel est le dernier état authentique des *Essais* de Montaigne?', *Bibliothèque d'Humanisme et Renaissance*, 40 (1978): 85–103.

Maslen, R. W. *Elizabethan Fictions: Espionage, Counter-Espionage, and the Duplicity of Fiction in Early Elizabethan Prose Narratives* (Oxford: Clarendon Press, 1997).

—— 'Sidney, Gascoigne and the "Bastard Poets"', in Constance C. Relihan and Goran V. Stanivukovic, eds., *Prose Fiction and Modern Sexualities in England, 1570–1640* (Basingstoke and New York: Palgrave Macmillan, 2003), 215–35.

—— 'The Afterlife of Andrew Borde', *Studies in Philology*, 100.4 (2003): 463–92.

—— 'William Baldwin and the Politics of Pseudo-Philosophy in Tudor Prose Fiction', *Studies in Philology*, 97 (2000): 29–60.

—— 'William Baldwin and the Tudor Imagination', in Mike Pincombe and Cathy Shrank, eds., *The Oxford Handbook of Tudor Literature, 1485–1603* (Oxford: Oxford University Press, 2010) 291–306.

Mason, Roger A. *Kingship and the Commonweal: Political Thought in Renaissance and Reformation Scotland* (East Linton: Tuckwell, 1998).

Matthiessen, F. O. *Translation: An Elizabethan Art* (Cambridge, MA: Harvard University Press, 1931).

Mayer, T. F. *Thomas Starkey and the Commonweal: Humanist Politics and the Religion of Henry VIII* (Cambridge: Cambridge University Press, 1989).

Melnikoff, Kirk, and Edward Gieskes, eds. *Writing Robert Greene* (Aldershot: Ashgate, 2008).

Mendelson, Sara Heller. 'Stuart Women's Diaries and Occasional Memoirs', in Mary Prior, ed., *Women in English Society, 1500–1800* (London and New York: Methuen, 1985), 181–210.

Menn, Stephen. 'The Intellectual Setting', in Daniel Garber and Michael Ayers, eds., *The Cambridge History of Seventeenth-Century Philosophy* (Cambridge: Cambridge University Press, 1998), 33–86.

Mentz, Steve. 'Forming Greene: Theorizing the Early Modern Author in the *Groatsworth of Wit*', in Kirk Melnikoff and Edward Gieskes, eds., *Writing Robert Greene* (Aldershot: Ashgate, 2008), 115–31.
—— *Romance for Sale in Early Modern England: The Rise of Prose Fiction* (Aldershot: Ashgate 2006).
Miller, Daniel. *Stuff* (Cambridge: Polity Press, 2010).
Miller, Jacqueline. 'Lady Mary Wroth in the House of Busirane', in Patrick Cheney and Lauren Silberman, eds., *Worldmaking Spenser* (Lexington: University Press of Kentucky, 2000), 115–24.
Miller, Naomi. *Changing the Subject* (Lexington: University of Kentucky Press, 1996).
—— and Gary Waller, eds. *Reading Mary Wroth* (Knoxville: University of Tennessee Press, 1991).
Millet, O. *La première reception des* Essais *de Montaigne* (Paris: Champion, 1995).
Milward, Peter. *Religious Controversies of the Elizabethan Age: A Survey of Printed Sources* (Aldershot: Scolar Press, 1977).
Mitchell, Linda C. 'Letter-Writing Instruction Manuals in Seventeenth-Century and Eighteenth-Century England', in Carol Poster and Linda C. Mitchell, eds., *Letter-Writing Manuals and Instruction from Antiquity to the Present: Historical and Bibliographical Studies* (Columbia, SC: University of South Carolina Press, 2007), 178–99.
Monta, Susanna Brietz, and Margaret W. Ferguson, eds. *Teaching Early Modern English Prose* (New York: Modern Language Association of America, 2010).
Montalvo, Garci Rodríguez de. *Amadís de Gaula*, ed. Juan Manuel Cacho Blecua, 2 vols. (Madrid: Ediciones Cátedra, 1991).
Moore, Helen. 'Of Marriage, Morals and Civility', in Jennifer Richards, ed., *Early Modern Civil Discourses* (Palgrave Macmillan, 2003), 35–50.
—— 'The Eastern Mediterranean in the English *Amadis* Cycle, Book V', *Yearbook of English Studies*, 41 (2011): 113–25.
Morgan, J. R., and Richard Stoneman, eds. *Greek Fiction: The Greek Novel in Context* (London: Routledge, 1994).
Morini, Massimiliano. *Tudor Translation in Theory and Practice* (Aldershot: Ashgate, 2006).
Morison, Stanley. *English Prayer Books: An Introduction to the Literature of Christian Public Worship* (Cambridge: Cambridge University Press, 1945).
Morrissey, Mary. *Politics and the Paul's Cross Sermons, 1558–1642* (Oxford: Oxford University Press, 2011).
Morrissey, Matt. 'Scripture, Style and Persusasion in Seventeenth-Century English Theories of Preaching', *Journal of Ecclesiastical History*, 53.4 (2002): 686–706.
Mortimer, Ian. 'Tudor Chronicler or Sixteenth-Century Diarist: Henry Machyn and the Nature of His Manuscript', *Sixteenth-Century Journal*, 33 (2002): 981–98.
Moss, Ann. *Printed Commonplace Books and the Structuring of Renaissance Thought* (Oxford: Oxford University Press, 1996).
Mozley, J. F. *John Foxe and his Book* (London: SPCK, 1940).
Mueller, Janel, ed. *Donne's Prebend Sermons* (Cambridge, MA: Harvard University Press, 1971).
—— *The Native Tongue and the Word* (Chicago: University of Chicago Press, 1984).
—— and Joshua Scodel, eds. *Elizabeth I: Translations, 1592–1598* (Chicago: University of Chicago Press, 2009).
Mueller, William R. 'Robert Burton's Frontispiece', *PMLA*, 64 (1949): 1074–88.

Muggli, Mark Z. 'Ben Jonson and the Business of News', *Studies in English Literature*, 32 (1992): 323–40.

Mukherjee, Ayesha. 'Food and Dearth in Early Modern England: The Writings of Hugh Platt' (unpublished doctoral dissertation, University of Cambridge, 2007).

Müller, Wolfgang G. 'Directions for English: Thomas Wilson's *Art of Rhetoric*, George Puttenham's *Art of English Poesy*, and the Search for Vernacular Eloquence', in Mike Pincombe and Cathy Shrank, eds., *The Oxford Handbook of Tudor Literature, 1485–1603* (Oxford: Oxford University Press, 2009), 307–22.

Munro, Ian. 'Shakespeare's Jestbook: Print, Wit, Performance', *English Literary History*, 71.1 (2004): 89–113.

Murphy, James J. *Rhetoric in the Middle Ages: A History of Rhetorical Theory from Saint Augustine to the Renaissance* (Berkeley: University of California Press, 1974).

Murphy, Kathryn. 'Jesuits and Philosophasters: Robert Burton's Response to the Gunpowder Plot', *Journal of the Northern Renaissance*, 1 (2009): 109–28.

—— and Richard Todd, eds. *'A man very well studyed': New Contexts for Thomas Browne* (Leiden: Brill, 2009).

Neelands, David. 'Hooker on Scripture, Reason, and "Tradition"', in Arthur Stephen McGrade, ed., *Richard Hooker and the Construction of Christian Community* (Tempe, AZ: Medieval and Renaissance Texts and Studies, 1997), 75–94.

Nevitt, Marcus. 'Ben Jonson and the Serial Publication of News', in Joad Raymond, ed., *News Networks in Seventeenth-Century Britain and Europe* (London: Routledge, 2006), 51–66.

Newbold, W. Webster. 'Letter Writing and Vernacular Literacy in Sixteenth-Century England', in Carol Poster and Linda C. Mitchell, eds., *Letter-Writing Manuals and Instruction from Antiquity to the Present: Historical and Bibliographical Studies* (Columbia, SC: University of South Carolina Press, 2007), 127–40.

Newcomb, Lori Humphrey. *Reading Popular Romance in Early Modern England* (New York: Columbia University Press, 2002).

Nicholl, Charles. *A Cup of News: The Life of Thomas Nashe* (London: Routledge, 1984).

Nicholson, Marjorie Hope. *Pepys' Diary and the New Science* (Charlottesville: University of Virginia Press, 1965).

Nielson, J. 'Elizabethan Realisms' (Ph.D. dissertation, McGill University, 1990).

Nielson, James. 'Reading Between the Lines: Manuscript Personality and Gabriel Harvey's Drafts', *Studies in English Literature*, 33 (1993): 43–82.

Nochimson, Richard L. 'Studies in the Life of Robert Burton', *Yearbook of English Studies*, 4 (1974): 85–11.

Norbrook, David. *Writing the English Republic: Poetry, Rhetoric and Politics, 1627–1660* (Cambridge: Cambridge University Press, 1999).

North, Jonathan, ed. *England's Boy King: The Diary of Edward VI, 1547–1553* (Welwyn Garden City: Ravenhall, 2005).

North, Marcy. *The Anonymous Renaissance: Cultures of Discretion in Tudor-Stuart England* (Chicago: University of Chicago Press, 2003).

Nussbaum, Felicity. 'Toward Conceptualizing Diary', in James Olney, ed., *Studies in Autobiography* (Oxford: Oxford University Press, 1988), 128–40.

O'Reilly, Terence. 'The Erasmianism of *Lazarillo de Tormes*', in Richard Cardwell, ed., *Essays in Honour of Robert Brian Tate* (Nottingham: University of Nottingham, 1984), 91–100.

O'Rourke, Sean Patrick. 'The Most Significant Passage on Rhetoric in the Works of Francis Bacon', *Rhetoric Society Quarterly*, 26.3 (1996): 31–55.

Olmert, Wendy. *Rhetoric: An Historical Introduction* (Oxford: Blackwell Publishing, 2006).
Ong, Walter. *Ramus, Method, and the Decay of Dialogue* (Cambridge, MA: Harvard University Press, 1958).
Orgel, Stephen. *The Illusion of Power: Political Theater in the English Renaissance* (Berkeley and Los Angeles: University of California Press, 1975).
Osler, Margaret J., ed. *Rethinking the Scientific Revolution* (Cambridge: Cambridge University Press, 2000).
Osler, William. 'Robert Burton: The Man, his Book, his Library', in *A Way of Life and Other Selected Writings of Sir William Osler* (New York: Dover Books, 1958).
Ostermark-Johansen, Lene. 'The Death of Euphues: Euphuism and Decadence in Late-Victorian Literature', *English Literature in Translation, 1880-1920*, 45.1 (2002): 4-25.
Ostovich, Helen, and Elizabeth Sauer, eds. *Reading Early Modern Women: An Anthology of Texts in Manuscript and Print, 1550-1700* (London and New York: Routledge, 2004).
Paradis, James. 'Montaigne, Boyle, and the Essay of Experience', in George Levine, ed., *One Culture: Essays in Science and Literature* (Madison: University of Wisconsin Press, 1987), 59-91.
Parks, G. B. *Richard Hakluyt and the English Voyages* (New York: American Geographical Society, 1928).
Parmalee, Lisa Ferrarou. *Good Newes from Fraunce: French Anti-League Propaganda in Late Elizabethan England* (Rochester, NY: University of Rochester Press, 1996).
Passannante, Gerard. 'The Art of Reading Earthquakes: On Harvey's Wit, Ramus's Method, and the Renaissance of Lucretius', *Renaissance Quarterly*, 61 (2008): 792-832.
Patterson, Annabel. *Censorship and Interpretation: The Conditions of Writing and Reading in Early Modern England* (Madison: University of Wisconsin Press, 1984).
—— *Reading Holinshed's Chronicles* (Chicago: University of Chicago Press, 1994).
Patterson, Lee. 'Perpetual Motion: Alchemy and the Technology of the Self', *Studies in the Age of Chaucer*, 15 (1993): 25-57.
Patterson, W. B. 'Elizabethan Theological Polemics', in Torrance Kirby, ed., *A Companion to Richard Hooker* (Leiden: Brill, 2008), 89-119.
Pearlman, E. 'Typological Autobiography in Seventeenth-Century England', *Biography*, 8 (1985): 95-118.
Pebworth, Ted Larry. '"Real English Evidence": Stoicism and the English Essay Tradition', *PMLA*, 87 (1972): 101-2.
Peck, Linda Levy. 'Introduction', in Linda Levy Peck, ed., *The Mental World of the Jacobean Court* (Cambridge: Cambridge University Press, 1990), 1-17.
Peltonnen, Marku. *Classical Humanism and Republicanism in English Political Thought, 1570-1640* (Cambridge: Cambridge University Press, 1995).
Perelman, Lee. 'The Medieval Art of Letter Writing: Rhetoric as Institutional Expression', in Charles Bazerman and James Paradis, eds., *The Textual Dynamics of the Professions* (Madison: University of Wisconsin Press, 1991), 97-119.
Perry, Curtis. *Literature and Favouritism in Early Modern England* (Cambridge: Cambridge University Press, 2006).
Perry, Nandra. 'Imitatio and Identity: Thomas Rogers, Philip Sidney, and the Protestant Self', *English Literary Renaissance*, 35.3 (2005): 365-406.
Phillips, James E. *Images of a Queen: Mary Stuart in Sixteenth-Century Literature* (Berkeley: University of California Press, 1964).
Piggott, Stuart. *Ancient Britons and the Antiquarian Imagination: Ideas from the Renaissance to the Regency* (London: Thames and Hudson, 1989).

Plett, Heinrich F. *Rhetoric and Renaissance Culture* (New York: Walter de Gruyter, 2004).
Pollen, John Hungerford, SJ, and William MacMahon, SJ, eds. *The Ven. Philip Howard, Earl of Arundel, 1557–1595, English Martyrs*, 2, Catholic Record Society 21 (1919).
Pooley, Roger. *English Prose of the Seventeenth Century, 1590–1700* (London: Longman, 1993).
Popkin, Richard H. *The History of Scepticism from Erasmus to Descartes* (New York: Harper & Row, 1964).
Powell, William S. *John Pory, 1572–1636: The Life and Letters of a Man of Many Parts* (Chapel Hill, NC: University of North Carolina Press, 1977).
Prescott, A. L. 'Crime and Carnival at Chelsea: Widow Edith and Thomas More's Household', in Clara E. Murphy, Henri Gibaud, and Mario A. Di Cesare, eds., *Miscellanea Moreana: Essays for Germain Marc'hadour* (Binghampton, NY: Medieval and Renaissance Texts and Studies, 1989), 247–64.
—— 'Humanism in the Tudor Jestbook', *Moreana*, 24.95–6 (1987): 5–16.
—— 'The Ambivalent Heart: Thomas More's Merry Tales', *Criticism*, 45.4 (2003): 417–33.
Preston, Claire. 'In the Wilderness of Forms: Ideas and Things in Thomas Browne's Cabinets of Curiosity', in Neil Rhodes and Jonathan Sawday, eds., *The Renaissance Computer: Knowledge Technology in the First Age of Print* (London: Routledge, 2000), 170–83.
—— *Thomas Browne and the Writing of Early Modern Science* (Cambridge: Cambridge University Press, 2005).
Prewitt, Kendrick W. 'Gabriel Harvey and the Practice of Method', *Studies in English Literature*, 39 (1999): 19–39.
Principe, Lawrence W. 'Virtuous Romance and Romantic Virtuoso: The Shaping of Robert Boyle's Literary Style', *Journal of the History of Ideas*, 56.3 (1998): 377–97.
Prouty, Charles T. *George Gascoigne: Elizabethan Courtier, Soldier, and Poet* (New York: Columbia University Press, 1942).
—— and Ruth Prouty. 'George Gascoigne, *The Noble Arte of Venerie*, and Queen Elizabeth at Kenilworth', *Joseph Quincy Adams Memorial Studies* (Washington, DC: Folger Shakespeare Library, 1948): 639–64.
Quinn, D. B., ed. *The Hakluyt Handbook* (London: Hakluyt Society, 1974).
Quintero, Ruben. 'Introduction: Understanding Satire', in Ruben Quintero, ed., *A Companion to Satire: Ancient to Modern* (Oxford: Blackwell, 2007), 1–11.
Randall, David. 'Joseph Mead, Novellante: News, Sociability and Credibility in Early Stuart England', *Journal of British Studies*, 54 (2006): 293–312.
Ray, Sid. '"Those Whom God Hath Joined Together": Bondage Metaphors and Marital Advice in Early Modern England', in Kari Boyd McBride, ed., *Domestic Arrangements in Early Modern England* (Pittsburgh, PA: Duquesne University Press), 15–47.
Raymond, Joad. *Milton's Angels: The Early-Modern Imagination* (Oxford: Oxford University Press, 2010).
—— ed. *News Networks in Seventeenth Century Britain and Europe* (New York: Routledge, 2006).
—— *Pamphlets and Pamphleteering in Early Modern Britain* (Cambridge: Cambridge University Press, 2003).
—— *The Invention of the Newspaper: English Newsbooks, 1641–1649* (1996; Oxford: Oxford University Press, 2005).
—— ed. *The Oxford History of Popular Print Culture: Vol. 1, Cheap Print in Britain and Ireland to 1660* (Oxford: Oxford University Press, 2011).

Read, Sophie. 'Puns: Serious Wordplay', in Sylvia Adamson, Gavin Alexander, and Katrin Ettenhuber, eds., *Renaissance Figures of Speech* (Cambridge: Cambridge University Press, 2007), 81–96.

Rebhorn, Wayne. *The Emperor of Men's Minds: Literature and the Renaissance Discourse of Rhetoric* (Ithaca: Cornell University Press, 1995).

—— 'The Metamorphosis of Moria: Structure and Meaning in *The Praise of Folly*', *PMLA*, 89 (1974): 463–76.

Rees, D. G. 'Petrarch's "Trionfo Della Morte" in English', *Italian Studies*, 7 (1952): 82–96.

Relihan, Constance. *Fashioning Authority: The Development of Elizabethan Novelistic Discourse* (Kent, OH: Kent State University Press, 1994).

—— ed. *Framing Elizabethan Fictions: Contemporary Approaches to Early Modern Narrative Prose* (Kent, OH: Kent Sate University Press, 1996).

Relle, Eleanor. 'Some New Marginalia and Poems of Gabriel Harvey', *Review of English Studies*, NS 23 (1972): 401–16.

Renaker, David. 'Robert Burton and Ramist Method', *Renaissance Quarterly*, 24 (1971): 210–20.

Rhatigan, Emma. 'Preaching Venues: Architecture and Auditories', in Peter McCullough, Hugh Adlington, and Emma Rhatigan, eds., *The Oxford Handbook of the Early Modern Sermon* (Oxford: Oxford University Press, 2011), 87–119.

Rhodes, Neil. *Elizabethan Grotesque* (London: Routledge & Kegan Paul, 1980).

—— ed. *English Renaissance Prose: History, Language and Politics* (Tempe, AZ: Medieval and Renaissance Text Society, 1997).

—— *Shakespeare and the Origins of English* (Oxford: Oxford University Press, 2004).

—— *The Power of Eloquence and English Renaissance Literature* (New York: St. Martin's Press, 1992).

Richards, Jennifer. 'Male Friendship and Counsel in Richard Edwards' *Damon and Pythias*', in Thomas Betteridge and Greg Walker, eds., *The Oxford Handbook of Tudor Drama* (Oxford: Oxford University Press, 2012), 293–308.

—— *Rhetoric and Courtliness in Early Modern Literature* (Cambridge: Cambridge University Press, 2003).

Richardson, Malcolm. 'The *Ars Dictaminis*, the Formulary, and Medieval Epistolary Practice', in Carol Poster and Linda C. Mitchell, eds., *Letter-Writing Manuals and Instruction from Antiquity to the Present: Historical and Bibliographical Studies* (Columbia SC: University of South Carolina Press, 2007), 52–66.

Rigney, James. 'Sermons into Print', in Peter McCullough, Hugh Adlington, and Emma Rhatigan, eds., *The Oxford Handbook of the Early Modern Sermon* (Oxford: Oxford University Press, 2011), 198–212.

Roberts, Josephine A. 'The Life of Lady Mary Wroth', in Roberts, ed., *The Poems of Lady Mary Wroth* (Baton Rouge: Louisiana State University Press, 1983), 3–40.

Robertson, Jean. 'George Gascoigne and *The Noble Arte of Venerie and Hunting*', *Modern Language Review*, 37 (1942): 484–5.

Ronnick, Michele Valerie. 'A Note Concerning Elements of Tacitus's Depiction of Nero in Thomas More's *Historia Richardi Regis Angliae*', *Moreana*, 36 (December, 1999): 64–5.

Rosenberg, Eleanor. *Leicester, Patron of Letters* (New York: Columbia University Press, 1955).

Rosendale, Timothy. *Liturgy and Literature in the Making of Protestant England* (Cambridge: Cambridge University Press, 2007).

Rossi, Paolo. *Francis Bacon: From Magic to Science*, trans. Sacha Rabinovitch (Chicago: University of Chicago Press, 1968).
Ruutz-Rees, Caroline. 'Some Notes of Gabriel Harvey's in Hoby's Translation of Castiglione's *Courtier* (1561)', *PMLA*, 25 (1910): 608–39.
Sacks, David Harris. 'Richard Hakluyt's Navigations in Time: History, Epic, and Empire', *Modern Language Quarterly*, 67.1 (2006): 31–62.
Salter, F. R., ed. *Some Early Tracts on Poor Relief* (London: Methuen, 1926).
Salzman, Paul, ed. *An Anthology of Elizabethan Prose Fiction* (Oxford: Oxford University Press, 1998).
—— ed. *An Anthology of Seventeenth-Century Fiction* (Oxford: Oxford University Press, 1991).
—— *English Prose Fiction, 1558–1700: A Critical History* (Oxford: Oxford University Press, 1985).
—— 'John Barclay's *Argenis*: The Perfect Glass of State', in *Literary Culture in Jacobean England: Reading 1621* (Basingstoke and New York: Palgrave Macmillan, 2002), 75–9.
—— 'Mary Wroth: From Obscurity to Canonization', in *Reading Early Modern Women's Writing* (Oxford: Oxford University Press, 2006), 60–89.
Sanders, Norman. *The Revels History of Drama in English* (London: Methuen, 1981).
Santoyo, Julio-César. *Ediciones y traducciones inglesas del Lazarillo de Tormes* (Vitoria: Colegio Universitario de Alava, 1978).
Sawday, Jonathan. 'Shapeless Elegance: Robert Burton's Anatomy of Knowledge', in Neil Rhodes, ed., *English Renaissance Prose: History, Language and Politics* (Tempe, AZ: Medieval and Renaisance Texts and Studies, 1997), 173–202.
—— 'The Transparent Man and the King's Heart', in Claire Jowitt and Diane Watt, eds., *The Arts of Seventeenth-Century Science: Representations of the Natural World in European and North American Culture* (Aldershot: Ashgate, 2002), 12–24.
Sayce, R. 'L'édition des *Essais* de Montaigne de 1595', *Bibliothèque d'Humanisme et Renaissance*, 36 (1974): 115–41.
—— *The Essays of Montaigne: A Critical Exploration* (London: Weidenfeld & Nicolson, 1972).
—— and D. Maskell, *A Descriptive Bibliography of Montaigne's Essais* (London, 1983).
Schäfer, Jürgen. *Documentation in the O.E.D.: Shakespeare and Nashe as Test Cases* (Oxford: Clarendon Press, 1980).
Scherb, Victor I. 'Assimilating Giants: The Appropriation of Gog and Magog in Medieval and Early Modern England', *Journal of Medieval and Early Modern Studies*, 32 (2002): 59–84.
Schlatter, Richard, ed. *Hobbes's Thucydides* (New Brunswick, NJ: Rutgers University Press, 1975).
Schlauch, Margaret. *Antecedents of the English Novel, 1400–1600: From Chaucer to Deloney* (Warsaw: PWN and London: Oxford University Press, 1963).
Schmidt, Jermy. *Melancholy and the Care of the Soul: Religion, Moral Philosophy, and Madness in Early Modern England* (Aldershot: Ashgate, 2007).
Schneider, Gary. *The Culture of Epistolarity: Vernacular Letters and Letter Writing in Early Modern England, 1500–1700* (Newark, DE: University of Delaware Press, 2005).
Schoenfeldt, Michael. 'Reading Bodies', in Kevin Sharpe and Stephen Zwicker, eds., *Reading, Society, and Politics in Early Modern England* (Cambridge: Cambridge University Press, 2003), 215–43.

Schulz, E. 'Die englischen Schwankbücher bis herab zu *Dobson's Drie Bobs*', *Palaestra*, 117 (1912).
Schurink, Fred. 'An Elizabethan Grammar School Exercise Book', Bodleian Library Record, 18.2 (2003): 174–96.
—— 'Manuscript Commonplace Books, Literature and Reading in Early Modern England', *Huntington Library Quarterly*, 73 (2010): 453–69.
—— 'The Intimacy of Manuscript and the Pleasure of Print: Literary Culture from *The Schoolmaster* to *Euphues*', in Mike Pincombe and Cathy Shrank, eds., *The Oxford Handbook of Tudor Literature, 1485–1603* (Oxford: Oxford University Press, 2009), 671–86.
Schwyzer, Philip. 'Summer Fruit and Autumn Leaves: Thomas Nashe in 1593', *English Literary Renaissance*, 24 (1994): 583–619.
Scott, Sir Walter. *The Monastery* (Edinburgh: Adam and Charles Black, 1886).
Scott-Warren, Jason. *Early Modern Literature* (Cambridge: Polity Press, 2005).
Scragg, Leah. 'Edward Blount and the History of Lylian Criticism', *Review of English Studies*, 46.181 (1995): 1–10.
—— 'John Lyly and the Politics of Language', *Essays in Criticism*, 55.1 (January 2005): 17–38.
Screech, M. A. *Laughter at the Foot of the Cross* (London: Penguin, 1997).
Seaver, Paul. *Wallington's World: A Puritan Artisan in Seventeenth-Century London* (London: Methuen, 1985).
Seelig, Sharon Cadman. *Autobiography and Gender in Early Modern Literature: Reading Women's Lives, 1600–1680* (Cambridge: Cambridge University Press, 2006).
Seidel, Michael. *Satiric Inheritance: Rabelais to Sterne* (Princeton: Princeton University Press, 1979).
Serjeantson, R. W. 'Testimony: The Artless Proof', in Sylvia Adamson, Gavin Alexander, and Katrin Ettenhuber, eds., *Renaissance Figures of Speech* (Cambridge: Cambridge University Press, 2008), 181–96.
Shami, Jeanne. 'Donne and Discretion', *English Literary History*, 47.1 (1980): 48–66.
Shapin, Steven. *A Social History of Truth: Civility and Science in Seventeenth-Century England* (Chicago: University of Chicago Press, 1994).
—— 'Pump and Circumstance: Robert Boyle's Literary Technology', *Social Studies of Science*, 14 (1984): 481–520.
Shapiro, Barbara J. *A Culture of Fact: England, 1550–1720* (Ithaca: Cornell University Press, 2000).
Sharpe, Kevin. *Reading Revolutions: The Politics of Reading in Early Modern England* (New Haven: Yale University Press, 2000).
—— *The Personal Rule of Charles I* (New Haven and London: Yale University Press, 1992):.
—— 'Uncommon Places? Sir William Drake's Reading Notes', in Sabrina Alcorn Baron, ed., *The Reader Revealed* (Seattle and London: University of Washington Press, 2001), 59–65.
—— and Steven Zwicker, eds. *Writing Lives: Biography and Textuality, Identity and Representation in Early Modern England* (Oxford: Oxford University Press, 2008).
Sherman, William H. *John Dee: The Politics of Reading and Writing in the English Renaissance* (Amherst, MA: University of Massachusetts Press, 1995).
—— *Used Books: Marking Readers in Renaissance England* (Philadelphia: University of Pennsylvania Press, 2008).
Shleck, Julia. '"Plain Broad Narratives of Substantial Facts": Credibility, Narrative, and Hakluyt's *The Principall Navigations*', *Renaissance Quarterly*, 59.3 (2006): 768–94.

Shrank, Cathy. ' "This fatall Medea", "this Clytemnestra": Reading and the Detection of Mary Queen of Scots', *Huntington Library Quarterly*, 73 (2010): 523–41.
—— *Writing the Nation in Reformation England, 1530–1580* (Oxford: Oxford University Press, 2004).
Shuger, Deborah. 'Conceptions of Style', in Glynn P. Norton, ed., *The Cambridge History of Literary Criticism. Volume III: The Renaissance* (Cambidge: Cambridge University Press, 1999), 176–86.
—— 'The Laudian Idiot', in Reid Barbour and Claire Preston, eds., *Sir Thomas Browne: The World Proposed* (Oxford: Oxford University Press, 2009), 36–62.
Simon, Jean Robert. *Robert Burton et 'l'Anatomie de la mélancolie'* (Paris: Didier, 1964).
Simpson, Evelyn M. *A Study of the Prose Works of John Donne*, 2nd edn. (Oxford: Clarendon Press, 1948).
Sisson, C. J. *The Judicious Marriage of Mr. Hooker and the Birth of 'The Laws of Ecclesiastical Polity'* (Cambridge: Cambridge University Press, 1940).
Skinner, Quentin. 'Hobbes's Changing Conception of Civil Science', in *Visions of Politics. Volume III: Hobbes and Civil Science* (Cambridge: Cambridge University Press, 2002), 66–88.
—— 'Paradiastole: Redescribing the Vices as Virtues', in Sylvia Adamson, Gavin Alexander, and Katrin Ettenhuber, eds., *Renaissance Figures of Speech* (Cambridge: Cambridge University Press, 2007), 148–63.
—— *Reason and Rhetoric in the Philosophy of Hobbes* (Cambridge: Cambridge University Press, 1996).
Skretkowicz, Victor. *European Erotic Romance: Philhellene Protestantism, Renaissance Translation and English Literary Politics* (Manchester: Manchester University Press, 2010).
Skura, Meredith. '*A Mirror for Magistrates* and the Beginnings of English Autobiography', *English Literary Renaissance*, 36 (2006): 26–56.
—— *Tudor Autobiography: Listening for Inwardness* (Chicago: University of Chicago Press, 2008).
Slaughter, Mary. *Universal Languages and Scientific Taxonomy in the Seventeenth Century* (Cambridge: Cambridge University Press, 1982).
Sloane, Thomas O. *Donne Milton and the End of Humanist Rhetoric* (Berkeley: University of California Press, 1985).
—— 'Rhetorical Selfhood in Erasmus and Milton', in Walter Jost and Wendy Olmstead, eds., *A Companion to Rhetoric and Rhetorical Criticism* (Oxford: Blackwell Publishing, 2006), 112–27.
Smith, G. C. Moore. 'Gabriel Harvey's Letter-Book', *Notes and Queries*, 11.3 (1911): 261–3.
—— *Gabriel Harvey's Marginalia* (Stratford-upon-Avon: Shakespeare Head Press, 1913).
Smith, G. Gregory, ed. *Elizabethan Critical Essays*, 2 vols. (Oxford: Oxford University Press, 1904).
Smuts, Malcom. 'Court-Centred Politics and the Uses of Roman Historians, c.1590–1630', in Peter Lake and Kevin Sharpe, eds., *Culture and Politics in Early Stuart England* (Basingstoke: Macmillan, 1994), 21–44.
Smyth, Adam. 'Almanacs, Annotators and Life-Writing in Early Modern England', *English Literary Renaissance*, 38 (2008): 200–44.
—— *Autobiography in Early Modern England* (Cambridge: Cambridge University Press, 2010).
Somerville, J. P. *Politics and Ideology in England, 1603–1640* (Harlow: Longman, 1986).

Sowerby, R. 'Thomas Hobbes's Translation of Thucydides', *Translation and Literature*, 7 (1998): 147–69.
Staines, John D. *The Tragic Histories of Mary Queen of Scots, 1560–1690* (Farnham: Ashgate, 2009).
Starnes, D. T. 'Sir Thomas Elyot and the "Sayings of the Philosophers"', *Texas University Studies in English*, 13 (1933): 5–35.
Starobinski, Jean. 'La Mélancolie de l'Anatomiste', *Tel Quel*, 10 (1962): 21–9.
Staub, Susan C. '"According to My Source": Fictionality in *The Adventures of Master F.J.*', *Studies in Philology*, 87 (1990): 101–35.
Stephanson, Raymond. 'John Lyly's Prose Fiction: Irony, Humor and Anti-Humanism', *English Literary Renaissance*, 11 (1981): 3–21.
Stern, Virginia F. *Gabriel Harvey: His Life, Marginalia and Library* (Oxford: Oxford University Press, 1979).
Stewart, Alan. 'Gelding Gascoigne', in Constance C. Relihan and Goran V. Stanivukovic, eds., *Prose Fiction and Early Modern Sexualities in England, 1570–1640* (Basingstoke: Palgrave Macmillan, 2003), 147–70.
—— *Shakespeare's Letters* (Oxford: Oxford University Press, 2008).
—— and Heather Wolfe, *Letterwriting in Renaissance England* (Washington, DC: Folger Shakespeare Library, 2004).
Strassler, Robert B., ed. *The Landmark Thucydides* (New York: Free Press, 1996).
Sugimura, N. K. *'Matter of Glorious Trial': Spiritual and Material Substance in Paradise Lost* (New Haven: Yale University Press, 2009).
Sullivan, Ceri. *The Rhetoric of Credit: Merchants in Early Modern Writing* (London: Associated University Press, 2002).
Swart, J. 'Lyly and Pettie', *English Studies*, 23 (1941): 9–18.
Targoff, Ramie. *Common Prayer: The Language of Public Devotion in Early Modern England* (Chicago: University of Chicago Press, 2001).
Thomas, Sir Henry. *Spanish and Portuguese Romances of Chivalry* (Cambridge: Cambridge University Press, 1920).
Thornton, Alice. *The Autobiography of Mrs Alice Thornton*, ed. C. Jackson, *Surtees Society* 62 (1875).
Tilmouth, Christopher. 'Burton's "Turning Picture": Argument and Anxiety in *The Anatomy of Melancholy*', *Review of English Studies*, 56 (2005): 524–49.
Travitsky, Betty S. 'The Possibilities of Prose', in Helen Wilcox, ed., *Women and Literature in Britain, 1500–1700* (Cambridge: Cambridge University Press, 1996), 234–66.
Trevor, Douglas. *The Poetics of Melancholy in Early Modern England* (Cambridge: Cambridge University Press, 2004).
Tribble, Evelyn. 'The Peopled Page: Polemic, Confutation, and Foxe's Book of Martyrs', in George Bornstein and Theresa Tinkle, eds., *The Iconic Page in Manuscript, Print, and Digital Culture* (Ann Arbor, MI: University of Michigan Press, 1998), 109–22.
Truman, Ron. 'Lázaro de Tormes and the *Homus novus* Tradition', *Modern Language Review*, 64, (1969): 62–7.
Tuck, Richard. *Philosophy and Government, 1572–1651* (Cambridge: Cambridge University Press, 1993).
—— 'The Institutional Setting', in Daniel Garber and Michael Ayers, eds., *The Cambridge History of Seventeenth-Century Philosophy* (Cambridge: Cambridge University Press, 1998), 9–32.

Turner, Henry S. 'Nashe's Red Herring: Epistemologies of the Commodity in *Lenten Stuffe* (1599)', *English Literary History*, 68 (2001): 529–61.
Tyacke, Nicholas. *Anti-Calvinists: The Rise of English Arminianism, c.1590–1640* (Oxford: Clarendon Press, 1987).
—— 'Lancelot Andrewes and the Myth of Anglicanism', in Peter Lake and Michael Questier, eds., *Conformity and Orthodoxy in the English Church, c.1560–1660* (Woodbridge: Boydell Press, 2000), 5–33.
Ule, Louis. *A Concordance to the Works of Thomas Nashe*, 2 vols. (Hildesheim: Olms-Weidmann, 1997).
Underdown, David, ed. *William Whiteway of Dorchester: His Diary, 1618–1635* (Dorset: Dorset Record Society, 1991).
Underhill, John Garrett. *Spanish Literature in the England of the Tudors* (London: MacMillan, 1899).
Ungerer, Gustav. 'English Criminal Biography and Guzmán de Alfarache's Fall from Rogue to Highwayman, Pander and Astrologer', *Bulletin of Hispanic Studies*, 76 (1999): 189–97.
Upham, A. H. *The French Influence in English Literature* (New York: Columbia University Press, 1911).
Vaillancourt, Luc, ed. *La lettre familière au XVIe siècle: rhétorique humaniste de l'épistolaire* (Paris: Champion, 2003).
Van Dijk, Tuen A. *News as Discourse* (Hillsdale, NJ: Lawrence Erlbaum Associates, 1988).
Versini, Laurent. *Le roman épistolaire* (Paris: Presses Universitaires de France, 1979).
Vicari, E. Patricia. *The View from Minerva's Tower: Learning and Imagination in 'The Anatomy of Melancholy'* (Toronto: University of Toronto Press, 1996).
Vickers, Brian, ed. *English Renaissance Literary Criticism* (Oxford: Clarendon Press, 1999).
—— *Francis Bacon and Renaissance Prose* (Cambridge: Cambridge University Press, 1968).
—— ed. *Seventeenth Century Prose* (London: Longmans, Green and Co, 1969).
—— '"Words and Things"—or "Words, Concepts, and Things"? Rhetorical and Linguistic Categories in the Renaissance', in Eckhard Kessler and Ian Maclean, eds., *Res et Verba in der Renaissance* (Wiesbader: Harrassowitz Verlag, 2002), 289–335.
Vivo, Filippo de. *Information and Communication in Venice: Rethinking Early Modern Politics* (Oxford: Oxford University Press, 2007).
Voss, Paul J. *Elizabethan News Pamphlets: Shakespeare, Spenser, Marlowe, and the Birth of Journalism* (Pittsburgh, PA: Duquesne University Press, 2001).
Walker, Greg. 'Dialogue, Resistance and Accommodation: Conservative Literary Responses to the Henrician Reformation', in N. Scott Amos, Andrew Pettegree, and Henk van Niewp, eds., *The Education of a Christian Society* (Aldershot: Ashgtate, 1999), 89–111.
—— *Writing Under Tyranny: English Literature and the Henrician Reformation* (Oxford: Oxford University Press, 2005).
Walsham, Alexandra. *Providence in Early Modern England* (Oxford: Oxford University Press, 1999).
Walter, J., and S. J. Ong. *Rhetoric, Romance, and Technology: Studies in the Interaction of Expression and Culture* (Ithaca: Cornell University Press, 1971).
Warner, Christopher. 'Thomas More's *Utopia* and the Problem of Writing a Literary History of English Renaissance Dialogue', in Dorothea Heitsch and Jean-François Vallée, eds., *Printed Voices: The Renaissance Culture of Dialogue* (Toronto: University of Toronto Press, 2004), 63–76.
Warren, Austin. 'The Style of Sir Thomas Browne', *Kenyon Review*, 13 (1951): 674–87.

Watt, Ian. *The Rise of the Novel: Studies in Defoe, Richardson and Fielding* (Berkeley: University of California Press, 1957).

Wear, Andrew. *Knowledge and Practice in English Medicine, 1550–1680* (Cambridge: Cambridge University Press, 2000).

Webber, Joan. *Contrary Music: The Prose Style of John Donne* (Madison: University of Wisconsin Press, 1963).

—— *The Eloquent 'I': Style and Self in Seventeenth-Century Prose* (Madison: University of Wisconsin Press, 1968).

Weinbrot, Howard D. *Menippean Satire Reconsidered: From Antiquity to the Eighteenth Century* (Baltimore: Johns Hopkins University Press, 2005).

Weiss, Adrian. 'Shared Printing, Printer's Copy, and the Text(s) of Gascoigne's *A Hundreth Sundrie Flowres*', *Studies in Bibliography*, 45 (1992): 71–104.

Weiss, René. 'Was There a Real Shakespeare?' *Textual Practice*, 23.2 (2009): 215–28.

Whallon, William. 'Hebraic Synonymy in Sir Thomas Browne', *English Literary History*, 28 (1961): 335–52.

White, Hayden. *The Content of the Form: Narrative Discourse and Historical Representation* (Baltimore and London: Johns Hopkins University Press, 1987).

Whitlock, Keith. *Discourses of Poverty: Social Reform and the Picaresque Novel in Early Modern Spain* (Toronto: University of Toronto Press, 1999).

—— ed. *The Life of Lazarillo de Tormes*, trans. David Rowland (Warminster: Aris and Phillips, 2000).

Wilcox, H. '"Needy Nothing Trimmed in Jollity"', in J. M. Dutcher and A. L. Prescott, eds., *Renaissance Historicisms: Essays in Honor of Arthur F. Kinney* (Newark, DE: University of Delaware Press, 2008), 313–29.

—— ed. *Women and Literature in Britain, 1500–1700* (Cambridge: Cambridge University Press, 1996).

Williams, George Walton, ed. *The Complete Poetry of Richard Crashaw* (New York: Doubleday, 1970).

Williams, Grant. 'Disfiguring the Body of Knowledge: Anatomical Discourse and Robert Burton's *The Anatomy of Melancholy*', *English Literary History*, 68 (2001): 593–613.

—— 'Textual Crudities in Robert Burton's *Anatomy of Melancholy* and Thomas Browne's *Pseudodoxia Epidemica*', in Christopher Ivic and Grant Williams, eds., *Forgetting in Early Modern English Literature and Culture: Lethe's Leg* (London: Routledge, 2004), 67–82.

Williamson, George. *The Senecan Amble: Prose Form from Bacon to Collier* (Chicago: University of Chicago Press, 1951).

Wilson, F. P. 'The English Jest-books of the Sixteenth and Early Seventeenth Centuries', in *Shakespearian and Other Studies* (Oxford: Clarendon Press, 1969), 285–324.

Wilson, H. S. 'Gabriel Harvey's Orations on Rhetoric', *English Literary History*, 12 (1945): 167–82.

—— 'The Cambridge Comedy *Pedantius* and Gabriel Harvey's *Ciceronianus*', *Studies in Philology*, 45 (1948): 578–91.

Wilson, Katharine. *Fictions of Authorship in Late Elizabethan Narratives* (Oxford: Clarendon Press, 2006).

—— 'Revenge of the Angel Gabriel: Harvey's "A Nobleman's Suit to a Country Maid"', in Mike Pincombe, ed., *The Anatomy of Tudor Literature: Proceedings of the First International Conference of the Tudor Symposium* (Aldershot: Ashgate, 1998), 79–89.

Winzet, Ninian. *Niniane Winzet's Works*, ed. J. King Hewison (Edinburgh: Blackwood, 1888).

Wise, James N. *Sir Thomas Browne's 'Religio Medici' and Two Seventeenth-Century Critics* (Columbia: University of Missouri Press, 1973).

Withington, Phil. '"For This is True or else I Do Lye": Thomas Smith, William Bullein and Mid-Tudor Dialogue', in Mike Pincombe and Cathy Shrank, eds., *The Oxford Handbook of Tudor Literature, 1485–1603* (Oxford: Oxford University Press, 2012), 455–72.

Wolff, Samuel Lee. *The Greek Romances in Elizabethan Prose Fiction* (New York: Columbia University Press, 1912).

Womersley, David. 'Against Teleology of Technique', *Huntington Library Quarterly*, 68 (2005): 95–108.

—— *Divinity and State* (Oxford: Oxford University Press, 2010).

—— 'Sir Henry Saville's Translation of Tacitus and the Political Interpretation of Elizabethan Texts', *Review of English Studies*, NS 42 (1991): 313–42.

—— 'Sir John Hayward's Tacitism', *Renaissance Studies*, 6 (1992): 46–59.

—— 'Sir Thomas More's *History of King Richard III*: A New Theory of the English Texts', *Renaissance Studies*, 7 (1993): 272–90.

Woolf, D. R. 'Genre into Artifact: The Decline of the English Chronicle in the Sixteenth Century', *Sixteenth Century Journal*, 19 (1988): 321–54.

—— *The Idea of History in Early Stuart England: Erudition, Ideology, and 'The Light of Truth' from the Accession of James I to the Civil War* (Toronto: University of Toronto Press, 1990).

—— 'The Rhetoric of Martyrdom: Generic Contradictions and Narrative Strategy in John Foxe's *Acts and Monuments*', in Thomas F. Mayer and D. R. Woolf, eds., *The Rhetorics of Life Writing in Early Modern Europe: Forms of Biography from Cassandra Fedele to Louis XIV* (Ann Arbor, MI: University of Michigan Press, 1995), 243–82.

Worden, Blair. 'Ben Jonson Among the Historians', in Peter Lake and Kevin Sharpe, eds., *Culture and Politics in Early Stuart England* (Basingstoke: Macmillan, 1994), 67–90.

—— 'Republicanism, Regicide and Republic: The English Experience', in Martin Van Gelderen and Quentin Skinner, eds., *Republicanism: A Shared European Heritage*, 2 vols. (Cambridge: Cambridge University Press, 2002), Vol. I, 307–28.

—— *The Sound of Virtue: Philip Sidney's 'Arcadia' and Elizabethan Politics* (New Haven: Yale University Press, 1996).

—— 'Which Play was Performed at the Globe on 7 February 1601?', *London Review of Books*, 23.13 (10 July 2003): 22–4.

Wormald, Jenny. 'Godly Reformer, Godless Monarch: John Knox and Mary Queen of Scots', in Roger Mason, ed., *John Knox and the British Reformations* (Aldershot: Ashgate, 1998), 220–41.

—— *Mary Queen of Scots: A Study in Failure* (London: Collins & Brown, 1991).

Woudhuysen, Henry. *Sir Philip Sidney and the Circulation of Manuscripts, 1558–1640* (Oxford: Oxford University Press, 1996).

Wray, Ramona. 'Autobiography', in Laura Lunger Knoppers, ed., *The Cambridge Companion to Early Modern Women's Writing* (Cambridge: Cambridge University Press, 2009), 194–207.

Wright, Herbert G. *Boccaccio in England from Chaucer to Tennyson* (London: Athlone Press, 1957).

Wriothesley, Charles, and Windsor Herald. *A Chronicle of England during the reigns of the Tudors, from A.D. 1485 to 1559*, ed. William Douglas Hamilton (London: Royal Historical Society, 1875 and 1877).

Yamamoto-Wilson, John. 'James Mabbe's Achievement in his Translation of *Guzmán de Alfarache*', *Translation and Literature*, 8 (1999): 137–56.

Yates, Frances. *John Florio: The Life of an Italian in Shakespeare's England* (Cambridge: Cambridge University Press, 1934).

Yates, Julian. *Error Misuse Failure: Object Lessons from the English Renaissance* (Minneapolis: University of Minnesota Press, 2003).

Zachman, Randall. 'Calvin and Melanchthon on the Office of the Evangelical Teacher', in *John Calvin as Teacher, Pastor, and Theologian: The Shape of His Writings and Thought* (Grand Rapids, MI: Baker Academic, 2006): 29–54.

Zall, P. M., ed. *A Hundred Merry Tales and other Sixteenth-Century Jestbooks* (Lincoln: University of Nebraska Press, 1963).

——*A Nest of Ninnies and Other English Jestbooks of the Seventeenth Century* (Lincoln: University of Nebraska Press, 1970).

Zimbalist, Barbara. 'Critical Perspectives on Lady Mary Wroth's *The Countess of Montgomery's Urania*: An Annotated Bibliography', *Sidney Journal*, 24.1 (2006): 45–74.

Zurcher, Amelia A. 'Introductory Note' to Judith Man, *An Epitome of the History of Faire Argenis and Polyarchus* (1640), The Early Modern Englishwoman: Series 1, Printed Writings, 1500–1640, 3:2 (Aldershot: Ashgate, 2003).

——*Seventeenth-Century English Romance: Allegory, Ethics and Politics* (Basingstoke: Palgrave Macmillan, 2007).

Index

Adlington, William 113, 118
Aers, David 450
Aesop 118, 154, 348
Agger, Edward 80
Ainsworth, William 518
Alberic of Monte Casino 418
Alberti, Leon Battista 350
Alexander, Sir William 223
Alfred the Great 118, 324
Allen, Don Cameron 473
Almanacs 446–7
Alwes, Derek 193
Amadis de Gaule 59–76
Ames, William 336
Amyot, Jacques 111, 117, 119, 461
Anderson, Benedict 529
Andreae, Johann Valentin 262
Andrewes, Lancelot 560–4, 567, 571–4
Anglo-Saxon 16–17, 165
Anne of Denmark 238, 243
Apollonius of Tyre 118
Apuleius 118
Aquinas, Thomas 605
Archer, Jayne 164
Archer, Thomas 407, 408, 409
Arden of Faversham 318
Ariosto, Ludovico 157, 225, 246, 247, 248
Aristophanes 256, 570
Aristotle 21, 46, 117, 229, 254–5, 279, 363, 457, 605
    Aristotelianism 232, 272, 288–90, 360, 649
Armstrong, Archie 352–4
Arthur, King 299, 318, 324
Ascham, Roger 9–10, 92, 175, 179, 329, 422, 425
Astrology 326–33
Aubrey, John 220, 458, 465–6

Augustine, Saint 50–51, 109, 118, 170, 526, 566, 605
Austen, Jane 186
Aylmer, John 552

Bacon, Anthony 80
Bacon, Francis 263–4, 268–70, 272–4, 278, 282, 292, 302, 313–6, 318, 328, 336, 361, 363, 366–70, 426, 427, 468, 469–73, 474–5, 481–2, 550, 557, 666
Baker, Sir Richard 427
Baldwin, C. S. 30
Baldwin, William 29, 36, 45–54, 139–55, 157
Bale, John 530, 554
Bancroft, Richard 554, 555, 576–7, 600
Bandello, Matteo 93, 97, 191
Barbour, Reid 276
Barclay, Alexander 109, 110, 119, 236
Barclay, John 59–76
Barnaud, Nicholas 32, 33
Barrow, Henry 578–9
Barton, John 512
Bauthumley, Jacob 520
Baxter, Margery 536
Bayly, Lewis 484
Beadle, John 437
Beaumont, Francis 135
Beaumont, Joseph 683
Bebel, Heinrich 349
Bedford, Ronald 456, 463
Bell, Ilona 242
Belleforest, François de 296
Belsey, Catherine 437, 455
Bernard, Richard 340, 341, 568
Best, George 298
Bible 5, 44, 87, 117, 316, 437, 439, 462–3, 492, 505–21, 530–2, 560, 634, 635–6

Bible (*cont.*)
  Genesis 489–90
  Geneva Bible 14, 338, 348, 641, 643
  Proverbs 464, 513
  Psalms 578
Biondo, Flavio 320–1
Bird, Robert 588, 589
Black, Scott 468, 473
Blake, William 684
Blakeston, James 129
Blank, Paula 23
Blench, J. W. 561
Bloom, Harold 450
Blount, Edward 80, 172–3, 180, 185, 186
Boccaccio, Giovanni 91–4, 96, 98, 101, 161, 194, 357, 418
Boccalini, Trajano 369
Boemus, Johann 296
Boethius 118, 157, 226
Boleyn, Anne 436
Bonner, Archbishop Edmund 539, 541
Book of Common Prayer 5, 437, 560, 569, 576–91, 600
Booty, John 580–1, 602
Borde, Andrew 147, 149
Bosc, Jacques du 431
Bourchier, John, Lord Berners 428
Bourne, Nicholas 407, 409, 411
Boutcher, Warren 89
Bowen, Barbara C. 349
Bowers, Terence N. 142
Boyle, Robert 269, 271, 281–90, 505, 510, 514–5, 682, 683
Boyle, Robert, First Earl of Orrery 282
Bracciolini, Poggio 348, 350, 418
Braden, Gordon 460
Brandolino, Aurelio Lippo 419
Bredon, William 332
Brennan, Michael 297
Breton, Nicholas 431, 481–2
Bridges, Dean 599
Bridges, John 548–9
Bright, Timothy 346
Brinsley, John 44, 420
Browne, Thomas 269, 275–81, 669–85
Bruni, Leonardi 418
Bruno, Giordano 80

Bruster, Douglas 207–8
Bucer, Martin 577
Buchanan, George 361, 362, 375, 631–45
Buckingham, Duke of 367–8
Buellein, William 33
Bull, Henry 522
Burckhardt, Jacob 449
Burke, Kenneth 242
Burke, Peter 3, 317, 453, 455, 456
Burns, J. H. 640
Burton, Robert 56–8, 89, 263–4, 300, 646–68
Butler, Thomas 536
Butter, Nathaniel 407, 409, 411, 412
Butts, Thomas 302
Bynneman, Henry 123, 124, 129, 158

Cabot, John 257, 295
Caesar, Julius 292, 298, 321, 375
Caesar, Julius (lawyer) 44
Calvin, John 373, 593, 600, 605, 641
  Calvinist 374–7, 404, 437, 455, 563, 587, 603, 632, 635, 638
Camden, William 107, 109, 310, 320
Campanella, Tommaso 262
Campbell, Julie 244
Campion, Gaspar 302
Campion, Thomas 242
Careless, John 537
Carew, Richard 226
Carey, John 100, 232
Carleton, Sir Dudley 64
Carleton, George 330
Carpenter, John 443
Carr, Robert 341
Carrell, Jennifer 241
Cartier, Jacques 298, 307
Cartwright, Thomas 376, 551, 593–4, 596
Cary, Elizabeth 459
Casaubon, Meric 117
Castiglione, Baldassare 27, 28, 194, 228, 260, 350, 619
Catholics, Catholicism 52, 61, 79, 118, 121, 125, 129, 140, 144, 258, 336, 340, 354, 373, 375–7, 383, 401, 440, 459, 523, 529, 530, 536, 539, 551, 577, 632–3, 639, 643

Catullus 78
Cave, Terence 45
Cavendish, Christiana, Countess of
     Devonshire 240
Cavendish, Margaret 269, 271
Caxton, William 154, 348
Cecil, Sir Robert 300, 304
Cecil, William (Lord Burghley) 39, 163, 166,
     401, 427, 637
Celtis, Konrad 419
Chaloner, Thomas 382, 386
Chamber, John 332
Chamberlain, John 236, 400
Chapman, George 23
Chard, Thomas 549
Charles I 120, 240, 361, 368, 369, 377, 378,
     410–11, 432, 436, 450, 582
Charles II 432, 450
Charles V of Spain 127, 633
Charleton, Walter 269, 275, 284
Chaucer, Geoffrey 4, 150, 151–2, 161, 201, 350,
     522, 612, 625
Chettle, Henry 189
Christ, Christian, Christianity 255, 296, 305,
     316, 368, 383–4, 437–8, 479, 491–2, 494,
     497, 501, 530, 532, 566, 569, 580, 589, 674
Churchman, John 594
Churchman, Thomas 594
Churchyard, Thomas 161
Cicero 10, 13–14, 20, 30, 94, 109, 117, 211, 274,
     344, 345–6, 348, 349–50, 362, 371, 373,
     376, 391, 392, 418, 420, 526, 527, 532
   Ciceronian 20, 31, 114, 117, 211, 274, 276,
     345, 362, 365, 367–8, 372, 375, 376, 506,
     562, 671
Clarendon, Edward Hyde, 1st Earl of 239–40
Clark, Danielle 69
Clark, Henry 328
Clark, Stuart 381
Clarke, Samuel 463
Claudian 350
Cleaver, Robert 485, 488, 489–90, 492, 495, 498
Clegg, Cyndia 162–3
Cleland, John 89
Clifford, Lady Anne 442, 444–5
Clucas, Stephen 274
Codrington, Robert 283

Coeffeteau, Nicolas 66
Colclough, David 508
Colie, Rosalie 479
Collenuccio, Pandolfo 37
Collinson, Patrick 372, 523, 552, 563
Columbus, Christopher 257
Colwell, Thomas 123
Coke, Edward 366
Constantine 532–3, 566
Contarini, Gaspar 372
Conti, Bruno 674
'cony-catching literature' 132, 203
Cooper, Thomas 336, 340, 341, 404, 544–5,
     551, 554, 600
Cornwallis, William 80, 347, 473–7
Corro, Antonio del 124
Cortes, Toledan 122
Coryat, Thomas 307
Cotta, John 335, 340
Cotton, Robert 320
Cotton, Thomas 399
Covell, William 606
Cox, Leonard 10–11, 13
Cox, Virginia 36
Crane, Mary 54
Cranmer, George 551, 594, 600, 601
Cranmer, Thomas 540, 577, 580, 584
Crashaw, Richard 112
Crawford, Julie 435
Crawley, Richard 116
Cressy, David 587
Croll, Maurice 365–6, 561, 563
Cromwell, Oliver 347, 370, 432
Cromwell, Thomas 447, 539
Crosse, Robert 271
Culpepper, Nicholas 330
Cummings, Robert 63

Dangerfield, Thomas 135
Daniel, Samuel 16, 89, 323–4
Dante, Alighieri 94, 157, 357
Davies, Horton 561
Davis, John 303, 307, 322
Davis, Walter 190
Day, Angel 109, 118, 423–4
Day, John 523

Day, Matthew 299
Dee, John 117, 337, 446
Deakins, Roger 28
Defoe, Daniel 135, 308
De Grazia, Margareta 442
Dekker, Thomas 135, 380–1
Delaval, Lady Elizabeth 439
Deloney, Thomas 164
Democritus, Democritean 56–8, 653–6, 666
Denny, Sir Edward 236, 237
Derrida, Jacques 3
Deutsch, Helen 482–3
De Vere, Edward, Earl of Oxford 180, 201
Devereux, Robert, 2nd Earl of Essex 366
Diaries 399, 434–51
Digby, Kenelm 669–70, 678
Digges, Dudley 427
Digges, Leonard 328, 331
Diodati, Thomas 81
Dockwra, William 432
Domestic Manuals 484–502
Donne, John 282, 477–9, 560–7, 570–1, 572, 574
Downes, Bartholomew 409
Drake, Francis 295
Drake, William 54
Drayton, Michael 206, 227–8, 458
Dudley, John, Earl of Warwick 11
Dudley, Robert, Earl of Leicester 168, 427
Duffy, Eamon 581, 587
Duigdale, Sir William 445
Dyer, Edward 425

Earle, John 481
Eden, Richard 297
Edward IV 362, 364
Edward VI 39, 143, 435, 580, 581, 634
Edwards, Richard 196
Elderton, William 616
Elizabeth, Queen 3, 33, 39, 68, 92, 109, 118, 170, 297, 313, 316, 354, 367, 369, 446, 461, 469, 532–5, 545, 554, 560, 611, 635
Elliot, Sir John 369
Eliot, T. S. 562, 566–7
Eloquence 9–26
Elyot, Sir Thomas 9, 12, 16, 20, 22, 31, 36, 37, 40, 55, 259, 265, 367

England, Englishness 9–26, 45, 226
Erasmus, Desiderius 44, 46, 47, 48, 49, 50, 146, 213, 256, 257, 350, 381–6, 390, 391, 418–9, 421, 425, 612, 627, 663
  Erasmian 125
Essays 468–83
Evelyn, John 271, 444, 445, 447

Fabri, Pierre 421
Farrow, Kenneth 644
Featley, John 437
Felch, Susan 634, 641, 642
Feltham, Owen 479
Fenlon, Dermot 364
Fenner, Dudley 549
Fenton, Geoffrey 92, 190–1, 193
Ferguson, Robert 515–7
Fergusson, James 506
Ferrar, Robert 537
Ferrell, Lori Anne 564
Ficino, Marsilio 425
Field, John 552
Fielding, Henry 135, 432
Filmer, Robert 378
Fincham, Kenneth 563
Fish, Stanley 646, 672
Fitch, Ralph 298
Fitzgeffrey, Charles 206
Fleming, Abraham 422, 524
Fletcher, John 328, 331
Florio, John 79, 80–90, 298, 426
Fludd, Robert 332–3
Folger Library 577
Forman, Simon 448
Forster, Richard 328, 329
Fortesque, Thomas 92
Fortune, John 537
Foster, William 332
Fox, Adam 399
Foxe, John 322, 463–4, 522–43
Frame, Donald 79
France, French 16, 32–3, 37, 60, 74, 117, 123, 259, 374, 406
  French Wars of Religion 407
Fraunce, Abraham 222, 227
Frisch, Andrea 305

Frobisher, Martin 295
Froude, James A. 296
Frye, Northrop 646
Fuller, Mary 299
Fulwood, William 421–2
Furse, Robert 440

Gainsford, Thomas 409, 410, 424
Galen, Galenic 649, 660, 661
Garber, Marjorie 358
Garnier, Robert 239
Gascoigne, George 23–4, 25, 129, 156–71, 174–6, 191, 192, 193, 401–3, 428–9, 615, 619, 625
Gataker, Thomas 486, 489–90, 491, 493, 494, 497, 498, 500
Gellius, Aulus 348
Genre 3, 479
Geoffrey of Monmouth 299, 317
Gesta Romanorum 118
Geuffroy, Antoine 37
Gibson, Sir John 440, 450
Gifford, George 340
Gilbert, Sir Humphrey 158, 159, 295
Giles, Peter 34, 47
Gill, Alexander 23
Glaisyer, Natasha 485
Glanville, Joseph 681–2
Godwin, Francis 264, 265
Goodcole, Henry 404
Goodman, Christopher 374
Goodwin, John 394, 518
Googe, Barnabe 161
Gosson, Stephen 92, 381, 386–90, 391
Gouge, William 484, 485, 486, 488, 489, 490, 491, 492, 493, 496, 497, 499, 500, 501
Gournay, Marie de 79
Grafton, Richard 316, 363, 580
Graham, Elspeth 453, 455, 465
Grange, John 164
Greece, Greek 9–12, 18, 20, 21, 45, 60, 70–71, 109, 120, 165, 190, 220, 225, 253, 384, 389, 510, 513, 572, 615
Green, Ian 564, 578
Greenblatt, Stephen 304

Greene, Robert 2, 132, 135, 164, 184–5, 188–203, 215, 218, 307, 428, 555, 557, 616–7
Greene, Thomas 54
Greenwey, Richard 109, 115, 365
Gregory, Saint of Nazianzene 528
Gresham, Sir Thomas 124, 127
Greville, Fulke 220, 221, 222, 459–50
Grey, Lady Jane 464
Gribben, Crawford 642
Grimald, Nicholas 109, 117
Grimeston, Arthur 118
Grymeston, Elizabeth 480
Guazzo, Stephano 32–3, 41, 55, 102, 619
Guez, Jean-Luis, Sieuer de Balzac 426–7
Guicciardini, Francesco 638
Gustavus Adolphus 411
Gwinne, Matthew 81

Hackett, Helen 238
Haddon, Walter 422
Hadfield, Andrew 92, 96
Hainhofer, Jerome 431–2
Hakluyt, Richard the Younger 80, 292–309
Hall, Edward 436
Hall, John 338
Hall, Joseph 264–5, 300, 426, 480, 569–70
Hamilton, Patrick 539
Hamlin, William 89
Hamling, Tara 487
Hannay, Margaret 238
Harcourt, Lady Anne 449
Harington, Sir John 246, 346
Harpsfield, Nicholas 530, 532
Harrington, Anne 81
Harrington, James 266
Harris, Jonathan Gil 207–8
Harrison, Peter 269
Harrison, Richard 10
Harvey, Gabriel 22, 123–4, 173, 184, 189, 211, 213, 214, 217, 219, 299, 425–6, 556–7, 611–30
Harvey, Mercy 622–9
Harvey, Richard 211, 212, 217, 329, 556, 627
Hastings, Sir Edward 436
Hausted, Peter 172, 173, 185
Hawkins, John 295, 298

Hay, William 483
Hayward, Sir John 313, 366–7, 368, 460
Hazlitt, W. Carew 343
Hazlitt, William 675
Healey, John 109, 264
Hebrew 510, 572
Hegendorph, Christoph 419
Heliodorus 75, 118, 194, 220, 225
Henri III 68, 79
Henri IV 68, 79, 412, 461
Henri de Navarre 79
Henrietta Maria 59, 60
Henry II 323–4
Henry VII 257, 295, 314–6, 368–70
Henry VIII 37, 256, 331, 362, 364, 371, 392, 396, 398, 436, 541, 544, 577, 580
Henry, Prince 426, 589
Herberay, Nicholas de 61, 63
Herbert, George 567–8
Herbert, Philip 60, 241
Herbert, William, Third Earl of Pembroke 238, 239–41, 248
Herodotus 118
Hester, John 614
Heton, Sir Thomas 168
Heydon, Sir Christopher 332
Heylyn, Peter 682–3
Heywood, Thomas 110, 114
Hidalgo, Gaspar 477
Hill, Thomas 446–7
Hind, James 132
Hobbes, Thomas 109, 115–6, 120, 274, 360
Hoby, Lady Margaret 44, 434–7, 438, 449
Hoby, Sir Thomas 350, 437
Hodgkins, John 204–5
Holinshed, Raphael 221, 310–25, 363, 524
Holland, Guy 682
Holland, Henry 337, 340
Holland, Philemon 71, 106–10, 112, 113, 117, 118, 119, 321, 461
Holsinger, Bruce 590
Homer 279
Hooker, Richard 376–7, 548, 551, 592–608
Hooper, John 540
Hopkins, Matthew 339
Hopton, Arthur 446
Horace 78

Hoskins, John 39, 223, 225, 227, 232
Howard, Frances 341, 480
Howard, Sir George 100
Howard, Henry, Earl of Northampton 627–8
Howard, Henry, Earl of Surrey 213, 304, 391–2, 396
Howard, Philip, Earl of Arundel 626–7
Howleglas 146, 613, 618
Howell, James 426
Howell, Joseph 684
Hunt, Arnold 564, 566
Hunter, Michael 283
Hutchinson, Lucy 457
Hutson, Lorna 92, 387

Ireland 33, 34, 142–4
Isham, Elizabeth 448
Italy, Italian 37, 168

Jack, R. D. S. 643
Jackson, Arthur 513
James VI and I 39, 64, 164, 241, 340, 352, 361, 367–9, 377–8, 409, 410, 469, 480, 554, 564, 581, 582, 640, 648
Jeake, Samuel 439
Jenkin, William 518
Jenkinson, Anthony 301
Jestbooks 146–8, 343–59
Jewel, John 594
Johnson, Samuel 186, 471, 670, 675
Jones, Emrys 573
Jonson, Ben 21, 64, 89, 115, 217, 239, 240, 243, 245, 265, 355–6, 365, 400–1, 473
Josselin, Ralph 438, 440
Joubert, Lawrence 346–7

Katherine of Aragon 117, 125
Kay, Billy 643
Keach, Benjamin 506
Kempe, William 420
Kepler, Johannes 264
Kernan, Alvin 387
Killeen, Kevin 278, 279
King, Henry 571–2

King, John N. 51, 524
Kinney, Arthur 388
Kinney, Claire 249
Kirby, W. J. 598, 603–4
Kirk, James 640
Kitson, Anthony 34
Knox, John 361, 362, 374–5, 631–45
Kushner, Tony 671
Kyle, Richard 638

Lake, Peter 563, 603–4
Lambarde, William 321, 322
Lander, Jesse M. 387
Lane, Edward 506
Langland, William 523
Latin 9–12, 18, 19, 20, 21, 28, 31, 46, 60, 61, 109, 112, 165, 176, 348, 510, 526, 572, 615, 635
Lazarillo de Tormes 121–36, 613
Le Blon, Christoph 652
Lee, Sir Henry 166
Le Grys, Robert 64, 68
Le Roy, Louis 117
Leigh, Edward 512
Lekpreuilk, Robert 32
Letters 417–33
Lettisham, Elizabeth 588
Lever, Ralph 15–16
Levett, Timothy 588
Levine, Joseph 318, 320
Levy, F. J. 312
Lewin, William 618
Lewis, C. S. 91, 92, 207–8, 579
Lewkenor, Lewis 372
Libanius 419
Libell of English Pollicie 303
Life Writing 452–67
Lightfoot, John 511
Lilley, Kate 479–80
Lilly, William 331, 335
Lily, William 174
Lindsay, Maurice 645
Lindsay, Robert of Pitscottie 643–5
Lipsius, Justus 365, 419, 658
Livy 71, 92–3, 97, 102, 118, 119, 312, 613, 617
Locke, Anne 641

Locke, John 271, 377
Lodge, Thomas 107, 114, 117, 164, 185
Lok, Michael 302
Lollards, Lollardy 535–6, 538
Longinus 513–4
Longus 109, 118, 193
Lowth, William 487, 489, 493
Lucan 64
Lucian 256, 302, 384–5
Lucretius 78
Lukin, Henry 513
Lund, Mary Ann 56
Lupset, Thomas 36
Lupton, Thomas 261
Luther, Martin 256, 382, 398
 Lutheran 374
Lyall, R. J. 644
Lyly, John 86, 164, 172–87, 189, 190, 191, 192, 193, 195, 197, 226–7, 292–3, 428, 551, 555–6, 619

Mabbe, James 134–5
McCabe, Richard 563
MacCullough, Diarmaid 577
McGrade, A. S. 598, 602
Machiavelli, Niccolo 312, 315, 365, 366, 638
Machyn, Henry 436, 448
Mack, Peter 565
McKeon, Michael 132
Macrobius 348
Macropedius, Georgius 419
Magic 334–7
Maitland, Thomas 635–6
Maltby, Judith 578
Man, Judith 66
Mancall, Peter 304
Mandeville, Sir Thomas 305
Manningham, John 448
Marcus Aurelius 117
Marcus, Laura 445
Marguerite of Navarre 93, 97, 161
Markham, Gervase 225
Marlowe, Christopher 216
Marot, Clement 355
Marotti, Arthur 242

Marprelate, Martin 204–6, 213, 391, 394, 406, 544–59, 576, 599, 604
Martyr, Peter 297, 594
Mary I 39, 127, 297, 318, 363, 373, 375, 590, 632, 633, 642
Mary Stuart (Queen of Scots) 32, 35, 39, 376, 631–2, 634–9, 642
Mascuch, Michael 464
Maslen, R. W. 92, 154, 164
Mason, Roger 633, 642
Massinger, John 424
Matthew, Tobie 427
Matthiesson, F. O. 81, 83, 107, 111, 115
May, Thomas 64
Mayer, T. F. 37
Meade, Joseph 400, 408–9
Medina, Juan de 131
Melanchthon, Philip 526
Mellis, John 443
Melton, John 332
Mendelson, Sara Heller 449
Menippus of Gadara 256
　Menippian satire 381, 384, 386, 646
Mentz, Steve 189
Merbecke, John 581
Mercator, Gerald 304
Meres, Francis 49
Middleton, Henry 158
Mildmay, Lady Grace 439
Millanges, Simon 78
Miller, Daniel 207, 208
Milton, John 324, 362, 363, 370, 376, 378, 653
Milward, Peter 594
Minsheu, John 126
Mitchell, W. F. 561
Molyneux, Edmund 221, 222, 228
Montaigne, Michel de 45, 77–90, 257–8, 304, 365, 468, 472, 482, 658, 559, 664
Montalvo, Garci Rodriguez de 61, 62
Montemayor, Jorge de 225, 226, 246, 247, 428
Mordaunt, Viscountess Elizabeth 441
More, Henry 683
More, Sir Thomas 29, 30, 33, 36, 253–66, 302, 311–4, 348, 352, 361, 362–4, 366, 368, 370, 523
　History of Richard III 370–1
　Utopia 28–9, 33–5, 140, 253, 370–1, 384
Morgan, Matthew 283
Morini, Massimiliano 111
Morison, Stanley 580, 581
Morrisey, Mary 567–8
Moss, Ann 44, 45, 46
Mueller, Janel 528, 565
Mulcaster, Richard 347
Muller, Wolfgang 12
Munday, Anthony 61
Munster, Sebastian 296
Murner, Thomas 123
Muscott, Francis 590

Nabokov, Vladimir 186
Napea, Osep 301
Napier, Richard 330
Nashe, Thomas 10, 22, 23, 134, 135, 164, 173, 189, 204–18, 304, 380–1, 387, 390–4, 445, 555, 556, 611–2, 614, 619, 627
Neville, Henry 302
Newberry, Ralph 298
Newdigate, Anne 484
News 397–414
News from the North 38, 41
Newton, Isaac 271
Newton, Thomas 117
Nicholls, Mark 40
Nicolls, Thomas 115, 116, 298, 300
Nielson, James 617
North, Sir Thomas 107, 111, 112, 113, 119, 460, 461–2
Norton, Thomas 33
Novel 1

Odoricus, Friar Beatus 302
Oldcastle, Hugh 443
Ong, Walter J., SJ 43, 44
Oresme, Nicolas 117
Orrery, see Robert Boyle, 1st Earl of Orrery
Overbury, Thomas 480–1
Overton, Richard 558
Ovid 279, 388, 417
Oxford English Dictionary 24, 31, 216, 253

Page, Matthew 446
Painter, William 91–101, 190–1
Palfreyman, Thomas 49
Paracelsian 288–90, 333
Paradis, Vanessa 288
Parker, John 593
Parks, G. B. 303
Parliament 39
Parsons, Robert 338, 377, 523
Pater, Walter 186
Patterson, Annabel 68
Paynell, Thomas 109
Peacham, Henry 482
Peck, Linda Levy 60
Pecke, Samuel 400
Pecock, Reginald 540
Pecocke, Edward 627
Pelham, Lady Frances 449
Pennell, Sara 485
Pepys, Samuel 441–2
Perkins, William 329–30, 336, 340, 341, 488, 489, 494, 495, 500, 567
Perne, Andrew 551, 614–5
Peters, Helen 477
Petrarch, Francesco 212, 320, 418
Pettie, George 32, 33, 101–4, 164, 174–5
Petty, William 271
Philip II 70, 122, 130
Piccolomini, Aeneas Sylvius 538
Pigman, G. W. 157
Pindar 528
Plantin, Christoph 117
Plast, Hugh 212
Plato 46, 51, 117, 229, 254–6, 261, 370
  Platonism 272, 514, 649, 679
Plattes, Gabriel 266
Pliny 71, 106, 107, 112, 176, 279, 296
Plutarch 46, 48, 49, 71, 78, 107, 112, 117, 350, 389, 454, 460, 461–2
Pole, Cardinal Reginald 37, 364, 371–2
Politics 360–79
Polo, Gaspar Gil 246, 247, 248
Polybius 118
Poliziano, Angelo 421
Ponet, John 373
Popular Culture 3
Pory, John 400

Potts, Thomas 340
Power, Henry 683
Powle, Sir Stephen 476
Presbyterian 548, 552, 553, 558, 594–6, 604, 606
Preston, Thomas 617
Priest, William and Anne 588
Principe, Lawrence 283
Print, printing 1
Protestant, Protestantism 14, 80–81, 83, 118, 121, 125, 143, 240, 322, 326, 348, 355, 375, 401, 404, 409, 437, 456, 487, 530, 537, 565, 567, 631–2, 637, 642, 643
  Proto-Protestantism 536
Prudentius 528
Ptolemy 296
Purchas, Samuel 25, 306
Purfoote, Thomas 446–7
Purgatory 326
Puritan, Puritanism 261, 438, 440, 449, 578
Puttenham, George 17, 21, 22–3, 25, 164, 227, 228, 355, 380–1

Quintilian 10, 14, 21, 227, 345, 351

Rabelais, François 259, 265, 348
Ralegh, Sir Walter 39–40, 89, 295, 297, 306, 318, 435
Ramus, Peter (Petrus Ramus) 222, 613, 651
  Ramism 509, 651
Rastell, William 363
Reisner, Noam 568
Reynolds, Henry 206
Rhetoric 9–26, 209, 272–4, 350, 488–9, 527–8, 572, 663, 676–7
Rhodes, Richard 435
Rich, Barnabe 118, 161, 164
Rich, Mary, Countess of Warwick 449
Richard II 313, 366, 373, 535
Richard III 362–5, 368, 476
Richardson, Samuel 432
Rio, Martin del 338
Roberts, Alexander 340, 341
Roberts, Francis 510, 512
Roberts, Mary 449

INDEX

Robins, John 328
Robinson, Ralph 28–9, 262
Roebuck, Graham 394
Romance 2, 200, 202, 225, 235–50
Rosenberg, Eleanor 168
Rosendale, Timothy 580
Ross, Alexander 672
Rous, John 399, 435
Rowland, David 126–9

Sacks, David Harris 299
Saker, Austen 184
Sale, Sarah 445
Sallust 109, 110, 114, 119, 274, 312, 363
Salutati, Coluccio 418
Salzman, Paul 68
Sandys, Edwin 594, 600, 601, 602
Sanford, Hugh 248
Sanford, John 126
Sannazaro, Jacopo 158, 225, 226–7
Satire 380–95
Saville, Sir Henry 109, 114–5, 118, 119, 365–7
Schneider, Gary 426
Schoenfeldt, Michael 55
Schulz, Ernst 344
Science 268–91
Scot, Reginald 328, 334, 336, 338, 339–40
Scott, Thomas 369
Scott, Sir Walter 186
Scott, William 226–9, 232
Screech, Michael 79
Seelig, Sharon Cadman 436
Selden, John 320
Seneca 78, 114, 117, 212, 287, 362, 365
 Senecan 274, 362, 561, 562, 671
Sermons 560–75
Seyssel, Claude de 115, 117
Shakespeare, William 89, 92, 95, 98, 109, 111–2, 118, 135, 157, 185–6, 189, 191, 194, 216, 237, 240, 303, 331, 343, 363, 370, 448, 450, 454, 466, 544, 612, 619
Shapin, Steven 305
Shapiro, Barbara 305
Sharpe, Kevin 54
Sheffard, William 409
Sherman, William 44, 297, 301

Sherry, Richard 12, 20–21
Shuger, Debra 509, 607
Shrank, Cathy 149
Sidney, Mary (Philip's mother) 191
Sidney, Mary (Philip's sister), Countess of Pembroke 220, 236–7, 239, 241, 248
Sidney, Sir Philip 31, 32, 44, 59, 70–71, 73, 86, 93, 157, 164, 165, 185, 213, 219–34, 236, 271, 282, 293, 295, 374, 425, 429–30, 459–60, 588, 613, 629
Sidney, Robert 220, 238, 241
Simpson, Evelyn M. 562
Singer, Samuel 343
Skelton, John 124, 354–5, 397, 613
Skura, Meredith 452, 466
Smith, G. C. Moore 613, 618, 627
Smith, Henry 486, 492, 501
Smith, John (colonist) 307
Smith, John (rhetorician) 677
Smith, Richard 162
Smith, Sir Thomas 29, 30, 33, 34, 41, 260–1, 372, 427, 611, 613, 614–5, 628
Smith, Walter 352
Smollet, Tobias 135
Smyth, Adam 453, 466
Smyth, John 518–9
Smythe, Robert 92
Socrates 46, 47, 55, 118, 256, 483, 570, 616
Solinus 279
Somerville, J. P. 378
South, Robert 271
Sowerby, Robin 115
Spain, Spanish 4, 59, 63, 74, 121–36, 295
Speed Hill, W. 607
Speght, Thomas 612
Spenser, Edmund 70–71, 117, 123–4, 135, 157, 206, 217, 219, 372–3, 425–6, 611, 613, 617, 618, 629
Sprat, Thomas 269, 270, 278
Squier, Adam 338
Stanhope, Charles 128
Stanley, Thomas 117
Stanwood, Paul 592
Staper, Thomas 298
Stapleton, Thomas 529–30
Starkey, Thomas 32, 36, 37, 260, 371–3

INDEX

Stationers's Company 406, 410, 412, 424
   Stationers's Register 600
Sterne, Lawrence 304
Stow, John 316, 321–2, 356, 524
Strada, Famiano 112
Streater, John 370
Stubbes, Katherine 464
Stubbes, Philip 329
Sturm, Johann 420
Stuteville, Sir Martin 408
Suetonius 107, 363, 364, 461
Swift, Jonathan 265

Tacitus 114–5, 119, 274, 312, 313, 362–6, 368, 369–70
   Tacitean 322, 362
Tadmor, Naomi 510
Taitus, Achilles 194
Talbot, Lady Mary 239, 241
Tanner, Robert 329
Targoff, Ramie 585
Tarlton, Richard 356–7, 358, 551
Tasso, Torquato 83
Tatius, Achilles 118
Taverner, Richard 50
Taylor, Jeremy 512
Taylor, John 346, 357–8
Terence 419
Tertullian 580, 674
Thevert, Andre 296, 300
Thirty-Nine Articles 437
Throkmorton, Job 545
Thucydides 109, 115–6, 312
Tibullus 350
Tirwhyt, William 426
Todorov, Tzvetan 3
Translation 4, 406–12
Travers, Walter 549, 595
Troyes, Chretien de 74
Tuck, Richard 362
Turberville, George 92, 124, 127, 161
Turkey, Turks, Turkish 24
Turner, William 554
Twysden, Lady Isabella 445, 449
Tyacke, Nicholas 563
Tyndale, William 510, 526, 528, 540

Unton, Sir Henry 454
Ussher, James 513
Utopianism 253–67

Valdes, Fernando de 120
Valerius Maximus 350
Valla, Lorenzo 115
Valleriolus, Francis 338
Vasari, Giorgio 461
Vaughan, Sir William 206
Vespucci, Amerigo 257
Vickers, Brian 272, 287, 563
Virgil 20, 78, 228, 229, 388, 523, 628
   Virgilian 20, 225
Vives, Juan Luis 125, 131, 419

Wadsworth, Jacob 426
Waldegrave, Robert 548
Walker, Elizabeth 439
Waller, Sir William 439–40
Wallington, Nehemiah 399, 439–40, 484
Walkley, Thomas 128, 411
Walsingham, Sir Francis 295, 300, 304, 427
Walwyn, William 377
Ward, Samuel 438
Warner, Christopher 39
Warren, Austen 671
Watson, Christopher 118
Watt, Ian 432
Webbe, George 347
Webbe, William 164
Webber, Joan 562, 563
Webster, John 331
Webster, Noah 675
Weiss, Adrian 158
Weiss, Rene 460
Wentworth, Anne 66
Westfall, T. W. 276
Whately, William 485, 486, 490–1, 493, 494, 495, 496, 499, 500
Whetstone, George 92, 104, 164
Whitaker, Richard 426
Whitchurch, Edward 580
White, Hayden 446
White, William 536

Whiteway, William 435
Whitgift, John 376, 551, 554, 593–5, 600, 603, 606
Wiclif, John 535
Wilkins, John 271, 272, 278, 561
Willes, Richard 297
William the Conqueror 16
Williams, Grant 56–7
Williams, John 513
Williams, Penry 40
Williamson, George 561
Wilson, F. P. 344
Wilson, John 506
Wilson, Katharine 164, 194
Wilson, Thomas 10–19, 23, 38, 345, 349–50, 506
Winstanley, Gerrard 266
Winthrop, John 261
Winzet, Ninian 643
Wishart, George 639
Witchcraft 337–41
Withie, William 625
Wodenote, Theophilus 505
Wolfe, John 406, 407, 425
Wolfe, Reyner 318
Wolsey, Cardinal 354
Womersley, David 322

Woolf, D. R. 319, 322
Woolf, Virginia 628–9
Worden, Blair 374
Wormald, Jenny 639
Wotton, Sir Edward 81
Wray, Ramona 465
Wright, Gilbert 335
Wriothesley, Charles 436
Wroth, Mary 235–50
Wroth, Sir Robert 239, 241
Wyatt, Sir Thomas 20, 117
Wyer, Robert 147

Xenophon 70–71, 107, 220, 261, 461

Yates, Dame Frances 81, 83
Yong, Bartholomew 102, 246, 428
Yonge, Walter 435
Young, John 616
Young, Richard 89

Zall, Paul 343, 356
Zuccolo, Lodovico 262–3
Zwinger, Theodor 651